PAST WORLDS

THE  TIMES
ATLAS OF ARCHAEOLOGY

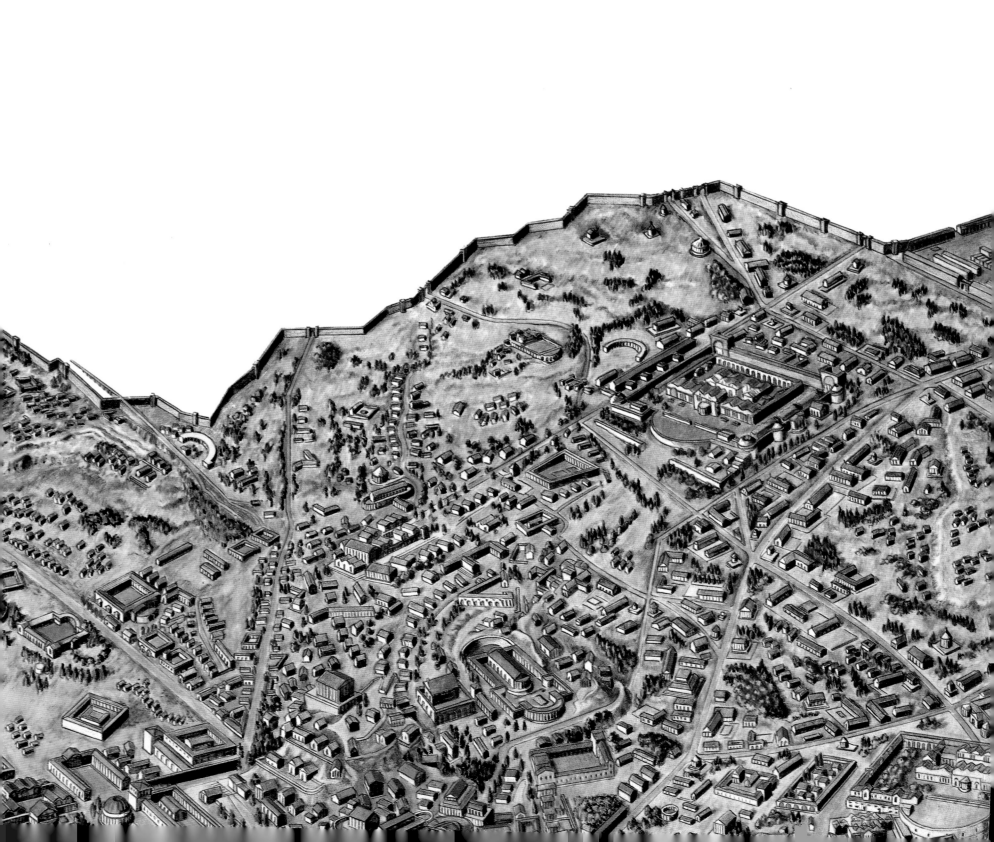

PAST WORLDS

THE TIMES ATLAS OF ARCHAEOLOGY

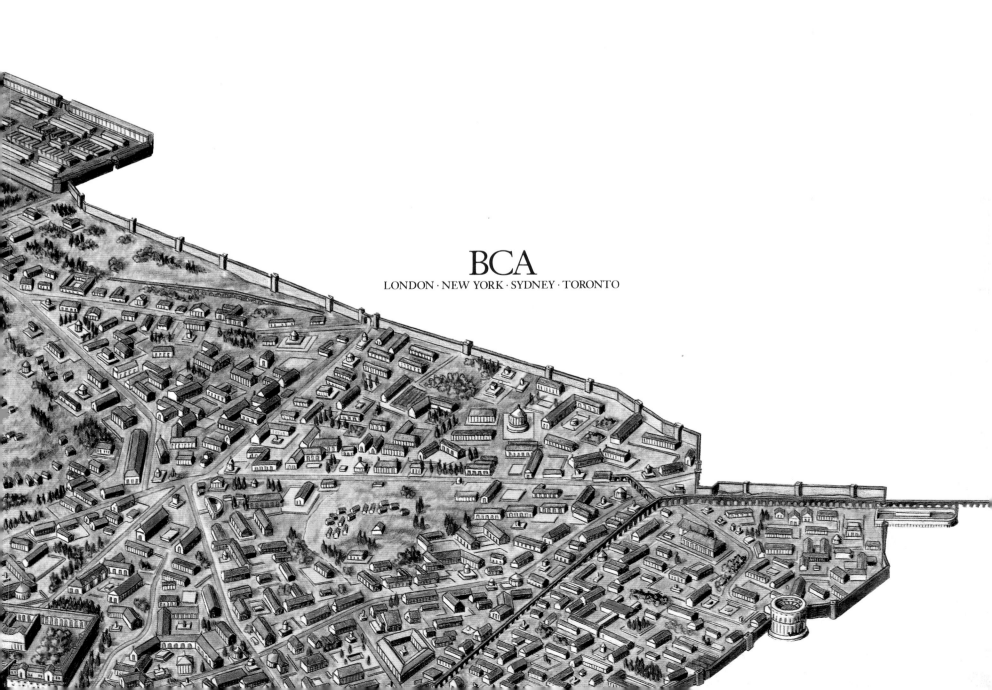

BCA

LONDON · NEW YORK · SYDNEY · TORONTO

**This edition first published
1989 by BCA
by arrangement with
Times Books
A division of HarperCollins***Publishers*
**77-85 Fulham Palace Road
London W6 8JB**
Reprinted 1992, 1993

© Times Books 1988, 1989, 1990, 1991, 1992, 1993

Maps, illustrations, typesetting
Swanston Graphics, Derby
Malcolm Swanston
Andrea Fairbrass
Mel Pickering
James Mills-Hicks
Andrew Bright
Jeanne Radford

Duncan Mackay
Tony Hoyle
Rex Nicholls
Cheryl Wilbraham

Colour processing
Ensign Graphics, Hull

Design
Ivan Dodd

Editorial direction
Elizabeth Wyse
Barry Winkleman

Rosemary Aspinwall
Ailsa Heritage
Andrew Heritage
Candida Hunt
Olivia Landry
Paul Middleton

Place names consultant, index
P J M Geelan

Picture research
Caroline Lucas

Glossary
Liv Gibbs and Andy Brown

Printed in Italy by
Arnoldo Mondadori, Verona

CN 5693

INTRODUCTION

AN ATLAS OF WORLD ARCHAEOLOGY is a challenging enterprise. World archaeology has only recently become a reality. Indeed only for the past thirty years has it technically even been a possibility. When dealing with the early human past, the first question which one must answer, and the very crux of the matter when trying to discover what actually happened, is 'when'? When did the significant changes, which we are trying to understand, take place in different parts of the world? If the human species first developed in Africa, as now seems to be the case, when did people first move from Africa to Asia, and then to Europe? When were the Americas first peopled? When did the ancestors of the aborigines first arrive in Australia? These are questions which can, at last, be answered, even though some of these answers are still provisional. Coherent views are emerging on these topics (and are surveyed in Section two of this Atlas).

Another great question for archaeologists during this century, has been one of independence. Did the major developments in one part of the world (for instance the emergence of civilisation in the Americas) take place without any significant impetus from the earlier heartlands of civilisation in the Old World, for instance in Mesopotamia, in Egypt or in China? A sound answer to this question also can only come if we can tell *when* these developments occurred in each part of the world.

Progress in archaeological science has, in recent decades, allowed us to answer such questions with confidence for the first time, and on a global scale. Hitherto a firm date could only be established by demonstrating the existence of some contact between the area in question and a region already historically dated. Any reliable chronology could only be based upon such links. But, of course, to be 'historically dated' inevitably implied that written records had to be available. The oldest in Egypt and Mesopotamia, dated back only to about 3000 BC. China has historical records going back to about 1500 BC which form the basis for a historical chronology. But in most other parts of the world such records were not created until very much later. History in that sense depends upon literacy. So that, if a region which at the time in question was non-literate (such as South America, or Australia, prior to the first European contact), and was independent and lacking in contacts with the literate world, it had to remain undated. Thus, no true world archaeology could be written, and no soundly-based survey of world archaeology was conceivable.

All this has now changed. Laboratory developments, based on advances in nuclear physics, allow the dating of events in the past, quite without any reference to written records or to calendars established in ancient times. Radiocarbon dating is the most useful of these laboratory techniques. By its application, the date of death can be established for any plant or animal remains which may be found, back to an age limit of about 40,000 years ago. This is precise to within a century or so. Wood from burials in the Americas, or bone from early refuse tips in Australia, or carbonised rice grains from East Asia, can, of course, be dated as readily in the laboratory as materials from Europe or the Near East. It is now possible to develop a chronology, a timetable for the sequence of events in every part of the world, in each case without being obliged to make reference to information derived from other areas. A coherent world archaeology has, at last, become possible.

This Atlas reaps the benefits of these advances. It concentrates on some of the greatest themes of human existence. First, the emergence of humankind. Section two deals with humanity's colonisation of the Earth. Then, in Section three, comes that momentous series of developments from which agriculture, and a settled way of life, developed in several parts of the world. Not only are the maps themselves new; they are accompanied by illustrations which present and interpret, in a fresh and original way, a whole range of archaeological evidence.

If the agricultural revolution constitutes a landmark in the human story, so, too, does the 'urban revolution', in which cities and civilisations arose in certain areas. Again, as indicated in Section four, (and in Section six for the Americas) there seem to have been independent developments in different parts of the world. Urban organisation and state government, and, in some cases, literacy, also made their appearance at different times upon the different continents.

It is clear, however, that once communities are organised to acquire the centralised control typical of state societies, further expansion, often military expansion, is possible. Section five documents and illustrates the way in which the world's early empires were formed.

But archaeology does not stop with the development of written records and the inception of literate history, such as are encountered in the world of Classical Greece and Rome, or with the rise of the European and Islamic Middle Ages. Increasingly, scholars are coming to realise that the *things* produced at the time – the settlement remains, the monuments, the artefacts – can, if properly interpreted, yield as much, if not more, information about the life of their times as a written chronicle. So it is that the archaeology of the mediaeval world, examined in Section seven, plays an increasingly important role in mediaeval studies. Even industrial archaeology is a growing object of study today. It is appropriate, therefore, that the last maps in the Atlas should be concerned with the Industrial Revolution.

This volume, then, is more than just an atlas, more than just a compendium of maps designed to show where places are; it is, in effect, an entirely new vision of world history, from the beginning of human life down to the emergence of the modern world. It is, thus, a significant new work of interpretation, not merely one of cartographic record. With its global sweep, the Atlas offers us an unrivalled opportunity of taking in rapidly, the outline of what is now known of human origins, of the emergence of various technologies, and of the development of human social organisation. We can begin to contemplate, through its pages, questions of long-term change in human history, of the timescale of human achievement and of the relationships between the human societies and their environments.

Happily, archaeological evidence is now becoming available from parts of the world where little was formerly known of the early past. The early hominids of Australia have already been mentioned. Another example is the early history of Polynesia, where recent archaeological research has made the picture much clearer. In sub-Saharan Africa too, archaeology is now on the move. The new states of Africa, like those in other areas, are anxious to establish their own archaeology and their own history on the basis of material sources found mainly within their own frontiers. The archaeological evidence is accumulating. In consequence, it is now possible to offer an account of such societies in their own right, without constant reference to Europe or to other parts of the Old World.

World archaeology has come of age. This original volume allows us to celebrate that new maturity, and to profit from it by forming, for ourselves, our own global view of the human experience across time and across space. That is this work's particular contribution, and its enduring fascination.

Colin Renfrew
Disney Professor of Archaeology
and Master of Jesus College,
University of Cambridge

CONTENTS

CONTRIBUTORS

GENERAL EDITOR
DR. CHRIS SCARRE
Wolfson College
University of Cambridge

CONSULTANT EDITORS
DR. WARWICK BRAY
Reader in Latin American Archaeology
Institute of Archaeology
University of London

DR. JILL COOK
Head of Quaternary Section
Prehistoric and Romano – British Antiquities
British Museum

The late GLYN E. DANIEL
Former Disney Professor of Archaeology
University of Cambridge

JEREMY A. SABLOFF
University Professor of Anthropology and the
History and Philosophy of Science
University of Pittsburgh

CONTRIBUTORS
DR. JOHN ALEXANDER
Department of Archaeology
University of Cambridge

DR. F. RAYMOND ALLCHIN
Reader in Indian Studies
University of Cambridge

CAROL ANDREWS
Curator
Department of Egyptian Antiquities
British Museum

JAN AUTON
New Hall
University of Cambridge

CHARLES A. AYLMER
Chinese Librarian
Cambridge University Library

DR. PAUL G. BAHN
Writer and Translator of Archaeology
Hull

DR. G. N. BAILEY
Department of Archaeology
University of Cambridge

DR. GINA L. BARNES
St. John's College
University of Cambridge

IRIS BARRY
Former Research Student
Institute of Archaeology
University of London

DR. PETER BELLWOOD
Department of Prehistory and Anthropology
Australian National University
Canberra

DR. J. BINTLIFF
Senior Lecturer
School of Archaeological Sciences
University of Bradford

DR. A. D. H. BIVAR
Near and Middle East Department
School of Oriental and African Studies
University of London

KEITH BRANIGAN
Professor of Archaeology and Prehistory
University of Sheffield

DR. NOEL BROADBENT
Centre for Arctic Cultural Research
Umeå University
Sweden

A. A. M. BRYER
Professor of Byzantine Studies
University of Birmingham

DR. L. A. S. BUTLER
Director of Archaeological Studies
University of Leeds

DEBORAH CAMPBELL
Department of Anthropology
University of Pittsburgh

DR. J. WISSEMAN CHRISTIE
Centre for South-East Asian Studies
University of Hull

DR. HELEN CLARKE
Senior Lecturer
Department of Mediaeval Archaeology
University College
London

DR. JOHN CLEGG
Department of Anthropology
University of Sydney

DR. J. M. COLES
Formerly Professor of European Archaeology
University of Cambridge

MELISSA CONNOR
Midwest Archaeological Centre
Lincoln
Nebraska

ELIZABETH CRUWYS
Scott Polar Research Institute
Cambridge

RICHARD D. DAUGHERTY
Professor Emeritus
Washington State University

DR. JEREMY H. C. S. DAVIDSON
Lecturer in Vietnamese
School of Oriental and African Studies
University of London

T. DILLEHAY
Professor of Anthropology
University of Kentucky

CORINNE DUHIG
Bone Technician
Department of Biological Anthropology
University of Cambridge

DONALD D. F. EASTON
Clare Hall
University of Cambridge

DR. GEORGE ERDOSY
Wolfson College
University of Cambridge

KATE FERNIE
Selwyn College
University of Cambridge

JOHN FISHER
Professor of Latin American Studies
University of Liverpool

MARY FRASER
Girton College
University of Cambridge

MARTIN FUESS
Department of Anthropology
University of Pittsburgh

YURIKO FUKASAWA
Archaeological Researcher
Tokyo

PETER GATHERCOLE
Darwin College
University of Cambridge

JAMES P. GEISS
Department of East Asian Studies
Princeton University

DR. IAN S. GLOVER
Department of Prehistoric Archaeology
University of London

DR. JEREMY GREEN
Department of Maritime Archaeology
Western Australian Maritime Museum
Fremantle

D. W. HARDING
Professor of Archaeology
University of Edinburgh

CHARLOTTE HERXHEIMER
Institute of Archaeology
University of London

DR. CATHERINE HILLS
Department of Archaeology
University of Cambridge

DR. MARK HORTON
Pitt Rivers Museum
University of Oxford

WENDY HORTON
Darwin College
University of Cambridge

KENNETH HUDSON
Social and Industrial Historian
Bath

I. NOËL HUME
The Colonial Williamsburg Foundation
Virginia

HENRY R. HURST
Museum of Classical Archaeology
University of Cambridge

J-F. JARRIGE
Mission Archéologique de l'Indus
Musée Guimet
Paris

ROGER JOUSSAUME
Chargé de Recherches au CNRS
Université Beaulieu
Rennes

BARRY J. KEMP
Lecturer in Egyptology
University of Cambridge

DR. R. G. KILLICK
Former Secretary/Librarian.
British Archaeological Expedition
Iraq

DR. PETER S. KORNICKI
Lecturer in Japanese
University of Cambridge

WOLFGANG LIEBESCHÜTZ
Professor of Classics
University of Nottingham

DR. ROGER J. LING
Department of the History of Art
University of Manchester

DR. MICHAEL LOEWE
Faculty of Oriental Studies
University of Cambridge

PETER MARSDEN
Museum of London

DR. COLIN MARTIN
Director of Scottish Institute of Maritime Studies
University of St. Andrews

MALCOLM McLEOD
Keeper of Ethnography
British Museum

JAMES MELLAART
Lecturer in Anatolian Archaeology
Institute of Archaeology
University of London

DR. GEORGE MITCHELL
Specialist in Indian Archaeology
London

DR. PETER MITCHELL
Donald Baden-Powell Quaternary Research
Centre
Department of Ethnology and Prehistory
University of Oxford

JANE A. MOON
Former Senior Research Associate
British Archaeological Department
Iraq

DR. ELIZABETH H. MOORE
School of Oriental and African Studies
University of London

DR. A. E. NORTHEDGE
Specialist in Islamic Archaeology
London

DR. JOAN OATES
Girton College
University of Cambridge

DR. YOUNGSOOK PAK
School of Oriental and African Studies
University of London

GEOFFREY PARKER
Professor of Modern History
University of Illinois

CHRISTOPHER S. PEEBLES
Glenn A. Black Laboratory of Archaeology
Bloomington
Indiana

DR. DAVID W. PHILLIPSON
Curator
University Museum of Archaeology and
Anthropology
University of Cambridge

STUART PIGGOTT
Former Professor of Archaeology
University of Edinburgh

DR. J. N. POSTGATE
Reader in Mesopotamian Studies
University of Cambridge

JESSICA RAWSON
Acting Keeper
Department of Oriental Antiquities
British Museum

DR. JANE RENFREW
Lucy Cavendish College
University of Cambridge

TIMOTHY E. G. REYNOLDS
Department of Archaeology
University of Cambridge

DR. DEREK A. ROE
Donald Baden-Powell Quaternary Research
Centre
University of Oxford

DR. PETER ROWLEY-CONWY
Clare Hall
University of Cambridge

DR. SANDER VAN DER LEEUW
Department of Archaeology
University of Cambridge

DOUGLAS SCOTT
Regional Archaeologist
Rocky Mountain Regional Division
Midwest Archaeological Centre

DR. ANDREW SHERRATT
Department of Antiquities
Ashmolean Museum
University of Oxford

R. C. SIMMONS
Professor of American History
University of Birmingham

A. M. SNODGRASS
Laurence Professor of Classical Archaeology
University of Cambridge

CHRISTOPHER SYKES
Wolfson College
University of Cambridge

THURSTAN SHAW
Formerly Professor of Archaeology
University of Ibadan
Nigeria

MARY TREGEAR
Keeper
Department of Eastern Art
Ashmolean Museum
University of Oxford

DENIS C. TWITCHETT
Gordon Wu Professor of Chinese History
Department of East Asian Studies
Princeton University

DR. MICHAEL URSINUS
Centre for Byzantine Studies and Modern Greek
University of Birmingham

ERICA UTSI
Lucy Cavendish College
University of Cambridge

SHELAGH VAINKER
Department of Oriental Antiquities
British Museum

DR. J. P. WILD
Department of Archaeology
University of Manchester

We would also like to thank:
Greig W. Arnold Professor J. Baines
Pauline Batchelor Matthew Bennett
Dr. H. A. W. Burl Amanda Claridge
Dr. John Collis Dr. A. R. David Dr. Mark Elvin
Dr. Andrew Goudie Hero Granger-Taylor
Dr. G. Herrmann Dr. D. Hughes John J. Hurst
Dr. John Irwin Simon Kaner
Dr. James Lewthwaite Dr. F. M. Meddens
Dr. Joan Oates Gwil Owen Dr. Neil Roberts
Dr. R. Rodden David Sekers
Professor Stuart Struever Lord William Taylour
H. P. Willmott

CHRONOLOGY

In the chronology table which follows, the world is divided into five geographical regions: Europe, Africa, western Asia (including the Steppe lands and the Indian subcontinent), eastern Asia (including Australia and the Pacific Islands), and the Americas. In this way the pace of human social, cultural and economic achievement in these different regions of the world can be compared and contrasted, from the emergence of the earliest human ancestors some 2.5 million years ago to the dawn of the modern industrial age.

The time-scale of archaeology stretches back far into the past, beginning with the creation of the first tools. By 800,000 years ago early humans had spread from their African homeland into Europe and Asia, and their descendants colonised Australia in about 50,000 BC and the New World by 12,000 BC, if not earlier. The centuries which followed witnessed a series of major innovations which transformed almost every aspect of human existence: the adoption of agriculture, the development of cities, states and empires, and the invention of metals and writing, leading ultimately to the Industrial Revolution and the nuclear age of today. Many of these inventions and innovations arose independently in different places through parallel processes of development.

EUROPE

AFRICA

WEST ASIA & SOUTH ASIA

EAST ASIA & OCEANIA

NEW WORLD

4–5 MILLION YEARS BC
Earliest known bipedal hominids (Australopithecines) in the East African Rift Valley and southern Africa.

2.5 MILLION YEARS BC
First fossil finds of genus *Homo habilis* in East and southern Africa.

2.5 MILLION YEARS BC
Earliest stone tools at Hadar in Ethiopia.

1.75 MILLION YEARS BC
Earliest known man-made shelter at Olduvai Gorge, Kenya.

1.5 MILLION YEARS BC
First finds of *Homo erectus*.

1.5 MILLION YEARS BC
Diversification of stone tools: handaxes, cleavers, scrapers and choppers. (Acheulian and Developed Oldowan industries).

900,000 BC
Earliest hominid settlement of western Asia.

850,000 BC
Earliest hominids reach Europe from Africa; beginning of European Lower Palaeolithic. Struck pebble tools used.

600,000 BC
Acheulian stone industries appear in Europe, including the first handaxes.

450,000 BC
Beginning of occupation at Zhoukoudian, northern China.

400,000 BC
Introduction of 'prepared-core technique' for making stone tools.

300,000 BC
The lakeside site of Bilzingsleben, Germany: well preserved organic materials including wooden tools.

200,000 BC
Middle Palaeolithic begins in Europe.

200,000 BC
Middle Stone Age industries with blades and triangular points for attachment to wooden hafts.

125,000 BC
First exploitation of shellfish for food in southern Africa (Klasies River Mouth).

120,000 BC
Neanderthals present from western Europe to Soviet Central Asia; frequent use of Mousterian stone tools; first humans to bury their dead.

120,000 BC
Neanderthals present in western Asia. Evidence of frequent use of Mousterian tools and first intentional burials (Shanidar, Iraq).

120,000 BC
First archaic *Homo sapiens* in East Asia, at Ngandong, Java.

100,000 BC
Earliest evidence of modern man *Homo sapiens sapiens* in eastern and southern Africa.

90,000 BC
First secure evidence for hominids in East Asia.

50,000 BC
Settlement of Australia by groups probably originating in South-East Asia.

42,000 BC
Mines for red ochre at Lion Cave, Swaziland.

40,000 BC
Earliest flaked stone tools appear in island South-East Asia, mainly made of chert.

35,000 BC
Beginning of Upper Palaeolithic. Modern man appears for first time in Europe, with advanced social structures and innovations in tool manufacture.

30,000 BC
Earliest cave art in south-west France and northern Spain; also portable art objects such as Venus figurines.

30,000 BC
Earliest evidence for human settlement in the Americas, from Pedra Furada, Brazil

25,000 BC
Rapid expansion of settlement of Australia, including the south-east coast, Tasmania and the New Guinea Highlands.

14,000 BC
Development of microliths in Europe.

13,000 BC
Occupation of Bluefish Cave, the earliest site in the Alaska and Yukon region.

12,000 BC
First grindstones used in Upper Egypt and Nubia, for making flour from wild grass seeds.

12,000 BC
First secure traces of human occupation in North America, from Meadowcroft Rock Shelter, Pennsylvania.

11,000 BC
Late Palaeolithic village of Monte Verde, southern Chile, well-preserved in peat with remains of timber buildings, artefacts, food and medicines.

10,500 BC
Earliest known pottery in the world in southern Japan (Fukui Cave).

10,000 BC
Natufian communities of Palestine harvest wild emmer wheat and use grindstones to produce flour.

10,000 BC
Human settlement reaches the southern tip of America (Fell's Cave, Patagonia).

10,000 BC
North American ice-sheets retreat. Settlements become more abundant.

10,000 BC
Palaeo–Indian stage begins in North America. Nomadic big-game hunters using first Clovis and later Folsom stone projectile points.

9000 BC
Einkorn wheat harvested in northern Syria.

9000 BC
Early Chinese pottery from Xianrendong and other sites.

9000 BC
Sheep domesticated in northern Mesopotamia.

8500 BC
Microlithic tools used by first postglacial inhabitants of the Sahara.

8500 BC
Beginnings of Saharan rock art depicting wild and later domesticated animals.

8500 BC
Earliest, tentative evidence for the cultivation of grasses, beans, peppers and squash (Peru).

8300 BC
Glaciers retreat, many lowland areas flooded. New fauna and flora give new opportunities for hunter-gatherers. Use of microlithic tools increased. Beginning of Mesolithic period.

EUROPE

8000 BC
Hunter groups move into Lappland from the east, south and west; ancestral Saami.

6500 BC
Adoption of farming in the Balkans signals the beginning of the European Neolithic. Domesticated cereals, sheep and goat spread, probably from Anatolia.

6500 BC
Britain separated from the Continent by rising sea level.

6200 BC
Farming villages established in the west and central Mediterranean.

5200 BC
First farmers of central Europe spread north-west as far as the Netherlands; distinctive pottery (Bandkeramik), with linear incised decoration found throughout this area.

5000 BC
Gold and copper objects made in the Balkans.

4500 BC
Copper smelted in eastern Europe; copper objects used as status symbols.

4500 BC
Rich individual burials in eastern and central Europe, some containing spectacular metalwork (Varna).

4500 BC
Cattle used as plough animals: lower Danube.

4500 BC
First megalithic tombs built in western Europe.

4200 BC
Copper mines in eastern Europe (Aibunar and Rudna Glava), the earliest known copper mines in the world.

4000 BC
Intensified procurement of high quality flint from mines (western and northern Europe).

3800 BC
Ditched enclosures around settlements in western Europe, forming defended villages.

3500 BC
New farming practices: animals increasingly used for traction, wool and milk.

3500 BC
The simple plough (ard) now used in northern and western Europe.

AFRICA

7500 BC
First pottery manufactured in Sahara and its southern fringes, with characteristic wavy line decoration.

6500 BC
Domestication of native North African cattle in the Saharan region.

6000 BC
First African plant domestication – native millet in the Sahara. Sheep, barley and wheat introduced to Egypt from western Asia.

6000 BC
First use of microliths in southern Africa.

4100 BC
Native sorghum and rice cultivated in Sudan.

4000 BC
Use of sail (Egypt)

WEST ASIA & SOUTH ASIA

8000 BC
Fully domesticated wheat, barley and pulses cultivated in Fertile Crescent (Jericho).

7000 BC
Wheat, barley and pulses cultivated from Anatolia to Pakistan. Goat becomes the main domesticated animal.

7000 BC
Pig domesticated in southern Anatolia.

7000 BC
Foundation of Çatal Hüyük, Anatolia, largest Neolithic site in the Near East, famous for impressive mud-brick architecture, craftsmanship and art.

7000 BC
Independent development of farming in the Indian subcontinent between River Indus and Baluchistan Hills. Barley the principal crop.

7000 BC
First pottery in the Near East.

6500 BC
Earliest known textiles (linen) in the Old World, from Çatal Hüyük (Anatolia).

6200 BC
Copper smelting on a limited scale begins at Çatal Hüyük .

6000 BC
Farming well established in north and central Mesopotamia (Hassuna and Samarra cultures). Painted kiln-fired pottery appears for first time, along with copper and lead smelting.

6000 BC
Pottery production at Mehrgarh, Pakistan.

5500 BC
Earliest known irrigation system in the world at Choga Mami, Mesopotamia.

5500 BC
Halaf culture appears in Mesopotamia, characterised by domed round houses and fine painted pottery.

5000 BC
'Ubaid culture established in Mesopotamia. Irrigation agriculture supports large concentrated populations.

4500 BC
Earliest plough marks found in Mesopotamia.

4500 BC
Agriculture begins just south of Ganges Valley (eg. Mahagara and Chopani–Mando). Native rice cultivated, pottery with corded decoration made.

4500 BC
First use of sail in Mesopotamia.

4400 BC
Domestication of horse on Eurasian Steppes (Dereivka); used for meat and riding.

3650 BC
Earliest vehicle burials in the world (southern Russia); ox-drawn wagons.

3500 BC
Development of first urban civilisation in the world in Sumer, southern Mesopotamia; rise of Uruk.

EAST ASIA & OCEANIA

8000 BC
Sea level rise at the end of the Ice Age creates new islands and more coastline in South-East Asia.

7000 BC
Agriculture begins in New Guinea; root crops such as taro.

6000 BC
Established farming villages in China; millet cultivated, pigs and dogs kept.

6000 BC
First pottery in mainland South-East Asia, also quadrangular adzes and polished slate knives. Agriculture slowly adopted.

5000 BC
Wet-rice farming established at Hemudu near the east coast of China.

5000 BC
Sea level rise culminates in the flooding of coastal settlements in Australia and the detachment of New Guinea and Tasmania.

4000 BC
Jade, imported from 3000 kilometres away, used for ornaments and weapons in China.

3500 BC
Wide-ranging exchange of luxury items in China and evidence for increased social stratification.

NEW WORLD

8000 BC
Archaic stage in North America. Greater variety of food sources – smaller game animals, plants, fish and shellfish. New tool types.

8000 BC
First burials in North America, often with red ochre.

7000 BC
Beginning of crop cultivation in the Tehuacán Valley, Mexico.

7000 BC
Manioc cultivation in the upper Amazon.

7000 BC
Semi-permanent settlements emerge in North America; plant foods play an increasing role in the diet.

6300 BC
Special high-altitude grains domesticated in Peru (Ayacucho); evidence for potato cultivation.

5400 BC
Herding of camelid species in Ayacucho region, Peru.

5000 BC
First cultivation of maize in the Tehuacán Valley, Mexico.

5000 BC
Cultivation of bottle gourd (a species of Mesoamerican origin) in eastern North America; used as a container.

5000 BC
Beginning of limited cultivation in the lower Amazon.

4000 BC
First pottery in the Americas from the Amazon Basin (Guyana); a little later in Colombia and on the Ecuador coast.

3500 BC
Llama used as a domestic pack animal in the highlands and coastal plains of southern Peru. Many other llama products also used.

3500 BC
Cultivation of cotton in southern Peru (Chilca and Ancón). Fishing nets and twilled textiles manufactured.

EUROPE	AFRICA	WEST ASIA & SOUTH ASIA	EAST ASIA & OCEANIA	NEW WORLD

3400 BC
First walled towns in Egypt.

3400 BC
Sumerian trading post at Habuba Kabira, Syria, evidence of long-distance trade.
3250 BC
Earliest writing in the world from Mesopotamia (Tell Brak and Uruk). Pictographic clay tablets used for commercial accounts.

3200 BC
Maize first cultivated in South America.

3200 BC
First wheeled vehicles in Europe: models found in Hungary.
3200 BC
Circles of megalithic standing stones, principally in the British Isles and north-west France.
3200 BC
Introduction of comb-dented pottery to Lappland.

3100 BC
Emergence of Egyptian state; new capital at Memphis.

3100 BC
Developed cuneiform script in Mesopotamia.

3000 BC
Construction of walled citadels in Mediterranean Europe for an increasingly powerful elite; development of a successful metal industry.

3000 BC
First evidence of Egyptian hieroglyphic.

3000 BC
Finds of possible ploughshares in Hangzhou area of China.
3000 BC
First evidence for agriculture in Korea: millet cultivation.
3000 BC
New types of hafted stone tools in Australia and introduction of the dingo – probably from South-East Asia.

2900 BC
Appearance of the Corded Ware pottery assemblages in northern Europe.

2800 BC
Village societies appear in Amazonia, based on horticulture.

2700 BC
Beginning of Egyptian Old Kingdom.
2650 BC
First Egyptian pyramid (stepped Pyramid of Zoser) built at Saqqara.
2600 BC
Pyramid of Maidum, Egypt; the earliest true pyramid.
2530 BC
Construction of Great Pyramid of Khufu at Giza.
2500 BC
Increasing desiccation of Sahara region.

2700 BC
Silk weaving in China.
2700 BC
First Chinese bronze artefacts.

2600 BC
Use of plough in the Indus Valley (Kalibangan).

2600 BC
Large temple mounds and other ritual complexes built on central coast of Peru.

2500 BC
Characteristic bell beakers found in western Europe, often associated with individual burials, which also contain copper daggers.

2500 BC
Development of urban civilisation on the Indus Plain. Substantial towns at Mohenjo-Daro and Harappa surrounded by defensive walls of baked brick. Pictographic script, used mainly on seals.
2500 BC
Earliest known woven cotton cloth found at Mohenjo-Daro.
2500 BC
Earliest syllabic script used in Sumerian literature, from Abu Salabikh, Mesopotamia.
2500 BC
Emergence of city-states in northern Mesopotamia and the Levant, each dominated by large palace complex.
2500 BC
The Royal Graves at Ur, Sumer; spectacular array of imported and locally manufactured objects buried with the dead, occasionally also sacrificed retainers.
2500 BC
Use of four-wheeled war wagon in Mesopotamia.

2500 BC
Early bronze metallurgy in South-East Asia.
2500 BC
Emergence of walled settlements in Longshan China; production of wheel-thrown pottery.
2500 BC
First domesticated animals and pottery on the islands of South-East Asia.

2500 BC
Great improvements in crop yields in South America due to selection and hybridisation of maize leading to population growth and appearance of large permanent villages.
2500 BC
Technological innovations in South America – loom weaving, ground and polished stone tools and simple irrigation works.
2500 BC
Long-distance trade throughout South America, mainly of valuables, some deposited in rich burials.

2300 BC
Beginning of the full European Bronze Age.

2300 BC
City-states of southern Mesopotamia united under Sargon of Agade: first Old World empire.

2300 BC
Earliest ceramics in Mesoamerica.

2150 BC
Collapse of the Egyptian Old Kingdom.
2040 BC
Establishment of Egyptian Middle Kingdom.

2000 BC
Main phase of Stonehenge.
2000 BC
Fortified settlements in east and central Europe point to increasing social and economic pressures.
2000 BC
Formation of states on Minoan Crete, with the construction of palaces at Knossos, Malia, Zakro and Phaistos, each the centre of a town.

2000 BC
Collapse of Indus civilisation. Occupation ceases at Mohenjo-Daro.

2000 BC
Earliest ceramics and large-scale cultivation of maize in the Peruvian Andes.
2000 BC
The Arctic Small Tool tradition, an early Inuit (Eskimo) culture, found from Siberia to Greenland.

1990 BC
New Egyptian capital founded at El-Lisht; Middle Kingdom rulers buried in desert-edge pyramids nearby.

1900 BC
Cretan hieroglyphic writing.

1950 BC
Foundation of Assyrian trading colonies in Anatolia (eg. Kültepe).
1850 BC
Horses used for first time to pull light carts in the western Steppes.

1800 BC
Introduction of the horse to Egypt.
1783 BC
Fall of the Middle Kingdom (Egypt).

1800 BC
New innovations in military weaponry and defences in Near East: two-wheeled war chariot, battering ram and glacis-rampart.
1775 BC
Construction of Palace of Zimri-Lim at Mari, the largest in Mesopotamia at the time, with archive of 17,500 clay tablets.
1760 BC
Babylon temporarily pre-eminent in Mesopotamia.
1700 BC
Bronze body armour used in Near East.
1650 BC
City-states of central Anatolia unified to form the Hittite kingdom, with a strongly fortified capital at Boğazköy.

1800 BC
Emergence of Shang civilisation in north-east China; urban settlements.

1650 BC
Linear A script (Crete and the Cyclades).

EUROPE

1550 BC
Beginning of the Myce naean period in Greece.

1450 BC
Mycenaeans take over Minoan Crete.

1400 BC
Linear B script (mainland and islands of Greece).

1300 BC
Westward spread of urnfield cemeteries.

1150 BC
Collapse of Mycenaean Greece: palaces and towns abandoned.

1085 BC
Fall of the New Kingdom of Egypt.

1000 BC
Hillforts in western Europe.

1000 BC
Iron industry established in the Aegean and Central Europe.

900 BC
End of the Greek dark age and beginning of the Geometric period: upsurge of trade with Near East.

850 BC
First settlement at Rome: cluster of huts on Palatine Hill.

800 BC
Establishment of Celtic culture north and east of the Alps, marking the first phase of the Celtic Iron Age, known as Hallstatt.

800 BC
Rise of the Etruscan city-states in central Italy.

750 BC
First Greek alphabetic inscription.

750 BC
Iron-working spreads to Britain.

750 BC
Earliest Greek colonies set up from the western Mediterranean to the eastern shores of the Black Sea.

700 BC
Beginning of the Archaic period in Greece: cities develop with grand civic buildings such as temples, theatres and gymnasia. Many were the centres of city-states.

690 BC
Etruscan script developed from Greek.

AFRICA

1570 BC
Rise of the powerful New Kingdom of Egypt. Rulers buried in rock-cut tombs in the Valley of the Kings.

1500 BC
Foundation of Deir el-Medina, village of craftsmen responsible for Egyptian royal tombs.

1350 BC
Short-lived Egyptian capital of El-Amarna.

1337 BC
Egyptian king Tutankhamun buried in rich tomb in Valley of the Kings.

1200 BC
Chariot rock-carvings in the Sahara.

1166 BC
Death of Ramesses III, last great pharaoh of Egypt.

c.900 BC
Foundation of Kingdom of Kush.

750 BC
Earliest archaeological evidence for Phoenician settlement at Carthage.

WEST ASIA & SOUTH ASIA

1595 BC
Hittites sack Babylon.

1500 BC
Competition between Egyptians, Hittites and Mitannians for control of Levantine city-states.

1400 BC
Development of first alphabets in Sinai and the Levant.

1400 BC
Development of pastoral nomadism on the Steppes: cattle herded from horseback.

1200 BC
Sophisticated bronze industry established in central Steppes. Its knives, axes and spearheads found in Shang China.

1200 BC
Collapse of Levantine states due to maritime raids.

1200 BC
Collapse of Hittite empire.

1000 BC
Phoenicians become main maritime trading power of Levant. Phoenician alphabet introduced.

1000 BC
Emergence of Kingdom of Israel; capital at Jerusalem.

1000 BC
A full nomadic economy on the Steppes, based on rearing horses, cattle and sheep.

950 BC
Foundation of powerful Assyrian empire, which ultimately unified almost all the Near East.

950 BC
Megiddo becomes important royal fortress and administrative centre in Israel.

900 BC
Establishment of Kingdom of Urartu in Armenia. Powerful and militaristic, it resists Assyrian rule.

880 BC
Capital of Assyria moved to Nimrud; palace of Ashurnasirpal II.

800 BC
Rise of cities and states in Ganges Valley supported by rice farming.

722 BC
Israel absorbed into Assyria.

710 BC
Khorsabad replaces Nimrud as capital of Assyria.

705 BC
Capital of Assyria moves to Nineveh.

700 BC
Permanent settlements on western Steppes, some fortified, belonging to the Scythians, a rich and hierarchical warrior people.

650 BC
First coins in use in Lydia (Asia Minor).

612 BC
Fall of Assyrian empire: Nimrud and Nineveh sacked.

EAST ASIA & OCEANIA

1500 BC
Wet-rice agriculture begins in Korea.

1500 BC
Expansion of the Lapita people (ancestors of the Polynesians) to Melanesia and western Polynesia from their origin in central and eastern Indonesia.

1400 BC
Anyang succeeds Zhengzhou as the last Shang capital of China.

1400 BC
First written inscriptions in China, on oracle bones and bronze ritual vessels.

1027 BC
The Chou dynasty replaces the Shang in China; beginning of Western Chou period.

1000 BC
Long-distance exchange networks in Australia for ornaments and raw materials.

1000 BC
Large villages of round stone houses in south-east Australia.

1000 BC
Lapita settlers well-established on the Tongan and Samoan Islands of western Polynesia.

1000 BC
Bronze technology reaches the Korean peninsula from northern China.

770 BC
The beginning of the Eastern Chou in China; capital moved to Luoyang.

NEW WORLD

1500 BC
First metalworking in Peru.

1200 BC
Beginning of Formative period in Mesoamerica, marked by the first urban civilisations, especially the Olmec.

1000 BC
Beginning of the Adena culture in the eastern woodlands of North America, characterised by rich burials beneath mounds.

1000 BC
Early Horizon in the central and southern Andes – development of large-scale societies.

900 BC
Beginning of the Chavín civilisation (Early Horizon) in the Andes.

900 BC
La Venta replaces San Lorenzo as the principal ceremonial centre of the Mesoamerican Olmec.

800 BC
First writing in the Americas (Zapotec).

800 BC
Introduction of intensive maize cultivation on the Amazon flood plain. Denser, hierarchical societies leave black-midden deposits.

EUROPE	AFRICA	WEST ASIA & SOUTH ASIA	EAST ASIA & OCEANIA	NEW WORLD
600 BC Foundation of the Greek colony Massilia (Marseilles). **600 BC** Trade between the Celts north-west of the Alps and the Greek colonies of the west Mediterranean. Rich wagon burials reflect wealth and power of Celtic elite. **600 BC** Latin script. **600 BC** Rome becomes an urban centre. **600 BC** Central lowlands of northern Europe settled for first time, leaving settlement mounds known as *terpen* or *Wierden*. **600 BC** First Greek coins.	**600 BC** Nubian capital moves to Meroë; soon becomes a major iron-working centre.	**600 BC** Use of elephant in warfare in India.		
		563 BC Birth of Siddhartha Gautama (Sakyamuni), founder of Buddhism, in northern India. **550 BC** Foundation of the vast Achaemenid empire of Persia, stretching from Egypt to the Indus. **550 BC** Immense stone-faced dam, part of an irrigation system built at Marib, capital of south Arabian kingdom of Sabaea. **550 BC** Rise of states around Red Sea and Gulf of Aden based on overland export of frankincense and myrrh from southern Arabia to east Mediterranean. **550 BC** Zoroastrianism becomes official religion of Persia. **521 BC** Darius I (the Great) rules Persian empire.	**550 BC** First significant iron production in China; manufacture of cast iron.	
510 BC Completion of Temple of Jupiter Optimus Maximus on the Capitol, Rome. **500 BC** Rich burial at Vix in Burgundy, France, containing dismantled wagon and Greek and Etruscan imports including the famous Vix crater.	**500 BC** First copper smelting in sub-Saharan Africa (Niger and Mali). **500 BC** Darius I completes canal connecting Nile and Red Sea. **500 BC–AD 200** Period of Nok culture in northern Nigeria.	**500 BC** Persian Royal Road from Sardis to Susa, with posting stations. **500 BC** Tribute reliefs at palace of Persepolis, portraying the diverse people of Achaemenid empire and the tribute they donated. **500 BC** Taxila and Charsadda become important trading cities. Persian, and later Hellenistic influence passes through them to India.	**500 BC** Beginning of coinage in China; miniature bronze spade and knife coins. **500 BC** Wet-rice agriculture in Japan. **500 BC** Production of bronze Dong Son drums in northern Vietnam.	**500 BC** Early hieroglyphic inscription from Monte Albán, Oaxaca.
480 BC Second stage of the European Iron Age, known as La Tène due to its characteristic art style. Burials included chariots and weapons but were less wealthy than those in the Hallstatt period. **480 BC** Emergence of the Classical period of Greek art and architecture; city-states reach their apogee. **478 BC** Foundation of Confederacy of Delos, later transformed into Athenian empire.				
450 BC Athens, the centre of the largest and most powerful of the Greek city-states, reaches its peak. **432 BC** Completion of the Parthenon, the principal temple of Athens.	**450 BC** Earliest known iron metallurgy in sub-Saharan Africa (Jos Plateau, Nigeria).	**460 BC** Parchment replaces clay tablets for Achaemenid administrative documents (written in Aramaic).		
400 BC Celtic settlement of northern Italy. **390 BC** Celts sack Rome. **380 BC** The defences of Rome greatly improved by the building of the massive Servian Wall.	**400 BC** Carthage dominates west Mediterranean; city reorganised on grid-plan and massive new defences constructed.		**403 BC** Warring States period in China; finds of bronze and iron weapons and city defences. **400 BC** Iron-working introduced into Korea.	**400 BC** Florescence of Chavín de Huantar (Peru), a great temple complex with cult objects.
			350 BC The crossbow invented in China.	
	331 BC Foundation of Alexandria.	**334–329 BC** Alexander the Great (of Macedonia) invades Asia Minor, conquers Egypt and Persia and reaches India. Hellenism established in Asia. **322 BC** Chandragupta founds Mauryan empire in India.		**310 BC** Hopewell culture in the eastern woodlands of North America. Burials become more impressive, chiefdoms and a long-distance trade network develop.
300 BC Appearance of Celtic coinage and the formation of incipient Celtic states. **250 BC** All of peninsular Italy controlled by Rome.		**250 BC** Brahmin alphabetic script in India. **250 BC** Mauryan empire in northern and central India reaches its height; capital at Pataliputra. **250 BC** Appearance of earliest Buddhist monuments in India: *stupas*, stone columns and wheels. **250 BC** Buddhism reaches Ceylon; first monuments at Anuradhapura.	**250 BC** First urban sites in mainland South-East Asia with walls or moats, eg. Co Loa, Vietnam.	**300 BC** Typical features of Maya civilisation established (ceremonial centres and writing system).

EUROPE

206 BC
Rome gains control of Spain.

200 BC
The first use of concrete in Rome in the construction of the Porticus Aemilia; a great innovation in the fields of architecture and engineering.

146 BC
Romans destroy the Greek states, but Greek culture still important and Greek artists brought to Rome.

100 BC
Development of *oppida* in western Europe – large fortified settlements with houses, craft workshops and storehouses.

46 BC
Introduction of Julian calendar (replaced by Gregorian calendar from AD 1582).

27 BC
Augustus sole ruler of Roman empire.

AD 1
Roman pottery traded beyond the Roman empire to northern Europe and southern India.

AD 42
Construction of artificial harbour at Portus, near Ostia.

AD 50
Rome the largest city in the world with a population of one million.

AD 79
Pompeii and Herculaneum entombed by the devastating eruption of Mount Vesuvius.

AD 100
The Roman army contains 300,000 soldiers and reaches its peak. Network of forts and legionary fortresses concentrated along the frontiers.

AD 110
Construction of Trajan's Forum in Rome.

AD 117
The Roman empire reaches its greatest extent.

AD 125
Building of Hadrian's Wall, northern Britain, to defend against northern barbarians.

AD 130
The Pantheon in Rome and palace at Tivoli built by emperor Hadrian.

AD 275
A defensive wall built around Rome by Aurelian.

AD 285
Administrative separation of the eastern and western halves of the Roman empire.

AD 300
Large-scale iron production in northern Europe, possibly connected to the rise of small kingdoms and increased centralisation.

AFRICA

146 BC
Roman destruction of Carthage.

100 BC
Camel introduced into Saharan Africa.

46 BC
Foundation of Roman colony of Carthage on site of earlier city.

AD 50
Expansion of Kingdom of Axum (Ethiopia) begins.

AD 162
Construction of Zaghouan aqueduct to supply Carthage.

WEST ASIA & SOUTH ASIA

240 BC
Beginning of the Parthian dynasty in northern Persia.

185 BC
Bactrian conquest of north-west India.

115 BC
Parthians take control of Persia, Mesopotamia and parts of Central Asia.

100 BC
Spectacular rock-cut city of Petra, capital of Nabataean kingdom in Arabia, reaches its apogee.

90 BC
Ctesiphon established as Parthian capital.

53 BC
Parthians halt eastward expansion of Rome.

50 BC
Development of Mahayana Buddhism in central India; first human images of Buddha.

AD 1
Extensive irrigation schemes in Ceylon.

AD 1
Discovery of monsoon winds increases trade between Indian Ocean and Red Sea; Roman pottery and coins found in southern India.

AD 60
Rise of Kushan empire.

AD 100
Gandharan Buddhist art from Peshawar Valley shows strong Hellenistic influence.

AD 116
Roman conquest of Mesopotamia.

AD 132
Failure of Jewish rebellion against Rome leads to *diaspora* (dispersal of Jews) from Judaea.

AD 200
Cities appear for first time on Deccan Plateau, India.

AD 226
Sasanians defeat the Parthians and found Sasanian empire.

AD 300
Decline of south Arabian kingdoms as overland trade replaced by maritime trade. Axum takes their place.

EAST ASIA & OCEANIA

221 BC
Unification of China by the Qin dynasty. Shih Huang-ti, the first Emperor, builds the Great Wall.

210 BC
Emperor Shih Huang-ti interred in a vast mausoleum with terracotta army.

206 BC
Accession of the Han dynasty of China; capital at Chang'an.

200 BC
Probable use of water-buffalo as draught animal in South-East Asia.

200 BC
Marquesas Islands settled by Lapita colonists.

119 BC
Chinese iron industry becomes state monopoly.

108 BC
Chinese take control of North Korea, establishing military posts.

100 BC
Spread of Indian religions and ideas to South-East Asia along maritime trade routes.

50 BC
Chinese silk traded to the Romans.

AD 100
First metallurgy on the islands of South-East Asia.

AD 105
Paper comes into use in China.

AD 150
Buddhism reaches China.

AD 200
Disappearance of Lapita culture in the western Pacific, along with pottery-making skills.

AD 220
Collapse of Han dynasty; China divided into three independent states.

AD 271
Magnetic compass in use in China.

AD 300
Florescence of native states in Korea – Paekche, Shillas and Koguryo.

AD 300
Formation of the Yamato state in Japan; rulers buried in huge keyhole-shaped burial mounds.

AD 300
Spread of wet-rice agriculture to whole of Japan, except Hokkaido.

NEW WORLD

200 BC
Rise of Nazca civilisation on the south Peruvian coast.

200 BC
The Nazca Lines. Geometric and animal motifs scratched out on a large scale on the desert plain of southern Peru.

AD 1
Moche, famous for their gold and pottery, dominate the north Peruvian coast.

AD 1
Basketmaker II period in the North American Southwest. Hamlets with up to eleven circular houses.

AD 1
Emergence of complex cultures on the north Pacific coast; sophisticated craftsmanship in wood and bark.

AD 50
The city of Teotihuacán, central Mexico, laid out on a rectangular grid-plan.

AD 150
Construction of Pyramid of the Sun at Teotihuácan – the largest structure in the Americas before the arrival of the Europeans.

AD 300
Classic period of Maya civilisation begins. Appearance of true cities and city-states.

EUROPE

AD 313
Edict of Milan: Christianity granted toleration in Roman empire.

AD 330
Constantine founds the new eastern capital of the Roman empire at Constantinople.

AD 410
Sack of Rome by Visigoths, leading to the collapse of the western Roman empire.

AD 449
Angles, Saxons and Jutes begin invasion of Britain.

AD 500
Economic and urban decline throughout the areas of the old Greek and Roman worlds.

AD 500
The villages of northern Europe abandoned due to flooding. Landless Germanic people migrate eastwards and settle in eastern England and parts of France.

AD 532
St. Sophia, the great domed cathedral of Constantinople, built by the Emperor Justinian.

AD 542
Bubonic plague in Europe.

AD 610
Accession of east Roman Emperor Heraclius; east Roman empire henceforward known as Byzantine empire.

AD 625
Sutton Hoo boat burial in Suffolk, England, contains grave-goods from Sweden, France and Constantinople.

AD 680
Bulgars invade Balkans.

AD 711
Muslim invasion of Spain.

AD 717
Unsuccessful Muslim attack on Constantinople.

AD 737
Phase I of the Danevirke, the Danish defence which cross the neck of the Jutland peninsula.

AD 787
First recorded Viking raid.

AFRICA

AD 325
Axum destroys Kingdom of Meroe (Kush).

AD 400
First towns in sub-Saharan Africa (Jenne-jeno).

AD 429
Germanic (Vandal) kingdom in North Africa.

AD 500
Arrival of Bantu in southern Africa with iron and domesticated cattle.

AD 600
Ancient Kingdom of Ghana, the first known state in West Africa.

AD 641
Arabs conquer Egypt and spread into North Africa.

AD 750
Great increase in trans-Saharan trade between Muslim North Africa and the West African savanna.

WEST ASIA & SOUTH ASIA

AD 320
Chandragupta I founds Gupta empire in north India.

AD 475
Wall paintings in Buddhist cave-temples at Ajanta.

AD 480
Gupta empire overthrown.

AD 550
New defensive works built by Sasanians including Alexander's Barrier on the Gorgan Plain.

AD 622
Hegira of Mohammed, beginning of the Muslim era.

AD 636–7
Arabs overrun Syria and Iraq.

AD 642
Sasanian empire conquered by the Arabs.

AD 661
Umayyad Caliphate comes to power. Islamic empire covers one third of the Old World.

AD 712
Arabs conquer Sind and Samarkand.

AD 750
Muslims control maritime trade from the Red Sea to China.

AD 750
Umayyads displaced by Abbasid Caliphate. Boundaries of empire stabilised and trade and craftsmanship flourish.

AD 750
Abbasid Caliphate established.

AD 751
Paper making spreads from China to Muslim world.

AD 766
Foundation of Baghdad as Abbasid capital.

EAST ASIA & OCEANIA

AD 304
Hsiung-nu (Huns) invade China.

AD 350
Invention of stirrup in China; metal-reinforced wooden stirrups at Wanbaoting.

AD 400
Buddhist cave-temples constructed along the Silk Road. Buddhism becomes established in China.

AD 400
Shilla and Koguryo royal tombs in Korea.

AD 427
Tomb of Yamato Emperor Nintoku, the largest keyhole tomb in Japan.

AD 550
Buddhism arrives in Japan from Korea. Temples replace mound tombs.

AD 589
China temporarily unified by the Sui dynasty.

AD 610
Canals built in China linking the Yangtze River to Chang'an and Luoyang, enabling the transport of grain to the capitals.

AD 618
Tang dynasty unifies China. The empire based on Chang'an, the world's largest city (one million inhabitants).

AD 645
Buddhism reaches Tibet (first temple founded 651).

AD 650
All major island groups of Polynesia now settled except New Zealand.

AD 668
The Shilla state controls Korea.

AD 710
Beginning of the Nara period in Japan. A centralised state based on the Chinese system of administration.

AD 784
Japanese capital moves from Nara to Kyoto, marking the beginning of the Heian period.

NEW WORLD

AD 400
Beginning of Marajoara culture on Marajó Island in the mouth of the Amazon, one of the earliest of the powerful Amazonian chiefdoms.

AD 450
Teotihuacán influence found in Maya territory over 100 kilometres away: trading posts and cities set out in Teotihuacán style (eg. Kaminaljuyú).

AD 500
Teotihuacán the sixth largest city in the world, with a population of c.200,000; a major pilgrimage centre.

AD 500
Beginning of the Middle Horizon in the central and southern Andes, dominated by two vast, authoritarian empires – Tiahuanaco and Huari.

AD 500
Basketmaker III period in the North American Southwest. Villages of up to 50 semi-sunken houses.

AD 600
City of Tiahuanaco, Bolivia, the highest ancient city in the Andes, population c.35,000.

AD 700
Domination of North American Southeast by Hohokam, Mogollon and Anasazi cultures. Production of high quality ceramics.

AD 700
Temple-mounds of the Mississippi region, sometimes forming towns, eg. Cahokia, the earliest town in North America.

AD 700
Rebuilding of Maya city of Tikal, with five temple pyramids.

AD 700
Northern coast of Peru dominated by the Chimú state; capital at Chan Chan.

AD 750
Sacred Cenote at Chichén Itzá, Yucatán, used for ritual offerings. Continued in use for 1000 years.

EUROPE	AFRICA	WEST ASIA & SOUTH ASIA	EAST ASIA & OCEANIA	NEW WORLD

AD 800
Trading emporia develop in north-west Europe.

AD 800
Romanesque style of architecture develops in Frankish Europe.

AD 800
Charlemagne crowned Holy Roman Emperor.

AD 862
Novgorod founded by Rurik the Viking.

AD 863
Creation of Cyrillic alphabet.

AD 882
The Swedish Vikings set up a state in Russia, centred on Kiev.

AD 972
Beginning of Hungarian state under Duke Geisa.

AD 983
Beginning of German eastward expansion.

AD 1000
Sacrificial sites in Lappland containing metal items (eg. crosses and birds) from Russia and north-west England.

AD 1016–1035
Empire of Cnut includes England, Denmark, Norway.

AD 1066
The Norman conquest of England.

AD 1088
Construction of Cluny III, the church of Cluny Abbey, Burgundy.

AD 1100
Benign climatic conditions in Europe lead to new villages being set up on previously unworked land. Population increases.

AD 1100
First universities in Christian Europe.

AD 1150
Gothic architecture develops in the Ile de France and spreads to the rest of Europe.

AD 1150
Paper-making spreads from Muslim world.

AD 1236–41
Mongols invade Russia, Poland, Hungary, Bohemia.

AFRICA

AD 900
Arab merchants settle on East African coast (Manda and Kilwa).

AD 969
Fatimids seize Egypt and found Cairo.

AD 1067
Almoravids destroy Kingdom of Ghana.

AD 1200
Rock-hewn churches of Ethiopia (Lalibela and Tigre region).

AD 1200
Rise of Mali in West Africa.

AD 1200
Emergence of Hausa city states (Nigeria).

AD 1228
Hafsid dynasty established at Tunis.

AD 1250
Stone enclosures in south-east Africa, including the elliptical building at Great Zimbabwe.

AD 1250
Emergence of empire of Benin (Nigeria).

WEST ASIA & SOUTH ASIA

AD 836
Samarra, stretching 40 kilometres along the River Tigris, becomes new Abbasid capital.

AD 850
Great mosque of al-Mutawakkil, the largest mosque known in Islam, built in Samarra.

AD 892
Abbasids revert to Baghdad as capital.

AD 900
Cholas the dominant power in southern India: much building of Hindu temples and emergence of God-King cult.

AD 1096
First Crusade: Franks invade Anatolia and Syria and found Crusader states.

AD 1100
Polonnaruwa replaces Anuradhapura as capital of Ceylon.

AD 1175
Foundation of first Muslim empire in India.

AD 1206
Sultanate of Delhi founded.

EAST ASIA & OCEANIA

AD 800
Construction of Buddhist temple at Borobudur, Java.

AD 800
Kingdoms emerge in South-East Asia, characterised by monumental architecture, eg. the Khmer state centred on Angkor.

AD 850
Settlement of New Zealand by tropical Polynesian colonists – the ancestors of the Maori.

AD 868
The Diamond Sutra, the world's first printed book (Dunhuang, western China).

AD 907
End of Tang empire.

AD 935
State of Koryo founded in Korea.

AD 979
Sung Dynasty takes power in China, capital at Luoyang. Overseas trade important.

AD 1000
Carving and erection of stone statues begins on Easter Island.

AD 1044
Creation of first Burmese state at Pagan.

AD 1050
Printing with clay moveable type invented in China.

AD 1126
Qin overrun north China; Sung rule restricted to south.

AD 1150
Construction of Angkor Wat, royal sepulchre and shrine, at the city of Angkor, Cambodia.

AD 1161
Chinese invention of gunpowder.

AD 1170
Apogee of Srivijaya Kingdom on Java.

AD 1180
Angkor empire at greatest extent.

AD 1185
Zen Buddhist order founded in Japan.

AD 1195
Feudal system of government replaces centralised administration in Japan. Beginning of the Kamakura Shogunate.

AD 1200
Construction of the Bayon, the temple inside Angkor Thom.

AD 1200
Rise of the Polynesian chiefdoms.

AD 1206
Mongols under Genghis Khan begin conquest of Asia.

AD 1220
Emergence of first Thai kingdom.

AD 1250
Burial of Roy Mata, a powerful Melanesian ruler, on the island of Retoka, with 40 sacrificial victims.

NEW WORLD

AD 800
First use of bow and arrow in the Mississippi Valley, making game-hunting more efficient.

AD 800
Beginning of Dorset culture in Greenland and north-east Canada, an Inuit (Eskimo) group depending substantially on sea-ice hunting.

AD 900
Hohokam of the American Southwest build irrigation canals up to 16 kilometres long. Influence from Mexico shown through imports and building style.

AD 900
A hiatus in Maya civilisation, first in the southern lowlands and then in the north.

AD 950
The Toltecs rise to power in central Mexico, and found their capital, Tula.

AD 1000
Shortlived Viking settlements on coasts of Labrador and Newfoundland.

AD 1000
Moulds used in Central and North America for pottery manufacture.

AD 1050
Anasazi settlements of the North American Southwest move to well defended positions, eg. Pueblo Bonito in Chaco Canyon.

AD 1100
Thule culture of Arctic America, its economy based on whaling, expands eastwards dominating the area from Siberia to Greenland.

AD 1150
Anasazi dominate the North American Southwest, forming a general Pueblo culture; most famous sites on Mesa Verde.

AD 1170
Fall of the Toltecs in central Mexico. Internecine warfare ensues.

AD 1250
The Southern Cult, covering much of south-eastern North America reaches its height; marked by special motifs on funerary artefacts.

EUROPE	AFRICA	WEST ASIA & SOUTH ASIA	EAST ASIA & OCEANIA	NEW WORLD

AD 1258
Mongols sack Baghdad; end of Abbasid Caliphate.

AD 1251
Tripitaka Koreana: complete Buddhist canon carved of woodblocks.

AD 1261
Greek empire restored in Constantinople.

AD 1275
Marco Polo reaches China.

AD 1290
Spectacles invented in Italy.

AD 1299
Ottoman Turks begin expansion in Anatolia.

AD 1300
European climate deteriorates. Some newly-settled land becomes unviable for farming.

AD 1309
Papacy moves from Rome to Avignon.

AD 1300
New Zealand Maoris hunt the giant moa bird and other fauna to extinction; reliance on agriculture in North Island.

AD 1300
Revival of Maya civilisation. Capital at Mayapán.

AD 1300
Inca tribe base themselves in a valley of the Peruvian Andes; foundation of capital at Cuzco.

c.AD 1341
Black Death starts in Asia.

AD 1345
Arrival of Aztecs in central Mexico; foundation of capital Tenochtitlán on the site of Mexico City.

AD 1348
Black Death from Asia ravages Europe.

AD 1350
Foundation of the spectacular temple-city Vijayanagara, southern India: a royal Hindu capital.

AD 1350
Classic Maori period begins on North Island, New Zealand; earthwork fortifications (*pa*).

AD 1350
Collapse of Pueblo cultures of the North American Southwest caused by warfare or climatic decline.

AD 1368
Establishment of the Ming dynasty in China.

AD 1380
Timur (Tamerlane) begins conquests in Central Asia.

AD 1397
Earliest surviving books printed with moveable type in Korea.

AD 1398
Timur invades India and sacks Delhi.

AD 1400
Peking, the Ming capital, the largest city in the world.

AD 1400
Manufacture of bronze heads in the Kingdom of Benin, southern Nigeria.

AD 1400
Collapse of the Khmer kingdom and many of its contemporaries in South-East Asia.

AD 1405
Beginning of Ming maritime expeditions, reaching the east coast of Africa, where Ming porcelain traded.

AD 1415
Portuguese capture Ceuta; beginning of Portugal's African empire.

AD 1428
Aztec state very powerful; militarism spurred by need for human sacrificial victims; defeat of neighbouring state of Atzcapatzalco.

AD 1434
Portuguese explore south of Cape Bojador.

AD 1438
The Inca state becomes a vast, centralised empire.

AD 1455
Gutenberg prints first book in Europe. using moveable type.

AD 1450
Apogee of Songhay empire; university at Timbuktu.

AD 1450
Depopulation and abandonment of towns in the Middle Mississippi area, possibly owing to disease.

AD 1453
The Byzantine empire falls to the Ottoman Turks.

AD 1476
Conquest of the Chimú by the Incas.

AD 1478–1480
Ivan III, first Russian tsar, subdues Novgorod and throws off Mongol yoke.

AD 1492
Fall of Granada; Arabs and Jews expelled from Spain.

AD 1492
Spanish begin conquest of North African coast.

AD 1492
Columbus navigates to the Caribbean and discovers New World.

AD 1493
Inca empire reaches its height, extending 3500 kilometres north-south.

AD 1493
First Spanish settlement in New World, at Hispaniola.

AD 1493
Treaty of Tordesillas divides New World between Portugal and Spain.

AD 1498
The discovery of world sea routes (Columbus and Vasco da Gama) sets the stage for integrated world trade.

AD 1500
Europeans build forts on the coasts of West and East Africa to exploit natural resources.

AD 1500
Vijayanagara empire reaches its peak: now controlling almost all southern India.

AD 1500
Portuguese lay claim to Brazil.

AD 1500
Shah Ismail founds Safavid dynasty in Persia.

AD 1505
Portuguese establish trading posts in East Africa.

AD 1509
Watch invented by Peter Henle (Nuremberg).

AD 1511
Portuguese seize control of Malacca.

AD 1516–17
Ottomans overrun Syria, Egypt and Arabia.

AD 1519
Magellan crosses Pacific.

AD 1519
Spaniards under Hernán Cortez arrive in central Mexico. Aztecs overthrown in two years.

AD 1520
Beginning of slave trade from West Africa to New World.

AD 1525
Introduction of potato from South America.

AD 1526
Babur conquers Kingdom of Delhi and founds Mughal dynasty.

AD 1532
Inca empire destroyed by the Spaniards under Francisco Pizarro.

AD 1539
Printing reaches Mexico.

AD 1542
Foundation of Spanish South American capitals at Lima, Santa Fé de Bogotá and Santiago.

AD 1545
Discovery of silver mines in Peru and Mexico.

AD 1546
Destruction of Mali empire by Songhay

EUROPE

AD 1581
Yemak begins Russian conquest of Siberia.

AD 1588
Shipwrecks of Spanish Armada around coasts of Britain and Ireland.

AD 1602
Formation of Dutch East India Company.

AD 1609
Telescope invented (Holland).

AD 1620
First weekly newspapers in Europe (Amsterdam).

AD 1703
Foundation of St Petersburg, capital of Russian empire.

AD 1712
Invention of the atmospheric steam-engine by Thomas Newcomen.

AD 1779
Construction of the first iron bridge in the world at Ironbridge on the River Severn.

AD 1836
Needle-gun invented (Prussia), making breech-loading possible.

AD 1838
First electric telegraph (Britain).

AD 1840
First postage stamp (Britain).

AD 1850
Rapid expansion of the European railway network, mainly used for transporting freight.

AD 1856
Bessemer process permits mass-production of steel.

AFRICA

AD 1550
Portuguese traders penetrate Zambezi Valley.

AD 1591
Moroccans destroy Songhay empire.

AD 1652
Foundation of Cape Colony by Dutch.

AD 1659
French found trading station on Senegal coast.

AD 1700
Rise of Asante (Gold Coast).

AD 1807
Slave trade abolished within British empire.

AD 1869
Suez Canal opens.

WEST ASIA & SOUTH ASIA

AD 1550
The Ottoman empire grows to include Asia Minor, Egypt, Levant and south-east Europe.

AD 1565
Fall of Vijayanagara, through Mughal invasions from the north.

AD 1570
Foundation of Fatehpur Sikri as Mughal capital.

AD 1598
Safavids of Persia move their capital to Isfahan.

AD 1600
The Ottoman, Mughal and Safavid empires at their height.

AD 1616
Construction of the magnificent Masjid-i Shah mosque in Isfahan; main dome covered with decorated glazed tiles.

AD 1632
Construction of the Taj Mahal at Agra, the marble covered mausoleum of Mumtaz-i Mahal.

AD 1638
Delhi replaces Agra as Mughal capital; new constructions – Red Fort and Friday Mosque.

AD 1690
Calcutta founded by English.

AD 1760
British win control of eastern India.

AD 1818
British defeat Marathas becoming effective rulers of India.

AD 1853
First railway and telegraph lines in India.

EAST ASIA & OCEANIA

AD 1557
Portuguese established in Macao; first European colony in China.

AD 1571
Spanish conquer Philippines.

AD 1603
Beginning of Tokugawa Shogunate in Japan.

AD 1619
Foundation of Batavia; beginning of Dutch colonial empire in East Indies.

AD 1620
Burial of the Emperor Wanli near Peking, the most spectacular Ming tomb.

AD 1629
First Europeans on Australian soil.

AD 1644
Manchus found Ch'ing dynasty in China.

AD 1645
Tasman circumnavigates Australia and discovers New Zealand.

AD 1649
Russians reach Pacific.

AD 1650
Classic Maori period begins on South Island, New Zealand.

AD 1697
Chinese occupy Outer Mongolia.

AD 1788
Foundation of British penal colony at Sydney Cove, Australia.

AD 1863
France establishes protectorate in Indo-China.

AD 1868
End of Tokugawa Shogunate in Japan. Beginning of modernisation.

NEW WORLD

AD 1560
Portuguese begin sugar cultivation in Brazil.

AD 1607
First permanent English settlement in America (Jamestown, Virginia).

AD 1608
French colonists found Quebec.

AD 1625
Dutch colonists found New Amsterdam (New York).

AD 1692
Port Royal, a colonial harbour town in Jamaica, destroyed by an earthquake.

AD 1728
Bering begins Russian reconnaisance of Alaska.

AD 1775–1776
American Revolution and Declaration of Independence.

AD 1834
Invention of first mechanical reaper.

AD 1859
First oil well drilled, Pennsylvania.

AD 1861–1865
American Civil War, first modern war to extensively use telegraph, railways.

AD 1869
First trans-continental railway completed.

21

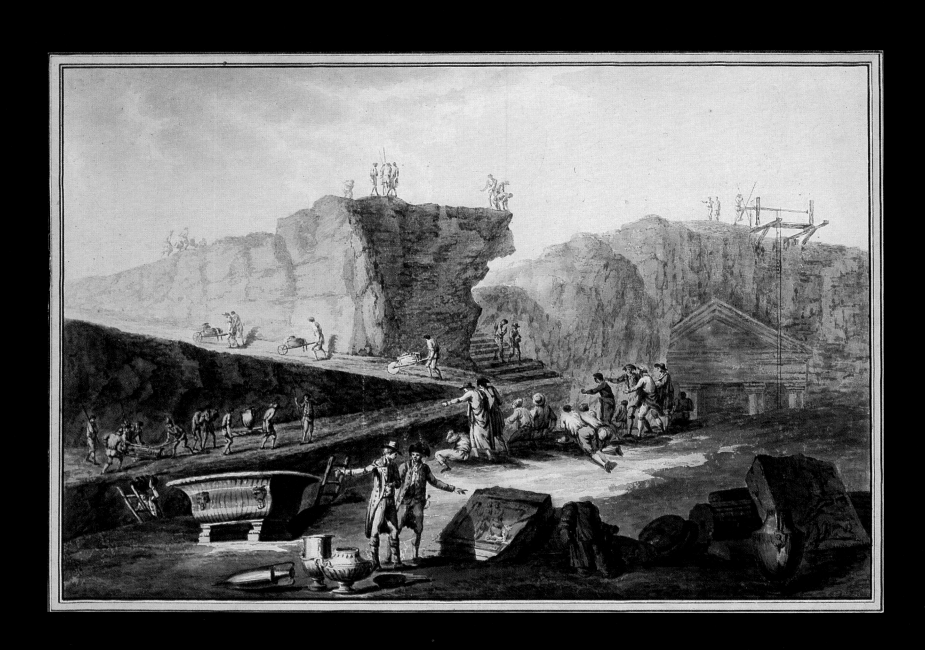

ONE
ARCHAEOLOGY: UNDERSTANDING THE PAST

CURIOSITY ABOUT THE ORIGINS and development of human society is a distinctive feature of our species which can be traced back thousands of years. As early as the 6th century BC the Babylonian princess Ennigaldi-Nanna had a collection of antiquities in a room of her palace at Ur. For most of the human past archaeology is the only source of information, as written records are a comparatively recent innovation.

Our knowledge of the vast period stretching back from the present day to the emergence of the first tool-making hominids some 2.5 million years ago is based predominantly on the remains of settlements, burials and artefacts. It is the study of these traces that is the domain of archaeology. From it we learn of the gradual but increasing mastery of the environment, beginning with the first tools, the building of shelters and the knowledge of fire – early steps along a path of successive innovations such as pottery and metallurgy which has led to the nuclear power and microchip technologies of the present day. We learn also of the development of the hunting and gathering way of life, of farming, and of the increasing social complexity which accompanied these changes, eventually leading to the formation of states and empires. The archaeological record of more recent periods is enriched by the survival of lavishly furnished tombs, temples and palaces which are among the greatest human cultural and artistic achievements. Yet archaeology is not only the study of the grandiose and spectacular, but documents the everyday circumstances of ordinary people, their food and clothing, their appearance and customs, their tools and utensils, their dwellings and burial places.

Archaeology's unique perspective ensures its importance in the study even of recent periods, alongside history, covering major aspects of life on which historical records may be silent. The development during the last 50 years of post-mediaeval and industrial archaeology has extended its scope virtually down to the present day. Within the same 50 years the increasing application of new techniques for the analysis of ancient materials has given rise to a more professional and scientific archaeology, far removed from the treasure-hunting of previous centuries. New methods for dating remains have shown for the first time the true age of many sites and artefacts, and the extreme antiquity of the crude stone tools which are the earliest evidence of human culture. But though scientific techniques have transformed archaeology, the aim of the subject remains what it always was – the study of human culture, society and economy in all its many forms from the very earliest times.

Picture of the excavations at Pompeii showing the discovery of the Temple of Isis.
1793-4, Jacob Phillipp Hackert.

Dating the past

The world we live in today is surrounded by the remains of past ages, from the simple stone tools of the first humans to industrial remains of modern times. It is the task of the archaeologist to interpret these traces, constructing an account of human social, cultural and economic development. Dating methods and the establishment of a reliable chronology are crucial to the successful performance of that task. It is only within the last 50 years that scientific methods have become available which allow the true antiquity of prehistoric sites and artefacts to be determined with confidence.

In the 18th century it was widely believed in western Europe that the world had been created by divine ordinance in 4004 BC. This date was based on the evidence of the Bible, and it was only after considerable debate that the existence of geological and archaeological remains more than 6000 years old was accepted. The discovery of early stone tools and bones of extinct mammals buried in the gravel terraces of European rivers was one of the important discoveries which forced this change of opinion.

Various methods were used to establish the relative date of different types of artefacts. A landmark in this respect was the development of the so-called Three Age system, according to which stone tools were replaced by bronze and then iron tools. A system of successive stone, bronze and iron ages had in fact already been suggested by earlier Chinese and Roman writers, and it is still a major feature of prehistoric chronology. The use of stratigraphy (a chronological sequence formed by accumulated deposits) was also important from the 19th century on. Sites with a deep accumulation of layers – such as tell sites or caves – could sometimes show a long succession of cultural and technological change extending over many centuries or millennia. But it was still only possible to give an absolute date where historical records or inscriptions were available, or where a site or layer contained imports from a historical civilisation of known age.

Scientific dating methods have been developed only in the present century. The first of these techniques – dendrochronology and varves – took advantage of natural rhythmic processes. Dendrochronology (tree-ring dating) relied on the pattern of annually produced rings which can be seen even in ancient pieces of wood. Dating by varves is a similar method, using the annual layers of sediment laid down on lake-beds at the edge of glaciers. It was varves that first allowed the melting of the ice sheets at the end of the last Ice Age to be dated with precision.

The greatest revolution in dating, however, has taken place within the last 50 years, and is a by-product of research in nuclear physics. The principal methods are radiocarbon dating, potassium–argon dating and thermoluminescence dating. Radiocarbon dating, which measures the steady decay of radioactive substances, was developed in the late 1940s, and its impact on prehistoric archaeology was profound. The method allows the dating of a variety of materials which are fairly common on archaeological sites, such as bone, shell, charcoal and plant remains, and can be applied anywhere in the world. However, the method is limited in time, and can only be applied to remains which are less than 40,000 years old. For earlier periods, there is the potassium–argon method, another radioactive dating method which is, however, restricted to volcanic materials. In regions such as East Africa where suitable volcanic rocks are found, potassium–argon dating has proved an invaluable tool, however, and it was this method that first demonstrated the true age of the early stone tools and hominid remains from the Olduvai Gorge (page 54).

All these methods have provided the framework for a truly world-wide archaeology. By constructing a detailed chronology which stretches from the present day back to the earliest stone tools some 2.5 million years ago, archaeologists have been able to chart the gathering pace of human achievement.

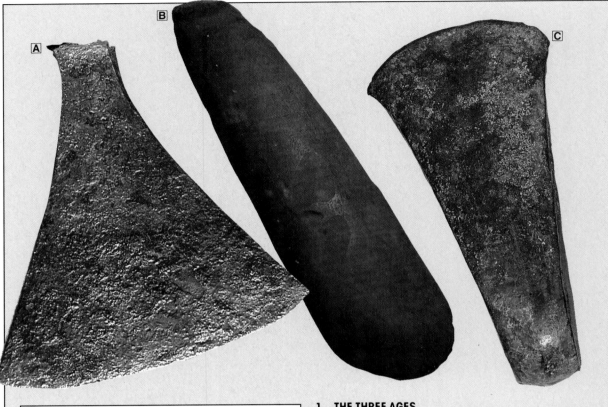

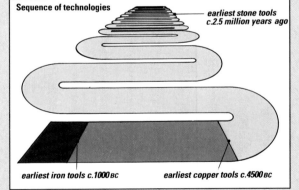

1 THE THREE AGES

The study of human technology from the earliest times to the present day demonstrates the continual refinement of tools and materials, and the development of increasingly sophisticated manufacturing methods. Technological features have long been recognised as a means of dating archaeological remains. In about 100 BC the Chinese scholar Yuan Kang wrote of successive ages of stone, jade, bronze and iron, and in the century that followed the Roman writer Lucretius described the use first of stone, then of bronze and finally of iron for weapons. With modifications – notably the subdivision of the Stone Age into the Palaeolithic, Mesolithic and Neolithic periods – this sequence has remained an important feature of archaeological chronology over the centuries.

A *Viking carpenter's axe from Coppergate, York. 10th century AD, iron, length 20cm.* B *Axe from Blaye, France. 3000 BC, polished stone, length c.25cm.* C *Shaft-hole axe from Kythnos, Greece. Mid-3rd millennium BC, arsenical bronze, length 15.6cm.*

2 TECHNOLOGY AND STYLE

The Three Age system, the division into stone, bronze and iron ages, was refined by the careful analysis of stylistic features. It was possible to develop a chronology by considering the ways in which a particular type of tool or weapon developed, over a given time period, often starting with a relatively crude form and undergoing progressive modification to produce a more efficient or effective design. Stylistic schemes of a similar kind were used to arrange pottery types in a chronological sequence. This method can be applied not only to tools, weapons and pottery, but also to sculpture and works of art.

Below *The changing form of the Chinese Ko halberd (ge), particularly the elaborations in the haft and rear end, demonstrates a time sequence from the Shang dynasty to the Warring States period (c.1400–200 BC).*

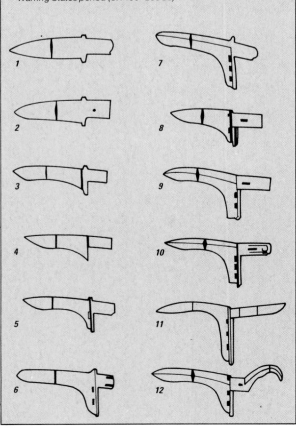

3 HISTORICAL RECORDS

Writing was first invented in Mesopotamia around 3200 BC, and soon began to be used for historical records such as lists of kings. Finds of clay tablets and monumental inscriptions are useful in dating archaeological sites and layers. Where preservation is particularly good, remains of letters or accounts written on wood, cloth, parchment or paper may survive, and these sometimes contain references to historical events or individuals which allow them to be dated precisely. Writing spread only slowly throughout the rest of the world, however, and it is often necessary to use scientific methods such as radiocarbon dating to establish the age of particular remains.

A *List of kings from Sumer and Akkad, cuneiform. c.1817 BC, clay, height 20cm.* B *Tablets from the Roman garrison at Vindolanda, addressed to Lucius decurion saying 'A friend sent me 50 oysters from Cordonovi...' AD 105–115, width 9cm.*

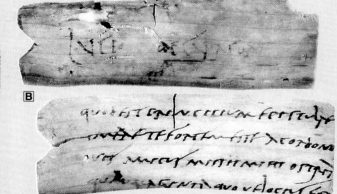

4 THERMOLUMINESCENCE

One of the most common finds on archaeological sites from the Neolithic period to the present day is pottery and other objects of fired clay. Thermoluminescence provides a means of dating these materials, and can also be applied to burned flints. The method relies on the effect of low-level radioactivity within the pottery. Over a period of time, this radioactivity frees electrons which, however, remain trapped within the clay until it is heated, when they are released as light. Reheating the object in the laboratory and measuring the amount of light emitted allows the time that has elapsed since it was originally fired to be determined. The method has been used with great success to distinguish works of art such as Chinese pottery horses of the Tang period from recent fakes.
Right *Pottery horse from China, Tang dynasty (AD618–906). The antiquity of this figurine was confirmed by thermoluminescence.*

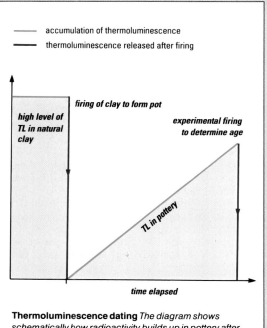

accumulation of thermoluminescence
thermoluminescence released after firing

high level of TL in natural clay

firing of clay to form pot

experimental firing to determine age

TL in pottery

time elapsed

Thermoluminescence dating *The diagram shows schematically how radioactivity builds up in pottery after firing.*

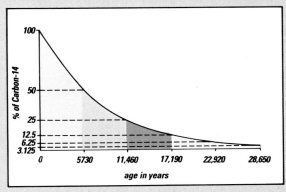

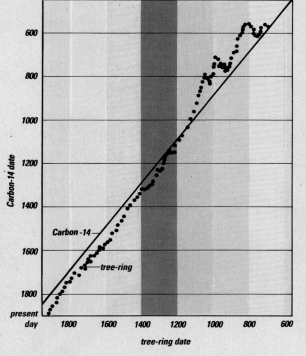

5 RADIOCARBON DATING

Radiocarbon dating is based on the radioactive decay of the carbon isotope, Carbon-14, which is produced by cosmic rays in the atmosphere. Carbon-14 is absorbed by all living things, but on the death of an organism it begins to decay at a gradual but steady rate, halving every 5730 years. Measurement of the amount of Carbon-14 remaining indicates the time that has elapsed since the organism died – be it the bone of an animal killed for its meat, charcoal from wood burned on a hearth, or timber used in the construction of a building. Early results of the method, which was introduced in the late 1940s, were inaccurate owing to past fluctuations in cosmic ray activity. A calibration procedure is now applied, using reliable dendrochronological dates from the Californian Bristlecone pine and Irish bog oaks to correct the radiocarbon dates.
Above *Californian Bristlecone pine, the world's oldest living tree.*

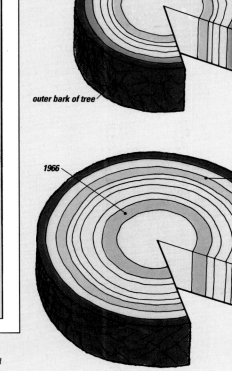

1975   1971

outer bark of tree

1966   1971

cross-section of tree-trunks showing variations in width of annual growth rings caused by fluctuations in climate.

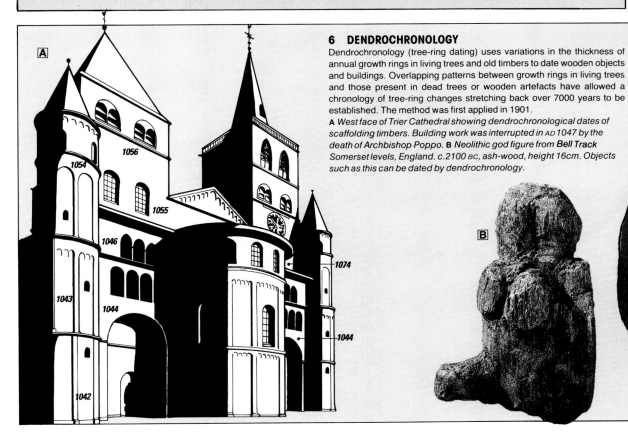

[A]

1056
1054
1055
1046
1043   1044
1042
1074
1044

6 DENDROCHRONOLOGY

Dendrochronology (tree-ring dating) uses variations in the thickness of annual growth rings in living trees and old timbers to date wooden objects and buildings. Overlapping patterns between growth rings in living trees and those present in dead trees or wooden artefacts have allowed a chronology of tree-ring changes stretching back over 7000 years to be established. The method was first applied in 1901.
A *West face of Trier Cathedral showing dendrochronological dates of scaffolding timbers. Building work was interrupted in AD 1047 by the death of Archbishop Poppo.* **B** *Neolithic god figure from Bell Track Somerset levels, England. c.2100 BC, ash-wood, height 16cm. Objects such as this can be dated by dendrochronology.*

[B]

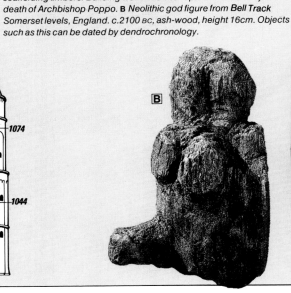

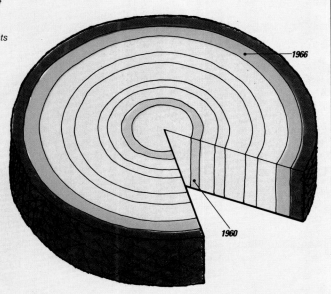

1966

1960

Survival from the past

Archaeology is the study of the material traces of our past; the archaeologist's ability to learn about all aspects of the past is made much easier if all the remains have survived intact. However, this is exceptional. In the huge majority of sites, only a minute fraction survives of what originally existed. So much material has been lost through normal decomposition, the ravages of nature and the wilful or accidental damage done by man, that great importance is attached to sites with excellent conditions of preservation.

Owing to their different physical and chemical compositions, the materials that people leave behind have widely differing chances of being preserved. A number of factors play a part: the climate, the kind of soil in which they are deposited, how quickly they become buried, and whether they undergo any disturbance before or after burial. The age of a site is also a critical factor. In recent years a number of experiments have assessed how various types of material survive burial. This enables archaeologists to anticipate the degree of decay in the artefacts they are likely to encounter.

At most sites only durable inorganic objects survive, above all, the various kinds of stone used for tools or construction. Fired clay, such as pottery, is also hard-wearing, though an acid soil can damage its surface and ploughing can crumble it to fragments. Some metals, such as gold, silver and lead, also survive well, whereas copper and low-quality bronze are attacked by acid soils and can become so oxidised that only a green deposit or stain is left. Iron rusts even more easily and may simply become a discolouration in the soil. Since even metals decay in this way, it is not surprising that perishable materials such as textiles are much more rarely preserved. Good survival of organic materials is limited to cases involving extremes of moisture: that is, arid, frozen or waterlogged conditions. The nature of the soil is also important. Chalk, for example, preserves bone well, whereas acid soils destroy bone and wood within a few years, but leave telltale discolourations where postholes or hut-foundations once existed. Caves, if undisturbed by floods or trampling feet, can preserve not only bones but even fragile traces like footprints and plant fibres.

Freak events such as violent storms or volcanic eruptions may provide extraordinarily good preservation. The coastal Neolithic village of Skara Brae on the Orkneys (*page 108*) was completely submerged and preserved by sand during a violent storm. The eruption of Vesuvius on the Italian coast buried the towns of Pompeii and Herculaneum with volcanic ash, preserving them at the moment of their destruction (*page 176*).

Archaeologists purposely seek sites, either to rescue them in the face of imminent destruction or to improve their own knowledge of particular cultures or settlement patterns. The simplest way to find sites is to talk to locals, or to consult maps, place-names or historical texts. Some sites may be perfectly visible (walls, burial mounds and so on), though vegetation may hide them or affect their accessibility. Many sites, however, survive only as faint surface traces, which need to be sought out. This can be done by systematic site-survey within a given area; prior study of geological maps and geomorphology can help in several ways. From these studies it is possible to assess the factors influencing a site's location, for example where the best soils for ancient cultivation are as well as where circumstances are most conducive to the preservation and exposure of sites.

Surface fieldwork is often supplemented (and often preceded) by survey from the air. Photographs from satellites are also proving useful in some areas: for example, false-colour satellite imagery recently found an extensive network of Maya fields and settlements in Yucatán. High-altitude radar mapping from aircraft has also begun to be applied to the discovery of sites in the New World, though its great expense limits its potential.

In the past, many sites were destroyed through ignorance of their archaeological value (*see illustration right*): for example, farmers removed monuments that obstructed their work, and builders quarried ancient structures for stone. Today, wilful damage is largely restricted to the work of clandestine diggers, though much is still destroyed accidentally in the course of ploughing, quarrying, construction, and so forth. Conversely, these same activities, all of which disturb the ground surface, have also led to the discovery of many previously unknown sites. Nature, too, can sometimes expose sites, through earthquake, wind action or erosion. It was erosion that revealed the terraces of Africa's Rift Valley with their invaluable evidence of the very earliest stages of human evolution (*page 54*).

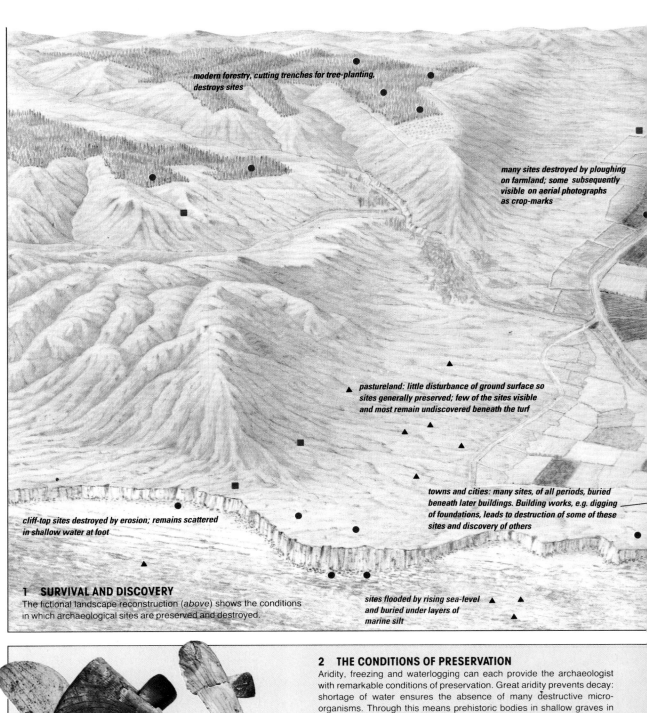

modern forestry, cutting trenches for tree-planting, destroys sites

many sites destroyed by ploughing on farmland; some subsequently visible on aerial photographs as crop-marks

pastureland: little disturbance of ground surface so sites generally preserved; few of the sites visible and most remain undiscovered beneath the turf

towns and cities: many sites, of all periods, buried beneath later buildings. Building works, e.g. digging of foundations, leads to destruction of some of these sites and discovery of others

cliff-top sites destroyed by erosion; remains scattered in shallow water at foot

sites flooded by rising sea-level and buried under layers of marine silt

1 SURVIVAL AND DISCOVERY
The fictional landscape reconstruction (*above*) shows the conditions in which archaeological sites are preserved and destroyed.

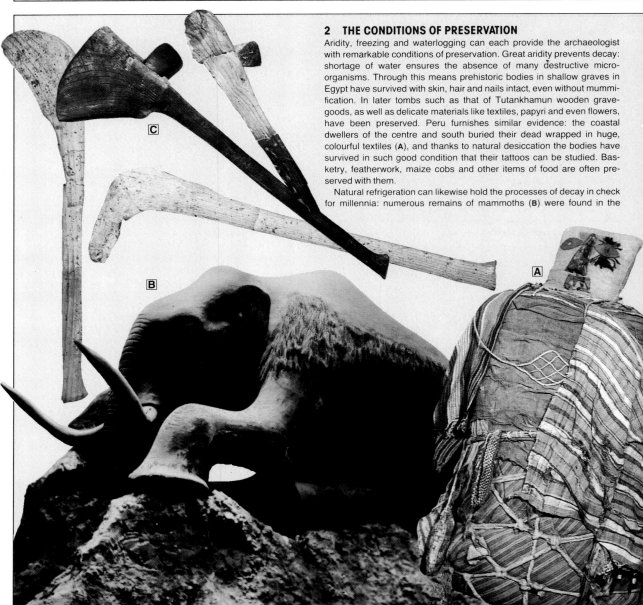

2 THE CONDITIONS OF PRESERVATION
Aridity, freezing and waterlogging can each provide the archaeologist with remarkable conditions of preservation. Great aridity prevents decay: shortage of water ensures the absence of many destructive micro-organisms. Through this means prehistoric bodies in shallow graves in Egypt have survived with skin, hair and nails intact, even without mummification. In later tombs such as that of Tutankhamun wooden grave-goods, as well as delicate materials like textiles, papyri and even flowers, have been preserved. Peru furnishes similar evidence: the coastal dwellers of the centre and south buried their dead wrapped in huge, colourful textiles (**A**), and thanks to natural desiccation the bodies have survived in such good condition that their tattoos can be studied. Basketry, featherwork, maize cobs and other items of food are often preserved with them.

Natural refrigeration can likewise hold the processes of decay in check for millennia: numerous remains of mammoths (**B**) were found in the

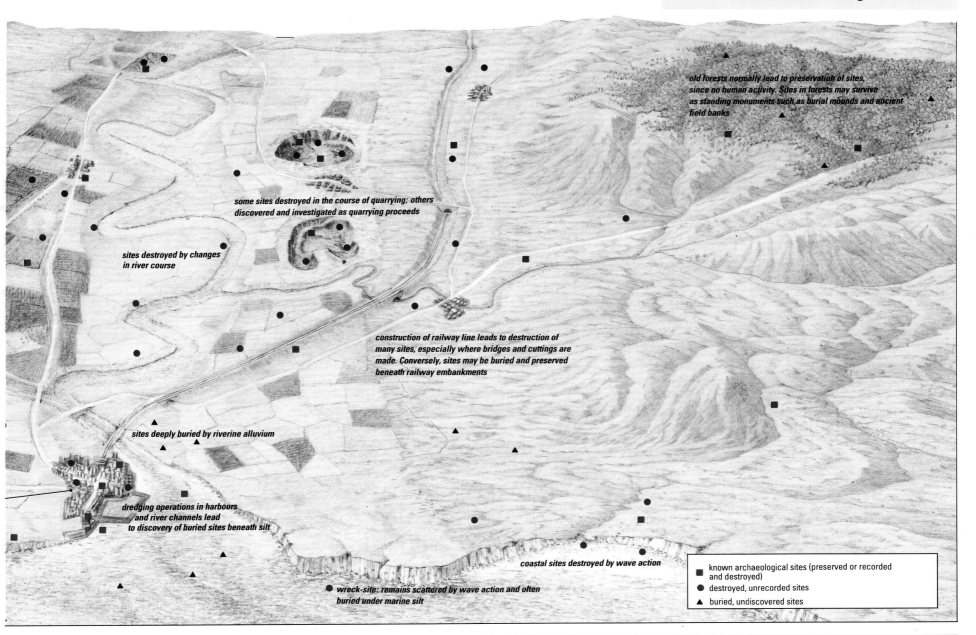

old forests normally lead to preservation of sites, since no human activity. Sites in forests may survive as standing monuments such as burial mounds and ancient field banks

some sites destroyed in the course of quarrying; others discovered and investigated as quarrying proceeds

sites destroyed by changes in river course

construction of railway line leads to destruction of many sites, especially where bridges and cuttings are made. Conversely, sites may be buried and preserved beneath railway embankments

sites deeply buried by riverine alluvium

dredging operations in harbours and river channels lead to discovery of buried sites beneath silt

coastal sites destroyed by wave action

wreck-site: remains scattered by wave action and often buried under marine silt

■ known archaeological sites (preserved or recorded and destroyed)
● destroyed, unrecorded sites
▲ buried, undiscovered sites

permanently frozen soil of Siberia, many with their flesh, hair and stomach contents intact. Humans are also preserved by refrigeration – there are frozen Eskimo bodies from Greenland and Alaska, as well as well-preserved Scythian burials from southern Siberia (*page 182*). Natural freeze-drying shrinks and discolours the tissues, but the features and even tattoos survive, as well as clothing and other grave-goods.

Organic materials deposited in waterlogged conditions (in lakes, fens or peat bogs) are sealed and preserved in a wet and airless tomb. The bog bodies of north-west Europe are the most famous examples of preservation in wet conditions, but a wide range of wooden artefacts (**C**), from spoons to trackways, are also preserved in waterlogged sites such as the lake villages of the Swiss Alps. In a wetland site the percentage of organic finds is often 75–90% of the whole, and can even be 100%, whereas on dryland sites little if any of this material would leave any trace at all (*see graph*).

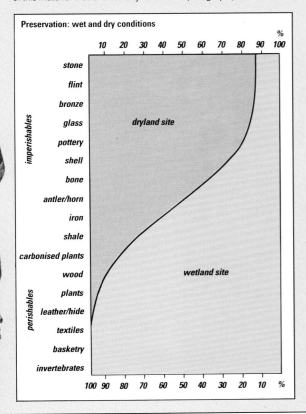

Preservation: wet and dry conditions

%
10 20 30 40 50 60 70 80 90 100

stone
flint
bronze
glass   dryland site
pottery
shell
bone
antler/horn
iron
shale
carbonised plants
wood   wetland site
plants
leather/hide
textiles
basketry
invertebrates

100 90 80 70 60 50 40 30 20 10 %

imperishables / *perishables*

3 THE USES OF AERIAL SURVEY

Aerial photography is used for recording, mapping and interpreting sites. It is only from the air that one can really make sense of large-scale site layouts, such as the Serpent Mound in the USA (**A**), or the figures drawn on the Nazca desert of Peru. Oblique aerial photographs enable sites to be recognised through the play of light and shadow on features above ground (such as walls or earthworks), or from the height, vigour and type of vegetation (**B**), which reflect what lies buried beneath the surface. Over pits or ditches the soil is richer in moisture and phosphates, so crops are taller and more dense: the opposite occurs over buried walls. Infra-red film (**C**) can be used to enhance the differences in colour, especially in cereal crops.

Excavation

Excavation is the principal method of discovering and retrieving the material remains of the past. From a haphazard and damaging treasure hunt it has developed into a slow, painstaking and complex operation which is generally used for only two purposes: to examine a site which is about to be destroyed, or to answer specific questions about the past.

In the early days sites were dug like potato fields, with artefacts quarried out, and only the finest of the discoveries selected for display or publication. Little attention was paid to precisely where they came from. Today, however, archaeologists are no longer interested simply in acquiring objects; what matters is solving problems, and that demands noting the exact provenance of all pieces of evidence, and their distribution, density and associations within the site.

Interpretation of an excavation relies heavily on the law of superposition, or 'stratigraphy'; this means that, in general, where one layer overlies another, the lower is older than the upper. Hence, a vertical profile shows a series of layers that has accumulated through time. In the past many excavators – particularly in caves and rock shelters – were simply concerned with exposing such profiles, and extracting a sample of tools from each of the layers as they were removed one by one. The different cultures represented in the chronological sequence were each characterised by 'type fossils', or diagnostic artefact forms. There is, however, another dimension which has taken on increasing importance in recent decades: the exposure of horizontal areas, or 'slices of time', in order to investigate the spatial configurations of objects, the position of features such as hearths, and the plan and layout of structures, buildings and even villages.

In practice, most digs will involve both vertical and horizontal aspects to obtain both types of information. Much depends on the size and type of site, the time, equipment and labour available, and the particular questions that must be answered. These factors will also decide whether all the site or only a fraction of it is dug. Total excavation is rare today, partly because of the exorbitant costs and slow dissection involved in modern work, and partly because it is always sensible to leave part of a site for investigation by future archaeologists with improved techniques and different questions.

The decision about which part of a site to dig is largely determined by survey, involving examination of material lying on the surface (page 26) and a wide range of 'remote sensing' methods which use electrical or magnetic fields to detect buried features such as hearths, walls, ditches and pits, and thus produce a picture of what lies beneath the surface. Test pits and trenches can also be dug to check these results before proceeding.

All excavation involves destruction; even if only a small part of a site is dug, nobody can ever repeat the investigation of that unique little piece of our past. It is therefore imperative to keep the fullest possible record of the excavation and its results and finds. The excavation of a site is not a casual hobby; it is an unrepeatable opportunity, and carries great responsibilities.

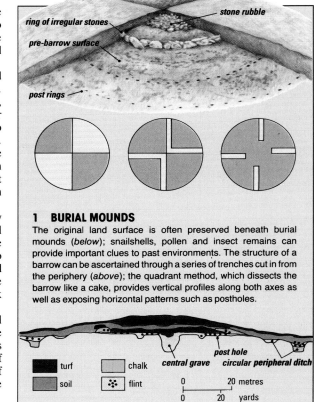

1 BURIAL MOUNDS

The original land surface is often preserved beneath burial mounds (below); snailshells, pollen and insect remains can provide important clues to past environments. The structure of a barrow can be ascertained through a series of trenches cut in from the periphery (above); the quadrant method, which dissects the barrow like a cake, provides vertical profiles along both axes as well as exposing horizontal patterns such as postholes.

| | turf | | chalk |
| | soil | | flint |

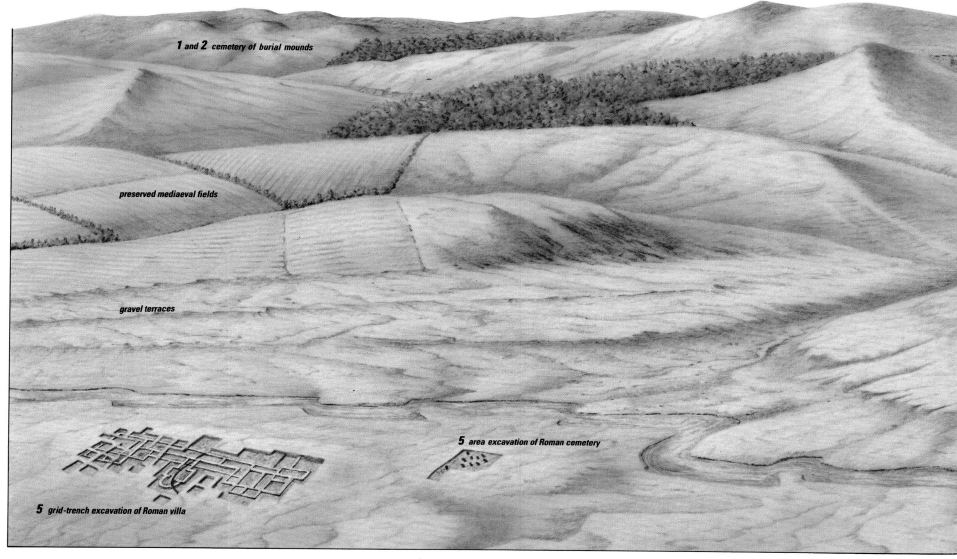

1 and 2 cemetery of burial mounds

preserved mediaeval fields

gravel terraces

5 area excavation of Roman cemetery

5 grid-trench excavation of Roman villa

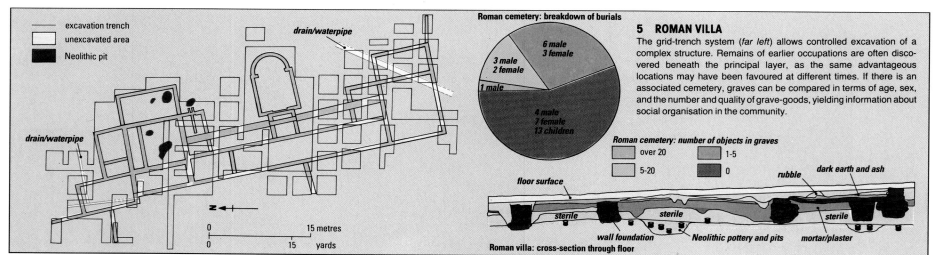

	excavation trench
	unexcavated area
	Neolithic pit

drain/waterpipe

drain/waterpipe

Roman cemetery: breakdown of burials

6 male 3 female

3 male 2 female

1 male

4 male 7 female 13 children

5 ROMAN VILLA

The grid-trench system (far left) allows controlled excavation of a complex structure. Remains of earlier occupations are often discovered beneath the principal layer, as the same advantageous locations may have been favoured at different times. If there is an associated cemetery, graves can be compared in terms of age, sex, and the number and quality of grave-goods, yielding information about social organisation in the community.

Roman cemetery: number of objects in graves

| | over 20 | | 1-5 |
| | 5-20 | | 0 |

floor surface

rubble

dark earth and ash

sterile

sterile

sterile

wall foundation

Neolithic pottery and pits

mortar/plaster

Roman villa: cross-section through floor

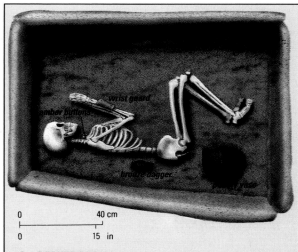

2 BEAKER BURIAL

The excavation of individual burials can provide clues to ritual and social organisation. How was the grave constructed? Was it enclosed by stone slabs, as in the Beaker burial illustrated here, or was there a wooden mortuary structure, or a coffin? How many skeletons are present, of what age and sex, and in what position – extended, flexed or crouched? In what direction is the body orientated? Does the skeleton display any pathological features, or an indication of cause of death? And, finally, what objects accompany the body – clothing, food, ornamentation, tools or weapons? In a case such as a typical Beaker burial, archaeologists can expect to find particular objects, as shown here.

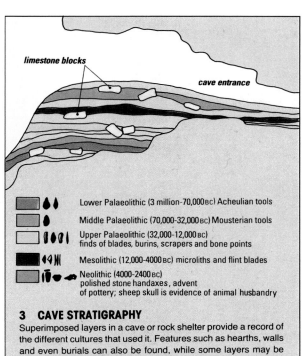

3 CAVE STRATIGRAPHY

Superimposed layers in a cave or rock shelter provide a record of the different cultures that used it. Features such as hearths, walls and even burials can also be found, while some layers may be sterile, showing that there were gaps in occupation. The cave floor indicates changing temperatures: large, angular pieces of the walls and roof result from frost action; temperate conditions produce rounder, weathered fragments.

Key:
- Lower Palaeolithic (3 million-70,000 BC) Acheulian tools
- Middle Palaeolithic (70,000-32,000 BC) Mousterian tools
- Upper Palaeolithic (32,000-12,000 BC) finds of blades, burins, scrapers and bone points
- Mesolithic (12,000-4000 BC) microliths and flint blades
- Neolithic (4000-2400 BC) polished stone handaxes, advent of pottery; sheep skull is evidence of animal husbandry

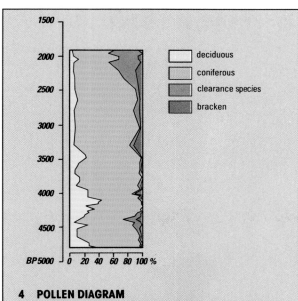

4 POLLEN DIAGRAM

Pollen grains are virtually indestructible and can be extracted either in a core (from wet sites such as bogs) or in a series of samples from different layers in the site. Under the microscope the distinctive shape and surface ornamentation of the pollens of different families and genera of plants can be identified, quantified and then plotted as a curve. Such curves reflect climatic fluctuations, as well as the impact of human interference, such as forest clearance or the intrusion of crop plants.

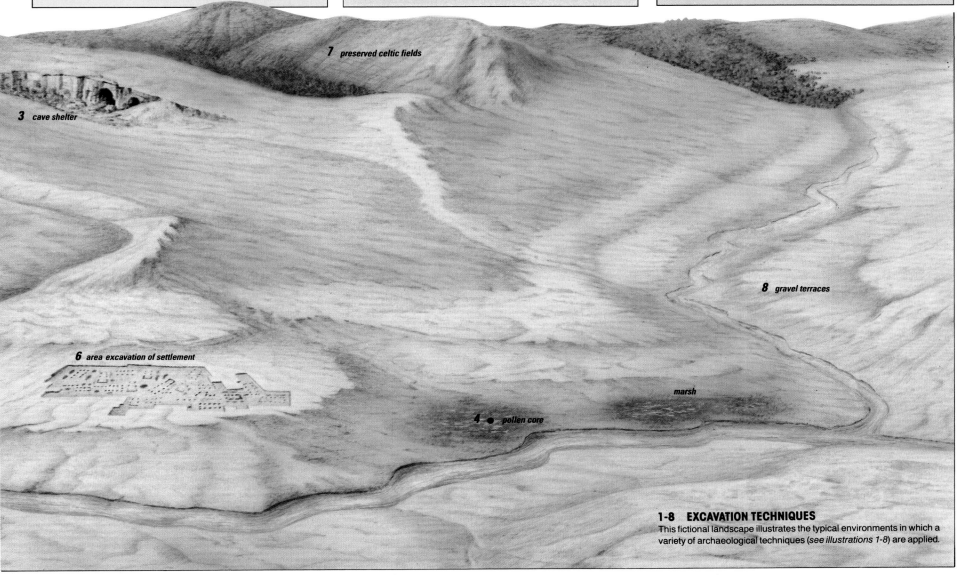

1-8 EXCAVATION TECHNIQUES

This fictional landscape illustrates the typical environments in which a variety of archaeological techniques (see illustrations 1-8) are applied.

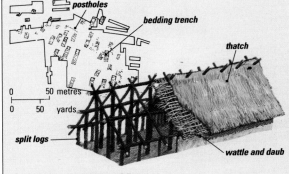

6 NEOLITHIC VILLAGE

A large-scale area excavation can be used to expose the ground plans, visible as postholes and bedding trenches, within a Neolithic village. In a site occupied for a long time, houses may be rebuilt many times, with slightly different orientations.

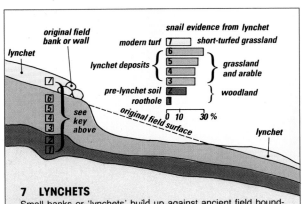

7 LYNCHETS

Small banks or 'lynchets' build up against ancient field boundaries, through the movement of the soil down the slope. The frequencies of a particular type of snail from the different layers within the lynchet can help to pinpoint vegetation and land use.

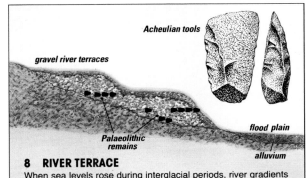

8 RIVER TERRACE

When sea levels rose during interglacial periods, river gradients became less steep and gravels and silt were deposited; when ice sheets advanced and sea levels fell again, the rivers cut into their beds, leaving terraces in the valley sides. The sequence of these terraces can often be dated by the ancient artefacts they contain – either deposited in situ, or carried there by the river.

INTERPRETATION
Settlement

The archaeology of settlement can be defined as the study of the spatial relationship between human activities and occupation. The fundamental aim of these studies is to assess the evidence for human behaviour, whether domestic, economic or social. In the Palaeolithic period, for example, there are sites that seem to have been devoted entirely to the killing or butchering of animals, others to the extraction or working of stone tools, and base-camps with evidence of many different types of activity. In later periods, a wide range of specialised sites are found, reflecting the greater organisation and complexity of society. These include fortresses, mines and workshops,

all of which played a vital role in the economic or political life of a state or empire.

It is extremely difficult to disentangle successfully the separate activities which took place at complex sites. One important procedure is to plot the precise position of every object on a living floor, as it is sometimes possible to ascertain in which parts of the site different activities such as food preparation or toolmaking were carried out; where people sat around hearths and what they did there; even the spatial positioning of entrances to their tents or huts can be estimated from the scatters of material and the empty spaces in between. In sites that have been little disturbed stone blades and flakes can be fitted together again, an exercise that not only provides information on the techniques used but also shows how the craftsman who

was making the tools moved around the site.

In villages much can be learned from the distribution and density of features such as storage pits. In towns and cities individual workshops can be identified, or even whole districts of artisans. Other parts of the settlement may be classed as residential areas or commercial sectors, quite apart from the more obvious features such as cemeteries or rubbish dumps. Large towns and cities usually have a ceremonial centre, comprising temples and palaces, with stelae, altars, inscriptions. There may also be special features like theatres or defensive works.

The materials used in the construction of a settlement may range from hides, wood or mammoth bone in the Palaeolithic, to timber, stone, brick or adobe in later periods, and give some idea of whether the occupation

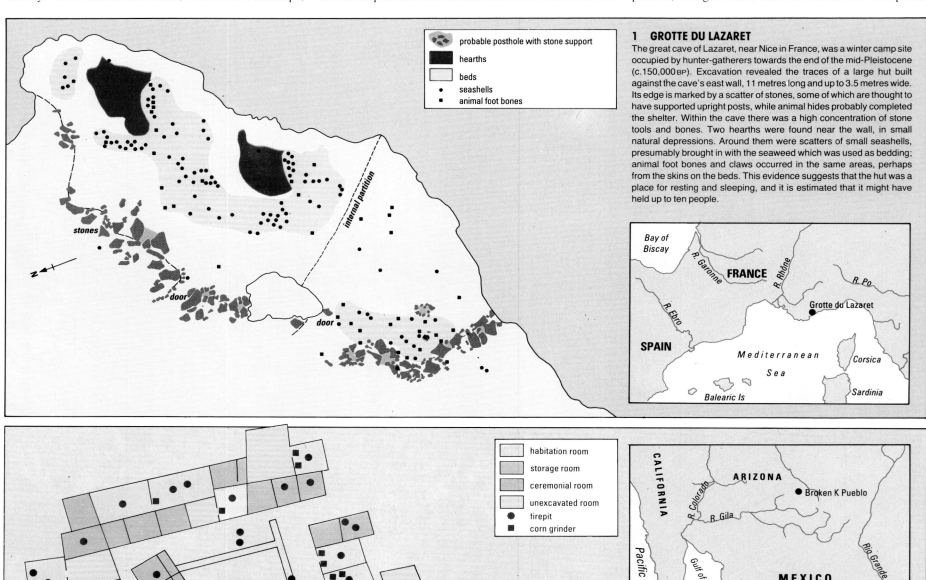

Key:
- probable posthole with stone support
- hearths
- beds
- • seashells
- ■ animal foot bones

stones / door / door / internal partition

1 GROTTE DU LAZARET

The great cave of Lazaret, near Nice in France, was a winter camp site occupied by hunter-gatherers towards the end of the mid-Pleistocene (c.150,000 BP). Excavation revealed the traces of a large hut built against the cave's east wall, 11 metres long and up to 3.5 metres wide. Its edge is marked by a scatter of stones, some of which are thought to have supported upright posts, while animal hides probably completed the shelter. Within the cave there was a high concentration of stone tools and bones. Two hearths were found near the wall, in small natural depressions. Around them were scatters of small seashells, presumably brought in with the seaweed which was used as bedding; animal foot bones and claws occurred in the same areas, perhaps from the skins on the beds. This evidence suggests that the hut was a place for resting and sleeping, and it is estimated that it might have held up to ten people.

Map showing: Bay of Biscay, R. Garonne, R. Rhône, FRANCE, R. Po, R. Ebro, Grotte du Lazaret, SPAIN, Mediterranean Sea, Corsica, Balearic Is, Sardinia

Key:
- habitation room
- storage room
- ceremonial room
- unexcavated room
- • firepit
- ■ corn grinder

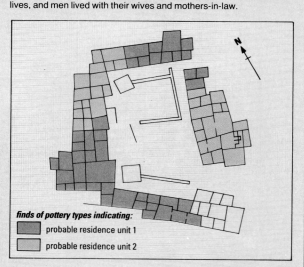

2 BROKEN K PUEBLO

This large 95-room pueblo (village) of the 13th century AD is situated in Arizona. There were three categories of rooms: the larger rooms, with firepits and corn grinders, were probably used for daily domestic activities; smaller rooms for storage; while the rare kind, sunk below ground level with benches and wall niches, were ceremonial. Analysis of pottery from excavated rooms showed a correlation between distinctive styles and certain sectors of the site, suggesting that the rooms belonged to two social groups or residence units. As the potters were probably women, the residences were arranged in matrilocal groupings; generations of women remained together throughout their lives, and men lived with their wives and mothers-in-law.

Map showing: CALIFORNIA, ARIZONA, Broken K Pueblo, R. Colorado, R. Gila, Pacific Ocean, Gulf of California, Rio Grande, MEXICO

finds of pottery types indicating:
- probable residence unit 1
- probable residence unit 2

0   10 metres
0   10 yards

was temporary or permanent. In the former case analysis of plant and animal remains found in the site can help to pinpoint the seasons in which people were present.

The internal organisation of a settlement is often closely related to the organisation of the society as a whole. Early settlement sites, such as the Grotte du Lazaret, are small and often appear to have been occupied only seasonally. They are characteristic of hunter-gatherer societies, where groups consisting of only a few individuals moved from camp to camp in an annual cycle. Agricultural settlements, on the other hand, tend to be larger, permanent villages. The greater size and stability of farming settlements is directly reflected in the archaeological record by their more extensive remains and more substantial architecture. Early Jericho, for example,

covered 1.6 hectares. Social differentiation may be indicated by differences in size and location of individual houses. These tendencies become still more pronounced in the remains of ancient cities, with striking differences between rich and poor areas. The very size of cities indicates the existence of a sophisticated economic and political organisation able to ensure the supply of food, drinking water and other essential commodities to such large populations. Centralised planning at its most obvious and extreme may be seen in the grid-iron plans of a large number of cities, from the Chinese capital, Chang'an, and the cities of the Greek and Roman world to the Meso-american metropolis of Teotihuacán. Such planned cities are naturally a hallmark of powerful state societies.

While it might be possible to excavate the whole of a

rock shelter or house, it is rarely feasible to uncover all of a village, let alone a large town. Since various sectors of a town may differ greatly in their role and their remains, it is desirable to obtain a representative sample of all the varieties of structure or groups of buildings, together with some idea of their extent as well as that of the whole town.

Short-lived, purpose-built settlements like El-Amarna in Egypt, or towns destroyed suddenly like Pompeii, are exceptional. The vast majority grew from more humble origins, experienced considerable development and change, and declined slowly. Archaeologists have to take this into account, and attempt to trace the history of renewal, demolition and replacement from the confusing picture they encounter, frequently disturbed by the recycling of older materials.

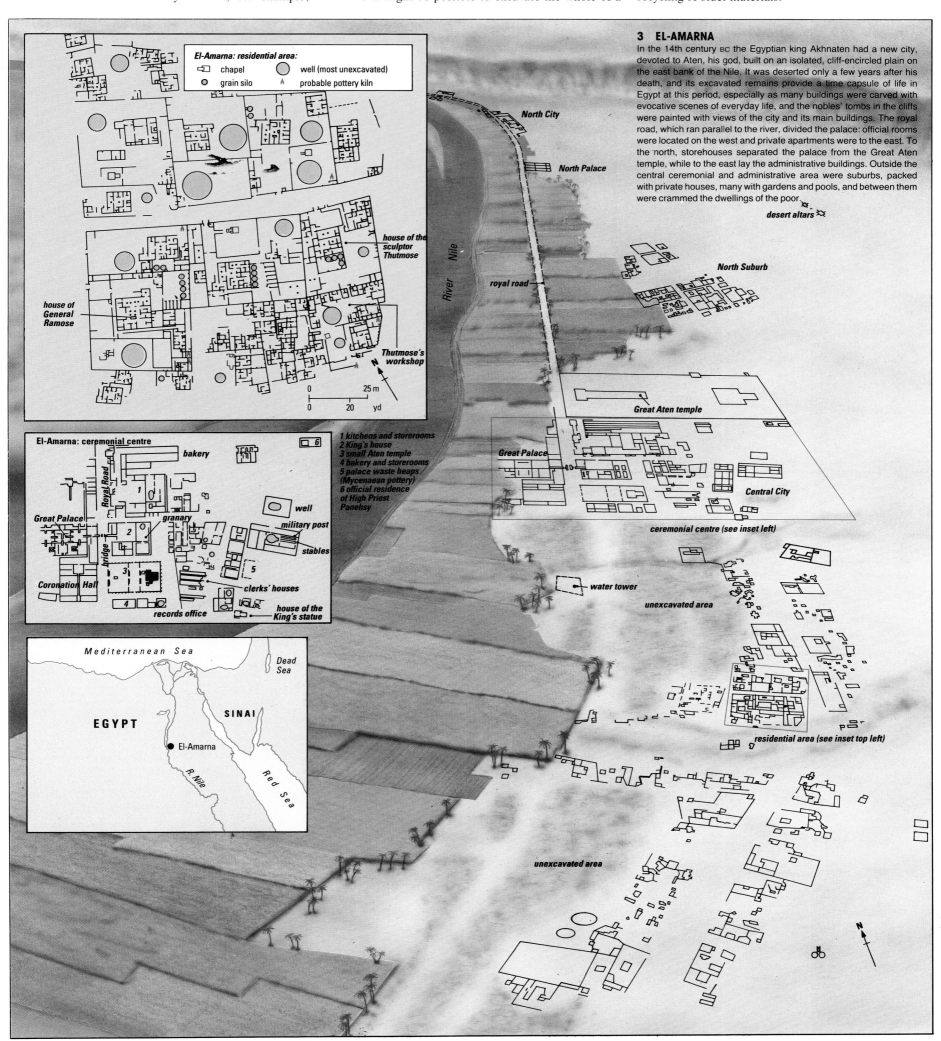

3 EL-AMARNA

In the 14th century BC the Egyptian king Akhnaten had a new city, devoted to Aten, his god, built on an isolated, cliff-encircled plain on the east bank of the Nile. It was deserted only a few years after his death, and its excavated remains provide a time capsule of life in Egypt at this period, especially as many buildings were carved with evocative scenes of everyday life, and the nobles' tombs in the cliffs were painted with views of the city and its main buildings. The royal road, which ran parallel to the river, divided the palace: official rooms were located on the west and private apartments were to the east. To the north, storehouses separated the palace from the Great Aten temple, while to the east lay the administrative buildings. Outside the central ceremonial and administrative area were suburbs, packed with private houses, many with gardens and pools, and between them were crammed the dwellings of the poor.

El-Amarna: residential area:
- chapel
- grain silo
- well (most unexcavated)
- probable pottery kiln

house of the sculptor Thutmose
house of General Ramose
Thutmose's workshop

0 — 25 m
0 — 20 yd

El-Amarna: ceremonial centre

1 kitchens and storerooms
2 King's house
3 small Aten temple
4 bakery and storerooms
5 palace waste heaps (Mycenaean pottery)
6 official residence of High Priest Panehsy

bakery
Great Palace
Royal Road
granary
Coronation Hall
bridge
records office
well
military post
stables
clerks' houses
house of the King's statue

Mediterranean Sea
Dead Sea
EGYPT
SINAI
El-Amarna
R. Nile
Red Sea

North City
North Palace
royal road
River Nile
North Suburb
desert altars
Great Aten temple
Great Palace
Central City
ceremonial centre (see inset left)
water tower
unexcavated area
residential area (see inset top left)
unexcavated area

Settlement patterns

No community was ever totally isolated from others, and human settlements are never scattered either regularly or haphazardly over the landscape. Instead, people deliberately choose to occupy spots that have some advantage for subsistence, defence, transport, manufacture, trade, or a combination of all these factors. The archaeology of settlement patterns deals with the interaction between people and their environment (as opposed to an examination of the internal layout and contents of a single site.) It can involve the study of an individual site's position within the landscape, the relationships between groups of contemporary sites, or the relationship between a group of sites and the landscape.

In the past, scholars worked from distribution maps that were often incomplete or distorted and reflected the location of previous archaeological exploration rather than a true picture of past settlement. Today far more survey is carried out with the aim of locating as many settlements as possible within a given region. Even the most thorough survey, however, cannot hope to find everything: some sites simply elude all efforts, only to turn up unexpectedly later, while untold numbers have already been destroyed. Moreover, only excavation can really produce a firm date for each site, and thus establish which were truly contemporaneous – 'archaeological contemporaneity' is a relative concept, as it can rarely be proved that any two sites were actually occupied at the same time. All deductions about interrelationships and patterns of settlements in the landscape are thus founded on assumptions rather than certainties.

Territorial analysis of individual sites investigates either the total area from which their contents have been derived (their 'site catchment'), or the area surrounding the site that would have been most frequently or intensively used (the 'site exploitation territory'). For hunter-gatherer sites such analysis involves a study of the landscape and of the location of water supply, fords, raw material sources, natural passages for game, natural corrals or traps for herds, and so forth. For farming settlements analysis is more complex, and entails an attempt to reconstruct what land would have been exploitable in different periods with different farming technologies. The effects of erosion, irrigation or terracing also need to be taken into account. One basic assumption is that people will generally try to minimise effort of any kind, such as the distance which has to be travelled between their home and key resources.

When sites are grouped, and their archaeological contemporaneity is established, settlement patterns can be assessed. Sites can sometimes be ascribed to a number of mobile groups, as in the Tehuacán Valley in Mexico, with hunter-gatherers moving between them in order to take full advantage of the resources available in different areas at different times of year. If sites of different sizes are grouped in this way, it may mean that people were dispersing or coming together seasonally according to the availability of food and space.

In addition, there may be specialised sites, visited for

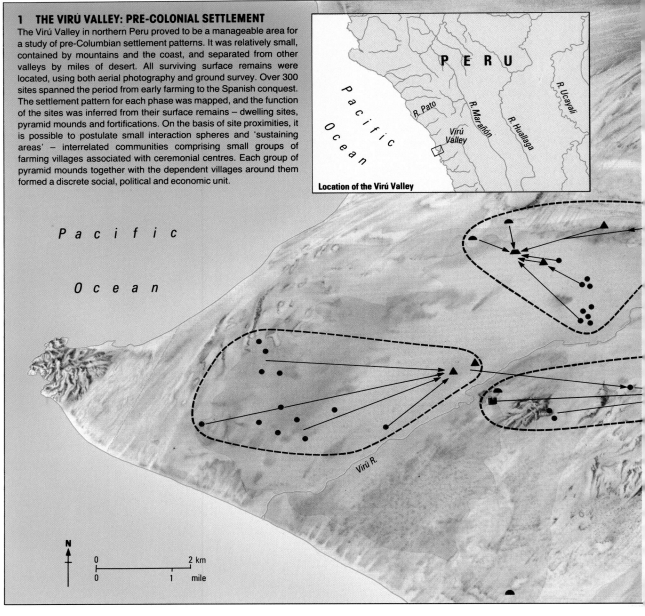

1 THE VIRÚ VALLEY: PRE-COLONIAL SETTLEMENT

The Virú Valley in northern Peru proved to be a manageable area for a study of pre-Columbian settlement patterns. It was relatively small, contained by mountains and the coast, and separated from other valleys by miles of desert. All surviving surface remains were located, using both aerial photography and ground survey. Over 300 sites spanned the period from early farming to the Spanish conquest. The settlement pattern for each phase was mapped, and the function of the sites was inferred from their surface remains – dwelling sites, pyramid mounds and fortifications. On the basis of site proximities, it is possible to postulate small interaction spheres and 'sustaining areas' – interrelated communities comprising small groups of farming villages associated with ceremonial centres. Each group of pyramid mounds together with the dependent villages around them formed a discrete social, political and economic unit.

Location of the Virú Valley

such purposes as extracting or working raw materials, military operations, ritual practices, or trade. The remains left by these activities usually show what the site was used for, but the location in the landscape can often be a valuable additional clue. Where subsistence is concerned, village settlements surrounded by rough ground with poor agricultural potential may have depended more on animal husbandry than on crop cultivation. A much stronger case for agriculture can be made out where remains of field boundaries, cultivation terraces or irrigation systems have survived; these labour-demanding works are almost always associated with intensive crop cultivation.

In more sedentary societies, settlement patterns often become increasingly complex as the effects of politics

and religion become traceable in the size, layout, function and distribution of sites. There may now be a settlement hierarchy with smaller sites grouped around larger centres, as in the Virú Valley in Peru. Great ceremonial centres served as regional religious foci, often combined with political organisation. Maya settlements, for example, were laid out in segments that were dictated by both religious and political requirements.

Trade, too, often played a major part in settlement distribution; settlements were located not only near key resources but also along trade routes and important arteries such as rivers. Regional centres served as redistribution points, facilitating the transport of goods and services from the major concentrations of population to the hinterland.

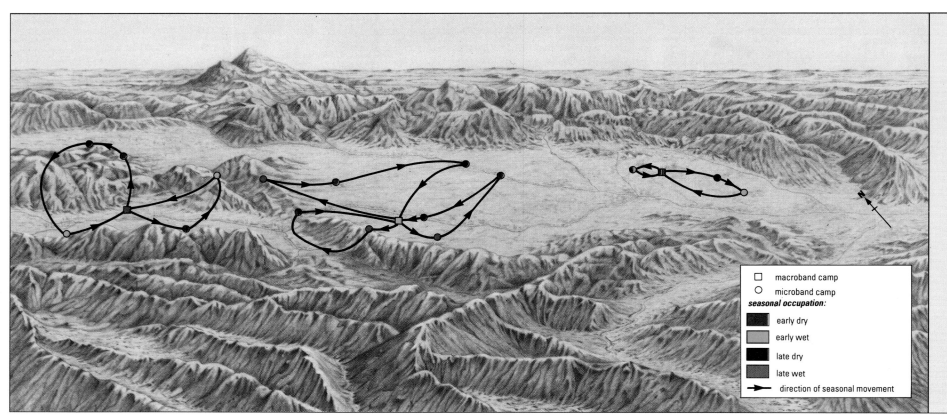

macroband camp
microband camp
seasonal occupation:

early dry
early wet
late dry
late wet
→ direction of seasonal movement

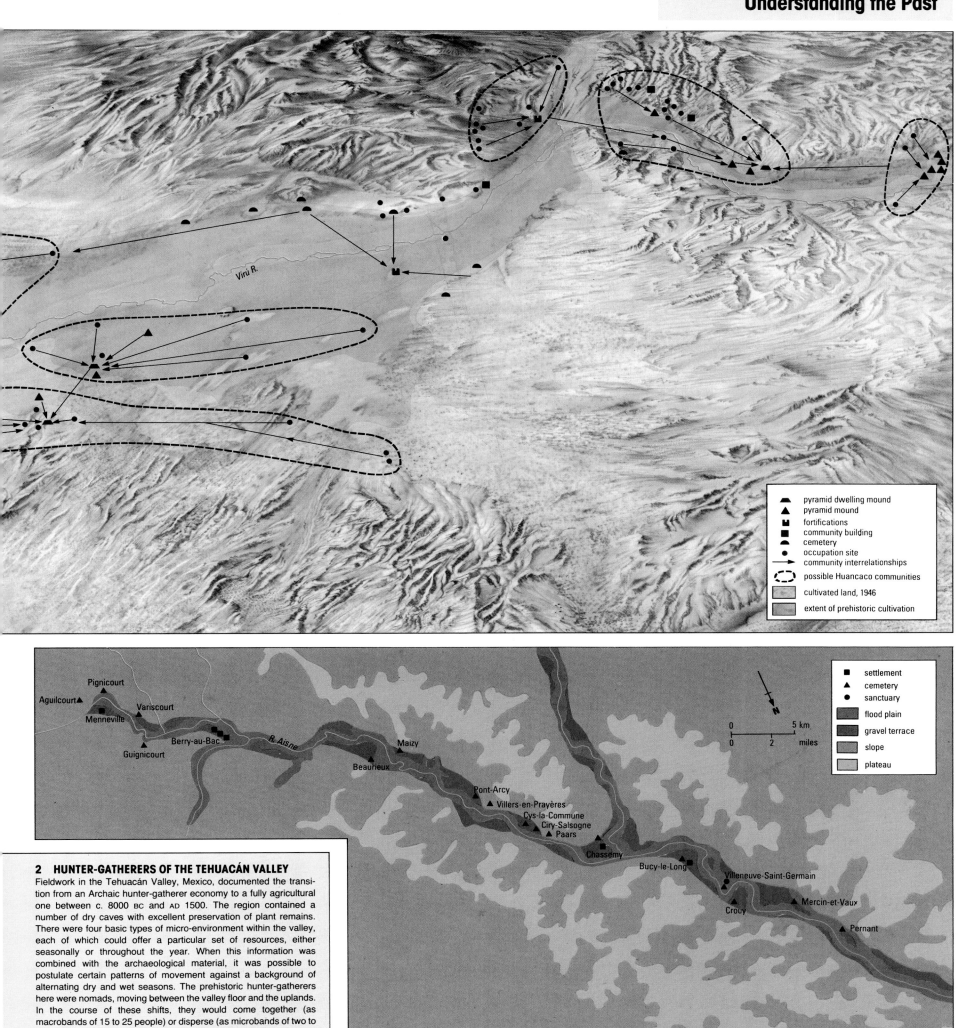

pyramid dwelling mound
pyramid mound
fortifications
community building
cemetery
occupation site
community interrelationships
possible Huancaco communities
cultivated land, 1946
extent of prehistoric cultivation

Virú R.

■ settlement
▲ cemetery
● sanctuary
flood plain
gravel terrace
slope
plateau

0   5 km
0   2   miles

N

Pignicourt
Aguilcourt
Variscourt
Menneville
Berry-au-Bac
Guignicourt
R. Aisne
Maizy
Beaurieux
Pont-Arcy
Villers-en-Prayères
Cys-la-Commune
Ciry-Salsogne
Paars
Chassemy
Bucy-le-Long
Villeneuve-Saint-Germain
Crouy
Mercin-et-Vaux
Pernant

2 HUNTER-GATHERERS OF THE TEHUACÁN VALLEY

Fieldwork in the Tehuacán Valley, Mexico, documented the transition from an Archaic hunter-gatherer economy to a fully agricultural one between c. 8000 BC and AD 1500. The region contained a number of dry caves with excellent preservation of plant remains. There were four basic types of micro-environment within the valley, each of which could offer a particular set of resources, either seasonally or throughout the year. When this information was combined with the archaeological material, it was possible to postulate certain patterns of movement against a background of alternating dry and wet seasons. The prehistoric hunter-gatherers here were nomads, moving between the valley floor and the uplands. In the course of these shifts, they would come together (as macrobands of 15 to 25 people) or disperse (as microbands of two to five people) in different seasons as the resources permitted.

MEXICO
Gulf of Mexico
R. Balsas
YUCATÁN
Tehuacán Valley
Pacific Ocean
Location of the Tehuacán Valley

3 THE AISNE VALLEY: IRON AGE FARMING

The flat-bottomed valley of the Aisne, in the Paris basin, cuts through a region of limestone plateaux. It is fairly narrow (average width three kilometres). A stretch some 80 kilometres in length has been surveyed, building up an interesting picture from the first settlements of the Neolithic, comprising small groups of large timber houses, to the denser occupation of the Iron Age, shown here. The picture is incomplete, as many sites have probably been destroyed through gravel extraction and agriculture: this would account for the gaps between settlements, and for the cemeteries that are not associated with occupation sites. It can be seen, however, that the inhabitants placed their villages on the gravel terraces overlooking the river and the flood plain, but out of reach of the effects of flooding. The result was a linear arrangement of fairly regularly spaced settlements along what was probably an important corridor for trade and traffic.

ENGLAND
English Channel
FRANCE
R. Somme
R. Seine
R. Oise
R. Aisne
Aisne Valley
Location of the Aisne Valley

33

INTERPRETATION
Burials

The care lavished on the dead by peoples of the past has been of immense importance to archaeology. Indeed, the very appearance of deliberate burial in the Middle Palaeolithic (c.80,000–35,000 BP) is seen as a major mile stone in human development, and is often taken as proof of belief in a soul or an afterlife. If archaeologists can learn little about specific ancient beliefs from burials alone, they can nevertheless extract a great deal of varied and useful information from them. Archaeology's principal interest lies in the reconstruction of past behaviour, and burials provide us with the remains of the very people who produced the archaeological record.

Human remains – which range from fully preserved frozen, desiccated, waterlogged or mummified bodies to skeletons, cremated fragments and even soil-stains – may provide information about age at death, sex, height, weight and appearance. The cause of death, state of health, and evidence for parasites, disease or trauma are all also of interest. Stomach contents, if they survive, reveal the composition of the last meal, while analysis of tooth wear and of isotopic ratios in bone or tissue can tell us a great deal about diet. If blood groups can be established, it is occasionally possible to reconstruct family relationships between individuals, as in the Hungarian cemetery of Mözs. The position and orientation of the body is often significant, Islamic burials, for instance, always face towards Mecca. The particular treatment of the body, which may be interred, cremated, mummified,

or even intentionally dismembered, also provides a vital clue to funerary ritual. But even where the body has completely decayed, a considerable amount may be deduced from the structure and form of the tomb (ranging from a simple pit to a vast stone monument) and from the objects placed to accompany the dead: the grave-goods can range from a joint of meat and a simple vessel to the incredibly lavish collections known from tombs such as that of Tutankhamun, or the Royal Graves at Ur. They may provide information about the dead person's age and sex (for instance, weapons in male graves), as well as occupation, wealth and social rank. Tombs that required large numbers of people for their construction may also reflect the wealth of their occupants, and the power and influence they wielded within the community.

Where groups of bodies are concerned burial studies become even more ambitious. Some tombs are collective graves, used over long periods by a family or other community, with the older remains being pushed to one side to make room for the new. However, it is in cemeteries, where individual graves can be compared, that social organisation can be analysed. The age and sex of the deceased, the location of the grave and the richness and quantity of grave-goods can provide some invaluable indications about status and class. In some cemeteries, certain areas seem to have been reserved for people by sex, age-group or social rank as at Moundville in North America. Cemeteries also allow us to estimate the incidence of conditions such as arthritis in an ancient community and to establish the general life-expectancy of people of the period.

There are two major problems today concerning ancient burials. Tomb robbery has existed since at least the time of the pharaohs, and indeed is known as the world's second oldest profession. Archaeology's low manpower and resources, together with the remote locations of ancient tombs in many countries, make it easy for robbers to operate. They are generally interested only in gold and silver, and everything else – for example pottery and bones – is destroyed and left behind. The irreplaceable information to be derived from an intact burial is consequently destroyed forever. Today, however, the archaeologist's worst enemies are not the robbers so much as the international dealers and collectors, whose appetite for antiquities ensures that the looting is increasingly profitable.

The second problem, which has only recently become an issue, is that both the morality and legality of archaeological excavation of burials is being seriously questioned by indigenous people (primarily North American Indians and Aborigines) and religious groups (such as ultra-orthodox Jews), some of whom object passionately to the disturbance, study and display of the remains of their ancestors. As a result, archaeologists in many parts of the world have had to curtail burial excavation, or at least carry it out with the consent and cooperation of local indigenous communities. Some skeletons dug up in the past have been returned to descendants who have, in certain cases, reburied or cremated the remains in accordance with their ancestors' wishes. Archaeologists will have to accept that they are not the only group with a valid interest in the remains of ancient humans.

---

1 SUNGIR: A PALAEOLITHIC BURIAL

On present evidence, deliberate burial began during the Middle Palaeolithic period (c.80,000–35,000 BP) but became more common in the Upper Palaeolithic (35,000–10,000 BP), when there is increasing evidence of decorative items being placed in burials (*see table*), indicating the existence of an incipient hierarchy. Upper Palaeolithic burials at Sungir, near Moscow, date to 24,000 BP. The old man buried there (*below*) had two dozen perforated fox canines sewn on the back of his cap, and about 20 ivory armlets and bracelets. The burials of two boys, aged 7–9 and 10–12, also contained fox canines, ivory ornaments, pendants, animal carvings, and a series of weapons including some unique spears of mammoth ivory, over two metres in length. With each of these bodies were found about 3500 beads of mammoth ivory, arranged in rows across the forehead and the body, down the arms and legs, and around the ankles. It is estimated that each bead would have taken about 45 minutes to make, adding up to 2625 hours of 'beadwork' for each body.

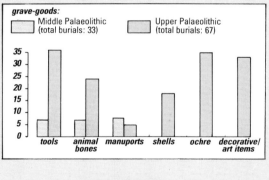

grave-goods:

Middle Palaeolithic (total burials: 33) ▫ | Upper Palaeolithic (total burials: 67) ▪

Bar chart categories: tools, animal bones, manuports, shells, ochre, decorative/art items (y-axis 0–35)

Mözs: plan of cemetery

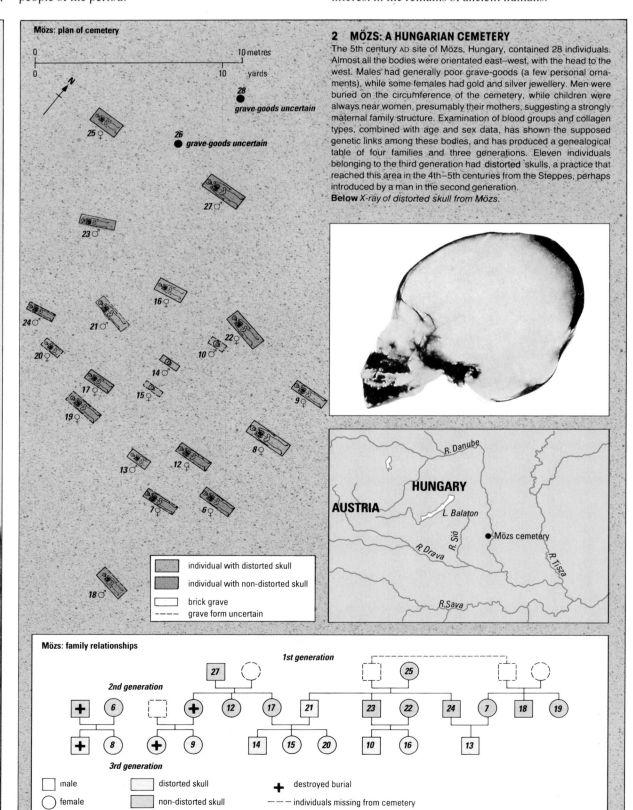

0 ————————— 10 metres
0 ————————— 10 yards

N

28 ● grave-goods uncertain

26 ● grave-goods uncertain

25 ♀
27 ♂
23 ♂
16 ♀
24 ♂   21 ♂   22 ♀
20 ♀   10 ♂
14 ♀
17 ♀ 15 ♀   9 ♂
19 ♀
8 ♀
13 ♀ 12 ♂
7 ♀   6 ♀
18 ♂

individual with distorted skull
individual with non-distorted skull
brick grave
---- grave form uncertain

---

2 MÖZS: A HUNGARIAN CEMETERY

The 5th century AD site of Mözs, Hungary, contained 28 individuals. Almost all the bodies were orientated east–west, with the head to the west. Males had generally poor grave-goods (a few personal ornaments), while some females had gold and silver jewellery. Men were buried on the circumference of the cemetery, while children were always near women, presumably their mothers, suggesting a strongly maternal family structure. Examination of blood groups and collagen types, combined with age and sex data, has shown the supposed genetic links among these bodies, and has produced a genealogical table of four families and three generations. Eleven individuals belonging to the third generation had distorted skulls, a practice that reached this area in the 4th–5th centuries from the Steppes, perhaps introduced by a man in the second generation.
Below X-ray of distorted skull from Mözs.

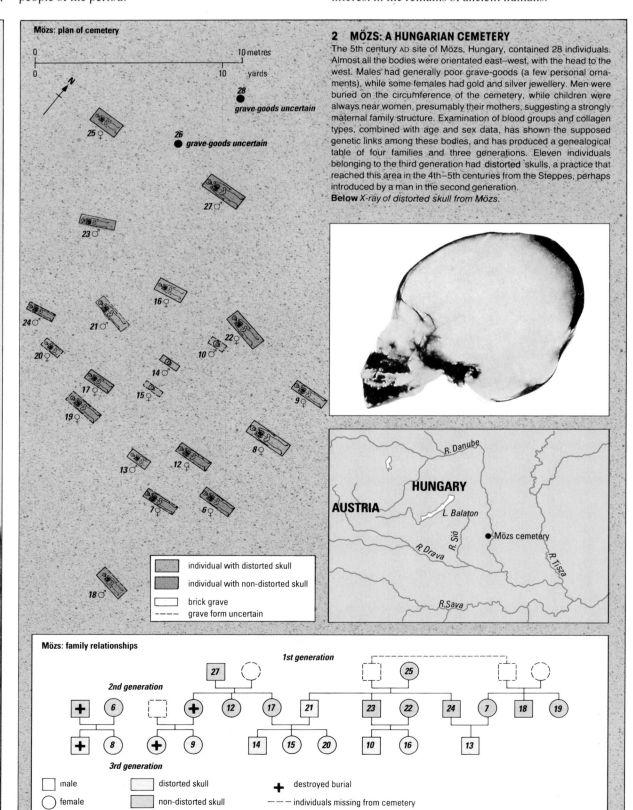

HUNGARY
AUSTRIA
R. Danube
L. Balaton
R. Sió
● Mözs cemetery
R. Drava
R. Tisza
R. Sava

Mözs: family relationships

1st generation
27 □—○ ◌ □—25 ○ ◌ □—○

2nd generation
✚ 6 — ◌ ✚ 12 — 17 — 21 — 23 — 22 — 24 — 7 — 18 — 19

3rd generation
✚ 8 — ✚ 9 — 14 — 15 — 20 — 10 — 16 — 13

□ male | ▨ distorted skull | ✚ destroyed burial
○ female | ▨ non-distorted skull | --- individuals missing from cemetery

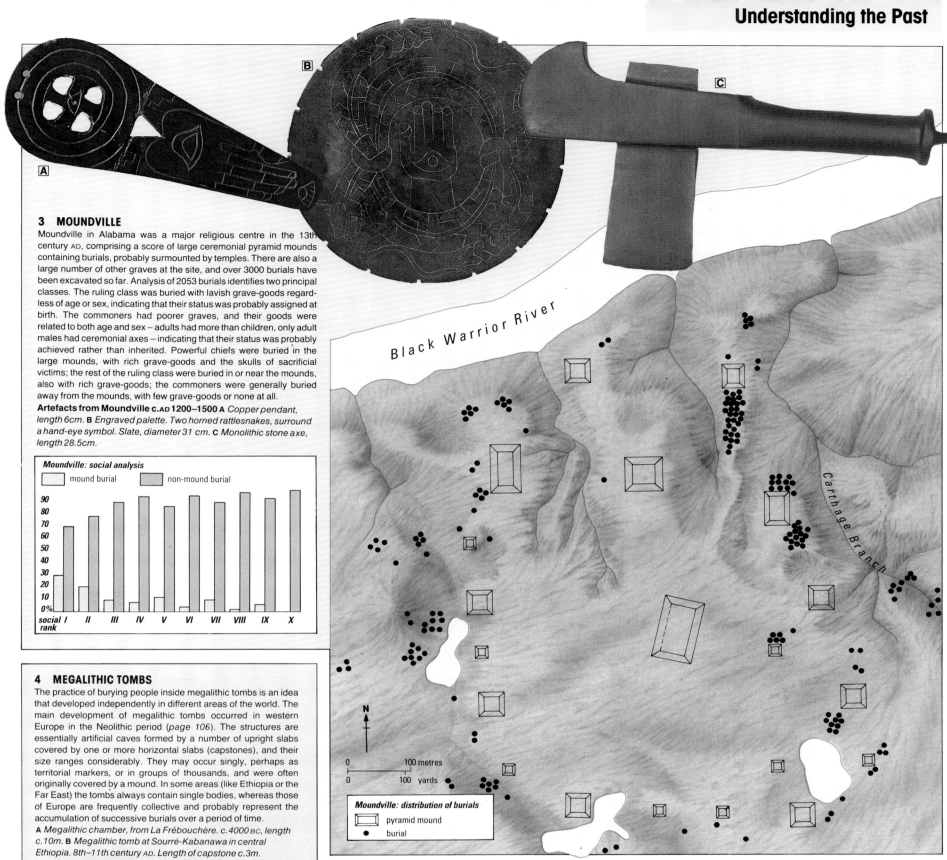

3 MOUNDVILLE

Moundville in Alabama was a major religious centre in the 13th century AD, comprising a score of large ceremonial pyramid mounds containing burials, probably surmounted by temples. There are also a large number of other graves at the site, and over 3000 burials have been excavated so far. Analysis of 2053 burials identifies two principal classes. The ruling class was buried with lavish grave-goods regardless of age or sex, indicating that their status was probably assigned at birth. The commoners had poorer graves, and their goods were related to both age and sex – adults had more than children, only adult males had ceremonial axes – indicating that their status was probably achieved rather than inherited. Powerful chiefs were buried in the large mounds, with rich grave-goods and the skulls of sacrificial victims; the rest of the ruling class were buried in or near the mounds, also with rich grave-goods; the commoners were generally buried away from the mounds, with few grave-goods or none at all.

Artefacts from Moundville c.AD 1200–1500 A *Copper pendant, length 6cm.* **B** *Engraved palette. Two horned rattlesnakes, surround a hand-eye symbol. Slate, diameter 31 cm.* **C** *Monolithic stone axe, length 28.5cm.*

Moundville: social analysis

mound burial   non-mound burial

| social rank | I | II | III | IV | V | VI | VII | VIII | IX | X |

(bar chart y-axis: 0%, 10, 20, 30, 40, 50, 60, 70, 80, 90)

4 MEGALITHIC TOMBS

The practice of burying people inside megalithic tombs is an idea that developed independently in different areas of the world. The main development of megalithic tombs occurred in western Europe in the Neolithic period (*page 106*). The structures are essentially artificial caves formed by a number of upright slabs covered by one or more horizontal slabs (capstones), and their size ranges considerably. They may occur singly, perhaps as territorial markers, or in groups of thousands, and were often originally covered by a mound. In some areas (like Ethiopia or the Far East) the tombs always contain single bodies, whereas those of Europe are frequently collective and probably represent the accumulation of successive burials over a period of time.

A *Megalithic chamber, from La Frébouchère. c.4000 BC, length c.10m.* **B** *Megalithic tomb at Sourré-Kabanawa in central Ethiopia. 8th–11th century AD. Length of capstone c.3m.*

Moundville: distribution of burials

▱ pyramid mound
● burial

0 — 100 metres
0 — 100 yards

Megalithic tombs distribution

GREENLAND

NORTH AMERICA

SIBERIA

EUROPE

ASIA

western Europe: 5th – 3rd millennium BC

Caucasus: 3rd – 2nd millennium BC

China and Korea: 1st millennium BC

North Africa and Mediterranean: 3rd–1st millennium BC

Palestine: 4th – 3rd millennium BC

Japan: 300 BC – AD 700

AFRICA

Ethiopia: 1st/2nd millennium AD

India: late 2nd and 1st millennium BC

Colombia: 6th century BC – 15th century AD

SOUTH AMERICA

Madagascar: 7th – 20th century AD

Atlantic Ocean

Pacific Ocean

Pacific Ocean

Indian Ocean

AUSTRALIA

Underwater sites

Underwater archaeology has tackled a wide variety of sites, from wells and springs to submerged lakeside settlements, and of course marine sites, including drowned cities, sunken harbours and shipwrecks. Although it was originally an activity largely associated with treasure-hunting, it has developed into a valuable complement to terrestrial archaeology.

The first recorded underwater excavation took place in 1854, when Adolphe Morlot, with a glass-fronted bucket over his head, used a pick and butterfly net to recover remains from the bottom of Lake Geneva. The systematic investigation of wreck sites, however, only really began after the Second World War. This was due largely to new technology. The invention of miniature submarines, other submersible craft and, above all, of scuba-diving gear greatly improved the archaeologist's ability to locate and study sites. Underwater sites can be found in many different ways: through information from fishermen and divers; by dredging operations in rivers and harbours; through aerial survey; and from actual exploration. Suspected wrecks containing metal can be investigated from the surface using side-scanning sonar, as iron and steel cause anomalies in the magnetic field. For wooden wrecks with little metal, however, it is necessary for divers to approach to within a few metres, and use metal detectors or a portable magnetometer to produce a detailed plan. Even buried clay jars or Roman amphorae have been detected in this way from the iron oxide impurities in their clay.

Settlement sites are usually less deeply submerged and hence pose fewer technical problems for their excavators, though working on a sea or lake bed is nonetheless costly and time-consuming. At sites such as these, however, the organic remains such as timber and textiles are considerably better preserved than at normal dry land excavations. The Alpine lakes, for instance, have provided a fuller picture of Neolithic life than almost any other part of Europe.

Since it is rarely feasible to lift an entire vessel to the surface or transport it to land, even on wreck sites, much of the archaeological work has to be done underwater. This can often be hazardous and difficult, but the rewards are great; the yield of well-preserved organic remains has been tremendous, while every wreck adds to our knowledge of shipbuilding, trade routes, and of the importance of maritime traffic at different periods. Coming suddenly to grief in the midst of their everyday operations, shipwrecks can act as time capsules. The merchantman of the 4th century BC discovered at Kyrenia, for example, had amphorae from Samos and Rhodes, grindstones from Cos, and a large cargo of almonds from Cyprus, and was probably leaving the latter island when disaster struck. Like any archaeological site, each wreck poses new problems. The condition of vessels can range from almost totally destroyed to virtually intact, from freestanding to completely buried. Much depends on how and why they sank, the type of bed they lie on, the depth of water and the existence of currents. Strong tides and currents can cause rapid burial by sand, which helps to preserve the remains. Few underwater sites are easy to see at first, since sediments, growths and concretions make excellent camouflage.

The position of the cargo on the sea bed results from the way in which the ship went down, its impact on the bottom and the angle of tilt. Test cores in different parts of the site can help to assess the nature, extent and number of layers of cargo, and the axis and orientation of the vessel. Cargo is usually stowed solidly from wall to wall, so it can often provide a clear idea of the ship's width, and sometimes of the length, though the vessel may not have had the same cargo from stem to stern.

The excavation of an entire vessel is rarely undertaken, because underwater work is long, complex and expensive, and if a ship has become buried under a mound there are vast quantities of sand and sediment to be removed. Apart from cargoes the most frequent remains encountered are the bottoms of ancient boats, usually preserved in good condition through the double protection of cargo and sand. Even though they are waterlogged, and often distorted by the shape of the sea bed, specialists may still be able to reconstruct something of the vessel's overall form and lines, and how its sections fitted together.

From this evidence it is slowly becoming possible to chart the history of maritime technology from the dugout canoes of the prehistoric period down to the invention of the three-masted ocean-going vessel in the 15th century and beyond. Indeed many of the best-studied shipwrecks date from the relatively recent period of European colonial expansion, and they too have a great deal to tell us about ship construction which is not available from other sources.

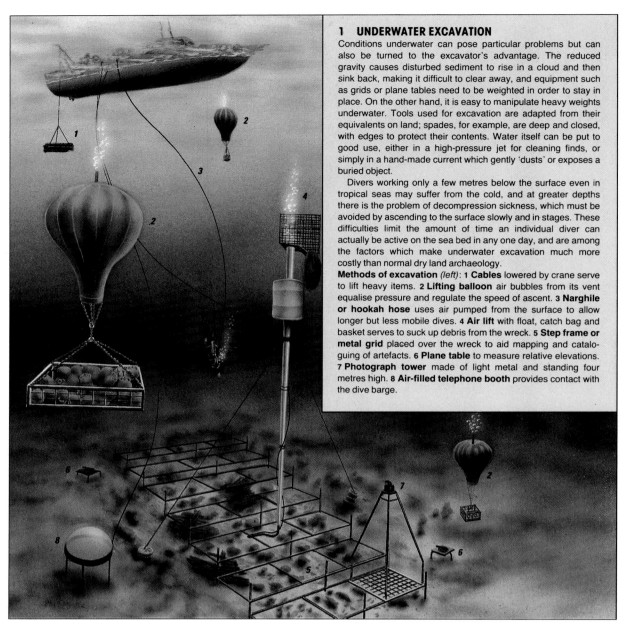

1 UNDERWATER EXCAVATION

Conditions underwater can pose particular problems but can also be turned to the excavator's advantage. The reduced gravity causes disturbed sediment to rise in a cloud and then sink back, making it difficult to clear away, and equipment such as grids or plane tables need to be weighted in order to stay in place. On the other hand, it is easy to manipulate heavy weights underwater. Tools used for excavation are adapted from their equivalents on land; spades, for example, are deep and closed, with edges to protect their contents. Water itself can be put to good use, either in a high-pressure jet for cleaning finds, or simply in a hand-made current which gently 'dusts' or exposes a buried object.

Divers working only a few metres below the surface even in tropical seas may suffer from the cold, and at greater depths there is the problem of decompression sickness, which must be avoided by ascending to the surface slowly and in stages. These difficulties limit the amount of time an individual diver can actually be active on the sea bed in any one day, and are among the factors which make underwater excavation much more costly than normal dry land archaeology.

Methods of excavation (left): **1 Cables** lowered by crane serve to lift heavy items. **2 Lifting balloon** air bubbles from its vent equalise pressure and regulate the speed of ascent. **3 Narghile or hookah hose** uses air pumped from the surface to allow longer but less mobile dives. **4 Air lift** with float, catch bag and basket serves to suck up debris from the wreck. **5 Step frame or metal grid** placed over the wreck to aid mapping and cataloguing of artefacts. **6 Plane table** to measure relative elevations. **7 Photograph tower** made of light metal and standing four metres high. **8 Air-filled telephone booth** provides contact with the dive barge.

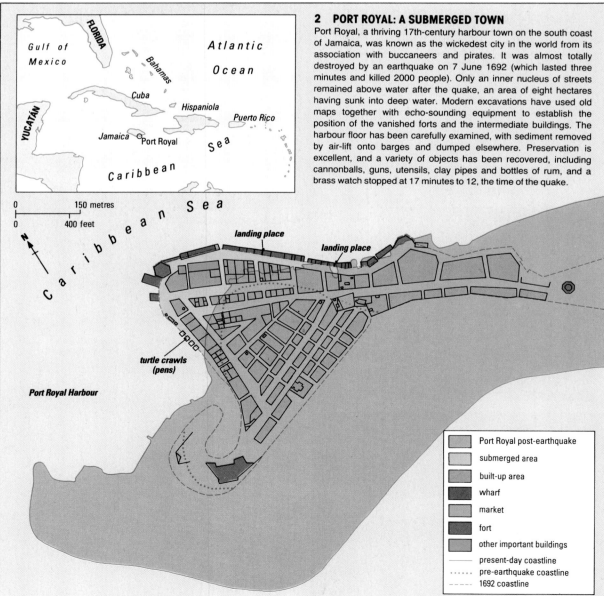

2 PORT ROYAL: A SUBMERGED TOWN

Port Royal, a thriving 17th-century harbour town on the south coast of Jamaica, was known as the wickedest city in the world from its association with buccaneers and pirates. It was almost totally destroyed by an earthquake on 7 June 1692 (which lasted three minutes and killed 2000 people). Only an inner nucleus of streets remained above water after the quake, an area of eight hectares having sunk into deep water. Modern excavations have used old maps together with echo-sounding equipment to establish the position of the vanished forts and the intermediate buildings. The harbour floor has been carefully examined, with sediment removed by air-lift onto barges and dumped elsewhere. Preservation is excellent, and a variety of objects has been recovered, including cannonballs, guns, utensils, clay pipes and bottles of rum, and a brass watch stopped at 17 minutes to 12, the time of the quake.

landing place

landing place

turtle crawls (pens)

Port Royal Harbour

0 — 150 metres
0 — 400 feet
N

Gulf of Mexico

Atlantic Ocean

Bahamas

Cuba

Hispaniola

Puerto Rico

Jamaica — Port Royal

Sea

Caribbean

YUCATÁN

FLORIDA

Caribbean Sea

Port Royal post-earthquake
submerged area
built-up area
wharf
market
fort
other important buildings
— present-day coastline
····· pre-earthquake coastline
----- 1692 coastline

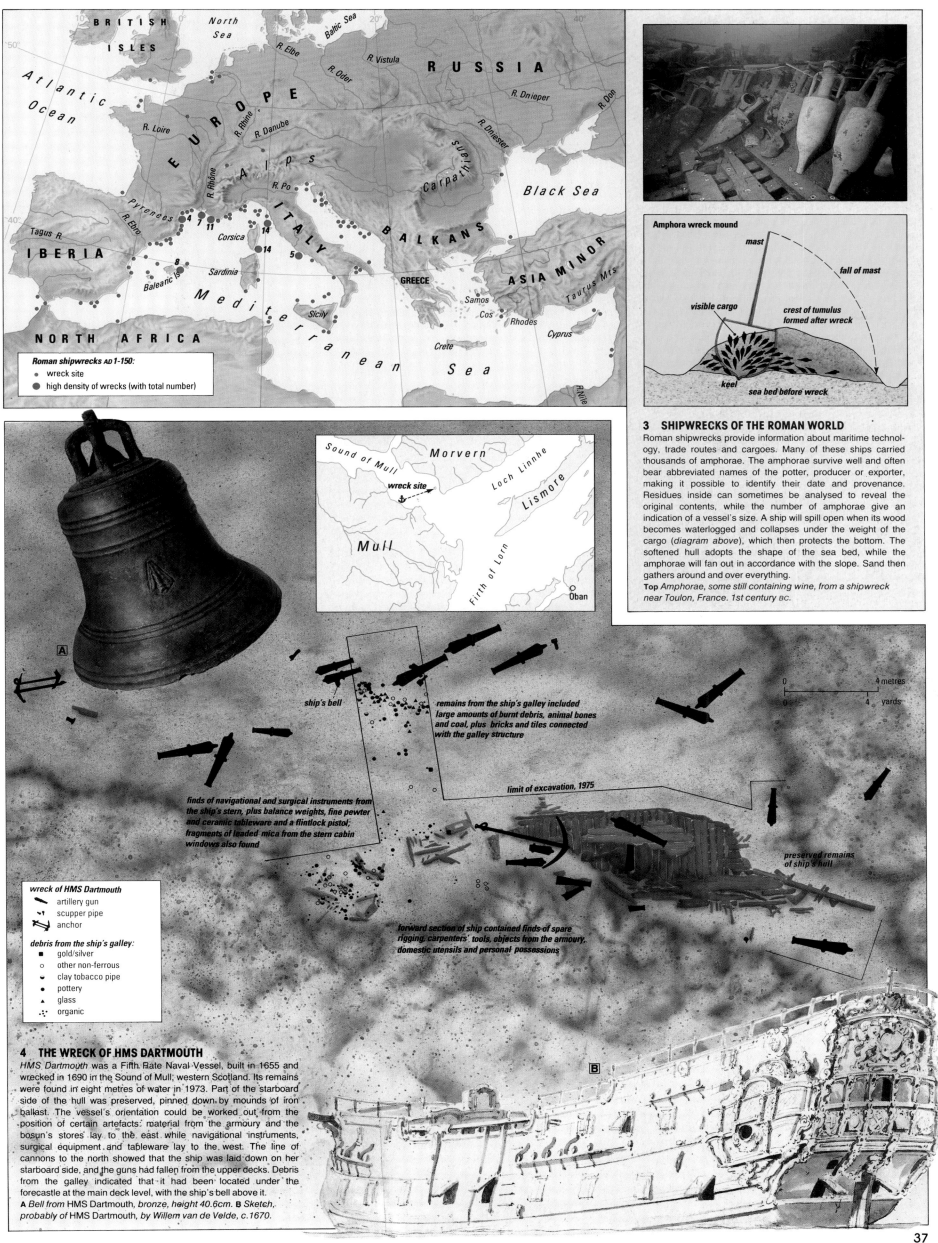

3 SHIPWRECKS OF THE ROMAN WORLD

Roman shipwrecks provide information about maritime technology, trade routes and cargoes. Many of these ships carried thousands of amphorae. The amphorae survive well and often bear abbreviated names of the potter, producer or exporter, making it possible to identify their date and provenance. Residues inside can sometimes be analysed to reveal the original contents, while the number of amphorae give an indication of a vessel's size. A ship will spill open when its wood becomes waterlogged and collapses under the weight of the cargo (*diagram above*), which then protects the bottom. The softened hull adopts the shape of the sea bed, while the amphorae will fan out in accordance with the slope. Sand then gathers around and over everything.

Top *Amphorae, some still containing wine, from a shipwreck near Toulon, France. 1st century* BC.

Roman shipwrecks AD 1-150:
- wreck site
- high density of wrecks (with total number)

Amphora wreck mound
- mast
- fall of mast
- visible cargo
- crest of tumulus formed after wreck
- keel
- sea bed before wreck

wreck of HMS Dartmouth
- artillery gun
- scupper pipe
- anchor

debris from the ship's galley:
- gold/silver
- other non-ferrous
- clay tobacco pipe
- pottery
- glass
- organic

ship's bell

remains from the ship's galley included large amounts of burnt debris, animal bones and coal, plus bricks and tiles connected with the galley structure

finds of navigational and surgical instruments from the ship's stern, plus balance weights, fine pewter and ceramic tableware and a flintlock pistol; fragments of leaded mica from the stern cabin windows also found

limit of excavation, 1975

preserved remains of ship's hull

forward section of ship contained finds of spare rigging, carpenters' tools, objects from the armoury, domestic utensils and personal possessions

4 THE WRECK OF HMS DARTMOUTH

HMS Dartmouth was a Fifth Rate Naval Vessel, built in 1655 and wrecked in 1690 in the Sound of Mull, western Scotland. Its remains were found in eight metres of water in 1973. Part of the starboard side of the hull was preserved, pinned down by mounds of iron ballast. The vessel's orientation could be worked out from the position of certain artefacts: material from the armoury and the bosun's stores lay to the east, while navigational instruments, surgical equipment and tableware lay to the west. The line of cannons to the north showed that the ship was laid down on her starboard side, and the guns had fallen from the upper decks. Debris from the galley indicated that it had been located under the forecastle at the main deck level, with the ship's bell above it.

A *Bell from HMS Dartmouth, bronze, height 40.6cm.* **B** *Sketch, probably of HMS Dartmouth, by Willem van de Velde, c.1670.*

Food

There can be few aspects of life more fundamental to human existence than food. For much of the past 3 million years the life of the hunter-gatherer was largely devoted to the food quest, and usually there were no means of storing food supplies. The change from reliance on wild foods to domestic animals and crops was a very recent development, beginning only about 10,000 years ago. The ability to provide a stable food supply and to create a storable surplus of food, soon led to the development of more complex societies.

When archaeologists recover the remains of our distant ancestors and their tools, they also look for clues about their foods. The process is essentially one of detective work, and direct evidence may survive in a variety of different forms: animal bones, sometimes showing butchery marks, or traces of burning during cooking, and plant remains, preserved as charred seeds or fruits, or buried in conditions which favour preservation, such as waterlogged soil, desiccated environments and permanent frost (permafrost), or as impressions in mud-brick or pottery. Only in rare instances do prepared foods such as loaves of bread or large vessels filled with mead or wine survive. The study of the tools used for food preparation – cutting, grinding, pounding and cooking – enables us to understand the range of cooking techniques which were available to a given society, and to see how they developed through time. Representations of foods and of food preparation in contemporary art, wall paintings and pottery may also supplement this information.

Human remains also provide evidence of diet. Careful excavation of the stomach regions of skeletons may reveal the contents of the last meal. The Iron Age bodies recovered from the bogs in Scandinavia and Britain had their stomachs preserved intact; their last meals consisted of a range of cereals, linseed and a great number of weed seeds – some possibly added as flavourings. Human coprolites (fossil faeces) are another important source of information in waterlogged or desiccated conditions. The most important crops were those which supplied the farmers with easily storable supplies of carbohydrate – wheat, maize, rice, barley, oats, rye, millet, sorghum. In parts of the tropics carbohydrates are supplied by the sweet potato, taro, yam, manioc, banana and bread fruit. In addition to carbohydrates the human diet must contain fats and proteins. Domestic animals provide the main sources of these. Vegetable proteins are found mainly in the legumes, the most important in the Old World being beans, peas and lentils, which were domesticated at the same time as cereals.

The present-day distribution of foods owes much to trade and the introduction of domestic plants and animals to new areas. The Greeks and Romans built up extensive trade in plant foods, olive oil and wine, and imported spices from the Far East. The next influx of food plants into Europe was brought by the Arabs to Spain. They introduced lemons and oranges, peaches, pomegranates, bananas, figs, aubergines, asparagus, rice, liquorice and sugar cane. The discovery of America brought further new crops to Europe: maize, potatoes, tomatoes, beans, red and green peppers and peanuts. In exchange Columbus carried vegetable seeds, wheat, chickpeas and sugarcane to the Caribbean islands.

Alcoholic beverages were traded early in human history. The first known recipe for beer comes from a clay tablet in southern Mesopotamia dating to c.2500 BC. Mildly alcoholic drinks have been made throughout history using a wide range of ingredients: honey, rice, agave, cereal fruits, grapes. The keeping qualities of some of these drinks allow them to be transported over long distances without deterioration. Wine was perhaps the first to be traded extensively round and from the Mediterranean, providing one of the sources of income on which the civilisations of Greece and Rome were based.

Animals were domesticated for a number of different purposes – for draught, wool and hair, as beasts of burden, for riding and for food. As sources of food, animals provide meat, and may also be used for milk and milk products, and for blood. A total of only about 50 animals have been truly domesticated, if the honey bee, the silkworm and fish such as carp and trout are included. Of these only cattle, pigs, goats and water buffalo have a wide global distribution. Fish and seafood have also played an important role in man's diet. From the Palaeolithic period onwards people valued the harvest of the seashore, and the remains of shellfish are found in huge middens around many temperate coastlines.

Availability and distribution of different types of food has had a powerful influence on the ways in which human societies have organised their annual round of everyday activities. The study of food is a critical element in the understanding of these societies and their development.

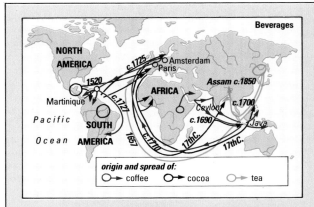

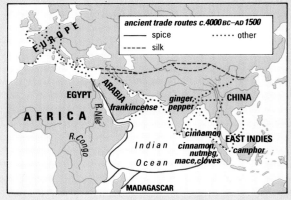

1 FOOD, TRADE AND COLONISATION
The spread of crops across the world reflects the expansion of trade and colonisation from the period of the first civilisations to the European conquest of America (*see maps right*). One group of plants – the spices – have themselves been responsible for stimulating much early exploration (*above*). They were highly prized by early civilisations in China, Greece, Rome and Egypt. Even earlier, in c.3000 BC, the Sumerians were using cloves from the Moluccas, and the Old Testament refers to cinnamon from Ceylon. Spices added variety to the diet, concealed the flavour of meat that was not fresh, and increased the rate of perspiration thus having a cooling effect on the body. They have always been rated as an expensive luxury, and indeed were so valuable that the one surviving shipload returning to Europe from Magellan's ill-fated voyage round the world (1519–22) paid for the entire expedition.

3 THE ARCHAEOLOGY OF FOOD
Both contemporary representations of food and food production and preserved remains can tell us much about prehistoric diet. Egyptian tombs are a particularly rich source, with detailed wall paintings showing harvesting, baking, brewing and feasting scenes, and elaborate models of bakers and brewers at work. In South America pots were modelled in the shapes of maize cobs, peanuts, bean pods and potatoes. Remains of food are rarely preserved, and normally due to waterlogged, arid or exceptionally cold conditions, although in some instances an extraordinary occurrence such as the eruption of Vesuvius at Pompeii can also lead to remarkable preservation.

A *Corn cob figure from Peru. Mochica culture, AD 400–600, height 16.5cm.* **B** *Model from Egypt, of three servants making bread: the woman kneeling is grinding grain, the man is kneading dough, and the other woman is tending the oven, while shielding herself from the heat with her hand. 6th Dynasty, c.2250 BC, wood, length 40.8cm.* **C** *Sun-dried fish in a bowl from Thebes, Egypt. New Kingdom c.1250 BC.* **D** *Seeds and walnuts preserved under layers of volcanic ash after the eruption of Vesuvius at Pompeii in AD 79.*

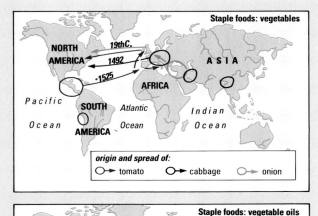

Staple foods: vegetables

origin and spread of:
- ◯→ tomato
- ◯→ cabbage
- ◯→ onion

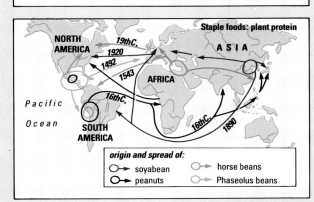

Staple foods: vegetable oils

origin and spread of:
- ◯ cottonseed
- ◯ sunflower
- ◯→ palm oil

Staple foods: plant protein

origin and spread of:
- ◯→ soyabean
- ◯→ peanuts
- ◯ horse beans
- ◯ Phaseolus beans

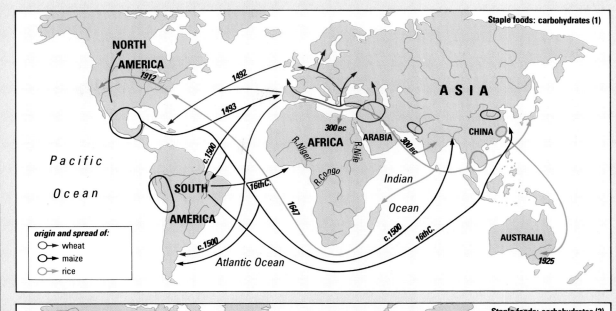

Staple foods: carbohydrates (1)

origin and spread of:
- ◯→ wheat
- ◯→ maize
- ◯→ rice

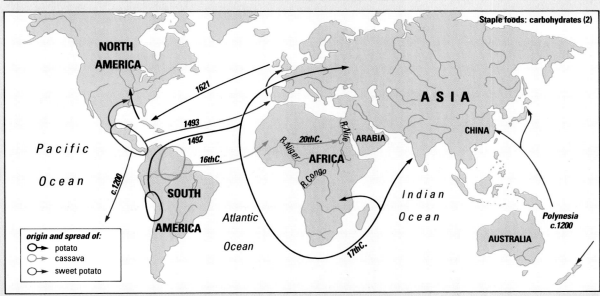

Staple foods: carbohydrates (2)

origin and spread of:
- ◯→ potato
- ◯→ cassava
- ◯→ sweet potato

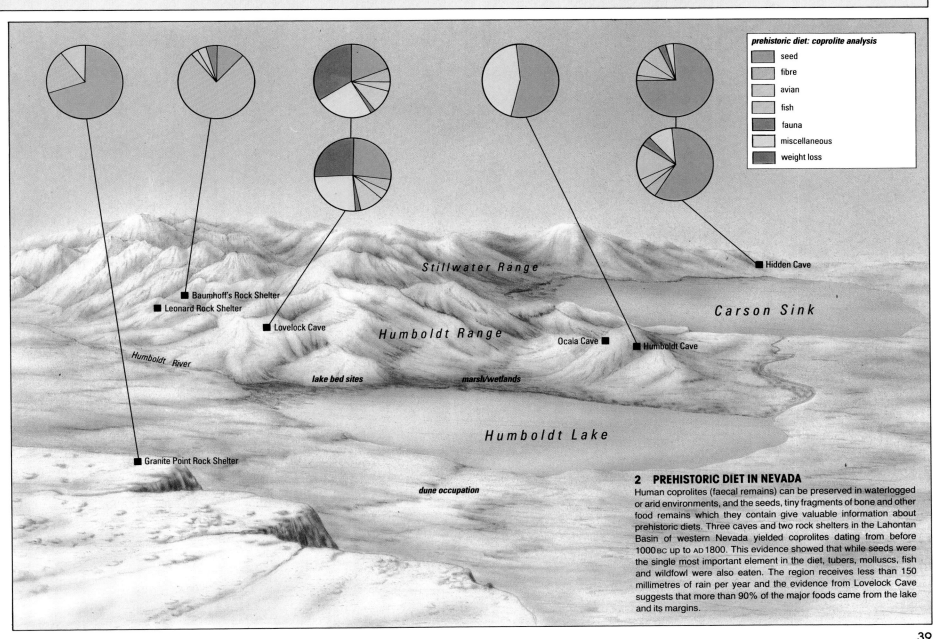

prehistoric diet: coprolite analysis
- seed
- fibre
- avian
- fish
- fauna
- miscellaneous
- weight loss

Stillwater Range

Hidden Cave

Carson Sink

Baumhoff's Rock Shelter

Leonard Rock Shelter

Lovelock Cave

Humboldt Range

Ocala Cave

Humboldt Cave

Humboldt River

lake bed sites

marsh/wetlands

Granite Point Rock Shelter

Humboldt Lake

dune occupation

2 PREHISTORIC DIET IN NEVADA

Human coprolites (faecal remains) can be preserved in waterlogged or arid environments, and the seeds, tiny fragments of bone and other food remains which they contain give valuable information about prehistoric diets. Three caves and two rock shelters in the Lahontan Basin of western Nevada yielded coprolites dating from before 1000 BC up to AD 1800. This evidence showed that while seeds were the single most important element in the diet, tubers, molluscs, fish and wildfowl were also eaten. The region receives less than 150 millimetres of rain per year and the evidence from Lovelock Cave suggests that more than 90% of the major foods came from the lake and its margins.

Textiles

Clothing and textiles have been among the most important products of human skill for well over a million years. It is only because of clothing that man has been able to spread beyond his original tropical homeland into cooler and less hospitable regions. Clothing and textiles have also played a crucial role in social life. Particular woven designs in carpetry, for example, are sometimes the mark of a clan or tribe, and fine or expensive clothing has always been a major expression of social status.

The character of early textile production was closely related to regional climatic conditions, and methods of spinning and weaving were adapted to locally available fibres. Climate has also directly influenced the survival of textile remains – cold, dry and waterlogged conditions are ideally suited to the preservation of fabrics.

Plant fibres were the first to be utilised by prehistoric man. The earliest known Old World textiles are linens from Çatal Hüyük in Anatolia dated to c.6500 BC; the first northern European textiles do not appear until 3500 BC. In China silk was being woven by c.2700 BC, while in the New World there are textiles in Peru before 1000 BC.

After man's domestication of animals it was found that the wool and hair of sheep, goats and members of the camel family could readily be spun, their surface scales interlocking to give a stable yarn. The animals were plucked or, after the introduction of metal tools, shorn. In China, on the other hand, it was discovered that the domesticated silkworm, *Bombyx mori*, extrudes a filament that requires no spin to give it strength.

Vegetable fibres, in contrast, require more labour to convert into textiles; they have to be extracted from the stem or bark of the host plant, and vigorously pounded and combined before they can be spun. Until the introduction of the spinning wheel (in the Middle Ages in Europe, but earlier in China) raw fibre was converted into yarn on the hand-spindle, a short wooden stick that could be rolled on the thigh to give the yarn twist, or rotated between finger and thumb, either supported in a bowl or hanging free. The free-hanging spindle was normally weighted with a whorl, a pierced disc of bone or pottery, to give it momentum. Spinners – notably in ancient Egypt and Inca Peru – were capable of creating extraordinarily fine yarn. The direction in which the spindle was rotated, either clockwise or anticlockwise, was dictated by local social tradition.

Weaving, the act of interlocking weft and warp threads, required a loom, if only a simple one. A range of immensely complex patterned fabrics was woven on the Peruvian backstrap loom. A similar loom, mounted at ground level, was characteristic of Dynastic Egypt, and is still in use among the Bedouin. Much of our knowledge of ancient Egyptian weaving techniques comes to us from wall paintings and tomb models. The first vertical frame loom, in which the warp was extended between two beams, appeared in Egypt in 1200 BC. The best-known loom of Europe and the Near East was the warp-weighted vertical loom, on which a set of weights tied to groups of warp threads replaced the lower beam and gave the loom great flexibility.

In the last three centuries BC Chinese weavers were experimenting with raised horizontal or obliquely mounted looms on which elaborate warp-patterned designs were achieved. Independently, craftsmen in western Asia had learnt by AD 200 to weave damask and other patterned silks on a raised horizontal loom with multiple heddle rods. Rapid technical evolution between AD 300 and 1000 led to the development of the drawloom for structurally complex silks, and to the basic handloom for everyday silks.

Pattern weaves gave each region its distinctive textile imprint. Check patterns, whether in Iron Age Europe, the Islamic East or Inca Peru, relied on planned use of contrasting colours in both warp and weft. Hand-plaited braids, abundant in the New World, also involved pre-planned patterning. Tapestry weaves, popular in Central America and the Mediterranean, were freehand designs in weft yarn over bare warp. More complex weft-faced weave structures, especially in silk, were associated with the Chinese and Byzantine horizontal looms; but Peruvian weavers were noted for double-cloth, made from two separate fabrics with interlocked patterns. Various forms of looped or knotted pile for cloaks, carpets and hangings are recorded. Embroidery, however, despite its versatility, took second place to woven patterns, and both were ultimately in competition in some regions with tie-dyed, resist-dyed or printed fabrics.

The dyer's craft depended on colouring agents extracted from plants, molluscs and insects. A branch of empirical chemistry, it helped the weaver to satisfy the urge of humans to adorn as well as to cover themselves.

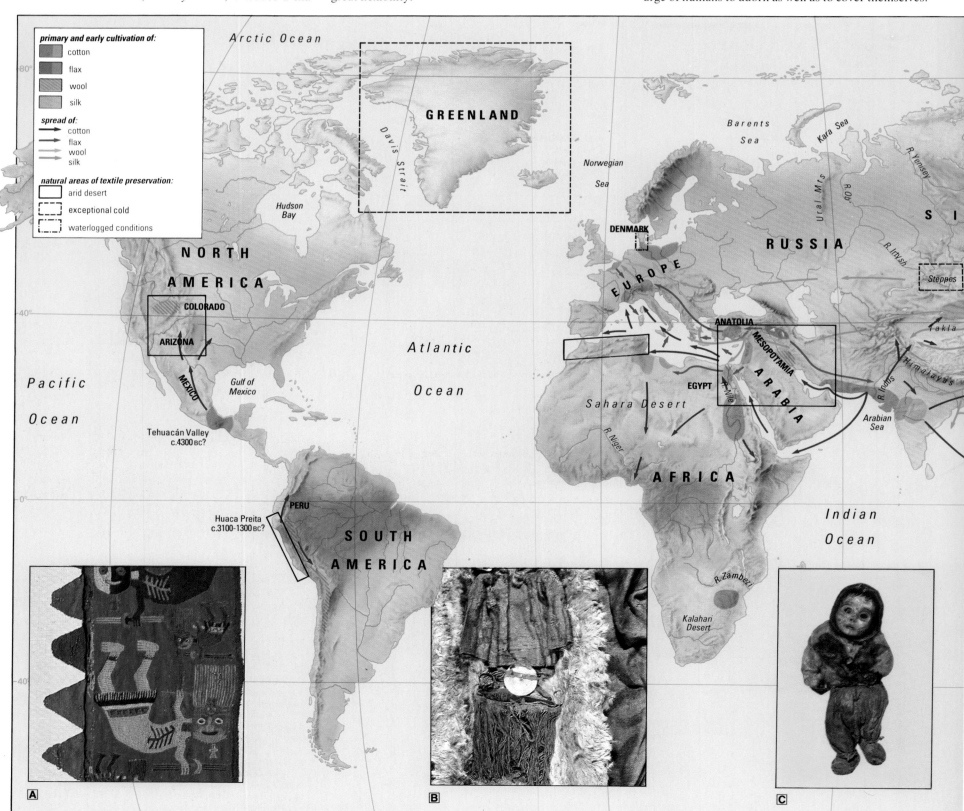

primary and early cultivation of:
cotton
flax
wool
silk

spread of:
cotton
flax
wool
silk

natural areas of textile preservation:
arid desert
exceptional cold
waterlogged conditions

Arctic Ocean

GREENLAND

Davis Strait

Barents Sea

Kara Sea

R. Yenisey

Norwegian Sea

Hudson Bay

DENMARK

RUSSIA

R. Ob

R. Irtysh

S I

NORTH AMERICA

EUROPE

Steppes

Takla

COLORADO

ARIZONA

ANATOLIA

MESOPOTAMIA

ARABIA

Himalayas

R. Indus

MEXICO

Atlantic Ocean

EGYPT

R. Nile

Arabian Sea

Pacific Ocean

Gulf of Mexico

Sahara Desert

R. Niger

Tehuacán Valley c.4300 BC?

AFRICA

Indian Ocean

PERU

Huaca Preita c.3100–1300 BC?

SOUTH AMERICA

R. Zambezi

Kalahari Desert

A

B

C

2 TEXTILES: RANGE AND USES

Not content with wearing the skins of other mammals, early man experimented with every conceivable source of natural fibre that grew around him. The use of an extraordinary range of strong fibres (mainly of vegetable origin) for ropes, netting and basketry has been attested. Linen, the earliest known Old World textile, was transported, with the spread of Neolithic farming techniques, far from its centre of discovery in Mesopotamia. Cotton, which grew both in the Near East and in the Americas, later became more important. For woven textiles only a limited number of fibres proved over time to be fully satisfactory. The cultivated silk of China was highly prized, and traded vast distances along the trans-Asian Silk Road to the markets of the Mediterranean. Sheep and goats were important wool-bearing animals in the Old World, and vicuña, llama and alpaca in the New.

1 TEXTILES: PRESERVATION AND AVAILABILITY

Cultivated flax (*Linum usitatissimum*) had been developed from the wild flax of Mesopotamia by the 7th millennium BC, and subsequently its use spread into Europe and the Indus Valley. Indigenous species of cotton are found in both the Old and the New World, and the potential of the cotton boll's fibres was discovered independently in several centres. Sheep had been domesticated in western Asia by 9000 BC, but were not wool-bearing until perhaps 3000 BC: woolly sheep are found everywhere in Europe by the beginning of the Bronze Age. Yarn was spun from the cocoons of several varieties of wild silk moth throughout Asia but sericulture did not reach the eastern Mediterranean until the 6th century AD.

Preserved textiles A *An embroidered cloak fringe from the Peruvian coastal desert. c.200 BC, height 59cm, width 15cm.*
B *The woollen dress of a Bronze Age girl buried in a mound at Egtved, Denmark. c.1120 BC.* **C** *A fully clothed baby of about six months buried in the permafrost at Qilakitsoq, western Greenland. c.AD 1475.*

Natural materials used in textile production

function	animal skins		animal fibres		plant fibres	
	Old World:	New World:	Old World:	New World:	Old World:	New World:
cloth and clothing	*wolf*	*moose*	*silkworm*	*guanoco*	*cotton*	*cotton*
	bear	*dog*	*sheep*	*vicuna*	*flax*	*yucca leaves*
	ox	*rabbit*	*goat*	*alpaca*	*ramie*	*apocynum*
	deer	*buffalo*	*camel*	*llama*	*jute*	*maguey*
	wildcat	*musk ox*	*rabbit*	*dog*	*mallow*	*cabuya*
	sable	*caribou*	*dog*	*rabbit*	*nettles*	*puya*
	otter	*seal*	*mollusc (pinna marina)*	*human hair*	*hemp*	*tillandsia*
	leopard	*deer*	*horse*	*bear*		
	colt	*bear/polar bear*	*cow*	*buffalo*		
	sheep	*jaguar*	*beaver*	*mountain goat*		
			mineral – asbestos	*feathers*		
matting, basketry and cordage			*goat*	*human hair* *bast from lime*	*flax* *hemp* *esparto grass* *mallow* *nettles* *corn-straw*	*apocynum* *yucca leaves* *shredded juniper* *bark* *willow* *ixtle* *agave* *junco* *totora* *pisa* *penca* *milkweeds* *vines*

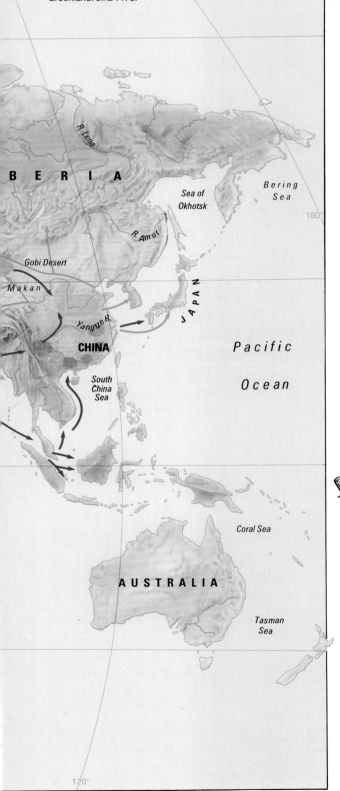

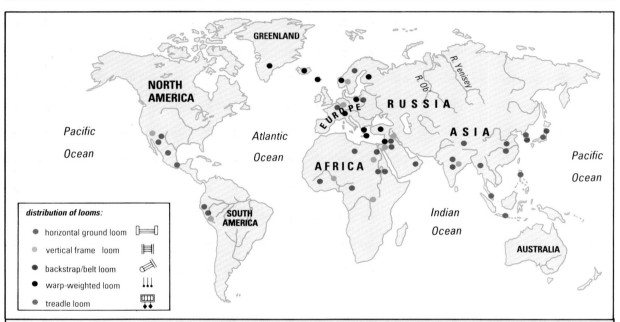

distribution of looms:
- horizontal ground loom
- vertical frame loom
- backstrap/belt loom
- warp-weighted loom
- treadle loom

3 ANCIENT EGYPT: WEAVING METHODS

The horizontal ground loom of ancient Egypt, reconstructed below, illustrates the main principles of weaving. The warp threads, spanned between the warp beam and the breast beam, are divided into two layers. Odd-numbered yarns (blue) are raised by a heddle rod linked to them by string loops to open the first shed through which the weft yarn is passed on a spool. The weaver compacts the new weft against the cloth already woven with a sword-beater. The second (counter) shed is opened with a shed rod alone. The same principles are used in the vertical warp-weighted and two-beam frame looms of Europe and the simple backstrap looms of the Americas and South-East Asia (see map above for global distribution of looms).
Below left *tomb painting from Beni Hasan, Egypt, showing weavers. c.1890 BC, 10.4 x 6.7m.*

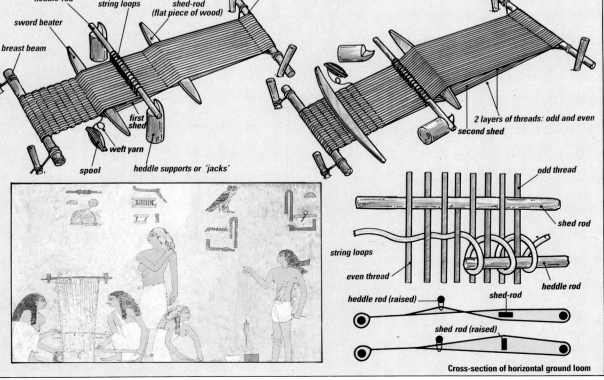

ANALYSIS
Disease

Palaeopathology is the study of disease in ancient peoples. Human remains are perhaps the closest we can get to ancient people, closer to their experience than their artefacts or settlements, and while archaeology strives to be objective, we need to remind ourselves that we are researching the lifestyle of real individuals from the past. A small amount of work with skeletons can indicate many things: the age and sex of the individual and the height and build can frequently be estimated. It is even possible to reconstruct facial features, as forensic scientists do in crime cases. The faces of many early human types, such as Neanderthal man, have been reconstructed, and as part of the work of the Manchester Mummy Project a medical illustrator produced paintings, drawings and models of the heads of several of the mummies.

A surprising amount of information can be gained from human bones about a person's genetic inheritance, natural environment and social conditions. Bones present evidence of sickness, deformity, inadequate diet, injury – accidental or as a result of violence – early death or a suffering old age. On the other hand, we can often find evidence of robust good health, sound healing of severe injuries or long survival through serious illness.

Bone changes throughout life. The skeleton is an organ of the body, and bone contains within itself, not only structural cells (*osteocytes*), but also cells that can break the structure down (*osteoclasts*) and others that rebuild it (*osteoblasts*). A membrane called the *periosteum* surrounds every bone, and this contains many *osteoblastic* cells, which contribute to bone growth in the earlier years and to repair in later life. The *periosteum* disappears after death, but evidence of its activity in response to infection or injury can be found in many diseased bones.

In the foetus and growing child, the skeleton develops according to its hereditary constitution, and some pathologies result from inherited disease, for example brittle bone disease and congenital deformation of the hip. Thus family relationships can sometimes be identified. Palaeopathologists also look for a number of 'non-metric traits' (harmless variations in bone size and shape, position of nerves, etc.) which can run in families: the additional 'Wormian' bones, for example, found in the skulls of the so-called Princes in the Tower of London suggest that they were closely related. Environmental influences can affect normal growth in the child, one of the commonest effects being slowing or halting of growth due to sickness or inadequate diet. The lines of faulty bone production at the growing ends of a long bone show up on X-rays; these are called Harris lines.

The bones of an adult constantly renew and repair themselves. Fractures are often found in ancient skeletons, some are cleanly healed, some have occurred shortly before death and show no signs of healing. Splinting appears to have been uncommon in the past, so we find many broken limb bones shortened or twisted by the tightening of powerful muscles. Even horrific head wounds have been survived: some ancient Egyptian skulls have had the braincase shattered – presumably by blows from a heavy weapon such as a mace – but the injuries have healed well and the person has lived on into old age. Trepanation, the cutting of holes in the skull for relief of pressure, or perhaps for magical reasons, is known from archaeology and ethnography, and the recovery rate is extraordinary; the largest number known in one skull is seven, all well-healed. On the other hand, in societies where medical and dental treatment was poor, severe illness or death could result from apparently trivial causes, for example dental abscesses. The dental health of the ancient Egyptians was appalling, and more than one pharoah suffered from abscesses which would have caused great pain, and may even have hastened death.

Disease patterns change through time. When looking at a particular group – from one grave, from a burial ground or even from a whole area or country – it is useful to look at the pattern of disease and mortality. How and at what age did people die, and are there status- or occupation-linked differences in disease patterns? For example, it was common for sailors in the past to suffer or even die of scurvy, a deficiency of Vitamin C resulting from a lack of fresh fruit and vegetables. We also have to consider whether the group being studied was representative of a wider population, or was distinctive in some way, such as an isolated community where genetic variants might be found. Palaeopathology shows that early populations were subject to disease on a scale which makes it a significant factor in human history.

Archaeology is able to produce ancient bone material – and occasionally mummified soft tissue – which allows the nature, development and prevalence of disease to be charted. The resulting picture makes the cultural achievements of disease-affected and undernourished early societies even more impressive.

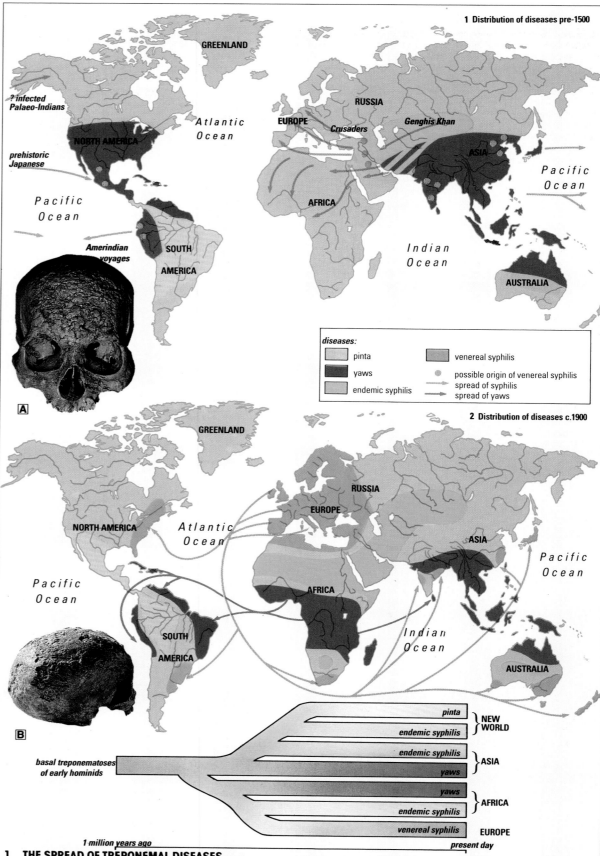

1 Distribution of diseases pre-1500

2 Distribution of diseases c.1900

diseases:
- pinta
- yaws
- endemic syphilis
- venereal syphilis
- possible origin of venereal syphilis
- spread of syphilis
- spread of yaws

1 million years ago ... **present day**

basal treponematoses of early hominids

pinta / endemic syphilis — **NEW WORLD**
endemic syphilis / yaws — **ASIA**
yaws / endemic syphilis — **AFRICA**
venereal syphilis — **EUROPE**

1 THE SPREAD OF TREPONEMAL DISEASES

It has long been thought (map 2) that veneral syphilis spread through Europe in the 1st century AD, and throughout the world from the 16th century AD. Recent research (map 1) suggests, however, the spread of an ancestral disease from Asia into the Americas. The diagram (*above*) suggests that multiple forms have evolved from a common ancestor.

A *Facial view of skull with widespread inflammation of forehead due to treponemal disease. From Cueva de Cendelaria, Mexico, pre-Columbian.* B *Cranium of mediaeval woman from London, showing the characteristic bone erosion of the late stages of syphilis.*

The archaeology of disease

Congenital and developmental	Deficiency diseases
dwanism and gigantism *Down's syndrome* *hydrocephaly* *spina bifida* *cleft palate* *congenital dislocations (such as hip joint)* *additional or missing bones* *congenital anaemias (radiographic 'hair on end' appearance to skull)*	*rickets (childhood)/osteomalacia (adulthood) (light and brittle bones, long bones bowed and/or fractured)* *scurvy (calcified haemorrhages below the bone surface)* *iron deficiency anaemia ('hair on end' radiographic appearance, possible sieve-like appearance within eye orbits)*
Trauma and surgery	**Non-communicable diseases**
fractures *cuts and puncture wounds (from sword or arrow perhaps)* *trepanation* *amputation* *deliberate deformation of bones (such as head flattening and foot binding)*	*osteoarthritis* *rheumatoid arthritis* *gout*
	Dental diseases
	caries (tooth decay) *periodontal disease (gum infections, often leading to erosion of the bony support of the teeth and tooth loss)* *abscesses* *impaction (usually wisdom teeth)*
Communicable diseases	**Neoplasia – tumours**
leprosy (destruction of small bones) *treponemal diseases (such as syphilis, yaws: destruction and regeneration of bone)* *tuberculosis (septic arthritis at joints)* *poliomyelitis (restricted bone growth in a paralysed limb)* *periostitis/osteomyelitis (reaction to infection – appears as rough, irregular areas of bone destruction and regeneration)*	*malignant tumours of bone or other tissues (such as bone marrow cartilege and connective tissue)* *benign tumours and cysts (variously sized and shaped outgrowths of bone or bone cavities)* *secondaries (metastases) from primary malignant tumours (small, irregular perforations throughout skeleton)*

2 SOFT TISSUE: THE MANCHESTER MUMMIES

Mummified tissue can be even more informative than skeletal. A team at Manchester, England, has been working on a collection of Egyptian mummies using techniques such as radiography, electron microscopy, fingerprinting, rehydration of desiccated tissues and facial reconstruction.

A *The jaw of Nekht Ankh shows tooth wear, probably due to coarse bread. Severe dental decay was very rare.* **B** *Fingerprint taken from Asru, Chantress of Amun, which indicates that she died in her early 40s having done little or no manual work. However, she could not avoid arthritis in her fingerjoints (X-ray (*C*)) or intestinal parasites (electron micrograph (*D*)).* **E** *The unwrapping of mummy 1770 showed that this teenage girl had lost her lower legs before death – perhaps by crocodile bite – but the embalmers had replaced them with false ones.*

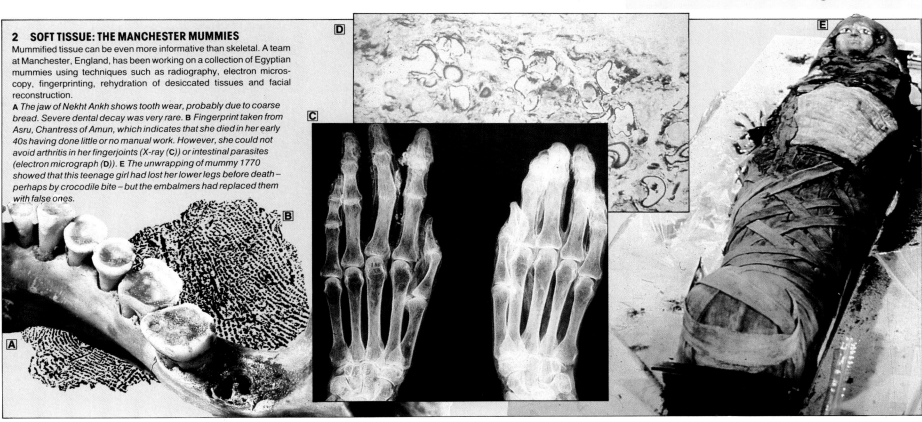

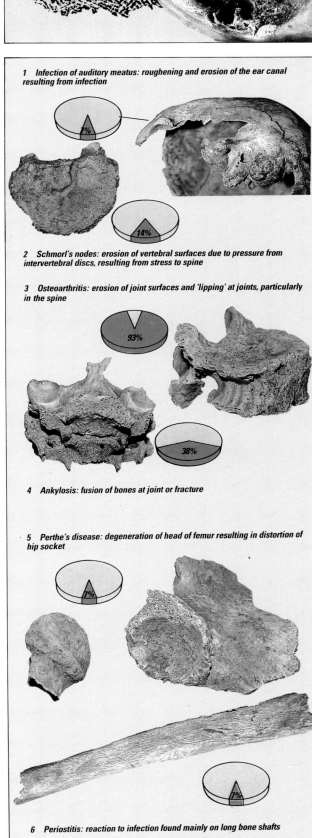

1 *Infection of auditory meatus: roughening and erosion of the ear canal resulting from infection*

2 *Schmorl's nodes: erosion of vertebral surfaces due to pressure from intervertebral discs, resulting from stress to spine*

3 *Osteoarthritis: erosion of joint surfaces and 'lipping' at joints, particularly in the spine*

4 *Ankylosis: fusion of bones at joint or fracture*

5 *Perthe's disease: degeneration of head of femur resulting in distortion of hip socket*

6 *Periostitis: reaction to infection found mainly on long bone shafts*

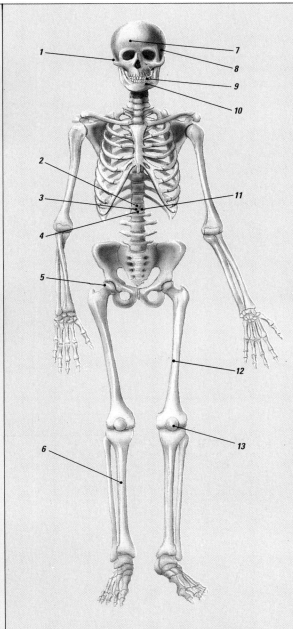

3 GRAFTON REGIS: A MONASTIC COMMUNITY

The 14th-century burial ground of the monastery of Grafton Regis contained a roughly contemporaneous group of skeletons, 14 men between 30 and 55. The majority of these men had arthritis, and many showed resultant changes such as eburnation and ankylosis. More than half had broken bones, several multiple. Although documentary evidence tells us that the monks of this period did not do manual labour, a heavy workload is implied by stress fractures of the feet and compression fractures of the spine. Compared with the ancient Egyptians they had little tooth wear, but they had even higher rates of dental decay than most mediaeval people.

Above *The relative percentages of diseases suffered by the monks of Grafton Regis in Northamptonshire, England.*

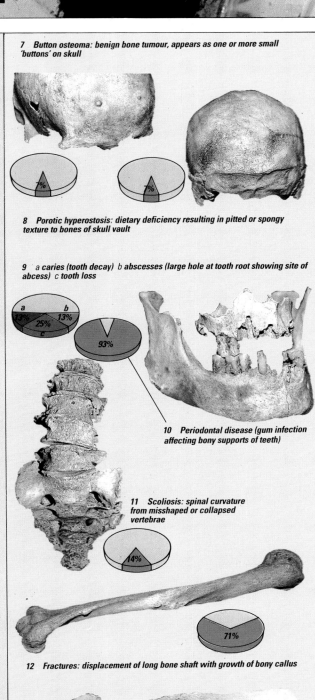

7 *Button osteoma: benign bone tumour, appears as one or more small 'buttons' on skull*

8 *Porotic hyperostosis: dietary deficiency resulting in pitted or spongy texture to bones of skull vault*

9 *a caries (tooth decay) b abscesses (large hole at tooth root showing site of abcess) c tooth loss*

10 *Periodontal disease (gum infection affecting bony supports of teeth)*

11 *Scoliosis: spinal curvature from misshaped or collapsed vertebrae*

12 *Fractures: displacement of long bone shaft with growth of bony callus*

13 *Eburnation: polishing of bone surface when cartilage has been destroyed, resulting in direct bone-to-bone contact*

Warfare

Aggression has long been an integral part of human nature, perhaps ever since the emergence of the earliest hominids in Africa over two million years ago. However, organised group conflict is first attested only about 10,000 years ago, from evidence in a prehistoric cemetery just north of Wadi Halfa near the Egyptian–Sudanese border. Here no fewer than 24 of the 58 individuals – men, women and children – appear to have met a violent end, in some cases with stone blades actually embedded in the bones. A little later, rock art in south-eastern Spain shows groups of Mesolithic archers firing arrows at each other.

The development of group conflict was closely linked to changes in economy and society, and probably became more serious after the adoption of agriculture. Larger populations placed greater pressure on land and resources, and thus increased tension between neighbours. Settled farmers also had food stores, herd animals and standing crops to steal. The stresses associated with the emergence of more hierarchical societies ruled over by chiefs and kings may also have played an important part in the growth of inter-group conflict.

As human communities became organised into larger units the warfare they waged became ever more lethal. States had greater resources available for aggression, defence and the development of new weapons. Clay tablets from Greece and Mesopotamia tell of full-time specialists employed by the state to produce armour and weaponry, and expensively equipped elite forces such as chariotry and armoured cavalry came into being. Sometimes the whole social and economic order was moulded around the demands of warfare; the feudal system of mediaeval Europe had as one of its principal objectives the maintenance of a force of armoured knights.

Changes in weaponry and equipment had a dramatic effect on warfare, and archaeology can unravel the development of such innovations. Much can be learnt from armaments deposited as grave-goods or as offerings to the gods. Skeletal remains are a further source of evidence, the wounds made by sword cuts sometimes indicating the nature of combat; almost all the cuts in the 14th-century Japanese war cemetery of Zaimokuza, for instance, had been made from horseback against victims who do not appear to have worn helmets.

The use of the horse has been one of the most versatile and important factors in the history of warfare up to modern times. First domesticated in the south Russian Steppes in about 4400 BC, its earliest military use seems to have been as a draught- and later as a chariot-animal. The light, two-wheeled war chariot, pulled by a pair of horses, developed in the Near East after 2000 BC and chariotry formed the elite arm of both the Egyptian and the Hittite armies during the 2nd millennium BC. In about 1000 BC light cavalry was developed, followed a few centuries later by heavy armoured cavalry, though the cavalry charge only reached its full potential after the adoption of the stirrup in the 1st millennium AD. Another innovation that had a great impact on warfare is the Chinese invention of gunpowder, conventionally dated to AD 1161. Military application soon followed, with the development during the 13th century of the first rockets and cannon. The new invention soon spread to the west, and by 1500 western Europe and the Arab world had both heavy cannon and smaller handguns. The military superiority conferred by firearms was a significant factor in the success of European colonial ventures.

Archaeology can also throw considerable light on the course of individual battles and military operations. The most common examples are sieges where the excavation of a city or fortress may encounter evidence of attack or destruction. In some cases these archaeological traces can be linked with a known historical event. The fortress of Masada in Israel, ringed by Roman siege works and with a massive siege ramp built up against one side, is a spectacular example. The archaeological investigation of battlefields is less common. The Battle of the Little Bighorn, however, is an excellent illustration of the way in which archaeology can supply details of a military action that are missing from the historical record, even of a battle that took place only a little over a hundred years ago.

In the study of warfare archaeology is circumstantial and is thus, to some extent, able to avoid the bias inherent in historical accounts written by victor or vanquished. It also provides detailed information about military technology, on which written records are often vague or uninformative. Archaeology's greatest strength is that it is able to fill in details about periods for which there are no historical documents, allowing us to look back into the remote past of our hunter-gatherer ancestors and chart the progress of human conflict from small-scale tribal skirmishes down to the present nuclear age.

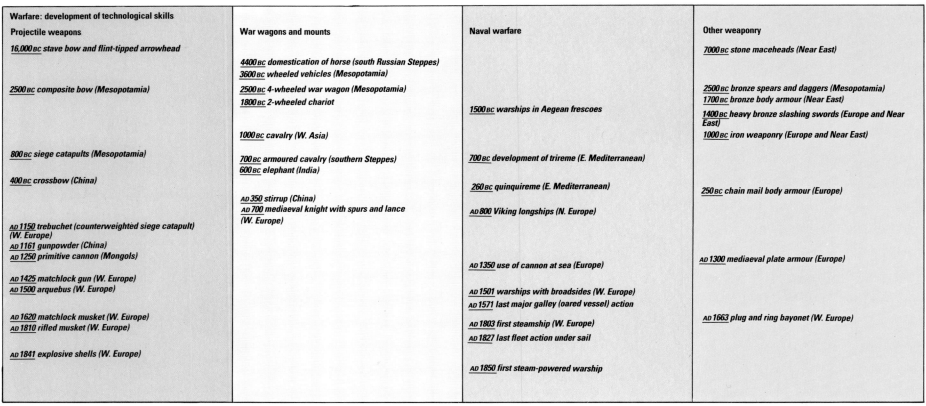

Warfare: development of technological skills			
Projectile weapons	**War wagons and mounts**	**Naval warfare**	**Other weaponry**
16,000 BC stave bow and flint-tipped arrowhead			*7000 BC stone maceheads (Near East)*
	4400 BC domestication of horse (south Russian Steppes)		
	3600 BC wheeled vehicles (Mesopotamia)		
2500 BC composite bow (Mesopotamia)	*2500 BC 4-wheeled war wagon (Mesopotamia)*		*2500 BC bronze spears and daggers (Mesopotamia)*
	1800 BC 2-wheeled chariot		*1700 BC bronze body armour (Near East)*
		1500 BC warships in Aegean frescoes	*1400 BC heavy bronze slashing swords (Europe and Near East)*
	1000 BC cavalry (W. Asia)		*1000 BC iron weaponry (Europe and Near East)*
800 BC siege catapults (Mesopotamia)	*700 BC armoured cavalry (southern Steppes)*	*700 BC development of trireme (E. Mediterranean)*	
400 BC crossbow (China)	*600 BC elephant (India)*		
		260 BC quinquireme (E. Mediterranean)	*250 BC chain mail body armour (Europe)*
	AD 350 stirrup (China)		
	AD 700 mediaeval knight with spurs and lance (W. Europe)	*AD 800 Viking longships (N. Europe)*	
AD 1150 trebuchet (counterweighted siege catapult) (W. Europe)			
AD 1161 gunpowder (China)		*AD 1350 use of cannon at sea (Europe)*	*AD 1300 mediaeval plate armour (Europe)*
AD 1250 primitive cannon (Mongols)			
AD 1425 matchlock gun (W. Europe)		*AD 1501 warships with broadsides (W. Europe)*	
AD 1500 arquebus (W. Europe)		*AD 1571 last major galley (oared vessel) action*	
AD 1620 matchlock musket (W. Europe)		*AD 1803 first steamship (W. Europe)*	*AD 1663 plug and ring bayonet (W. Europe)*
AD 1810 rifled musket (W. Europe)		*AD 1827 last fleet action under sail*	
AD 1841 explosive shells (W. Europe)		*AD 1850 first steam-powered warship*	

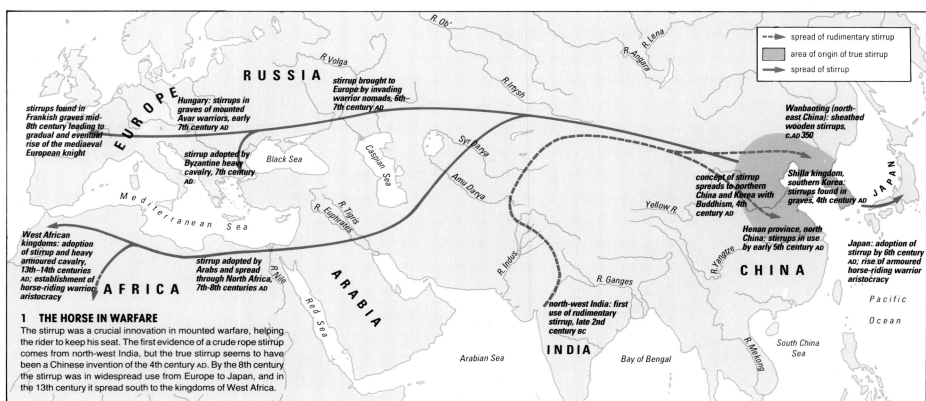

1 THE HORSE IN WARFARE
The stirrup was a crucial innovation in mounted warfare, helping the rider to keep his seat. The first evidence of a crude rope stirrup comes from north-west India, but the true stirrup seems to have been a Chinese invention of the 4th century AD. By the 8th century the stirrup was in widespread use from Europe to Japan, and in the 13th century it spread south to the kingdoms of West Africa.

2 THE BATTLE OF THE LITTLE BIGHORN

In June 1876 the US Seventh Cavalry was defeated by a large force of Cheyenne and Sioux Indians on the banks of the Little Bighorn River. The battle lasted less than an hour, and left some 210 men under the command of Lt. Col. Custer dead. Archaeologists have attempted to reconstruct that single hour's action. The soldiers were issued with Springfield carbines and Colt revolvers, and by mapping spent cartridges fired from these weapons it was possible to identify their posi-

tions. By studying the position of cartridges fired from the same weapon it was possible to show the progress of the battle, with the collapse of the various positions, and finally the convergence on Last Stand Hill. Several years after the battle, markers were erected over the graves of the soldiers. Although the bodies had later been exhumed and reburied in a mass grave, it was thought that if a man had ever been buried near one of the markers, small bones, buttons, boot nails and other items might remain. At marker number 128 archaeologists found an articulated lower leg en-

cased in an eroding cavalry boot. A little deeper lay most of the skeleton. The soldier was between 19 and 22 years old, and about 5' 8" tall. He had one wound on each side of his rib cage, and a bullet wedged in his wrist. These wounds may not have been immediately fatal, and it is likely that this soldier had ridden down the ridge, out of the firing line. As he lay in the grass, bleeding badly and dead or dying, the battle line above him was quickly breached and his death was ensured with a swift savage blow from a rifle butt or tomahawk.

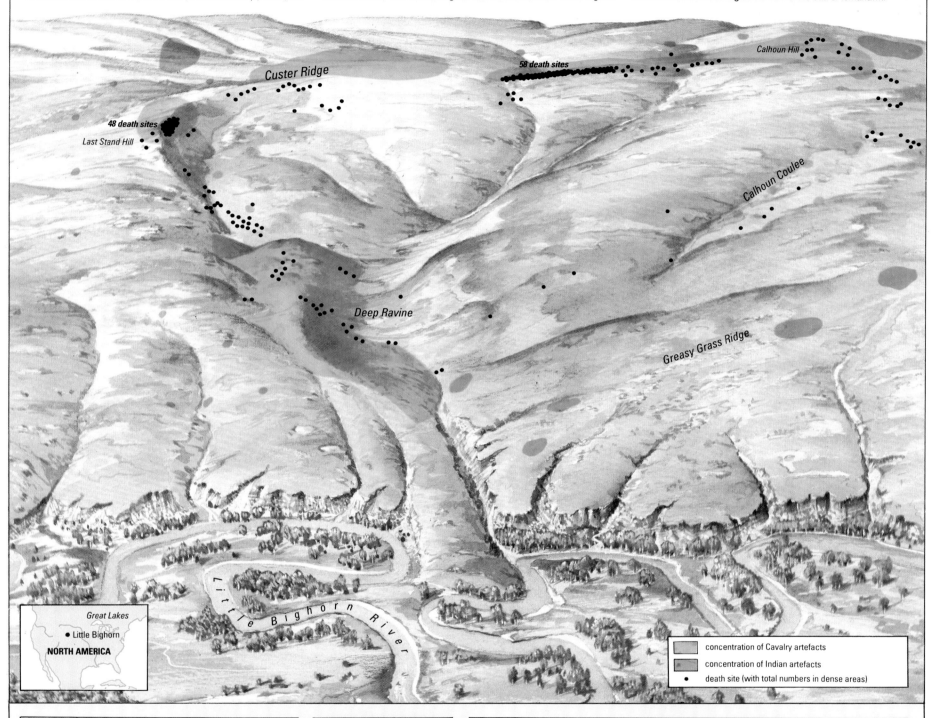

concentration of Cavalry artefacts

concentration of Indian artefacts

• death site (with total numbers in dense areas)

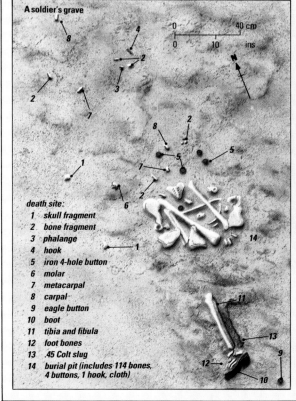

A soldier's grave

death site:
1 skull fragment
2 bone fragment
3 phalange
4 hook
5 iron 4-hole button
6 molar
7 metacarpal
8 carpal
9 eagle button
10 boot
11 tibia and fibula
12 foot bones
13 .45 Colt slug
14 burial pit (includes 114 bones, 4 buttons, 1 hook, cloth)

Above *tibia and fibula with boot in situ from grave (left).*

Above *(left to right) .50/.70 Indian cartridge case, .45/.55 Indian carbine cartridge, .45/.55 Army cartridge case.*

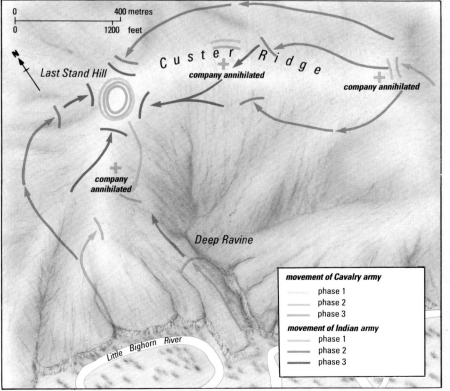

movement of Cavalry army
phase 1
phase 2
phase 3
movement of Indian army
phase 1
phase 2
phase 3

ANALYSIS
Valuables

The first creature we regard as truly human, *Homo habilis*, was distinguished from his ancestors by his capacity to create stone tools. Other animals were more agile, fleet of foot or stronger, but it was the tool-making ability that ultimately prevailed. Far from being restricted to utilitarian objects, however, from the earliest times onwards humans have devoted enormous effort and energy to the creation and acquisition of items that have little practical use but are nonetheless highly valued for their cultural, symbolic or religious significance. Such items often play a major part in social organisation by acting as indicators of rank and power, and sometimes

serve as repositories of wealth. These valuables, as they may be termed, form a prominent part of the archaeological record.

Many of the materials considered valuable by ancient and prehistoric communities came to be regarded as precious independently, and at different times, in several parts of the world. Jade is an example, valued in prehistoric Europe, in Central America until the Spanish conquest, and in China and New Zealand up to relatively recent times. Gold, similarly, became highly valued both throughout most of Eurasia and, independently, in parts of Central and South America. This tendency for widely separated communities to attribute value to the same substances clearly demonstrates that all these materials possess special qualities. Among these special qualities

three of the most important are attractiveness, durability and rarity.

Precious materials are intended to be seen and to impress, and appearance is therefore a prime consideration. Many, such as metals or precious stones, are brightly coloured, translucent or shiny. Durability is also vital, which explains why minerals and metals predominate. The especially high value placed on gold is due to the fact that if it is sufficiently pure in composition it does not tarnish or discolour like other metals. Finally, rarity or limited access is necessary if a material or craft product is to retain its value. For this reason the sources of many valuables are geographically remote and often distant from the places where they are used. Gold, amber, turquoise and jade are all scarce, and the high cost of their

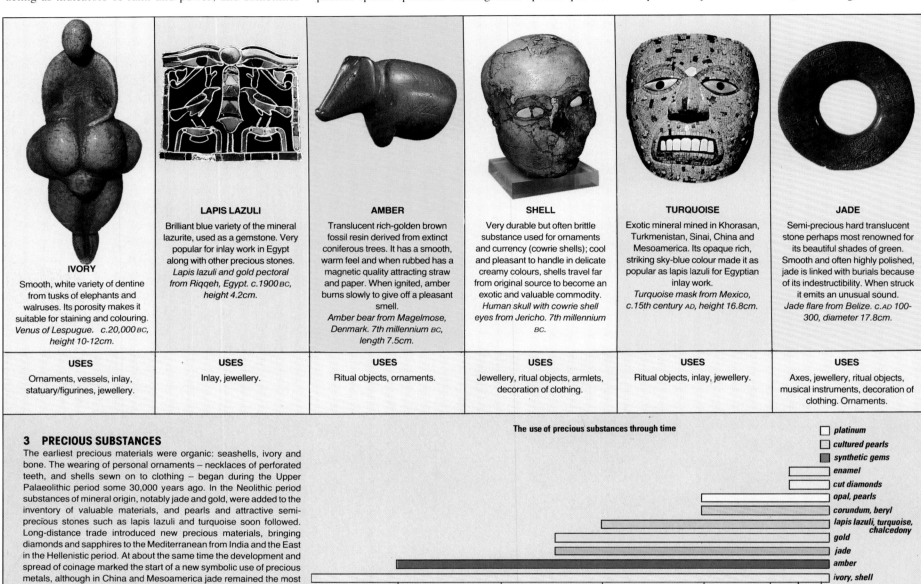

IVORY
Smooth, white variety of dentine from tusks of elephants and walruses. Its porosity makes it suitable for staining and colouring. *Venus of Lespugue. c.20,000 BC, height 10-12cm.*

LAPIS LAZULI
Brilliant blue variety of the mineral lazurite, used as a gemstone. Very popular for inlay work in Egypt along with other precious stones. *Lapis lazuli and gold pectoral from Riqqeh, Egypt. c.1900 BC, height 4.2cm.*

AMBER
Translucent rich-golden brown fossil resin derived from extinct coniferous trees. It has a smooth, warm feel and when rubbed has a magnetic quality attracting straw and paper. When ignited, amber burns slowly to give off a pleasant smell. *Amber bear from Magelmose, Denmark. 7th millennium BC, length 7.5cm.*

SHELL
Very durable but often brittle substance used for ornaments and currency (cowrie shells); cool and pleasant to handle in delicate creamy colours, shells travel far from original source to become an exotic and valuable commodity. *Human skull with cowrie shell eyes from Jericho. 7th millennium BC.*

TURQUOISE
Exotic mineral mined in Khorasan, Turkmenistan, Sinai, China and Mesoamerica. Its opaque rich, striking sky-blue colour made it as popular as lapis lazuli for Egyptian inlay work. *Turquoise mask from Mexico, c.15th century AD, height 16.8cm.*

JADE
Semi-precious hard translucent stone perhaps most renowned for its beautiful shades of green. Smooth and often highly polished, jade is linked with burials because of its indestructibility. When struck it emits an unusual sound. *Jade flare from Belize. c.AD 100-300, diameter 17.8cm.*

USES	USES	USES	USES	USES	USES
Ornaments, vessels, inlay, statuary/figurines, jewellery.	Inlay, jewellery.	Ritual objects, ornaments.	Jewellery, ritual objects, armlets, decoration of clothing.	Ritual objects, inlay, jewellery.	Axes, jewellery, ritual objects, musical instruments, decoration of clothing. Ornaments.

3 PRECIOUS SUBSTANCES

The earliest precious materials were organic: seashells, ivory and bone. The wearing of personal ornaments – necklaces of perforated teeth, and shells sewn on to clothing – began during the Upper Palaeolithic period some 30,000 years ago. In the Neolithic period substances of mineral origin, notably jade and gold, were added to the inventory of valuable materials, and pearls and attractive semi-precious stones such as lapis lazuli and turquoise soon followed. Long-distance trade introduced new precious materials, bringing diamonds and sapphires to the Mediterranean from India and the East in the Hellenistic period. At about the same time the development and spread of coinage marked the start of a new symbolic use of precious metals, although in China and Mesoamerica jade remained the most valued material. Only with the spread of European influence during the last 500 years did gold become the world-wide standard of value.

The use of precious substances through time

- □ platinum
- □ cultured pearls
- ■ synthetic gems
- enamel
- cut diamonds
- opal, pearls
- corundum, beryl
- lapis lazuli, turquoise, chalcedony
- gold
- jade
- amber
- ivory, shell

	8000		3-6000		3000		300 BC	AD 400	1500 1900
Upper Palaeolithic		Mesolithic		Neolithic		Near Eastern civilisations		Graeco-Roman	mediaeval modern

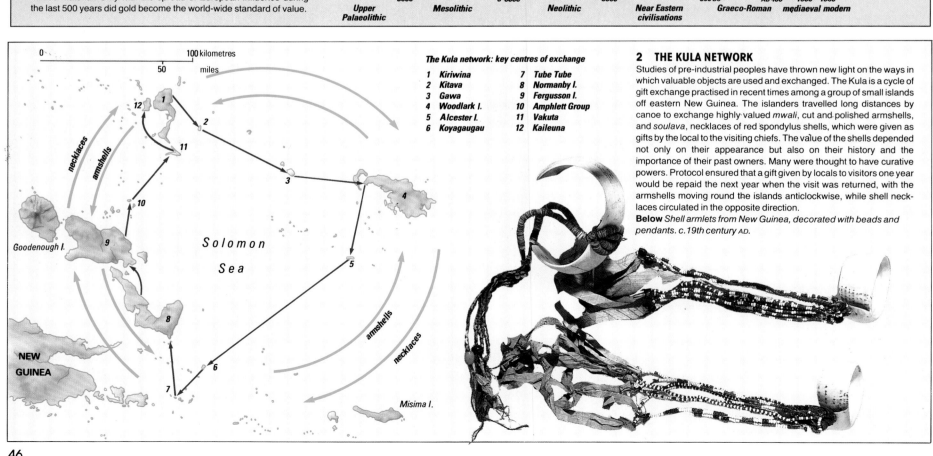

0 — 100 kilometres / 50 miles

Solomon Sea

NEW GUINEA

Goodenough I.

Misima I.

The Kula network: key centres of exchange
1. Kiriwina
2. Kitava
3. Gawa
4. Woodlark I.
5. Alcester I.
6. Koyagaugau
7. Tube Tube
8. Normanby I.
9. Fergusson I.
10. Amphlett Group
11. Vakuta
12. Kaileuna

2 THE KULA NETWORK

Studies of pre-industrial peoples have thrown new light on the ways in which valuable objects are used and exchanged. The Kula is a cycle of gift exchange practised in recent times among a group of small islands off eastern New Guinea. The islanders travelled long distances by canoe to exchange highly valued *mwali*, cut and polished armshells, and *soulava*, necklaces of red spondylus shells, which were given as gifts by the local to the visiting chiefs. The value of the shells depended not only on their appearance but also on their history and the importance of their past owners. Many were thought to have curative powers. Protocol ensured that a gift given by locals to visitors one year would be repaid the next year when the visit was returned, with the armshells moving round the islands anticlockwise, while shell necklaces circulated in the opposite direction.
Below Shell armlets from New Guinea, decorated with beads and pendants. c.19th century AD.

long-distance transport added greatly to their value. In the case of many minerals the expense and labour of mining or extracting the material from the earth had to be added to the cost of transport. It was this high cost, which meant that only the richer and more powerful members of society could acquire these materials, that led to their recognition as symbols of rank and power, a role that many of them have retained down to the present day.

Precious materials were generally worked by skilled craftsmen to produce ornaments or regalia. In the process, the symbolic value of the raw material was sometimes used to convey a message in the object produced. Thus gold in Egypt and jade in China, both materials symbolic of eternity, are especially common in the graves of the rulers, a good example being the gold sarcophagus

and mask from the tomb of Tutankhamun. These two materials were often conspicuous in royal regalia, as in the gold crowns and sceptres of historical Europe and the jade sceptres of ancient China. Precious materials also figured prominently where contact with the supernatural was being made or sought: on the western wall of the Temple of the Sun at Cuzco the Spanish invaders found a huge gold plate engraved with a representation of the Sun god. Gold, lapis lazuli and carnelian were all buried as foundation offerings beneath Mesopotamian temples and gold chalices are still used in Christian churches today. Historical examples lead us naturally to suppose that precious materials had similar roles in prehistoric societies. The finely polished jade axes from Neolithic Europe, for instance, may well have been symbols of

authority. Placed in the graves with the dead, such objects provide an important clue to the social position occupied in life by the deceased.

The increasing use of precious materials since the Upper Palaeolithic period not only reflects the increasingly hierarchical nature of human society, but may actually have helped to bring it about. Striking in appearance and limited in availability, these symbols of wealth and power strengthened the social position of their owners and made their political authority more natural and acceptable. As society became more complex and sophisticated, a continuing search for material symbols of power and privilege ensued. This quest provided a further stimulus to long-distance trade and brought with it advances in both technology and craft skills.

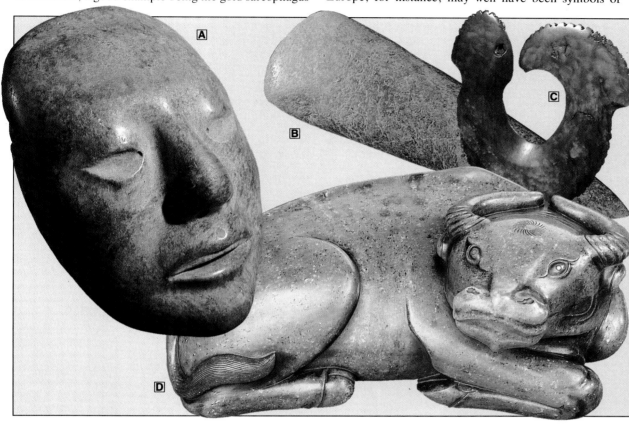

1 THE VALUE OF JADE

Jade was highly prized in widely separated parts of the world in ancient times, notably China, New Zealand, Mesoamerica and Europe. Its smooth texture and translucency when polished have always made it a particularly attractive material. It exists in a variety of forms, the three principal ones being nephrite, jadeite and chloromelanite, and colour varies according to its mineral composition – it can be green, red, blue or black. In China and Europe the earliest jade objects date to about 4000 BC. This early date is especially remarkable both because of the hardness of the material, which would have made it exceedingly difficult to work without the benefit of metal tools, and because of its rarity; sources are limited and often lie far from the places where it came to be so important. China, the principal consumer of jade, had no source within its ancient frontiers, and had to import the material from Central Asia, over 3000 kilometres away. The jade used in Aztec Mexico and prehistoric western Europe was also traded over long distances, indicating the value placed on it by these far-flung communities.

Jade had both ritual and symbolic uses, especially in China and Mesoamerica. Caches of jadeite objects, mainly axes but in one case including human figurines, were deposited at the Olmec centre of La Venta in the early 1st millennium BC, and plaques and other jade objects figure prominently among the offerings found in the sacred *cenote* or water hole at Chichén Itzá (*page 48*). In China, jade became associated with immortality; in the Han period, royal burial suits were made consisting of over 2000 jade plates joined together by gold, silver or bronze wire.

A *Maya jade mask from Central America. c.AD 100-300, height 17.8cm.*
B *Jadeite axe from Sweet Track, Somerset. c.4000 BC, length 20.3cm.* **C** *Jade peka peka pendant for ears and neck from Maori New Zealand, width 5.7cm.* **D** *Jade water buffalo. c.AD 1280-1640, width 43cm.*

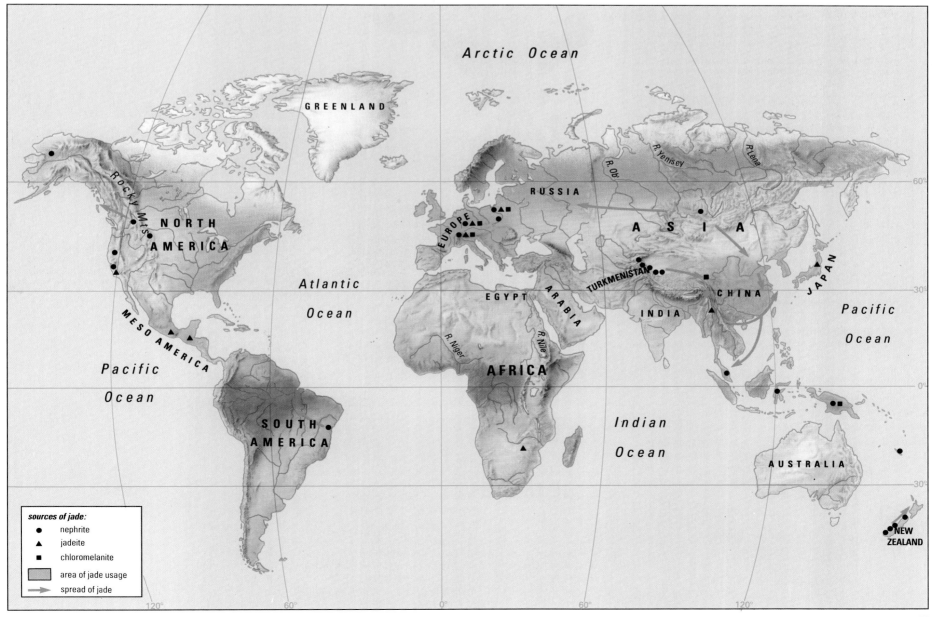

sources of jade:
● nephrite
▲ jadeite
■ chloromelanite
▨ area of jade usage
→ spread of jade

ANALYSIS
Ritual

For at least the last 35,000 years, ritual and religion have been a universal feature of human society. Burials from Neanderthal sites in Israel and south-western France take the origins of ritual back to 50,000 BP. It is difficult to say what beliefs were held by these early human communities, though it is thought that some of the scenes from cave art were connected with hunting magic and the fertility of the herds on which these early hunters depended. Even at this relatively remote period people were prepared to devote considerable time and energy to the creation of works of ritual or religious significance. This basic human impulse can be traced throughout the archaeological record down to recent times in temples, tombs and iconography. This record of ritual and religion can be divided into two parts: the remains of the special structures constructed for religious purposes; and the surviving traces of the ritual activities themselves, in the form of offerings, sacrifices and cult objects.

Temples have a prominent place in the archaeology of many parts of the world. One of the earliest and simplest was found at the base of the tell at Jericho. This was a roughly rectangular structure only 3.5 x 6.5 metres in size. Two large stone blocks with holes bored right through them are thought to have held totem poles, and the interior of the structure had been kept scrupulously clean, though the adjacent area was littered with debris. If the interpretation is correct, this modest affair was a spring-side shrine of hunter-gatherer groups who occupied the region in about 11,000 BP.

The development of agriculture led to the growth of larger settlements with more substantial architecture. Around 3500 BC there is the first evidence of an institutionalised priesthood, and the first monumental temples. In the early cities of Mesopotamia temples on raised platforms dominated the urban skyline, and extensive temple precincts frequently occupied a very large part of the walled area. Monumental religious structures were not restricted to states and empires, however, and some of the most famous examples, such as Stonehenge in southern Britain, were built by non-state societies. The power of religious beliefs and institutions is reflected in the scale and grandeur of these structures: often religious buildings, rather than the palaces of secular rulers, are an ancient society's most impressive remains.

Religion is not restricted to impressive public buildings, and archaeology can throw light on many other types of ritual site. Natural features were often endowed with religious significance by particular communities, and became the focus of elaborate sacrificial rituals. These include sacred pools and lakes, such as the Sacred Cenote or Well of Sacrifice at Chichén Itzá, or Lake Guatavita in Colombia with its rich offerings of gold. Perhaps the most famous examples of this kind of offering are the bog bodies of north-western Europe, the majority of which appear to have been ritually killed before deposition in peat bogs (*page 180*). Other bog finds include musical instruments, wooden boats, and whole suits of armour taken from defeated enemies and sacrificed to the gods.

Human sacrifice, the ultimate offering to the gods, is well illustrated by the European bog bodies and by the skeletons from the Sacred Cenote of Chichén Itzá. Frequently, sacrifice played a part in the dedication of buildings, as at Anyang and other important Chinese sites of the Shang period. Sacrifices also often feature in the burials of wealthy or powerful individuals. The tomb of one early ruler in southern Egypt was surrounded by the graves of 338 sacrificed retainers. More recently, on the opposite side of the world, subjects of the Polynesian ruler Roy Mata accompanied their lord to the next world. It is often from burial practices such as these that we gain the clearest information about the religions of the past.

The use of statues and other pictorial representations can make it possible to identify the type of deity or cult associated with a particular shrine. The iconography of the shrines at Çatal Hüyük, for instance, suggests that there was a fertility cult associated with a female deity, a bull cult with a male deity, and a death cult (*page 82*). The offerings made at a shrine can also throw light on the nature of the cult. At the Celtic shrine at the Sources de la Seine, a collection of carved wooden votive objects was discovered representing heads, limbs, eyes, internal organs and breasts. The intention was to solicit a cure by offering the deity a replica of the diseased organ or limb.

Without written records, archaeology can never give us the names of the gods and goddesses worshipped by ancient societies, nor the details of their mythology, but it does illustrate the pervasive and powerful influence of religious beliefs throughout human history, and the repeated recourse to supernatural agencies to protect against disease, natural disaster and fear of the unknown.

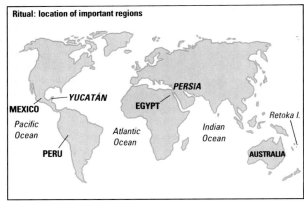

Ritual: location of important regions

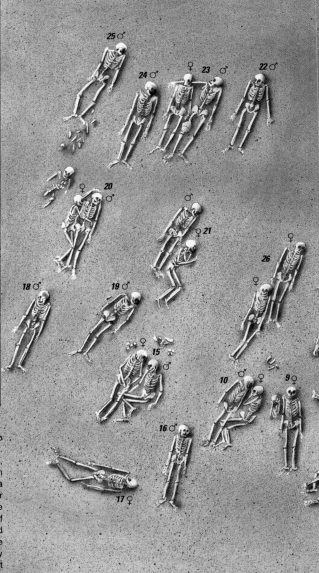

AD	phases of cenote ritual	offerings
1539		Chichén Itzá becomes the focus of a more purely Maya ritual: pilgrimage made from Mayapán (new capital founded in 13th century AD), and there is more concern with deities and ancestors. Objects are poorer and more parochial. Less ritual 'killing' of objects than in earlier phases. Most common: copal and rubber incense (often in tripod bowls), wooden idols, copper bells, cotton textiles, and wooden sceptres associated with lineage rituals. At this time jade was rare and ancient carved jades and jade beads were taken from the tombs and votive caches of the early period (c.3000 BC–AD 800) and deposited in the cenote.
1461	LATE PHASE	
1283	(founding of Mayapán)	
1145		Chichén Itzá apparently abandoned by its elite population in 12th century AD; no offerings for over 100 years.
899	EARLY PHASE II	Items offered are more identifiably Toltec in style, frequently warrior regalia, which reflects the warrior cult of the Toltec people and the Toltec glorification of militarism. Items include: cast gold bells and pendants, sheet gold discs and masks and cast copper bells. Offerings become sparser and less exotic towards the end of this period.
770	EARLY PHASE I	Most objects found in the cenote appear to have been offered at elite ceremonies: valuable imported objects were ritually broken, crushed, melted and burnt before being cast in. The Toltec, central Mexicans who are thought to have been founding a new capital here at this time, consecrated the Sacred Cenote by their offerings, and many objects depict or symbolise their military victories, for example sheet and cast gold alloy figurines, brought back from Central America by warlords. Jade objects carved in Maya style, brought to Chichén Itzá from the Maya area outside Yucatán, were sometimes broken and thrown into the cenote. Domestic jars and basins indicate rain-making ceremonies.

The chronology of the Sacred Cenote ritual at Chichén Itzá

Some human sacrifice also took place: the bones of 42 individuals have been found, more than half of which were younger than 20, and 14 were younger than 12 years old, but we do not know whether this practice was associated with the early or the late period of ritual.

3 THE SACRED CENOTE OF CHICHÉN ITZÁ
Several of the *cenote* or natural water holes of Yucatán became the subject of a religious cult, the most famous being that at Chichén Itzá. For roughly a thousand years, objects were thrown into its greenish black waters as offerings to the rain god.

Offerings from the Sacred Cenote A Bell surmounted by owl, from Panama. AD 900–1150, gold, height 4.6 cm. **B** Tripod vessel of tecali, a translucent stone from Oaxaca, with painted decoration. AD 800–900, height 18.9 cm. **C** Skull of young man converted into incense burner. AD 1250–1539, height 16 cm.

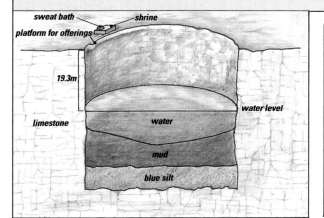

2 THE BURIAL OF ROY MATA
Oral tradition tells of Roy Mata, a powerful ruler of central Melanesia who was buried with members of his retinue on the small island of Retoka. Excavations at the site have uncovered the graves of over 40 individuals, buried singly and in couples around their master in about the mid-13th century AD. Roy Mata himself was buried in a deeper rectangular pit, with a young woman at his feet, a secondary burial between his legs, his *avati* or keeper of the peace to his right, and another couple to his left. Many of the retinue buried in the surrounding graves were probably representatives of tribes and clans that owed him allegiance. The dead wore shell beads and perforated animal teeth. The table (*right*) represents the number and type of artefacts found within individual burials. The men had been heavily drugged before sacrifice. Memorial stones were raised over the most important of the graves, and the whole island was declared *tabu*.

48

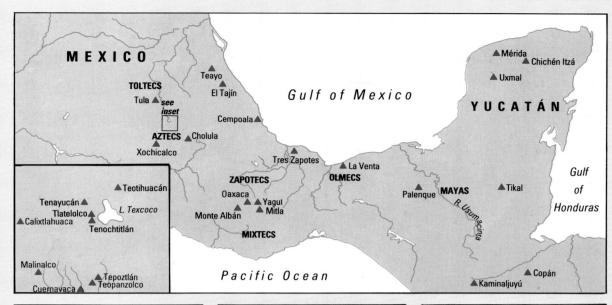

The distribution of pyramids

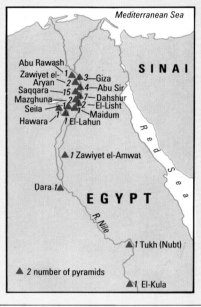

▲ *2 number of pyramids*

1 PYRAMIDS AND TEMPLE PYRAMIDS

The pyramid form was developed independently in different parts of the world for religious buildings serving two distinct functions. True pyramids, with four smooth sides culminating in a point, are restricted to Egypt, where they replaced an earlier stepped pyramid in about 2600 BC. Egyptian pyramids were closed structures containing the burial chamber of the god-king, but in Mesoamerica, Mesopotamia and Peru monuments of a similar form were built to serve as raised temple platforms. In Mesopotamia and the New World they are stepped or terraced, and are known as ziggurats and temple pyramids respectively. The similarity between the Egyptian, Mesopotamian and American examples is partly coincidental, but nevertheless demonstrates the importance of certain common requirements in the design, function and symbolism of monumental ritual structures. One important consideration was structural stability; the tapering pyramid shape reduced the risk of collapse and at the same time enhanced the impression of height. Height had a strong symbolic significance, raising the religious rituals above the secular events of everyday life and bringing them nearer to the heavens where the gods were thought to reside. The spatial separation between the priests and privileged individuals allowed access to the top of the temple pyramids and the watching populace below emphasised the status of the priesthood. The very size of all these structures is evidence of the great power of the religious establishment, closely associated with that of the state.

grave–goods table

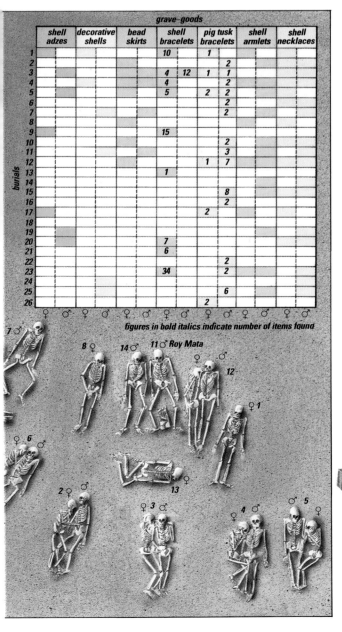

	shell adzes	decorative shells	bead skirts	shell bracelets	pig tusk bracelets	shell armlets	shell necklaces
1	▓			10	1		
2							2
3				4	12	1	1
4				4			2
5		▓		5	2		2
6							2
7							2
8							
9			15				
10							2
11							3
12					1		7
13				1			
14							
15							8
16							2
17					2		
18							
19							
20		▓		7			
21				6			
22							2
23				34			2
24							
25						6	
26							2

burials

figures in bold italics indicate number of items found

Pyramid sections

The step pyramid of Saqqara, Egypt c.2650 BC **A**

- 6-step pyramid
- further extension
- 4-step pyramid
- original mastaba tomb
- extension
- main burial chamber
- shaft to subsidiary burial chambers
- underground passages

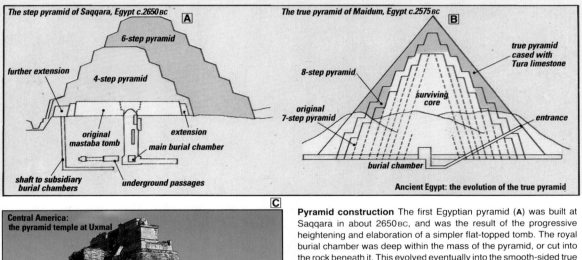

The true pyramid of Maidum, Egypt c.2575 BC **B**

- true pyramid cased with Tura limestone
- 8-step pyramid
- surviving core
- original 7-step pyramid
- entrance
- burial chamber

Ancient Egypt: the evolution of the true pyramid

Pyramid construction The first Egyptian pyramid (**A**) was built at Saqqara in about 2650 BC, and was the result of the progressive heightening and elaboration of a simpler flat-topped tomb. The royal burial chamber was deep within the mass of the pyramid, or cut into the rock beneath it. This evolved eventually into the smooth-sided true pyramid at Maidum (**B**). Mesoamerican pyramids sometimes also contained burials, but were primarily temple platforms, with a long flight of steep stairs leading to the sanctuary at the summit. The fine Mayan example at Uxmal (**C**) dates from the Late Classic period (AD 600–900), but has fewer terraces than most. Mesopotamian *ziggurats* (**D**) were also usually of terraced construction, as shown below by the reconstruction of the example at Choga Zanbil.

Central America: the pyramid temple at Uxmal **C**

- temple
- covered flight of steps
- sacrificial tables
- cart gate

Mesopotamia: the Ziggurat at Choga Zanbil **D**

TWO
HUMAN ORIGINS
16 million – 10,000 BC

THE EARLY development of the human species is a long and complicated story, made all the more difficult to untangle by the scattered nature of the fossilised remains which provide most of the evidence. It is now clear, however, that the ancestors of modern man, first diverged from the African apes between eight and five million years ago. The upright posture of these early hominids left their hands free for carrying, manipulating and tool-making. The first known tools are chipped pebbles from East Africa, which are dated to around two million years ago.

The earliest human ancestors (hominids) are found only in Africa, and were adapted to life in a tropical climate. The development of tool-making and the gradual increase in brain size eventually allowed the early hominids to spread beyond their original African homeland into Asia and Europe. The ability to make clothing and shelter was essential to this gradual expansion, as world climate was cooling during this period and around 1,500,000 years ago the first full-scale ice age occurred. Ice ages recurred at fairly regular intervals of 80,000 to 100,000 years: dramatic falls in temperature and the formation of extensive ice sheets, especially in the northern hemisphere, alternated with warmer periods when temperatures were similar to those of the present day. With his larger brain, increasingly sophisticated tools, use of fire, and improved hunting and gathering strategies, early man was able to survive and spread even in periods of adverse climate.

The final stage in human biological evolution came with the development of modern man – *Homo sapiens sapiens* – in Africa around 100,000 years ago. Modern man has a still larger brain than his predecessors, and a corresponding greater ability in tool-making, food-gathering, the organisation of social life and not least the urge and ability to colonise. By 30,000 years ago *Homo sapiens sapiens* was present throughout the greater part of the world, including the Americas and Australia, which had been beyond the range of earlier hominids. The cave art of western Europe illustrates the new level of cultural achievement. By the time the last ice age came to an end, around 10,000 BC, modern man was one of the world's most widespread and successful species.

Wall painting from the Lascaux cave in France depicting a man and bison
c. 14,000 BC, length of bison 1.1m.

Humanity's ancestors

Humans are closely related to the living great apes, sharing the same basic structure and a similar genetic make-up. This suggests that both also shared a common ancestor several million years ago. Since that time some of the characteristics of that ancestor have been retained, others changed, in one direction in the evolution of the apes and in another in human evolution.

Apes and humans together are known as hominoids. The first known representatives of the hominoids have been found only in Africa and were very different from living apes and humans. The oldest finds belong to a group of species in the genus *Proconsul*, whose skeletons are described as generalised. This means that they show none of the particular features such as thickened tooth enamel or adaptation for knuckle-walking which characterise the later apes. Some of these specialisations began to appear in a hominoid known as *Kenyapithecus*, which showed modifications in the teeth and limb bones making them more like those of the living great apes. *Kenyapithecus* can be regarded as part of the combined great ape and human group but cannot be linked directly to any one of the living hominoids. Apes and humans had not yet split off onto their separate evolutionary paths.

Outside Africa, the oldest identified hominoid fossils are known as *Ramapithecus* and *Sivapithecus*. These have been found in the same deposits dating to between 11 and 13 million years old. For several years many anthropologists believed that the jaws and teeth of *Ramapithecus* showed basic human features, and that it could be regarded as a member of the human branch of hominoids. This would mean that the divergence of apes and humans took place some 14 million years ago – a view contested by scientists working on the molecular evidence for evolution. Their research indicates that organisms which have evolved from a common ancestor become genetically more distinct through time, making it possible to estimate when divergence occurred even without any fossil evidence. Despite obvious physical differences, the living African great apes (chimpanzees and gorillas) are genetically almost identical to humans, indicating a divergence from a common ancestor a mere 5 to 6 million years ago. There was some scepticism about this 'molecular clock' approach until research proved that *Ramapithecus* could not be a hominoid. Finds from Anatolia and Pakistan, in which much of the skull, face and teeth are preserved, show that *Sivapithecus* differs from *Ramapithecus* only in size. Both share some of the characteristics of *Kenyapithecus*, as well as particular features which show they must be related exclusively to the orang-utan and not to humans. This evidence indicates that the orang-utan was the first to split away from the general hominoid pool, and that this split occurred before the divergence of the African great apes and humans. Removing *Ramapithecus* from human ancestry means that the divergence of the African apes and humans must be pushed forward in time – in accordance with the molecular evidence – to the period between 5 and 8 million years ago. Unfortunately, virtually no fossils relevant to the evolution of either apes or humans have been found in deposits dating to this time, and a picture of the common ancestor must be built up from the existing evidence.

The common ancestor of chimpanzees, gorillas and humans probably lived in open woodland or wooded savanna habitats in the tropics of Africa. It would have been a medium-sized (10–30 kilograms) active primate adapted to a mixture of tree-climbing and ground-living. On the ground it would have moved about on all fours, occasionally standing upright on two legs. Its body was probably covered in hair but lacking a tail, and it would have had a short face with widely set eyes, a flattened, upturned nose and strong jaws. The chance of finding fossils of this primate are extremely remote as it was fairly rare and existed for a relatively short time.

By 4 million years ago, however, the characteristics which distinguish humans from the apes had evolved in Africa. Rapid and fundamental changes in the anatomy of the hips and feet enabled the first hominoids to stand upright and walk on two legs (bipedalism). In conjunction with this remarkable and important reconstruction of the body, brain size increased and the jaw was modified to a continuous curve with no projecting canines at the corners. Since the time of this major evolutionary event only minor details in the human skeleton have changed to produce anatomically modern humans like ourselves. In contrast, the archaeological record documents the dramatic evolution of the intelligence and culture, which above all distinguish humans from the rest of the animal kingdom.

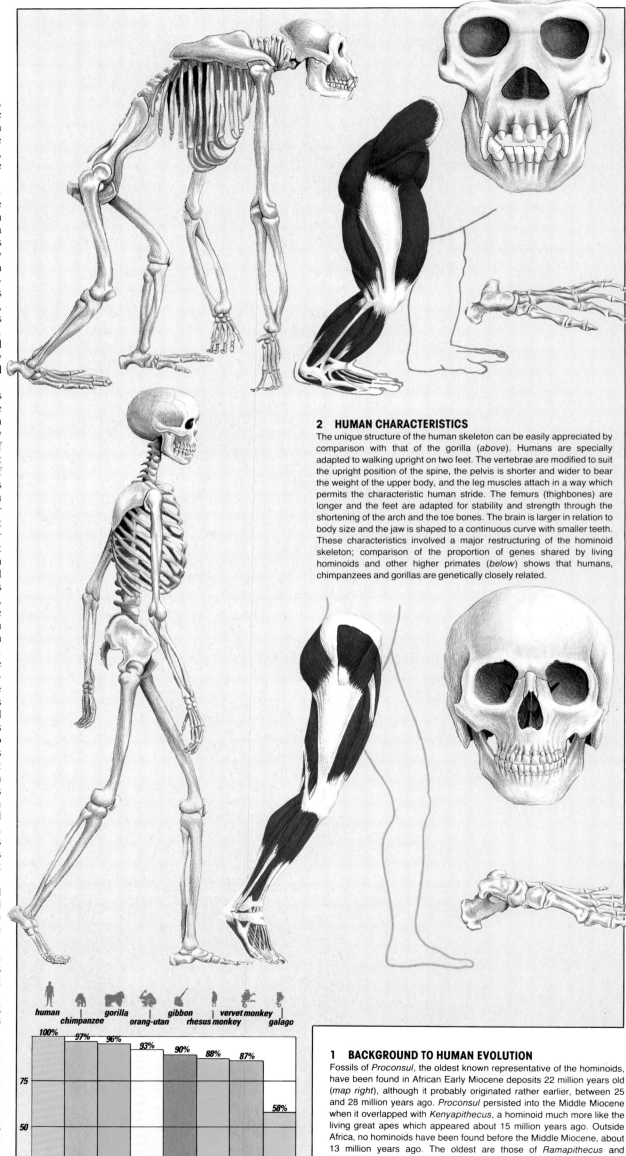

2 HUMAN CHARACTERISTICS
The unique structure of the human skeleton can be easily appreciated by comparison with that of the gorilla (*above*). Humans are specially adapted to walking upright on two feet. The vertebrae are modified to suit the upright position of the spine, the pelvis is shorter and wider to bear the weight of the upper body, and the leg muscles attach in a way which permits the characteristic human stride. The femurs (thighbones) are longer and the feet are adapted for stability and strength through the shortening of the arch and the toe bones. The brain is larger in relation to body size and the jaw is shaped to a continuous curve with smaller teeth. These characteristics involved a major restructuring of the hominoid skeleton; comparison of the proportion of genes shared by living hominoids and other higher primates (*below*) shows that humans, chimpanzees and gorillas are genetically closely related.

human chimpanzee gorilla orang-utan gibbon rhesus monkey vervet monkey galago

100%	97%	96%	93%	90%	88%	87%		58%

Genetic similarity among primates

1 BACKGROUND TO HUMAN EVOLUTION
Fossils of *Proconsul*, the oldest known representative of the hominoids, have been found in African Early Miocene deposits 22 million years old (*map right*), although it probably originated rather earlier, between 25 and 28 million years ago. *Proconsul* persisted into the Middle Miocene when it overlapped with *Kenyapithecus*, a hominoid much more like the living great apes which appeared about 15 million years ago. Outside Africa, no hominoids have been found before the Middle Miocene, about 13 million years ago. The oldest are those of *Ramapithecus* and *Sivapithecus* from Anatolia and Pakistan; they are closely related to the orang-utan, whereas the more recent European finds of *Dryopithecus* are more like *Proconsul* and cannot be related to any of the living hominoids. Humans are closest to the African great apes with whom they shared their last common ancestor 5 to 8 million years ago. This ancestor lived in the tropics of Africa where chimpanzees and gorillas still occur, and where the first distinctly human fossils have been found.

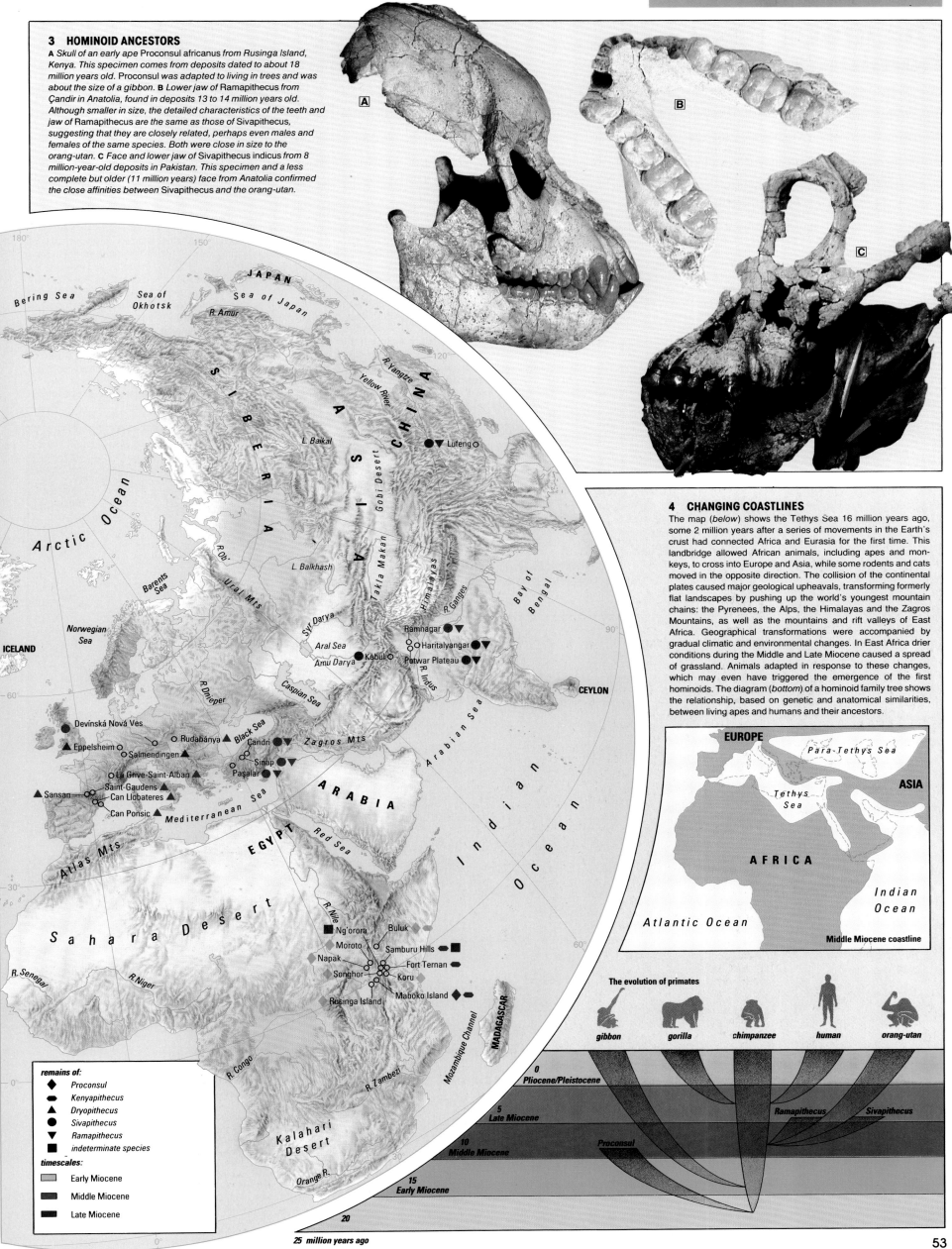

3 HOMINOID ANCESTORS

A *Skull of an early ape Proconsul africanus from Rusinga Island, Kenya. This specimen comes from deposits dated to about 18 million years old. Proconsul was adapted to living in trees and was about the size of a gibbon.* **B** *Lower jaw of Ramapithecus from Çandir in Anatolia, found in deposits 13 to 14 million years old. Although smaller in size, the detailed characteristics of the teeth and jaw of Ramapithecus are the same as those of Sivapithecus, suggesting that they are closely related, perhaps even males and females of the same species. Both were close in size to the orang-utan.* **C** *Face and lower jaw of Sivapithecus indicus from 8 million-year-old deposits in Pakistan. This specimen and a less complete but older (11 million years) face from Anatolia confirmed the close affinities between Sivapithecus and the orang-utan.*

4 CHANGING COASTLINES

The map (*below*) shows the Tethys Sea 16 million years ago, some 2 million years after a series of movements in the Earth's crust had connected Africa and Eurasia for the first time. This landbridge allowed African animals, including apes and monkeys, to cross into Europe and Asia, while some rodents and cats moved in the opposite direction. The collision of the continental plates caused major geological upheavals, transforming formerly flat landscapes by pushing up the world's youngest mountain chains: the Pyrenees, the Alps, the Himalayas and the Zagros Mountains, as well as the mountains and rift valleys of East Africa. Geographical transformations were accompanied by gradual climatic and environmental changes. In East Africa drier conditions during the Middle and Late Miocene caused a spread of grassland. Animals adapted in response to these changes, which may even have triggered the emergence of the first hominoids. The diagram (*bottom*) of a hominoid family tree shows the relationship, based on genetic and anatomical similarities, between living apes and humans and their ancestors.

Middle Miocene coastline

The evolution of primates

gibbon   gorilla   chimpanzee   human   orang-utan

Ramapithecus   Sivapithecus

Proconsul

0
Pliocene/Pleistocene
5
Late Miocene
10
Middle Miocene
15
Early Miocene
20

remains of:

◆ Proconsul
◗ Kenyapithecus
▲ Dryopithecus
● Sivapithecus
▼ Ramapithecus
■ indeterminate species

timescales:

Early Miocene
Middle Miocene
Late Miocene

25 million years ago

The first hominids in Africa

The critical determining factor in early human evolution was the restructuring of the anatomy to allow upright walking (bipedalism). Evidence that this fundamental adaptation had evolved in Africa by at least 4 million years ago has been found at Laetolil, northern Tanzania, where footprints preserving the unmistakable outlines of the human foot were discovered in 1978. Forensic investigation suggests that the largest trail of about 30 footprints was made by two adults between 1.1 and 1.4 metres tall, each weighing about 27 kilograms, and a child. However, to discover more about these earliest humans it is necessary to turn to the evidence provided by their fossilised teeth and bones.

Most of the fossils dating to between 3 and 4 million years old are fragmentary and their significance would be difficult to interpret but for the discovery of most of the skeleton of a single individual, nicknamed Lucy, found at Hadar in the Afar region of Ethiopia. Dated to about 3.4 million years BP, this skeleton of a small but sturdy adult female is clearly adapted to upright walking, and her teeth show certain human characteristics although she retains many features similar to those of apes. This combination of human and ape traits places Lucy in the group of hominids known as the australopithecines, or southern apes. The australopithecines existed in Africa between

about 4 and 1.7 million years ago, and four species are currently recognised on the basis of variation in the detailed characteristics of their skulls and teeth. Lucy belongs to the oldest known species, *Australopithecus afarensis*, present between 4 and 3.2 million years ago. Her lightly built (gracile) skeleton and small brain resemble those of *Australopithecus africanus* (c.3 to 2 million years BP), well known from cave sites in southern Africa, but the latter has a more robust, forwardly pronounced face and larger molar teeth. In contrast, the face of *Australopithecus robustus* (c.2 to 1 million years BP) has a concave profile, massive jaws, brow ridges, a bony crest along the top of the skull with strong muscles attached, and a larger brain than the other australopithecines, including *Australopithecus boisei* (c.2.7 to 1.7 million years BP), a similarly robust species found in East Africa. Detailed comparison of species shows that they are closely related to each other, and it is possible that *A. afarensis* is ancestral to both the gracile *A. africanus* and the more robust forms. However, it is uncertain whether any of these upright walkers with small brains belong to the evolutionary line which leads to modern humans.

The oldest known fossils referred to as *Homo* (Man) date from c.2.5 million years BP. The first was discovered at the Olduvai site in Tanzania. The fossil, *Homo habilis*, was distinguished by its larger brain, rounded skull and distinctly human face. Since this discovery, further finds from East and southern Africa, including a well-preserved skull from Koobi Fora in Kenya, have been referred to this species. These show a lot of variation in detailed characteristics, but in general the skulls, hips and legs

show marked differences from those of the australopithecines. In the cases of the *Homo* skeletons, the structure of the pelvis and the hip joints are very similar to those of modern humans, whereas in *A. afarensis* and *A. africanus* the neck of the femur (the top of the thighbone) is longer, so that body weight and the stresses placed on the joints by upright walking were differently distributed. It is possible that this made the australopithecines more efficient bipeds than modern humans, but the adaptations seen in the pelvis of *H. habilis* were essential to allow the birth of infants with larger brains. Some scientists believe that the new features seen in *H. habilis* could have evolved from *A. afarensis*, either directly or via *A. africanus*, while others consider that the differences indicate two diverging evolutionary lines, one leading to the australopithecines, the other to *Homo*, both stemming from a common ancestor. Only new fossil finds will solve this problem.

It is clear, however, that the earliest representatives of *Homo* show a progressive trend towards modern anatomical characteristics. This is evident in fossils from Koobi Fora, which demonstrate changes in the size and shape of the skull to encase a larger, more developed brain, and in the remains of a 12-year-old boy found at Nariokotome, Kenya, whose skeleton differs only slightly from that of a modern boy, although it is 1.7 million years old. Some scientists refer to these early humans as *Homo erectus*, a species first defined from later fossils found in South-East Asia and China. However, their characteristics differ significantly and only the African fossils can be regarded with any certainty to be on a course set towards the evolution of fully modern humans.

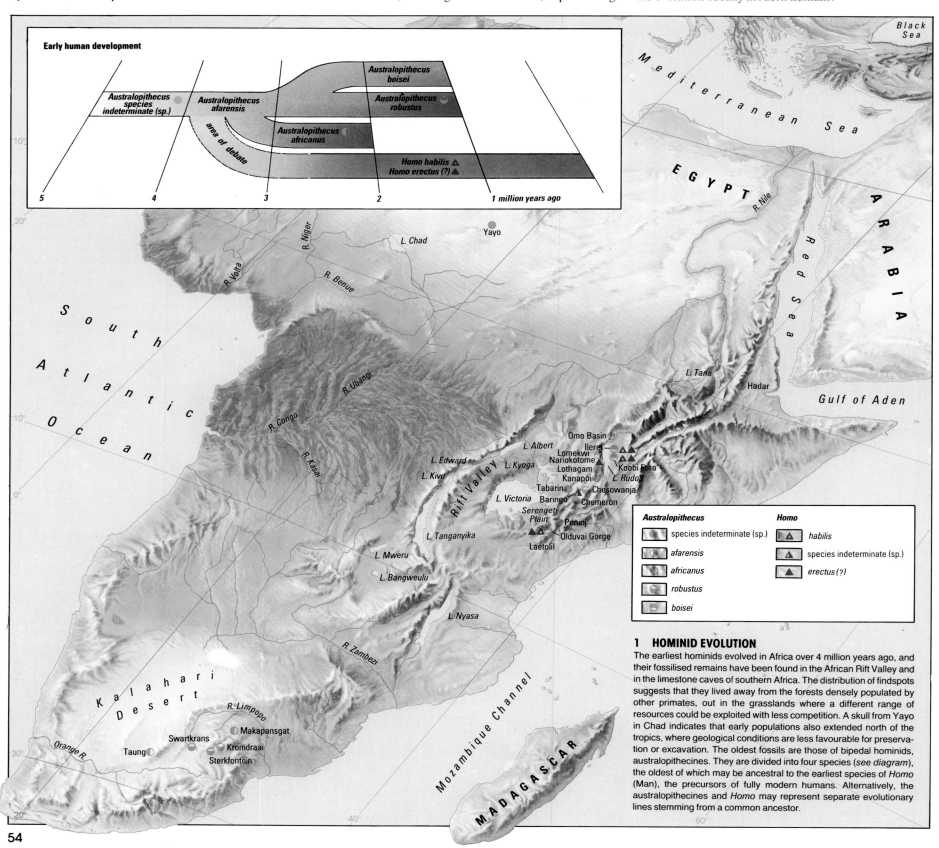

1 HOMINID EVOLUTION

The earliest hominids evolved in Africa over 4 million years ago, and their fossilised remains have been found in the African Rift Valley and in the limestone caves of southern Africa. The distribution of findspots suggests that they lived away from the forests densely populated by other primates, out in the grasslands where a different range of resources could be exploited with less competition. A skull from Yayo in Chad indicates that early populations also extended north of the tropics, where geological conditions are less favourable for preservation or excavation. The oldest fossils are those of bipedal hominids, australopithecines. They are divided into four species (see diagram), the oldest of which may be ancestral to the earliest species of *Homo* (Man), the precursors of fully modern humans. Alternatively, the australopithecines and *Homo* may represent separate evolutionary lines stemming from a common ancestor.

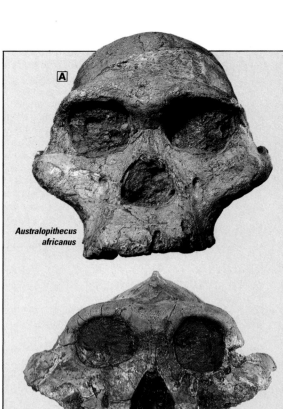

Australopithecus africanus

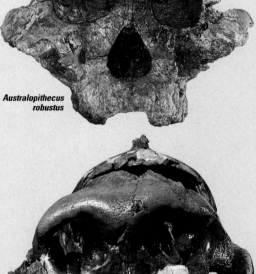

Australopithecus robustus

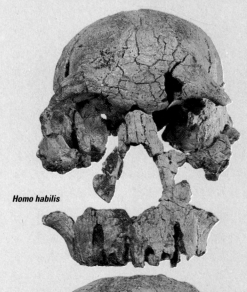

Australopithecus boisei

Homo habilis

Homo erectus

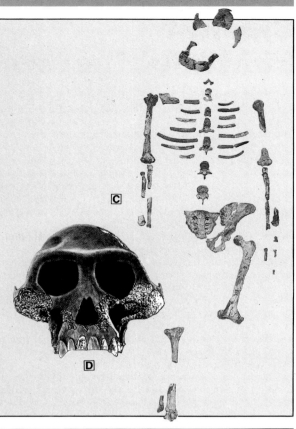

3 HOMINID REMAINS

A *To date, four species of australopithecine have been distinguished on the basis of clearly observable differences in their skulls and teeth.* **Left (top to bottom)** *adult female* Australopithecus africanus *from Sterkfontein, southern Africa, c.2 million years BP; adult male* Australopithecus robustus *from Koobi Fora, Kenya, c.2 million years BP. Adult male* Australopithecus boisei *from Olduvai Gorge, Tanzania, c.1.9 to 1.7 million years BP; adult male* Homo habilis *and (bottom)* Homo erectus *(sex indeterminate) from Koobi Fora, c.2 to 1.5 million years BP.* B *Hominid footprints 3.8 to 3.5 million years old discovered at Laetolil, northern Tanzania. The footprints were made in soft volcanic ash which hardened to a cement-like layer after a shower of rain, revealing the unmistakable outlines of the human foot.* C *Skeleton remains of* Australopithecus afarensis *found at Hadar, Ethiopia. Nicknamed Lucy, this adult female skeleton shows clear adaptations to upright walking and is about 3.4 million years old.* D *Reconstruction of Lucy's skull.*

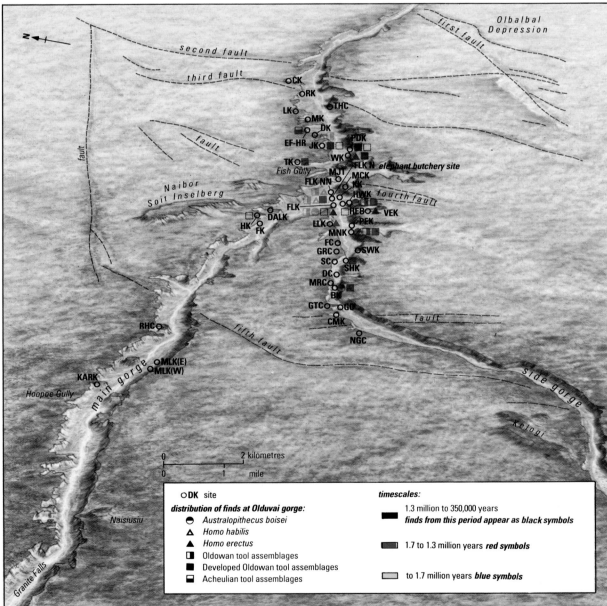

○DK site

distribution of finds at Olduvai gorge:
- ◓ *Australopithecus boisei*
- △ *Homo habilis*
- ▲ *Homo erectus*
- ▣ Oldowan tool assemblages
- ■ Developed Oldowan tool assemblages
- ▱ Acheulian tool assemblages

timescales:

▬ 1.3 million to 350,000 years *finds from this period appear as black symbols*

▬ 1.7 to 1.3 million years *red symbols*

▬ to 1.7 million years *blue symbols*

2 OLDUVAI GORGE

The fossil deposits of the Olduvai Gorge on the south-eastern edge of the Serengeti Plain, Tanzania, contained the first discovered examples of both *Australopithecus boisei* and *Homo habilis*, as well as numerous concentrations of hominid remains, animal bones and stone tools. The sites at which these remains were found were known by abbreviated names such as FLK, in which FL refers to Frida Leakey (the Leakey family started excavations there), and K stands for Korongo, meaning gully. Fossils and tools accumulated on the low-lying shores of a lake before the gorge was formed, and were then buried by lake sediments and volcanic lava. Within the last 500,000 years geological faulting created a depression to the east, diverting a stream which started to cut down through the layers of deposit, exposing the archaeological material and providing information about biological and cultural evolution over a crucial period of time.

The first hunter-gatherers

One of the fundamental distinguishing features of the human species is the ability to make tools, and the appearance of stone tools around 2.5 million years ago marks the critical first step in human cultural development. Tools enabled early hominids to widen the range of food available to them, for instance to cut meat from carcasses, and enabled materials such as wood, bark, reeds and hides to be cut and sharpened into useful everyday items. It is with the creation of the first tools that archaeological study can really begin.

The oldest stone tools found so far come from Hadar in Ethiopia and date to as much as 2.5 million years ago. Similar tools have been discovered at other well-dated but younger contexts in East Africa, notably at the famous site of Olduvai Gorge, and are therefore known as Oldowan. These tools consist of pebbles with irregular sharp edges created by using one stone as a hammer to chip a series of flakes off the other. A variety of raw materials was employed (basalt, lava, quartz and quartzite) and both the chipped stones and the flakes could be used as implements.

One of the main uses of these sharp flakes was in butchering animals. Studies under microscopes of the marks on some of the bones from early sites indicate they were made by such flakes, and other evidence of damage on bones is interpreted as the result of smashing them to get at the marrow inside. Meat was evidently an important part of the diet of early humans, but it seems likely that it was obtained mostly through the scavenging of carnivore kills and naturally dead carcasses rather than by hunting. Early humans were probably highly social animals living in fairly permanent groups. The sharing of food, and the beginnings of a division of labour between males (concentrating on providing meat) and females (concentrating on providing plant foods), may have come about only gradually as hunting became more important. Shelters found within the Olduvai Gorge may indicate that the idea of home bases, occupied for substantial periods of time and to which food was brought back, had already developed 1.8 million years ago.

About 1.5 million years ago significant changes in tool types coincided with the appearance of a new hominid, *Homo erectus*, replacing the earlier, smaller-brained *Homo habilis*. The most important change in stone implement technology at this period was the development of the Acheulian industry, characterised by handaxes and cleavers worked on both faces. The Acheulian was not the only new industry to appear about 1.5 million years ago, and a new diversity in the types of stone tool being produced was a significant feature of the period. In the Koobi Fora area of Kenya there was the Karari industry, characterised by large core-scrapers, while at Olduvai the earlier Oldowan gave place to a new industry known as the Developed Oldowan.

Acheulian industries remained in use for well over a million years, spreading beyond Africa into Europe and Asia. Handaxes were probably more efficient butchery tools than simple flakes, and may also have been used for other purposes. During the Acheulian period in Africa, there is some evidence that larger animals were being consumed, and in some cases the discovery of remains of many animals of a single species together at the same site suggests that they were all killed in one operation. This may indicate that scavenging was beginning to give way to active hunting as the major source of meat in the human diet. An unknown factor, however, is the degree to which plants were used as foods. Although it seems likely that they, rather than meat, have always formed the basic staple of human subsistence in Africa, practically the only direct evidence is the presence of the seeds of some edible plants in the late Acheulian site at Kalambo Falls. This site is also important because its waterlogged deposits have preserved evidence of the use of wood, for example in making clubs and digging sticks. Many of the stone tools found there may have been used to work wood rather than to butcher or hunt animals.

It is not known for certain when fire began to be used in Africa, and traces of it may have been lost at many sites. It seems to have been used at Kalambo Falls, but other sites, such as Chesowanja, may put its origins at more than 1 million years ago. Fire would have been important not only in cooking, thereby extending the range of edible foods, but also in making tools from wood and as protection from predators.

By the end of the Acheulian some 120,000 years ago many aspects of human behaviour were probably already in existence, among them the combination of hunting and gathering as a successful way of life, the use of fire, and a simple but effective technology in both stone and wood.

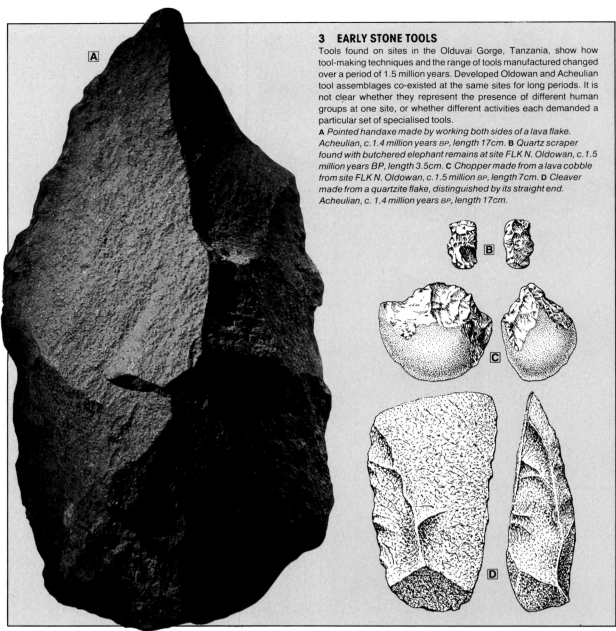

3 EARLY STONE TOOLS
Tools found on sites in the Olduvai Gorge, Tanzania, show how tool-making techniques and the range of tools manufactured changed over a period of 1.5 million years. Developed Oldowan and Acheulian tool assemblages co-existed at the same sites for long periods. It is not clear whether they represent the presence of different human groups at one site, or whether different activities each demanded a particular set of specialised tools.
A *Pointed handaxe made by working both sides of a lava flake. Acheulian, c.1.4 million years BP, length 17cm.* **B** *Quartz scraper found with butchered elephant remains at site FLK N. Oldowan, c.1.5 million years BP, length 3.5cm.* **C** *Chopper made from a lava cobble from site FLK N. Oldowan, c.1.5 million BP, length 7cm.* **D** *Cleaver made from a quartzite flake, distinguished by its straight end. Acheulian, c. 1.4 million years BP, length 17cm.*

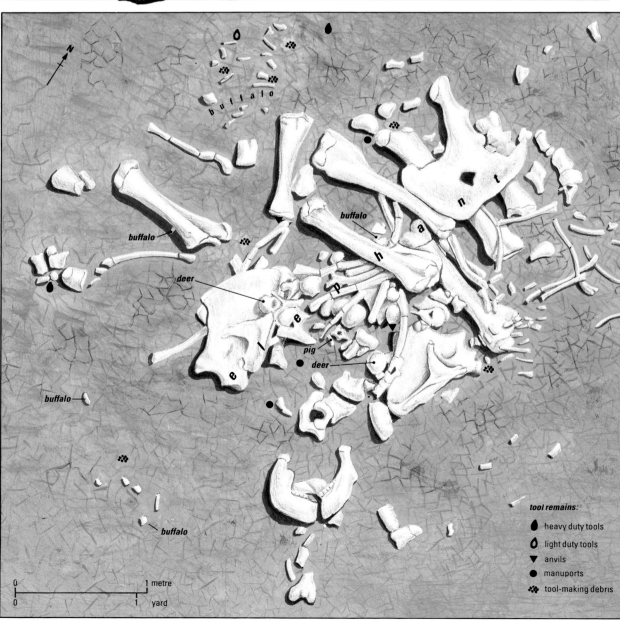

tool remains:
- heavy duty tools
- light duty tools
- anvils
- manuports
- tool-making debris

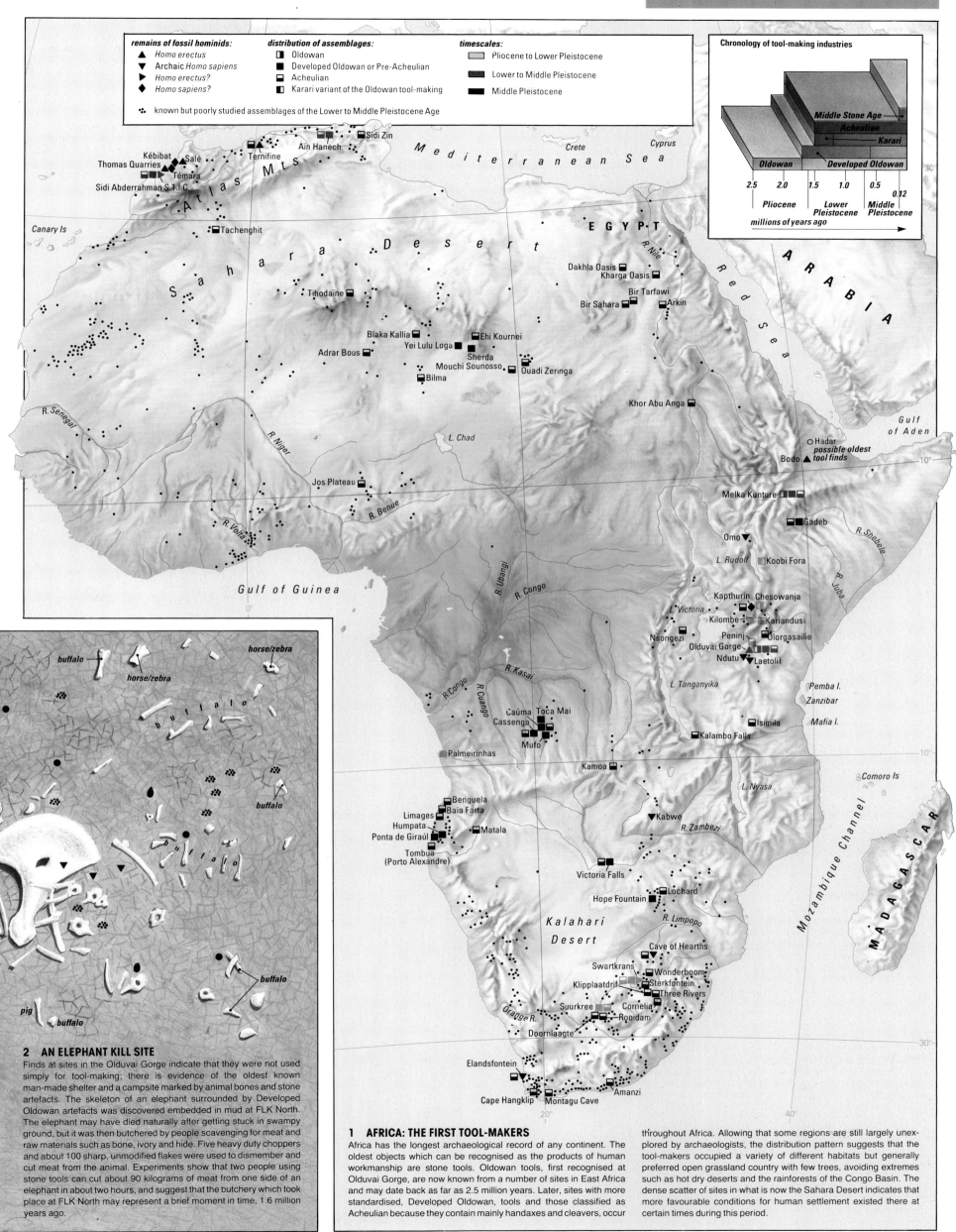

remains of fossil hominids:
- ▲ *Homo erectus*
- ▼ Archaic *Homo sapiens*
- ▶ *Homo erectus?*
- ◆ *Homo sapiens?*

distribution of assemblages:
- ▫ Oldowan
- ▪ Developed Oldowan or Pre-Acheulian
- ▢ Acheulian
- ■ Karari variant of the Oldowan tool-making

timescales:
- ▨ Pliocene to Lower Pleistocene
- ▨ Lower to Middle Pleistocene
- ■ Middle Pleistocene

∵ known but poorly studied assemblages of the Lower to Middle Pleistocene Age

Chronology of tool-making industries

Middle Stone Age
Acheulian
Karari
Oldowan   Developed Oldowan

2.5   2.0   1.5   1.0   0.5   0.12
Pliocene   Lower Pleistocene   Middle Pleistocene

millions of years ago

2 AN ELEPHANT KILL SITE

Finds at sites in the Olduvai Gorge indicate that they were not used simply for tool-making; there is evidence of the oldest known man-made shelter and a campsite marked by animal bones and stone artefacts. The skeleton of an elephant surrounded by Developed Oldowan artefacts was discovered embedded in mud at FLK North. The elephant may have died naturally after getting stuck in swampy ground, but it was then butchered by people scavenging for meat and raw materials such as bone, ivory and hide. Five heavy duty choppers and about 100 sharp, unmodified flakes were used to dismember and cut meat from the animal. Experiments show that two people using stone tools can cut about 90 kilograms of meat from one side of an elephant in about two hours, and suggest that the butchery which took place at FLK North may represent a brief moment in time, 1.6 million years ago.

1 AFRICA: THE FIRST TOOL-MAKERS

Africa has the longest archaeological record of any continent. The oldest objects which can be recognised as the products of human workmanship are stone tools. Oldowan tools, first recognised at Olduvai Gorge, are now known from a number of sites in East Africa and may date back as far as 2.5 million years. Later, sites with more standardised, Developed Oldowan, tools and those classified as Acheulian because they contain mainly handaxes and cleavers, occur throughout Africa. Allowing that some regions are still largely unexplored by archaeologists, the distribution pattern suggests that the tool-makers occupied a variety of different habitats but generally preferred open grassland country with few trees, avoiding extremes such as hot dry deserts and the rainforests of the Congo Basin. The dense scatter of sites in what is now the Sahara Desert indicates that more favourable conditions for human settlement existed there at certain times during this period.

The impact of climate

Over the past 16 million years the world's climate has undergone a succession of dramatic changes probably resulting from oscillations in the Earth's rotation. The best known of these is the so-called Ice Age (the Pleistocene) which is in fact made up of a series of colder and warmer phases and began about 2 million years ago. The most striking evidence of the action of the ice in these colder phases are the deep U-shaped valleys found across northern latitudes. Less obvious but just as important are vast deposits of boulders, clays and wind-blown dust – the refuse produced by the scouring effects of the ice – which can be found right across North America, northern Europe and as far east as China. The climatic changes had dramatic effects not just on the landscape but also on sea levels, plants and animals. At different times Britain, for example, was host to animals now associated with Africa and with the Arctic.

Recent studies of cores taken from the ocean beds show that climate changes were highly complex and involved a succession of cold, 'glacial' periods and warmer, 'interglacial' periods. Some of the interglacial periods were warmer than today. Ocean cores show the climatic changes more effectively than land-based deposits because the ocean bed is not so eroded. Each glacial period had a different impact, depending on how far south the ice extended, how long it lasted and consequently how much effect it had on the landscape and the plant and animal life located there. Within each of the major glacials smaller-scale warmer and colder periods occurred.

Although most striking in northern and southern latitudes, these climatic changes also had effects in the tropics. When the ice sheets advanced they locked away large amounts of water, reducing the amount of moisture in the atmosphere that could fall as rain or snow. As a glacial established itself the amount of rainfall consequently decreased. In tropical and sub-tropical latitudes this increased aridity led to the expansion of the deserts. Similarly, when the ice melted more water became available and rainfall could increase. These changes are seen in dramatically changing coastlines. As the glacials locked away large amounts of water, the average sea level fell, exposing areas of land where the sea is to be found today. In the interglacials the sea level could actually be higher than it is today, resulting in stranded beach lines above the present sea level.

This changing climate had a major effect on the landscape of prehistoric man. The vast ice sheets cut deep valleys, laid down thick deposits of clay, boulders and wind-blown dust, and altered the paths of rivers. Additionally, the changes in the amount of free water and rainfall affected the amount of land available for feeding the herds and growing the plants upon which prehistoric man depended. Colonisation of areas that are now islands was feasible; in Europe it was possible to walk from France to England, while in East Asia both Japan and Java were joined to the mainland, and Siberia and Alaska were linked across the Bering Strait.

The changing climate also had profound effects on plant and animal life. Polar species moved south with the advance of the ice, retreating north again as conditions warmed up. In colder phases Britain was home to lemmings, reindeer, mammoths and woolly rhinoceros, while in warmer times elephants, hippopotamus and lions could all be found. The tropical rainforest, on the other hand, showed little change, with the same types of plants and animals living there, though the area it occupied shrank and expanded.

One creature that appears to have coped well with all the environmental changes is prehistoric man, who could be found living in the grasslands of Africa, the tropical rainforest of South-East Asia and the more temperate areas of southern Europe, from where he spread into more northerly regions as suitable conditions arose. The changes in plant and animal life were reflected in the diet of prehistoric peoples, but it was the development of technology to cope with different environments which enabled humans to survive while other species moved or became extinct. Climatic changes may have been important in the evolution of man himself. The harsher conditions of glacial times may have made human intelligence vital for survival, favouring larger brains, more inventive and flexible behaviour, forward planning and better communication through the use of speech. Such changes in the prehistoric populations would have taken many generations, and the development of stone tools, site organisation, the building of shelters and the use of clothing may all reflect this evolution.

2 CLIMATIC CHANGE: DOCUMENTATION

Documenting the climatic changes of the Ice Age (Pleistocene) is a complex problem, since the record of ice sheet advances and retreats is incomplete. This is partly the result of erosion and the burial of evidence in the post-Pleistocene period, but more dramatically each ice advance scours the deposits of the previous ones as it passes over them. Scientists believed for a long time that only five cold, glacial phases existed, and that these periods were simple advances and retreats of ice sheets. Boring deep holes into the ocean bed produces long cores of deposits which show a different picture. The deposits of the deep-sea floor usually accumulate without interruption and therefore show a finer degree of resolution than is found on land. These deposits are made up of the detritus of dead sea creatures; of particular importance for studying the ice ages are the microscropic plankton which have skeletons of calcium carbonate (coccoliths). If left for long enough in shallow tropical seas such deposits can build up to form chalk. Studies of the composition of coccoliths which lived in surface sea waters can tell us about the temperatures present at given times by radiometrically dating the marine deposits trapped in the core. These data are then used to draw up a sequence of temperature fluctuations through time. The dating of the core can be compared to evidence for reversals in the Earth's magnetic field, which are relatively well-dated and also show up in the marine deposits. The study of coccoliths and the ratios of two isotopes of oxygen in their bodies quite accurately inform us about the sea temperature changes and the volume of ice present at any given time, because ice preferentially locks away the heavier oxygen isotope. It may be seen from the illustration (right) that the temperature fluctuations of the Pleistocene are extremely complex, and that each major cold phase comprises a series of warmer and colder stages.
Right *Planktonic formanifera of the marine protozoan type. Since they are found in fossil beds they are useful in dating.*

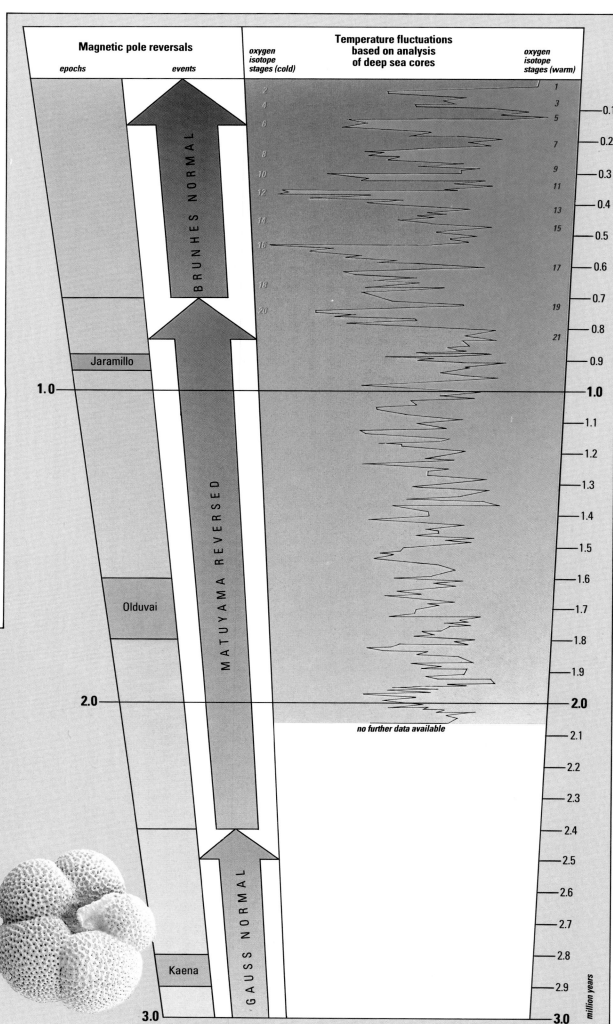

Magnetic pole reversals

epochs   events

BRUNHES NORMAL

Jaramillo

1.0

Olduvai

MATUYAMA REVERSED

2.0

Kaena

GAUSS NORMAL

3.0

Temperature fluctuations based on analysis of deep sea cores

oxygen isotope stages (cold)

oxygen isotope stages (warm)

no further data available

million years

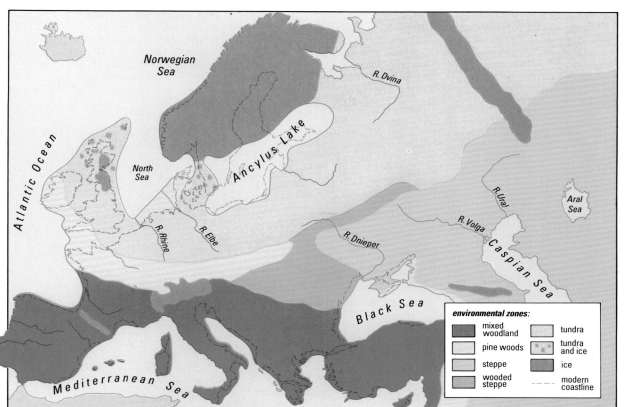

1   ICE AGE EUROPE: CHANGING ENVIRONMENTS

The map (*left*) depicts Europe in a period when the ice sheets were not at their fullest extent but when conditions were colder than those of the present day. Features to be noted are the extension of the coastal plains as a result of the lowered sea level – the British Isles, for instance, are joined to the continent. Equally, woodland is absent from northern Europe, which would have been covered by tundra and, in more sheltered parts, pine woods. Deciduous trees would have been restricted to the south of Europe although dwarf varieties of them may have survived in some northern areas. As conditions improved the vegetation zones would move north. The Baltic Sea was cut off from the North Sea and formed a deep, brackish lake. The warm waters of the Gulf Stream would have been diverted southwards during colder times, enhancing the cooling of the land in north-western Europe. Just as the vegetation zones changed to reflect the variations of climate so too did animal distribution. Present-day patterns became established only 10,000 years ago.

3   LONDON: THE ANIMAL POPULATION

Animals are frequently associated with certain environmental conditions. Animal fossils, revealed when building work was being undertaken in London (*map below*), show times when conditions were warmer than those of the present day – open country species like lions and elephants were present, and hippopotamus lived in marshy areas. Similarly, finds of woolly rhinoceros and mammoth fossils show times when the climate was much colder and the London area was open steppe, similar to Siberia. Creatures such as the horse, bison, lion and hyena may be found at different times in many different climatic conditions. As the climate changed, some species, such as lions and hyenas, moved to more suitable areas, and some, such as the horse, simply adjusted to their new surroundings. Others – the giant deer, mammoth and woolly rhinoceros – failed to do either and over the last 10,000 years have become extinct.

environmental zones:
- mixed woodland
- pine woods
- steppe
- wooded steppe
- tundra
- tundra and ice
- ice
- --- modern coastline

1   reindeer antler, Twickenham

2   skull of woolly rhinoceros, Battersea Power Station

3   straight-tusked elephant tooth, Pall Mall

4   partial skull of bison, Trafalgar Square

5   canine tooth of hippopotamus, Trafalgar Square

6   mammoth jaw, Salisbury Square

Fossil remains in Greater London

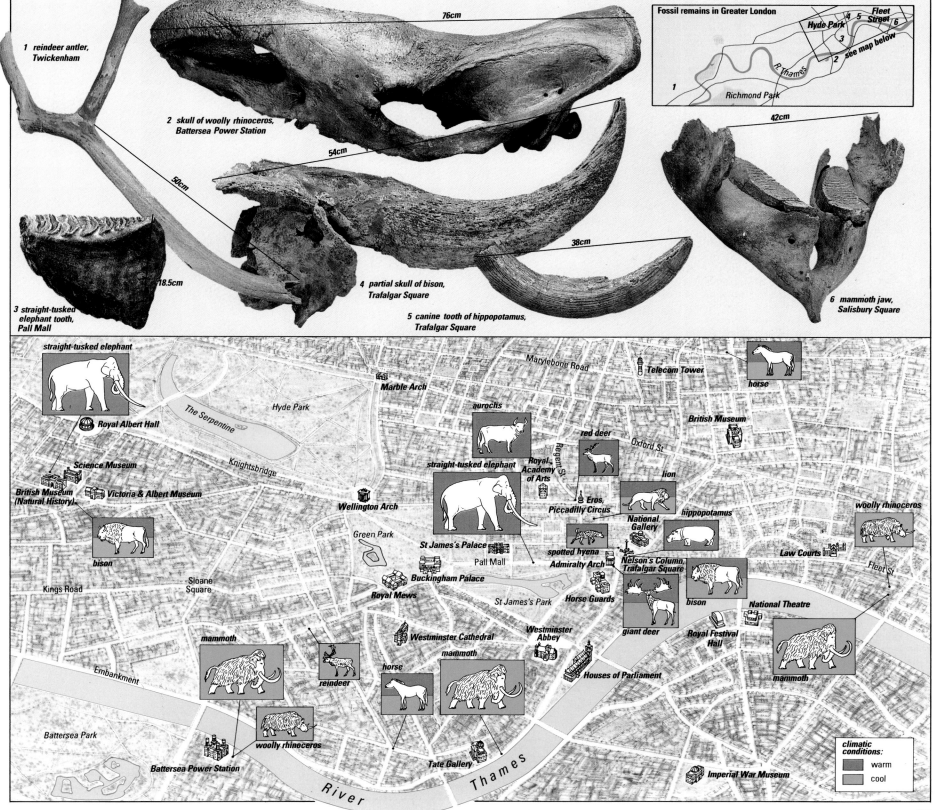

climatic conditions:
- warm
- cool

Early hominids in East Asia

The earliest hominids evolved in Africa, and it was only when *Homo erectus* appeared some 1.7 million years ago that an expansion out of Africa occurred. Once this stage was reached, however, hominids spread out into the Middle East, Asia and Europe, adapting to very different conditions of climate, food sources and geography. Clothing, the use of fire and the construction of artificial shelters were all crucial to this process. As little information is available about this period, understanding of the lifestyles of the time hinges upon a few well-known sites, most particularly that of Zhoukoudian in China.

In contrast to other parts of the world, the early settlers of East Asia used very irregularly shaped stone tools that are difficult to recognise as artefacts. In addition, they exploited the versatile plant resources such as bamboo and rattan to make their equipment. Fire as a means of heating and for cooking was clearly important, and traces of it have been found at every Early Palaeolithic site in China. It may also have been used as a means of clearing the dense tropical vegetation in the south of the region, stimulating the growth of useful food plants as the jungle regenerated.

The earliest evidence for human occupation in East Asia derives from two regions; the first, dated to 1.7 million years ago, is at Yuanmou in western China, and the second, at Sangiran in Java, is dated to 1.3 million years ago. Both sites yielded remains of *Homo erectus*, and Yuanmou also had stone tools and charcoal debris, indicating the use of fire. In Java no stone tools have been discovered that can be connected with the known skeletal remains. It is possible that this scarcity of stone tools shows a different type of adaptation by *Homo erectus* to the humid tropics of Indonesia that contrasted with the way of life that developed in the more temperate climate of northern China.

The Chinese record shows rich evidence of stone tools, fire, animal bones and occasional plant remains, often associated with limestone caves. The best known cave site in China is Zhoukoudian, where there is an archaeological deposit over 50 metres thick, divided into eleven layers which span the period 450,000 to 350,000 BP. The stone tools recovered from it are mostly of coarse materials such as quartz and quartzite, and include a variety of picks, points and scrapers made from flakes, in addition to choppers and chopping tools made from river pebbles. An interesting discovery at Zhoukoudian was a large number of burnt hackberries indicating, for the first time in the region, the part vegetables played in the diet. Archaeological work in China has been carried out mainly in the north, so markedly fewer sites are known from the south. Whether this reflects a preferred occupation of the temperate woodland and grassland over the tropical zone or simply a lack of archaeological exploration in the more southerly regions remains to be seen. Many of the areas settled by early humans now lie under the South China Sea on what were then rich coastal plains.

The tropical zone is now being explored more thoroughly, however, and this has recently resulted in the discovery of three sites in Thailand, thought to be at least 600,000 years old, as well as finds of *Homo erectus* among accumulations of animal bones in caves in Lang Son province, Vietnam. To the north, Korea also has a number of sites dating to this period. The tools from the Korean sites are more distinctively shaped than those from South-East Asia and include handaxes worked on both faces, points and scrapers. The earliest dated occupation of Japan is more recent.

The first modern humans in the East Asian area have been found in the same two key regions, Java and China. The finds of a number of skulls at Ngandong in Java represent an early form of *Homo sapiens* dating to 120,000 BP (*page 68*). In China, early modern people are to be found at Zhoukoudian, where they show an advance over their predecessors in having more refined stone tools, burials and ornaments such as pierced animal-tooth beads. They still lived by hunting and gathering, but a more complex social organisation meant that specific tasks were allocated to individual work groups. By 30,000 years ago the occupants of the Zhoukoudian Upper Cave were physically identical to ourselves. In South-East Asia further remains of humans identical to ourselves have been found at Niah Cave in Borneo, dated to 40,000 years ago, and at Wadjak in Java. Slightly more recent than these is Tabon Cave in the Philippines dated to 23,000 BP (*page 68*). All these finds are associated with poorly developed stone tools resembling those of earlier periods. It was, however, with the coming of fully modern man to the region that the stage was set for the last major human expansion into Australia and the Americas.

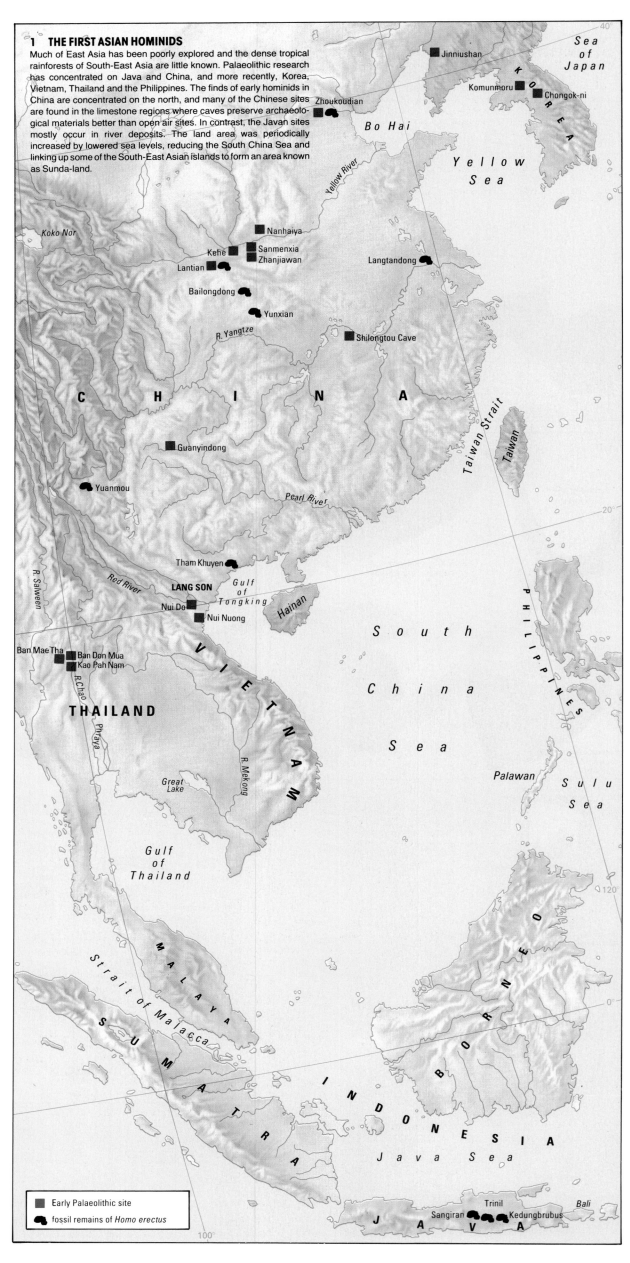

1 THE FIRST ASIAN HOMINIDS
Much of East Asia has been poorly explored and the dense tropical rainforests of South-East Asia are little known. Palaeolithic research has concentrated on Java and China, and more recently, Korea, Vietnam, Thailand and the Philippines. The finds of early hominids in China are concentrated on the north, and many of the Chinese sites are found in the limestone regions where caves preserve archaeological materials better than open air sites. In contrast, the Javan sites mostly occur in river deposits. The land area was periodically increased by lowered sea levels, reducing the South China Sea and linking up some of the South-East Asian islands to form an area known as Sunda-land.

■ Early Palaeolithic site

fossil remains of *Homo erectus*

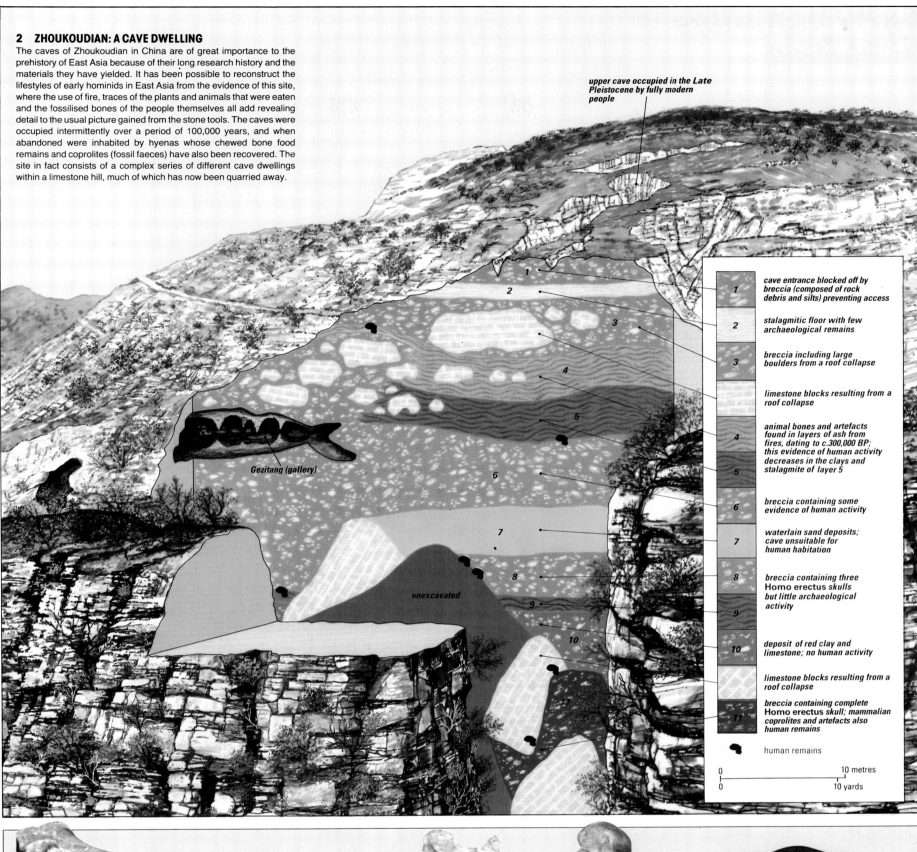

2 ZHOUKOUDIAN: A CAVE DWELLING

The caves of Zhoukoudian in China are of great importance to the prehistory of East Asia because of their long research history and the materials they have yielded. It has been possible to reconstruct the lifestyles of early hominids in East Asia from the evidence of this site, where the use of fire, traces of the plants and animals that were eaten and the fossilised bones of the people themselves all add revealing detail to the usual picture gained from the stone tools. The caves were occupied intermittently over a period of 100,000 years, and when abandoned were inhabited by hyenas whose chewed bone food remains and coprolites (fossil faeces) have also been recovered. The site in fact consists of a complex series of different cave dwellings within a limestone hill, much of which has now been quarried away.

upper cave occupied in the Late Pleistocene by fully modern people

Gezitang (gallery)

unexcavated

1	cave entrance blocked off by breccia (composed of rock debris and silts) preventing access
2	stalagmitic floor with few archaeological remains
3	breccia including large boulders from a roof collapse
	limestone blocks resulting from a roof collapse
4	animal bones and artefacts found in layers of ash from fires, dating to c.300,000 BP; this evidence of human activity decreases in the clays and stalagmite of layer 5
5	
6	breccia containing some evidence of human activity
7	waterlain sand deposits; cave unsuitable for human habitation
8	breccia containing three Homo erectus skulls but little archaeological activity
9	
10	deposit of red clay and limestone; no human activity
	limestone blocks resulting from a roof collapse
11	breccia containing complete Homo erectus skull; mammalian coprolites and artefacts also human remains

● human remains

0   10 metres
0   10 yards

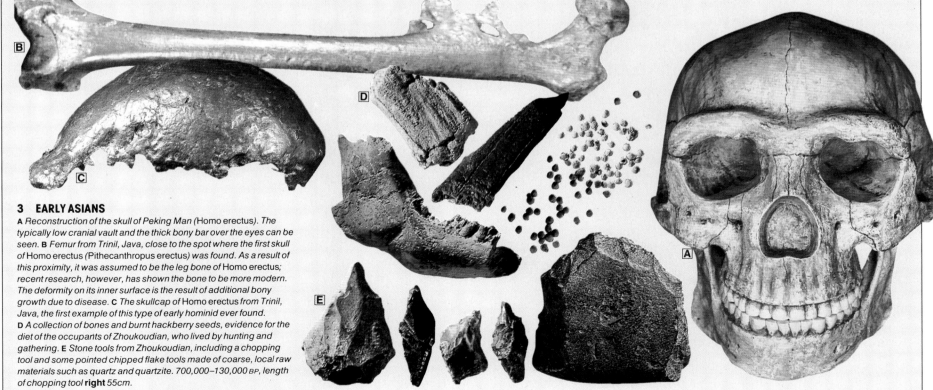

3 EARLY ASIANS

A *Reconstruction of the skull of Peking Man* (Homo erectus). *The typically low cranial vault and the thick bony bar over the eyes can be seen.* B *Femur from Trinil, Java, close to the spot where the first skull of* Homo erectus (Pithecanthropus erectus) *was found. As a result of this proximity, it was assumed to be the leg bone of* Homo erectus; *recent research, however, has shown the bone to be more modern. The deformity on its inner surface is the result of additional bony growth due to disease.* C *The skullcap of* Homo erectus *from Trinil, Java, the first example of this type of early hominid ever found.* D *A collection of bones and burnt hackberry seeds, evidence for the diet of the occupants of Zhoukoudian, who lived by hunting and gathering.* E *Stone tools from Zhoukoudian, including a chopping tool and some pointed chipped flake tools made of coarse, local raw materials such as quartz and quartzite.* 700,000–130,000 BP, *length of chopping tool* **right** 55cm.

Early hominids in Europe

The earliest hominids in Europe arrived from Africa some time after one million years ago, so beginning the phase known as the Lower Palaeolithic, which lasted until the Middle Palaeolithic 200,000 years ago. Throughout this time the climate of Europe was fluctuating between warm and cold phases, and periods of low sea level were an important factor in enabling humans to expand into the region. The earliest European colonists were closely related to *Homo erectus*, and may even have been members of this group, though as human fossils of this era are rare, this is uncertain. These groups lived by hunting and gathering, and probably depended heavily upon seasonal resources, moving about regularly within their territories to get food. Their principal remains are stone tools, which include refined types such as handaxes. Woodworking and wooden tools are also known from some of these early sites. Fire and clothing would have been necessary before the temperate zone could be occupied, especially during the colder, glacial phases.

The precise date of the first colonisation of Europe is not yet known. The evidence for hominid occupation in Europe before 700,000 years ago is scanty, but at a number of sites in France, Czechoslovakia and Yugoslavia struck pebble tools have been found, and it would appear from this evidence that they were occupied earlier

than 700,000 BP. After 700,000 BP, however, the evidence becomes unequivocal, and sites from all over Europe have been dated to between 700,000 and 400,000 BP. Most of these sites were located by rivers or lakesides, where the debris of stone tool manufacture is often found together with the discarded tools themselves and the bones of large mammals. The tools of this period are primitive in appearance and often made by striking off a few flakes from river pebbles to produce a rough chopping tool. Sometimes the flakes themselves would be chipped into points or scrapers. There is also evidence of actual human fossils from this period. One of the best known is the Mauer jaw, a very robust jaw with large teeth, which lacks a marked chin. Experts disagree as to whether these people should be considered as members of the *Homo erectus* group or some early form of *Homo sapiens*.

It was during the period 700,000–400,000 BP that the first handaxes were used in Europe. These were an advance over the earlier pebble tools, being portable and multi-purpose. With time handaxes became more refined and varieties with distinctly differing shapes can be discerned. Assemblages of tools which include handaxes are called Acheulian after the site of St. Acheul in France. A number of sites dating from about 400,000 BP offer a more detailed picture of the activities of these early Europeans. In southern France at the coastal site of Terra Amata a number of simple wooden huts and a human footprint were discovered. Further information came from the study of human coprolites (fossil faeces) from the site, which contained pollen showing the time of year of the occupation, and also revealed the presence of intestin-

al parasites. The site seems to have been occupied only briefly some time in the late spring or early summer, and revisited at about the same time in succeeding years.

Big-game hunting dominated the economy of this period. In Spain, elephants were driven into boggy ground using torches at the sites of Torralba-Ambrona. In the Channel Islands, at La Cotte of St. Brelade, evidence shows that big-game animals, including rhinoceros, were driven over cliffs. Evidence from the important site of Bilzingsleben in Germany reinforces this picture of big-game hunting – bones of animals were recovered there which bear the marks of butchery. Bilzingsleben was a lakeside site where wooden tools were preserved, and where distinct occupation zones – huts, flint-working areas and wood-working areas – have all been identified. There is clear evidence for the use of fire at many of these sites.

Between 400,000 and 120,000 BP a new method for working stone was introduced, called the prepared-core technique, which involved the shaping of the block of flint so that the shape of the tools which were then struck could be closely controlled. This development reflects the demand for specialised tools for specific tasks and remained an important feature of stone tool technology during the Middle Palaeolithic which succeeded the Lower Palaeolithic in about 200,000 BP.

Important evolutionary changes had occurred since the first hominids colonised Europe. By the time of the last interglacial (120,000 years ago), the early European population had begun to exhibit many of the physical characteristics which were to appear still more strongly in the following Neanderthal phase.

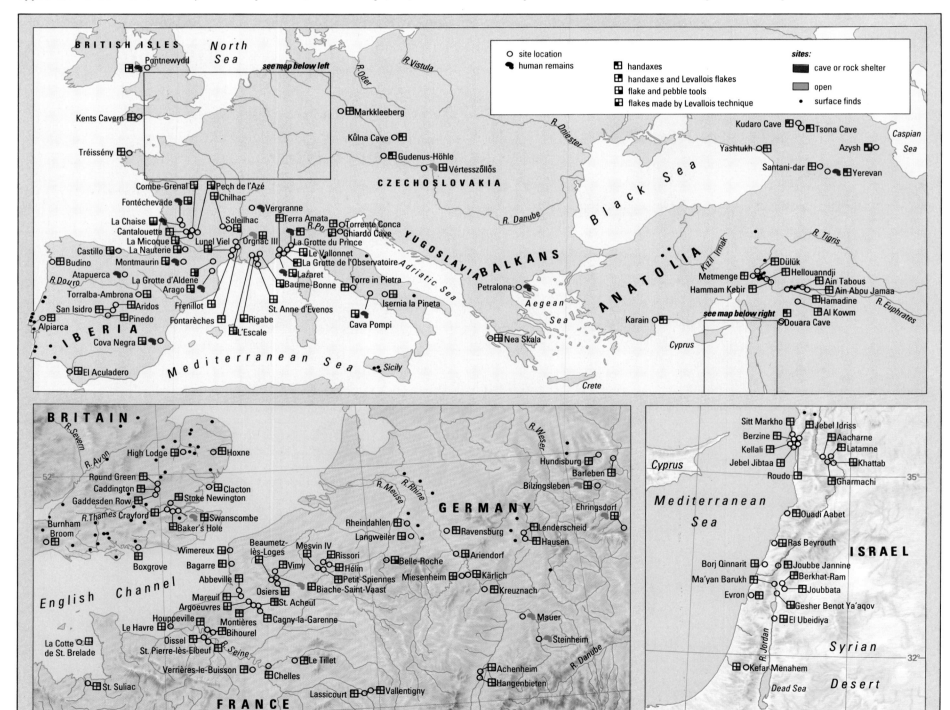

1 THE EARLY HOMINIDS OF EUROPE

Early hominids were widely distributed throughout Europe, with the earliest sites located around the Mediterranean. More northerly areas were only accessible periodically when the climate was warmer. Sites with stone tools are more common discoveries than the fossils of the

people themselves. The distribution of sites reflects which areas of Europe have been most thoroughly investigated archaeologically – the north-western corner of Europe is particularly rich. Many sites are concentrated along the major rivers: these areas offered a reliable water supply, and good hunting opportunities. There is no evidence for the highland zones

such as the Alps and the Apennines at this time, perhaps because the early hominids were unable to adapt to the harsher conditions. Another factor in this pattern may be the formation of glaciers on these high areas which would remove any evidence of previous occupation during warmer times.

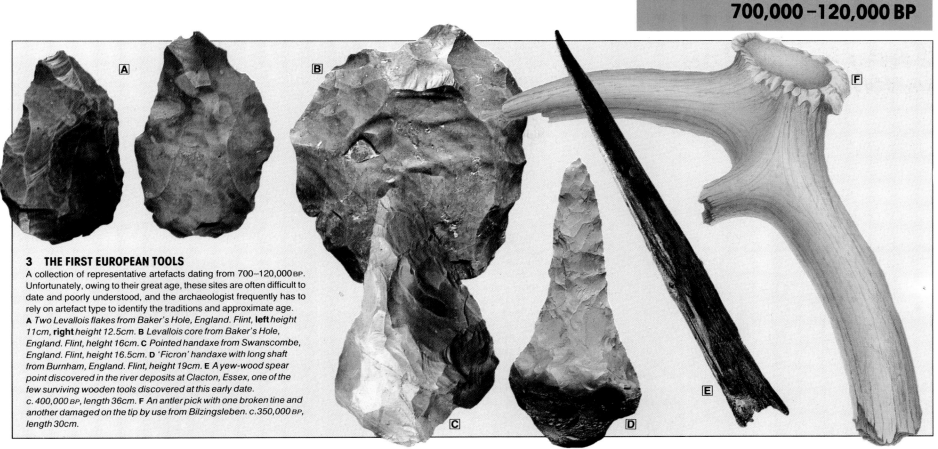

3 THE FIRST EUROPEAN TOOLS

A collection of representative artefacts dating from 700–120,000 BP. Unfortunately, owing to their great age, these sites are often difficult to date and poorly understood, and the archaeologist frequently has to rely on artefact type to identify the traditions and approximate age. **A** *Two Levallois flakes from Baker's Hole, England. Flint,* **left** *height 11cm,* **right** *height 12.5cm.* **B** *Levallois core from Baker's Hole, England. Flint, height 16cm.* **C** *Pointed handaxe from Swanscombe, England. Flint, height 16.5cm.* **D** *'Ficron' handaxe with long shaft from Burnham, England. Flint, height 19cm.* **E** *A yew-wood spear point discovered in the river deposits at Clacton, Essex, one of the few surviving wooden tools discovered at this early date.* c. 400,000 BP, *length 36cm.* **F** *An antler pick with one broken tine and another damaged on the tip by use from Bilzingsleben.* c. 350,000 BP, *length 30cm.*

Bilzingsleben: environmental resources

environmental zones	gathering	snaring/scavenging/hunting		
marsh	reeds/rhizomes	water birds, waders and eggs		
copse (mainly willow)	herbs	aurochs		
parkland (alder, poplar, ash, willow, lime, oak)	wild honey, resins, nuts, berries, bark	wild pigs, red and roe deer	elephants	small mammals/predators (lion, wolf, fox) omnivores (bears)
deciduous woodland (oak, maple, lime)				
scrub (hazel, box, pyracanthus, rose, dogwood, elder)	nuts, berries, roots	rhinoceros		
open ground (no trees or bushes)		herds of bison, horse, deer		
green pasture				
river, streams and pools		fish		

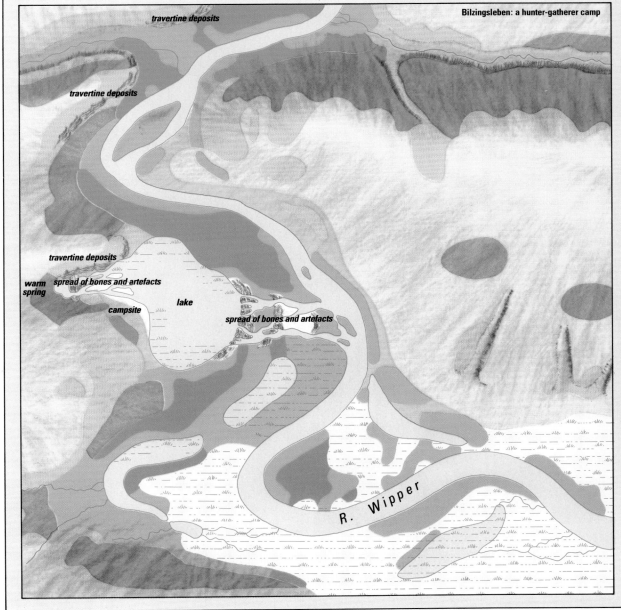

Bilzingsleben: a hunter-gatherer camp

travertine deposits
travertine deposits
travertine deposits
warm spring
spread of bones and artefacts
campsite
lake
spread of bones and artefacts
R. Wipper

2 BILZINGSLEBEN: A LAKESIDE SITE

The lakeside site of Bilzingsleben in East Germany is important because of the quality of information it has yielded. The remarkable conditions of preservation at the site have even led to the survival of wooden tools. Amongst the wooden tools which were discovered at the site were both wooden rods and the chips and shavings produced in making them. Recent dating evidence suggests that the remains of a human skull from Bilzingsleben date to more than 400,000 years ago, and research indicates that the skull is a specimen of Archaic *Homo sapiens*. Bilzingsleben was occupied by a group of hunter-gatherers who used the site primarily for big-game hunting, but its location was especially favourable because it gave them access to a great variety of resources. The nearby scrub offered nuts and berries, as well as rhinoceros, elephants and small mammals. From the parkland and deciduous woodland wild honey, resin, nuts, berries, bark, wild pigs, red and roe deer, rhinoceros, elephants and small mammals were available. The river and marsh were rich in fish and water birds, while the open ground and pasture were grazed by herds of bison, horse and deer.

Bones and tools were discovered at the site, and it was possible to identify areas of stone tool production, butchery and shelters. Large stone and bone anvils were found along with collections of hammerstones. The bones of the large animals bore the chopping and cutting marks of the stone tools used to butcher the carcasses. Of the hunted animals, rhinoceros was most common, providing large amounts of meat, bone marrow, and also bone for use as fuel for fires, props for shelters and as material for making tools. The next most common species was the beaver, which was probably hunted for its fur.

Many other early sites in Europe resemble Bilzingsleben; they have similar stone tools and were also located in places with access to different environments and resources. Unfortunately, only at Bilzingsleben have working areas, shelters and wooden tools been found in a sufficiently well-preserved state to offer a rare glimpse into the details of early hominid life.

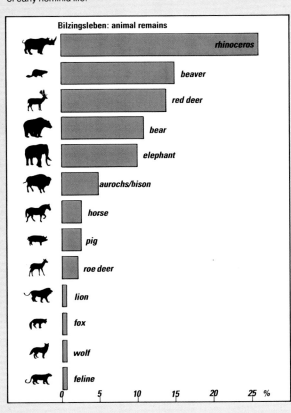

Bilzingsleben: animal remains

rhinoceros
beaver
red deer
bear
elephant
aurochs/bison
horse
pig
roe deer
lion
fox
wolf
feline

0   5   10   15   20   25 %

The Neanderthals

The Neanderthals, generally associated with the typical image of primitive 'cave-men', are first known some 120,000 years ago and lived in western Eurasia until some 35,000 years ago. The Neanderthals are distinguished from fully modern man by a strong and heavy skeleton and a projecting face with a large, broad nose and large teeth. Casts of their brains show little difference from those of modern man, and their brain size is as large. The Neanderthals are the first type of human known to have buried their dead, and display a variety of ritual behaviour. Some dismiss Neanderthals from the direct line of modern human ancestry, but given the close chronological and physical similarities between Neanderthals and modern man it is difficult to accept that they made no contribution to the succeeding European populations.

The Neanderthals lived in a variety of environments ranging from the relatively arid Middle East to the cold central European region. They lived by hunting in central and eastern Europe, where groups of them probably joined together to hunt large animals such as mammoths. These animals provided them not only with meat and hides but also with large bones, which were used as fuel for fires in areas so cold that trees would not grow, and also could be used as supports and frames for tents. In the slightly less harsh environment of western Europe the Neanderthals could live by more haphazard hunting, killing deer, horse or wild ox as they encountered them, and possibly also river fishing.

The floors of Neanderthal sites have been examined by archaeologists for evidence of huts, and for special areas where stone and hides were worked. Neanderthal living places were the site of diverse activities, including the making and use of stone tools, the butchering of animal carcasses, cooking over hearths, and a variety of wood-working tasks. The edges of stone tools have been studied under microscopes for evidence of their use. Large numbers of these tools were used in working wood, both for chopping up large branches and for whittling away at smaller pieces. Other tools were used in the preparation of meat and vegetables, while some were also used to work hides – some of the tools resemble implements used today for making suede. The stone for making the tools was mostly obtained locally, although some flint may have been transported up to 30 kilometres from its source. Few bone or antler tools are known from Neanderthal sites, and when they do occur they are fairly primitive.

Neanderthals are best known as the manufacturers of Mousterian stone tools, predominantly made from flakes, and including a large number of scrapers and points. They frequently used a prepared-core technique, where the intended flake is preformed on the core before removal. This marked an important technological advance over their predecessors. The Micoquian industry is contemporary with the Mousterian, and characterised by fine, pointed handaxes as well as a wide range of flake-based tools. These industries are termed Middle Palaeolithic (200,000 to 30,000 BP) and are similar to the tool industries of the preceding Lower Palaeolithic.

The Neanderthals have often been considered as brutish and primitive, but the archaeological evidence suggests that of all the earlier fossil human groups, such as *Homo erectus* and archaic *Homo sapiens*, they most resemble modern man. This evidence includes the discovery of cemeteries at La Ferrassie in France and at Shanidar in Iraq. At the grave of one old man at Shanidar flowers had been laid with the body. This was discovered by sampling the grave for pollen. This man had been handicapped in life by the loss of one arm and blindness in one eye, and his legs were so injured that walking would have been very difficult. It is likely that he was cared for by the other members of the group. Further east still, a young Neanderthal child was found buried with a deposit of ibex horns at Teshik-Tash in Central Asia.

Recently, Neanderthal remains have been discovered associated with the earliest Upper Palaeolithic industries in south-western France. It had long been assumed that the differences between the tool industries of the Middle and the Upper Palaeolithic were attributable to the differences in the intellectual ability of their manufacturers (the Upper Palaeolithic being produced by modern man, while the Middle Palaeolithic was associated with Neanderthal and other hominids). This new discovery supports the image of the Neanderthals as very like the earliest modern populations: robust, well adapted to a rigorous lifestyle in harsh environments, but showing signs of modern humanity in the burial of their dead, their ritual and social organisation.

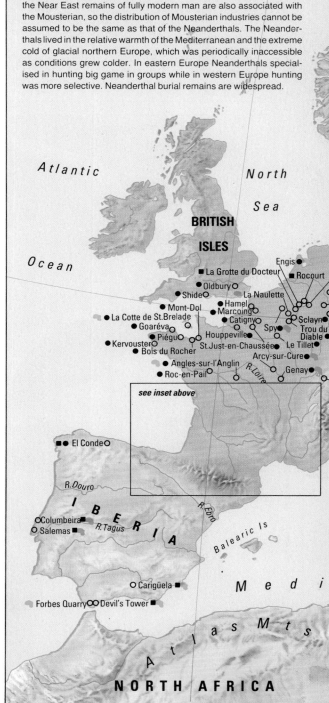

3 THE LOST EURASIANS
Mousterian tools *(120,000BP–35,000BP)* **A** *Side-scraper from Le Moustier, France. Flint, length 9cm.* **B** *Convex side-scraper from Le Moustier. Flint, length 7.5cm.* **C** *Levallois point from Le Moustier. Flint, length 6cm.* **D** *Double convex side-scraper from Le Moustier. Flint, length 8.5cm.* **E** *Handaxes from Le Moustier. Flint,* **left** *8.5cm,* **right** *6cm.* **F** *Handaxe from Bois du Rocher, Brittany. Quartzite, length 7.5cm.* **G** *Single straight side-scraper from Le Moustier. Flint, length 8.5cm.* **H** *The skull and some post-cranial bones of the 'Old man' of La Chapelle-aux-Saints, France. These specimens were used to reconstruct Neanderthals as stooping and primitive. The bones are, however, deformed by arthritis. The skull shows many typical Neanderthal traits including large teeth, a projecting snout, a large nose and heavy ridges of bone over the eye sockets.* **I** *Large Neanderthal skull from Tabun, Mount Carmel, Israel. It was broken into many fragments after it was buried over 35,000 years ago.*

1 NEANDERTHAL EURASIA
Neanderthals are found widely dispersed through Eurasia, over an area from the Portuguese coast in the west to Soviet Central Asia in the East. The richest areas for Neanderthal finds are the caves of south-western France and Israel (*see inset maps*). Mousterian stone tool assemblages, which in Europe were produced solely by Neanderthals, are more widely spread and include finds in the British Isles. In the Near East remains of fully modern man are also associated with the Mousterian, so the distribution of Mousterian industries cannot be assumed to be the same as that of the Neanderthals. The Neanderthals lived in the relative warmth of the Mediterranean and the extreme cold of glacial northern Europe, which was periodically inaccessible as conditions grew colder. In eastern Europe Neanderthals specialised in hunting big game in groups while in western Europe hunting was more selective. Neanderthal burial remains are widespread.

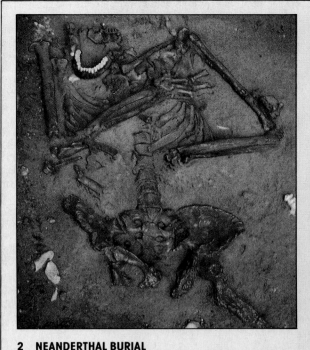

adult female flexed into crouched position

adult male in crouched position

burnt animal bones and flint tools in pits

pits each containing skeleton of 3-5 year old child and flint implements

low mounds

burial containing remains of foetus

5 year old child buried with head resting on animal bone fragments and 3 flint tools

possible burial

2 NEANDERTHAL BURIAL
At La Ferrassie, France, two adults and three children (*right*), were buried in a crouched position, characteristic of Neanderthal sites.
Above *The burial of an elderly Neanderthal at Shanidar in Iraq.*

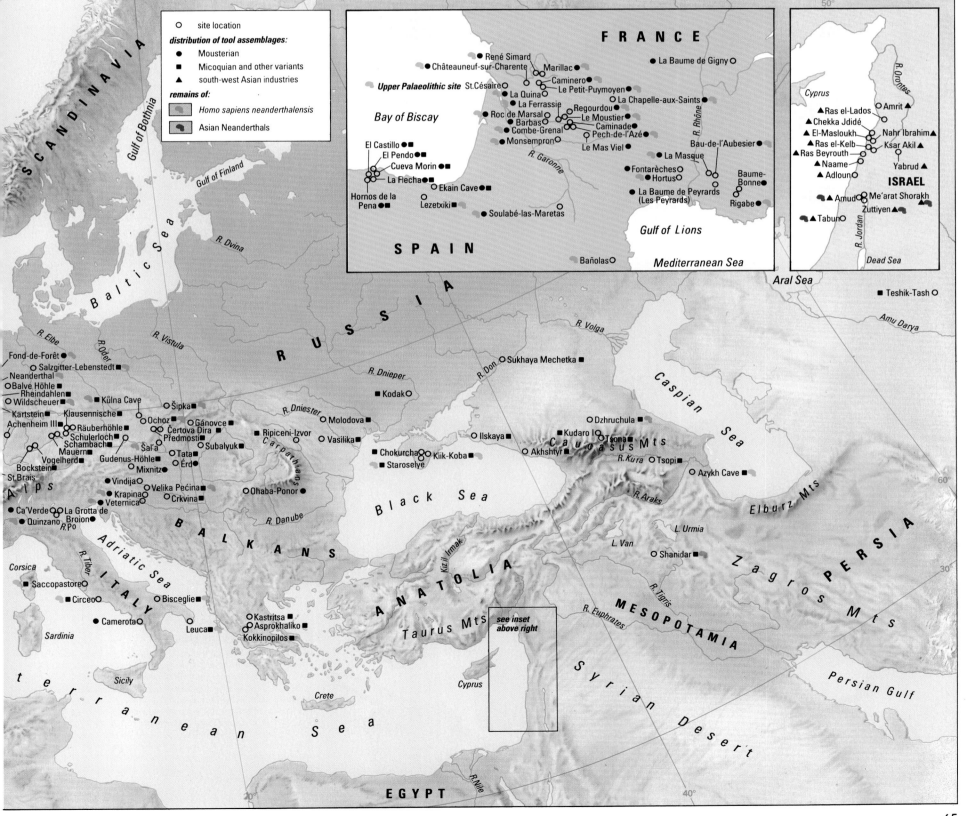

○ site location

distribution of tool assemblages:
● Mousterian
■ Micoquian and other variants
▲ south-west Asian industries

remains of:
Homo sapiens neanderthalensis
Asian Neanderthals

FRANCE

● René Simard
● Châteauneuf-sur-Charente   ● Marillac
● La Baume de Gigny ○
Upper Palaeolithic site St.Césaire
● Caminero
● Le Petit-Puymoyen
● La Quina
● La Chapelle-aux-Saints
Bay of Biscay
● La Ferrassie
● Regourdou
● Roc de Marsal   ● Le Moustier
● Barbas   ● Caminade
● Combe-Grenal   ● Pech-de-l'Azé
● Monsempron   Le Mas Viel
● Bau-de-l'Aubesier
● El Castillo ●■
● El Pendo ●
● Cueva Morin   ■■
● La Masque
● La Flêcha
● Fontarèches
● Hortus ○
● Baume-
Bonne ●
Hornos de la ●■   ● Ekain Cave ●■
Pena ●■   ● Lezetxiki   ● La Baume de Peyrards
(Les Peyrards)
● Rigabe ■
● Soulabé-las-Maretas

SPAIN   Gulf of Lions
● Bañolas   Mediterranean Sea

Cyprus
▲ Ras el-Lados   ▲ Amrit
▲ Chekka Jdidé
▲ El-Masloukh   ▲ Nahr Ibrahim ▲
▲ Ras el-Kelb   ○ Ksar Akil ▲
▲ Ras Beyrouth
▲ Naame   ▲ Yabrud
▲ Adloun
ISRAEL
▲ Amud   ○ Me'arat Shorakh
Zuttiyen
▲ Tabun

SCANDINAVIA
Gulf of Bothnia
Gulf of Finland
Baltic Sea
R. Elbe   R. Oder   R. Vistula   R. Dvina
Fond-de-Forêt ●
Salzgitter-Lebenstedt ■
Neanderthal   R. Volga
Balve Höhle ○
Rheindahlen
Kartstein   Külna Cave ■
Klausennische   ○ Šipka   R. Don   ■ Sukhaya Mechetka
Wildscheuer   R. Dnieper   ○ Kodak
Achenheim III   ○ Ochoz   R. Dniester
Räuberhöhle   ○ Gánovce   ○ Molodova
Schulerloch   ● Čertova Dira   Ripiceni-Izvor ●   ○ Vasilika
Schambach   ● Predmosti   Dzhruchula ○
Mauern   Šal'a ■   ○ Ilskaya   Kudaro I ○   ○ Tsona   Caspian Sea
Bockstein   ● Tata   ● Érd   ○ Chokurcha   Akhshtyr ○   R. Kura   ○ Tsopi
Vogelherd   ○ Gudenus-Höhle   ● Subalyuk   ○ Kiik-Koba   Azykh Cave ■
St Brais   ○ Mixnitz   ● Staroselye   Caucasus Mts
Alps   ● Vindija   R. Araks
● Krapina   ○ Ohaba-Ponor   R. Danube   Black Sea   Elburz Mts
● Veternica   ○ Velika Pećina
● Crkvina
Ca'Verde ●   ○ La Grotta de   BALKANS   L. Urmia
Quinzano ●   Broion   L. Van   Zagros   PERSIA
R. Po   Adriatic Sea   ○ Shanidar   Mts
Corsica
● Saccopastore   ANATOLIA   MESOPOTAMIA
● Circeo ■   ITALY   R. Tigris
Bisceglie ■   Kastritsa ■   Taurus Mts
● Camerota ○   ○ Asprokhaliko   R. Euphrates   30°
Sardinia   Leuca ○   Kokkinopilos ○
see inset
above right
Sicily   Cyprus   Syrian Desert   Persian Gulf
Crete
Mediterranean Sea

Aral Sea   50°

■ Teshik-Tash ○   Amu Darya

60°

EGYPT   R. Nile   40°

The first modern humans

The Middle Stone Age of Africa lasted from about 120,000 to 35,000 years ago, and was a period marked by major changes in the abilities and behaviour of early hominids. Their increasing mastery of the problems and possibilities offered by the natural environment is shown by their colonisation of some of the less hospitable areas of Africa, such as the tropical rain forests. There is also evidence for the use of a wider range of foodstuffs, including shellfish, and for the earliest African art. But

without doubt the most important development in Middle Stone Age Africa was the emergence of the first anatomically modern humans, *Homo sapiens sapiens*, in the south of the continent around 100,000 years ago.

The Middle Stone Age is distinguished from earlier periods by significant improvements in the manufacture of stone tools. One such improvement was the development of a technique of shaping the core by careful preliminary flaking. This so-called prepared-core technique made it possible to produce more regular flakes, including triangular points and parallel-sided blades. These were suitable for mounting in hafts of bone or wood to form more efficient composite tools. Composite tools, which combined the use of stone for the cutting edge and organic materials for the remainder, are not known before

this period and represent an important advance in human technology. The numerous tanged points and scrapers of the Atèrian industry of the Sahara, produced at a time when the desert region was much more hospitable than today, are among the best examples of stone tools which were probably hafted in this way.

There is widespread evidence from sites in many parts of Africa that Middle Stone Age peoples hunted a great diversity of animals, although detailed work at Klasies River Mouth in southern Africa suggests that particularly dangerous species, such as bush pig, may have been avoided. At both Klasies River Mouth and Haua Fteah on the Libyan coast extensive accumulations of shell middens provide some of the earliest evidence in the world for the use of marine resources such as shellfish. Thick ash layers

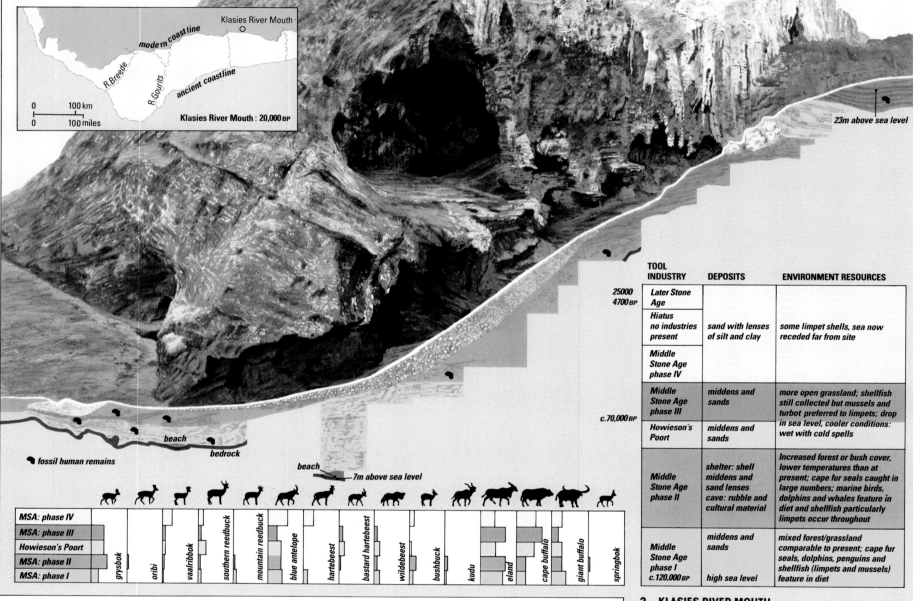

TOOL INDUSTRY	DEPOSITS	ENVIRONMENT RESOURCES
Later Stone Age		
Hiatus no industries present	sand with lenses of silt and clay	some limpet shells, sea now receded far from site
Middle Stone Age phase IV		
Middle Stone Age phase III	middens and sands	more open grassland; shellfish still collected but mussels and turbot preferred to limpets; drop in sea level, cooler conditions: wet with cold spells
Howieson's Poort	middens and sands	
Middle Stone Age phase II	shelter: shell middens and sand lenses cave: rubble and cultural material	Increased forest or bush cover, lower temperatures than at present; cape fur seals caught in large numbers; marine birds, dolphins and whales feature in diet and shellfish particularly limpets occur throughout
Middle Stone Age phase I c.120,000 BP	middens and sands / high sea level	mixed forest/grassland comparable to present; cape fur seals, dolphins, and shellfish (limpets and mussels) feature in diet

(scale markers on photo: 25000 4700 BP; c.70,000 BP; 23m above sea level; 7m above sea level)

Map inset: Klasies River Mouth. modern coastline, ancient coastline, R.Breede, R.Gourits. 0–100 km, 0–100 miles. Klasies River Mouth: 20,000 BP

Labels on photo: fossil human remains, beach, bedrock, beach

	grysbok	oribi	vaalribbok	southern reedbuck	mountain reedbuck	blue antelope	hartebeest	bastard hartebeest	wildebeest	bushbuck	kudu	eland	cape buffalo	giant buffalo	springbok
MSA: phase IV															
MSA: phase III															
Howieson's Poort															
MSA: phase II															
MSA: phase I															

2 KLASIES RIVER MOUTH

The caves and rock shelters of Klasies River Mouth, southern Africa, were occupied intermittently from 125,000 to 70,000 BP. During this time the sea was never far from the site, and the inhabitants were able to collect limpets, periwinkles and mussels from the rocky shore and to hunt Cape fur seals, possibly as much for their furs as for their meat. This is the earliest known evidence for the exploitation of sea foods, and their importance may be reflected in the abandonment of the site when sea levels dropped during the last glaciation and the coastline receded some 64 kilometres (*see inset*). Although antelope and eland were the main animals hunted or scavenged, a wide range of other prey was also hunted (*see table*). The inhabitants were fully modern humans whose tools were made from skilfully produced flakes and blades which were probably fixed into wooden shafts and handles. Their fossilised bones are some of the oldest known remains of modern humans in the world.

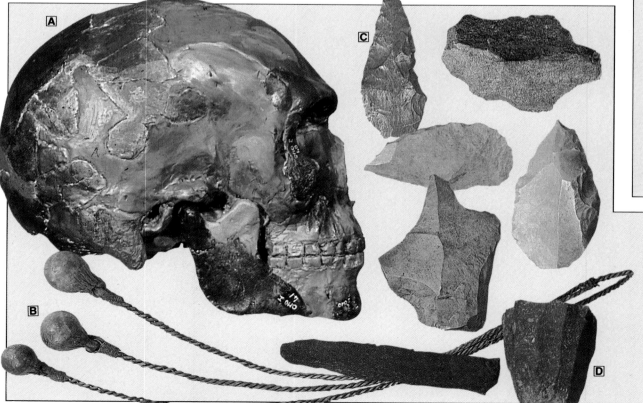

3 MIDDLE STONE AGE AFRICA

A The Omo I skull from East Africa, dated to c.130,000 BP, one of the earliest known examples of modern man. This reconstruction shows that the skull shape and size is completely modern.
B A bola made up of a weighted rope, which was whirled around the head and thrown at game animals. The spinning stone weights covered in rawhide wrap the rope around the animal's legs and bring it to the ground. Diameter of weight 6cm. **C** Five flake tools from the Howieson's Poort tradition, including two points, one chipped on both sides. c.70,000 BP, length of average point 4cm. **D** A long, regular blade-flake and a core for removing such blades from Klasies River Mouth. Middle Stone Age, length of flake 18.6cm.

in many southern African caves suggest that extensive meat-drying was being practiced; this would have been an important potential source of storable food. Clearly recognisable hearths at many sites demonstrate the controlled use of fire, and also suggest that Middle Stone Age people would have been able to practice 'firestick-farming': increasing the yields, and controlling the distribution, of important plant foods by burning the vegetation in the same way as recent hunter-gatherers.

The distribution of Middle Stone Age sites differed from that of the Acheulian (*page 56*) in covering a wider range of African environments, including, for the first time, the tropical rain forests. Stone tool assemblages also showed a more marked regional pattern and were designed to respond to the needs of specific environmental conditions. Studies suggest that Middle Stone Age populations were less tied to the availability of permanent water sources than their predecessors, and that their perception of the environment and the resources it offered was similar to that of modern hunter-gatherers.

The Middle Stone Age also provides the first evidence for developments in the human capacity for abstract thought. There is widespread evidence for the use of ochre, which was mined on a large scale at Lion Cave in Swaziland by at least 42,000 years ago. Ochre was probably used for body decoration, but in a very late Middle Stone Age assemblage from Apollo 11 Cave, Namibia, four painted rock slabs foreshadow the richness of Africa's Later Stone Age rock art. The possibility that some of the human bones recovered from sites such as

Klasies River Mouth and Border Cave are the remains of burials is another indication of the essentially modern character of Middle Stone Age behaviour.

The most significant of all developments in the Middle Stone Age may lie in the field of human evolution. Recent genetic studies of modern populations suggest that our own species, *Homo sapiens sapiens*, developed around 100,000 years ago, point in particular to the long isolation of southern African populations from other racial groups. Human remains from sites such as Klasies River Mouth in southern Africa and Omo in Ethiopia, which date to at least 100,000 years ago, are of anatomically modern people. Because they are much older than similar remains from Europe or Asia they strengthen the case for Africa having been the birthplace of modern humans.

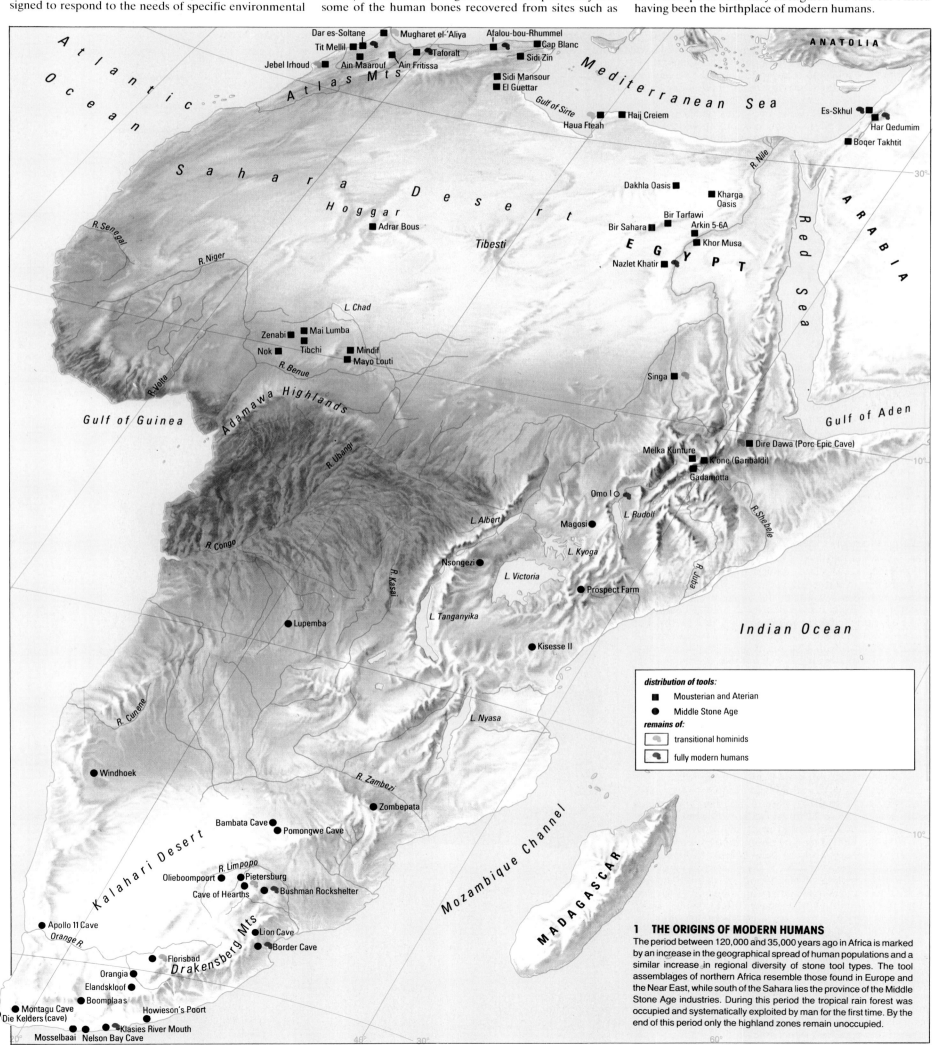

1 THE ORIGINS OF MODERN HUMANS

The period between 120,000 and 35,000 years ago in Africa is marked by an increase in the geographical spread of human populations and a similar increase in regional diversity of stone tool types. The tool assemblages of northern Africa resemble those found in Europe and the Near East, while south of the Sahara lies the province of the Middle Stone Age industries. During this period the tropical rain forest was occupied and systematically exploited by man for the first time. By the end of this period only the highland zones remain unoccupied.

The peopling of Australia

The peopling of Australia was a long-term process involving numerous movements of people out from Asia. Two routes were possible, one from southern China through the Philippines and into New Guinea, the second from South-East Asia through the islands of Indonesia and into northern Australia. At periods of low sea level islands often became joined; however, the Australian landmass, a unit comprising Australia, Tasmania, New Guinea and surrounding coastal areas known as Sahul-land, was never linked to South-East Asia. Both of the colonisation routes, therefore, involved crossing at least 60 kilometres of open sea, so sea-going crafts would have been essential. The archaeology of these groups, however, does not reflect this innovation, and the remains so far discovered comprise mostly crudely made stone tools. Both New Guinea and Tasmania were severed from Australia only 10,000 years ago. Australia's isolation prevented almost all mammals reaching there; the only species to cross the sea barrier successfully were man, the dingo and the rat.

The cultural evidence for the migration routes into Australia is sparse and simple. The important sites of Lake Mungo and Keilor are both older than 30,000 BP, and have revealed human skeletal remains and stone tools. At Lake Mungo, a site situated on a sand dune overlooking the now dried up lake, cremation burials were discovered, and food remains including freshwater molluscs, fish and small marsupials were excavated. The Keilor site lies in river deposits and has yielded human skull bones. The bones from both sites are fully modern in appearance, and it is clear that the earliest settlers of Sahul-land were *Homo sapiens sapiens* (modern humans). Evidence for settlement older than 40,000 BP has been suggested for some sites, and it is likely that the first colonisation took place at the time of lowered sea levels between 60,000 and 50,000 years ago. Settlement expanded rapidly, and a number of sites dating from 25,000 years ago or less are known in the southern and eastern coastal areas of Australia, along the coast and mountains of Tasmania and in the New Guinea highlands. During this time the environment changed quite dramatically, becoming increasingly dry and reaching a peak of aridity 18,000–16,000 years ago, followed by a slight improvement in conditions.

The changing climate and environment are critical in understanding the distribution of sites in this region. The early hunter-gatherer sites of Australia are found mainly on the coasts and along major rivers, and this may be explained by the fact that the early settlers tended to cluster in these areas, where food sources would have been more readily available. Visits into the hinterland were occasional and brief. The rise in sea level since about 10,000 BP, however, covered the rich coastal sites, leaving evidence only of the occasional inland sites. The changing climate was also a factor in the extinction of the giant marsupials, which occurred around 16,000 years ago. Some have claimed that hunting was the cause for this, but few archaeological sites have yielded any bones of these large creatures, and it seems that smaller kangaroos, shellfish and fish were preferred for food. The human role in the demise of the giant marsupials is more likely to have been indirect: the results of firing the bush to clear the dense vegetation, thus stimulating the growth of food plants as the bush regrows. This affected the balance of food plants on which the giant marsupials depended and may have exacerbated the difficulties already posed by the increasing aridity.

Large ground-stone axes recovered from New Guinea have been interpreted as tools for clearing some of the natural vegetation, to allow wild forms of sago, taro, banana and yam to produce more. All these food plants grow on the edges of the forest, so by cutting down trees it is possible to increase their productivity. It is only a short step from this kind of manipulation of the environment to proper agriculture, and the New Guinea highlands are likely to have been one of the areas in which it began.

Towards the close of this period, at about 10,000 BP, another variety of human type appeared in Australia, fully modern but with a heavy robust skull. These individuals may be a later wave of immigrants, but it is also possible that they are the result of local breeding effects in a small isolated community. By this time humans had colonised the whole continent. As the low-lying areas between Tasmania and Australia, and between Australia and New Guinea were inundated by the rising sea level many fertile coastal areas were lost, which posed new problems of adaptation. By 10,000 BP the arid hinterland had been settled and early man in Australia had adapted successfully to a desert environment.

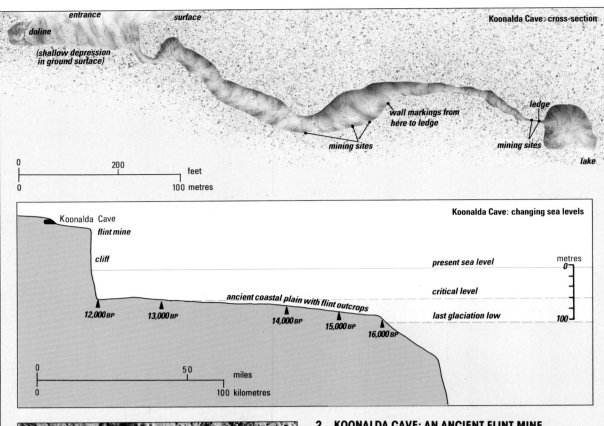

2 KOONALDA CAVE: AN ANCIENT FLINT MINE

Koonalda Cave is situated on the southern coast of Australia and is dated to at least 20,000 BP. This limestone cave was exploited by the early Australians as a flint mine. The cave is over 305 metres long and was reached by a difficult descent of 60 metres down from the plain above. Artificial lighting would have been needed, as the cave lies beyond the reach of sunlight. Only a few chipped stone tools were found at the site. Deep inside the cave at its farthest end a series of marks on the cave wall were found (*left*). These marks were produced by the fingers of the ancient miners pressing into the soft limestone, and some of the grooves were criss-crossed to form lattice-work patterns. These wall markings are at least 20,000 years old. Outcrops of flint were available when the adjacent coastal plain was exposed, but as the sea level rose and fell these sources were periodically covered and uncovered (*see cross-section above*).

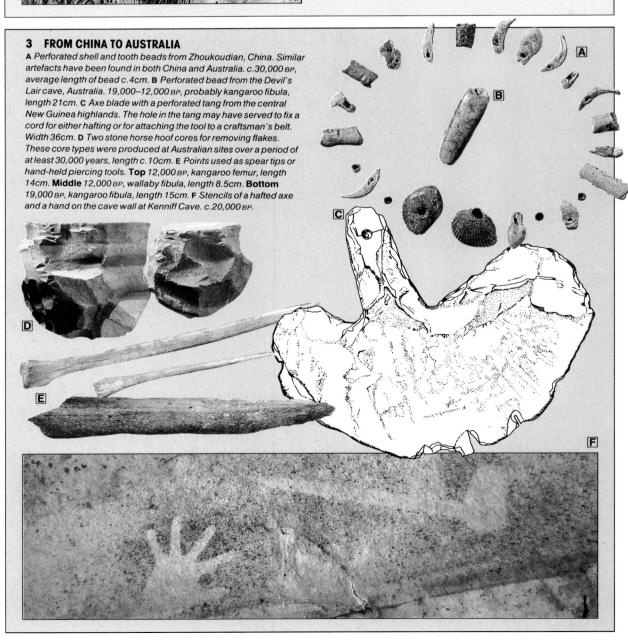

3 FROM CHINA TO AUSTRALIA

A *Perforated shell and tooth beads from Zhoukoudian, China. Similar artefacts have been found in both China and Australia. c.30,000 BP, average length of bead c.4cm.* B *Perforated bead from the Devil's Lair cave, Australia. 19,000–12,000 BP, probably kangaroo fibula, length 21cm.* C *Axe blade with a perforated tang from the central New Guinea highlands. The hole in the tang may have served to fix a cord for either hafting or for attaching the tool to a craftsman's belt. Width 36cm.* D *Two stone horse hoof cores for removing flakes. These core types were produced at Australian sites over a period of at least 30,000 years, length c.10cm.* E *Points used as spear tips or hand-held piercing tools.* **Top** *12,000 BP, kangaroo femur, length 14cm.* **Middle** *12,000 BP, wallaby fibula, length 8.5cm.* **Bottom** *19,000 BP, kangaroo fibula, length 15cm.* F *Stencils of a hafted axe and a hand on the cave wall at Kenniff Cave. c.20,000 BP.*

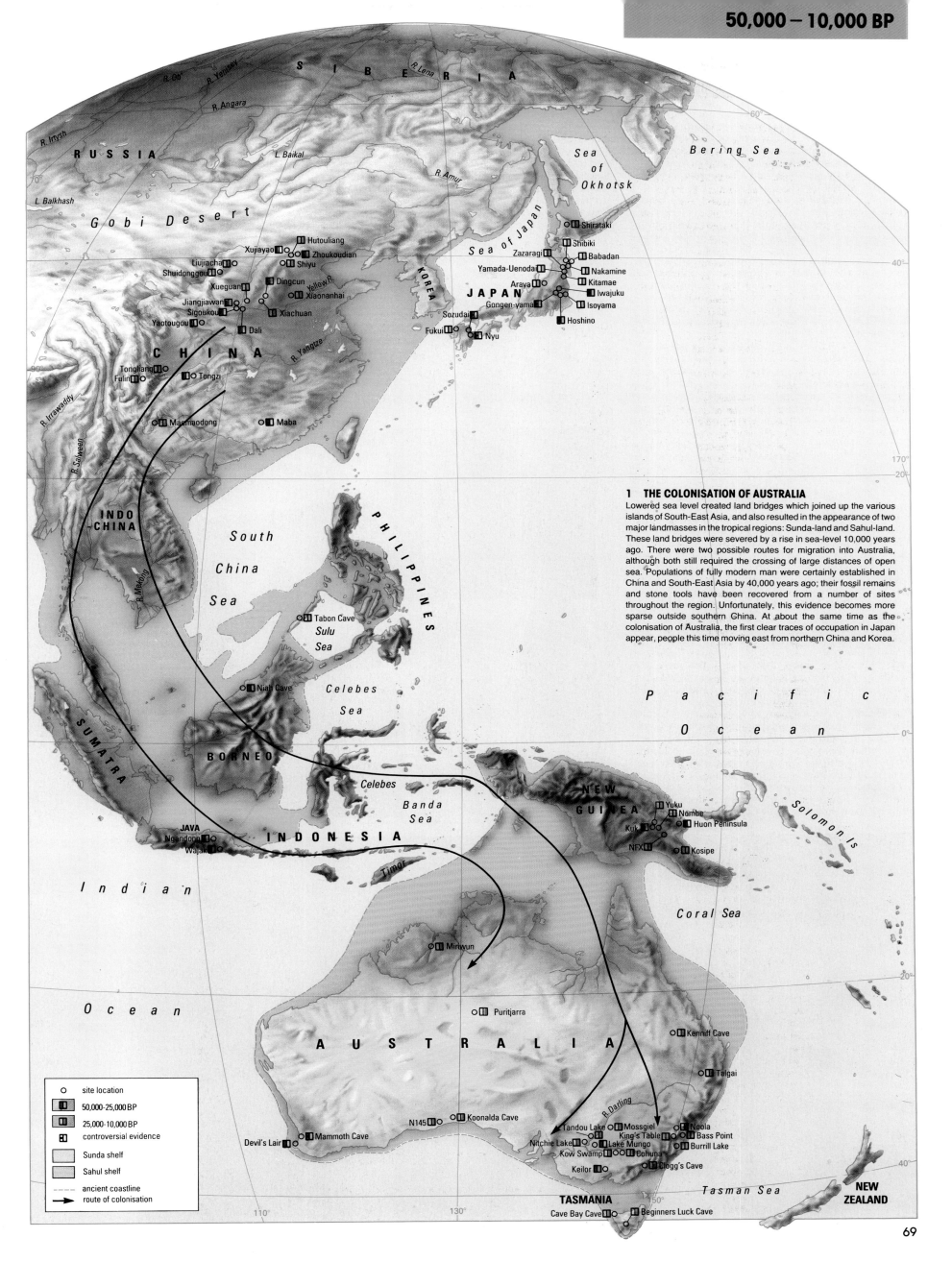

R. Irtysh
R. Ob'
R. Yenisey
L. Baikal
R. Lena
R. Angara
R. Amur
RUSSIA
S I B E R I A

Bering Sea

L. Balkhash

Sea of Okhotsk

G o b i   D e s e r t

Shirataki

Sea of Japan

Hutouliang
Xujiayao
Zhoukoudian
Liujiachang
Shiyu
Shuidonggou
Dingcun
Xueguan
Yellow R.
Xiaonanhai
Jiangjiawan
Xiachuan
Sigoukou
Yaotougou
Dali
C H I N A
R. Yangtze

KOREA

Shibiki
Zazaragi
Babadan
Yamada-Uenodai
Nakamine
Araya
Kitamae
JAPAN
Gongen-yama
Iwajuku
Isoyama
Sozudai
Fukui
Hoshino
Nyu

Tongliang
Fulin
Tongzi

R. Irrawaddy
R. Salween

Maomaodong
Maba

INDO-CHINA

R. Mekong

South China Sea

P H I L I P P I N E S

Tabon Cave
Sulu Sea

1   THE COLONISATION OF AUSTRALIA
Lowered sea level created land bridges which joined up the various islands of South-East Asia, and also resulted in the appearance of two major landmasses in the tropical regions: Sunda-land and Sahul-land. These land bridges were severed by a rise in sea-level 10,000 years ago. There were two possible routes for migration into Australia, although both still required the crossing of large distances of open sea. Populations of fully modern man were certainly established in China and South-East Asia by 40,000 years ago; their fossil remains and stone tools have been recovered from a number of sites throughout the region. Unfortunately, this evidence becomes more sparse outside southern China. At about the same time as the colonisation of Australia, the first clear traces of occupation in Japan appear, people this time moving east from northern China and Korea.

P a c i f i c   O c e a n

Niah Cave
Celebes Sea

S U M A T R A

B O R N E O

Celebes

Banda Sea

NEW GUINEA
Yuku
Nombe
Kuk
Huon Peninsula
NFX
Kosipe

Solomon Is

JAVA
Ngandong
Wajak
INDONESIA

Timor

Indian Ocean

Coral Sea

Miriwun

Puritjarra

A U S T R A L I A

Kenniff Cave

Talgai

N145
Koonalda Cave
R. Darling
Tandou Lake
Mossgiel
Noola
Nitchie Lake
King's Table
Bass Point
Devil's Lair
Mammoth Cave
Lake Mungo
Burrill Lake
Kow Swamp
Cohuna
Keilor
Cloggs Cave

TASMANIA
Cave Bay Cave
Beginners Luck Cave

Tasman Sea

NEW ZEALAND

Legend:
○ site location
▣ 50,000–25,000 BP
▣ 25,000–10,000 BP
▣ controversial evidence
Sunda shelf
Sahul shelf
- - - ancient coastline
→ route of colonisation

The peopling of the Americas

There is little doubt that present-day North American Indians are descended from people of Asian stock who entered North America across the Bering Strait. This migration probably occurred at a time when sea levels were lowered by glaciation and a landbridge known as 'Beringia' joined Siberia to Alaska. This created a continuous, cold but ice-free plain from eastern Europe across central Asia to North America. The oldest evidence for the peopling of the Americas might thus be expected in Alaska and the Yukon, with the sites in Central and South America becoming progressively more recent to allow time for people to spread gradually south across thousands of kilometres to inhabit both continents. However, because of the random nature of preservation and discovery, the archaeological record does not match this prediction and the result is a controversial debate about when people first entered the New World.

Very few sites have been discovered in Alaska and Yukon. The oldest known evidence from that region is from Bluefish Cave in the Keele Range, where stone artefacts are between 15,000 and 12,000 years old. These artefacts include 'microblades' struck from small cores to be set into grooves along the sides of bone points, making spear-tips. This technology originated in Siberia as many as 30,000 years ago, and its presence in the American Northwest is evidence of west to east migration across Beringia. As people moved south, new environments brought technological change and such links with Siberia disappear from the archaeological record. The hunters of Beringia were cut off to the south by the Laurentide and Cordilleran ice sheets which covered most of Canada during the last glaciation. In North America archaeological evidence becomes abundant only with the retreat of the ice sheets some 11,500 years ago. This coincides with the appearance of the so-called Clovis tradition of tool manufacture and suggests that the users of these distinctive stone points were the first colonists south of Beringia.

However, there is now convincing evidence for human activity south of the ice sheets in late glacial times. Sites in Missouri, Idaho and Oregon are reliably dated to between 14,000 and 13,000 years old. Radiocarbon dating of a wooden point used to kill a giant tortoise at Little Salt Spring shows that people had arrived in Florida by 12,000 BP. These sites imply that colonisation began with the first signs of postglacial warming about 14,500 years ago, but at Meadowcroft rock shelter, in Pennsylvania, stone artefacts have been dated back to about 16,000 BP. To have reached the Northeast by this time, people must have migrated from Beringia at a much earlier date, possibly moving through an ice-free corridor between the ice sheets, which may have been passable during a brief warm phase around 19,000 BP.

The evidence of the colonisation of South America points to even earlier dates of entry into North America. Stone artefacts found at Fell's Cave in Patagonia reveal that people had reached the southernmost tip of South America by 12,000 BP, while sites in Peru, Argentina and Colombia all contain artefacts dating from about 14,000 BP. The settlement of Monte Verde shows that hunter-gatherers had an intimate knowledge of the forest, coast and mountain resources of southern Chile by 13,000 BP. Such successful adjustment could not have been achieved by the first wave of colonists as they spread into the region, and implies that the area had been inhabited for some time prior to the date of the site. Five flaked stones and a possible hearth found beneath the main settlement at Monte Verde and dated to 33,000 BP remain to be substantiated as proof of this, but there is little doubt about the early occupation of the rock shelter of Pedra Furada in north-east Brazil.

Radiocarbon dates on charcoal taken from hearths have dated human occupation at Pedra Furada to 32,000 BP. This early evidence consists of a hearth surrounded by flake and pebble tools and fragments of painted rock fallen from the shelter walls, which may represent the oldest evidence of art in the Americas.

To have reached South America by 32,000 years ago, people might have entered North America between 45,000 and 40,000 years ago. However, there is no known occupation of Siberia at this time and such early dates also require reappraisal of dental and linguistic evidence, which suggests colonisation c.20,000 BP. There is, as yet, no trace of human activity in North America before 15,000 BP. There is still much to be discovered about the peopling of the Americas.

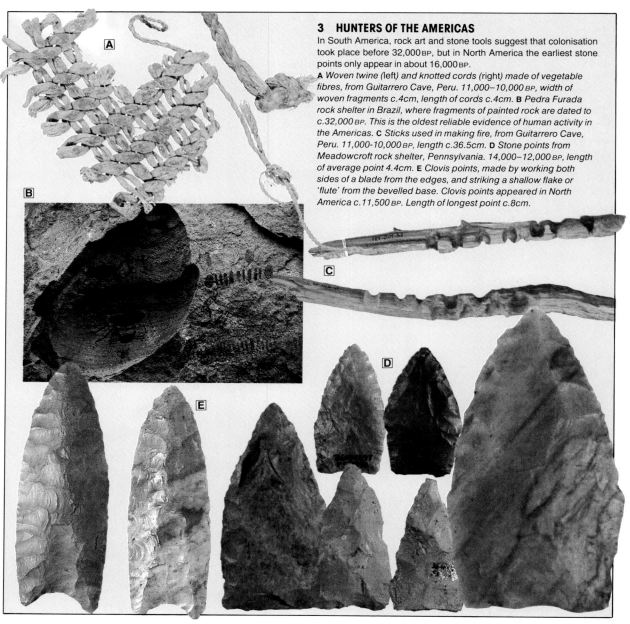

3 HUNTERS OF THE AMERICAS

In South America, rock art and stone tools suggest that colonisation took place before 32,000 BP, but in North America the earliest stone points only appear in about 16,000 BP.

A Woven twine (left) and knotted cords (right) made of vegetable fibres, from Guitarrero Cave, Peru. 11,000–10,000 BP, width of woven fragments c.4cm, length of cords c.4cm. **B** Pedra Furada rock shelter in Brazil, where fragments of painted rock are dated to c.32,000 BP. This is the oldest reliable evidence of human activity in the Americas. **C** Sticks used in making fire, from Guitarrero Cave, Peru. 11,000-10,000 BP, length c.36.5cm. **D** Stone points from Meadowcroft rock shelter, Pennsylvania. 14,000–12,000 BP, length of average point 4.4cm. **E** Clovis points, made by working both sides of a blade from the edges, and striking a shallow flake or 'flute' from the bevelled base. Clovis points appeared in North America c.11,500 BP. Length of longest point c.8cm.

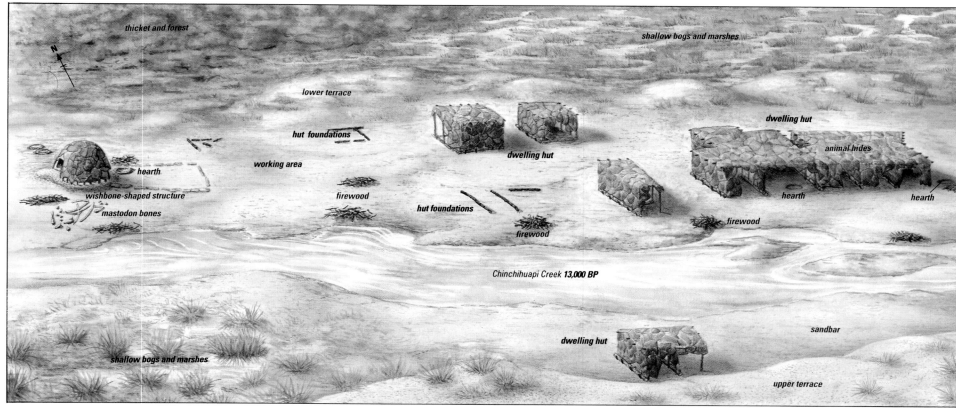

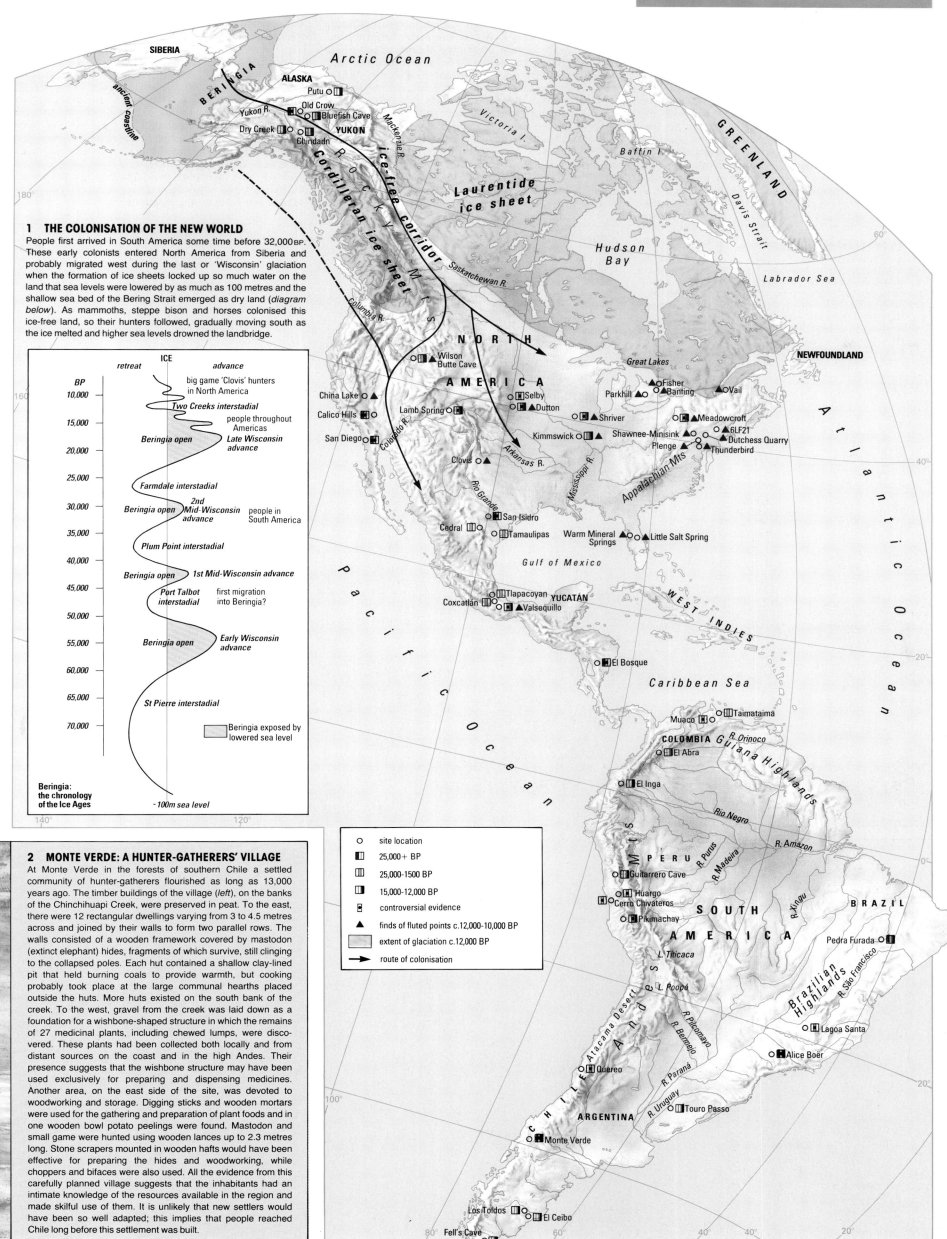

SIBERIA

Arctic Ocean

ALASKA

BERINGIA

ancient coastline

Putu

Old Crow

Yukon R.

Bluefish Cave

YUKON

Dry Creek

Chindadn

GREENLAND

Victoria I.

Baffin I.

Davis Strait

ice-free corridor

Rocky Mts

Cordilleran ice sheet

Mackenzie R.

Saskatchewan R.

Columbia R.

Laurentide ice sheet

Hudson Bay

Labrador Sea

60°

1 THE COLONISATION OF THE NEW WORLD

People first arrived in South America some time before 32,000 BP. These early colonists entered North America from Siberia and probably migrated west during the last or 'Wisconsin' glaciation when the formation of ice sheets locked up so much water on the land that sea levels were lowered by as much as 100 metres and the shallow sea bed of the Bering Strait emerged as dry land (diagram below). As mammoths, steppe bison and horses colonised this ice-free land, so their hunters followed, gradually moving south as the ice melted and higher sea levels drowned the landbridge.

NEWFOUNDLAND

ICE

retreat   advance

BP

10,000 — big game 'Clovis' hunters in North America

Two Creeks interstadial

15,000 — people throughout Americas

Beringia open   Late Wisconsin advance

20,000 —

25,000 —

Farmdale interstadial

30,000 — 2nd Mid-Wisconsin advance   people in South America

Beringia open

Plum Point interstadial

35,000 —

40,000 — 1st Mid-Wisconsin advance

Beringia open

45,000 — Port Talbot interstadial   first migration into Beringia?

50,000 —

55,000 — Early Wisconsin advance

Beringia open

60,000 —

65,000 —

St Pierre interstadial

70,000 —

Beringia exposed by lowered sea level

Beringia: the chronology of the Ice Ages

-100m sea level

140°   120°

180°   160°

N O R T H   A M E R I C A

Wilson Butte Cave

Great Lakes

Fisher   Vail

China Lake   Parkhill   Banting

Calico Hills   Selby   Dutton

Lamb Spring   Shriver   Meadowcroft

San Diego   Kimmswick   Shawnee-Minisink   6LF21

Dutchess Quarry

Clovis   Plenge   Thunderbird

Colorado R.   Arkansas R.

Mississippi R.   Appalachian Mts

Rio Grande

San Isidro

Cedral   Tamaulipas   Warm Mineral Springs   Little Salt Spring

Gulf of Mexico

Tlapacoyan   YUCATÁN

Coxcatlán   Valsequillo

Atlantic Ocean

40°

Pacific Ocean

WEST INDIES

20°

El Bosque

Caribbean Sea

Muaco   Taimataima

COLOMBIA   Guiana Highlands

El Abra   R. Orinoco

El Inga   Rio Negro

R. Amazon

R. Purus   R. Madeira

Legend

○ site location

⊞ 25,000+ BP

⊞ 25,000-1500 BP

⊞ 15,000-12,000 BP

⊟ controversial evidence

▲ finds of fluted points c.12,000-10,000 BP

extent of glaciation c.12,000 BP

→ route of colonisation

P E R U

Guitarrero Cave

Huargo   R. Xingu

Cerro Chivateros

Pikimachay

S O U T H   A M E R I C A

B R A Z I L

Brazilian Highlands

Pedra Furada

R. São Francisco

2 MONTE VERDE: A HUNTER-GATHERERS' VILLAGE

At Monte Verde in the forests of southern Chile a settled community of hunter-gatherers flourished as long as 13,000 years ago. The timber buildings of the village (left), on the banks of the Chinchihuapi Creek, were preserved in peat. To the east, there were 12 rectangular dwellings varying from 3 to 4.5 metres across and joined by their walls to form two parallel rows. The walls consisted of a wooden framework covered by mastodon (extinct elephant) hides, fragments of which survive, still clinging to the collapsed poles. Each hut contained a shallow clay-lined pit that held burning coals to provide warmth, but cooking probably took place at the large communal hearths placed outside the huts. More huts existed on the south bank of the creek. To the west, gravel from the creek was laid down as a foundation for a wishbone-shaped structure in which the remains of 27 medicinal plants, including chewed lumps, were discovered. These plants had been collected both locally and from distant sources on the coast and in the high Andes. Their presence suggests that the wishbone structure may have been used exclusively for preparing and dispensing medicines. Another area, on the east side of the site, was devoted to woodworking and storage. Digging sticks and wooden mortars were used for the gathering and preparation of plant foods and in one wooden bowl potato peelings were found. Mastodon and small game were hunted using wooden lances up to 2.3 metres long. Stone scrapers mounted in wooden hafts would have been effective for preparing the hides and woodworking, while choppers and bifaces were also used. All the evidence from this carefully planned village suggests that the inhabitants had an intimate knowledge of the resources available in the region and made skilful use of them. It is unlikely that new settlers would have been so well adapted; this implies that people reached Chile long before this settlement was built.

L. Titicaca

L. Poopó

Atacama Desert

ANDES

CHILE   Querero

R. Pilcomayo

R. Bermejo

R. Pilcomayo

Lagoa Santa

Alice Boër

Touro Passo

R. Paraná

R. Uruguay

ARGENTINA

Monte Verde

Los Toldos   El Ceibo

Fell's Cave

100°   80°   60°   40°   20°

European hunter-gatherers

The period between 35,000 and 12,000 years ago is known as the Upper Palaeolithic and is associated with the appearance in Europe of anatomically modern humans who first evolved in Africa some 100,000 years ago, and moved into Europe to replace the Neanderthals 35,000 years ago. It is in the Upper Palaeolithic that complex social structures may be first recognised in the archaeological record; communal graves have been discovered at Předmostí, and there are remains of organised settlements in eastern Europe. Art objects, Venus figurines, cave paintings and personal ornaments are all characteristic of this period, while trade carried raw materials and exotic objects such as marine fossils over long distances.

The Upper Palaeolithic was a time of rapid technological innovation and change, including the introduction of the pressure flaking technique, which produced very finely shaped tools, spear throwers, bows, and items such as fish nets, hooks and spears. Broadly speaking, Upper Palaeolithic stone industries are based on blades rather than flakes (a blade being a flake that is more than twice as long as it is wide), and feature a great variety of end scrapers and burins (a type of engraving tool). The blade technology was an early form of mass production, for many more or less identical blades could be produced from a single core. The large numbers of burins were probably used in the working of bone and antler.

The timespan of the Upper Palaeolithic encompasses the end of the last Ice Age, and includes a series of climatic fluctuations, the most dramatic being the peak of the last Ice Age, 20,000–16,000 years ago. After this time, an increasing number of relatively small (microlithic) tools began to be made, and the use of bone in tool and weapon manufacture became common. The climate may have played an important role in these changes: bone and antler tools are less affected by cold (unlike flint which becomes brittle), while wood would have been scarce – there was a change at this period from temperate woodland to open, less wooded grassland.

There was an overall increase in the number, size and

1 UPPER PALAEOLITHIC EUROPE
Parts of northern Europe were occupied for the first time with the arrival of fully modern man at about 35,000 BP. Portable art objects are found distributed throughout the region, while painted cave walls were concentrated in the limestone areas of France and Iberia. Artefacts of this period show the development of regional traditions, although communications between the groups were probably important, both for obtaining raw materials and mates. Many sites are found along rivers – fish were a crucial part of the diet, and river valleys were often the routes taken by migrating herds of deer.

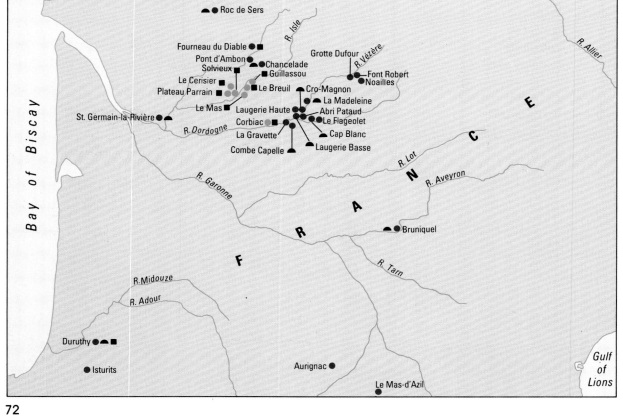

complexity of sites during this period. Traces of large huts and tents are found, and a few settlements even had storage pits. Some settlements have evidence for year-round occupation while others were used only in one season, indicating that there was specialisation of the roles of various sites. Upper Palaeolithic sites were sometimes located at the narrow entrances to valleys so that hunters could intercept the herds as they passed by during their seasonal migrations. If they were successful, hunters would not be forced to follow the herds but could live on stored meat, plants and smaller animals such as rabbits, fish and birds until the herds returned. Hunters and gatherers evolved flexible social groupings, which allowed parties to set out to obtain more distant resources while permitting most of the people to stay at single sites (base

camps) for longer. The changing climate caused periods of hardship within certain territories, and contacts between the different groups was essential for survival. The Venus figurines found across Europe at this time testify to the range of these contacts. Widespread finds of exotic raw materials also represent the first signs of trade.

Broadly based hunting was the mainstay of the Upper Palaeolithic economy, although there were concentrations on single species (often reindeer) at specific locations. Many thousands of mammoth bones have been excavated in certain eastern European sites, such as Předmostí in Czechoslovakia, that represent the results of organised community hunting. In western Europe equally large accumulations of horse bones are known at Solutré. The increasing use of stable resources such as shellfish

becomes apparent after the height of the last Ice Age, and these secondary resources could help food supplies when the hunting was going badly. The gathering of plant foods is likely to have been of great importance, but plant remains are only rarely preserved.

Different stone tool types can be identified from each geographical region, showing a succession of more locally based forms or 'cultures'. This regionalism contrasts strongly with earlier times and probably reflects the importance of increasing group identification or 'ethnicity'. This was a result of increased group size, specialisation of roles within the group and increased competition between groups. The emphasis on group identity, with its accompanying rites and symbols, marks the appearance of fully modern human behaviour.

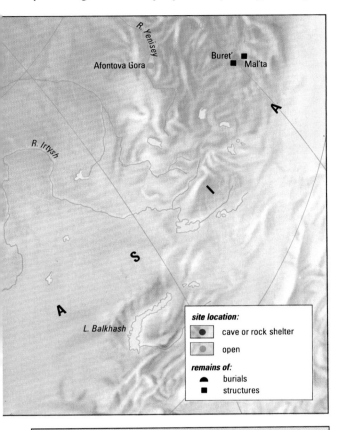

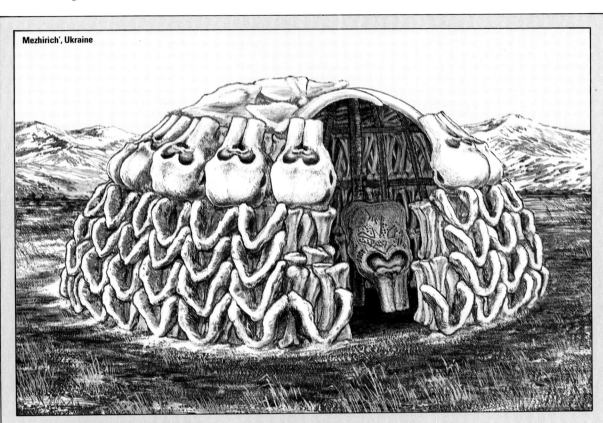

Mezhirich', Ukraine

3 HUNTERS OF THE UPPER PALAEOLITHIC

A *Three barbed points, probably used as the armatures of harpoons for river fishing. c.17,000–10,000 BP, average length 12.5cm.*
B *A bone point which would have served as the tip of a spear, and an eyed bone needle from La Madeleine, France. Such tools are a particular feature of the latter part of the last glacial when river fishing, particularly for salmon, became important. 13,000–11,000 BP, length of point c.15cm, length of needle c.5cm.* C *Three Solutrean leaf points from Laugerie Haute, France. 21,000–18,000 BP, flint, length (left to right) 7cm, 6.5cm, 5.4cm.* D *Endscraper and burin on one blade from Laugerie Haute, France. 15,000–10,000 BP, flint, length 6.2cm.* E *Burin from La Madeleine, France. 15,000–10,000 BP, flint, length 6cm.* F *Blade core from La Madeleine, France. 15,000–10,000 BP, flint, length 10.5cm.*

2 UPPER PALAEOLITHIC DWELLINGS

Pincevent (*below*) in the Seine Valley, northern France was occupied at about 10,000 BP. Studies of animal remains show the site was used between mid-summer and mid-winter on several different occasions. The occupants were hunter-gatherers whose main source of meat was reindeer but fish bones and eggshells have also been found. Excavations revealed a series of 4.5 x 3 metre spreads of debris with a hearth at one end and red ochre staining showing the area of occupation. As no post or stake holes were found it is thought that the people lived in portable tents constructed of wooden poles with animal skins lashed to them. Examination of the edges of stone tools demonstrates some of the activities carried out there – butchery, hide-working, the making of wooden hafts for tools and the manufacture of arrows. Well-made, stone-lined hearths were used; the stones of an earlier hearth sometimes re-used during a later occupation. It is probable that each hut was occupied by a nuclear family group.

A total of 385 mammoth bones, closely packed into a circular area of 4–5 metres in diameter, was excavated at Mezhirich' in the Ukraine (*above*). Beneath these bones, occupation remains were found in a circular pit which also contained ash and charcoal and may have been a hearth. Two other hearths were found outside the area of the mammoth bones. In the main hearth some bones had been stood vertically, possibly to support cooking equipment. The arrangement of the bones suggests that most of them are the collapsed walls of a structure. In the Ukraine many such bone structures have been excavated. This use of bone is probably due to the lack of wood in the harsh, windswept environment. At Mezhirich' a dome-shaped structure was reconstructed, with mammoth skulls at the base to support upright long-bones, more skulls, pelves and vertebrae. Animal hides would have been stretched over this structure, and the hides would have been held down by mammoth jaws to prevent them from tearing in the strong winds.

Pincevent, France

The art of the hunter-gatherers

The first modern humans in Europe, the hunter-gatherers of the Upper Palaeolithic, produced the continent's earliest recorded art (35,000–30,000 BP). It is thought that Palaeolithic art played an important part in religious rituals involving hunting, fertility and the initiation of the young. Earlier sites have yielded colouring materials such as ochre, but what was being coloured has yet to be discovered. The art of the prehistoric hunter-gatherers falls into two categories: mural art – the painting and engraving of the walls of caves and rock shelters, and portable art – painting, engraving or carving portable objects.

The decoration of portable objects was widespread throughout Europe, but cave art was concentrated in south-western France and northern Spain. Wall art was produced using various techniques: in south-western France there is bas-relief sculpting in the Venus images of Laussel, engraving at the site of Combarelles, painting at Font de Gaume, and a combination of these techniques at Lascaux. Occasionally, natural features of the wall itself were exploited – at Rouffignac a flint nodule in the cave wall was used to form the eye of an engraved mammoth. The paintings were made using natural colouring pigments, like ochre, which were treated to produce paints ranging from red to brown and yellow, and manganese oxides, which made black and violet. No blue or green colourings are yet known from the Upper Palaeolithic. Large animals such as bison, deer, wild oxen and horses predominate in the cave art with, more occasionally, mammoths, lions and even sometimes fish. Human figures are shown only very rarely. Some images appear to represent people wearing masks, animal skins and antlers. These latter may be camouflage for hunting or ceremonial dress for hunting rituals worn by shamans. In a few instances, the animals have marks which may be wounds, but there is no strong evidence to suggest that all this early art was closely associated with hunting. In a very few caves the wall paintings of animals were supplemented by clay models, the most famous being the two clay bison, each almost a metre long, from the cave of Le Tuc d'Audoubert. Wall art also includes a series of abstract images such as lines, dots and combinations of these. There are also hand stencils in some caves, made by holding the palm against the wall with fingers spread out and spraying paint around them. It has been suggested that some abstract images are male and female symbols used in fertility and initiation rites.

Cave paintings are very difficult to date because it is rare for the sediments which build up inside a cave to reach the level of the art, and there is, therefore, usually no clear relationship between the occupation layers and the wall paintings or engravings. Occasionally, however, slabs of rock fall off the wall and pencils of colouring material may also be found in stratified levels. The principal method for dating the wall art is to compare it with the portable art of the same period. A sequence of art styles has been proposed using these methods, and the earliest wall art is dated to the Aurignacian culture of France (about 30,000 BP).

Portable art begins slightly earlier than the wall art and is more easily dated as it occurs in archaeological occupation layers. This art includes sculptures and engravings of animals on bone and antler, and thousands of engravings on small plaques of stone. Very occasionally the engravings take the form of abstract patterns of lines and dots, or sequences of notches or grooves, which might conceivably have been hunting tallies or even calendars for plotting the movements of the moon. Decorated ornaments were also made, such as fine carved amber swan pendants from Russia, or cut beads of ivory and antler from the same region. Venus figurines are particularly striking. These pieces are carved in the round and are representations of a highly stylised female form with exaggerated breasts and buttocks. An analogous style is found in wall art where bas-relief engravings of Venuses, perhaps representations of the mother goddess, have been discovered.

The cave art of the Upper Palaeolithic is often located in extremely inaccessible places where few could have seen it and where artificial lighting and occasionally ladders or scaffolding would have been required. The fact that cave art was inaccessible suggests that strong religious beliefs motivated the artists. It is possible that the wall art formed the backdrop to rituals partly concerned with hunting, perhaps intended to encourage the fertility of the herd, and possibly as a means of initiating younger members of the group into their adult roles (footprints and fingermarks of young children have been found at certain sites). Whatever the explanation, Palaeolithic art is an outstanding and evocative monument to the full humanity achieved by the early hunters of Europe.

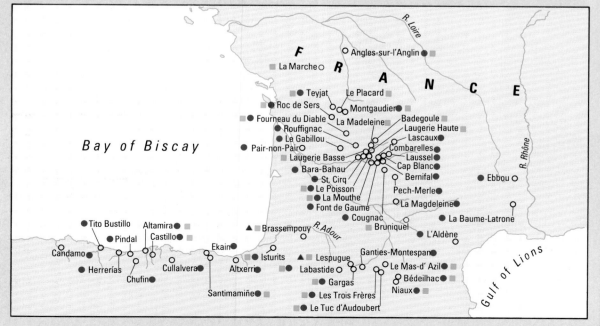

1 THE ART OF UPPER PALAEOLITHIC EUROPE
Small or 'portable' works of art occur throughout the area inhabited by European hunters between 30,000 and 10,000 BP. In western and central Europe, animals and abstract signs decorate equipment and plaques. Further east, carved or modelled animals decorated with abstract designs and often perforated as pendants are more common. Stylised human female figurines occur in both areas. Most cave art is found in the valleys of the Vézère and Dordogne in south-west France, the Pyrenees and the Cantabrian Mountains of Spain, though paintings and engravings are known from sites far beyond these areas.

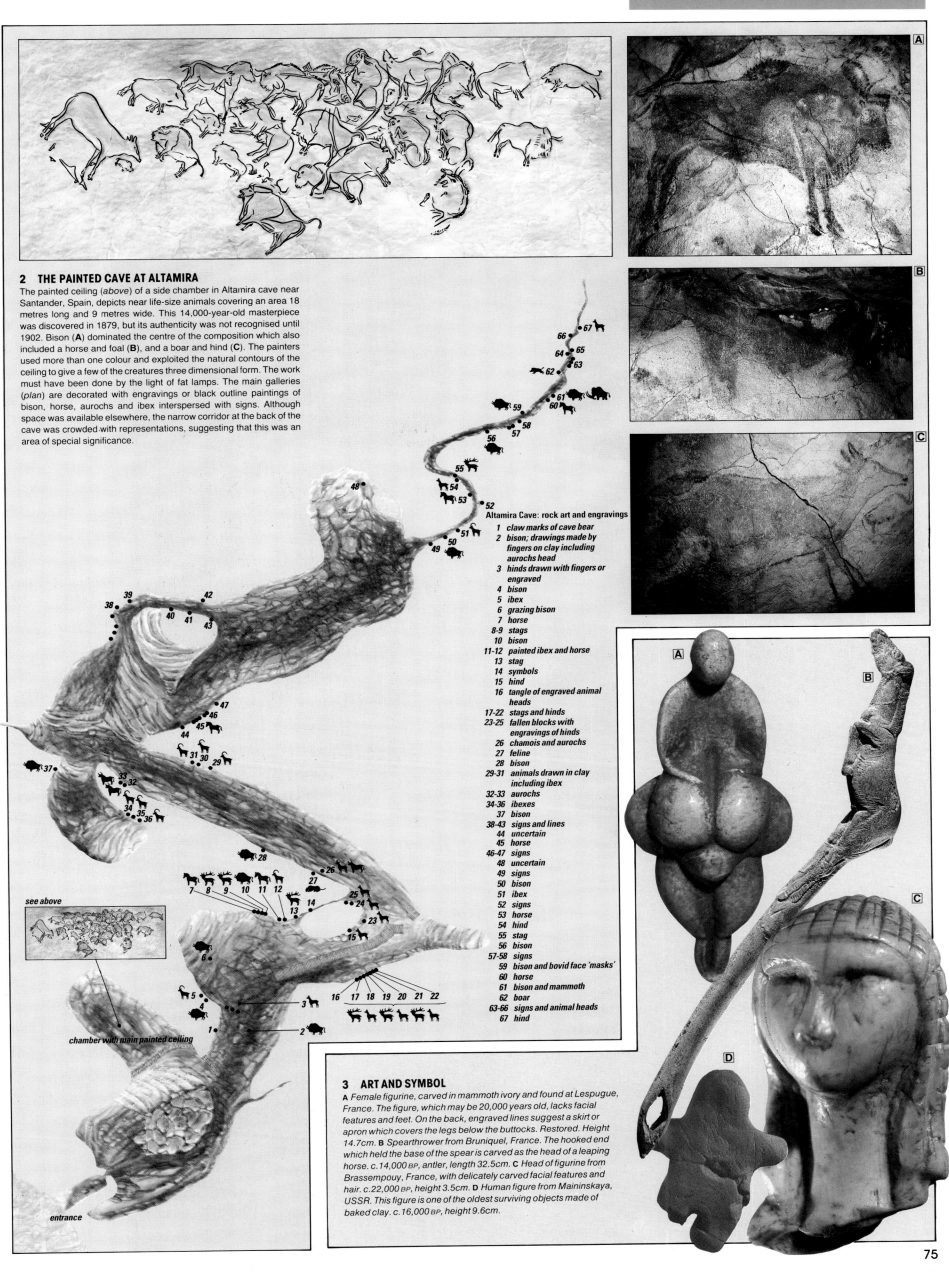

2 THE PAINTED CAVE AT ALTAMIRA

The painted ceiling (*above*) of a side chamber in Altamira cave near Santander, Spain, depicts near life-size animals covering an area 18 metres long and 9 metres wide. This 14,000-year-old masterpiece was discovered in 1879, but its authenticity was not recognised until 1902. Bison (**A**) dominated the centre of the composition which also included a horse and foal (**B**), and a boar and hind (**C**). The painters used more than one colour and exploited the natural contours of the ceiling to give a few of the creatures three dimensional form. The work must have been done by the light of fat lamps. The main galleries (*plan*) are decorated with engravings or black outline paintings of bison, horse, aurochs and ibex interspersed with signs. Although space was available elsewhere, the narrow corridor at the back of the cave was crowded with representations, suggesting that this was an area of special significance.

Altamira Cave: rock art and engravings

1 claw marks of cave bear
2 bison; drawings made by fingers on clay including aurochs head
3 hinds drawn with fingers or engraved
4 bison
5 ibex
6 grazing bison
7 horse
8-9 stags
10 bison
11-12 painted ibex and horse
13 stag
14 symbols
15 hind
16 tangle of engraved animal heads
17-22 stags and hinds
23-25 fallen blocks with engravings of hinds
26 chamois and aurochs
27 feline
28 bison
29-31 animals drawn in clay including ibex
32-33 aurochs
34-36 ibexes
37 bison
38-43 signs and lines
44 uncertain
45 horse
46-47 signs
48 uncertain
49 signs
50 bison
51 ibex
52 signs
53 horse
54 hind
55 stag
56 bison
57-58 signs
59 bison and bovid face 'masks'
60 horse
61 bison and mammoth
62 boar
63-66 signs and animal heads
67 hind

see above

chamber with main painted ceiling

entrance

3 ART AND SYMBOL

A Female figurine, carved in mammoth ivory and found at Lespugue, France. The figure, which may be 20,000 years old, lacks facial features and feet. On the back, engraved lines suggest a skirt or apron which covers the legs below the buttocks. Restored. Height 14.7cm. **B** Spearthrower from Bruniquel, France. The hooked end which held the base of the spear is carved as the head of a leaping horse. c.14,000 BP, antler, length 32.5cm. **C** Head of figurine from Brassempouy, France, with delicately carved facial features and hair. c.22,000 BP, height 3.5cm. **D** Human figure from Maininskaya, USSR. This figure is one of the oldest surviving objects made of baked clay. c.16,000 BP, height 9.6cm.

75

THREE
THE AGRICULTURAL REVOLUTION
10,000 – 4000 BC

AS THE ICE AGE came to an end, around 10,000 BC, the world underwent a series of dramatic changes which had far-reaching effects on human communities. Temperatures rose, and the ice sheets which had covered almost a quarter of the earth's land surface melted, allowing plants and animals to spread northwards into latitudes which for several thousand years had been too cold to support them. At the same time, the deserts which had occupied about half the land between the tropics receded as much of the water which had been locked up in the ice sheets was released to fall as rain. Human communities adapted to these changed circumstances in a variety of ways. In many areas, milder temperatures meant that resources were more abundant and varied than before, and hunter-gatherer groups were able to intensify their quest for food. The new abundance of marine resources, for example, is well illustrated by the large shell middens which developed in coastal regions. Populations grew rapidly in these favourable circumstances, and settlements gradually became larger and more permanent.

Many of these changes were of considerable importance, but it was the development of agriculture which was to have the most dramatic impact on human society. In certain restricted areas of the Old World – the Fertile Crescent of the Near East, the hill country of Pakistan, the plains of northern China, and the Yangtze delta – hunter-gatherer communities began to experiment with locally available plants and animals in a way which ultimately led to their domestication. Farming, though a labour-demanding way of life, offered several important advantages, notably the ability to feed a larger population than was usually possible with hunting and gathering alone. Agriculture soon spread to neighbouring areas, sometimes by the process of migration and settlement, sometimes by virtue of imitation, and in its wake spread certain features which became characteristic of farming communities in most parts of the world – pottery, for cooking or storage; village settlements, made possible by the high yields of plant and aninal husbandry; and traded items such as obsidian or semi-precious stone.

Farming was not, however, adopted by all hunter-gatherer communities immediately. In some regions, such as Japan, north-western Europe and sub-Saharan Africa, wild food sources were sufficiently abundant to support relatively large populations without recourse to agriculture, and village settlements and pottery became common before the adoption of domesticated plants and animals. As population levels rose in these regions, however, farming began to be adopted, so that ultimately hunting and gathering were restricted to those areas where farming could not become established, such as the deserts of Australia and the Kalahari, and the Arctic wastes.

Clay figurine of standing woman, from Nea Nikomidhia, Greece.
Late 7th millennium BC, height 17cm.

The birth of agriculture

About 10,000 years ago the ice sheets which had covered vast areas of the Earth's land surface were in retreat. As temperatures rose, the former arctic wastes and deserts around the equator were recolonised by forests and grasslands, both rich in game. Taking advantage of the improvement in climate, hunter-gatherers were able to move into latitudes that for several thousand years had been too inhospitable, and human communities everywhere had to develop new ways of benefiting from the resources of the postglacial world. The most important of those new adaptations, one which was to transform the face of the Earth, was the adoption of farming.

Hunting and gathering relied simply on the productivity of the natural environment. Nevertheless, hunters and gatherers were also aware of the manner of reproduction of the plants and animals on which they relied, and often took steps to increase or safeguard yields by activities which may loosely be termed agricultural. The aborigines of north-east Australia, when digging up a yam, would cut off a part and replant it to ensure its propagation, while the Shoshoni Indians of North America built dams and canals to irrigate natural stands of bulb- and seed-bearing plants. Hunter-gatherers normally avoid killing young animals or pregnant females and concentrate instead on mature males, a strategy designed to obtain maximum yields and safeguard the continuation of the herd.

These techniques for managing and improving the available resources developed over many thousands of years. These were the backdrop to the development of early farming. The shift to a full-scale reliance on cultivated plants and domestic animals which marks the beginning of true agriculture was, however, a revolutionary development, occurring within the last 10,000 years. Surprisingly, agriculture developed, apparently independently, in widely distant parts of the world, yet at approximately the same time: in the Near East by around 8000 BC, in China by 6000 BC, by at least the 7th millennium in Mesoamerica. In each of these areas a range of different plants was cultivated: wheat, barley and pulses in the Near East and Europe, rice and millet in south and east Asia, maize, beans and potato in the New World, to name only some of the most important species involved. These new species proved particularly suitable for domestication and high in yields. At the same time, animal husbandry was developed to provide a secure source of high quality protein, especially in the Old World: sheep, goat, pig and cattle.

Together, the combination of plants and animals provided an economy of vast potential, able to support much higher populations and substantially larger settlements than hunting and gathering. Yet primitive farming made great demands on time and effort: breaking the ground, sowing, weeding and harvesting were all carried out by hand. For this reason hunters and gatherers only turned to agriculture when their natural resources were no longer adequate – the improved conditions of the early Postglacial meant that populations grew to levels which the traditional way of life could no longer support. The transition to the new economy was not always a sudden development, however, and frequently took the form of an increasing dependence on cultivated plants which were at first only a supplement to traditional hunting and gathering.

Food, however, was not the only reason for the domestication of plants and animals. Flax, for example, was grown for its fibre, from which clothing and textiles could be made. Other cultivated plants had medicinal qualities, while animals could be used for pulling or carrying heavy loads. In South America the domesticated llama appears to have been used primarily as a beast of burden rather than a meat source.

Agriculture soon began to spread from its centres of origin, gradually displacing hunting and gathering, until today when it is only in inhospitable regions such as deserts or the arctic which are completely unsuitable for agriculture that the earlier way of life survives. The greater productiveness of the new economy soon led to the appearance of larger settlements. In these settled conditions, early farmers invested more time and energy in building houses and other structures, and in producing a much greater quantity of material goods and equipment: pottery, ornaments, ground stone tools, and ultimately metal objects. Essentially, agriculture was a change in subsistence, but its consequences were enormous, transforming virtually all aspects of human life, and laying the foundations on which all the subsequent achievements were to rest.

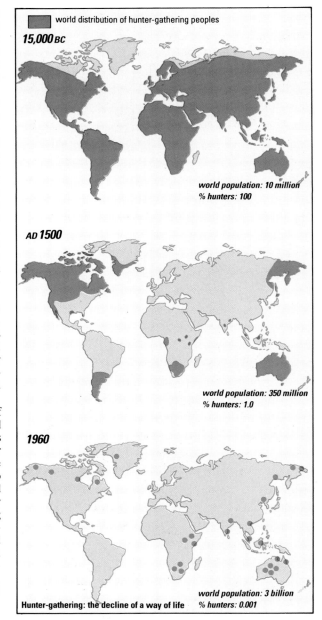

world distribution of hunter-gathering peoples

15,000 BC

world population: 10 million
% hunters: 100

AD 1500

world population: 350 million
% hunters: 1.0

1960

world population: 3 billion
% hunters: 0.001

Hunter-gathering: the decline of a way of life

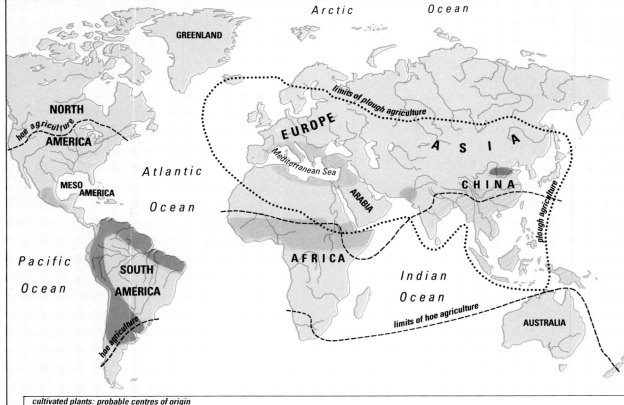

1 THE DOMESTICATION OF PLANTS

Many of the cultivated plants with which we are familiar today were first domesticated in one of a limited number of widely separated geographical regions, each of which can claim to be a centre of agricultural origins. Some species were independently brought into cultivation in more than one of these regions by a process of parallel domestication. The principal centres of agricultural origin lie in the tropical and sub-tropical belt on either side of the equator. In some of these centres, such as Mesoamerica, the Near East, or northern China, preserved remains, particularly the grains of cereal plants such as wheat, rice and maize, provide direct evidence of the early cultivation of certain species. Where agriculture relied heavily on tubers and root crops, as for example in Amazonia or parts of tropical Africa, archaeology is less able to document the early history of cultivation as these plants lack hard seeds or kernels which are resistant to decay, and few remains of these species have survived the passage of time. The domestication of important root crops such as yams and manioc may, however, be of considerably greater antiquity than we today suppose.

The techniques used in early plant cultivation may be divided into two categories. The first farmers probably used simple hoes and digging sticks to plant and weed their crops, and these remained the principal agricultural tools of much of Africa and the Americas up to the period of European contact and in some cases up to the present day. Throughout most of Eurasia, however, the use of human labour in the fields was supplemented from a relatively early stage by the invention of the plough, powered by animal traction. Though the animals used, usually cattle, were expensive to feed and maintain, the plough enabled larger areas and heavier soils to be cultivated, and this fruitful combination of crop and livestock remained a dominant feature of Eurasian farming systems until the introduction of mechanisation in the present century.

cultivated plants: probable centres of origin

Near East and Mediterranean: wheat, barley, pea, lentil, olive, grape, carrot, turnip, leek, broadbean, flax, chickpea, rapeseed, plum, pear, cabbage, lettuce, onion, date palm

Africa: yam, oil palm, sorghum, millet, baobab, ensete, groundnut, cowpea, African rice

north-west India/Pakistan: cotton, wheat, barley

north China: millet, soybean, turnip, adzuki bean, tea

rapeseed, peach, cucumber, ginger

South-East Asia: rice, taro, arrowroot, coconut, breadfruit

grapefruit, lemon, banana, sago palm, sugar cane, jute, nutmeg

Mesoamerica: maize, amaranth

manioc, common bean, sweet potato, cotton, tomato, squash, bottle gourd

South America: amaranth, peanut

common bean, manioc, potato, cotton, chili pepper, squash, bottle gourd, tobacco

eastern America: sunflower, sumpweed

3 THE EFFECTS OF DOMESTICATION

One of the most important consequences of farming was the separation of the domestic species from the wild, so that cross-breeding was minimal or absent. Early farmers, like their successors, positively managed the reproduction of their crops and livestock. In many cases, the objective was an increased yield, which could be achieved by selecting only the largest strains for breeding or re-seeding. The long early history of maize (*right*) illustrates this process. The twisted horns of Bronze Age goats from Jericho (*below left*), may have merely been a passing preference of the breeders, or could have been the accidental consequence of breeding strategies really designed to increase size or body weight. Other changes following from domestication were unintentional, and probably undesirable, for example the reduced size of domestic cattle, perhaps originally the result of restricted grazing and poor winter feed. Domestic cattle today are still substantially smaller than their wild ancestor the aurochs (*below*).

Below:
The evolution of the corn cob.
The examples shown all come from the
Tehuacán Valley of Mexico. Actual size.

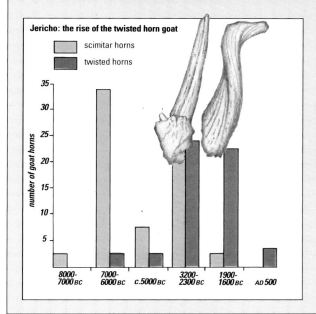

Jericho: the rise of the twisted horn goat
- scimitar horns
- twisted horns

number of goat horns

8000-7000 BC · 7000-6000 BC · c.5000 BC · 3200-2300 BC · 1900-1600 BC · AD 500

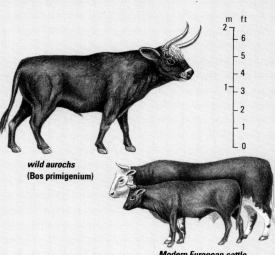

wild aurochs
(Bos primigenium)

Modern European cattle

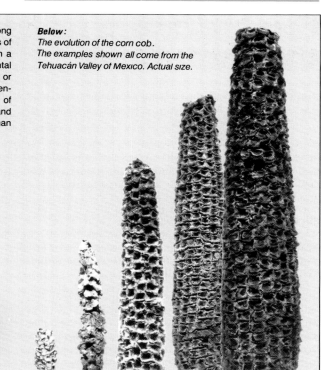

5200–3400 BC · 3400–2300 BC · 200 BC–AD 700 · AD 700–1540

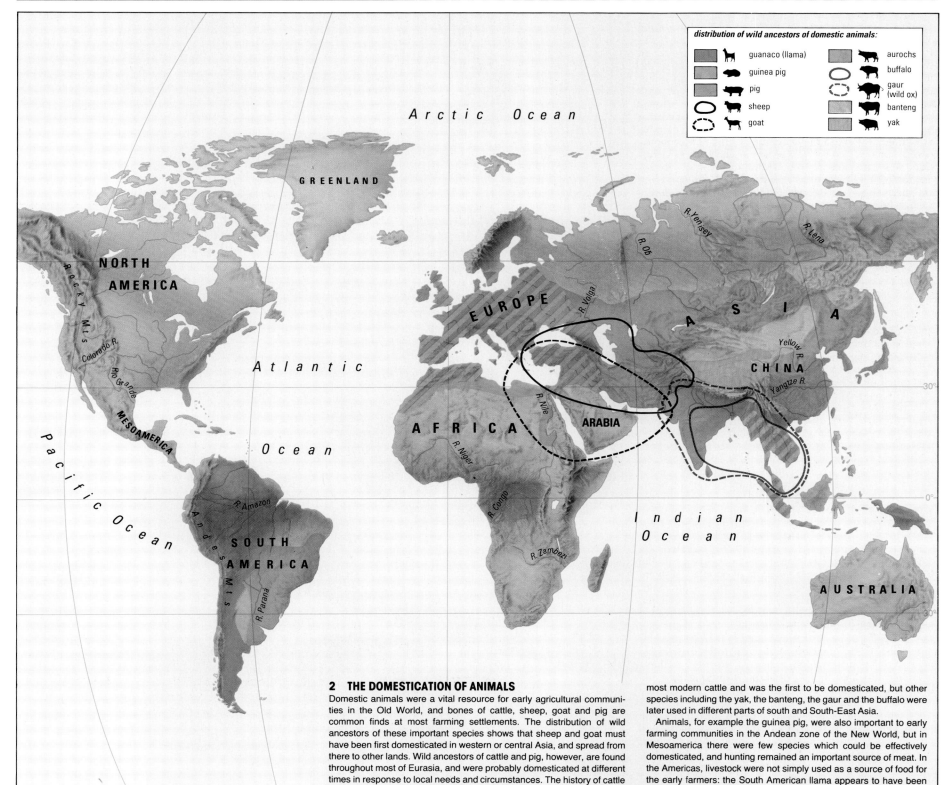

distribution of wild ancestors of domestic animals:
- guanaco (llama)
- guinea pig
- pig
- sheep
- goat
- aurochs
- buffalo
- gaur (wild ox)
- banteng
- yak

2 THE DOMESTICATION OF ANIMALS

Domestic animals were a vital resource for early agricultural communities in the Old World, and bones of cattle, sheep, goat and pig are common finds at most farming settlements. The distribution of wild ancestors of these important species shows that sheep and goat must have been first domesticated in western or central Asia, and spread from there to other lands. Wild ancestors of cattle and pig, however, are found throughout most of Eurasia, and were probably domesticated at different times in response to local needs and circumstances. The history of cattle domestication is complicated by the existence of a number of separate species. The principal Old World variety, the aurochs, is the ancestor of most modern cattle and was the first to be domesticated, but other species including the yak, the banteng, the gaur and the buffalo were later used in different parts of south and South-East Asia.

Animals, for example the guinea pig, were also important to early farming communities in the Andean zone of the New World, but in Mesoamerica there were few species which could be effectively domesticated, and hunting remained an important source of meat. In the Americas, livestock were not simply used as a source of food for the early farmers: the South American llama appears to have been used principally as a pack animal, while the alpaca was valued for its woolly coat.

First farmers of the Near East

Agriculture in the Near East had its beginnings in the Fertile Crescent, a broad arc of territory curving from the head of the Persian Gulf around the northern edge of the Syrian Desert to Palestine and the borders of Egypt. On its hilly flanks the moist conditions following the end of the last Ice Age led to the spread of open woodland and large-seeded grasses, ancestors of modern wheats and barleys. These grasses, with their nutritious and easily-stored grain, naturally attracted the attention of local hunter-gatherers, who used flint-bladed knives to harvest them. Increasing reliance on wild wheat and barley soon led to attempts to improve nature, by scattering grain so as to enlarge the area or density of natural cereal growth. In this gradual way the foundations of Near Eastern agriculture were laid.

The initial stage of this development, the intensive collection of wild cereals, is best known in Palestine, where small villages of circular stone-walled huts dating to around 10,000BC have been found. These 'Natufian' communities hunted, herded goat and gazelle and harvested wild emmer wheat. Grindstones were used to convert the grain to flour, and skeletons show evidence of the heavy tooth wear resulting from the inclusion of small fragments of grit in the flour during grinding.

The intensive collection of wild cereals was followed by the sowing of cereals outside their natural habitat, a practice first traceable to northern Syria in c.9000BC. Einkorn, a wheat which grew wild in the foothills of the Taurus and Zagros Mountains to the north and east, was found as far away as Mureybat and Tell Abu Hureira, on the banks of the River Euphrates, showing that the inhabitants must have been cultivating the plant intentionally. The first cereals of fully domesticated type, with larger grains and a seed-head which did not shatter readily on ripening, are those from Jericho in the Jordan Valley, dated to around 8000BC. With such obvious advantages for expanding communities the new economy spread rapidly, and by 7000BC wheat and barley cultivation was established from Anatolia to the Zagros Mountains and beyond to Pakistan. With the spread of cereal farming went the cultivation of pulses and legumes such as peas and lentils.

As communities became larger, major changes in the exploitation of animals also became necessary. Before the introduction of agriculture, many Near Eastern communities depended for meat on gazelle or goat. Most of the early Levantine farming communities still relied principally on gazelle, which may have been herded in a domesticated or at least semi-domesticated state. By 7000BC, however, goats had replaced gazelle – they grazed on a wider range of plant-foods, so the land was able to support a larger number of animals, and they could also be milked. Other animals were domesticated at this time: pigs in southern Turkey c.7000BC, cattle in North Africa and around the Aegean c.6000BC, while sheep had already been domesticated, perhaps as early as 9000BC, in northern Mesopotamia.

While hunter-gatherers were dependent on wild resources which were not normally sufficiently dense or abundant to allow them to live in large settlements all year round, early farming villages were often both permanent and substantial, frequently covering several acres. The houses were commonly of mud-brick, and as they weathered and collapsed would be rebuilt many times in the same place, a practice leading to the formation of a mound of settlement debris, known variously as a 'tell', 'tepe' or 'hüyük', which is a characteristic feature of ancient Near Eastern sites (p82).

Agriculture enabled communities to increase the amount of food they could produce, and made it possible for them to support larger numbers of people who were not directly involved full-time in work on the land, notably specialist craftsmen. This in turn stimulated trade between communities. Among the items traded were obsidian, a black volcanic glass, and shells and semi-precious stones sometimes used in the manufacture of necklaces. The great prosperity which this wide range of material goods reflects appears, however, to have been accompanied by less desirable consequences, and the powerful defences of Jericho suggest an increased level of conflict and violence.

By 6000BC many of the staple plants and animals on which we rely today had been domesticated, and prosperous farming villages had sprung up throughout the Near East. During the following three millennia, populations continued to grow, trade and craftsmanship developed still further, and new types of settlement and society began to form – a process which eventually was to culminate in the development of the first literate civilisations of the Old World.

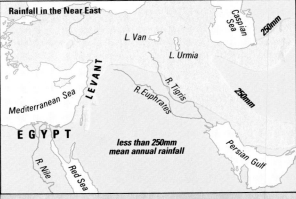

Rainfall in the Near East

less than 250mm mean annual rainfall

1 THE FERTILE CRESCENT

Large areas of the Near East are dry steppe or desert, but rainfall (left) is more plentiful in the broad arc of uplands from the Levant to the Zagros mountains, south of the Caspian Sea, which forms the backbone of the Fertile Crescent. Here, wheat and barley grew wild, and its fringes were also home to the ancestors of domestic sheep and goat (below). This natural availability of suitable plants and animals was a major reason for the early development of agriculture in the region. The successful combination of wheat and barley with sheep and goat, supplemented where conditions allowed by pulses, cattle and pig, led rapidly to a dramatic increase in the size and stability of settlements, which in turn stimulated new levels of craftsmanship and trade. One of the best-documented trade materials was obsidian, volcanic glass used instead of flint in cutting-tools and much prized for its lustrous black appearance. Obsidian from sources in central and eastern Anatolia occurs in small quantities at early farming sites over 800 kilometres to the south (right).

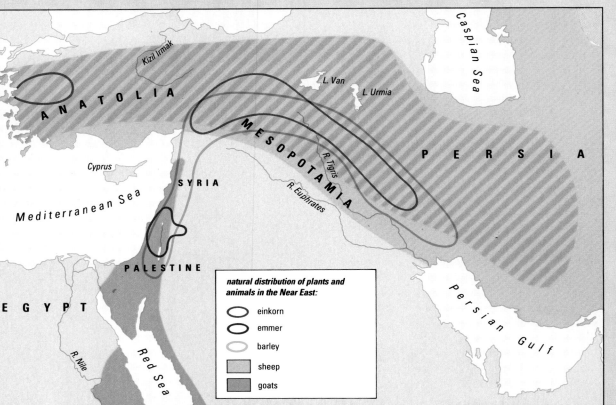

natural distribution of plants and animals in the Near East:

- einkorn
- emmer
- barley
- sheep
- goats

3 THE ARTS OF THE FARMER

A Skull of a young woman from Jericho, probably placed on display and used in rituals. The features were modelled in plaster, with cowrie shells inset as eyes. The skull had been intentionally deformed during life by lengthening backwards. 7th millennium BC, height 18cm. **B** Sickle haft with end carved in form of goat's head from Mugharet Kebara, Israel. A groove down one side of the haft originally held flint blades. Over 1000 flint blades were found here, some with the characteristic gloss resulting from the cutting of grasses or cereals. Natufian, c.9000BC, bone, length 32cm. **C** Carved spouted bowl with decoration of chevrons and rows of rectangular knobs, from grave of 8-year-old child at Khirokitia, Cyprus. This valued item had been repaired in antiquity. c.6000BC, dark grey andesite, length 30.5cm. **D** Necklace of dentalium shells and carnelian beads from grave of middle-aged woman at Khirokitia. c.6000BC, length of longest shell c.4.5cm.

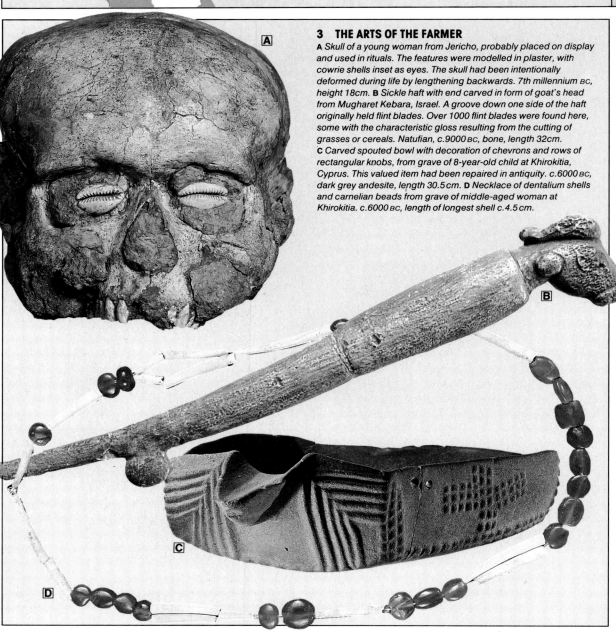

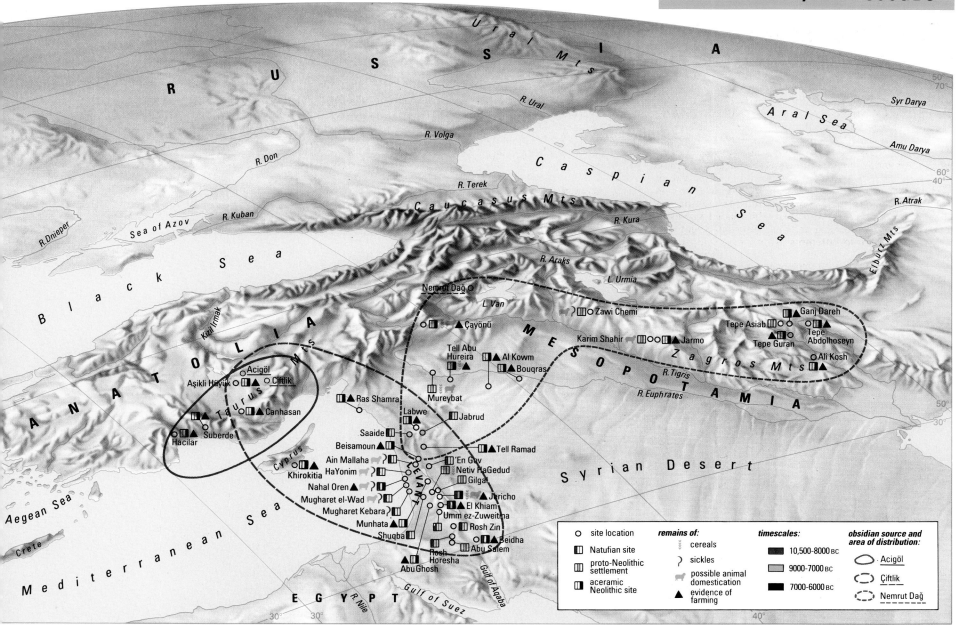

site location ○
Natufian site ▯
proto-Neolithic settlement ▯
aceramic Neolithic site ▮

remains of:
cereals ⸚
sickles ⸝
possible animal domestication 🐑
evidence of farming ▲

timescales:
10,500-8000 BC
9000-7000 BC
7000-6000 BC

obsidian source and area of distribution:
Acigöl
Çiftlik
Nemrut Dağ

2 JERICHO: AN EARLY FARMING COMMUNITY

Situated beside a perennial spring, the ancient site of Jericho, marked by a tell or settlement mound, began as a Natufian shrine c.9000BC. Muddy land, watered by the spring, provided excellent conditions for cereal farming in an otherwise arid environment, and by 8000BC the Jericho settlement had grown to a size of 1.6 hectares. For greater security, the prosperous farming community built a stone perimeter wall 3 metres thick, strengthened at one point by a circular stone tower over 9 metres high, with an internal stairway (*below*). By 7000BC new developments in religion are evident, and plastered skulls, the faces perhaps modelled in the likeness of venerated ancestors, are found at the site. This economy was based on cultivated wheat and barley, with domestic sheep and goat finally replacing gazelle as the dominant meat source in around 7000BC (*below far right*). The development of Jericho, adjacent to excellent arable land, may be contrasted with that of nearby Nahal Oren (*far right*). There was very little land suitable for cereal growing around the latter site, and though it had long been used by hunters and gatherers it never grew beyond a small group of huts. and in the 7th millennium BC was finally abandoned.

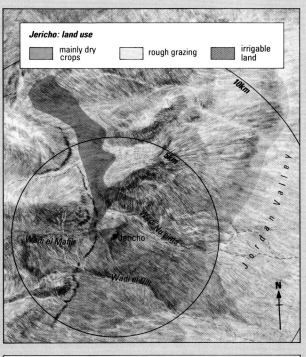

Jericho: land use
mainly dry crops
rough grazing
irrigable land

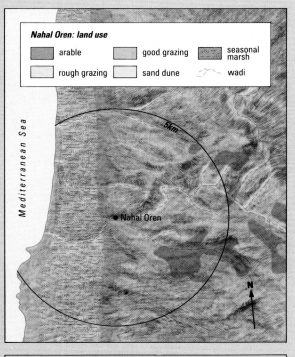

Nahal Oren: land use
arable
good grazing
seasonal marsh
rough grazing
sand dune
wadi

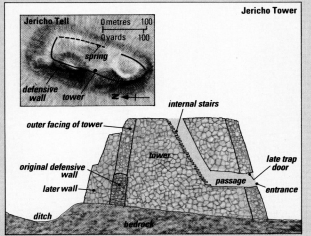

Jericho Tower

Jericho Tell
0 metres 100
0 yards 100
spring
defensive wall
tower

internal stairs
outer facing of tower
original defensive wall
late trap door
later wall
passage
entrance
tower
ditch
bedrock

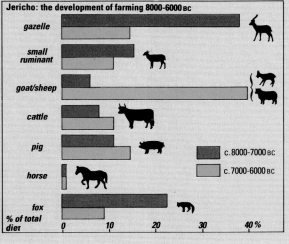

Jericho: the development of farming 8000-6000 BC
gazelle
small ruminant
goat/sheep
cattle
pig
horse
fox
% of total diet

c. 8000-7000 BC
c. 7000-6000 BC

0   10   20   30   40 %

Çatal Hüyük: a farming village

Situated on the banks of the Çarşamba river on the Konya Plain of central Anatolia, the village of Çatal Hüyük is the largest Neolithic site in the Near East covering 13 hectares. Founded c.7000 BC, the settlement grew rapidly and became prosperous, well-organised and culturally sophisticated, with wide-ranging trade networks and impressive craftsmanship. Outstanding shrines, wall paintings, figurines and burials give a detailed picture of the mysterious religious life of this early farming community.

Carbonised remains found at Çatal Hüyük indicate that staple crops were wheat, barley and peas, although lentils and vetches were also grown. These crops were supplemented by apples, pistachios, hackberries, almonds and acorns, which were collected locally. The principal meat source was cattle, which featured prominently in the religious life of the community. Wild animals were still important – the hunting of red deer, boar and onager is frequently portrayed on wall paintings. From skeletal remains it is possible to assess the health and life expectancy of the inhabitants of Çatal Hüyük. There is evidence in some cases of arthritis and of anaemia, the latter perhaps caused by malaria, which may have been endemic in the marshy environment around the site. Life expectancy was short; an average of 34 years for men, 29 for women, although some individuals lived to over 60.

With the exception of obsidian, available from the nearby volcano of Hasan Dağ, raw materials had to be imported. Çatal Hüyük became the centre of a trading complex, dealing in a wide range of items – timber, obsidian, flint, copper, shells. Cowrie shells were imported from as far afield as the Red Sea. With access to raw materials assured, the craftsmen of Çatal Hüyük became increasingly skilled and specialised, producing a wide variety of goods: arrowheads, lanceheads and daggers of flint and obsidian, stone maceheads, baked clay and carved stone figurines, textiles, wooden vessels and coil-built pottery. Trinkets such as copper beads and lead pendants were also produced, and copper-smelting

Çatal Hüyük: settlement 6500-5720 BC

III c.5790
II c.5750
I c.5720
IV c.5830
V c.5880
VI A c.5950
VI B c.6050
VII c.6200
VIII c.6280
IX c.6380
X c.6500
XI
XII-XIII

unexcavated lower levels

2 ÇATAL HÜYÜK
Reconstruction of excavated area, only one thirtieth of whole site. **1 Clay hearth** raised circular fireplace with curb to prevent embers spilling. **2 Clay bench** covered with reed or rush matting used for sleeping; the area beneath was often used as a burial place. **3 Built-in clay oven**; adjacent area served as kitchen. **4 Ladder**; these were the only method of gaining access to the village and of entering the house interior from the roof. **5 Roof**; stout oak beams and smaller timbers covered with reeds and thick mud, with matting underneath. **6 Shrine** with human skulls found on benches beneath reliefs of bulls' and rams' heads and human breasts. One breast had the massive lower jaw bone of a wild boar protruding symbolically from it. **7 Drainage area** inside the house; rushes cover the bare earth. **8 Storeroom** with low open doorway (c.70cm high) perhaps for foodstuffs.

at Çatal Hüyük provides some of the earliest evidence of metallurgy in the Near East.

The houses at Çatal Hüyük were closely packed together, without intervening streets and lanes, and access to the interiors was by wooden ladder from the flat roofs. Built of mud-brick covered with plaster, the standard plan comprised a living room (c.4x5m), with subsidiary rooms. The main room contained benches and platforms for sitting and sleeping, a raised rectangular hearth and a vaulted bread oven. As well as houses there were shrines, similar in size and construction but distinguished from ordinary dwellings by their wall-paintings, plaster reliefs and animal-head decorations.

The dead were buried beneath the sleeping platforms in both houses and shrines; the burials were communal and new bodies were added over the years. Several generations of one family may have been buried together, suggesting that some form of ancestor worship was practised. Before burial, the bodies were exposed until the flesh had been removed by vultures and insects. Most of the burials lack grave-goods, although bodies have been found beneath the shrines interred with precious objects such as obsidian mirrors, ceremonial daggers and metal beads, suggesting that these were the burials of the community leaders.

Wall paintings, decorations and figurines provide an evocative picture of the religious life of Çatal Hüyük. Goddesses, often associated with leopards, and frequently represented as pregnant or giving birth – sometimes to rams and bulls – suggest a fertility cult. Gods are symbolised by bulls, which occur repeatedly in the art of Çatal Hüyük, especially in the shrines, where plaster reliefs incorporate actual bulls' horns. Some of the decorations at Çatal Hüyük point to a death cult; vultures are shown attacking headless human corpses (perhaps a representation of mortuary rituals) and female breasts modelled in the walls of shrines and containing the bones of scavenging species – fox, weasel, vulture – suggest some symbiosis between life and death.

Many features of Çatal Hüyük are puzzling. However, although we know little of this highly sophisticated early town's political and social development, or the precise nature of its inhabitants religious beliefs, it serves as a vivid illustration of the huge new potential offered by the adoption of agriculture.

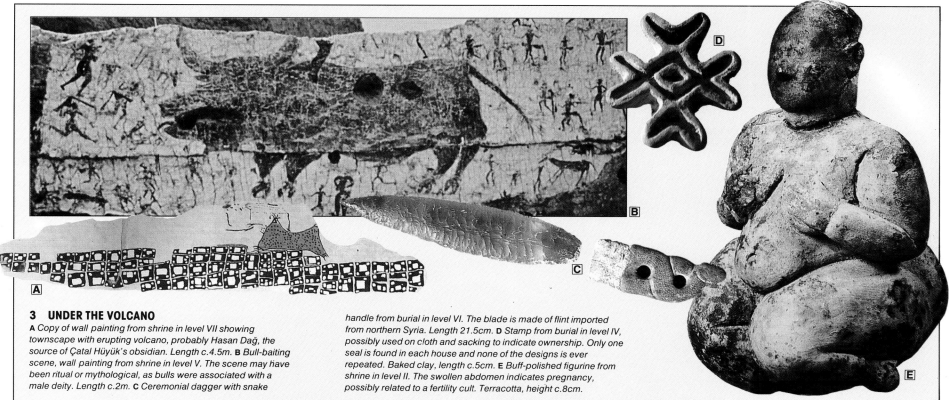

3 UNDER THE VOLCANO

A Copy of wall painting from shrine in level VII showing townscape with erupting volcano, probably Hasan Dağ, the source of Çatal Hüyük's obsidian. Length c.4.5m. B Bull-baiting scene, wall painting from shrine in level V. The scene may have been ritual or mythological, as bulls were associated with a male deity. Length c.2m. C Ceremonial dagger with snake handle from burial in level VI. The blade is made of flint imported from northern Syria. Length 21.5cm. D Stamp from burial in level IV, possibly used on cloth and sacking to indicate ownership. Only one seal is found in each house and none of the designs is ever repeated. Baked clay, length c.5cm. E Buff-polished figurine from shrine in level II. The swollen abdomen indicates pregnancy, possibly related to a fertility cult. Terracotta, height c.8cm.

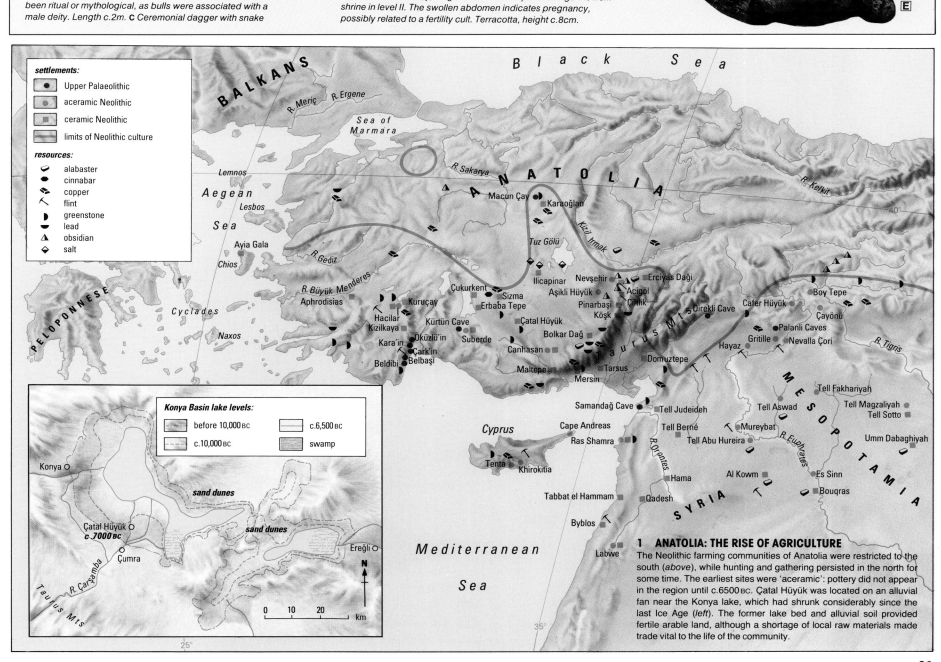

1 ANATOLIA: THE RISE OF AGRICULTURE

The Neolithic farming communities of Anatolia were restricted to the south (above), while hunting and gathering persisted in the north for some time. The earliest sites were 'aceramic': pottery did not appear in the region until c.6500 BC. Çatal Hüyük was located on an alluvial fan near the Konya lake, which had shrunk considerably since the last Ice Age (left). The former lake bed and alluvial soil provided fertile arable land, although a shortage of local raw materials made trade vital to the life of the community.

Europe
after the ice

The end of the last Ice Age (the Postglacial period) brought with it dramatic changes in the European landscape. Ice sheets, melting in the higher temperatures, flooded many coastal lowlands, while changes in fauna and vegetation – particularly the spread of forest – brought on by the more temperate climate offered many opportunities which hunter-gatherers exploited to the full, developing a new tool technology and new hunting, fishing and gathering strategies. Populations grew, and settlements became larger and more permanent. This transitional period between the end of the last glacial (c.8300 BC), and the adoption of farming, (6th millennium BC) is known as the Mesolithic – a period when the Ice Age hunters of Upper Palaeolithic Europe gradually changed their way of life to cope with different environmental conditions.

The main technological change in the Mesolithic was the increase in use of microlithic flints, frequently mounted in bone or wood hafts, and used as arrowheads, knives, and other 'composite' tools. These tools helped the Mesolithic hunter-gatherers exploit the wide range of animal and plant foods becoming available. Styles of microlith manufacture vary greatly, probably indicating local population groups, although cutting across these local styles are three major chronological divisions each lasting a millennium or more, and each characterised by different kinds of microliths. Tools of the third major phase (starting around 5750 BC) never spread into Britain, as in around 6500 BC sea levels rose, cutting off Britain from the Continent.

The wider range of food resources which became available after the last Ice Age meant that seasonal movements of the Mesolithic hunter from one camp to the next were generally over shorter distances. Special-purpose camps, for trapping fur-bearing animals or mining high-quality flint, were also established. In areas which were particularly well-endowed with food sources settlement size increased, and some settlements were even occupied throughout the year, with only small

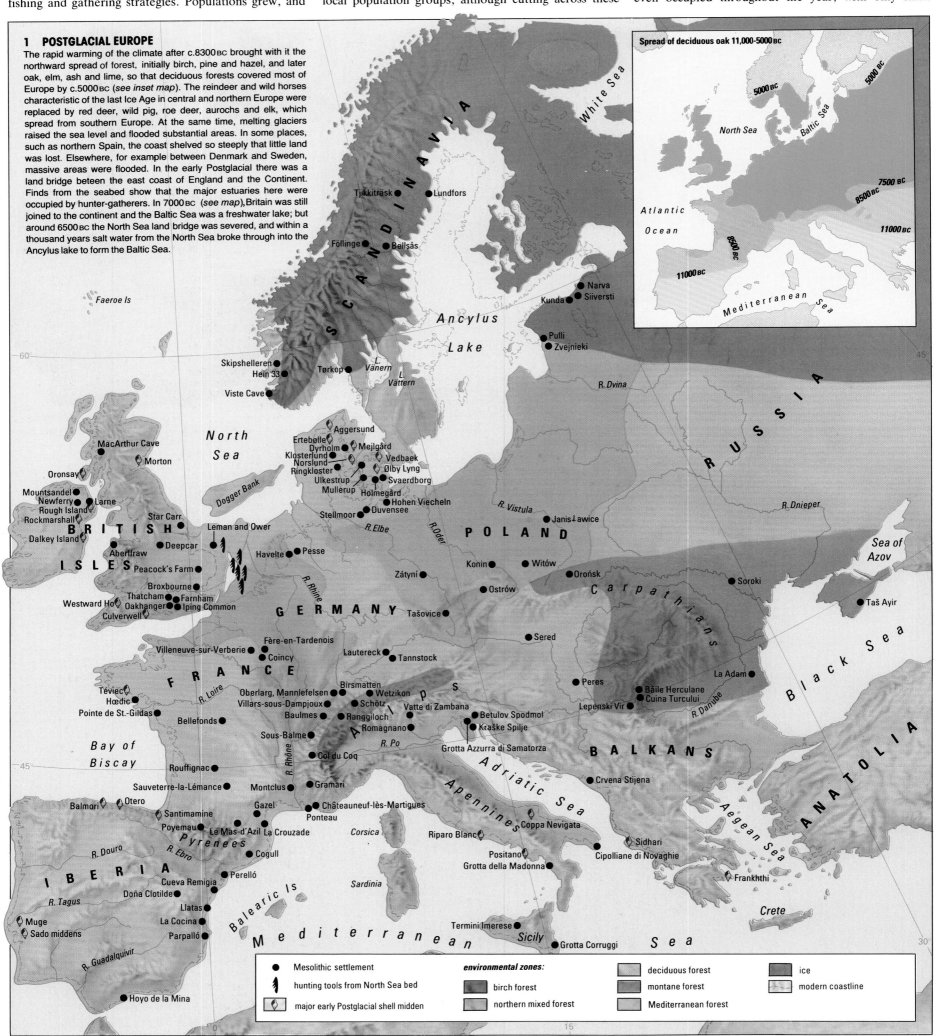

1 POSTGLACIAL EUROPE
The rapid warming of the climate after c.8300 BC brought with it the northward spread of forest, initially birch, pine and hazel, and later oak, elm, ash and lime, so that deciduous forests covered most of Europe by c.5000 BC (see inset map). The reindeer and wild horses characteristic of the last Ice Age in central and northern Europe were replaced by red deer, wild pig, roe deer, aurochs and elk, which spread from southern Europe. At the same time, melting glaciers raised the sea level and flooded substantial areas. In some places, such as northern Spain, the coast shelved so steeply that little land was lost. Elsewhere, for example between Denmark and Sweden, massive areas were flooded. In the early Postglacial there was a land bridge beteen the east coast of England and the Continent. Finds from the seabed show that the major estuaries here were occupied by hunter-gatherers. In 7000 BC (see map), Britain was still joined to the continent and the Baltic Sea was a freshwater lake; but around 6500 BC the North Sea land bridge was severed, and within a thousand years salt water from the North Sea broke through into the Ancylus lake to form the Baltic Sea.

Spread of deciduous oak 11,000-5000 BC

Mesolithic settlement

hunting tools from North Sea bed

major early Postglacial shell midden

environmental zones:
birch forest
northern mixed forest
deciduous forest
montane forest
Mediterranean forest
ice
modern coastline

groups moving from the base camp to the outlying special purpose camps. These large, permanent settlements were usually situated on coasts or major rivers, particularly in eastern Europe. Despite this reduced mobility, local groups maintained contact with each other. The new tool types of each major phase spread very quickly, and where distinctive raw materials such as obsidian were used, they can be traced at great distances from their points of origin. Canoes and paddles have been found, indicating one way in which neighbouring groups could maintain contact.

Some of the parts of Europe richest in food resources were the coasts, where settlement would have been most dense. Relatively little is known about these areas, as rising sea levels have flooded most of the Mesolithic shoreline, rendering it beyond the reach of archaeologists. However, there are a few regions, notably in northern Europe, where the rise in land masses outstripped the rise in sea level, leaving late Mesolithic coastlines preserved. Settlements in these areas show that coastal groups depended on both the forest and a variety of marine resources including fish of many species, water birds such as migrating swans and ducks, and seals. In areas where shellfish were a staple food, for example in Denmark, northern Spain and Portugal, the discarded shells piled up to form large shell middens, which often also contain the bones of fish.

Inland, several species of large animal – red deer, wild pig, aurochs, elk, roe deer – flourished and these probably provided the main meat source for most hunting groups. The spread of deciduous forest, rich in plant foods, was also important. Charred hazelnut shells are often found in settlements, and while many other plant foods must also have been eaten, they usually leave no trace in the archaeological record. The bones of smaller animals such as pine martens are also found; these were probably killed for their pelts.

Mesolithic hunter-gatherers probably experimented with the use of natural resources in order to safeguard or increase their productiveness. Husbandry of certain plant species may have begun at this period, while some communities relied very heavily for meat on a single species, red deer. It is possible, therefore, that some aspects of the agricultural way of life had already been adopted by the indigenous communities of Mesolithic Europe before the introduction of domestic crops and livestock from the Near East (*page 86*).

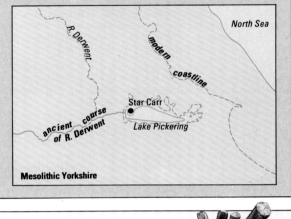

Star Carr: a Mesolithic settlement

Mesolithic Yorkshire

2 STAR CARR: A HUNTER-GATHERER CAMP

Star Carr, situated by the side of ancient Lake Pickering in Yorkshire, was occupied around 7500 BC. It was repeatedly visited in early summer by small groups of hunters, whose main quarries were red deer, elk, aurochs, roe deer and wild boar. Objects deposited in the lake were sealed into the growing peat and many were well preserved.

A *Flint scraper, possibly used for cleaning and preparation of hides. Length 5.1cm.* **B** *Barbed antler point with sharp cutting edge. Length 8.6cm.* **C** *Stag frontlet with antlers, perforated so it could be tied on as headgear. Probably worn in rituals, or as a disguise to enable hunters to get closer to their quarry. Width c.32.9cm.*

3 LEPENSKI VIR: A VILLAGE ON THE DANUBE

Lepenski Vir, first occupied c.6000 BC, lies on the Danube where it runs through the Iron Gates gorge. The settlement was permanent and substantial – perhaps 100 people – and the larger central house may indicate social stratification. These developments were possible because of the resources available: fish, including catfish and carp, were an important addition to red deer, roe deer, aurochs, wild pigs, and plant foods.

Below *Fish-head sculpture. Similar sculptures were found close to the hearth in many houses. They reflect the importance of fish in the diet and economy, and may have represented a fish-deity, c.5500 BC, height 36cm.*

The village of Lepenski Vir

Early farming in Europe

The spread of farming into temperate Europe did not make steady progress, since farming strategies had to be adapted to the more northerly climate. It was necessary to rely more heavily on cattle and pigs, and new strains of cereal had to be developed to cope with the cooler and more moist conditions. In some areas, particularly on the peripheries of temperate Europe, the success of existing hunter-gatherer groups and their high population density also slowed the spread of the new economy.

Agriculture first reached the Balkans in the 7th millennium BC, probably spreading from Anatolia. The villages of these early farmers often formed tells similar to those in the Near East, and were larger, more substantially built and longer-lived than the early farming settlements of the west Mediterranean or the temperate forest zones. Craftsmanship was more sophisticated here than in other areas of Europe, and included elaborate painted pottery and figurines. The Balkan farmers practiced mixed agriculture not unlike that of the Near East with wheat and barley, lentils, peas and vetch, while sheep, goats, pigs and cattle were bred.

Farming villages first appeared in southern Italy and Sicily in c.6200 BC, possibly as a result of direct immigration from the Balkans across the Adriatic. These villages consisted of groups of hut-compounds within large ditched enclosures. Further west, the Mediterranean coast was occupied by small hunter-fisher-gatherer communities, mainly known from caves and rock shelters, who adopted agriculture gradually. Wild resources remained important, and it seems that the herding of sheep and goats, and some cereal cultivation, was integrated with hunting, fishing and gathering. These communities made pottery decorated with impressions of cockle shells (*Cardium*), known as Cardial pottery which is found among virtually all the Neolithic groups in the west Mediterranean. The new economy became progressively more important: by 5000 BC cereal agriculture was well established and the first farming villages had developed in the south of France.

In central Europe the earliest farming culture is called the Bandkeramik, after the distinctive linear incised decoration which characterises their pottery. Here, immigration was probably the major means by which farming spread, and the process was rapid, beginning around 5400 BC and carrying farming from Hungary to the Netherlands within two or three centuries. Villages of substantial longhouses, which may have contained both families and cattle, were characteristic settlements. The fertile soils of river terraces and easily cultivated loess soils of central Europe were all well suited to agriculture, while the forested hinterland was rich in wild resources and suitable for pig and cattle herding. Farming practices were very different from the Mediterranean or Near East, however, with much less reliance on sheep and goat.

These early farming communities of Europe buried their dead in a variety of ways. Along the Atlantic coast, in southern Iberia, Brittany, the British Isles and southern Scandinavia, communal burial in megalithic tombs was usual, while in central and eastern Europe individual graves, sometimes grouped in small cemeteries, were customary. A Bandkeramik cemetery at Elsloo, in the Netherlands, consists of 113 graves, containing a variety of grave-goods – polished stone axes and adzes, pottery, flint blades and arrowheads and shell ornaments. The distribution of these items shows no evidence of a hierarchically ordered society. Many of the items in these Bandkeramik graves were traded; spondylus shells reached the Bandkeramik area from the Aegean and Adriatic. Essential raw materials, such as hard stones, often not available locally, were also traded.

The hunter-gatherer way of life persisted around the northern fringes of Europe, and along the east European rivers; concentrated in favourable locations, it sometimes supported high population densities, and large settlement sites were occupied on a fairly permanent basis. Some groups developed pottery, possibly imitating neighbouring farmers. Farming was often not adopted until problems arose with the local economy – for example, the disappearance of the oyster in Denmark, an important winter and spring food resource.

By the end of the 5th millennium BC, farming was well established. As settlements increased in size and number, trade networks widened and craft-skills improved. These developments led to the appearance of new types of society and technology, as the early farming communities gave way to the hierarchical, metal-using societies of the Copper and Bronze Ages.

wattle and daub

livestock pen possibly for sheep

faunal remains:
— Müddersheim (Rhineland)
— Anza (Balkans)

cattle · sheep/goat · pig · dog · hunted animals

3 THE CRAFTS OF THE EUROPEAN FARMERS

During the early centuries of farming, eastern Europe was characterised by larger and more permanent settlements and more complex craftsmanship. In the centre and west, pottery was relatively simple, with impressed or incised designs. In the east, painted pottery was more elaborate, and ritual models and figurines were also made.
A Finely polished shaft-hole adze, probably for woodworking, from Hamburg. c. 4700 BC, length 24 cm. **B** Pottery model of seated figure, perhaps a deity, holding a sickle, from Szegvár-Tüzköves, Hungary, c. 4500 BC, height 25.6 cm. **C** Face-pot with pedestal, from Szegvár-Tüzköves. c. 4500 BC, height 16.5 cm. **D** Bandkeramik pot with linear decoration from Langweiler 9, West Germany. c. 4300 BC, clay; height 14.2 cm. **E** Clay figurines and models of furniture from shrine at Ovcharovo, Bulgaria. c. 4500 BC.

1 EUROPE: AGRICULTURAL INROADS

The spread of agriculture throughout Europe can be mapped archaeologically by the distribution of different pottery styles, each corresponding to a major grouping of early farming communities. In the south-east, environmental conditions were similar to those of the Near East, and west Asiatic crops and livestock could be raised without difficulty. In temperate Europe, however, farming strategies had to be adapted to the more northerly climate; new strains of cereal were developed, and greater reliance was placed on cattle and pigs, which unlike sheep and goats were to be found wild in the temperate forests. Hence the central European forest environment had a profound impact upon the nature of early farming settlement, and upon the speed with which the new economy was adopted. Along the coasts and estuaries of the Baltic and Atlantic the abundance of wild resources and the success of existing Mesolithic communities meant that hunting, fishing and gathering continued to prosper long after the appearance of domestic plants and animals further inland.

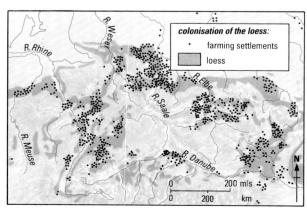

colonisation of the loess:
— farming settlements
— loess

R. Weser · R. Rhine · R. Elbe · R. Saale · R. Meuse · R. Danube

0   200 mls
0   200 km

2 LANGWEILER 2: AN EARLY FARMING VILLAGE

The forests of temperate Europe had a major impact on building methods and farming practices, with timber being used extensively in the construction of the longhouses characteristic of Bandkeramik settlements. Up to 45 metres in length, these houses were usually divided into three parts. The main dwelling area was in the middle section, with cattle stalls in the north, and in the south a raised loft – possibly for storing cereals. Longhouses were usually built in groups of two to five, accompanied by ancillary buildings, rubbish pits and animal pens. These hamlets were spaced out at intervals along watercourses with access to fertile, easily cultivated loess soils, and each settlement probably had a number of small fields of cereals or legumes. Nearby woodland provided a rich variety of wild plants and hunted animals (more important in temperate Europe than further south-east, *see table*), as well as fodder for the domestic cattle and pigs kept by these early farmers.

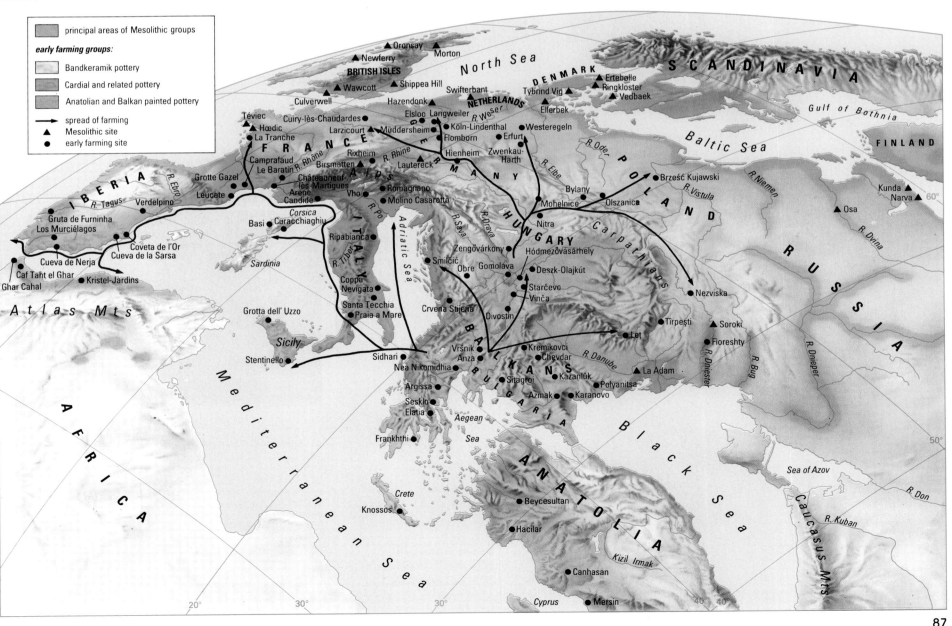

87

Early farming in South Asia

The earliest farmers of the Indian subcontinent have now been dated to the beginning of the 7th millennium BC, as a result of recent excavations in the Kachhi Plain. This transitional zone between the hills of Baluchistan and the Indo-Gangetic Plains offers a wide range of resources: the highland areas are suitable for summer grazing, while the perennial streams draining the Kachhi Plain can be dammed in order to trap fresh silts and regulate the flow of water, thereby permitting the cultivation of cereals.

The wild progenitors of wheat, barley, cattle, sheep and goats are all found in this area, flint nodules carried by the River Bolan provided raw materials for tools, and trade routes opened the way to Central Asia as well as to the Indo-Gangetic Plains.

With a natural environment so full of exploitable potential, it is likely that agriculture was a separate indigenous development on the Kachhi Plain. The gradual evolution of herding and cereal cultivation, reflected in the composition of faunal and floral remains at Mehrgarh – the principal site of the Kachhi Plain – certainly suggests autonomous development. In addition, the richness of even the earliest remains which predate pottery dispels the long-held belief that Baluchistan was a cultural backwater in comparison with

the Near East. Already in the 7th–6th millennia BC cereals, in particular 6-row barley, were cultivated, and herding of sheep, goats and cattle supplemented – and soon replaced – the livelihood gained from hunting. Villages of mud-brick houses were built, and blades, microliths, polished axes, grinding stones and bone tools were all manufactured. Lapis lazuli, marine shells, and turquoise were imported from as far as Persia and Badakhshan to meet the demand for luxury goods.

The numerous burials found in open areas within the settlement at Mehrgarh yielded a rich variety of bone, shell, and stone ornaments. Sometimes even infants were buried with elaborate grave-goods, which demonstrate that their high status was inherited. By the 6th millennium BC ceramics were in use, and storehouses were

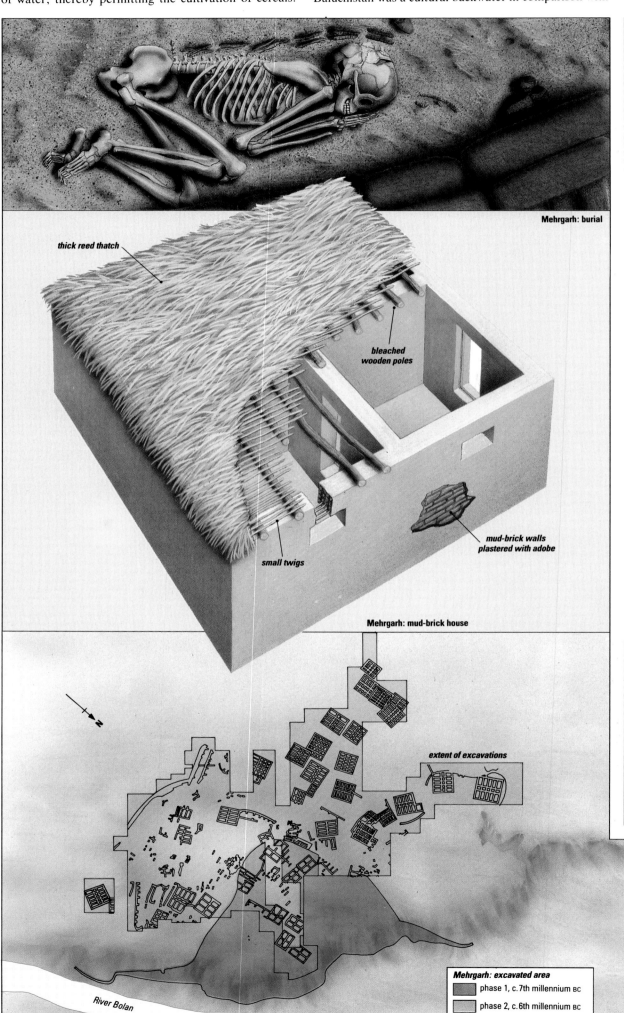

thick reed thatch

bleached wooden poles

small twigs

mud-brick walls plastered with adobe

Mehrgarh: burial

Mehrgarh: mud-brick house

extent of excavations

N

River Bolan

Mehrgarh: excavated area
- phase 1, c. 7th millennium BC
- phase 2, c. 6th millennium BC

3 FIRST FARMERS IN INDIA

A *The numerous burials found at Mehrgarh yielded the best sample of artefacts from the Neolithic phase. The grave illustrated opposite contained a polished stone axe, three flint cores, nine geometric microliths, and 16 unretouched flint blades (illustrated below), in addition to four turquoise beads and an asphalt coated basket (not illustrated below). 7th–6th millennium BC.* **B** *Painting of a herd of goats from the Mesolithic rock shelter of Morhana Pahar, which also yielded an abundance of microliths. Such sites as this, occupied by hunter-gatherer groups, have a wide distribution in central India.* **C** *A selection of bone, shell and limestone beads from Mehrgarh. 7th–6th millennium BC.*

A

B

C

2 MEHRGARH: AN EARLY FARMING COMMUNITY

The Neolithic village of Mehrgarh, situated on a terrace cut by the River Bolan, is the earliest yet discovered in South Asia. Its inhabitants lived in mud-brick houses. Burials were located in the open spaces within the settlement; the dead were placed in a flexed position and were often accompanied by rich grave-goods, which indicate distinctions in status. From 6000 BC onward storehouses – mud-brick buildings divided into small compartments which often contained grains and tools – were built. Society was becoming more highly organised, and the storehouses acted as a central point for the redistribution of food for general consumption, raw materials for specialised craftsmen, and manufactured goods for trade. The remains indicate growth in population in the 7th–6th millennia BC, following the invention of agriculture.

built in the village. Raw materials for specialised crafts such as the manufacture of bone tools and steatite ornaments were stored there – the emergence of a class of specialised craftsmen demonstrates a high level of social and administrative organisation. The sophisticated societies of the Kachhi Plain must have formed the prelude to the eventual colonisation of the Indus Valley; the first flowering of civilisation in South Asia was clearly an independent development.

Evidence of early agricultural communities – possibly from the 6th–5th millennia BC – also comes from the Vindhyan Hills just south of the Ganges Valley. Mesolithic hunter-gatherer groups, traceable by their tool assemblages and rock paintings, were already widely distributed in central India. Although the Vindhyan Hills

do not offer as great a range of habitats as the Kachhi Plain, they were equally abundant in raw materials, and in the wild progenitors of domesticated plants and animals, including rice, which must have made them attractive to settlers. A gradual transition from hunting and gathering to agriculture and animal husbandry is observable at such sites as Chopani-Mando and Mahagara, with rice cultivation beginning by perhaps the 5th millennium BC. This period also reveals the beginnings of social stratification, reflected in the differing sizes of individual houses and contrasting amounts of artefacts found within them. At the same time, sites such as Sarai-Nahar-Rai and Mahadaha are evidence of the first exploitation of the alluvial plains of the Ganges Valley by seasonal migrants based in the Vindhyas.

The indigenous development of Vindhyan agriculture should not be ruled out; the economy was based on rice, rather than on wheat or barley, so it is unlikely that it was derived from a western source. While the technological and subsistence base of the Vindhyan Neolithic parallels that of the Kachhi Plain (except for the dominance of rice among cultivated plants), the sites appear to be much poorer. Settlements consisted of wattle-and-daub huts with floors of beaten earth and pit-hearths. Artefacts consisted mainly of Corded Ware pottery and some bone and terracotta beads. Nevertheless, the economic and social changes which took place in the Vindhyas were as crucial a springboard to Ganges civilisation as the Neolithic villages of Baluchistan had proved to be for the cities of the Indus.

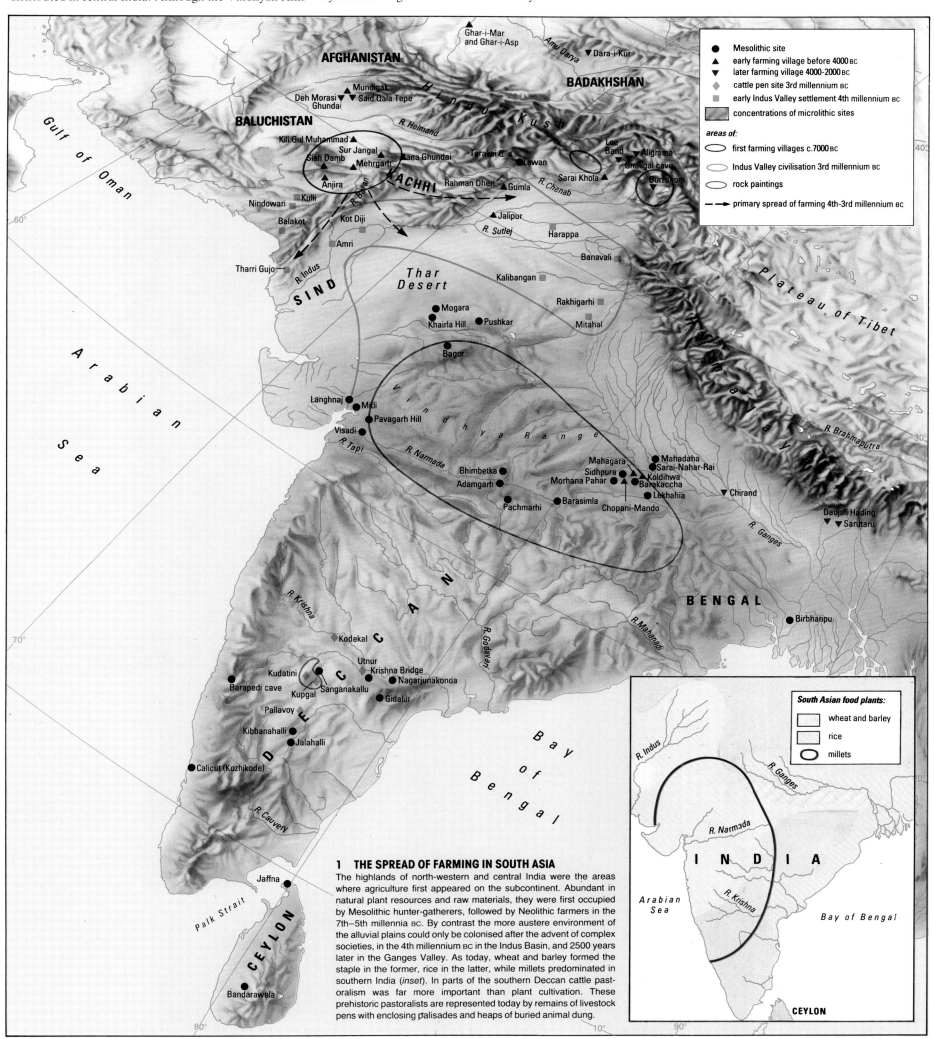

1 THE SPREAD OF FARMING IN SOUTH ASIA
The highlands of north-western and central India were the areas where agriculture first appeared on the subcontinent. Abundant in natural plant resources and raw materials, they were first occupied by Mesolithic hunter-gatherers, followed by Neolithic farmers in the 7th–5th millennia BC. By contrast the more austere environment of the alluvial plains could only be colonised after the advent of complex societies, in the 4th millennium BC in the Indus Basin, and 2500 years later in the Ganges Valley. As today, wheat and barley formed the staple in the former, rice in the latter, while millets predominated in southern India (inset). In parts of the southern Deccan cattle pastoralism was far more important than plant cultivation. These prehistoric pastoralists are represented today by remains of livestock pens with enclosing palisades and heaps of buried animal dung.

Legend:
- ● Mesolithic site
- ▲ early farming village before 4000 BC
- ▼ later farming village 4000-2000 BC
- ◆ cattle pen site 3rd millennium BC
- ■ early Indus Valley settlement 4th millennium BC
- concentrations of microlithic sites

areas of:
- first farming villages c.7000 BC
- Indus Valley civilisation 3rd millennium BC
- rock paintings
- → primary spread of farming 4th-3rd millennium BC

South Asian food plants:
- wheat and barley
- rice
- millets

From hunting to farming: South-East Asia

The melting of the ice sheets at the end of the last Ice Age transformed the landscape and ways of life of South-East Asia. Rising sea levels submerged the Sunda shelf, a large landmass which had linked mainland South-East Asia to the islands of western Indonesia, and created many new islands and estuaries, increasing the proportion of coastline to land over threefold. The rise in temperatures also led to a greater density and variety of plants. All these changes were particularly beneficial to hunter-gatherer communities, the coasts and estuaries being especially rich in food resources, and many of the sites where stone tools of this period have been found are coastal or estuarine shell middens.

Other favourable habitats were caves and rock shelters found in the distinctive limestone karst formations which stretch from Burma to Vietnam, and south into Indonesia. These sites often reveal lengthy sequences of human occupation, extending back to the beginning of the postglacial period and beyond: Nam Tun and Tham Hoi in northern Vietnam and Padah-lin in Burma, for example, were first occupied some 12,000 years ago. The most common remains from South-East Asia during this period are stone tools. Most of them are fairly unspecial-

ised, and designed for simple cutting, pounding and scraping. The tools fall into two broad traditions, the Hoabinhian of the mainland and the contemporary flake tradition of the islands.

The Hoabinhian is named after the flaked cobble tools found in the limestone caves of the Hoa Binh region of Tongking. Similar tools are found throughout South-East Asia in Burma, Thailand, Laos, Cambodia, Vietnam, Malaya and on northern Sumatra. Most of these were made from river-worn pebbles of basic and volcanic rocks, which were worked on one or two faces or were truncated to make short axes. Some tools were also made of shell and bone.

The earliest flaked stone tools of island South-East Asia originated in Indonesia, Borneo and the Philippines, and are at least 40,000 years old. Island tools are frequently made of chert, though obsidian tools have also been found in the central Philippines, western Java and southern Sumatra. Chert tools sometimes have a polish or gloss suggesting that the prehistoric cave dwellers were working silica-rich plants, such as palms, which left a permanent polish on the edge of the tools. Study of the traces shows that a variety of plants were being used, including rattan palm and pandanus leaves, probably for making mats, rope and baskets.

Many sites of this period have yielded important animal and plant remains. Plant remains from Spirit Cave in northern Thailand have been identified as plants which are cultivated today, such as peas and beans, but it is difficult to distinguish wild from domestic species, and impossible to establish a sequence of farming activities

based on the small sample of seed remains recovered. Carbonised seeds found on Timor and Celebes also indicate that plants such as *Piper* and *Areca* (the two main ingredients of betel chewing), *Canarium*, *Prunus* and *Aleurities* (nut-producing trees), and *Lagenaria* (bottle gourds), were being used well over 5000 years ago. Most of the preserved remains are stimulants, medicinal or poisonous plants, and tree fruits. There is little indication of staple foods such as roots or grains.

Despite the ambiguity of the evidence, it is probable that the adoption of agriculture in South-East Asia was a gradual process, with communities beginning to plant and harvest a few species as a supplement to hunting and gathering. The introduction of pottery, however, around 6000 BC on the mainland and c.2500 BC on the islands, marked a significant change throughout South-East Asia. From this time ceramics, quadrangular adzes and polished slate knives are found on mainland sites, while on the islands the introduction of fine, hard, red-burnished pottery coincides with the arrival of domesticated and exotic animals. Pottery, being a fragile commodity, is rarely produced by migratory hunter-gatherer communities, so its appearance probably coincided with increasingly permanent settlements.

This period also saw an increasing contact between communities and wider trading networks. These wider contacts, combined with the diversification of the economic base – simple agriculture supplementing hunting and gathering – point to a growing sophistication, which was ultimately to result in the development of bronze technology by the end of the 3rd millennium BC.

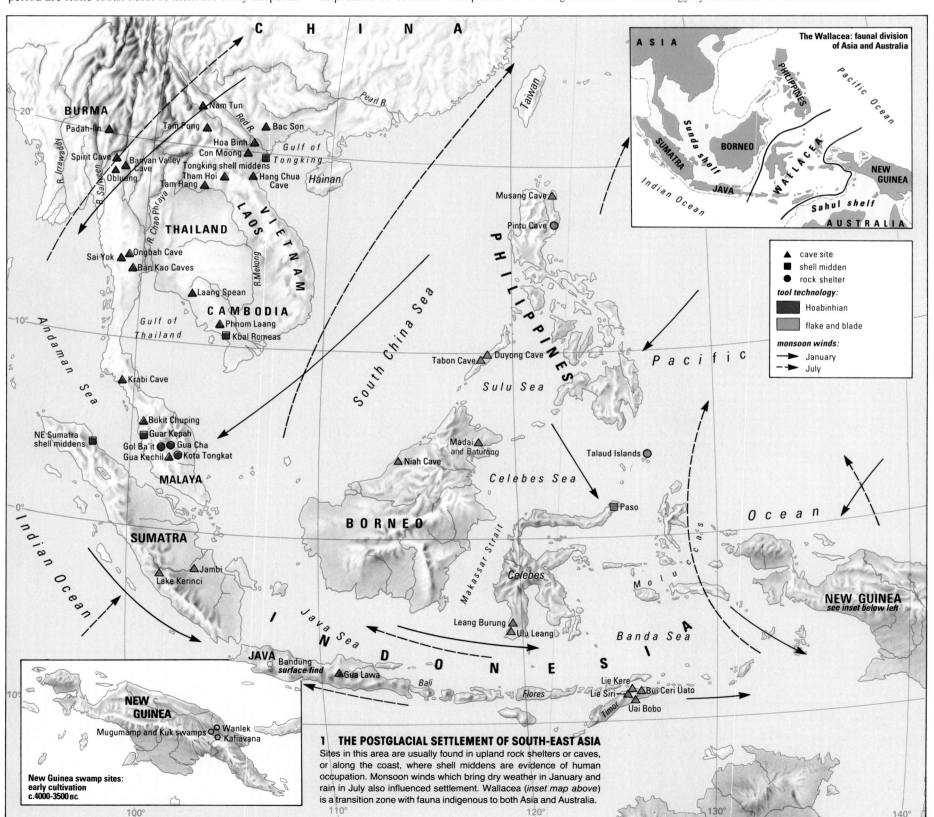

1 THE POSTGLACIAL SETTLEMENT OF SOUTH-EAST ASIA
Sites in this area are usually found in upland rock shelters or caves, or along the coast, where shell middens are evidence of human occupation. Monsoon winds which bring dry weather in January and rain in July also influenced settlement. Wallacea (inset map above) is a transition zone with fauna indigenous to both Asia and Australia.

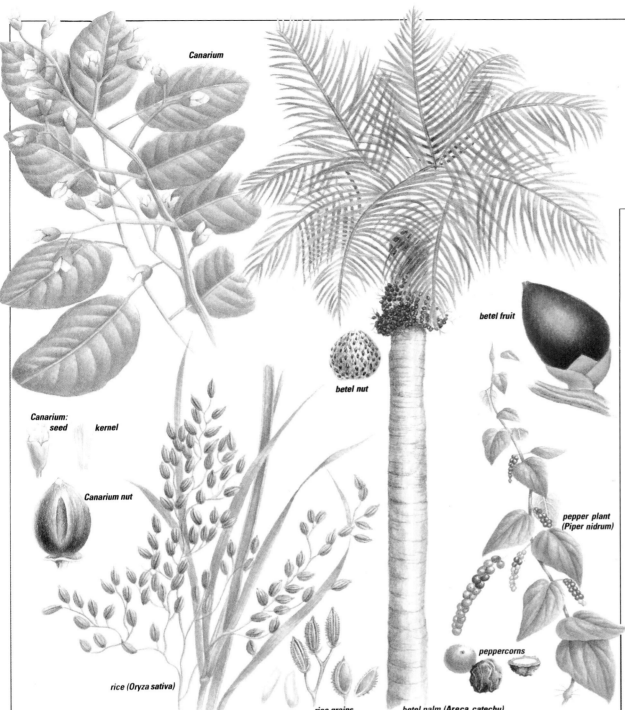

Canarium

betel fruit

betel nut

Canarium:
seed   kernel

Canarium nut

pepper plant
(Piper nidrum)

peppercorns

rice (Oryza sativa)

rice grains

betel palm (Areca catechu)

3 THE DOMESTICATED PLANTS OF SOUTH-EAST ASIA

South-East Asian agriculture today is dominated by a single crop, rice (*Oryza sativa*). However, carbonised grains were only found in the more recent occupation layers at Banyan Valley Cave, in Thailand, and it is difficult to distinguish between cultivated and wild rice. The remains of *Areca catechu* (betel palm), and *Piper nidrum* (pepper plant) – the two main ingredients of betel chewing – are found at several sites. The *Areca* nut is gathered from tall palm trees, while the peppercorns, red when ripe, grow on a vine. Seeds of the *Canarium* have also been found widely distributed throughout the region. *Canarium* is a large genus of trees, producing resins which can be used for medicines, for oil lamps, as an incense or as a caulking material. The kernels of the oil seed and of the delicately flavoured wild *Canarium* nut can also be eaten.

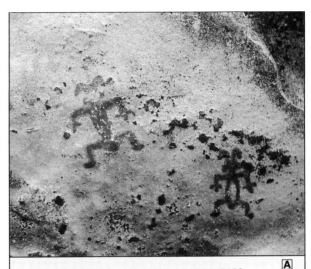

A

4 HUNTER-GATHERERS OF THE EAST INDIES

A *Prehistoric rock art from Lie Kere, Timor. Height of figure c.8cm.* **B** *Shells from Uai Bobo, c.4000 BC.* **Left to right** *Anadara granosa shell, length 5cm. Four olive shells, height 2-2.5cm. Five Nautilus shell discs, diameter 0.5-1cm. Pierced Anadara pilula shell, height 2.2cm.* **C** *Hoabinhian tool from northern Vietnam c.8000-6000 BC, height 15cm.* **D** *Tools from Bui Ceri Uato c.3000-500 BC.* **Left to right** *Fish hook, diameter 2.5cm. Shell beads, length 0.5cm. Shellfish hook, length 3cm.* **E** *Bone points from Ulu Leang c.4000-2000 BC.* **Left** *length 2cm.* **Right** *length 5cm.* **F** *Stone tools from Timor c.5000-2000 BC.* **Top to bottom** *Blade, length 8cm. Chert flake, length 13cm. Scraper, length 5cm.*

B

C

D

E

F

2 BUI CERI UATO: A TIMORESE ROCK SHELTER

The cave at Bui Ceri Uato, on eastern Timor, is a long but shallow shelter which was occupied from about 8000 to 2000 BC. The artefacts found at the site show little change over a period of several thousand years, with stone tools such as steep-edged scrapers and flaked pieces the most common objects. The early inhabitants ate a range of animals, and enjoyed a varied diet. The remains of land animals are dominated by several species of now extinct giant rats, as well as fruit bats, snakes and reptiles. Molluscs were obviously an important part of the diet, and were found throughout the deposits. Some molluscs would have been exposed on the coral reef flats at spring tides, others came from the rocky shores or from mangrove swamps. Shells were also used for beads and fish-hooks. After 3000 BC, new objects were brought to the cave, marking important changes in the way of life. Most significant are finds of pottery and new domesticated animals such as pigs – evidence of the transition from a purely hunter-gatherer community to a more sedentary lifestyle. At the same time, the number of stone tools increased, perhaps reflecting a growth in population supported by ever-improving horticulture. Earlier practices of shifting cultivation were gradually supplanted by fixed field cultivation of tubers and grains such as yams and rice. Both the pottery and the exotic animals may have been introduced by immigrants familiar with agriculture and animal husbandry.

Bui Ceri Uato: horizons

	pottery	stone tools	shells	land molluscs	sea molluscs	giant rat	pig	economic status
X-IX	BP							
VIII	1000							improved horticulture
VII	2000							metal tools
VI	3000			few remains only				
V	4000							horticulture
IV	5000							
III	6000							hunting and gathering
II	7000							
I	8000							

Bui Ceri Uato: cross-section of cave

cave overhang

trench

stone rubble wall

| 0 | 3 metres |
| 0 | 3 yards |

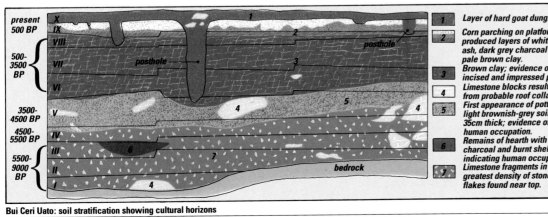

present 500 BP	X
	IX
	VIII
500-3500 BP	VII
	VI
3500-4500 BP	V
4500-5500 BP	IV
5500-9000 BP	III
	II
	I

posthole

posthole

bedrock

1 Layer of hard goat dung.
2 Corn parching on platforms produced layers of white ash, dark grey charcoal and pale brown clay.
3 Brown clay; evidence of incised and impressed pottery.
4 Limestone blocks resulting from probable roof collapse.
5 First appearance of pottery in light brownish-grey soil 25-35cm thick; evidence of human occupation.
6 Remains of hearth with charcoal and burnt shell indicating human occupation.
7 Limestone fragments in clay; greatest density of stone flakes found near top.

Bui Ceri Uato: soil stratification showing cultural horizons

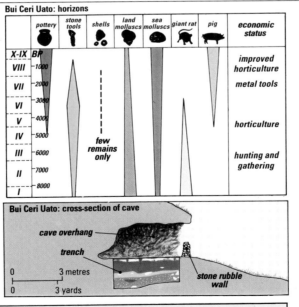

From hunting to farming: East Asia

The end of the last Ice Age around 10,000 BC was accompanied by far-reaching changes in the landscape and vegetation of East Asia. Hunter-gatherers exploited the rich marine resources around the coasts of southern China, Japan and Korea, while elsewhere in China experimentation with locally available plants and animals led to the development of agriculture in some areas.

In central China, limestone cave sites such as Xianrendong were occupied between 9000 and 5500 BC. A wide range of tools, including choppers, scrapers, awls, grinding-stones, arrow- and harpoon-heads, has been found there, suggesting that there was a hunting, fishing and gathering way of life in these areas – a variety of wild animal and shellfish remains was also found. The accumulation of debris – hearths, pots and kitchen waste – within the caves suggests that these were at least semi-permanent homes or bases from which specialised hunting and gathering expeditions set out.

From around 6000 BC in northern China, there are numerous sites, such as Banpo, with evidence of well-established agriculture – the cultivation of foxtail and broomcorn millets, domesticated pigs and dogs, houses with walls, roofs and fireplaces, and excavated pits for grain storage. Other plant remains include cabbage, jujube, plums and hazelnuts. By c.1100 BC soyabeans were grown as part of a rotational crop system with the millets. The discovery of rice husks, chaff and charred seeds at Hemudu, dated to the 5th millennium BC, shows that wet-rice farming was already well-established, and the early stages of plant cultivation must have been going on for some time before then.

From the 4th millennium onwards, there is increasing evidence of contact between various groups. The painted pottery from Yangshaocun in the north-west, the distinctive black-burnished pots of Longshan in the east (page 146), and the jade of the south-east were all items of exchange, though these groups retained their individual identity. Rich burials containing delicate jade carvings – adzes, cups, beads – have been discovered, particularly in the Shanghai and Hangzhou Bay area, revealing growing social stratification; these societies were evidently the precursors of Shang dynasty China.

In Korea, pottery was being made by c.6000 BC, though hunting and gathering continued to be the basis of subsistence. The rich fishing resources of the coasts and estuaries, reflected in finds of substantial shell middens, were even able to support small permanent villages. It is difficult to say precisely when farming began, but millet was in cultivation by 3000 BC, and rice was introduced – like millet, from China – during the 2nd millennium, if not earlier.

The Jomon peoples of Japan were hunter-fishers and gatherers, living on the great diversity of resources available throughout the mountains, rivers and coasts of the Japanese archipelago. Animal and plant remains reflect the seasonal round of activities: spring and early summer saw the height of the fishing and shell-fishing season, when deep-sea species such as tuna and bonito and aquatic mammals frequent the rocky shores and estuaries of the Pacific coast to feed and breed. In autumn, fruits and seeds were collected: chestnut, walnut, hazelnut and acorn were all important – abundant, nutritious and easily stored, as underground pits containing various nuts and acorns demonstrate. Animals such as deer and wild boar were hunted during late autumn and winter. In the more densely populated east, people lived in permanent settled villages in pit-houses with large, communal buildings. There is, however, no evidence of plant domestication at these sites.

Pottery manufacture in Japan dates back to c.10,500 BC, the earliest yet known anywhere in the world. It spread throughout the southern islands from south-western Kyushu to northern Honshu, finally reaching Hokkaido c.6500 BC. This style of cord-marked 'Jomon' pottery was manufactured in the Japanese islands for over 10,000 years. Tools were also made during this period, with a predominance of chipped stone adzes and axes, grinding stones and querns in the inland and western forested areas, and specialised fishing tackle including harpoons, fish-hooks, projectile points and net-sinkers throughout the riverine and coastal regions.

Hunting, fishing and gathering was a way of life in Japan for several thousand years. Ultimately, however, it was farming, which could support denser populations, that prevailed, and by the last few centuries BC cultivation of plants – especially rice – had become the mainstay of life throughout East and South-East Asia.

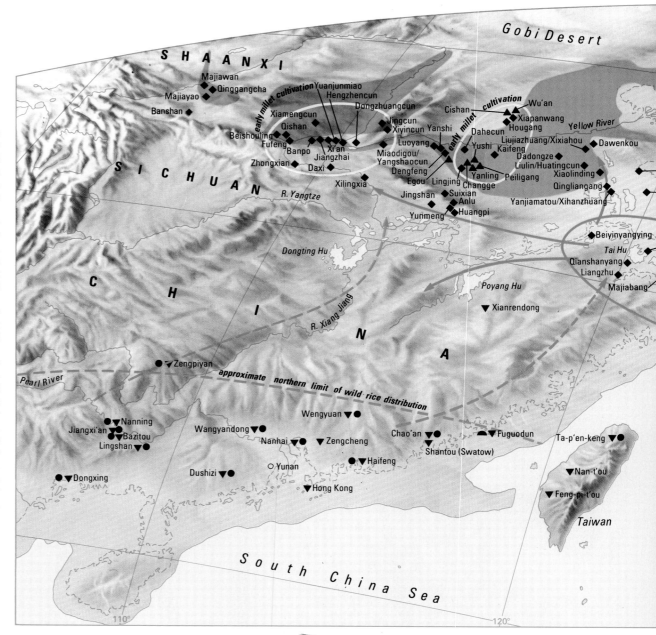

3 EARLY CRAFTS OF EAST ASIA

A *Pointed-base Jomon pot from Tatehira. Initial Jomon. c.10,500–7500 BC, height 42cm.* B *Harpoon heads from Banpo, 5th-4th millennium BC, bone, length 6.1cm.* C *Amphora with cord markings from Banpo. Yangshao culture, 5th millennium BC, height 31.7cm.*

D *Fish-hooks from Numazu shell mound, Japan. Middle Jomon, c.3000 BC, shell, height of hook on left 4.4cm, right 3.6cm.* E *Knob and lid of painted pottery vessel decorated with an image of a human face. From Banshan (Gansu). Banshan phase of the Yangshao culture, c.2500 BC, diameter 20.5cm.*

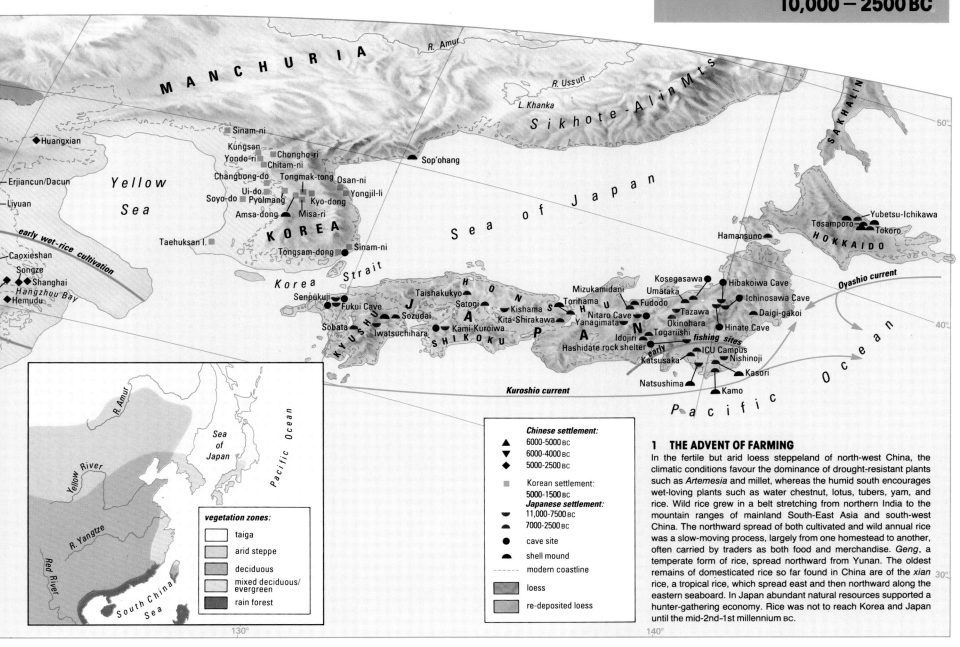

1 THE ADVENT OF FARMING

In the fertile but arid loess steppeland of north-west China, the climatic conditions favour the dominance of drought-resistant plants such as *Artemesia* and millet, whereas the humid south encourages wet-loving plants such as water chestnut, lotus, tubers, yam, and rice. Wild rice grew in a belt stretching from northern India to the mountain ranges of mainland South-East Asia and south-west China. The northward spread of both cultivated and wild annual rice was a slow-moving process, largely from one homestead to another, often carried by traders as both food and merchandise. *Geng*, a temperate form of rice, spread northward from Yunan. The oldest remains of domesticated rice so far found in China are of the *xian* rice, a tropical rice, which spread east and then northward along the eastern seaboard. In Japan abundant natural resources supported a hunter-gathering economy. Rice was not to reach Korea and Japan until the mid-2nd-1st millennium BC.

2 BANPO: A CHINESE FARMING VILLAGE

Banpo is situated near the River Zhuan in northern China. The village was probably used for several separate occupations. Agriculture followed a shifting pattern, known as swidden, where the land is left fallow for a long period after cultivation. Pollen data (*below*) indicates two distinct phases when land was cleared and planted. The houses were square, oblong or round, with plastered floors. They were either semi-subterranean or built on ground level with wattle-and-daub foundations, and their roofs and upper walls were supported by wooden posts. During a later phase of occupation, a large communal longhouse was built in the village centre. Beyond the ditch which surrounds the village lay a pottery-making centre with six kilns, anticipating the later creation of separate workshop areas. Next to this lay the village cemetery which contained only adult burials. Children were buried in pottery urns between the houses.

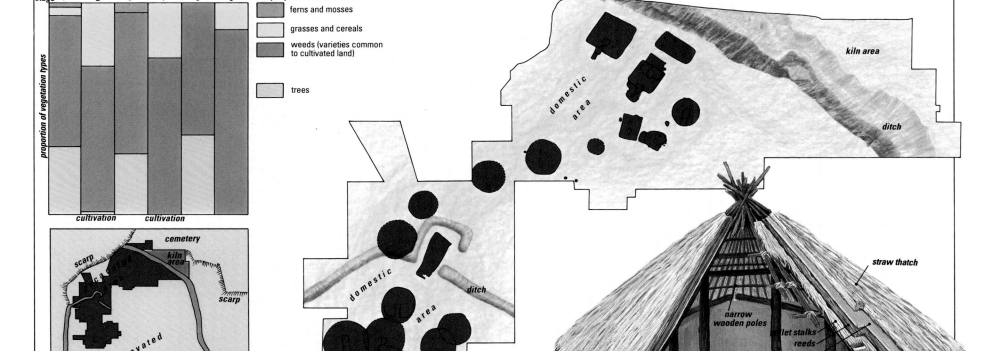

Africa: hunters and herders

Africa, unlike Europe, Asia and North America, was not affected by ice sheets during glacial periods, nor did it suffer the extreme cold experienced at more northerly latitudes. Instead, Ice Age Africa was a dry continent, since much of the Earth's water was frozen in the ice sheets, leaving less available to fall as rain. At the height of the last Ice Age (20,000 BC–10,000 BC), much of the Sahara was much drier even than today, and completely hostile to human settlement. As the ice sheets retreated in more northerly latitudes, however, conditions in the Sahara improved, lakes appeared in many places, and around 9000 BC human groups were able to move back into the area. For the following 5000 years the Sahara experienced lengthy periods with a rainfall slightly higher than that of the present, allowing Mediterranean-type woodland to develop in upland regions, and grasslands to spread along the Saharan fringes and around the central massifs. These improved conditions attracted wildlife from neighbouring areas, and elephant, lion, rhinoceros and even hippopotamus were to be found in some places.

The effects of postglacial climatic changes were not limited to North Africa but were felt, in one form or another, throughout the whole continent. The development of a more sophisticated stone tool technology, based on the production of small blades or microliths only a centimetre or two in length, played a crucial part in the response of human communities to environmental changes. The ubiquity of microliths indicates that they could be used in a range of tools for a wide variety of purposes. Mounted in a handle of bone or wood, they could make an effective sickle for the harvesting of wild grasses. Others were fixed as the points and barbs of arrows, and in some cases traces of the mastic, an aromatic resin obtained from the mastic tree, and used to hold the microliths in place, have survived. Highly adaptable, the microlith played an important part in the development of postglacial communities, not only in Africa, but also in Europe and parts of Asia.

The appearance of sites with microliths marks the first postglacial colonisation of the Sahara in about 8500 BC. They were probably the temporary encampments of hunting and gathering communities spreading into the desert from the Mediterranean coastlands and from the savanna to the south. Within a short time a series of more permanent settlements became established around the lakes and rivers of the central Saharan massifs and in a wide band along its southern fringe from the River Niger to the Kenya Rift Valley. These settlements were occupied by people who hunted with bone harpoons and used shell fish-hooks. They lived on fish, crocodile and hippopotamus. Around 7000 BC they began to manufacture pottery, decorated with a distinctive 'wavy-line' pattern made by dragging a catfish spine across the surface of the wet clay. The introduction of pottery, too fragile and heavy to be carried, reflects the more permanent nature of the settlements at this period. This type of pottery was probably first produced in the central Sahara, but soon spread westwards to the River Niger and eastwards to the Nile and the Rift Valley. The distribution of wavy-line pottery is closely matched by that of the Nilo-Saharan language group today, suggesting that Nilo-Saharan speakers are the linguistic descendants of the fishing peoples of the early postglacial period.

Together with fishing in the lakes and rivers the early settlers of the Sahara also hunted local fauna and collected plant foods – dry grasslands are the natural habitat of many cereals. By the end of the 7th millennium BC there is evidence that sorghum and millet may already have been domesticated in these areas, while barley was introduced to the eastern Sahara from western Asia. Attempts were also made to domesticate some of the local wild fauna, but only in the case of cattle does this seem to have met with success. Bones of domestic cattle dated to 6500–4000 BC have been found at several Saharan sites, and they also figure prominently in the contemporary rock art of the region. Saharan rock art gives a vivid picture of the range of wild animals to be seen in the region at this time – elephant, rhinoceros, hippopotamus, giraffe – while the frequent portrayal, after 6000 BC, of domestic cattle reflects the transition which was being made during this period towards pastoralism.

Lake Chad reached its fullest postglacial extent in about 4000 BC, but these more temperate conditions were not to last, and soon the inexorable process of desiccation began. As the lakes dried up and the grasslands withered, human communities withdrew to more hospitable areas, leaving only their tools and rock art as testimony to the less harsh Sahara of the early postglacial period.

2 THE ROCK ART OF THE SAHARA

The hunters of the Sahara during the early postglacial period were the creators of a prolific rock art. The earliest phase (c.8500 BC) consisted exclusively of representations of wild animals – the now extinct *Bubalus antiquus* (a large African buffalo), giraffe, elephant, rhinoceros and hippopotamus. In c.6000 BC herds of domestic cattle began to be portrayed with increasing frequency, supplanting the hunting scenes and wild animals. The art illustrates experiments made at about this time in taming and domesticating other Saharan species, such as the giraffes, though none of these achieved lasting success. With drier conditions after 3000 BC many species gradually disappeared from the rock art as they became extinct, and new animals more suited to desert conditions, notably the camel, were depicted.

Giraffe rock painting (below) from Jabbaren, 6000–4000 BC. Tassili fresco (right) from Tissoukaï, 6000–4000 BC.

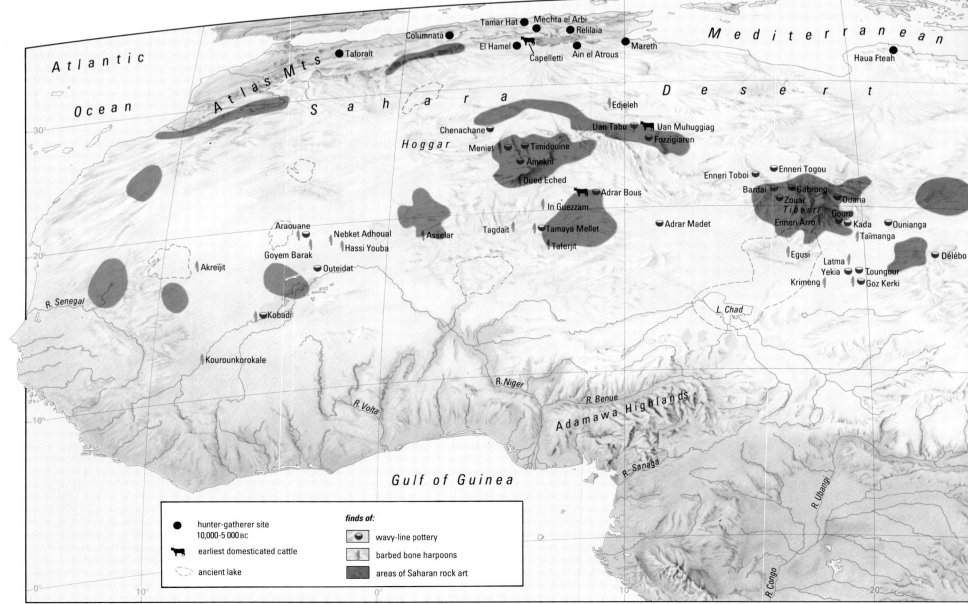

hunter-gatherer site
10,000–5 000 BC

earliest domesticated cattle

ancient lake

finds of:

wavy-line pottery

barbed bone harpoons

areas of Saharan rock art

94

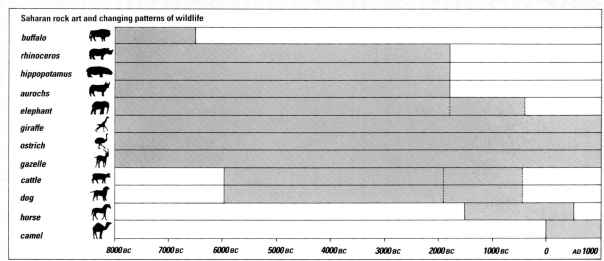

Saharan rock art and changing patterns of wildlife

- buffalo
- rhinoceros
- hippopotamus
- aurochs
- elephant
- giraffe
- ostrich
- gazelle
- cattle
- dog
- horse
- camel

8000 BC 7000 BC 6000 BC 5000 BC 4000 BC 3000 BC 2000 BC 1000 BC 0 AD 1000

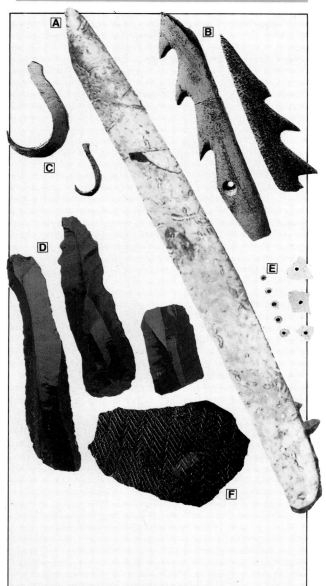

3   TOOLS OF HUNTING AND GATHERING

A Reaping knife with microliths set in grooved bone shaft from Columnata, Algeria, probably used for harvesting wild grasses and cereals. Only three of the original microlithic blades of flint remain in place. 6th millennium BC, length 21.15cm. **B** Barbed harpoons from Esh Shaheinab, Sudan. Harpoon on left has perforation for attachment of the line. c.4400 BC, bone, length of longer harpoon c.12.3cm. **C** Fish-hooks from Esh Shaheinab. c.4400 BC, shell, length of larger example c.4.9cm. **D** Obsidian tools from Gamble's Cave, Kenya. Tools of this general type were in use in the Rift Valley area of East Africa from c.10,000 BC to at least the end of the 1st millennium AD. Length of longest tool c.10.5cm. **E** Ostrich egg-shell beads, found throughout East Africa, and usually associated with hunter-gatherers. The earliest examples date to 3500 BC. Average 4mm. **F** Potsherd from Early Khartoum, Sudan, with characteristic wavy-line decoration, produced by dragging a catfish spine over the surface of the wet clay. This is the earliest type of pottery found in Africa and predates the introduction of farming. 8th–7th millennium BC.

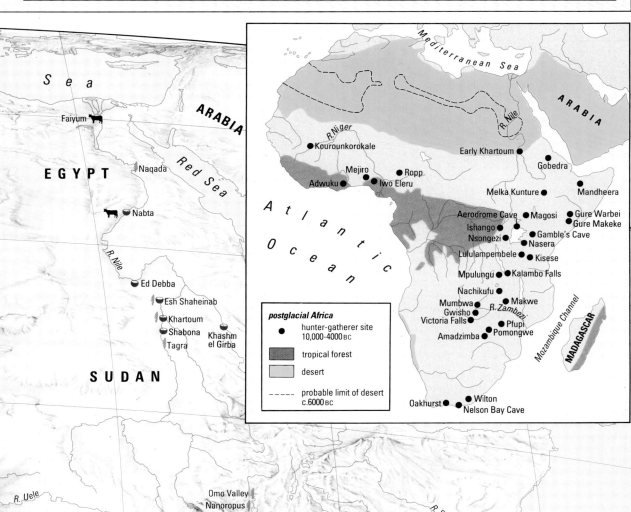

postglacial Africa
- ● hunter-gatherer site 10,000-4000 BC
- tropical forest
- desert
- - - - probable limit of desert c.6000 BC

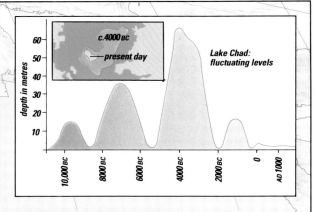

c.4000 BC
→ *present day*

Lake Chad: fluctuating levels

depth in metres

10,000 BC 8000 BC 6000 BC 4000 BC 2000 BC 0 AD 1000

1   THE SAHARA AFTER THE ICE

For much of the postglacial period the Sahara benefited from more moist climatic conditions than at present, and the area of full desert was significantly smaller than today. On the central Saharan massifs, Mediterranean-type woodland became established, and lakes and grassland formed on the lower ground around their edges. These changes in environment are reflected in the fluctuating level of Lake Chad. This lake disappeared completely about 20,000 BC because of the aridity of the tropical latitudes at the height of the last Ice Age. In about 11,000 BC the lake re-formed and, fed by rainwater from the Tibesti massif, it grew eventually to over one million square kilometres in area, several times its present size. The pattern of lake levels shows that the wetter periods alternated with dry interludes, and after 4000 BC there was a rapid fall in level, indicating the onset of the desiccation which has resulted in the arid Sahara of today.

Aboriginal Australia

When Captain Cook sailed into Botany Bay in 1770, the Australian continent was occupied by nearly half a million Aborigines whose ancestors had arrived more than 30,000 years previously. They lived as hunters and gatherers, although the richness of their ritual life, the complexity of their social organisation and the diversity and skill of their subsistence economy, as recorded at the time of European contact, are all the more remarkable for the capricious and often inhospitable environments in which they flourished. Their culture was not static: the expansion of population, the development of new technologies, and the more intensive use of food resources and raw materials, can be plotted in the preceding millennia, along with the development of more complex and diverse patterns of social and ceremonial organisation and the extension of exchange networks across the full length and breadth of the continent.

The rise of sea level from its maximum lowering 18,000 years ago must have had a dramatic impact on the geography of settlement. By 7000 years ago extensive coastal plains had been flooded, Australia severed from New Guinea, and the population of Tasmania isolated beyond the reach of the mainland. By 5000 years ago the sea level had stabilised to create a rich inshore environment of estuaries, shallow lagoons and rock platforms with abundant marine food. Shell middens representing the rubbish accumulated at coastal camps and settlements are common from this time onwards. In the interior of the continent the drying out of lakes had by the end of the Pleistocene, about 10,000 years ago, already resulted in a concentration of settlement along the major rivers. In these areas seeds of wild millet were harvested in large quantities and processed with grinding stones. Subsequently occupation extended into the most extreme environments of the desert interior and the mountains of the south-east.

About 5000 years ago new types of hafted stone tools were introduced. Although the Australians were burying their dead as early as 25,000 years ago, by this period both inhumation and cremation were more widespread. Rock art also became more common. The dingo was introduced to Australia at this time, and as its nearest relative is the pariah dog of India, its introduction is clear evidence for contact between Australia and the mainland of South-East Asia.

From about 3000 years ago long-distance exchange networks developed in raw materials and ornaments. There was greater regional diversity in styles of material culture, and increased population density in some areas, with settled villages of up to 700 people, living in round stone houses, in the most productive areas such as the swamp regions of inland Victoria. Ritual life was centred on ceremonial gatherings, on sacred sites, such as the painted rock shelters associated with the concept of dreamtime – a mythical golden age of the past – and on the use of bora grounds – stone arrangements used for religious ceremonies. Hundreds of people drawn from large areas would gather together for short periods, and the ceremonies were often associated with the harvest of special foods such as the cycad nut, which needs elaborate preparation by soaking or fermentation to remove the poison, and the bogong moth, which can be found in large numbers in the Snowy Mountains at certain seasons.

By the time of European contact the Aborigines had successfully occupied every available environmental niche, ranging from small nomadic groups moving over hundreds of thousands of square kilometres in the desert interior to permanent villages in the richer areas, and from the tropical estuaries and offshore islands of the north to the snow-covered mountains of the south-east. Their diet encompassed every conceivable item of plant and animal food, from the witchetty grub to the dugong, and the poisonous cycad nut to the kangaroo, from oysters and turtle eggs to the roots of daisy yams, from fish caught by line, spear or net to flying foxes and bogong moths. A detailed knowledge of the environment extended to simple measures for increasing the natural harvest; simple stone constructions were built for trapping fish on sea coasts, and canals were dug to concentrate eels in inland swamps. Occasionally grass seeds and root cuttings were replanted, and fire was used to open up the landscape to fresh growth of grasses and shrubs. Absence of agriculture was due not to the lack of knowledge or of potential plant cultigens, but most likely to lack of incentive to invest in crop cultivation in one of the world's most erratic rainfall regimes. Artificial harvests would have been scarcely more abundant or more predictable than those of nature.

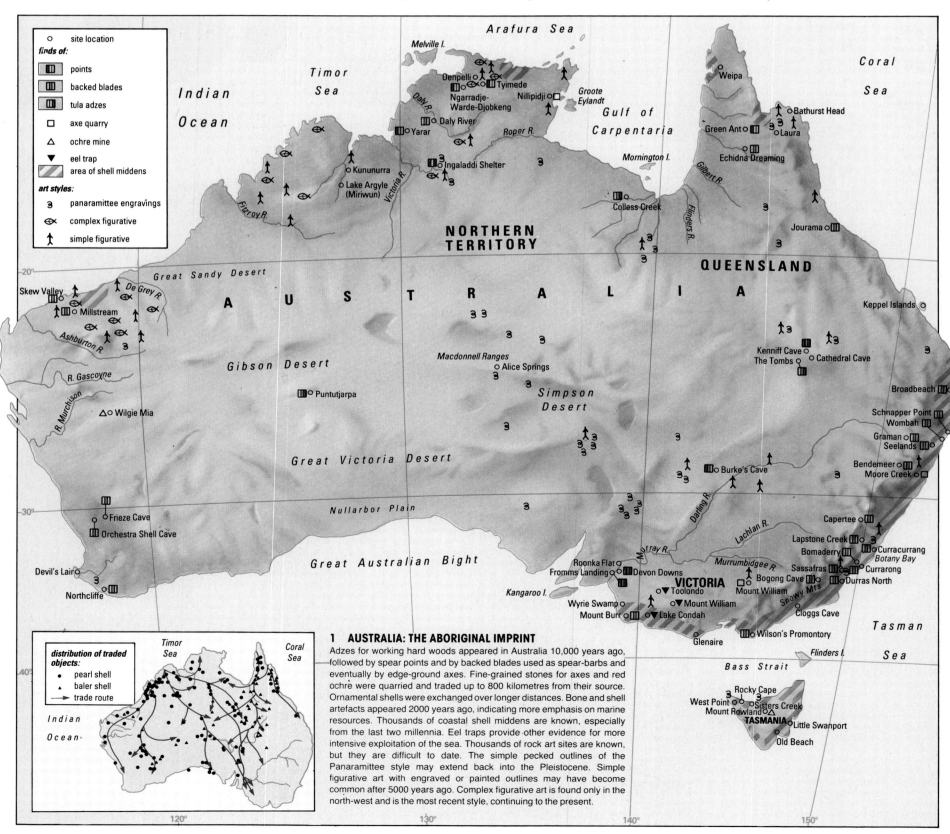

1 AUSTRALIA: THE ABORIGINAL IMPRINT

Adzes for working hard woods appeared in Australia 10,000 years ago, followed by spear points and by backed blades used as spear-barbs and eventually by edge-ground axes. Fine-grained stones for axes and red ochre were quarried and traded up to 800 kilometres from their source. Ornamental shells were exchanged over longer distances. Bone and shell artefacts appeared 2000 years ago, indicating more emphasis on marine resources. Thousands of coastal shell middens are known, especially from the last two millennia. Eel traps provide other evidence for more intensive exploitation of the sea. Thousands of rock art sites are known, but they are difficult to date. The simple pecked outlines of the Panaramitee style may extend back into the Pleistocene. Simple figurative art with engraved or painted outlines may have become common after 5000 years ago. Complex figurative art is found only in the north-west and is the most recent style, continuing to the present.

3 ART AND ARTEFACTS

A Perforated pearl shell from north-west Australia with incised geometric designs, worn as a pubic ornament. Length 17.5cm. **B** Rock painting of Wandjina spirit beings, from north-west Australia, discovered in 1837, reconstruction. Height 156cm. **C** Bark painting in X-ray style of a Kakadu hunter spearing a crane, from the Northern Territory, discovered 1912, height 1.68m. **D** Trident fish spears collected by Captain Cook in AD 1770. The points at the ends are made of fish spines or marsupial bones held together with grass fibre and resin. Length of prong c.60cm. **E** Ground-edge axe made of greenstone from the Mount William quarry, Victoria. Holocene era from 8000 BC, length c.4cm. **F** Stone spear pirri point found in one of the graves at Roonka Flat. 3000–4000 BC, chert, length 6.5cm. **G** Shell middens on the east bank of the Hey River, near Weipa in Queensland. The mounds are up to 9 metres high and were used for hundreds of years.

2 ROONKA FLAT: AN AUSTRALIAN BURIAL SITE

The Roonka Flat Dune is a low mound of wind-blown sands in a bend of the lower Murray River. It is named after the roongko grub, a food delicacy found in the rotting timbers of gum trees. The arrival of Europeans in the mid-19th century initiated progressive tree clearance of the surrounding area, partial erosion of the dune, and subsequent exposure of the archaeological remains. People first camped there at least 18,000 years ago, but did not bury their dead there until later. The earliest burials are a distinctive series of 12 graves dated to the period between 7000 and 4000 years ago. The bodies were placed vertically in a shaft-hole and accompanied by pendant ornaments of drilled oyster shell and bone. There is evidence that some of the bones of the buried skeletons were rearranged, suggesting that the graves were reopened or revisited at a later date as part of the burial rite. One body was found with a bone dagger 29 centimetres long, apparently used to prise open the rib-cage. From the later period, after 4000 years ago, there are 70 burials, indicating a change in burial practices. The bodies of mature adults were fully extended or contracted, and graves contained food offerings, bone awls and bodkins or stone artefacts. Some individuals were buried in elaborate clothing and jewellery and accompanied by an infant, suggesting a differentiation in social status.

A Grave 108 at Roonka Flat contained the partially contracted skeleton of an adult male and a child. The man was buried in a cloak of animal skins pinned at the shoulder, with a fringe of bird feathers. The child wore a bone pendant and necklace and had traces of ochre staining on the feet. c. 200 BC. **B** Around the skull of the adult in grave 108 was a headband with two rows of carefully matched and notched wallaby incisor teeth, and a second similar headband lay nearby.

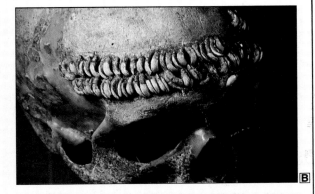

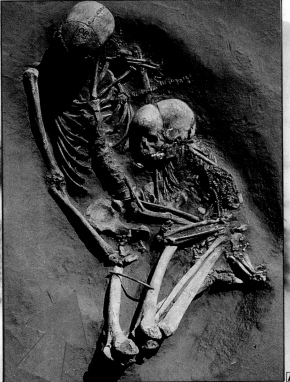

Mesopotamia: towards civilisation

The arrival of farming in the fertile lowlands of Mesopotamia transformed human society, demonstrating for the first time the revolutionary potential of the agricultural way of life. During the 7th millennium, farming villages, hitherto confined to the Zagros Mountains, began to appear on the rain-fed north Mesopotamian plain. Within a few centuries the development of irrigation allowed settlement to spread into central Mesopotamia, ultimately reaching the rich alluvial lands of the south, where the first cities were eventually to emerge. The expansion of farming settlement is reflected in a sequence of prehistoric cultures, each characterised by a distinctive pottery style: Hassuna, Samarra, Halaf and 'Ubaid.

The earliest of these cultures, Hassuna (6000–5500 BC), was centred on northern Mesopotamia. Subsistence was based on cereal crops – emmer, einkorn, two-rowed hulled barley – and domestic sheep, goats, cattle and pigs, supplemented by hunting cattle, gazelle and onager. Houses, originally simple structures of sun-dried mud, gradually evolved into more spacious and sophisticated dwellings, with work and living rooms, storerooms and internal court yards. The first appearance of painted pottery, the earliest two-chambered pottery kiln, and

evidence for copper and lead smelting all demonstrate that the Hassuna culture was both innovative and technologically sophisticated. Finds of imported carnelian and turquoise beads and the first use of stamp seals – a device for indicating personal ownership – suggest that economic horizons were also widening.

The Samarran culture, partly contemporary with the Hassuna, was based in the mid-Tigris region. Many Samarran settlements are located beyond the limits of the rain-fed zone, and it was in these areas that simple irrigation techniques, essential for successful agriculture, were first developed. At Choga Mami the remains of a disused canal system and finds of irrigated hybrid crops such as six-row barley, bread wheat and large-seeded flax are the earliest evidence of irrigation so far discovered. Samarran pottery was painted in a dynamic style, depicting dancing girls with streaming hair, goats, deer, scorpions and many other animals. Highly sophisticated female figurines were also made, decorated with face paint or tattoo marks, and crowned with an elaborate coiffure.

By the mid-6th millennium BC the Halaf culture had appeared in northern Mesopotamia. Halaf was unrelated to earlier north Mesopotamian cultures, and may represent the arrival of new settlers from elsewhere. Its architecture was distinctive, characterised by domed round houses built of sun-dried clay, the largest exceeding ten metres in diameter. New burial customs are associated with the Halaf culture: many people were now buried in shaft graves (deep, narrow pits), and there is also evidence for complex cremation rites which included the ritual smashing of grave-goods and the burial of ashes in a

pot below the house floor.

The fourth of these pottery styles, the 'Ubaid, was made from about 5500 BC and remained in use for about 1500 years. It was in this period that settlements first appeared in the arid southern plains of Mesopotamia and depended on irrigation agriculture. The destructive spring floods of the River Euphrates were harnessed to provide vastly improved crop yields, which in turn sustained larger populations – Eridu may have been ten hectares in area in the 'Ubaid period, with as many as 4000 inhabitants. Larger populations brought an increased demand for raw materials which were not locally available, and trade networks expanded. At Tell Abbada small clay counters found inside pots suggest that a primitive accounting system was already in operation – out of such humble beginnings writing eventually developed. Communal religious activity was another important feature of this period. The earliest 'Ubaid temple at Eridu, a simple one-roomed shrine, had all the basic features of later Mesopotamian temples: an ornamented facade, an altar niche and an offering table.

By the end of the 'Ubaid period, after the long march of prehistory, the threshold of a new age had been reached on the plains of Mesopotamia. Settlements were larger, richer and more numerous than ever before. Society was becoming increasingly centralised and hierarchical. Craftsmanship in stone, ceramics and metal had reached new heights of sophistication, and trade networks were expanding. Impressive though they were, however, these achievements proved to be only a foretaste of the cultural explosion which was to follow: the rise of civilisation.

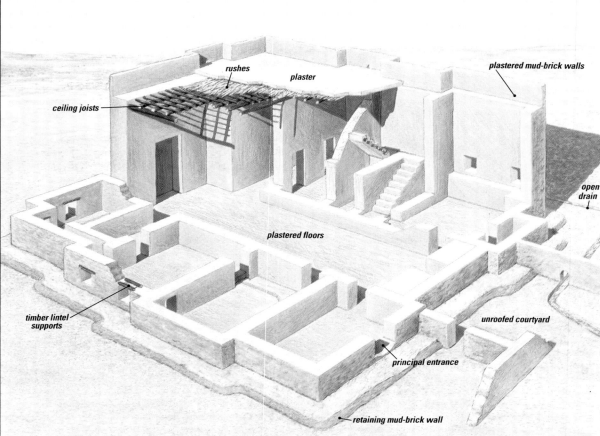

2 AN 'UBAID HOUSE

'Ubaid houses were characterised by a distinctive plan. The main part of the house consisted of a central cruciform area with an entrance hall, staircase and living rooms on either side. The house found at Tell Madhhur (above) had been destroyed by fire: the charred remains of the timbers and reed matting which made up the roof were found collapsed in the debris of destruction. The domestic utensils of the household lay where they had been abandoned 6500 years ago: painted pots, grindstones and they included hoes, and over 3800 sling bullets were scattered across the floors. Beneath the floor of one of the side-rooms the body of an infant had been buried in a pottery jar. Burial within the family living quarters was a common practice among these early settlers.

3 TELL ES-SAWWAN: A SAMARRAN VILLAGE

Tell es-Sawwan lies on a bluff above the left bank of the Tigris. There were three levels of occupation between the 6th and 5th millennia BC. The earliest houses of level I were protected by a rectangular ditch, which was soon built over as the village expanded. By level III there were more elaborate fortifications – a buttressed wall and ditch. Many houses were T-shaped with up to 14 rooms, separated by streets and courtyards. With the aid of simple irrigation techniques the villagers cultivated wheat, barley and flax, herded sheep and goat, fished and occasionally hunted gazelle, deer and onager. Many graves were found within the settlement, containing a wealth of personal ornaments: beads of turquoise and carnelian, alabaster vessels and superbly worked alabaster figurines of standing and squatting women.

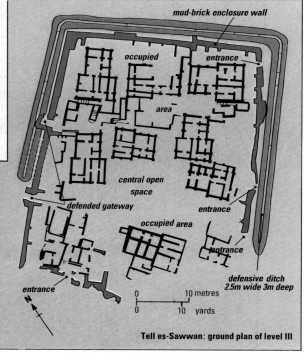

Tell es-Sawwan: ground plan of level III

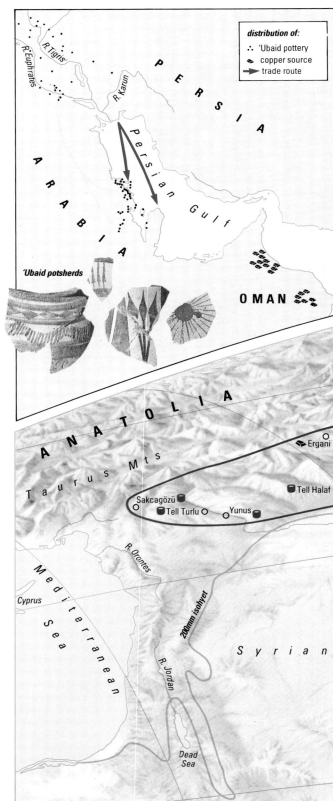

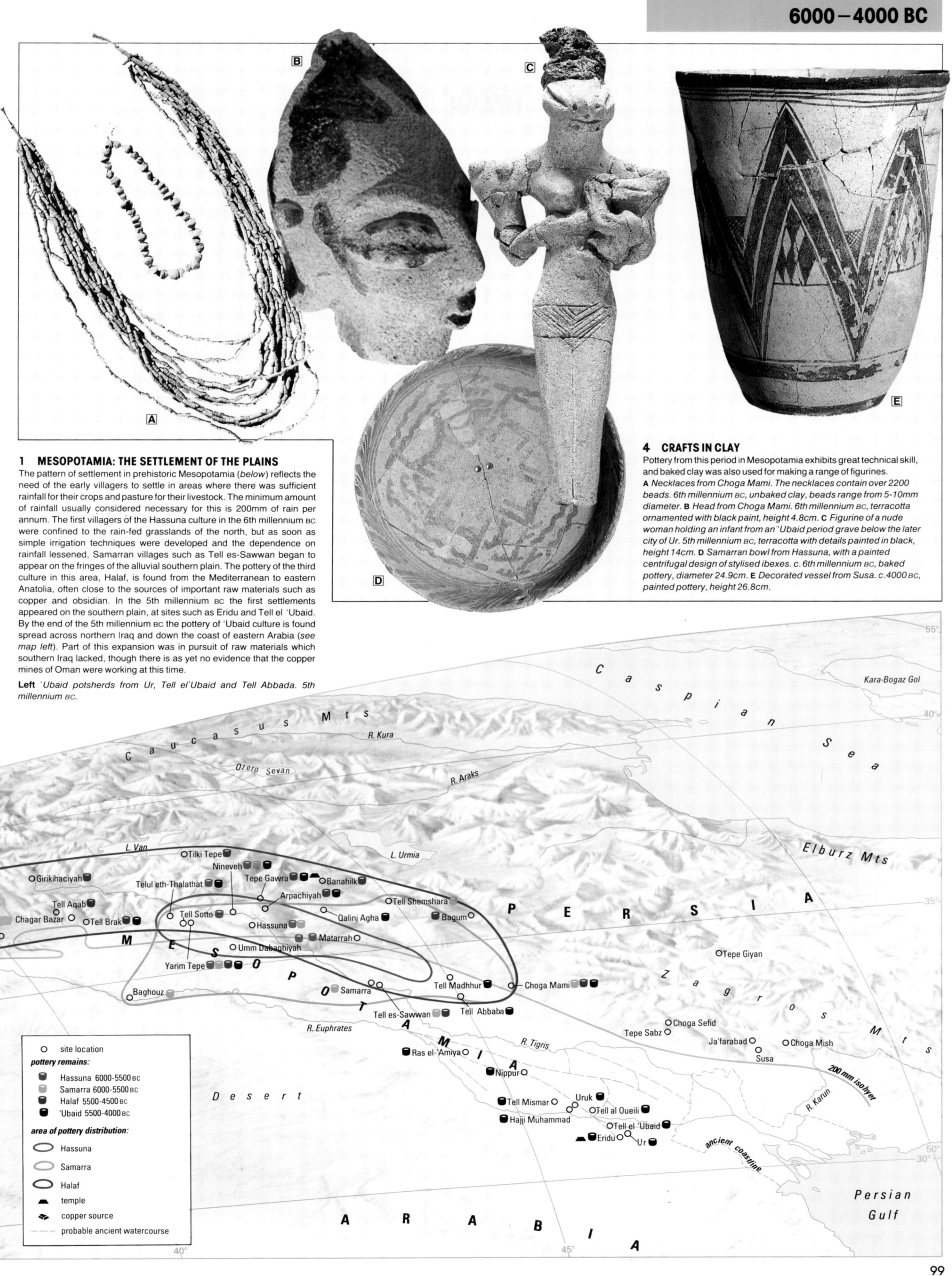

1   MESOPOTAMIA: THE SETTLEMENT OF THE PLAINS

The pattern of settlement in prehistoric Mesopotamia (*below*) reflects the need of the early villagers to settle in areas where there was sufficient rainfall for their crops and pasture for their livestock. The minimum amount of rainfall usually considered necessary for this is 200mm of rain per annum. The first villagers of the Hassuna culture in the 6th millennium BC were confined to the rain-fed grasslands of the north, but as soon as simple irrigation techniques were developed and the dependence on rainfall lessened, Samarran villages such as Tell es-Sawwan began to appear on the fringes of the alluvial southern plain. The pottery of the third culture in this area, Halaf, is found from the Mediterranean to eastern Anatolia, often close to the sources of important raw materials such as copper and obsidian. In the 5th millennium BC the first settlements appeared on the southern plain, at sites such as Eridu and Tell el 'Ubaid. By the end of the 5th millennium BC the pottery of 'Ubaid culture is found spread across northern Iraq and down the coast of eastern Arabia (*see map left*). Part of this expansion was in pursuit of raw materials which southern Iraq lacked, though there is as yet no evidence that the copper mines of Oman were working at this time.

Left 'Ubaid potsherds from Ur, Tell el'Ubaid and Tell Abbada. 5th millennium BC.

4   CRAFTS IN CLAY

Pottery from this period in Mesopotamia exhibits great technical skill, and baked clay was also used for making a range of figurines.
A *Necklaces from Choga Mami. The necklaces contain over 2200 beads. 6th millennium BC, unbaked clay, beads range from 5-10mm diameter.* **B** *Head from Choga Mami. 6th millennium BC, terracotta ornamented with black paint, height 4.8cm.* **C** *Figurine of a nude woman holding an infant from an 'Ubaid period grave below the later city of Ur. 5th millennium BC, terracotta with details painted in black, height 14cm.* **D** *Samarran bowl from Hassuna, with a painted centrifugal design of stylised ibexes. c. 6th millennium BC, baked pottery, diameter 24.9cm.* **E** *Decorated vessel from Susa. c.4000 BC, painted pottery, height 26.8cm.*

Map legend:

○ site location

pottery remains:
- Hassuna 6000-5500 BC
- Samarra 6000-5500 BC
- Halaf 5500-4500 BC
- 'Ubaid 5500-4000 BC

area of pottery distribution:
- ◯ Hassuna
- ◯ Samarra
- ◯ Halaf
- ▲ temple
- ⚒ copper source
- --- probable ancient watercourse

Map labels: Caspian Sea, Kara-Bogaz Gol, Caucasus Mts, R. Kura, Ozero Sevan, R. Araks, Elburz Mts, L. Van, L. Urmia, Tilki Tepe, Nineveh, Tepe Gawra, Banahilk, Girikihaciyah, Telul eth-Thalathat, Arpachiyah, Tell Shemshara, Tell Aqab, Tell Sotto, Qalinj Agha, Bagum, Chagar Bazar, Tell Brak, Hassuna, Matarrah, Umm Dabaghiyah, Yarim Tepe, Tepe Giyan, Baghouz, Samarra, Tell Madhhur, Choga Mami, Tell es-Sawwan, Tell Abbada, Tepe Sabz, Choga Sefid, Ja'farabad, Choga Mish, Ras el-'Amiya, Susa, R. Tigris, Nippur, R. Euphrates, Tell Mismar, Uruk, Tell al Oueili, Hajji Muhammad, Tell el 'Ubaid, Eridu, Ur, R. Karun, 200 mm isohyet, ancient coastline, Desert, MESOPOTAMIA, PERSIA, ZAGROS Mts, ARABIA, Persian Gulf

Ceramics: the mastery of clay

Pottery-making, one of the oldest crafts known to man, was invented independently in different parts of the world at different times. The earliest known pottery comes from Japan, and is dated to about 10,500 BC; China and Indo-China follow shortly afterwards. The earliest dates in the Indian subcontinent fall in the 6th millennium BC. In the western Old World, pottery first appears in the 8th millennium BC in Africa and the Near East, and in southern Europe a thousand years later. In the Americas, pottery was a still later, but completely independent development: c.4000 BC on the coast of Guyana, and about 2000 BC in Peru and Mesoamerica. Since pottery is both heavy and fragile, and therefore unsuitable for mobile hunter-gatherer people, its introduction always coincides with the beginnings of settled life.

The earliest pottery was probably made by the 'coiling' technique (fashioning the pot by hand from a lump or strips of moist clay). Once the vessel was complete, the wall could be smoothed, and decorated with incised or painted designs. The pots were then fired, probably only briefly, in an open fire. Such a simple technique would have been accessible to almost all members of society, demanding no specialist skills, tools, or selection and preparation of the clay. Thus almost everybody would have been able to make their own pots at this stage.

Another early technique was the moulding of relatively stiff clay by beating it into shape using a 'hammer' or 'paddle' on the outside against an 'anvil', a round stone held inside the pot. A third basic technique was the use of a mould, around or within which the pot could be shaped. This could be a basket, a fishnet, or a mould of pottery, stone or wood. The use of pottery moulds was very widespread, and they have remained in common use until very recently. With the passage of time, a number of other techniques were invented for the shaping and firing of ceramics, including moulds, *tournettes*, wheels and kilns. Where these techniques were adopted, pottery-making usually became a specialist occupation, with a few potters supplying the needs of whole populations.

It is not always possible to determine precisely where these innovations were first used. In Mesopotamia,

Egypt, China and the Indus Valley, the pivoted *tournette* appeared relatively early, around the middle of the 4th millennium BC. The *tournette* was a small wheel which improved pottery-making but did not rotate with sufficient speed to make full use of the centrifugal forces which were harnessed by the later fast wheel. The *tournette* facilitated the rapid production of large numbers of identical pots, found all across the Near and Middle East from Persia to northern Mesopotamia. This development led to the innovation of the 'true' potter's wheel or fast wheel, where the centrifugal force of the wheel is balanced by pressure of the potter's fingers on the clay.

In the New World, the pivot was never introduced. Here the only form of rotating device until recent times was the *kabal*, a wooden cylinder which was turned between the feet while the potter shaped the pottery with his hands. Potters in the Americas, however, made extensive use of moulds in shaping their vessels. In this way they achieved both speed and standardisation of production. The 'vertical' mould, where the parts of the mould join along the vertical axis of the vessel, seems to have been an exclusively New World invention.

Remains of potters' kilns are virtually unknown outside Eurasia. Firing elsewhere must often have been done in the open air – it is possible to achieve temperatures of 800–900°C by this method. Open-air firing must have been (indeed still is) adequate for common types of earthenware pottery in most parts of the world. It was probably the availability of special clays, such as kaolin, that led to experiments with high firing temperatures (1000°C and more) in the Far East. Reaching these temperatures required well-designed kilns, and led to the manufacture of porcelain, and the discovery of glaze. When firing to such temperatures, the pores in the clay fill up with molten paste, and the resulting product is watertight. In Egypt, the Near East and much of the Indian subcontinent, kilns were also used at an early date, but in general the firing temperatures were lower because most clays could not stand high temperatures.

Pottery is one of the most common archaeological finds, and the study of pottery types found at sites is one of the most basic ways of establishing when a settlement was occupied and for how long. The full significance of pottery goes far beyond this, however, and enables us to chart both the progress of technological change over thousands of years, and the role of new skills and their products in the development of early societies.

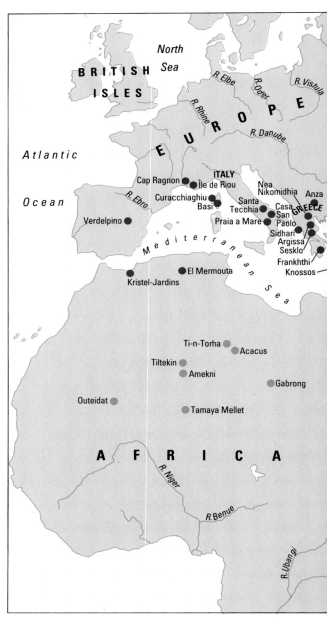

Coil technique: stages of shaping procedure

2 POTTERY: SHAPING AND FIRING

Coiling is one of the simplest ways of making a pot: the base is moulded by hand from a lump of clay, or a thin roll of clay is coiled into a spiral to form the bottom of a pot. The body is then formed by rolling strips of moist clay between the hands, and stacking them on top of each other in circles or spirals (*illustation above*). Many such pots have an S-shaped profile because the first part of the pot is made with the thumbs inside, while the upper part is made with the thumbs outside. Smoothing both the interior and the exterior surface keeps the coils together and creates a surface ready for decoration. If the pot is large, construction can be made easier by standing it on a support which can turn. The better pivoted such a support, the heavier the pot can be, creating momentum and freeing one of the potter's hands from continuously turning the pot. Eventually, this momentum generates enough centrifugal force to permit true 'throwing' of the pottery.

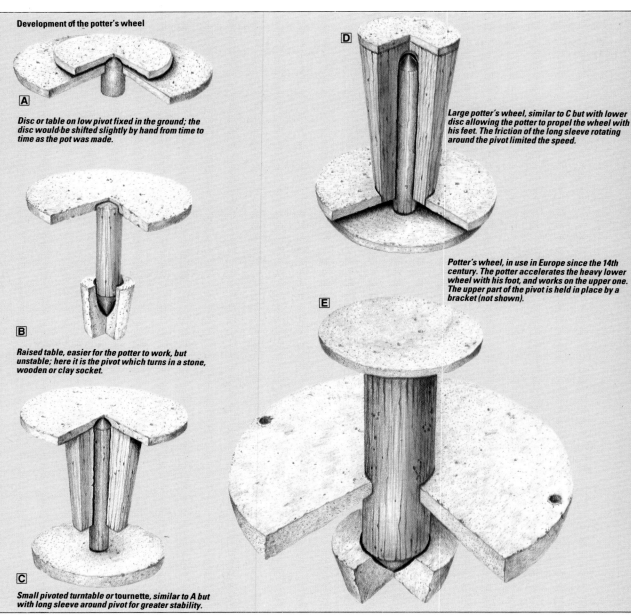

Development of the potter's wheel

A Disc or table on low pivot fixed in the ground; the disc would be shifted slightly by hand from time to time as the pot was made.

B Raised table, easier for the potter to work, but unstable; here it is the pivot which turns in a stone, wooden or clay socket.

C Small pivoted turntable or tournette, similar to A but with long sleeve around pivot for greater stability.

D Large potter's wheel, similar to C but with lower disc allowing the potter to propel the wheel with his feet. The friction of the long sleeve rotating around the pivot limited the speed.

E Potter's wheel, in use in Europe since the 14th century. The potter accelerates the heavy lower wheel with his foot, and works on the upper one. The upper part of the pivot is held in place by a bracket (not shown).

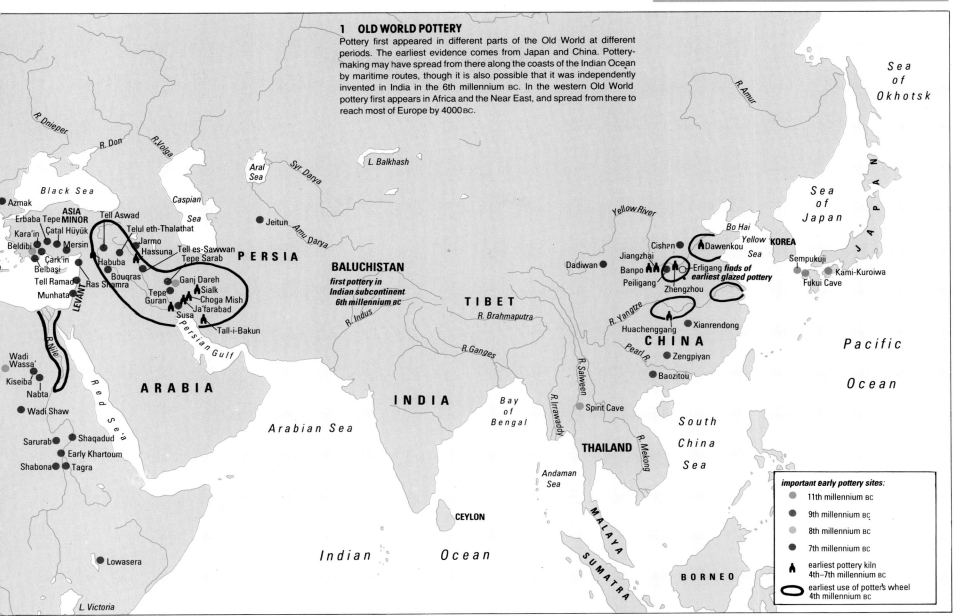

1 OLD WORLD POTTERY

Pottery first appeared in different parts of the Old World at different periods. The earliest evidence comes from Japan and China. Pottery-making may have spread from there along the coasts of the Indian Ocean by maritime routes, though it is also possible that it was independently invented in India in the 6th millennium BC. In the western Old World pottery first appears in Africa and the Near East, and spread from there to reach most of Europe by 4000 BC.

BALUCHISTAN
first pottery in Indian subcontinent 6th millennium BC

Erliang finds of earliest glazed pottery

important early pottery sites:
- 11th millennium BC
- 9th millennium BC
- 8th millennium BC
- 7th millennium BC
- ⋏ earliest pottery kiln 4th–7th millennium BC
- ⬭ earliest use of potter's wheel 4th millennium BC

Simple updraught kiln from Banpo, China c. 4500 BC

baked earth
baking floor
kiln chamber
ceramic grate
flue
wattle and daub
firing chamber
fire

Pottery kilns are usually dug out of the ground or built of clay. In the illustration (*above*) the kiln consists of two chambers, a firing chamber and a chamber in which the pottery is stacked. The draught generated raises the temperature of the fire to that necessary for firing the pots. The potter probably covered the upper chamber with potsherds from earlier firings after stacking his pots inside to keep the hot air around the pots for as long as possible. In the absence of a fixed roof over the kiln and a flue, the temperatures cannot have reached much more than 800–900°C without using an inordinate amount of fuel. Once such a roof was invented, the distribution of the heat in the kiln would be the potter's next worry. If the distribution was uneven, a part of each kiln would either be underfired or overfired. Modifications in the placing of the fire, the flow of hot air, the location of the flue and the shape of the kiln can all create particular firing characteristics.

3 THE DEVELOPMENT OF POTTERY

A *Round-based pot from Nasunahara, Japan, with linear relief decoration; one of the earliest known pottery vessels. Incipient Jomon, 11th–9th millennium BC, height 23.5cm.* B *Potter's wheel from Lachish, Israel. 2200 BC, diameter 75cm.* C *Limestone statuette of woman working a pot on a disc or tournette, from Egypt. New Kingdom period, late 2nd millennium BC, length 11cm.* D *Glazed vessel with angular profile from Mingkunglu, Zhengzhou, China; one of the oldest known glazed vessels. Shang period, 16th–15th century BC, height 28.2cm.*

FOUR
THE FIRST CITIES AND STATES
4000 – 1000 BC

6000 YEARS ago agricultural communities flourished throughout much of Eurasia. Agriculture was able to support increasingly large groups of people, and over the next three millennia this led to new forms of political and social organisation. Societies became more hierarchical, the leaders buried with marks of their special status ranging from the modest treasures of the richer graves in the Tiszapolgár cemetery to the splendour of the Egyptian pyramids. Craftsmanship thrived in this new social milieu. Greater sophistication was shown in the working of traditional materials such as wood and stone, and many new materials came into use – gold, copper and its alloy bronze, lacquer and semi-precious stones such as lapis, turquoise and jade. But it was with the development of advanced techniques of processing these materials – the smelting and casting of metals, the blending of alloys and glazing of pottery, that the period came to maturity. The application of new technologies in the development of wheeled vehicles, the sailing ship, the irrigation of the land and the construction of monuments is clear evidence of this great advance.

In the fertile valleys of the Nile, the Tigris and the Euphrates, the Indus and the Yellow River, intensive agriculture could support very high levels of population and it is in these regions that the first cities and states were born. Great temples and other public buildings dominate many of these sites, and kings and princes were buried in large tombs with an astonishing wealth of grave offerings. The administrative demands of the growing populations led to the rise of bureaucracies and encouraged the adoption of writing. Professional priestly classes came into being to regulate relations with the gods. The growth of these wealthy cities and states stimulated the development of warfare, and important sites were provided with stronger defences. Large armies struggled for land and power, and new weaponry came into use making armed conflict ever-more deadly. This inexorable rivalry led to the creation of larger and larger states as smaller kingdoms were conquered by their more powerful neighbours, a process culminating in the great Old World empires of the 1st millennium BC.

Statue of Khafre from Egypt, depicted with the hawk-god Horus spreading its wings around the king's head. 4th dynasty. c. 2500 BC, black, white and yellow grained diorite, height 1.68m.

Agricultural intensification

By 4000 BC agriculture had become the basis of life throughout many parts of the Old World. As population levels rose, the simple farming methods used by the earliest agricultural societies came under increasing strain. The solution lay in various forms of intensification which would increase the amount of food produced.

The methods used to increase agricultural yields varied considerably depending on soils, water availability, topography and population density. In much of Asia considerable energy and ingenuity were devoted to the creation and maintenance of irrigation systems. In the Nile and Indus Valleys, the water was provided by the annual flooding of the river, or inundation, and it was necessary simply to build dykes and basins to hold back the water as the flood receded. Only later did water-lifting devices such as the *shaduf* or *sakia* come into use in Egypt. In Mesopotamia, on the other hand, the annual flood of the Tigris and Euphrates was insufficient, and costly networks of radial canals had to be constructed and maintained, involving a huge input of manpower. Indeed, the earliest known irrigation canals are in Mesopotamia, at Choga Mami, dating from around 5000 BC. Radial canal systems were also used in other parts of the Old World where aridity limited land which could be cultivated, for instance in Turkmenia, where it

enabled the early farmers to cultivate the dry lowlands on the edge of the Karakum desert.

Terraced fields are a characteristic feature of the landscape in mountainous areas such as the Peruvian Andes, the Philippines, and parts of Greece, where the slopes would normally be too steep to allow cultivation. Like irrigation, the heavy costs involved in constructing and maintaining the extensive dry-stone walls used for terracing meant that only where population was relatively dense, and pressure on land high, would terraced field systems have been a worthwhile investment. Terraced fields are often fed by irrigation systems, and the combination of the two techniques can produce high agricultural yields where seasonal drought is a problem or where water-demanding crops such as wet-rice are grown. The ultimate development of this combination was the terraced pond-fields of South-East Asia, not only irrigated but flooded to form raised paddies suitable for the cultivation of wet-rice. In the northern Philippines these pond-fields are thought to predate the Spanish occupation of the 16th century AD, and lowland paddies had been in use in China since at least 4000 BC.

Another important innovation was the increased use of animals, not only for meat but also as sources of milk, wool and traction. Farmers with herds of sheep, goat and cattle soon learned to make use of the renewable resources which live animals could provide – milk, butter and cheese, wool and hair, manure for fields, and muscle power. The use of the plough, particularly when pulled by cattle, made cultivation of open fields much more efficient and increased agricultural yields.

Irrigation, terracing and plough agriculture increased the efficiency with which food could be produced, and allowed agriculture to become established in hitherto marginal zones. But there proved to be significant drawbacks. Where populations were especially high, or where the environment was particularly vulnerable, the long-term ecological effects of the more intensive agricultural practices soon became apparent. Southern Mesopotamia, where large-scale irrigation quickly led to increasing salinity, is a notable case. Written records of the last three thousand years BC show periods of salinity coinciding with a substantial decline in crop yields and a shift from wheat to the more salt-tolerant barley. The effect was felt first, and most severely, in the south, where cultivation of wheat virtually ceased around 2000 BC. By 500 BC cereal farming in central Mesopotamia was also suffering from salination, but here the problem was less severe and there was continued agricultural expansion into the early 7th century AD. These changes in agricultural potential are mirrored by political developments; southern Babylonia was replaced as the centre of power by central and northern Babylonia at the beginning of the 2nd millennium BC.

Over the centuries agricultural intensification has transformed much of the Earth's surface, whether by obvious works of landscape engineering such as terracing and irrigation, or by the common consequences of these innovations – salination, erosion and soil exhaustion. The scale of these works – and their impact on the landscape – is an enduring testimony to the labour and ingenuity of past societies.

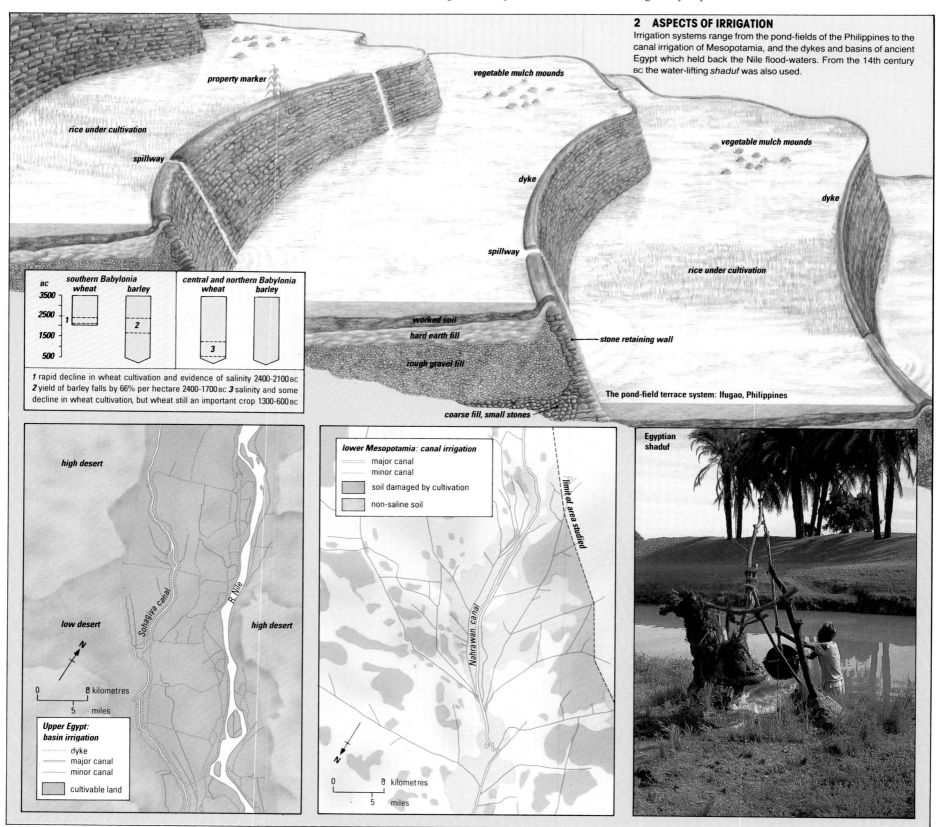

2 ASPECTS OF IRRIGATION

Irrigation systems range from the pond-fields of the Philippines to the canal irrigation of Mesopotamia, and the dykes and basins of ancient Egypt which held back the Nile flood-waters. From the 14th century BC the water-lifting *shaduf* was also used.

property marker

vegetable mulch mounds

rice under cultivation

spillway

BC	southern Babylonia		central and northern Babylonia	
	wheat	barley	wheat	barley
3500				
2500	1	2		
1500				
500			3	

1 rapid decline in wheat cultivation and evidence of salinity 2400-2100 BC
2 yield of barley falls by 66% per hectare 2400-1700 BC 3 salinity and some decline in wheat cultivation, but wheat still an important crop 1300-600 BC

vegetable mulch mounds

dyke

dyke

spillway

rice under cultivation

worked soil

hard earth fill

stone retaining wall

rough gravel fill

The pond-field terrace system: Ifugao, Philippines

coarse fill, small stones

high desert

low desert

high desert

Upper Egypt: basin irrigation
- - - - dyke
——— major canal
——— minor canal
cultivable land

R. Nile

Sohagiya canal

0   8 kilometres
0   5 miles

N

lower Mesopotamia: canal irrigation
——— major canal
——— minor canal
soil damaged by cultivation
non-saline soil

Nahrawan canal

limit of area studied

N

0   8 kilometres
0   5 miles

Egyptian shaduf

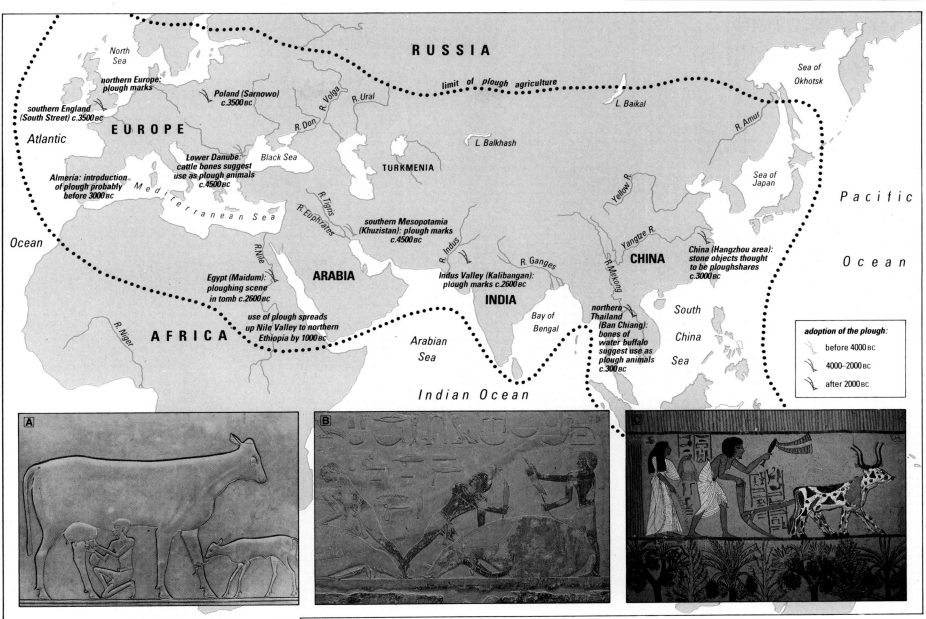

northern Europe: plough marks

Poland (Sarnowo) c.3500 BC

southern England (South Street) c.3500 BC

Almería: introduction of plough probably before 3000 BC

Lower Danube: cattle bones suggest use as plough animals c.4500 BC

southern Mesopotamia (Khuzistan): plough marks c.4500 BC

Egypt (Maidum): ploughing scene in tomb c.2600 BC

use of plough spreads up Nile Valley to northern Ethiopia by 1000 BC

Indus Valley (Kalibangan): plough marks c.2600 BC

China (Hangzhou area): stone objects thought to be ploughshares c.3000 BC

northern Thailand (Ban Chiang): bones of water buffalo suggest use as plough animals c.300 BC

limit of plough agriculture

adoption of the plough:
- before 4000 BC
- 4000–2000 BC
- after 2000 BC

North Sea · RUSSIA · Sea of Okhotsk · R. Volga · R. Ural · L. Baikal · R. Amur · EUROPE · Atlantic · R. Don · Black Sea · TURKMENIA · L. Balkhash · Sea of Japan · Pacific Ocean · Mediterranean Sea · R. Tigris · R. Euphrates · R. Nile · ARABIA · R. Indus · R. Ganges · R. Mekong · Yellow R. · Yangtze R. · CHINA · INDIA · AFRICA · R. Niger · Arabian Sea · Bay of Bengal · South China Sea · Indian Ocean

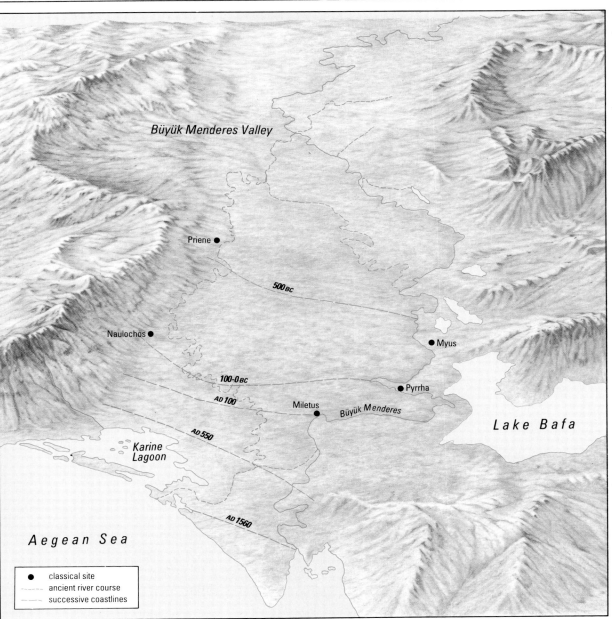

classical site
ancient river course
successive coastlines

Büyük Menderes Valley · Priene · 500 BC · Naulochos · Myus · 100-0 BC · AD 100 · Pyrrha · Miletus · Büyük Menderes · AD 550 · Karine Lagoon · Lake Bafa · AD 1560 · Aegean Sea

1 AGRICULTURE: THE POTENTIAL OF ANIMALS

The introduction of the ard or simple scratch plough made cultivation much more efficient, especially when cattle were used to pull them. No early ploughs have been preserved, but the scratch marks they made are occasionally found buried beneath later structures. Together with other evidence they enable the spread of the plough to be traced far from its origins in Mesopotamia or south-east Europe (*see map above*).

Above Wall paintings from Egyptian tombs illustrate the various uses of animals – for milk, meat and traction – in ancient agriculture.

A *Relief on sarcophagus of Queen Kawit from Deir el-Bahri, showing a man milking a cow. 2040-1991 BC.* **B** *Relief from tomb of Princess Sesh-Seshet Idut at Saqqara showing the slaughtering of an ox. 2323-2150 BC.* **C** *Wall painting from tomb of Sennedjem, Thebes, showing cattle pulling a plough. c.1300 BC.*

3 AEGEAN ANATOLIA: THE IMPACT OF SOIL EROSION

A side-effect of plough agriculture was soil erosion, caused by the clearing of the protective vegetation cover and by the annual breaking up of the ground preparatory to sowing the crop. Rainstorms then carried the loosened sediment down into neighbouring valleys, leaving only a thin and degraded soil cover on the hills. In Aegean Anatolia agriculture intensified with the growth of the Greek coastal cities during the last few centuries BC, resulting in severe soil erosion. Sediment gradually filled in the open estuaries, landlocking the cities and their harbours as the coastline moved inexorably westwards. Cut off from profitable maritime trade, and with falling agricultural yields, the cities slowly declined.

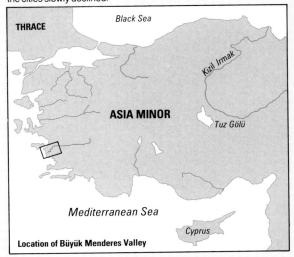

THRACE · Black Sea · Kızıl Irmak · ASIA MINOR · Tuz Gölü · Mediterranean Sea · Cyprus

Location of Büyük Menderes Valley

Europe: the megalith age

The spread of agriculture through Europe was a gradual process, and it was several millennia after the earliest farming in the Near East that the first agricultural communities appeared in north-west Europe. One reason for the delay was the need to adapt an agricultural economy originally developed in the Near East to the climate and soils of temperate Europe, while the continuing success of existing hunting and gathering ways of life made labour-intensive farming an uneconomic alternative in some areas. As population levels rose, however, communities in the fertile lowlands of western Europe turned to agriculture – a development reflected in the tombs and settlements of the early farmers.

Most of these settlements are marked today only by scatters of broken pots, flints and animal bones, with little evidence of houses or other buildings. Tell sites like those of south-east Europe and the Near East are unknown, as mud-brick was not suitable for the temperate European climate and settlements were not occupied for long enough to form mounds of occupation debris. Only in exceptional conditions has clear evidence survived: in the Alps, rising lake-levels have preserved the wooden posts and floors of rectangular houses, and at Skara Brae in the Orkneys the lack of suitable timber meant that dry-stonework was used for walls, beds and built-in cupboards.

Remains of tombs are, however, much more conspicuous than those of early farming settlements. These consisted of a dry-stone or megalithic (large stone slab) entrance passage and burial chamber, covered by a circular or elongated mound of earth or rubble. In general, the tombs were intended for repeated use, as at West Kennet (below). These barrows were burial places for groups of people rather than individuals; the communal nature of the burials and the division of labour involved in building such structures indicates a growing degree of social organisation. In some cases, the size of the mounds covering the burial chambers suggests that they may have served as temple platforms or territorial markers. On the island of Arran in Scotland, each tomb appears to be associated with a sepa-

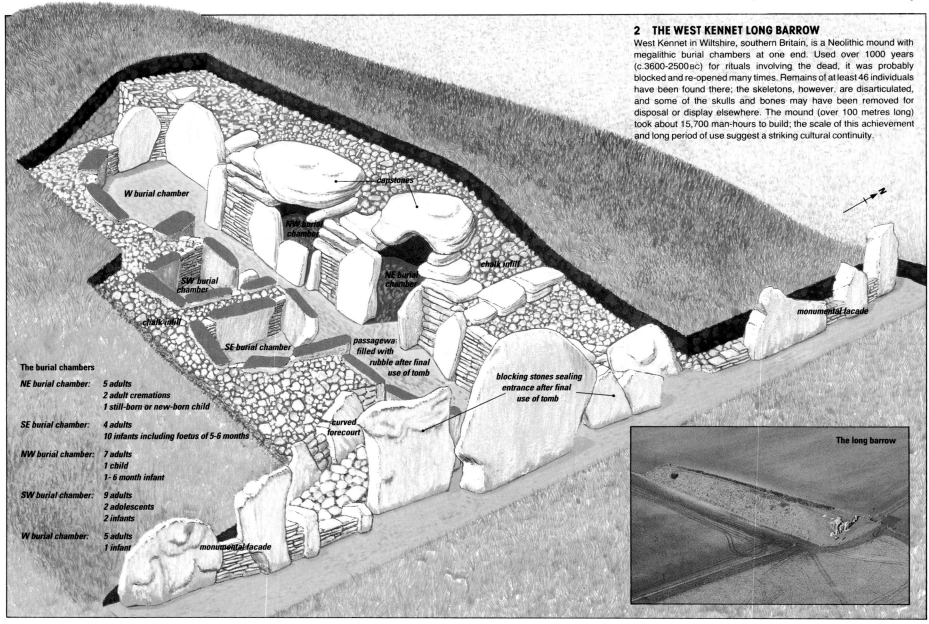

The burial chambers

NE burial chamber:
5 adults
2 adult cremations
1 still-born or new-born child

SE burial chamber:
4 adults
10 infants including foetus of 5-6 months

NW burial chamber:
7 adults
1 child
1-6 month infant

SW burial chamber:
9 adults
2 adolescents
2 infants

W burial chamber:
5 adults
1 infant

2   THE WEST KENNET LONG BARROW

West Kennet in Wiltshire, southern Britain, is a Neolithic mound with megalithic burial chambers at one end. Used over 1000 years (c.3600-2500 BC) for rituals involving the dead, it was probably blocked and re-opened many times. Remains of at least 46 individuals have been found there; the skeletons, however, are disarticulated, and some of the skulls and bones may have been removed for disposal or display elsewhere. The mound (over 100 metres long) took about 15,700 man-hours to build; the scale of this achievement and long period of use suggest a striking cultural continuity.

The long barrow

3   CRAFTS AND RITUALS

The sedentary lifestyle which developed with the establishment of farming communities saw a growth in ritual and artistic activity, and the production of a greater range and quantity of tools and household equipment.
A Bowl from ditched enclosure of Chaillot-de-la-Jard in western France. c.3250 BC, decorated pottery, height c.14.6cm. B Bowls from long barrow at Fussell's Lodge, southern Britain. c.4000 BC, pottery, left height 16.5cm, right height 11.2cm. C Stone decorated with geometric and other non-representational motifs from Newgrange megalithic tomb, eastern Ireland. c.3350 BC, c.3.5m long. D Polished axes from Staby, west Jutland, Denmark. c.3000 BC, flint, c.20-25cm. E Low-relief sculpture of (goddess?) female figure from the Razet cemetery of rock-cut tombs, north-east France. c.2500 BC, height c.45cm.

rate patch of arable land and may have been the burial place of the people farming there, serving to legitimise their descendants' rights to these patches of land.

The appearance of ditched enclosures in western Europe early in the 4th millennium BC also reflects the communal nature of Neolithic society. Small farming communities gathered into regional groupings, accompanied by the construction of defensive enclosures in western France with rock-cut ditches and out-turned entrances, and the 'causewayed camps' of southern Britain. These enclosures, with their ditches and causeways, show little evidence of permanent settlement, and were probably religious centres and communal meeting places. This process of centralisation became even more marked in southern Britain with the appearance of very large henges (ritual monuments), less

numerous than the causewayed camps, suggesting that some of the earlier ritual centres had been amalgamated into larger units. These developments culminated in southern England with the emergence of paramount centres, first Avebury, then Stonehenge (page 108), both demanding millions of man-hours to construct.

At the beginning of the 5th millennium BC most of temperate western Europe was covered by forest. However, by 3000 BC cleared agricultural land was to be found throughout western and northern Europe. Agricultural production was improved by the introduction of the ard or simple plough; ard marks have been preserved beneath some Neolithic burial mounds. Flint and hard stone were essential for axes and agricultural tools, and mine shafts were sunk to exploit rich or high-grade deposits – the mines

at Grimes Graves in Norfolk had over 360 shafts. Since sources of these commodities were rare in the agricultural lowlands, they were often traded over long distances; flint from Grand Pressigny in western France has been found in graves in the Low Countries. Contacts over wide areas between different communities are also shown by similarities in pot forms, decorations and tomb types.

Stimulated by the new agricultural economy, population levels rose and farming communities spread beyond their early centres in the fertile river valleys to the less productive uplands. As Europe reached the threshold of the Bronze Age, a marked increase in the number of defended sites suggests that competition and stress between communities were growing as the amount of new land available for colonisation diminished.

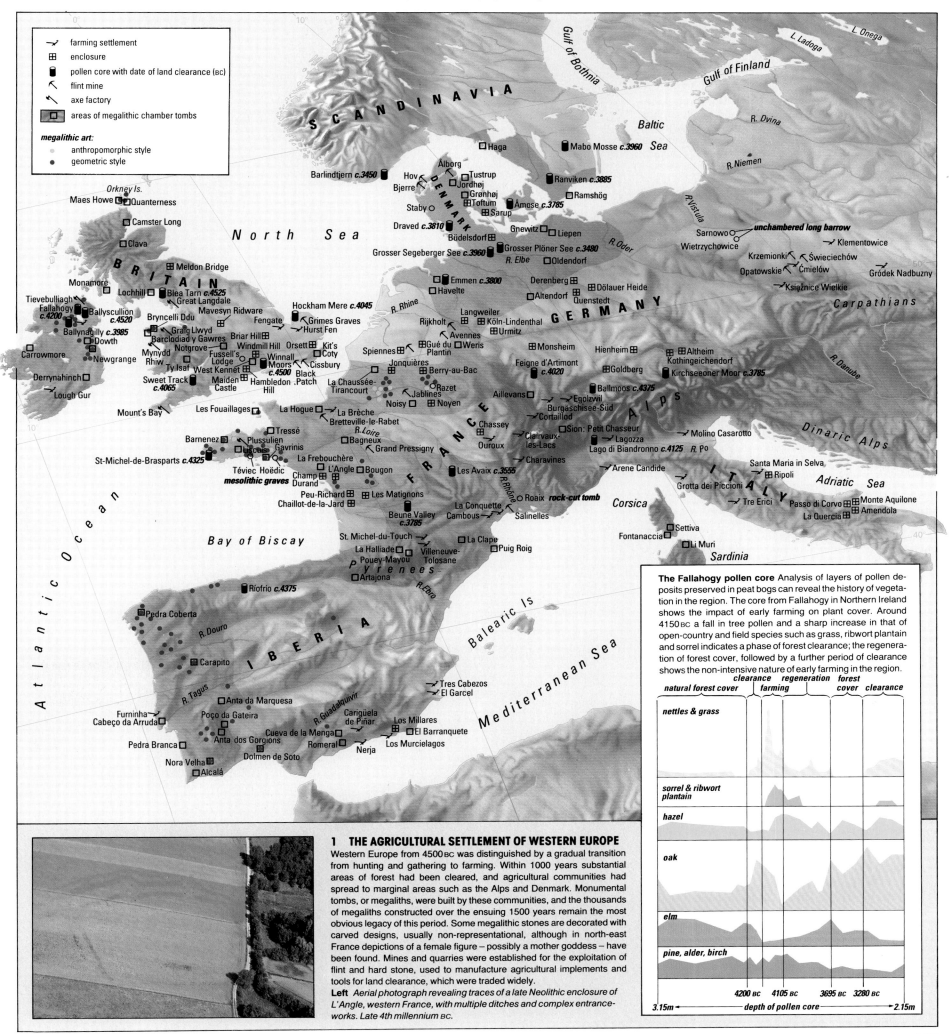

1 THE AGRICULTURAL SETTLEMENT OF WESTERN EUROPE
Western Europe from 4500 BC was distinguished by a gradual transition from hunting and gathering to farming. Within 1000 years substantial areas of forest had been cleared, and agricultural communities had spread to marginal areas such as the Alps and Denmark. Monumental tombs, or megaliths, were built by these communities, and the thousands of megaliths constructed over the ensuing 1500 years remain the most obvious legacy of this period. Some megalithic stones are decorated with carved designs, usually non-representational, although in north-east France depictions of a female figure – possibly a mother goddess – have been found. Mines and quarries were established for the exploitation of flint and hard stone, used to manufacture agricultural implements and tools for land clearance, which were traded widely.
Left Aerial photograph revealing traces of a late Neolithic enclosure of L'Angle, western France, with multiple ditches and complex entrance-works. Late 4th millennium BC.

The Fallahogy pollen core Analysis of layers of pollen deposits preserved in peat bogs can reveal the history of vegetation in the region. The core from Fallahogy in Northern Ireland shows the impact of early farming on plant cover. Around 4150 BC a fall in tree pollen and a sharp increase in that of open-country and field species such as grass, ribwort plantain and sorrel indicates a phase of forest clearance; the regeneration of forest cover, followed by a further period of clearance shows the non-intensive nature of early farming in the region.

Standing stones

Standing stones – arranged in circles or aligned in rows – are among the most impressive prehistoric monuments of north-western Europe, and their nature and purpose have been the subject of considerable speculation. The principal ritual monuments associated with the first farming communities were long barrows and megalithic tombs (*page 106*), used for burials and rituals connected with the dead. These continued throughout the 3rd millennium, but by 3200 BC a different kind of ritual orientation had developed with the appearance of various types of stone circles which, with their skyward emphasis, were not so closely connected with burial rituals. Stone circles usually consist of a ring of large stones, while alignments are single or multiple rows of standing stones. These, along with circular ditched enclosures (henges) and single standing stones known as menhirs, form a group of ritual monuments involving the use of (megalithic) standing stones which were built in large numbers in the British Isles and north-western France during the period 3200-1500 BC.

The British Isles alone possess some 1000 stone circles of different types and over 80 henges, while on the opposite side of the Channel in Brittany and adjacent areas there are further circles and alignments and over 1200 menhirs. This distribution demonstrates the importance of the western seaways as an artery for the movement of people, ideas and traded goods – quantities of stone axes have been found at henge sites. Traffic along the sea-routes from Brittany to Wales and south-west Britain, and around the Irish Sea and Scottish islands, bound these regions together; and it seems likely that during this period the British Isles and north-western France formed a cultural entity with similar religious practices.

The labour involved in building even the smallest henges and circles was considerable; the digging of ditches and the quarrying, transport and erection of the stones were only possible with co-operation between communities. Estimates of man-hours required to construct these monuments show an interesting progression; in Wessex, the earlier 'causewayed camps', from which henges may have originated, required around 50,000-70,000 man-hours, while the large henges of the mid-3rd millennium BC such as Durrington Walls and Mount Pleasant required perhaps 500,000 man-hours. However, it is estimated that the third phase of Stonehenge (with sarsen circle and trilithons) took as many as 2,000,000 man-hours to complete; succeeding Avebury as the ritual focus of the Wessex region, its pre-eminent importance is highlighted not only by its size but also by the local concentration of rich barrow burials containing bronze tools and weapons and gold ornaments. The famous Grand Menhir Brisé (which may have stood over 20 metres high) and the elaborate stone rows at Carnac form part of a comparable major group of ritual monuments, the largest in north-western France, around the Gulf of Morbihan. This ritual centre also included huge burial mounds, and reached its fullest development towards the end of the 3rd millennium BC. The complex arrangement of circles and rows at Callanish in the Hebrides may have served as a similar social, economic and religious centre for western Scotland. It is likely that the construction of these large monuments during this period represents an ever-increasing tendency towards political – and hence ritual – centralisation.

Although little is known of the religious beliefs that inspired these monuments, astronomical and seasonal events were undoubtedly important. At Newgrange in Ireland, sunlight only strikes the central chamber of the passage grave which stands within the stone circle at the midwinter solstice. The rising sun on midsummer day aligns with the axis of Stonehenge, while the central standing stone of the Ballochroy alignment defines the point on the horizon at which the midsummer sun sets. There are many other astronomical observations which can be made from these monuments, involving not only the sun and moon (which may well have had religious importance for these early farming communities), but also the stars, particularly the dog-star Sirius. It has been suggested that the stone rings, few of which are true circles, were laid out using Pythagorean triangles, and it has even been argued that a common unit of length, the 'megalithic yard' (0.83 metres), was used from the Orkneys to Brittany when these monuments were built.

Around the middle of the 2nd millennium BC the construction of stone circles and alignments in the British Isles and north-western France ceased, and the centres of power and prosperity shifted away from southern Brittany and Wessex to the agriculturally richer areas of the major river valleys, especially the Seine and the Thames. During this period, stone circles with their skyward orientation fell into disuse: instead, ritual deposits of bronze weaponry in rivers, lakes and bogs became common, suggesting the emergence of religious beliefs focusing on deities of earth and water.

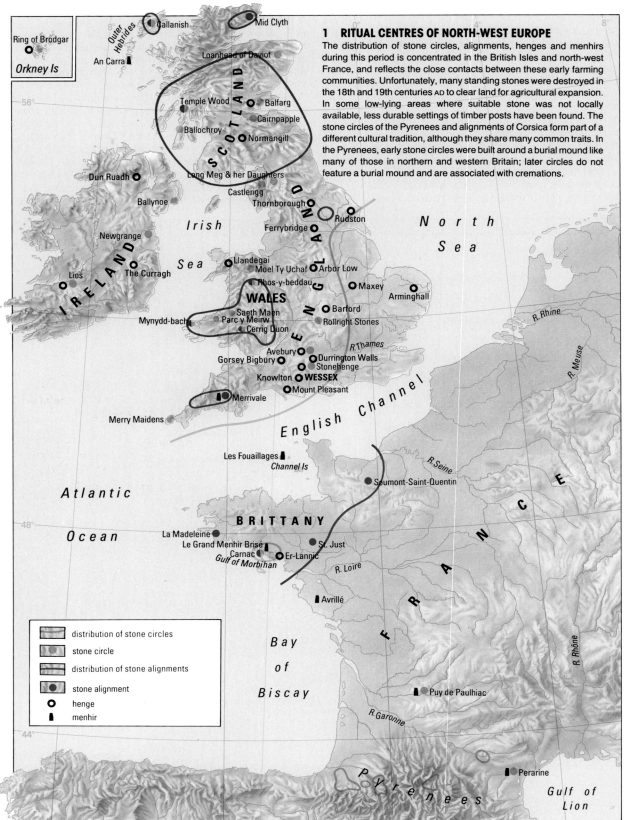

1 RITUAL CENTRES OF NORTH-WEST EUROPE

The distribution of stone circles, alignments, henges and menhirs during this period is concentrated in the British Isles and north-west France, and reflects the close contacts between these early farming communities. Unfortunately, many standing stones were destroyed in the 18th and 19th centuries AD to clear land for agricultural expansion. In some low-lying areas where suitable stone was not locally available, less durable settings of timber posts have been found. The stone circles of the Pyrenees and alignments of Corsica form part of a different cultural tradition, although they share many common traits. In the Pyrenees, early stone circles were built around a burial mound like many of those in northern and western Britain; later circles do not feature a burial mound and are associated with cremations.

distribution of stone circles
stone circle
distribution of stone alignments
stone alignment
○ henge
▮ menhir

3 STONE CIRCLES AND ALIGNMENTS

The structures built of standing stones in north-west Europe during the period 3200-1500 BC take a wide variety of forms. Alongside the impressive stone rings of Stonehenge and Avebury are smaller circles such as Moel Ty Uchaf where none of the uprights is more than one metre high. On the other hand, at Callanish, a circle of only modest diameter (11.3-13.1 metres), the stones are tall and thin, made of gneiss quarried only a mile to the north-east; the central stone of the circle is no less than 4.5 metres high. Near the cardinal points of the Callanish circle there are lines of stones leading away from the monument, the northern line being double and forming an avenue or processional approach. The most impressive of all stone rows are those near Carnac in Brittany; the Le Menec alignments consist of no fewer than 12 nearly parallel lines of stones running for over 950 metres

between two fragmentary stone circles. On a smaller scale, the alignment at Ballochroy in Argyll consists of only three tall standing stones together with a slab-built burial cist. Many stone circles also involve a burial, for example, the stone cist at Moel Ty Uchaf in northern Wales, illustrating the close link between funerary ritual and standing stones in northern and western Britain.

A *The Callanish stone circle in the Hebrides lies at the centre of three single and one double set of stone rows, and also contains a chambered barrow burial.* B *The stone alignments at Le Menec, Carnac, are part of a cluster of sites in Brittany, including another major alignment at Kermario and many menhirs.* C *The stone setting at Moel Ty Uchaf, North Wales, is composed of a series of arcs of different diameters.* D *In Argyll, Scotland, the central standing stone of the Ballochroy alignment defines the midwinter and midsummer sunset (see diagram E, right).*

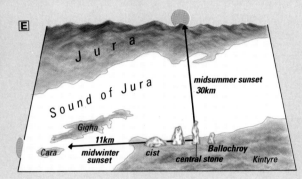

2 STONEHENGE

In the late 3rd and early 2nd millennium BC, Wessex seems to have been the ritual centre of southern England, and it is here that most of the major monuments and rich burials are found. By 2100 BC, Stonehenge – originally a simple henge consisting of a circular ditch and bank – had displaced nearby Avebury as the pre-eminent ritual centre of southern Britain. Within the bank and ditch of the early henge, over 100 metres in diameter, a complex arrangement of ritual pits, abandoned stone holes and blue stone and sarsen circles and trilithons was created, approached by an avenue. Sarsen blocks averaging 26 tonnes each, were brought from the Marlborough Downs some 29 kilometres to the north, probably on sledges using rollers and ropes. It is estimated that it would take 1000 men to haul one stone. Bluestones were quarried from the Prescelly Mountains in Wales, over 217 kilometres away; the area of origin must have had some significance, since the distance involved, in terms of manpower, was massive. Possibly the stones originally formed part of a ritual monument which was dismantled and transported to Wessex; alternatively the source of the stones may have been a sacred mountain (*see map below*). The stones were probably quarried by levering wooden wedges into natural cracks, which – when wetted – expanded and split off the rocks. Cracks could also be produced by lighting fires along the breakage lines; rapid cooling with water caused internal stress, and the rock could then be broken off with hammers. The stones were raised by positioning the lower edge over the posthole – reinforced with wooden stakes – and pulled upright using ropes. While Stonehenge is aligned so that the midsummer sunrise can be seen along the axis of the site, little is known of the rituals enacted there. There is little evidence to support the popular tradition that the so-called 'Altar Stone' was used for human sacrifice. Burials have, however, been found in various parts of the monument; they may have been connected with rituals of consecration and possibly even with some kind of sacrifice.

Stonehenge plan labels

pits and stoneholes
- bluestone
- sarsen

0   10   20 metres
0   10   20 yards

burial of young male with flint arrowheads in his back, c.2200 BC

Heel Stone, c.3000-2300 BC

avenue to R. Avon (2.5km)

site of station stone

entrance

ditch

Slaughter Stone c.2000 BC

N

station stone

bluestone horseshoe c.1550 BC

bank of chalk rubble, 1.8m high, c.3200 BC

sarsen trilithon

ditch cut into chalk, c.2m deep, 6m wide, c.3000 BC, containing some 20 cremations

Aubrey holes; ritual pits containing cremations, c.2300 BC

ditch

bluestone circle c.1550 BC

sarsen circle c.2100 BC; several uprights had carvings of Bronze Age axes and daggers

bank

Altar Stone c.1550 BC

station stone

skeleton found here

axis aligned towards position of sunrise at the summer solstice

ditch

site of station stone

Map labels

probable route for transport of:
- bluestones
- sarsens

WALES

Prescelly Mts

Milford Haven

Marlborough Downs

Avebury

Bristol Channel

R. Avon

Devizes

Stonehenge

52°

51°

5°   4°   3°   2°

Diagram E labels

Jura

Sound of Jura

midsummer sunset 30km

Gigha

11km

Cara

midwinter sunset

cist

central stone

Ballochroy

Kintyre

Copper Age Europe

During the 6th and 5th millennia BC farming spread northwards and westwards from the Balkans, replacing hunting, fishing and gathering as a way of life from the Atlantic to the western fringes of the Steppes. North of the Danube, the flourishing farming villages of the 'Cucuteni-Tripolye' group appeared – sometimes containing as many as 150 houses – and it was there that the first instance of European horse domestication occurred, in the 4th millennium BC. By c. 2500 BC, use of the horse had spread as far west as Newgrange in Ireland. During this period, wheeled vehicles also came into use in eastern Europe, indicated by finds of pottery cart models and wooden wheels, and by 2800 BC the wheel was being used further west in Denmark and Holland. Farming became increasingly productive with the introduction of the scratch-plough or ard (plough-marks have been found under burial mounds), and the greater use of animal traction and of animal products such as milk and wool. This agricultural intensification was accompanied by an increase in population and consequently in settlement size, and new, hitherto unfarmed areas were colonised.

One of the most important developments of the period was the appearance of specialist craftsmen engaged in the mining and working of copper and other materials. The development of metallurgy marked a new level of control by man over his environment and its resources (*page 120*). In Europe, the earliest copper- and gold-working was in the Balkans, the first objects (beads and awls) produced by hammering dating to around 5000 BC. Later in the 5th millennium BC smelting – the extraction of the metal from its ore – was introduced; this required temperatures of around 800°C and was made possible by the development of high-temperature kilns originally intended for firing fine pottery. Smelting was followed by the invention of casting: heating the metal to melting point and pouring it into a mould – a technique which enabled larger objects and more complex shapes such as shaft-hole axe-adzes and hammer-axes to be produced. Crucibles and slag have been found in the 4th millennium levels at Balkan tell sites, while in the highlands copper mines have been found at Aibunar in Bulgaria and Rudna Glava in Yugoslavia which were already being exploited around 4500 BC. Use of metal objects, designed to display the status of the owner, spread rapidly from the Balkans to neighbouring areas, and metallurgical skills developed even in areas devoid of metal sources, such as Moldavia. Wide reaching trade networks were established during this period; copper axes which probably originated in the Balkans appear in the early 4th millennium cemetery of Tibava in Hungary, while copper objects were being traded as far afield as Denmark.

The development of more hierarchical societies dominated by wealthy elites is best illustrated by the evidence of graves and cemeteries. In the 5th and 4th millennium cemeteries of eastern and east-central Europe, the richest burials are accompanied by metalwork while the poor contain only flints, pottery vessels and animal bones or, in some cases, nothing at all. The most spectacular of these cemeteries is at Varna, in Bulgaria, where the wealthier burials contain diadems, earrings, plaques and sceptre-mounts of gold; one grave contained no less than 1.5 kilograms of bracelets, beads and other objects of gold. A contemporary grave at Tărtăria contained inscribed clay tablets, and may have been the burial of a priest or shaman, the tablets symbolising his mystical power.

At a slightly later date in western and northern Europe, similar rich burials appeared associated with the 'Beaker' and 'Corded Ware' groups, so called because of their distinctive decorated pottery. In the north, male skeletons are buried with Corded Ware pots and battle axes. In the west, Beaker pottery is found in male graves, along with copper knives, stone archers' wristguards and flint arrowheads. These individual burials contrast with the earlier tradition of communal, undifferentiated burial in megalithic tombs (*page 106*); the emphasis on the individual and rich grave-goods indicates the development of a stratified society. The distribution of Beaker and Corded Ware assemblages reflects both the scale and distance of cultural contact, and the widespread recognition of these distinctive symbols of rank.

By the end of the 3rd millennium the increased sophistication of the European way of life was a fact established by the expansion of farming settlement and improvements in agricultural techniques, and in craftsmanship – with fine objects of gold and copper appearing throughout Europe. Impressive advances in technology transformed the character of these prehistoric communities, paving the way for the still greater social complexity and skilled craftsmanship of the European Bronze Age.

3 IN COPPER, GOLD AND CLAY
A Ornament in form of bull from grave in the Varna cemetery, Bulgaria. Later 5th millennium BC, gold sheet, 5.8cm. **B** Collar or 'lunula', probably worn on ritual occasions, from Orbliston, Scotland. c.2250 BC, sheet gold with incised decoration, outer diameter 19.5cm. **C** Circular tablet with incised signs interpreted as a form of proto-writing from tell site of Tărtăria, Romania. c.5000 BC, unbaked clay, diameter 6.1cm. **D** Square-mouthed cup with handle in form of a wagon from grave in Szigetszentmárton cemetery, Hungary. Late 4th millennium BC, pottery, height 9cm. **E** Model of a pair of long-horned oxen, originally yoked, from Bytyń, Poland. 4th millennium BC, copper, 13cm long and 10cm high. **F** Beaker grave assemblage from Culduthel Mains, Scotland, late 3rd millennium BC, comprising: polished archer's wristguard of stone with gold-capped rivets; decorated beaker (height 22.6cm); fire-lighting flint; eight flint arrowheads; amber bead; looped bone tube or toggle.

2 TISZAPOLGÁR: A COPPER AGE CEMETERY

The prehistoric cemetery of Tiszapolgár is typical of many Copper Age cemeteries in eastern and central Europe. The cemetery is regularly laid out, and although the graves do not have covering mounds, their location was probably indicated by grave markers, now vanished. Most of the 156 graves investigated there contained individual burials, though a few multiple burials of adults and small children were also found. The quantity and nature of the objects deposited with the dead varied considerably from grave to grave, probably reflecting the different wealth and status of the deceased before death, and it is likely that the graves containing copper and gold objects belonged to the wealthiest individuals. The poorest graves, by contrast, contained only flints and a small number of pots; a few contained no accompanying objects at all. The age and sex of the skeletons in the rich graves indicate that males of middle age and above were the wealthiest and most powerful members of society. Several of the burials with copper artefacts were, however, those of children suggesting that in this community wealth and status could be passed on from one generation to the next. Few people survived into what we would nowadays term old age, and child mortality was high, perhaps even higher than the numbers from Tiszapolgár suggest, as dead infants may not always have been given formal burial.

Copper Age metalwork from central Europe:

spiral bracelets (A), shaft-hole axe-adzes (B) and daggers or knives of copper (C) are found at settlements and in cemeteries, where they mark the graves of the wealthier section of society.

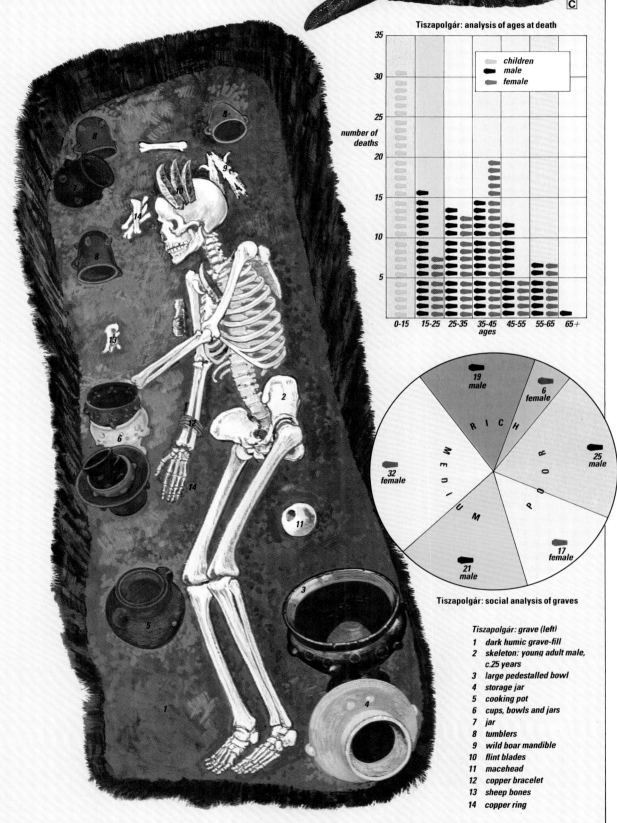

Tiszapolgár: analysis of ages at death

Tiszapolgár: social analysis of graves

Tiszapolgár: grave (left)
1. dark humic grave-fill
2. skeleton: young adult male, c.25 years
3. large pedestalled bowl
4. storage jar
5. cooking pot
6. cups, bowls and jars
7. jar
8. tumblers
9. wild boar mandible
10. flint blades
11. macehead
12. copper bracelet
13. sheep bones
14. copper ring

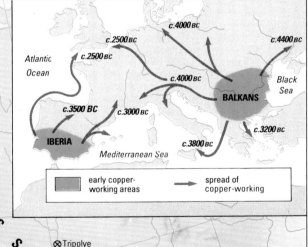

early copper-working areas → spread of copper-working

Balkans:
- tell settlement
- Copper Age cemetery
- early copper mine

south-east Europe:
- ⊗ Cucuteni-Tripolye village

northern Europe:
- Corded Ware groups
- ● Corded Ware settlement
- Corded Ware burial

western Europe:
- distribution of Beakers showing areas of concentration
- Beaker burial

resources:
- copper
- gold

1 THE METALLURGICAL REVOLUTION

Copper and gold metallurgy are thought to have been invented independently in at least two separate regions of Europe, the Balkans and southern Iberia. From the Balkans metalworking spread east, west and north to cover most of Europe east of the Rhine and southern Britain by the 3rd millennium BC. In Atlantic Europe, on the other hand, the earliest metalworking was probably the result of contact with Iberia via the western seaways. Some areas, such as Denmark and the western Ukraine, lacked metal deposits of their own, and remained dependent on raw materials obtained by trade from other regions. The wide dissemination of Balkan metallurgy and its products and the spread of Beaker and Corded Ware material in northern and western Europe illustrate the long-distance links which had developed by the end of the Copper Age.

The dawn of Mediterranean civilisation

The most important settlements of 4th millennium Greece were in the north, on the fertile plains of Thessaly and Macedonia. However, by the 3rd millennium there was a dramatic shift, with the south and the islands taking the lead in the development of a thriving bronze industry, the production of luxury and ritual items and the construction of walled palace-citadels. The growth of populations around the Aegean was accompanied by the development of increasingly sophisticated societies resulting in the emergence of particular families or individuals as chiefs or rulers. These rulers lived in palaces, and one of their primary roles was to collect, store and redistribute dues of agricultural produce within their domain.

Social elites also supported sophisticated craftsmanship in metal and stone, and craft areas are commonly found within palace precincts. Manufactured goods were valuable commodities, used by the ruling class to display their wealth and separateness. A characteristic product of the early Aegean bronze industry was the dagger, deposited in many graves as a symbol of social status. A wide-reaching trading network was established, exchanging agricultural produce and manufactured goods for exotic materials such as ivory, or valued scarce metals such as

gold. Palaces therefore had two functions, acting as centres of stored wealth – local agricultural produce, manufactured and imported goods – as well as centres of power. They became natural targets for envious or acquisitive neighbours; fortifications were vital, and are found throughout the Aegean.

At the opposite end of the Mediterranean, in southern Iberia, similar changes were taking place. More land was being taken into cultivation to feed growing populations, and the plough came into use in the 4th millennium BC. A series of fortified settlements with bastioned stone walls was built along the Tagus estuary (c. 3000 BC), associated with elaborate tombs which reveal an increasing distinction between rich and poor. The leaders of this more stratified society in the west created a demand for luxury goods – notably ivory and ostrich eggshell from North Africa. Sophisticated metallurgy also catered for the demand for status symbols such as copper knives; copper-working in Iberia may have been an independent development based on pyrotechnic experimentation in firing high-temperature ceramics. Most striking of the Iberian sites is Los Millares; here the settlement is defended by a bastioned stone wall, with a series of outpost forts on nearby hilltops. There is also a large cemetery of well-built tombs containing burials of groups of people, probably families, many with rich grave-goods.

The evidence from Italy, southern France and the west Mediterranean basin is not so striking, but there is little doubt that social elites were also developing in these areas. Enclosures, some with bastions, are found in southern France and Corsica, the Balearic Islands and

Sicily, and copper metallurgy became established in much of the region during the 3rd millennium BC. In Italy, an important centre of copper-using developed in Tuscany based on local ores, and copper tools and weapons occur in the flat grave cemeteries of northern and central Italy and in the rock-cut tombs of the south.

With increasing social complexity, ritual also became more elaborate; emerging social elites and rulers often played the leading role in religious life, incidentally strengthening their position in society. During this period, an extraordinary range of ritual objects appear all along the Mediterranean. In the east, there are stylised marble figurines from the Cycladic islands, and the so-called Cycladic 'frying pans' whose representations of the female genitalia possibly indicate a fertility cult. The temple complexes of Malta are decorated with stone-carvings of the ample figure of a mother goddess – depicted sitting, standing and even sleeping. The graves of the Iberian peninsula contain stylised geometric plaques with eye designs which are thought to represent a deity.

Throughout the Mediterranean, the years 4000-2000 BC witnessed a consolidation of skill and resources, both in craftsmanship and agricultural efficiency. Horizons were widened, with an increasing frequency of sea-borne traffic bringing together hitherto separate communities. It was in the east that these developments were to have their most profound effect. In about 2000 BC the first and greatest of the Cretan palaces was founded at Knossos (*page 140*), and within 500 years the Minoan civilisation of Crete had been joined across the Aegean by the Mycenaean civilisation of the Greek mainland.

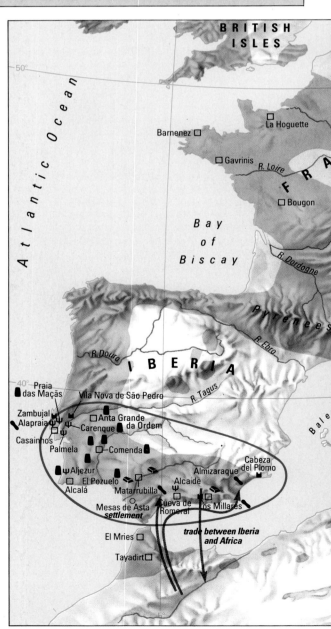

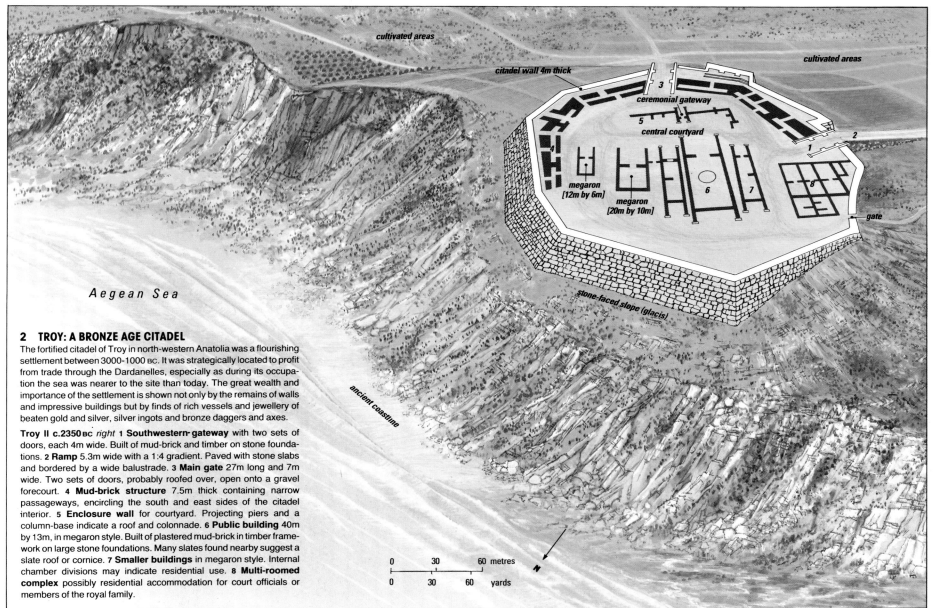

2 TROY: A BRONZE AGE CITADEL

The fortified citadel of Troy in north-western Anatolia was a flourishing settlement between 3000-1000 BC. It was strategically located to profit from trade through the Dardanelles, especially as during its occupation the sea was nearer to the site than today. The great wealth and importance of the settlement is shown not only by the remains of walls and impressive buildings but by finds of rich vessels and jewellery of beaten gold and silver, silver ingots and bronze daggers and axes.

Troy II c.2350 BC *right* **1 Southwestern- gateway** with two sets of doors, each 4m wide. Built of mud-brick and timber on stone foundations. **2 Ramp** 5.3m wide with a 1:4 gradient. Paved with stone slabs and bordered by a wide balustrade. **3 Main gate** 27m long and 7m wide. Two sets of doors, probably roofed over, open onto a gravel forecourt. **4 Mud-brick structure** 7.5m thick containing narrow passageways, encircling the south and east sides of the citadel interior. **5 Enclosure wall** for courtyard. Projecting piers and a column-base indicate a roof and colonnade. **6 Public building** 40m by 13m, in megaron style. Built of plastered mud-brick in timber framework on large stone foundations. Many slates found nearby suggest a slate roof or cornice. **7 Smaller buildings** in megaron style. Internal chamber divisions may indicate residential use. **8 Multi-roomed complex** possibly residential accommodation for court officials or members of the royal family.

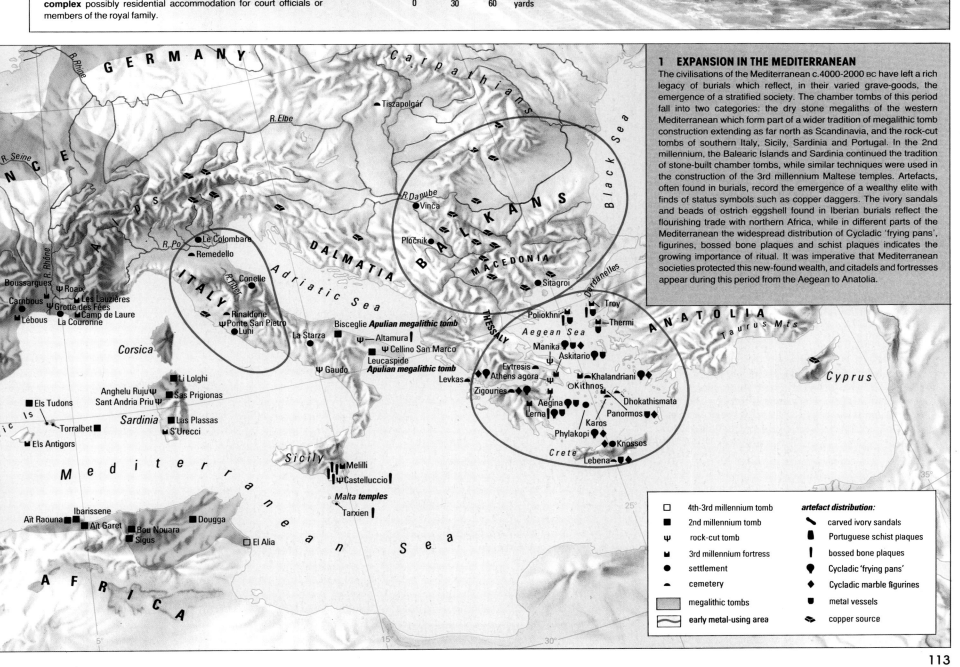

1 EXPANSION IN THE MEDITERRANEAN

The civilisations of the Mediterranean c.4000-2000 BC have left a rich legacy of burials which reflect, in their varied grave-goods, the emergence of a stratified society. The chamber tombs of this period fall into two categories: the dry stone megaliths of the western Mediterranean which form part of a wider tradition of megalithic tomb construction extending as far north as Scandinavia, and the rock-cut tombs of southern Italy, Sicily, Sardinia and Portugal. In the 2nd millennium, the Balearic Islands and Sardinia continued the tradition of stone-built chamber tombs, while similar techniques were used in the construction of the 3rd millennium Maltese temples. Artefacts, often found in burials, record the emergence of a wealthy elite with finds of status symbols such as copper daggers. The ivory sandals and beads of ostrich eggshell found in Iberian burials reflect the flourishing trade with northern Africa, while in different parts of the Mediterranean the widespread distribution of Cycladic 'frying pans', figurines, bossed bone plaques and schist plaques indicates the growing importance of ritual. It was imperative that Mediterranean societies protected this new-found wealth, and citadels and fortresses appear during this period from the Aegean to Anatolia.

	artefact distribution:
☐ 4th-3rd millennium tomb	⟍ carved ivory sandals
■ 2nd millennium tomb	⊫ Portuguese schist plaques
Ψ rock-cut tomb	❙ bossed bone plaques
⬚ 3rd millennium fortress	◗ Cycladic 'frying pans'
● settlement	◆ Cycladic marble figurines
▬ cemetery	⬛ metal vessels
megalithic tombs	⬧ copper source
early metal-using area	

Bronze Age Europe

The appearance of bronze objects in tombs and settlements heralds the beginning of the European Bronze Age at around 2300 BC. An alloy of copper with approximately 10% tin, the bronze in use was considerably harder than pure copper, and a much more useful material for tools and weapons. By 1200 BC even everyday objects were being manufactured in bronze, with hard stone and flint falling into disuse. Large mining complexes developed: at the Mitterberg in the Austrian Alps it is estimated that the 32 mine shafts would have produced 10,000 metric tons of crude copper. Long-distance trade routes supplied areas without natural deposits of metal ores, such as Denmark, and also distributed highly prized tin from its sources in western and south-western Europe to bronze-smiths throughout the continent. Manufactured bronze goods also travelled great distances – Hungarian swords have been found in Denmark, and Breton axes in Switzerland. The result of these long-distance contacts was a considerable degree of cultural and technological uniformity.

Throughout Europe this period was distinguished by increasing social stratification; the emergence of an elite class of rich chieftains is reflected in changing burial practices. In central Europe, the burials of individuals under large mounds mark a significant transition from the earlier flat grave cemeteries of Copper Age Europe (*page 110*). The most famous is at Leubingen in northern Germany, where a massive timber mortuary house at the centre of the mound held the dead man, who was accompanied by a young girl, and rich grave-goods of gold and bronze. Set apart from the burials of the rest of the community – this segregation emphasised the exclusiveness of the new aristocracy – these large burial mounds demanded considerably more communal labour to construct than a simple flat grave, while the richness of the grave-goods testifies to the wealth and the status of the individuals. These barrow burials were widespread, frequently appearing in areas such as Brittany and Wessex which had access to vital tin sources. It is very likely that control of tin sources is one of the factors which account for the emergence of a wealthy and powerful elite class.

Settlement in north-western Europe was restricted to small farmsteads or hamlets, while in eastern and central Europe tell sites were frequently quite substantial. However, the lakeside villages of the Alps give the most evocative picture of Bronze Age life. The timber houses of these villages have yielded remains of wheat, barley, flax, a large selection of wild fruits – including apples, plums, strawberries and raspberries–a loaf of bread, and bones of fish, game and wild animals. Evidence of the use of the plough – remains of ploughs, plough-marks preserved beneath barrows and depictions of ploughing in Alpine and Scandinavian rock art – is widespread. As the population grew, pressure on the land increased and there was a marked decline in the fertility of long-cultivated and over-exploited lowlands, so agriculture gradually spread to marginal upland areas such as Dartmoor in south-west England, and Bavaria in southern Germany. In many parts of north-western Europe, field boundaries were laid out at this time – clear evidence of the rising value of land and the need to define ownership.

In eastern and central Europe, these social and economic pressures led, in the centuries following 2000 BC, to an increasing emphasis on the fortification of settlements. Hillforts were built in the Carpathians, one of the most impressive being Spišský Štvrtok, with a stone-faced rampart four metres high and a bastioned gateway. The massacred bodies found at the fortified settlement of Blučina vividly illustrate the importance of such defences. Other types of fort included island villages such as the Wasserburg in southern Germany. Society was becoming increasingly militaristic; by 1250 BC new types of weaponry were adopted throughout Europe – including bronze slashing swords and sheet-bronze greaves, helmets and cuirasses, and the use of fortifications spread to western Europe. A warrior elite had replaced the chieftains of the earlier Bronze Age.

The emergence of warrior elites was accompanied by the adoption and spread of a new type of burial and cemetery–the urnfield, where the body was cremated and the remains placed in a funerary urn. The scale of urnfield burials – with cemeteries of up to 10,000 graves – is surprising, and the widespread adoption of this method of burial further indicates a remarkable cultural conformity, conditions which favoured trade and exchange of ideas. It was in these conditions that use of a new metal – iron – began to spread throughout Europe. By 700 BC, iron was in common use, replacing bronze even on the fringes of Europe. By a process of gradual transition, the age of iron had arrived.

3 ARMOUR AND ADORNMENT
A *Helmet with cheek-pieces, part of a hoard from Pass Lueg near Salzburg, Austria. 13th century BC; bronze, height c.41cm.* B *Greave (leg armour) with embossed decoration, one of a pair from Pergine Valsugana, northern Italy. Sheet-bronze metalworking was a feature of the Urnfield period in central Europe. c.1100 BC, bronze, height 29cm.* C *Necklace from a cremation burial at Upton Lovell, Wiltshire. The amber probably came by trade from the Baltic. 18th-17th century BC; faience, shale and amber, length of largest amber bead c.2cm.* D *Engraved solid-hilted dagger from Bresinchen, East Germany. The hilt is attached to the blade by metal rivets. Part of a large hoard comprising a total of 30 kg of metal. c.2200 BC, bronze, length 27.1cm.* E *Ornaments from chieftain's grave at Leubingen, East Germany, including a gold bracelet, spiral bead and finger rings, and long pins with eyelets, probably used to fasten a cloak. c.2000 BC, gold, diameter of bracelet 8.3cm, length of longest pin 10cm.*

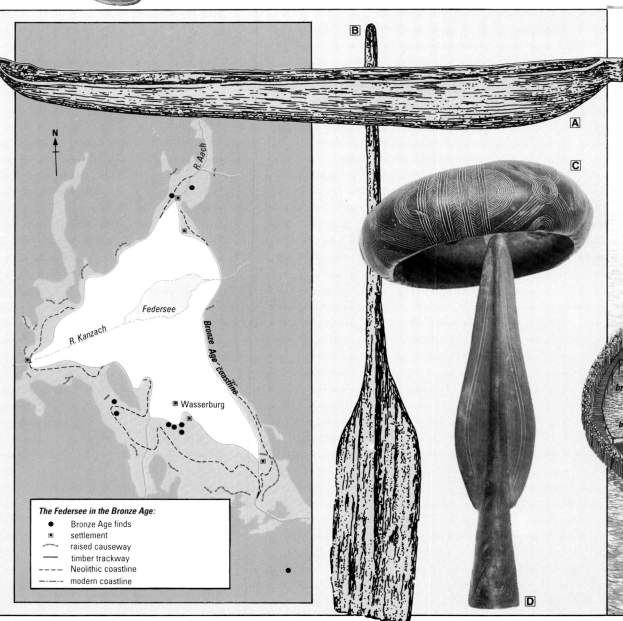

The Federsee in the Bronze Age:
- Bronze Age finds
- settlement
- raised causeway
- timber trackway
- Neolithic coastline
- modern coastline

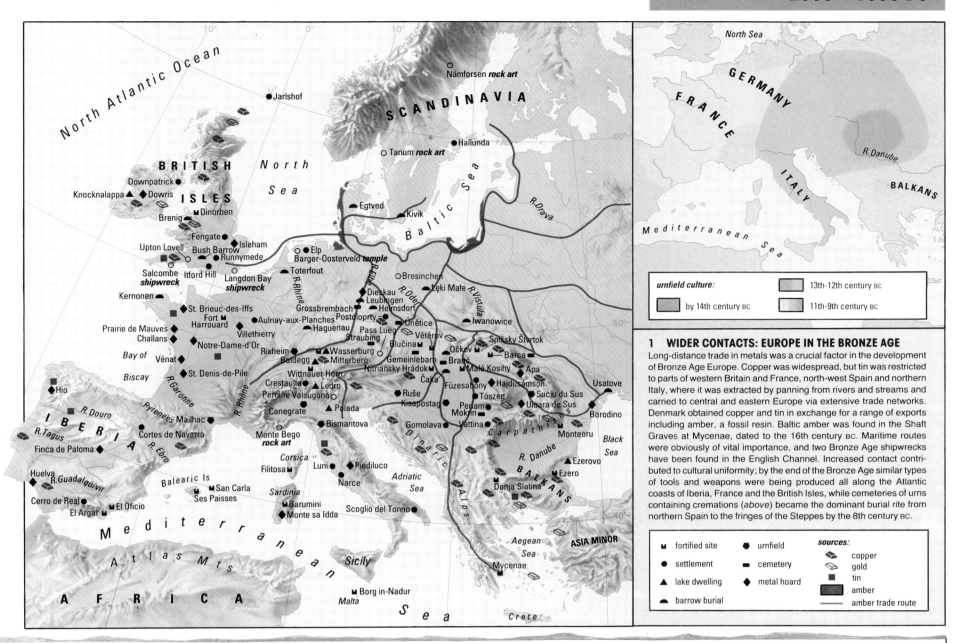

1 WIDER CONTACTS: EUROPE IN THE BRONZE AGE

Long-distance trade in metals was a crucial factor in the development of Bronze Age Europe. Copper was widespread, but tin was restricted to parts of western Britain and France, north-west Spain and northern Italy, where it was extracted by panning from rivers and streams and carried to central and eastern Europe via extensive trade networks. Denmark obtained copper and tin in exchange for a range of exports including amber, a fossil resin. Baltic amber was found in the Shaft Graves at Mycenae, dated to the 16th century BC. Maritime routes were obviously of vital importance, and two Bronze Age shipwrecks have been found in the English Channel. Increased contact contributed to cultural uniformity; by the end of the Bronze Age similar types of tools and weapons were being produced all along the Atlantic coasts of Iberia, France and the British Isles, while cemeteries of urns containing cremations (*above*) became the dominant burial rite from northern Spain to the fringes of the Steppes by the 8th century BC.

		sources:	
■ fortified site	● urnfield	◇ copper	
● settlement	▭ cemetery	■ tin	
▲ lake dwelling	◆ metal hoard	▭ amber	
▬ barrow burial		— amber trade route	

2 THE WASSERBURG: AN ISLAND VILLAGE

The Wasserburg is a Late Bronze Age settlement founded around the 12th century BC on an island in the Federsee lake in southern Germany. The settlement was initially occupied by 40 or more small, one-roomed houses, surrounded by a palisade of over 15,000 substantial posts. After a time, the rising lake level flooded the outer margins of the settlement, and eventually it was abandoned. The site was re-occupied c.1000 BC, when nine large tripartite houses were built (*see illustration below*). These were of log-cabin construction, with internal dividing walls of wattle and daub. One of the largest houses had an entrance porch and may have been the residence of the village headman. Smaller buildings were probably workshops and granaries. This second settlement, like the first, was surrounded by a palisade, though owing to the encroachment of the lake the area enclosed by the second palisade was smaller. Despite its defensive island position, the houses of the second settlement were burned to the ground around 800 BC and the site was abandoned. Within and around the site a large number of objects were found, including pottery and bronzes and evidence of craft activities such as clay spindle whorls. The villagers kept domestic cattle, pigs, sheep, goats and horses. They also had a species of large wolfhound, and hunted deer, elk, wild pig, bear and beaver, while the waters of the Federsee provided pike and catfish. The Wasserburg was only one of several Late Bronze Age settlements around the Federsee, most lying on the lake edge. The area was marshy and causeways and timber trackways were built to ease passage across the more difficult stretches.

Objects from the Wasserburg (*left*)
A *Dug-out canoe, wood, length c.5.2m and* **B** *paddle, length c.90cm.* **C** *Decorated bracelet, 10th century BC, bronze, outer diameter c.10.7cm.* **D** *Spearhead, 10th century BC, bronze, length c.18.8cm. These last two items are part of a hoard of bronzes intentionally buried, presumably for safe-keeping, on the northern shore of the Wasserburg, but for some reason never retrieved.*

Bronze Age Scandinavia

Scandinavia underwent a cultural florescence in the 2nd millennium; a flourishing export trade developed – mainly in Baltic amber – with central Europe, while Scandinavia imported copper and tin. Craftsmanship in bronze was revolutionised during this period, and with it a hierarchical society emerged. Rich burials in tree-trunk coffins covered by mounds have been extraordinarily well preserved by waterlogging, and finds of organic remains such as clothing, as well as more durable grave-goods, give a vivid impression of Scandinavian culture.

In contrast to the exceptional condition of many of the mound burials, the remains of settlement sites are much less well preserved. Wooden dwellings were in use – timber, especially oak, was widely available, and a high standard of woodworking craftsmanship is evident in the tree-trunk coffins in which the dead were buried. Agriculture was obviously the basis of subsistence: plough marks have been found preserved under barrows, and wooden scratch ploughs (ards) have been found in bogs. Scenes showing oxen drawing ploughs are sometimes depicted in rock carvings, often associated with fertility symbolism. Wheat, barley and millet were grown during this period, and pollen cores indicate that much of the land was open, and probably used for stock rearing – cattle or dairy products may well have been exported to central Europe. Throughout Scandinavia, more marginal land first came into use at this time in response to the pressure on productive land caused by rising population.

Scandinavia possesses no natural tin sources, and its copper was not exploited at this period. As it was entirely dependent on imports of these metals, bronze had great rarity value, and was a highly prized and prestigious commodity. Baltic amber from the west coast of Jutland, valued in the ancient world for beads and jewellery, was widely traded with the metal-producing countries of Europe. The volume of the metal imported is so great in comparison with the amount of traded amber found elsewhere that it seems likely that other commodities (which have not been as well preserved) were also traded; these probably included furs, skins, animals and slaves. Ships were of vital importance, both for negotiating the rugged coastline and islands of Scandinavia itself, and also for trade – across the Baltic Sea to northern Europe, and over the North Sea to the British Isles. Ships are a recurring motif, both in rock carvings and on bronze articles; they are shown as oar-propelled long-boats with flat keels and a high prow and stern.

At first, when bronze was not widely available, imitations of bronze articles were made in less costly materials such as flint; however, skilled and distinctive native metalwork developed quickly after the appearance of the first imports. Large hoards of metalwork were deposited in bogs – probably as ritual offerings – preserving some fine examples of Scandinavian bronze work; the Smørumøvre hoard contained 60 spearheads and over 80 axes, while six bronze *lurer* (horns which were probably blown at religious ceremonies) were found in a deposit at Brudevaelte. The high degree of skill necessary to produce these items goes together with other evidence to suggest that Bronze Age Scandinavia was a hierarchical society, with agricultural labourers, craftsmen, sailors, and an elite class who controlled trade and whose rich burials advertise their status.

At the beginning of the period, the usual method of burial for wealthier members of society was to wrap the body in an ox hide before placing it in an oak coffin with grave-goods of bronze, flint and wood, covering it with a burial mound or barrow. After some centuries, people began to cremate their dead, and grave-goods became smaller and fewer – miniaturised weapons or toilet articles such as tweezers or razors which could be placed in the pottery urns which were used instead of coffins to hold the cremated remains. Among the remains in the earlier barrows are fine examples of clothing – mostly of woollen cloth. The men were dressed in simple wrap-round cloths and cloaks, while women wore short corded skirts or longer woollen skirts and short-sleeved tunics, with long woven belts and rich bronze jewellery. This may have been burial garb with religious significance, as corded skirts are also depicted on bronze ritual figurines.

Despite its wealth and sophistication, the Scandinavian Bronze Age was a fragile edifice, dependent on trade for its supply of many raw materials. From the 8th century BC the harmful effects of cooler and wetter conditions on agriculture and the realignment of the trade routes caused by the introduction of a new metal, iron, plunged these northern regions into a period of decline which lasted until the 1st century BC.

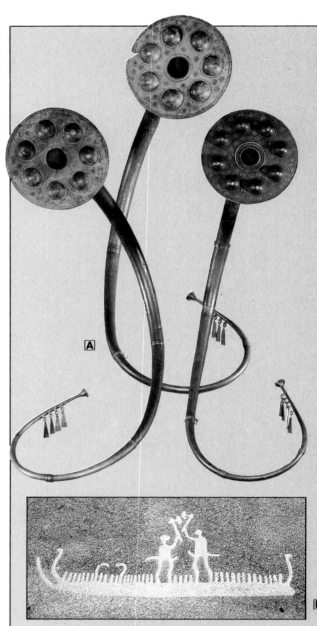

2 BORUM ESHØJ: A BRONZE AGE BURIAL

The Bronze Age burial mound at Borum Eshøj contained three oak tree-trunk coffins protected by the water-retentive nature of the inner core of the mound which preserved both the coffins themselves, and the human remains, clothing and objects they contained. The main burial at the centre of the mound was that of an elderly man; a woman and a younger man, possibly kinsfolk, lay in separate coffins towards the eastern edge. The woman's grave in particular was richly equipped, containing a bronze dagger, neck ring, finger-rings, decorated fibula and belt-disc. The coffins were probably prepared *in situ*, and were constructed of oak tree-trunk sections, split lengthways.
A *Young man's burial in tree-trunk coffin. Length 2.35m.* B *Old man's round-cut woollen cape and kilt secured by girdle. Total length 1.26m.* C *Elaborate tassel of woman's woollen waist-belt. Length 15cm.* D *Woman's hairnet of woollen thread. Length 18.7cm.*

3 ART AND RITUAL

The sun was probably worshipped by the people of Bronze Age Scandinavia, and sun symbolism is widespread, for example the Trundholm sun chariot. Other rituals centred on bogs and lakes, suggesting the worship of different deities – of earth and water. Rock carvings vividly depict ritual scenes; beating of drums, blowing of *lurer*, ship ceremonies, fertility rites, chariot races, stallion fights, and possibly human sacrifice. Sorcery was clearly practised: a burial at Hvidegård yielded a small leather bag containing a bizarre collection of items including amber beads, the tail of a grass snake, a falcon's claw, a squirrel's jaw and dried roots, suggesting that a shaman or priest was buried there. Other ritual finds include bronze figures of horned gods, goddesses in short corded skirts, and goddesses with snakes.

A *Lurer (ritual musical instruments) from Brudevaelte, NE Jutland. The left and central lurer are a pair, each capable of producing 14 notes. The right-hand lur can produce twelve notes. c.1000 BC, bronze, diameter of decoration plates c.28cm, length of tubes c.195cm.* **B** *Rock engraving from Fossum, Sweden, depicting fight or ritual axe dance between ithyphallic warriors on board ship. Late 2nd/early 1st millennium BC, length of ship c.130cm.* **C** *Miniature sword from Gedebjerg, Zealand, produced for placing with the ashes of the dead in pottery urn. c.1250 BC, bronze, length 9.4cm.* **D** *Sword from Torupgaarde, Lolland; Hungarian import into Denmark. c.1900 BC, bronze, length 84.5cm.* **E** *Figurine of man or deity wearing horned helmet found at Grevensvaenge, Zealand; one of a matching pair, originally brandishing an axe in its right hand. c.1250 BC, bronze, height c.9cm.* **F** *Wheeled model of horse drawing a disc, gold-plated on one side, found in the Trundholm bog, Zealand. The disc probably represented the sun and moon. c.1650 BC, bronze, diameter of disc 25.9cm, length of vehicle c.59cm.* **G** *Razor with ship engravings from burial at Solbjerg, N Jutland. c.1000 BC, bronze, length 15.8cm.*

1 BRONZE AGE CULTURE

In comparison with central Europe, bronze-using came late to Scandinavia. Even after the introduction of the first bronze daggers, stone tools continued to be used in Norway and Sweden. Farming was also slow to spread northwards, and hunting, fishing and gathering persisted as a way of life in the northern peripheries of the region. In the south, however, agriculture flourished and a sophisticated bronze-using society developed, closely linked by trade with central Europe and Britain. As copper and tin were not available locally, these metals had to be imported, and in exchange amber was widely exported from Scandinavia.

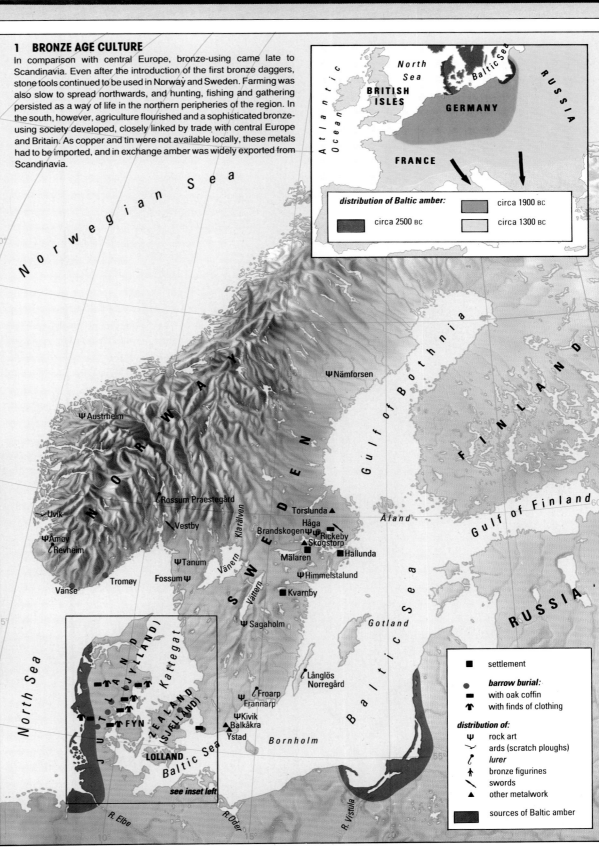

Early farming in Africa

Agriculture today supports the bulk of the African population, but it is difficult to say exactly when it began, and its development and spread throughout the whole of the continent was clearly a long and gradual process. In many parts of eastern and southern Africa, pastoralism was more important than arable farming. Indeed, herding, based on the domestication of the local wild cattle, began in the Sahara at about the same time as the first African plant cultivation, though its subsequent spread to the south took many centuries and involved several different breeds.

While grindstones came into use in Nubia and Upper Egypt in around 12,000 BC, probably reflecting the making of flour from the seeds of local wild grasses, the first definite evidence of plant cultivation, however, dates only to about 6000 BC, when wheat and barley were introduced to north-east Africa from western Asia. They soon spread down the Nile Valley to the Sudan and Ethiopia, and with them spread the use of the plough. These cereals, dependent on winter rainfall, were, however, unable to penetrate the tropics, where most of the rain falls in the summer. Other cereals such as millets, rice and sorghum were native to the grasslands of the Sahara, and were independently domesticated in the desert and its fringes. Evidence of cultivation of these crops survives in archaeological deposits as carbonised grains or impressions in pottery, indicating that bulrush millet may have been cultivated in the central Sahara as early as 6000 BC, and by 4000 BC finger millet was being grown alongside sorghum in the Sudan. The cultivation of African rice may have begun at about the same time.

In the woodland savanna and tropical forests to the south, a different range of plant species was brought into cultivation, consisting not of grasses and cereals but of tubers and tree crops. Tubers leave virtually no archaeological remains, while tree crops also present problems; even where seeds or husks are found, it is usually impossible to say whether the trees they came from were wild or whether they had been intentionally planted and tended. However, it is likely that the domestication of major African food plants such as the yam and the oil palm is of considerable antiquity, and probably first took place in the woodland and forest zones where their wild relatives are still found.

Almost all these indigenous African cultivated plants – cereals, tubers and tree crops – were first domesticated in the band of territory between the Sahara and the Equator. The reason for this may have been the gradual desiccation of the Sahara. As conditions became ever drier, communities living in the desert and its fringes were forced to cultivate the local grasses and cereals to improve the security of their food supply. Eventually, most of the Sahara had to be abandoned, and its inhabitants were forced to move into neighbouring areas such as the Nile Valley and the savanna grasslands. As a result, the population density around the periphery of the Sahara increased, perhaps leading to the adoption of agriculture in this region. The density of population supported by African agriculture was lower on the whole than in most of Europe, western Asia or the Far East, however, and the systems of farming were correspondingly less intensive – over most of the continent agriculture relied on hoes and digging sticks.

South of the Equator, hunting and gathering continued to be the basis of subsistence long after farming and pastoralism had been established further north. The pre-agricultural way of life was well adapted to the local environment, and the relatively low population density made cultivation and domestication unnecessary. The remains from the camp site of Gwisho in Zambia show how well the inhabitants made use of the available plant resources. The staple food plants were the shrub *Bauhinia* and the ivory palm, but alongside these were other species which were used for more specialised purposes – the bottle gourd provided organic containers, while *Commiphora* and *Swartzia madagascarensis* were used for poisoning the tips of arrows. The success of hunting and gathering in southern Africa is demonstrated by its long survival. Even when the expansion of the Bantu brought agriculture and animal husbandry south of the River Limpopo in the early centuries AD, hunting and gathering communities continued to thrive in the extreme south and south-west. The spread of agriculture through Africa has been a long process, only completed in recent times with the relegation of non-agricultural peoples to arid wastes and dense forests where farming can make little headway.

2 NATIVE AFRICAN CROPS

African domesticated plants include cereals, root crops and trees. **A** *Yam, the most nutritious African tuber, and the staple food in the forest and woodland savanna areas of West Africa today.* **B** *Finger millet and* **C** *Bulrush millet, two of the six species of cultivated African millets. Bulrush millet is particularly valuable because of its high tolerance of drought, and may already have been domesticated in the central Sahara by 6000 BC.* **D** *Sorghum, the most important indigenous cereal; different varieties are grown today throughout sub-Saharan Africa.* **E** *Oil palm, source of oil which is rich in protein and vitamins. Remains of palm nuts at Esh Shaheinab in the Sudan c.4400 BC, outside the tree's supposed area of origin, suggest it may already have been domesticated.* **F** *Ensete or 'false banana', cultivated not for its fruit but for its stem and tap root. Ensete, noog and tef are Ethiopian domesticates which never achieved importance outside their country of origin.*

3 FARMERS AND FORAGERS

Study of traditional African farming, hunting and fishing practices today (*above and right*) provides useful information about prehistoric food procurement, which supplements the evidence from preserved remains of ancient tools and equipment.
A *Wooden digging stick from Gwisho, used for grubbing up roots and tubers. c.2000 BC, overall length 61cm.* **B** *Wooden arrow-point from Gwisho, originally probably mounted in the end of a reed arrow shaft and armed with poison. c.2000 BC, length 17cm.* **C** *Stone tool from Iwo Eleru, possibly for attachment to a wooden shaft as a hoe. c.3000 BC, sandstone, length c.12cm.* **D** *Ground stone axe, from Iwo Eleru, perhaps used to clear forest for farming. c.3000 BC, sillimanite, length c.13cm.* **E** *Reconstructed reaping knife from Iwo Eleru. The small chalcedony blades were fixed into the slotted wooden stick by binding or mastic. c.55cm.*

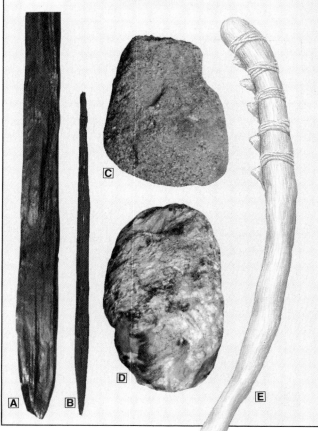

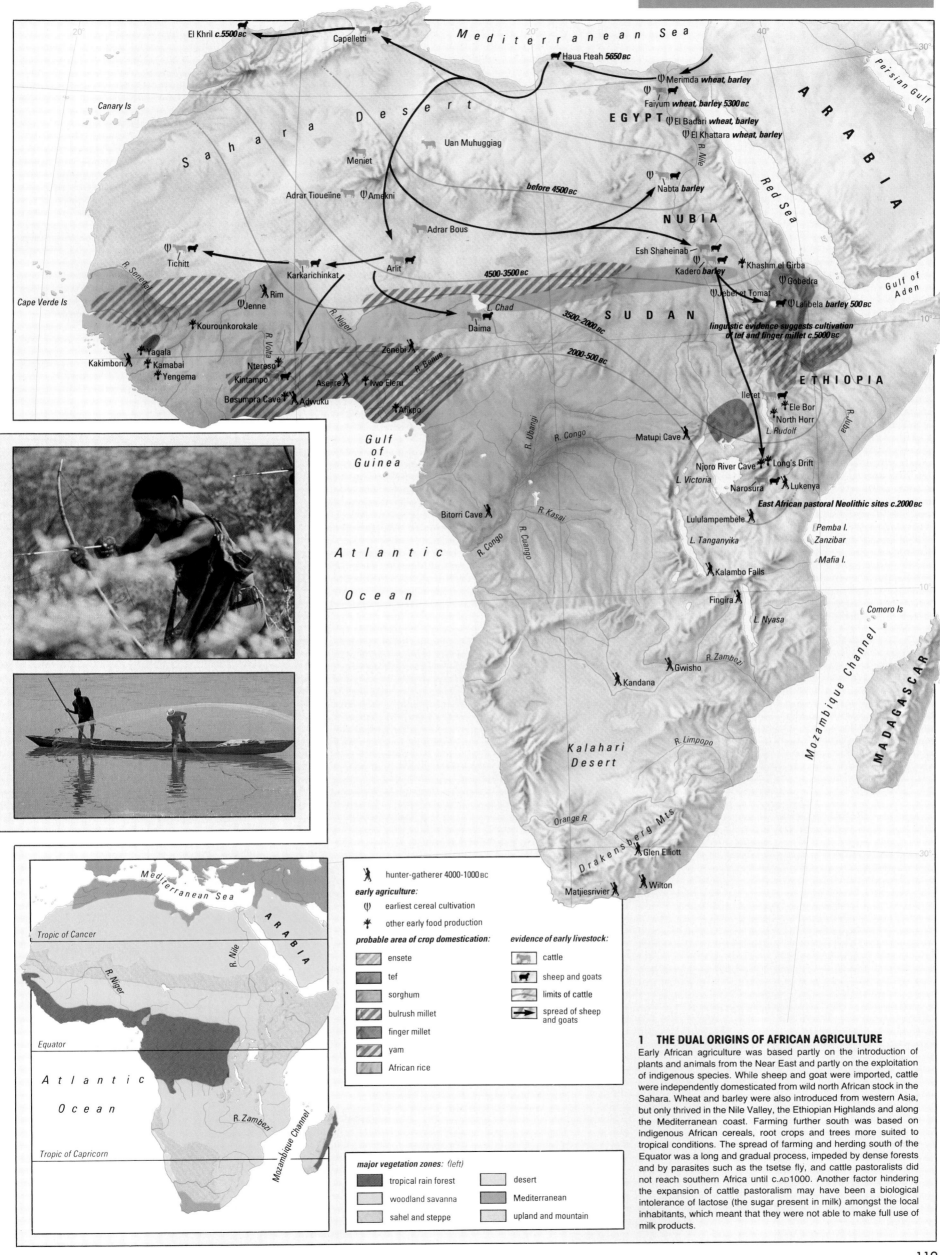

Mediterranean Sea

El Khril *c.5500 BC*

Capelletti

Haua Fteah *5650 BC*

Merimda *wheat, barley*

Faiyum *wheat, barley 5300 BC*

EGYPT

El Badari *wheat, barley*

El Khattara *wheat, barley*

ARABIA

Persian Gulf

Canary Is

Sahara Desert

Uan Muhuggiag

Meniet

before 4500 BC

Nabta *barley*

NUBIA

Red Sea

Adrar Tiouejine

Amekni

Adrar Bous

Gulf of Aden

Tichitt

Karkarichinkat

Arlit

4500–3500 BC

Esh Shaheinab

Khashm el Girba

Kadero *barley*

Gobedra

Jebel et Tomat

Lalibela *barley 500 BC*

R. Senegal

R. Niger

Rim

Jenne

Kourounkorokale

3500–2000 BC

L. Chad

Daima

SUDAN

linguistic evidence suggests cultivation
of tef and finger millet *c.5000 BC*

Cape Verde Is

R. Volta

2000–500 BC

Zenebi

R. Benue

ETHIOPIA

Kakimbon

Yagala

Kamabai

Yengema

Ntereso

Kintampo

Busumpra Cave

Adwuku

Aselire

Iwo Eleru

Afikpo

Ileret

Ele Bor

North Horr

L. Rudolf

Gulf
of
Guinea

R. Ubangi

R. Congo

Matupi Cave

Njoro River Cave

Long's Drift

L. Victoria

Narosura

Lukenya

East African pastoral Neolithic sites *c.2000 BC*

Bitorri Cave

Lululampembele

Pemba I.

Zanzibar

Atlantic

R. Kasai

R. Cuango

R. Congo

L. Tanganyika

Mafia I.

Ocean

Kalambo Falls

Fingira

Comoro Is

L. Nyasa

Mozambique Channel

MADAGASCAR

R. Zambezi

Gwisho

Kandana

Kalahari
Desert

R. Limpopo

Orange R.

Drakensberg Mts

Glen Elliott

Matjiesrivier

Wilton

Key / legend:

- hunter-gatherer 4000–1000 BC

early agriculture:
- (!) earliest cereal cultivation
- other early food production

probable area of crop domestication:
- ensete
- tef
- sorghum
- bulrush millet
- finger millet
- yam
- African rice

evidence of early livestock:
- cattle
- sheep and goats
- limits of cattle
- spread of sheep and goats

1   THE DUAL ORIGINS OF AFRICAN AGRICULTURE

Early African agriculture was based partly on the introduction of plants and animals from the Near East and partly on the exploitation of indigenous species. While sheep and goat were imported, cattle were independently domesticated from wild north African stock in the Sahara. Wheat and barley were also introduced from western Asia, but only thrived in the Nile Valley, the Ethiopian Highlands and along the Mediterranean coast. Farming further south was based on indigenous African cereals, root crops and trees more suited to tropical conditions. The spread of farming and herding south of the Equator was a long and gradual process, impeded by dense forests and by parasites such as the tsetse fly, and cattle pastoralists did not reach southern Africa until c.AD1000. Another factor hindering the expansion of cattle pastoralism may have been a biological intolerance of lactose (the sugar present in milk) amongst the local inhabitants, which meant that they were not able to make full use of milk products.

Inset map (lower left):

Mediterranean Sea

ARABIA

Tropic of Cancer

R. Nile

R. Niger

Equator

Atlantic

Ocean

R. Zambezi

Mozambique Channel

Tropic of Capricorn

major vegetation zones: *(left)*
- tropical rain forest
- woodland savanna
- sahel and steppe
- desert
- Mediterranean
- upland and mountain

The mastery of metals

The discovery that metals can be isolated from certain rocks by heating, and then hammered or moulded into useful shapes, was a great human intellectual triumph. The use of copper, bronze and iron has revolutionised control of the environment. Study of mines, smelting processes, equipment of smiths and artefacts produced has shown that knowledge of metals was discovered independently in several parts of the world. Copper was being used for making tools and weapons as early as 9000 years ago. Except for Australia, where metals were unknown before the coming of the Europeans, metal technology was established throughout the world by the 1st millennium AD and its development in each continent can be outlined.

The earliest metals in use were copper and gold, probably because attractive nuggets of these occur naturally and were soft enough to be hammered flat and cut with stones. This process required no knowledge of metallurgical chemistry. Pure deposits of metal are, however, limited in their distribution, and a major threshold was crossed when it was discovered that heating produced chemical changes in metal ores and could help separate out pure metal from them. This discovery may have been made by craftsmen using attractive varieties of copper ore such as malachite and azurite for making jewellery or decorating pottery. Heating also allowed metals to be cast when molten. This was the beginning of true metallurgy. The discovery seems to have been made separately in western Asia and south-east Europe (7000–6000 BC) and eastern Asia (before 2000 BC). The rest of Europe, Asia and North Africa acquired this knowledge from these centres between 4000 and 2000 BC. Most of the early use of metal was for ornament and display, as tools and weapons of pure copper proved of limited use.

This changed with the discovery of bronze, an alloy, or combination of copper and tin which could be given a much harder cutting edge and also made better castings; like copper it could also be recycled. It was discovered in western Asia between 4000 and 3000 BC, and the knowledge spread through the Old World between 3000 and 2000 BC. Its spread was helped by the development of long-distance trade routes for metals, especially as deposits of tin and gold were rare. Bronze was probably discovered separately in eastern Asia (2000 BC), the technology then spreading south. Bronzesmiths in each continent became steadily more skilled after 3000 BC, and where metal supplies were plentiful bronze began to be used to make utilitarian items such as agricultural implements, which greatly increased the potential of farming.

The most important of all discoveries was that of iron-working, for this is by far the most common metal, and with the addition of carbon to make steel it has the best cutting edge of all. It was discovered later than the other metals, the earliest evidence coming from western Asia, where it was being smelted and forged into tools and weapons between 2000 and 1500 BC. From that time bronze was increasingly restricted to ornaments. Between 1500 and 600 BC knowledge of iron spread in all directions from western Asia to Europe, North Africa and Central and southern Asia. In Europe it became common enough by 500 BC to be found in small farming settlements, and iron was used extensively in forest clearance, which changed the face of the European landscape. The introduction of iron also led to the appearance of better craft tools and better armed warriors. Before 150 BC steel-making had already begun to be practised.

In sub-Saharan Africa there was almost no use of metal before c. 500 BC. At that date both iron and copper came into use in the West African savannas and forests, and large quantities of iron were being smelted in the Middle Nile Valley. Iron was known in eastern Africa by 200 BC and had reached southern Africa by AD 200. The great gold and copper deposits of Zimbabwe, Zaire and Zambia were not utilised until AD 800–1000.

In eastern Asia iron technology probably developed independently and differently from elsewhere. In China, where iron was first smelted in about 600 BC, the new metal was cast in the same way as bronze had traditionally been cast. This required very high temperatures and did not happen elsewhere for more than a thousand years. In the western Old World iron-working relied on smithing (hammering and forging). Casting of iron began in Europe in the Middle Ages, however, and large-scale production of cast-iron subsequently became an important part of the Industrial Revolution of the 18th and 19th centuries. It was, indeed, the technological potential of iron for harnessing steam power that propelled the world into the modern age.

4 TOOLS AND TECHNIQUES

Metal artefacts may be divided into those that need hard sharp edges, mainly tools and weapons, and those made for display, religious purposes and currency, which do not. For edged weapons and tools bronze and iron are the most suitable metals, although it was only with the discovery of iron that metal weapons and tools became common. The non-edge artefacts were usually made from gold, silver and copper, with bronze becoming a favourite when the *cire perdue* (lost-wax) technique was discovered – a wax model was used to form a clay mould, and then melted and drained off.

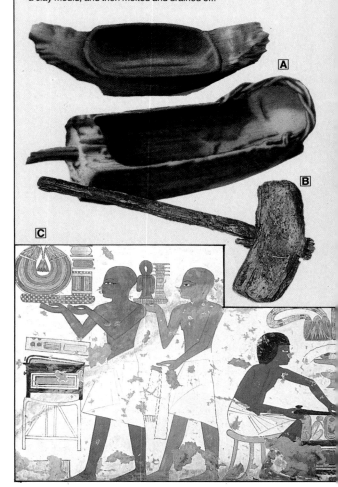

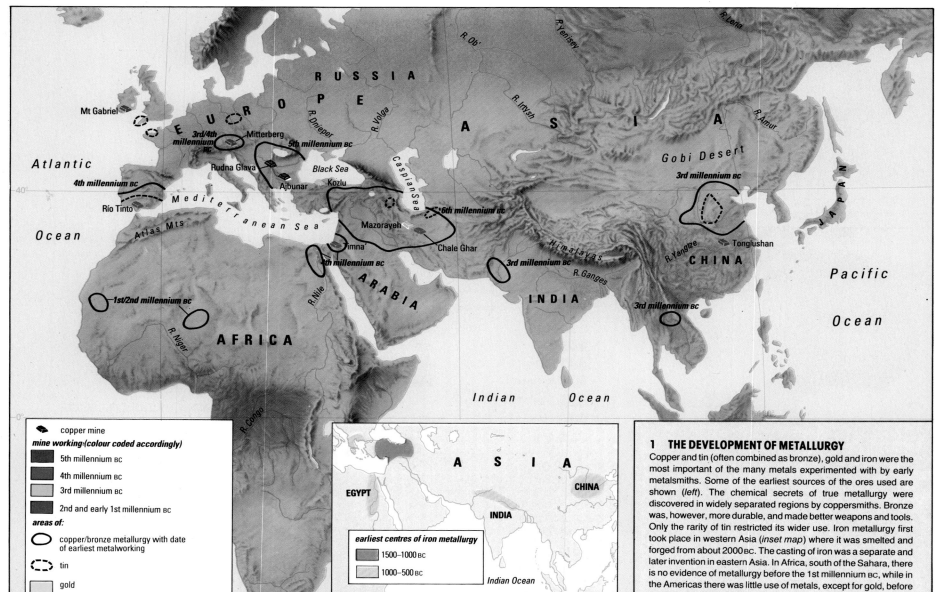

copper mine

mine working: (colour coded accordingly)

- 5th millennium BC
- 4th millennium BC
- 3rd millennium BC
- 2nd and early 1st millennium BC

areas of:

- copper/bronze metallurgy with date of earliest metalworking
- tin
- gold

earliest centres of iron metallurgy

- 1500–1000 BC
- 1000–500 BC

1 THE DEVELOPMENT OF METALLURGY

Copper and tin (often combined as bronze), gold and iron were the most important of the many metals experimented with by early metalsmiths. Some of the earliest sources of the ores used are shown (*left*). The chemical secrets of true metallurgy were discovered in widely separated regions by coppersmiths. Bronze was, however, more durable, and made better weapons and tools. Only the rarity of tin restricted its wider use. Iron metallurgy first took place in western Asia (*inset map*) where it was smelted and forged from about 2000 BC. The casting of iron was a separate and later invention in eastern Asia. In Africa, south of the Sahara, there is no evidence of metallurgy before the 1st millennium BC, while in the Americas there was little use of metals, except for gold, before the European conquest.

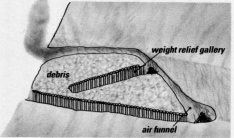

A *Troughs from copper mines at Tonglushan, China, probably for carrying water used in fire-setting within the mine. Late 1st millennium BC, wooden.* B *Hammer from the copper mines at Mitterberg, Austria. c. 1000 BC.* C *Wall painting from the tomb of Nebamun and Ipuky, Thebes, showing goldsmiths and joiners. 1300 BC, height 50cm.* D *Double-axe and mould from Knossos, Crete. 1900–1700 BC, bronze and stone, length 15cm.* E *Model of a chariot drawn by four onagers from the Shara temple, Tell Agrab. This is the earliest known example of the cire perdue (lost-wax) process. c. 2700 BC, copper, height 7cm.*

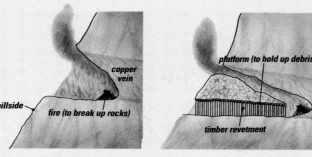

Austrian Alps: operation of a prehistoric copper mine

2 MINING

Copper mining took place in the Salzberg region of Austria between c.1500 and 800 BC (*illustrations above*). The deposits of ore would have been recognised by prospectors from their colour and texture, and the veins exploited by simple tunnels (adits). Labour could be reduced by 'fire-setting' – lighting fires against the vein to fracture it and make removal of the ore easier. As the tunnels became longer the fires at the working face needed a circulation of air to burn properly, and wooden passages with strong ceilings were built. The ceilings kept the air passages clear and held the broken ore. When the tunnels penetrated deep underground a passageway for the miners and fuel was necessary and the timber contructions became more elaborate.

The broken lumps of ore were taken outside, pulverised and washed to remove impurities. The ore was then roasted and smelted in furnaces, the local forests supplying the fuel. The cakes (ingots) of copper were carried elsewhere for casting. As many as 200 men may have been needed to service one mine as miners, foresters, smelters and porters.

The map (*below*) shows one of the greatest concentrations of early copper mines in Europe, in the Mitterberg region of Austria in the later 2nd millennium BC. It is estimated that by 800 BC some 13,000 tons of copper had been produced by this group of mines.

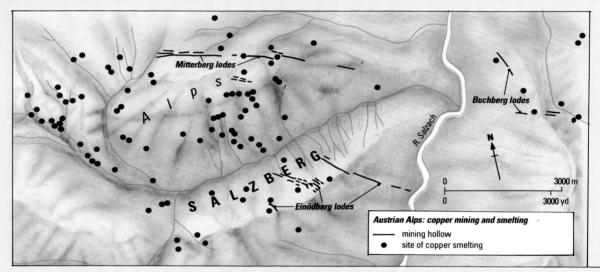

Austrian Alps: copper mining and smelting
— mining hollow
• site of copper smelting

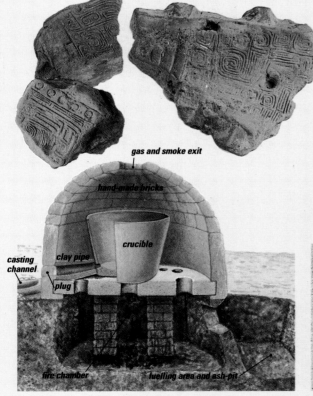

iron ore and charcoal mixture

bag bellows

tuyère

3 SMELTING

Reconstruction of Chinese bronze-casting furnace from late Shang period (*above*). Here, copper and tin which had already been smelted were combined in the desired proportion (usually 10% tin and 90% copper). The furnace was fuelled by charcoal. When molten, bronze was transferred from the crucible through the clay pipe to the casting channel. It is thought that when the metal within the crucible was molten a small section of the crucible wall was broken to release the metal into the clay channel. Gas and smoke escaped through an opening at the top of the dome. The alloy which was the end-product of this process was tapped into ingots (shaped moulds) which could later be re-melted in crucibles and poured into artefact moulds (*top*).

Top fragments of clay moulds for casting bronze vessels, from Anyang, China. c.1000 BC, average length 5cm.

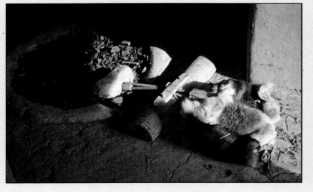

The iron smelting furnace (*above*) shows how simply iron ore can be smelted to produce a 'bloom', a lump of spongy but usable iron. Within this stone-built, clay-lined bowl furnace the ore, already broken into small pieces and cleaned of obvious impurities, was packed in alternate layers with charcoal. One or more bellows made of skin connected with the interior through long clay nozzles (tuyères) and holes in the walls. When the charcoal was fired the bellows were worked for many hours to raise the temperature to c.1200°C and to maintain it. The metal becomes nearly molten at this temperature, leaving more impurities as 'slag'. The iron coagulated at the bottom of the furnace as the bloom. Special smithing tools, particularly tongs, were needed to forge artefacts from the reheated bloom.
Left reconstruction of iron smelting furnace. The bellows of animal skin are attached to clay pipes, which carry the bellows' draught to the charcoal fire.

The first civilisations

The development of the first urban, literate civilisation, in southern Mesopotamia in about 3500 BC, was to have profound consequences on subsequent human history. Within a few centuries, a similar independent process of development led to the emergence of civilisation in Egypt (c.3200 BC), the Indus Valley (c.2500 BC) and northern China (c.1800 BC). These were the four primary civilisations of the Old World. The remains of their cities, tombs and temples reflects a new level of cultural and economic achievement, while through writing, perhaps their single most revolutionary innovation, they have left inscriptions and clay tablets which are the earliest historical records in the world.

All four civilisations shared certain features. Each was centred on a fertile alluvial plain with the rich agricultural potential necessary to support high populations. In each case, a part of the population lived in cities, ruled over as independent states or as parts of a larger kingdom or empire. However, agricultural practices varied significantly. In Egypt and the Indus Valley, the annual flooding of the Rivers Nile and Indus brought both water and fertile alluvium. Crops could be planted on flooded land as the waters receded, and good regular harvests were assured. In Mesopotamia, on the other hand, extensive and costly systems of irrigation canals had to be built to take water from the Rivers Tigris and Euphrates to the fields. Irrigation canals also played an important part in the agriculture of Shang China. In all four areas, productive agriculture was essential for the rise of the cities.

The development of cities was the culmination of a long process of settlement expansion. The early cities had populations thousands or even tens of thousands strong, much larger than the earlier farming settlements which had numbered their inhabitants only in hundreds. The appearance of settlements of this size precipitated major changes in government, social organisation and economic activity. All of the early civilisations were characterised by centralised state or city-state administrations. In Egypt, a unified state, power was concentrated in the hands of the king, reflected in the colossal size of the royal tombs, the pyramids. Shang China, too, appears to have had a single supreme ruler, though with a number of vassal states, and centralisation was less marked. In Mesopotamia, by contrast, each city was originally independent, and the landscape was divided among city-states engaged in a constant struggle for hegemony. The Indus Valley may also have been divided into city-states, though the greater size of Harappa and Mohenjo-Daro suggests that they were either capitals of two separate kingdoms or successive capitals of the same state.

Writing was a crucial development in the administration of early civilisations, and with it emerged a new class of specialist, the scribe. The growth of this and other specialised occupations was an important feature of all the first civilisations. Many city dwellers were not directly involved in tasks related to subsistence because of the high productivity of the farming in these regions. Part of the 'surplus' wealth was in the hands of ruling elites, and their demand for luxury items created a growing market for craftsmanship. Crafts became more sophisticated, and often used raw materials which had to be imported from distant sources. Large urban populations also led to the establishment of full-time specialists producing everyday items such as pottery and textiles. Workshops and markets must have been a dominant feature of many early cities.

Hand in hand with craftsmanship went trade. The river basins were deficient in many of the essentials of everyday life, such as hard stone and metals. These had to be imported from neighbouring regions, and the size of the lowland populations created a demand that could be met only by organised trade on a substantial scale. In return for raw materials, the lowland populations exported manufactured goods, thus spreading their influence to far-flung communities.

Trade brought Mesopotamia into direct contact first with Egypt, then with the Indus. Sealstones used by Indus merchants have been found at several Mesopotamian cities, and it is possible that other influences and ideas also spread in this way. Nevertheless, each civilisation must be seen as an independent growth, with its roots fixed firmly in local development stretching back to the adoption of agriculture. The ultimate impact of the four Old World civilisations was nothing less than revolutionary. Together, they mark the beginning of a new phase in the development of human society.

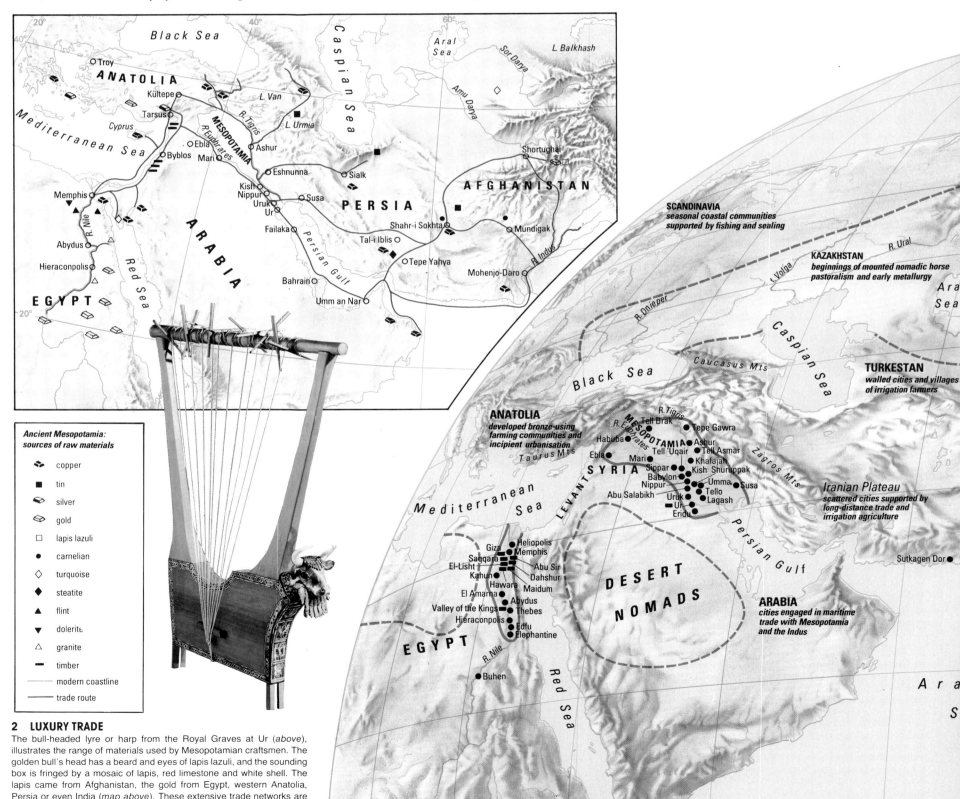

**Ancient Mesopotamia:
sources of raw materials**

- copper
- tin
- silver
- gold
- lapis lazuli
- carnelian
- turquoise
- steatite
- flint
- dolerite
- granite
- timber
- — modern coastline
- — trade route

2 LUXURY TRADE

The bull-headed lyre or harp from the Royal Graves at Ur (*above*), illustrates the range of materials used by Mesopotamian craftsmen. The golden bull's head has a beard and eyes of lapis lazuli, and the sounding box is fringed by a mosaic of lapis, red limestone and white shell. The lapis came from Afghanistan, the gold from Egypt, western Anatolia, Persia or even India (*map above*). These extensive trade networks are attested by records on clay tablets, and Egyptian tomb paintings show Semitic merchants leading caravans of donkeys laden with panniers.

3 THE ROLES OF LITERACY

The administration of city-states and kingdoms was transformed by the development of writing. Inscriptions and clay tablets from Mesopotamia and Egypt show that writing was used for keeping accounts and records, codifying laws and correspondence. In China and the Indus, however, writing seems to have had a more limited use. The surviving texts from China consist principally of inscriptions on 'oracle bones' which were used in royal divination, while in the Indus short inscriptions on steatite sealstones and other small objects are the only traces of writing that have survived.
A The law code of Hammurabi, king of Babylon, engraved on a diorite stela. The scene at the top of the stela shows Hammurabi receiving the commission to compile the law code from Shamash, the sun-god and god of justice. c.1760 BC, diorite, height of scene at top of stela 71cm. **B** Shang oracle bone from Anyang, China. The inscription records the question posed of the oracle, the response, and sometimes whether this was subsequently confirmed by events. The divination was achieved by interpreting the cracks resulting from the application of a heated object to the rear of the bone. Shang dynasty, 3000–1000 BC, length c.23cm. **C** The Instruction of the Vizier Ptah-hotep, an Egyptian moralising text purporting to be the advice of a 5th Dynasty vizier (c.2400 BC) to his son and successor. c.1900 BC. **D** Indus sealstone from Mohenjo-Daro, showing a horned bull standing before a brazier, with a short inscription in the Indus script above. Seal impressions on clay which had been attached to bales of merchandise may indicate ownership, and the inscriptions may record personal names or titles. Later 3rd millennium BC, steatite, height c.4.5cm.

1 THE GEOGRAPHY OF CIVILISATION

The first civilisations of the Old World developed in four separate river valleys which were capable of providing the regular high agricultural yields needed to support large urban populations. Other major valleys, such as the Ganges and the Mekong, were too heavily forested and unsuitable for dense occupation at this period. These early civilisations took on an importance out of all proportion to their comparatively limited geographical extent. Their influence spread with their need to obtain many raw materials from neighbouring regions. This contact, coupled with in-digenous processes of development, soon led to the appearance of cities, writing and other features of civilisation in areas which bordered the urban heartlands, such as the Iranian Plateau, Syria and the Levant. Further afield, in Europe and South-East Asia, village farming communities continued to flourish at this period, developing advanced technological skills such as metal-working, while on the Eurasian Steppes a new way of life, based on pastoralism and use of the horse, became established during the 2nd millennium BC.

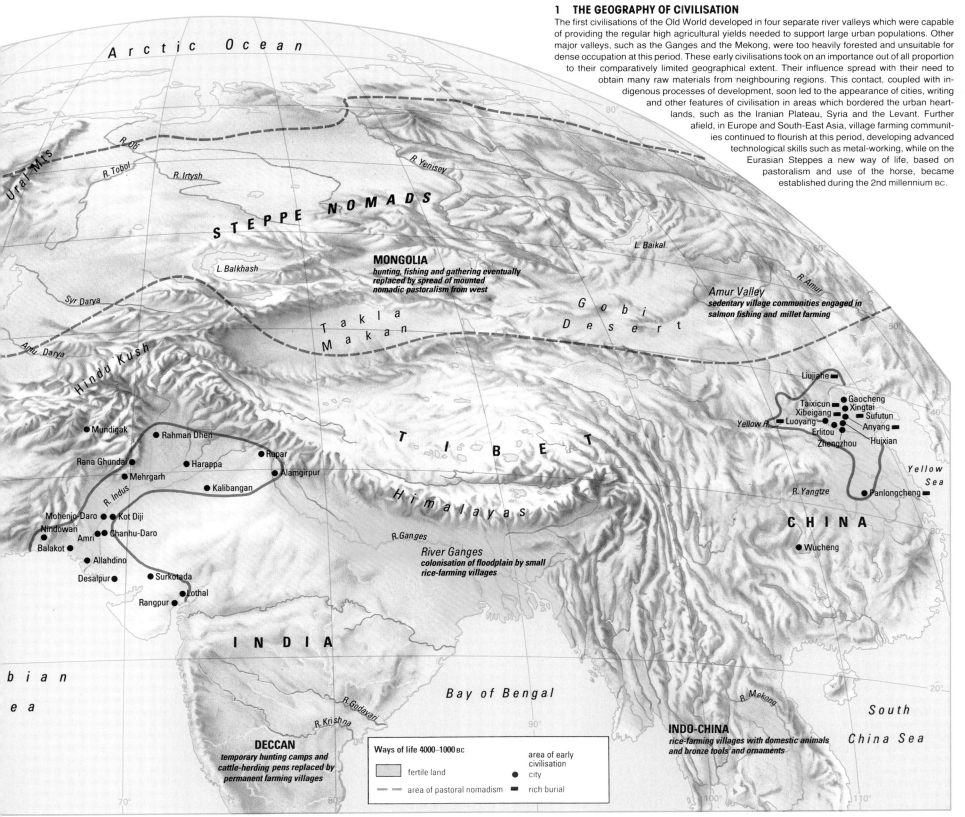

STEPPE NOMADS

MONGOLIA
hunting, fishing and gathering eventually replaced by spread of mounted nomadic pastoralism from west

Amur Valley
sedentary village communities engaged in salmon fishing and millet farming

River Ganges
colonisation of floodplain by small rice-farming villages

DECCAN
temporary hunting camps and cattle-herding pens replaced by permanent farming villages

INDO-CHINA
rice-farming villages with domestic animals and bronze tools and ornaments

Ways of life 4000–1000 BC

- fertile land
- - - - area of pastoral nomadism
- ● city
- area of early civilisation
- ■ rich burial

Mesopotamia: the first cities

One of the most important developments in human history – the emergence of the first cities – took place in southern Mesopotamia in the 4th millennium BC. The earliest cities were the culmination of increases in population and agricultural output which had taken place since the adoption of farming, and their massive remains today dominate the landscape of southern Iraq. This development was not merely one of size and number of inhabitants, however, but resulted in radical changes in society, religion, politics, intellectual experience, and indeed almost every aspect of life.

The first cities grew up in southern Mesopotamia during the late 4th millennium BC, the 'Late Uruk' period. Life in the dry, resourceless southern plain depended on irrigation, agriculture and foreign trade, and it may be that these special requirements eventually produced not only particular administrative or organisational skills but also sufficient economic surplus to support a concentrated population, larger settlements and, since some of the inhabitants were not directly involved in subsistence farming, craft specialists. These factors, along with the centralised authority necessary to create and maintain the canal systems, are directly associated with the emergence of the first cities. During most of the 3rd millennium (the 'Early Dynastic' period)

a number of city-states co-existed that were finally united under Sargon of Agade in 2300 BC.

Each city was under the protection of a particular god, housed in the splendidly fitted main temple along with his numerous human retinue. These attendants also performed an economic role, for the temple owned much of the city's land and livestock. Rainfall is scant and unreliable in southern Mesopotamia, and the rivers flood too late in the year for the planting season. The crops – barley, sesame and onions – were therefore watered by deliberate inundation from artificial canals. Sheep, goats, pigs and cattle were kept, and dairy farming, wool production and brewing were major industries. Produce was redistributed as rations to artisans and craftsmen.

The temple complex dominated the city physically as well as socially, and included spacious courtyards, storerooms and living quarters as well as cult rooms. Rebuilding on the same site often created a *temenos* area raised above the tightly packed dwellings of the lower town. Winding alleys and narrow main streets, sometimes divided by precinct walls, led to the gates in the outer defensive wall.

It was the increasing complexity of temple accounts that gave birth to the first written receipts: the earliest pictographic clay tablets from Uruk date to about 3100 BC. Gradually a syllabic script developed – the earliest known works of Sumerian literature, from Abu Salabikh, date to about 2500 BC. Most of the population remained illiterate, however, and writing skills stayed in the hands of the scribes, for whom training schools operated in the temples. It is to the practice of copying

documents at such establishments that we owe our knowledge of the traditions of these early cities, enshrined in later Akkadian texts. Some, such as the story of the Flood, go on into Hebrew legend, and others find their way into Classical mythology.

Little is known of the secular social organisation of these early cities. There were certainly slaves, and dynastic kings existed by the middle of the 3rd millennium – many are named in a later document called the Sumerian King List, which reckons back to the Flood. The city-states were usually in a state of petty rivalry with each other over land and water rights, and raids resulted in the taking of tribute and prisoners. Relations could be friendly too, with rulers sending each other occasional gifts. The fortunes of individual states waxed and waned, but Nippur and Kish always retained a certain cultural dominance. In the south the wealthy state of Ur, along with Lagash, dominated the region, squabbling continually with their northern neighbour, Umma.

Urbanism soon spread beyond the area of its first appearance, to the rain-fed country of northern Mesopotamia. Sites such as Nineveh and Tepe Gawra, Tutub, Eshnunna and Tell Agrab on the Diyala, Mari on the Euphrates (*page 132*) and Susa in western Persia exhibit strong cultural links with the cities of the south. Further afield, parallel processes of population increase and agricultural growth led to the emergence of cities in the Nile Valley, the Indus Plain and northern China. Within two thousand years, the city was an established feature in many parts of Eurasia, marking a further important advance towards the modern world.

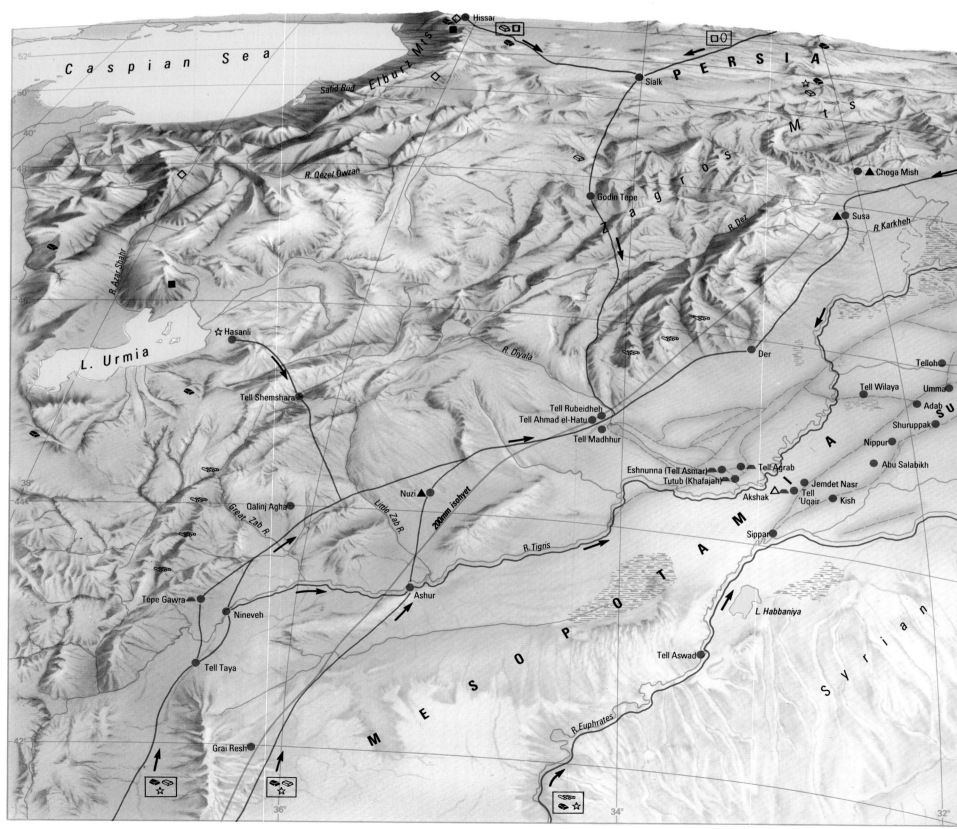

1 MESOPOTAMIA: THE GROWTH OF URBANISM

The river plain of the Tigris and Euphrates (below), the heartland of the early cities, is flat and featureless, alternatively parched and liable to sudden flooding. The 200-millimetre isohyet represents the limit below which rain-fed agriculture is not possible. Every city was situated on a major river, or joined to it by canal, and it was these waterways which connected Mesopotamia with the Gulf and countries beyond. Boats of the kind still used today in the marshy regions of Iraq often appear in mythology and art, and places such as Ur and Lagash were ports, connected to the open sea by a network of canals. Trade was essential, providing basic raw materials such as stone which were lacking in southern Mesopotamia, as well as the exotic luxuries characteristic of Sumerian culture. Goods were carried upstream by donkey and downstream by water. Detail is lacking for this early period, but it seems that temples had a monopoly where foreign trade was concerned. The Sumerians traded over impressive distances: to Afghanistan for lapis lazuli, to the Indus for precious stones such as carnelian and rare hardwoods, to the mountains of Anatolia and Persia for metal ores, and to the Zagros and the Lebanon for timber. Timber was an important commodity needed for the pole-and-mat roofs of the mud-brick buildings. The only native tree, the date palm, is too flexible for this purpose. Many goods entered Sumer via Bahrain (ancient Dilmun) which acted as an entrepôt for the Gulf region, with its own system of weights and measures. Recently, an actual trading post has been discovered at Habuba Kabira in Syria, dating to the end of the 4th millennium. Here many of the trappings of southern civilisation appear, including characteristic pottery and clay *bullae* (hollow balls containing tokens representing goods exchanged or despatched). At the same time, in Godin Tepe in western Persia, southern traders had their own quarter in the city. There was frequent rivalry between the cities of Sumer, often erupting into armed conflict, but a constant, and more serious, threat was posed both by the inhabitants of the mountain regions surrounding the plain and by the nomadic peoples of the desert.

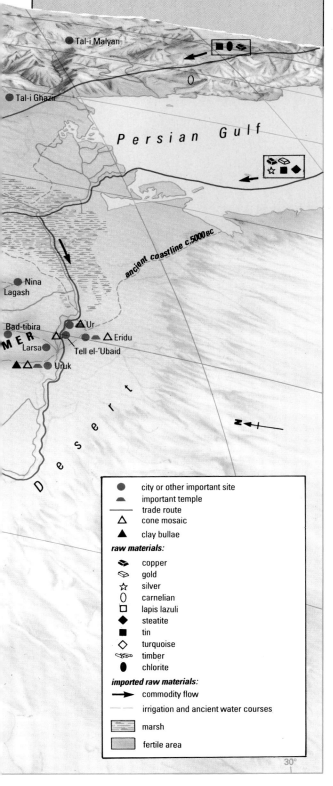

Key:
- ● city or other important site
- ▲ important temple
- — trade route
- △ cone mosaic
- ▲ clay bullae

raw materials:
- ⬙ copper
- ⬨ gold
- ☆ silver
- ◌ carnelian
- ▢ lapis lazuli
- ◆ steatite
- ■ tin
- ◇ turquoise
- ∿ timber
- ● chlorite

imported raw materials:
- → commodity flow
- --- irrigation and ancient water courses
- ▨ marsh
- ▨ fertile area

3 WRITING AND WORSHIP

A Bulla *from Susa, with the tokens (calculi) it contained, which represented items of merchandise. The contents of the bulla were recorded as a series of marks on the surface of the clay sphere: an early step towards the development of writing. c.3300 BC, clay, diameter c.5–6cm.* B *Cuneiform tablet from Jemdet Nasr giving details of areas of fields and crops. The signs were made by impressing the end of the reed into the wet clay, giving the* characteristic wedge-shaped marks. c.2900 BC, clay, height 7.5cm. C *Votive statues from early temples at Tell Asmar, placed in the sanctuary to intercede with the deity on behalf of the worshipper. c.2900–2600 BC, limestone, alabaster and gypsum, height of tallest figurine 55cm.* D *Vase from early temple at Uruk showing a procession of naked priests bringing offerings to Inanna, goddess of fertility, and friezes of sheep and goats, cereals and date palms. c.3000 BC, alabaster, height c.90cm.*

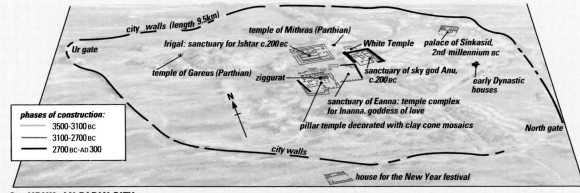

- city walls (length 9.5km)
- Ur gate
- temple of Mithras (Parthian)
- Irigal: sanctuary for Ishtar c.200 BC
- temple of Gareus (Parthian)
- White Temple
- palace of Sinkasid, 2nd millennium BC
- ziggurat
- sanctuary of sky god Anu, c.200 BC
- early Dynastic houses
- sanctuary of Eanna: temple complex for Inanna, goddess of love
- pillar temple decorated with clay cone mosaics
- city walls
- North gate
- house for the New Year festival

phases of construction:
- — 3500-3100 BC
- — 3100-2700 BC
- — 2700 BC-AD 300

2 URUK: AN EARLY CITY

The important early city of Uruk (*see photograph above*) has yielded some of the finest architecture and art objects of the period. It is here that the earliest Sumerian written tablets were found. By the end of the 4th millennium the already ancient settlements of Eanna and Kullaba had combined and attained truly urban proportions. A columned hall, 30 metres wide, in the huge ceremonial complex of Eanna is the first example of the use of columns to support a roof. These and the walls of adjacent buildings were covered with a mosaic made of coloured stone cones set into the mud plaster. In other buildings decorative techniques such as niches and engaged columns were used to relieve the drab mud exteriors. The best known king of Uruk was Gilgamesh, who set out from here on his quest for eternal life. The so-called *Epic of Gilgamesh* describes his many adventures, including an encounter with the Sumerian Noah, and mentions the Eanna precinct, the famous city walls, and the gardens and orchards which were said to form a third of the town.

Ur: a Sumerian city

The city of Ur, famous for its royal tombs and ziggurat, became, in the 3rd millennium BC, one of the most important states of Sumer, in southern Mesopotamia. It began at around 4500 BC as a small settlement in the marshy lowlands of southern Iraq (*page 124*), but within a few centuries parts of the site were overwhelmed by a massive flood, once thought to be the great flood described in the Bible and in Mesopotamian legend, now thought to have been only one of many periodic inundations. Ur recovered and grew in size, becoming the capital of a Sumerian empire extending as far north as the Anatolian highlands by the end of the 3rd millennium.

The early rulers of Ur were buried, with their retinues, in richly furnished royal tombs; many of the objects from the royal graves are made of costly materials obtained from sources hundreds of kilometres distant, and it is clear that by 2500 BC Ur had developed into a major centre of trade and manufacture – a role it retained for over 700 years. Ancient texts describe Ur as 'on the sea', indicating that the shoreline was nearer the city than it is today, and it was in maritime trade that the merchants of Ur excelled. On the northern and western sides of the city, within the walls, were artificial harbours linked to the Euphrates by canal – providing access for shipping from the Gulf. A bill of lading from the early 2nd millennium BC lists gold, copper ore, hardwoods, ivory, pearls and precious stones among the contents of one ship's hold. Ur's main trading partner was Dilmun (Bahrain) where a flourishing entrepôt was established; many merchants' seal stones from Bahrain and the Gulf have been found at Ur. Wider links were also established; seal stones bearing Indus script indicate lively commercial contacts with South Asia.

Ur reached the height of its political power under Ur-Nammu in around 2100 BC, when the city was rebuilt substantially. Foremost were the defences, consisting of a massive sloping mud-brick rampart against the side of the city-mound, surmounted by walls of more weather-resistant baked-brick. Within the walls, the famous ziggurat was rebuilt, standing in a sacred precinct containing other temples and a royal palace. The ziggurat was a typically Mesopotamian form, comprising a pyramidal series of ascending mud-brick terraces, decorated by buttresses and recesses, inset with mosaics and planted with trees. Each ziggurat was dedicated to the deity of the city – here the structure was topped by the temple of Nanna, the moon god and patron deity of Ur. The kings of Ur ruled their empire through an impressive bureaucracy, and archives of clay tablets from Ur and from several subject cities illustrate a passion for detailed accountancy. These tablets also reflect economic activity, recording for instance that in one particular year, one government department alone handled as much as 6000 tons of wool.

Ur was sacked by an invading army in 2000 BC, but in the ensuing 250 years the city attained its greatest size and economic prosperity. A new defensive wall was soon built, enclosing the temples and harbours and a dense network of winding streets and alleys. The population of the 60-hectare walled city may have exceeded 20,000 at this time, and beyond the walls were extensive suburbs, in some directions extending well over a mile. Between and beyond these suburbs lay the irrigated fields which supplied Ur with agricultural produce.

The wealthy burials of the rulers and their entourages in royal tombs preserve an evocative image of courtly life at Ur. Musical instruments, such as harps and lyres made of elaborately inlaid wood (*page 122*), and decorated gaming boards give some indication of the leisure pursuits of the courtiers. The ladies wore intricate headdresses and jewellery fashioned of gold, silver and semi-precious stones; cosmetics, toilet-boxes and wooden chests thought to have contained clothes have also been found in the graves. Banquets took place at court – perhaps celebrating victory in battle – where wine was drunk out of gold and silver vessels, to the accompaniment of harp music. All these objects reveal the skill and innovation of the Sumerian craftsmen in techniques such as metal casting, engraving and riveting.

In the 18th century BC, Ur declined in prosperity and political power and the initiative shifted further north, in particular to the city of Babylon. One reason for this may have been the collapse of the Indus civilisation, which deprived Ur of its control of a major trade route, while Babylon was better placed for trade with the Iranian Plateau to the east. Despite some restoration in the 14th century BC, Ur failed to recover its prosperity or prestige, and by 1000 BC it was important only for its temples and shrines. Although in the 6th century BC major restoration work was undertaken, the city was already moribund, and by the 4th century BC had been completely abandoned.

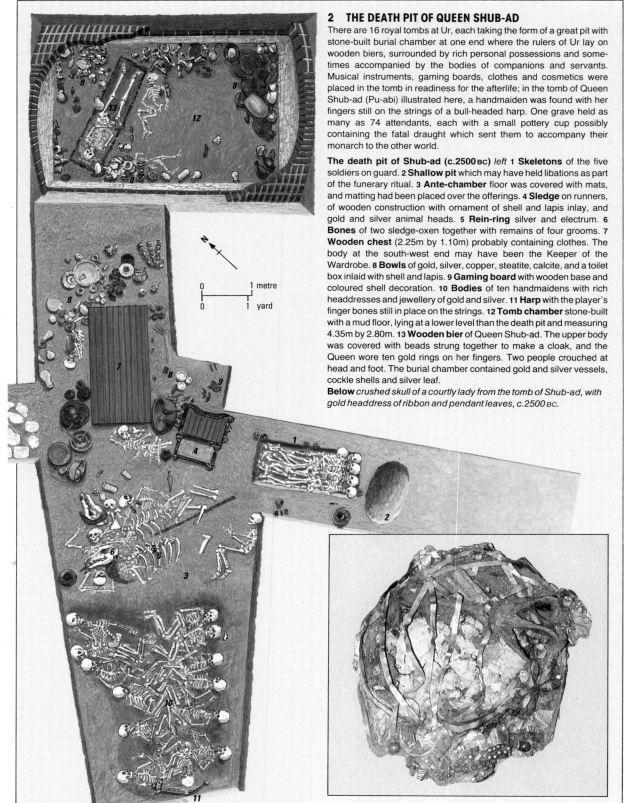

2 THE DEATH PIT OF QUEEN SHUB-AD

There are 16 royal tombs at Ur, each taking the form of a great pit with stone-built burial chamber at one end where the rulers of Ur lay on wooden biers, surrounded by rich personal possessions and sometimes accompanied by the bodies of companions and servants. Musical instruments, gaming boards, clothes and cosmetics were placed in the tomb in readiness for the afterlife; in the tomb of Queen Shub-ad (Pu-abi) illustrated here, a handmaiden was found with her fingers still on the strings of a bull-headed harp. One grave held as many as 74 attendants, each with a small pottery cup possibly containing the fatal draught which sent them to accompany their monarch to the other world.

The death pit of Shub-ad (c.2500 BC) *left* **1 Skeletons** of the five soldiers on guard. **2 Shallow pit** which may have held libations as part of the funerary ritual. **3 Ante-chamber** floor was covered with mats, and matting had been placed over the offerings. **4 Sledge** on runners, of wooden construction with ornament of shell and lapis inlay, and gold and silver animal heads. **5 Rein-ring** silver and electrum. **6 Bones** of two sledge-oxen together with remains of four grooms. **7 Wooden chest** (2.25m by 1.10m) probably containing clothes. The body at the south-west end may have been the Keeper of the Wardrobe. **8 Bowls** of gold, silver, copper, steatite, calcite, and a toilet box inlaid with shell and lapis. **9 Gaming board** with wooden base and coloured shell decoration. **10 Bodies** of ten handmaidens with rich headdresses and jewellery of gold and silver. **11 Harp** with the player's finger bones still in place on the strings. **12 Tomb chamber** stone-built with a mud floor, lying at a lower level than the death pit and measuring 4.35m by 2.80m. **13 Wooden bier** of Queen Shub-ad. The upper body was covered with beads strung together to make a cloak, and the Queen wore ten gold rings on her fingers. Two people crouched at head and foot. The burial chamber contained gold and silver vessels, cockle shells and silver leaf.

Below *crushed skull of a courtly lady from the tomb of Shub-ad, with gold headdress of ribbon and pendant leaves, c.2500 BC.*

1 A SUMERIAN CAPITAL

Like many Mesopotamian cities of its day, the centre of Ur (*see plan below*) was dominated by a sacred enclosure containing temples and related buildings; the most famous of these was the three-storeyed ziggurat, the lowest storey alone standing some 15 metres high. Clay tablets found within the sacred enclosure were given in receipt of goods – butter, oil and gold – suggesting that offerings were brought here. Food for the god was prepared in a kitchen within the precinct; inscribed copper cylinders speak of the 'evening and morning meals' of the god. To the south of the sacred enclosure lay the burial area of

the kings of Ur. Still further south an area of private houses of c.1800 BC has been exposed, probably typical of those to be found throughout the whole city, crossed by a network of unpaved streets, too narrow for wheeled vehicles. Like most buildings at Ur, the houses were built largely of mud-brick, though baked-brick was used for foundations and the street frontage. The lower storey was devoted to the kitchen, guest room, storerooms and servants' quarters, arranged around an open court, while the living rooms were on the first floor. Clay tablets identify one of the houses as that of Igmil-Sin, headmaster of a boys' school. Another house belonged to Ea-nasir, a merchant in the copper trade.

Right *aerial view of ziggurat and sacred enclosure at Ur.* **Below** *reconstruction of Ziggurat at Ur.*

1	ziggurat	3	temple of Nin-gal
2	court of Nanna	4	baked-brick city walls

R. Euphrates

northern harbour
palace (6th century BC)
shrine of Nanna
harbour temple (6th century BC)
houses
temple of E-nun-makh
fortress
palace of E-Khursag
royal mausolea
western harbour
houses (c.1800 BC)
temple of Enki
late Babylonian quarter (6th century BC)

0   200 metres
0   yards

temple
royal palace
other building

3 THE SUMERIAN LEGACY

The rulers buried in the royal tombs at Ur were accompanied on their journey into the afterlife by slaughtered retainers and by objects of exquisite craftsmanship using materials obtained from sources as far afield as eastern Persia and Afghanistan.

A 'Royal Standard' from the largest of the royal tombs, with panels depicting on each side the activities of the king in peace and war. The war side (illustrated here) shows helmeted infantry, four-wheeled battle wagons pulled by asses or onagers, and prisoners presented to the king. It was possibly the sounding box of a musical instrument. Lapis lazuli mosaic inlaid with shell and red limestone, originally fixed with bitumen to a wooden base. 56 x 23cm.
B Headdress from the grave of Queen Shub-ad. Gold with beads of lapis lazuli and carnelian. c.30–35cm. **C** 'Ram in a thicket'. One of a pair originally serving as supports, perhaps for a table. The head and legs are of gold, the belly of silver, the fleece of shell and lapis lazuli attached to a wooden body with bitumen. Height 46.5cm. **D** Silver rein-ring surmounted by an electrum onager. The onager is a type of ass domesticated in ancient Mesopotamia and used as a draught animal. The rein-ring was attached to the pole of the sledge in Queen Shub-ad's tomb. Height 12cm.

Egypt: the pyramid age

Ancient Egypt, a narrow valley bordered on either side by extensive deserts, was the gift of the Nile. The river, bringing water and rich alluvium in its annual floods, transformed desert into prosperous agricultural land, while the surrounding arid expanses provided strong natural frontiers. Secure, rich in agricultural and mineral resources, Egypt sustained a unique confidence and cultural purity for over three thousand years.

At the end of the last Ice Age, around 10,000 years ago, the inhabitants of the Nile Valley were hunter-gatherers; with the milder postglacial conditions population grew and local plants and animals were domesticated. In the late 6th millennium BC farming villages appeared in the Nile Valley, cultivating wheat and barley and rearing sheep and goats, introduced from the Near East. The ensuing two millennia saw the gradual formation of a unified Egyptian state. After 4000 BC there was a substantial increase in population and village size accompanied, during the second half of the 4th millennium, by great advances in craftsmanship and technology, culminating in the regular working of copper and the fashioning of ceremonial stone maceheads and slate palettes for grinding cosmetics. The first walled towns appeared at Naqada and Hieraconpolis (c.3300 BC). These were associated with rich tombs, probably the resting-places of the rulers of Upper Egypt, one of whom was the first to

unite the whole of the valley, from the first cataract to the Mediterranean, as a single kingdom in about 3100 BC. The unification was consolidated by the foundation of a new capital at Memphis, strategically situated at the junction of valley and delta. Memphis remained a major administrative centre, if not the capital, until supplanted by Cairo in the 7th century AD.

During the Old Kingdom Egypt was a theocratic state dominated by a divine king. Belief in life after death was a fundamental religious tenet, and both kings and courtiers built elaborate tombs to secure an afterlife by protecting the body, surrounded by as many comforts as they could afford. Non-royal tombs were decorated with reliefs and wall paintings of everyday scenes, often episodes from the owner's life, such as the supervision of craftsmen, or activities he wished to relive after death, for instance hunting in the marshes bordering the Nile. The daily tasks which were depicted included food production – farming, herding, harvesting, baking and brewing – which would magically provide sustenance for the dead. All furnish an extraordinarily comprehensive picture of life in ancient times (page 138).

Around 2650 BC, a revolutionary new type of royal tomb appeared. A stone stepped pyramid, 62 metres high, was built for Zoser in the Saqqara necropolis opposite Memphis – the first structure of its size in the world. Soon afterwards, in the 4th Dynasty, the true pyramid developed from the stepped form, and it was during this period that the largest pyramids of all were built. The Great Pyramid of Khufu at Giza (c.2540 BC) is 147 metres high and consists of an estimated 2.3 million blocks, each weighing an average of

2.5 tonnes. Work on the pyramid would have been carried out during the annual Nile floods – between July and October – when the majority of the farming population was idle; it can be estimated that, over the 23 years of Khufu's reign, 1100 blocks would have to be quarried, transported and erected in each working day in order to complete the pyramid in time for Khufu's burial. This startling achievement is the ultimate testament to the control exerted over the Egyptian populace by the ruler.

Egypt was governed by ministers, who were answerable to the king and headed by the vizier, responsible for administration, justice and taxation. The country was divided into provinces (nomes), each ruled by a provincial governor, who became increasingly independent of central control. By 2400 BC royal power was in decline and the size of the pyramids diminished accordingly. Before 2400 BC governors were buried in court cemeteries, beside the pyramids of their royal masters. As royal power diminished, the governors treated their provinces as petty kingdoms, and were buried in impressive rock-cut tombs at provincial centres up and down the Nile Valley, these changed burial practices reflecting their increasing power. But the final blow to the enfeebled monarchy was delivered by the Nile itself. The annual floods were always erratic, and the area of fields bordering the river which were watered and fertilised by the Nile inundations varied. Around 2150 BC, a period of consistently low floods precipitated half a century of disastrous famine which finally tore the old order apart. Nevertheless, the norms and values of Egyptian civilisation were deeply rooted and enduring, so that within a century centralised royal power was restored and a new age of stability and prosperity began.

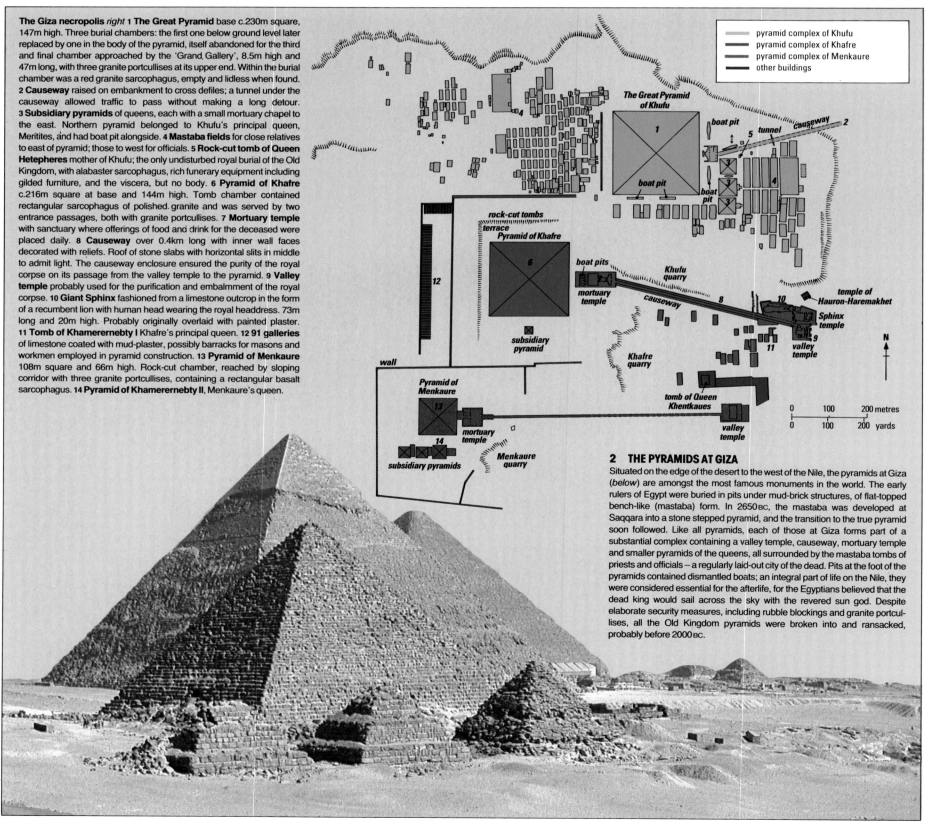

The Giza necropolis right **1 The Great Pyramid** base c.230m square, 147m high. Three burial chambers: the first one below ground level later replaced by one in the body of the pyramid, itself abandoned for the third and final chamber approached by the 'Grand Gallery', 8.5m high and 47m long, with three granite portcullises at its upper end. Within the burial chamber was a red granite sarcophagus, empty and lidless when found. **2 Causeway** raised on embankment to cross defiles; a tunnel under the causeway allowed traffic to pass without making a long detour. **3 Subsidiary pyramids** of queens, each with a small mortuary chapel to the east. Northern pyramid belonged to Khufu's principal queen, Meritites, and had boat pit alongside. **4 Mastaba fields** for close relatives to east of pyramid; those to west for officials. **5 Rock-cut tomb of Queen Hetepheres** mother of Khufu; the only undisturbed royal burial of the Old Kingdom, with alabaster sarcophagus, rich funerary equipment including gilded furniture, and the viscera, but no body. **6 Pyramid of Khafre** c.216m square at base and 144m high. Tomb chamber contained rectangular sarcophagus of polished granite and was served by two entrance passages, both with granite portcullises. **7 Mortuary temple** with sanctuary where offerings of food and drink for the deceased were placed daily. **8 Causeway** over 0.4km long with inner wall faces decorated with reliefs. Roof of stone slabs with horizontal slits in middle to admit light. The causeway enclosure ensured the purity of the royal corpse on its passage from the valley temple to the pyramid. **9 Valley temple** probably used for the purification and embalment of the royal corpse. **10 Giant Sphinx** fashioned from a limestone outcrop in the form of a recumbent lion with human head wearing the royal headdress. 73m long and 20m high. Probably originally overlaid with painted plaster. **11 Tomb of Khamerernebty I** Khafre's principal queen. **12 91 galleries** of limestone coated with mud-plaster, possibly barracks for masons and workmen employed in pyramid construction. **13 Pyramid of Menkaure** 108m square and 66m high. Rock-cut chamber, reached by sloping corridor with three granite portcullises, containing a rectangular basalt sarcophagus. **14 Pyramid of Khamerernebty II**, Menkaure's queen.

pyramid complex of Khufu
pyramid complex of Khafre
pyramid complex of Menkaure
other buildings

The Great Pyramid of Khufu
1
boat pit
5 tunnel causeway 2
boat pit
boat pit
rock-cut tombs terrace
Pyramid of Khafre
boat pits
Khufu quarry
mortuary temple
causeway
8
temple of Hauron-Haremakhet
Sphinx temple
subsidiary pyramid
Khafre quarry
10
11 valley temple
9
wall
Pyramid of Menkaure
13
mortuary temple
tomb of Queen Khentkaues
valley temple
14
subsidiary pyramids
Menkaure quarry

N

0   100   200 metres
0   100   200 yards

2 THE PYRAMIDS AT GIZA

Situated on the edge of the desert to the west of the Nile, the pyramids at Giza (below) are amongst the most famous monuments in the world. The early rulers of Egypt were buried in pits under mud-brick structures, of flat-topped bench-like (mastaba) form. In 2650 BC, the mastaba was developed at Saqqara into a stone stepped pyramid, and the transition to the true pyramid soon followed. Like all pyramids, each of those at Giza forms part of a substantial complex containing a valley temple, causeway, mortuary temple and smaller pyramids of the queens, all surrounded by the mastaba tombs of priests and officials – a regularly laid-out city of the dead. Pits at the foot of the pyramids contained dismantled boats; an integral part of life on the Nile, they were considered essential for the afterlife, for the Egyptians believed that the dead king would sail across the sky with the revered sun god. Despite elaborate security measures, including rubble blockings and granite portcullises, all the Old Kingdom pyramids were broken into and ransacked, probably before 2000 BC.

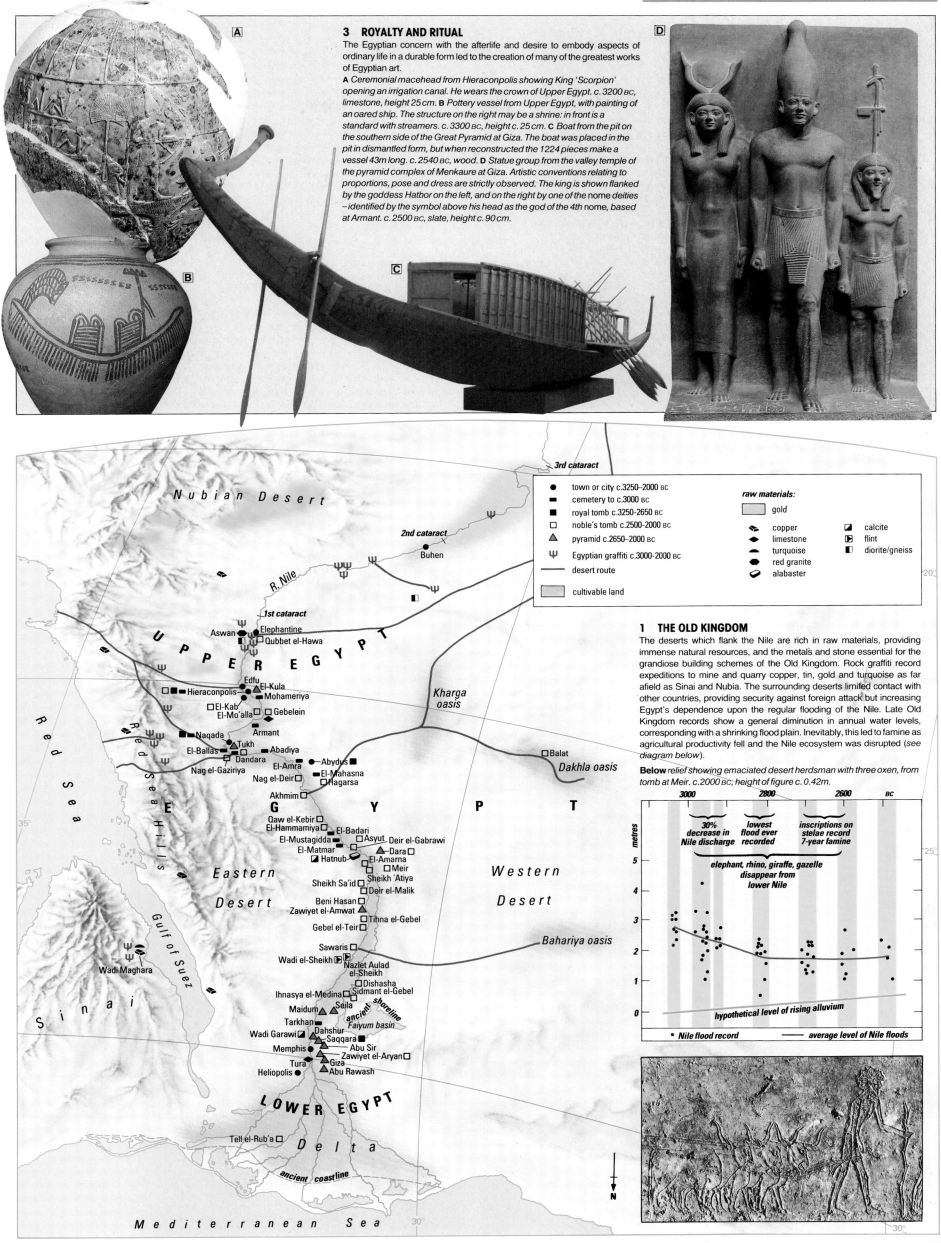

3 ROYALTY AND RITUAL

The Egyptian concern with the afterlife and desire to embody aspects of ordinary life in a durable form led to the creation of many of the greatest works of Egyptian art.

A Ceremonial macehead from Hieraconpolis showing King 'Scorpion' opening an irrigation canal. He wears the crown of Upper Egypt. c.3200 BC, limestone, height 25 cm. **B** Pottery vessel from Upper Egypt, with painting of an oared ship. The structure on the right may be a shrine: in front is a standard with streamers. c.3300 BC, height c. 25 cm. **C** Boat from the pit on the southern side of the Great Pyramid at Giza. The boat was placed in the pit in dismantled form, but when reconstructed the 1224 pieces make a vessel 43m long. c. 2540 BC, wood. **D** Statue group from the valley temple of the pyramid complex of Menkaure at Giza. Artistic conventions relating to proportions, pose and dress are strictly observed. The king is shown flanked by the goddess Hathor on the left, and on the right by one of the nome deities – identified by the symbol above his head as the god of the 4th nome, based at Armant. c. 2500 BC, slate, height c. 90 cm.

1 THE OLD KINGDOM

The deserts which flank the Nile are rich in raw materials, providing immense natural resources, and the metals and stone essential for the grandiose building schemes of the Old Kingdom. Rock graffiti record expeditions to mine and quarry copper, tin, gold and turquoise as far afield as Sinai and Nubia. The surrounding deserts limited contact with other countries, providing security against foreign attack but increasing Egypt's dependence upon the regular flooding of the Nile. Late Old Kingdom records show a general diminution in annual water levels, corresponding with a shrinking flood plain. Inevitably, this led to famine as agricultural productivity fell and the Nile ecosystem was disrupted (see diagram below).

Below relief showing emaciated desert herdsman with three oxen, from tomb at Meir. c.2000 BC; height of figure c. 0.42m.

Map key:

- town or city c.3250–2000 BC
- cemetery to c.3000 BC
- royal tomb c.3250-2650 BC
- noble's tomb c.2500-2000 BC
- pyramid c.2650-2000 BC
- Egyptian graffiti c.3000-2000 BC
- desert route
- cultivable land

raw materials:
- gold
- copper
- limestone
- turquoise
- red granite
- alabaster
- calcite
- flint
- diorite/gneiss

Diagram labels:
- 30% decrease in Nile discharge
- lowest flood ever recorded
- inscriptions on stelae record 7-year famine
- elephant, rhino, giraffe, gazelle disappear from lower Nile
- hypothetical level of rising alluvium
- Nile flood record
- average level of Nile floods

Cities of the Indus

The first urban communities of the Indian subcontinent developed around 2500 BC in the north-west, where the River Indus and its tributaries flow through a broad plain between the Thar Desert and the highlands of Baluchistan. This fertile alluvial lowland was first settled by farming groups around 3500 BC, and during the following thousand years (the Early Indus period), walled towns with extensive trading networks and increasingly sophisticated craftsmanship developed. This formative phase culminated in the Mature Indus period (2500-2000 BC), when earlier regional diversity was replaced by cultural uniformity, and a single province was created which encompassed the whole of the Indus plain. By 2500 BC a sophisticated urban civilisation, broadly comparable to those of Egypt and Mesopotamia but with its own individual character, had developed.

About a hundred settlements of the Mature Indus period are known, most of them substantial towns enclosed by defensive walls of baked-brick, with the largest sites, at Harappa and Mohenjo-Daro, each covering some 60 hectares. Their plan, repeated at certain of the smaller sites, consists of a raised mound or citadel overlooking a more extensive residential area. The citadels seem to have contained buildings of a religious, ceremonial and administrative character, but there are no remains of any palace.

At some sites town planning is apparent, with traces of a regular network of criss-cross streets. The larger houses at Mohenjo-Daro consisted of a series of rooms arranged around one or more open courtyards, with stairs leading to an upper storey or flat roof. The poorer inhabitants lived in single-roomed tenements. Almost all the buildings were of baked brick, and the bricks were of a standard size, found throughout the Indus Valley at this period: 28 x 14 x 7 cm. Many of the streets and lanes had drains, roofed in brick with regular inspection holes. Individual houses had bathrooms and lavatories discharging either into a pottery receptacle or direct into the street drain.

Mohenjo-Daro was clearly a major centre of trade and manufacture, with workshops of potters, dyers, metal-workers, shell-workers and bead-makers. Other Indus sites have yielded similar evidence, and surviving products indicate the high level of skill which was achieved. Some of the items made use of imported materials, while others may have been intended for export. Finds in Mesopotamia of Indus seals, used for securing bales of merchandise, and of Mesopotamian cylinder seals at Mohenjo-Daro demonstrate that a lively maritime trade linked the Indus Valley with the Persian Gulf and Mesopotamia at this time. As well as the maritime trade there were also important overland routes from the Indus Valley to Persia and Afghanistan. Shortughai was probably the site of a small Indus trading colony on the Amu Darya, over 1000 kilometres north of Harappa, perhaps supplying Persian tin and lapis lazuli from Badakhshan. Models of bullock-carts illustrate one of the main methods of land transport, while the ships used in river and maritime trade are represented by models and by carvings on seals and amulets.

Little is known of the social and political organisation of the Indus civilisation, or of its religious beliefs. The Indus script was used only for short inscriptions on seals, amulets and other small objects, and furthermore is as yet undeciphered. There are relatively few pieces of statuary which might represent rulers, and no buildings which can be interpreted as palaces, though the Great Bath and adjacent 'college' building at Mohenjo-Daro may have been for the use of a priestly elite. Priestly or secular, there must have been a strong central authority. Uniformity in weights, brick sizes, script and other cultural features suggests that the Indus area was a single state, with Harappa and Mohenjo-Daro the twin or successive capitals and towns such as Amri and Kalibangan provincial centres, although the evidence is not conclusive.

The Indus civilisation came to an end around 2000 BC, for reasons which are still unclear. At Mohenjo-Daro, the critical event was probably the shift in the course of the River Indus, which left the fields around the city desolate, no longer replenished by the annual flood. Epidemic disease, chronic flooding, disruption of trade and hostile incursions may also have upset the delicate balance between the urban communities of the plain and their agricultural base, trade networks and neighbours. After city life came to an end there was a return to a society based on agricultural village settlements. By around 1000 BC, however, the focus of interest had shifted eastwards to the basin of the River Ganges, where a new and more lasting episode of urban development was about to begin.

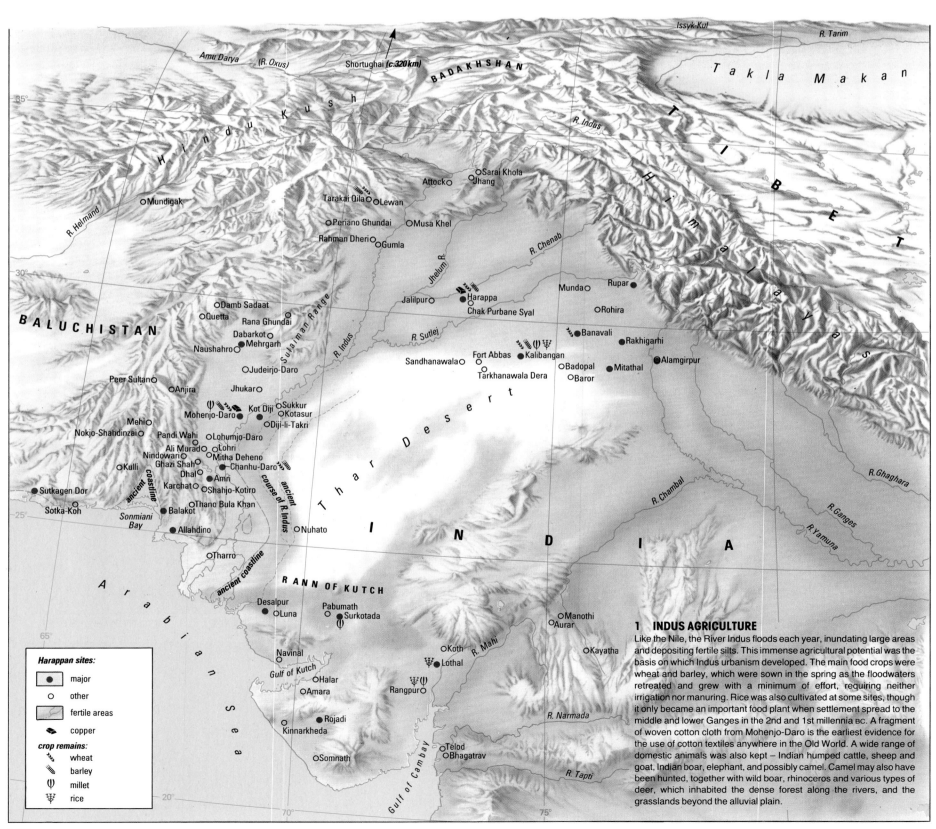

1 INDUS AGRICULTURE

Like the Nile, the River Indus floods each year, inundating large areas and depositing fertile silts. This immense agricultural potential was the basis on which Indus urbanism developed. The main food crops were wheat and barley, which were sown in the spring as the floodwaters retreated and grew with a minimum of effort, requiring neither irrigation nor manuring. Rice was also cultivated at some sites, though it only became an important food plant when settlement spread to the middle and lower Ganges in the 2nd and 1st millennia BC. A fragment of woven cotton cloth from Mohenjo-Daro is the earliest evidence for the use of cotton textiles anywhere in the Old World. A wide range of domestic animals was also kept – Indian humped cattle, sheep and goat, Indian boar, elephant, and possibly camel. Camel may also have been hunted, together with wild boar, rhinoceros and various types of deer, which inhabited the dense forest along the rivers, and the grasslands beyond the alluvial plain.

Harappan sites:

- ● major
- ○ other
- ▨ fertile areas
- ◆ copper

crop remains:

- 🌾 wheat
- 🌿 barley
- ⚘ millet
- ✿ rice

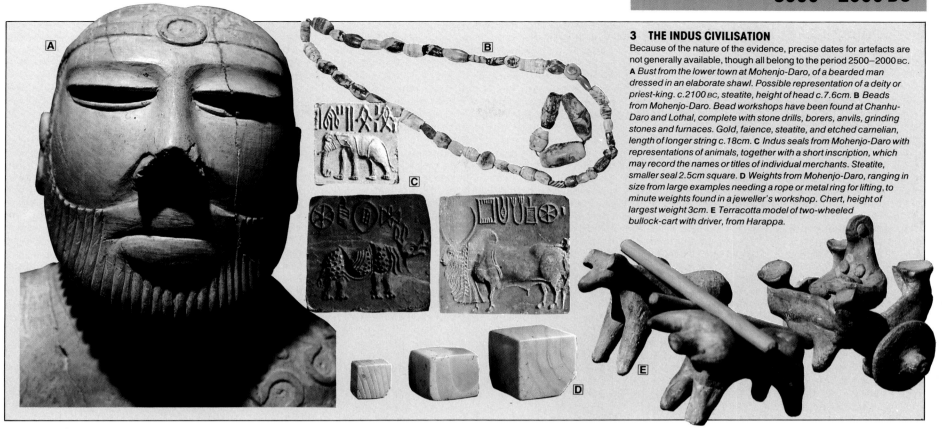

3 THE INDUS CIVILISATION

Because of the nature of the evidence, precise dates for artefacts are not generally available, though all belong to the period 2500–2000 BC. **A** *Bust from the lower town at Mohenjo-Daro, of a bearded man dressed in an elaborate shawl. Possible representation of a deity or priest-king. c.2100 BC, steatite, height of head c.7.6cm.* **B** *Beads from Mohenjo-Daro. Bead workshops have been found at Chanhu-Daro and Lothal, complete with stone drills, borers, anvils, grinding stones and furnaces. Gold, faience, steatite, and etched carnelian, length of longer string c.18cm.* **C** *Indus seals from Mohenjo-Daro with representations of animals, together with a short inscription, which may record the names or titles of individual merchants. Steatite, smaller seal 2.5cm square.* **D** *Weights from Mohenjo-Daro, ranging in size from large examples needing a rope or metal ring for lifting, to minute weights found in a jeweller's workshop. Chert, height of largest weight 3cm.* **E** *Terracotta model of two-wheeled bullock-cart with driver, from Harappa.*

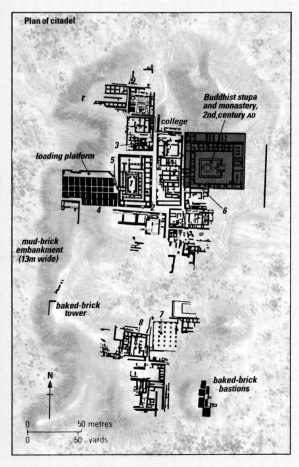

The city of Mohenjo-Daro

excavated areas

principal street of lower town, almost 10m wide, with brick-built drains

(see plan below)

excavated areas

citadel

N

l o w e r   t o w n

excavated areas

| 0 | | 200 metres |
| 0 | | 200 yards |

Plan of citadel

r

Buddhist stupa and monastery, 2nd century AD

college

3

loading platform

5

7

mud-brick embankment (13m wide)

4

2

6

baked-brick tower

7

8

N

baked-brick bastions

| 0 | | 50 metres |
| 0 | | 50 yards |

2 MOHENJO-DARO: AN INDUS CITY

Covering an area of 60 hectares, Mohenjo-Daro was a substantial city, with a population which may have reached 40,000. The lower town (*above*) was the main residential area, with houses of various sizes divided into nine blocks by regularly laid-out streets. The citadel was a religious, ceremonial and administrative centre; the so-called college building may have been the residence of a priestly elite.

Mohenjo-Daro citadel mound *above right* **1 Great Bath** 12m long, 7m wide and 3m deep, possibly for ritual bathing; steps into the bath on north and south sides had timber treads set in bitumen. Water supplied by indoor well. **2 Rooms** surrounding bath; on the east side, possible changing rooms. **3 Ancillary building** eight small bathrooms with runnels discharging into a central drain in the corridor. **4 Granary** (probable), built of timber, originally 45m long and 23m wide, later extended; massive

baked-brick podium divided into 27 blocks by a criss-cross arrangement of ventilation channels. **5 Brick corbelled drain** leading from Great Bath, length c.30m. **6 Building** with open court 10m square; possible residence for priests. **7 Assembly hall** 27.5m square, with 20 brick plinths, 1.5m by 0.9m, for the wooden pillars which supported the roof. **8 Possible temple complex**, including smaller aisled hall with finely paved floor.

Palace-cities of the Near East

In northern Mesopotamia and the Levant the period between 2500 and 1500 BC was dominated by the emergence of a network of city-states engaged in a continual struggle for political and economic supremacy. With the development of the first cities in Sumer at around 3500 BC large urban populations generated an increased demand for raw materials, which led to intensified contacts with neighbouring regions – Syria to the north-west and the Iranian plateau to the east. To secure supplies of essential raw materials the early states of southern Mesopotamia founded a number of substantial colonies in the north, soon to be followed by the indigenous development of cities in Syria and adjacent regions. By the middle of the 3rd millennium BC several powerful states had become established, each centred on a city with temples and a royal palace. Much of our knowledge of these kingdoms comes from the palaces with their valuable archives of clay tablets, which record their commercial, administrative and diplomatic activities.

The sites which have yielded the most important finds of architectural and archival material are Ebla and Mari, cities which achieved their greatest prosperity between 2400 and 1750 BC. At the heart of each city stood a palace complex and temples surrounded by private houses – only small areas have been excavated. The city was protected by powerful mud-brick walls or beaten earth ramparts – at Ebla the rampart was 50 metres wide at the base, and still stands 20 metres high above the surrounding plain. It enclosed an area of 50 hectares, while other cities were still larger – Hazor and Qatna some 70 hectares, and Mari over 100 hectares. It is estimated that the population of Hazor in the 18th century BC may have exceeded 25,000.

The largest collections of clay tablets come from the palaces of Ebla and Mari, numbering around 16,000 and 17,500 documents respectively. Many of the Ebla tablets are economic texts relating to the administration of palace and state, control of trade, and collection of tolls and taxes. Others are letters between the king and his governors, wives and officials. The Ebla tablets show that the city's major export was cloth. They also record considerable quantities of gold and silver received as tribute: in its heyday, Ebla's rule probably stretched from the River Euphrates to the Orontes, and as far north-west as the Taurus Mountains. The Mari tablets provide intimate details of life in a Syrian palace in the 18th century BC: pursuit of runaway slaves, measures to control an outbreak of epidemic disease, the collection of tolls from river traffic on the Euphrates. They also show the important position occupied by the royal ladies in the palace administration, who held keys to many of the stores and had control over important officials. Control was also exercised over the activities of artisans, who generally worked outside the confines of the palace. Finds from Mari and other palaces illustrate the high standard achieved in the working of metals, stone and ivory.

Trade was vital to the economies of these early city-states. The most impressive evidence of long-distance trade in the early 2nd millennium BC comes from the Anatolian site of Kültepe where, in c.1950 BC, Assyrian traders founded a colony on the edge of the native Anatolian city of Kanesh. Thousands of clay tablets from the business archives record the trade between this colony – one of some two dozen patronised by the merchants of the Ashur region – and the mother-city roughly 1500 kilometres to the south-east. The texts deal with a range of matters including the fixing of prices, the organising of trade caravans and the settling of debts. The object of this prodigious long-distance trade venture was the rich metal resources of Anatolia. Tin and textiles were sent west from Ashur by pack-ass, and payment returned in the form of gold and silver. The Anatolian colonies continued to function for 200 years, until the political power of Ashur went into temporary eclipse around 1750 BC.

This period was characterised by the persistent attempts of the most powerful cities to extend their rule over their rivals. A letter from Mari illustrates a fairly typical situation, with the kings of Babylon, Larsa, Eshnunna and Qatna each commanding a following of some 10-15 lesser rulers, while the King of Aleppo had as many as 20. Around the middle of the 18th century BC, Babylon achieved a measure of overall supremacy, defeating and destroying the cities of Mari and Eshnunna. This was only a further stage in the pattern of shifting hegemonies, however, and the first enduring attempts to unite substantial parts of the Near East in a single empire came only with the imperialist expansion of the Egyptian and Hittite states in the 16th century BC.

2 MARI: A MESOPOTAMIAN PALACE

The palace of Mari (below) dates in its present form from the reign of Zimri-Lim (c.1775-1760 BC) and is the largest of its period in Mesopotamia, covering 2.5 hectares in area and containing over 300 rooms. Built mainly of mud-brick, the palace is arranged around two courtyards. The larger outer court had an open-fronted audience chamber on its southern side, decorated with wall paintings of the 21st century BC. On the southern side of the inner court were two reception rooms: a throne room, with throne-base facing out onto the court; and behind the throne room a great hall with a sanctuary at one end and a throne-base at the other. The private apartments of the king and his queens, more simply decorated than the public rooms, lay at the north-west corner of the inner court. In the south-western corner of the palace were ranges of small, cell-like rooms on either side of a central corridor, which may have been slaves' quarters. Outside the main rectangle of the palace were supplementary storerooms and offices, while beyond the powerful perimeter wall on the east was a sacred area with a cult terrace and a series of temples, including one to Dagan, the principal Syrian deity of this period. The prosperity of Mari was based largely on control of river traffic on the Euphrates and on local agriculture, though in periods of political strength tribute was an important additional source. Cultivation was restricted largely to the river terrace on which the city stood; with irrigation, its fertile loam would have yielded a good harvest. Many tablets refer to the care of canals and the equitable distribution of irrigation waters. The flood plain itself was probably too wet for regular cultivation, while the plateau behind the site was too dry; these areas may have been used for pasturing livestock. Several ancient tells in the vicinity mark the location of smaller settlements within the kingdom of Mari (see map right).

Mari and its environs
▲ tell site

R. Euphrates

Wadi as Sawab

▲ Tell Halim Asra Hajin

▲ Tell Abu Hassan

lower terrace: pastureland subject to periodic flooding

middle terrace: cultivable land, irrigation essential

plateau: pastureland, no irrigation

Wadi Bir al Ahmar

▲ Mari

upper terrace: pastureland, too high for much irrigation

0   5   10 km
0   5   miles

Abu Kamal ○

temple of Ishtar

EARLY CITY

shops and workshops surrounding an open courtyard c.2500 BC

'schoolroom'
living quarters
first throne room
king's rooms
archive containing over 15,000 tablets
bathrooms
mud-brick outer walls
inner courtyard
entrance
possible slaves' quarters
second throne room
courtyard
kitchens with mud-brick ovens

PALACE OF ZIMRI-LIM (c.1775-1760 BC)

audience chamber
storerooms
palace temple
outbuilding housing chariots and stores
raised sacred terrace
temple of Dagan
temple of hamash
courtyard
courtyard
SACRED AREA

0   25   50 metres
0   25   50 yards

temple of Ninhursag

3 RULERS AND MERCHANTS

A Cylinder seal from Syria, with the impression of its sealing. Seals were used by merchants to identify their merchandise and guarantee the contents of containers, and were also used as 'signatures' on clay tablets. 18th or 17th century BC, haematite, height of seal 2cm. **B** Statue of Ishtup-Ilum, ruler of Mari. The pose is characteristic of statues of this period. Found in the palace of Mari. c.2100 BC, diorite or basalt; height 1.52m. **C** Exotic raw materials found at Ebla: obsidian from Anatolia, fragments of diorite and alabaster vessels from Egypt, sea shells from the Persian Gulf, basalt offering-tables, and pieces of unworked lapis lazuli from Afghanistan. c.2300 BC. **D** Donkey with panniers from Cyprus. Pack-asses were used widely in Near Eastern trade. 3rd millennium BC, pottery, length 8.8cm. **E** Cuneiform tablet from the business archives at Kültepe, recording the safe arrival of certain monies. Early 2nd millennium BC, clay, height 10cm. **F** Detail of polychrome fresco showing a procession of figures leading sacrificial bulls. Such frescos adorned the walls of the courtyards and many of the principal rooms at Mari. Early 2nd millennium BC, painted plaster, height of detail c.45cm.

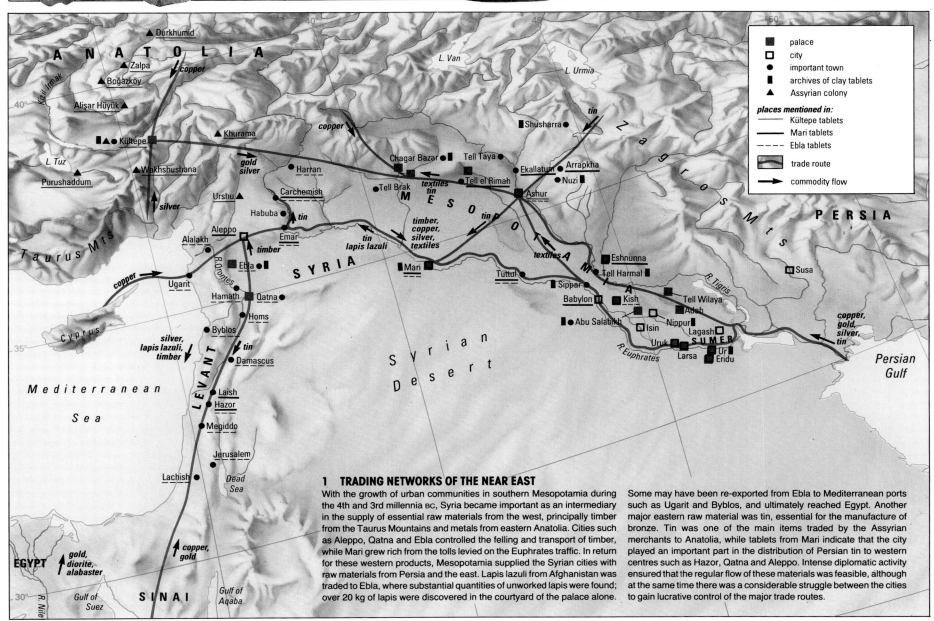

1 TRADING NETWORKS OF THE NEAR EAST

With the growth of urban communities in southern Mesopotamia during the 4th and 3rd millennia BC, Syria became important as an intermediary in the supply of essential raw materials from the west, principally timber from the Taurus Mountains and metals from eastern Anatolia. Cities such as Aleppo, Qatna and Ebla controlled the felling and transport of timber, while Mari grew rich from the tolls levied on the Euphrates traffic. In return for these western products, Mesopotamia supplied the Syrian cities with raw materials from Persia and the east. Lapis lazuli from Afghanistan was traded to Ebla, where substantial quantities of unworked lapis were found; over 20 kg of lapis were discovered in the courtyard of the palace alone.

Some may have been re-exported from Ebla to Mediterranean ports such as Ugarit and Byblos, and ultimately reached Egypt. Another major eastern raw material was tin, essential for the manufacture of bronze. Tin was one of the main items traded by the Assyrian merchants to Anatolia, while tablets from Mari indicate that the city played an important part in the distribution of Persian tin to western centres such as Hazor, Qatna and Aleppo. Intense diplomatic activity ensured that the regular flow of these materials was feasible, although at the same time there was a considerable struggle between the cities to gain lucrative control of the major trade routes.

Writing

Writing was invented to keep business accounts in the Near East in the late 4th millennium BC. The use of clay counters, or tokens, to help record transactions was already common, and the next stage was keeping those tokens inside a sealed clay 'envelope' marked with symbols indicating what was inside. The first actual texts consisted of numbers only, the next development being numbers with representations of domestic animals, probably receipts. Records of the most primitive kind come from Uruk and Nineveh in Mesopotamia, Habuba Kabira and Tell Brak in Syria, and Susa, Choga Mish and Godin Tepe in Persia. The most important subsequent develop-

ments took place in Mesopotamia. The writing was done by inscribing wet cakes of clay (tablets) with the end of a hollow reed stem, or stylus, which produced wedge-shaped marks. The cuneiform script developed from this (*cuneus* is Latin for wedge). Once dry, these tablets became very hard and brittle; many still survive today.

Gradually a whole pictographic script developed, with stylised drawings used to make up words. Although the language of these early texts is not known for sure it is likely that those from Susa are an early form of Elamite, and that those from Mesopotamian sites are in Sumerian. Each pictograph represents a syllable, and abstracts are conveyed by using concrete notions close in meaning ('mouth' for 'speak') or sound. Literary compositions are known from about 2400 BC, and after the accession of

Sargon of Akkad (2300 BC) the Akkadian language began to be written in cuneiform too. Sumerian has no relations, but Akkadian is Semitic, like Aramaic, Hebrew and Arabic. Assyrian and Babylonian are dialects of Akkadian, and over the next two thousand years they were used to record all manner of things in the cuneiform script, from royal chronicles to private letters, lawsuits, poetry and magic spells. A long literary tradition was established, and copies of old texts were frequently made and preserved. After the conquests of Alexander the Great cuneiform rapidly lost popularity in favour of the much more convenient Aramaic alphabetic script. The last cuneiform text dates to AD 75.

During its long lifetime cuneiform writing was borrowed to express other languages: Eblaite (from

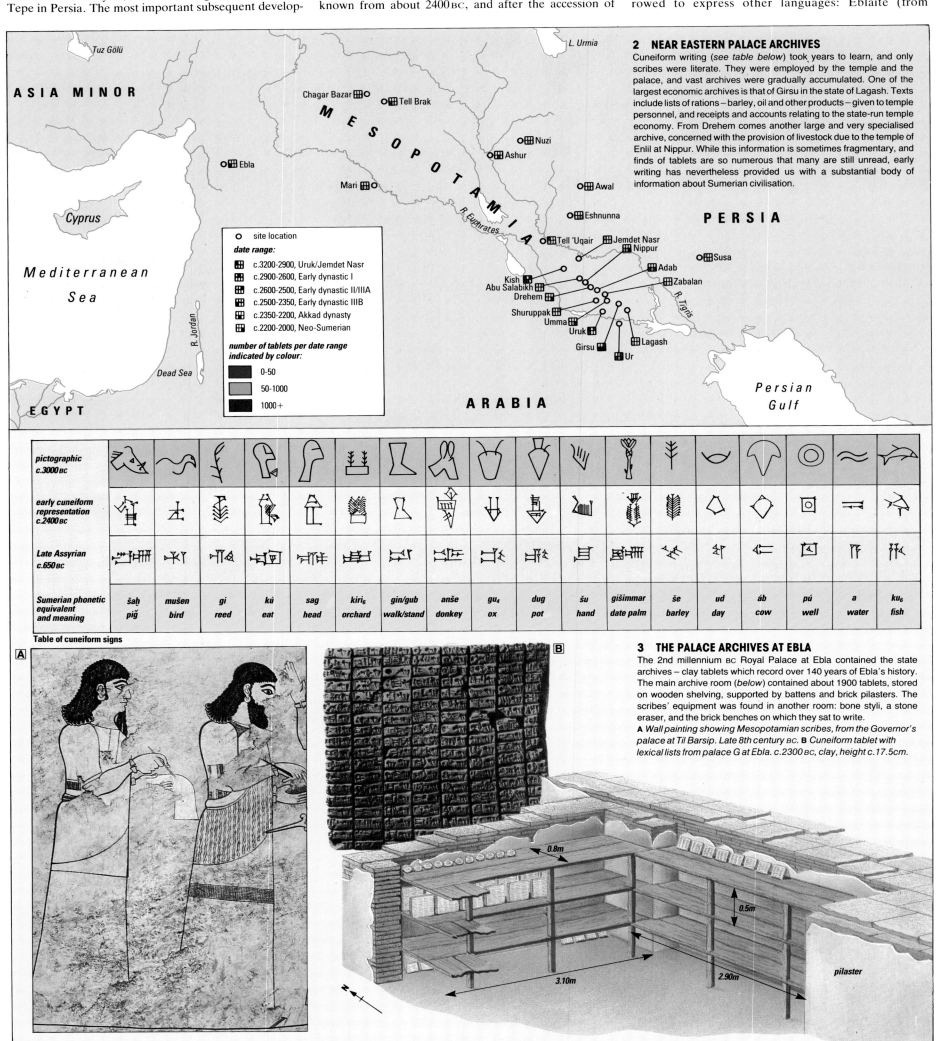

2 NEAR EASTERN PALACE ARCHIVES

Cuneiform writing (*see table below*) took years to learn, and only scribes were literate. They were employed by the temple and the palace, and vast archives were gradually accumulated. One of the largest economic archives is that of Girsu in the state of Lagash. Texts include lists of rations – barley, oil and other products – given to temple personnel, and receipts and accounts relating to the state-run temple economy. From Drehem comes another large and very specialised archive, concerned with the provision of livestock due to the temple of Enlil at Nippur. While this information is sometimes fragmentary, and finds of tablets are so numerous that many are still unread, early writing has nevertheless provided us with a substantial body of information about Sumerian civilisation.

Legend:
- o site location
- date range:
  - c.3200-2900, Uruk/Jemdet Nasr
  - c.2900-2600, Early dynastic I
  - c.2600-2500, Early dynastic II/IIIA
  - c.2500-2350, Early dynastic IIIB
  - c.2350-2200, Akkad dynasty
  - c.2200-2000, Neo-Sumerian
- number of tablets per date range indicated by colour:
  - 0-50
  - 50-1000
  - 1000+

Table of cuneiform signs

pictographic c.3000 BC																	
early cuneiform representation c.2400 BC																	
Late Assyrian c.650 BC																	
Sumerian phonetic equivalent and meaning	šaḫ piĝ / pig	mušen / bird	gi / reed	kú / eat	sag / head	kiri₆ / orchard	gin/gub / walk/stand	anše / donkey	gu₄ / ox	dug / pot	šu / hand	gišimmar / date palm	še / barley	ud / day	áb / cow	pú / well	a / water	ku₆ / fish

3 THE PALACE ARCHIVES AT EBLA

The 2nd millennium BC Royal Palace at Ebla contained the state archives – clay tablets which record over 140 years of Ebla's history. The main archive room (*below*) contained about 1900 tablets, stored on wooden shelving, supported by battens and brick pilasters. The scribes' equipment was found in another room: bone styli, a stone eraser, and the brick benches on which they sat to write.
A *Wall painting showing Mesopotamian scribes, from the Governor's palace at Til Barsip. Late 8th century BC.* **B** *Cuneiform tablet with lexical lists from palace G at Ebla. c.2300 BC, clay, height c.17.5cm.*

c.2500 BC), Elamite (from c.1285 BC), various Indo-European languages such as Hittite and its relatives Palaic and Luwian, and Hurrian and Urartian. A new reduced form, using only thirty signs as a primitive alphabet, was used to write Ugaritic from about 1400 BC; this is the first alphabet for which there is much evidence. Alphabetic writing was subsequently applied to such major languages as Hebrew, Aramaic, Arabic, Phoenician and Greek. Egypt almost certainly imported the idea of writing from Mesopotamia, though the Egyptian hieroglyphic script is unique. The earliest Egyptian writings were on stone, but papyrus ('paper' made by pressing flattened reeds together) survives from about 2600 BC.

None of the Near Eastern scripts was developed independently; all reflect the spread of the concept of writing, and sometimes the actual borrowing of written characters, from the original centre of origin in Mesopotamia. However, in other parts of the world writing was developed independently. In Mesoamerica, first Zapotec, and later Maya scripts were invented without any contact with the literate civilisations of the Old World. At the eastern limit of Eurasia, Chinese writing may also have been an independent invention. Though originally pictographic, the Chinese language it was used to represent was totally different from those of West Asia and the script developed along individual lines. The nature of the Chinese script, in which each character was simultaneously phonetic, syllabic and ideographic (expressing both a sound and a concept) was crucial in enabling it to unify a nation divided among many mutually unintelligible dialects. The political, cultural and military power of China led to the adoption of the Chinese script and derivatives of it over much of East Asia. Classical Chinese was until recently the *lingua franca* of the educated classes in Vietnam, Korea and Japan, while the vernacular was transcribed phonetically using modified Chinese characters.

With the adoption of writing it was possible, for the first time, to record business transactions, laws, histories and literature in a durable form that did not rely on human memory. Yet diffusion of literacy throughout society was also critical. While knowledge of writing was restricted to a small class of scribes, bureaucrats and priests its impact was necessarily limited. It was only in those societies where literacy became general – at Roman Pompeii, for example, where walls carried written graffiti and electoral slogans – that the true potential of this keystone of the modern world began to appear.

	oracle bone inscriptions c.1400-1200 BC	bronze inscriptions c.1500-700 BC	small seal script standardised after 221 BC	chancery script c.200 BC-AD 200	standard script c.AD 200 onwards	standard printed style c.AD 1400 onwards	cursive script c.AD 200 onwards	draft or 'grass' script c.200 BC onwards	simplified script standardised AD 1956	English translations
pictograph										horse
differentiated pictograph										up, to ascend
pictographic compound										sunset; negation
phonetic compound										willow
receptive medium	bone (ox scapulae) shell (turtle plastra)	bronze vessels	stone; metal plaques	wooden strips; silk	paper (traditionally soft, thin, absorbent hand-made rag paper, in modern times also machine-made, hard, sized wood-pulp paper)				paper (mostly machine-made wood pulp)	
writing materials	brush and ink; incised with a sharp instrument	inscriptions cast by lost-wax method	incised with a chisel: sometimes inlaid	writing brush red and black ink	hand-written text carved in reverse on wood blocks, printed sheets folded and sewn into books		brush and ink; in modern times pencil, fountain or ball-point pen		moveable metal type set horizontally from right to left	
contents	divinatory text; mostly formulaic	dedicatory texts	official texts; names on seals	general administration and literary texts	all kinds of texts		rough notes, letters, drafts etc		all kinds of texts	

The evolution of the Chinese script

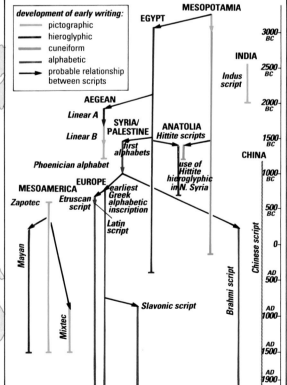

A

4 THE EVOLUTION OF CHINESE SCRIPT

Inscriptions on Chinese oracle bones (used for divination) of c.1400–1200 BC are written in a fully developed script whose structural principles still underlie that in use today, despite superficial variations. Four basic types of script units (characters) occur; pictographs, more or less stylised representations of concrete objects; differentiated pictographs, in which a marker indicates a portion of a pictograph; pictographic compounds, two or more pictographic elements combined to show the action or influence of one on the other and phonetic compounds in which two elements, chosen respectively from sets of semantic and phonetic signs, are combined, giving a broad indication of meaning and pronunciation. The last is by far the most productive group, accounting for some 90% of characters in existence today. The total number of characters has grown from c.9000 in AD 100 to c.60,000 today, of which 3500–4000 are in common use.

A *Oracle bone from Anyang, China. c.1200–1400 BC, height 30cm.*

The origin and spread of early scripts

area of origin	date of origin	comments
Mesopotamia	c.3500 BC	earliest writing
Egypt	c.3000 BC	
Scandinavia	c.3rd century BC	runes (script of northern Germanic tribes, maybe connected with northern Etruscan alphabet)
Indus Valley	c.2500–1700 BC	scripts
Greece	1700 BC–1200 BC	Linear A and B
Asia Minor and northern Syria	c.1500–600 BC and 1200 BC	hieroglyphic and cuneiform alphabet respectively
China	c.1400 BC	—
Syria and Palestine	c.1400 BC	early alphabets
Mesoamerica	c.600 BC (Zapotec) – AD 500 (Aztec)	—
Italy	1000–0 BC	Etruscan and (superseded by) Latin
Easter Island	AD 1500	—
Ireland and England	4th century AD	mostly bilingual Latin and Celtic

development of early writing:
- pictographic
- hieroglyphic
- cuneiform
- alphabetic
- → probable relationship between scripts

1 THE DEVELOPMENT OF SCRIPTS

Most of the early scripts used in different parts of the world were pictographic, hieroglyphic or cuneiform. The alphabet originated as an adaptation of Egyptian script in Sinai and the Levant in the 2nd millennium BC. By 1000 BC the Phoenicians had a fully developed alphabet of 22 consonants. This passed in the 8th century BC to the Greeks, who changed the sound-equivalence of certain characters and added vowels. The ancient Greek alphabet formed the basis of the later alphabets of both western and eastern Europe. The alphabet used a much smaller number of signs than earlier systems, in which separate characters were needed to represent whole words or syllables. It was thus more versatile and easier to master, and its adoption encouraged the spread of literacy in European and Near Eastern society during the 1st millennium BC.

Egypt: the imperial age

The people of ancient Egypt were obsessed with death, burial and the afterlife; remains of tombs and mortuary temples abound, and are much better known and more conspicuous than the houses and palaces of everyday life. The Egyptians believed that the tomb was to be the home of the deceased's spirit throughout eternity, and should be virtually indestructible. Tomb chambers were usually rock-cut, contrasting with everyday buildings which needed to survive no longer than a lifetime, and could be of less solid materials such as mud-brick. As a home for all eternity, the tomb was equipped with as many furnishings, everyday items and luxuries as possible.

The cemeteries of ancient Egypt are among the most substantial and impressive anywhere in the world, and the greatest of the Egyptian cemeteries are those of the successive royal capitals. The earliest court cemeteries were in the north, on the west bank of the Nile opposite Memphis and, after 2000 BC, around the Middle Kingdom capital of El-Lisht. The most famous of all, however, is the cemetery of Thebes in southern Egypt, which dates mainly from the New Kingdom (c.1560–1085 BC) when Thebes was the centre of an empire stretching from northern Syria to southern Nubia. The wealth generated by the empire enabled the Egyptians to adorn eastern Thebes, the city of the living, with monumental temples. On the opposite bank of the Nile, a necropolis or city of the dead was created to house the tombs of nobles, courtiers and officials and, in secluded valleys behind, the burial places of the kings and queens.

The construction of the royal tombs in the Valley of the Kings was designed to increase the security of the burial. Prior to the New Kingdom, most Egyptian kings had been buried in pyramids, which despite their impressive size did little to deter robbers, and often served only to make them more conspicuous and vulnerable to attack. The New Kingdom rulers adopted a new solution, based on secrecy. Instead of building large monumental tombs, designed to impress, they hid their burial places in a little-frequented valley, cutting them deep into the rock, giving them only a single access passage with no external superstructure, and concealing the entrance after the burial was complete. The mortuary temple in which the cult of the dead king was practised was not built next to the tomb, where it would serve to betray its location, but up to 2.5 kilometres away against the western Nile cliff. However, the royal tombs in the Valley of the Kings did not remain a secret for long, and ultimately it proved impossible to prevent their violation by tomb-robbing, which became particularly common in the 12th and 11th centuries BC, when the power of the monarchy was in decline. Documents tell of legal proceedings against bands of tomb-robbers, which sometimes included even the royal workmen themselves. Eventually, in the 11th century BC, the priests gathered together the surviving royal mummies from their desecrated tombs and secretly reburied them in two hidden caches, where they remained undisturbed, though without any of the lavish equipment which had accompanied their original burials, until the late 19th century AD.

One of the royal tombs managed to escape the ravages of tomb-robbers, and its virtually intact treasures have justly made it the most famous of them all: the tomb of Tutankhamun. It vividly illustrates the staggering luxury of the New Kingdom monarchy: it includes inlaid chests and gaming boards, jewellery, ostrich-feather fans, fly-whisks, a gold-plated and inlaid throne, alabaster vases and four dismantled chariots of gilded wood. The greatest riches of all lay around the mummified body of the king: the innermost coffin and death mask were of solid gold inlaid with semi-precious stones and glass. Yet Tutankhamun was a relatively minor New Kingdom ruler; one can only guess at the riches buried with the greatest kings of the dynasty.

Western Thebes also contains over five hundred rock-cut tombs belonging to nobles and lesser officials. Here mortuary chapel and burial chamber were combined in a single design; the chapel was entered direct from the outside, and the burial chamber was at a lower level usually reached by a shaft. Most of these tombs have also suffered badly at the hands of robbers, and few have retained even a part of their original contents. Only the paintings and reliefs which decorated their walls have survived, showing scenes from the life of the deceased which he might wish to re-enact after death. Ironically, western Thebes, the city of the dead, tells us more about the lives of the ancient Egyptians than the city of the living across the river.

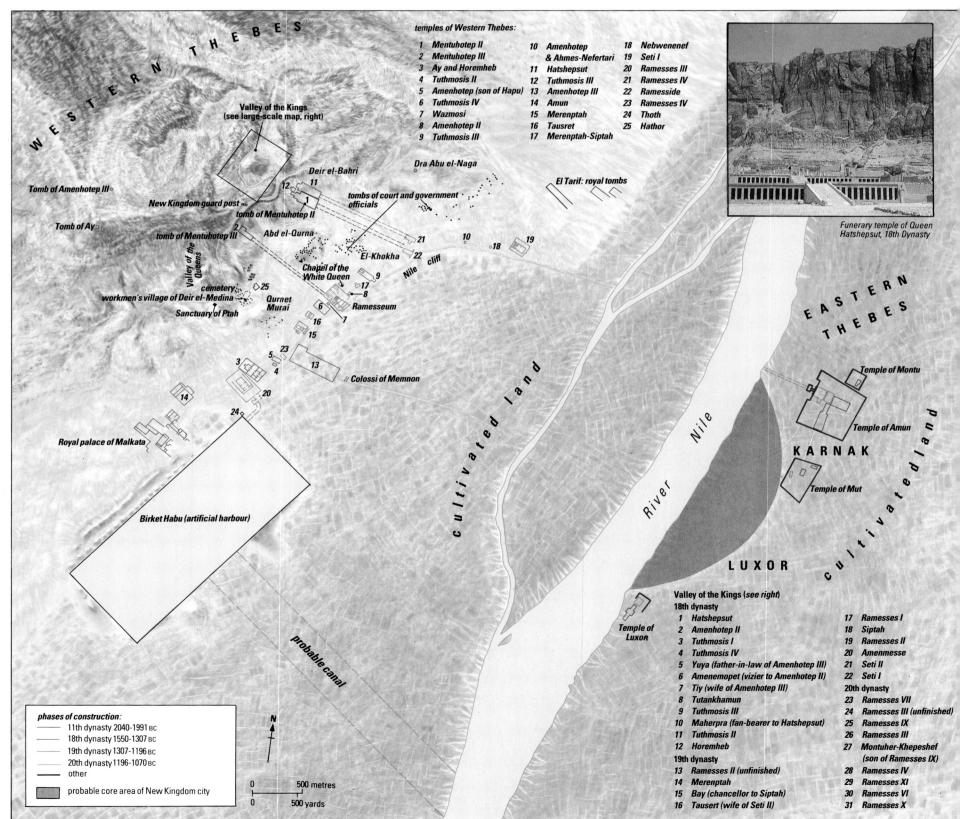

temples of Western Thebes:

1	Mentuhotep II	10	Amenhotep	18	Nebwenenef
2	Mentuhotep III		& Ahmes-Nefertari	19	Seti I
3	Ay and Horemheb	11	Hatshepsut	20	Ramesses III
4	Tuthmosis II	12	Tuthmosis III	21	Ramesses IV
5	Amenhotep (son of Hapu)	13	Amenhotep III	22	Ramesside
6	Tuthmosis IV	14	Amun	23	Ramesses IV
7	Wazmosis	15	Merenptah	24	Thoth
8	Amenhotep II	16	Tausret	25	Hathor
9	Tuthmosis III	17	Merenptah-Siptah		

Funerary temple of Queen
Hatshepsut, 18th Dynasty

Valley of the Kings (see right)

18th dynasty

1	Hatshepsut	17	Ramesses I
2	Amenhotep II	18	Siptah
3	Tuthmosis I	19	Ramesses II
4	Tuthmosis IV	20	Amenmesse
5	Yuya (father-in-law of Amenhotep III)	21	Seti II
6	Amenemopet (vizier to Amenhotep II)	22	Seti I
7	Tiy (wife of Amenhotep III)		**20th dynasty**
8	Tutankhamun	23	Ramesses VII
9	Tuthmosis III	24	Ramesses III (unfinished)
10	Maherpra (fan-bearer to Hatshepsut)	25	Ramesses IX
11	Tuthmosis II	26	Ramesses III
12	Horemheb	27	Montuher-Khepeshef
	19th dynasty		(son of Ramesses IX)
13	Ramesses II (unfinished)	28	Ramesses IV
14	Merenptah	29	Ramesses XI
15	Bay (chancellor to Siptah)	30	Ramesses VI
16	Tausert (wife of Seti II)	31	Ramesses X

phases of construction:
— 11th dynasty 2040-1991 BC
— 18th dynasty 1550-1307 BC
— 19th dynasty 1307-1196 BC
--- 20th dynasty 1196-1070 BC
— other

▢ probable core area of New Kingdom city

N

0   500 metres
0   500 yards

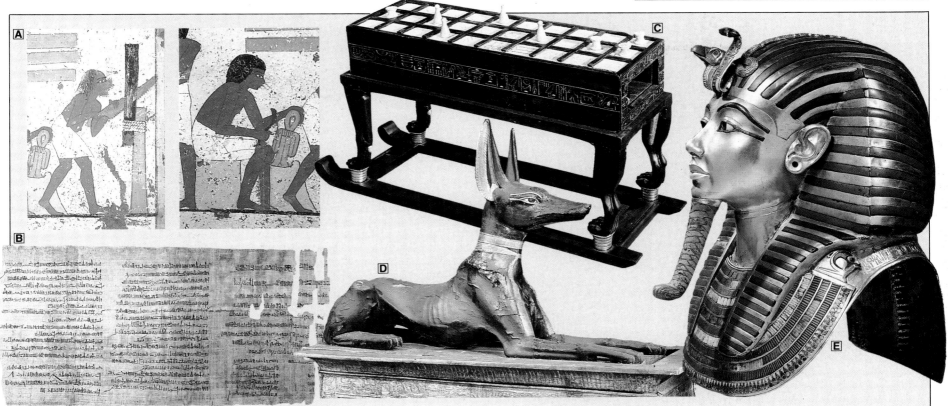

3 WEALTH OF THE DEAD

A *Craftsmen sawing ebony and carving wood to make decorations for a funerary catafalque. From the tomb of Nebamun and Ipuky, head sculptors of the king. c.1400 BC, painted wall plaster.* **B** *The Abbott Papyrus, an account of the special commission of high officials set up to investigate reports of tomb robberies in the Theban necropolis c.1090 BC* **C** *Gaming board from the tomb of Tutankhamun. The playing pieces were kept in a drawer at one end. c.1340 BC, ebony and inlaid ivory, length 46cm.* **D** *Figure of Anubis, the jackal-god of embalming, from the tomb of Tutankhamun. c.1340 BC, plastered wood painted with black resin, height 57cm.* **E** *Funerary mask of Tutankhamun. The king wears the vulture and cobra side by side on his forehead, symbolising sovereignty over Upper and Lower Egypt respectively. c.1340 BC, beaten gold, coloured glass and semi-precious stones. Life-size.*

2 THEBES

Thebes, the southern capital of Egypt during the New Kingdom (c.1560-1085 BC),was divided by the River Nile into two parts. On the eastern side of the river lay the core of the ancient city, dating back to around 3000 BC, and on the opposite bank lay the cemetery areas of western Thèbes. Little remains on the east bank today of what was once an imposing city – only the huge Karnak temple-precincts of Amun and Mut and the smaller enclosure of Luxor built in the 2nd millennium. On the west bank lay the palace of Malkata and the artificial harbour of Birket Habu. This harbour may have fed canals to the mortuary temples, giving access to funerary vessels, but it also demonstrates that Thebes was an important trading centre within easy reach of the rich mineral resources of Nubia, and with access via trade routes to the Levant. Also on the west bank, mortuary temples lined the impressive Nile cliff, surrounded by the lavishly decorated rock-hewn tombs of nobles and courtiers. The New Kingdom monarchs were not buried among them but in a valley behind the cliff – the Valley of the Kings (*see below*). To the south lay the village of Deir el-Medina (*page 138*) which housed the craftsmen who built the royal tombs, while further small communities along the west bank served the royal mortuary temples.

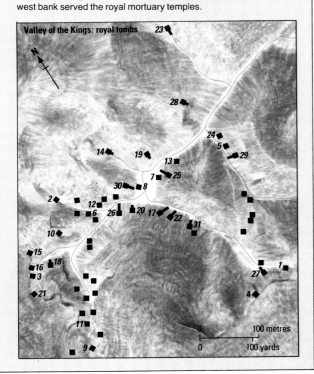

Valley of the Kings: royal tombs

100 metres
100 yards

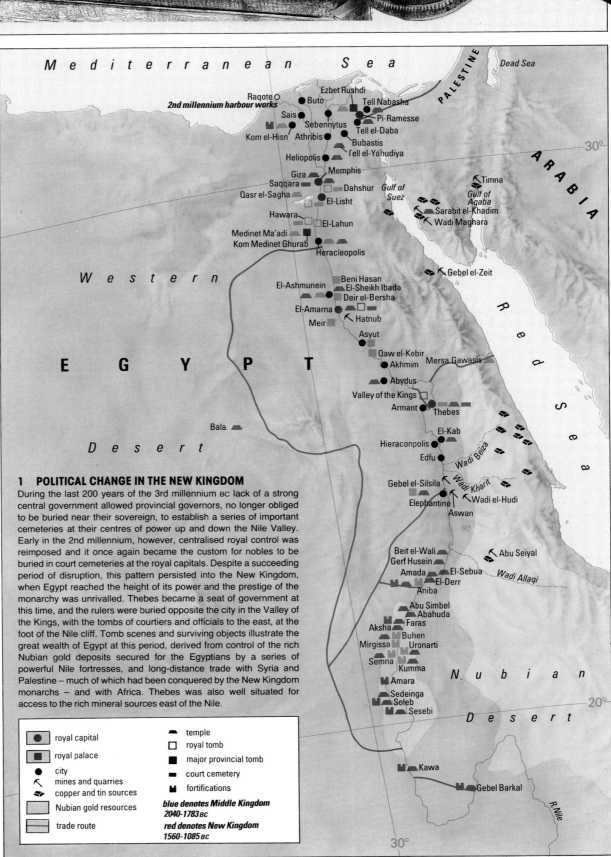

1 POLITICAL CHANGE IN THE NEW KINGDOM

During the last 200 years of the 3rd millennium BC lack of a strong central government allowed provincial governors, no longer obliged to be buried near their sovereign, to establish a series of important cemeteries at their centres of power up and down the Nile Valley. Early in the 2nd millennium, however, centralised royal control was reimposed and it once again became the custom for nobles to be buried in court cemeteries at the royal capitals. Despite a succeeding period of disruption, this pattern persisted into the New Kingdom, when Egypt reached the height of its power and the prestige of the monarchy was unrivalled. Thebes became a seat of government at this time, and the rulers were buried opposite the city in the Valley of the Kings, with the tombs of courtiers and officials to the east, at the foot of the Nile cliff. Tomb scenes and surviving objects illustrate the great wealth of Egypt at this period, derived from control of the rich Nubian gold deposits secured for the Egyptians by a series of powerful Nile fortresses, and long-distance trade with Syria and Palestine – much of which had been conquered by the New Kingdom monarchs – and with Africa. Thebes was also well situated for access to the rich mineral sources east of the Nile.

Legend:

- ● royal capital
- ■ royal palace
- ● city
- ⚒ mines and quarries
- ⛏ copper and tin sources
- Nubian gold resources
- trade route
- ▬ temple
- □ royal tomb
- ■ major provincial tomb
- ▬ court cemetery
- ▲ fortifications

blue denotes Middle Kingdom 2040-1783 BC

red denotes New Kingdom 1560-1085 BC

Ancient Egypt: life on the Nile

The ancient Egyptians understood the concept of life after death in a literal sense, providing the deceased with everyday objects and luxury items, decorating the walls of their tombs with scenes of harvests, hunts and feasts. From the tomb scenes, we are able to see the Egyptians as they saw, or would have liked to see, themselves, while the objects provide direct evidence of technology, trade and craftsmanship. The large numbers of documents which have been found and the actual remains of villages and cities also throw valuable light on the operation of law and government, and the living conditions – not only of the rich and privileged, but also of the artisans and peasant farmers, whose labour underpinned the Egyptian cultural achievement.

The Nile, bordered by fertile land and surrounded by uninhabited desert, was the principal artery of trade and communications, and the main cities and towns were situated on or near its banks. Built of mud brick, they were frequently destroyed by later overbuilding, and there are few substantial remains. Where excavations have been possible, as at El-Amarna in Upper Egypt, they have revealed haphazard, cramped settlements: the general impression must have been similar to the crowded and bustling towns of Egypt today. The stratified nature of Egyptian society is evident in the distinction between wealthy neighbourhoods with broad thoroughfares and substantial houses and poorer districts with small houses crowded together.

The craftsmen of ancient Egypt were highly skilled, and their workshops were a common feature of both cities and villages. Tomb paintings depict a wide variety of craft activities including pottery, weaving, carpentry, jewellery-making, stone-carving, joinery and leather and metalworking. Craftsmen were employed in the royal workshops to produce tomb-furnishings, and it is tombs, fully equipped with chests, chairs, beds, vases, cups, dishes and toilet objects, which illustrate most vividly the everyday life of the Egyptians and the craftsmen's skill. Craftsmen were not exempt from the Egyptian hierarchy. Highly trained scribes, whose services were essential for the administration of the state, occupied an especially privileged position. In one manuscript the scribe looks down on other trades, including the back-street coppersmith who is contemptuously dismissed as smelling 'worse than fish eggs'.

The foundation of Egyptian society, supporting scribe, priest and craftsman, was the peasant farmer. Egypt lies within a desert band, with arid wastes to east and west, and it was only the annual Nile inundation, bringing a fertile deposit of silt, which made cultivation within the river valley possible. The season of inundation or *akhet* (August to October) was followed by that of *peret* or 'coming forth' when the waters receded and crops could be sown (November to February). Then followed the dry, pre-inundation season of *shemu* or 'drought'. (March to August.) The yearly agricultural cycle is well illustrated by tomb-paintings. Various activities – ploughing, sowing, reaping – are shown in idealised form, although a vivid note of realism often slips in; young girl gleaners quarrel and pull each other's hair, a labourer exhorts his colleagues to 'speed up the work so that we can go home in good time'. Tomb paintings also give us a clear indication of what the Egyptians were cultivating; wheat and barley were the staple crops, although vegetables such as beans, lentils, chick peas and onions, and fruit such as grapes, figs and dates were also grown. Flax was cultivated for the Egyptian textile industry. Domestic cattle were bred for meat and ploughing, while the donkey was used for pack-transport. The horse was only introduced to Egypt c.1750 BC, and was then used principally in warfare.

The Egyptian economy was at the mercy of the Nile, and a series of low Nile floods could cause widespread famine and political crisis (*page 136*). One such period of famine coincided with the collapse of royal authority at the end of the Old Kingdom, c.2200 BC. A period of prosperity, accompanied by a re-assertion of royal authority followed, but in the 12th century BC grain prices rose to 24 times their former level. In 1153 BC even the privileged royal craftsmen of Deir el-Medina rioted because of food shortage. It was this crisis which finally marked the end of the period of greatest power and prosperity for the ancient Egyptian state. Although Egypt survived the joint onslaught of famine, foreign attack and internal unrest, and experienced a modest artistic and economic revival in the 6th century BC, the country never regained its former glory.

1 URBAN LIFE

The village of Deir el-Medina in western Thebes (*below*) was founded around 1500 BC to house the workmen employed on the construction of the royal tombs. The village was surrounded by a substantial mud-brick wall, which was extended as the population grew. At its peak in the 13th century BC, there were some 70 houses within the enclosure and a further 40–50 outside. The houses were built of mud-brick, sometimes on a stone foundation, and were generally long and narrow. In a typical house, the front room opened directly off the street and contained an enclosed brick-built shrine or a birthing-bed in one corner, reached by steps. The second or main room was higher and had in its walls a niche and false door, which served as shrines. There was also a built-in divan with steps below leading to a storage cellar. Behind, on one side, was a bedroom, on the other, a corridor/workroom, a stairway to the roof and an enclosed covered court used as a kitchen, containing a grain storage bin and an oven for baking bread. At the rear of the house there was sometimes a cellar for storing pottery. The walls and floors of the principal rooms were sometimes plastered, and the walls were also sometimes decorated with mural paintings.

Many thousands of casual writings on *ostraca* (limestone fragments and potsherds) have been found in the village and its surroundings. Some had been disposed of in a great pit outside the walls to the north, which served as a kind of scribal rubbish dump. More important documents would have been on papyrus, which could be easily stored for later reference, and, if necessary, erased for re-use. The abundance of *ostraca* shows that the standard of literacy in the village was exceptionally high, but this was a community of skilled craftsmen, and it is probable that only a small minority of the normal rural population could read and write.

Right A *Linen chest,* **B** *chair and* **C** *wooden lavatory stool, from the tomb of Kha, a foreman of the workmen at Deir el-Medina, c.1440 BC.*

accumulation of rubbish

mud-brick wall enclosing an area of 0.6 hectares

palm logs and thatch

branches and straw

vent

door to bedroom

niche

boxed bed

kitchen

false door (shrine)

limestone column or palm trunk roof support

bench

workroom and adjacent bedroom

mud-brick oven

floors of hard-packed earth

cellar

cellar

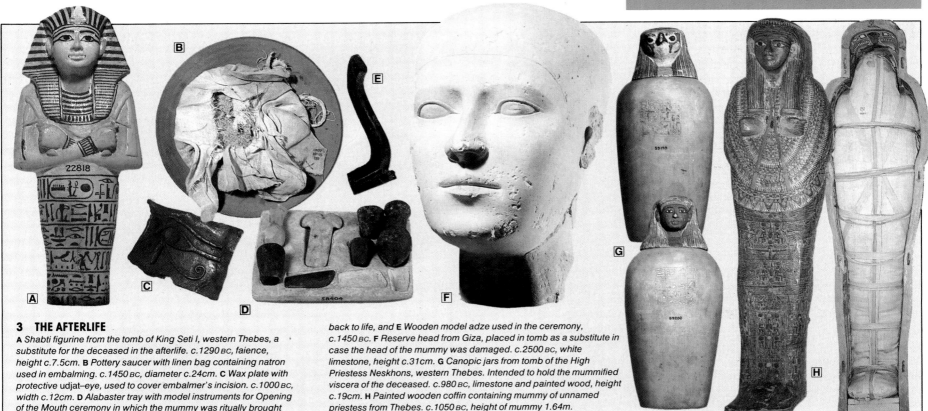

3 THE AFTERLIFE

A *Shabti figurine from the tomb of King Seti I, western Thebes, a substitute for the deceased in the afterlife. c.1290 BC, faience, height c.7.5cm.* B *Pottery saucer with linen bag containing natron used in embalming. c.1450 BC, diameter c.24cm.* C *Wax plate with protective udjat–eye, used to cover embalmer's incision. c.1000 BC, width c.12cm.* D *Alabaster tray with model instruments for Opening of the Mouth ceremony in which the mummy was ritually brought* back to life, and E *Wooden model adze used in the ceremony, c.1450 BC.* F *Reserve head from Giza, placed in tomb as a substitute in case the head of the mummy was damaged. c.2500 BC, white limestone, height c.31cm.* G *Canopic jars from tomb of the High Priestess Neskhons, western Thebes. Intended to hold the mummified viscera of the deceased. c.980 BC, limestone and painted wood, height c.19cm.* H *Painted wooden coffin containing mummy of unnamed priestess from Thebes. c.1050 BC, height of mummy 1.64m.*

2 RURAL LIFE

Documentary sources, paintings and models from tombs, and surviving agricultural implements give a detailed picture of rural life in ancient Egypt. Water was the critical resource, and for the greater part of the year farmers were dependent on water held back from the previous inundation. The Faiyum Basin (*right*) was one of the more favoured areas, and here the Egyptians were able to extend the area under cultivation by careful control of water through canals and sluices. A tax assessment of 1156 BC (the Wilbour papyrus) gives details of land ownership in one section of the Nile Valley (*far right*), and indicates that generally arable farming was less important in this area than pastoralism – reflected in the larger numbers of herdsmen and stable-masters. All the principal towns and administrative centres lay in or near the arable areas, where they could easily be supplied with foodstuffs.

A *Sickle with flint blades and wooden hoe, 1150-1070 BC.* B *Wall painting of the biennial goose count from the tomb of Neb Amun at Thebes. 1400 BC, limestone and plaster, height 71cm.* C *Funerary model of two men ploughing with oxen. 2000 BC, wood.*

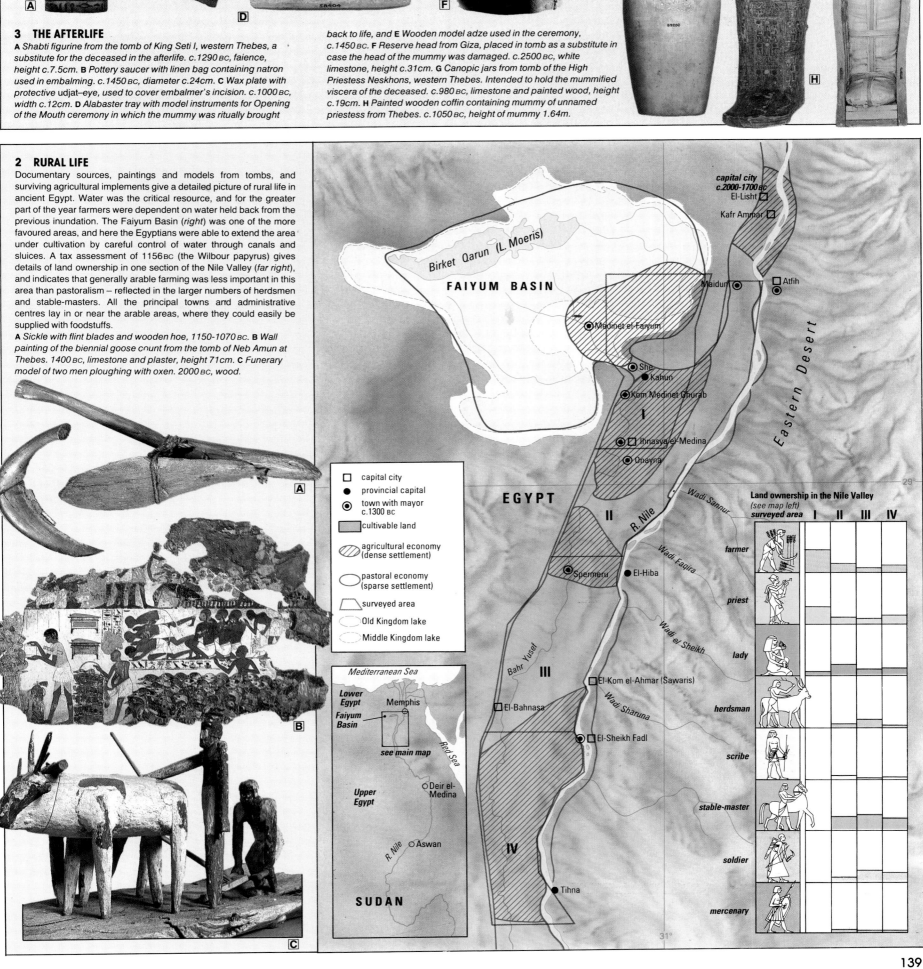

capital city c.2000-1700 BC
El-Lisht
Kafr Ammar

FAIYUM BASIN
Birket Qarun (L. Moeris)

Maidum
Atfih

Medinet el-Faiyum
She
Kahun
Kom Medinet Ghurab
I
Ihnasya el-Medina
Oneyna

EGYPT
II
R. Nile
Wadi Sannur
29°

Spermeru
El-Hiba
Wadi Faqira

Eastern Desert

Wadi el Sheikh

III
Bahr Yusef
El-Kom el-Ahmar (Sawaris)
Wadi Sharuna
El-Bahnasa
El-Sheikh Fadl

IV
Tihna

□ capital city
● provincial capital
◉ town with mayor c.1300 BC
cultivable land
⬱ agricultural economy (dense settlement)
⬭ pastoral economy (sparse settlement)
⬔ surveyed area
⬯ Old Kingdom lake
⬯ Middle Kingdom lake

Mediterranean Sea
Lower Egypt
Memphis
Faiyum Basin
see main map
Upper Egypt
Deir el-Medina
Red Sea
R. Nile
Aswan
SUDAN

Land ownership in the Nile Valley
(*see map left*)
surveyed area

	I	II	III	IV
farmer				
priest				
lady				
herdsman				
scribe				
stable-master				
soldier				
mercenary				

Minoan Crete

Classical Greek legend tells of Minos, a king of Crete who dominated the Aegean with his powerful navy and dwelt in a palace where the double-axe was a sacred symbol. It cannot be said whether Minos was actually a historical ruler, or merely a mythical character; however, there can be no doubt about the sophistication and prosperity of the Bronze Age palace civilisation which takes its name from the Cretan king.

Crete, a mountainous and wooded island, was first settled around 6000 BC. Remains of one of the earliest villages have been found buried beneath the later palace of Knossos. By the 3rd millennium BC, larger settlements began to develop; the village of Knossos became a town, while in the south the inhabitants of the Mesara Plain began to bury their dead in well-built circular stone tombs. The first palace at Knossos was built in around 2000 BC; over the next 300 years palaces appeared at Phaistos, Mallia and Zakro. The construction of these palaces marks the establishment of the first Cretan states. Later Greek legend suggests that these states were ruled over by royal houses, and suites of rooms thought to have been royal apartments have been found at all four Cretan palaces. The Cretan palaces had several functions; serving as royal households, ceremonial and ritual centres, and the foci of a flourishing redistributive economy. Built of local limestone, palace buildings were grouped around a courtyard – probably used for sacred rituals. The royal apartments were situated on the first floor, and these and the other principal rooms of the palace were decorated with vivid and naturalistic frescoes depicting a wide range of subjects – leaping dolphins and flying fish, crowd spectacles such as bull-leaping and boxing, and aspects of courtly life, such as rituals and processions. On the ground floor and basement were storerooms, filled with stone-lined boxes and *pithoi* (large jars) containing surplus produce collected from the agricultural hinterland – grain, olive oil, wine. The workshops of the palace craftsmen were also situated here; a bronzesmith's furnace was found at Phaistos, a lapidary's workshop at Knossos, and raw materials such as elephant tusks and copper ingots at Zakro. The Knossos tablets, written in Linear B, an archaic form of Greek developed to facilitate the palace administration, suggest that in the 14th century BC as many as 4300 people were receiving rations from the palace storerooms. The tablets also record that, with flocks of around 80,000 sheep under its control, the palace was the centre of a thriving textile industry.

During the Minoan period a network of towns developed throughout the populated parts of Crete, and around each of the major palaces. At Gournia, there is a planned settlement with paved streets and, at the centre, a public square and small palace. The town was packed with modest-sized houses; living quarters were frequently on the first floor, reached by stairs direct from the street, while the ground floor was devoted entirely to storerooms and, in some instances, workshops – a coppersmith's forge and a carpenter's bronze saw, axes, chisels and drill bit have been found. Undoubtedly the Cretans were outstanding craftsmen, excelling in pottery – the potter's wheel was introduced to Crete c.1900 BC, and was used to produce finely decorated, eggshell-thin vessels which were in great demand throughout the east Mediterranean, and have been found in Egypt, Cyprus and the Levant. Other skills included metalworking, gemstone carving, faience (an Egyptian pottery technique), ivory carving and the production of stone bowls.

The Minoans did not build public temples; they worshipped a variety of deities, possibly a Great Earth Mother, a God of the Beasts and a Goddess of the Hunt, at hilltop sanctuaries and in sacred caves. In one of these, models of pests were offered, presumably with a prayer for their eradication; in another, models of the limb or organ the supplicant wished to have healed. Domestic shrines in ordinary houses were often associated with the snake goddess – revered as the guardian spirit of the house. The double-axe (*labrys*) was a common sacred emblem; in Greek mythology Minos' palace is described as the 'labyrinth' or house of the double-axe, and at the palace of Knossos the basement rooms contain pillars decorated with the double-axe design – probably symbols of a particular deity.

In about 1450 BC Minoan Crete suffered a major disaster, the causes of which are still unclear. The palaces of Zakro, Mallia and Phaistos were destroyed, and though Knossos survived there were important changes. The script introduced after this disaster, Linear B, shows that the rulers of Knossos now spoke Greek, and suggests a changed regime, possibly even a takeover by Mycenaeans from the mainland. In about 1370 BC a great fire also destroyed the palace at Knossos. Henceforth it was the Mycenaean states of mainland Greece which were the major power in the Aegean.

2 KNOSSOS: THE PALACE ECONOMY

The present palace of Knossos (*illustration, left*) dates from c.1700 BC when it was rebuilt after an earthquake destroyed the original palace of c.2000 BC. Like all the major Cretan palaces it was arranged around a central courtyard, while a second western courtyard was probably used for spectator sports such as bull-leaping. The royal apartments were to the south-east of the palace, located to catch the cooling mountain winds in the summer; they were three to four storeys high, with light-wells and an elaborate water supply and drainage system, and were reached by a grand staircase. A throne room with a carved gypsum throne and griffin frescoes was located on the west side of the main courtyard. The extensive storerooms and workshops of the palace craftsmen indicate the important role the palace played in a flourishing regional economy (*see below*); collecting and redistributing agricultural produce, housing craftsmen and supplying them with local and imported raw materials, and exporting manufactured goods to the Aegean and east Mediterranean.

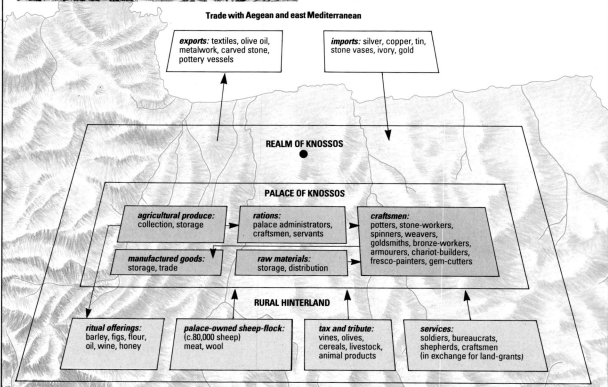

Trade with Aegean and east Mediterranean

exports: textiles, olive oil, metalwork, carved stone, pottery vessels

imports: silver, copper, tin, stone vases, ivory, gold

REALM OF KNOSSOS

PALACE OF KNOSSOS

agricultural produce: collection, storage

rations: palace administrators, craftsmen, servants

craftsmen: potters, stone-workers, spinners, weavers, goldsmiths, bronze-workers, armourers, chariot-builders, fresco-painters, gem-cutters

manufactured goods: storage, trade

raw materials: storage, distribution

RURAL HINTERLAND

ritual offerings: barley, figs, flour, oil, wine, honey

palace-owned sheep-flock: (c.80,000 sheep) meat, wool

tax and tribute: vines, olives, cereals, livestock, animal products

services: soldiers, bureaucrats, shepherds, craftsmen (in exchange for land-grants)

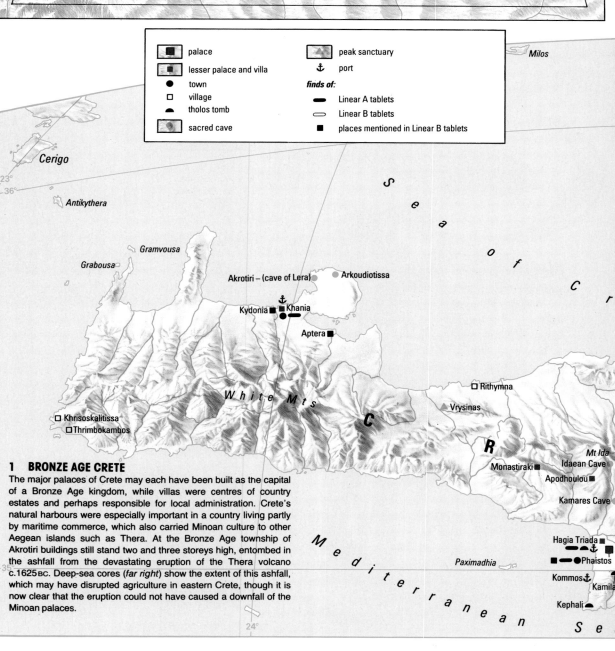

■ palace	🔺 peak sanctuary
▨ lesser palace and villa	⚓ port
● town	**finds of:**
□ village	▬ Linear A tablets
◗ tholos tomb	◖ Linear B tablets
🕳 sacred cave	■ places mentioned in Linear B tablets

Milos

Cerigo

Antikythera

Gramvousa

Grabousa

Akrotiri – (cave of Lera)   *Arkoudiotissa*

Kydonia   *Khania*

Aptera

White Mts

Khrisoskalitissa

Thrimbokambos

Rithymna

Vrysinas

C R E

Monastiraki   *Mt Ida*   *Idaean Cave*

Apodhoulou

Kamares Cave

Hagia Triada

Mediterranean   *Paximadhia*   *Phaistos*

Kommos   *Kamilari*

Kephali

Sea of   *Cr*

Mediterranean Sea

1 BRONZE AGE CRETE

The major palaces of Crete may each have been built as the capital of a Bronze Age kingdom, while villas were centres of country estates and perhaps responsible for local administration. Crete's natural harbours were especially important in a country living partly by maritime commerce, which also carried Minoan culture to other Aegean islands such as Thera. At the Bronze Age township of Akrotiri buildings still stand two and three storeys high, entombed in the ashfall from the devastating eruption of the Thera volcano c.1625 BC. Deep-sea cores (*far right*) show the extent of this ashfall, which may have disrupted agriculture in eastern Crete, though it is now clear that the eruption could not have caused a downfall of the Minoan palaces.

3 MINOAN ART

A *Late Minoan pithos amphora with octopus design – close links with the sea are reflected in the recurring use of marine motifs on Cretan pottery. c.1500 BC, height c.0.7m.* **B** *Wine press from a Minoan country villa at Vathypetro, including a clay basin for crushing the grapes and a great pithos for collecting the must. Wine produced at country estates was sent to the major palaces for storage, redistribution, and export. Late 16th century BC.* **C** *Statuette of a goddess holding a snake in either hand, possibly a household deity, from the palace of Knossos. c.1600 BC, faience, height 19.5cm.* **D** *Engraved votive double-axe – an important religious symbol – from the Minoan sacred cave of Arkalochori. c.1500 BC, gold, height 8.5cm.* **E** *Tablet from Knossos with Linear B text recording livestock kept by the Greek-speaking rulers who took control of the palace c.1450 BC. The animals listed include sheep, whose wool supplied the textile workers of Knossos. 14th century BC, length 23.9cm.* **F** *Bull-leaping fresco from the east wing of the palace of Knossos. Men are shown red, women white, an artistic convention borrowed from contemporary Egypt. 15th century BC, height 0.7m.*

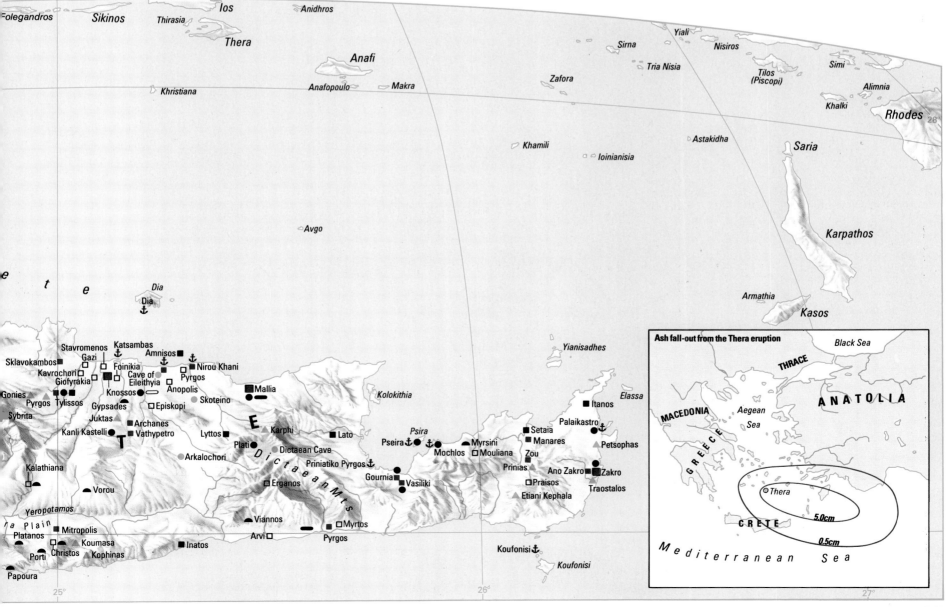

The struggle for the Levant

During the 2nd millennium BC the Levant, the east Mediterranean coastline between Anatolia and Egypt, was divided up among a network of prosperous city-states. Essentially disunited, they were a tempting target for the expansionist ambitions of the powerful kingdoms around the edges of the region. Egypt, the oldest of these states, had a tradition of strong centralised government stretching back to around 3000 BC. After a period of temporary eclipse, it reached a new peak of power and prosperity in the later 2nd millennium BC. At the same time the kingdom of Mitanni, centred on the steppelands of northern Mesopotamia, was also at the height of its power, its authority extending from the Zagros Mountains to the Syrian coast. The Hittite kingdom, with its capital at Boğazköy on the Anatolian plateau, was the third major power. The Hittite state had developed during the early 2nd millennium BC from a group of city-states, and during the 14th century BC it supplanted Mitanni as Egypt's principal rival.

Innovations were made in both weaponry and warfare as the Egyptians, Hittites and Mitannians vied for control of the Levant. The fast two-wheeled war chariot, sturdily built but so light that it could be carried by one man, was introduced to the Near East in around 1800 BC, and its use gradually spread throughout the region. Pulled by a team of horses, and manned by archers clad in bronze armour and equipped with powerful bows and bronze-tipped arrows, the chariot became a vital component of Near Eastern armies until its replacement by cavalry a thousand years later. However, open warfare was only one aspect of military operations. By the 2nd millennium BC the Levant was a land of many cities, and sieges became increasingly frequent. New types of offensive equipment were introduced, such as battering rams and siege towers, only to be countered by changes in the design of city defences. An important development was the glacis-rampart – the city wall was built beyond the reach of attackers on top of a long, steep slope faced with smooth plaster or stone. Substantial defences could not always prevent a city falling, however, and evidence of destruction dating from this period has been found at several sites.

Hand in hand with the endemic warfare of the period went constant diplomatic activity, recorded on clay tablets from Egyptian and Hittite state archives. The diplomatic language of the day was Akkadian, and among the archives found at the Hittite capital, Boğazköy, are records of a 13th-century peace treaty between the Hittite and Egyptian kings. The same treaty is known from a hieroglyphic version on the temple walls of Karnak in Egypt. Karnak is also decorated with large-scale reliefs portraying the prowess of the Egyptian king in battle against the Hittites, and such state propaganda, in texts or monuments, was a feature of the period. At Boğazköy some of the gateways had grandiose guardian figures of lions or sphinxes, while at another gate the monolithic door jamb bore the imposing figure of an armed Hittite god carved in bold relief.

One of the prizes in the contest for the Levant was control over the coastal cities and their lucrative commerce. Trading in gold, Cypriot copper and Mycenaean pottery, the leading maritime merchants in the east Mediterranean were Canaanites from the Levant and Mycenaeans from Greece. The coast of Syria and Palestine is relatively poor in natural harbours, and large, sheltered anchorages were artificially created by civil engineering works on offshore reefs and islands. The discovery of a shipwreck off Cape Gelidonya in southern Anatolia has yielded valuable information about maritime trade during this period. Little survived of the ship itself, but its cargo of copper ingots and scrap metalwork, which had probably been taken on board at Cyprus, was recovered. Scarab talismans, a cylinder seal, and haematite weights graduated in Egyptian and Syrian units suggest that the vessel was of Canaanite origin.

The maritime trade of the Levant reached its peak in the 1st millennium BC under the Phoenicians. By that time, however, the political geography of the Near East had undergone a transformation. During the 12th century BC the major states of the region had been prey to powerful onslaughts from maritime raiders of uncertain origin, the so-called 'Sea Peoples'. In the face of these attacks the Levantine empires crumbled and the Hittite state was destroyed, while Egypt survived only in a seriously weakened condition. When, shortly after 1000 BC, this Dark Age came to a close, the stage was set for the appearance of the great Near Eastern empires of the 1st millennium BC (*page 156*).

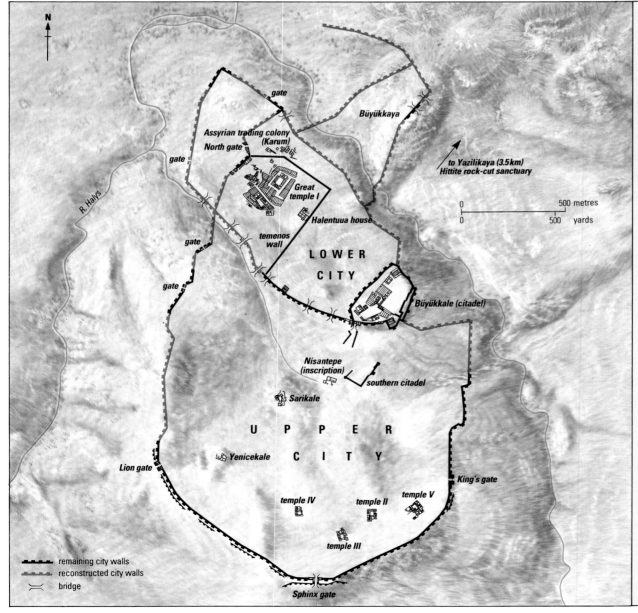

remaining city walls
reconstructed city walls
bridge

2 BOĞAZKÖY: A HITTITE CAPITAL

Boğazköy, ancient Hattushash, in north-central Anatolia was the capital of the powerful Hittite kingdom from 1650 to 1200 BC. The attraction of the site was twofold: the presence of water in a generally arid region, and the rocky terrain which could be exploited in conjunction with man-made defences to create a strongly fortified city. The naturally defensive outcrop of Büyükkale was the original core of the city, when Boğazköy was only one of a number of independent city-states in central Anatolia. However, these were combined by conquest into a single Hittite kingdom, and around 1650 BC Boğazköy became its capital. As the power of the Hittites grew the city was rebuilt and extended. Around 1500 BC it consisted of the Büyükkale citadel and the lower city to the north-west. A century later, the walled area was almost doubled by the construction of the upper city, and in the 13th century the fortifications were further extended to include the hill of Büyükkaya to the north-east. During this period Boğazköy was embellished with grandiose buildings. On the citadel the royal palace was rebuilt, and excavations there have revealed a pillared audience hall almost 32 metres square and two royal archives yielding some 3000 cuneiform tablets. Five monumental temples were built in different parts of the city, while at Yazilikaya, 3.5 kilometres outside the city, there was another important religious centre: deep natural rock-clefts decorated with friezes showing processions of deities in relief, with offering benches beneath. The walls of the imperial city were powerful and sophisticated, especially on the south. Here, the wall stood atop a massive stone-faced rampart, while projecting towers at regular intervals, twin-towered gateways, and a lower and less massive outer wall completed the defensive arrangements, making Boğazköy one of the most strongly fortified cities of the ancient Near East.

Above *View from Sphinx gate over upper city, with Temple III in foreground and Temple II to right.*

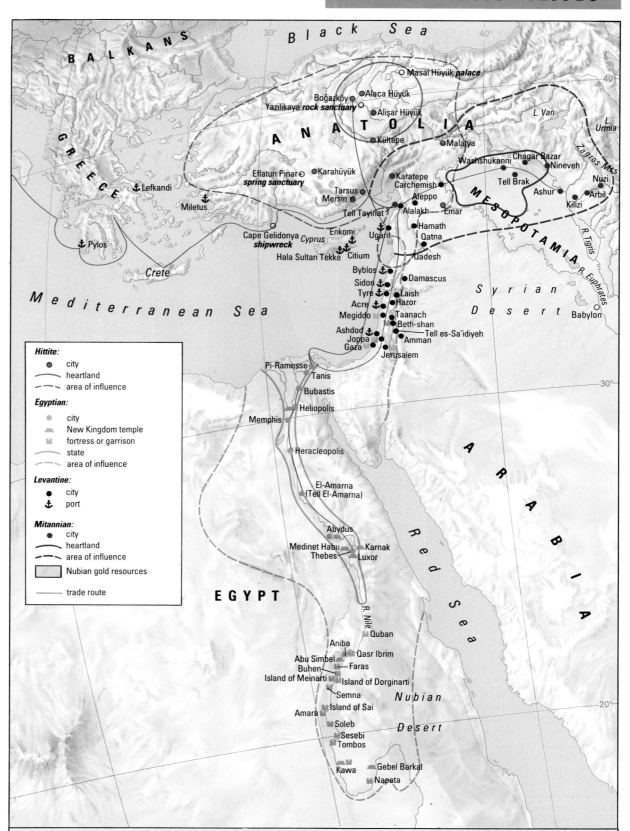

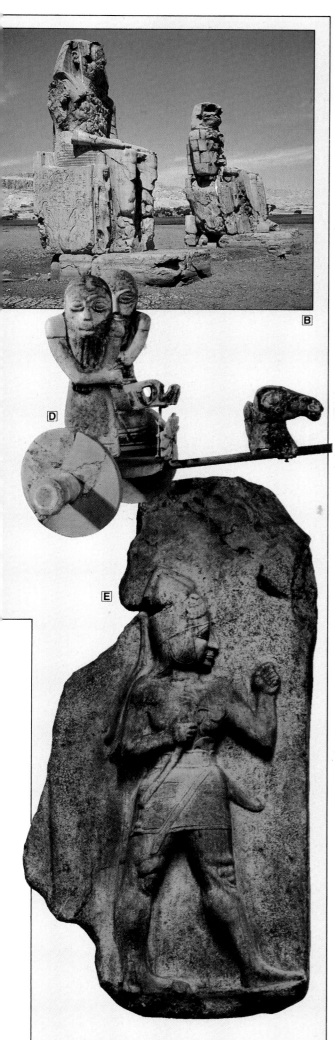

3 IMAGES OF EMPIRE

A *Fragment of plaque from Megiddo, probably used as an inlay on furniture, showing a woman in a long robe holding a staff. The style shows strong Egyptian artistic influence, paralleling their political domination of the southern Levant. 14th-12th century BC, ivory with glass inlay, height 20.3cm.* **B** *The Colossi of Memnon, gigantic seated statues of the Egyptian ruler Amenhotep III, originally part of his mortuary temple at Thebes. 14th century BC, sandstone, height 21.3m.* **C** *Ox-hide ingot from shipwreck off Cape Gelidonya. Contemporary Egyptian tomb paintings show Syrian merchants carrying ingots on their shoulders. c.1250 BC, copper, weight 23.4kg, length 66cm.* **D** *Fragmentary model chariot from Ugarit. c.14th century BC, faience.* **E** *Relief of armed figure, possibly a Hittite god, from the King's gate at Boğazköy. 14th-13th century BC, crystalline limestone, height 2.25m.*

1 POWER POLITICS IN THE NEAR EAST

The Hittite, Egyptian and Mitannian states of the 2nd millennium Near East each consisted of a core region surrounded by a fluctuating area under less permanent control. The three states came into direct competition and conflict in the Levant, but they were also engaged in military and diplomatic activity on their other frontiers. In Anatolia the Hittites had to deal with the kingdoms of Arzawa and Ahhiyawa to the west and the turbulent Kaska to the north. The power of Mitanni was threatened not only in the Levant but also in northern Mesopotamia, where important city-states such as Ashur were continually trying to break free. For Egypt, the attractions of a Levantine empire were balanced by an interest in the gold deposits of Nubia, and during the 15th century BC the Egyptians extended their control southwards, building a series of forts along the Nile bank. Even gold, however, was unable to secure the complete allegiance of the Levantine princes, as clay tablets found at the Egyptian capital of El-Amarna illustrate. This group of some 150 documents from the state archives consists principally of letters from Palestinian princes to the pharaoh, protesting their loyalty, accusing their neighbours, and beseeching assistance. The cities mentioned in the letters enable us to determine the extent of territory under Egyptian control (*right*). In some parts of the region, however, this control was precarious. The northern principality of Amurru, with ports at Irqata and Simyra, appears to have been particularly troublesome. One ruler was assassinated by an Egyptian expedition, and his successor Aziru proved no more reliable, ultimately defecting to the Hittites – an example of the shifting allegiances which were a feature of 2nd millennium Levantine diplomacy.

Right *Letter from Aziru, prince of Amurru, from Egyptian archive at El-Amarna. c.1370 BC, height 13.5cm.*

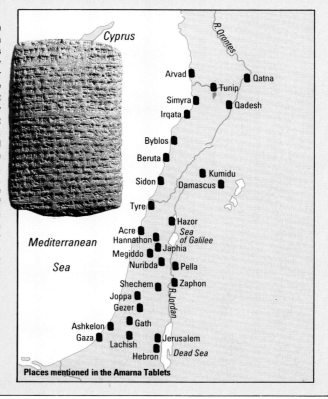

Places mentioned in the Amarna Tablets

Mycenaean Greece

The late 2nd millennium BC was a period of tension in the east Mediterranean, with political and commercial rivalry between a number of states, some already relatively ancient, others comparative newcomers. Among the latter, one of the most important was Mycenaean Greece. A new opulence was unmistakable in the burials of the earliest rulers of Mycenae; one skeleton alone was laden with five kilograms of gold – reflecting the rising power of Mycenae itself (c.1550 BC), which coincided with increased trade and prosperity throughout Greece and marks the beginning of the Mycenaean age (1550-1150 BC). The epics of Homer, although much later in date (c.800 BC), incorporate oral history and traditions about the Mycenaean age. According to legend, at the time of the Trojan War Mycenae was the residence of Agamemnon, overlord of all Greece, and the Mycenaeans are portrayed as heroic warlords and enterprising sailors and traders, characteristics amply borne out by the archaeological record. However, the Mycenaeans were also able administrators, with palace bureaucracies regulating the everyday activities of their kingdoms.

Mycenaean Greece consisted of a number of small kingdoms, each centred on a palace or citadel. The excavated Mycenaean palaces all have rooms arranged around a series of open courts. Floors and walls were plastered and often painted, with frescoes depicting scenes from daily life in some of the most important rooms. The focus in each palace was a megaron, a large hall with central circular hearth and a roof supported on four wooden columns; here the ruler and his court assembled. In addition to reception rooms and private accommodation, workshops and storerooms were an integral part of each palace, housing military equipment, agricultural produce, and craftsmen who made pottery, metalwork and finely carved ivory.

The best evidence for the administrative structure of Mycenaean Greece is provided by substantial archives of clay tablets from the palaces of Pylos and Knossos (*page 140*). These indicate a strongly centralised government controlling a wide range of workers: bronze-craftsmen, sheep- and cattle-herders, coastguards, oarsmen, weavers and priests are all mentioned, as well as kings, viziers and military personnel. The use of clay tablets for administrative records was derived from the palace bureaucracies of the Levant (*page 132*) but the script, Linear B, was a development of Minoan Linear A, adopted by the Mycenaeans for writing an early form of Greek. Other important aspects of Mycenaean culture were also derived from the Cretans, including the fresco technique used to decorate the palaces, and the shapes of pottery vessels and their painted designs. The inhabitants of the Greek mainland took control of the island of Crete c.1450 BC, possibly in the wake of the disastrous Thera eruption. The ensuing two centuries were the period of greatest Mycenaean power and commercial success, with a trading network extending from the Levantine ports in the east to Sicily and southern Italy in the west.

The substantial defensive wall at Mycenae illustrates the importance of warfare in Greece at this period. Painted pottery, frescoes, sword inlays and carved ivories show foot-soldiers armed with long spears and figure-of-eight shields, sometimes wearing helmets made of sawn boars' tusks. A rich early Mycenaean tomb at Dendra contained a complete bronze cuirass, a pair of bronze greaves, and a boar's tusk helmet with metal earflaps. This was probably the equipment of an aristocratic chariot-warrior. The war chariot reached the Mycenaeans from the Near East. However, the rugged and mountainous terrain of Greece was not ideal for such fighting vehicles, and the movement of troops and chariots was made possible by the construction of extensive roads, remains of which survive in the area of Mycenae and in Boeotia around the ancient Lake Kopais. Ships were also vital for Mycenaean military supremacy, and were used in overseas expeditions such as the attack on Troy recounted by Homer.

In such a militaristic society the more important Mycenaean centres were inevitably fortified; Mycenae itself was probably originally defended by a wooden palisade, but in the early 13th century BC this was replaced by a massive Cyclopean wall up to seven metres thick. Around 1250 BC these defences were extended to the south-west, and the monumental Lion Gate was added. The defences of other Greek citadels were also strengthened at this period, suggesting increasingly troubled conditions, but ultimately to little avail. Through internal disturbance, coupled perhaps with foreign invasion, all Mycenaean palaces and towns were sacked or abandoned by the end of the 12th century BC.

3 A WARRIOR ELITE

A *Funeral mask (the so-called 'Mask of Agamemnon') from grave circle A, Mycenae. Later 16th century BC, gold, width 26.5cm.* **B** *Bronze cuirass and boar's tusk helmet with metal earflaps from tholos tomb at Dendra. Nearby lay a pair of bronze greaves, two swords, and the remains of a wooden-framed leather shield. c.1400 BC.* **C** *Relief plaque of warrior wearing boar's tusk helmet,* possibly an inlay for a casket, from a chamber tomb at Mycenae. 14th or 13th century BC, ivory, height 8.5cm. **D** *Mycenaean stemmed goblet decorated with stylised cuttlefish, found at Lalgos, Rhodes. 14th century BC, pottery, height 20.7cm.* **E** *Bath-shaped coffin (larnax) with painted fish inside and a fish-scale design on the outside, from Pakhiammos, Crete, a feature of Cretan burials after the Mycenaean takeover. c.1350 BC, pottery, height 48cm.*

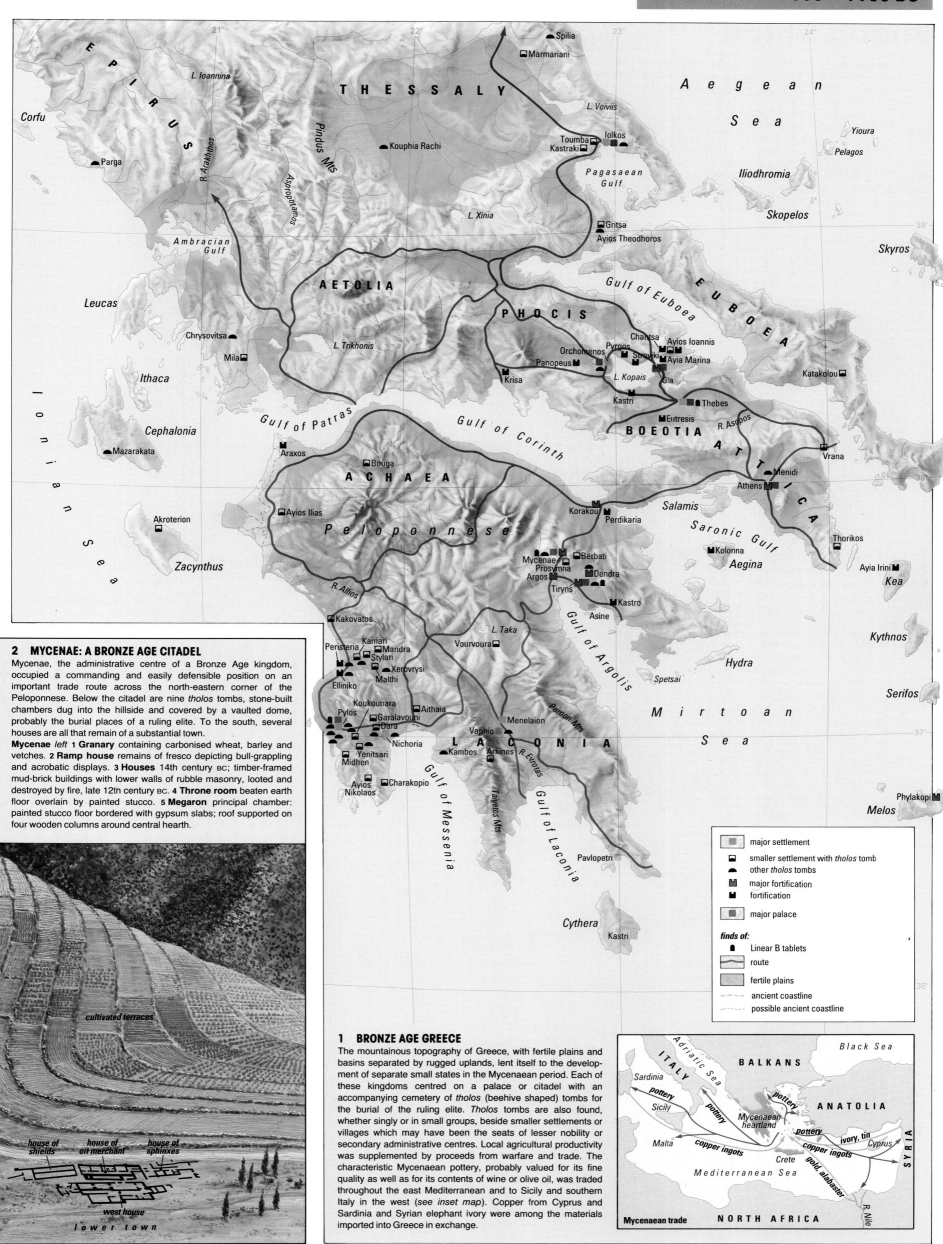

2 MYCENAE: A BRONZE AGE CITADEL

Mycenae, the administrative centre of a Bronze Age kingdom, occupied a commanding and easily defensible position on an important trade route across the north-eastern corner of the Peloponnese. Below the citadel are nine *tholos* tombs, stone-built chambers dug into the hillside and covered by a vaulted dome, probably the burial places of a ruling elite. To the south, several houses are all that remain of a substantial town.

Mycenae *left* **1 Granary** containing carbonised wheat, barley and vetches. **2 Ramp house** remains of fresco depicting bull-grappling and acrobatic displays. **3 Houses** 14th century BC; timber-framed mud-brick buildings with lower walls of rubble masonry, looted and destroyed by fire, late 12tn century BC. **4 Throne room** beaten earth floor overlain by painted stucco. **5 Megaron** principal chamber: painted stucco floor bordered with gypsum slabs; roof supported on four wooden columns around central hearth.

Map legend

- major settlement
- smaller settlement with *tholos* tomb
- other *tholos* tombs
- major fortification
- fortification
- major palace

finds of:
- Linear B tablets
- route
- fertile plains
- ancient coastline
- possible ancient coastline

1 BRONZE AGE GREECE

The mountainous topography of Greece, with fertile plains and basins separated by rugged uplands, lent itself to the development of separate small states in the Mycenaean period. Each of these kingdoms centred on a palace or citadel with an accompanying cemetery of *tholos* (beehive shaped) tombs for the burial of the ruling elite. *Tholos* tombs are also found, whether singly or in small groups, beside smaller settlements or villages which may have been the seats of lesser nobility or secondary administrative centres. Local agricultural productivity was supplemented by proceeds from warfare and trade. The characteristic Mycenaean pottery, probably valued for its fine quality as well as for its contents of wine or olive oil, was traded throughout the east Mediterranean and to Sicily and southern Italy in the west (*see* inset map). Copper from Cyprus and Sardinia and Syrian elephant ivory were among the materials imported into Greece in exchange.

Mycenaean trade

Shang China

The last of the four great civilisations of the Old World developed in north-east China in around 1800 BC. It takes its name from the Shang, the dynasty of kings who ruled in the middle valley of the Yellow River and established a powerful state which survived without serious rival until the 11th century BC. Remains of cities, rich tombs and luxury artefacts clearly demonstrate that the rulers and aristocracy were highly sophisticated and partly urbanised. However, much less is known of the ordinary people who provided the economic basis of Shang power and prosperity, farming the land and fighting numerous wars. The origins of this first Chinese civilisation date to about

3000 BC, when a growing discrepancy between rich and poor burials in the east of the country indicates the rise of a hierarchical society. Critical developments took place during the following 'Longshan' period (2500–1800 BC) (*map, below right*), when walled settlements were built and more sophisticated crafts – metalworking and wheel-thrown pottery – were developed. Though similar in some ways to those of India and the Near East, the resulting civilisation which formed in about 1800 BC was distinctively Chinese, owing little to contact with other regions.

The Shang capital was moved on several occasions, and the successive capitals of Zhengzhou and Anyang are the most important archaeological sites of Shang China. Each of the cities has a rammed-earth platform on which palace buildings stood, surrounded by lesser dwellings, work-

shops, and extensive suburbs. However, smaller settlements are probably more typical; at Panlongcheng in the Yangtze basin the central area was also surrounded by a rammed-earth wall, though here the space enclosed was less than a quarter of that at Zhengzhou. Around these cities and towns lie cemeteries, containing graves of both rich and poor. The richest of all are the Xibeigang graves at Anyang which date from the period when it was the Shang capital (14th–11th century BC), and are thought to have been the resting places of the last Shang kings. They consist of a large rectangular pit with a descending ramp on each side, and although robbed in antiquity the few surviving grave-goods hint at the incredible wealth they must once have contained. The more modest burial of a Shang queen in another part of Anyang yielded 16

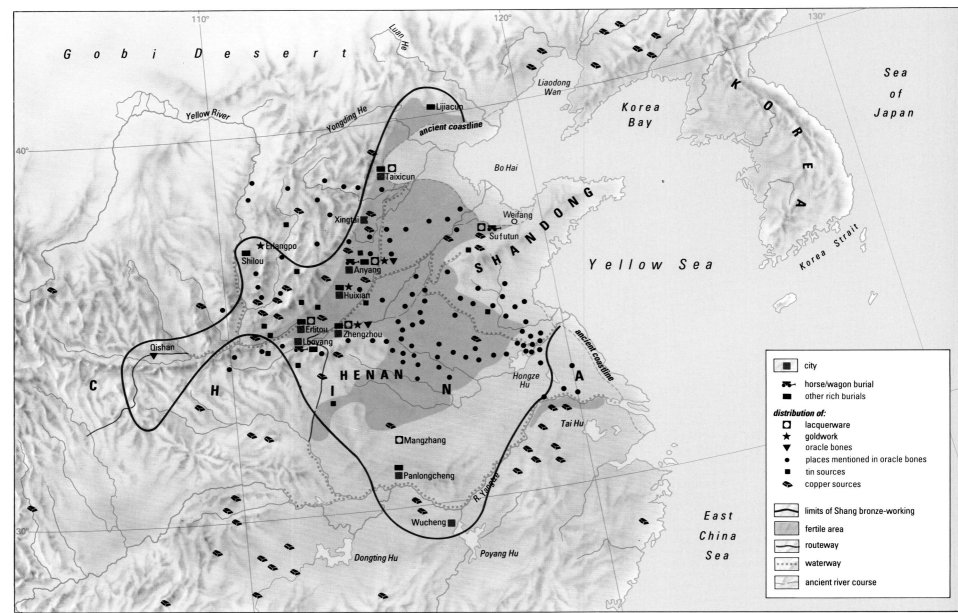

city
horse/wagon burial
other rich burials

distribution of:
□ lacquerware
★ goldwork
▽ oracle bones
• places mentioned in oracle bones
■ tin sources
copper sources

limits of Shang bronze-working
fertile area
routeway
waterway
ancient river course

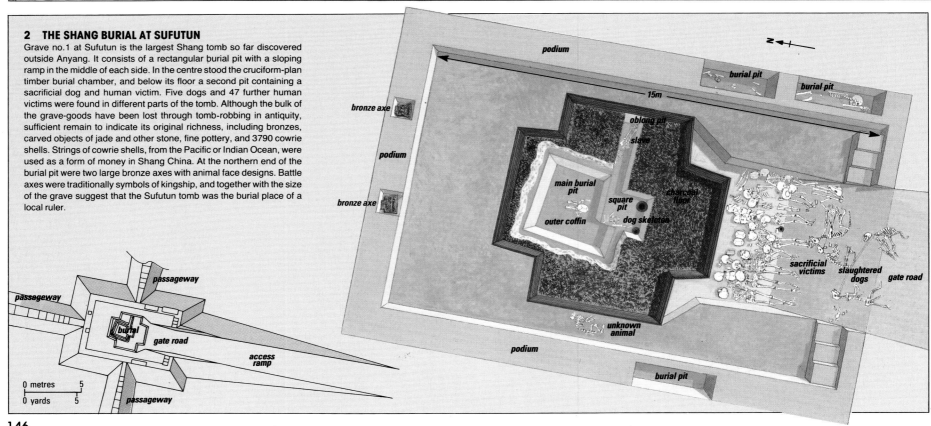

2   THE SHANG BURIAL AT SUFUTUN

Grave no.1 at Sufutun is the largest Shang tomb so far discovered outside Anyang. It consists of a rectangular burial pit with a sloping ramp in the middle of each side. In the centre stood the cruciform-plan timber burial chamber, and below its floor a second pit containing a sacrificial dog and human victim. Five dogs and 47 further human victims were found in different parts of the tomb. Although the bulk of the grave-goods have been lost through tomb-robbing in antiquity, sufficient remain to indicate its original richness, including bronzes, carved objects of jade and other stone, fine pottery, and 3790 cowrie shells. Strings of cowrie shells, from the Pacific or Indian Ocean, were used as a form of money in Shang China. At the northern end of the burial pit were two large bronze axes with animal face designs. Battle axes were traditionally symbols of kingship, and together with the size of the grave suggest that the Sufutun tomb was the burial place of a local ruler.

sacrificed humans, six sacrificed dogs, over 440 bronzes, some 590 jades, 560 bone objects and approximately 7000 cowrie shells. Sacrificed dogs and humans are a regular feature of the richest Shang graves; one Xibeigang tomb contained 165 human sacrifices, thought to have been prisoners of war sacrificed to the spirit of the deceased. They are also found in large numbers of building foundations and in sacrificial pits. The importance of warfare in Shang culture is reflected in the light two-wheeled chariots found in some of the graves; it seems likely that the war chariot reached China from the Near East, though there is little evidence to indicate the extent of such trans-Asian contact.

Religion, particularly ancestor worship, clearly played an important part in Shang China, and the rituals were probably carried out within ordinary houses and palaces. Ancestors were consulted through oracle bones; shoulder blades of cattle and water-buffalo or, more rarely, turtle shells were heated to produce cracks, which were then interpreted. The entire process of divination – the questions asked of the oracle, the answers given and the verification of the answer by the course of future events – was recorded on the bone in writing, and form an invaluable written record of the geographical and political organisation of the Shang state. Towards the end of the Shang period inscriptions also appeared on bronze ritual vessels, but we have no bureaucratic records comparable to those of the Near East and we must assume that these, if they existed, were written on perishable materials.

The Shang period saw great advances in craftsmanship – a response to the demand of a wealthy and privileged aristocracy for sophisticated goods, and many traditional Chinese crafts developed during this period. Elaborate bronze ritual vessels were cast from ceramic moulds, and decorated with animal motifs, imaginary beasts and abstract designs. Shang craftsmen were also skilled at stone and jade carving, while at the Xibeigang tombs the wooden ceilings were painted in lacquer, and vessels with lacquered surfaces have been found at several sites. By the end of this period, Chinese cultural traditions were already well established; although the Shang dynasty collapsed in the 11th century BC, the essential continuity of these traditions remained unbroken, and the foundations laid during this period remained the basis of Chinese civilisation in later times.

1 THE EVOLUTION OF SHANG CHINA

During the 3rd millennium BC prosperous farming communities developed in parts of northern and eastern China. Two of these, the Longshan groups of Henan and Shandong, formed the basis of the Shang state in around 1800 BC (map left). The heart of this state lay at the western edge of the North China Plain, near the point where the Yellow River leaves the mountains. This strategic area was made extremely fertile by the rich deposits of alluvium brought down by the river, and was also conveniently situated for the metal-rich uplands. Successive Shang capitals were situated here; Zhengzhou (below) has been identified as one of the earliest, while nearby Erlitou may mark the location of the very first capital. Anyang was probably the last residence of the Shang rulers, from the 14th to the 11th century BC. Oracle bone inscriptions mention many places on the plain, suggesting that this was an area of considerable importance, but few archaeological sites have been found here; they may lie buried beneath the alluvium, or have been destroyed by changes in river courses. The principal crop in the plain of the Yellow River was millet, but south of the Shandong peninsula rice grown in water-fed paddy fields was the staple cereal. Shang cultural influence, and perhaps political control, extended for a time as far south as the Yangtze basin, where the walled town of Panlongcheng displays typical Shang characteristics. However, by the time of the oracle bone inscriptions (c.1350 BC), Shang power was in decline, and the Yangtze Valley was clearly beyond the immediate control of the Anyang rulers.

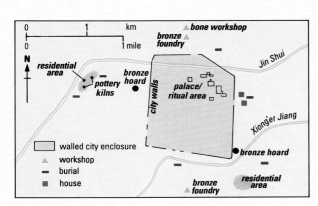

ZHENGZHOU: A SHANG CAPITAL

Zhengzhou (above) is the site of one of the successive capitals of the Shang state. It was founded around 1700 BC, and consisted of a large walled enclosure (320 hectares) surrounded by a network of residential areas and workshops. The rammed-earth enclosure wall was 7 kilometres long, and in places still survives to a height of over 9 metres. Outside the walls lay residential zones, together with the city cemeteries and specialist workshops for bone, pottery and bronze.

Late Neolithic China
sites:
- ▲ early Longshan c.3200-2500 BC
- ■ Longshan c.2500-1850 BC
- ▣ with rammed earth enclosure
- ◀ early copper-working, with date

regions:
- Shaanxi Longshan
- Henan Longshan
- Shandong Longshan
- southern Longshan
- peripheral

3 FROM THE SHANG DYNASTY

A *Three bronze halberds, the principal weapon of war in Shang China, the topmost with a jade blade set in a bronze tang inlaid with turquoise. These blades would have been mounted at right angles on a long wooden pole. Late Shang period, c.11th century BC, lowermost halberd 27cm long.* B *Stone buffalo, of uncertain provenance. 13th or 12th century BC, limestone, length 19.2cm.* C *Vessel for ritual offerings, in form of tiger protecting a man, decorated with feline and serpent designs. 13th or 12th century BC, cast bronze, height c.35cm.* D *Tripod jug from Weifang in the Shandong peninsula. c.2500 BC, white pottery, height 29.7cm.* E *Figurine of cormorant holding fish, a small amulet or plaque perhaps made for attachment to a wood or textile backing. Jade was probably not available within China and had to be imported, perhaps from the Baikal area of Central Asia. Late Shang, jade, height 4cm.*

The settlement of the Steppes

The Steppes of Eurasia cover a vast tract of territory from the eastern fringes of the Carpathians in the west to Manchuria in the east. Given the scarcity of rainfall and seasonal climatic variations from intense winter cold to the baking heat of summer it is hardly surprising that agriculture was slow to make any headway here. It was only after 4500 BC that communities depending on animal domestication and cereal cultivation began to appear in the southern Russian Pontic Steppe, around the mouth of the Amu Darya south of the Aral Sea, and further east around the River Yenisey north of the Gobi Desert. These early Steppe farmers relied more heavily on animals than on plants. Crop cultivation was difficult because of the general aridity, but the Steppes provided extensive grasslands, and rich seasonal pastures were found in mountainous uplands such as the Altai and Pamirs.

The best evidence for the animal-based economy of the early Steppe agriculturalists comes from the west, in southern Russia, where extensive excavations have been carried out. The key site is Dereivka, a settlement and cemetery on the middle Dnieper belonging to the Sredny Stog culture (c. 4400–3500 BC). Here, the surprising feature is the abundance of domestic horse bones (74%, as compared with 19% cattle and only 7% sheep, goat and pigs), a preponderance repeated at other sites of the Sredny Stog group. This is the earliest known domestication of the horse. At Dereivka the horses were primarily used for food, although finds of antler cheek pieces from soft-mouthed bits demonstrate that horse riding had already developed. The people of the Sredny Stog group lived in permanent settlements of large, rectangular timber-framed houses.

The Sredny Stog culture was followed in the western Steppes by a number of groups named after their burial practices. The first of these was the Pit Grave culture, with its later variant the Catacomb Grave culture. In these 'groups' or 'communities' burials were in pits or chambers beneath mounds. Disc-wheeled ox-drawn wagons were often among the objects placed in the grave, and are the earliest known remains of wheeled vehicles. During this period in the 3rd millennium BC, a flourishing copper industry based on local ores developed in the Caucasus, and copper objects are also found with these burials.

By about 1850 BC the Timber Grave phase, named after the characteristic timber burial chambers, had begun in the western Steppes. Finds of horse-bit cheek pieces show that horse riding was still practiced, and for the first time horses were used to pull wheeled vehicles. Near Chelyabinsk in the southern Urals a cemetery has been discovered with graves containing the remains of light horse-drawn carts with two spoked wheels. These contrast with the heavy ox-drawn wagons with four solid disc wheels of the previous period, and are clearly ancestral to the two-wheeled chariots that revolutionised Near Eastern warfare in the 2nd millennium BC.

The Andronovo culture, which covered a huge area from the Urals to Lake Baikal and south-west into Fergana, originated in about 1500 BC and developed from the earlier agricultural communities of the region. The Andronovo culture was fully bronze-using, obtaining tin from the Altai Mountains and tin and copper from the Urals and the mountains of Turkestan. Bronze-working was developed still further in the succeeding Karasuk phase, which began in about 1200 BC. The development of the Karasuk bronze industry demonstrates that for the first time Steppe culture was orientated towards China rather than the west. Bronzes from the Steppes have been found in Shang China: knives with ringed or ram's head butts from the Karasuk area, and socketed axes and spearheads from as far west as the Urals. One important result of this contact was probably the introduction, in the later Shang period, of the two-wheeled chariot into China – either from or via Central Asia.

The prehistoric agricultural communities of the Steppes played a vital part in the domestication of the horse, and subsequently in the development of wheeled vehicles. Both innovations were to have a major impact on world history. By the 2nd millennium BC, a new development was taking place: communities who had hitherto lived in small permanent villages herding livestock and growing crops gradually became pastoral nomads. Andronovo communities, for instance, herded cattle from horseback, and moved them between seasonal pastures. By the 1st millennium BC full pastoral nomadism had developed, and horse-riding warrior-nomads such as the Scythians began to gain notoriety through their fierce raids on neighbouring settled peoples.

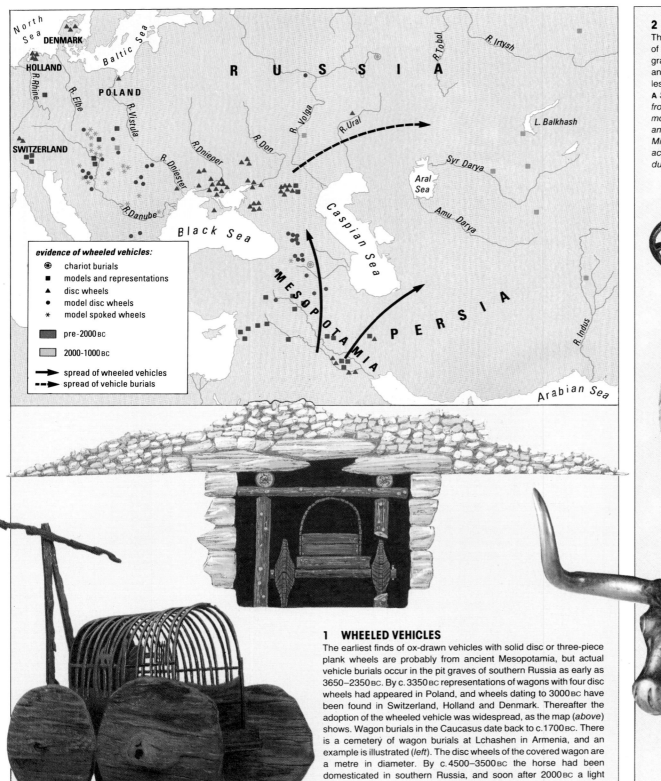

1 WHEELED VEHICLES

The earliest finds of ox-drawn vehicles with solid disc or three-piece plank wheels are probably from ancient Mesopotamia, but actual vehicle burials occur in the pit graves of southern Russia as early as 3650–2350 BC. By c. 3350 BC representations of wagons with four disc wheels had appeared in Poland, and wheels dating to 3000 BC have been found in Switzerland, Holland and Denmark. Thereafter the adoption of the wheeled vehicle was widespread, as the map (above) shows. Wagon burials in the Caucasus date back to c. 1700 BC. There is a cemetery of wagon burials at Lchashen in Armenia, and an example is illustrated (left). The disc wheels of the covered wagon are a metre in diameter. By c. 4500–3500 BC the horse had been domesticated in southern Russia, and soon after 2000 BC a light horse-drawn vehicle with two spoked wheels developed into the war-chariot and used throughout the Near East.

evidence of wheeled vehicles:
- ⊛ chariot burials
- ■ models and representations
- ▲ disc wheels
- ● model disc wheels
- ✳ model spoked wheels

▬ pre-2000 BC
▭ 2000–1000 BC

→ spread of wheeled vehicles
--▶ spread of vehicle burials

2 METALWORKING

The richly furnished burial barrow at Maykop in the Kuban region of the western Caucasus dates from about 2500 BC. Among the grave-goods were copper tools, and cups and bowls of gold, silver and fine stone. The find as a whole is uniquely rich, but similar, less spectacular tombs exist elsewhere in the region.
A Silver cup with frieze of wild cattle, goats and snow leopards from Maykop barrow. Height 11cm. **B** Gold bull originally mounted on a metal-cased rod; one of six wild bulls, two silver and four gold, from Maykop. Height 7.5cm. **C** Dagger from the Minusinsk area of the Upper Yenisey. It demonstrates that accomplished bronze casting was current in southern Siberia during the Karasuk period (13th–8th centuries BC).

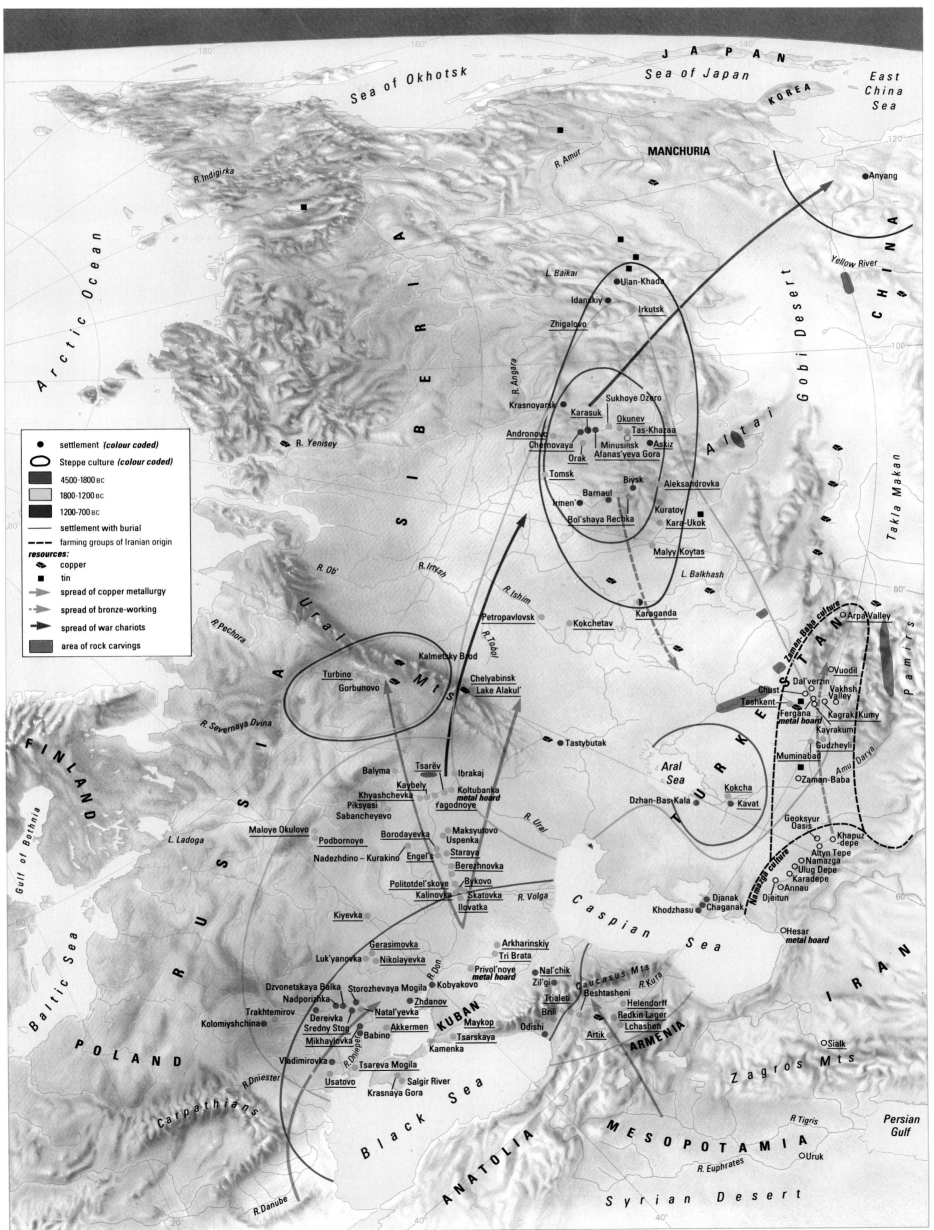

Sea of Okhotsk

Sea of Japan

J A P A N

KOREA

East China Sea

R. Indigirka

Arctic Ocean

R. Amur

MANCHURIA

Yellow River

• Anyang

C H I N A

S   I   B   E   R   I   A

Gobi Desert

L. Baikal

• Ulan-Khada

Idanskiy •
Irkutsk

Zhigalovo

R. Angara

Krasnoyarsk •

Sukhoye Ozero

Karasuk

Okunev
Tas-Khazaa

Andronovo
Chernovaya

Minusinsk • Askiz
Afanas'yeva Gora

Altai Mts

Orak

Tomsk

Biysk

Aleksandrovka

Takla Makan

Irmen'

Barnaul

Bol'shaya Rechka

Kuratoy

Kara-Ukok

R. Yenisey

R. Ob'

R. Irtysh

R. Ishim

Malyy Koytas

L. Balkhash

R. Pechora

R. Tobol

Petropavlovsk •

Kokchetav •

Karaganda

Zaman-Baba culture

Arpa Valley

U R A L   M t s

Kalmetsky Brod

Turbino
Gorbunovo

Chelyabinsk
Lake Alakul'

T U R K E S T A N

Vuodil •
Dal'verzin •

Chust
Tashkent •

Vakhsh
Valley

Fergana
metal hoard

Kagrak Kumy

Kayrakum

Gudzheyli

Pamirs

R. Severnaya Dvina

R. Don

Tastybutak •

Aral Sea

Muminabad •

Zaman-Baba

Amu Darya

FINLAND

Balyma
Tsarëv
Ibrakaj

Kaybely
Khyashchevka
Piksyasi
Sabancheyevo

Koltubanka
metal hoard
Yagodnoye

R. Ural

Dzhan-Bas Kala

Kokcha

Kavat

Geoksyur
Oasis

Khapuz-
depe

L. Ladoga

Maloye Okulovo

Podbornoye
Nadezhdino – Kurakino

Borodayevka
Maksyutovo
Uspenka

Engel's
Staraya

Berezhnovka

Politotdel'skoye
Bykovo

Kalinovka
Skatovka
Ilovatka

R. Volga

Altyn Tepe
Namazga
Ulug Depe
Karadepe
Annau

Djeitun

Namazga culture

Gulf of Bothnia

Kiyevka

Caspian Sea

Djanak
Chaganak

Khodzhasu

Hesar
metal hoard

I R A N

Baltic Sea

Gerasimovka
Luk'yanovka
Nikolayevka

Arkharinskiy
Tri Brata

Priv'nolnoye
metal hoard
Kobyakovo

Nal'chik
Zil'gi

Caucasus Mts
Beshtasheni

R. Kura

Dzvonetskaya Belka
Nadporizhka
Trakhtemirov
Kolomiyshchina •

Storozhevaya Mogila
Zhdanov

Dereivka
Sredny Stog Natal'yevka
Mikhaylovka Babino

Akkermen

Maykop

KUBAN

Tsarskaya

Kamenka

Trialeti
Brili

Odishi

Helendorff
Redkin Lager
Lchashen

Artik

ARMENIA

Sialk •

R U S S I A

P O L A N D

Vladimirovka
Tsareva Mogila

Salgir River
Krasnaya Gora

Usatovo

Carpathians

R. Dniester

R. Dnieper

Black Sea

ANATOLIA

MESOPOTAMIA

Zagros Mts

R. Tigris

Persian Gulf

Uruk •

R. Danube

Syrian Desert

R. Euphrates

Legend:

• settlement (colour coded)

⬭ Steppe culture (colour coded)

▪ 4500–1800 BC

▪ 1800–1200 BC

▪ 1200–700 BC

— settlement with burial

--- farming groups of Iranian origin

resources:

⬧ copper

▪ tin

→ spread of copper metallurgy

→ spread of bronze-working

→ spread of war chariots

▪ area of rock carvings

Bronze Age South-East Asia

In South-East Asia technological and cultural innovations tended to supplement rather than supplant past traditions. Thus it is not always possible to demonstrate a continuous technological evolution from the Late Stone Age through the Neolithic to the earliest metal ages. At Malayan sites such as Gua Cha and Gua Kechil (*page 96*) hunting and gathering may have lasted until the 3rd millennium BC and Neolithic farming traditions into the early centuries AD. The transition from hunting and gathering to simple farming was slow. Pottery (its fragility possibly indicating more permanent settlements) first appeared on the mainland in the 7th millennium BC and on the islands by the 3rd millennium BC. Chipped stone tools began to be supplanted by ground-edge and then fully polished Neolithic implements.

Metallurgy was also only gradually introduced to South-East Asia, appearing in the mainland in the 3rd millennium BC at sites such as Phung Nguyen in northern Vietnam and Ban Chiang in north-east Thailand. On the islands the first metallurgy is dated to the end of the 1st millennium BC. Older ways of life such as hunting, fishing and gathering persisted alongside these innovations. However, the advance of bronze-working marks an important change – the presence of bronze objects in some, but not all, of the burials of this period indicating greater social complexity. Excavations at Non Nok Tha and Ban Chiang in Thailand have uncovered bronze artefacts produced by sophisticated techniques similar to those of northern China, such as closed moulds and lost-wax casting. These bronzes may have been imported: however, earthenware crucibles have been found which suggest that local bronze-working took place quite early. At Ban Na Di, for example, remains of crucibles were found from the 1st millennium BC.

The most sophisticated artefacts, found in the Red River Valley of northern Vietnam, are the distinctive Dong Son drums, unique for both their technical and aesthetic qualities. Named after the famous site of Dong Son, some were grave-offerings in high-status burials. The motifs on the drums suggest a ritual function but their exact usage remains unknown. The sequence of early bronze-working in northern Vietnam can be divided into three phases: Dong Dau (1500 BC), Go Mun (1000 BC) and Dong Son (500 BC). The last style is considered to be the culminating or classic era. The drums were made using sophisticated lost-wax and casting-on methods, and their intricate decorative friezes depict geometric, human, and animal designs. Dong Son drums are also among the earliest metal objects found on the islands, and finds throughout South-East Asia are very widespread – numerous sites in Vietnam, Malaya and the islands of Indonesia such as Java and Sumatra. It is possible that the highly valued drums continued to be traded long after their date of manufacture, their final distribution marking early trading contacts.

The richness of the grave-goods in the burials at Dong Son shows that this was a highly stratified society. The burials were placed around wooden houses built on piles and contained large bronze drums as well as axes, halberds, daggers, spears and arrowheads, spitoons (perhaps for betel chewing), buckets, small sculptures and jewellery and ornamental belt buckles. In north-east Thailand the majority of bronze finds are also ornamental, including bracelets, anklets, neck ornaments and bells. Jewellery was sometimes fashioned from stone and from shell. By 200 BC large quantities of glass beads, commonly orange or blue, are also found in burials. Abundant pottery finds are characteristic of all phases of the burials.

With improved farming techniques, settlement gradually extended into hitherto unexploited areas – for example the lowland plains of north-east Thailand. Wet-rice farming appears to have become widespread during this period. The bones of buffalo, animals directly linked to the more intensive ploughing requirements of rice cultivation, are found for the first time. At the same time, finds of utilitarian iron artefacts, which could have been used to make ploughs, and iron slag show that iron was locally manufactured. Further evidence of intensive rice production, and hence of wet-rice farming, can be traced in the greater percentage of rice chaff found in the clay mixture used to make pottery.

The development of bronze metallurgy in South-East Asia coincided with an increasingly hierarchical society, firmly based on agricultural village settlements. It was these crucial changes, the introduction of new technologies, new social forms, and a new economic base, which culminated in the foundation of the proto-urban settlements of the 1st millennium AD.

2 BAN NA DI: A THAI BURIAL

Ban Na Di is a village located in the Sakon Nakhon Basin, in north-east Thailand. The village was built on a mound situated close to two small streams, with access to soils well suited to the cultivation of rice. Occupation at the site dates back to 1500 BC. Burial no. 47 (*above*) was of an adult male laid out on his back. He was aged between 30 and 34. The vessel at his head contained some fishbone fragments, shell, and a piece of bronze. On the right wrist was a stone bracelet which had been broken prior to the burial and repaired with bronze wire. Among the clay figurines found with the body were representations of cattle, deer, elephants and humans. Around the neck was a necklace made up of shells and one large stone bead. **A** *Human clay figurines. Height 7-8cm.* **B** *Shell bracelets. Outer diameter c.100cm.* **C** *Marble bracelet repaired with bronze wire. Outer diameter c.100cm.* **D** *Repaired bracelet in situ. c.1500 BC.*

3 FROM CERAMICS TO METALWORKING

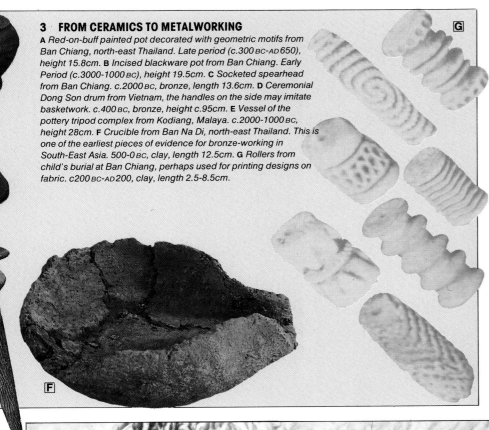

A Red-on-buff painted pot decorated with geometric motifs from Ban Chiang, north-east Thailand. Late period (c.300 BC-AD 650), height 15.8cm. B Incised blackware pot from Ban Chiang. Early Period (c.3000-1000 BC), height 19.5cm. C Socketed spearhead from Ban Chiang. c.2000 BC, bronze, length 13.6cm. D Ceremonial Dong Son drum from Vietnam, the handles on the side may imitate basketwork. c.400 BC, bronze, height c.95cm. E Vessel of the pottery tripod complex from Kodiang, Malaya. c.2000-1000 BC, height 28cm. F Crucible from Ban Na Di, north-east Thailand. This is one of the earliest pieces of evidence for bronze-working in South-East Asia. 500-0 BC, clay, length 12.5cm. G Rollers from child's burial at Ban Chiang, perhaps used for printing designs on fabric. c200 BC-AD 200, clay, length 2.5-8.5cm.

4 A SOUTH-EAST ASIAN HOUSE

Traditionally, most South-East Asian houses had living floors raised 2-3 metres above ground. All that remains of these early structures are post hole patterns. The reconstruction of an early house (above) is based on post holes from Nong Chae Sao, Thailand.

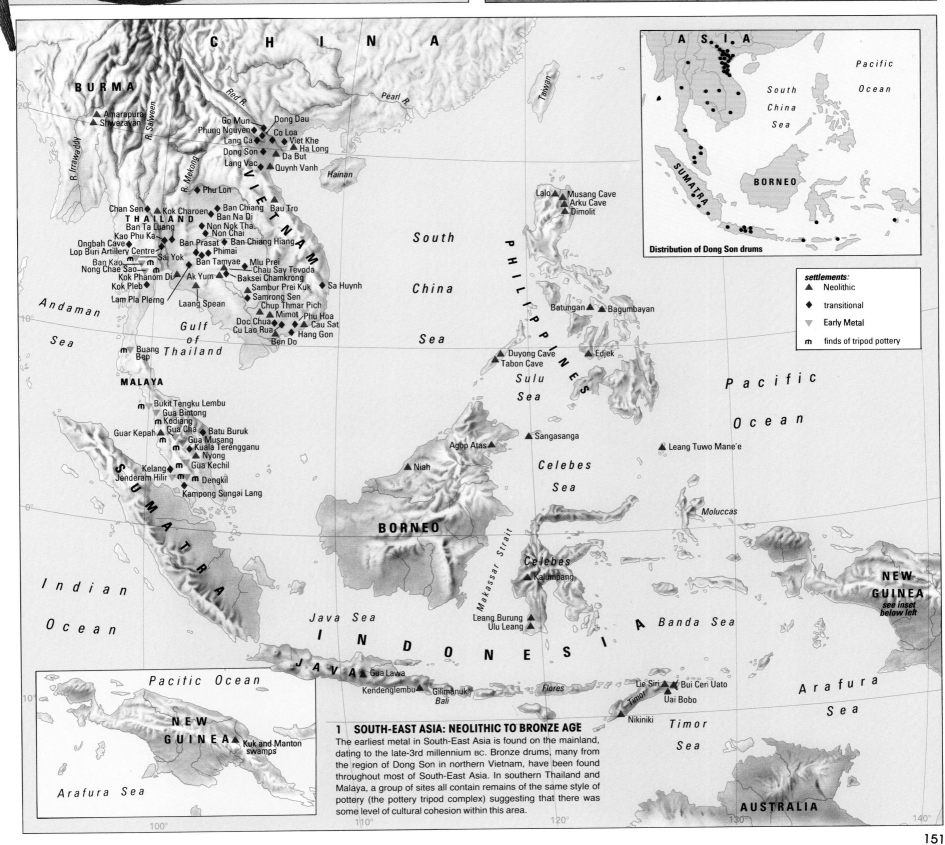

Distribution of Dong Son drums

settlements:
▲ Neolithic
◆ transitional
▽ Early Metal
m finds of tripod pottery

1 SOUTH-EAST ASIA: NEOLITHIC TO BRONZE AGE

The earliest metal in South-East Asia is found on the mainland, dating to the late-3rd millennium BC. Bronze drums, many from the region of Dong Son in northern Vietnam, have been found throughout most of South-East Asia. In southern Thailand and Malaya, a group of sites all contain remains of the same style of pottery (the pottery tripod complex) suggesting that there was some level of cultural cohesion within this area.

FIVE
EMPIRES OF
THE OLD WORLD
1000 BC – AD 650

THE CENTURIES following 1000 BC were a time of great changes throughout virtually the whole of the Old World. Since the first states arose – in about 3000 BC – there had been a continual tendency for larger and larger units to develop, involving ever more sophisticated systems of administration and control. This process culminated in the 1st millennium BC with the appearance of empires of hitherto unparalleled size and power. In the Near East, the Assyrian empire, whose military might is presented so vividly in the bas-reliefs of the royal palaces, was followed by the larger Achaemenid empire of Persia and that in turn by the still larger but short-lived empire of Alexander the Great. A little later, the greater part of the Indian subcontinent was united for the first time under the Mauryan empire while the Mediterranean world and most of western Europe fell under the sway of the powerful Roman empire. China also witnessed a period of empire-building in the last few centuries BC, when a number of warring kingdoms were combined into a single unified state under the Han dynasty.

The archaeology of these empires illustrated both the wealth which they brought to the ruling elites and the systems of administration and defence by which they governed their extensive territories. Remains of the impressive Roman road network show the importance that was placed on communications, while the Great Wall of China indicates the effort that could be devoted to imperial frontier defence. In the heartlands of these empires, vast palaces and rich tombs which have lost none of their power to stun the onlooker illustrate more directly the power and wealth of the rulers.

The fruits of empire clearly brought immense wealth to the elite, but in providing peace and protection such powerful states also brought considerable benefits to their subject populations. Trade and manufacture flourished as never before, and cities grew to record sizes – the imperial capitals of Rome and Chang'an may have had close on a million inhabitants at their peak. To support the huge urban populations agricultural systems became increasingly intensive. The introduction around 1000 BC of a new metal, iron, played an important role, as it was much cheaper than the earlier bronze; cheap enough, indeed, to be used in agricultural equipment. Imperial governments were also able to deploy vast resources of manpower on large-scale irrigation and land-reclamation schemes and the administration such civic works required.

Trade was an essential part of the economic life of the empires, supplying both raw materials and luxuries to the centres of population and power. Much of the bulk tranport – notably of foodstuffs – took place by ship, and most of the major cities of the period were located on coasts or waterways. Long-distance land routes were also developed, notably the great Silk Road linking East and West Asia. Such extensive trade networks brought the different empires into contact with each other, and also spread their political and cultural influence far afield. Beyond their reach however, in Polynesia, Australasia, northern Asia and sub-Saharan Africa, traditional societies continued to develop along their own independent lines, unaffected by the imperial theme.

Etruscan sarcophagus from the Banditaccia cemetery at Caere, Italy.
Late 6th century BC, terracotta, length 2m.

The archaeology of empire

During the last 3000 years the Old World has seen the rise and fall of a series of powerful empires, and their remains dominate the archaeological record of those countries where they held sway. The impressive ruins of cities, palaces and temples which have been left by the great civilisations of Persia, China and the Mediterranean are eloquent testimony to the wealth, grandeur and power of empire. The ways in which this power was exercised, by bringing and keeping subject territories under control, exacting tribute and taxation, and governing far-flung colonies, are reflected in the remains of fortresses, roads and administrative systems. While empires may vary greatly in size, antiquity and cultural traditions, they are all characterised by these common features.

Since most empires were established and maintained through the use of military power, it is not surprising that military activities and achievements are prominent on the temple and palace reliefs and victory monuments which record and celebrate imperial conquests. Most empires had professional standing armies which gave them a great advantage over their less powerful neighbours. Military professionalism often enabled them to conquer and absorb new areas with relatively small forces. Imperial armies also maintained control over the subject territories and protected them from invasion. Troops were stationed in strategic locations throughout an empire and especially along the imperial frontiers. These military dispositions are frequently evident in the remains of fortresses and frontier works – from Hadrian's Wall in northern Britain and Alexander's Barrier near the Caspian Sea to the Great Wall of China.

Roads also played a vital role in the maintenance of imperial control: an adequate road system was vital for the speedy transmission of messages across great distances. It could also enable imperial armies to reach even the most inaccessible areas of the empire quickly, allowing the government to respond immediately to any threat of invasion or insurrection. The Persian Royal Road from Sardis to Susa (6th–5th century BC) was one of the earliest of these, though for the most part it was merely a beaten track with inns and posting stations at regular intervals. The Roman road network was much more elaborate, and well-preserved stretches of road have survived, as well as bridges and milestones. The Romans used roads as a means of integrating new territories into their empire, and also developed post systems to speed the transmission of messages and commands.

The government of such large realms with their cultural and ethnic heterogeneity was nevertheless a problem. Most empires attempted to solve this by division into provinces. Each province was under the control of a centrally appointed governor, supported by an administrative staff and a military detachment. One of the most important functions of these provincial adminstrations was the collection of tax and tribute for the central government. Lists of tribute owed by individual cities and provinces have sometimes survived, while in the Assyrian royal palaces and at Persepolis in Persia, relief sculptures depict processions of subject peoples bringing tribute to the king. The diverse tribute shown in these reliefs includes agricultural produce, exotic animals such as ostriches and gazelles, and craft products such as goldwork and textiles. Tribute, however, was not the only way of collecting revenues from the subject population. In Han China, the income of the state was supplemented by the profits from the imperial monopolies in salt and iron. Harbour dues and forced labour were also exacted, but many empires, including Rome and the Han, relied above all on a fiscal tax.

Military control created peaceful conditions in which craftsmanship, trade and industry could flourish relatively free from the threat of war or invasion. Many imperial governments invested in public works projects which must have increased the prosperity of the subject peoples, for example the Achaemenid construction of a 'Suez canal' linking the Nile with the Red Sea. The great resources – both in manpower and wealth – of imperial governments meant that they were also able to assist areas struck by disasters such as invasion or famine, and the more secure conditions seem to have led to population growth in many areas. However, empires were concerned primarily with increasing their own revenues, and much of the wealth that was generated by promoting economic development in their subject territories was drained away to the imperial heartland. The monuments that the great empires left behind should therefore be seen as reminders, not only of the grandeur and scale of the imperial achievement, but also of the harsh military rule and economic exploitation by which it was so often supported.

3 SYMBOLS OF EMPIRE
A Edicts of the Mauryan emperor Asoka carved on a polished limestone pillar at Dalhi-Topra, India. The edicts, carved in important locations on smoothed rock faces as well as pillars, promulgate an ethical code which was designed to give greater unity to the culturally and ethnically heterogeneous Mauryan empire. 3rd century BC. **B** Relief sculpture showing barbarian captives, possibly offered as tribute to Rome, from Mainz, West Germany. 2nd–3rd century AD, limestone, height 0.84m. **C** Part of the model army of 6000 terracotta soldiers armed with spears, swords, bows and crossbows providing ritual protection for the tomb of Shih Huang-ti, the first emperor of China, at Mount Lishan, Shaanxi province, China. Late 3rd century BC. Height of figures c.1.8m. **D** Statue of the Roman emperor Augustus from the Villa of Livia, Prima Porta. The confident and commanding pose symbolises the effortless power of empire. c.AD 19 BC, marble, height 2.04m.

2 IMPERIAL PROPAGANDA: ASSYRIA
The power of art as imperial propaganda is well illustrated in the low relief friezes decorating the palaces of the Assyrian empire. At Khorsabad (far right) the subject of the reliefs was fitted to the function of each room and the classes of people who would have been received there. The facades of the palace courtyards were decorated with reliefs showing the king accompanied by his vizier and attendants and subject peoples bearing tribute. Visiting delegations would have been escorted through the passageway into the courtyard and from there into the large eastern reception room where scenes showed the king presiding over the torture and execution of rebels. Similar scenes were found in the adjoining room, which may have been used for entertaining foreign delegations, leaving no doubt of the inevitable consequences of revolt against Assyrian rule. Privileged guests may have entered the smaller room, decorated with peaceful scenes of hunting and feasting. Reliefs showing Assyrian military successes were restricted to rooms on the opposite side of the reception wing, where Assyrian courtiers could glory in their conquests.

Reliefs from Khorsabad (c.710 BC) A The chariots of Sargon II's army trampling fallen enemies (721–705 BC). **B** Subject peoples bearing model cities and tribute in token of their submission. **C** The king attended by his fan-bearer and arms-bearer facing a procession of Assyrian dignitaries.

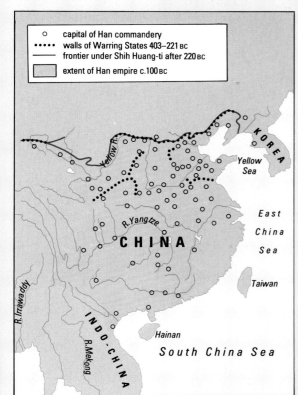

Legend (top left map):
- ○ capital of Han commandery
- ••• walls of Warring States 403–221 BC
- — frontier under Shih Huang-ti after 220 BC
- ▨ extent of Han empire c.100 BC

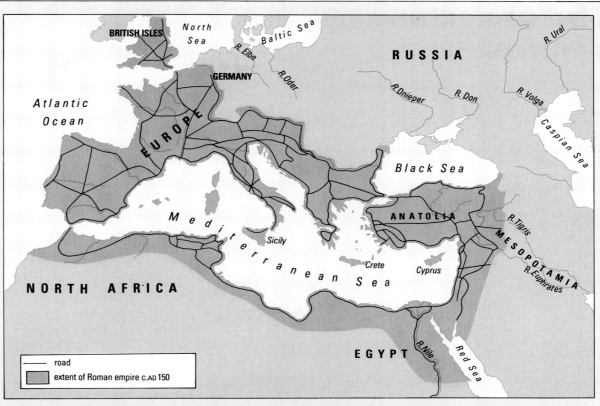

- — road
- ▨ extent of Roman empire c.AD 150

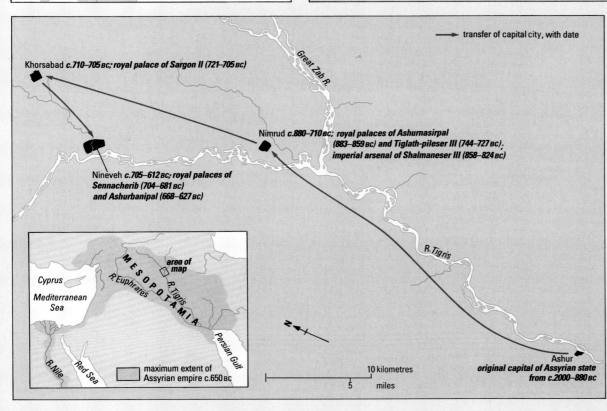

→ transfer of capital city, with date

Khorsabad c.710–705 BC; royal palace of Sargon II (721–705 BC)

Nimrud c.880–710 BC; royal palaces of Ashurnasirpal (883–859 BC) and Tiglath-pileser III (744–727 BC); imperial arsenal of Shalmaneser III (858–824 BC)

Nineveh c.705–612 BC; royal palaces of Sennacherib (704–681 BC) and Ashurbanipal (668–627 BC)

Ashur original capital of Assyrian state from c.2000–880 BC

▨ maximum extent of Assyrian empire c.650 BC

area of map

10 kilometres
5 miles

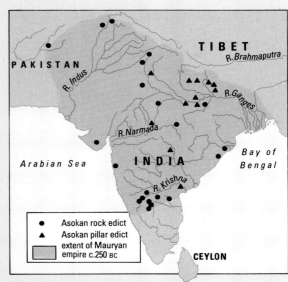

Legend (India map):
- ● Asokan rock edict
- ▲ Asokan pillar edict
- ▨ extent of Mauryan empire c.250 BC

1 GEOGRAPHY OF EARLY EMPIRES

The Mauryans (*above*) attempted to unify their realm by the erection of rock and pillar edicts. The military organisation of Han China included not only the Great Wall but also a system of military provinces or commanderies (*top left*). The Roman empire was also divided into provinces for civil and military administration, linked together by an extensive road network (*top right*). An important feature of all the empires was the flow of wealth towards the centre, and in Assyria lavish palaces were built at the imperial capitals (*left*).

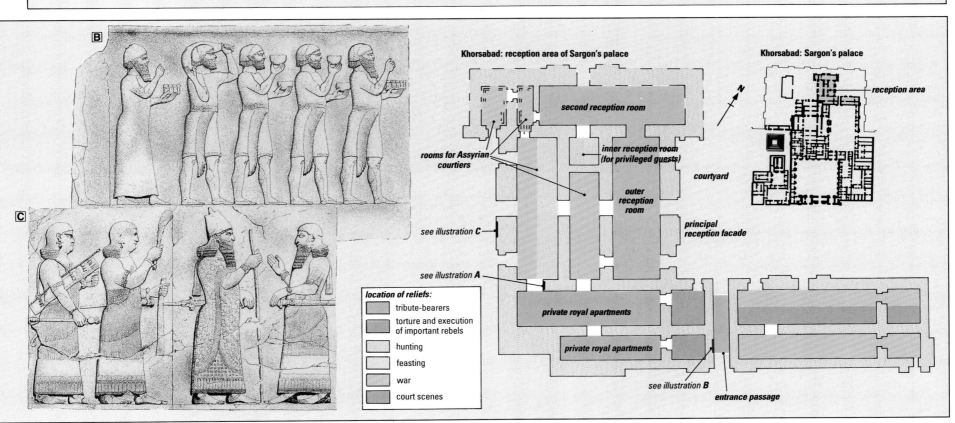

Khorsabad: reception area of Sargon's palace

Khorsabad: Sargon's palace

- second reception room
- rooms for Assyrian courtiers
- inner reception room (for privileged guests)
- courtyard
- outer reception room
- principal reception facade
- see illustration C
- see illustration A
- private royal apartments
- private royal apartments
- see illustration B
- entrance passage
- reception area

location of reliefs:
- tribute-bearers
- torture and execution of important rebels
- hunting
- feasting
- war
- court scenes

The Assyrian empire

The decline of the contending powers of Egypt and the Hittites at the end of the 2nd millennium BC left a patchwork of kingdoms and city-states in the Near East. There were many changes in the ensuing five hundred years: the emergence of the kingdom of Israel with Jerusalem as its capital, the growth of Phoenician trading cities along the Levantine coast, and the appearance of the powerful kingdom of Urartu in the mountains of Armenia. The mighty empire of Assyria originated in northern Mesopotamia and succeeded in uniting for the first time almost the whole of the Near East.

The heartland of the Assyrian empire was the fertile plains around Arbil and Nineveh, and it was here that the capital and main royal residence was moved in the early 9th century BC, first to Nimrud, and later to Khorsabad, and finally to Nineveh itself. These grandiose and impressive capitals were all dominated by a citadel containing temples and palaces, with a lower town housing the bulk of the city's population; attached to or outside the citadel was a palace-arsenal for housing military equipment and booty from foreign campaigns. The royal palaces of these Assyrian capitals contained elaborate networks of reception halls and throne rooms where officials and courtiers, foreign embassies and representatives of the subject peoples were received and entertained. The walls of these rooms were decorated with scenes showing Assyrian victories, courtly ceremonials and lion hunts, while entrances were guarded by colossal lions and winged bulls – obviously designed to impress visitors with the might of Assyrian arms.

The Assyrians dominated the Near East through relentless and ruthless military conquest; their success was largely due to their ingenuity and innovation in the art of war. Much of our knowledge of Assyrian warfare comes from palace reliefs. Here we find depicted several classes of infantry, including heavily armed lancers with mail coats and large shields, cavalry – the riders had neither saddles nor stirrups, but both they and their horses were protected by armour – and chariots with a driver, shield-bearers and archers, pulled by two or even three horses. Assyrians are also shown besieging and capturing heavily fortified cities: digging tunnels, swinging battering rams, mounting scaling ladders, ruthlessly plundering the captured city and carrying off booty and prisoners. Assyrian power was further consolidated by the introduction of a formal imperial structure, with a system of provinces and provincial governors; this reorganisation was marked by the construction of palaces to serve as the residences of the new governors, often imitating – though somewhat crudely – the reliefs and decorative motifs of the metropolitan centres. Throughout the empire stelae proclaim imperial achievements, boasting of military victories, celebrating and recording the successful completion of building and irrigation works.

Throughout the Levant and southern Palestine, cities were obliged to acknowledge Assyrian supremacy and offer tribute. The kingdom of Israel, established by 1000 BC, was protected by a network of strategically placed fortress-cities and initially resisted Assyrian domination. However, by the late 8th century BC it was absorbed into the Assyrian empire. North of Israel, the wealthy Phoenician cities of the Levant such as Tyre, Sidon, Byblos and Aradus traded over vast distances – from the Straits of Gibraltar to the east African coast – in timber from the Lebanese mountains, metals and metalwork, fine cloth and agricultural produce. These cities were also forced to acknowledge Assyrian hegemony and to pay tribute to their Assyrian overlords. The Phoenicians were famous for their ivory-carving; at Nimrud a large number of Phoenician ivories have been found, probably booty or tribute from military campaigns.

The only power in the region which successfully resisted Assyrian expansion and remained a wealthy and sophisticated rival was the highland kingdom of Urartu. Skilled in hydraulic and military technology, Urartu maintained a flourishing self-sufficiency boosted by the exploitation of local raw materials such as iron, and was famous for its fine horses raised on the lush pasturelands.

At the end of the 7th century BC, Assyria's enemies joined forces to overthrow the empire. Both Nimrud and Nineveh – the last and the greatest of the Assyrian capitals – were finally sacked and destroyed in 612 BC. Although Assyrian power was destroyed, and Assyria itself suffered a depopulation from which it did not recover for many centuries, the structure of the empire survived, to be taken over first by the Babylonians and then by the Persians, who incorporated it in a vast realm extending from the Aegean to the borders of India. The age of empire had arrived.

3 SYMBOLS OF POWER

A Winged human-headed lion, a guardian figure from the gate of the palace of Ashurnasirpal at Nimrud. 9th century BC, limestone, height 3.5m; B Relief slab from the North Palace at Nineveh, the last and greatest of the successive Assyrian capitals. The scene is a royal lion hunt, with the king, Ashurbanipal, firing arrows from the front of his speeding chariot, while two attendants armed with spears ward off an attack from a wounded animal. c. 640 BC, limestone, height 1.6m.

C Fragment of a model fortress from the Urartian capital of Toprakkale near Lake Van. Massive fortifications are a feature of many Urartian sites. Late 8th or 7th century BC, bronze, height 30.5cm.
D Open-work panel with sphinx from one of the main reception-rooms at Fort Shalmaneser, Nimrud, probably of Phoenician origin. Originally a furniture ornament, perhaps one of a matching pair attached to the back of a throne. 8th century BC, ivory with traces of gilding, 19 x 15 cm.

Megiddo, northern Israel
1 palace with deep and large foundations of stone indicating an upper storey
2 walls enclosing lime mortared courtyard constructed with rubble
3 administration building truncated by the construction of the stable block
4 southern stables built of stone blocks 1.5m thick; stone pillars and mangers divide the stables into three aisles
5 northern stables. Stabling facilities covered one fifth of the city and housed about 450 horses
6 city walls ran 820m round the flat top of the mound, built with offsets at 6m intervals
7 6-chambered gateway probably built by Solomon

well
shaft
rock-cut water tunnel

phases of building:
Ahab c.850 BC
Solomon c.965-928 BC

0   25   50 metres
0   25   50 yards

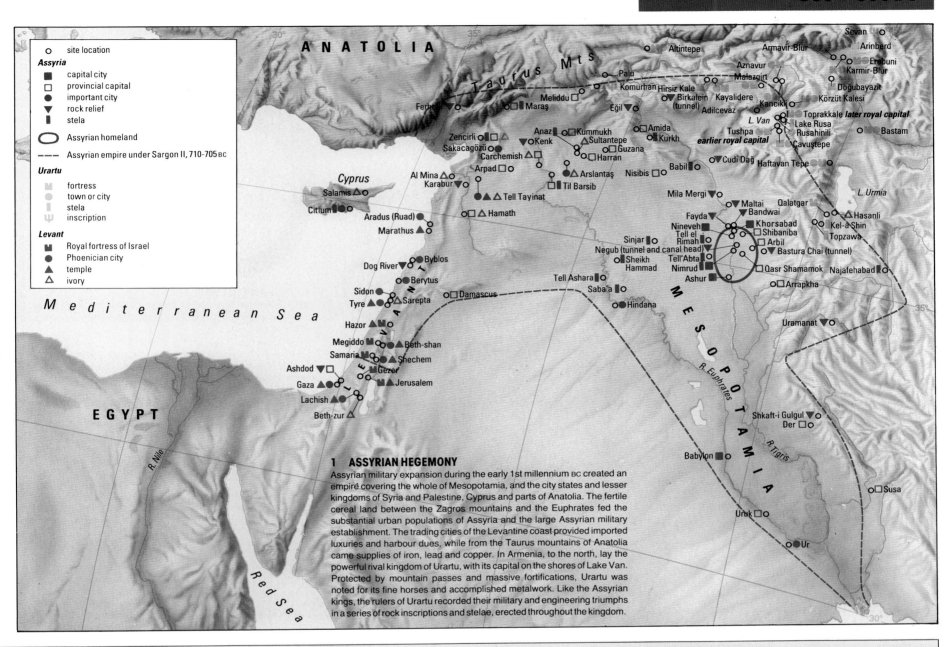

1 ASSYRIAN HEGEMONY

Assyrian military expansion during the early 1st millennium BC created an empire covering the whole of Mesopotamia, and the city states and lesser kingdoms of Syria and Palestine, Cyprus and parts of Anatolia. The fertile cereal land between the Zagros mountains and the Euphrates fed the substantial urban populations of Assyria and the large Assyrian military establishment. The trading cities of the Levantine coast provided imported luxuries and harbour dues, while from the Taurus mountains of Anatolia came supplies of iron, lead and copper. In Armenia, to the north, lay the powerful rival kingdom of Urartu, with its capital on the shores of Lake Van. Protected by mountain passes and massive fortifications, Urartu was noted for its fine horses and accomplished metalwork. Like the Assyrian kings, the rulers of Urartu recorded their military and engineering triumphs in a series of rock inscriptions and stelae, erected throughout the kingdom.

2 ROYAL CITIES

In about 880 BC the capital of Assyria was transferred from its original home at Ashur to the city of Nimrud, which remained pre-eminent for 150 years. The site consists of a vast roughly rectangular enclosure some 350 hectares in area, with massive mud-brick defences bordered on the west by the old course of the River Tigris and on the south by a wide canal. Most of the city area is unexplored; it was once occupied by the houses of the ordinary inhabitants. The total population is estimated to have been over 80,000. The citadel in the south-west was crowned by a 60-metre high ziggurat, and here Assyrian monarchs built a succession of temples and palaces as well as administrative buildings. The North West Palace (completed 879 BC) was the first Assyrian palace to be decorated with wall reliefs and colossal human-headed figures of lions and winged bulls. In the south-east corner of the city was Fort Shalmaneser, the royal arsenal, which yielded grisly evidence of the end of the city – a mass burial of people killed in the final sack of 612 BC.

In comparison, the ancient tell site of Megiddo was small, a mere six hectares in area. It was nevertheless a place of some importance, capital of a Levantine city state in the 2nd millennium BC, and in the early 1st millennium a royal fortress and administrative centre under the Israelite kings. There were two major phases of building under Solomon and Ahab; by the 9th century BC the city was defended by a fortification wall, and the interior was reserved for military and administrative buildings. These included storerooms and stables, with space for a contingent of the Israel chariotry; the stables of Megiddo housed as many as 450 horses. However, these precautions did not prevent the city falling to the Assyrian army in 733 BC. As an Assyrian provincial capital Megiddo remained a prosperous town to the end of the 7th century.

Right aerial view of citadel of Nimrud in northern Iraq, capital of the Assyrian empire c. 880–707 BC. On the left is the ancient course of the River Tigris; the lower city lies to the right.
Left aerial view of Megiddo in northern Israel, an important royal fortress and administrative centre in the early 1st millennium BC.

Nimrud, northern Iraq

Fort Shalmaneser (below), built 859-824 BC as the imperial arsenal

1 reception rooms and treasuries of the king
2 raised dais for the reviewing and inspecting of troops
3 stepped throne base
4 residential quarters
5 administrative offices
6 courtyards surrounded by workshops and magazines
7 barracks
8 magazines
9 walls with buttresses and projecting towers

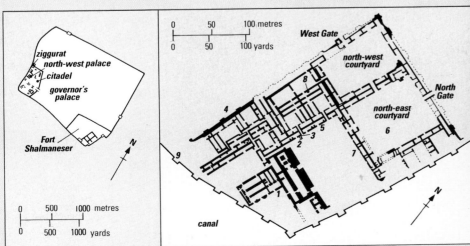

The first Persian empire

The Achaemenid empire of Persia which came into being in the middle of the 6th century BC was the largest the world had yet seen, covering not only the old imperial heartland of Egypt, Babylonia and Assyria but also Asia Minor, the Iranian Plateau and the Indus Valley. Its scale is illustrated by the remains of several elaborate royal palaces, spectacular finds of rich metalwork such as the Oxus Treasure, and numerous cuneiform tablets which provide an insight into the government of this vast realm. However, excavation and research have concentrated for the most part on the study of major public buildings, and relatively little is known about the way of life of the ordinary people.

Although remains of several Achaemenid palaces have survived, only those at Persepolis, Pasargadae and Susa have been the subject of extensive excavations. The palace at Susa occupies a commanding position at the heart of a city which was old even before the Persians began to build. At Persepolis and Pasargadae, on the other hand, the sites chosen were spacious and unencumbered by earlier buildings, with room for extensive gardens and walkways. Building inscriptions found at Susa and Persepolis record that peoples from many different parts of the empire were involved in the construction work, and a variety of architectural styles is represented ranging – at Persepolis – from Lydian or Greek columns to Egyptian cornices.

The cosmopolitan nature and administrative complexity of the Achaemenid realm are also demonstrated by the reliefs carved on the ceremonial stairway leading to the *apadana* or principal audience hall at Persepolis. Delegations from 23 peoples bring gifts or tribute including clothing, metal vessels, elephant tusks, gold and exotic animals such as antelope, okapi and camels. Cliff reliefs at Behistun and Naqsh-i Rustam and building inscriptions from Susa and Persepolis give lists of the principal peoples of the Persian empire, while clay tablets record the issue of provisions to provincial governors (satraps), usually naming the city or palace serving as the satrapal centre, which in some cases can be equated with a known archaeological site. Several thousand clay tablets found during excavations at Persepolis clearly demonstrate that the Achaemenid palaces were also administrative centres. The tablets, once part of the official archives, record payments in foodstuffs or silver to members of the royal family, officials and workmen. One category of tablet concerns the issue of rations to people travelling on official business, and cities as far away as Sardis, Kandahar and Bactra are named as starting-points or destinations. Most of the tablets deal only with local affairs around Persepolis; clearly the real centre of government was the palace at Susa.

Good communications were essential for the successful control of so large and heterogeneous a state, but of the Achaemenid road system few traces survive. Greek writers refer to the 'Royal Road' from Sardis to Susa, with regularly spaced posting stations and official inns, but the only evidence of this is a short stretch of metalled road at the eastern approach to Gordium; for the greater part of its length the road was probably an unmetalled track. It is likely that other highways would have linked Susa to Egypt and important eastern centres such as Bactra, and although there are no remains of these roads there is some archaeological evidence for the courier system which operated along them. A leather bag containing correspondence between Arsam, the governor of Egypt, who was at court at Susa or Babylon, and his subordinate officials and administrators in Egypt, was discovered early this century. The documents date to c.410 BC, and are written in Aramaic, the official language under the later Achaemenids, on parchment – which replaced the more cumbersome cuneiform tablets around the middle of the 5th century.

Despite the heavy burden of taxation required for the administration of such an empire, archaeological evidence shows that the Achaemenid rulers strove in a variety of ways to increase the prosperity of their lands. Three stelae from Egypt record the completion under royal direction around 500 BC of a 'Suez canal' linking the Nile with the Red Sea. At the opposite extremity of the empire, Russian excavations at the site of Ura-Tyube have uncovered remains which are thought to be one of seven forts built along the Syr Darya frontier in the 6th century to protect the inhabitants of Sogdiana. Nearby along the Amu Darya, and in the Diyala Plain of Mesopotamia, this period saw the development and elaboration of irrigation systems and an increase in the density of settlements, and it is likely that this, too, owed something to Achaemenid patronage.

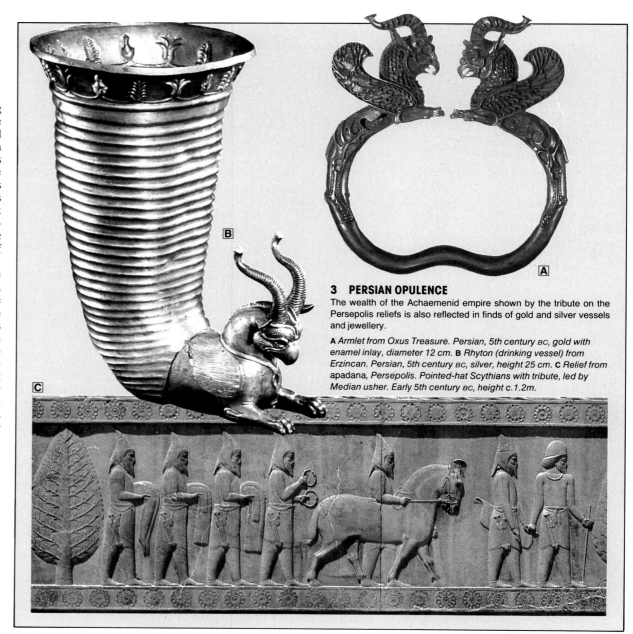

3 PERSIAN OPULENCE

The wealth of the Achaemenid empire shown by the tribute on the Persepolis reliefs is also reflected in finds of gold and silver vessels and jewellery.

A Armlet from Oxus Treasure. Persian, 5th century BC, gold with enamel inlay, diameter 12 cm. **B** Rhyton (drinking vessel) from Erzincan. Persian, 5th century BC, silver, height 25 cm. **C** Relief from apadana, Persepolis. Pointed-hat Scythians with tribute, led by Median usher. Early 5th century BC, height c.1.2m.

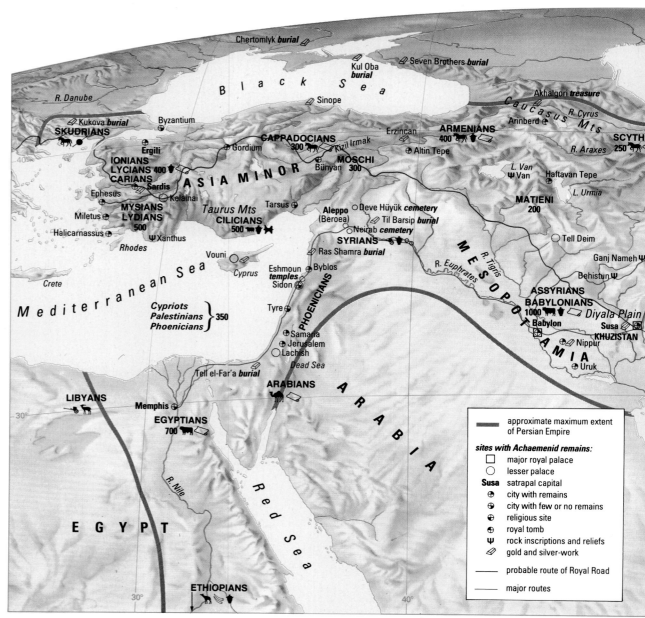

2 PERSEPOLIS: A ROYAL PALACE

Persepolis *below* **1 Principal stairway** to terrace, gently graded to allow ascent on horseback. **2 Gate tower** leading via processional way to Hall of 100 Columns (10) and to courtyard in front of principal audience hall (4). **3 Eastern stairway** to *apadana*, sides decorated with tribute reliefs. **4 Apadana** principal audience hall of Darius I, with open colonnades on 3 sides and a timber ceiling supported by 36 slender columns nearly 20m tall. **5 Tripylon** small central palace or vestibule. **6 Tachara** or 'winter palace' of Darius I, notable for the use of Egyptian architectural features. **7 Hadish** or Palace of Xerxes, with reception hall and fine carvings. **8 Palace of Artaxerxes I. 9 Unfinished gate-tower** leading to courtyard facing Hall of 100 Columns. **10 Hall of 100 Columns** or 'throne hall'; larger in floor area but only half the height of the *apadana*. **11 Hall of 32 Columns** small reception hall. **12 Royal stables** and chariot-house. **13 Offices and storerooms** of the Royal Treasury. **14 Additional treasury warehouses** and storerooms. **15 Garrison quarters. 16 Rock-cut royal tomb**, attributed to Artaxerxes III (c.340BC). **17 Remains of mud-brick fortification wall** with projecting towers. **18 Remains of mud-brick fortification wall** separating palace buildings from probable citadel area on higher ground to east.

0   50   100 metres
0   50   100 yards

phases of construction:
515–480 BC
479–450 BC
449–330 BC

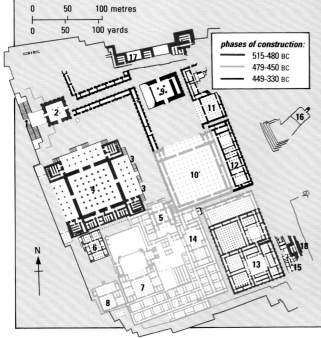

The great palace of Persepolis overlooks an extensive fertile plain in the Persian homeland of south-western Iran, and was a principal residence of the Achaemenid kings. Work began in the late 6th century BC with the construction of a terrace some 500 metres x 300 metres in area and 12 metres high. The buildings erected on this terrace over the following 50 or 60 years included high-columned audience halls and reception rooms, storerooms for tribute and other valuables, and quarters for a military garrison. Of these structures, only the stone columns and doorways survive, the walls of sun-dried brick and timber ceilings having perished long ago. Much of the stonework is decorated with fine low-relief sculptures depicting the Great King enthroned, Persian courtiers and soldiers, and, on the stairways leading to the *apadana*, a procession of delegations from different parts of the empire bearing gifts or tribute. The buildings on the Persepolis terrace, surrounded by a massive fortification wall of sun-dried brick, were probably used by royalty only on formal occasions or in times of danger. The customary royal residences were on the plain around the terrace, where remains have been found of several palaces, including one with an extensive walled hunting park and a vast ornamental lake. A sprawling town lay beyond the palace area, while 6 kilometres to the north at Naqsh-i Rustam are the 5th-century rock-cut tombs of the Achaemenid kings. Persepolis was only one of several major Achaemenid palaces between which the court moved at different seasons of the year. Susa, in the sultry lowlands of Khuzistan, was the administrative centre of the empire, and remains of a palace rivalling Persepolis in size and sophistication have been found there, while from material traces or written records others are known at Hamadan, Pasargadae and Babylon. The cosmopolitan architecture and monumental scale of these royal palaces clearly reflect the grandiose aspirations of the Achaemenid realm.

1 THE ACHAEMENID EMPIRE

The wealth and variety of the Achaemenid empire is well illustrated by the relief sculptures carved on the ceremonial stairways leading to the *apadana* at Persepolis, which portray delegations from the different subject peoples bringing gifts or tribute for the Great King. Study of the dress, weapons and tribute offerings on these reliefs has allowed a tentative identification of the delegations pictured there with the principal peoples of the empire listed in the building inscriptions at Susa and Persepolis and cliff reliefs at Behistun and Naqsh-i Rustam. Some of the peoples may correspond to the provinces or satrapies through which the empire was governed, though neither the reliefs nor the inscriptions were intended to constitute an official inventory of the administrative units of the Persian empire, and it remains difficult to reconstruct the provincial organisation beyond the identification of major administrative centres such as cities and palaces. The tribute brought by the delegations on the Persepolis reliefs reflects the cultural and natural resources of the regions from which they came: for example, lions from Elam, camels from Arabia and Bactria, gold from India, horses from Scythia. As well as tribute in kind, the Achaemenid rulers exacted a tax assessed in silver, the amounts for each province being recorded by the Greek historian Herodotus, and the resulting pattern provides an excellent illustration of the relative wealth of the different parts of the Achaemenid realm. Actual finds of Achaemenid metalwork demonstrate the rich resources and sophisticated craftsmanship of the empire. Objects similar to those depicted as tribute offerings on the reliefs were among a hoard of fine metalwork found near the Syr Darya (River Oxus), of which over 170 pieces survive, including gold armlets (3A) and a model chariot. Finely crafted objects of gold and silver have been found in other areas, including a silver rhyton from Armenia (3B) and silver armlets from Cyprus and Mesopotamia. The frequent occurrence of animal motifs in Achaemenid metalwork is a feature shared with the art of the steppe peoples to the north, and may reflect the nomadic or pastoralist origins of the Persian aristocracy.

Map labels:

Aral Sea — Syr Darya — Amu Darya — Caspian Sea

CASPIANS 200

SOGDIANS

Ura-Tyube *frontier fortress line of seven 6th century BC frontier forts*

Samarkand (Maracanda)

Merv (Margush) — Kobadian-I — *probable location of Oxus Treasure* — Altin-X

Tureng Tepe

CHORASMIANS

BACTRIANS 360 — Bactra (Zariaspa)

MEDES 450 — Elburz Mts

PARTHIANS

Parthians Arians Chorasmians 300

ARIANS — Herat (Haraiva)

Hamadan (Hagmatana)

GANDARIANS 170 — Hindu Kush — Charsadda

Salt Desert

PERSIA

Taxila (Bhir Mound)

Masjid-i Sulaiman

Dariush Kabir *remains of bridge and causeway*

Naqsh-i Rustam — Istakhr

ELAM — SUSIANS 300

Nad-i Ali *fortified palace*

Kandahar

Jinjan — Takht-i Rustam — Pasargadae — Borazjan

DRANGIANIANS — Dahan-i Ghulaman — ARACHOSIANS

Zohak

Shahr-i Dakyanus — SAGARTIANS — Tepe Yahya 600

INDIANS — Au

Bampur

Persian Gulf

PARIKANIANS 400

Indian Ocean

50° — 60° — 70°

IONIANS	satrapal people		Au	gold
400	tax in talents of silver			elephant tusks
articles of tribute				vessels
	okapi			daggers
	lionesses			bows
	Bactrian camels			textiles
	dromedaries			leather goods
	horse chariots			battle axes
	bulls			swords
	rams			lances and shields
	asses			rings
	antelopes			horses

Classical Greece

The cultural achievement of Classical Greece, perhaps the highest and most influential peak of early western civilisation, depended on a number of major developments in economy and society: the sophistication of political thought, the formation of cities, the resurgence of trade and industry, the growth of population, and the foundation of overseas colonies. These developments were crucial in the progress of Greece from the dark age of the post-Mycenaean decline to the remarkable florescence of the 5th century BC.

The political and economic structure of Mycenaean Greece collapsed in the 12th century BC, and the country remained relatively poor and isolated, with very little overseas trade, for over 200 years. This situation began to change in around 900 BC, as trade links with Italy and the Levant were re-established. As prosperity increased, population levels started to rise once again, and the political structure of Classical Greece emerged. The combination of political fragmentation with cultural and linguistic unity was a basic feature of Greece during most of the 1st millennium BC, as it had been in the Mycenaean age. Rugged mountains divided the country into a series of fertile basins, each of which formed the core of a small state. With the emergence of urban centres in around 700 BC the typical political unit of the classical period, the city-state, had developed (*page 162*).

Many of the cities of Classical Greece started as small settlements in the shelter of a naturally defensible citadel or acropolis. As wealth and security increased, fine buildings were erected, funded partly by state revenues and partly by private donations, which served as expressions of civic pride, and reflected all the key aspects of Greek city life. The main temple was the place of worship of the city's patron deity and a symbol of political power; it was often especially grandiose in scale and built of fine materials. The gymnasium represented the importance placed on fitness and physical recreation in Greek society. The theatre and odeon were for plays, poetry and musical recitals, while in the law courts and council chambers the private and public affairs of the city and its citizens were discussed and regulated. Finally there was the agora or market-place, in which the all-important commercial transactions were conducted.

The development of urban society was accomplished by far-reaching changes in economic organisation. With growing urban populations, imports of food and raw materials were vital, and pottery, metalwork and other manufactures were produced in ever-increasing numbers to pay for these imports. Greek products, such as Black- and Red-figure pottery, are found in large quantities at sites outside the area of Greek settlement – underlining the scale and success of the export trade. A widespread network of colonies was established from the west Mediterranean to the eastern shores of the Black Sea during the 8th and 7th centuries BC. Initially these towns acted as trading posts, for example Al Mina in Syria, which was strategically situated at the head of an important overland route to Mesopotamia. Many of the later colonies, however, also served as overspill towns for the cities of the Greek homeland – by the 5th century BC Athens and Corinth may have had as many as 50,000 or even 100,000 inhabitants. Colonies relieved the pressure on land created by these increasing populations.

Frequently, the colonies were located in positions where merchants could benefit from trade with non-Greek peoples. Merchants from Massilia travelled up the Rhône and across into the Danube basin, leaving gifts to smooth their passage, such as the huge bronze cauldron found in a Celtic aristocrat's grave at Vix, which was probably manufactured at a Greek colony in southern Italy. At Black Sea colonies such as Olbia, the Greek merchants exchanged luxury goods for grain to ship back to the cities of the Greek homeland. Such long-distance traffic depended almost entirely on sea and river transport, the only effective method for the carriage of bulk goods at this period. Access to the sea was of prime importance, and almost all the Greek colonies were consequently located on or near the coast.

The outstanding remains of Greece's autocratic eastern neighbours, the Assyrian and Achaemenid empires, are grandiose and luxurious imperial palaces. In Greece, by contrast, it is temples, theatres and other civic buildings of an essentially communal nature which are most conspicuous, reflecting the less centralised quality of Greek political institutions. Ruling dynasties and individuals are much less apparent in the material remains, and are largely replaced by symbols of the power of the community as a whole. This difference in emphasis gives ancient Greece much of its distinctive character, was perhaps partly responsible for its remarkable artistic achievement, and has survived as a key feature of Western ideology to the present day.

3   THE GREEK ACHIEVEMENT

A Stater of Metapontum showing ear of barley in relief. This Greek colony derived its prosperity from cereal cultivation. c.540 BC, silver, diameter 2.5cm. **B** Statue of Zeus, looted by the Romans from a temple in Greece in the late 2nd century BC, lost off sea at Cape Artemesion. c.460 BC, bronze, height 2.09m. **C** Temple of Poseidon at Posidonia (Paestum), an important Greek colony in southern Italy. The external columns are 8.8m tall. **D** Figurine of carpenter at work with saw, from the Boeotia region of Greece. Such small sculptures provide vivid images of everyday life which contrast with the formality of the larger works of Classical Greek art. c.500 BC, terracotta, height 8.15cm. **E** Two-handled Black-figure cup, or kylix, made in Attica and bearing the signature of Nikosthenes, a pottery producer active in the later 6th century BC. It shows a pair of warships in full sail, each furnished with a sturdy ram and a painted eye device on the bows. Diameter 28cm.

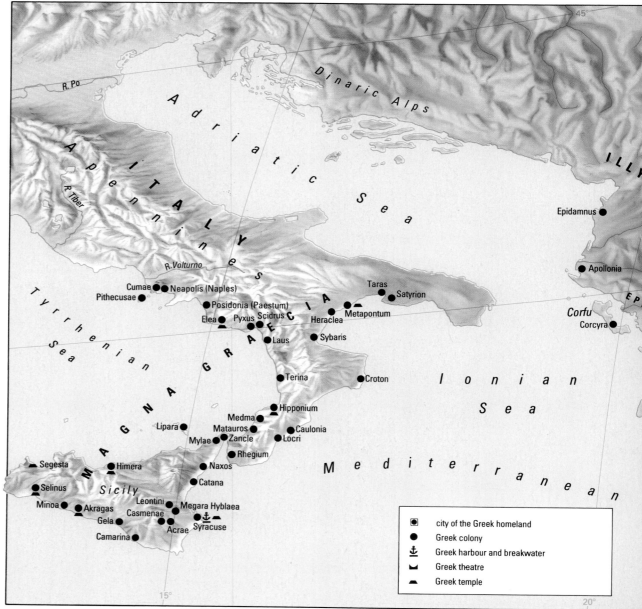

	city of the Greek homeland
●	Greek colony
⚓	Greek harbour and breakwater
⌣	Greek theatre
▲	Greek temple

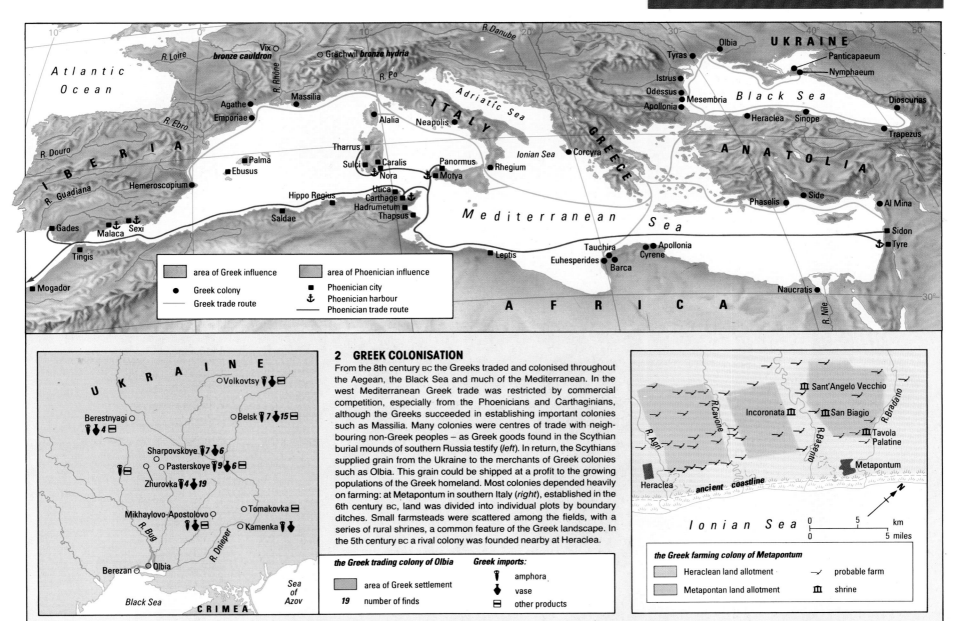

2 GREEK COLONISATION

From the 8th century BC the Greeks traded and colonised throughout the Aegean, the Black Sea and much of the Mediterranean. In the west Mediterranean Greek trade was restricted by commercial competition, especially from the Phoenicians and Carthaginians, although the Greeks succeeded in establishing important colonies such as Massilia. Many colonies were centres of trade with neighbouring non-Greek peoples – as Greek goods found in the Scythian burial mounds of southern Russia testify (*left*). In return, the Scythians supplied grain from the Ukraine to the merchants of Greek colonies such as Olbia. This grain could be shipped at a profit to the growing populations of the Greek homeland. Most colonies depended heavily on farming: at Metapontum in southern Italy (*right*), established in the 6th century BC, land was divided into individual plots by boundary ditches. Small farmsteads were scattered among the fields, with a series of rural shrines, a common feature of the Greek landscape. In the 5th century BC a rival colony was founded nearby at Heraclea.

the Greek trading colony of Olbia
- area of Greek settlement
- **19** number of finds

Greek imports:
- ▼ amphora
- ◆ vase
- ▭ other products

the Greek farming colony of Metapontum
- Heraclean land allotment
- Metapontan land allotment
- ⌐ probable farm
- Ⅲ shrine

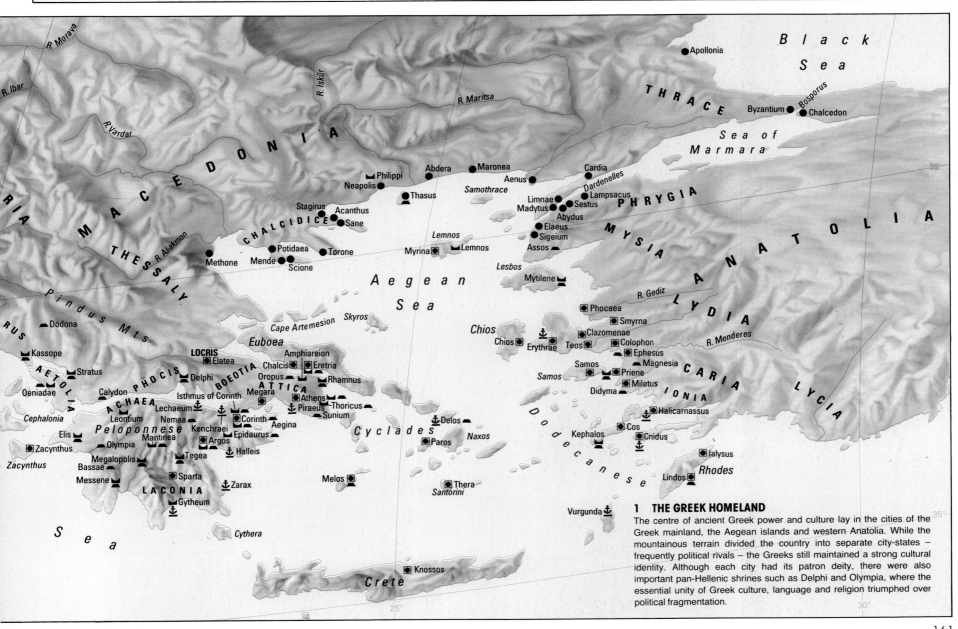

1 THE GREEK HOMELAND

The centre of ancient Greek power and culture lay in the cities of the Greek mainland, the Aegean islands and western Anatolia. While the mountainous terrain divided the country into separate city-states – frequently political rivals – the Greeks still maintained a strong cultural identity. Although each city had its patron deity, there were also important pan-Hellenic shrines such as Delphi and Olympia, where the essential unity of Greek culture, language and religion triumphed over political fragmentation.

Athens: a Greek city-state

The ancient Greek city of Athens reached its apogee in the 5th century BC when it became the cultural and intellectual centre of the Classical Greek world, the largest and wealthiest Greek city-state (or *polis*) and a leading military and maritime power. This Athenian florescence was curtailed by Sparta's defeat of Athens in 404 BC at the end of the Peloponnesian War, but Athens retained its cultural and symbolic pre-eminence for the next four centuries, and remains the most famous example of the Greek city-state.

The cultural and political development of ancient Greece was closely related to the geography of the country. The irregular coastline is punctuated by natural harbours and small plains, separated from each other by mountains. These fertile plains attracted agricultural settlement, and their isolation helped to form the self-contained political units which characterise Classical Greece. The main settlement usually formed around a natural outcrop (*acropolis*) which could be fortified as a retreat in emergencies. Around the main centre were farms, hamlets and villages. Athens was, until the 8th century, just such a cluster of small farming villages. A dramatic population explosion during this period – improved farming techniques were probably a contributing

factor – was accompanied by the political unification of the independent villages of Attica; Athens, with its steep, fortified *acropolis* rising to 100 metres, became a natural political centre, and in c.750 there was a sudden increase in the population of Athens itself.

The focus of Athenian city life was the market-place (*agora*) – with shops, temples, market halls, and law courts; it was also the meeting place for the city council until 500 BC. The process of ostracism, whereby citizens voted for the expulsion of public figures to prevent political strife, was carried out here; inscribed potsherds (*ostraka*) with which they voted have been found. The Acropolis, on the other hand, was the military and religious centre of the city. Surrounded by a massive wall, it contained many temples and shrines, most of which were dedicated to

3 THE ATHENIAN ACHIEVEMENT

The early Geometric style of Greek art was superseded first by the Archaic style, then by monumental Classical sculpture, with masterpieces such as the Parthenon frieze.

A *Dipylon vase, originally one of several standing over graves in the Kerameikos cemetery at Athens. A scene on the side shows a corpse on a bier and mourners. Mid-8th century BC, pottery, height 1.55m.* B *Detail from the Parthenon frieze showing part of the annual Panathenaic procession in honour of Athena, the city's patron deity. c.440 BC, Pendelic marble, originally painted, height of frieze 1.09m.* C *Athenian 'owl' coin, Attic tetradrachm minted from Laurium silver and used in payment for public works and services. The owl was a symbol of Athena. 479 BC, silver, diameter 2.5cm.* D *Statue of Athena from Piraeus, the port of Athens. c.350 BC, bronze, height 2.44m.*

The Acropolis

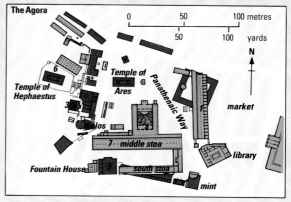

The Agora

Agora *inset right* 1 **Stoa of Attalus** a two-storeyed colonnaded market hall, 112m long and 20m wide, with small rooms (probably shops) at the rear on each floor. 2 **Old Bouleuterion** council chamber with inclined rows of seats around three walls. From c.400 BC it was used to house state archives, and was replaced by 3 **New Bouleuterion**. 4 **Odeum of Agrippa** hall for music concerts. The semicircular seating was backed and flanked by colonnades and faced a narrow stage. Originally roofed. 5 **Heliaia** principal law court of Athens. 6 **Temple of Hephaestus** square pits dug out of the rock surround the temple containing fragments of plant pots, the remains of a garden. 7 **Middle stoa** colonnaded hall of stone and sun-dried brick. At the rear were small square dining rooms with stone emplacements for couches.

2 THE BUILDING OF ATHENS

The sack of Athens by the Persians (480 BC) was followed by a major programme of public building in the 5th century BC, the age of the great Classical monuments. Athens is dominated by the rocky summit of the Acropolis, crowned by the city's greatest temple, the Parthenon (*above top*), and approached by the monumental Propylea entrance. The commercial and civic quarter, the Agora (*above*), was frequently rebuilt and expanded, and is remarkable for its spacious colonnaded market halls (*stoas*). The Panathenaic Way, a ceremonial avenue, entered the city through the main gateway, the Dipylon, and crossed diagonally to the Acropolis. The city was fortified by a wall of the 5th century BC, as well as the Long Walls which led to the nearby harbour town of Piraeus. The graves of the Kerameikos cemetery lined the Sacred Way, leading to the Sanctuary of Demeter at Eleusis.

Athens *left* 1 **Acropolis** rocky citadel of Athens, over 300m long, 130m wide, rising 100m above the surrounding plain. 2 **Temple of Athena** foundations of archaic temple. 3 **Propylaea** monumental entrance to the Acropolis, approached by a sloping ramp 20m wide and 80m long leading up to the religious buildings on the summit. 4 **Erechtheum** Ionic temple, notable for its caryatid porch. 5 **Parthenon** the principal temple of Athens, built entirely of marble, including the roof tiles. Within the Doric colonnade the interior was divided into two parts: to the east the *cella* or sanctuary, and to the west a rear chamber serving as a treasury. 6 **Odeum of Herodes Atticus** straight rear wall 28m high, semicircular rows of seats for 5000 spectators. Originally roofed in cedar. 7 **Stoa of Eumenes** a two-storeyed colonnaded hall. 8 **Roman agora** an open rectangular area surrounded by colonnaded market halls with ranges of shops at rear. 9 **Pnyx** semicircular structure of theatre-like design; assembly place for the citizens. 10 **Olympeium** the largest temple in Greece, 108m long and 41m wide. 11 **Agora** market and civic centre (*see inset above*).

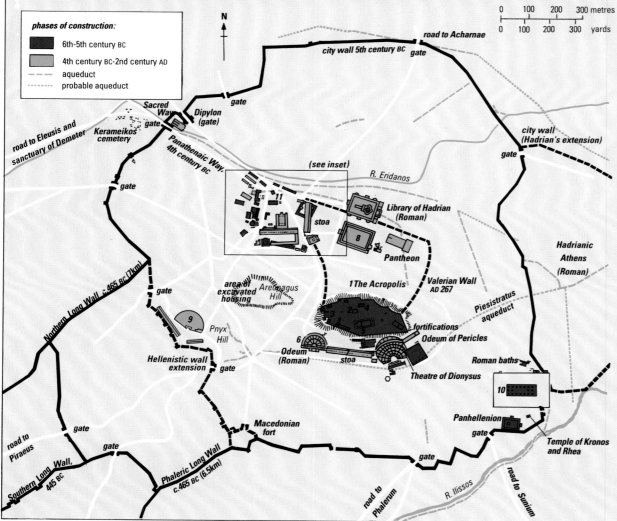

Athena, goddess of wisdom, the city's patron deity. From 432 BC, the Acropolis was dominated by the imposing silhouette of the Parthenon, which replaced an earlier Temple of Athena destroyed by the Persians in 480 BC. One of the largest Greek temples, it was constructed from local marble and decorated with a remarkable frieze depicting the procession which was the climax of the Panathenaea, Athens' greatest religious festival which took place every four years. Another important aspect of civic life is reflected in the theatre of Dionysus, the setting for performances of works by Athenian playwrights such as Sophocles and Aristophanes, as well as for religious ceremonies and public meetings.

In contrast to the imposing public buildings of Classical Athens, most private houses were small, irregular buildings with earth floors, clustered around courtyards. Country houses were more substantial, with fortified stone buildings surrounding rectangular yards. The streets of the city were narrow, winding, unpaved alleyways, with inadequate sewage, and private houses depended upon rainwater or wells and on cesspools for drainage. From the 6th century BC burials were not allowed within the city, and graves were placed along the roads leading out of Athens. At the Kerameikos, or potters' quarter, remains of workshops have been found among the tombs where decorated vases were used to mark the graves. In the 6th century BC, funerary stelae replaced the amphorae.

During this period, Athens became one of the first states to introduce coinage, and exploited the Laurium silver mines for suitable metal. These coins were used initially for state payments, in particular for massive public works programmes, as well as for financing regular civic festivals. During Athens' great expansion, increasing numbers of these coins were minted to finance defence; ships were purchased, mercenaries were recruited and massive new building projects were initiated in Piraeus, Athens' port and naval base. Vast fortifications (the Long Walls) were constructed to ensure secure communications betweeen Athens and its fleet.

Despite the defeat by Sparta in 404 BC Athens retained much of its prestige, and grandiose buildings such as the Odeum of Herodes and the Library of Hadrian were constructed during the next six centuries. When however, the city was finally sacked in the 3rd century AD, it lost its importance until the 19th century.

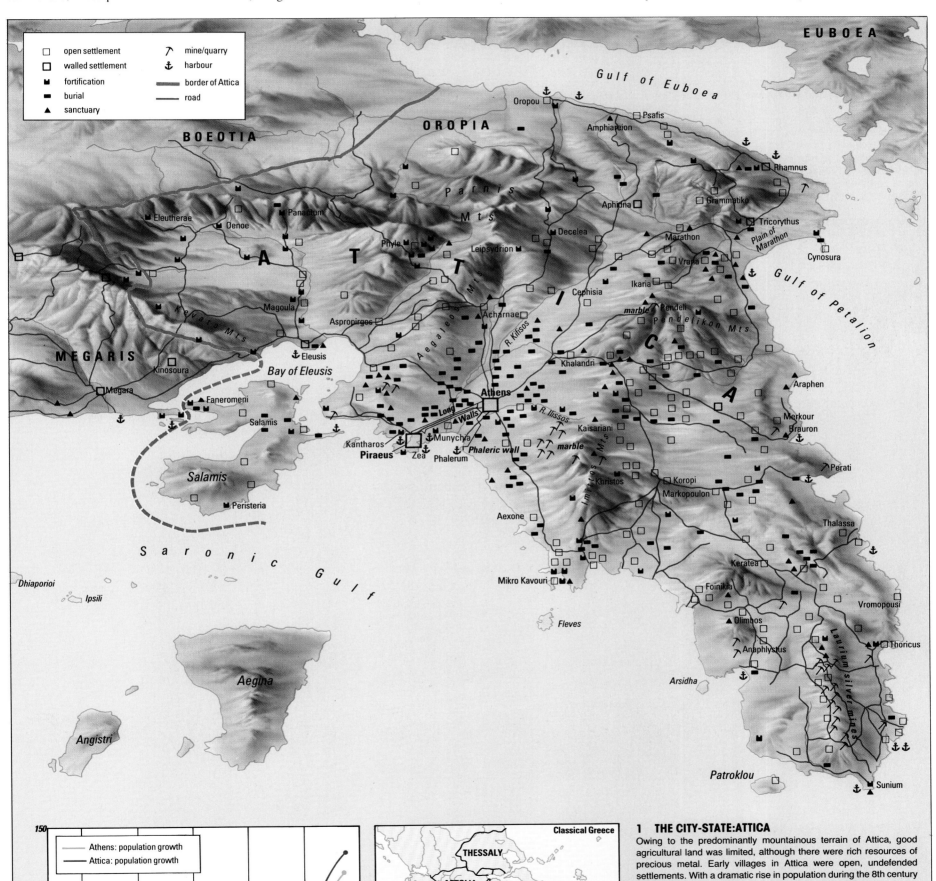

1 THE CITY-STATE: ATTICA

Owing to the predominantly mountainous terrain of Attica, good agricultural land was limited, although there were rich resources of precious metal. Early villages in Attica were open, undefended settlements. With a dramatic rise in population during the 8th century BC, reflected in an increase in burials throughout the region (*left*), villages expanded and more settlements were walled. The defences of the region were reinforced by strategically placed border and coastal forts; most were little more than signalling stations, but their impregnable positions enabled small garrisons to defend them. Attica's many harbours were an important factor in the development of trade and defence which, with building works, were financed by the profits from mining; Athenian coinage was minted from Laurium silver. Marble quarries, for example, in the Pendelikon mountains, were extensively exploited for the ambitious building projects of the 5th century BC. Richly endowed shrines and sanctuaries are found throughout Attica, both in towns and in the countryside.

Hellenism in Asia

Communities around the eastern Mediterranean in the middle of the 4th century BC experienced an acceleration in economic growth and the beginning of an era of prosperity that lasted well into the Roman period. The cultural influence of the Greek world had earlier spread to the west Mediterranean and the Black Sea through maritime trade and colonisation (*page 160*). It now reached overland in the wake of Alexander's eastern conquests as far as Afghanistan and the borders of India. The wealth and power provided by these territorial gains found expression in a spate of new buildings and monuments, both in existing cities of Asia Minor and the Near East such as Miletus, and in new foundations such as Antioch and Alexandria.

The founding of new cities was a significant feature of the Hellenistic age. Many of these were settlements of colonists established to strengthen military and political control over recently conquered territories. Economic developments in the eastern Mediterranean led several communities to abandon or reduce their earlier settlement and to build a new city in a location more accessible to trade routes. The new cities built during the Hellenistic period almost all adopted a grid-plan arrangement of streets and buildings, using the potential of a new site to conform as closely as possible to the notion of a model city. The grid-pattern layout even spread beyond the margins of the east Hellenistic states, for example to Bulgaria, where the Thracian planned city of Seuthopolis was founded in about 300 BC.

Centuries of later occupation have hidden or destroyed the remains of many of the principal Hellenistic cities, but sufficient sculpture, statuary and monuments have survived to demonstrate the artistic achievements of this period. Hellenistic art and architecture was a development of the artistic tradition of Classical Greece, but differed from earlier Greek art in a variety of ways. Statuary became more realistic: the imposing bronze figure of a 2nd-century Hellenistic ruler found in the Baths of Constantine at Rome is a good example. The so-called 'Alexander Sarcophagus' is also a notable example of early Hellenistic sculpture: reliefs around the sides show scenes of hunting and war with a mixture of Greek and Persian protagonists, while the lid of the sarcophagus is decorated with stylised ornamentation typical of the Hellenistic east. This artistic tradition carried great prestige and was frequently adopted in a relatively pure form by remote colonies such as Ai Khanum in Afghanistan. Neighbouring non-Greek peoples often used Hellenistic motifs, giving rise to hybrid styles, such as that of the massive funerary statues erected at Nemrut Dağ in eastern Asia Minor which betray clear traces of their Hellenistic cultural ancestry. The Hellenistic states in turn borrowed useful oriental features; the war elephant, illustrated on a Graeco-Bactrian silver disc and shown equipped with a fighting tower and soldiers, was a military innovation adopted from India.

The Hellenistic monarchs also encouraged learning – the famous library of Pergamum was reputed to contain 200,000 works. The cultural level maintained even by the more remote outposts of the Graeco-Bactrian kingdom is demonstrated by a recent discovery at Ai Khanum. A papyrus with three columns of Greek text – probably a philosophical text of Aristotelian affinities – was found in a room that may have been the palace library.

Archaeological studies of Hellenistic remains have concentrated largely on major sites, important buildings and works of art, and comparatively little research has been directed towards the living and working conditions of the ordinary people. Despite the growth of trade and industry, the economic base remained essentially agricultural. In western Asia Minor the bulk of the population, even those who worked on the land, probably lived in cities. A survey of irrigation works and settlement remains in the Diyala Plain of Mesopotamia however, shows a completely different pattern, with many small sites of hamlet or village size. In the alluvial plain north of Ai Khanum an extensive system of irrigation canals has been discovered, while in Egypt the 3rd-century rulers carried through an ambitious programme of lake drainage and land reclamation in the Faiyum Basin that was accompanied by the foundation of new villages and townships. The impressive advances in engineering, manufacturing and commerce that characterised this period survived the fall of the Hellenistic kingdoms to form a basis of Roman and Parthian prosperity in the early centuries AD.

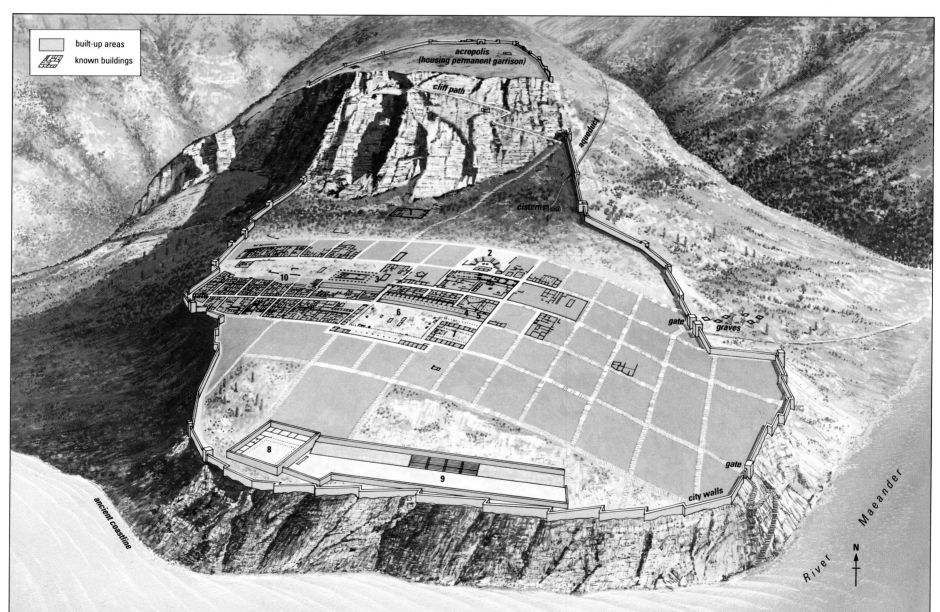

2 PRIENE: A HELLENISTIC CITY

One of the best examples of a planned Hellenistic city is Priene in western Asia Minor, where there has been little later building to obscure the remains. Today the site lies on the edge of the Maeander Valley (*page 104*), but originally – before the estuary silted up – it overlooked the sea. The city was moved to its present location from an earlier site in the mid-4th century BC, probably for access to the maritime trade which, together with agriculture, became its main source of wealth. All the characteristic buildings of a Greek city can be seen here. Municipal buildings such as the council chamber (*bouleuterion*), town hall (*prytaneion*) and market-place (*agora*) are grouped together at the centre of the street grid. At the southern end of the city was the recreation area with a *gymnasion* and *stadion*, while a steep cliff whose summit served as a citadel rose to a height of 200 metres to the north. By the end of the 1st century BC, however, the silt carried by the Maeander had shifted the coastline further to the west, and Priene went into decline.

Priene *above* 1 **Temple of Demeter and Kore** deities of earth and underworld. An irregular building at the west end of a rectangular enclosure. Outside the temple is a square, masonary-lined sacrificial pit for offerings. 2 **Theatre** with curving rows of stone seats facing a D-shaped acting area and a 2-storey stage-building with dressing and property rooms. The theatre was probably also used for public assemblies and as a law court. 3 **Temple of Athena** the principal temple of Priene. An antechamber at the east led into the *cella* or main chamber; a cult statue stood at the far end, while to the west a shallow room may have held the temple treasures. Only priests and celebrants entered the temple; the lay congregation remained in the sacred precinct, which contained an impressive altar with columns and relief carvings. 4 **Bouleuterion (council chamber)** with seats on three sides, alcove with bench for presiding officials, and altar in the centre; sacrifices were made at the beginning of every public assembly. 5 **Prytaneion (town hall)** municipal offices arranged around a small colonnaded court. 6 **Agora (market-place)** with bases for altars and statues, surrounded by porticoes. To the north, a spacious covered hall (*stoa*), 12 metres by 116 metres with one open side. 7 **Sacred precinct and temple of Zeus** small temple with antechamber and *cella*, base of altar and porticoes to north and south. 8 **Gymnasion** open court for sport and recreation, surrounded by porticoes, backed by ranges of small rooms. Lecture room on north side, with benches around the walls and students' graffiti. To north-west, a washroom with foot basins on either side of the entrance, and a row of basins at the back. 9 **Stadion** open racetrack, with remains of starting sill. Embankment to north, with stone seating for spectators in middle, and a long portico above. 10 **The average town house** of a prosperous citizen focused around a courtyard reached from the street door through a vestibule. The main rooms had high ceilings (c.5 metres), and there may have been an upper storey in part of the building.

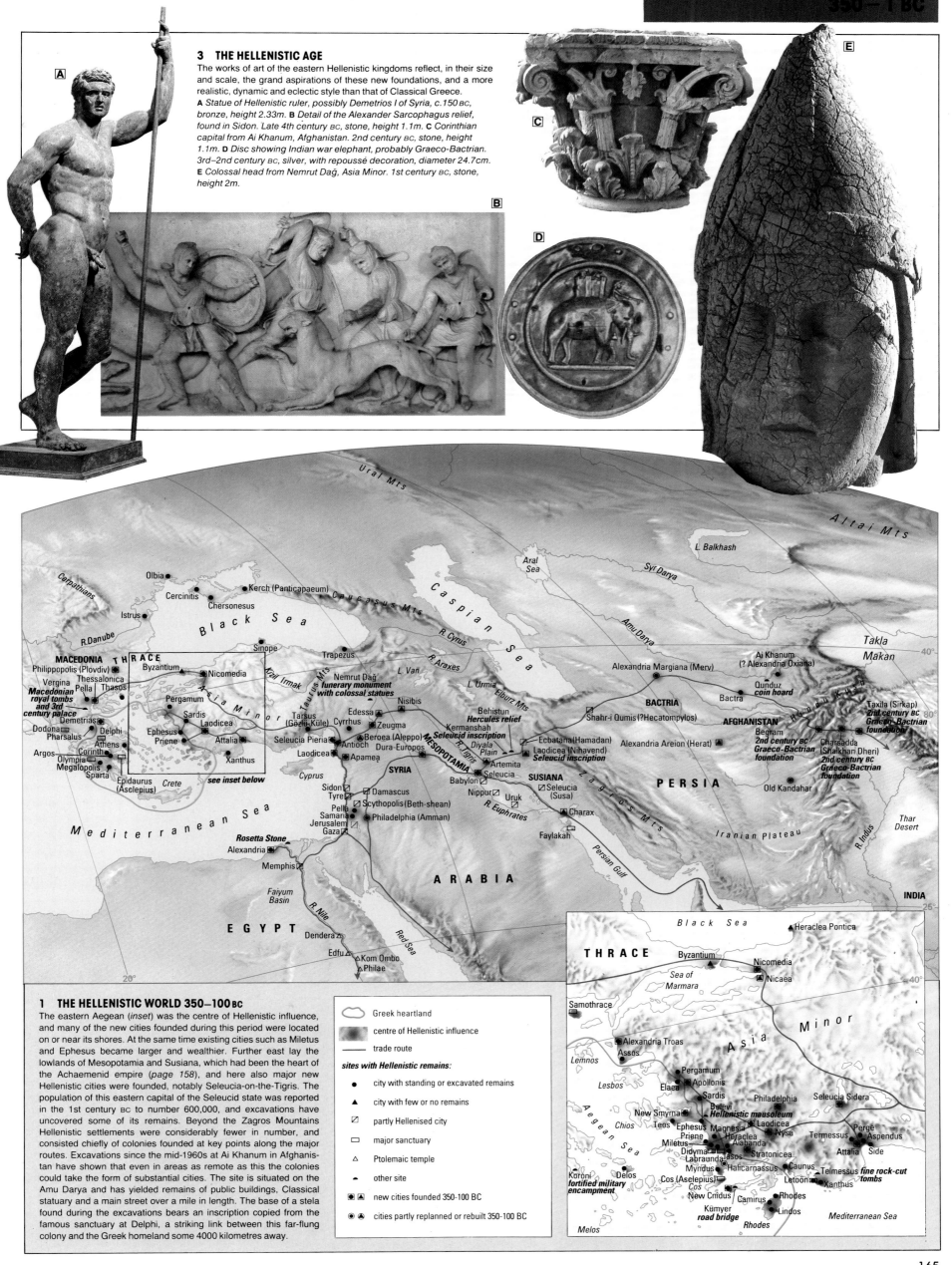

3 THE HELLENISTIC AGE

The works of art of the eastern Hellenistic kingdoms reflect, in their size and scale, the grand aspirations of these new foundations, and a more realistic, dynamic and eclectic style than that of Classical Greece.
A Statue of Hellenistic ruler, possibly Demetrios I of Syria, c.150 BC, bronze, height 2.33m. **B** Detail of the Alexander Sarcophagus relief, found in Sidon. Late 4th century BC, stone, height 1.1m. **C** Corinthian capital from Ai Khanum, Afghanistan. 2nd century BC, stone, height 1.1m. **D** Disc showing Indian war elephant, probably Graeco-Bactrian. 3rd–2nd century BC, silver, with repoussé decoration, diameter 24.7cm. **E** Colossal head from Nemrut Dağ, Asia Minor. 1st century BC, stone, height 2m.

1 THE HELLENISTIC WORLD 350–100 BC

The eastern Aegean (inset) was the centre of Hellenistic influence, and many of the new cities founded during this period were located on or near its shores. At the same time existing cities such as Miletus and Ephesus became larger and wealthier. Further east lay the lowlands of Mesopotamia and Susiana, which had been the heart of the Achaemenid empire (page 158), and here also major new Hellenistic cities were founded, notably Seleucia-on-the-Tigris. The population of this eastern capital of the Seleucid state was reported in the 1st century BC to number 600,000, and excavations have uncovered some of its remains. Beyond the Zagros Mountains Hellenistic settlements were considerably fewer in number, and consisted chiefly of colonies founded at key points along the major routes. Excavations since the mid-1960s at Ai Khanum in Afghanistan have shown that even in areas as remote as this the colonies could take the form of substantial cities. The site is situated on the Amu Darya and has yielded remains of public buildings, Classical statuary and a main street over a mile in length. The base of a stela found during the excavations bears an inscription copied from the famous sanctuary at Delphi, a striking link between this far-flung colony and the Greek homeland some 4000 kilometres away.

Legend

Greek heartland

centre of Hellenistic influence

trade route

sites with Hellenistic remains:

● city with standing or excavated remains

▲ city with few or no remains

☑ partly Hellenised city

□ major sanctuary

△ Ptolemaic temple

⬩ other site

◉ ▣ ▲ new cities founded 350-100 BC

◉ ▲ cities partly replanned or rebuilt 350-100 BC

Celtic Europe

Classical authors refer to Celtic communities occupying most of temperate Europe during the 1st millennium BC. Although the Celts as an ethnic group had probably occupied central Europe already for several hundreds if not thousands of years, remains normally associated with the emergence of Celtic culture appear only around 800 BC in southern Germany and the eastern Alps. Today these peoples are known to us mainly from the remains of their fortresses, burials and distinctive art style.

One of the key developments in temperate Europe during the early part of the 1st millennium BC was the introduction of iron metallurgy. Among the earliest iron objects found north of the Alps are swords, such as those from the cemetery at Hallstatt in Austria. Iron-working was already established in Central Europe by 1000 BC and spread gradually westwards, reaching Britain by the end of the 8th century BC. Warrior graves with horse-riding harness and iron swords were widespread in Europe in the 8th and 7th centuries BC. Iron goods were at first rare and highly prized, but the abundant sources of iron meant that it gradually replaced bronze for weapons and eventually for tools such as nails and hoes. This also led to changes in warfare, agriculture and craftsmanship.

The first part of the Celtic Iron Age (8th–5th centuries BC) takes its name from the important Hallstatt cemetery in Austria. During this period rich burials indicate the emergence of a new aristocracy and greater social distinctions. These distinctions became more pronounced in the

6th century BC, when Europe north and west of the Alps came into direct trading contact with recently founded Greek colonies in the west Mediterranean. The Rhône–Saône corridor became a major artery for this trade, and at Mont Lassois in eastern France an important Celtic centre and fortress developed on the profits derived from it. Princely hilltop fortresses also appeared in south-west Germany, notably the Heuneburg on the Danube and the Hohenasperg. These sites have many Mediterranean imports, including pottery and bronze vessels for serving and drinking wine – a habit the Celtic aristocracy seems to have adopted from the Greeks. At the Heuneburg there is evidence of a different type of Greek influence: a mud-brick fortification wall on limestone foundations, with rectangular towers at regular intervals, which closes one side of the site. The profit and power accruing from trading contacts are reflected in the rich burials which surround such princely residences including, at Vix, vehicles, fine Greek pottery, Etruscan bronzes, and even, at the Hohmichele barrow below the Heuneburg, textile made with silk perhaps from China.

The Hallstatt princely fortresses were abandoned in the 5th century BC, and the centre of wealth and power shifted northwards to the Hunsrück-Eifel area of West Germany. This change is associated with the development of the Celtic 'La Tène' art style which marks the second phase of the European Iron Age, lasting from the 5th century to the Roman conquest. The burials of the period often contain weapons and chariots, and while Mediterranean imports continue to be found there seems to be a considerable decrease in wealth, particularly after 400 BC.

This 'dark age' lasted until around 250 BC, and coincides with the period of the Celtic invasions referred to by Classical historians. Celts sacked Rome in c.390 BC, and Delphi in c.272 BC. Bands of Celtic warriors also conquered territories in Asia Minor, the Balkans and northern Italy.

The last three centuries BC saw considerable changes in Celtic Europe, with the appearance of coinage, the development of states and the foundation of large settlements known as *oppida*. The earliest Celtic coins, of the 3rd century BC, were based on Greek types. They were issued by the emergent Celtic states from Romania to Gaul and may have been used for official payments to individuals. The fortified *oppida*, which developed around the middle of the 2nd century BC, were defended by timber-framed ramparts and some, such as Manching, were of considerable size. Excavations have revealed a variety of timber buildings – houses, workshops, warehouses, barns, and elite residences in palisaded enclosures – as well as traces of bronze- and iron-working, weaving, pottery and coin production. In some respects the *oppida* were not unlike the later towns of mediaeval Europe.

Mediterranean imports became increasingly common at *oppida* and other sites during this period but it was now Roman Italy rather than Greece that was the source of the products, mainly wine amphorae and tableware. Thus Roman economic infiltration preceded the eventual imperial takeover; by the middle of the 1st century AD only Ireland and northern Scotland were left outside the boundaries of the Roman empire to carry Celtic culture undiluted into the early Middle Ages.

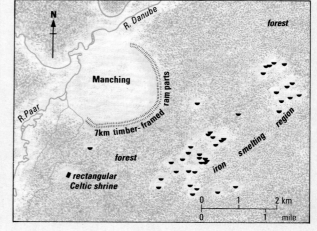

1 CELTIC SETTLEMENT

The Celtic peoples who dominated temperate Europe in the 1st millennium BC may well have been the long-established inhabitants of France, Germany and the Alpine region, but during the later centuries BC Celtic invasions reached into Iberia, Italy, Greece and Anatolia (inset map). Settlements, hillforts, *oppida*, and the rich artefacts, including 4-wheeled wagons and 2-wheeled chariots, found in burials, all reflect the distinctive character of Celtic culture. Little is known of Celtic religion, though wooden figurines have been found at sacred springs, such as the Sources de la Seine, and there are Celtic shafts and wells with ritual deposits, sometimes associated with shrines.

The *oppidum* of **Manching in Bavaria** (right) grew from a small settlement in the 2nd century BC, to become the largest centre in the region, covering 200 hectares. The earth and timber ramparts are 7 kilometres long and were held together by vast quantities of iron nails. There were four gateways, paved in stone, one with a double entrance for carts and wagons and smaller side passages for pedestrians. The streets within the *oppidum* were up to 10 metres wide. Remains of buildings include a row of small workshops, storerooms or warehouses, and elite dwellings within palisaded enclosures. Evidence of iron-working, leather-working and coin minting was also found. Many iron smelting sites have been found outside the *oppidum*.

3 CELTIC ART

The finest products of Celtic art, found in rich graves, are largely restricted to portable objects such as weapons, jewellery and vessels. **A** *Engraved mirror from female grave at Birdlip, Gloucestershire, England. Early 1st century BC, bronze, diameter 27cm.* **B** *La Tène scabbard plate from Lisnacrogher, Co. Antrim, Ireland. 2nd–1st century BC, bronze, length c.0.75m.* **C** *Torc from rich female grave at Waldalgesheim, West Germany. Late 4th century BC, gold, diameter 19.9cm.* **D** *Wooden ex voto ritual figurine from the Sources de la Seine, eastern France. 1st century BC–1st century AD, oak, height 46.5cm.* **E** *One of a pair of flagons from Basse-Yutz, eastern France. Late 5th century BC, bronze with enamel and Mediterranean coral inlay, height c.40cm.* **F** *Textile fragment from Hohmichele barrow, West Germany. Wool with silk thread, the latter possibly imported from China. Early 6th century BC, fragment length 11cm.*

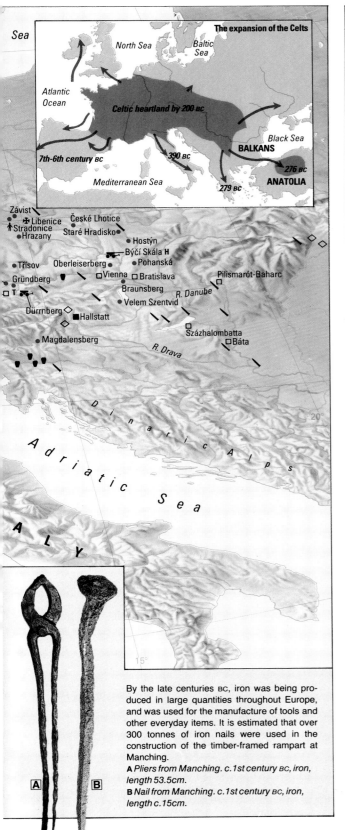

The expansion of the Celts

Celtic heartland by 200 BC

7th-6th century BC

390 BC

BALKANS

279 BC

276 BC

ANATOLIA

Závist
Libenice
Stradonice
Hrazany
České Lhotice
Staré Hradisko
Hostýn
Býčí Skála **H**
Třísov
Oberleiserberg
Pohanská
Gründberg
Vienna
Bratislava
Pilismarót-Baharc
Braunsberg
R. Danube
Dürrnberg
Velem Szentvid
Hallstatt
Magdalensberg
Százhalombatta
Báta
R. Drava

Dinaric Alps

Adriatic Sea

ITALY

By the late centuries BC, iron was being produced in large quantities throughout Europe, and was used for the manufacture of tools and other everyday items. It is estimated that over 300 tonnes of iron nails were used in the construction of the timber-framed rampart at Manching.
A *Pliers from Manching. c.1st century BC, iron, length 53.5cm.*
B *Nail from Manching. c.1st century BC, iron, length c.15cm.*

2 DANEBURY: A CELTIC HILLFORT

In southern Britain several hillforts were constructed on the South Downs in the 6th century BC (*map below*). Gradually power became centralised and fewer hillforts continued in occupation, though those that did, such as Danebury (*above*), were more heavily fortified. Within its ramparts was an area for livestock grazing, houses with thatched conical roofs and raised timber granaries. Around 100BC the occupation of Danebury came to a sudden end, probably as a result of hostilities; bodies were thrown into charnel pits and the east gate burned down.

1 Timber-framed rampart, c.550BC, fronted by a flat-bottomed ditch (**2**). **3 Middle and outer earthworks** (2nd century BC), enclosing 5.3 hectares. **4 East entrance**, probably with a timber platform or tower above. Slingstones were found along the entrance passage and over 1000 were stored in a pit nearby.

shrines
road
south-west entrance

- ● house
- ■ granary
- ⋯ rampart

Hillforts on the South Downs

- ● 6th century BC
- ◉ 1st century BC

Yarnbury
Salisbury Plain
Danebury
Woolbury
R. Itchen
St Catherine's Hill
R. Arun
R. Ouse
Whitsbury
Old Winchester Hill
Harting Beacon
South   Downs
R. Test
R. Avon
Devil's Dyke
R. Stour
The Trundle
Cissbury
Mount Caburn
Hengistbury Head
The Solent
Seaford Head
English Channel

The rise of Rome

The traditional cultural and political centres of the eastern Mediterranean were, by the end of the 1st millennium BC, overshadowed and subsumed by the might of Rome, which had built up a power base in and around the western and central Mediterranean. This remarkable achievement was closely linked with the gradual penetration of the west Mediterranean by Phoenician and Greek colonists from early in the millennium (*page 160*) and their influence upon the indigenous populations. The rich resources of the region – copper ore deposits in Sardinia, and silver, iron and lead in Italy and Iberia – and their exploitation and trade provided both the key and conduit to power.

The Etruscans, the indigenous peoples of Tuscany, founded cities in central Italy in about 800 BC. This development probably owed much to the richness of the agricultural land and extensive copper and tin deposits in the mountains of central Italy. The scope and extent of Etruscan influence is reflected in finds of traded goods, such as pottery vessels and bronze flagons, as far afield as the Levant, North Africa and the Danube and Rhine basins. Within Italy an extensive road system must have facilitated this trade. At the same time, Spina, Adria, Pyrgi and other ports were founded and developed, often strategically placed close to major Etruscan cities, such as Tarquinii and Caere (Cerveteri). Fortified hilltop cities were characteristic, but most of our knowledge of the Etruscans comes from the extensive cemeteries of rock-cut tombs, which were architecturally sophisticated and filled with rich grave offerings of gold, bronze and iron. The Etruscans were famous for their metalworking, beautiful wall paintings and pottery. While Greek influence is apparent in the grid-plan model of the new cities which the Etruscans founded, and also in the use of the Greek alphabet in the Etruscans' own script, the individual artistic style, particularly noticeable in bronze and terracotta statuary, is original. By the 6th century BC the influence of Etruscan art and culture had extended over most of central Italy.

It was during the period of Etruscan dominance, in the 7th century BC, that Rome developed from a small village – whose principal remains are the cemeteries of 'hut urns' in which the ashes of the dead were buried – to a city of some importance, although probably still under Etruscan control. As the power of the Etruscans declined, that of Rome increased: Etruscan influence was undermined by Celtic incursions from the north in the 5th century BC while, despite a temporary setback from the Celts c.390 BC, the power of Rome grew through a mixture of force and diplomacy, until by 250 BC it controlled the whole of peninsular Italy. This process was marked by the great achievements of Roman engineering: the building of the defensive 'Servian' Wall around Rome and the construction of elaborate road and aqueduct systems, while in the 3rd century BC the development of concrete revolutionised Roman engineering capabilities.

The dominant maritime power in the Mediterranean during this period was Carthage, which had close links with the other Phoenician trading posts and colonies of northern Africa, southern Italy and Spain. Carthage gradually consolidated its power throughout the region, uniting the Phoenician colonies into a confederation, controlling the north African coast, all the west Mediterranean islands and Iberia south of the Ebro. By the 4th century BC Carthage was the wealthiest city in the region, issuing enormous quantities of currency; the city itself underwent a major expansion in the 4th century, with new areas of grid-plan streets and houses, and a triple line of massive new landward fortifications with stables for war elephants and horses. Two harbours were also built, one for commercial shipping and one for the navy, an indication of the essentially maritime nature of Carthaginian power.

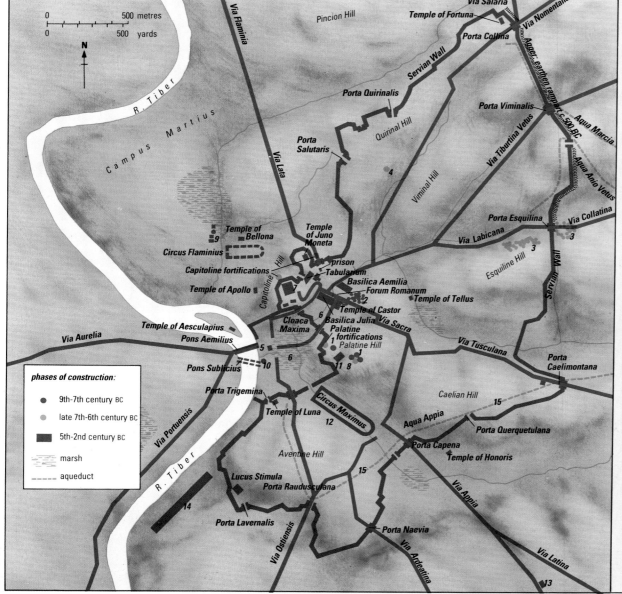

2 THE DEVELOPMENT OF REPUBLICAN ROME

The city of Rome began life around the 9th century BC as a cluster of small huts on the Palatine hill with a cremation cemetery in the marshy valley below. During the late 7th century Rome began to acquire distinct urban characteristics, when the marshland was cleared and laid out as a public square (*forum*). Stone fortifications were built on the Palatine and Capitoline hills, the Cloaca Maxima (a natural stream) was canalised to drain the valley floors, and earth and timber defences (the *agger*) were thrown up to protect the eastern side of the city. The defences of Rome were considerably strengthened in the early 4th century BC by the construction of the Servian Wall, a massive masonry barrier 3.6 metres thick, encircling the whole settlement and pierced by gates; later in the century the Aqua Appia, the city's first aqueduct, was built to supply the growing urban population. During the last few centuries BC the expansion of Roman power throughout the Mediterranean was reflected in the buildings of the capital, with the appearance of oriental cults (for example, that of the Mother goddess, centred on the temple of Magna Mater) and the introduction of Hellenistic architectural styles, including Corinthian columns and exotic marble decoration, which became a conspicuous feature of the high imperial period.

Early Rome *left* **1 Early hut remains** pits and postholes of two separate settlements, from which early Rome grew. **2 Forum cemetery** rock-cut graves with cremations and inhumations. In c.600 BC this area was laid out as the main public square of the city. **3 Esquiline cemetery** principal cemetery of early Rome from c.700 BC with rich and varied grave offerings including bronze and iron spearheads, bronze pins and razors, and silver earrings and bracelets. **4 Villino Hüffer** votive deposit containing a ritual vessel with a Latin inscription, one of the earliest known examples of the language. **5 Forum Boarium** sacred area occupied by an open-air sanctuary with votive deposit, followed in 5th century BC by a podium supporting two archaic temples. **6 Cloaca Maxima** natural stream canalised c.570 BC to serve as a major drain to the low-lying valleys and Forum area. **7 Temple of Jupiter Optimus Maximus** main temple of ancient Rome, built to an Etruscan plan with three adjoining chambers or *cellae* on a raised podium. **8 Palatine water system** two underground cisterns connected by galleries. **9 Largo Argentina** sacred area with four temples, each on a podium approached by a staircase. **10 Temple of Hercules Victor** oldest surviving marble temple in Rome. **11 Temple of Magna Mater** (the Great Mother) a cult of oriental origin, brought to Rome during the Carthaginian invasion under Hannibal, reflecting widening cultural horizons. **12 Circus Maximus** stadium or race track. **13 Tomb of the Scipio family** rock-cut galleries and burial chambers; part of the traditional burial ground along the Via Appia. **14 Porticus Aemilia** market hall trading in goods brought up the Tiber. The roof was supported on 50 stepped barrel vaults using concrete for the first time and fronted by arcades. **15 Aqua Appia** Rome's first aqueduct (312 BC), less than a mile long and largely underground.

The expansion of Rome inevitably led to conflict with Carthage; their struggle for control of the west Mediterranean, the Punic Wars, continued for over a century. Supremacy at sea was crucial in these conflicts, and at Marsala in Sicily remains of two Carthaginian ships have been found which were evidently sunk by ramming in battle. Gradually Rome took over Carthaginian island holdings and invaded Iberia and North Africa, finally capturing Carthage itself in 146 BC. Thereafter Rome expanded rapidly; the construction of increasingly grandiose buildings in the city itself reflected its military might and ushered in the imperial era. The Mediterranean became a Roman lake, and – until its disintegration in the 5th century AD – the heart of the Roman empire.

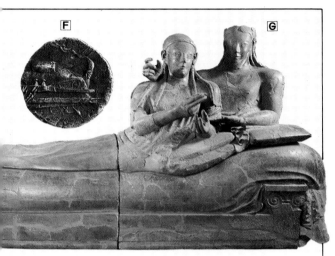

3 THE PRE-CLASSICAL WEST

A *Statuette of Etruscan warrior. Late 5th century BC, bronze, height 28cm.* B *Roman denarius probably depicting the 6th century temple of Jupiter, Rome. c.37 BC, silver, diameter 1.9cm.* C *Funerary urn in the form of a hut, from the Forum cemetery, Rome. 9th-8th century BC, pottery.* D *Funeral mask from Punic necropolis at Carthage. 7th-6th century BC, terracotta.* E *The 'Lady of Elche', bust from La Alcudia de Elche, Spain. The rich jewellery reflects Carthaginian influence. 4th or 3rd century BC, painted limestone, height 56cm.* F *Carthaginian half shekel showing prow of warship with ram. c.200 BC, silver, diameter 2.1cm.* G *Etruscan sarcophagus from the Banditaccia cemetery at Caere, Italy. Late 6th century BC, terracotta, length 2m.*

1 ROME AND CARTHAGE

The 1st millennium BC saw the emergence of the first cities and states in the west Mediterranean, with the rise of the Etruscan city-states and of Rome, both essentially indigenous developments. These urban civilisations soon began to extend their control over their less powerful neighbours, such as the Iberians, the Berbers of North Africa and the Sardinians with their dry-stone fortresses (*nuraghi*), and to vie with each other for supremacy. The expansion of the Carthaginians, absorbing Phoenician colonies in the west, is reflected in the distribution of their settlements, coinage, burials and terracotta funerary masks. Roman power in Italy was extended by the establishment of a network of colonies linked by roads. The struggle between Rome and Carthage ended in victory for Rome, and the gradual spread of Roman hegemony during the last two centuries BC is shown by the widening distribution of Roman coin hoards.

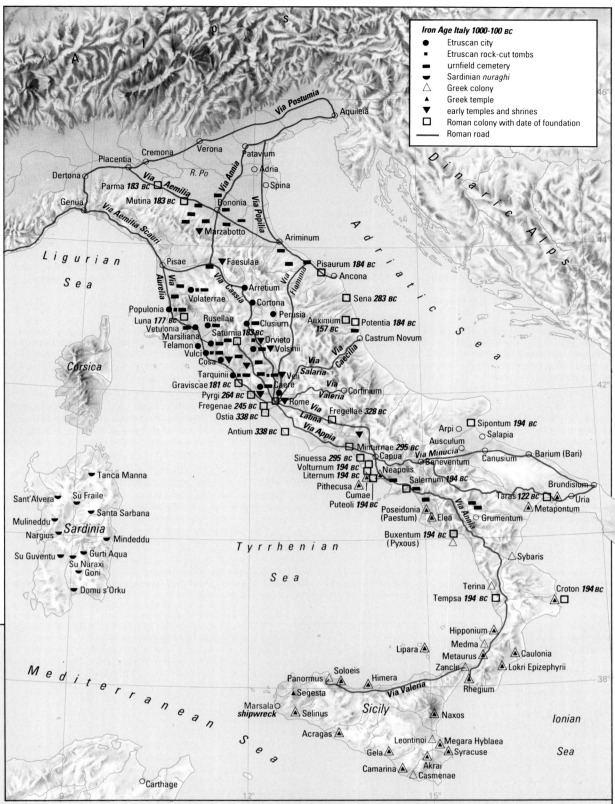

Iron Age Italy 1000-100 BC

- ● Etruscan city
- ■ Etruscan rock-cut tombs
- ◖ urnfield cemetery
- ◡ Sardinian *nuraghi*
- △ Greek colony
- ▲ Greek temple
- ▼ early temples and shrines
- ▢ Roman colony with date of foundation
- — Roman road

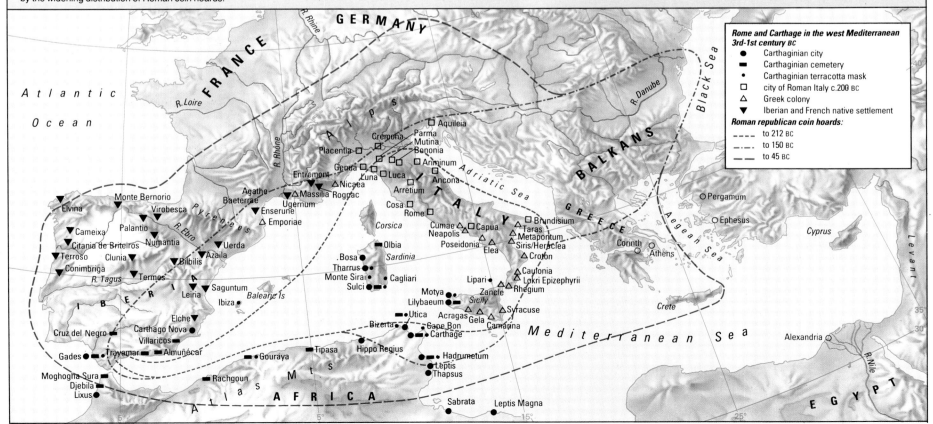

Rome and Carthage in the west Mediterranean 3rd-1st century BC

- ● Carthaginian city
- ■ Carthaginian cemetery
- • Carthaginian terracotta mask
- ▢ city of Roman Italy c.200 BC
- △ Greek colony
- ▼ Iberian and French native settlement

Roman republican coin hoards:
- – – – to 212 BC
- –·–·– to 150 BC
- – – to 45 BC

The Roman empire

At its largest, in the 2nd century AD, the Roman empire extended for some 4000 kilometres east–west and 3700 kilometres north–south, and its population was about 50–60 million. A major agent in both the formation and maintenance of the empire was the systematically organised and efficient Roman army. In the first two centuries AD it amounted to about 300,000 soldiers, concentrated at the fringes of the empire, although there were vast tracts of the Roman world where soldiers were never seen.

The bulk of the empire's population lived in locally self-governing communities, which were ranked in status from those whose inhabitants enjoyed the full rights of Roman citizenship, down to those who bore the heaviest burden of taxation and had fewest privileges. A system of inducements encouraged communities and their leading citizens to seek higher status, thereby increasing their devotion to Rome. Even the very highest offices in the Roman world, such as membership of the Senate in Rome, the consulship or the role of emperor were accessible to provincials, and as time went on were occupied by them – the emperor Trajan (AD 98–117) was a Spaniard, Septimius Severus (AD 192–211) a North African and Diocletian (AD 284–303) was from Dalmatia (modern Yugoslavia).

Agriculture was the main source of wealth in the Roman empire. Commerce was also important, and staple crops were traded around the Mediterranean where the largest cities depended on food brought by sea. Between the 1st and 4th centuries AD Rome depended for its survival almost entirely on grain and olive oil imported from overseas, mainly from the North African provinces. A basic supply of these items was distributed free of charge to the city's population. This supply represented a major shift of resources throughout the Mediterranean and it had a distorting effect on the economy of the whole area: different regions prospered according to their importance as producers – first Italy, then Spain, then North Africa. At the fringes of the empire, the Roman army had a strong impact on the economy. Frontiers were often in areas of marginal agricultural value; both at the Sahara fringe and in the area of Hadrian's Wall in Britain, elaborate efforts were made to develop agriculture, and the population increased well beyond the region's normal capacity.

Trade within and beyond the Roman empire can be traced primarily through finds of pottery. Table wares made in central Italy between the late 1st century BC and early 1st century AD were supplied to the Roman army in Gaul and Germany, and were traded beyond the limits of the empire to Britain and northern Europe; in another direction some of these wares travelled as far afield as southern India. In the 5th century AD wares made in Africa Proconsularis (modern Tunisia) are found in sites, however remote and rural, throughout the Mediterranean. These and many other examples highlight the fact that even low-value goods travelled far in the Roman empire, but how far trade was an important means of creating wealth, as in the modern world, is less certain. Most goods were undoubtedly moved by water where possible, since this was far easier than by land, despite the superb network of roads. Roman roads were primarily built for administrative purposes, for the movement of soldiers and for those engaged in official business, and, like many other monuments in the Roman world, as a visible symbol of Roman power.

Culturally the Roman empire always had an eastern part, in which Greek was the dominant language, and a western, Latin part: the dividing line was approximately along the west coast of Dalmatia and half way between Leptis Magna and Cyrene in North Africa, with all of the more northerly provinces lying in the western part. Politically these two parts began to separate and to fragment internally in the 3rd century AD. For most of the 4th century they were formally divided under eastern and western emperors. During the course of the 5th century Rome's control in the west collapsed, while the eastern empire continued with its capital at Constantinople. In the west the break was strongest in northern Europe, which had weak economic and cultural ties with Rome, while the provinces towards the south remained within the economic system of the Mediterranean and life continued in a recognisably Roman tradition for another two centuries or more. In the 6th century most of this area was reabsorbed into the Byzantine empire based on Constantinople (*page 238*). The east evolved gradually into the Christian, Greek world of mediaeval Byzantium. Constantinople's political independence was to last another thousand years until the capture of the city by the Ottoman Turks in 1453.

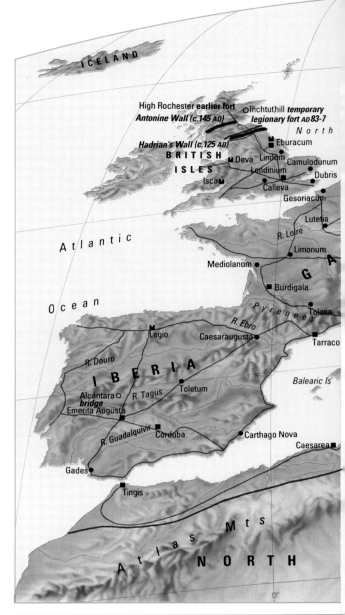

3 CIVIL AND MILITARY POWER
A Mosaic of a charioteer from Tunis. Roman pastimes, such as chariot racing, were transplanted to all parts of the empire. 3rd–5th century AD, width c.1m. **B** Inscription of the 20th Legion flanked by the figures of Mars and Hercules, from the outpost fort at High Rochester, England. c. early 3rd century AD, sandstone, height 76cm. **C** Relief of four-wheeled horse-drawn carriage with passengers from Vaison, southern France. c.1st century BC–1st century AD, height 1m. **D** Wall painting of a merchant ship being loaded with grain from the Piazzale delle Corporazione, Ostia. 2nd–3rd century AD.

2 INCHTUTHILL: A LEGIONARY FORTRESS
By the end of the first century AD the Roman army consisted of 300,000 soldiers and had reached the height of its organisation. That moment is to some extent 'frozen' in the remains of the legionary fortress at Inchtuthill, Perthshire. It was built between c.AD 83 and 87 as a permanent 'winter quarters' fortress, where the legion was based when not on active duties. The internal organisation of the legion as a unit is closely reflected in the layout of buildings. The 6000 or so men who made up the legion were divided into ten cohorts or regiments, each composed of six 'centuries' of 80 men and their centurions or officers. These in turn were divided into ten groups of eight men, who shared the same barracks room (*contubernia*). The numbers of the legion were made up with about 120 cavalry, headquarters and other specialist staff. Other buildings included granaries, a workshop and a hospital. The small cells with a colonnaded front lining the main streets were probably stores buildings. Most of the buildings were timber and clay, the walls supported by vertical posts set in trenches. The fortress was enclosed by an earthen rampart faced by a stone wall.

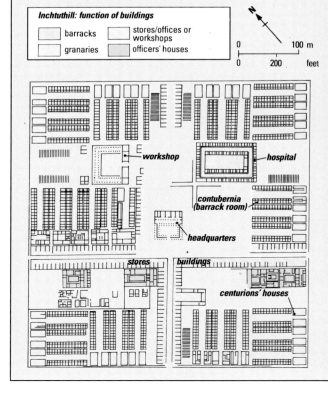

Inchtuthill: function of buildings
- barracks
- granaries
- stores/offices or workshops
- officers' houses

0   100 m
0   200   feet

workshop · hospital · contubernia (barrack room) · headquarters · stores buildings · centurions' houses

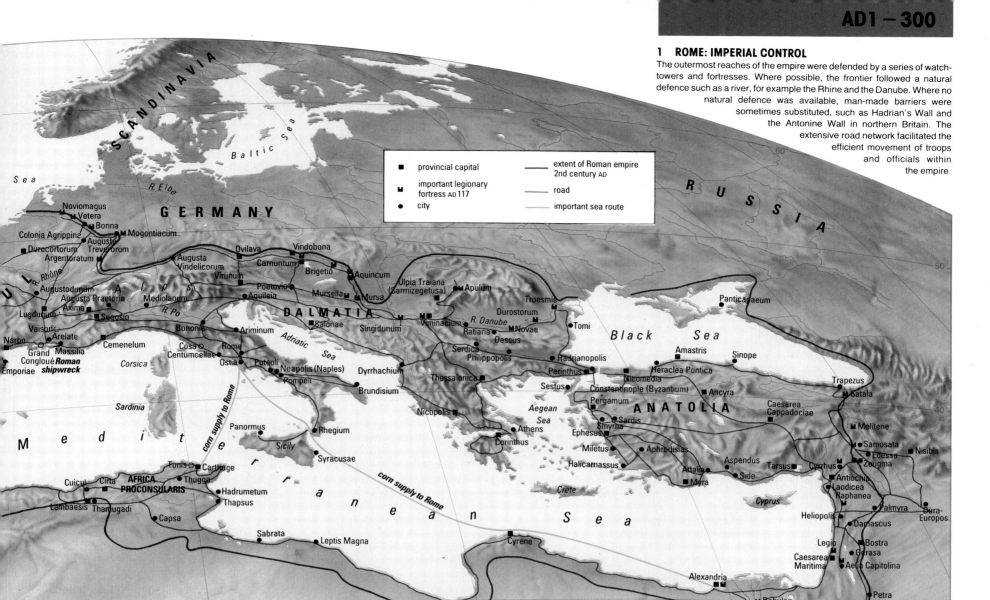

1 ROME: IMPERIAL CONTROL

The outermost reaches of the empire were defended by a series of watch-towers and fortresses. Where possible, the frontier followed a natural defence such as a river, for example the Rhine and the Danube. Where no natural defence was available, man-made barriers were sometimes substituted, such as Hadrian's Wall and the Antonine Wall in northern Britain. The extensive road network facilitated the efficient movement of troops and officials within the empire.

■ provincial capital	extent of Roman empire 2nd century AD
⊡ important legionary fortress AD 117	road
● city	important sea route

River Tay

temporary camp for troops constructing fortress

gate-tower

officers' temporary compound

gate-tower

cohort
cohort
cohort
cohort
officers' houses
gate-tower
stone wall
cohort

principia (*headquarters*)

fabrica (*workshop*)
court
cohort

court

stores compound

valetudinarium (*hospital*)

cohort

cohort
cohort

gate-tower

N

Rome: an imperial city

Between the 1st and 4th centuries AD the city of Rome had a population of about a million people. Its growth mirrored the expansion of Roman power, with the most dramatic change coming in the last two and a half centuries BC. The Romans had extended their sphere of political control outside Italy, first around the shores of the Mediterranean and then towards north-western Europe. Prior to Rome's foundation, traditionally dated at 753 BC, there had been a farming population living in village communities housed in simple huts (*page 168*). It was the Etruscans who first organised these peoples into an urban community. The Etruscans drained the marsh on what would later be the site of the Roman forum, enabling it to become a focus for the settlements on the surrounding hills. They also built the first streets and masonry houses and gave the city its first public buildings, such as the temple of Capitoline Jupiter. Etruscan political power ended with the creation of the Republic in 510–509 BC.

Rome at this stage was still a small community much preoccupied with regional politics in central Italy, and having little contact with the wider Mediterranean world. By the early 3rd century BC, however, Rome dominated the whole of the Italian peninsula, including most of the Greek cities of southern Italy and Sicily, and was forced into full contact with the wider world. Greece was still the principal artistic and cultural centre of the Mediterranean, and Greek ideas on everything from literature and philosophy to urban planning and the visual arts had a major impact. Rome as a city was backward at this time: it had grown rapidly and chaotically as its population exploded. There were no local sources of marble or fine building stones, so many of the buildings were in timber or mud or of rubble using the local volcanic tufa. Indeed, among the aristocracy there was a moral ethos supporting austere simplicity, opposed to the corrupting effects of 'eastern luxury'. Some Greek envoys in the early 2nd century BC were unwise enough to be amused at the contrast between Rome and the cities to which they were accustomed.

3 IMAGES OF ROME

A Equestrian statue of Marcus Aurelius, now on the Capitoline Hill, Rome. AD 161–180, bronze with traces of original gilding, height 5.08m. **B** Roman coin showing the legendary founders of Rome, the twins Romulus and Remus, who were suckled by a she-wolf in the 8th century BC. AD 330–335, bronze. **C** Cloaca Maxima, a natural stream canalised in order to drain marshy low-lying ground for the building of the forum. c.6th century BC, stone. **D** Wall painting showing a garden scene from the Villa of Livia, Prima Porta. Late 1st century BC.

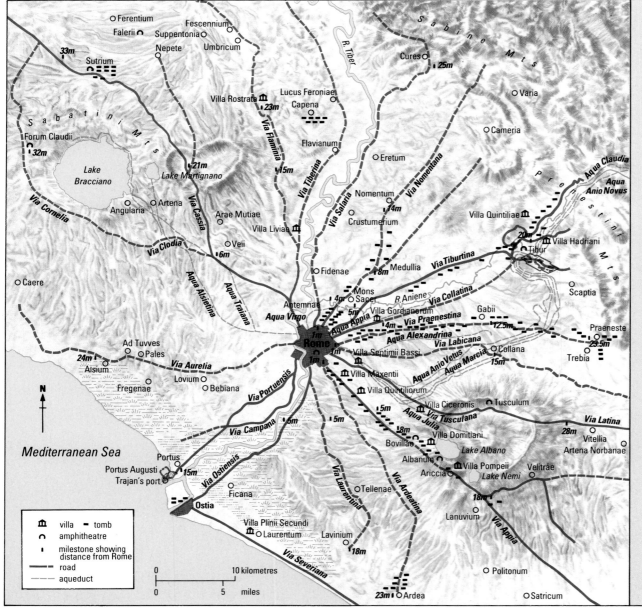

🏛	villa
⌂	amphitheatre
▮	milestone showing distance from Rome
—	road
---	aqueduct

— tomb

0   10 kilometres

0   5 miles

1 ROME AND THE TIBER VALLEY

The Tiber Valley, with Rome at its centre, was the heart of the Roman empire. The River Tiber was the main artery of trade to the city, and a substantial part of the river frontage at Rome was devoted to quaysides and landing stages, with warehouses and market halls such as the Porticus Aemilia and Horrea Galbae behind to receive the incoming wares. Near the waterfront is Mons Testaceus, a mound 50 metres high consisting of the debris of broken amphorae discarded after transfer of their contents. All the large cities of the empire depended heavily on imported food-stuffs. Some, such as Alexandria and Carthage, had a rich agricultural hinterland close by, but Rome itself had to import grain from further afield, particularly from Egypt. The original river port at Ostia could not handle the large freighters involved in this trade, and Puteoli on the Bay of Naples some 190 kilometres south of Rome provided the nearest suitable harbour. At Puteoli goods were unloaded either onto carts for transport along the Via Appia or in the case of bulky goods onto smaller boats to complete their journey up the Tiber. To improve these arrangements a large artificial harbour was built in the 1st century AD at Portus, near the mouth of the Tiber. A large basin was sheltered behind long curving moles made of *pozzolana*, a concrete invented by Roman engineers which hardens under water.

The city which this supply system served had far outgrown its Republican limits, and to meet the needs of the growing popula-tion aqueducts were built, bringing water from sources in the hills surrounding Rome to the baths and public fountains of the city as well as to private houses. The earliest of the aqueducts was the Aqua Appia, built in 312 BC, but by the 2nd century AD there were ten major aqueducts supplying over a million cubic metres of water per day. Several aqueducts were built up on arches as they entered the city.

The area around Rome was dotted with the country villas built by the richer citizens to avoid the worst of the summer heat and the diseases of the Tiber lowlands. The largest and grandest was the pleasure palace built by the emperor Hadrian at Tivoli between AD 125 and 138. This vast complex of exquisitely designed buildings set among ornamental lakes and gardens stretched for over a kilometre across the hillside. Two residential blocks – the Great Palace and Little Palace formed the core, but there were also bathing establishments, at least three theatres, a stadium, and a huge rectangular lake.

The principal cemeteries of the capital were located along the major roads just outside the city limits. The most famous were those of the Via Appia, which stretched for over 16 kilometres and included both underground burial complexes – the catacombs – and above-ground monuments ranging from simple tombstones to massive circular mausolea. Beyond these cemeteries the Roman road system continued, linking the metropolitan heartland of the Tiber Valley to the furthest corners of the empire.

In the 2nd and 1st centuries BC, however, Greek artists and works of art were imported and fine Italian building stones began to be exploited. Roman building technology overtook the Greek world through the structural use of concrete for walls, arches and vaults. This was accompanied by the development of characteristic Roman building forms – the triumphal arch, the bath building with its huge vaulted and domed spaces, the theatre, amphitheatre and circus with their seating artificially raised up on series of concrete vaults. The use of concrete also revolutionised the pace and organisation of major public building projects, since large unskilled forces could now supplement skilled masons. In periods of internal strain Roman politicians turned increasingly to monumental building as a device for expressing their aspirations. All these factors

led to a transformation of the city in the late 1st century BC. Augustus' claim that he found Rome a city of brick and left it one of marble was well founded.

Just as the growth of Rome was linked to the growth of the empire in the west, so was its decline. A period of political instability in the 3rd century is reflected in a lack of major monuments, and when order returned at the end of the century the main focus of the empire had shifted eastwards. Appropriately Rome's greatest monument of this period is a military one – the defensive wall with which the emperor Aurelian enclosed the city in the 270s after nearly six centuries in which it had been unwalled. Constantine the Great, who briefly reunited the eastern and western halves of the empire, brought Rome's era as the capital of the empire to a close by the foundation of his

'new Rome' at Constantinople in AD 330 (*page 238*). However, he also provided Rome with one of its most magnificent monuments in the arch which bears his name. This incorporates sculptures from monuments of the reigns of Trajan, Hadrian and Marcus Aurelius and thus looks back to the 'golden age' of the 2nd century, when the whole empire was politically united and Rome basked in its unrivalled glory.

Rome's future was now as a Christian centre, and already under Constantine some magnificent churches were being built. It remained a great city for another century or more, but its population declined and although it never disappeared altogether, Rome was still a modest city of a few tens of thousands when it was selected as the capital of a united Italy in 1870.

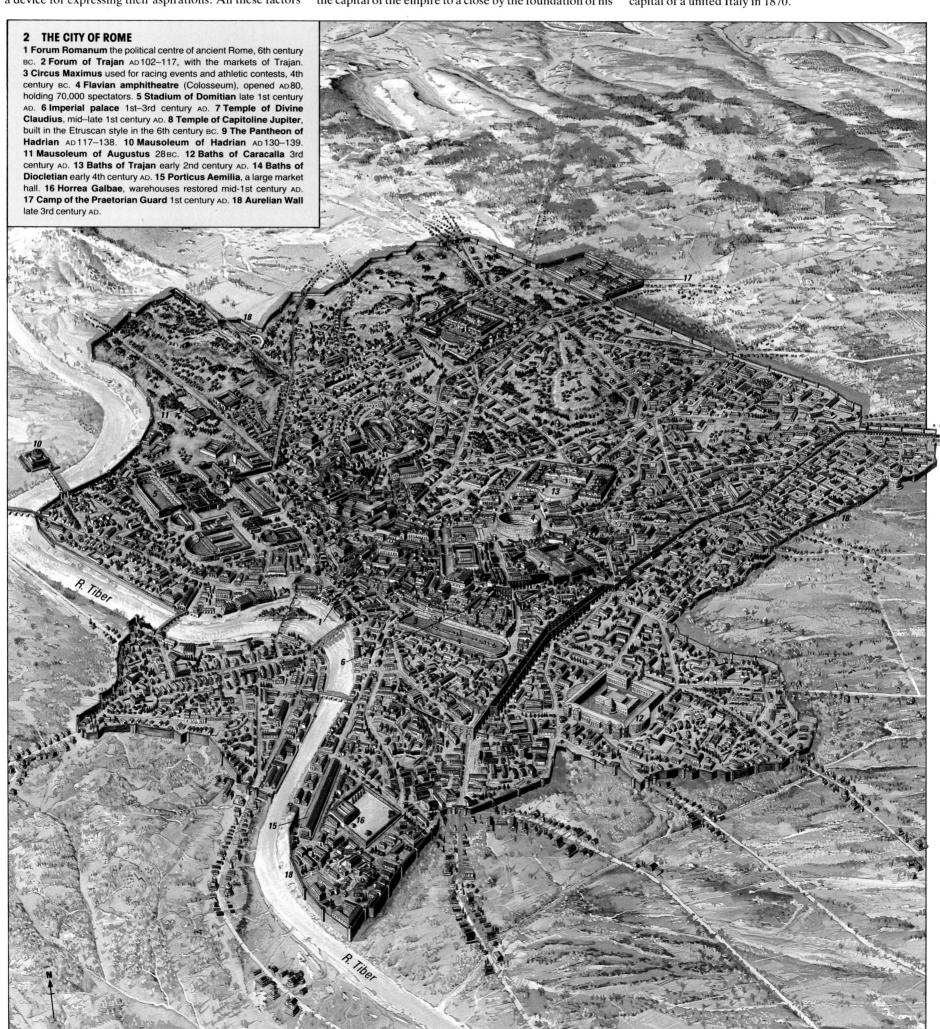

2 THE CITY OF ROME

1 Forum Romanum the political centre of ancient Rome, 6th century BC. **2 Forum of Trajan** AD 102–117, with the markets of Trajan. **3 Circus Maximus** used for racing events and athletic contests, 4th century BC. **4 Flavian amphitheatre** (Colosseum), opened AD 80, holding 70,000 spectators. **5 Stadium of Domitian** late 1st century AD. **6 Imperial palace** 1st–3rd century AD. **7 Temple of Divine Claudius**, mid–late 1st century AD. **8 Temple of Capitoline Jupiter**, built in the Etruscan style in the 6th century BC. **9 The Pantheon of Hadrian** AD 117–138. **10 Mausoleum of Hadrian** AD 130–139. **11 Mausoleum of Augustus** 28 BC. **12 Baths of Caracalla** 3rd century AD. **13 Baths of Trajan** early 2nd century AD. **14 Baths of Diocletian** early 4th century AD. **15 Porticus Aemilia**, a large market hall. **16 Horrea Galbae**, warehouses restored mid-1st century AD. **17 Camp of the Praetorian Guard** 1st century AD. **18 Aurelian Wall** late 3rd century AD.

R. Tiber

R. Tiber

N

A Roman landscape

Despite the centralised political structure of the empire, the Roman way of life was extremely adaptable and varied considerably from province to province. Some insight into the colonial Roman world is provided by the archaeology of the Trier area in West Germany.

The bulk of the surviving material dates from the first three centuries AD, when the strength of the empire brought peace and security even to frontier areas, and supply of the Rhine armies may indeed have been a major source of local income. The structure of settlement (*below*) was based primarily on small towns and villages (*vici*), linked by an extensive road network. Scattered across the countryside were villas or farmsteads. A further important element in the landscape were numerous shrines, many of them fairly small and usually consisting of one or more temples within a sacred precinct, commonly located at springs or on prominent hilltops. Excavations show that despite the adoption of Roman architectural styles, the people of the north-west provinces continued to venerate traditional Celtic nature deities. At the centre of the region lay Colonia Augusta Treverorum (modern Trier), one of the principal cities of the Roman empire, a walled area of 285 hectares with a population of over 80,000 at its height in the 4th century AD, when it became an imperial capital.

Archaeological research in the countryside has concentrated on the villas, and has shown that these varied considerably in size and comfort. Some were merely stone houses set in a yard, the equivalent of the earlier Celtic wattle-and-daub farmsteads. With increasing prosperity, however, buildings became more elaborate and luxury features were introduced. At the upper end of the range stood the great 3rd-century villa of Nennig, with mosaics, hypocausts, peristyle courts, fountains, and a substantial bath house. The entrance hall was decorated with a large rectangular mosaic, a complicated geometric pattern framing a central fountain and hexagonal panels depicting man and animal combats but also including a water organist and a horn player. Nennig is,

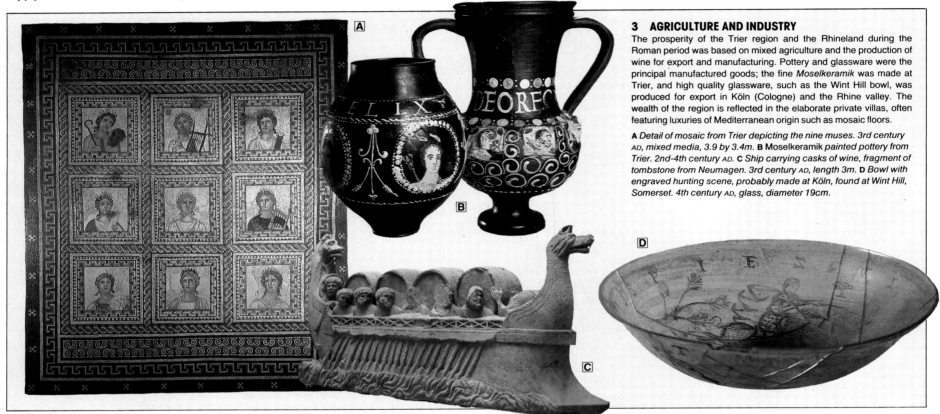

3 AGRICULTURE AND INDUSTRY

The prosperity of the Trier region and the Rhineland during the Roman period was based on mixed agriculture and the production of wine for export and manufacturing. Pottery and glassware were the principal manufactured goods; the fine *Moselkeramik* was made at Trier, and high quality glassware, such as the Wint Hill bowl, was produced for export in Köln (Cologne) and the Rhine valley. The wealth of the region is reflected in the elaborate private villas, often featuring luxuries of Mediterranean origin such as mosaic floors.

A *Detail of mosaic from Trier depicting the nine muses. 3rd century* AD, *mixed media, 3.9 by 3.4m.* B *Moselkeramik painted pottery from Trier. 2nd-4th century* AD. C *Ship carrying casks of wine, fragment of tombstone from Neumagen. 3rd century* AD, *length 3m.* D *Bowl with engraved hunting scene, probably made at Köln, found at Wint Hill, Somerset. 4th century* AD, *glass, diameter 19cm.*

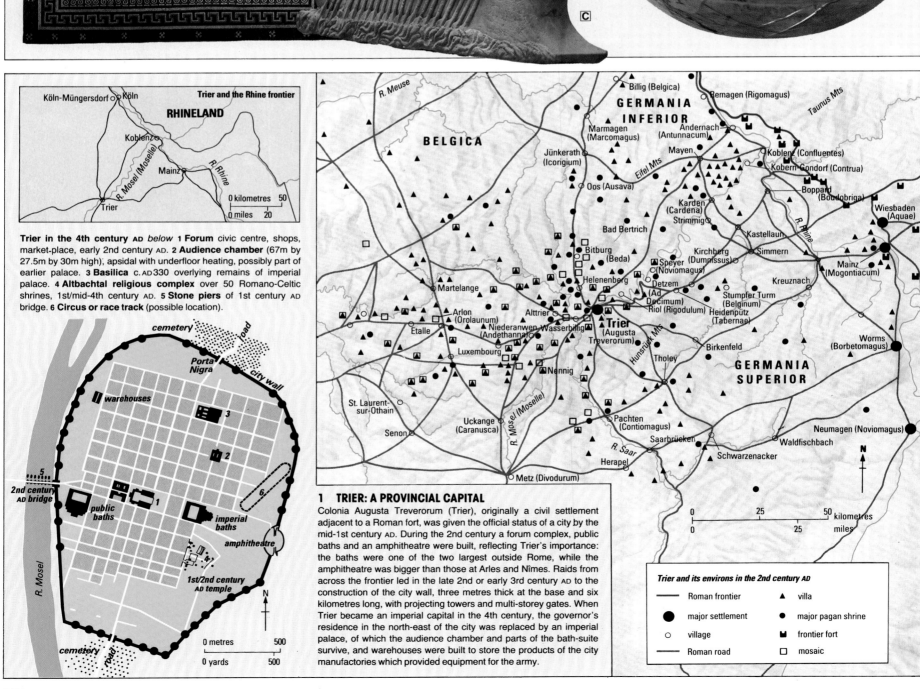

Trier in the 4th century AD *below* **1 Forum** civic centre, shops, market-place, early 2nd century AD. **2 Audience chamber** (67m by 27.5m by 30m high); apsidal with underfloor heating, possibly part of earlier palace. **3 Basilica** C. AD 330 overlying remains of imperial palace. **4 Altbachtal religious complex** over 50 Romano-Celtic shrines, 1st/mid-4th century AD. **5 Stone piers** of 1st century AD bridge. **6 Circus or race track** (possible location).

1 TRIER: A PROVINCIAL CAPITAL

Colonia Augusta Treverorum (Trier), originally a civil settlement adjacent to a Roman fort, was given the official status of a city by the mid-1st century AD. During the 2nd century a forum complex, public baths and an amphitheatre were built, reflecting Trier's importance: the baths were one of the two largest outside Rome, while the amphitheatre was bigger than those at Arles and Nîmes. Raids from across the frontier led in the late 2nd or early 3rd century to the construction of the city wall, three metres thick at the base and six kilometres long, with projecting towers and multi-storey gates. When Trier became an imperial capital in the 4th century, the governor's residence in the north-east of the city was replaced by an imperial palace, of which the audience chamber and parts of the bath-suite survive, and warehouses were built to store the products of the city manufactories which provided equipment for the army.

174

however, exceptional in its scale and elaboration, and smaller establishments like that at Köln-Müngersdorf in the Rhineland (*below*) were more usual.

Much of the land around Trier probably remained under forest during the Roman period, and was used as a source of timber, material for basketry and pasturage for swine. Funerary monuments show that woollen cloth was being produced and traded, so substantial herds of sheep must have been kept. A survey of a small area near Mayen has revealed traces of a field system associated with a modest, native-style farm. These fields were long and narrow, about 180 metres by 20-25·metres. Wheat, barley and oats were grown, some of the wheat probably for consumption by the Rhine armies, and the Mosel valley was above all important for its vineyards.

Although agriculture was the basis of the economy of the region throughout the Roman period, the Trier area and the Rhineland were also famous for manufacture of glass and pottery. The principal centre of glassmaking was Köln (Cologne), where remains have been found of several furnaces which were in production as early as AD 50. By the 4th century Köln had become the major glass producer of the Roman empire, and glass vessels began to be manufactured also at Mayen, near Trier. Late Roman glassware from these centres frequently displays an impressively high level of skilled workmanship. Trier was a pottery manufacturing centre, with groups of kilns situated on the bank of the Mosel just outside the walled area. *Terra sigillata*, a luxury orange-red ware often with moulded Classical decoration, was

produced here from the 2nd century AD, and like the glassware was traded to neighbouring provinces, including Britain. A second type of pottery manufactured at Trier and exported in large quantities from the 2nd century is the fine dark-brown or black ware with raised, cream-painted decoration known as *Moselkeramik*.

Although the Roman road system was used for trade in these products, overland transport was costly, and it was the rivers which were the principal trade arteries. Having begun as a net importer of luxury goods from the Mediterranean world, by AD 200 the region had become an active supplier both to the military on the Rhine frontier and to the north-western provinces generally. With the break-up of the western Roman empire at the close of the 4th century AD its prosperity came to an end.

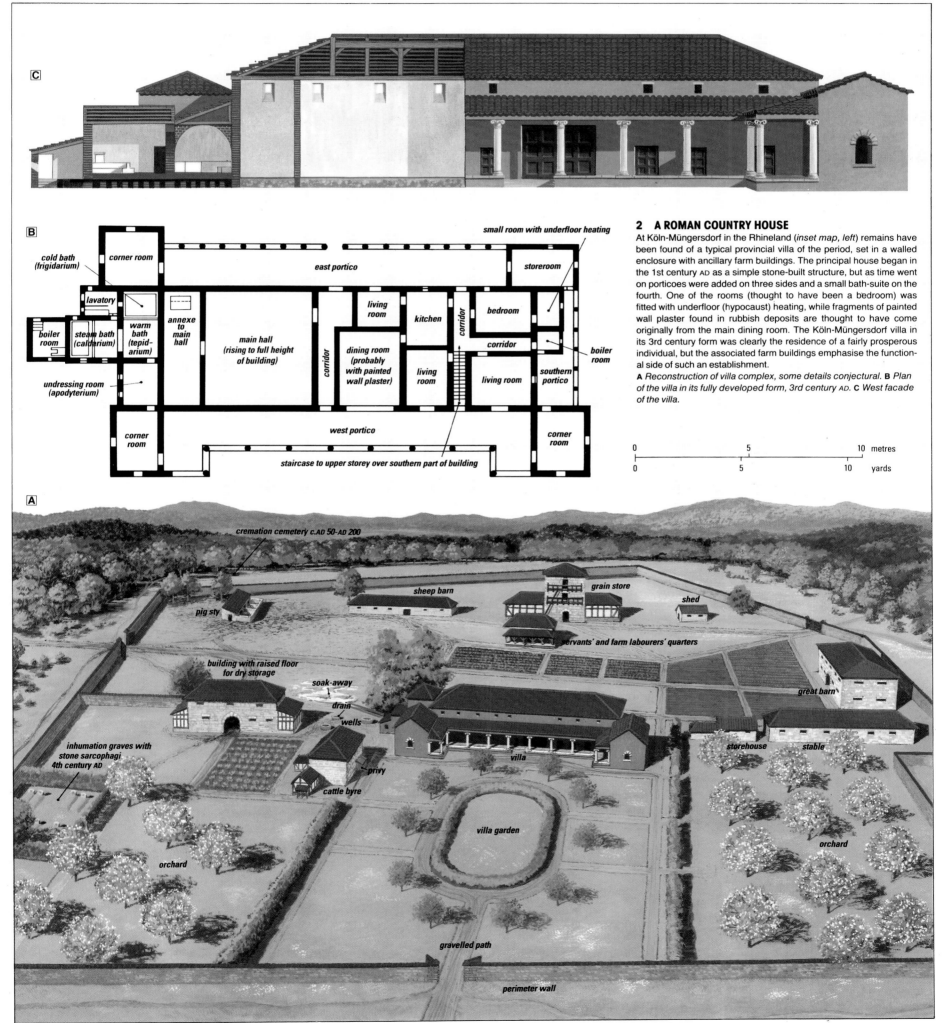

2 A ROMAN COUNTRY HOUSE

At Köln-Müngersdorf in the Rhineland (*inset map, left*) remains have been found of a typical provincial villa of the period, set in a walled enclosure with ancillary farm buildings. The principal house began in the 1st century AD as a simple stone-built structure, but as time went on porticoes were added on three sides and a small bath-suite on the fourth. One of the rooms (thought to have been a bedroom) was fitted with underfloor (hypocaust) heating, while fragments of painted wall plaster found in rubbish deposits are thought to have come originally from the main dining room. The Köln-Müngersdorf villa in its 3rd century form was clearly the residence of a fairly prosperous individual, but the associated farm buildings emphasise the functional side of such an establishment.

A *Reconstruction of villa complex, some details conjectural.* B *Plan of the villa in its fully developed form, 3rd century AD.* C *West facade of the villa.*

Pompeii: a Roman town

The town of Pompeii, along with its neighbours Herculaneum and Stabiae, is an exceptional archaeological site because of its destruction by the eruption of Mount Vesuvius on 24 August AD 79. The volcanic material that buried it and killed thousands of its inhabitants preserved a vivid record of a flourishing town of the early Roman empire. Whole houses, complete with decorations and furnishings, with graffiti and painted slogans on their walls, and with remains of hapless householders lying where they fell, can be disinterred and restored.

It is easy, however, to overemphasise Pompeii's importance. It was a minor Italian town, relatively prosperous but not a major force in Roman politics or culture. What makes it interesting is the light that it sheds on the life and taste of ordinary people during a momentous period in world history. Its origins can be traced back to at least the 6th century BC. It apparently developed as a native settlement of Oscans, the indigenous population of Campania, and its name is derived from an Oscan word, but it came under strong cultural influence from nearby Greek colonies such as Herculaneum and Naples. The nucleus of the early settlement, a small area of about nine hectares in the south-west quarter of the later town, had a street-system that appears to be a native imitation of the more methodical grid layouts of the Greek cities. The

temple built at its south-eastern corner, designed in the Doric order, was thoroughly Greek in style.

In the late 6th and early 5th centuries Pompeii shows evidence of the extension of Etruscan power into Campania; the characteristic Etruscan *bucchero* pottery has been found in excavations of early levels in various parts of the town. But direct rule by the Etruscans is unlikely; the pottery almost certainly arrived as a result of trade. Greek wine-jars have also been found, suggesting that Pompeii then, as later, acted as an intermediary for trade between parts of inland Campania and the Greek cities of the coast. At some stage in the 5th century this commercial activity declined as much of Campania came under the domination of the Samnites, groups of tribes from central Italy who absorbed first the old Etruscan settlements and ultimately the Greek coastal cities, except for Naples. Pompeii, too, was probably taken over. It was perhaps in response to the influx of new settlers that the town was enlarged to its present area of 63 hectares, with defensive walls built of local sedimentary limestone.

From the 5th to the early 1st century BC Pompeii remained an autonomous Samnite city, retaining its native language and organs of government. It enjoyed considerable prosperity as an agricultural producer, market town and port, and the new residential areas built up in the 2nd century BC included grand mansions with coloured stuccowork and mosaic pavements. The House of the Faun, named after a bronze statuette found in it, was 3150 square metres in area, larger than the contemporary royal palace at Pergamum. Important public buildings, too, such as the theatre, the Stabian baths, the

basilica, and the Temple of Jupiter, belong in all essentials to this period. These buildings and their decorations are overwhelmingly Greek in style, reflecting the cultural climate prevailing in much of central and southern Italy.

Effective political power in Italy had by now passed to the Romans, and Pompeii, like many other Italian cities, enjoyed its nominal independence within the framework of an alliance with Rome. However, after Pompeii became involved in the so-called Social War, a struggle by the Italians for increased political rights (91-89 BC), the town was besieged and captured by the Roman general Sulla, who subsequently established a colony of veteran soldiers to administer it and ensure its loyalty. New buildings, such as the forum baths, the concert-hall (*odeum*) and the amphitheatre were added by the colonists, and many houses were rebuilt or redecorated in the so-called Second Style of wall painting, apparently introduced from the capital at this time.

The subsequent history of Pompeii is marked by no important political and social changes. The old native families gradually reappeared among the holders of municipal office, and the town profited from the general economic prosperity brought by the consolidation of the Roman empire under Augustus (31 BC-AD 14). The rise of new commercial classes led to the break-up of some of the old aristocratic dwellings into smaller residential units. An earthquake caused extensive structural damage in AD 62, and many of the buildings affected by this earthquake, including the temple of the city's chief goddess, Venus, were still in ruins and awaiting reconstruction when the final cataclysm overtook the city 17 years later.

1 IN THE SHADOW OF VESUVIUS

Pompeii was a medium-sized town of about 10,000 inhabitants. Situated about ten kilometres south of the volcano of Vesuvius, it controlled a fertile hinterland suitable for wine production and fruit-growing. Its position on the coast and at the mouth of the River Sarno also made it a natural focus of regional communications and trade (though the eruptions of AD 79 and subsequent centuries have altered the course of the river and pushed the coastline over a mile to the west). The town walls followed the terrain, running along an escarpment at the south and west and cutting across a low saddle on the north-east. Roads radiated from each of seven gates: westwards to a port at the rivermouth, north-west to Herculaneum and Naples, north to the farmland on the slopes of Vesuvius, north-east to Capua, east to Nola, south-east to Nuceria, and south to Stabiae. The town-plan shows signs of a long and piecemeal development. The old quarter in the south-west corner focused round the *forum* and chief municipal buildings – the council chamber, magistrates' offices, Temples of Apollo and Jupiter, market buildings, and *basilica* (stock exchange and law court combined). The remaining quarters are successive planned developments, and the built-up regular blocks in the eastern quarter probably represent the latest construction stage. Just inside the Stabiae gate are the theatre and *odeum*, with fan-shaped auditoria; the former, open to the air, housed pantomimes and dramatic performances; the latter, originally roofed, was used for concerts and recitations. At the eastern corner was the elliptical amphitheatre, where gladiatorial combats and wild-beast hunts were staged; and next to it was the *palaestra*, a vast open-air drill ground and exercise area for the youth of the town. Other public buildings were the Turkish-style baths, two of which go back to the Republican period, while a third was begun after the earthquake of AD 62. Much of the remaining area comprised houses, shops and small industrial premises, the grandest and most humble establishments often juxtaposed in a way that would be barely thinkable today.

4 POMPEII: ASPECTS OF EVERYDAY LIFE

A *Carbonised loaf. Remains of food are well preserved, especially at Herculaneum where the hot volcanic mud hermetically sealed them against decomposition.* B *Painting of lovemaking. Sketchy erotic scenes are found above the doors of cubicles in the local brothels.* C *Public notices were painted directly on walls rather than posted as bills. Many survive from the last years of the city, either proclaiming support for candidates in local elections or advertising festivals and entertainments.* D *A bronze lamp-stand. Terracotta lamps fuelled with olive oil would have been suspended from the four hooks at the top. A great variety of decorated stands has been found, often with three or four feet in the form of animals' hooves or paws. Height c.1m.*

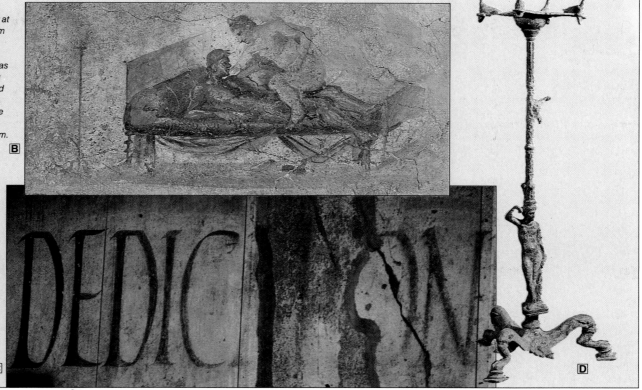

B

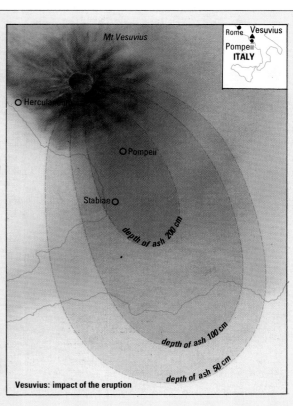

D

A

C

2 FROZEN IN TIME

When Vesuvius erupted a mass of volcanic material was initially thrown upwards to form a mushroom-shaped cloud ('like an umbrella pine', the eye-witness Pliny described it), then was carried south-eastwards directly over Pompeii and the villa-resort of Stabiae. For the first day the fallout was in the form of *lapilli*, small pumice stones that accumulated quickly in gardens and open spaces to a depth of nearly three metres, but were not lethal to the inhabitants. During this period many were able to escape by sea or inland. Later came a dense rain of ash and poisonous gases, which asphyxiated those who had re-mained behind. At the same time earthquake shocks destroyed many buildings. When, on the third day, the eruption ceased, the town was interred to a depth of four metres, and only the tops of walls remained visible to guide salvage-teams and plunderers. Subsequent eruptions have raised the modern level to about six metres above the ancient. The bodies of the victims have decayed but can be recovered by pouring plaster into the voids left by their imprints in the volcanic ash which hardened round them. Many were found lying in cellars or bedrooms where they had taken refuge; others had fallen in the open while seeking to escape over the deep banks of *lapilli*.

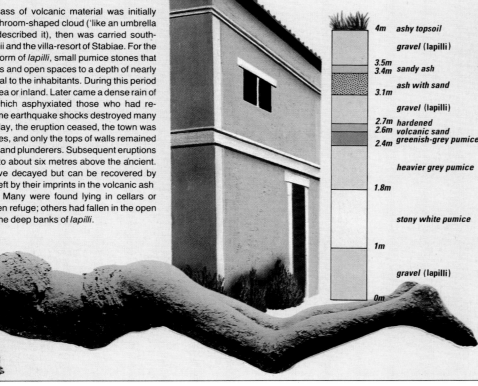

4m	ashy topsoil
	gravel (lapilli)
3.5m	sandy ash
3.4m	ash with sand
3.1m	gravel (lapilli)
2.7m	hardened
2.6m	volcanic sand
2.4m	greenish-grey pumice
	heavier grey pumice
1.8m	
	stony white pumice
1m	
	gravel (lapilli)
0m	

Vesuvius: impact of the eruption

3 THE HOUSE OF THE VETTII

The typical Pompeian town-house was focused round the *atrium* (a hall with a central roof-opening and a catchwater basin in the floor) and the *peristyle* (a colonnaded garden at the rear).

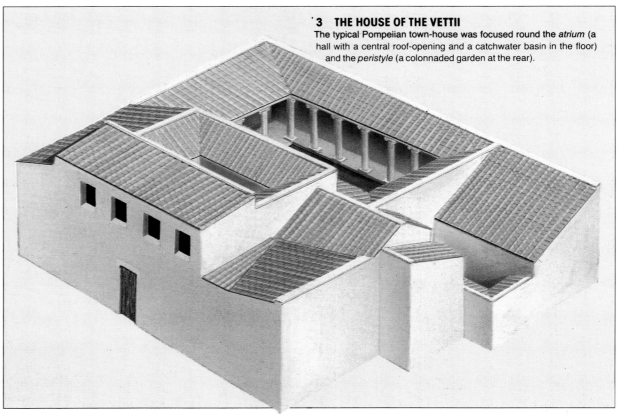

Greek and Roman technology

Major developments in agriculture, manufacturing, transport and technology transformed the Mediterranean world at the end of the 1st millennium BC. Marked increases in the number, size and prosperity of cities, an expansion in trade, advances in engineering, the increasing application of theoretical ideas to practical problems, and a greater exploitation of natural resources were all factors which revolutionised Mediterranean society at this period.

The population of the average city in Classical Greece was only around 10,000, although by the 5th century BC the population of Athens may have reached 200,000. As economies flourished, city populations grew, and in the 1st century AD Rome and Alexandria had around a million inhabitants. The supply of basic commodities to these vast population centres demanded the development and application of new engineering skills. Three crucial developments were the construction of larger merchant ships (some of 1000 tonnes carrying capacity) to transport foodstuffs; the Roman invention of concrete, which made possible many large-scale architectural and engineering projects; and the development of efficient systems for supplying water in bulk to both cities and farmland. The 2nd century BC water supply of Pergamum made use

of a siphon for the final three kilometres of its course, following the contours of the ground through pressure pipes across two valleys before reaching the citadel. Though occasionally used by Roman engineers, for example at Lyon, siphons tended to leak because of the high pressures involved. Most aqueducts simply used gradient to ensure a steady flow, the water channel supported on arches or piers where a defile had to be crossed. The Zaghouan aqueduct at Carthage runs mainly at ground level, making use of costly arcading only for short stretches. Where necessary, tunnels were dug to maintain a steady and gentle slope: the aqueduct of Samos, built by a Greek engineer in the 6th century BC, incorporates a tunnel two metres square cut through limestone for one kilometre. The water was sometimes

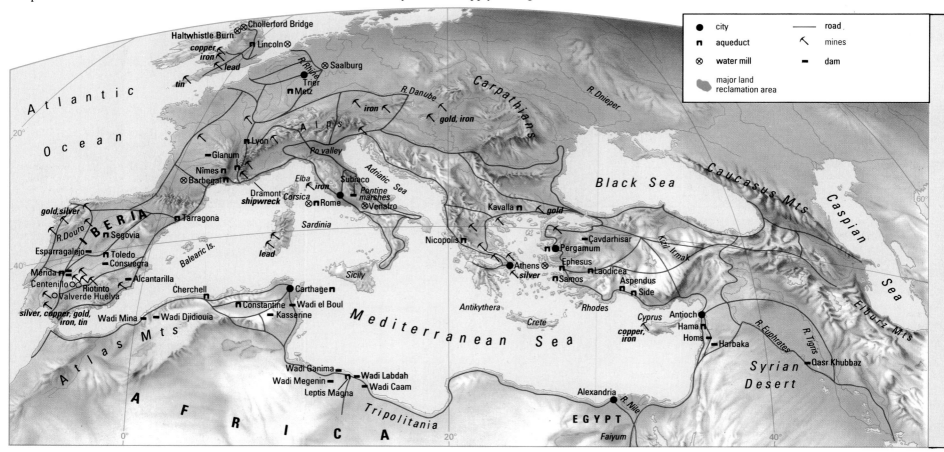

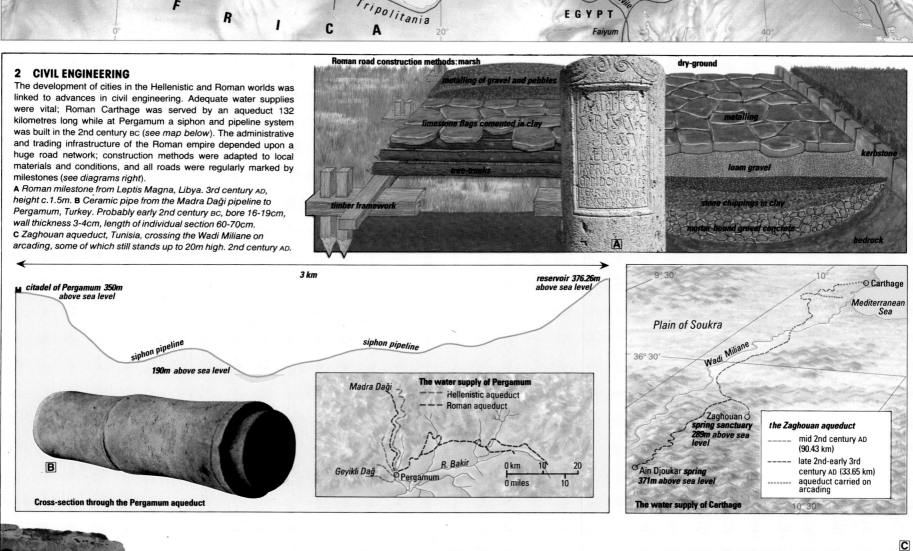

2 CIVIL ENGINEERING

The development of cities in the Hellenistic and Roman worlds was linked to advances in civil engineering. Adequate water supplies were vital; Roman Carthage was served by an aqueduct 132 kilometres long while at Pergamum a siphon and pipeline system was built in the 2nd century BC (see map below). The administrative and trading infrastructure of the Roman empire depended upon a huge road network; construction methods were adapted to local materials and conditions, and all roads were regularly marked by milestones (see diagrams right).

A Roman milestone from Leptis Magna, Libya. 3rd century AD, height c.1.5m. **B** Ceramic pipe from the Madra Daği pipeline to Pergamum, Turkey. Probably early 2nd century BC, bore 16-19cm, wall thickness 3-4cm, length of individual section 60-70cm.
C Zaghouan aqueduct, Tunisia, crossing the Wadi Miliane on arcading, some of which still stands up to 20m high. 2nd century AD.

Roman road construction methods: marsh

metalling of gravel and pebbles
limestone flags cemented in clay
tree-trunks
timber framework

dry-ground
metalling
kerbstone
loam gravel
stone chippings in clay
mortar-bound gravel concrete
bedrock

A

citadel of Pergamum 350m above sea level

3 km

reservoir 376.26m above sea level

siphon pipeline

siphon pipeline

190m above sea level

B
Cross-section through the Pergamum aqueduct

Madra Daği

The water supply of Pergamum
— Hellenistic aqueduct
— Roman aqueduct

Geyikli Daği

R. Bakir

Pergamum

0 km   10   20
0 miles   10

Plain of Soukra

Mediterranean Sea

Wadi Miliane

Zaghouan spring sanctuary 289m above sea level

Ain Djoukar spring 371m above sea level

the Zaghouan aqueduct
----- mid 2nd century AD (90.43 km)
----- late 2nd-early 3rd century AD (33.65 km)
.... aqueduct carried on arcading

The water supply of Carthage

C

carried in pipes, but more usually ran in cement-lined surface channels, covered to keep out dirt and limit evaporation. Regular water supplies fed public and domestic buildings, and also provided power for industrial uses and water mills.

The Hellenistic and Roman periods also witnessed major changes in the scale and organisation of manufacturing and in the exploitation of natural resources, including mines and agriculture. Pottery began to be mass produced, shapes became standardised, and many vessels carried a stamp showing where they had been manufactured. The exploitation of minerals, notably iron, copper and lead, increased substantially as the Roman empire grew to encompass such mineral-rich areas as Iberia and western Britain. By employing

water-lifting equipment such as screw- and force-pumps Roman engineers were able to increase the output of mines and exploit deeper mineral deposits. Agriculture underwent similar changes. Large, regularly laid-out estates (*latifundia*), often manned by slaves, were established. Both labour and capital were invested in ambitious land-improvement schemes such as the drainage of the Faiyum Basin in Egypt and parts of the Po plain in Italy. Improvements to Faiyum were begun in the 3rd century BC under state direction. These included the construction of canal irrigation systems around the arid edges of the basin. Lake Moeris was lowered to release large fertile areas of former lake bed for cultivation. On the reclaimed land around the lake a series of towns was founded, and the overall result of the

scheme was an increase, perhaps as much as five-fold, in the Faiyum population. Land improvement and the introduction of new irrigation devices such as the Archimedean screw (screw-pump) and the water wheel or *sakia* made Egypt one of the most populous countries of the Roman world, with possibly as many as five million people at the beginning of the Christian era.

The development of technology in Mediterranean lands slowed when the Roman economy went into decline in the 4th and 5th centuries AD. In the west, cities shrank or were abandoned, and roads and aqueducts were not maintained. Few of the innovations and advances were permanently lost, however, as most were adapted and developed during the Middle Ages in the Byzantine and Islamic states.

1 THE IMPACT OF TECHNOLOGY

The technological innovations which made such an impact on southern and western Europe in the first few centuries AD originated in Italy and the east Mediterranean, but with the expansion of Roman power were soon applied to a wide range of problems in very varied geographical circumstances. Among the most impressive was the system of all-weather roads which reached over widely contrasting terrains to the farthest corners of the empire. The method of road construction was adapted to the nature of the subsoil and the local availability of raw materials, and could cope with both arid desert and unstable marsh; in the latter case, the road might be laid on a timber foundation pinned to the ground by stakes, whereas on solid ground the foundation consisted of layers of gravel and clay. Technological solutions were also applied to the practical problems generated by rapidly increasing urban populations. Techniques for improving agricultural yields – irrigation, drainage and land reclamation – ensured an adequate food supply. In the drier Mediterranean lands, where rainfall was not always adequate, reservoirs of irrigation water were created by building large and sophisticated dams, as for example at Mérida in Spain and Homs in Syria. In Tripolitania the remains of a larger number of smaller dams dating from this period illustrate an alternative solution to the same problem. By way of contrast, in areas such as the Fenlands of eastern England or the Po plain agricultural improvement took the form of the reclamation of marshy lowland through extensive systems of drainage canals. New machinery was also introduced for the more efficient processing of agricultural produce. Water mills are known from Rome itself, the Athenian agora, Hadrian's Wall in northern Britain and the remarkable battery of water mills at Barbegal (*illustration F below*). Where suitable water sources were not available, rotary mills driven by human or animal power must have continued in use as before; the windmill was not used in this area until the 12th century AD. Finally, advances in technology changed the face of European settlement: mining and quarrying transformed remote but mineral-rich regions into areas which were both economically and strategically important.

3 MACHINERY

Improvements in machinery played a major part in the economic development of the Hellenistic and Roman periods. Writers such as Hero of Alexandria (1st century AD) describe experiments in mechanics. Hero gives an account of an elementary steam turbine, which does not appear to have passed the experimental stage. On the other hand the 'dioptra' surveying instrument, known only from Hero's description, may have been used to lay out roads, aqueducts and other structures. Certainly such undertakings required the use of accurate surveying methods. Water power and water-lifting devices are better represented by extant remains. The battery of Roman water mills at Barbegal in southern France may have been capable of producing enough flour for 80,000 people in their final form. Water-lifting devices, including the screw-pump, were used for irrigation and for draining mines. Remains of several screw-pumps have been found in the Roman workings of the Riotinto area of Spain, together with a bronze force-pump. Four Roman force-pumps were found at the site of the 'Dramont D' wreck, probably the ship's bilge-pumps. The most sophisticated piece of machinery known from the ancient world, the Antikythera astronomical calculator, also comes from a wreck site; a navigational aid, it used differential gearing only rediscovered in the late 16th century AD.

A *Force pump from Roman mine at Valverde Huelva in southern Spain. Probably early centuries AD, bronze, height 95cm.*
B *Diagram showing the operation of a screw-pump or Archimedean screw, based on remains found in the Roman mine at Centenillo in southern Spain. Length 4.25m, diameter 0.5m.* C *Reconstruction of the 'dioptra', a surveying instrument, based on the writings of Hero of Alexandria. 1st century AD.* D *Fragment of an astronomical calculator found in shipwreck off the Cycladic island of Antikythera. Central workings with main drive wheel. Early 1st century BC, bronze, height 16cm, width 13.5cm.* E *Reconstruction drawing showing differential gearing of Antikythera calculator.*
F *Reconstruction of the Roman water mills at Barbegal, France, as they appeared in the 4th century AD.*

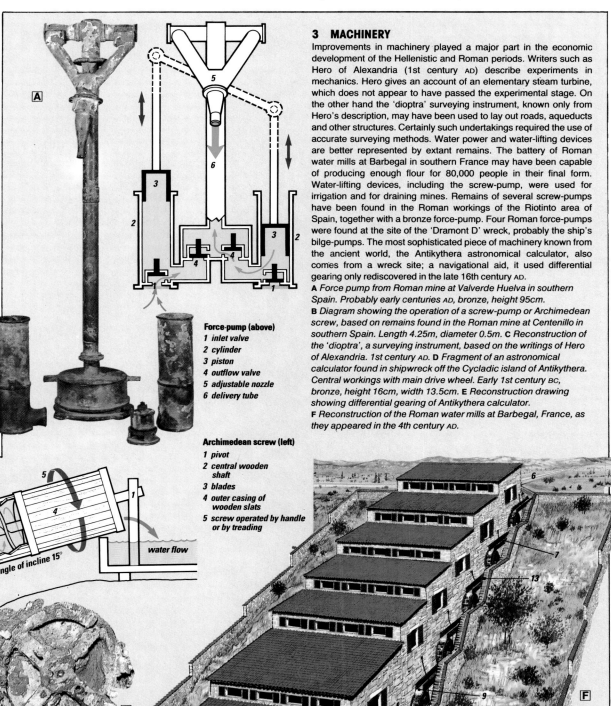

Force-pump (above)
1 inlet valve
2 cylinder
3 piston
4 outflow valve
5 adjustable nozzle
6 delivery tube

Archimedean screw (left)
1 pivot
2 central wooden shaft
3 blades
4 outer casing of wooden slats
5 screw operated by handle or by treading

angle of incline 15°

water flow

water flow

The Barbegal water mill
1 principal doorway
2 loading area for carts and wagons
3 concrete platform for drying grain
4 central passageway with access to milling chambers
5 milling chamber
6 aqueduct feeding triangular reservoir
7 mill race
8 overshoot water wheel c. 2.2m diameter
9 wooden spout with panels which can be raised
10 wooden gearing mechanism
11 millstone 0.9m diameter
12 wooden trough for collecting flour
13 stairway

The Germanic world

Lying beyond the northern limits of the Celtic world and the Roman empire, Germanic Europe from 500 BC to AD 650 was a region of small farming settlements gradually developing towards statehood. Although Roman imports occur frequently in the richer Germanic graves of the early centuries AD, developments in northern Europe were indigenous and on a small scale. Many perishable items survived in the bogs and marshes of Denmark and northern Germany, including wooden ships, tools and weapons and sacrificed bodies, making this one of the most interesting regions of Europe at this period.

The typical inhabitant of the Germanic world was a peasant farmer living in a single farmstead or small village of wattle-and-daub houses. Many of the coastal lowlands were settled for the first time at this period; hamlets and villages developed into mounds known as *terpen* (Dutch) or *Wierden* (German), through natural accumulation of debris and the intentional laying down of clay to raise house floors above the flood-level. In most areas arable farming was important, as finds of wooden ards (scratch ploughs) and systems of small fields testify. Agriculture and craftsmanship benefited considerably from the introduction of iron-working in the middle of the 1st millennium BC. The new technology developed slowly, probably because of the rarity of suitable deposits of iron ore in northern Europe; in the lowlands only inferior bog iron was available. By the 3rd and 4th centuries AD, however, iron was being produced on a large scale in several areas – notably Bohemia, Schleswig-Holstein and southern Poland. In the Lysa Góra area of Poland some 50 iron-smelting sites have been found, with batteries of kilns laid out in close-set rows. The iron produced here was traded extensively to neighbouring areas, possibly even south to the Roman empire.

Bog finds are a conspicuous feature of the Germanic Iron Age, and throw particular light on the religious practices of the period. Several large deposits of war equipment have been found, probably offerings to a deity in thanksgiving for victory; at Hjortspring (3rd century BC) a warship was surrounded by a mass of weapons and equipment including 150 wooden shields, 138 iron spear-heads and 20 coats of mail. Danish votive deposits of the early centuries AD accumulated in sacred locations over several decades or centuries and often contained Roman weapons – an indication of the combatants in at least some of the hostilities. Other ritual deposits include vessels of precious metal: the most remarkable is the massive silver Gundestrup cauldron, decorated with scenes of stags, elephants, snakes, warriors and deities. The best-known ritual deposits are, however, the corpses whose skin, clothing and facial features have been preserved by bog water. Most appear to have been ritually murdered, by hanging, strangulation, decapitation or stabbing. The most famous bog body, from Tollund in Denmark, had a noose round his neck, while the unworn state of the fingertips suggests that he had been exempt from manual work, perhaps a high-ranking individual or a priest.

By the 3rd century AD the Germanic world was changing, and the next two centuries were characterised by the emergence of small kingdoms and the development of maritime ventures – especially the invasion and colonisation of much of Britain. As the Roman empire weakened, Germanic peoples crossed the frontier and took over large parts of western Europe and North Africa. In Scandinavia a few wealthy cemeteries emerged, focal centres for quite substantial areas, indicating the gradual centralisation of power. The massive 5th century funeral mounds at Old Uppsala, Sweden, were probably burials of the leaders of this type of early kingdom. From the 7th century, these barrows were succeeded by rich cemeteries at Valsgärde and Vendel, the latter containing 26 elaborately furnished boat burials. The most impressive boat burial of this period is at Sutton Hoo in Suffolk (c. AD 625), where an East Anglian ruler was buried in a ship accompanied by a remarkable range of grave-goods. A sword, shield and helmet are Swedish in style, while the burial also contained 37 gold coins minted in Merovingian France, and silver ware from the Byzantine empire, as well as fine examples of local craftsmanship.

The cosmopolitan character of the Sutton Hoo grave-goods clearly demonstrates the extensive trading contacts between the Germanic world and the rest of Europe. By the 7th century AD the Germanic world had evolved from a series of dispersed farming villages on the fringes of the Roman empire to a number of small kingdoms with wealthy rulers and international trading contacts; the foundations of the nation states of mediaeval Scandinavia and of Anglo-Saxon England had been laid.

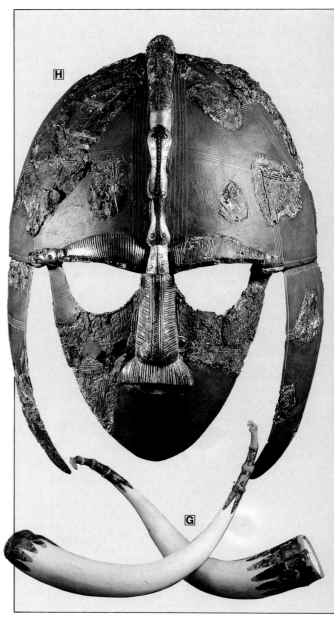

1 THE ANGLO-SAXON INVASIONS

The farming villages (or *terpen*) which were the main settlements of the coastal lowlands of northern Germany and Holland appear to have suffered severe marine flooding c. AD 500 and were abandoned at about this time. The land hunger which was the result of these environmental changes, as well as rising levels of population, led to a general raiding and colonising movement westwards; eastern Britain was subject to Anglo-Saxon invasions in the 5th and 6th centuries AD. The long indented coastline of northern Europe, with its many rivers and inlets, encouraged the development of boats and ships; several have been found preserved in Danish bogs, while boat finds from, for example, Nydam and Sutton Hoo give us some indication of the kind of oar-powered vessels in which the invaders crossed the North Sea. This movement of the Germanic peoples across to Britain is reflected in the widespread distribution of traded goods: for example the cruciform brooches which originated in Denmark and northern Germany, and Rhenish 'claw' beakers.

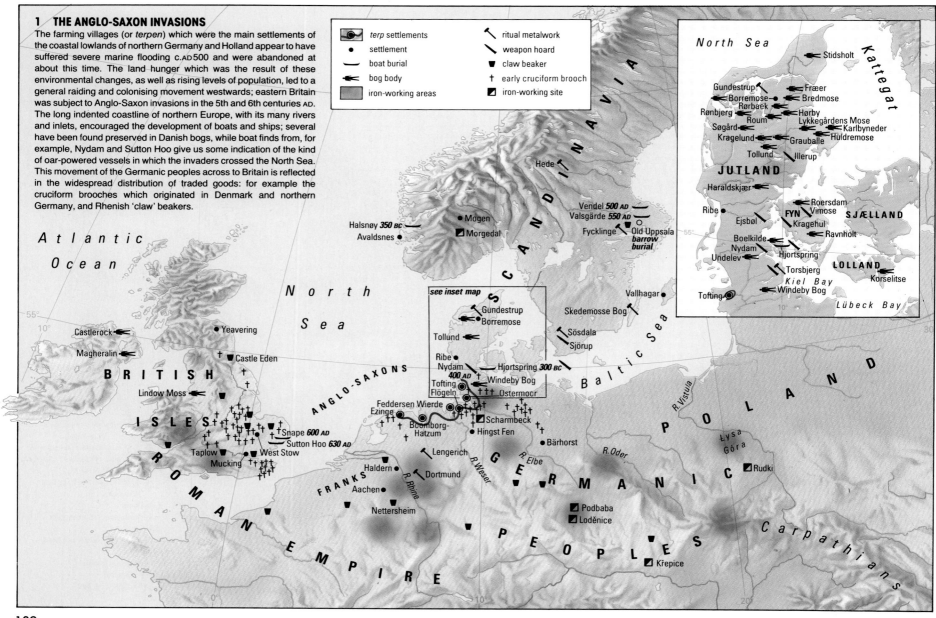

3 RITUALS AND BURIALS

A *Tollund Man, head of bog body with leather hat and thong fastening. He had been garrotted. Late 3rd century BC.* **B** *Gundestrup cauldron, decorated with ritual scenes, gods and exotic animals. c.2nd century BC, embossed silver-gilt, diameter 97cm.* **C** *Nydam ship, part of a ritual deposit. Clinker-built vessel of oak, fixed by iron nails. Probably rowed by a crew of 30 oarsmen. Late 4th century AD, 23m long, 3m wide.* **D** *Germanic cruciform brooch from Haslingfield, Cambridgeshire. 6th century AD, bronze, length 9.2cm, width 6cm.*
Objects from Sutton Hoo boat burial, early 7th century AD:
E *Purse-lid, originally attached to leather or cloth bag holding 37 gold coins. Gold, inset with garnet and millefiori glass – a late Roman style. Length of lid 19.05cm.* **F** *Great belt buckle. Gold, length 13.2cm.* **G** *Pair of drinking horns with silver-gilt mounts, diameter at mouth 10cm.* **H** *Reconstruction of helmet. Iron, with gilding, silver wire and garnets, lined with leather. Circumference 75.5cm.*

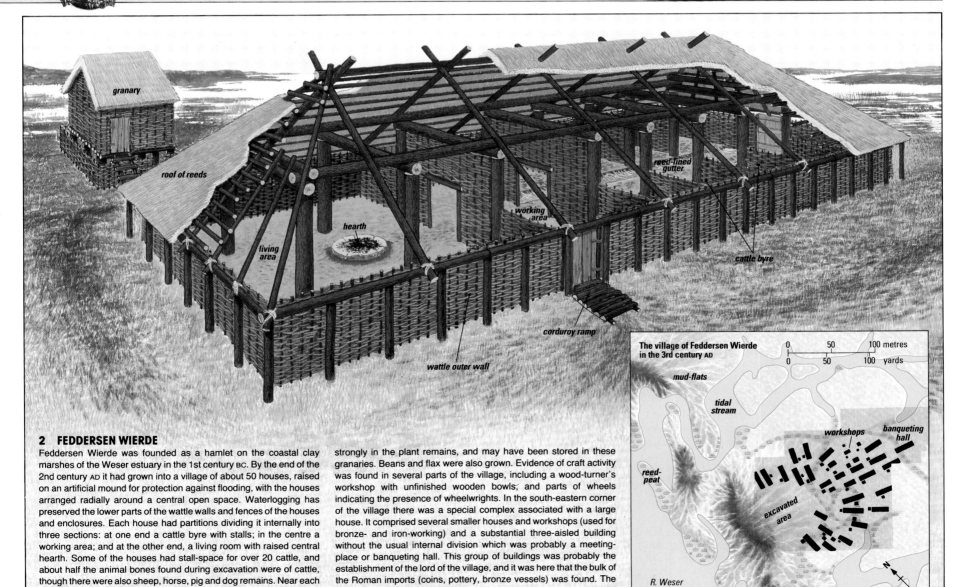

2 FEDDERSEN WIERDE

Feddersen Wierde was founded as a hamlet on the coastal clay marshes of the Weser estuary in the 1st century BC. By the end of the 2nd century AD it had grown into a village of about 50 houses, raised on an artificial mound for protection against flooding, with the houses arranged radially around a central open space. Waterlogging has preserved the lower parts of the wattle walls and fences of the houses and enclosures. Each house had partitions dividing it internally into three sections: at one end a cattle byre with stalls; in the centre a working area; and at the other end, a living room with raised central hearth. Some of the houses had stall-space for over 20 cattle, and about half the animal bones found during excavation were of cattle, though there were also sheep, horse, pig and dog remains. Near each large house was a small rectangular granary with a floor raised on posts to allow ventilation and keep out vermin. Barley and oats figure

strongly in the plant remains, and may have been stored in these granaries. Beans and flax were also grown. Evidence of craft activity was found in several parts of the village, including a wood-turner's workshop with unfinished wooden bowls, and parts of wheels indicating the presence of wheelwrights. In the south-eastern corner of the village there was a special complex associated with a large house. It comprised several smaller houses and workshops (used for bronze- and iron-working) and a substantial three-aisled building without the usual internal division which was probably a meeting-place or banqueting hall. This group of buildings was probably the establishment of the lord of the village, and it was here that the bulk of the Roman imports (coins, pottery, bronze vessels) was found. The site was abandoned in the middle of the 5th century AD, when coastal flooding made the lowlands too wet and salty to support agriculture.

The Steppe nomads

The Steppes are a vast belt of grassland stretching from Manchuria in the east to European Russia in the west. They are broken in places by desert and upland, and fringed on the north by forests and on the south by mountain ranges and arid zones. The more temperate parts of this region were colonised as early as the 5th millennium BC by groups of farmers, and remains of their villages have been found in the Dnieper Valley, but many parts of the Steppes were too dry for early agriculture. During the 2nd millennium BC, however, specialised nomadic economies developed based on the horse, so that by 1000 BC most of this zone was occupied by pastoral groups.

Much of our knowledge of these Steppe nomads comes from burials, notably the rich Scythian barrows of southern Russia and the exceptionally well-preserved cemeteries of the Altai Mountains, Pazyryk and Noin Ula. Remains of settlements are relatively rare, partly because the nomadic lifestyle depended on tents and temporary dwellings rather than substantial buildings. Large permanent settlements which have been found in the Ukraine reflect both the sedentary nature of western Scythian society and its more highly developed political structure. Kamenskoye, north of the Black Sea, had a fortified area of almost eight square kilometres, and was occupied from the 5th to the 2nd century BC.

During the 1st millennium BC life on the Steppes was based on rearing herds of cattle, sheep and horses, supplemented by some agriculture and hunting. Hunting scenes, frequently featuring stags, are common in Steppe art, and bones of wild animals are often found among the food offerings in the graves. Horse riding became widespread during the 2nd millennium BC and many graves contain remains of horses, some of them thoroughbreds, slaughtered to accompany their owner in death. Wheeled carts from the Steppes date from as early as the 3rd millennium, and one of the Pazyryk barrows contained a complete, though dismantled, wagon. Seasonal movement between pastures meant that horses and wagons were essential. It was also vital that equipment was portable: bronze cauldrons, carried on horseback, have been found throughout the region.

Naturally, there were certain limitations on Steppe craftsmanship but this did not prevent the development of a distinctive art style, in which wild animals and hunting scenes figured prominently. Weaponry, textiles, riding tack and small ornaments were the principal products, worked in gold, bronze, antler and wood. Most of the finds of woodwork and textiles come from the Pazyryk and Noin Ula barrows, where they were well-preserved by permafrost and waterlogging. Barrow 2 at Pazyryk contained the corpse of a chieftain with traces of extensive tattooing, while bronze mirrors were found in this and two of the other barrows, suggesting that these nomadic people paid considerable attention to personal appearance. This even extended to binding the skulls of babies to produce an elongation of the cranium, common to human remains throughout the Steppes.

Written accounts by neighbouring peoples – the Greeks, the Persians and the Chinese – describe Steppe society as hierarchical, with warrior chiefs and tribesmen. Rich graves such as Kostromskaya and Kul Oba in southern Russia, with gold ornaments, weaponry and slaughtered horses and retainers, probably represent the burial places of important chiefs. Some of the gold and bronze ornaments were made in the Greek colonies of the Black Sea coast, or by Greek craftsmen working for Scythian chieftains. Further east, the Pazyryk barrows contained silks and a bronze mirror from China, and coriander seeds from southern Asia. Chinese silk makes its appearance in the Mediterranean and central Europe at this period, and it is likely that the Steppe chieftains acted as middlemen in this long-distance trade.

Greek and Chinese sources indicate that warfare was an endemic feature of Steppe life. The warriors generally fought on horseback using the bow, the Hunnish reflex bow being the most powerful form. Swords and long lances were also used. Herodotus describes how the Scythians of the Ukraine scalped their enemies, retaining the hair as a trophy, and this is borne out by the disfigured head of one of the Pazyryk chieftains.

The fierceness and mobility of the Steppe warriors made them a redoubtable force, especially when united under a strong leader. During the last centuries BC and early centuries AD the settled peoples of China, India and Europe suffered a series of major incursions from the Steppes, culminating in those of the Huns, which left a trail of death and devastation and foreshadowed in scale and violence the later campaigns of the Mongols.

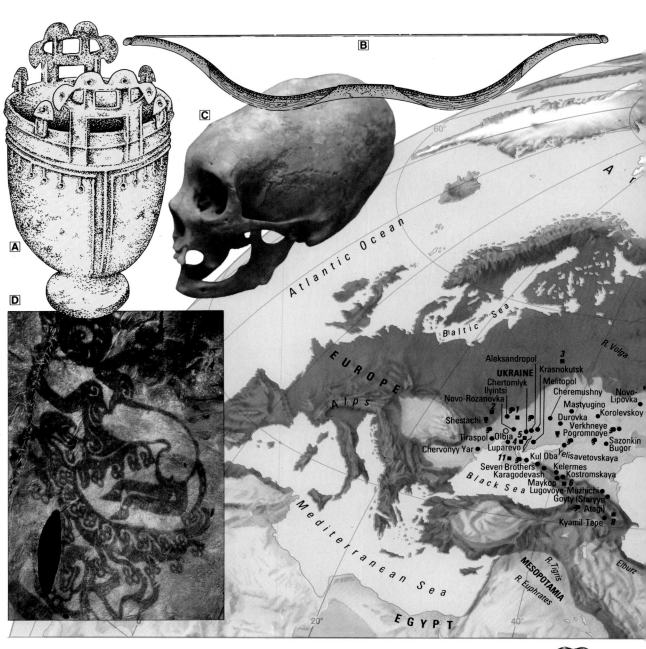

2 THE KOSTROMSKAYA BARROW

The Kostromskaya barrow, in the Kuban region to the east of the Black Sea, was probably the burial place of an important Steppe chieftain. The square wooden burial chamber had a pyramidal roof supported on massive corner posts 3.2 metres apart and had been set alight before earth was heaped over it to form the barrow. The principal burial had been placed in a small underground chamber, but this was empty when found. At higher levels were skeletons of 13 people, probably the dead man's servants or retainers, and 22 horses, illustrating both the great wealth of the buried chieftain and the importance of the horse in Steppe life. Among the grave-goods weapons were prominent, including an iron shield, its hub decorated by a gold plaque in the form of a crouching stag. From the style of this piece the burial may be dated to the 7th–6th century BC.

A *Stag, centrepiece of shield, from burial at Kostromskaya, USSR. 6th century BC, gold, length 31.7cm.*

plan of horse level (below):

1 leather quivers   6 potsherds
2 iron shield   7 bronze arrowheads
3 iron spear heads   8 grindstone
4 bits
5 scale armour

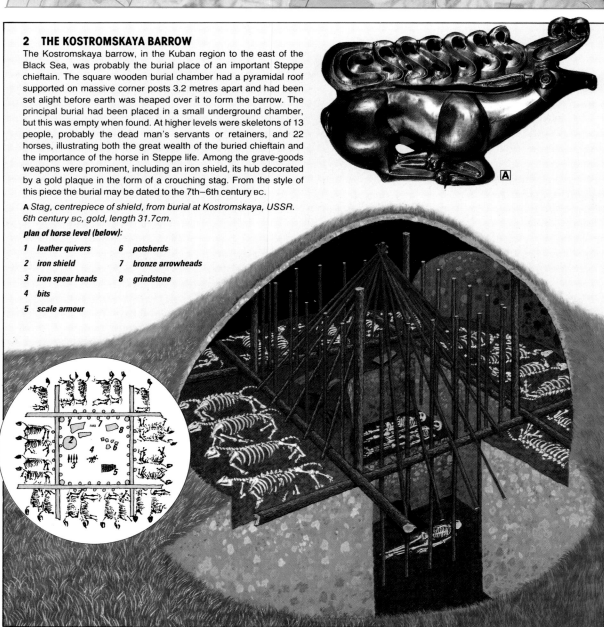

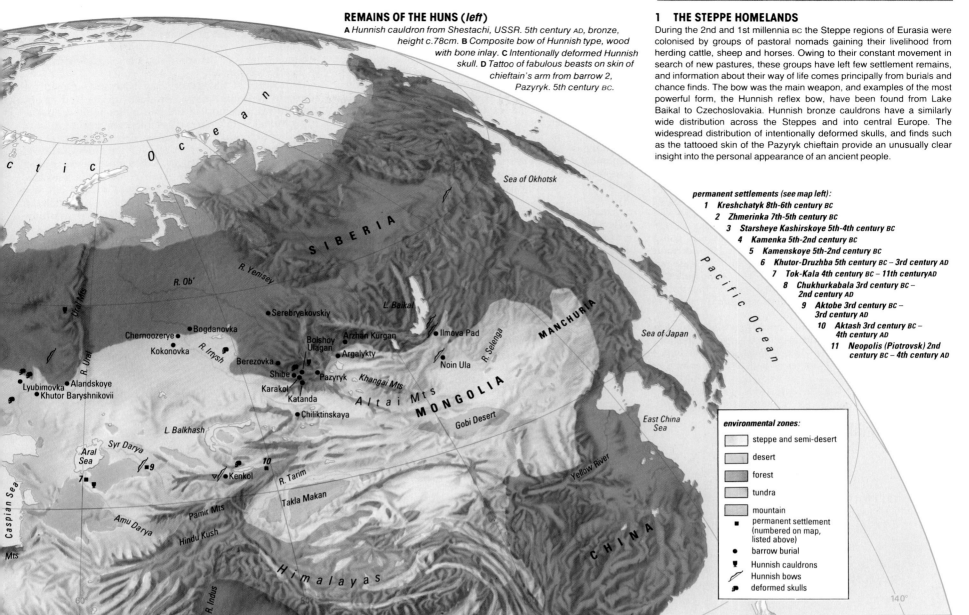

REMAINS OF THE HUNS (left)

A *Hunnish cauldron from Shestachi, USSR. 5th century AD, bronze, height c.78cm.* B *Composite bow of Hunnish type, wood with bone inlay.* C *Intentionally deformed Hunnish skull.* D *Tattoo of fabulous beasts on skin of chieftain's arm from barrow 2, Pazyryk. 5th century BC.*

1 THE STEPPE HOMELANDS

During the 2nd and 1st millennia BC the Steppe regions of Eurasia were colonised by groups of pastoral nomads gaining their livelihood from herding cattle, sheep and horses. Owing to their constant movement in search of new pastures, these groups have left few settlement remains, and information about their way of life comes principally from burials and chance finds. The bow was the main weapon, and examples of the most powerful form, the Hunnish reflex bow, have been found from Lake Baikal to Czechoslovakia. Hunnish bronze cauldrons have a similarly wide distribution across the Steppes and into central Europe. The widespread distribution of intentionally deformed skulls, and finds such as the tattooed skin of the Pazyryk chieftain provide an unusually clear insight into the personal appearance of an ancient people.

permanent settlements (see map left):
1   Kreshchatyk 8th-6th century BC
2   Zhmerinka 7th-5th century BC
3   Starsheye Kashirskoye 5th-4th century BC
4   Kamenka 5th-2nd century BC
5   Kamenskoye 5th-2nd century BC
6   Khutor-Druzhba 5th century BC – 3rd century AD
7   Tok-Kala 4th century BC – 11th century AD
8   Chukhurkabala 3rd century BC – 2nd century AD
9   Aktobe 3rd century BC – 3rd century AD
10   Aktash 3rd century BC – 4th century AD
11   Neopolis (Piotrovsk) 2nd century BC – 4th century AD

environmental zones:
- steppe and semi-desert
- desert
- forest
- tundra
- mountain
- ■ permanent settlement (numbered on map, listed above)
- ● barrow burial
- Hunnish cauldrons
- Hunnish bows
- deformed skulls

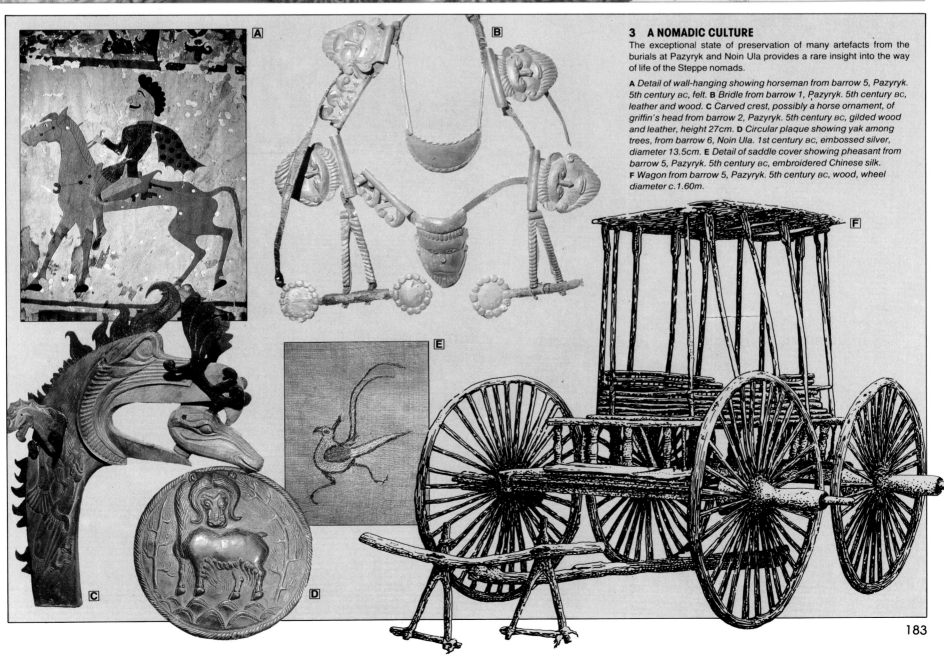

3 A NOMADIC CULTURE

The exceptional state of preservation of many artefacts from the burials at Pazyryk and Noin Ula provides a rare insight into the way of life of the Steppe nomads.

A *Detail of wall-hanging showing horseman from barrow 5, Pazyryk. 5th century BC, felt.* B *Bridle from barrow 1, Pazyryk. 5th century BC, leather and wood.* C *Carved crest, possibly a horse ornament, of griffin's head from barrow 2, Pazyryk. 5th century BC, gilded wood and leather, height 27cm.* D *Circular plaque showing yak among trees, from barrow 6, Noin Ula. 1st century BC, embossed silver, diameter 13.5cm.* E *Detail of saddle cover showing pheasant from barrow 5, Pazyryk. 5th century BC, embroidered Chinese silk.* F *Wagon from barrow 5, Pazyryk. 5th century BC, wood, wheel diameter c.1.60m.*

183

Red Sea states

A number of prosperous states developed around the trading corridor of the Red Sea during the 1st millennium BC. These included the 'incense kingdoms' of Sabaea, Qataban, Hadhramaut and Ma'in in Arabia, the Ethiopian state of Axum and to the north-east of the Red Sea, the kingdom of Nabataea, with Petra as its capital. The reason for their rise to wealth was the control of the overland caravan trade between southern Arabia and the eastern Mediterranean, a trade based largely on the growth and export of the aromatic gums, frankincense and myrrh. Both were in great demand in ancient times; Egypt, in particular, used frankincense in religious ceremonies and for embalming, while myrrh was widely used throughout the Near East as an ingredient of costly incense, perfumes and cosmetics, and was also sought after for its medicinal qualities. In the late 1st millennium BC there was a dramatic increase in the scale and importance of this trade, when the appearance of prosperous new Hellenistic kingdoms in the eastern Mediterranean created a new and accessible market for the Arabian traders.

Frankincense and myrrh, which produce a pleasant odour when burned, are the product of separate species of large bush or tree and are obtained by cutting the bark in summer and allowing globules of gum to form, which can then be collected in the autumn when they have hardened. Today, myrrh and frankincense trees are found only in limited areas of Somalia and southern Arabia, but there is evidence that in ancient times myrrh was widely grown in southern Arabia in irrigated plots. The main area of Arabian frankincense production lay in Hadhramaut, the easternmost of the kingdoms, and incense from this source passed through several other states on its way to the markets of the east Mediterranean. Irrigation systems were essential for the survival of communities in these exceptionally arid regions, and areas of ancient irrigated fields have been found in many parts of southern Arabia, for instance in the Wadi Beihan at the heart of the kingdom of Qataban. The Sabaean capital of Ma'rib depended on an impressive feat of early engineering: a massive stone-faced dam almost 600 metres in length, built in the 6th century BC. The city of Ma'rib itself covered over 100 hectares, and was surrounded by irrigated fields which drew water from the dam: cereals were the staple crop, and there were probably irrigated groves of myrrh trees. The success of the irrigation works of southern Arabia is evident in the prosperity and sophistication of the communities they supported: new kingdoms embarked on ambitious building projects, constructing temples, palaces and tombs which, while they were clearly influenced by Classical Greek and Roman architectural styles, retained a native identity.

The last of the kingdoms through which the camel caravans passed on their northward journey to the ports of the Mediterranean was Nabataea, and it is the impressive remains of the capital city, Petra, which provide the most striking illustration of the extraordinary impact of this lucrative trade on the desert cities. Situated in a mountainous area with few natural resources and little capacity for agriculture, Petra (a city of about 30,000 people) relied almost entirely on its control of the overland traffic between the frankincense and myrrh producing areas of the south and the expanding markets of the Mediterranean.

Difficulties of navigation may have discouraged the transport of south Arabian products up the Red Sea by boat throughout most of the first millennium BC, but as navigational skills improved an increasing proportion of trade began to use the sea routes. This development was revolutionised by the discovery of the monsoon wind system in the first century AD, which made direct contact by sea between southern Arabia and India possible. Slower and more expensive overland routes, and the kingdoms which depended upon them, declined, and the balance shifted in favour of states involved in maritime trade. Merchant ships plied their way along the coasts of India, the Gulf and the Red Sea and by the 4th century AD the kingdom of Axum in northern Ethiopia had become the dominant mercantile power in the Red Sea. Axum acted both as an exporter of ivory and other East African products, and as an intermediary in the maritime trade via the Red Sea between the Mediterranean world and the spice markets of India. Finds at Axum of Roman coins from the Mediterranean and Kushan coins from the borders of India testify to the extent of its commercial contacts. The site of Axum itself is marked today by an imposing series of over one hundred monolithic funerary stelae. This period of Axumite prosperity came to an end when the control of Red Sea trade passed to Islamic sailors in the 8th century AD.

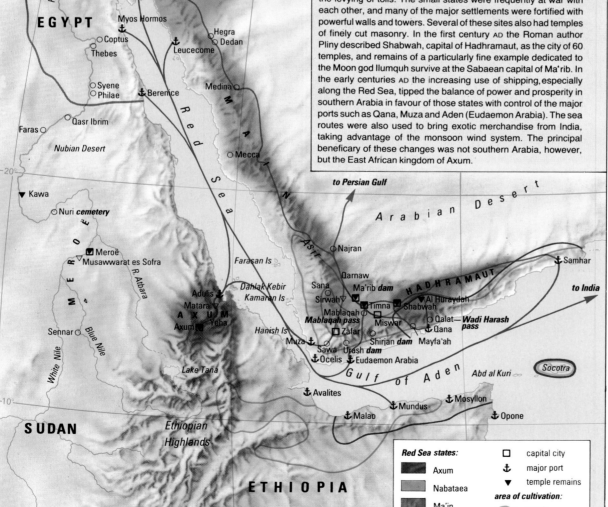

1 THE INCENSE STATES

The incense states of southern Arabia were linked to the prosperous cities of Egypt and the east Mediterranean by overland routes. Use of the overland routes through arid regions became more regular after the introduction of camels which could travel for longer periods without water than pack-asses and donkeys. For the most part the routes consisted of dusty desert tracks between settlements or waterholes, but within the kingdoms themselves paved roads were built in some places. These roads eased overland trade, especially where there was rough ground to be negotiated, but they also performed an important secondary function in channelling the traffic and levying tolls. The road over the Mablaqah pass from the kingdom of Qataban was paved for five kilometres, with a small reservoir for camels and travellers at each end. Another important route linked the principal frankincense areas of Hadhramaut with the port Qana through the Wadi Harash pass. The pass was blocked at the frontier of Hadhramaut by a wall with a single gate, both for defence and for the levying of tolls. The small states were frequently at war with each other, and many of the major settlements were fortified with powerful walls and towers. Several of these sites also had temples of finely cut masonry. In the first century AD the Roman author Pliny described Shabwah, capital of Hadhramaut, as the city of 60 temples, and remains of a particularly fine example dedicated to the Moon god Ilumquh survive at the Sabaean capital of Ma'rib. In the early centuries AD the increasing use of shipping, especially along the Red Sea, tipped the balance of power and prosperity in southern Arabia in favour of those states with control of the major ports such as Qana, Muza and Aden (Eudaemon Arabia). The sea routes were also used to bring exotic merchandise from India, taking advantage of the monsoon wind system. The principal beneficary of these changes was not southern Arabia, however, but the East African kingdom of Axum.

2 PETRA: A DESERT CAPITAL

The desert city of Petra, carved out of the sandstone mountains to the north-east of the Red Sea, is situated in a cliff-bound valley crossed by numerous wadis. Petra was the capital of the Nabataean kingdom, which at its height controlled a large area on the desert fringe of the Near East reaching from Sinai north towards Damascus. It may have been a trading centre as early as the 5th century BC, but the city reached its greatest prosperity between c. 100 BC and AD 150, and it is to this period that most of the visible remains belong, such as the monumental tombs cut into the cliffs which surround the site. Classical facades of these tombs reflect Petra's close trading links with the Hellenistic world. Of the city itself, relatively little is visible today apart from the public buildings of the central area, notably the colonnaded street dating from the period of Roman control. A reliable water supply was assured by numerous cisterns and an elaborate system of channels and earthenware pipes which brought the water of the Wadi Musa spring through the Siq to the heart of the city. Trade was the basis of Petra's prosperity, and when the trade routes went into decline during the 2nd–3rd centuries AD the city atrophied, and by the mid 6th century was effectively abandoned.

1 *Colonnade Street*	15 *Kasr el Bint Temple*
2 *Wadi Musa*	16 *altar*
3 *nymphaeum (public drinking fountain)*	17 *small temple*
4 *shrine*	
5 *upper market*	
6 *camel tethering ground*	
7 *lower market*	
8 *shops*	
9 *palace*	
10 *Atagartis Temple*	
11 *Great Temple*	
12 *pottery painter's workshop*	
13 *Temenos Gate*	
14 *Temenos (sacred precinct)*	

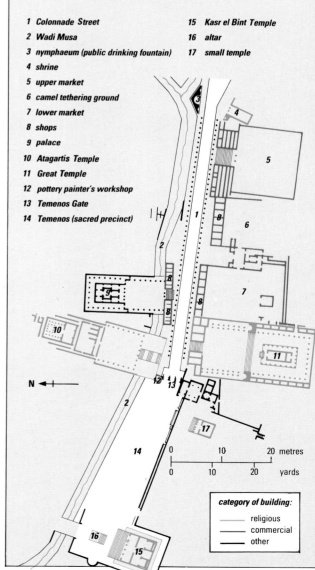

category of building:
— religious
— commercial
— other

Red Sea states:
- Axum
- Nabataea
- Ma'in
- Sabaea
- Qataban
- Hadhramaut

□ capital city
⚓ major port
▼ temple remains

area of cultivation:
⬭ myrrh
⬯ frankincense
— trade route
∿ Roman empire

3 RED SEA REMAINS

A Funerary statuette from south Arabian kingdom of Qataban, with name of deceased carved on base. 1st–2nd century AD, alabaster, height 27cm. B Axumite coin showing head of ruler, Emperor Ousanas, with cross in margin indicating that it post-dates the conversion of the kingdom to Christianity (c. AD 300). AD 286-317, gold, diameter 1.7cm. C Nabataean bowl, fine painted pottery vessel of a type found throughout the northern Red Sea area and southern Levant in the last centuries BC/1st century AD, illustrating the widespread trade carried out by the merchants of Nabataea. D Incense burner from southern Arabia, sides inscribed with names of four different kinds of incense. 2nd–1st century BC, stone, height 9.5cm.

The rock-cut tombs at Petra (above). E Palace Tomb one of the largest of the monuments of Petra, with a broad and complex facade (c.1st century AD). F Urn Tomb tall Classical facade with large tomb-chapel and three burial chambers. Probably the burial place of one of the last of the Nabataean kings (1st century AD). G Corinthian Tomb an early Nabataean experiment with the Hellenistic style of architecture, perhaps the burial place of a 1st century BC king of Petra.

These extraordinary tombs form part of a complex (below) cut into the cliffs to the east of the city.

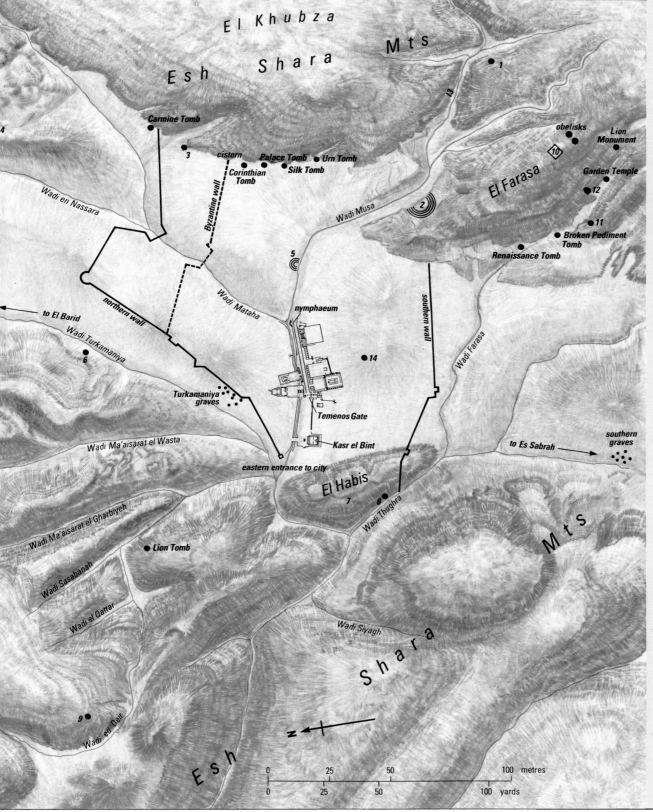

The remains of Petra (left) lie largely on a terrace in a broad valley which runs on a north–south axis. The valley is contained by a series of steep sandstone escarpments, which are veined with shades of purple, red and yellow. The landscape has been dissected by numerous seasonal watercourses or wadis, the principal of these being the Wadi Musa.

1 Khasneh or Treasury one of the first Hellenistic-inspired monuments of Petra (1st century BC), with rock-cut facade 28m wide and 40m high. **2 Theatre** with 33 rows of seats cut in the rock, faced by remains of stage and dressing rooms. Roman (2nd century AD). **3 Sextus Florentinus Tomb** a simple facade with inscription showing it to be the tomb of a Roman governor of Arabia of the early 2nd century AD. **4 Moghar en Nassara** an important suburb of Petra. Tomb facades are carved into the low cliffs of this area. **5 Small theatre. 6 Turkamaniya Tomb** with Nabataean inscription which lists the elements of the tomb complex, including garden, terrace, triclinium (chamber for funeral feasts 12), dwelling places, courtyard and porticoes in addition to the rock-cut facade and tomb chambers which are all that survive today. **7 Convent Group** buildings of various dates on the summit of the rocky outcrop of El Habis, centred on a garden area and sunken courtyard. **8 El Habis High Place** a shrine or offering-place with block altar on the western edge of the El Habis outcrop overlooking the wadi below. **9 The Deir** largest of the rock-cut monuments of Petra, probably built late 1st century AD. A boldly carved temple facade with central doorway 8m high leading to large rock-cut chamber. A stepped processional way led up to the levelled court in front of the Deir. **10 Attuf Ridge** 'High Place of Sacrifice', a shallow rectangular levelled area reached by three steps with raised altar equipped with rock-cut drains and basins for the blood of sacrifices and for washing. Reached from the city below by a stepped rock-cut processional way. **11 Roman Soldier Tomb** Classical facade with three statue-niches at 1st floor level, the central one holding a figure in Roman armour. The principal tomb chamber has arched recesses for corpses or coffins. **12 Triclinium** (2nd century AD) decorated internally with half-columns and pilasters. **13 The Siq** a narrow ravine lined with monuments which was the eastern entrance to Petra. Along the sides of the Siq are remains of earthenware pipes and a rock-cut channel, which brought water into the city from the east. **14 Faroun Pillar** originally one of a pair of ritual pillars in front of a temple of which little survives.

Imperial Persia

Two Iranian dynasties, the Parthians (c. 240 BC–AD 226) and Sasanians (AD 226–642) preserved in Iraq and Iran (ancient Mesopotamia and Persia) the cultural heritage of the great empires of the Near East – Assyrian, Babylonian and Achaemenid (pages 156–159). Despite the spread of Hellenism into Asia (page 164) and a long period of Roman domination, these dynasties brought about an impressive Persian renaissance.

The Parthians were of Iranian nomadic tribal stock from east of the Caspian Sea, with an early capital at Nisa, in Turkmenistan. From about 240 BC, the Parthians spread first east into Bactria, then west into Mesopotamia, consolidating their control of the region by 115 BC. The capital was established at Ctesiphon, opposite the great Hellenistic city of Seleucia-on-the-Tigris, the political centre of southern Mesopotamia. The Parthian state seems to have been feudal in its organisation, consisting of an aristocracy under the direct rule of the king. Substantial Parthian palaces, probably belonging to the aristocracy, have been excavated at Qal'eh-i Yazdigerd in western Persia, and at Ashur, Khirbat Jaddala and Nippur in Mesopotamia.

In these palaces and at Seleucia excavations have shown that the Hellenistic architectural legacy was supplanted by the indigenous iwan, a barrel-vaulted reception room open to a courtyard. Iwans were built in pairs facing one another, or symmetrically on all four sides of a courtyard. This architectual development reflects a more general tendency – Hellenistic art and culture was replaced in the 1st century AD by the revival of the indigenous tradition of the Near East.

The Parthians fought successfully against Rome in the 1st century, greatly benefiting from the use of heavily armoured cavalry, hitherto unknown in the Near East. In the 2nd century, however, internal disputes and economic recession loosened the grip of the central government. Ardashir, who was to become the first Sasanian King of Kings (shahanshah), led a rebellion in Fars in AD 224. In defeating the Parthians, Ardashir established his empire roughly along the frontiers of his predecessors – Mesopotamia, Persia and parts of Central Asia. Ctesiphon was again the capital, with royal cities at Istakhr, Bishapur and Gor (Firuzabad) in Fars.

Contrasting with the loose confederation of the Parthians, the Sasanian state was organised increasingly hierarchically; below the King of Kings there were numerous grades of nobles, priests, warriors, bureaucrats and peasantry. Zoroastrianism, a Persian monotheist religion founded by the prophet Zoroaster dating back to Achaemenid times, was established as a state religion – numerous fire-temples demonstrate its importance. Coming from Fars, the Sasanians emphasised the heritage of Persian kingship, descending from the Achaemenids. Monumental rock reliefs in their homeland celebrated the early achievements of the dynasty. Many other Sasanian artefacts – silver plates, seals and stucco statuary – show the King of Kings in glorious regalia or involved in royal pastimes such as hunting.

The Parthian and Sasanian empires were both funda-mentally agrarian. But there was also an important intermixture of nomads – Arab camel-herders on the western frontier of Mesopotamia, Luri and Kurdish sheep-herders in the Zagros highlands, Iranian and, later, Turkish nomads on the Central Asian frontier. Mesopotamia was the economic and cultural centre of gravity, although there was only a ruling class of Persians. The remaining population were Assyrians, Babylonians, Greeks, Babylonian Jews and Arabs.

After setbacks in the 5th century, the empire was re-formed by Khusrau Anushirvan (531–578). The land and its revenue was reorganised; in Mesopotamia the irrigation system, which dated back more than 3000 years, was extensively reworked. This development, which led to the highest density of settlement in ancient times, is now thought to have ruined the delicate natural drainage of lower Mesopotamia, and was partly responsible for the extensive depopulation of the Islamic period. Military administration was also reformed – the empire was divided into four zones, each with its own commander (marzban). An extensive ditch protected by forts was dug to protect the western frontier, and it was probably Anushirvan who built Alexander's Barrier, the great wall in the Gorgan Plain.

His grandson, Khusrau Parviz, the last great Sasanian king, conquered Syria and Egypt (614–628), before being defeated by the East Roman emperor Heraclius. A decade after his death, the empire was lost to Islam. But Sasanian culture lived on in the Abbasid Caliphate, and Iran was a dominant influence in the mediaeval Islamic world.

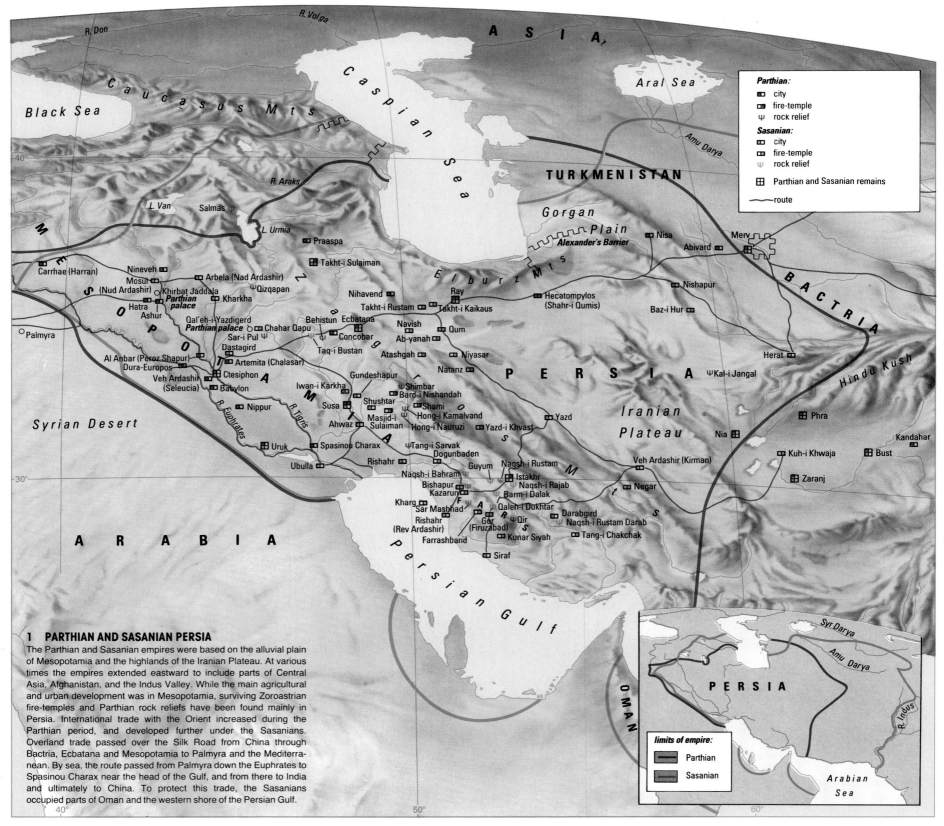

1 PARTHIAN AND SASANIAN PERSIA

The Parthian and Sasanian empires were based on the alluvial plain of Mesopotamia and the highlands of the Iranian Plateau. At various times the empires extended eastward to include parts of Central Asia, Afghanistan, and the Indus Valley. While the main agricultural and urban development was in Mesopotamia, surviving Zoroastrian fire-temples and Parthian rock reliefs have been found mainly in Persia. International trade with the Orient increased during the Parthian period, and developed further under the Sasanians. Overland trade passed over the Silk Road from China through Bactria, Ecbatana and Mesopotamia to Palmyra and the Mediterranean. By sea, the route passed from Palmyra down the Euphrates to Spasinou Charax near the head of the Gulf, and from there to India and ultimately to China. To protect this trade, the Sasanians occupied parts of Oman and the western shore of the Persian Gulf.

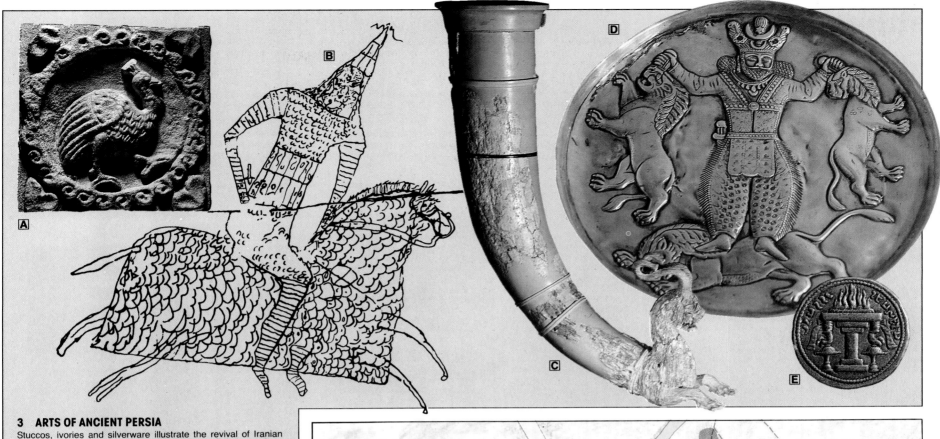

3 ARTS OF ANCIENT PERSIA

Stuccos, ivories and silverware illustrate the revival of Iranian and Near Eastern artistic traditions in the early centuries AD. The imperial ideology of Achaemenid Persia (*page 158*) re-surfaced in the Parthian and Sasanian period with the appearance of rock reliefs and *rhyta*(C).

A *Sasanian stucco relief with guinea fowl from the west iwan of a house at Ctesiphon. 6th century* AD, *width 25.5cm.* B *Graffito of an armoured cavalryman from Dura-Europos. c.2nd–3rd century* AD. C *Parthian rhyton (horn-shaped vessel) from Nisa, southern Turkmenistan. 2nd–1st century* BC, *ivory, length c.30cm.* D *Sasanian dish, with a portrait of either Bahram V (*AD*421–439) or Peroz (*AD*458–484) and a lion-hunting scene. Silver, diameter c.30.5cm.* E *Sasanian coin showing a Zoroastrian fire-altar. From the reign of Ardashir I (*AD*224–243), silver, diameter 2.5cm.*

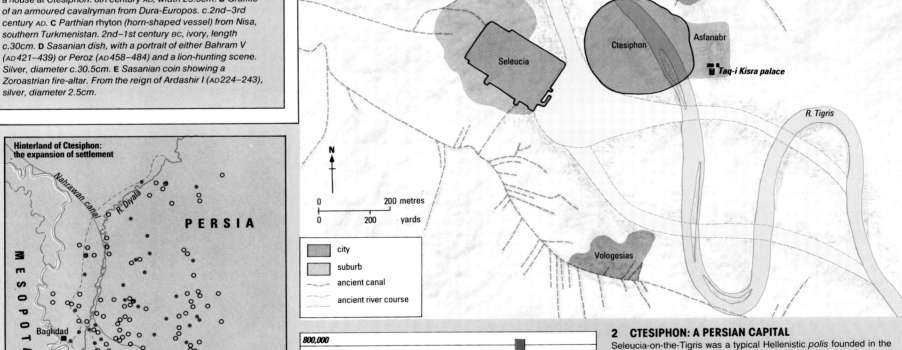

Hinterland of Ctesiphon: the expansion of settlement

PERSIA

MESOPOTAMIA

Baghdad

Ctesiphon
Seleucia

R. Tigris

Nahrawan canal

R. Diyala

- • town c.2100–625 BC
- ○ town c.AD 226–637
- *ancient river courses:*
- – – – c.2100–625 BC
- ——— c.AD 226–637

city
suburb
- – – ancient canal
——— ancient river course

Veh Antiokh Khusrau

Ctesiphon

Asfanabr

Taq-i Kisra palace

R. Tigris

Seleucia

Vologesias

N

0   200 metres
0   200   yards

Hinterland of Ctesiphon: population and settlement

- capital city
- urban
- town
- village and hamlet
- limited or doubtful data

800,000
600,000
400,000
200,000
100,000

3000 BC   2000 BC   1000 BC   BC/AD   AD 1000   AD 1857

2 CTESIPHON: A PERSIAN CAPITAL

Seleucia-on-the-Tigris was a typical Hellenistic *polis* founded in the 3rd century BC, laid out in a grid-pattern on the west bank of the river. Ctesiphon, on the east bank, became the main Parthian capital in the 1st century BC and the Sasanian capital from the 3rd century AD. The east bank was irrigated by the Nahrawan canal, the greatest Sasanian irrigation project, which led to the highest density of settlement in Mesopotamia in ancient times (*far left*), abandoned when it ran dry in c.1150. Comparison with earlier periods shows the great expansion of settlement in the Sasanian period (*see graph*). The round city, now cut by the Tigris, where the Sasanian White Palace was once located, was probably the old city. Asfanabr, the site of the Taq-i Kisra palace, and Veh Antiokh Khusrau, built for Roman captives, were both suburbs. The Taq-i Kisra (*below*) is a grand *iwan*, probably built in the 6th century.

0   5 m
0   5 yd

Buddhist India

With the demise of the Harappan cities at the beginning of the 2nd millennium BC the cultural centre of northern India shifted eastwards to the Yamuna and upper Ganges valleys, where townships such as Hastinapura and Ahicchatra flourished. Colonisation of the middle and lower Ganges had already begun in the 2nd millennium BC, and though at first hindered by dense monsoon forests and heavy alluvial soils, by c.1000 BC this movement had gained momentum with the introduction of iron tools which were used for both land clearance and cultivation. Rice farming was one of the principal factors in the settlement of the Ganges Plain; although the early villages

of the middle valley have also yielded remains of wheat, the communities of the lower Ganges depended exclusively on rice, and the build-up of population and the appearance of cities is directly related to its growing importance as a staple crop.

By 600 BC no fewer than 16 small states had developed in northern India, concentrated chiefly around the urban centres of the Ganges Plain. The cities were protected by great mud-brick ramparts some of which have been dated to the 5th or 6th century BC, for example at Kausambi in the middle Ganges and Ujjain to the south-west. A series of wars led finally to the absorption into the Mauryan empire of the Ganges city-states, together with the north-west, Nepal and a large part of the Deccan. The Empire, centred on the earlier Ganges kingdom of

Magadha, reached the peak of its power and prosperity in the 3rd century BC. The Mauryan capital at Pataliputra, near Patna, was a large and luxurious city, defended by a substantial timber-framed rampart and said by contemporary writers to have stretched for 14 kilometres along the Ganges. Excavations have revealed foundations of columned halls, and a stone column-capital showing strong Persian stylistic influence. In an attempt to unify his culturally and ethnically diverse realm, the Mauryan emperor Asoka developed a moral and ethical code which he promulgated throughout the empire by issuing a series of edicts incorporating Buddhist principles which were carved on stone pillars and smoothed rock surfaces. Their distribution indicates the wide extent of Asoka's rule which, though based in the urban sophisticated heartland

2 THE TEMPLES OF AJANTA

The rock-cut temples and monasteries at Ajanta are among the most important and impressive Buddhist remains in India. Set within a spectacular horseshoe cliff (*right*), they contain reliefs and wall paintings of superb quality. The site first became important in the late 2nd or 1st century BC, when two temples and three monasteries were cut into the cliff and decorated with fine wall paintings. It was during the later 5th century AD, however, that all the remaining caves were cut. The 21 monasteries of the second phase are more complex in form, with pillared halls, colonnades and verandahs, and in some the internal structures are on two levels. A pair of apsidal temples also belong to the later phase, and both they and the 21 monasteries are richly decorated. The relief carvings and wall paintings depict scenes from the life of the Buddha, and are among the greatest examples of early Indian art. **Above right** *palace scene from Ajanta. 5th–6th century AD.*

3 FROM THE IRON AGE TO BUDDHISM

A *Preaching Buddha seated on a throne, with a Bodhisattva carved against the drapery below, from Mardan. Gandhara, 2nd–3rd century AD, schist, height 95cm.* **B** *Relief from Nagarjunakonda (Amaravati school) showing, on the upper register, women sleeping and on the lower, a Bodhisattva about to leave the mortal world. 3rd century AD, height c.1.30m.* **C** *Two piece snaffle bit from Nagpur. 6th century BC, iron, length 26cm.* **D** *Axehead with crossed bands from Nagpur. 6th century BC, iron, length 28.3cm.* **E** *Yakshi (tree spirit) sculpture from Didarganj, Patna. Mauryan. 3rd century BC, height 1.6m.* **F** *Asokan column erected at Lauriya-Nandangarh. c.242 BC, polished sandstone, height 9.75m.*

of the Ganges Valley, also included large areas of southern India where political and economic organisation was less developed.

During the final centuries BC the prosperity of the northern cities was greatly increased by trade, and Magadha benefited from its strategic position on both the river route leading to the port of Tamluk in the Ganges delta, and the important overland routes to the trading cities of Taxila and Charsadda in the north-west. In southern India maritime trade based on the exploitation of the newly discovered monsoon wind system, and geared largely to the demand of the Roman world for ivory, spices and other Indian products, developed more slowly. Roman coins have been found at the ancient ports of southern India such as Muzirs and Kaveripattinam,

while at Arikamedu part of a Roman trading station has been unearthed. The stimulus of these trading contacts contributed to the rise of cities and states in southern India and Ceylon in the late 1st millennium BC.

The earliest Indian irrigation systems may be dated to this period, and today the most impressive remains are to be found in the south, in particular in Ceylon. In the 1st and 2nd centuries BC these systems were small-scale and local in character, but during the first five centuries AD large-scale irrigation projects were carried out under state direction around the island's main cities, notably Anuradhapura. Schemes such as the impressive Kalava reservoir, which supplied an area of 466 square kilometres around Anuradhapura with water, contributed greatly to the growing prosperity of Ceylon and the south.

By the end of the 1st millenium BC Buddhism had become the most prominent religion in northern India (page 260). The oldest remains at many of the great sites associated with the Buddha (such as Sarnath and Sravasti) date from the 3rd century BC, and it was at this time that Buddhism spread to Ceylon and the first of the monasteries at Anuradhapura were founded. Conspicuous among these early monuments is the *stupa*, a domed mound containing relics, and the focal point of many religious complexes such as Sanchi. The golden age of early Buddhist art came in the first five centuries AD, when the important monasteries of Amaravati, Ajanta and Nagarjunakonda were founded and embellished, while in the north-west Buddhist themes figure prominently in Indo-Hellenistic Gandharan culture.

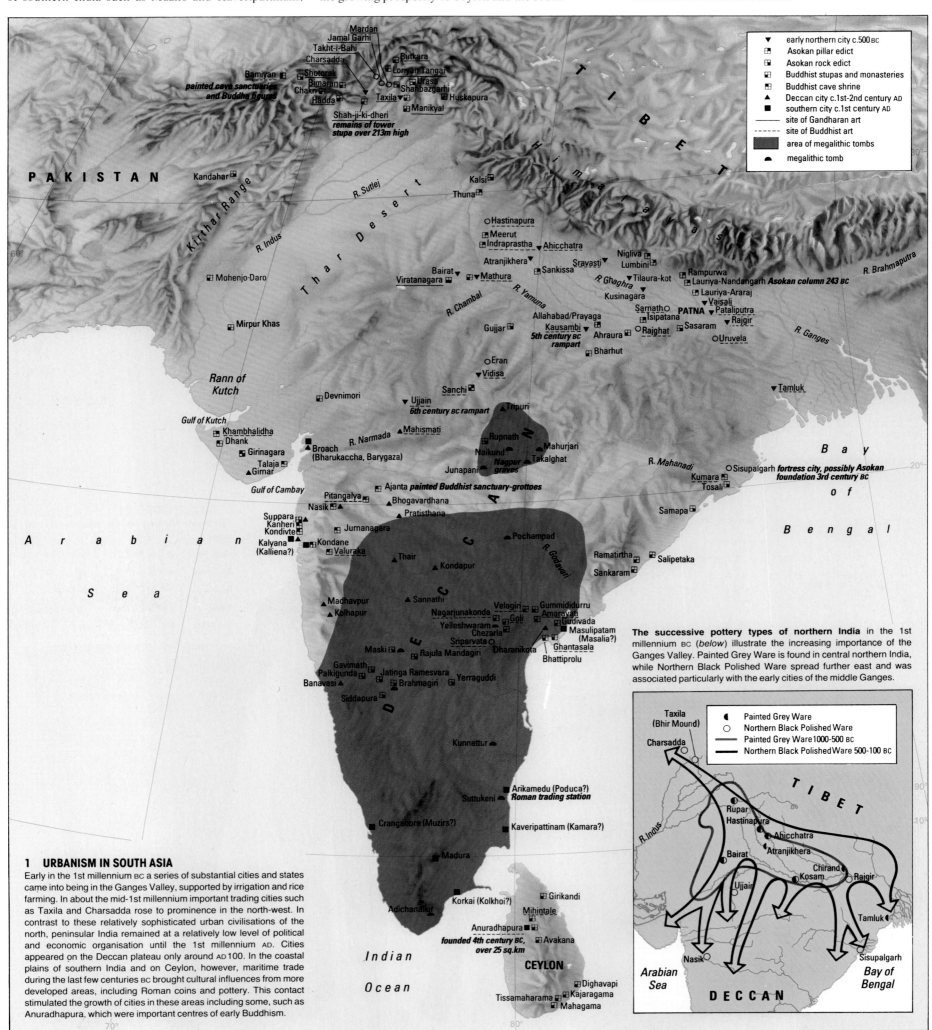

The successive pottery types of northern India in the 1st millennium BC (*below*) illustrate the increasing importance of the Ganges Valley. Painted Grey Ware is found in central northern India, while Northern Black Polished Ware spread further east and was associated particularly with the early cities of the middle Ganges.

1 URBANISM IN SOUTH ASIA

Early in the 1st millennium BC a series of substantial cities and states came into being in the Ganges Valley, supported by irrigation and rice farming. In about the mid-1st millennium important trading cities such as Taxila and Charsadda rose to prominence in the north-west. In contrast to these relatively sophisticated urban civilisations of the north, peninsular India remained at a relatively low level of political and economic organisation until the 1st millennium AD. Cities appeared on the Deccan plateau only around AD 100. In the coastal plains of southern India and on Ceylon, however, maritime trade during the last few centuries BC brought cultural influences from more developed areas, including Roman coins and pottery. This contact stimulated the growth of cities in these areas including some, such as Anuradhapura, which were important centres of early Buddhism.

Trans-Asian trade

During the 1st millennium BC both eastern and western Asia witnessed a dramatic urban expansion: cities such as Chang'an and Alexandria may have had populations exceeding 500,000. The expansion of trade stimulated by such huge populations culminated in extensive trans-Asian networks linking China to the east Mediterranean.

Long-distance trade across Asia followed two principal routes: overland and maritime. The best known crossed the steppes and deserts of Central Asia, linking China with western Asia and Europe. Although it has been called the Silk Road it did not carry silks alone, nor was it a single road, but a diverse group of caravan routes between oasis towns. Chinese silks appeared in the West as early as 550 BC. Fragments have been found in the Kerameikos cemetery at Athens, and in northern Europe silk furnished Hallstatt burials at Hohmichele and Hochdorf (Eberdingen). Finds of Han bronze mirrors in the Ukraine and of rich silk-clothed burials at Panticapaeum (Kerch), suggest a route to the Black Sea. Chinese goods also reached the far north through the nomadic Steppe peoples of Central Asia.

During the Han dynasty silks were sent westwards by the Chinese, not for commercial gain, but mainly to pacify the nomadic tribes along the border. A little later, silk became especially fashionable in the Roman empire; Pliny the Elder complained about the lavish and decadent use of the new material. Silk fragments have even been found as far afield as the British Isles. Other items were also sent west: spices, furs, lacquer and especially bronze objects. It is uncertain what products from the West were sent eastwards in exchange – traded goods probably included gold and silver coins, ivory, precious stones, coral, amber and manufactured glass vessels.

The journey across Asia was exceptionally dangerous and few traders traversed the whole distance, most travelling instead only certain stages between well-established towns. These desert 'ports' grew wealthy through their control of the trade, and flourished during the Tang dynasty (AD 618–906), perhaps the only time when formal caravans of traders travelled westwards. Remains from Turfan and the margins of the Takla Makan desert, demonstrate great achievements in art and culture after the conversion to Buddhism in the 6th century AD. Long-distance trade across Central Asia finally ended during the Sung dynasty (960–1279), by which time very much cheaper and safer maritime routes were offering a viable alternative.

Trade by sea between the Indus and the Persian Gulf was established by the 3rd millennium BC, while maritime societies had developed in South-East Asia, the Bay of Bengal and the Gulf of Aden by about 500 BC. Indonesians may have settled on the African island of Madagascar by the early 1st century AD. Much information about this commerce comes from a Greek trading manual of the 1st century AD, called *The Periplus of the Erythraean Sea*. The seasonal reversals of the monsoon winds, which made it possible to sail direct from the Red Sea to India, were well known by the 1st century AD, when there was a massive expansion in Roman trade with the East. Many hoards of Roman gold coins have been found in southern India, while other Roman coin finds extend from Indo-China to East Africa. Two trading ports at either end of the route, Poduca (Arikamedu) in southern India and Leucos Limen (Quseir el-Qadim) on the Red Sea, contained similar Roman pottery despite their distance apart. The main products of India, according to *The Periplus of the Erythraean Sea*, were spices and cloth. Chinese silks also reached India overland and were sent on by sea to the West. Maritime trade in silk was probably as important as the overland route in Central Asia.

Several groups developed as specialist traders in the Indian Ocean during the late classical period. In the 6th century, merchants from Axum in Ethiopia traded in silk between Ceylon and the Mediterranean. The Sasanians from Persia operated an active commercial network throughout the western Indian Ocean, and may be identified with the Possu, who are documented in Chinese ports by 671. However, direct sailing to China was not started until the late 8th century, when Muslim merchants travelled from the Persian Gulf.

The future lay with Islam. During the 8th century AD Muslim merchants gained control of maritime trade from the Red Sea to India and beyond, spreading Islamic culture and religion around the rim of the Indian Ocean from East Africa to South-East Asia. Their supremacy was to remain unbroken until the intrusion of European shipping in the 16th and 17th centuries AD.

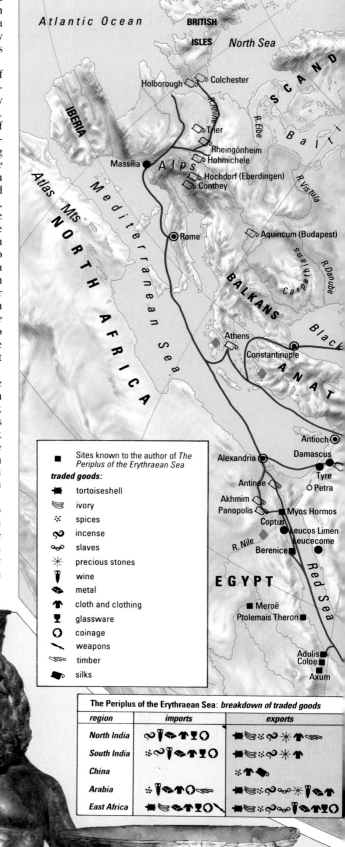

Sites known to the author of *The Periplus of the Erythraean Sea*

traded goods:
- tortoiseshell
- ivory
- spices
- incense
- slaves
- precious stones
- wine
- metal
- cloth and clothing
- glassware
- coinage
- weapons
- timber
- silks

The Periplus of the Erythraean Sea: *breakdown of traded goods*

region	imports			exports		
North India						
South India						
China						
Arabia						
East Africa						

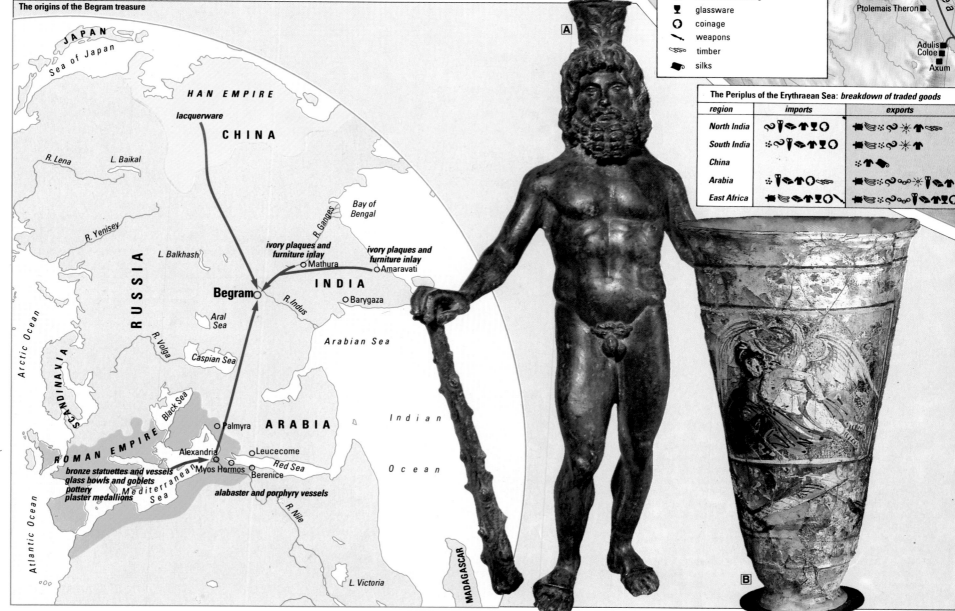

The origins of the Begram treasure

HAN EMPIRE — lacquerware

CHINA

ivory plaques and furniture inlay (Mathura)

ivory plaques and furniture inlay (Amaravati)

Begram

INDIA

ROMAN EMPIRE

bronze statuettes and vessels
glass bowls and goblets
pottery
plaster medallions

alabaster and porphyry vessels

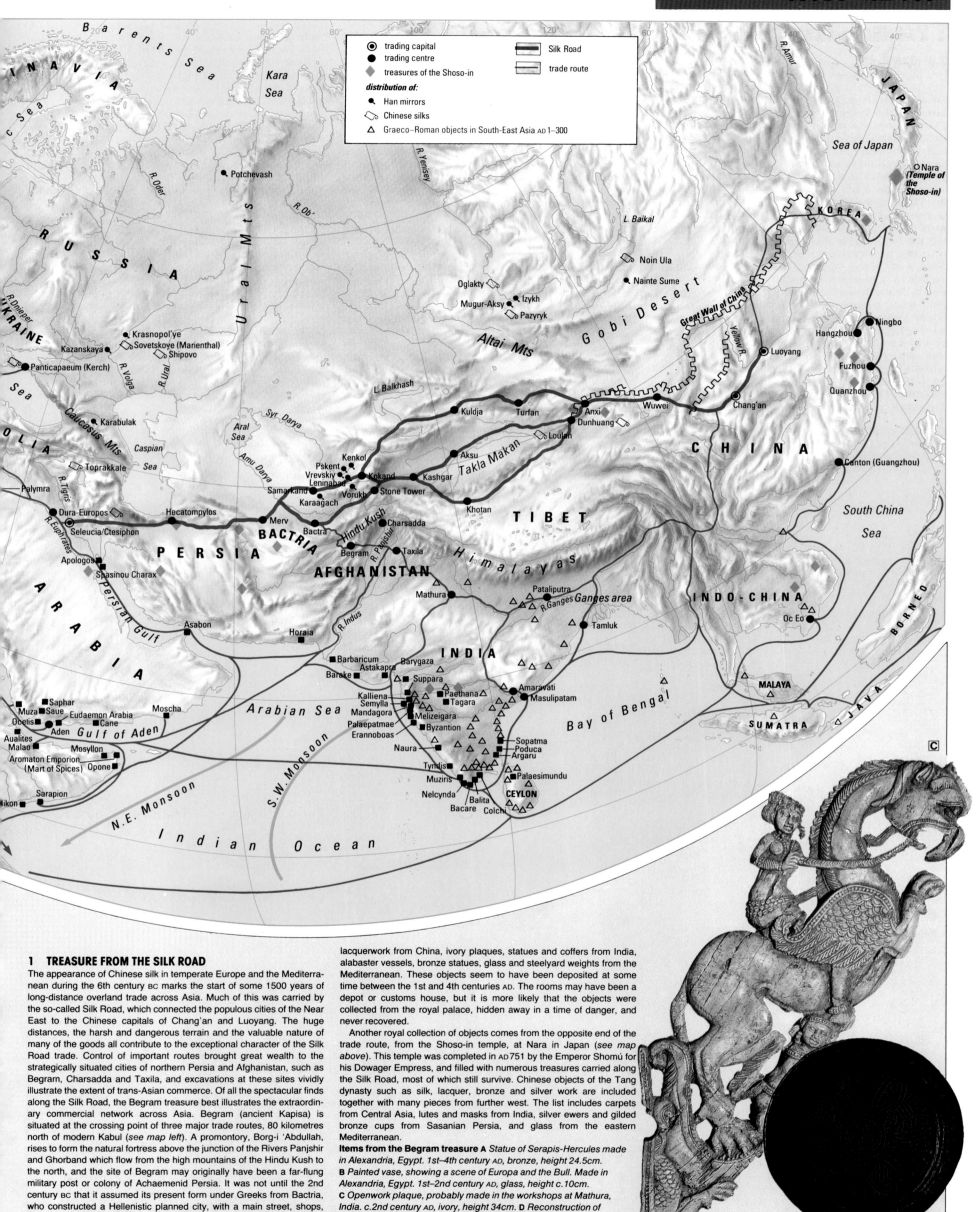

KEY

- ⊙ trading capital
- ● trading centre
- ◆ treasures of the Shoso-in
- ▬ Silk Road
- ▭ trade route

distribution of:
- ● Han mirrors
- ◠ Chinese silks
- △ Graeco–Roman objects in South-East Asia AD 1–300

1 TREASURE FROM THE SILK ROAD

The appearance of Chinese silk in temperate Europe and the Mediterranean during the 6th century BC marks the start of some 1500 years of long-distance overland trade across Asia. Much of this was carried by the so-called Silk Road, which connected the populous cities of the Near East to the Chinese capitals of Chang'an and Luoyang. The huge distances, the harsh and dangerous terrain and the valuable nature of many of the goods all contribute to the exceptional character of the Silk Road trade. Control of important routes brought great wealth to the strategically situated cities of northern Persia and Afghanistan, such as Begram, Charsadda and Taxila, and excavations at these sites vividly illustrate the extent of trans-Asian commerce. Of all the spectacular finds along the Silk Road, the Begram treasure best illustrates the extraordinary commercial network across Asia. Begram (ancient Kapisa) is situated at the crossing point of three major trade routes, 80 kilometres north of modern Kabul (*see map left*). A promontory, Borg-i 'Abdullah, rises to form the natural fortress above the junction of the Rivers Panjshir and Ghorband which flow from the high mountains of the Hindu Kush to the north, and the site of Begram may originally have been a far-flung military post or colony of Achaemenid Persia. It was not until the 2nd century BC that it assumed its present form under Greeks from Bactria, who constructed a Hellenistic planned city, with a main street, shops, houses and public buildings. In 1938, a Belgian expedition discovered two bricked-up storerooms filled with objects of enormous value;

lacquerwork from China, ivory plaques, statues and coffers from India, alabaster vessels, bronze statues, glass and steelyard weights from the Mediterranean. These objects seem to have been deposited at some time between the 1st and 4th centuries AD. The rooms may have been a depot or customs house, but it is more likely that the objects were collected from the royal palace, hidden away in a time of danger, and never recovered.

Another royal collection of objects comes from the opposite end of the trade route, from the Shoso-in temple, at Nara in Japan (*see map above*). This temple was completed in AD 751 by the Emperor Shomú for his Dowager Empress, and filled with numerous treasures carried along the Silk Road, most of which still survive. Chinese objects of the Tang dynasty such as silk, lacquer, bronze and silver work are included together with many pieces from further west. The list includes carpets from Central Asia, lutes and masks from India, silver ewers and gilded bronze cups from Sasanian Persia, and glass from the eastern Mediterranean.

Items from the Begram treasure A *Statue of Serapis-Hercules made in Alexandria, Egypt. 1st–4th century AD, bronze, height 24.5cm.*
B *Painted vase, showing a scene of Europa and the Bull. Made in Alexandria, Egypt. 1st–2nd century AD, glass, height c.10cm.*
C *Openwork plaque, probably made in the workshops at Mathura, India. c.2nd century AD, ivory, height 34cm.* **D** *Reconstruction of Chinese lacquerware cup, based on fragments found in the Begram treasure. Han dynasty (206 BC–AD 220), estimated diameter c.13cm.*

Chou China

In the 11th century BC political power in China passed from the Shang dynasty to the Chou (Zhou), a rival state lying to the north of the Shang capital at Anyang. The 800-year period which follows takes its name from the Chou dynasty, though in fact central authority collapsed in the 8th century BC and thenceforth the Chou were only one of a number of states contending for political and military supremacy. By the 5th century seven major kingdoms had emerged, and over the next 250 years these engaged in a violent struggle which culminated in the victory of the Ch'in and the unification of China by Shih huang-ti, the first emperor, in 221 BC. Despite these unsettled conditions the lst millennium BC was a time of major cultural, economic and technological advances, with the introduction of iron and the spread of Chinese urban civilisation to new areas.

The early Chou state, or Western Chou (11th–8th centuries BC), was very much a continuation of the Shang period. This is shown by similarity in building techniques, tomb types, bronze vessels, and the use of the same writing system. The Chou kings maintained power by granting fiefdoms (feudal estates) to relatives and worthies on whose allegiance they could rely. The feudal organisation of the Chou period is documented by bronze vessels which bear inscriptions recording the granting of lands to vassals in return for political and military allegiance. The famous Kang Hou *gui* (urn), for example, records the grant of territory to Marquis Kang in return for his part in quelling a rebellion.

The capital moved east to Luoyang in 770 BC, an event which marks the beginning of the Eastern Chou, and a period of struggle for supremacy among many small states. The fragmentation of the Chou state in the 8th century also marked the beginning of a period of change and innovation. One of the most important new features was the development of iron metallurgy. Meteoric iron had been used in the cutting edges of bronze axes in the Shang period, but it was only in the 6th century BC that iron-smelting from local ores began on a significant scale. Chinese iron-working used casting from around 500 BC to manufacture huge quantities of iron tools and weapons. The introduction of cast-iron agricultural tools and wooden tools with iron tips greatly increased the productivity of the land and helped feed the growing population.

Towns and cities were increasing in both size and number, though since the buildings were largely of wood little survives except the rammed-earth foundations. Remains also survive of the walls, gates and ditches which protected the cities in these troubled times. Wherever possible, the rectangular city-plan was favoured, as in the Shang period, but the density of occupation within the walls was much higher than at Shang sites, and included not only ceremonial and aristocratic buildings but also industrial quarters and the houses of ordinary individuals.

Some of the most vivid evidence for life in 1st millennium China comes from tombs, especially the richly furnished burials of kings and aristocrats. The form of the tombs varies from region to region: in central China they consisted of a deep shaft with a timber chamber at the bottom, while in the east and north multi-chambered tombs of brick or stone are found, and in the west, rock-cut graves are common. The high level of craft skill available to the wealthy is well illustrated by tombs in the Chu kingdom of the Yangtze valley, which contained musical instruments, lacquerware, elaborately carved and painted wooden figurines and paintings on silk.

Coinage first came into use in China around 500 BC, the earliest coins being miniature bronze spades and knives with an inscription recording their place of origin. Their form reflects an earlier stage when full-sized knives and spades were used in barter. By the 3rd century BC the simpler disc-shaped bronze coin had replaced the older types. Disc coins with a central hole so that they could be threaded on a cord became the standard Chinese coin of the Han period (*page 194*).

City defences and finds of bronze and iron weaponry reflect the endemic warfare of the Warring States period, 403–221 BC. An important new invention was the crossbow, probably first used in the 4th century BC. For greater security several of the states of northern China built frontier walls, some for protection against neighbouring states, others against the ever-present threat of the nomadic peoples to the north. The concept of a frontier wall reached its fullest expression only after the unification of China in 221 BC, however, when the first emperor, **Shih Huang-ti**, incorporated parts of earlier walls into a continuous barrier over 1000 miles long. Repaired, rebuilt and extended, the Great Wall (*page 154*) continued to stand as a symbol of Chinese power throughout the long imperial age which followed.

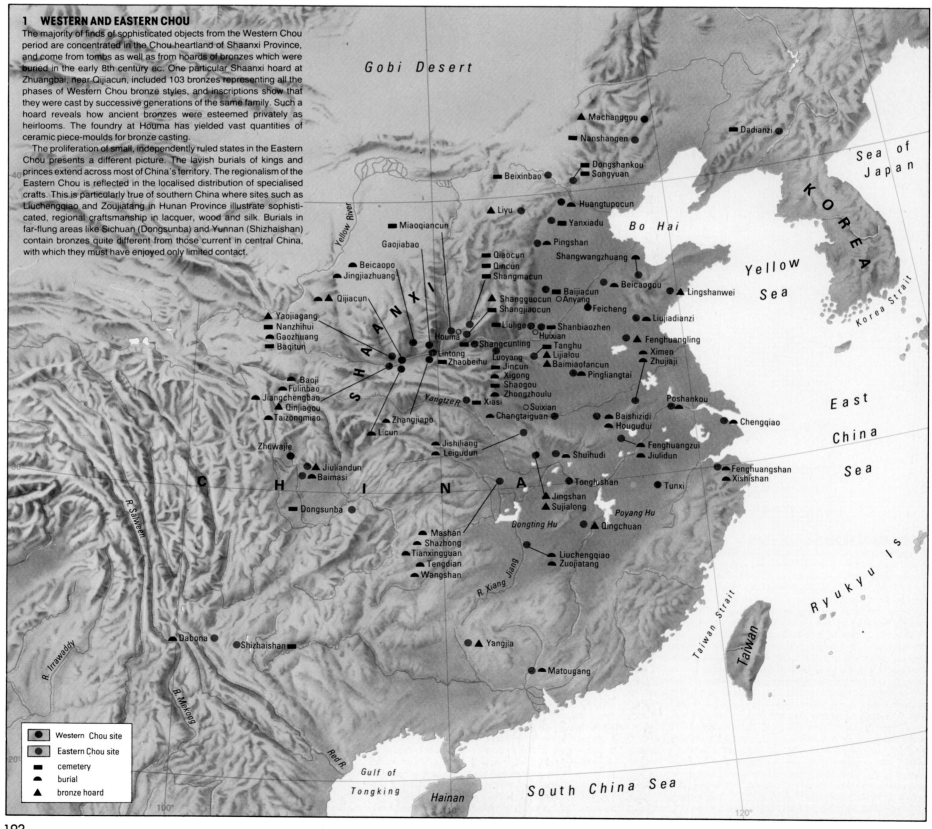

1 WESTERN AND EASTERN CHOU
The majority of finds of sophisticated objects from the Western Chou period are concentrated in the Chou heartland of Shaanxi Province, and come from tombs as well as from hoards of bronzes which were buried in the early 8th century BC. One particular Shaanxi hoard at Zhuangbai, near Qijiacun, included 103 bronzes representing all the phases of Western Chou bronze styles, and inscriptions show that they were cast by successive generations of the same family. Such a hoard reveals how ancient bronzes were esteemed privately as heirlooms. The foundry at Houma has yielded vast quantities of ceramic piece-moulds for bronze casting.

The proliferation of small, independently ruled states in the Eastern Chou presents a different picture. The lavish burials of kings and princes extend across most of China's territory. The regionalism of the Eastern Chou is reflected in the localised distribution of specialised crafts. This is particularly true of southern China where sites such as Liuchengqiao and Zoujiatang in Hunan Province illustrate sophisticated, regional craftsmanship in lacquer, wood and silk. Burials in far-flung areas like Sichuan (Dongsunba) and Yunnan (Shizhaishan) contain bronzes quite different from those current in central China, with which they must have enjoyed only limited contact.

Western Chou site
Eastern Chou site
cemetery
burial
bronze hoard

3 CHOU CRAFTSMANSHIP

A *Winged beast from the royal tombs of Zhonghsan, at Pingshan. 4th century BC, bronze inlaid with silver, height 24cm.* **B** *Bi-valve mould for casting a tiger from Houma. 5th–4th century BC, pottery, length 18cm.* **C** *Bo bell from Chìn state. 5th century BC, bronze, height 54cm.* **D** *The Kang Hou gui (urn) and inscription. 11th–10th century BC, bronze, height 54cm.* **E** *Cast-iron agricultural implement from Huixian. 481–221 BC.* **F** *Three coins. c.250 BC, bronze, length of knife coin 14 cm. Length of spade coin 4.6cm, diameter of round coin 3.3cm.* **G** *Seated stag from the tombs of Marquis Yi of Zeng at Suixian. 5th century BC, lacquer, height 86.5cm.* **H** *Eastern Chou swords. 4th–3rd century BC, bronze, length c. 50cm.*

2 TONGLUSHAN: A CHINESE COPPER MINE

The mining and refining of copper ore on a large scale was essential to the high output of bronze vessels, weaponry and fittings in the Shang and Chou periods. The most extensive ancient mines known are those at Tonglushan close to the Yangtze River which were mined during the Eastern Chou and Han periods. Pottery sherds dating from the Western Chou have also been found at the site, suggesting that the mines may have been exploited even earlier. Mining galleries reach more than 50 metres below the surface. Each deposit was worked from the lowest level upwards, so first an inclined shaft was sunk to the bottom of the ore seam. A horizontal gallery was then excavated and worked in rising sections until the seam had been exhausted. The ores were roughly graded in the initial stages of mining, and rock and poor quality pieces were used to fill the gaps left by material already extracted. Vertical shafts were erected for conveying ore to the surface in buckets, which were also used to drain water from the galleries through wooden channels. Ventilation was maintained by blocking disused galleries in order to control the air flow produced by the different level of shaft openings. Burnt bamboo slips adhering to the walls in some galleries indicate the means of lighting the mines. Wooden hammers and shovels, and bronze axes were found in the earlier shafts, while those of Han dynasty date were mostly made of iron. Bronze was widely used in China at this period, and its composition varied from a copper–tin alloy with occasional lead traces, to a copper–lead–tin alloy, or even simply copper and lead. Copper was in all cases the principal component, however, and copper mines such as those at Tonglushan must have played an important role in the metallurgy of early China.

Han China

The Warring States period (403-221 BC), a time when seven major states contended for supremacy (*page 192*), was followed by the unification of the whole of China, under the Ch'in (Qin) dynasty. New systems of law and administration were set up and the empire was divided into provinces, or commanderies, which continued almost unchanged throughout the succeeding Han dynasty. The authoritarian Ch'in government encouraged new technology, which in turn increased production. New roads and canals were constructed and the first Great Wall was built. However, the regime was short-lived – its rule was harsh and a rebellion led to its downfall.

The Han dynasty, which succeeded the Ch'in, was divided into two periods: the Former Han (206 BC–AD 2) with its capital at Chang'an, and the Later Han (AD 25–220) based at Luoyang. The most spectacular archaeological remains of the Han period are tombs. The luxurious way of life of the elite is reflected in their burials, which contained rich artefacts in gold, bronze, jade, silk and lacquer. Material conditions in the next world were thought to be much the same as on Earth, so an array of everyday items was also buried with the deceased. These give a fascinating insight into Chinese life, and include clay models of farmsteads, carts, boats, cooking stoves, and even individual servants. Impressed and painted decorations on tomb walls depict everyday scenes such as farming and industries such as salt mining. Documents, providing useful historical information, are also often found in Han tombs. Written on silk, bamboo slips or paper, which was invented in the 1st century BC, they cover religious subjects such as Confucianism and Taoism, as well as military and administrative matters. Stelae erected at the mausoleum entrances often identify the tomb occupants – giving the ancestry and official status of the individual.

One of the most important industries in Han China was iron-working, nationalised in 119 BC. There were 49 state foundries, with enormous blast furnaces built of heat-resistant bricks. Cast iron had been manufactured in China since 500 BC, but new techniques for creating higher smelting temperatures improved products, enabling more resilient weapons and a greater variety of everyday items to be manufactured. Agriculture also benefited; the ploughshare was redesigned and improved and the seed machine was introduced. Dykes and canals were built to irrigate farm land and prevent flooding. One canal was 125 kilometres long and linked the Yellow River to Chang'an. It was used for transporting grain to the capital to feed the large urban population.

China's main export item was silk, traded overland through Central Asia along the Silk Road, although in later Han times there was an increase in the volume of sea trade. Shipyards have been found at Canton in the south and goods were transported from there to the north by river. Imports included wool, glass, pearls, jade, fur and spices – and by land, horses. Silk reached as far afield as Rome in the 1st century BC, and was traded there by land and sea. Western influences were brought to China by the Greek, Persian and Indian merchants who travelled along the Silk Road, and Chinese art styles, as well as Buddhism (*page 260*), spread to Central Asia by the same route.

Chang'an, the first Han capital of China, was more like an enormous imperial court than a city, with two thirds of the space inside the walls taken up by palace complexes. There were also two markets and residential areas, while outside the walls were parks, hunting grounds and further housing. Unfortunately, there are few standing remains – just fragments of the rammed-earth wall, which would have had a perimeter of 25 kilometres, and twelve gates. High pavilions became popular during the Former Han period, and Chang'an is said to have boasted one 115 metres high.

Under the Later Han, there was a move towards decentralisation; the nationalised industries and state monopolies were relaxed and ownership passed into private hands. Trade flourished, especially by sea, and land-owners, merchants and the upper classes became increasingly rich and powerful. There was a marked movement of population towards the south, and the capital was moved east to Luoyang. From the mid-2nd century AD, however, the empire was weakened by an increasing number of power struggles at Court, while in the countryside there were constant uprisings due to the poverty and oppression of the peasants. The resulting anarchy caused the demise of the Han dynasty in AD 220, and China was divided into three independent states. It was not to be unified again until the 6th century, when Chinese civilisation rose to new heights under the Sui and Tang dynasties (*page 262*).

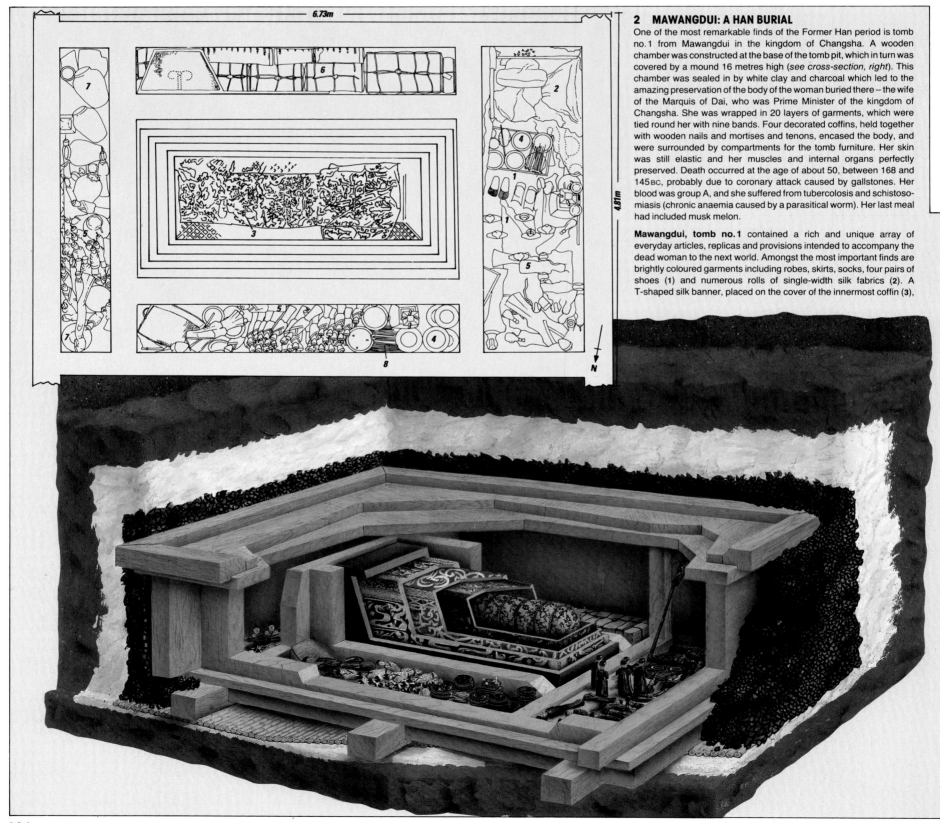

2 MAWANGDUI: A HAN BURIAL

One of the most remarkable finds of the Former Han period is tomb no. 1 from Mawangdui in the kingdom of Changsha. A wooden chamber was constructed at the base of the tomb pit, which in turn was covered by a mound 16 metres high (*see cross-section, right*). This chamber was sealed in by white clay and charcoal which led to the amazing preservation of the body of the woman buried there – the wife of the Marquis of Dai, who was Prime Minister of the kingdom of Changsha. She was wrapped in 20 layers of garments, which were tied round her with nine bands. Four decorated coffins, held together with wooden nails and mortises and tenons, encased the body, and were surrounded by compartments for the tomb furniture. Her skin was still elastic and her muscles and internal organs perfectly preserved. Death occurred at the age of about 50, between 168 and 145 BC, probably due to coronary attack caused by gallstones. Her blood was group A, and she suffered from tuberculosis and schistosomiasis (chronic anaemia caused by a parasitical worm). Her last meal had included musk melon.

Mawangdui, tomb no. 1 contained a rich and unique array of everyday articles, replicas and provisions intended to accompany the dead woman to the next world. Amongst the most important finds are brightly coloured garments including robes, skirts, socks, four pairs of shoes (**1**) and numerous rolls of single-width silk fabrics (**2**). A T-shaped silk banner, placed on the cover of the innermost coffin (**3**),

3 HAN CHINA: EVERYDAY LIFE

A *Tomb model of a house. Such tomb models provide valuable evidence of the construction and appearance of Chinese houses. Han dynasty, pottery, height c.20cm.* **B** *Brick relief depicting ploughing from tomb structure at Yangzishan, Sichuan. Han dynasty, AD 100-200.* **C** *Horse-drawn chariot from the tomb of a general at Leitai, Wuwei. Such carriages were used by the upper strata of society. Later Han dynasty, bronze, 2nd century AD, height 43.5cm.*

Key:
- ■ city
- ◣ burial
- ▨ kingdom
- ▭ commandery
- 〰 defensive wall
- — Han empire

1 IMPERIAL CHINA: THE HAN DYNASTY

Han China was divided into commanderies, each run by a civil governor and a military general. Up until the 1st century AD, most of China's population of 58 million was concentrated in the north.

FROM A HAN DYNASTY BURIAL

Burial goods at Mawangdui include A *Group of painted peachwood musicians; their instruments include zithers and 12-pitch pipes. Height 30-38cm.* **B** *Polychrome painting on silk, which acted as a banner at the head of the woman's funerary procession. The top section represents heaven, with the gates manned by two guardians. In the centre is the tomb occupant with her attendants, and below, scenes of the underworld, including a sacrifice, perhaps to help the woman's soul on the journey to heaven. Length 205cm.* **C** *Lacquerware tray, bearing plates, mugs and a cup, with a typical cloud design. Lacquer utensils were frequently used by the upper classes. Length 60cm.* **D** *Silk shoes with ties, length 24cm.*

Mawangdui: cross-section of tomb

- tomb mound
- 20 metres
- packed earth tomb pit
- packed earth tomb walls
- original earth
- charcoal
- tomb chamber
- white clay
- 2.8 metres

depicts the dead person's journey to the afterworld. The tomb also contained the largest and best-preserved group of lacquerware (**4**) ever unearthed in China, including toilet boxes, tripods, vases, spoons, ladles, cups and trays, pitchers, armrests and screens. A total of 162 wooden tomb figures were discovered (**5**), including female attendants, musicians and dancers all in silk costumes. The musical instruments included a zither 1.16 metres in length, with its 25 strings and bridges still intact, an organ with 22 pipes arranged in two rows and twelve pitch pipes of varying length. One side compartment was completely filled with bamboo cases (**6**) c.48-50 centimetres in length, containing a variety of garments, silk fabrics, foodstuffs, herbal medicines and funerary models. Elsewhere, pottery boxes and vases (**7**), were found and food remains from these vessels included grains such as rice, wheat, millet, and fruit such as pears and plums. Hare, dog, chicken, sparrow, carp and bream bones were also found. Scattered throughout, were bamboo fans, baskets and mats, bronze mirrors, tin bells, clay imitations of bronze and gold coins, toilet articles and seals. Over 300 bamboo slips (**8**), each c.28 centimetres in length, listed name, size and quantity of funerary object plus a summary of each type of tomb furniture.

Korea and Japan

The introduction of bronze and iron technology to Japan and Korea in the 1st millennium BC, and the firm establishment of millet and rice agriculture, ended long periods of Postglacial foraging and horticulture. In 108 BC north-western Korea was colonised by the Han dynasty, and Chinese commanderies – centres of military control – were established in the north of the Korean peninsula and Manchuria. Trade generated by the Chinese colonists in precious goods such as bronze mirrors, and raw materials such as iron, greatly increased cultural and commercial contact throughout Korea, western Japan and the Yellow Sea region in the first few centuries AD.

Bronze technology first reached the Korean peninsula from Manchuria in c.1000 BC, long before the Han period. The Manchurian connection is reflected in the style of some of the earliest Korean bronzes, although distinctive Korean variants soon developed; the lute-shaped dagger was transformed in the hands of Korean craftsmen into a sharp, functional weapon. Other early Korean bronze items included mirrors with incised line decoration and carriage-horse trappings. Bronze technology was restricted to the manufacture of weapons and ornaments that probably served as status symbols for elite groups, and are frequently found in burials. Dolmens – simple stone structures placed over burials – are also thought to be status symbols, and two regional styles are known: large table-shaped dolmens in the north, and later, capstones set on cobbles on the ground in the south. In the north, both dolmens and pit-houses – so called because they were usually slightly sunken below ground level – have yielded very few bronzes, although ring-shaped axes of polished stone and plain pottery have been found in northern dolmens.

A north–south division is also apparent in the subsistence patterns of Korea during this period, largely due to the climatic differences. In the north, millet and soya-beans were staples, whereas wet-rice cultivation was important in the south. Wet-rice probably spread to southern Korea from China in around the middle of the 2nd millennium BC and may have been established in western Japan by the middle of the 1st millennium BC, when a new rice-farming culture, the Yayoi, spread from Kyushu throughout central and western Honshu. These agricultural communities developed a bronze industry under Korean influence, producing weapons and ceremonial *dotaku* bells. Bronze was not used for everyday items; Yayoi rice farmers used stone reaping knives (*ishibocho*) for snapping the seed heads from rice plants, and wooden hoes and spades. Bronze ceremonial goods testify to the emergence of a sophisticated society, while the building of defended hilltop enclosures demonstrates increasing conflict and warfare, possibly related to the development of a more hierarchical society ruled by powerful chieftains. The Jomon coastal fishers of north-eastern Japan initially resisted the agricultural way of life, but rice-farming was finally adopted throughout Honshu by c. AD 300. This isolated region used little bronze and retained a distinctive character, while in the northern island of Hokkaido the Jomon tradition and way of life continued, untouched by Yayoi culture.

Iron-working was introduced into the Korean peninsula in the 4th century BC. The eastward expansion of the Han frontier, and the establishment of commanderies in Korea and Manchuria, greatly increased Chinese cultural influence on Japan and Korea, stimulating wealth and trade, especially in new luxury products. Native states, founded in the 1st century BC, developed steadily in the early centuries AD: Koguryo in the mountainous isolation of the northern Korean peninsula, Paekche and Shilla in the south, and Yamato in Japan. All four polities are marked archaeologically by the monumental mounded tombs constructed by their elites. The unusual construction of the Shilla tombs – a wooden chamber and coffin mounded over with stones and then earth – has prevented looting, and stupendous gold articles such as crowns and pendant belts have been recovered. Contemporary Chinese texts tell of many minor chieftains and much internal warfare in Japan; however, the Yamato state gradually extended its hegemony over much of the country from AD 300 to 700. The core area of the Yamato state was the Kinai region, and here unique keyhole-shaped tombs are found – burial places of the first emperors – reaching up to 32 hectares in area.

By the end of this period both Japan and Korea were no longer isolated and had become integrated into the international scene. Diplomatic contacts were established, and Buddhism reached Japan through Korea in the 6th century AD. Thereafter, resources were re-directed from tomb-building into temple construction, which became characteristic of Buddhist Japan.

2 MOZU: AN IMPERIAL CEMETERY

The Yamato cemetery at Mozu contains the impressive burial monuments of the rulers of this ancient state, surrounded by the graves of their nobles and courtiers. The largest tomb (*photograph below*) is attributed to Nintoku, the 15th emperor (early 5th cent. AD). Measuring 485m in length, it consists of an estimated 1,405,866 cubic metres of earth and is of characteristic keyhole plan (*below left*). It is located in a cemetery of tombs, some also keyhole-shaped

(*below right*). On the slopes of the mound and on the inner greenbelt between the moats there originally stood some 23,000 *haniwa* or pottery objects providing ritual protection for the tomb. Many were cylindrical; others were in the shape of houses, waterfowl, dogs, horses and warriors. The principal burial has never been located, but a landslip in 1872 revealed an ancillary stone-lined burial chamber. Here a large stone sarcophagus was surrounded with iron swords, a helmet with visor, a cuirass and a glass plate and bowl.

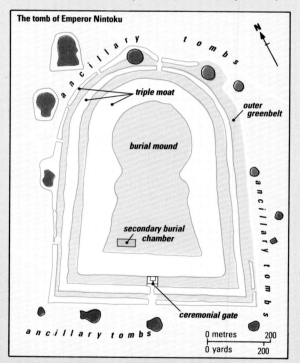

The tomb of Emperor Nintoku

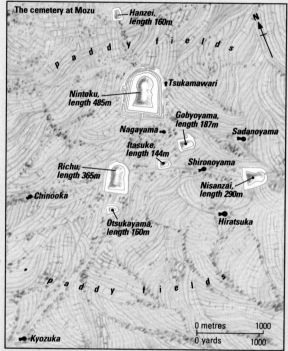

The cemetery at Mozu

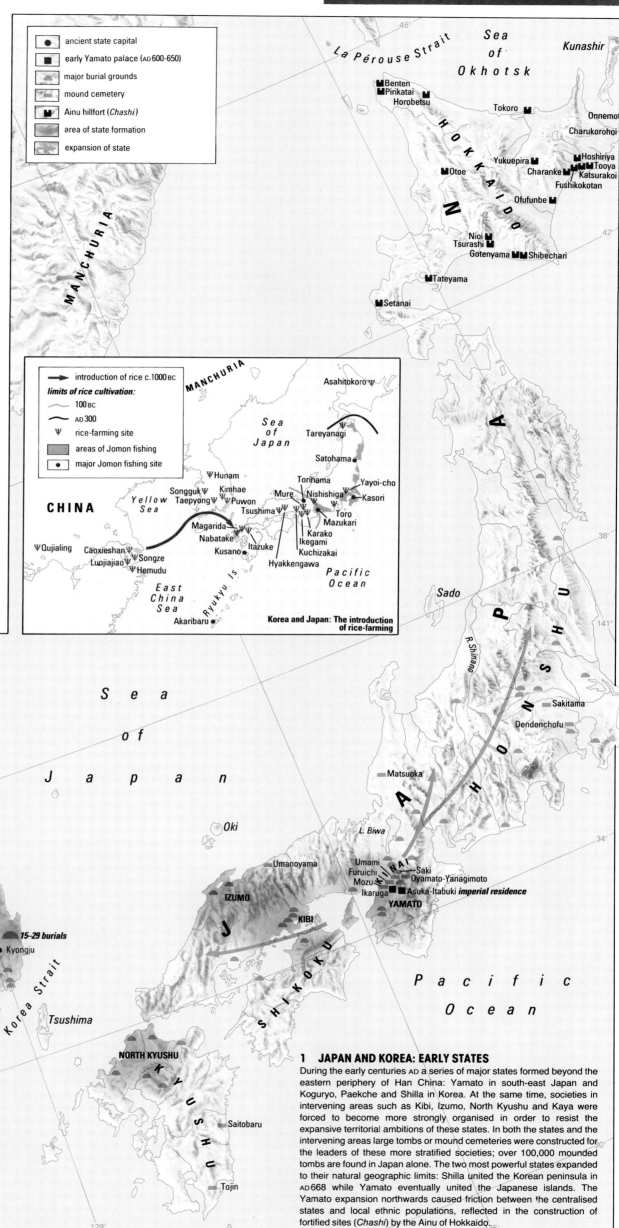

3 ACROSS THE SEA OF JAPAN

A *Diadem with six pendants, from north mound of the Great Tomb of Hwangnam-ni, Kyongju, capital of the early Korean state of Shilla. c.5th century AD, gold with jade ornaments, length of longest pendant 30.3cm.* **B** *Circular mirror with decorated back. Mirrors of this type originated in Han China but were imported to Japan and Korea. 2nd–3rd centuries AD, bronze, diameter 16.6cm.* **C** *Haniwa figure of armoured warrior, placed on burial mounds to provide protection for the deceased and their grave furnishings. 5th century AD, terracotta, height 38cm.* **D** *Ceremonial dotaku bell, from Kinai region, Japan, a characteristic product of the early Japanese bronze industry. 2nd–3rd centuries AD, bronze, height 48.5cm.* **E** *Reconstruction of granary at the Yayoi rice-farming settlement of Toro, Japan. The structure was raised on stilts to ensure that the contents remained dry and to place them beyond the reach of rodents.*

Korea and Japan: The introduction of rice-farming

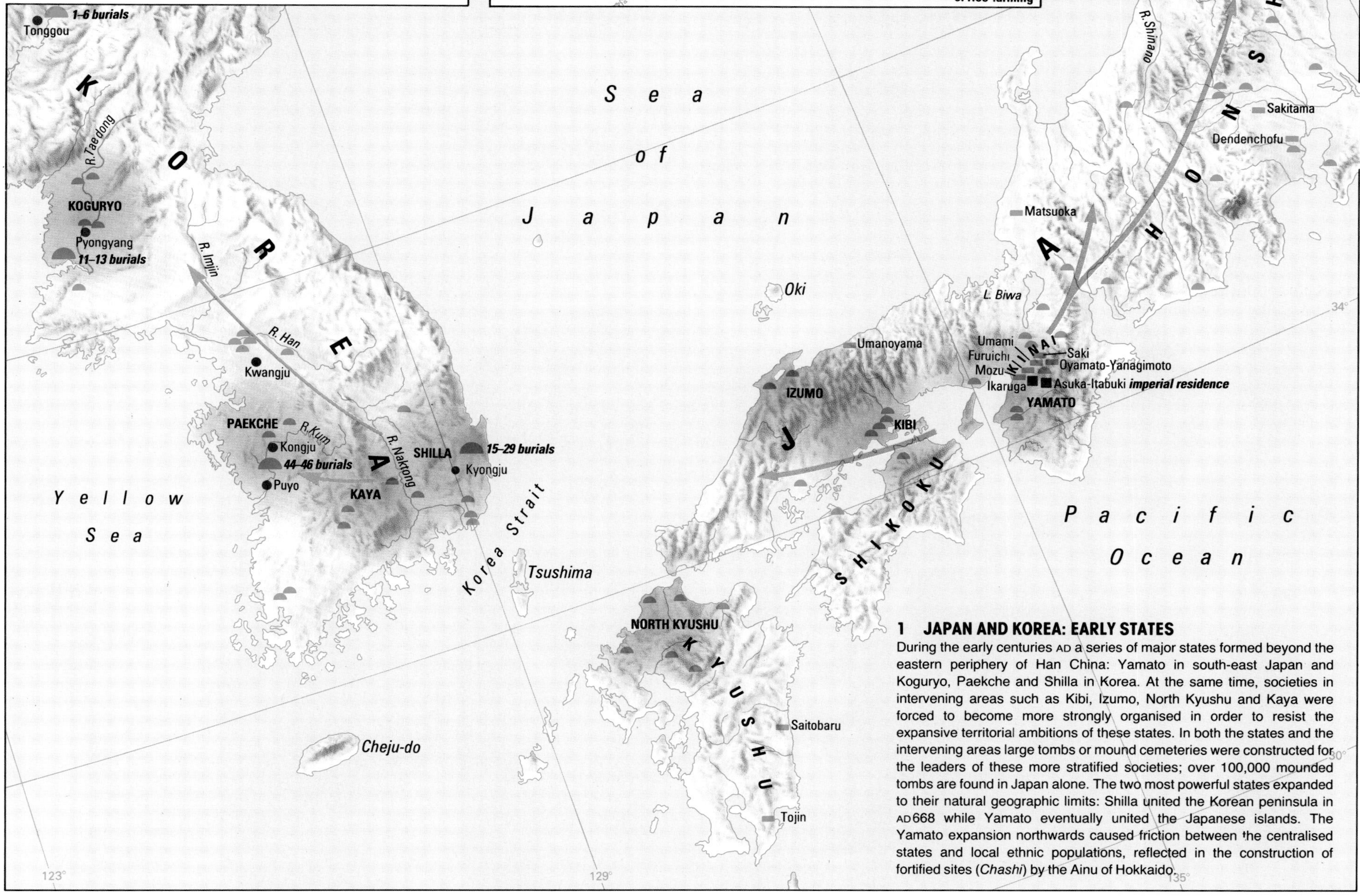

Legend:
- introduction of rice c.1000 BC
- limits of rice cultivation:
  - 100 BC
  - AD 300
- rice-farming site
- areas of Jomon fishing
- major Jomon fishing site

Map legend (top)

- ancient state capital
- early Yamato palace (AD 600–650)
- major burial grounds
- mound cemetery
- Ainu hillfort (*Chashi*)
- area of state formation
- expansion of state

1 JAPAN AND KOREA: EARLY STATES

During the early centuries AD a series of major states formed beyond the eastern periphery of Han China: Yamato in south-east Japan and Koguryo, Paekche and Shilla in Korea. At the same time, societies in intervening areas such as Kibi, Izumo, North Kyushu and Kaya were forced to become more strongly organised in order to resist the expansive territorial ambitions of these states. In both the states and the intervening areas large tombs or mound cemeteries were constructed for the leaders of these more stratified societies; over 100,000 mounded tombs are found in Japan alone. The two most powerful states expanded to their natural geographic limits: Shilla united the Korean peninsula in AD 668 while Yamato eventually united the Japanese islands. The Yamato expansion northwards caused friction between the centralised states and local ethnic populations, reflected in the construction of fortified sites (*Chashi*) by the Ainu of Hokkaido.

South-East Asia

During the 1st millennium AD, South-East Asian cultures were profoundly affected by their contacts with two major powers, China, and more particularly, India. Expanding trade brought not only exotic material goods but also new ideas to the prehistoric Bronze and Iron Age inhabitants (*page 150*). There is little evidence from which to reconstruct the political and religious world of these earlier prehistoric peoples. This situation changed during the 1st millennium AD when the first truly urban settlements appeared in South-East Asia.

The earliest urban sites in South-East Asia are thought to have been located in Vietnam, where the fortifications at Co Loa have been dated to the 3rd century BC. The monumental stone remains at these sites tell only part of the story, as the majority of the dwellings and utilitarian goods were made from perishable materials like wood or bamboo – stone and brick were reserved for religious buildings. At individual sites Hinduism and Buddhism either co-existed or were popular at different periods – Peikthano, in Burma, is Buddhist, but its name means 'Vishnu city'. Many so-called protohistoric sites from this period are considered to be urban although they were not densely populated cities, but instead served as trading and religious centres for large regions. They were often surrounded by a wall or, in some cases a moat. It is impossible to generalise about their functions; moats, for example, served many different purposes. At trading entrepôts such as Oc Eo, they were used for drainage, irrigation and transportation. However, moats are also found at what appear to have been ceremonial centres such as Muang Fa Daet and surround agricultural villages like Ban Muang Fai.

South-East Asia was receptive to important aspects of Indian civilisation, such as Indian concepts of kingship and law, the Hindu and Buddhist religions with their styles of art and architecture, and Sanskrit, the language of the earliest known inscriptions found in South-East Asia which has had an influence on the modern languages of the region. Indian customs were adopted by local rulers because they strengthened the hierarchical political and economic systems that were already established. Contact with India undoubtedly already existed during

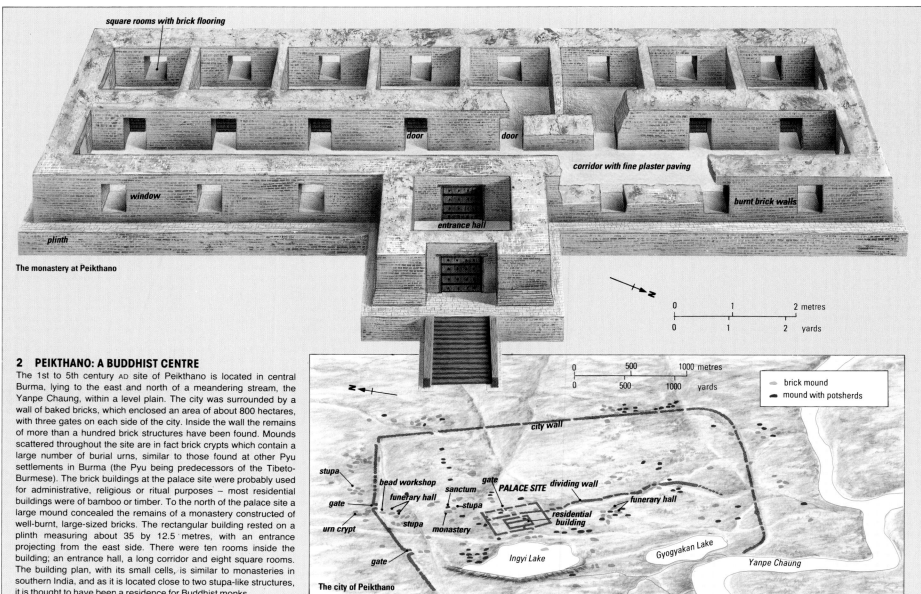

The monastery at Peikthano

2 PEIKTHANO: A BUDDHIST CENTRE

The 1st to 5th century AD site of Peikthano is located in central Burma, lying to the east and north of a meandering stream, the Yanpe Chaung, within a level plain. The city was surrounded by a wall of baked bricks, which enclosed an area of about 800 hectares, with three gates on each side of the city. Inside the wall the remains of more than a hundred brick structures have been found. Mounds scattered throughout the site are in fact brick crypts which contain a large number of burial urns, similar to those found at other Pyu settlements in Burma (the Pyu being predecessors of the Tibeto-Burmese). The brick buildings at the palace site were probably used for administrative, religious or ritual purposes – most residential buildings were of bamboo or timber. To the north of the palace site a large mound concealed the remains of a monastery constructed of well-burnt, large-sized bricks. The rectangular building rested on a plinth measuring about 35 by 12.5 metres, with an entrance projecting from the east side. There were ten rooms inside the building; an entrance hall, a long corridor and eight square rooms. The building plan, with its small cells, is similar to monasteries in southern India, and as it is located close to two stupa-like structures, it is thought to have been a residence for Buddhist monks.

The city of Peikthano

3 THE ECLECTIC CULTURES OF SOUTH-EAST ASIA

A *Statue of Uma ('Light'), the consort of the Hindu god Siva, from Cambodia. Late 7th century AD, sandstone, height 95cm.* B *Beads from Ban Don Ta Phet, central Thailand.* **Top left** *Black onyx bead with pale blue band, diameter 2.7cm.* **Lower left** *Etched black onyx bead, diameter 2.5cm.* **Right** *Cylinder-shaped black onyx bead with etched white design, length 5.5cm.* **Bottom** *Carved chalcedony (carnelian) pendant bead in the shape of a lion, length 7cm. 1st millennium BC.* C *Stela from Sri Ksetra, central Burma. The Buddha is seated on a lotus throne, the left hand touching the earth, calling it to witness his challenge to the forces of evil, the right hand holding a begging bowl. 6th-7th century AD, sandstone, height 35.5cm.* D *Pyu coins from southern and central Burma. 8th century AD, silver, diameter 3.5cm.* E *Boundary stone from north-east Thailand, with detail of a graceful figure dancing above several buildings. 9th-11th century AD, sandstone, height of figure 40cm.*

the prehistoric period. Nonetheless, during the 1st millennium AD trade increased radically, both within South-East Asia and with other regions, using both overland and maritime routes. Products traded between inland and coastal settlements throughout South-East Asia included timber, oils and resins, mineral resources and plants which had a variety of uses: dye, medicine, poison, food. For example, excavations at Gilimanuk, on the island of Bali in Indonesia, have yielded evidence of a coastal settlement linked to inland sites in mountainous areas by similar objects such as pottery, metal and beads, these last being made of various materials, including glass, shell, and precious stones such as carnelian.

In contrast to the widespread Indian cultural influence during this period, Chinese contact was more political

and military, and took the very different form of tribute payments to the Chinese court by South-East Asian polities, and the political annexation of northern Vietnam, which was ruled as a Chinese province from about 100 BC to AD 900. Chinese texts, which mention an active sea trade with South-East Asia from the beginning of the 2nd century BC (the Han period), indicate an awareness of the maritime skills of the southern natives, and an eagerness to utilise them for the export of Chinese silks and spices. Ships from Indonesia carried goods from China as far as Malaya, from where they would continue westward on Indian vessels.

On the islands of South-East Asia finds of pottery with copper, bronze and iron artefacts are abundant during this period. However, in contrast to the large settlement

concentrations on the mainland such as Co Loa, Oc Eo, Angkor, and Peikthano, there is an apparent lack of large cities dating from this era. In Java, for example, the only early monumental remains are the enigmatic stone monuments found on the Dieng Plateau, in the central part of the island. On the other hand, finds of metal artefacts from the islands, often in jar burials, indicate a sophistication not echoed in the remains of large cities or even the monumental stone temple complexes which are found on the mainland. It was only towards the end of the 1st millennium AD, when there were true states with cities of sometimes more than 1000 hectares throughout the mainland, that large ceremonial complexes such as Borobodur and Prambanan (*page 258*) were built on the Indonesian island of Java.

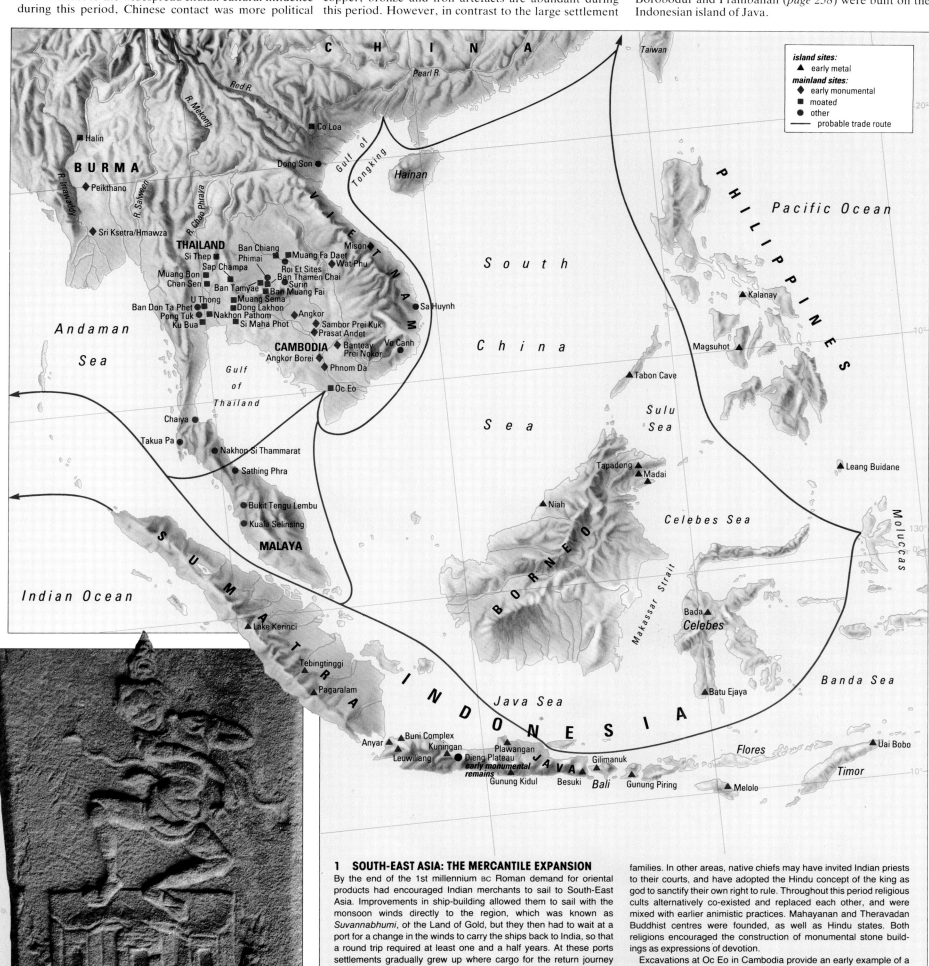

1 SOUTH-EAST ASIA: THE MERCANTILE EXPANSION

By the end of the 1st millennium BC Roman demand for oriental products had encouraged Indian merchants to sail to South-East Asia. Improvements in ship-building allowed them to sail with the monsoon winds directly to the region, which was known as *Suvannabhumi*, or the Land of Gold, but they then had to wait at a port for a change in the winds to carry the ships back to India, so that a round trip required at least one and a half years. At these ports settlements gradually grew up where cargo for the return journey could be collected. Indian traders may have intermarried with the local population, further disseminating Indian culture, and ultimately transforming these small commercial settlements into Hindu-Buddhist kingdoms. In some early cases, Indian princes may have followed in the traders' wake, been readily accepted by the local population, and legitimised their presence by marrying into the local

families. In other areas, native chiefs may have invited Indian priests to their courts, and have adopted the Hindu concept of the king as god to sanctify their own right to rule. Throughout this period religious cults alternatively co-existed and replaced each other, and were mixed with earlier animistic practices. Mahayanan and Theravadan Buddhist centres were founded, as well as Hindu states. Both religions encouraged the construction of monumental stone buildings as expressions of devotion.

Excavations at Oc Eo in Cambodia provide an early example of a trading city from this period. Here, both indigenous and foreign artefacts were found, in particular Indian and Roman objects, including a gold signet ring with a Sanskrit inscription and coins of Marcus Aurelius and Antoninus Pius. The richness of these finds, along with the discovery of a vast network of canals, has led to its identification as the early historical kingdom called Funan in Chinese annals.

The settlement of Polynesia

In AD 1000 the Polynesians were the most widespread ethnic group on Earth, having colonised all the major islands within a vast triangular segment of the Pacific Ocean, stretching from New Zealand to Easter Island and on to the Hawaiian Islands, an area of approximately 20 million square kilometres, twice the size of the USA. Since less than 1% of this area is dry land, the Polynesians must be seen as the greatest navigators in history of mankind.

The question of Polynesian origins has been fiercely disputed since the late 18th century. It is now clear that the Polynesians share a close genetic and linguistic heritage with the peoples of central eastern Indonesia and the Philippines (also speakers of Austronesian languages) and that they have also been influenced by contacts with Melanesian populations in the western Pacific. New Guinea and adjacent islands had been settled by Melanesians at least 30,000 years ago, and quite large agricultural populations may have existed as far east as the Solomon Islands by the start of the Polynesian dispersal c.1500 BC.

There can be no doubt that the biological, linguistic and technological roots of later Polynesian culture lie in the eastern islands of South-East Asia. The development of rice cultivation in southern China about 7500 years ago gave rise, after c.4000 BC, to a population expansion through Taiwan and the Philippines into the islands of central and eastern Indonesia, and it was this expansion which formed the basis of the Polynesian dispersal. Around 1500 BC, the so-called Lapita culture spread rapidly over a distance of some 4000 kilometres into the Pacific, from the Admiralty Islands in the west to Tonga and Samoa in the east. Lapita colonists made intricately decorated red-slipped pottery, used obsidian tools from volcanic sources in Melanesia, and manufactured a range of shell ornaments and tools, including fish-hooks – sea fishing and shellfish were important. They also used stone adzes, and cultivated tubers such as yam and taro, and fruits such as coconut, breadfruit and banana. They kept pigs and fowl (and possibly dogs), and were undoubtedly skilled navigators, sailing canoes perhaps similar to the Hawaiian double canoe. The Lapita peoples were the ancestors of the Polynesians, and also contributed a great deal to the genetic and cultural heritage of the Melanesian populations in the Solomons, Vanuatu, New Caledonia and Fiji.

The Lapita population which had established itself in Tonga and Samoa by 1000 BC was still confronted by a vast unsettled region to the east. It took the Polynesians over 2000 years to complete their migrations after entering the Polynesian triangle. The Marquesas Islands were probably settled from Samoa in around 200 BC, and after a brief pause colonists set out for Easter Island, the Hawaiian Islands, Tahiti and the Society Islands in the early–mid 1st millennium AD. New Zealand was perhaps the last major region to be reached, around AD 900. It is hard to visualise the hardships endured by these early Polynesian colonists. Most settlement was intentional, and the partially open canoes were therefore laden with livestock and seed plants, as well as men, women and children. It was under these conditions that the Polynesian settlers embarked on remarkable journeys of up to 4000 kilometres.

Although the original Lapita colonists were relatively homogeneous in culture, language and physique, this was not true of their descendants. Polynesians certainly retain a striking homogeneity, but Melanesia has witnessed major interaction between peoples of quite different biological and cultural origins. Furthermore, not all Pacific island environments are alike: the cultural adaptations on volcanic tropical islands have often differed from those on relatively barren atolls. The cool temperate climate of New Zealand imposed severe constraints, since most cultivated plants could not successfully be transplanted there, while the isolation of Easter Island provided the setting for one of the most remarkable cultural episodes in human prehistory (*page 268.*)

By AD 1000 the Polynesians had completed an extraordinary undertaking – reaching virtually every island in the Polynesian triangle, and permanently settling a large number of them. They had introduced new crops and livestock, and developed new systems of horticulture which were supporting ever-increasing populations. New forms of social organisation emerged as populations increased, and by AD 1200 the next chapter in the history of these far-flung islands was about to begin: the rise of the first Polynesian chiefdoms.

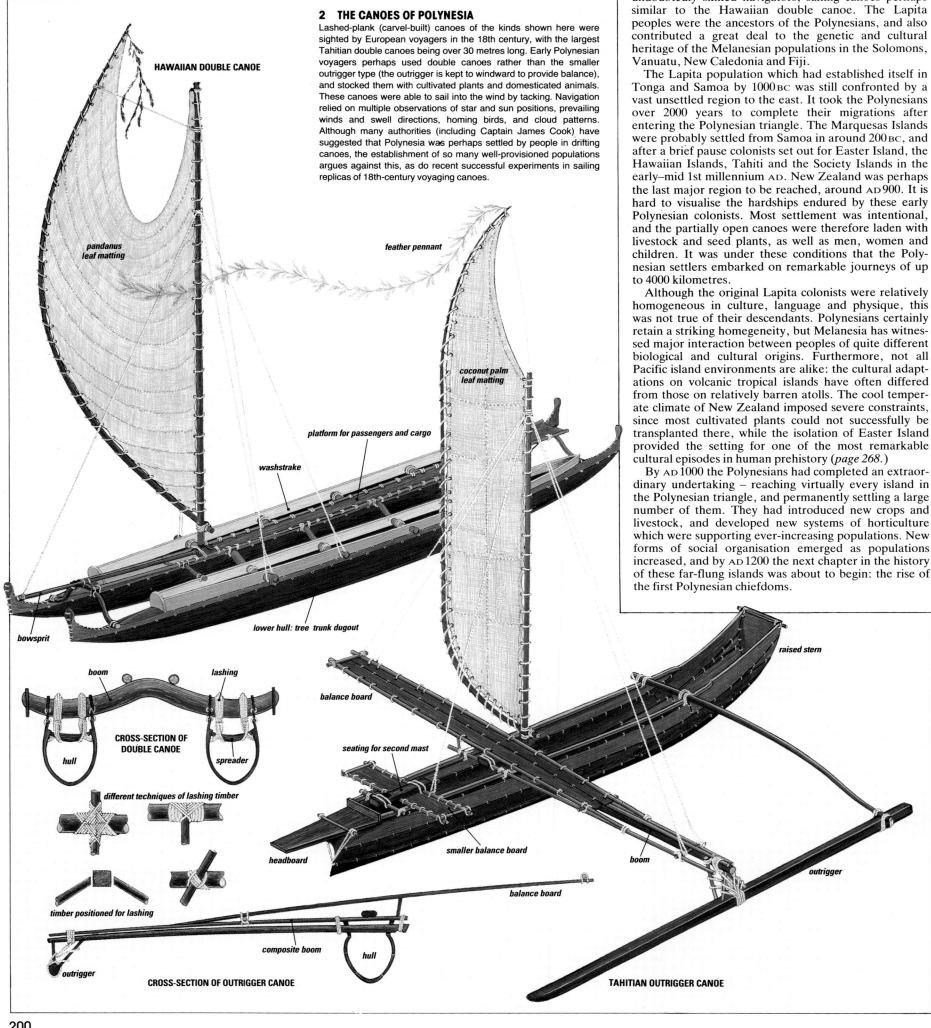

2 THE CANOES OF POLYNESIA

Lashed-plank (carvel-built) canoes of the kinds shown here were sighted by European voyagers in the 18th century, with the largest Tahitian double canoes being over 30 metres long. Early Polynesian voyagers perhaps used double canoes rather than the smaller outrigger type (the outrigger is kept to windward to provide balance), and stocked them with cultivated plants and domesticated animals. These canoes were able to sail into the wind by tacking. Navigation relied on multiple observations of star and sun positions, prevailing winds and swell directions, homing birds, and cloud patterns. Although many authorities (including Captain James Cook) have suggested that Polynesia was perhaps settled by people in drifting canoes, the establishment of so many well-provisioned populations argues against this, as do recent successful experiments in sailing replicas of 18th-century voyaging canoes.

HAWAIIAN DOUBLE CANOE

pandanus leaf matting

feather pennant

coconut palm leaf matting

platform for passengers and cargo

washstrake

bowsprit

lower hull: tree trunk dugout

CROSS-SECTION OF DOUBLE CANOE

boom

lashing

hull

spreader

different techniques of lashing timber

timber positioned for lashing

CROSS-SECTION OF OUTRIGGER CANOE

outrigger

composite boom

hull

balance board

seating for second mast

headboard

smaller balance board

balance board

raised stern

boom

outrigger

TAHITIAN OUTRIGGER CANOE

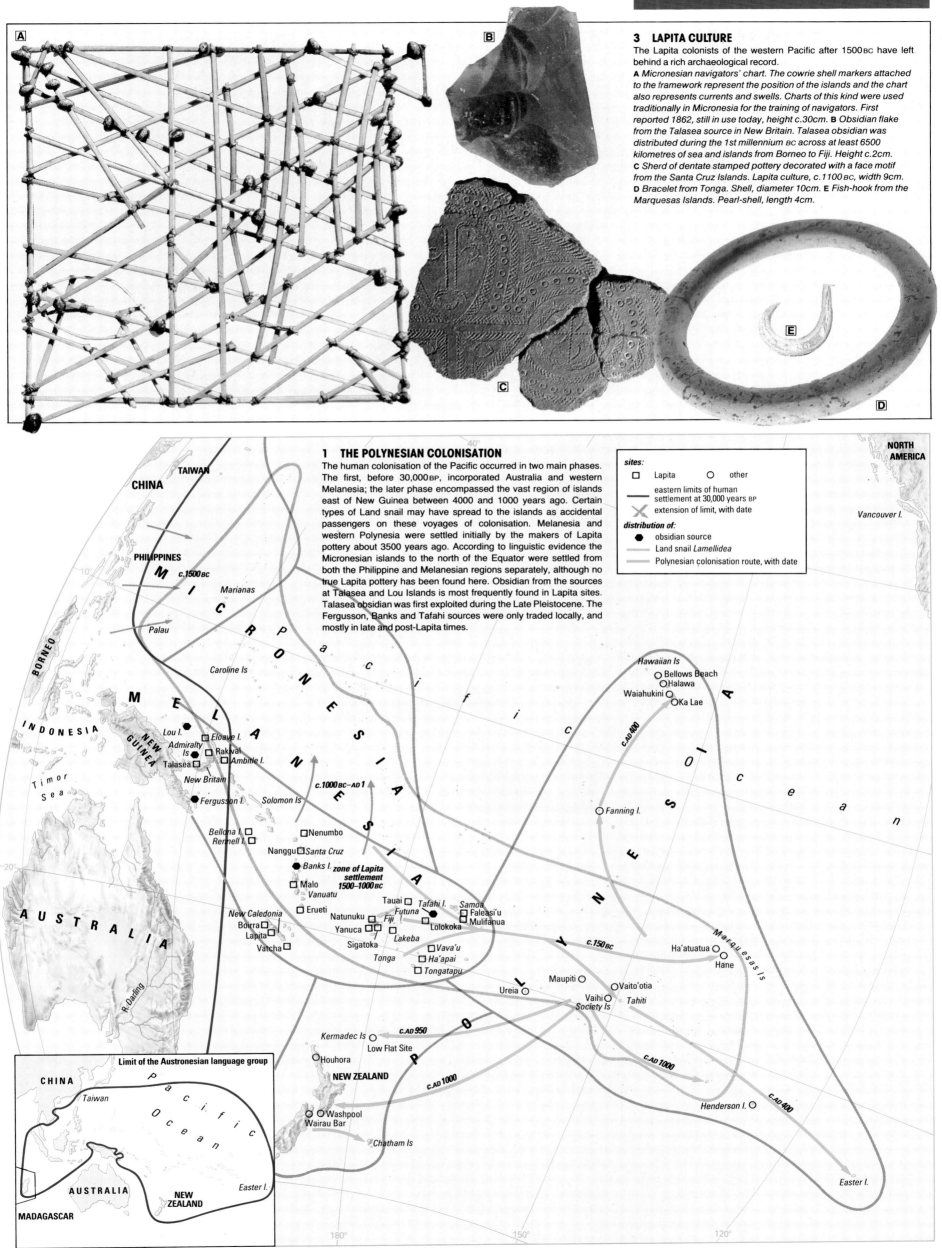

3 LAPITA CULTURE

The Lapita colonists of the western Pacific after 1500BC have left behind a rich archaeological record.

A Micronesian navigators' chart. The cowrie shell markers attached to the framework represent the position of the islands and the chart also represents currents and swells. Charts of this kind were used traditionally in Micronesia for the training of navigators. First reported 1862, still in use today, height c.30cm. **B** Obsidian flake from the Talasea source in New Britain. Talasea obsidian was distributed during the 1st millennium BC across at least 6500 kilometres of sea and islands from Borneo to Fiji. Height c.2cm. **C** Sherd of dentate stamped pottery decorated with a face motif from the Santa Cruz Islands. Lapita culture, c.1100BC, width 9cm. **D** Bracelet from Tonga. Shell, diameter 10cm. **E** Fish-hook from the Marquesas Islands. Pearl-shell, length 4cm.

1 THE POLYNESIAN COLONISATION

The human colonisation of the Pacific occurred in two main phases. The first, before 30,000BP, incorporated Australia and western Melanesia; the later phase encompassed the vast region of islands east of New Guinea between 4000 and 1000 years ago. Certain types of Land snail may have spread to the islands as accidental passengers on these voyages of colonisation. Melanesia and western Polynesia were settled initially by the makers of Lapita pottery about 3500 years ago. According to linguistic evidence the Micronesian islands to the north of the Equator were settled from both the Philippine and Melanesian regions separately, although no true Lapita pottery has been found here. Obsidian from the sources at Talasea and Lou Islands is most frequently found in Lapita sites. Talasea obsidian was first exploited during the Late Pleistocene. The Fergusson, Banks and Tafahi sources were only traded locally, and mostly in late and post-Lapita times.

sites:
□ Lapita   ○ other
— eastern limits of human settlement at 30,000 years BP
✕ extension of limit, with date

distribution of:
● obsidian source
— Land snail *Lamellidea*
— Polynesian colonisation route, with date

Limit of the Austronesian language group

Iron Age Africa

The 1st millennium BC marked the opening of a new epoch in the development of Africa. Among the most important innovations of this period was the introduction of iron metallurgy – the key to manufacturing more effective tools and weapons – first in the west and the Great Lakes area, then spreading gradually southward. In the west, the use of iron may relate to the emergence of a more hierarchical society. It was pastoralists, however, ancestors of the present-day Bantu people, who carried iron-working southwards, together with farming, into lands previously occupied by hunters and gatherers. In contrast to the incipient development of complex societies in West Africa south of the Sahara, farming was only just reaching southern Africa during this period.

In most of Africa, the Iron Age succeeded the Late Stone Age without an intervening Copper or Bronze Age. Indeed, only in the Nile Valley and in parts of West Africa (Niger and Mauritania) is there evidence that copper was worked before the introduction of iron. The sudden development of metallurgy during the 1st millennium BC suggests that iron-working must have been brought to sub-Saharan Africa from the Phoenician colonies of the North African coast. Chariot engravings found in the desert show light, two-wheeled chariots drawn by horses – a type thought to have been made in the 1st millennium BC. The distribution of the engravings along the routes which traverse the desert suggests that these vehicles may have been used in trans-Saharan trade, and it is quite possible that knowledge of iron-working was transmitted in this way. However, the strength and individuality of the sub-Saharan iron-working traditions vividly demonstrate the skill and inventiveness of the earliest African craftsmen.

The earliest evidence for iron-working in Africa south of the Sahara comes from the area just north of the Niger–Benue confluence, notably from the sites of Taruga and Samun Dukiya. The iron smelting furnaces at Taruga date to around 450 BC. These are settlements of the so-called Nok culture, which flourished in this part of Nigeria from the 5th century BC until the early centuries AD. Its most characteristic and intriguing remains are a series of terracotta heads, some of which are life-size, which were faithfully modelled, even to the representation of hairstyles and physical abnormalities and deformities. Although their function and significance are unknown, they must have been used for ritual and religious purposes, like the Ife and Benin heads of later periods (*page 248*).

To the west of Lake Victoria, in western Tanzania and adjacent parts of Rwanda, sophisticated brick-built furnaces were used on a large scale to produce what was technically a high-carbon steel. It is clear that this industry was thriving by the last four centuries BC, and it may have been established significantly earlier. Further east, however, the pastoral peoples of the Rift Valley highlands continued to use only stone tools for another thousand years.

In West Africa and the Great Lakes region, iron-using was first adopted by established farming communities, but in more southerly regions, the situation was totally different. Over the huge area to the south and east of the equatorial forest, farming and metallurgy spread both rapidly and concurrently. This major transition from hunter-gathering to farming was probably initiated by a series of rapid and substantial movements of Bantu-speaking people who then staked their claim to the more fertile regions by incorporating or displacing ealier inhabitants. This led to periods of productive contact and interaction between the settled peoples and the new arrivals. In the extreme south-west of Africa, general aridity or a winter-rainfall pattern discouraged the full adoption of the agricultural way of life. However, as early as the beginning of the 1st millennium AD domestic animals (sheep and probably cattle) were kept, and techniques of pottery manufacture were known by the inhabitants.

The developments which took place during the thousand years following the introduction of iron-working laid the foundations of historical Africa. By the end of the period, iron-using farmers had established themselves far to the south, and hunting and gathering were restricted to the arid south-west. In the savanna grasslands south of the Sahara, more sophisticated settlements developed, anticipating the first of the great West African kingdoms. There were also major social changes in the east, with the emergence of elite groups marking the beginning of a process which was ultimately to lead to the construction of monumental centres such as Great Zimbabwe. Thus, when the first Arab traders arrived on the east coast in the 8th century AD (*page 252*), Africa south of the Sahara was already entering a new phase in its development.

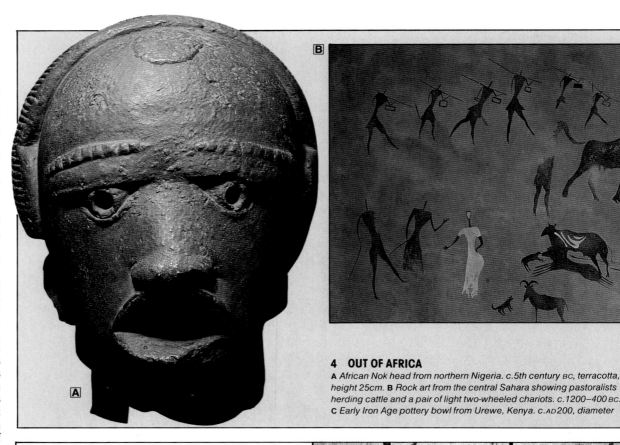

4 OUT OF AFRICA
A African Nok head from northern Nigeria. c.5th century BC, terracotta, height 25cm. **B** Rock art from the central Sahara showing pastoralists herding cattle and a pair of light two-wheeled chariots. c.1200–400 BC. **C** Early Iron Age pottery bowl from Urewe, Kenya. c.AD 200, diameter

3 AN AFRICAN IRON SMELTING FURNACE
African iron-smelting furnaces vary from simple pits or trenches to large funnel-shaped or domed structures. The iron ore was placed within the furnace with charcoal fuel in alternate layers. Although many were fired with the aid of bellows, others were designed so that the high temperatures needed to smelt iron (over 1100°C) could be attained by means of natural draught, directed into the centre of the furnace through clay pipes or *tuyères*. The resulting metal was generally of high quality. Although African iron smelting was labour-intensive and consumed huge quantities of charcoal fuel, abundant remains of furnaces, together with ancient mines and quarries for extracting the ore, illustrate the massive scale of iron production.
Right Dome-shaped furnace from Chipata, south-east Zambia.

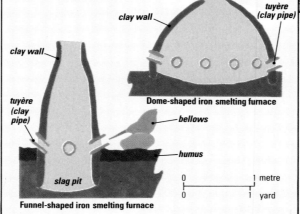

clay wall

clay wall

tuyère (clay pipe)

Dome-shaped iron smelting furnace

tuyère (clay pipe)

bellows

humus

slag pit

Funnel-shaped iron smelting furnace

0   1 metre
0   1 yard

2 AN AFRICAN DWELLING
Excavations at Broederstroom, west of Pretoria in the Transvaal region of South Africa, have revealed the remains of a substantial village occupied by farming peoples in around the 5th century AD. At least 13 huts were set in an area of about two hectares. They were dome-shaped structures of grass applied to a light wooden framework, and plastered inside and outside with clay. Scattered among the houses were a number of burials. In one case the dead man had been placed seated in a shallow pit; in two others, cranial fragments, teeth and an arm bone were found in pottery vessels. The inhabitants of Broederstroom cultivated cereals, herded cattle, sheep and goats, smelted iron and made finely decorated pottery. They were probably the first farming people to settle in the Transvaal highlands, and they were responsible for starting the exploitation of South Africa's mineral wealth.

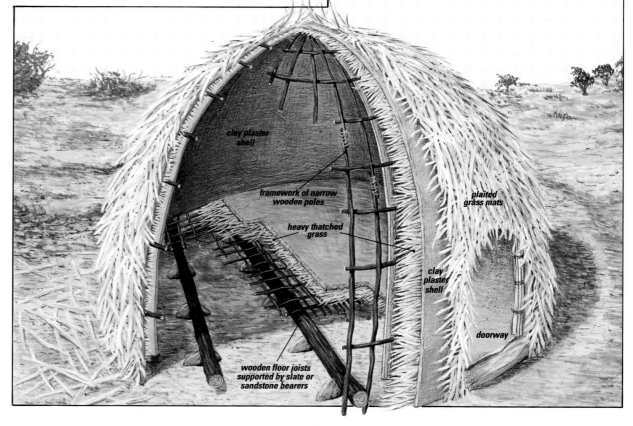

clay plaster shell

framework of narrow wooden poles

heavy thatched grass

plaited grass mats

clay plaster shell

doorway

wooden floor joists supported by slate or sandstone bearers

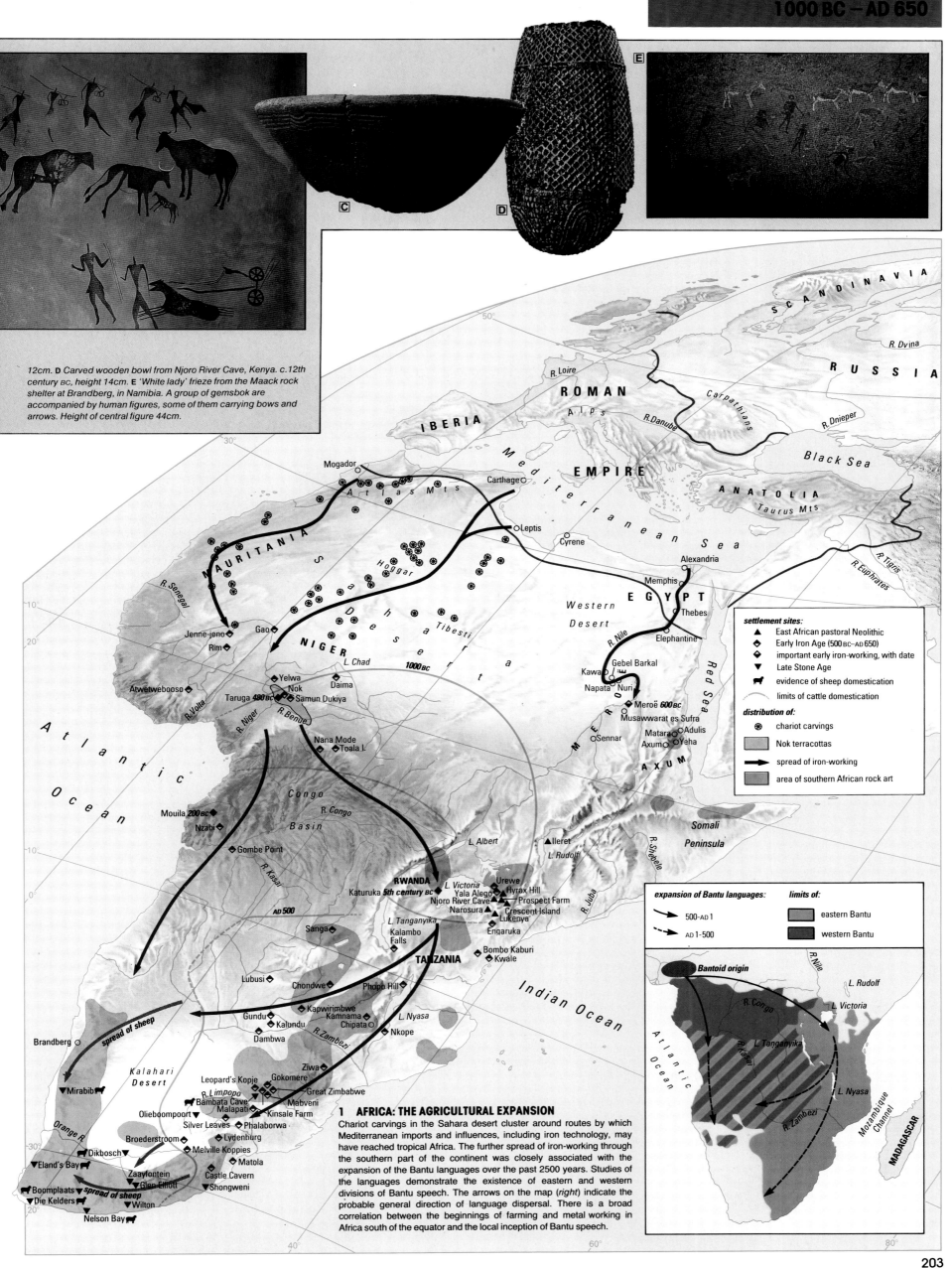

E

C D

12cm. **D** Carved wooden bowl from Njoro River Cave, Kenya. c.12th century BC, height 14cm. **E** 'White lady' frieze from the Maack rock shelter at Brandberg, in Namibia. A group of gemsbok are accompanied by human figures, some of them carrying bows and arrows. Height of central figure 44cm.

settlement sites:

▲ East African pastoral Neolithic
◆ Early Iron Age (500 BC–AD 650)
⬖ important early iron-working, with date
▼ Late Stone Age
🐑 evidence of sheep domestication
⌇ limits of cattle domestication

distribution of:

✳ chariot carvings

▨ Nok terracottas

➡ spread of iron-working

▨ area of southern African rock art

expansion of Bantu languages:

→ 500–AD 1
⇢ AD 1–500

limits of:

▨ eastern Bantu
▨ western Bantu

Bantoid origin

1 AFRICA: THE AGRICULTURAL EXPANSION

Chariot carvings in the Sahara desert cluster around routes by which Mediterranean imports and influences, including iron technology, may have reached tropical Africa. The further spread of iron-working through the southern part of the continent was closely associated with the expansion of the Bantu languages over the past 2500 years. Studies of the languages demonstrate the existence of eastern and western divisions of Bantu speech. The arrows on the map (right) indicate the probable general direction of language dispersal. There is a broad correlation between the beginnings of farming and metal working in Africa south of the equator and the local inception of Bantu speech.

203

SIX
THE NEW WORLD
10,000 BC — AD 1600

HUMAN GROUPS probably first entered the Americas from Siberia during the last glacial period, 40,000–10,000 BC, when lowered sea levels uncovered a broad land bridge called Beringia, where the Bering Strait now lies, between Asia and Alaska. Rising sea levels then isolated the continent: it seems likely that American societies thereafter evolved independently, without significant outside contact. Despite this, however, many New World developments parallel those of the Old World: the adoption of agriculture, the rise of cities and the innovation of metallurgy and writing.

By about 9000 BC settlers had reached the southern tip of South America. They lived by hunting and gathering, a way of life which continued in many areas, and especially in North America, until European contact began in the 16th century. However, climatic changes and the extinction of several animal species forced many communities to become more dependent on plant food. From about 8000 BC native plants, particularly maize, squash, beans, cotton, manioc and high altitude grains and tubers, were cultivated.

In Central America, and in South America on the Pacific Coast and in the Andes, villages based on agriculture developed from about 3000 BC. Cultural traits, which reappeared in all subsequent major American civilisations, were already apparent; these included elaborate irrigation works and massive artificial mounds crowned with temples grouped round open plazas. The first major cultures, the Olmec in Mexico and Chavín in the northern highlands of Peru, emerged during the 2nd millennium BC. Both had highly distinctive art styles, probably linked to their religions, which continued to pervade American iconography until the European conquest. From these cultures sprang the famous civilisations of Teotihuacán, the Maya, the Toltecs and Aztecs and, in South America, the Moche, Nazca, Chimú and Inca. Of these, only the Maya were fully literate, using a hieroglyphic writing which has only recently been deciphered. The development of the New World civilisations was brutally arrested by the invasion of Europeans in the 16th century AD.

The earth goddess Coatlicue (Lady of Serpents) from the courtyard of the temple of Tenochtitlán AD 1325–1521, height 2.5m.

North America after the ice

Between 10,000 BC and 4000 BC there was an increasing diversity in environment and human adaptation all over North America. The last major glacial advance, the Wisconsin (*page 70*), reached its maximum southward extent at a latitude of approximately 43° North. The period immediately following the glacial retreat is known as the Palaeo–Indian. It is characterised by rapidly changing environments, more clement climates, and the widespread extinction of certain species of plants and animals, or their displacement to other, more suitable terrain. The Palaeo–Indian peoples are known as big-game hunters because they preyed on large animals, many of which – the mammoth, mastodon, ground sloth, and more robust forms of bison than are found today – became extinct. All these species migrated seasonally, and the Palaeo–Indian groups that followed the herds were also nomadic. It has been suggested that the big-game extinctions were the results of 'overkill' by Palaeo–Indian groups. However, it seems likely that this was not the primary factor; a combination of shrinking habitats and reproductive stress are more probable causes.

By 8000 BC nomadic big-game hunting gave way to a much more varied way of life, based on a wider range of smaller game animals. An increase in the use of plant resources was also an important development. This period is known as the Archaic Stage and extends until c. 1000 BC. It is characterised by intensive hunting and gathering by groups who were far less nomadic than the big-game hunters. For the first time food processing equipment, such as *manos* and *metates* for grinding seeds and other plant foods are abundant, together with ground stone tools for woodworking. Marine and lake species were also exploited, demonstrating that more diverse natural resources were coming into use.

The big-game hunters of the earlier period were characterised by two very widespread forms of projectile point, Clovis and Folsom, whereas the projectile point types of the Archaic were much more diversified. Archaic peoples used a much wider range of stone tools, as well as making tools from bone, shell, clay, and later copper. Human burials have been found for the first time during the Archaic period. Many, especially in the Northeast, contained red ochre, possibly indicating a ritual identification of red pigment with blood and life itself.

Over the centuries, Archaic groups became very specialised hunters and gatherers and settled into more precise territories, especially in areas where abundant year-round food resources were available. Group size increased, and vast territories which had previously been uninhabited began to be settled.

The hunters of the Northeast relied heavily upon caribou, but as the caribou moved north Archaic groups turned to the diverse resources of the deciduous forests and lakes. At Lamoka Lake site they depended seasonally on nuts, berries, deer, and shellfish. In the Southeast many areas were rich in wild food supplies throughout the year – a potential that was tapped by Archaic groups. These rich habitats allowed the inhabitants of a few areas to become more sedentary very early on, and to remain as hunters and gatherers for much longer than in other parts of the continent. A more settled way of life was also possible in certain areas along the Northwest Coast as well as some areas of the Southwest. Although these areas were very different, they both had a wide range of natural resources which Archaic groups were able to exploit.

In the Midwest there are a number of deeply stratified sites which have some of the longest cultural sequences found in North America. The Koster site in Illinois has yielded substantial information about changes in human adaptation from 7000 BC to AD 1200. This site was first inhabited during the period of rapid environmental adjustment at the end of the last glacial period. The climate was unpredictable and variable, tending to cool moist conditions between 7000 and 5000 BC and hot arid conditions between 5000 and 2500 BC. Animal and plant resources were equally unreliable, and there was a trend away from concentration on one or two species towards hunting a wider range of smaller game. Intensive foraging for nuts, fish and shellfish began. During much of the middle Archaic (8000–5000 BC) tools and weapons were all-purpose, generalised types, but gradually complex specialised tools developed including heavy grinding stones for processing plant foods. By 3500 BC a permanent village of log-built houses existed. Although many groups, such as those of the Northwest coast, continued an Archaic way of life until forced to change by European contact, others, such as that at Koster, were able to make the crucial leap from food collection to food production.

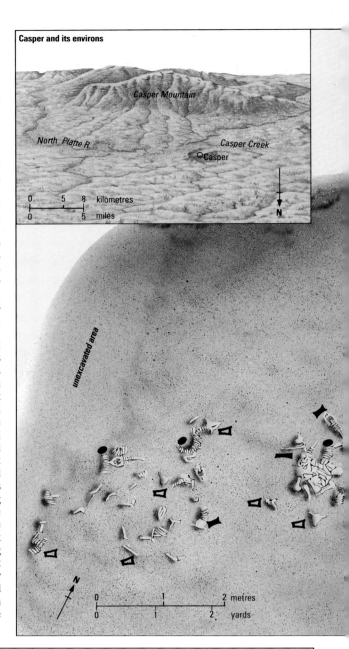

Casper and its environs

Casper Mountain

North Platte R.

Casper Creek

Casper

0 5 8 kilometres
0 5 miles

unexcavated area

3 HUNTERS OF THE PLAINS

A Moccasin from Danger Cave, Utah, made in one piece and stitched together with sinew, the hair inside. c. 6000 BC, antelope hide, length 25cm. **B** Rectangular net bag with drawstring fastening from Danger Cave, possibly a snare for small game or ground-feeding birds. c. 6000 BC, Apocynum (hemp) fibre, width 70cm. **C** Skinning–fleshing tool from Casper site, Wyoming, used to remove the hide and muscles from bones. c. 8000 BC, bison bone, length 22cm. **D** Hafted lanceolate projectile point from Casper site. c. 8000 BC, length of point 6cm. **E** Hammer stones with pointed ends used in butchering to break bison bones, from Casper site. c. 8000 BC, weight 0.57–1.19kg. **F** Rounded-end cobble stone used to break off spines from bison vertebrae, from Casper site. c. 8000 BC, weight 0.57–1.19kg. **G** Flaked stone Clovis point, with short flute scar at base. 10,000–9000 BC, length 10cm.

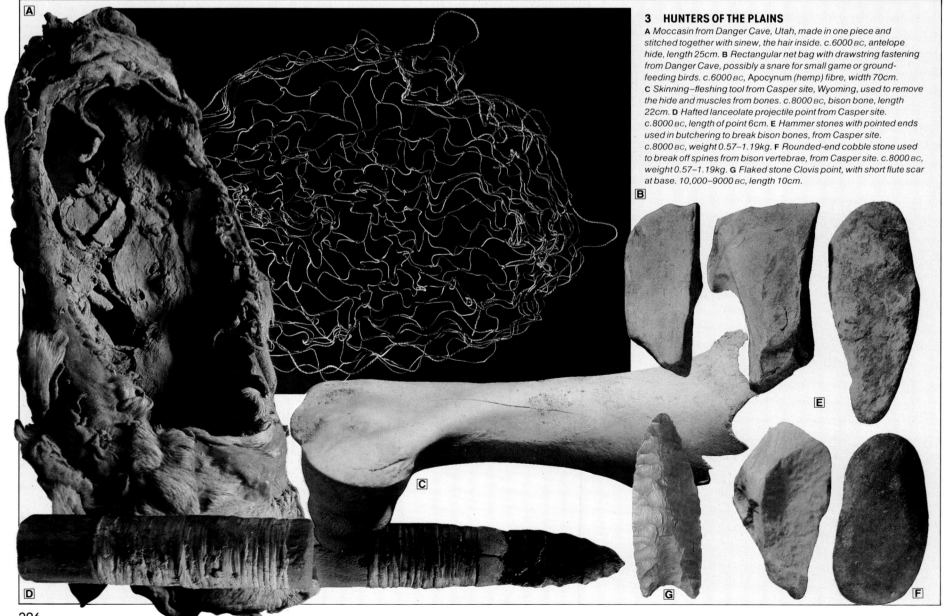

Sequence of butchering bison:

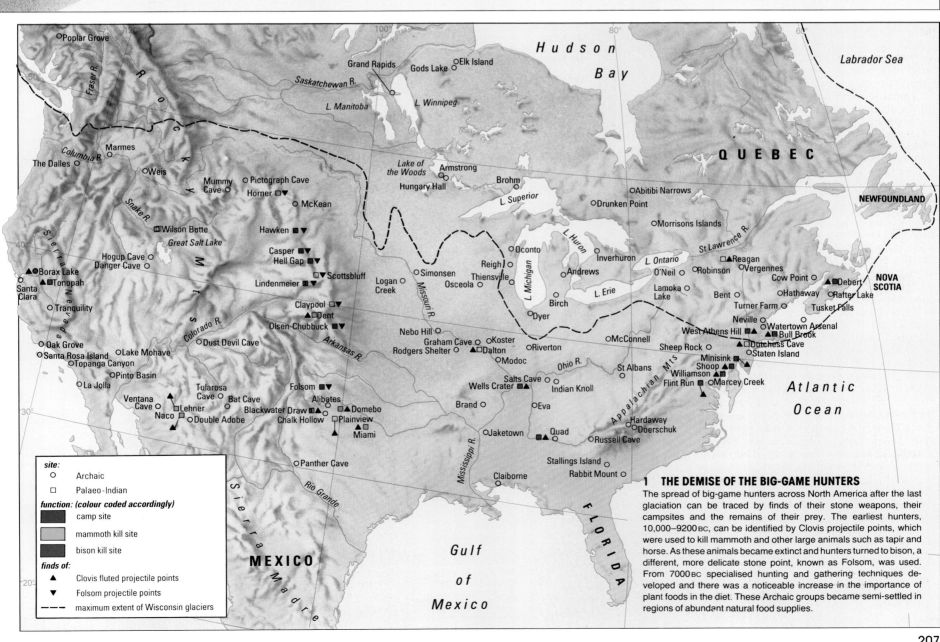

1 'blanket of flesh' and front legs

2 hump meat

3 rib meat and inner organs

4 pelvic girdle

5 hind legs

6 neck meat and tongue

unexcavated area

finds of:
- bison humerus tools
- bison tibia
- femur choppers
- fetal remains

number of bison found

estimated population

50 40 30 20 10

·6 1·6 2·6 3·6 4·6 5·6 6·6 7·6 8·6 9·6 10·6 11·6

age in years and months

2 CASPER: A BISON KILL SITE

In about 8000 BC, near Casper, Wyoming, a group of 15–20 hunters trapped 75 *Bison antiquus*, and butchered them on the spot. Analysis of the age of the animals indicates that the hunt took place in autumn. The animals were driven into a sand dune where they were immobilised and killed by spears tipped with stone points of the Hell Gap type. The bison skeletons had been efficiently stripped of at least 19,000 kilograms of meat. Much of this was presumably dried and made into pemmican for the winter months. At the Olsen–Chubbuck site, Colorado, a herd of *Bison occidentalis* was stampeded into an arroyo (gully) in about 6500 BC. Excavation revealed the logical sequence in which the animals were dismembered (*diagram*).

Poplar Grove

Grand Rapids • Gods Lake • Elk Island

Hudson Bay

Labrador Sea

Saskatchewan R.

L. Manitoba • L. Winnipeg

QUEBEC

Fraser R.

Columbia R. • Marmes

The Dalles • Weis

Snake R. • Mummy Cave • Pictograph Cave • Horner

Lake of the Woods • Armstrong

Hungary Hall • Brohm

L. Superior • Abitibi Narrows

Drunken Point • Morrisons Islands

NEWFOUNDLAND

McKean

Hawken

Wilson Butte

Great Salt Lake

Hogup Cave • Danger Cave

Borax Lake • Tonopah

Santa Clara

Tranquility

Oak Grove

Santa Rosa Island • Lake Mohave

Topanga Canyon

Pinto Basin

La Jolla

Tularosa Cave • Bat Cave

Ventana Cave • Lehner

Naco • Double Adobe

Casper • Hell Gap

Scottsbluff

Lindenmeier

Claypool

Dent

Olsen-Chubbuck

Dust Devil Cave

Colorado R.

Arkansas R.

Folsom

Alibates

Blackwater Draw

Chalk Hollow • Plainview

Miami

Domebo

Logan Creek

Simonsen

Osceola

Nebo Hill

Graham Cave • Koster

Rodgers Shelter • Dalton

Modoc

Brand

Missouri R.

Reigh

Oconto

L. Michigan

Thiensville

Andrews

Birch

L. Huron

Inverhuron

O'Neil

L. Ontario

Robinson

Lamoka Lake

L. Erie

Dyer

Riverton

Ohio R.

McConnell

St Lawrence R.

Reagan • Vergennes

Cow Point • Debert

Hathaway • Rafter Falls

Bent • Turner Farm

Neville • Tusket Falls

West Athens Hill • Watertown Arsenal

Sheep Rock • Dutchess Cave • Bull Brook

Minisink • Staten Island

Shoop

Williamson

Flint Run • Marcey Creek

NOVA SCOTIA

Atlantic Ocean

Appalachian Mts

St Albans

Salts Cave

Wells Crater • Indian Knoll

Eva

Hardaway • Doerschuk

Jaketown • Quad

Russell Cave

Stallings Island

Claiborne • Rabbit Mount

Panther Cave

Rio Grande

MEXICO

Sierra Madre

Gulf of Mexico

FLORIDA

1 THE DEMISE OF THE BIG-GAME HUNTERS

The spread of big-game hunters across North America after the last glaciation can be traced by finds of their stone weapons, their campsites and the remains of their prey. The earliest hunters, 10,000–9200 BC, can be identified by Clovis projectile points, which were used to kill mammoth and other large animals such as tapir and horse. As these animals became extinct and hunters turned to bison, a different, more delicate stone point, known as Folsom, was used. From 7000 BC specialised hunting and gathering techniques developed and there was a noticeable increase in the importance of plant foods in the diet. These Archaic groups became semi-settled in regions of abundant natural food supplies.

site:
- ○ Archaic
- □ Palaeo-Indian

function: (colour coded accordingly)
- camp site
- mammoth kill site
- bison kill site

finds of:
- ▲ Clovis fluted projectile points
- ▼ Folsom projectile points
- - - - maximum extent of Wisconsin glaciers

First farmers of the Americas

In the difficult search for the origins of agriculture in the New World, excavations at dry cave sites in Tamaulipas, and later in the Tehuacán Valley were important. They provided the first tangible evidence of where and when humans were thought to have begun the domestication of the vitally important crop, maize.

The wild ancestor of domesticated maize may well have been *teosinte*, a grass native to semi-arid and sub-tropical zones of Mexico and Guatemala. It is possible to study the changes in shape and size of the ears of corn as human selection of natural mutations, which gave more food per cob, modified the plant and so domesticated it. Much information has been extracted from sites where there is good preservation of plant remains, such as dry cave sites in highland Mexico and Peru, but data are lacking in the moist, lowland areas where the climate has destroyed the evidence. It is thought that maize was domesticated by at least 5000 BC in the Tehuacán Valley. Other domesticated plants dated to between 7000 and 5000 BC include squash, avocado, chilli peppers, beans and gourds. It was only many centuries later that cultivated plants became a dominant element in the diet.

In the lowland and highland areas of Peru evidence for the domestication of various grasses, squash, beans and peppers is tentatively dated at 8500 BC. According to pollen evidence, the principal New World crop, maize, appeared in South America in the 7th millennium BC. Grain crops suitable for high altitude cultivation had been developed some three thousand years before the arrival of maize. Quinoa, which with cañihua and tarwi was domesticated from hardy grasses that grew wild at heights of over 3000 metres, became an Andean staple food, and has been found in dry cave sites near Ayacucho dated c.6300 BC. Preservation of grain food plants is generally better than that of fleshy root plants, but root crops were of immense importance in the Andes, Amazon, and later in Mesoamerica, where yam, cocoyam and possibly manioc were cultivated at Cuello in Belize, around 2000 BC. Tubers and rhizomes related to oca and ulluco were being eaten by the inhabitants of Guitarrero Cave, Peru, by 6300 BC and possibly as early as 8500 BC. A similar date may be assigned to potatoes, which originated in the southern Andes. Manioc may have been cultivated in the Upper Amazon as early as 7000–5000 BC, but there is only indirect evidence: the pottery griddles, firedogs and huge beer-brewing vats which are necessary for its processing only appear at later sites.

Domesticated plants in North America seem to have been obtained mainly through contact from trade and migration. A few species, such as the bottle gourd *Cucurbita poro*, grown as a container and originating in Mesoamerica, reached eastern North America as early as 5000 BC. However, the spread of other crops, including maize, into eastern North America and the American Southwest did not occur until much later.

In contrast to the huge number of plant species available for intensive gathering and later domestication, particularly in the Andes where the variation in ecological zones is enormous, there were few animals which could be tamed and herded by humans. Most possible species, such as the horse, had become extinct at the end of the Pleistocene. In Mesoamerica only the Muscovy duck, stingless bee, turkey and dog were domesticated. Hunting dogs may have been brought by the Palaeo-Indian settlers of America as they entered the continent from Asia, and much later, in Mexico, a special breed of dog was kept, fattened on corn and used as a source of meat.

In the Central Andes wild camelids, guanacos – the ancestors of llamas – alpacas and vicuñas inhabited the cold grasslands over 3000 metres above sea level. By 5400 BC there were two distinct breeds of camelid, one large, one small, in the Ayacucho region of Peru, indicating that the transition from hunting to herding had been made. Two thousand years later llamas existed on the coastal plain, at Chilca, far away from their natural habitat. Llamas, the only beasts of burden in the whole of pre-Columbian America, could carry loads of up to 60 kilograms and provided many vital materials for their herders. Wool for cloth, meat, fat for lamps and candles, pelts, leather, sinews all came from llamas and alpacas, and their dung was important as domestic fuel and as fertiliser for potato fields. These animals were the only creatures which could turn the high *puna* grassland that comprises about 25% of the Andean area into an economically useful zone; tubers and quinoa cannot grow at such an altitude, but llamas and alpacas can graze there. The guinea pig was a native of the Andean valleys below 4000 metres, and by 7500 BC they provided up to 40% of the meat in highland Colombia and Peru.

potato

1 EARLY AMERICAN AGRICULTURE

The process of domestication in the Americas was slow. Archaic foragers, dependent on collected food, began to sow seeds from wild species and selected seed from the best cropping plants to use the following year. It is impossible to identify the first cultivated plants as they were identical to wild types, and so the birthplace of farming will never be pinpointed. The first areas of cultivation of individual species can, however, be roughly identified as they are located where the wild ancestors of the domesticates occur naturally.

Map legend — evidence of:
- early plant domestication
- early animal domestication
- growth of wild teosinte
- habitat of wild llama

the Americas: early domesticated plants and animals:
- amaranth
- tepary bean
- bottle gourd
- chilli pepper
- cotton
- maize
- cucurbit (squash)
- common bean
- pumpkin
- setaria
- lima bean
- potato
- sweet potato
- ulluco
- quinoa
- dog
- llama
- guinea pig

GUILÁ NAQUITZ: DIET

The well-preserved plant remains at Guilá Naquitz (*below*) show that the cave was in use between August and December each year, when the nuts, seeds, pods, edible fruits and fibrous parts of the vegetation of the thorn forest and mesquite grassland surrounding the site were ripe and abundant. At this time of year piñon nuts and curcurbit seeds, both high in protein, fat, carbohydrate and calories, were probably dietary staples together with *susí* nuts. They were augmented by acorn flour, roasted agave hearts and the jelly-like insides of acacia and mesquite pods. Prickly pear fruits (*tunas*) and the fruit of organ cactus were also eaten, as were the tender young stems of prickly pear cactus (*nopales*). *Nanche* fruits, hackberries and wild beans were also eaten in this predominantly vegetarian diet. Comparatively small quantities of meat were consumed; the principal species hunted and trapped are shown in the chart (*right*).

Subsistence: species hunted at Guilá Naquitz

Species	%
white-tailed deer	
cottontail rabbit	
mud turtle	
band-tailed pigeon	
dove	
barn owl	
songbirds	

% scale: 0 10 20 30 40 50

Subsistence: plants and diet

Plant	Apr	May	Jun	Jul	Aug	Sep	Oct	Nov	Dec	Jan	Feb	Mar	no. of grams consumed	no. of kilocalories represented
acorns													629	1812
agave													140	176
nopales													97	12
guaje seeds													54	19
nanches													30	21
mesquite pods					pods			stored seeds					14	42
hackberries													13	4
opuntia fruits													12	9
susi nuts													5	30
beans			flowers			seeds							3	4
piñon nuts													1	6
wild onions				flower				bulbs					1	0
cucurbit					flowers		seeds						1	4

2 EARLY FOOD PLANTS

The food plants shown here are only six of more than one hundred plants domesticated in pre-Columbian America. Potatoes, beans, chilli peppers, maize and squashes, today all plants of world-wide importance, were first cultivated in America during the period 8000–4000 BC. In many cases their early forms did not look much like their modern descendants. The wild ancestors produced far smaller edible parts: the earliest known maize cobs, from the Tehuacán Valley, Mexico, were only 3 centimetres long. Maize and beans were among the first cultivated plants in Mexico, a fortunate choice of early cultivars, as together they provide a complete, balanced diet: carbohydrates, protein and amino acids. In the Andes special food plants which flourished at altitudes of over 3000 metres were domesticated. Tubers included the familiar potato, also ulluco, mashua and oca, and grains such as quinoa, tarwi and cañihua.

runner bean *ulluco* *pepper* *cob* *pod* *flower* *maize plant* *squash plant* *seed* *kernels* *fruit*

3 GUILÁ NAQUITZ: A MEXICAN CAVE

Guilá Naquitz is a rock shelter in Oaxaca, Mexico, occupied by food foragers and incipient farmers from 8900 BC to 6700 BC. At Guilá Naquitz six preceramic living floors were found, and analysis revealed pathways, hearths, storage and dumping areas where plant food processing, butchering, cooking and tool-making took place. Men's and women's areas became more distinct over the 2200-year-long use of the cave, showing the emergence of a sexual division of labour which may be attributable to the adoption of primitive farming.

Finds from the site include: A *ground stone mano, length 9cm, and* **B** *ball of* Lemaireocerus *(organ cactus) gum, diameter 7cm. It was probably used for sticking stone points onto shafts.*

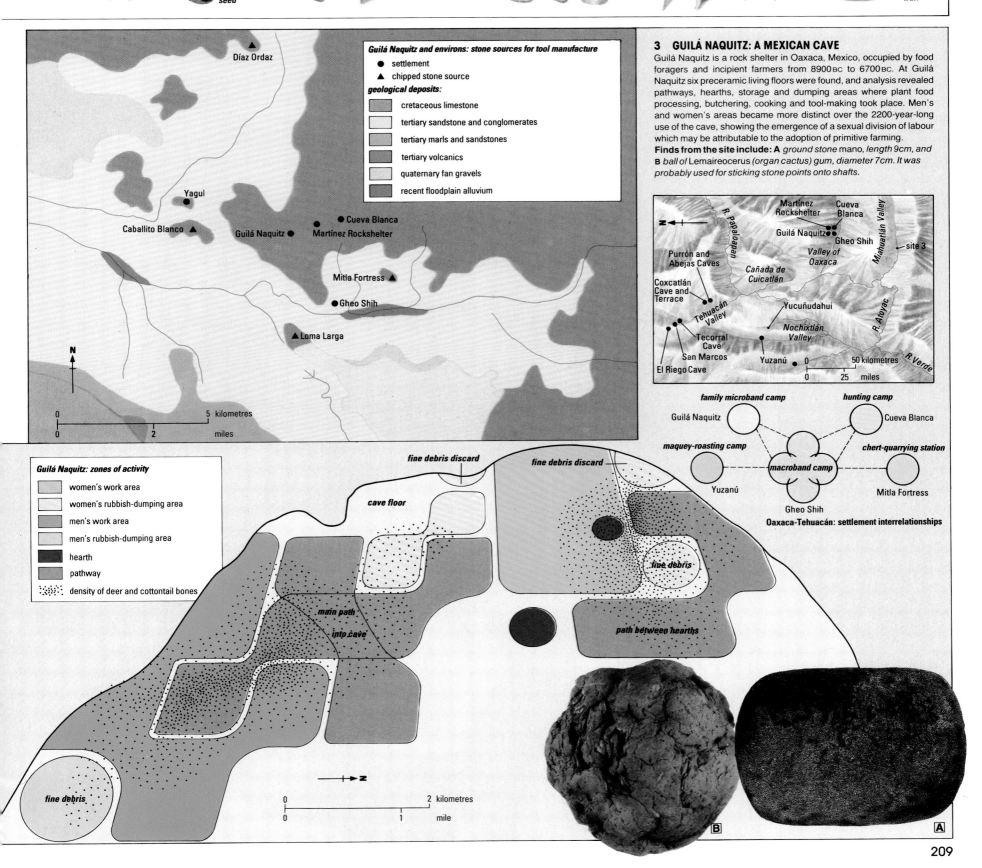

First villages of the Americas

The transition in the Americas from an incipient farming economy to a truly agriculture-based way of life was a slow one. During the millennia 4000–1000 BC farming based on plants such as maize, beans, squash, manioc, chilli peppers, sunflowers, amaranth, potatoes, cotton and bottle gourds gradually developed in Middle and South America and extended into parts of North America such as New Mexico, Kentucky, Missouri and the eastern woodlands.

In about 2500 BC, revolutionary improvements in plant yields resulting from selection and hybridisation meant that up to 25 times as many people could be supported by farming than had been possible by hunting and gathering in a comparable area, and there was a resulting population increase. The first permanent hamlets, villages and towns appeared, housing up to 4000 people; pottery was first made; loom weaving was invented; and ground and polished stone tools began to replace the chipped and flaked artefacts of the Archaic period. Female figurines modelled in clay were innovations, possibly representing belief in fertility cults. A growing stratification of society is evident: some graves, for example, contain only a body, while others, smaller in number, were furnished with beads, mirrors, marine shell ornaments, jewellery and exotic coloured feathers. By 2600 BC, on the central coast of Peru, large temple-mounds were being built, entailing the movement of thousands of tonnes of earth or dressed stone by well-organised teams of labourers.

The beginnings of this social complexity can be seen on the Peruvian coast between 5000 and 2000 BC, when hunting became less important as more reliance was placed on the abundant marine resources and the wild plant foods found in the river valleys. By 3500 BC at Chilca and Ancón, cotton was cultivated and used to make fishing nets and twilled textiles. Within two hundred years squashes were grown, and by 3000 BC bottle gourds were being grown for use as containers and floats for nets. Permanent villages such as Las Haldas grew up first on the coast. From about 2500 BC, when cultivation became more important, settlements moved to the river valleys to be near the fertile alluvium deposited during seasonal flooding, and small-scale irrigation works soon appeared. Large complexes of platforms, sunken courts and pits, made of adobe and stone, have been found at Aspero, Sechin Alto, Huaca de los Reyes and Garagay, dated 2600–2000 BC. Finds from both highland and lowland sites indicate that long-distance trade had been established by the mid-3rd millennium BC. Coloured marine shells, for example, were exchanged for Andean tubers or for brilliant feathers from Amazonia.

Most of the fundamental features of later Andean civilisations were well developed by 2500 BC. Two key elements lacking were pottery and widespread maize cultivation. Both appeared in about 2000 BC, and may be connected, as the new crop needed new storage and cooking containers. Elsewhere in South America pottery had been made for at least a thousand years. The earliest ceramics in the Americas have been found in Colombia and coastal Ecuador, and were made between 3600 and 3000 BC. It is curious that more complex societies did not evolve in this area, but in the desert coastlands and highlands of Peru.

In Mexico the best evidence for early agriculture comes from the Tehuacán Valley and from Oaxaca. Both these areas have dry climates, which are excellent for organic preservation. The story in the moist lowlands is much less clear, as plant remains have been destroyed. By 3400–2300 BC there were villages of 5–10 circular pit houses in the Tehuacán Valley. Bottle gourds, beans, black sapote, squash, maize and pumpkins were all under cultivation. Full dependence on agriculture developed only gradually, however, and even at this late stage, some food was still obtained by hunting and gathering. The earliest ceramics in Mesoamerica, however, appeared before this date, in about 2300 BC. Pottery had become widespread by 1500 BC, and noticeable similarities in decoration and shape between the ceramics found in coastal Guatemala, and the very early pottery from Colombia and Ecuador points to some contact, probably by sea, between these widely separated areas.

In Oaxaca large villages were established by 1150 BC. Differentiation in status was already developed. The rich were buried with mirrors, cut shell ornaments, jades, ear spools and grey and white ceramics. Even greater advances had been made on the Gulf coast, where very soon after the establishment of village life large ceremonial structures or public buildings were built by the Olmec, the civilisation sometimes referred to as the 'mother culture' of Mesoamerica.

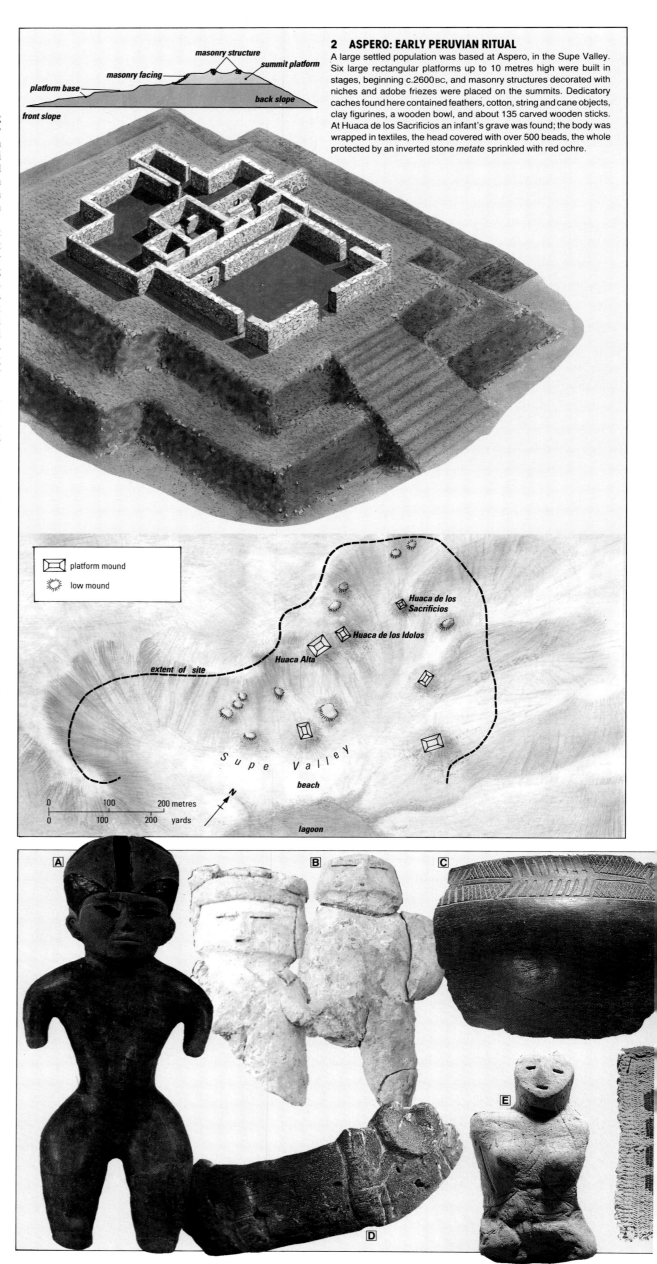

2 ASPERO: EARLY PERUVIAN RITUAL

A large settled population was based at Aspero, in the Supe Valley. Six large rectangular platforms up to 10 metres high were built in stages, beginning c.2600 BC, and masonry structures decorated with niches and adobe friezes were placed on the summits. Dedicatory caches found here contained feathers, cotton, string and cane objects, clay figurines, a wooden bowl, and about 135 carved wooden sticks. At Huaca de los Sacrificios an infant's grave was found; the body was wrapped in textiles, the head covered with over 500 beads, the whole protected by an inverted stone *metate* sprinkled with red ochre.

Legend:
- • early agricultural settlement
- ◯ important preceramic site
- ✕ public building
- ▬ oldest dated pottery

vegetation zones:
- tropical rainforest
- forest
- high altitude grassland
- alluvial flood plain
- grassland
- scrub and semidesert
- desert
- → possible trans-Andean route

1 THE FOUNDATIONS OF AMERICAN CIVILISATION

The nuclear area of Andean civilisation can be discerned by 2500 BC when, in a remarkable progression from simple village life, ceremonial centres were established along a 700 kilometre length of the Peruvian coast and in parts of the central highlands. This is the first monumental architecture in the Americas, and the massive platforms and mounds, on top of which stood temples, were built by people who did not yet make pottery. These preceramic ceremonial centres functioned both as religious and economic meeting places. River valleys formed the lines of communication over the difficult terrain between the coast, the highlands and the rain forest of the Upper Amazon, linking the vastly different ecological zones, each of which produced materials desired by the others. Cotton, marine shell and anchovetas came from the coast; wool and Andean root crops from the highlands; and coloured feathers and hallucinogenic snuffs from Amazonia. These materials have all been found in high-status graves and in dedicatory deposits within temple-mounds or at *huacas*, places such as caves which had supernatural significance. North–South routes were also open to early travellers and traders, either by sea, along the coastal plain or via the chain of Andean basins and valleys.

In Central America complex societies did not evolve until about one thousand years later than in the Andean area. Settled village life emerged in about 1500 BC, flourishing in the humid areas of the Pacific and Gulf coasts and in the fertile highland valleys of Oaxaca and Mexico. Although a very large number of early hamlets have been found (indicating a major population increase) it is, as yet, impossible to say where the transition to a fully settled agricultural economy took place. It has been suggested, based on evidence from Cuello, Belize, that it occurred in the Maya lowlands as early as 2000 BC. Excavations at the later Olmec site, San Lorenzo, show that in about 1500 BC it consisted of two small farming settlements of no great distinction, but that by 1350 BC a massive public works project began, together with the appearance of Olmec traits. The Olmec was to become the first great civilisation of Central America.

3 THE AMERICAS: EARLY VILLAGE CRAFTS

A Hollow painted pottery figurine of a dwarf with large head, elongated torso and stubby legs. Tehuacán Valley, Mexico, c.1000 BC, height 45cm. **B** Unfired clay figurines found in a dedicatory cache in Huaca de los Idolos, Aspero, Peru. 2300–1900 BC, height 80cm. **C** Fragments of a burnished Valdivia period bowl decorated with incised and excised motifs. c.1500 BC, diameter of complete bowl, c.25cm. **D** Side view of a fragmentary, burned wooden bowl with carved decoration in the shape of frogs. Huaca de los Sacrificios, Aspero, Peru, 2300–1900 BC, length 12cm. **E** Anthropomorphic clay figurine from Poverty Point, Louisiana. 1300–1000 BC, less than 5cm tall. **F** Twined cotton textile with pattern showing a condor with a snake in its belly. Huaca Prieta, Peru, 3000–2000 BC, width 21cm.

F

Map labels:

Mississippi R., Red R., Rio Grande, Poverty Point, Gulf of Mexico, Bahamas, Cuba, Hispaniola, Puerto Rico, Jamaica, Caribbean Sea

Gulf of Campeche, Pavón, Chupícuaro, El Arbolillo, El Trapiche, YUCATÁN, El Opeño, Valley of Mexico, Remojadas, Capacha, Tlatilco, Gualupita, Taxla Cerro de la Bomba, Cuello, Gulf of Honduras, Tlapacoya, San Lorenzo, Mezcala, Santa Marta, San Jerónimo, Chiapa de Corzo, Puerto Marquez, Santa Rosa, Zanja, Dainzu, Boca del Río, GUATEMALA, Juxtlahuaca, San José Mogote, Izapa, Monte Albán, La Victoria

La Pitia, Monsú, Puerto Hormiga, R. Orinoco, Cerro Mangote, Monagrillo, COLOMBIA, R. Amazon

ECUADOR, Agua Blanca, Machalilla, Valdivia, Cerro Narrío, Real Alto, El Encanto, Upper Amazon, R. Araguaia, R. Parnaiba

Huaca de los Reyes, La Galgada, Tutishcainyo, Huaca Prieta, Huaricoto, Huaca Negra, Cueva de las Lechuzas, Los Morteros, Sechín Alto, Las Haldas, Kotosh, Culebras, Shillacoto, Huarmey, R. São Francisco, Aspero, Huacho, Río Seco, PERU, Garagay, Ancón, El Paraíso, Wichquana, La Florida, Chupas, Mina Perdida, Asia, Chanapata, Chilca, Chapanata

Pacific Ocean, Andes Mts, Atlantic Ocean, R. Paraná, R. Uruguay, R. Plate, Falkland Is

Early civilisations: the Andes

The history of cultures in the central and southern Andes between 1000 BC and AD 650 is a complex one and not yet fully understood. However these cultures established features which appear in all subsequent Andean civilisations. Periods of widespread uniformity in the area (referred to as the Early and Middle Horizons) alternating with times of far greater regional diversity (the Intermediate Periods).

The Early Horizon period (1200-200 BC) was dominated by the Chavín culture, the earliest Andean civilisation. The first Chavín sites date from 1200 BC, but the culture is named after the type site at Chavín de Huantar, which was at its peak between 850 and 200 BC. Here a substantial temple complex has been found, its monumental stone-built platform honeycombed with passages and rooms. In these were concealed cult objects; the Great Image, a 4.5-metre-high stone carving of a deity with projecting fangs, a snarling mouth, and serpentine hair is still in place. The Chavín pantheon contains jaguars, eagles, caymans, snakes and anthropomorphic figures with these same features. The Chavín sphere of influence extended from the Lambayeque Valley in the North to Paracas on the south coast.

Artefacts in pottery, shell, wood, stone, silver and gold, and well-preserved woven and painted textiles, all decorated with images of the Chavín pantheon, have been found throughout the extensive area.

By 200 BC many Andean valleys had developed distinctive local cultures, heralding the return of regionalism. However, this Early Intermediate period also produced two main civilisations: Nazca and Moche. Nazca, on the south coast of Peru, continued the region's established traditions of fine textiles and pottery. The pots, painted before firing, depicted animals, birds, fish and plants, as well as human trophy heads and decapitated bodies. Similar motifs were also traced, in vast sizes, on the surface of the desert between Cahuachi and Palpa. These famous 'Nazca lines' were made by clearing away surface stones to reveal the underlying rock. The lines depict either animals such as monkeys, spiders, and birds, or outline geometric shapes. Their purpose is unknown, they may have been offerings to the gods.

The northern Peruvian coast, meanwhile, was dominated between c. AD 1-600, by the Moche culture. Centred on the Moche and Chicama Valleys and expanded by military conquest, Moche territory ranged from the Pacasmayo Valley to the Santa and Nepena Valleys. It produced impressive urban and religious centres. One such was the Pyramid of the Sun, a solid adobe structure 350 metres long and 40 metres high. Major public works were carried out, including irrigation schemes which enabled farmers to use desert land to grow maize, peanuts, peppers and sweet potatoes. Craftsmen produced some of the finest pottery and goldworking in pre-Columbian America – goldsmiths had mastered the techniques of gilding, making alloys, and casting by both the lost-wax process and using moulds. Potters used moulds to mass-produce vessels and also made thin-walled stirrup-spouted pots, decorated with scenes of everyday life, warfare, and ritual or mythological events.

Between AD 500-1000 (The Middle Horizon period) two empires emerged and dominated much of the central and southern Andes and parts of the coast. Their relationship is unknown but they shared a single art style which suggests a common religion. The first civilisation is named after its capital, Tiahuanaco, a populous city lying in the bleak altiplano of Bolivia, and a centre of religious pilgrimage throughout the Andes. Various motifs on its stone architecture, such as running winged figures and felines, are also depicted on polychrome painted pots and in multi-coloured textiles. Although these were executed in the local style, they can be traced back to the Chavín culture. Similar figures also appear, though more crudely expressed, on the pottery of the second empire, Huari. Both these empires administered their vast territories from deliberately created centres, where government officials supervised vast public works carried out as labour tax by the inhabitants.

These cultures laid down much for those that followed. It was on these methods of exploitation and control that succeeding cultures, especially the authoritarian Inca, depended for their existence. Firm political, religious and social foundations had thus been established a thousand years before the Inca rose to power and created the largest empire ever to exist in the Americas.

2 TIAHUANACO: AN ANDEAN CITY

At 3660 metres above sea level, Tiahuanaco, with a population of 30,000-40,000, was the highest ancient city of the Andes. Its outstanding stone architecture is dominated by temple complexes such as the Akapana and Kalasasaya, with sunken courts, monumental sculptures and megalithic gateways. The city rulers initiated large-scale land reclamation schemes to feed their citizens. At Pampa Koani (below), the Río Catari was canalised, and an extensive drained field system for intensive cultivation was created. Two regional administrative centres were situated at Luqurmata and Pajchiri, while farmers lived in small hamlets on raised mounds.

Lake Titicaca

see below
● Pajchiri
● Luqurmata
● Tiahuanaco

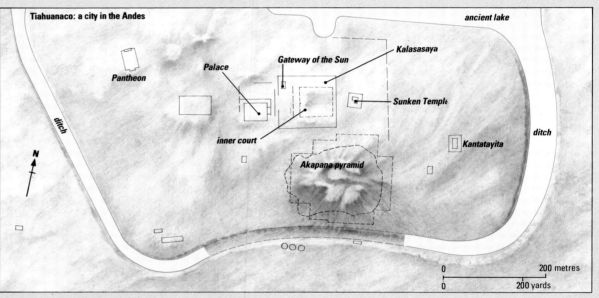

Tiahuanaco: a city in the Andes

ancient lake

Pantheon
Palace
Gateway of the Sun
Kalasasaya
Sunken Temple
inner court
Kantatayita
Akapana pyramid
ditch
ditch

0 — 200 metres
0 — 200 yards

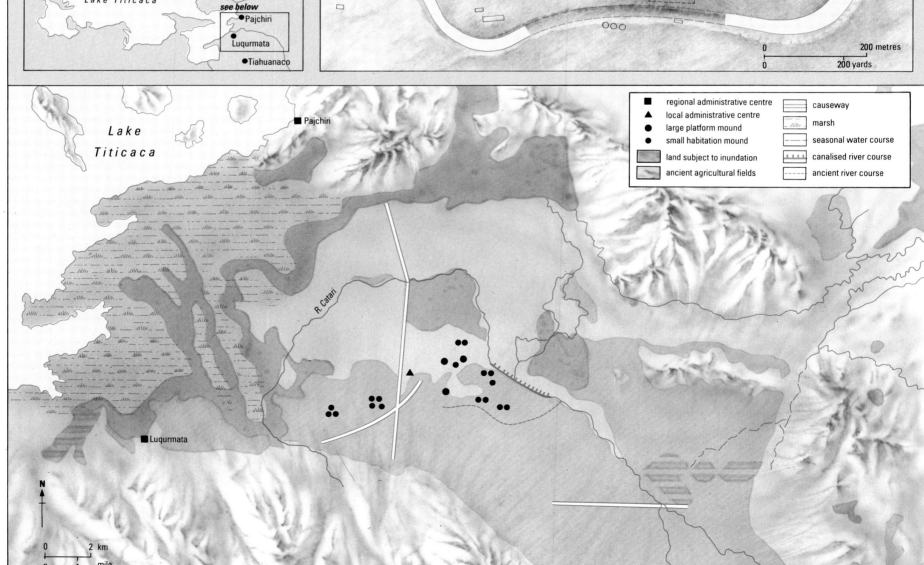

■ regional administrative centre
▲ local administrative centre
● large platform mound
● small habitation mound
land subject to inundation
ancient agricultural fields

causeway
marsh
seasonal water course
canalised river course
ancient river course

■ Pajchiri

Lake Titicaca

R. Catari

▲

■ Luqurmata

0 — 2 km
0 — 1 mile

Pampa Koani: an agricultural hinterland

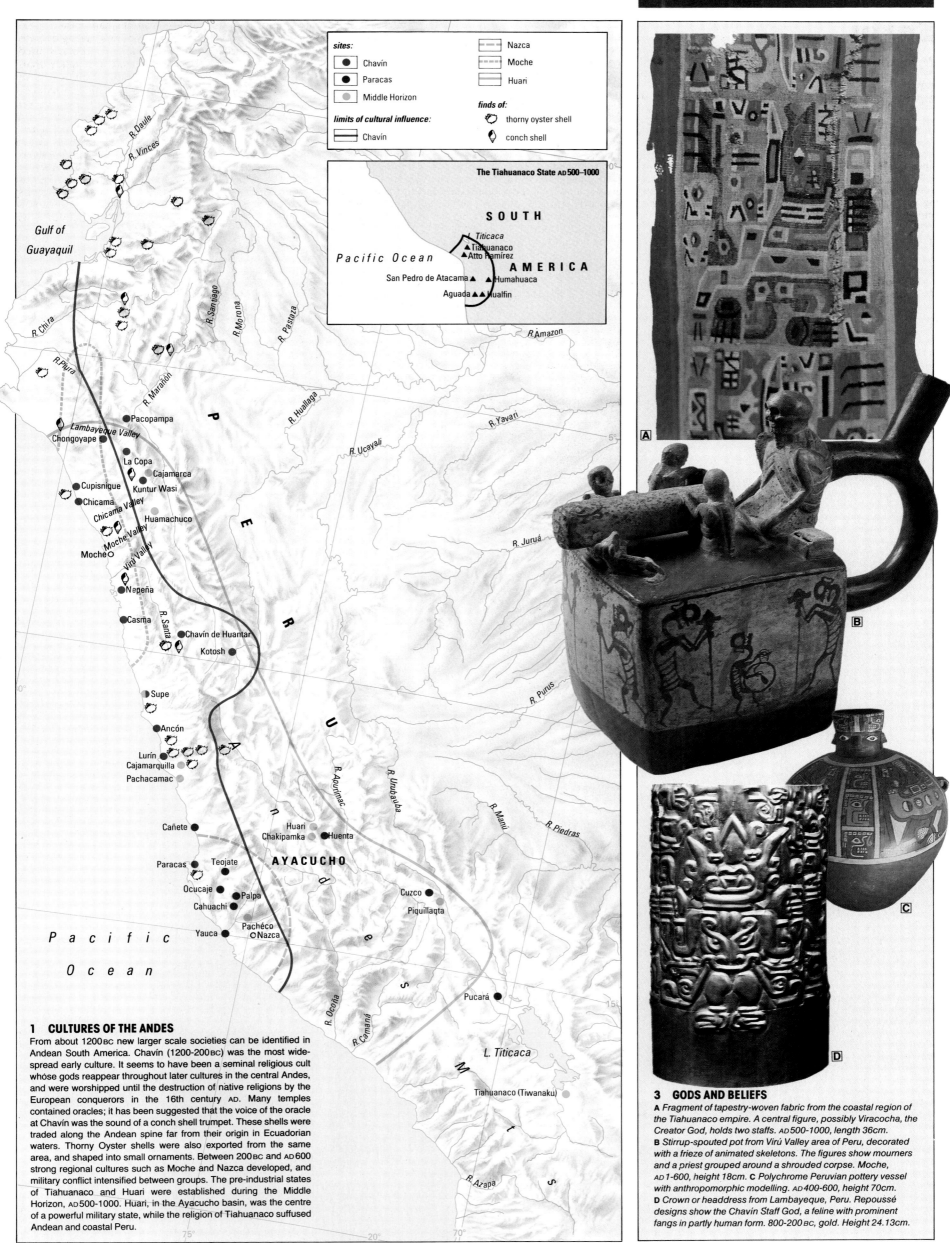

1 CULTURES OF THE ANDES

From about 1200 BC new larger scale societies can be identified in Andean South America. Chavín (1200-200 BC) was the most widespread early culture. It seems to have been a seminal religious cult whose gods reappear throughout later cultures in the central Andes, and were worshipped until the destruction of native religions by the European conquerors in the 16th century AD. Many temples contained oracles; it has been suggested that the voice of the oracle at Chavín was the sound of a conch shell trumpet. These shells were traded along the Andean spine far from their origin in Ecuadorian waters. Thorny Oyster shells were also exported from the same area, and shaped into small ornaments. Between 200 BC and AD 600 strong regional cultures such as Moche and Nazca developed, and military conflict intensified between groups. The pre-industrial states of Tiahuanaco and Huari were established during the Middle Horizon, AD 500-1000. Huari, in the Ayacucho basin, was the centre of a powerful military state, while the religion of Tiahuanaco suffused Andean and coastal Peru.

3 GODS AND BELIEFS

A Fragment of tapestry-woven fabric from the coastal region of the Tiahuanaco empire. A central figure, possibly Viracocha, the Creator God, holds two staffs. AD 500-1000, length 36cm.
B Stirrup-spouted pot from Virú Valley area of Peru, decorated with a frieze of animated skeletons. The figures show mourners and a priest grouped around a shrouded corpse. Moche, AD 1-600, height 18cm. C Polychrome Peruvian pottery vessel with anthropomorphic modelling. AD 400-600, height 70cm. D Crown or headdress from Lambayeque, Peru. Repoussé designs show the Chavín Staff God, a feline with prominent fangs in partly human form. 800-200 BC, gold. Height 24.13cm.

Early civilisations: Central America

Fundamental features of Central American civilisation first appeared between 1200 and 150 BC: stelae and monuments commemorating rulers and their reigns, the hieroglyphic writing system, a complex notation of calendrical calculations, and the ritual ball game, were all established. Towns and cities grew, outstripping earlier farming villages. The city of Monte Albán in Oaxaca had a population of up to 16,000 in 200 BC. Such cities were governed by elite groups capable of organising huge labour forces to construct temples, palaces and pyramids.

The most famous culture of the Early-Middle Formative period (1200-300 BC) in Central America is the Olmec, whose homeland lay in the wet tropical jungles of coastal Veracruz and Tabasco. The Olmec are known chiefly from their art carved in stone; few settlements have been discovered though recent excavations at Teopantecuanitlan (Tlacozotitlán), Guerrero, have revealed remains of a house belonging to a middle status family as well as a previously unknown ceremonial centre on the fringe of the Olmec world. Information comes principally from ceremonial centres such as San Lorenzo, La Venta and Tres Zapotes, where monumental basalt sculptures and small, exquisite hard stone carvings have been found *in situ*. The powerful art style of the Olmecs gives a glimpse of their religion, which was dominated by a pantheon of fearsome supernatural beings, part human, part animal. The animals, which are the prototype of later Central American deities, come from the fauna of the swampy forest and coast: harpy eagles, caimans, snakes and sharks. The most frequently represented god was a were-jaguar, conceived, according to a relief at Potrero Nuevo, when a woman copulated with a jaguar. The result of this union has puffy, infantile features and a snarling mouth with downturned corners, thick lips and fangs.

The Olmec homeland was an area measuring only 200 by 50 kilometres. San Lorenzo is the oldest known Olmec centre; it flourished from 1200 BC until 900 BC, when it was

1 CENTRAL AMERICAN CIVILISATION
Between 1200 and 300 BC simple village societies in some parts of Central America were transformed into the earliest hierarchical urban civilisations. This metamorphosis has been identified in three principal regions of Mexico: the Valley of Mexico, the Gulf Coast and the Valley of Oaxaca. In the Valley of Mexico Tlatilco, a town covering 65 hectares, was well established by 1200 BC. Richly furnished graves indicate a stratified society, which was in contact with the most influential culture ever to emerge in Central America, the Olmec. Traits established by the Olmec, whose homeland was the Gulf Coast of Mexico, were so strong throughout the area's prehistory that it has been called the 'Mother Culture' of this region. Finds of Olmec trade pieces indicate the great extent of their influence. In Oaxaca, the Middle Formative city of Monte Albán has yielded early Zapotec architecture, calendrical inscriptions and sculpture with slightly Olmec features.

3 MONTE ALBÁN: A ZAPOTEC TEMPLE
Excavations of the earliest Zapotec phases of settlement at Monte Albán, Oaxaca, have revealed the Temple of the *Danzantes* (Dancers), a large flat-topped mound flanked by more than 150 stone slabs decorated with low relief carved figures of naked men shown in strange postures as if dancing or swimming. They date to c.500 BC. Their distorted poses may indicate that they are corpses, probably the bodies of enemy leaders slain by the early rulers of the city. Although there are faint Olmec traits, for example the downturned mouths, the *Danzantes* are uniquely Zapotec in style. Sexual organs were emphasised, and some show blood pouring from genital mutilations. Brazen nudity was considered shameful and was frequently a sign of captivity in Central American cultures. Hieroglyphic inscriptions and calendrical notations using the 52-year Calendar Round associated with the figures are among the oldest examples of literacy in the Americas.

4 LA VENTA: A VOTIVE OFFERING
The burial of valuable and beautiful votive offerings in caches is a feature of major Olmec sites. Perhaps the most extraordinary of all caches was discovered at La Venta, Tabasco, where a group of stone figurines and axes had been arranged to represent a scene of ritual activity (*see photograph* D). When the offering was made (*see diagram below*) the bases of the figurines and axes were embedded in a mound of reddish-brown sand, while the whole cache was covered with white sand heaped up to conceal the figures. Some time later an elliptical-shaped hole the same size as the figure layout, and centred directly above it, was dug through the floors and down to the level of the heads of the figurines. It was then refilled. The purpose of this 'checking' operation is unknown, but indicates that precise records were kept of the position of caches so that they could be easily relocated.

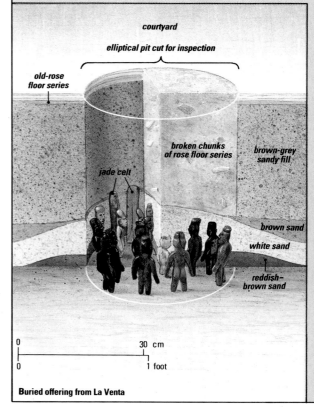

Buried offering from La Venta

destroyed. Its leading role was taken over by La Venta, located on a small island in coastal swamps. Here, a 34-metre-high clay pyramid, possibly in the shape of a fluted volcanic cone, was built, taking an estimated 800,000 work days to complete. Two plazas extended northwards from it, and rows of 3-metre-high basalt columns flanked one plaza. The layout of the ceremonial precinct has been interpreted as a massive stylised jaguar mask, and within its limits have been found three rectangular pavements each of approximately 480 serpentine blocks arranged to form jaguar masks. These pavements are one example of a dedicatory offering or 'cache' which are characteristic finds at Olmec sites.

Although the Olmecs were not a peaceful group, to judge from armed figures shown on some monuments, they were not empire builders. They established trade networks to obtain exotic raw materials such as basalt, obsidian, cinnabar, serpentine, jade and iron ore. Chalcatzingo in Morelos was probably a frontier trading station where the local populace were introduced to Olmec religion through the didactic rock-cut relief scenes. Olmec cultural influence was felt far afield – possibly even reaching Monte Albán in the Valley of Oaxaca where the Zapotecs had developed their own distinctive cultural identity and a characteristic style of monumental stone building. In Oaxaca or the Valley of Mexico Olmec influence may have been spread as much by diplomacy and marriage links as by trade, possibly strengthened by missionary activity. However, despite such evidence for widespread Olmec influence, recent archaeological research indicates that the development of complex towns and ceremonialism occurred in Oaxaca, at San José Mogote, and Morelos, at Chalcatzingo, as early as and relatively independently of Olmec growth in the Gulf coast lowlands.

Like San Lorenzo five centuries before, La Venta was defaced and abandoned in 400–300 BC, and the great days of the Olmec were over. At Tres Zapotes occupation continued, but as a derivative shadow. The site has, however, produced a stela with one of the oldest dates known in the New World, a Long Count (calendrical) inscription corresponding to 3 September 32 BC. The Gulf coast nurtured the seedlings of Mexican and Maya civilisations, establishing patterns of culture which endured for more than 2500 years.

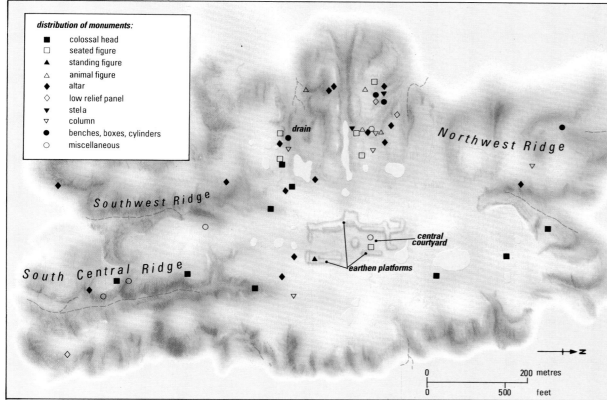

distribution of monuments:

- ■ colossal head
- □ seated figure
- ▲ standing figure
- △ animal figure
- ◆ altar
- ◇ low relief panel
- ▼ stela
- ▽ column
- ● benches, boxes, cylinders
- ○ miscellaneous

drain

Northwest Ridge

Southwest Ridge

central courtyard

South Central Ridge

earthen platforms

0 — 200 metres
0 — 500 feet

2 SAN LORENZO: AN OLMEC CEREMONIAL CENTRE

San Lorenzo is situated in the hot, moist homeland of the Olmecs, the Bay of Campeche. Flourishing from 1200 to 900 BC, it consists of a natural plateau which stands about 50 metres high and measures 1.25 kilometres north to south. The uppermost seven metres of the mound are composed of an artificial fill of earth and clay, and the long, finger-like ridges on the north-west, north and south sides are possibly part of an uncompleted scheme to shape the plateau into the giant figure of a flying bird. On the summit of the plateau stood a ceremonial complex of earthen platforms delimiting courtyards, a court for the sacred ball game, and pools for ritual bathing. Excess water from these was removed through a network of deeply buried drains up to 170 metres long, made of sections of U-shaped basalt troughs fitted with lids. Basalt was brought from the Tuxtla Mountains 80 kilometres distant. Sculpture at San Lorenzo includes stelae, reliefs, columns and eight colossal heads of rulers, up to 2.85 metres high, each wearing the helmet-like headdress used by players in the ball game, and 'altars' (probably thrones) – flat-topped basalt blocks weighing up to 40 tonnes and decorated with carvings of rulers holding were-jaguar babies. Most of the large monuments had been deliberately and brutally defaced in a frenzy of destruction which took place, for unknown reasons, in about 900 BC. The mutilated carvings were buried in rows along the tops of the ridges, eventually tumbling into the ravines.

Excavation of some of the 200 house mounds at San Lorenzo show that the centre was supported by the high agricultural productivity of the surrounding area, where crops – predominantly maize – were raised on the seasonally inundated fields. Animal bones from middens demonstrate that fish and domesticated dogs provided most of the first-class protein in the diet. Deer and wild pig were eaten occasionally, as, perhaps, was human flesh, suggested by finds of human bones bearing butchering and burn marks.

5 OLMEC ART

A *Standing figure of a were-jaguar, the eyes are inlaid with pyrites, and paw prints are carved on the bottom of the hind feet. Olmec, 800-300 BC, serpentine, height 8cm.* B *Large votive axe or 'celt', the butt carved in the form of the baby-faced god, characterised by a snarling downturned mouth, V-shaped cleft in the head and serrated eyebrows indicating a supernatural being. Olmec, 800-300 BC, jade, height 31cm.* C *Polished pottery vessel in the shape of an armadillo. From the Tlatilco cemetery, Valley of Mexico, 1200-900 BC, length 30cm.* D *Cache of 16 stone figurines and 6 celts arranged to show a ritual scene. Olmec, La Venta, 800-400 BC, jade, serpentine and granite, height 18cm.* E *Colossal head, of a ruler from San Lorenzo. The helmet-like headpiece has side straps and a central identifying glyph. Olmec, 1200-900 BC, basalt, height 2.85m.*

Teotihuacán: an American metropolis

In AD 500 Teotihuacán was the sixth largest city in the world with a population of c.200,000, and the centre of an empire which directly controlled some 25,000 square kilometres of central Mexico and dominated Mesoamerica. Sited on a natural cave (later encapsulated by the Pyramid of the Sun) it became a place of cosmic importance to the early inhabitants of the region. They may have believed it was the birthplace of the Sun and the Moon, the holy place where time itself began. Teotihuacán was the most important pilgrimage centre in the whole of Mesoamerica – hundreds of temples have been identified within the city limits, and altars have been found in all residential quarters, together with the remains of pottery incense burners and figurines of deities. Here the gods familiar from later Mexican civilisations are depicted: Tlaloc, the Rain God, his consort Chalchihuitlicue, the Water Goddess, and Quetzalcoatl, the Feathered Serpent, appear in brilliantly coloured murals decorating temples and palaces.

The decision to construct the Pyramid of the Sun, one of the largest artificial structures in pre-Columbian America, to mark this site of immense ritual importance, was made as part of the impressive urbanisation programme which took place at Teotihuacán during the 1st century AD. At this time the dispersed rural population was persuaded to relocate and become city dwellers. For the next 600 years approximately 90% of the inhabitants of the east and south valley of Mexico lived in Teotihuacán. More than 20 square kilometres of temples, palaces and residences were laid out on a rectangular grid plan. The organisation of workforces necessary to carry out such a rigid scheme, and the fact that for half a millennium the city plan was adhered to, demonstrate the great power of the rulers of Teotihuacán.

The precise nature of the government of the city is unknown; there are no written documents to enlighten us, only calendrical glyphs giving dates. Few military

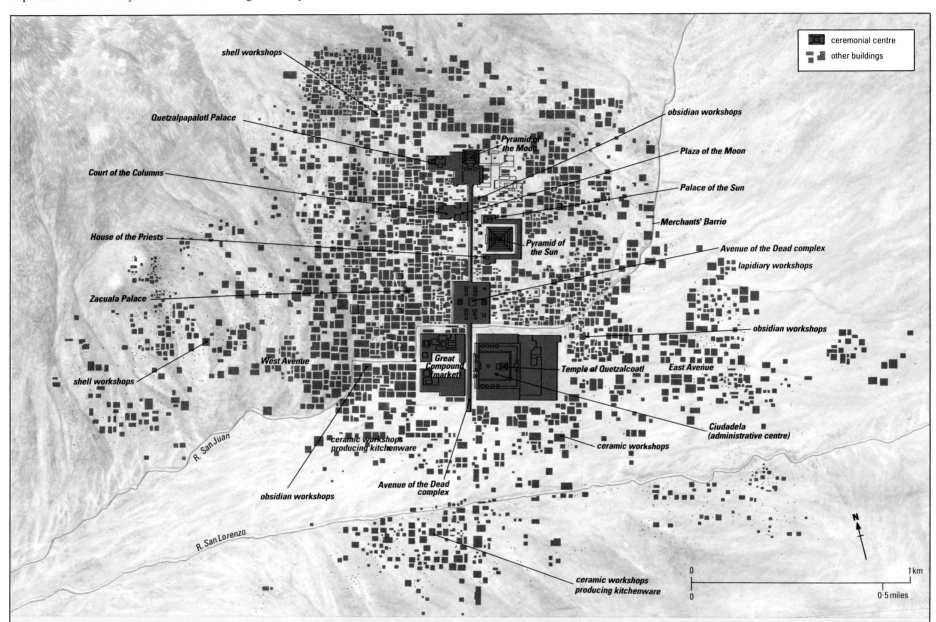

ceremonial centre
other buildings

shell workshops
Quetzalpapalotl Palace
Court of the Columns
House of the Priests
Zacuala Palace
West Avenue
shell workshops
obsidian workshops
ceramic workshops producing kitchenware
Avenue of the Dead complex
ceramic workshops producing kitchenware

Pyramid of the Moon
obsidian workshops
Plaza of the Moon
Palace of the Sun
Merchants' Barrio
Pyramid of the Sun
Avenue of the Dead complex
lapidary workshops
obsidian workshops
Great Compound market
Temple of Quetzalcoatl
East Avenue
ceramic workshops
Ciudadela (administrative centre)

R. San Juan
R. San Lorenzo

N

0   1km
0   0.5 miles

2 THE CITY OF TEOTIHUACÁN

The grid-pattern layout of Teotihuacán covered more than 20 square kilometres and was surveyed as one massive operation. The basic unit of measurement was approximately 57 metres. Even the Río San Juan was canalised to conform to the scheme. The core of the city was the ceremonial centre, whose main north–south axis was the 'Avenue of the Dead'. The northern end of the Avenue of the Dead is marked by the Pyramid of the Moon (*foreground right*), and the wide avenue over five kilometres long was lined with more than 75 temples constructed on flat-topped pyramid mounds of adobe, soil and rubble faced with stone. They were painted red and white and some were decorated with polychrome murals of mythological scenes. Designed to overawe and impress, the Avenue of the Dead contains the oldest and largest structure at Teotihuacán; the Pyramid of the Sun (*right*), which is 70 metres high and made of an estimated 1,000,000 cubic metres of fill.

At the intersection of the Avenue of the Dead with the principal east–west axis are the Great Compound and the Ciudadela, a vast complex forming the political, religious, administrative and military centre of the city. The rulers of Teotihuacán probably lived in palaces within the Ciudadela. The Great Compound may have served as the central marketplace of the city.

At the bottom of the hierarchy were a lower class who occupied one- or two-roomed adobe huts scattered throughout the city, while the intermediate group of skilled craftsmen, traders, and farmers inhabited one-storey apartment compounds, clustered in groups often associated with specific crafts. Windowless stone walls surrounded rectangular plots 50-60 metres square, inside which were sub-units of rooms, patios and passageways. The apartments were family residential units and a single compound housed 60-100 people. One district in the west of Teotihuacán was occupied by an ethnic group from Oaxaca and another, in the east, by Maya, and they may have been embassies or merchant enclaves.

figures are portrayed until the very last phases of Teotihuacán, yet it seems that a warrior-merchant group existed and that territory was won by force of arms. The large population was supported by produce from the intensively irrigated fields in the Teotihuacán Valley, and the fertile alluvial soils on the swampy edges of neighbouring Lake Texcoco may also have been drained and used to raise food crops. Salt came from the saline lake waters; clay for pottery and quarries of building stone were available in the valley. As the state expanded it acquired the control of sources of important raw materials further afield, such as the obsidian sources at Pachuca and Otumba, where volcanic glassy rock used for making razor-sharp tools and weapons is found.

More than 400 craft workshops have been found at Teotihuacán, about one third of which produced pottery. Other crafts included obsidian working, the grinding and polishing of semi-precious stones such as jade and onyx, and the carving of imported marine shell into ornaments. These goods were traded at local, regional and foreign levels. In return, exotic materials were sent to the city: copal, tree resin which can be burned as incense, came from the Gulf coast, while lustrous green tail feathers from the quetzal bird were supplied from the Maya area.

Teotihuacán influence is best seen in the distant Maya lands. Kaminaljuyú in the Guatemalan Mountains was partly re-designed in the Teotihuacán style. Beneath the temple platforms lay graves of warrior-merchants from Teotihuacán who had assumed control of this area, possibly by marrying into local ruling houses. At Tikal,

in the Maya lowlands, stela 31 shows three figures: in the centre is Stormy Sky, ruler of Tikal in AD 435; on either side stand Teotihuacán warriors carrying shields decorated with the face of Tlaloc.

Warriors appear with increasing frequency in the art of the final century of Teotihuacán's existence, 650-750. They may represent either a symptom or a cause of the city's ultimate collapse, when it was destroyed by fire. There may have been a split in the governing hierarchy, or the city may have been invaded. It is even possible that it was a ritual destruction. Whatever happened, the city, which still retained a large population, kept its mythological significance and remained a place of pilgrimage until the downfall of the last indigenous Mesoamerican state, the Aztec empire, in 1521.

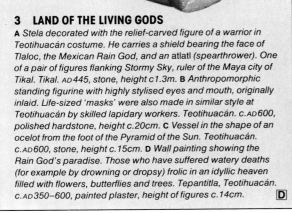

3 LAND OF THE LIVING GODS

A Stela decorated with the relief-carved figure of a warrior in Teotihuacán costume. He carries a shield bearing the face of Tlaloc, the Mexican Rain God, and an atlatl (spearthrower). One of a pair of figures flanking Stormy Sky, ruler of the Maya city of Tikal. Tikal. AD 445, stone, height c.1.3m. **B** Anthropomorphic standing figurine with highly stylised eyes and mouth, originally inlaid. Life-sized 'masks' were also made in similar style at Teotihuacán by skilled lapidary workers. Teotihuacán. c.AD 600, polished hardstone, height c.20cm. **C** Vessel in the shape of an ocelot from the foot of the Pyramid of the Sun. Teotihuacán. c.AD 600, stone, height c.15cm. **D** Wall painting showing the Rain God's paradise. Those who have suffered watery deaths (for example by drowning or dropsy) frolic in an idyllic heaven filled with flowers, butterflies and trees. Tepantitla, Teotihuacán. c.AD 350–600, painted plaster, height of figures c.14cm. **D**

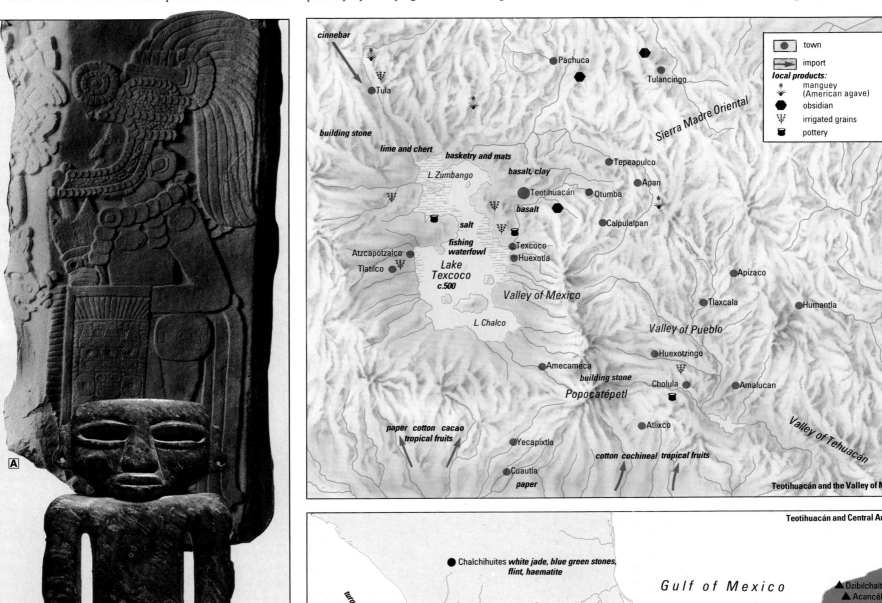

Teotihuacán and the Valley of Mexico

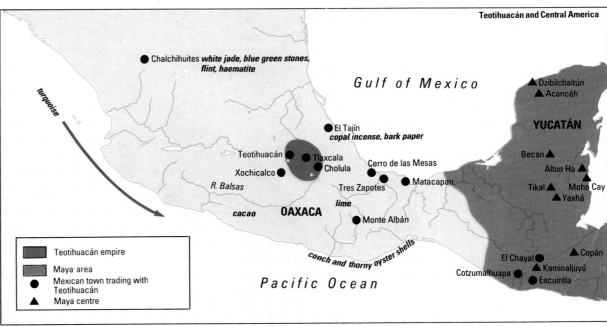

Teotihuacán and Central America

1 THE TEOTIHUACÁN EMPIRE

Teotihuacán controlled the eastern route into and out of the Valley of Mexico and the shallow lakes adjoining Lake Texcoco. For more than 600 years the city developed, managed and exploited the resources of its hinterland. Intensive agriculture was undertaken in the heavily irrigated valley, and manguey, a cactus whose leaves could be used for textiles and also making an intoxicating beverage, was an important crop. Vital staples such as salt, fish and waterfowl were taken from the lakes. Local clay was used for pottery, while quarries nearby supplied basalt, limestone and chert. A monopoly of obsidian deposits provided the raw material for tool manufacture. Long-distance trade links are shown by finds from Teotihuacán: turquoise and haematite from the north, marine shells from the Pacific and Gulf, and copal incense from the Gulf coast. Contact with the Maya some 1100 kilometres distant is demonstrated by Mexican trading posts in the southern Maya area and by finds of Teotihuacán ceramics at Tikal and Kaminaljuyú.

The Maya

The ancient Maya have been considered the most enigmatic of pre-Columbian civilisations ever since descriptions appeared in the 1840s of their ruined cities deep in the tropical rain forests of Mesoamerica. The Maya were the only truly literate civilisation of the Americas, but their hieroglyphic inscriptions remained impenetrable – only the numerals and dates could be read. Since the late 1950s, when major breakthroughs were made in deciphering the glyphs, however, our understanding of Maya culture has been revolutionised.

Large architectural complexes forming the centres of Maya cities were fundamental to their civilisation. The plan of such ceremonial centres was established in the earliest days of the Maya, dating back to 2000 BC. They were first built in a fully developed form, consisting of plazas surrounded by stone-built pyramids crowned by temples and palaces, during the Later Preclassic and Proto-Classic periods (300 BC–AD 300). These large politico-religious centres evolved into full-scale cities by the beginning of the Classic phase in AD 300, a period which is characterised by strong Mexican influences – evident in some temple architecture and burial offerings. The centuries AD 600–800 (the Late Classic) were a period of vigorous expansion. The city of Tikal was rebuilt and the major temples, palaces, plazas and ball courts were constructed at Palenque, Piedras Negras, Copán, Quiriguá, Naranjo and Cobá.

During the 9th century, Maya civilisation in the southern lowlands of Yucatán declined and collapsed. Cities were depopulated, and the last known stela was erected in 909. The collapse may have been caused by agricultural failures due to over-exploitation of a fragile ecosystem, flaws in the social system leading to internal unrest, or foreign invasion. At the same time, cities of the northern lowlands such as Uxmal, Kabáh, Sayil, and Labná, and the great urban centre of Chichén Itzá began to flourish. Strong central Mexican influences, some of which ultimately derived from the Toltec city of Tula, were present at this time, particularly at Chichén Itzá. However, these northern cities also declined after several centuries, and Chichén Itzá was abandoned in about 1200. After a period of diaspora the Maya founded the new city of Mayapán in northern Yucatán, which became their capital in 1328. However, the city was destroyed in the civil wars of the mid-15th century, and by the time of the first Spanish contact with Mesoamerica, from 1517 onwards, only a few small towns survived.

The seemingly undefended Classic Maya cities and the apparent purely ceremonial function of their central precincts led to the early idealisation of the Maya as a peaceful theocracy. However, the lowland Maya city-states did not exist in co operative tranquillity. They were constantly at war with each other, seeking tribute and captives destined to be sacrificial victims – blood-letting rituals which were commemorated on stone stelae. These aggressive city-states were led by hereditary dynasties of kings whose unity with the gods was proclaimed in the wall paintings, sculptures and inscriptions ornamenting official buildings. The so-called ceremonial centres were in fact the administrative and religious cores of true cities with populations of up to 50,000 people. Intensive agricultural techniques including raised field systems supplied maize, beans, squash, chilli peppers and root crops to feed the populace.

The Maya created the first comprehensive writing system in pre-Columbian America. They also excelled at astronomical observation and calendrical calculation, devising a numerical system based on units of 20 and including the concept of zero, with several calendars running simultaneously. The Long Count was also kept, a tally of the days elapsed from a base date, possibly August 3,114 BC, expressed in units of time ranging from 400 years to single days. Such great interest in time was partly for astrological reasons; the Maya believed that auspicious days under the control of suitable gods must be chosen for various activities.

Maya artists were masters of relief carving in stone and wood, wall painting and modelling in stucco. Potters produced not only everyday cooking pots but also fragile vessels covered with polychrome painted scenes from epic stories of the underworld, which were for use as grave-goods. Jade, the most precious material known to the ancient Maya, was traded throughout the region from its restricted sources such as the Motagua Valley, and was carved and polished to make ear-flares, pendants, plaques, tubular beads and anthropomorphic figures. Exquisitely flaked flints and obsidians were made to be buried in votive caches. The skills of the master craftsmen, the exemplification of Maya power and ideology in their temples, palaces and cities, and their impressive intellectual achievements all combined to make the Maya the New World's greatest civilisation.

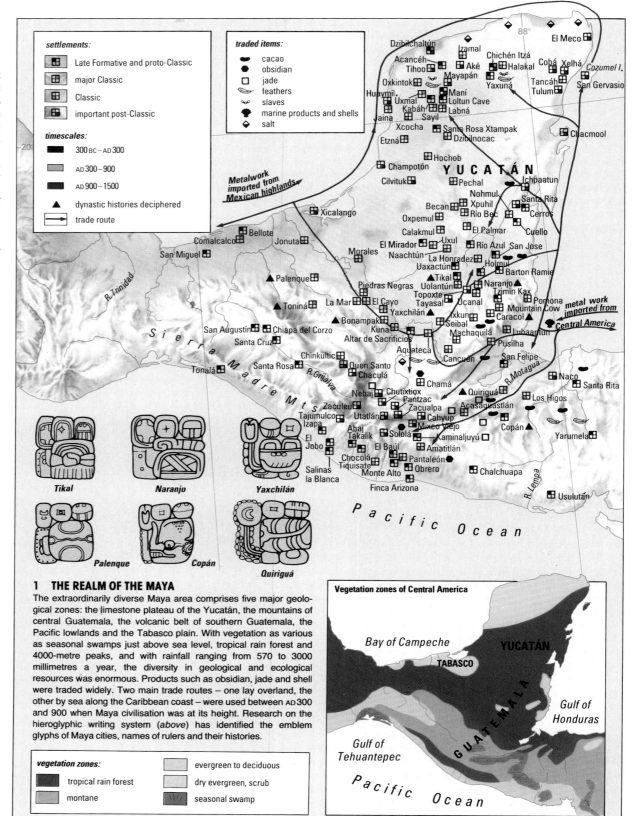

1 THE REALM OF THE MAYA
The extraordinarily diverse Maya area comprises five major geological zones: the limestone plateau of the Yucatán, the mountains of central Guatemala, the volcanic belt of southern Guatemala, the Pacific lowlands and the Tabasco plain. With vegetation as various as seasonal swamps just above sea level, tropical rain forest and 4000-metre peaks, and with rainfall ranging from 570 to 3000 millimetres a year, the diversity in geological and ecological resources was enormous. Products such as obsidian, jade and shell were traded widely. Two main trade routes – one lay overland, the other by sea along the Caribbean coast – were used between AD 300 and 900 when Maya civilisation was at its height. Research on the hieroglyphic writing system (*above*) has identified the emblem glyphs of Maya cities, names of rulers and their histories.

3 THE ENIGMA OF THE MAYA
A Ball court marker from Chinkultic, used to divide the playing area. It shows a player wearing protective clothing, and glyphs form the border. c.AD 650, stone, diameter c.55cm. **B** Wall painting from Bonampak, Mexico. Captives, some tortured by having fingernails removed, have been brought before a Maya lord clad in a jaguar skin. Late 8th century, painted plaster, height of figures c.60cm.

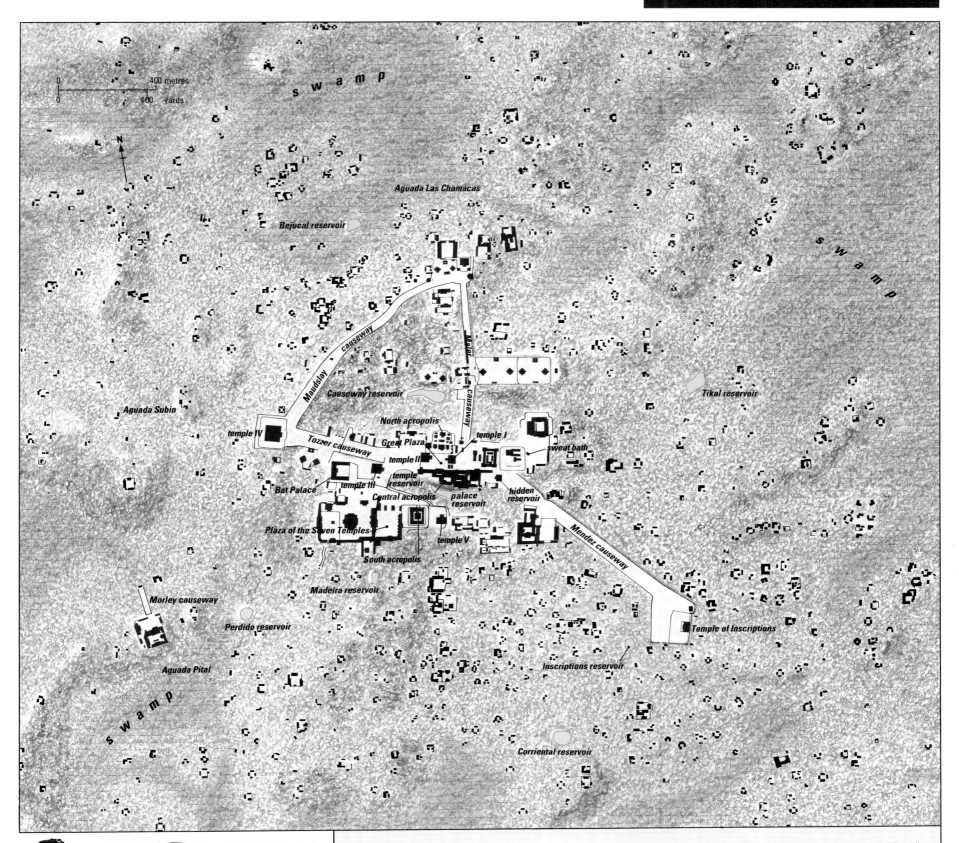

swamp

swamp

swamp

Aguada Las Chamacas

Bejucal reservoir

Maudslay causeway

Major causeway

Causeway reservoir

Tikal reservoir

Aguada Subin

North acropolis

temple IV

Tozzer causeway

Great Plaza

temple I

sweat bath

temple II

Bat Palace

temple III

temple reservoir

Central acropolis

palace reservoir

hidden reservoir

Plaza of the Seven Temples

South acropolis

temple V

Mendez causeway

Morley causeway

Madeira reservoir

Perdido reservoir

Temple of Inscriptions

Aguada Pital

Inscriptions reservoir

Corriental reservoir

2 TIKAL: A MAYA CITY

Tikal, a city of 50,000 people in the 8th century AD, contained five temple pyramids up to 70 metres tall covering the graves of the city rulers. Temple groups comprised pyramids, ball courts, temples and palaces, and were linked by broad causeways. The northern acropolis (*below*), consisting of stone courtyards, temples and buildings covering more than one hectare, was built over 500 years, revealing the sequence of architectural development at Tikal.

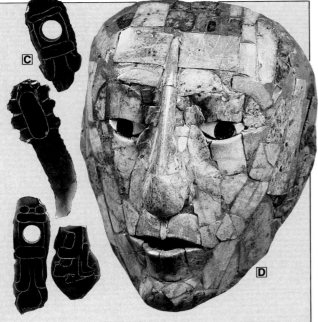

C Obsidian flakes and blades from Tikal, Guatemala, decorated with portraits of deities. Obsidian was thought to be a sacred material formed when lightning struck the earth. 8th century AD, length 5–10cm. D Death mask of Pacal, ruler of Palenque, from his stone sarcophagus. The jade mosaic pieces, with inlaid eyes of shell and obsidian, were fixed to a wooden backing. AD 684, life-size.

Early cultures of North America

In North America, the Archaic economy based on intensive hunting and gathering continued for several millennia alongside horticulture, and provided at least as important a portion of the diet as farming.

In the arid Southwest the dry climate has preserved food remains such as piñon nuts and rice grass seeds, together with basketry winnowing trays, conical baskets and bags used by foragers. Large animals, including deer, elk and mountain sheep, were hunted; small game such as rabbits were more commonly netted or snared. This economic pattern was modified during the period AD 1– 500 (Basketmaker II), when hamlets of up to eleven circular houses with slightly sunken floors were constructed on river bluffs overlooking fertile bottom lands where maize was cultivated. Most plant food was still gathered rather than grown, and settlements had access to many different environments containing an enormous variety of plant species.

After AD 500 (Basketmaker III), more radical changes occurred in the Southwest. Villages were moved to terraces near the river flood plains, where maize, squash and beans were cultivated, providing about 50% of the food intake. Basketmaker III villages were large, consisting of up to 50 shallow pit-houses 2–7 metres in diameter surrounded by grain storage cists. The bow and arrow was introduced, replacing the spearthrower and dart. Pottery making was also introduced from the neighbouring Mogollon (*page 228*) culture and developed, after 700, into the superb ceramics of the Pueblo Indians. Plain grey ware, occasionally decorated with painted designs in black, was made by coiling and smoothing techniques.

In the eastern woodlands the Adena culture, famous for its richly furnished burials beneath earthen mounds, flourished between 1000 and 300 BC in Ohio, Kentucky, Indiana, Pennsylvania and West Virginia. Several types of burial have been found. Important individuals were sometimes interred in log tombs, which were burned down in the funeral ceremony and then covered by conical mounds up to 20 metres high. Corpses were more often cremated in oval clay basins dug into the ground, and the ashes and bones were buried beneath mounds. Most burials were accompanied by grave-goods, including polished stone tools, cigar-shaped or tubular tobacco pipes, bracelets, rings, beads and spoons of copper, and beads made from marine shells. Thin stone tablets carved with curvilinear and zoomorphic designs may have been used for marking tattoo patterns. Adena earthworks also included large geometrically shaped ceremonial constructions, circles and the massive zoomorphic Great Serpent Mound (*page 26*), which is 217 metres long. The florescence of Adena probably depended on the production of reliable food surpluses to feed the labourers who built the massive mounds. Small villages were located in river valleys where many varieties of mammals, birds and fish as well as vegetable foods, were available. Horticulture began during this period; sunflowers, marsh elder, squashes, gourds and *chenopodium* were cultivated.

From c. 300 BC the pattern of elaborate burial rites and large earthwork constructions was continued and enriched during the Hopewell phase, named after the Hopewell site in Ohio. The biggest and most complex earthworks, possibly ceremonial centres, have been found in this region, where banks some five metres high enclose circular, rectangular and octagonal areas of up to 40 hectares. Finds from Hopewell graves are not only fine works of art but also indicators of the existence of a social or religious network through which exotic imported materials reached the eastern woodlands. Gulf Coast shells have been found in tombs in Michigan and Wisconsin; sharks' teeth occur in Illinois; copper was traded from its source at Lake Superior, and obsidian and grizzly bear teeth came from the far west to graves in Illinois and Ohio. Mica and favoured types of flint, such as that from Flat Ridge, Ohio, were traded over long distances.

The construction of large earthen monuments, the elaboration of burial rites and the existence of long-distance trade networks for the acquisition of exotic rare materials suggest that chiefdoms had developed during the Hopewell period. Although maize has been found in late Hopewell sites, it seems to have played a comparatively small part in the economy. Villages continued to be sited near many types of natural environment, each of which had different natural food resources which could be tapped. Foraging remained a significant method of obtaining food long after the arrival of maize, squash and beans in North America: natural resources were so abundant that they could support permanent villages.

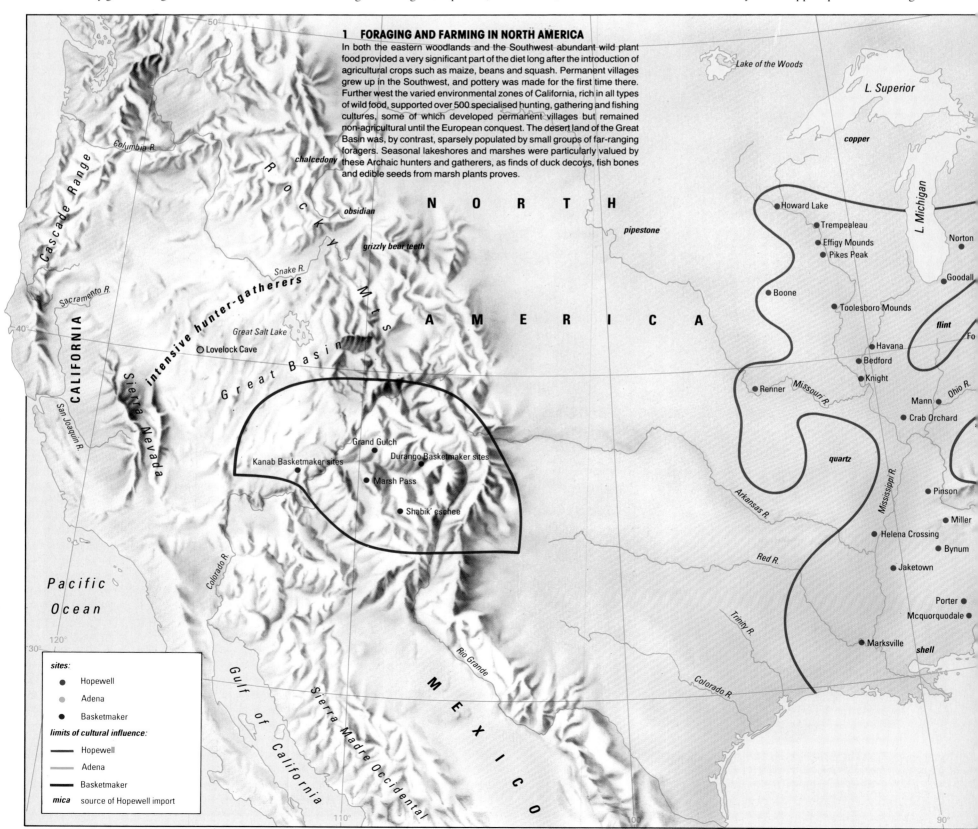

1 FORAGING AND FARMING IN NORTH AMERICA
In both the eastern woodlands and the Southwest abundant wild plant food provided a very significant part of the diet long after the introduction of agricultural crops such as maize, beans and squash. Permanent villages grew up in the Southwest, and pottery was made for the first time there. Further west the varied environmental zones of California, rich in all types of wild food, supported over 500 specialised hunting, gathering and fishing cultures, some of which developed permanent villages but remained non-agricultural until the European conquest. The desert land of the Great Basin was, by contrast, sparsely populated by small groups of far-ranging foragers. Seasonal lakeshores and marshes were particularly valued by these Archaic hunters and gatherers, as finds of duck decoys, fish bones and edible seeds from marsh plants proves.

sites:
● Hopewell
○ Adena
● Basketmaker

limits of cultural influence:
— Hopewell
— Adena
— Basketmaker

mica source of Hopewell import

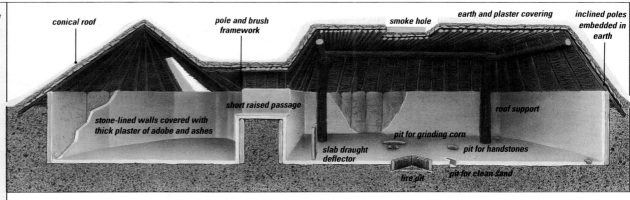

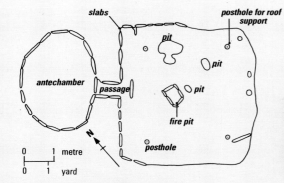

2 A BASKETMAKER HOUSE

Farming villages of up to 50 houses have been discovered from the Basketmaker III (AD 500–700) period in the Southwest, for example at Shabik'eschee Village, New Mexico. One well-preserved pit house there consisted of a rectangular, sunken room connected by a low passage to a circular antechamber (see plan). The entrance to the house was via the conical roof of the antechamber. Vertical stone slabs lined the plastered pit walls of the living room. Stone slabs also lined the rectangular fire pit. A deflector slab was set vertically in the house floor to control the draught. A small oval hole in the floor near the fire was the *sipapu*, a symbolic representation of the place from which man first emerged into the world. The house superstructure was a pole and brush framework supported on horizontal wooden roof beams. The roof and external wall surfaces were covered with earth and plaster. Outside the house were further work areas and a large *kiva* (circular ceremonial room).

3 EARLY CRAFTS OF NORTH AMERICA

A *Decoy duck made of tule (rush) and duck feathers, from Lovelock Cave, Nevada. c. 200 BC, length c. 30cm.* **B** *Gorget made from a human scalp covered with engraved designs of birds. Adena culture, Florence Mound, Ohio, 700 BC–AD 400, length 8.55cm.* **C** *Monitor pipe in the form of a bird. The tobacco cavity is in the bird's back, and at one end is the mouthpiece with a drilled smokehole; Hopewell culture, 100 BC–AD 600, length c. 6–8cm.* **D** *Silhouette of a hand cut from sheet mica. Hopewell site, Ohio, 100 BC–AD 600, length 29cm.*

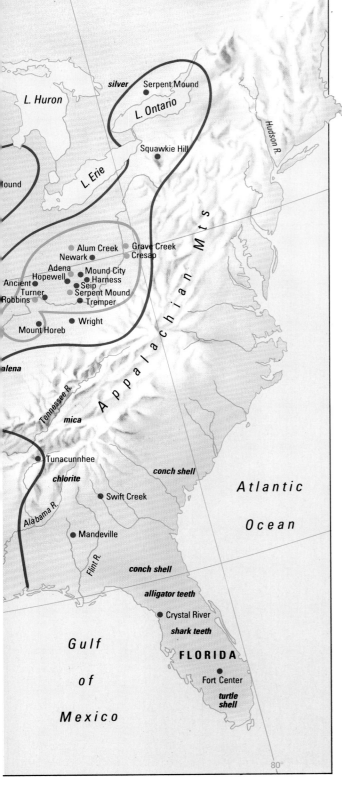

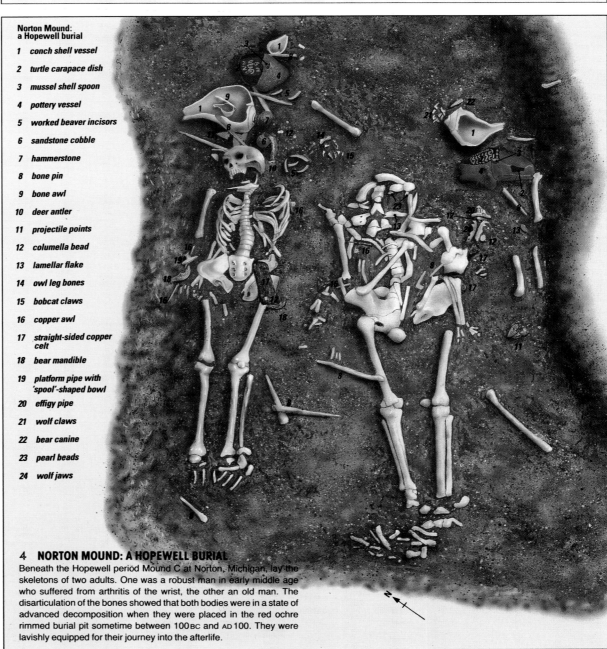

Norton Mound: a Hopewell burial

1. conch shell vessel
2. turtle carapace dish
3. mussel shell spoon
4. pottery vessel
5. worked beaver incisors
6. sandstone cobble
7. hammerstone
8. bone pin
9. bone awl
10. deer antler
11. projectile points
12. columella bead
13. lamellar flake
14. owl leg bones
15. bobcat claws
16. copper awl
17. straight-sided copper celt
18. bear mandible
19. platform pipe with 'spool'-shaped bowl
20. effigy pipe
21. wolf claws
22. bear canine
23. pearl beads
24. wolf jaws

4 NORTON MOUND: A HOPEWELL BURIAL

Beneath the Hopewell period Mound C at Norton, Michigan, lay the skeletons of two adults. One was a robust man in early middle age who suffered from arthritis of the wrist, the other an old man. The disarticulation of the bones showed that both bodies were in a state of advanced decomposition when they were placed in the red ochre rimmed burial pit sometime between 100 BC and AD 100. They were lavishly equipped for their journey into the afterlife.

Empires of the Andes

The Inca empire, the largest of all pre-Columbian states, rose to greatness in less than a century. In about AD 1300, the tribe settled a valley high in the Peruvian Andes where they built their capital, Cuzco. Initially, they were one group among several in the area engaged in local warfare, and it was not until after 1438, when Pachacuti Inca came to the throne, that the strongly centralised Inca state was established and vast territories won. Pachacuti's son, Topa Inca, conquered the kingdom of Chimor, on the north coast of Peru, in the 1470s, and lands continued to be added to the realm until shortly before the arrival of Francisco Pizarro in 1532 and its destruction by European conquerors.

The strictly regulated social hierarchy of the Inca state was designed in the form of a pyramid. At the apex was the Sapa Inca, the absolute ruler in political, religious and military matters. The aristocracy, principally his relatives, acted as councillors and provincial governors. Lower-ranking officials were ultimately responsible to the Sapa Inca through their representative in the rank above, ensuring control at all levels of society. This system had two major faults: the state crumbled without an effective head as there was no longer any cohesion between the classes of society, and there was no well-defined line of succession to the throne.

The Incas learned much from earlier cultures of the highlands (*page 212*) and more from the Chimú, whose civilisation dominated the north coast of Peru from c. 700 until their defeat by the Inca in 1476. The Chimú empire operated under a similar social framework, supported by an efficient colonial policy and communications network. The Inca took these over and also assimilated the more developed Chimú techniques of metal working, textiles and the mass-production of pottery. New towns were built in freshly conquered areas, acting as a base for state control of military and economic affairs. It was from these bases that the administrators exacted approximately 66% taxation on agricultural produce and processed goods such as cloth and maize beer. They also deployed the labour duty, *mit'a*, owed by the masses to the state, on projects such as road-building, irrigation and drainage systems, the construction of agricultural terraces, quarrying and mining as well as massive state fortress- and town-building schemes.

Inca military success was due to the training of young noblemen, who were instilled with warlike attitudes, and to the existence of a standing army which could rapidly reach all parts of the empire. The extensive road network meant that news travelled easily, and also enabled troops to reach trouble-spots quickly. Hostile peoples were forced to migrate from their homelands to regions safe in the well-protected Inca heartland, while loyal subjects were sent as *mitimaes* (colonists) to replace them.

These roads were also used for the transportation of huge cargoes which were carried on people's backs or by llamas to regional food stores. At Huánuco Pampa the granaries could hold 36 million litres of grain, and many such towns functioned as centres of industrial production where large weaving factories or potteries produced quantities of highly standardised goods. There was little room for individual creativity in the Inca empire. Inca ceramics, for example, show very little variation in form or decoration, and are all decorated with regularly spaced painted geometric designs. Metal and stone tools, decorative metalwork such as small human and animal figures, and textile designs were all similarly uniform.

It is surprising that this complex bureaucracy had no form of writing. Records were kept on *Quipus*, lengths of string which were knotted at significant intervals, and were looked after by a special class of administrator, the *Quipucamayoc*. These tallies of tribute and taxation were based on a decimal system of reckoning, but may also have served as *aides-mémoir* for historical and cultural information. The cult of the Sun God was the chief religion, directly linked with astronomical and calendrical observations and predictions. The Sapa Inca was believed to descend from the Sun, and was himself the initiator of the planting season. For the aristocracy Viracocha, the Creator God, was the chief deity, while peasants were allowed to worship local spirits found in springs and sacred stones, as long as the Sun cult was also observed.

In 1532, when Francisco Pizarro captured the Sapa Inca, the temples were stripped of their ornaments, which were nearly all melted down. Thus many works of art were destroyed, but more seriously the destruction of the Inca religious system had begun. Pizarro had delivered a death blow to the Andean socio-political system that had evolved over some five thousand years, from which it never recovered.

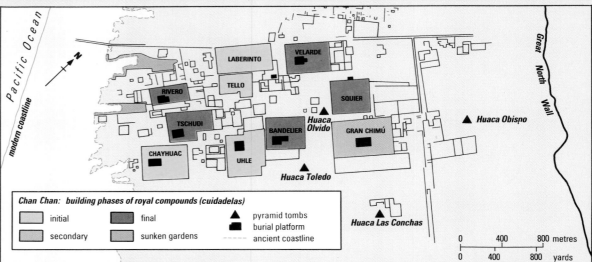

Chan Chan: building phases of royal compounds (cuidadelas)

initial — final — pyramid tombs
secondary — sunken gardens — burial platform — ancient coastline

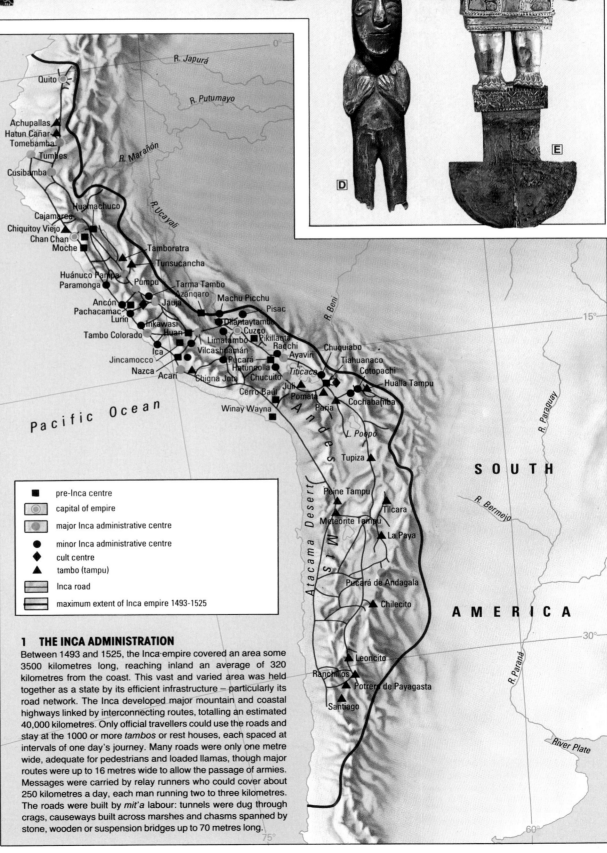

3 INCA ART

A *Man's sleeveless tunic worn over a loincloth and in cold weather covered with a large cloak. Inca, 13th-16th century AD, cotton and wool, length 95cm.* **B** *Highly polished Cuzco polychrome aryballus or water jar. Designed to be carried on the back, a cord passed through the vertical strap handles and below the neck. Inca, 13th-16th century AD, painted pottery, height 36cm.* **C** *Chimú 'burial-glove', one of a pair from a rich grave, with repoussé designs of warriors and birds. It has silver fingernails. 14th century AD, sheet cut gold, length 54cm.* **D** *Figurine of a naked woman holding her breasts. Many such figurines of men and women have been found, sometimes clothed in removable garments. Inca, 15th-16th century AD, hammered, cut and repoussé silver sheet, height 6cm.* **E** *Ceremonial knife or tumi. The handle is in the form of a richly dressed man wearing a headdress and large ear spools, indicating high status. Sicán style, AD 1200-1400, gold and turquoise, height 34cm.*

2 CITIES OF THE ANDES

Chan Chan The mud-brick walls, 12 metres high, which surrounded compounds at Chan Chan (*upper left*), capital of the kingdom of the Chimú, isolated the divine kings in the centre of the city and emphasised their superiority and power. The city covered more than 15 square kilometres of Pacific coastline and, from c.AD 700 until 1476, when the Chimú were conquered by the Incas, it was the capital of a state which stretched some 1600 kilometres along the northern coast of Peru. Ten royal compounds or *ciudadelas* built over a 250-year period lie at the heart of Chan Chan (*see plan, left*). It is probable that each of the compounds belonged to one of the Chimú kings. On the death of a king his *ciudadela* was sealed as a mausoleum and his successor had a new compound constructed. The compound was entered through a single doorway which led to a vast entrance courtyard. Beyond lay a maze-like complex of storerooms, small courtyards, U-shaped rooms probably used for the control and tallying of distribution of goods, and large roofed wells. In the northern part of the *ciudadela* lay the royal living quarters and, beneath a truncated pyramid, the royal burial platform. Chimú society was governed by a dynasty of kings and an hereditary elite. As territory was colonised, new centres were created from which governors controlled the economic exploitation of the provinces.

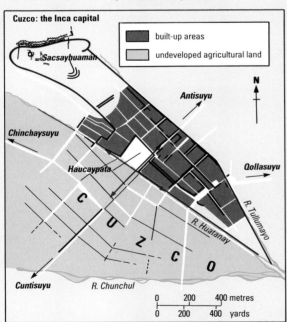

Cuzco: the Inca capital

built-up areas
undeveloped agricultural land

Cuzco The capital city of the Inca empire was tranformed into a planned metropolis after 1438 under Inca Pachacuti (*see plan above*). In the inner city great palaces of finely fitted and dressed masonry were inhabited by the nobility, administrators and academics, and the streets between the Rio Tullumayo and Rio Huatanay were laid out in the form of the body, legs and tail of a feline. The enormous fortress of Sacsayhuamán forms the head of the animal. The four cardinal quarters of the Inca realm, the underlying conceptual basis of its organisation, radiate from the central Haucaypata (Holy Place), emphasising the function of Cuzco as the hub of the world. **Machu Picchu**, a small Inca town, lies about 70 kilometres northwest of Cuzco, on the top of a ridge of land encircled by the River Urubamba 610 metres below (*see photograph, left*). The town was built by *mit'a* workers who smoothed the rock to form flat surfaces on which to construct the major temples. A sequence of small plazas ran along the top of the saddle of land, while the steep flanking slopes were terraced to support small thatched houses and for cultivation.

pre-Inca centre
capital of empire
major Inca administrative centre
minor Inca administrative centre
cult centre
tambo (tampu)
Inca road
maximum extent of Inca empire 1493-1525

1 THE INCA ADMINISTRATION

Between 1493 and 1525, the Inca empire covered an area some 3500 kilometres long, reaching inland an average of 320 kilometres from the coast. This vast and varied area was held together as a state by its efficient infrastructure – particularly its road network. The Inca developed major mountain and coastal highways linked by interconnecting routes, totalling an estimated 40,000 kilometres. Only official travellers could use the roads and stay at the 1000 or more *tambos* or rest houses, each spaced at intervals of one day's journey. Many roads were only one metre wide, adequate for pedestrians and loaded llamas, though major routes were up to 16 metres wide to allow the passage of armies. Messages were carried by relay runners who could cover about 250 kilometres a day, each man running two to three kilometres. The roads were built by *mit'a* labour: tunnels were dug through crags, causeways built across marshes and chasms spanned by stone, wooden or suspension bridges up to 70 metres long.

Farmers of the Amazon

The tropical lowlands of the Amazon Basin have traditionally been regarded as a cultural backwater in pre-Columbian America. Amazonia was dismissed as a region covered by dense rain forest with indigenous cultural development limited to shifting slash and burn agriculture. There is, however, archaeological and early ethno-historical evidence for intensive cultivation, complex societies with large settlements and extensive chiefdoms in the Amazon Basin, and the prehistory of this region has, in recent years, been radically reassessed.

The earliest traces of Palaeo-Indian occupation in Amazonia are widely scattered but poorly studied. At the Abrigo do Sol in the Mato Grosso, Brazil, tools used for cutting petroglyphs in the sandstone cave have been dated to between 10,000 and 7000 BC. Flaked stone tools from the Guiana Highlands of Venezuela and Guyana, and from the River Tapajós, lower Amazon, have been assigned, on stylistic grounds, to the period 8000–4000 BC. Lacking better evidence, it is not yet known what kinds of game these hunters were pursuing.

The transition from hunting and gathering to incipient agriculture took place between 4000 and 2000 BC. Plant and animal food remains dated to between 6000 and 4000 BC have been found in cave and rock shelter sites in Brazil and Venezuela, left behind by intensive foragers.

The development from foraging through incipient cultivation to agriculture can be traced in the many large shell middens discovered near the mouths of the Amazon and the Orinoco, on the Guiana coast, and along the lower Amazon. The earliest levels of these middens contain no pottery but very rare sherds occur in the later levels, dated c.4000 BC in Guyana and c.3000 BC at the Mina shell mounds south-east of the Amazon mouth. These finds and the ceramics from Taperinha shell mound near Santarem, Brazil, are at least a millennium earlier than the first pottery of Peru. Some time after 3000 BC small dispersed horticultural villages began to emerge. At the same time, ceramic styles which all feature zoomorphic motifs and modelled animal decoration, either incised or painted, began to appear throughout the region. It is thought that subsistence at this period was based on root crops such as manioc, which may have been cultivated as early as 5000 BC in the upper Orinoco.

The introduction of maize into the flood plain area during the 1st millennium BC was a crucial development. Remains of maize in the middle Orinoco region have been dated to c.800 BC. This crop, probably introduced from the northern Andes, was intensively cultivated in permanent fields along the banks, levees and deltas of rivers flowing from the Andes, and produced far larger storable food surpluses than did manioc. The rivers' seasonal flooding deposited rich silt, as well as supplying plentiful fish and aquatic mammals.

During this period, both populations and settlements expanded and hierarchical societies developed. Settlements extended for several kilometres along the riverside, housing thousands of people and building up deep, black midden deposits known as Indian Black Soil. The most famous region of Indian Black Soil sites is around Santarém in Brazil, which was the centre of the warlike Tapajos chiefdom in the 16th and 17th centuries AD. Such warring chiefdoms dominated territories of tens of thousands of square kilometres. They were headed by paramount chiefs who exacted tribute from those they controlled. Large workforces, including slaves, built massive defensive earthworks, habitation and ceremonial mounds, and dug canals. The biggest complexes of mounds are located on the widest stretches of alluvial soil in savanna zones such as the plains of the Bolivian Amazon, the middle Orinoco and Marajó Island at the mouth of the Amazon. Here groups of up to 40 mounds occur in a 10 to 15 square kilometre area. Few of these important settlements have been excavated, though the associated cemeteries have long attracted diggers seeking the superbly painted and modelled ceramics in which the bones of important people were placed. An ancestor cult centering on the mummified bodies of chiefs seems to have been an important belief in these societies, and it is at this time that anthropomorphic burial urns appear. The high quality of ceremonial ceramics indicates that they were produced by specialist craftsmen.

The Amazonian nations encountered and described by the first European intruders were rich and well-organised hierarchical societies. In the decades that followed contact, however, disease, slaving and land seizure helped to destroy them, and sent their survivors back to an earlier and far less elaborate way of life.

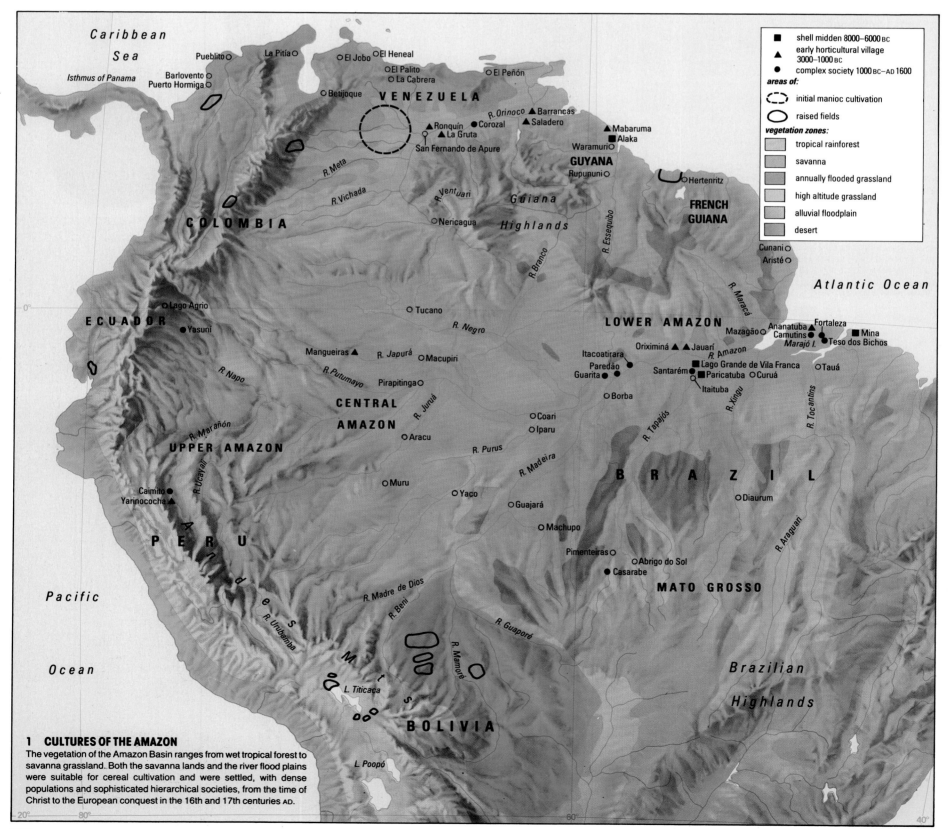

1 CULTURES OF THE AMAZON

The vegetation of the Amazon Basin ranges from wet tropical forest to savanna grassland. Both the savanna lands and the river flood plains were suitable for cereal cultivation and were settled, with dense populations and sophisticated hierarchical societies, from the time of Christ to the European conquest in the 16th and 17th centuries AD.

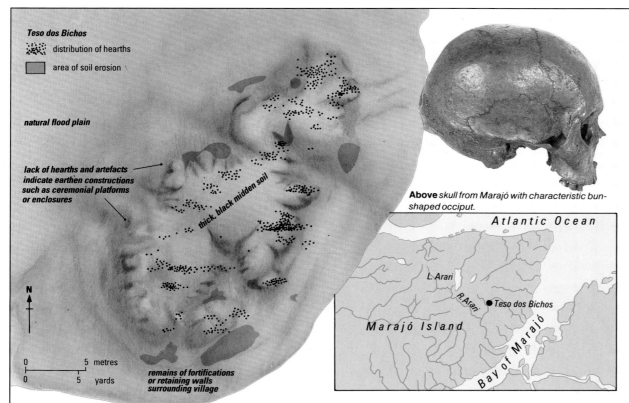

Teso dos Bichos

░ distribution of hearths

▓ area of soil erosion

natural flood plain

lack of hearths and artefacts indicate earthen constructions such as ceremonial platforms or enclosures

thick, black midden soil

N

| 0 | 5 metres |
| 0 | 5 yards |

remains of fortifications or retaining walls surrounding village

Above *skull from Marajó with characteristic bun-shaped occiput.*

Atlantic Ocean

L. Arari

R. Arari

● *Teso dos Bichos*

Marajó Island

Bay of Marajó

2 TESO DOS BICHOS: AN AMAZONIAN VILLAGE

The village of Teso dos Bichos is situated on Marajó Island at the mouth of the River Amazon. An early chiefdom flourished on Marajó Island between AD 400 and 1300. The mound of Teso dos Bichos is 7 metres high and covers 2.5 hectares. It was occupied continuously for about 900 years. Excavations revealed an oval village, ringed by massive earthworks at least 3 metres tall and 10 metres thick, either fortifications or retaining walls. About 20 large earth, pole and thatch houses were arranged in a concentric pattern around a central plaza. The dwellings contained fired clay hearths set in earth floors which were kept swept very clean. Rubbish was put on dumps. Semi-tubular cooking stoves of fired clay were found in clusters of 6–12. Plain cooking pots and sherds were found in the hearth debris, while decorated sherds, presumably used in ceremonies, came principally from the middens. This distribution of ceramics, together with the arrangement of the stoves, suggests a separation of male and female activities. Women shared food preparation and cooking in multi-family women's households, while men's lives centred around a men's house and the western area of the village, where a large ceremonial platform or enclosure was probably located. Population estimates suggest that 500–1000 people lived at Teso dos Bichos.

Examination of skeletons from Marajó revealed a people very like the present-day Amazonian Indians, but on average 10 centimetres taller. The shape of the skulls indicates an Amazonian rather than Andean origin for the population. Men were very muscular, but their bones bore no trace of arthritis caused by heavy agricultural labour, which was probably carried out by women. Analysis of the bone remains indicates that the ancient inhabitants had a mixed diet, eating an appreciable amount of animal protein, principally fish. Up to 30% of the diet was maize, which was supplemented by fruits and other crops. Study of plant remains shows that it was seed crops rather than root crops which were important.

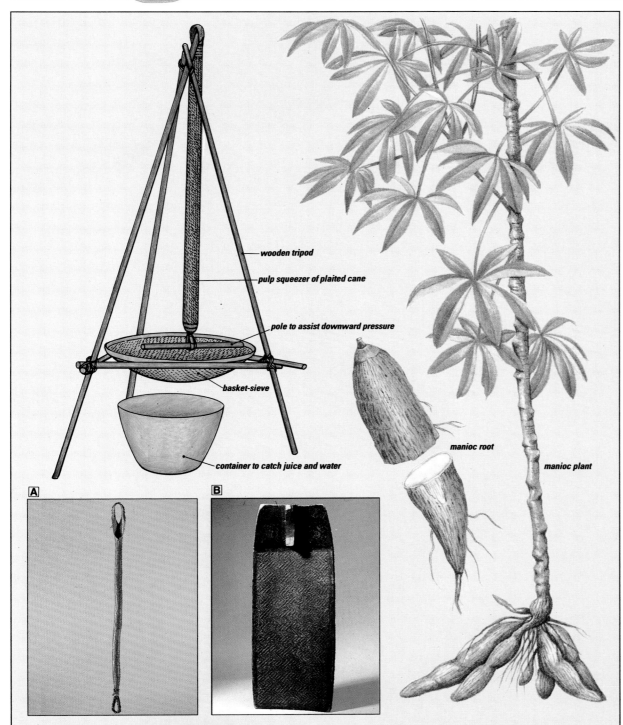

wooden tripod

pulp squeezer of plaited cane

pole to assist downward pressure

basket-sieve

container to catch juice and water

manioc root

manioc plant

A

B

3 MANIOC: AN AMAZONIAN STAPLE CROP

Manioc was, and still is, one of the most important staple foods of Amazonia. It was probably first domesticated in the Orinoco Basin, c.5000 BC. The bushy plant (*above right*) is up to 2.5 metres tall and contains poisonous Prussic acid. Bitter manioc needs processing to make it edible. The manioc was peeled and then grated to make a pulp, which was then put into a basketry squeezer (*above left*) so that the poison could be squeezed out (*diagram*). The juice was simmered, evaporating the acid and producing a syrup used as a stew base. The pulp was either made into unleavened bread or converted into small pellets of flour.
A *Manioc pulp squeezer. Basketry.* **B** *Manioc grater, set with stone chips from Tucano, north-west Amazon. Wood.*

4 CRAFTS OF THE AMAZON

A *Anthropomorphic burial urn, modelled and painted in polychrome colours, from Lago Agrio, Ecuador. Napo Phase, c. AD 1200, height 45cm.* **B** *Polished stone axe head from Playa Cardozo. Hardstone tools and weapons had to be traded hundreds of kilometres from their sources into the alluvial lands of Amazonia, and were comparatively scarce. Wood, bone and shell were commonly used for many cutting tools. Length 20cm.* **C** *Woman's pubic cover or ornament, tanga, made of painted pottery from Marajó Island, Brazil. AD 400–1300, height c. 13cm.* **D** *Large, shallow polychrome painted bowl from River Aguarico area, Ecuador. c. AD 1200, diameter 40cm.*

A

B

C

D

The Aztecs and their ancestors

During the 10th century AD, after the fall of Teotihuacán and the collapse of the Classic Maya, waves of barbaric tribes descended from their desert homelands in the north-west of Mexico into the central region. The most successful of these groups was the Toltecs, whose expansion was an organised military operation, the army supported by the confiscation of food surpluses as tribute. The Toltecs combined the settled city life of the peoples they conquered with elements of their own traditional culture; at Tula, the Toltec capital founded in about AD 950, the stepped pyramid of Quetzalcoatl was built in the style characteristic of Teotihuacán (*page 216*), and Quetzalcoatl, the Feathered Serpent, was a god adopted from earlier Mesoamerican cultures. Tradition has it that in about AD 987 the cult was outlawed in Tula, and Topiltzin, its leader, banished. It is said that he sailed with his followers from the Gulf of Mexico, possibly to refound the ceremonial centre at Chichén Itzá. The exile of Quetzalcoatl, representing traditional, theocratic power, was effected by the followers of a Toltec tribal god, **Texcatlipoca**, lord of life and death, master of sorcerors and patron of the knightly warrior orders of eagles, jaguars and coyotes. Texcatlipoca personified secular blood-thirsty power and for the first time overwhelming importance was given to human

sacrifice in Mesoamerican religion. They believed that although the days of this creation were numbered, the end could be postponed by feasting the gods with sacred nourishment, human blood and hearts.

Despite this ritual appeasement, the supremacy of the Toltecs ended in about 1170, when Tula was violently destroyed by the Chichimecs. Their arrival heralded a second period of confusion and internecine warfare in central Mexico, with many small city-states competing for political and military dominance. The last of the tribes to arrive in the area around Lake Texcoco was the Aztecs, a nomadic people who settled on the only unclaimed land, a swampy island in Lake Texcoco, and founded Tenochtitlán, their capital, in 1345. Under the influence of the neighbouring city-state, Atzcapotzalco,

the Aztecs were metamorphosed from a semi-civilised tribe to an organised state, and eventually defeated Atzcapotzalco in 1428. The Aztecs won many of the cities formerly paying tribute to the defeated enemy, and their subsequent history is one of conquest and reconquest until they occupied both the Gulf and Pacific coasts and controlled territory extending as far as Guatemala.

Aztec society was headed by a priest-king, educated, like all the nobility, at the elite seminary in Tenochtitlán, and elected from the members of the royal family by a council of nobles, priests and warriors who saw themselves, as the chosen people, continuing the traditions of the Toltecs. The Aztec state was a militaristic regime with a large, well-equipped professional army bent on acquiring territory and, more important, tribute. Gold,

1 THE HEART OF THE AZTEC EMPIRE

Tenochtitlán, the capital of the Aztec empire, was a stone-built city of up to 200,000 inhabitants, situated on an island and linked to the mainland by causeways. The key to the Aztecs' rise to power lay partly in their agricultural and hydraulic engineering skills. Extending and improving pre-existing systems of *chinampas* (reclaimed swampland), they developed the marshy lake shores into one of the most productive agricultural areas of the New World. Several crops of maize, beans, squash, chillies and other staples were harvested annually, and no fallow period was needed. The food surpluses produced from the *chinampas* fed both the city dwellers and the Aztec army – the bulk of which was made up by conscripts from conquered territory. The Dyke of Netzahualcóyotl protected the *chinampas* from the saline waters of Lake Texcoco, where many salt-making stations were located.

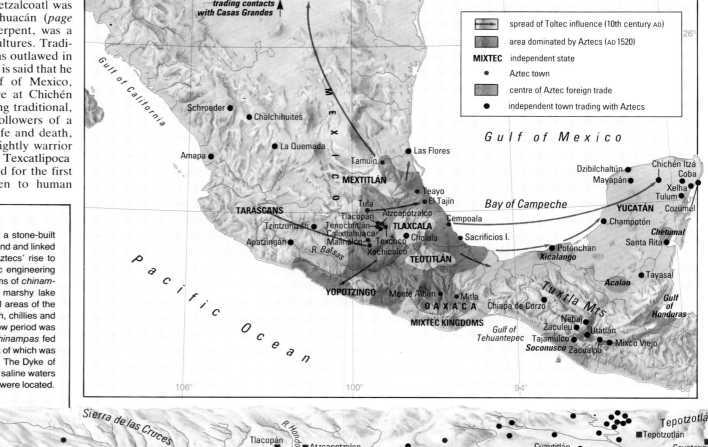

spread of Toltec influence (10th century AD)
area dominated by Aztecs (AD 1520)
MIXTEC independent state
Aztec town
centre of Aztec foreign trade
independent town trading with Aztecs

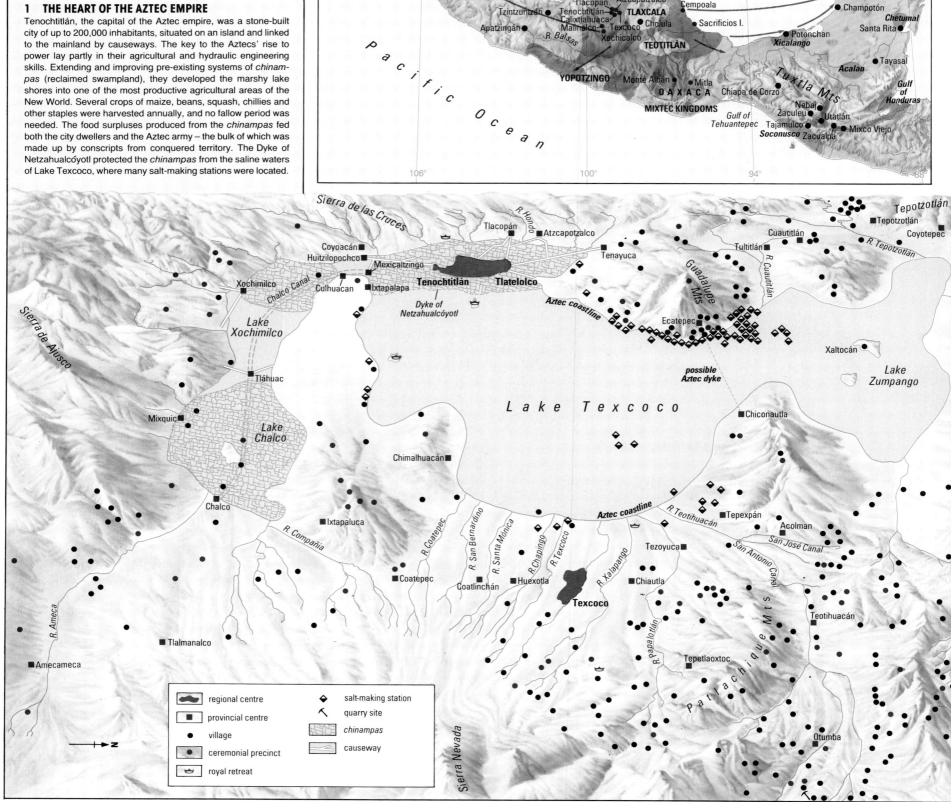

regional centre
provincial centre
village
ceremonial precinct
royal retreat
salt-making station
quarry site
chinampas
causeway

cotton, turquoise, feathers, incense and vast quantities of food, itemised on detailed tribute lists, were sent to Tenochtitlán. To the Aztecs, however, the most significant tribute exacted from conquered peoples was a vast number of human beings destined for sacrifice in the capital city. The principal underlying reason for Aztec militarism was the daily need of victims for the Sun God, Huitzilopochtli. He, like Tezcatlipoca, needed to be fed on human blood to prevent the end of the world. Most sacrifices were performed by cutting out the heart of the victim, who was stretched on a stone before the temple of the god. The scale of sacrifice was horrific; in the four-day long celebration of the enlargement of the Great Temple in Tenochtitlán, up to 20,000 prisoners met their deaths. Their hearts were offered to the gods, their bodies cast down the steep steps of the pyramid.

Aztec artists excelled in stone sculpture, carving vessels, statues and 'masks' portraying priests wearing the flayed skins of sacrificial victims. Other nations, particularly the Mixtec of Oaxaca, were employed to make multicoloured feather work, polychrome painted ceramics, superb gold jewellery and intricate mosaics.

The inadequacy of Aztec colonial policy led to the downfall of their empire. When Spanish colonists under Hernan Cortés arrived in 1519, the emperor, Montezuma II, suspected that the pale, bearded strangers were Quetzalcoatl and his followers returning in the prophesied year – suspicions confirmed by portentous natural phenomena. Within two years, the combined forces of the invaders, disaffected native groups and exotic diseases had brought the Aztec empire to an end.

3 MASTER CRAFTSMEN OF MEXICO

Many of the artefacts of Toltec and Aztec Mexico reflect all too clearly the militaristic nature and sanguinary religion of these empire-building peoples, combined with a love of brilliant colour and personal display.
A *Roof support in the form of a Toltec warrior from pyramid B, Tula. 10th century AD, basalt, height 4.5m.* B *Mixteca-Puebla polychrome painted tripod pot. 13th-16th century AD, fired clay, height 22cm.* C *Aztec sacrificial knife from the Templo Mayor, Tenochtitlán. 15th century AD, flint, shell and turquoise, length 17cm.* D *Manuscript illumination (Codex Florentino). This early colonial document shows priests and laymen sacrificing two victims in honour of the war god. 16th century AD, height 12cm.* E *Mixtec pendant earring, Mexico. 11th-15th century AD, gold, length 13.5cm.*

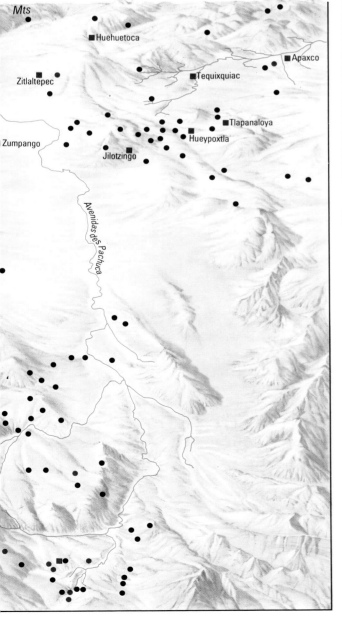

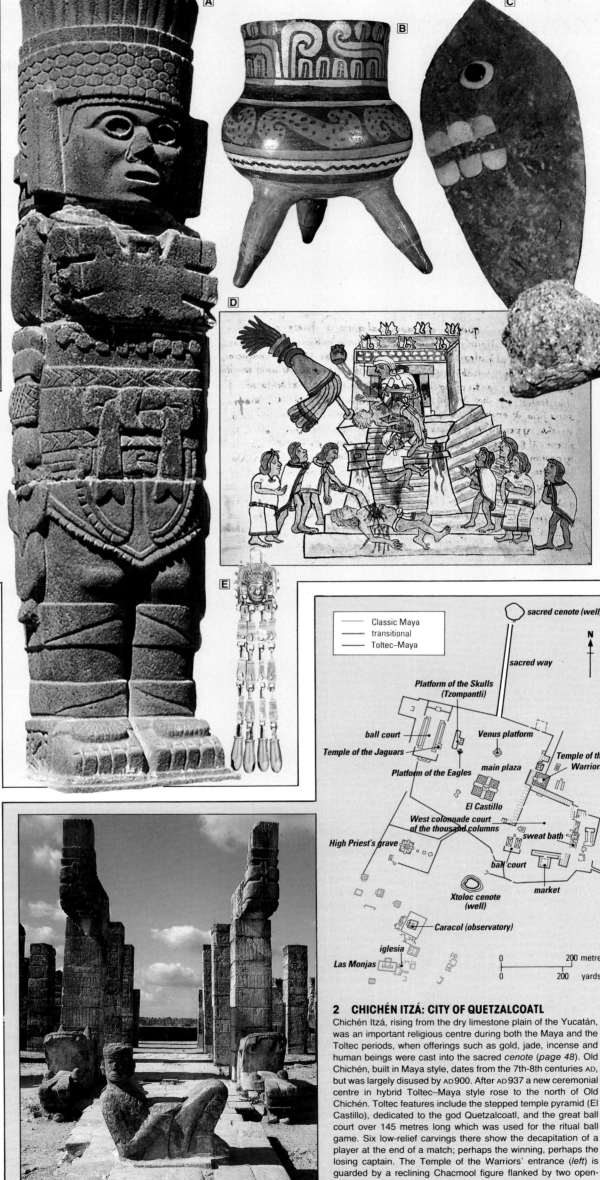

2 CHICHÉN ITZÁ: CITY OF QUETZALCOATL

Chichén Itzá, rising from the dry limestone plain of the Yucatán, was an important religious centre during both the Maya and the Toltec periods, when offerings such as gold, jade, incense and human beings were cast into the sacred *cenote* (*page 48*). Old Chichén, built in Maya style, dates from the 7th-8th centuries AD, but was largely disused by AD 900. After AD 937 a new ceremonial centre in hybrid Toltec–Maya style rose to the north of Old Chichén. Toltec features include the stepped temple pyramid (El Castillo), dedicated to the god Quetzalcoatl, and the great ball court over 145 metres long which was used for the ritual ball game. Six low-relief carvings there show the decapitation of a player at the end of a match; perhaps the winning, perhaps the losing captain. The Temple of the Warriors' entrance (*left*) is guarded by a reclining Chacmool figure flanked by two open-jawed feathered serpents, the symbol of Quetzalcoatl.

The Pueblo farmers of the Southwest

By AD 700 three principal cultural traditions had emerged in the southwestern part of North America: the Hohokam, Mogollon and Anasazi. Their territories covered much of present-day Utah, Colorado, Arizona and New Mexico, extending south into Sonora and Chihuahua. The region is diverse, ranging from hot, dry deserts to cooler, more moist elevations of over 3600 metres.

The earliest Southwestern culture, the Hohokam, was centred in the desert lands of southern Arizona and northern Sonora. Settlements consisted of shallow semi-subterranean pit houses located near rivers that could feed irrigation canals. Maize, beans, squash and cotton were the main crops: tobacco and amaranth were possibly also grown. By the Sedentary period (900–1200), canals up to 16 kilometres long were being constructed, and these irrigation schemes allowed two crops a year to be harvested. Gathered food such as prickly pears and seed pods from mesquite trees supplemented agriculture.

Strong Mexican influences are evident in the Hohokam. Excavations at Snaketown and Pueblo Grande have revealed ball courts and even rubber balls made of latex imported from Mexico. Mesoamerican-style platform mounds were built at several sites, including Gatlin where the platform base measures 29 x 22 metres. Copper bells made by the lost-wax method were acquired from Mexico, as were other artefacts including turquoise mosaics, carved shell bracelets and beads, ear spools, nose plugs, stone palettes, pyrite mirrors, effigy vessels and figurines. Local craftsmen also made Mexican-style jewellery. During the Classic period (1200–1400) the area was dominated by the Anasazi from the north, forming a generalised western Pueblo culture. Solid, high adobe walls were built to protect villages from raiders, possibly fierce nomadic tribes such as the Apache, and from AD 1400 many Hohokam sites were abandoned.

In New Mexico and eastern Arizona, Mogollon culture flourished. By the 9th century AD villages of many small pit houses had developed along the tributaries of main rivers. Agriculture, which depended on direct rainfall and floodwater, was supplemented by hunting and gathering. After 1000, stone houses with intercommunicating rooms were built above ground; *kivas*, semi-subterranean ceremonial rooms used by male kin-groups, also appeared. White-slipped pottery was produced, and decorated with black painted geometric motifs and stylised human and animal figures. Bowls were made to be used as grave-goods, and were often ritually 'killed' by piercing a hole in the base before they were interred with mats and shell and turquoise ornaments. Casas Grandes in Chihuahua, a town covering c.36.5 hectares and with 2200 inhabitants, may have been established by Mexicans as the economic, administrative and trading centre for the Mogollon area. During the 14th century, after a period of drought and raids by Athabascan nomads, Mogollon culture was assimilated into the western Pueblo sphere of influence.

The third and most extensive late prehistoric group was the Anasazi, which was centred on the area where the modern boundaries of Arizona, New Mexico, Utah and Colorado meet, and reached its greatest extent between 900 and 1100. At first the Anasazi depended on natural flooding, rainfall and flash storms during the hot summers, and settled near rivers or on uplands where there was fertile wind-blown soil. Sometime before 1100 the Anasazi left these villages and took refuge in well-defended positions. In the Mesa Verde area communal apartment houses, storerooms and *kivas* were constructed in rock shelters high in the canyon cliffs, guarded by watchtowers. Pueblo Bonito in Chaco Canyon flourished between 950 and 1300. Its population of about 1200 were housed in 800 rooms arranged within D-shaped outer walls four storeys high. The canyon contained more than 400 kilometres of roads, and was possibly an important ceremonial centre and a redistribution point both for food and for exotic goods such as turquoise and brightly coloured feathers from macaws and parrots.

Both the cliff-dwellings and the Chaco Canyon towns were abandoned soon after AD 1300. Crop failures caused by low rainfall have been suggested as the cause, as has the attack by ancestors of the Navajo and Apache. Each of the Southwestern cultures collapsed under similar pressures, but unlike many prehistoric peoples of the Americas there is a living legacy today. The Pueblo Indians are the descendants of the Anasazi; the Pima and Papago Indians of the Hohokam, and the Zuni Pueblo retain elements of Mogollon culture.

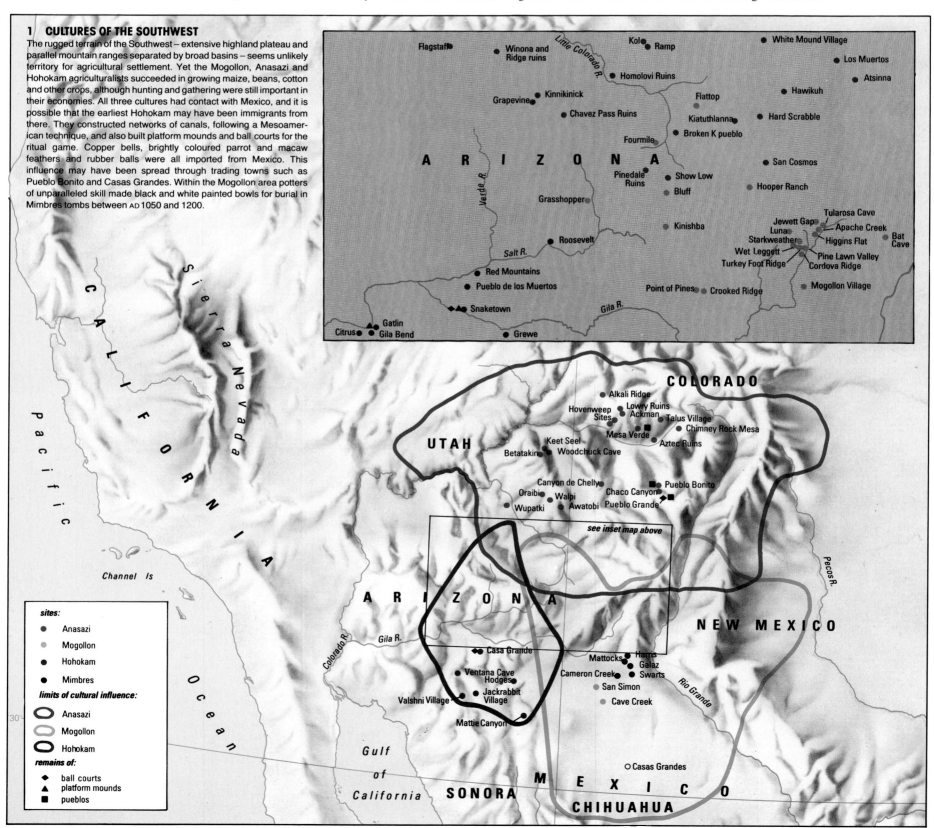

1 CULTURES OF THE SOUTHWEST

The rugged terrain of the Southwest – extensive highland plateau and parallel mountain ranges separated by broad basins – seems unlikely territory for agricultural settlement. Yet the Mogollon, Anasazi and Hohokam agriculturalists succeeded in growing maize, beans, cotton and other crops, although hunting and gathering were still important in their economies. All three cultures had contact with Mexico, and it is possible that the earliest Hohokam may have been immigrants from there. They constructed networks of canals, following a Mesoamerican technique, and also built platform mounds and ball courts for the ritual game. Copper bells, brightly coloured parrot and macaw feathers and rubber balls were all imported from Mexico. This influence may have been spread through trading towns such as Pueblo Bonito and Casas Grandes. Within the Mogollon area potters of unparalleled skill made black and white painted bowls for burial in Mimbres tombs between AD 1050 and 1200.

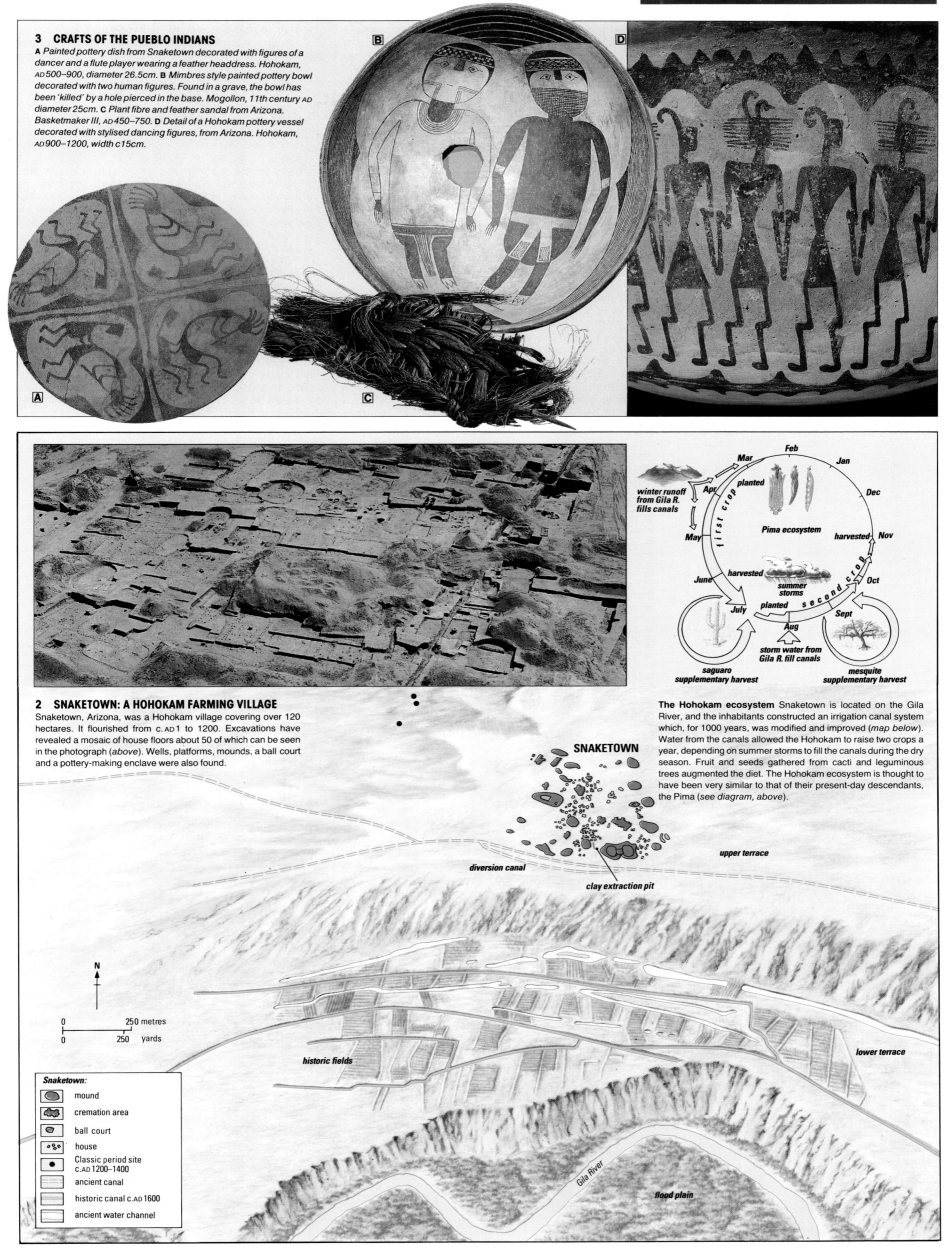

3 CRAFTS OF THE PUEBLO INDIANS

A *Painted pottery dish from Snaketown decorated with figures of a dancer and a flute player wearing a feather headdress. Hohokam, AD 500–900, diameter 26.5cm.* B *Mimbres style painted pottery bowl decorated with two human figures. Found in a grave, the bowl has been 'killed' by a hole pierced in the base. Mogollon, 11th century AD diameter 25cm.* C *Plant fibre and feather sandal from Arizona. Basketmaker III, AD 450–750.* D *Detail of a Hohokam pottery vessel decorated with stylised dancing figures, from Arizona. Hohokam, AD 900–1200, width c15cm.*

2 SNAKETOWN: A HOHOKAM FARMING VILLAGE

Snaketown, Arizona, was a Hohokam village covering over 120 hectares. It flourished from c. AD 1 to 1200. Excavations have revealed a mosaic of house floors about 50 of which can be seen in the photograph (*above*). Wells, platforms, mounds, a ball court and a pottery-making enclave were also found.

The Hohokam ecosystem Snaketown is located on the Gila River, and the inhabitants constructed an irrigation canal system which, for 1000 years, was modified and improved (*map below*). Water from the canals allowed the Hohokam to raise two crops a year, depending on summer storms to fill the canals during the dry season. Fruit and seeds gathered from cacti and leguminous trees augmented the diet. The Hohokam ecosystem is thought to have been very similar to that of their present-day descendants, the Pima (*see diagram, above*).

SNAKETOWN

diversion canal

clay extraction pit

upper terrace

historic fields

lower terrace

Snaketown:
- mound
- cremation area
- ball court
- house
- Classic period site c.AD 1200–1400
- ancient canal
- historic canal c.AD 1600
- ancient water channel

N

0   250 metres
0   250 yards

Gila River

flood plain

Pima ecosystem

winter runoff from Gila R. fills canals

first crop

second crop

planted

harvested

harvested

planted

summer storms

storm water from Gila R. fill canals

saguaro supplementary harvest

mesquite supplementary harvest

Temple-mounds of the Mississippi

The first true towns in North America appeared in the Middle Mississippi Valley in about AD 700, characterised by flat-topped, rectangular mounds, surmounted by temples and mortuary houses for the elite classes of society, and timber houses. A town centre typically consisted of up to 20 mounds grouped around a plaza and enclosed by a defensive wooden stockade. Traces of longhouses with walls of mud plaster and thatched roofs have also been found. Such towns were both administrative centres, for the collection and redistribution of food and materials, and ceremonial centres. They had substantial populations sometimes reaching urban proportions – Cahokia had at least 10,000 inhabitants.

In the fertile river valleys surrounding the towns there were unprecedentedly large rural populations living in permanent villages – about 200 people per square kilometre. Only a revolution in agriculture made such large populations possible. Mexican influence, arguably evident in the layout of the towns, may account for the change in the economic base of the south-east. Before 700, maize cultivation generally had been limited to the south of the region, as the varieties grown needed 200 frost-free days to ripen. After that date hardier, more productive strains were introduced that matured within a 120-day season – this allowed two crops to be harvested each year in some sheltered spots. Only the rich, seasonally inundated bottom lands of the Mississippi, Ohio, Tennessee, Arkansas and Red Rivers and their major tributaries were suitable for this intensive cultivation. The farmers were hoe agriculturalists, and hoes were not suitable for cultivating the grassy uplands.

In addition to maize cultivation, specialised gathering of plant foods such as nuts, which are high in protein and fat, and the cultivation of sunflowers, beans and squash were vital contributions to a balanced diet. More efficient hunting of the abundant game on the uplands became possible after 800, when the bow and arrow replaced the spear-thrower and dart.

16th-century French explorers who reached these towns described a ranked matrilineal society, headed by a chief who ruled four well-defined social classes. Archaeological evidence, particularly from burials, endorses this picture. Although funerary practices changed over the centuries, the elite tended to be buried on timber litters in mortuaries built on the top of mounds in town centres. Corpses were often kept in charnel houses until the flesh had rotted from the bones, which were then collected in bundles and given an elaborate second burial. Exotic valuables such as whelk or conch shell vessels, pearl and marine shell beads and embossed copper sheets were placed in mausolea. Sometimes retainers were killed, accompanying their masters to the grave.

A spectacular group of artefacts, decorated with highly distinctive motifs, has been found in major mortuary temple-mounds from Mississippi to Minnesota and from Oklahoma to the Atlantic coast, and bears witness to a widespread religion known as the Southern Cult. The ritual objects include marine shell discs used as gorgets (chest decorations) and complete conch shells decorated with incised designs such as a human eye in the palm of an open hand, forked and weeping eyes, elaborate crosses, flying winged human figures and sunburst motifs. These designs also appear on embossed copper sheets, stone palettes and polychrome painted textiles. Other objects connected with the Southern Cult include monolithic polished stone axes and maces and pottery vessels in the shape of effigy heads, which may be trophy heads or representations of ancestors. The Southern Cult reached its climax in about 1250. Little is known of its dogma or rituals, although certain Mexican traits can be detected; for example, the importance of the four cardinal directions, and the emphasis which the cult placed on death.

European explorers and settlers who reached the region in the 16th century, brought contagious diseases with them that carried off many of the native inhabitants. Others were violently killed. Deserted villages and towns are described, abandoned through fear or emptied by fatal illnesses. A century earlier, in about 1450, long before European contact, a similar depopulation occurred in the Middle Mississippi area around Cahokia. It is possible that the town dwellers of this region fell victim to diseases caused by unhealthy overcrowding and poor sanitation, probably tuberculosis or internal parasite infestations. Whatever the cause of the decline of North America's earliest towns, their demise was but a pale foreshadowing of the destruction that was to befall these cultures when Europeans arrived in the New World.

2 CAHOKIA: A MISSISSIPPIAN TEMPLE-MOUND

Cahokia lies in a large, fertile alluvial valley south of the confluence of the Mississippi, Missouri and Illinois Rivers. The light, rich soil was ideal for the hoe-using agriculturalists who built the first permanent villages there in about 800. The population of this region, the American Bottoms, grew rapidly, reaching an estimated 38,000 in the 12th and 13th centuries. The communities which developed here were headed by Cahokia itself, where over 100 flat-topped earthen mounds were constructed. The largest of these, Monks Mound, is more than 30 metres high, and like many others bears traces of timber structures on its summit. In about 1200 a bastioned timber stockade was erected around the central complex of Cahokia, enclosing some 120 hectares. This may have been a defensive structure or a massive screen. Some mounds contained burials (*photograph right*), which varied in type according to social status. A small ridge-topped mound contained two

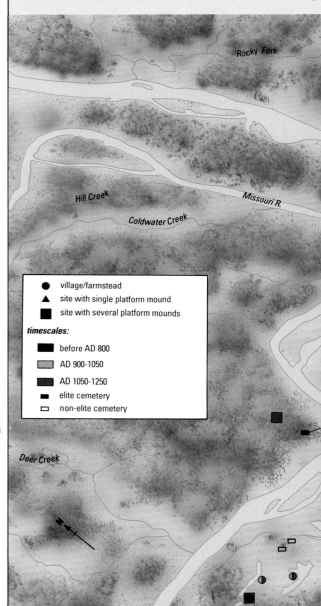

site legend:
- ● village/farmstead
- ▲ site with single platform mound
- ■ site with several platform mounds

timescales:
- ■ before AD 800
- ■ AD 900–1050
- ■ AD 1050–1250
- ■ elite cemetery
- □ non-elite cemetery

Map 1 legend

- ● site
- ⬭ extent of cultural influence

cultures: (colour coded accordingly)
- Middle Mississippi
- South Appalachian Mississippian
- Plaquemine Mississippian
- Caddoan Mississippian
- Fort Ancient
- Oneota

1 TEMPLES OF NORTH AMERICA

The central area of the Mississippian tradition, characterised by earthen mounds surmounted by important buildings and grouped around rectangular plazas, was the Middle Mississippi Valley. Peripheral groups known as the Caddoan, Plaquemine, Southern Appalachian Mississippian, Oneota and Fort Ancient cultures were coeval with the Middle Mississippian culture, developing along the same lines because of similar local conditions and events. There was contact between these different and distant groups by river. In the Ohio Valley the Fort Ancient culture is characterised by the construction of large earthwork fortifications, symptomatic of the apparent growth of warfare throughout the south-east during this period.

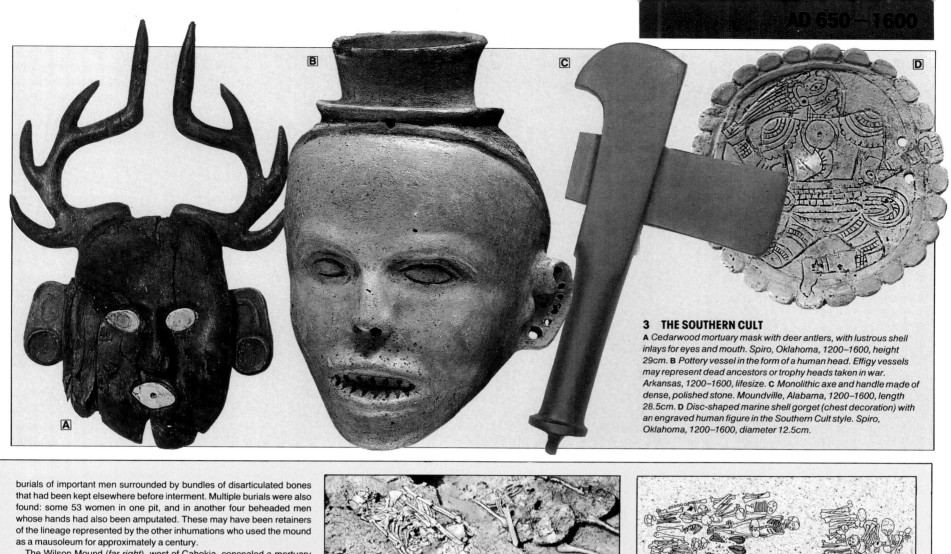

3 THE SOUTHERN CULT

A Cedarwood mortuary mask with deer antlers, with lustrous shell inlays for eyes and mouth. Spiro, Oklahoma, 1200–1600, height 29cm. **B** Pottery vessel in the form of a human head. Effigy vessels may represent dead ancestors or trophy heads taken in war. Arkansas, 1200–1600, lifesize. **C** Monolithic axe and handle made of dense, polished stone. Moundville, Alabama, 1200–1600, length 28.5cm. **D** Disc-shaped marine shell gorget (chest decoration) with an engraved human figure in the Southern Cult style. Spiro, Oklahoma, 1200–1600, diameter 12.5cm.

burials of important men surrounded by bundles of disarticulated bones that had been kept elsewhere before interment. Multiple burials were also found: some 53 women in one pit, and in another four beheaded men whose hands had also been amputated. These may have been retainers of the lineage represented by the other inhumations who used the mound as a mausoleum for approximately a century.

The Wilson Mound (*far right*), west of Cahokia, concealed a mortuary chamber 4.25 metres x 5.5 metres in size. Inside were hundreds of disarticulated human bones grouped to form bundles composed of several individuals. Cut-marks on some bones showed that tendons and ligaments had been severed to allow the bundles to be made, and that adhering flesh had been stripped off, indicating that the skeletons had been at different stages of decomposition before being reburied. A single dog skeleton was found in the mortuary, and among the human remains were scattered disc-shaped marine shell beads and large whelk shells.

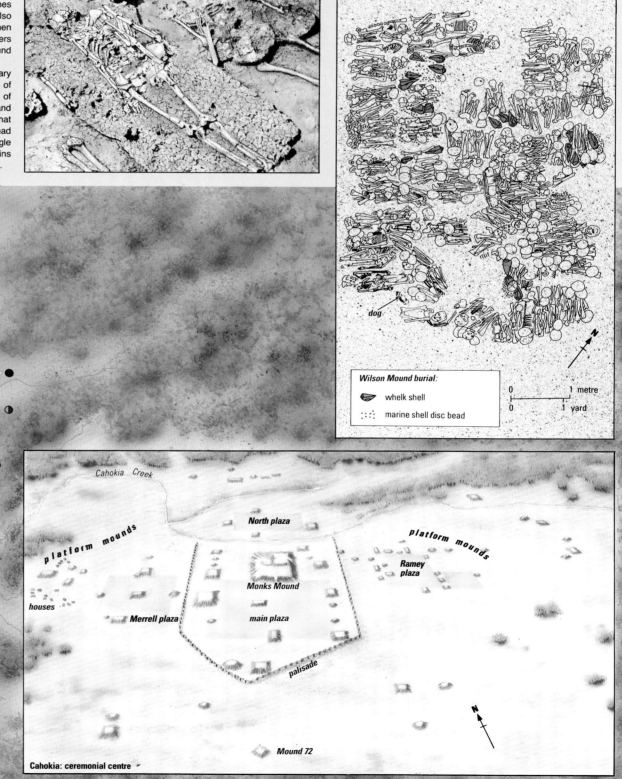

dog

Wilson Mound burial:

🐚 whelk shell

marine shell disc bead

| 0 | | 1 metre |
| 0 | | 1 yard |

Cahokia: ceremonial centre

Ozette: a hunting village

The north-west coast of America is one of the most bountiful areas in the world. Indigenous people exploited the rich land, river and marine sources of British Columbia, Washington and Oregon, and developed sophisticated cultures. These societies, which date back to the time of Christ, are famous for their elaborate material items – carved boxes, masks and house posts, as well as textiles and basketry. Since most of these artefacts were made of perishable materials such as wood and bark, these Northwest Coast cultures have left very little trace in the archaeological record. The discovery of a village midden with excellent organic preservation, representing some 2000 years of occupation, at Ozette, Washington, was therefore of enormous interest. Its importance was not truly realised until February 1970, when storm waves undercut a bank at Ozette, and the resulting landslip revealed the timbers of a longhouse buried beneath a two-metre-thick mudslide. The dense mud had created anaerobic conditions under which organic materials did not decay, forming a 'time capsule'. The local Makah people tell legends of mud sweeping into Ozette, flattening houses and burying their owners. The discovery of human skeletons together with complete house contents confirms these stories, and enables the catastrophe to be dated in the 15th century.

The ancient inhabitants of Ozette, like their successors until 1910, were whale-hunters, going out to sea from the shelter of Ozette Bay in dugout canoes 11 metres long, from which they harpooned grey, humpback and sperm whales. One kill could supply the whole village with meat, oil and massive bones. Fur seals, each weighing up to 200 kilograms, were less dangerous prey; in the spring up to a dozen a day could be caught as their migration route swung inshore at Ozette, and over 80% of the animal bones from the site consist of fur seal remains. Other marine mammals, such as sea lions, were also hunted; they were easier to hunt than land animals as their carcasses could be towed direct to the village, rather than carried laboriously overland. Both shallow- and deepwater fish were caught and dried, and shellfish, especially clams and mussels, were collected. Although elk and deer bones are scarcely represented in the bone sample from the site, it is probable that meat from these animals was cut from the carcass at the site of the kill and brought home in strips containing no bones and therefore leaving no trace. Ducks, geese, gulls and other birds were hunted and trapped, and plant food was collected from the forest. Analysis shows that 99% of the vegetable intake consisted of three types of wild berry (salmonberry, huckleberry and red elderberry).

The forest supplied raw materials for making houses, canoes, tools, containers and textiles. The straight-grained, knot-free timber from red cedar was split into planks, and was then dressed and carved with adzes and chisels. Most chisel blades were made from beaver teeth, and artefacts of remarkably high quality were being produced long before iron and steel blades became available with the arrival of the Europeans. Houses were constructed and almost entirely furnished with cedar-wood, which was also used to make boxes for storage and cooking. Watertight rectangular boxes were made by steaming and bending sheets of cedarwood; they were then filled with water, heated by hot stones, and meat or fish was placed inside to cook. The finds at Ozette are so complete that even the pairs of flat sticks used to lift hot stones from the hearth to the box have been found. Red alder and Oregon ash were used to make bowls for food and oil, as they do not impart a false flavour to their contents. Some bowls still smelt of fish and seal oil when they were found. Bows were made from springy big leaf maple and Pacific yew; cherry bark was used for binding handles to make non-slip grips, as it tightens when it dries. Fluff from seed heads of plants such as fireweed was collected to be spun and woven, and small dogs with poodle-like fleeces were also kept to provide wool. Most of the textiles at Ozette however, were made from cedar bark, which was stripped from the tree trunk each May and June in six-metre lengths. The pliable bark was split into narrow strips and woven into blankets and fringed skirts on upright looms. Cedar bark was also used to make a range of baskets for food storage and collection, as well as sleeping mats and conical rain hats.

These examples of remarkably good preservation at Ozette show how incomplete a picture of prehistoric life is normally available to archaeologists. Anticipating further advances in both theory and techniques of investigation, a large area of Ozette has been left untouched, in trust for future excavators, for this site may prove to be unique.

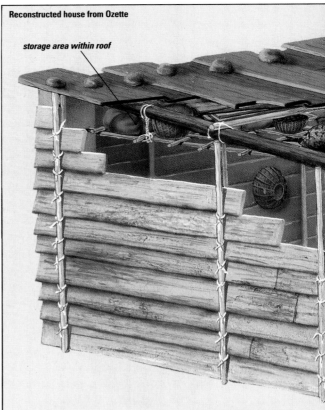

Reconstructed house from Ozette

storage area within roof

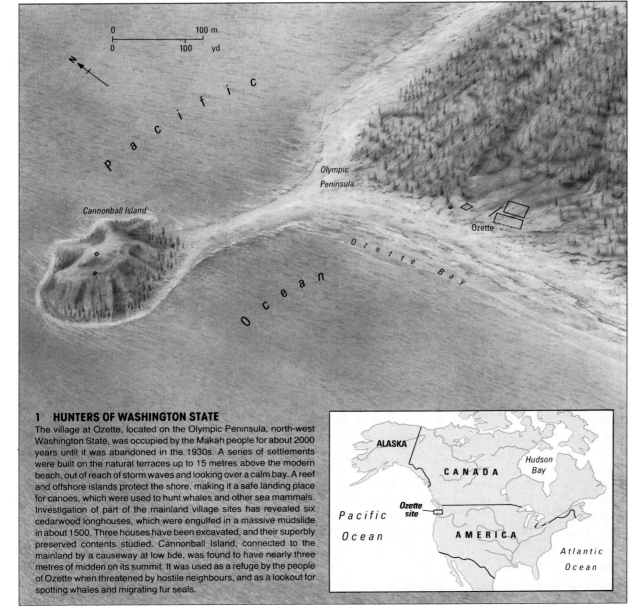

1 HUNTERS OF WASHINGTON STATE

The village at Ozette, located on the Olympic Peninsula, north-west Washington State, was occupied by the Makah people for about 2000 years until it was abandoned in the 1930s. A series of settlements were built on the natural terraces up to 15 metres above the modern beach, out of reach of storm waves and looking over a calm bay. A reef and offshore islands protect the shore, making it a safe landing place for canoes, which were used to hunt whales and other sea mammals. Investigation of part of the mainland village sites has revealed six cedarwood longhouses, which were engulfed in a massive mudslide in about 1500. Three houses have been excavated, and their superbly preserved contents studied. Cannonball Island, connected to the mainland by a causeway at low tide, was found to have nearly three metres of midden on its summit. It was used as a refuge by the people of Ozette when threatened by hostile neighbours, and as a lookout for spotting whales and migrating fur seals.

Diet: meat resources			
	common name	bone frequency	percentage
	rabbit	2	0.004
	beaver	23	0.043
	red squirrel	5	0.010
	mouse	5	0.010
	porpoise	1104	2.085
	dog	1974	3.729
	wolf	4	0.008
	black bear	21	0.040
	raccoon	32	0.060
	marten	8	0.015
	mink/weasel/skunk	23	0.043
	river otter	15	0.028
	sea otter	501	0.946
	fur seal/sea lion	29	0.055
	northern fur seal	47,296	89.342
	sea lion	930	1.757
	harbour seal	377	0.712
	northern elephant seal	2	0.004
	elk	100	0.189
	deer	485	0.916
	cow	2	0.004
	total	52,938	100.000

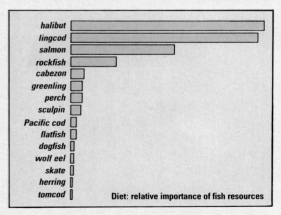

Diet: relative importance of fish resources

halibut
lingcod
salmon
rockfish
cabezon
greenling
perch
sculpin
Pacific cod
flatfish
dogfish
wolf eel
skate
herring
tomcod

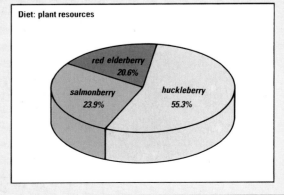

Diet: plant resources

red elderberry 20.6%
salmonberry 23.9%
huckleberry 55.3%

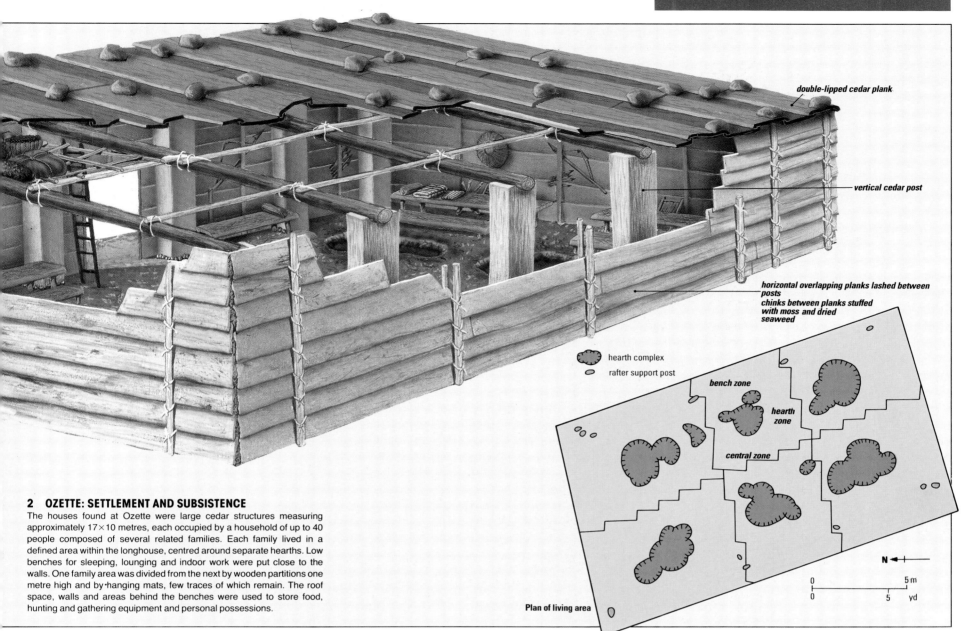

double-lipped cedar plank

vertical cedar post

horizontal overlapping planks lashed between posts
chinks between planks stuffed with moss and dried seaweed

hearth complex

rafter support post

bench zone

hearth zone

central zone

N

Plan of living area

0 ____ 5 m
0 ____ 5 yd

2 OZETTE: SETTLEMENT AND SUBSISTENCE

The houses found at Ozette were large cedar structures measuring approximately 17×10 metres, each occupied by a household of up to 40 people composed of several related families. Each family lived in a defined area within the longhouse, centred around separate hearths. Low benches for sleeping, lounging and indoor work were put close to the walls. One family area was divided from the next by wooden partitions one metre high and by·hanging mats, few traces of which remain. The roof space, walls and areas behind the benches were used to store food, hunting and gathering equipment and personal possessions.

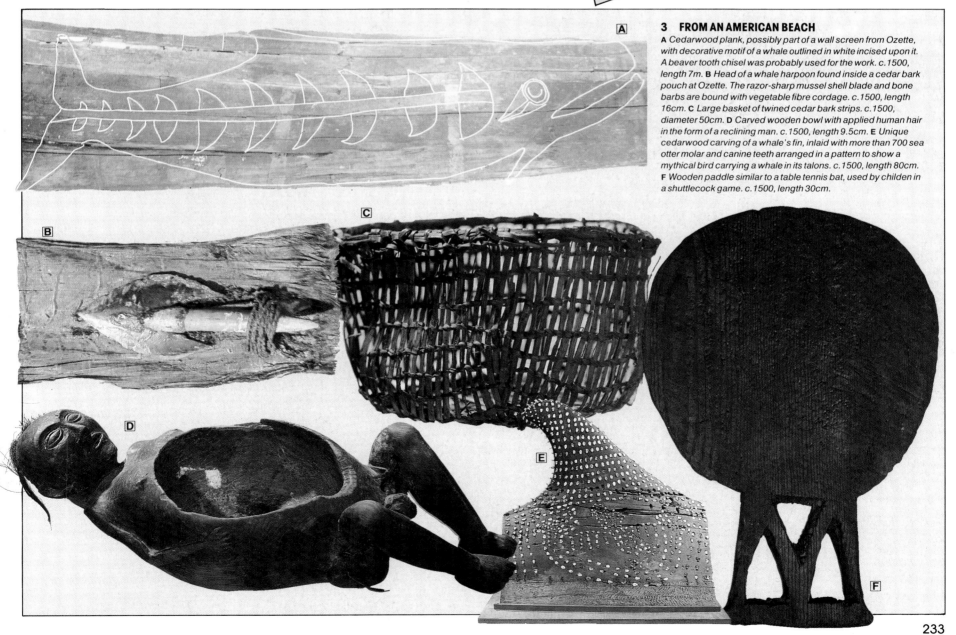

3 FROM AN AMERICAN BEACH

A Cedarwood plank, possibly part of a wall screen from Ozette, with decorative motif of a whale outlined in white incised upon it. A beaver tooth chisel was probably used for the work. c.1500, length 7m. **B** Head of a whale harpoon found inside a cedar bark pouch at Ozette. The razor-sharp mussel shell blade and bone barbs are bound with vegetable fibre cordage. c.1500, length 16cm. **C** Large basket of twined cedar bark strips. c.1500, diameter 50cm. **D** Carved wooden bowl with applied human hair in the form of a reclining man. c.1500, length 9.5cm. **E** Unique cedarwood carving of a whale's fin, inlaid with more than 700 sea otter molar and canine teeth arranged in a pattern to show a mythical bird carrying a whale in its talons. c.1500, length 80cm. **F** Wooden paddle similar to a table tennis bat, used by childen in a shuttlecock game. c.1500, length 30cm.

The first European settlements

Vikings from northern Europe had settled and explored the coasts of Labrador and Newfoundland by about AD 1000, but they were few in number and their settlements soon perished. For the next half millennium Europeans and Americans developed their separate cultures in total ignorance of the other's existence. The arrival in the Caribbean of Christopher Columbus in 1492, however, heralded a massive and sustained European invasion which would eventually wrest the entire continent from the hands of its native peoples.

The lands Columbus discovered were duly claimed for Spain, in spite of the fact that they were already the home of a large native Amerindian population. During the next quarter century, aided by the arrival of constant reinforcements from Europe, the Spaniards conquered all the Caribbean islands and founded their first city – at Santo Domingo on Hispaniola. It was laid out on the regular grid-iron plan which was to be copied all over Latin America. Each colonial town could boast a small but proud European population and a town council, running municipal affairs just as if it were in Spain, and organising the labour of captured Indians and (from 1505) imported Blacks to raise cattle, grow sugar and search for gold.

From this already prosperous base, a successful series of invasions of the mainland were mounted. In 1519, a small army of 500 settlers with horses and guns landed at Veracruz and, within two years, overthrew the powerful Aztec confederation (*page 226*), occupied its capital, Tenochtitlán, and soon dominated the central Mexican plateau. Panamá was founded in 1519, and from there the conquerors fanned out into modern Guatemala, Nicaragua and El Salvador. A mere 180 settlers toppled the Inca empire in Peru (*page 222*), substituting a Spanish regime. Lima, the new capital, was established in 1535. From Peru, the conquerors moved north-east, founding Santa Fé de Bogotá in 1536, and south into Chile, founding Santiago in 1542. By then, some two million square kilometres (four times the size of Spain) were under European control, containing some 50 million subjects, about seven times the population of Spain.

The European conquest had severe demographic consequences. On the one hand, the European population increased steadily, both through natural increase and through sustained immigration from Europe. More dramatic, however, was the fall of the native Indian population (largely due to disease) from perhaps 50 million in 1500 to no more than three million a century later. The Spaniards were numerous enough to populate some 225 towns and to maintain vast farmsteads (*haciendas*), worked by the servile labour of either local Indians or slaves imported from Africa. Slave markets and slave quarters became a feature of all colonial centres. The Spaniards felt no need to fortify their settlements against the threat of rebellions by the dwindling local population.

The sensational success of the *Conquistadores* in Central America had soon led Europeans from other lands to attempt invasions elsewhere. The Portuguese laid claim to Brazil in 1500, and imported African slaves in large numbers. By 1700 there were some 100,000 European and 200,000 Black inhabitants in Brazil, living either on the sugar plantations or in the 37 towns along the coastal plain. The French laid claim to the lands along the St Lawrence River from the 1530s, and when that failed to deliver sufficient quantities of gold ('Canada' meant 'worthless' in the local language), they tried to establish colonies in Brazil and in Florida.

The early English colonies in Virginia (Roanoke was founded in 1584) lived a highly precarious existence. The commercial possibilities of tobacco revolutionised the situation. There was a scramble for land suitable to raise tobacco, and in 1622 the colonists' greed provoked a major Indian attack. The Indian War proved to be a turning-point. As one Jamestown colonist gloated after the Indians' defeat: 'We, who hitherto have had possession of no more ground than their waste ... shall now enjoy their cultivated places.' The Indians, outnumbered and outgunned, were driven back into the wilderness.

Much the same progression took place in the early 17th century in the other colonies established in North America. By 1700, the total population of European origin in the New World must have exceeded one million, and there were almost as many European towns in North America between Québec and St Augustine as there were between St Augustine and Santiago in Chile. All remained firmly under European control until the revolt of 13 of the English colonies in 1776.

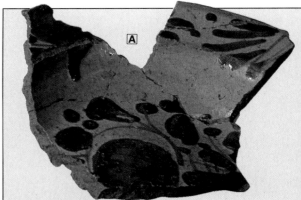

Diet: analysis of bone remains

food	low status	middle status	high status
	%	%	%
cow	62.6	77.2	60.3
pig	11.2	6.1	14.9
deer	1.0	7.1	11.5
sea catfish	4.9	0.6	0.9
drum	4.6	2.7	2.4
gopher tortoise	0.5	0.2	3.0
chicken	0.5	0.8	1.3
mullet	1.0	0.8	0.6

Pottery: analysis of social differences

ceramic type	low status	middle status	high status
	%	%	%
aboriginal	92.6	66.0	58.6
Spanish majolica	2.9	12.0	19.2
utilitarian earthenwares	1.5	11.0	14.4
other European wares	3.04	9.0	7.4
porcelain	0.15	0.2	0.2

households:
■ high and middle status
□ low status

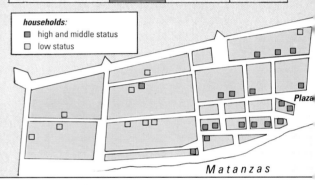

Plaza

Matanzas

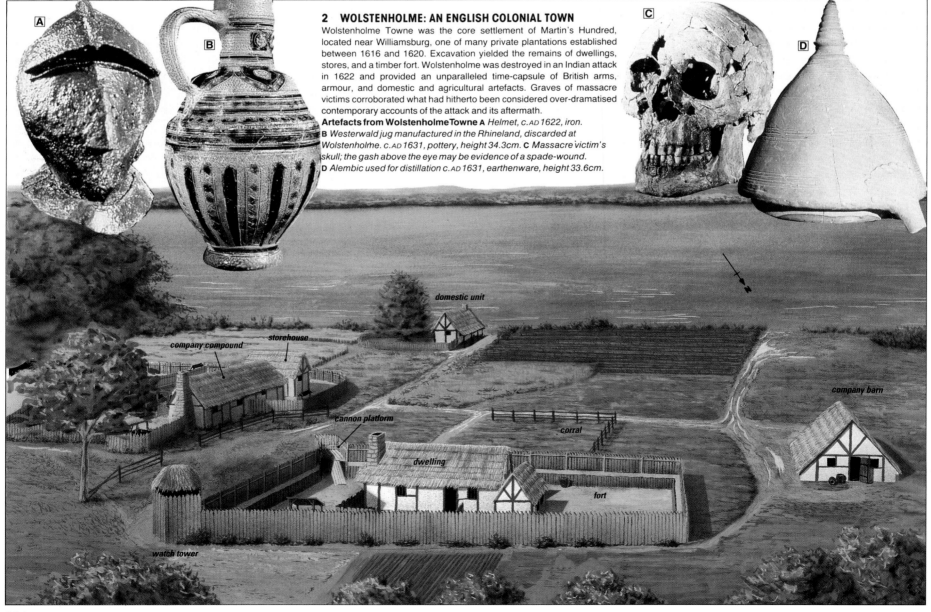

2 WOLSTENHOLME: AN ENGLISH COLONIAL TOWN

Wolstenholme Towne was the core settlement of Martin's Hundred, located near Williamsburg, one of many private plantations established between 1616 and 1620. Excavation yielded the remains of dwellings, stores, and a timber fort. Wolstenholme was destroyed in an Indian attack in 1622 and provided an unparalleled time-capsule of British arms, armour, and domestic and agricultural artefacts. Graves of massacre victims corroborated what had hitherto been considered over-dramatised contemporary accounts of the attack and its aftermath.
Artefacts from Wolstenholme Towne A *Helmet, c. AD 1622, iron.* **B** *Westerwald jug manufactured in the Rhineland, discarded at Wolstenholme. c. AD 1631, pottery, height 34.3cm.* **C** *Massacre victim's skull; the gash above the eye may be evidence of a spade-wound.* **D** *Alembic used for distillation c. AD 1631, earthenware, height 33.6cm.*

domestic unit
company compound
storehouse
cannon platform
corral
dwelling
fort
company barn
watch tower

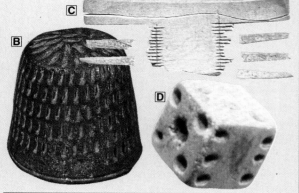

Castillo de San Marcos

town wall

Castillo de
San Marcos

Bay

3 SAINT AUGUSTINE: A SPANISH COLONIAL TOWN

Saint Augustine was founded by the Spanish on the Florida coast
in 1585. The oldest standing remains – the Castillo de San Marcos
(above) and the town gates – date from the 17th century. The
difference in status between the officials, military officers and
merchants, and the coloured (casta) inhabitants has been illustrated by excavation. High-status households imported their
pottery from Spain, but low-status households made do with locally
produced wares. Seafood was considered low status, but deer, a
prestigious hunted animal, was clearly high status (see tables).
Artefacts from Saint Augustine A *Puebla blue on white, a
traditional ware from Spain. 18th century, diameter 21cm.*
B *Thimble. Early 16th century, brass, height 1.5cm.* **C** *Comb. 16th
century, ivory, width c.2cm.* **D** *Die. Early 16th century, ivory,
height c.1cm.*

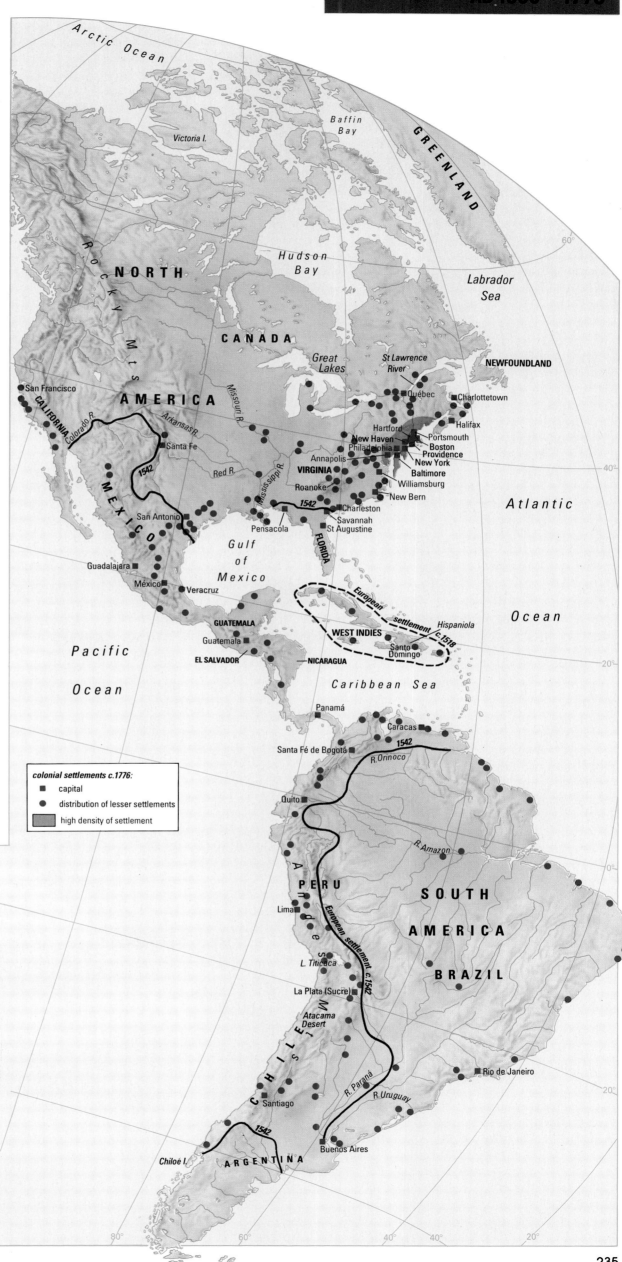

colonial settlements c.1776:
- ■ capital
- ● distribution of lesser settlements
- ▨ high density of settlement

1 THE COLONISATION OF THE AMERICAS

The careful efforts of the Europeans to consolidate conquests with
settlements and missions meant that by 1776 (see map) Europe
dominated an area of the New World that was far larger than its share
of the Old. There were four main zones of European occupation.
Along the Atlantic seaboard of North America, the English colonies
covered 2,072,000 square kilometres (15 times the size of England)
and boasted a population of just over two million – almost one-quarter
of them Blacks. There were virtually no descendants of the indigenous Amerindian population here. Immediately to the north and west
lay the considerably less populous towns and trading posts founded in
the St Lawrence and Mississippi River valleys by the French.

Far larger than either were the Spanish settlements: around the
Caribbean, up into California (where a chain of missions linked San
Francisco with Mexico City) and down into Chile and Argentina. By
1776, the populations of Spanish America approached twelve million:
one-fifth of them of pure European stock, almost one-half Indian, and
the rest either Black or half-caste. At this date, the Portuguese towns
and plantations of Brazil were inhabited by perhaps three million
people – about one million of them white and most of the rest Black.

Nevertheless, the peoples of European and African descent still
remained largely confined to the coastal plains of the continent, or to
upland plains adjacent to the sea. The conquest of the hinterland from
the surviving indigenous populations of America was to be the work of
those states which wrested their independence from Europe following
the rebellion of the English colonists in 1776.

SEVEN
TOWARDS THE MODERN WORLD
AD 650 – 1800

THE 7th CENTURY AD marks the beginning of a recovery from the collapse of the ancient world with the onset of a period of expansion in trade which has continued up to the present day. In Europe, the time of turmoil and readjustment following the collapse of the western Roman empire was gradually brought to a close by a modest economic recovery in the 9th and 10th centuries. In China, the imperial mantle of the Han was assumed by the Tang dynasty, who brought classical Chinese culture to a new peak, and extended their political control far into Central Asia. Perhaps the most startling development of this period, however, was the emergence of a new power – Islam – in the Near East, centred on the old Sasanian realms, but with an empire stretching across half of the Old World, from the shores of the Atlantic to Afghanistan and beyond.

The keynotes of these centuries are trade and world religion. In the west, Viking warrior-merchants dominated the seas and rivers from Novgorod to Newfoundland. In the east, overland trade along the Silk Road brought a wide variety of goods from as far afield as the Mediterranean to the cosmopolitan Tang capital of Chang'an. But the most successful merchants of the period were the Muslims, who not only followed the sea routes from the Red Sea to India and Indonesia, but also developed overland routes across the Sahara to trade with the developing kingdoms of Black Africa. Where trade and conquest led, religion followed. Islam spread rapidly until it reached from the Indies in the east to the Atlantic in the west, and south to the savanna kingdoms of West Africa and the trading cities of the east African coast. In eastern Asia, Buddhism spread from its northern Indian home to China and thence to Korea, Japan and Central Asia. In Europe, Christianity consolidated its hold and became the critical cultural force in the emerging nation-states.

The economic revival of Europe and the spread of European trade and colonisation from the 16th century onwards marks the final stage in the establishment of a single, inter-linked world economy. Innovations in maritime technology and nautical skills enabled European ships to transport silver from the Americas, porcelain from China and spices from the East Indies to the flourishing cities of western Europe. It was these processes which culminated in the European colonialism and imperialism of the 18th and 19th centuries which, together with industrialisation, mark the birth of the modern world.

Stone Buddha head from Wat Mahathat in Lop Buri, Thailand.
13th–14th century AD, height 20cm.

The Byzantine empire

The Byzantine empire is a modern term for the East Roman empire from 11 May 330, when Constantine the Great, the first Christian emperor, made Byzantium, renamed Constantinople, the capital of the eastern half of the empire until 29 May 1453 when it was conquered by the Ottoman Turks.

In the 5th and 6th centuries AD economic decline and unsettled conditions throughout the Greek and Roman worlds led to a reduction in the overall population and a marked decline in the importance and wealth of the cities. Most shrank to mere villages, and the civic institutions were abandoned, marking the transition from the Ancient to Byzantine worlds. A major hiatus ensued between the 6th and 10th centuries. It is unclear whether the Greek cities of the Mediterranean and Balkan shores died because of Slav, Avar, Persian and Arab attack and infiltration, or at the hands of their own citizens who found them an unwanted expense. At the capital of Roman Asia, Ephesus, the markets, arcades, baths, theatres and public spaces were replaced initially by Christian basilicas and shrunken walls. The city then moved inland to the garrison fortress and pilgrim church. On the other hand, settlement surveys in Macedonia and the Pontus (to the south of the Black Sea) paint a different picture, revealing that local rural economies flourished until a modest market-surplus led to an urban revival in the 10th century.

From the 4th-6th centuries, imperial patronage littered the east Mediterranean with vast aisled basilicas, culminating in Justinian's domed St Sophia (532-27), the last great Roman building. But from the 8th century local patrons housed the liturgy in more compact churches – typically, a quincunx (cross-in-square) nave, surmounted by a central dome – a basic plan which was adopted in the Balkans and Russia too. The hiatus in early Christian art was marked by Iconoclasm (726-843), a period when statues and images in religious buildings were banned and destroyed on the grounds that they were heretical. After this period a complex iconography was evolved in mosaics, wall paintings and icons.

Thereafter monasteries multiplied, sometimes in monastic republics such as Athos and Olympus, and sometimes perched on mountainsides, dominated by a keep. Within the walls, a refectory and an abbey church stood in courtyards of serried cells. Monasteries were a colossal spiritual and economic investment. In 1136 the leper-house, asylum and hospital of the Pantokrator monastery, Constantinople, employed 165 staff (including four gravediggers); its estates harvested over 20 million kilograms of corn a year. By 1321 Athos had some 3,000 dependent peasants (*paroikoi*) on 20,000 hectares of land, in a monastic economy which had reached almost Tibetan proportions.

Byzantium was put on a war footing against the Arabs and Slavs from the 7th century. In effect the state became the army, and provinces became regiments (*themata*), some of which manned a navy. Lacking harbours, their shallow galleys had to be beached in tideless seas. The 'lateen' sail brought shipping closer to the wind, but Byzantine boats hugged the coast and did not sail in winter. From the 10th century the land army levies were increasingly heavy – a response to enemies such as the Seljuk Turks and the Crusaders. The great *themata* garrison fortresses of the 7th century were replaced from the 10th by a network of castles.

Until the 11th century the army and bureaucracy were paid in the Byzantine solid gold coin, from taxes raised largely on land. Thereafter, the state maintained its army, church and bureaucracy, by granting land (and its *paroikoi*) direct. Despite its strategic position, Constantinople was a consumer rather than exporter; it was not exploited commercially until the advent of western merchants in the 12th century. Byzantine tracks contrasted with the extensive and well-maintained road-system of the West Roman empire: in the absence of much wheeled traffic, goods were carried on the backs of beasts or women, which made only the coast of the Empire economically accessible.

Byzantium survives in living archaeology: not just in every Orthodox church, but in the traditional agriculture and habits of the east Mediterranean. Western developments in tilling, harvesting and milling passed Byzantium by, and it remained impervious to new crops like Asiatic rice. Instead it preserved ancient methods which have been replaced only recently. Most vividly, Byzantium flourishes in the walled monasteries of Mounts Athos and Sinai, where at sunset the gates close upon the liturgical rhythm of the 10th century.

3 BYZANTIUM: CHURCH, LAND AND STATE
A *Mosaic from St Sophia of the Mother of God and Child, flanked by* left *Constantine presenting his City in 330, and* right *Justinian offering his Church in 537. Width at base 4.5m.* B *Gold* Hyperpyron *coin of Michael VIII, showing the Mother of God protecting the walls and gates of her City. 1261, gold, diameter 24mm.* C Boullotirion *pincers, used for striking lead seals. 6th century AD, length 20.9cm.* D *Manuscript showing Byzantine peasants disguised as the swineherds of the parable of the prodigal son. 10th century AD.*

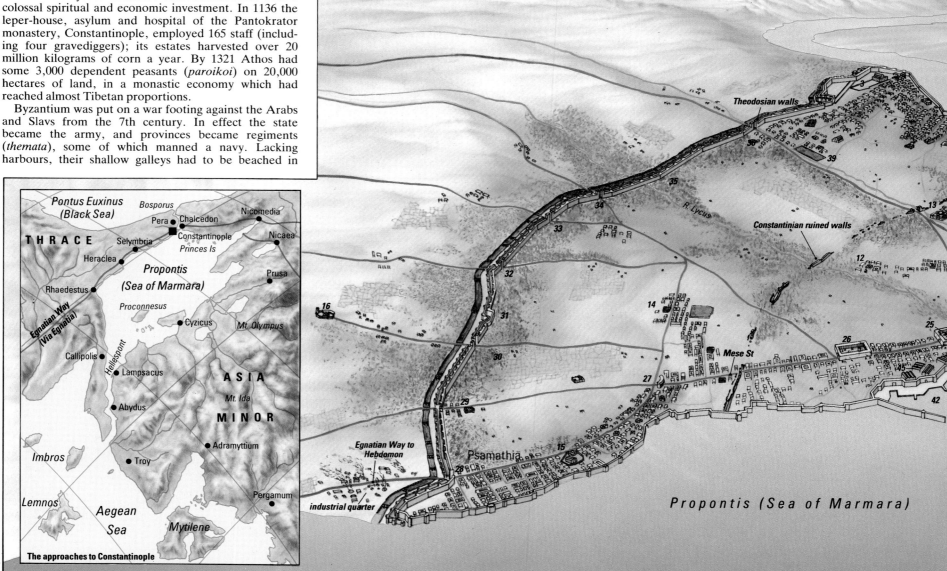

The approaches to Constantinople

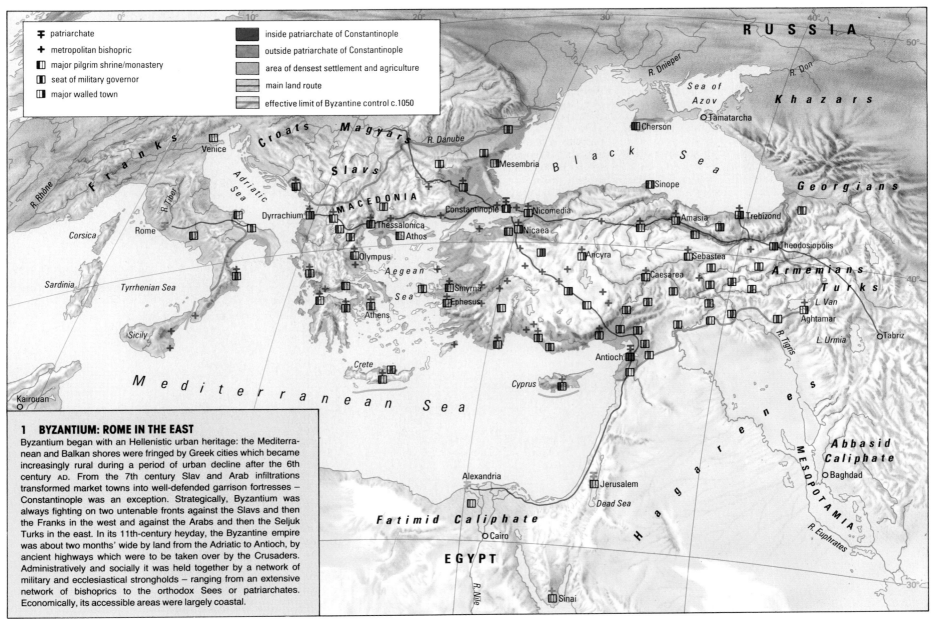

Legend:
- ☩ patriarchate
- + metropolitan bishopric
- 🏛 major pilgrim shrine/monastery
- 🏛 seat of military governor
- 🏛 major walled town
- inside patriarchate of Constantinople
- outside patriarchate of Constantinople
- area of densest settlement and agriculture
- main land route
- effective limit of Byzantine control c.1050

1 BYZANTIUM: ROME IN THE EAST

Byzantium began with an Hellenistic urban heritage: the Mediterranean and Balkan shores were fringed by Greek cities which became increasingly rural during a period of urban decline after the 6th century AD. From the 7th century Slav and Arab infiltrations transformed market towns into well-defended garrison fortresses – Constantinople was an exception. Strategically, Byzantium was always fighting on two untenable fronts against the Slavs and then the Franks in the west and against the Arabs and then the Seljuk Turks in the east. In its 11th-century heyday, the Byzantine empire was about two months' wide by land from the Adriatic to Antioch, by ancient highways which were to be taken over by the Crusaders. Administratively and socially it was held together by a network of military and ecclesiastical strongholds – ranging from an extensive network of bishoprics to the orthodox Sees or patriarchates. Economically, its accessible areas were largely coastal.

2 CONSTANTINOPLE: A CITY BETWEEN TWO WORLDS

Constantinople at the beginning of the 13th century was the last great Classical city. Always too extensive for its population, Constantine's walls of AD 330 were abandoned for the still awesome 5th-century Theodosian walls, which embraced over 1800 hectares – still not fully built up in Istanbul today. There was one 'city' and seven lay and monastic garden suburbs. Although by 1204 it was a city too large for its Empire, it was still the richest and most populous city in Christendom.

In 1204, the accumulated courts, barracks, shrines and offices of the Great Palace were still partly used, although the government had largely moved to the Blachernea complex on the walls. There were several hundred churches and monasteries, the most notable being the cathedral of the Holy Wisdom (St Sophia). Public monuments and markets lay along what was left of the arcades of a grandiose and largely 5th-century civic plan to rival Rome. The *Mese*, Constantinople's High Street, led to the Forum, and on to Constantinople's 'front door', the Golden Gate, passing through a noisome industrial quarter of potters and tanners, the imperial barracks, parade grounds and the largest of all cisterns, before heading across the Balkans. Constantinople's defences comprised 6.7 kilometres of triple and moated Land Walls, breached only in 1204 and 1453. They were punctuated in turn by military and civil gates. Constantinople is not the most convenient of capitals, for its river, the Lycus, is only a stream. Outside water ended in an aqueduct, inside there were cisterns. Constantinople also needed to import food as well as water, and the Golden Horn was fringed with harbours.

The approaches to Constantinople (*see map left*). Like the legendary Argonauts, mariners climbed against the current from the Aegean to the Euxine (Black) Sea, through the Hellespont straits and the Marmara (Marble) Sea, whose Proconnesus Island was quarried for Constantinople's fine white marble. By land, Constantinople was linked to the west by the last stages of the Via Egnatia.

Constantinople 1 Great Palace 2 Botaneiates palace enclosure 3 Blachernae palace complex and shrine 4 church of Hagia Sophia 5 church of St Eirene 6 church of Chalcoprateia 7 church of Sts Sergius and Bacchus and Bucoleum imperial landing stage 8 monastery of St Polyeuctus 9 monastery of Christ Pantocrator 10 church of Christ Pantepoptes 11 monastery of Myrelaium 12 monastery of Constantine Lips 13 mausoleum of the Holy Apostles 14 church and cistern of St Mocius 15 church of St John Studius 16 Pege monastery fountain 17 Acropolis 18 Augusteum square 19 Milion (the Empire's milestone) 20 hippodrome 21 forum of Constantine 22 tetrapylon 23 Theodosian forum 24 capitol 25 Butchers' forum 26 Arcadian forum 27 Sigma 28 Golden Gate 29 2nd military gate 30 Pege gate 31 3rd military gate 32 Rhegium gate 33 4th military gate 34 St Romanus gate 35 5th military gate 36 Charisius gate 37 Galata Tower and quarter of Genoa 38 aqueduct 39 Aetius cistern 40 Aspar cistern 41 Contoscalium harbour 42 Langa harbour 43 Italian quays 44 covered bazaar 45 granaries 46 districts of Pisa and Amalfi 47 Venetian district 48 Golden Horn chained across its mouth.

The Islamic world

Islam, one of the world's great monotheistic religions, began in Mecca in AD 610. In 622 the prophet Mohammed and a small group of followers moved to Medina, and this year marks the start of the Muslim era. The new religion quickly spread through the Arabian peninsula, and in the century that followed, Arab armies carried Islam to India in the east and Spain in the west. Under the Umayyad caliphs, who came to power in 661, Islam dominated one third of the Old World. Under the

Abbasids who replaced the Umayyads in 750 the boundaries of Islam remained relatively stable. Encouraged by more peaceful conditions, long-distance trade increased, with a corresponding rise in economic prosperity. The Abbasid Caliphate was distinguished by an impressive cultural florescence which successfully synthesised many of the achievements of subject peoples, and is reflected in magnificent building and skilled craftsmanship; a new unity of Arab culture had emerged.

New towns such as Kufa, Basra and Al Fustat were founded in the early days of Islam, originally serving as military encampments. A stipend was paid to Arab soldier settlers, encouraging immigration and economic growth. However, many aristocrats of the Umayyad period preferred to live in the Steppe, as their Arab

ancestors had done, and their grand palaces have been found on the edge of the desert in Jordan and Syria. These looked like fortresses from the outside, but the internal buildings were luxurious and often included a small mosque, bath and reception hall.

With the accession of the Abbasid Caliphate there was a change in cultural outlook – away from the Mediterranean towards Mesopotamia and Persia. The subsequent move of the capital from Damascus to the new city of Baghdad (founded in 766) marks the beginning of an empire with a true urban base; phenomena such as desert palaces were becoming more rare. Strategically sited on the Tigris, at the crossroads of the major east–west trade routes, Baghdad developed into a potent symbol of Abbasid power. The Round City, an administrative

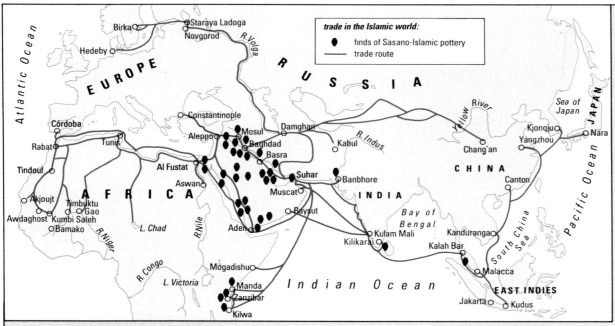

1 ISLAM: CONQUEST AND COMMERCE

The rapid expansion of the Islamic empire (see map right) during the Umayyad Caliphate (AD 661–750) is reflected in the construction of mosques and new towns. With the accession of the Abbasids in AD 750, expansion ceased and a period of internal consolidation followed. Defences were built in vulnerable areas, notably the *ribat* fortresses built on the North African coast against Byzantine maritime attacks. Maritime trade flourished, with major ports located on the Red Sea and the Persian Gulf. Islamic merchants mastered the monsoon winds of the Indian Ocean and sailed in *dhows* to India, Indonesia, China and East Africa, and widely dispersed finds of Sasano-Islamic pottery demonstrate the extent of this commerce (see map above).

3 EARLY ISLAMIC CRAFTS

A Bowl with lustre-painted decoration, Fatimid period, Egypt. Fatimid Egypt became the main centre for the production of Islamic wares at this time, supplanting the Persian Gulf area. European and Coptic Christian influences in style are common. 11th–12th century AD, diameter 23.7cm. B Leaf from a Koran showing Kufic script. 9th century AD, 43 x 34cm. C Sasano-Islamic pottery jar with turquoise glaze. These jars, which were manufactured around the Persian Gulf, were exported to places as far afield as East Africa and Malaya. 9th century AD, height 48cm. D Large flat plate with rim and slip painted decoration, Samarkand. 10th–11th century AD, diameter 36cm. E Silk band with figures, 8th–9th century AD.

2 SAMARRA: AN ABBASID CAPITAL

Samarra, stretching for 40 kilometres along the River Tigris, was the capital of the Abbasid Caliphate from 836–892. The city's elongated shape is probably due to the problem of water supply, although this led to communication and security difficulties. There was no outer wall, and the inhabitants (mainly soldiers and labour conscripts) were confined to self-sufficient, enclosed cantonments. Founded by Caliph al-Mu'tasim, the original city core was around Jawsaq al-Khaqani, while subsequent caliphs added new features. The caliph al-Mutawakkil added a new sector to the north, Ja'fariyya (859–861), including cantonments, palaces and the mosque, Abu Dulaf. After his murder, the court moved back to the south of the city where new structures were built. On the death of the eighth caliph, al-Mu'tamid, the Abbasid capital reverted to Baghdad.

Samarra *right* **1 Qadisiyya** unfinished octagonal copy of the Round City of Baghdad; built by Harun al-Rashid, father of the city's founder, Caliph al-Mu'tasim. **2 Jawsaq al-Khaqani** Mu'tasim's main palace. **3 Great Mosque of Samarra** built 849–50 by al-Mutawakkil. **4 Abu Dulaf** congregational mosque with small spiral minaret. **5 Qasr al-Ja'fari** Mutawakkil's new palace, over 1km in length. **6 Samarra** walled mediaeval city **7 Grand Avenue** 11km long and 98m wide, used by the troops. **8 Qasr al-'Ashiq** last palace built in Samarra, by Caliph al-Mu'tamid after 878. **9 Qubbat al-Sulaibiyya** earliest known Islamic monumental mausoleum, 862–3. **10 Al-Musharrahat** hunting palace overlooking artificial basin, with large game reserve.

Below *Great Mosque of al-Mutawakkil, the largest in Islam.*

complex, had double mud-brick defences, with four gates at the cardinal points, and the caliph sited his palace at the centre of the city, with officials in a ring of dwellings just inside the walls. The markets and the majority of the population were located outside, around the earlier centre of Al Karkh.

Mosques, the most important buildings of Islam, were built in every Islamic town. They vary greatly, but always consist of a courtyard and a covered prayer hall with a *mihrab*, a niche in the wall indicating the direction of prayer, towards Mecca. Another feature was the minaret, or tower, from which the call to prayer is given. Perhaps the most impressive early religious building is the Dome of the Rock in Jerusalem, which is still standing and houses the original mosaics, which portray fruits, vines

and trees – it is considered idolatrous to represent human and animal figures in a religious context.

Trade was of paramount importance, and commercial contact was established with the Vikings and the peoples of China, South-East Asia, India, East Africa and sub-Saharan West Africa. Overland caravan routes through Central Asia to China can be traced through remains of *caravanserais* – road stations providing food and shelter for travellers. The Arabs also ruled the seas at this time, sailing in *dhows*, lateen-rigged boats made of teak or coconut planks sewn together with coconut twine. A wide variety of goods were traded: spices and ceramics from the Far East, gold, ivory and slaves from Africa, amber, furs and wax from the Baltic. Luxury goods were exported in return; in 300 years the crafts of a

desert people had evolved into the specialised skills of the far-flung subjects of the caliph – wood-carving, metal and glass working, textile-weaving, tile-glazing and lustre-painted ceramics.

The 10th century was a time of political fragmentation, as power passed into the hands of ruling local dynasties. The power of the Abbasid caliphs declined and they became religious rather than political leaders. This marks the end of the Arab domination of the Islamic world. Although the ensuing centuries were disrupted by political strife, however, Islamic culture remained a unifying force, and merchants and missionaries continued to spread the Islamic religion, finding adherents as far afield as Indonesia, the southern Philippines, Nigeria and the eastern coast of Africa.

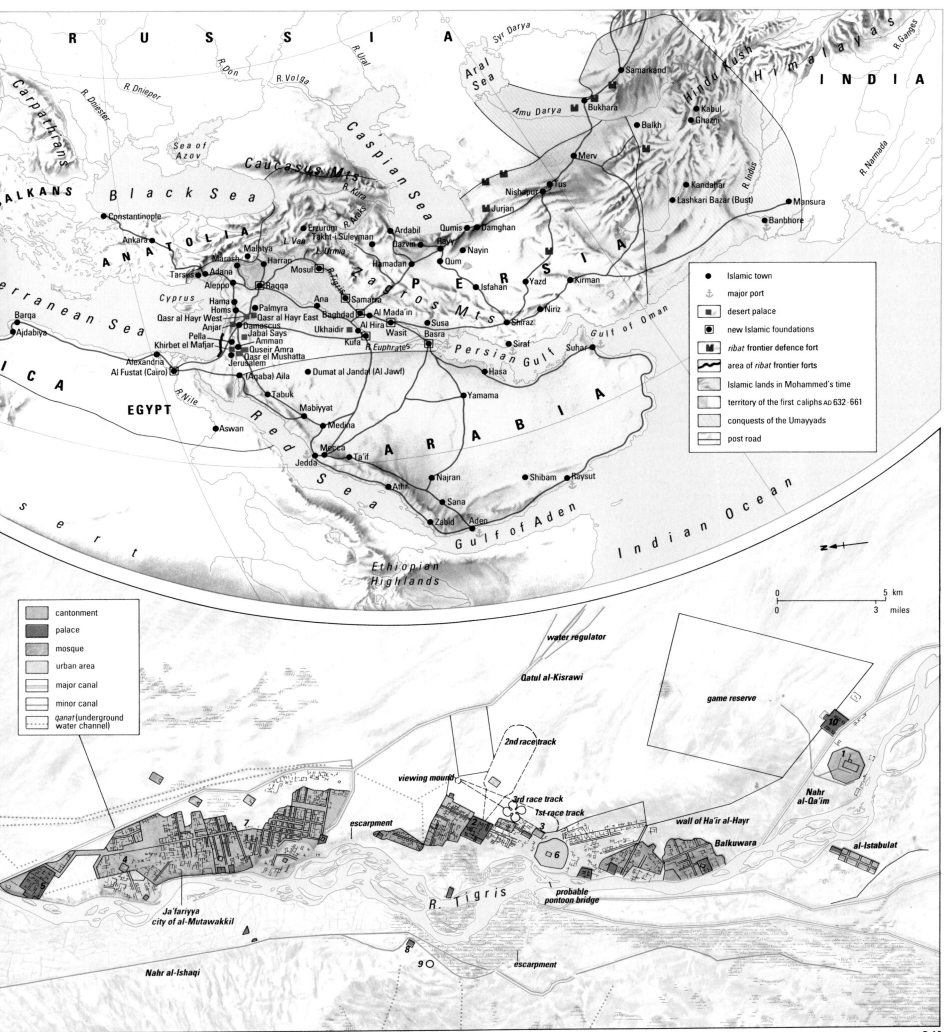

The Viking world

One symptom of the decline of the west Roman empire in the 4th–5th centuries AD was the movement of Germanic peoples from Jutland and northern Germany to France and Britain. Angles and Saxons settled in lowland Britain, while the Franks settled in northern Gaul and the Rhineland, taking over the Roman manufacturing centres. Under Charlemagne (c.768-814) the Frankish empire extended from the Pyrenees to the Baltic. At the same time, Arab expansion disrupted the Mediterranean trade of southern Europe, and north-west Europe became an independent trading unit. The Scandinavians, previously isolated from European trade, were now in a good position to conduct business with the Franks and, via the Russian rivers, with the Arabs and with Byzantium across the Black Sea. During the 9th century, the Scandinavians, or Vikings, became the dominant power in north-west Europe, and by 882 the Swedes had also established a state in Russia, which was centred on Kiev.

The majority of the Viking population were farmers growing rye, barley and oats and herding cattle – as well as hunting, fishing and trapping. The system of land inheritance through primogeniture meant that a supply of younger sons was available to become warriors, traders or craftsmen in towns. As population and the demand for land grew, settlements gradually spread to the outlying areas where farming could be supplemented by walrus hunting, fur-trapping and iron-ore extraction, providing a substantial trading base.

As a result of a large increase in the volume of trade in the 8th and 9th centuries, emporia or international trading and manufacturing centres developed. They were often on coasts or rivers near territorial frontiers, like Hedeby, which made them accessible to foreign merchants. Local and imported raw materials such as silver, wood, amber and soapstone were worked there by specialist craftsmen, and distributed to all parts of north-west Europe. There was fierce competition between Vikings and Franks for trade with the Arabs for silver bullion, but wealth could also be gained by raiding, piracy and plunder: the Norwegians and Danes found the Christian lands especially rich. Monasteries such as Lindisfarne and Iona were easy targets; hoards found in Scandinavia often contain plundered Christian relics, although Christianity did not actually reach the region until the 10th century AD. Viking maritime supremacy was accountable for the success of these expeditions. Longboats were fast and manoeuvrable, with a shallow draught, removing the need for deep harbours, and sails. Viking voyages were not always for plunder; they settled as farmers in foreign lands, colonising territory as far afield as Greenland, Iceland and L'Anse aux Meadows in Newfoundland.

Scandinavian paganism was not a unified system of beliefs, and this is illustrated by the varied nature of burial customs. From the 1st century AD, many wealthy individuals were buried in ships; the Oseberg lady, for example, was buried in Norway in a highly decorated ship 21.44 metres long and 5.1 metres wide. Her grave goods included horses, an ox, a cart, a sledge and a tent. The less wealthy sometimes had symbolic boat burials: stones were set out around the burial in the shape of a ship. Cremation was common, and all except the poor were buried with everyday items such as clothes, tools and trinkets. Such burial practices changed with the arrival of Christianity, which spread slowly, and initially co-existed with paganism.

By the 10th century AD, Denmark had become a unified state under Christian royal authority, with land no longer being held by ordinary families but by feudal lords. New towns were founded, such as Århus and Roskilde, which were under the king's control, and served as political and administrative centres. Many of the towns had mints; coins, imprinted with the heads of the Scandinavian kings, were now used in the market-place. Under royal direction, the towns were provided with defences, and the 8th century frontier dyke which stretched across the neck of the Jutland peninsula, the Danevirke, was extended. In north and east Denmark four circular forts were built, containing industrial workshops. It is probable that the taxes collected for the king, along with items manufactured in the workshops, were stored within the defences.

The Vikings were the most powerful force in north-west Europe in the 9th and 10th centuries, but in the 11th century they withdrew to the periphery of feudal Christendom. Although the Vikings were notorious for their plundering raids, their achievement was also substantial; by encouraging trade and industry they revitalised declining urban centres, and they founded urban communities as far afield as Russia and Ireland which have flourished to the present day.

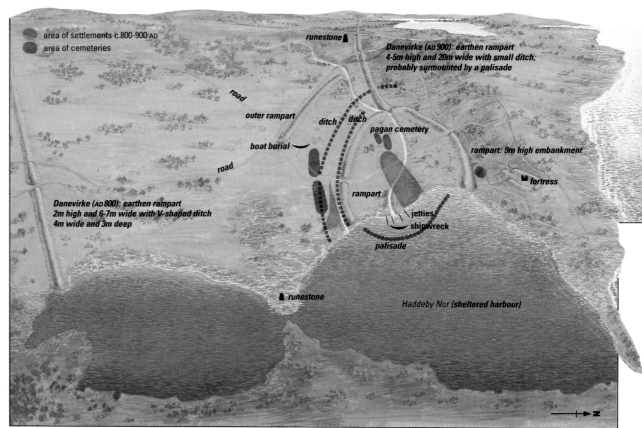

2 HEDEBY: A DANISH EMPORIUM

Hedeby was the largest of the Scandinavian emporia, occupying an important strategic position near the boundary between the Viking and Carolingian empires in southern Denmark, with access along rivers to both the North Sea and the Baltic. In the 8th century Hedeby consisted of diffuse merchants' settlements, but in 808 a large centralised settlement was founded, protected, in the 10th century, by an earthen rampart, which now stands 5–10 metres high, enclosing an area of 24 hectares, while wooden harbour defences prevented sea attacks. Most of the wooden houses within these defences were rectangular, and lay in planned plots. Workshops were dispersed amongst the dwellings, and there is evidence of a variety of crafts including glass, bone and horn working and bronze casting. Hedeby was destroyed in c.1050, when it was plundered and burnt by the Norwegians.

3 NORDIC CULTURE

A Wooden sledge from the Oseberg ship burial, Norway. Early 9th century, length c.2m. **B** Tating ware jug, from Birka, Sweden. These were manufactured in the Rhineland, and widely exported. Early 9th century, pottery, height 25cm. **C** Coin, a copy of an Arab dinar, issued in the name of Offa, King of Mercia (AD 757–796), probably used for overseas trade. AD 774, gold, diameter 2cm. **D** Hoard from Hon, Norway, containing 2.5kg of gold, silver and beads. The coins are Byzantine, Arab, Carolingian and Anglo-Saxon. Mid-9th century. **E** Runestone from Olsa, Uppland, Sweden, raised as a memorial over the burial of a wealthy individual by his wife and children. AD 1020, height c.0.8–1m. **F** Viking pagan cemetery at Lindholm, Denmark, containing several hundred cremations in boat-shaped stone-settings. AD 400–1000, height of stones 0.5-1m.

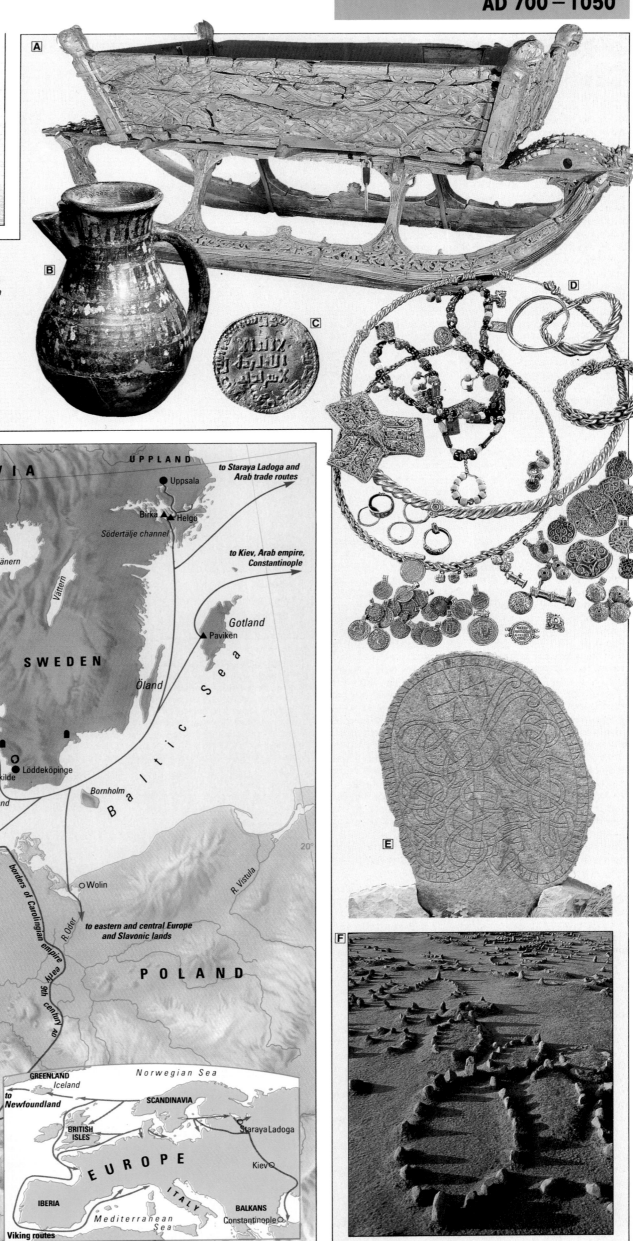

1 THE VIKINGS: RAIDERS AND TRADERS

Viking, Carolingian and Anglo-Saxon traders dominated the seaways and rivers of north-west Europe in the 8th and 9th centuries, dealing in utilitarian objects as well as luxury items. While the Swedes had contacts to the east, the Danes and Norwegians looked west, settling in England and making inroads into France, Scotland and Ireland.

Mediaeval Christendom

After the fall of the Roman empire in the 5th century AD, western Europe entered a dark age of economic decline and instability which lasted until the revival of the 11th–12th centuries. By this time, a new cultural identity had developed, derived partly from Roman roots but powerfully influenced by western Christianity. The greater prosperity, based both on agriculture and trade, encouraged the growth of existing cities and the foundation of new centres. The tangible remains of this cultural and economic revival survive today in great religious buildings of the age – churches, cathedrals and monasteries.

Politics, economics and religion were inseparable during this period. Mediaeval cities were both religious and economic centres, with their own manufacturing industries, strategically situated on trade routes, rivers or the coast. Many bishoprics and archbishoprics were set up in former Roman cities which already had an established function as regional centres of administration and law. In some parts of Europe, especially Germany, there were fewer Roman centres, so new cities were built in economically viable locations. These, too, often became the seat of bishoprics, with impressive cathedrals.

Monasteries, on the other hand, were often sited in secluded places away from the great population centres, such as forest clearings or rocky islands. The monasteries were both the guardians of holy relics and the home of learning. The Holy Land was not easily accessible to Christian travellers and many lesser centres became the object of pilgrimage. The great Benedictine abbeys also catered for companies of pilgrims by feeding and sheltering them, and gave noble benefactors the additional comfort of an impressive place of burial fortified by a continuous round of obituary prayers. Monasteries were also a major economic force, reclaiming and cultivating vast areas of barren wasteland.

Despite warring kingdoms and political rivalries, western Europe was unified through religion. From the 12th century, uniformity was stressed in church law, teaching and the rules of monastic orders. Christian pilgrimages meant contact between distant neighbours, and encouraged the spread of building styles and ideas. Between the 9th and 12th centuries, churches were generally built in the Romanesque style – heavy-looking buildings with characteristic rounded arches and barrel-vaulting. In the mid-12th century Gothic architecture was developed in the Ile de France (Paris basin) and spread rapidly throughout Europe, where many distinctive regional styles grew. It represented a considerable technological achievement: the weight of the building was carried only through skeletal members, such as the rib-vault and flying buttress. This allowed soaring edifices to be constructed, with large windows which flooded the interior with light. This in turn led to ever more sophisticated developments in stained glass; windows were often paid for by rich patrons or tradesmen who, not confined to religious subjects, sometimes had their profession depicted – as, for example, in the window of the vintagers of Chartres. The Gothic style eventually encouraged an effusion of elaborate sculptural decoration which threatened to engulf the singular purity of the architecture.

The revival of trade initially made its greatest impact in the Mediterranean, and particularly Italy. Venice and Genoa were the main entrepôts, with merchant fleets used extensively in crusading ventures to the east. In these north Italian cities European products were exchanged for imports from Africa and Asia. Constantinople, Antioch, Jerusalem and Cairo all became staging posts in a trading network that brought to Europe the silks of China, the spices of India, the gold of Africa, the precious stones of Arabia and the fine glassware of Syria. High in value but low in volume, these exotic commodities stimulated the production of a marketable surplus in western Europe. The grain of Sicily and France and the cloth of Flanders and eastern England were among the products that prompted rulers, whether kings, counts, bishops or abbots, to found towns, markets and fairs so that trade might be controlled, tolls levied and taxes collected. Mineral resources, both metals and salt, were further exploited and regular issues of coinage lubricated the processes of trade and taxation.

As population increased and towns grew throughout the 12th and 13th centuries, there was a movement into previously uninhabited rural areas; the Black Forest, for example, was colonised and settled by farmers for the first time. All this suffered a major set-back in the 14th century, when the Black Death carried off up to a third of the population. In time, however, the European economic revival continued to grow and flourish, culminating in the 15th century in the first major voyages of discovery.

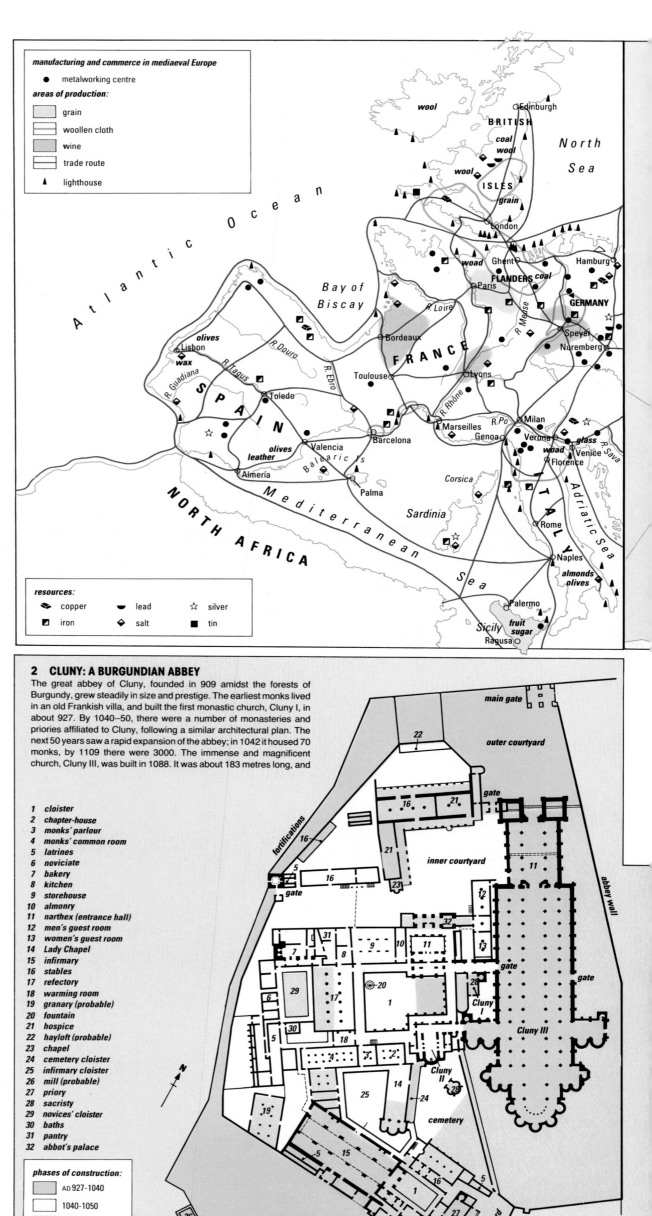

manufacturing and commerce in mediaeval Europe

- ● metalworking centre

areas of production:
- grain
- woollen cloth
- wine
- trade route
- ▲ lighthouse

resources:
- copper
- lead
- ☆ silver
- iron
- ◇ salt
- ■ tin

2 CLUNY: A BURGUNDIAN ABBEY
The great abbey of Cluny, founded in 909 amidst the forests of Burgundy, grew steadily in size and prestige. The earliest monks lived in an old Frankish villa, and built the first monastic church, Cluny I, in about 927. By 1040–50, there were a number of monasteries and priories affiliated to Cluny, following a similar architectural plan. The next 50 years saw a rapid expansion of the abbey; in 1042 it housed 70 monks, by 1109 there were 3000. The immense and magnificent church, Cluny III, was built in 1088. It was about 183 metres long, and

1 cloister
2 chapter-house
3 monks' parlour
4 monks' common room
5 latrines
6 noviciate
7 bakery
8 kitchen
9 storehouse
10 almonry
11 narthex (entrance hall)
12 men's guest room
13 women's guest room
14 Lady Chapel
15 infirmary
16 stables
17 refectory
18 warming room
19 granary (probable)
20 fountain
21 hospice
22 hayloft (probable)
23 chapel
24 cemetery cloister
25 infirmary cloister
26 mill (probable)
27 priory
28 sacristy
29 novices' cloister
30 baths
31 pantry
32 abbot's palace

phases of construction:
- AD 927-1040
- 1040-1050
- 1050-1150
- 1150-1160

0   50 metres
0   50 yards

1 CHRISTIAN EUROPE

Christianity created an international cultural sphere stretching from Sicily to Scotland. The period AD 650–1200 saw a florescence in centres of learning, with universities being founded throughout Europe. This may have been partly due to Arab influence – the Arabs had the first universities in the world – and early secular education in Europe combined Arabic, Greek and Latin traditions. The pilgrim routes which connected Christian shrines benefited towns along their path. More regular trade flourished at the great fairs of Flanders and France, where the manufactured goods of Italy and the Low Countries were exchanged for the raw materials of the north and British Isles.

Christian Europe
- ⌂ archbishopric
- ▲ major monastic foundation
- • distribution of bishoprics
- ⬟ pilgrimage centre
- ▦ known pilgrimage route
- ▣ university founded before 1300

3 CRAFTSMANSHIP AND COMMERCE

A *Statue of St. James of Compostela from the collegiate church at Santa Marta de Tera, Spain. The shrine of St. James at Compostela was one of the principal centres of pilgrimage in mediaeval western Europe. 12th century AD.* **B** *Stained glass window from Chartres Cathedral in France showing detail of the wine cart from the story of St. Lubin. 13th century AD, diameter 1m.* **C** *Civic seal of Colchester. The growth in the power and importance of mediaeval towns and cities is reflected in the adaption of such civic seals for use by municipal authorities. c.1413, bronze, diameter 8.5cm.* **D** *Wine jugs from the Bordeaux region. Large quantities of Bordeaux wines were shipped to England, especially during the 12th–15th centuries when this area was under English political control. c. 13th century AD.* **E** *Dunstable swan jewel. Early 15th century AD, gold decorated with white enamel, height c.3cm, length of chain 6.4cm.*

was highly decorated, with 15 towers on or around it. In contrast, the monks' living quarters were plain although well-built, with wooden roofs. The abbey became a small town, with a forest of towers and a complex of halls for monks, servants, novices, guests and the sick. Cluniac monastic houses were established in the neighbouring vicinity, and also throughout France, Germany, Switzerland, and to a lesser extent in England, Italy and Spain. They numbered 1450 at the height of Cluny's power and influence.

Feudal Yorkshire

Mediaeval England was fundamentally an agricultural country, with nearly as much land under cultivation as in 1914. The pre-Norman inhabitants, the Danes and Anglo-Saxons, all lived in parishes which were the basic unit of administration, and they worshipped in churches, often built of stone, with high towers. It is these substantial structures which are the most tangible remains of these local communities and the religion they practised. This system continued after the Norman conquest, but there was a marked increase in the number of churches, monasteries and especially villages. The Lord and his manor assumed a greater importance, and strong stone-built castles or defended manor houses were built to protect aristocratic families.

Yorkshire was a varied area. It ranged from the fertile Vale of York and the chalk Wolds, to high moorlands and the waterlogged Vale of Pickering. From 1000 to 1200, the climate became milder. New villages were set up on marginal or previously unworked land – woods, heavy clay lowland and moorland – and as more land was brought into cultivation the population increased. Monasteries played an important part in this process of land clearance. Although there had been monasteries in Anglo-Saxon England, new orders arrived from the Continent under the Normans. The Cistercians, who preached an ascetic life of hard physical work, settled in more desolate areas, and especially parts of Yorkshire. Rievaulx and Fountains were early Cistercian houses, followed by Jervaulx, Byland and Meaux. Lay brethren worked the land for agricultural or pastoral use, and often lived in monastic granges or monastery farms.

In the typical mediaeval village, houses stood within their individual enclosures and were organised around a main street and perhaps a village green. There was generally a church and a manor house. Most buildings, with the exception of the churches, were made of timber and daub, though from the 13th century the bases of the walls were often built of stone. They were frequently rebuilt, but their position usually remained the same.

By the 13th century, the open field system of farming had become common. Large open fields were divided into strips and worked by peasant families. Several strips of land made up a furlong, and these were the basic units of crop rotation. It is even possible to see the 'ridge and furrow' pattern created by mediaeval ploughing on the ground today, as well as the S-shaped bends, where the plough team (normally oxen or horses) turned. Wheat, barley and oats were the staple crops. Sheep, cattle and pigs were the principal livestock, though the sheep were kept for their wool rather than for meat and cattle were used as plough animals.

The number of towns rose during the mediaeval period, though the majority of the population still lived in the country. Towns became administrative, political and industrial centres, and also acted as markets, where surplus farm produce was brought and exchanged for manufactured goods and raw materials. Pottery was made in both rural and urban areas and some was even imported from Europe, perhaps via the North Sea ports of Scarborough, York and Hull. Iron slag is found on many sites, and a smithy seems to have been a feature of each village – iron keys, latches, hinges, buckles and horseshoes are often found. Other important industries were textiles, leather and wood working, although remains of these are preserved only at a limited number of waterlogged sites. Monasteries also played an important role in these manufacturing industries; there were leather tanning vats at Rievaulx, and a kiln for making floor-tiles at a grange connected with Meaux.

Many features of the rural economy changed in the 14th century when the climate became colder and wetter, with alternating floods and droughts. Much of the marginal land which had been newly inhabited was no longer viable for farming, especially the clay lowlands, which had become waterlogged. Sheep farming was more economically viable than agriculture, and this in turn required a smaller labour force. As a result, some villagers moved to isolated farmsteads to tend sheep, others moved to larger thriving villages, or towns. Many villages of the 11th–13th centuries were deserted, a trend that accelerated with the onset of the Black Death in the 14th century, which wiped out probably a third of the English population. These villages now present archaeologists with a fossilised picture of the past.

In the 15th century the wool trade grew in importance and pastoral farming became even more widespread. The great enclosure movement of the 15th and 16th centuries meant that the large open fields were broken up among the landlords and wealthier peasants. Enclosure brought concomitant and lasting changes in the distribution of settlements, and permanently transformed the face of the landscape throughout the British Isles.

3 MEDIAEVAL YORKSHIRE: A RURAL ECONOMY

The survival of everyday tools and utensils gives an insight into the crafts skills of mediaeval Yorkshire, and illustrates the living and working conditions in the home and in the fields at that time. The increasing importance of wool-production in the English economy is reflected in artistic representations of sheep and shearing.
A Reaping hook from Yorkshire. Wood and iron, length 50cm.
B Aquamanile (water pourer) in the shape of a ram, from Scarborough. 13th–14th century, clay, height 24cm. **C** Anglo-Saxon comb from Wharram Percy. Probably 7th–early 8th century, bone, length 18cm. **D** Waterjug embossed with seals from York. 13th-14th century, clay, height 35.5cm. **E** Sheep shearing manuscript illumination from the Luttrell Psalter. c.AD 1340, vellum, manuscript page 35 x 23.5cm.

2 WHARRAM PERCY: A MEDIAEVAL VILLAGE

The excavations conducted over the past 30 years at the deserted mediaeval village of Wharram Percy have enabled archaeologists to understand more clearly the appearance of a typical village, and the variety of changes it experienced. The location of this site was influenced by earlier Iron Age and Roman settlement and cultivation. The settlement may have started as a group of scattered farms which only gradually coalesced to form a village served by the church, established c.800. This church expanded over the next six centuries to meet the increasing needs of the population – for both worship and burial. The rectory stayed near the same site, but manor houses rose and fell as the resident lordly families of Chamberlain, Percy and Hilton prospered or decayed. The wealth of the village derived from a balance between crops and livestock, though on the high Wolds sheep were predominant. The village houses were generally well-built, constructed from chalk rubble, wattle and daub. Some were long houses accommodating men and beasts under the same roof. The village did not operate in isolation, but was linked to other hamlets within the parish and nearby villages by tracks (see map). There was regular access to weekly markets at Malton and Driffield, as well as to the more distant York, Beverley and Hull.

Wharram Percy and its environs

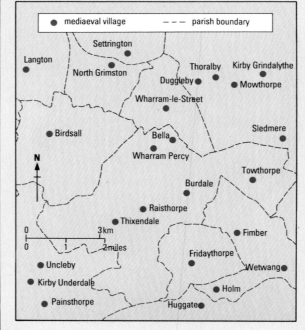

- ● mediaeval village – – – parish boundary

Settrington
Langton
Thoralby
Kirby Grindalythe
North Grimston
Duggleby
Mowthorpe
Wharram-le-Street
Birdsall
Bella
Sledmere
Wharram Percy
Towthorpe
Burdale
Raisthorpe
Thixendale
Fimber
Fridaythorpe
Uncleby
Wetwang
Kirby Underdale
Holm
Painsthorpe
Huggate

0   3km
0   2miles

N

arable land

North manor house

cultivated

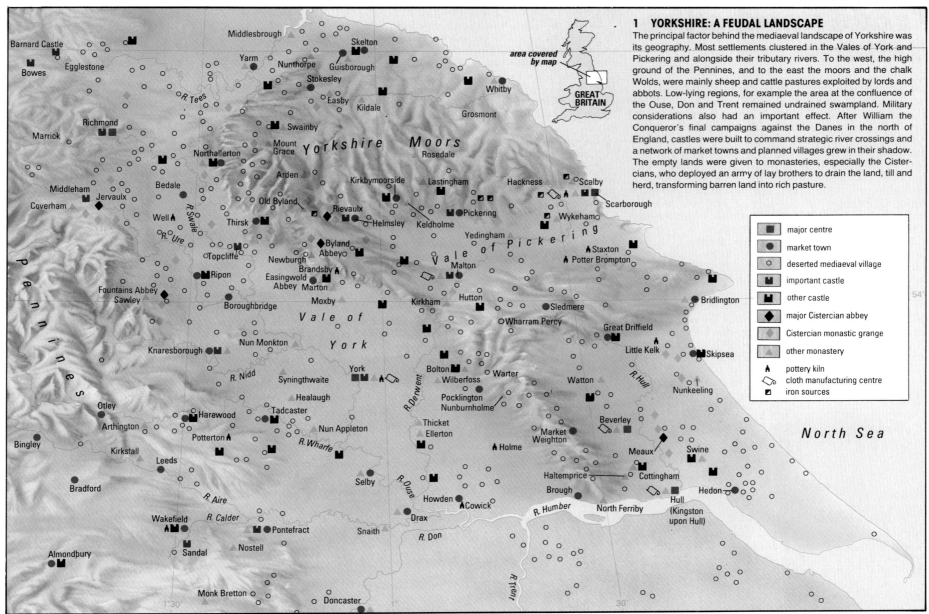

1 YORKSHIRE: A FEUDAL LANDSCAPE

The principal factor behind the mediaeval landscape of Yorkshire was its geography. Most settlements clustered in the Vales of York and Pickering and alongside their tributary rivers. To the west, the high ground of the Pennines, and to the east the moors and the chalk Wolds, were mainly sheep and cattle pastures exploited by lords and abbots. Low-lying regions, for example the area at the confluence of the Ouse, Don and Trent remained undrained swampland. Military considerations also had an important effect. After William the Conqueror's final campaigns against the Danes in the north of England, castles were built to command strategic river crossings and a network of market towns and planned villages grew in their shadow. The empty lands were given to monasteries, especially the Cistercians, who deployed an army of lay brothers to drain the land, till and herd, transforming barren land into rich pasture.

area covered by map

GREAT BRITAIN

■	major centre
●	market town
○	deserted mediaeval village
▣	important castle
♜	other castle
◆	major Cistercian abbey
◆	Cistercian monastic grange
▲	other monastery
⚲	pottery kiln
⬭	cloth manufacturing centre
⬓	iron sources

North Sea

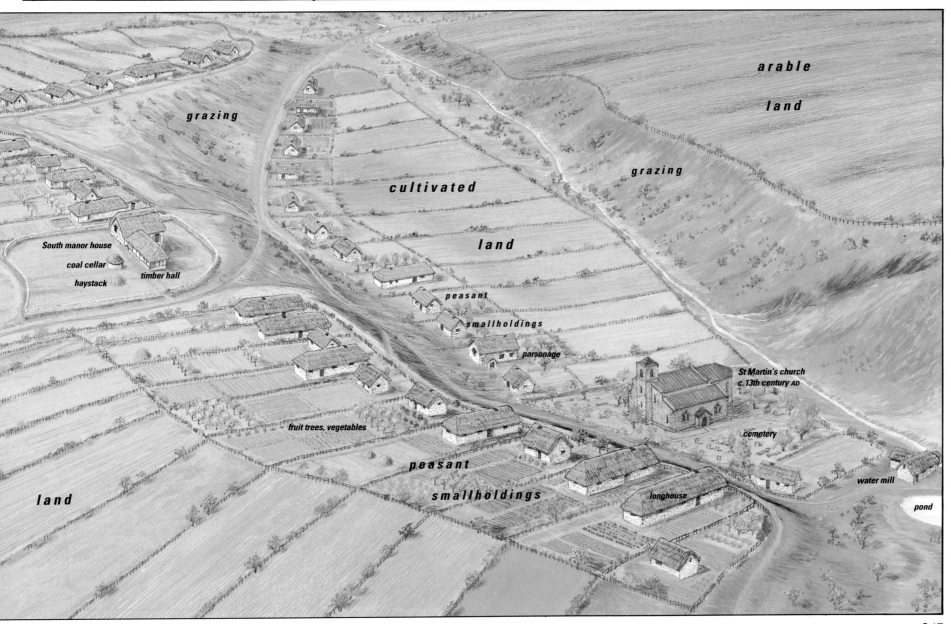

arable land

grazing

cultivated

grazing

land

South manor house

coal cellar

timber hall

haystack

peasant

smallholdings

parsonage

St Martin's church c. 13th century AD

cemetery

fruit trees, vegetables

peasant

smallholdings

land

longhouse

water mill

pond

Trade across the Sahara

The emergence of towns and states in West Africa during the 1st millennium AD was closely connected with an increase in the amount of trade across the Sahara with the urban communities of Mediterranean North Africa. Luxury goods were imported from North Africa and beyond, while the produce of the tropical forests and the minerals of the grasslands and southern desert were exported. Muslim merchants from the north controlled the trade across the Sahara, and while they probably greatly encouraged the growth of towns, urbanisation itself was an indigenous West African development predating their arrival in the 8th century.

As early as 1000BC rock carvings depicting chariots found in the desert indicate that there was contact between the Mediterranean and sub-Saharan Africa, and the use of iron probably spread into Africa from the Carthaginian cities on the North African coast. From the 8th century AD the tempo of contacts increased, when the Muslim traders began to penetrate the sub-Saharan regions from the North African coast. To these merchants the Sahara Desert was rather like an ocean, with 'trading ports' on its northern and southern fringes where they set up colonies or quarters. Luxury goods such as oil lamps, glass, fine pottery and cowrie shells were brought from the north, and exchanged for forest and savanna products like ivory, ebony and gold, as well as slaves.

Ghana, probably the earliest indigenous West African state, was strategically situated between the goldfields of the south-west and the North African consumers. Dense clusters of sites have been found on the extremely fertile land of the Niger Delta, each with a specialised function such as iron smelting. From these semi-urban clusters arose the earliest urban centre yet known in sub-Saharan Africa – Jenne-jeno, a true town from c.AD400. The arrival of the Arabs in the 8th century may have encouraged long-distance trade in luxury goods, but originally the town was primarily a centre for local trade, importing iron and grinding stones and exporting food, especially fish and cereals, to the new towns on the fringes of the desert. Among the recipients of these foodstuffs was Timbuktu, which developed as a major market for salt, a valuable trade commodity that was mined in the southern Sahara nearby.

New kingdoms also emerged further south, along the boundary of the tropical forest, with centres such as Ife and Igbo Ukwu. Indigenous elites emerged from about the 8th century AD, controlling the exploitation of forest resources, which were traded with African middlemen from the sahel and savanna belts, increasing the demand for prestige goods which served to legitimise their status. This demand led to specialisation and new manufacturing techniques. The *cire perdue* (lost-wax) method of brass and bronze casting may have spread down from the north along with Saharan copper. Ife, the capital city of the Yoruba people, was famous for its ritual brass heads. Iron-working was also highly developed, and the forest was a source of iron ore and wood for smelting.

Ancestor veneration was a significant element of traditional African religion. Human figurines, such as the hundreds carved of soapstone from Esie and the brass heads from Ife, are thought to represent ancestors, chiefs or other eminent people, and at Jenne-jeno the bodies of relatives were sometimes inhumed within houses or ritual buildings. Different elements of traditional religions are shown through megalithic burial monuments which are found right across West Africa; an exceptional number are known in the area between the Senegal and Gambia rivers. The 4000 tumuli found in Sine-Saloum each contained multiple burials with grave goods such as iron, copper and gold jewellery and carnelian beads. As Islam spread from the north traditional religious practices were gradually curtailed, though ancestor veneration has persisted in some areas to the present day. Sometimes religious practices were fused; in Mali, traditional tumuli were orientated east–west, Islamic-style, with stones at the ends. At the 12th-century cemetery in Gao the burials are Muslim, and the gravestones with Kufic inscriptions may have been brought there from Islamic Spain.

This was an important period in the development of West Africa: the emergence of the first indigenous kingdoms and towns, the appearance of elite ruling groups and the great progress made in manufacturing technology, all led to greater contact with the outside world. These developments were accompanied by the florescence of traditional African religion, but soon curbed by the advance of Islam and Christianity.

4 ART OF THE OBAS

A *Mask from the palace at Ife. Like many Ife figurines, the style is naturalistic, but it is unusual in being a real mask, with slits for the eyes and holes for the attachment of hair and a beard. It is said to represent an early Ife king called Obalufon. c.12th century AD, copper, height 33cm.* B *Roped pot probably used for holding water, from Igbo Ukwu. The vessel was made in sections and the rope, about 8mm in diameter, was made up of twisted bronze threads. c.9th century AD, leaded bronze, height 3..3cm.* C *Statuette of a Yoruba deity called Eshu, who personifies the spirit of unpredictability, from Igbaja. c.12th century AD, stone, height 61cm.* D *Fan-holder from the burial chamber at Igbo Ukwu, part of a dignitary's regalia. Feathers would originally have been attached to the perforations around the crescent. c.9th century AD, copper, height 56.4cm.*

3 JENNE-JENO: AN EARLY AFRICAN CITY

Jenne-jeno (*below*), situated on an island in the River Niger, is the oldest known city south of the Sahara. It was first occupied by about 200BC by iron-using people, but intensive settlement only began in about AD400, and it reached its peak 500 years later. The city wall, built of cylindrical bricks between AD400 and 800, was up to eleven metres wide, and its two kilometre circumference enclosed both round and rectilinear mud-brick houses (*see plan right*). The fertile alluvium of the Niger Delta meant that local agriculture could support Jenne-jeno and its large population. The city was also well placed for trade since bulky goods could easily be transported by water. Jenne-jeno was already a thriving urban centre before the arrival of Muslim traders in the 8th century, demonstrating the indigenous nature of West African urbanism. In about AD1300, the rulers of Jenne-jeno were converted to Islam and dissociated themselves from the old pagan religion by deserting Jenne-jeno and founding the new Islamic city of Jenne to the north.

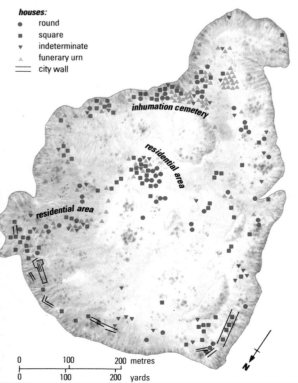

The city of Jenne-jeno

houses:
- round
- square
- indeterminate
- funerary urn
- city wall

inhumation cemetery

residential area

residential area

| 0 | 100 | 200 metres |
| 0 | 100 | 200 yards |

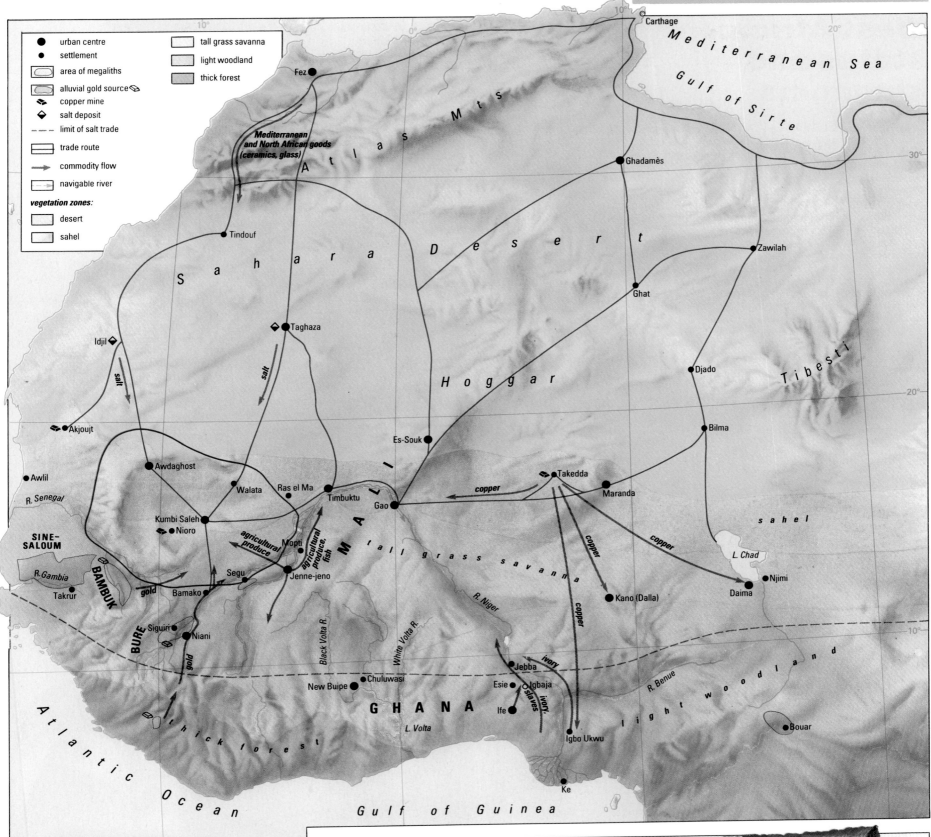

Legend:

- ● urban centre
- ● settlement
- area of megaliths
- alluvial gold source
- copper mine
- salt deposit
- --- limit of salt trade
- trade route
- → commodity flow
- navigable river

vegetation zones:
- desert
- sahel
- tall grass savanna
- light woodland
- thick forest

Mediterranean and North African goods (ceramics, glass)

---

1 WEST AFRICAN COMMERCE

The contrasting environments within West Africa, ranging from desert to forest, and the widely differing raw materials available from each area, was a major incentive to trade and commerce. Copper and salt were mined in the desert and were traded throughout the area, whereas the sources for gold were restricted to the savanna and forest of the south-west. The forest was also rich in other resources, especially ivory and ebony, iron ore and fuel for smelting. To obtain maximum advantage from these varied resources, many African towns grew up on the borders between environmental zones. The main export of the fertile land around the River Niger was food. This may have gone to support the populations of towns along the southern fringes of the desert such as Timbuktu, which developed as a major salt market. Much of the demand for West African produce came from the Muslims of North Africa.

2 IGBO UKWU: AN AFRICAN BURIAL

Igbo Ukwu was the burial place of a dignitary from a small kingdom of the 8th–9th century AD. The man was originally buried in a wooden chamber pit, in full ceremonial regalia, which included a bead-studded headdress and a copper crown, a pectoral plate, anklets, armlets and strings of beads. He was seated and held a fly-whisk. About five other bodies, probably of slaves, were placed on top of the chamber. When eventually the timbers decayed and the chamber collapsed, the dignitary and his regalia were scattered in disarray. A shrine or store was also found at Igbo Ukwu, containing many ritual items including a bronze altar stand and roped pot. All the objects are African in style, although some raw materials were traded from great distances; the carnelian may have been imported from as far away as Persia or India.

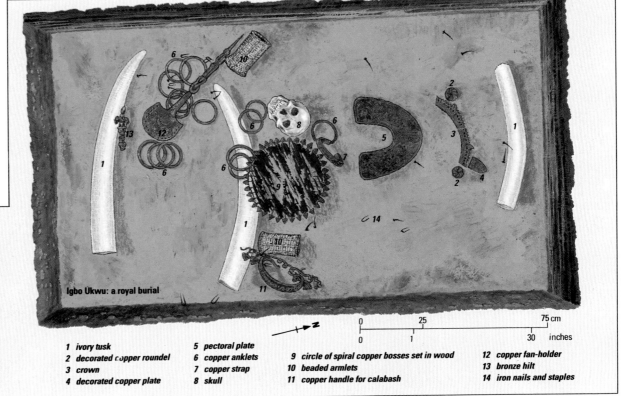

Igbo Ukwu: a royal burial

1 **ivory tusk**	5 **pectoral plate**
2 **decorated copper roundel**	6 **copper anklets**
3 **crown**	7 **copper strap**
4 **decorated copper plate**	8 **skull**

9 **circle of spiral copper bosses set in wood**
10 **beaded armlets**
11 **copper handle for calabash**
12 **copper fan-holder**
13 **bronze hilt**
14 **iron nails and staples**

West Africa: states and kingdoms

In the centuries following AD 1200 the states and urban centres of West Africa, which had first emerged before AD 1000 in the area south of the Sahara, developed on an unprecedented scale, continuing to derive much of their livelihood from trans-Saharan trade. Contact with the Islamic merchants of North Africa was still of paramount importance, as these towns took on the role of trading intermediaries between the southern forest belt and Mediterranean Africa, where slaves and other produce from the south was in great demand. Exploitation of local raw materials, especially copper and salt, and agriculture supplemented the wealth of these states. Their rise and fall is attributable to shifting economic and political circumstances; in the west, the Mali empire controlled the fertile Niger bend and the important trading cities sited there, ensuring its power and wealth. It was supplanted in the 15th century by Songhay – exploitation of new gold sources in Akan had led to an eastwards realignment of trade routes and centres of power. The powerful state of Borno, centred on Lake Chad, developed still further east, incorporating the earlier Kanem.

From the 13th century, powerful new states and chiefdoms also emerged to the south of the savanna, although little is known of their changing fortunes. Their wealth was based on Akan gold, and other commodities such as kola nuts, ivory and slaves. In Akan itself, there were several small states, and the towns of Bono Manso and Begho are known to have been important political centres. Begho, occupied from 1400–1750, was a market town which acted as a collection centre for gold and had close links with the Mali empire, especially the trading city of Jenne. The town was divided into several quarters, including one for local artisans and another which housed foreign merchants from the north. Initially, Islamic units of weight were used in the king's court, although a European standard was introduced by Portuguese traders, when they began to buy gold from Begho in about 1500.

Benin was the most impressive of the forest kingdoms of southern Nigeria. Founded in the 11th–12th century, it was centred on the city of Benin, where the political and religious ruler, the Oba, lived with his court retinue. The economy of Benin was based on trading, especially of slaves, first with the savanna people and later with the Europeans. Huge earthworks surrounded Benin city, including an inner defence measuring 17 metres from the bottom of the ditch to the top of the bank, which would have taken many man-hours to build. Benin is also renowned for its brass heads, which date from the 15th century, and show some similarity to the earlier terracotta and brass heads from Ife. They depict Obas, chieftains, court ceremonials, hunters, traders, and even Portuguese soldiers.

The construction of spectacular mud-brick mosques in the major towns of the savanna states, such as Jenne and Timbuktu in the 13th and 14th centuries points to the spread of Islam among the ruling and merchant classes. These mosques were often built under royal patronage. Further south, traditional religion persisted, mainly in the form of ancestor veneration. Although the Portuguese arrived in West Africa in the later 15th century, very few people were converted to Christianity until the colonial rule of the mid-19th century. The Portuguese built a series of fortified trading posts, the earliest example being the castle of São Jorge built at Elmina in 1482. Akan gold, the most sought after commodity, was exchanged by the Portuguese for slaves raided from the Bight of Benin. The Portuguese also traded with the Mali empire, using the River Gambia, and bought gold, gum and skins to be sold in Mediterranean Africa for horses, cloth and silver, which were in turn brought down to the markets of the south. At the site of Dawu there is a striking example of European influence – the appearance of tobacco pipes in the 17th century levels.

Contact with Europeans increased still further when the Portuguese lost their trade monopoly in the 17th century. By 1750 a number of European nationalities were trading with West Africans, but remained removed from their internal affairs. This situation changed completely with the onset of European colonialism and Christian missionary activity in the 19th century. In the north, however, traditional practices and Islam remained the dominant religions, and some of the cities of the early empires, such as Kano, are still thriving to this day.

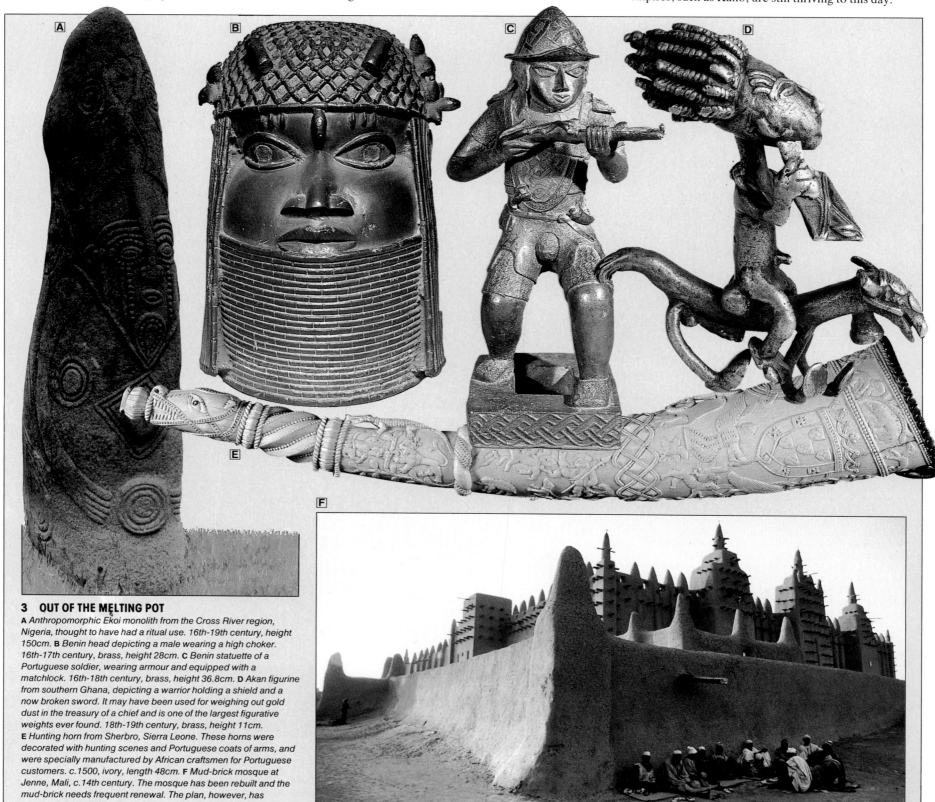

3 OUT OF THE MELTING POT

A Anthropomorphic Ekoi monolith from the Cross River region, Nigeria, thought to have had a ritual use. 16th-19th century, height 150cm. B Benin head depicting a male wearing a high choker. 16th-17th century, brass, height 28cm. C Benin statuette of a Portuguese soldier, wearing armour and equipped with a matchlock. 16th-18th century, brass, height 36.8cm. D Akan figurine from southern Ghana, depicting a warrior holding a shield and a now broken sword. It may have been used for weighing out gold dust in the treasury of a chief and is one of the largest figurative weights ever found. 18th-19th century, brass, height 11cm. E Hunting horn from Sherbro, Sierra Leone. These horns were decorated with hunting scenes and Portuguese coats of arms, and were specially manufactured by African craftsmen for Portuguese customers. c.1500, ivory, length 48cm. F Mud-brick mosque at Jenne, Mali, c.14th century. The mosque has been rebuilt and the mud-brick needs frequent renewal. The plan, however, has remained constant.

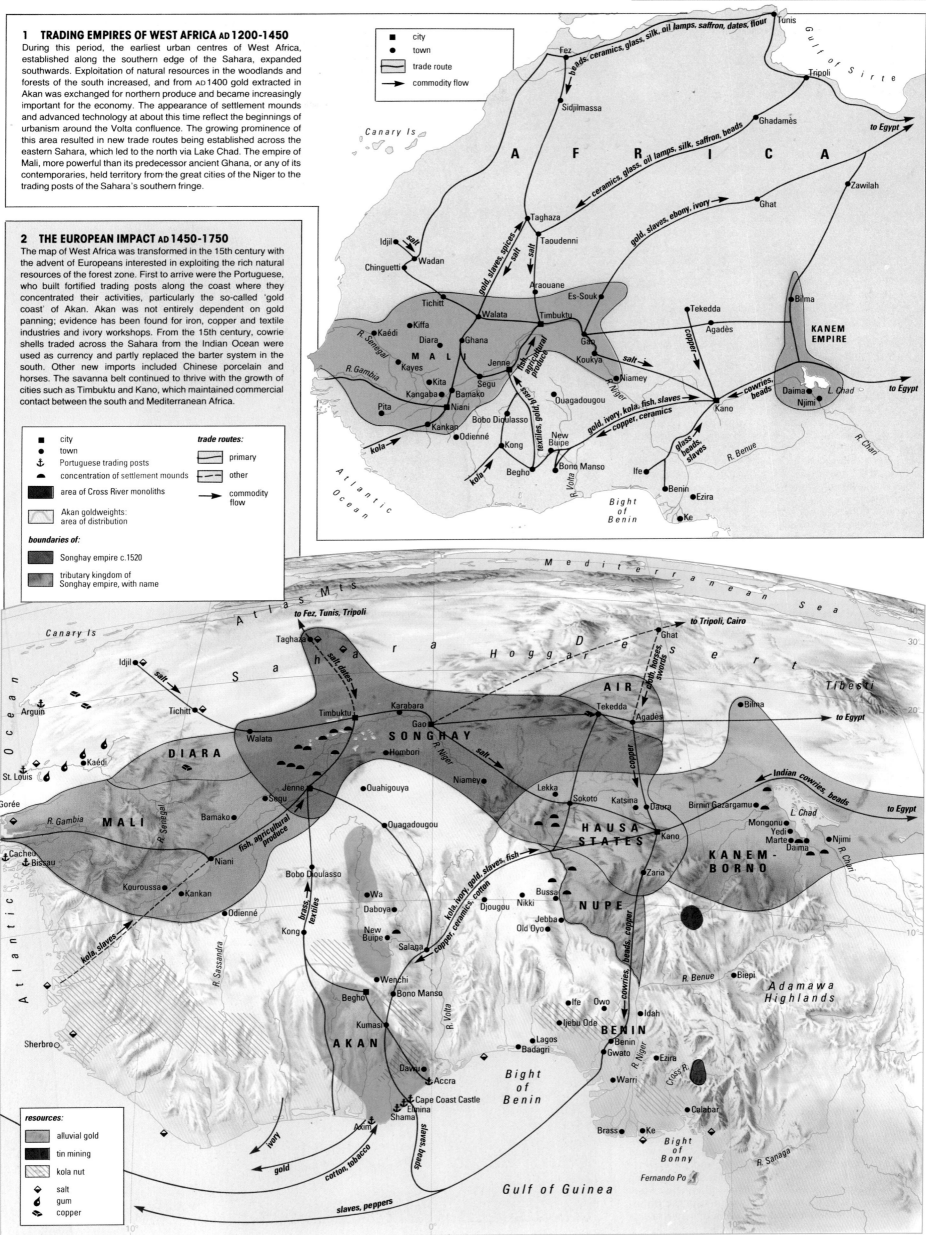

1 TRADING EMPIRES OF WEST AFRICA AD 1200-1450

During this period, the earliest urban centres of West Africa, established along the southern edge of the Sahara, expanded southwards. Exploitation of natural resources in the woodlands and forests of the south increased, and from AD 1400 gold extracted in Akan was exchanged for northern produce and became increasingly important for the economy. The appearance of settlement mounds and advanced technology at about this time reflect the beginnings of urbanism around the Volta confluence. The growing prominence of this area resulted in new trade routes being established across the eastern Sahara, which led to the north via Lake Chad. The empire of Mali, more powerful than its predecessor ancient Ghana, or any of its contemporaries, held territory from the great cities of the Niger to the trading posts of the Sahara's southern fringe.

2 THE EUROPEAN IMPACT AD 1450-1750

The map of West Africa was transformed in the 15th century with the advent of Europeans interested in exploiting the rich natural resources of the forest zone. First to arrive were the Portuguese, who built fortified trading posts along the coast where they concentrated their activities, particularly the so-called 'gold coast' of Akan. Akan was not entirely dependent on gold panning; evidence has been found for iron, copper and textile industries and ivory workshops. From the 15th century, cowrie shells traded across the Sahara from the Indian Ocean were used as currency and partly replaced the barter system in the south. Other new imports included Chinese porcelain and horses. The savanna belt continued to thrive with the growth of cities such as Timbuktu and Kano, which maintained commercial contact between the south and Mediterranean Africa.

Legend (top):
- city
- town
- trade route
- commodity flow

Legend (map 2):
- city
- town
- Portuguese trading posts
- concentration of settlement mounds
- area of Cross River monoliths
- Akan goldweights: area of distribution

trade routes:
- primary
- other
- commodity flow

boundaries of:
- Songhay empire c.1520
- tributary kingdom of Songhay empire, with name

resources:
- alluvial gold
- tin mining
- kola nut
- salt
- gum
- copper

The trading kingdoms of East Africa

Eastern Africa underwent a series of distinct developments between AD 650-1750, with a great expansion of trade, Arab contact along the coast, and the rise of more complex societies inland ruled over by chiefs and kings.

In Christian Ethiopia, the powerful mercantile kingdom of Axum had reached its peak in the 4th century AD. By the 8th century control of the Red Sea had passed to the Arabs, and it was finally overthrown by people from further south in the late 10th century. In the 12th century a new dynasty established their capital at Lalibela, famous for its churches, cut out of huge blocks of rock, and in some cases totally subterranean. The Ethiopians became isolated from the rest of the Christian world as Muslims made inroads to the south and east and the Christian kingdoms of the Middle Nile Valley were subdued.

Developments elsewhere in East Africa can be divided between the coast and the interior, although these were commercially interdependent. Merchants began to trade and settle along the coast in the 9th century. The most prosperous early trading town was Manda, which exported mangrove wood and probably iron and ivory in return for fine pottery and other luxury items. After 1050 its pre-eminence passed to other towns such as Kilwa, where the ruling Shirazi dynasty issued a coinage and in the early 14th century built themselves an impressive palace, 'Husuni Kubwa'. Kilwa relied heavily on exporting raw materials such as gold, ivory, horns, skins and tortoiseshell from the interior to Arabia and India, while Chinese and Islamic pottery, glass beads and cloth were traded inland.

In parts of the East African interior, the emergence of elite groups was accompanied by a rise in the volume of trade and production, especially of metal goods. The elites probably controlled trade in raw materials to the coast and used both imports and locally produced metal items as status objects. At such places as Ingombe Ilede, copper was cast into cross-shaped moulds and these ingots, probably used as currency, were traded widely. The impressive stone enclosures at Great Zimbabwe were almost certainly the headquarters for a ruling group who controlled the production and export of gold from the Zimbabwe plateau. Their position may have been legitimised by religion, since many ritual objects, including soapstone figures, are in evidence at the site. Great Zimbabwe was by far the largest settlement, covering about 40 hectares before its decline in the 15th century, but there were over one hundred such stone enclosures in the region. Some housed single families, while some, such as Chumnungwa and Manekweni, were territorial capitals. They all formed an integrated trading system which was linked to the coast. Developments in social complexity can be seen in the burials from Sanga, Zaire. Prior to 1300, graves contained pottery and metal implements including copper jewellery; the metal was mined some 300 kilometres to the south at Kansanshi and Kipushi. Later, richer grave goods included imports such as cowrie shells and glass beads, new types of pottery, cross-shaped copper ingots and occasionally iron gongs – traditional symbols of kingship in this area.

In many parts of East Africa, animal husbandry was a major aspect of the economy, and generally cattle were more important than sheep. Movement of cattle herds was determined by the influx of tsetse fly into the wet lowlands during the rainy season, forcing migration to higher ground. Sites such as Great Zimbabwe were situated on the plateau, accessible to both highland and lowland grazing areas. At Bigo, west of Lake Victoria, an earthwork enclosing 3.2 square kilometres has been found, which it is thought was used for corralling cattle, since the banks are outside the ditches, indicating their non-military function. Substantial cattle enclosures such as these point to a centralised control of herds, probably by an elite ruling class, for whom cattle were important status symbols as well as a good investment. Cereal remains are rarer, but sorghum was grown in Zambia and Zimbabwe from the 7th century and there is also evidence for beans, cowpeas and squashes. The coastal people, however, grew bananas, coconut palms and sugar cane, which had been imported from Indonesia.

The Portuguese reached Sofala in 1497 and founded forts there and in Kilwa. They discovered Zimbabwean gold when they explored the Zambezi, and set up forts such as Sena and Tete on the river. This shift in trading relations led to a decline in the coastal settlements, while independent states arose in the interior, with the Portuguese acting as new, but not dominant trading partners: a new era of European contact had arrived.

2 GREAT ZIMBABWE

Great Zimbabwe is the largest and most famous of a series of stone enclosures in East Africa dating from the 10th-15th centuries AD. The main enclosure, the Elliptical Building, is the largest stone structure of this period which has been found in sub-Saharan Africa, possibly housing the chief and his relatives. Luxury goods, including Chinese and Islamic pottery and cowrie shells and beads from coastal cities such as Kilwa were found at this site – probably traded up the Sabi river by Swahili merchants. Great Zimbabwe provided raw materials for the coastal settlements, especially gold, copper, tin and iron. The indigenous rulers probably levied food, goods and labour as tribute from the surrounding farming population. The decline of the site in c. AD 1450 roughly coincided with that of Kilwa – the fortunes of the two sites were closely related.

Great Zimbabwe *below* 1 **Hill ruins** built on and around natural granite boulders, bounded by two curved walls over 9m high capped with masonry monoliths possibly serving a ritual function. The earliest dwellings in the 10th century AD were found here; also soapstone columns, dishes and small human figurines. 2 **Elliptical Building or Great Enclosure** political and ritual focus of the whole settlement containing the *daga* (clay and gravel) huts of the king and his entourage. The outer wall was built later, increasing in size and quality as it progressed. At its latest stage it was 244m long, 5.2m thick and 9.8m high, topped by monoliths. 3 **Conical Tower** built during the later phase, 5.5m in diameter and 10.4m high with a truncated top. It was thought to represent a past chief or his power and may also have served a ritual function.

Right *Great Zimbabwe. In the foreground is the Elliptical Building.*

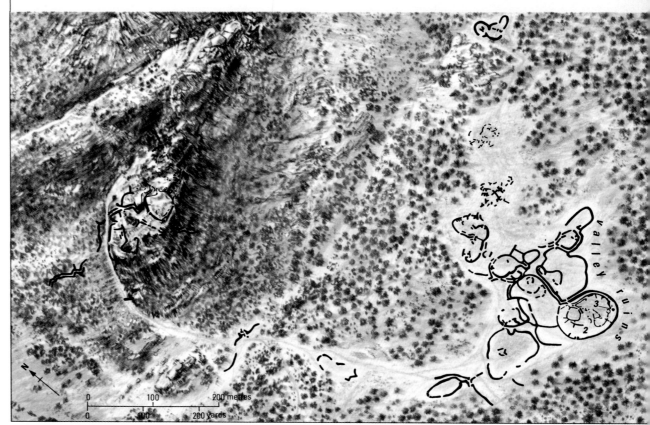

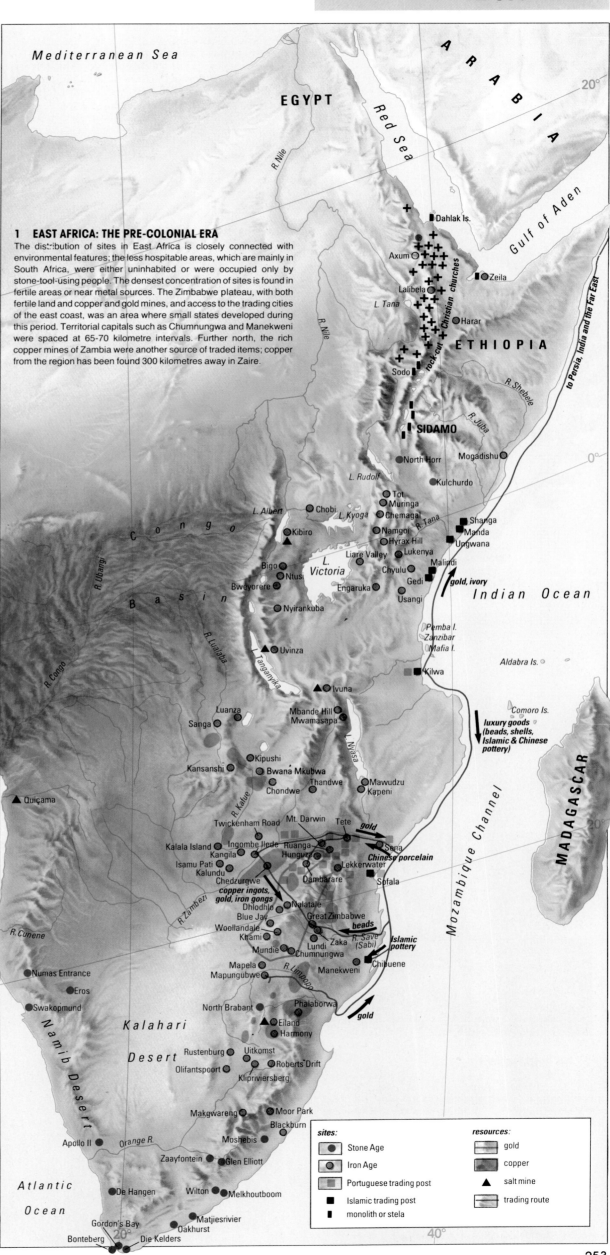

1 EAST AFRICA: THE PRE-COLONIAL ERA

The distribution of sites in East Africa is closely connected with environmental features; the less hospitable areas, which are mainly in South Africa, were either uninhabited or were occupied only by stone-tool-using people. The densest concentration of sites is found in fertile areas or near metal sources. The Zimbabwe plateau, with both fertile land and copper and gold mines, and access to the trading cities of the east coast, was an area where small states developed during this period. Territorial capitals such as Chumnungwa and Manekweni were spaced at 65-70 kilometre intervals. Further north, the rich copper mines of Zambia were another source of traded items; copper from the region has been found 300 kilometres away in Zaire.

3 CROSS-CULTURAL CONTACTS

A *Burial from Sanga, Zaire, containing 44 pottery vessels, copper and iron jewellery, two imported cowrie shells and an ivory pendant. The range and value of the grave-goods indicate that the society of this early state was stratified. Long-distance trade was important; the copper in the burial comes from 300km away, and cowries and glass beads from the east coast. 12th century AD.* B *Anthropomorphic figure, probably from Great Zimbabwe. Eight soapstone birds on monoliths and two anthropomorphic figures have been found at the site. The nearest source of soapstone is 24km away, and it is thought that the monoliths performed a ritual function. 13th-14th century AD, soapstone, 41cm.* C *Pot from Kilwa with low ridge decoration. This typical unglazed pot was probably made on a slow wheel, and fired in the open. Much of the fine decorated pottery found at Kilwa, however, was imported from China and the Islamic world. c. 14th century AD, height 16cm.* D *The rock-cut church of St George, Lalibela, Ethiopia. This free-standing cruciform church was cut into a single block of rock. 13th-14th century AD.*

sites:
- Stone Age
- Iron Age
- Portuguese trading post
- Islamic trading post
- monolith or stela

resources:
- gold
- copper
- salt mine
- trading route

Southern India and Ceylon

In the 3rd century BC Buddhism had spread widely throughout Mauryan India (*page 188*) under royal patronage. It had reached the Afghan borderlands in the north and had even been carried by missionaries beyond the frontiers of the empire to Ceylon (Sri Lanka). It still remained the dominant religion of the north and of Ceylon in the early centuries AD. However, in southern India, where Mauryan political control had never been strong, Hinduism, the traditional pre-Buddhist religion,

began to gain ground. This development is marked by the construction of an impressive series of elaborately decorated Hindu stone temples.

Stone temples are virtually the only remains of the early Hindu capitals of southern India, as domestic and secular buildings were constructed in ephemeral materials that have not survived southern India's tropical climate. Investment in temple building, sacred art and rituals were means by which rulers maintained their links with divine power, and depictions of gods and kings were sometimes interchangeable. Temple inscriptions often named the royal patron, and listed his military conquests. Thus they became secular symbols of royal power and grandeur.

Rivalries between the major dynasties or kingdoms are shown archaeologically through their different temple

styles. The Hoysalas, for instance, built temples of star-shaped plans, and decorated the outside with horizontal friezes depicting animals, flowers, entertainers and battle scenes. The early Chola period saw a great expansion in temple building; images of kings were worshipped within these temples, reflecting the emergence of the cult of the god-king. Agricultural estates belonged to temples, and landless labourers worked there. Inscriptions in the Brihadishvara temple at Thanjavur noted the land, agricultural produce and jewels donated, and mentioned the 400 dancing girls and attendants who worked and lived there. In the country, temples became the social and economic centre of the community and also acted as schools and banks. In the Vijayanagara period (from the middle of the 14th century), huge temple-cities came into

2 THE HINDU LEGACY

The kingdom of Vijayanagara, based in the Krishna Valley, gradually extended its power until the 16th century, when it controlled almost all the Hindu kingdoms of southern India. This was the great period of Hindu/Muslim tolerance, which also saw the rise of the temple city. Vijayanagara, the best-preserved Hindu royal site in southern India, is one of the most magnificent capitals anywhere in Asia. It was founded in the middle of the 14th century; in 1565 it was destroyed by invading Muslim armies (during the invasion of the subcontinent by the Mughals) and then abandoned. The ruins cover an area of 25 square kilometres; they include portions of a massive defensive system with concentric fortification walls which enclose a variety of religious, residential and civil structures. To the north of the royal palace is the sacred centre of the city, the original settlement, distinguished by its

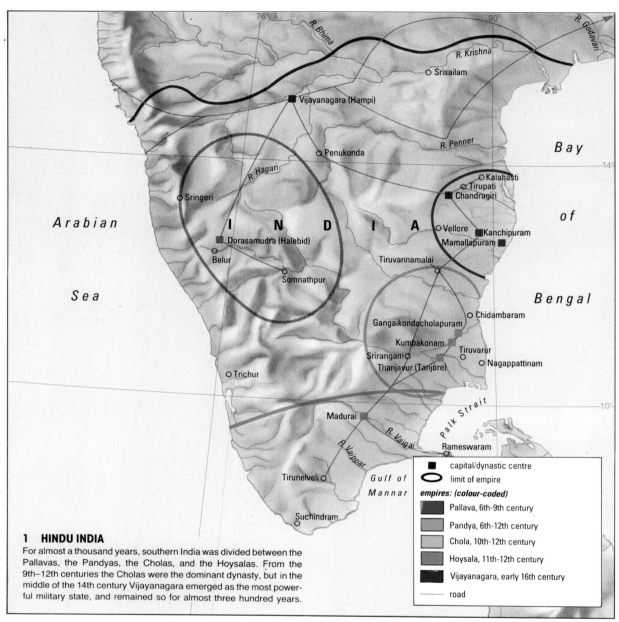

1 HINDU INDIA

For almost a thousand years, southern India was divided between the Pallavas, the Pandyas, the Cholas, and the Hoysalas. From the 9th–12th centuries the Cholas were the dominant dynasty, but in the middle of the 14th century Vijayanagara emerged as the most powerful military state, and remained so for almost three hundred years.

■	capital/dynastic centre
⬭	limit of empire

empires: (colour-coded)

- Pallava, 6th-9th century
- Pandya, 6th-12th century
- Chola, 10th-12th century
- Hoysala, 11th-12th century
- Vijayanagara, early 16th century
- road

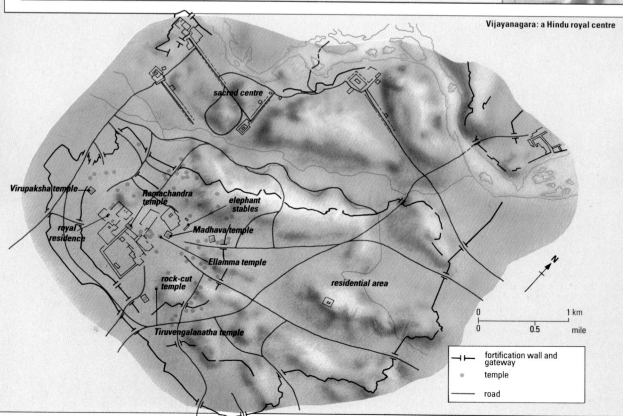

Vijayanagara: a Hindu royal centre

⊣⊢	fortification wall and gateway
•	temple
—	road

being covering up to 63 hectares.

As in southern India, the archaeological record of Ceylon is dominated by monumental religious structures. These are invariably associated with Buddhism, the religion that was brought by a royal missionary from India in the 3rd century BC. Monastic institutions were rapidly evolved to promote the new religion. Despite dynastic conflict, and even the invasions of Hindu rulers from southern India, Buddhism has been preserved on this island, more or less intact, up to the present day.

The rulers of Ceylon were also religious patrons; shrines served as memorials not only to Buddha and his disciples, but also to the kings themselves. Extensive monasteries were often incorporated into royal centres so that kings could maintain close links with religious communities. However, up to the 12th century most buildings were of wood – there was abundant timber in the centre and south of the island. It was not until Polonnaruwa became the capital that the first buildings made entirely of brick or stone appeared.

The religious architecture of Ceylon is conservative; the same structures were used repeatedly over many centuries and continuously renovated. The earliest architectural form associated with Buddhism was the *stupa (page 260)*: a solid hemispherical mound, sometimes constructed entirely of brick, in which relics connected with the Buddha or his disciples were enshrined. Residential halls raised on platforms were often grouped together into complexes, with shrines, *stupas*, eating halls and kitchens. Control of water was an important factor. Irrigation schemes were started in the 1st century AD, and by the 12th century there were 800 kilometres of canals, with a large concentration in the dry south. Most religious sites have extensive reservoirs and canal systems.

By the 7th century AD, Buddhism had been rejected in southern India and the earlier Hindu religion reinstated. In Ceylon, however, only 50 kilometres away, Buddhism remained dominant from the 3rd century BC. During the following 2000 years Hinduism at times has been the religion of a minority in the north of the island, as it is today. There are certainly points of similarity in the beliefs of the two faiths, notably the shared adherence to the doctrines of reincarnation, and though Buddhist *stupas* and Hindu temples are strikingly different in general form and appearance both religions were distinguished by their massive investment in the construction of impressive and lasting monuments to their beliefs.

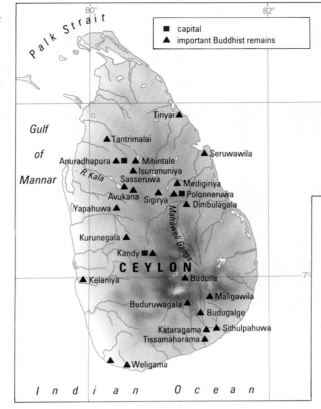

3 BUDDHIST CEYLON

The oldest religious centre of importance in Buddhist Ceylon is Anuradhapura, an extensive complex of shrines and monasteries, which flourished from the 6th to the 10th centuries AD, when various rulers made it their capital. It is still a religious centre today. The smaller royal site of Sigirya belongs to the 5th century; its spectacular rock fort was an impregnable citadel. By the 12th century, Polonnaruwa had emerged as the chief capital of the island, and a large royal complex is still preserved within the city walls. Some structures here were constructed by the invading Hindu Cholas of southern India. Other religious sites, of less importance politically, are found in Avukana and Mihintale. In later times the capital was shifted to Kandy, in the safety of the central highlands. It, too, was surrounded by temple centres which have maintained their importance up to the present day.

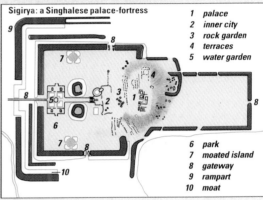

Sigirya: a Singhalese palace-fortress

1 palace
2 inner city
3 rock garden
4 terraces
5 water garden
6 park
7 moated island
8 gateway
9 rampart
10 moat

4 BUDDHIST ART AND ARCHITECTURE OF CEYLON

Sigirya, in Ceylon was a palace-fortress built by Kassapa (447–495), a usurper of power, who believed he was a god-king. Kassapa's palace was precariously sited at the summit of the rock (*below*). Residences, courts and alleys were arranged in a sequence of levels with what may have been the king's audience hall at the top. Access was by a walkway that clung to the side of the rock, where overhanging boulders were adorned with paintings. A planned garden complex with ponds and plantations extended to the west of the citadel.

A *Reclining Buddha from Polonnaruwa, Ceylon. c.12th century AD, length 14m.* B *Wall painting of aerial maidens from Sigirya, Ceylon. c.5th century AD, life-size.*

impressive planned temple complexes (*above*). Within the interior courts of the temples were sanctuaries dedicated to different deities, as well as subsidiary shrines, colonnades, kitchens and stores. These temples were responsible for land management and irrigation – water was transported and stored by elaborate systems of tanks and canals. A few of the secular monuments at Vijayanagara – for example the domed elephant stables (*top*) and some of the gateways – were built of stone, and are especially important because secular buildings were usually of wood and have rarely survived.

A *Shiva, Lord of the Dance, surrounded by a circle which represents the cycle of creation, destruction and rebirth. 11th century AD, bronze, height 96cm. Chola sculptures are unsurpassed for their technical virtuosity and delicacy of modelling.* B *The Brihadishvara temple at Thanjavur, an outstanding example of Chola architecture, dedicated to the god Shiva. Built by Rajaraja I in AD 1010.*

The Islamic empires

With the decline of the Abbasid Caliphate the Islamic world entered a new cultural phase marked by the emergence of Persia in the east as a major centre of gravity from the 11th–13th centuries AD. Here a high mediaeval civilisation developed, based on quasi-feudal land tenure. In the 13th century, however, and again at the end of the 14th, the Middle East was devastated by Mongol invasions, and it was only in the 15th and 16th centuries that a series of great new Islamic empires became established: the Ottomans in Anatolia and the Levant, the Safavids in Persia, and the Mughals in the Indian subcontinent.

The Ottoman empire, with capitals first at Bursa, then Edirne and finally Istanbul, began as a frontier warrior state, but as its power spread it developed a complex bureaucratic system of government. By the middle of the 16th century the empire covered not only Anatolia but also Egypt, the Levant and much of south-east Europe. Military success was due partly to the widespread use of firearms, especially huge siege cannon capable of destroying the walls of fortresses and cities. The centre of government was the imperial palace of Topkapi Saray in Istanbul, a sprawling complex of courtyards and pavilions overlooking the Bosporus, which has survived with its archives and treasure house intact. The most striking monuments of Ottoman power are not the palaces, however, but the great mosques. The Ottoman mosque design was derived from that of Byzantine churches, with large central domes and airy interiors. To this basic plan were added slender pencil-like minarets with extensive decoration of glazed tiles. The master architect Sinan brought the style to perfection in c. AD 1530 in the Selimiye mosque at Edirne. Sinan did not only build mosques, but was also responsible for baths, schools, hospitals, palaces, aqueducts, bridges and *caravanserais*; a total of more than 400 Ottoman buildings are attributed wholly or in part to him and his pupils.

As with the Ottoman empire, the principal remains of the Safavid realm are major works of architecture. The capital was finally established at Isfahan in 1598, and it is this city, extensively rebuilt by the Safavids, which contains many of the finest surviving buildings. A superb new official complex was constructed around the Maidan-i Shah with a monumental polo and review ground. The only surviving sections of the palace, however, are the 'Ali Qapu, which was the main gate and elevated viewing stand overlooking the Maidan, and a few garden pavilions. The principal mosque, the Masjid-i Shah, was built at the southern end of the Maidan between 1616 and 1620. The facades and main dome are covered in glazed tiles with abstract floral patterns in white and gold on a turquoise-blue background. Safavid architects made extensive use of glazed tiles, since their buildings were made not of stone but of brick. Some tiles were curved so as to fit the surface of the building exactly. Isfahan also had a grand central avenue, the Chahar Bagh, consisting of three separate streets and a canal and lined with the houses and gardens of the aristocracy.

The Mughal empire differed from the Ottomans and Safavids in its mixture of Islamic and Hindu artistic and architectural styles. This is vividly demonstrated in the combination of Islamic pavilions and massive Hindu-style buildings at the palace complex built at Fatehpur Sikri in about 1570. The greatest architectural achievements belong to the reign of Shah Jahan early in the following century. The most famous is the Taj Mahal, a domed mausoleum with four minarets built for his favourite wife, Mumtaz-i Mahal, between 1632 and 1654. The entire building is covered with white marble inlaid with coloured stones in abstract and floral patterns, creating an impression of splendour which has rarely been surpassed. Other important buildings followed Shah Jahan's transfer of the capital from Agra to Delhi in 1638. These include the large Friday Mosque and the Red Fort, built to serve as a palace, administrative headquarters, arsenal, treasury and manufacturing centre. The new capital's grand avenue, the Chandni Chowk, rivalled the Chahar Bagh of Isfahan in scale.

The magnificent public buildings and monumental architecture demonstrate the vitality of Islamic art and culture during these centuries. Craftsmanship in pottery, metalwork, glass and other materials also flourished. Isfahan, for example, was a commercial city as well as a capital, and had an impressive bazaar, in which each craft had its own particular area. One of its most important products, and a major export, was silk. A wealth of more everyday items also survives to illustrate life in these Islamic empires, but it is without doubt their great artistic and architectural achievements which are their most impressive legacy.

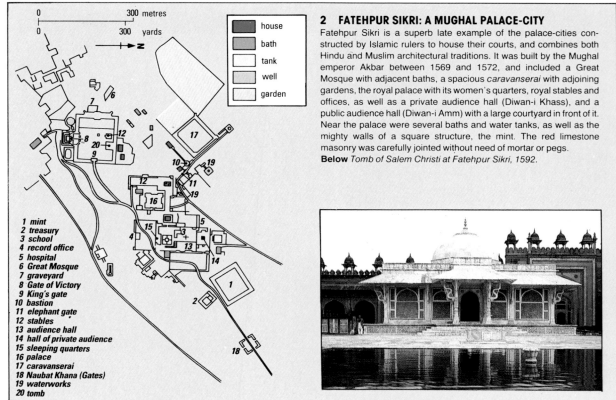

2 FATEHPUR SIKRI: A MUGHAL PALACE-CITY

Fatehpur Sikri is a superb late example of the palace-cities constructed by Islamic rulers to house their courts, and combines both Hindu and Muslim architectural traditions. It was built by the Mughal emperor Akbar between 1569 and 1572, and included a Great Mosque with adjacent baths, a spacious *caravanserai* with adjoining gardens, the royal palace with its women's quarters, royal stables and offices, as well as a private audience hall (Diwan-i Khass), and a public audience hall (Diwan-i Amm) with a large courtyard in front of it. Near the palace were several baths and water tanks, as well as the mighty walls of a square structure, the mint. The red limestone masonry was carefully jointed without need of mortar or pegs.
Below Tomb of Salem Christi at Fatehpur Sikri, 1592.

Key:
- house
- bath
- tank
- well
- garden

1 mint
2 treasury
3 school
4 record office
5 hospital
6 Great Mosque
7 graveyard
8 Gate of Victory
9 King's gate
10 bastion
11 elephant gate
12 stables
13 audience hall
14 hall of private audience
15 sleeping quarters
16 palace
17 caravanserai
18 Naubat Khana (Gates)
19 waterworks
20 tomb

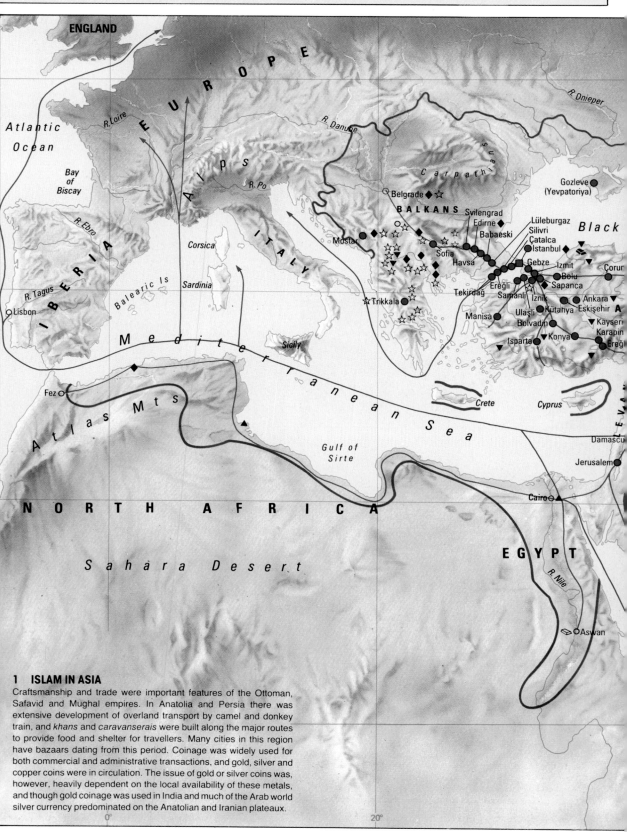

1 ISLAM IN ASIA

Craftsmanship and trade were important features of the Ottoman, Safavid and Mughal empires. In Anatolia and Persia there was extensive development of overland transport by camel and donkey train, and *khans* and *caravanserais* were built along the major routes to provide food and shelter for travellers. Many cities in this region have bazaars dating from this period. Coinage was widely used for both commercial and administrative transactions, and gold, silver and copper coins were in circulation. The issue of gold or silver coins was, however, heavily dependent on the local availability of these metals, and though gold coinage was used in India and much of the Arab world silver currency predominated on the Anatolian and Iranian plateaux.

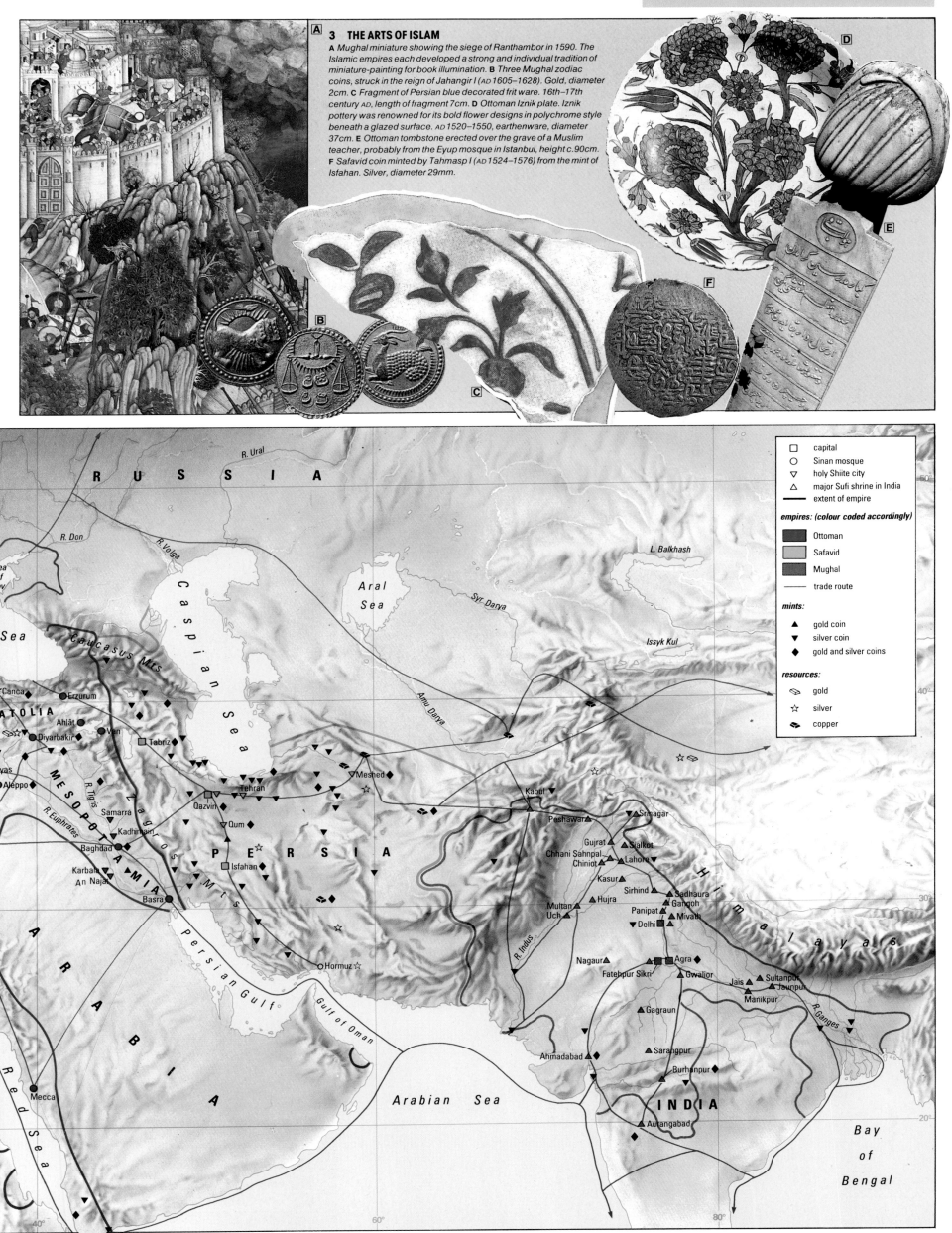

3   THE ARTS OF ISLAM

A Mughal miniature showing the siege of Ranthambor in 1590. The Islamic empires each developed a strong and individual tradition of miniature-painting for book illumination. **B** Three Mughal zodiac coins, struck in the reign of Jahangir I (AD 1605–1628). Gold, diameter 2cm. **C** Fragment of Persian blue decorated frit ware. 16th–17th century AD, length of fragment 7cm. **D** Ottoman Iznik plate. Iznik pottery was renowned for its bold flower designs in polychrome style beneath a glazed surface. AD 1520–1550, earthenware, diameter 37cm. **E** Ottoman tombstone erected over the grave of a Muslim teacher, probably from the Eyup mosque in Istanbul, height c.90cm. **F** Safavid coin minted by Tahmasp I (AD 1524–1576) from the mint of Isfahan. Silver, diameter 29mm.

Legend:

- □ capital
- ○ Sinan mosque
- ▽ holy Shiite city
- △ major Sufi shrine in India
- — extent of empire

empires: (colour coded accordingly)
- Ottoman
- Safavid
- Mughal
- — trade route

mints:
- ▲ gold coin
- ▼ silver coin
- ◆ gold and silver coins

resources:
- gold
- ☆ silver
- copper

Kingdoms of South-East Asia

The period from the 9th to the 14th centuries AD in South-East Asia was a time of powerful kingdoms and monumental architecture on an unprecedented scale. Major temple complexes are found throughout the region, from Borobudur and Prambanan in Java to Sukhothai in Thailand. Extensive irrigation systems were developed by rulers of mainland kingdoms such as the Khmer, allowing cultivation of rice on a large enough scale to provide a secure economic base. In contrast to the agricultural economies of the mainland, the islands – including the trading entrepôts of Java and Sumatra – depended on a flourishing maritime trade.

Though the intricate social hierarchy and religious system, as well as the art and architecture of the region, owed a great debt to India, they developed along uniquely South-East Asian lines. Stone temples were erected to glorify king, state and religion, and the rulers used Indian concepts of the king as god to increase their status. Theravada and Mahayana Buddhism as well as Hindu cults reached South-East Asia from India, and there is evidence that both Hinduism and Buddhism were often practiced simultaneously. Religion was a vital part of both cultural and economic development: when a temple was built by a king or important official he gained religious merit and also gave status to the area. The Khmer empire encouraged the construction of over 900 temples in Cambodia and neighbouring Thailand between the 9th and 13th centuries, representing an enormous investment of both materials and labour. At Angkor, the capital, a combination of brick, sandstone and, later, laterite was used to construct a complex of temples, each one a symbolic representation of Hindu or Buddhist cosmology. The Angkor complex eventually covered an area stretching more than 25 kilometres east to west and nearly 10 kilometres north to south. Pagan, on a vast plain near the Irrawaddy River, was second in urban area only to Angkor. Here, by the 11th and 12th centuries thousands of Buddhist temples covered an area of more than 60 square kilometres. At Borobudur, the massive 9th cen-

2 THE TEMPLES OF ANGKOR

Angkor, capital of the Khmer empire, was located on the vast alluvial flood plain just to the north of the Great Lake, known as the Tonle Sap. Angkor's prosperity depended on rice cultivation based on receding flood agriculture. During the dry season the Tonle Sap drained into the Mekong, but during the rainy season this process was reversed, greatly increasing the depth of the lake. When this process was once again reversed rich alluvial deposits were left behind by the receding flood, and the area could be used for rice cultivation, which supported an urban population of about one million people. Within the capital, the Khmer kings built a huge network of canals and water reservoirs (baray) for ritual purposes, irrigation, and for transporting the vast quantities of stone required for building new structures. Temples were built to honour the parents and other ancestors of these god-kings who also built temple-mountains, which were set aside to serve as royal mausoleums. The most impressive temple-mountains are the 12th-century Angkor Wat and the 13th-century Bayon, each decorated with bas-reliefs illustrating stories of battles and myths, as well as showing a wealth of details about everyday life.

Above *The 12th-century temple complex of Angkor Wat seen across one of the pools which surround it.*

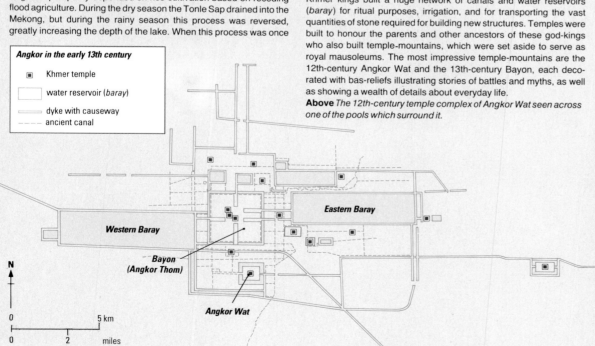

Angkor in the early 13th century

- ▣ Khmer temple
- ▭ water reservoir (baray)
- ━━ dyke with causeway
- ---- ancient canal

Western Baray

Eastern Baray

Bayon (Angkor Thom)

Angkor Wat

N

0　　　5 km

0　　2　miles

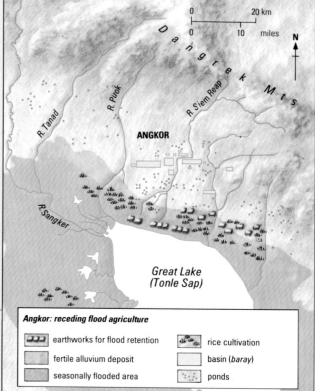

ANGKOR

Dangrek Mts

R. Tanad

R. Puok

R. Siem Reap

R. Sangker

Great Lake (Tonle Sap)

0　　　20 km

0　　10　miles

N

Angkor: receding flood agriculture

- earthworks for flood retention
- fertile alluvium deposit
- seasonally flooded area
- rice cultivation
- basin (baray)
- ponds

tury Buddhist temple, which is terraced and surmounted by *stupas*, contains 2500 square metres of stone bas-reliefs. In contrast, few remains of secular works or buildings have survived.

In the islands, numerous ports were constructed along the east coast of Sumatra and the north coast of Java as the exchange of goods between China and India was funnelled through the Straits of Malacca. However, by the end of the 14th century the maritime kingdom of Srivijaya, which was probably centred on Sumatra, succumbed to competition from the growing land-based states in eastern Java, such as Kediri and Singhasari.

Details of the everyday lives of the peoples of South-East Asia are known through bas-reliefs, literary works, stone inscriptions, and ceramics. At Angkor bas-reliefs not only show battles with weapons and armour, but also depict markets, fishing, and various forms of gambling such as cockfights. Khmer inscriptions inform us not only about great kings but also about everyday customs, such as the right to let pigs forage in ricefields, and the use of ginger and honey to make ritual foods. The life of common people in the agricultural states of South-East Asia was governed by the king, the six-month cycles of rain and drought, and adherence to religious custom, be it Hindu or Buddhist.

During the 13th and 14th centuries, however, the rise of new states and the over-exploitation of manpower and natural resources undermined the stability of many of the great kingdoms on both mainland and island South-East Asia. The technological and architectural wonders of the Khmer kingdom of Angkor, built up for over 500 years, rested on an agricultural base of rice cultivation. The kingdom finally collapsed in the 15th century when control of the manpower faltered and Angkor was sacked by the newly powerful Thai kingdom of Sukhothai. The Khmer were also threatened on the east by the Vietnamese, who gained independence from China in the 10th century, and absorbed the coastal kingdom of Champa (southern Vietnam).

The decline of these kingdoms by the 14th century ended what was the 'classical' period of South-East Asian history, not only in the florescence of art and architecture but also in the formation of economic, legal and social practices which were to guide the region until the arrival of European colonists many centuries later.

3 FROM THE TEMPLE KINGDOMS

A *Prajnaparamita statue from one of the Singhasari temples on eastern Java. c. AD 1350, height 126cm.* **B** *Bas-relief showing battle scene between Khmer and Cham warriors. From Bayon (Angkor Thom) 13th century AD, height of frieze 90cm.* **C** *Angkor-style three-headed naga or serpent. The naga guards the life energy stored in water. 12th century AD, bronze, height 34cm.* **D** *Vietnamese jar with a finely crackled cream glaze, decorated with brown leaf sprays within six panels. 10th-12th century AD, height 25cm.*

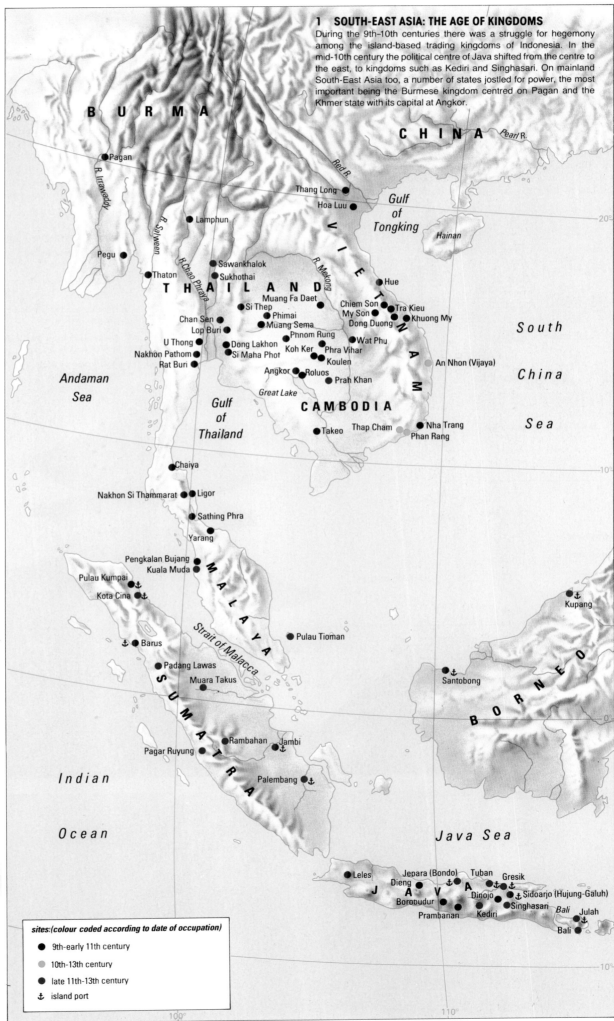

1 SOUTH-EAST ASIA: THE AGE OF KINGDOMS

During the 9th-10th centuries there was a struggle for hegemony among the island-based trading kingdoms of Indonesia. In the mid-10th century the political centre of Java shifted from the centre to the east, to kingdoms such as Kediri and Singhasari. On mainland South-East Asia too, a number of states jostled for power, the most important being the Burmese kingdom centred on Pagan and the Khmer state with its capital at Angkor.

sites: (colour coded according to date of occupation)

- ● 9th-early 11th century
- ● 10th-13th century
- ● late 11th-13th century
- ⚓ island port

Buddhist Asia

Buddhism, one of the world's great religions, is widely practised today. It was founded nearly 2500 years ago in north-east India by Siddhartha Gautama (the Buddha), who lived between 563 and 483 BC. From north-eastern India, his doctrine spread to the countries of East and South-East Asia, and many magnificent monuments to Buddhism remain throughout the region.

The essential aim of Buddhism is to achieve a release from the endless cycle of suffering and rebirth which is retribution for the misdeeds of previous existences. This release is sought through good works, discipline and meditation, and the final goal is to reach total enlightenment or *nirvana*. The spiritual quest is exemplified in the legendary life of Gautama himself. After his death, a group of his followers established a monastic order and began to collect the Buddha's preachings. Buddhist sects were divided according to principles. Theravada or Southern Buddhism which spread to Thailand and Indo-China concentrated on individual monastic discipline, while Mahayana or Northern Buddhism had a more universal nature, with the emphasis on the supernatural character of Buddhas and *Bodhisattvas* (semi-divine beings who helped mortals achieve salvation). It was mainly this form of Buddhism that spread to China, Japan and East Asia. Monasteries and monks formed an integral part of Buddhism. Originally monks were wanderers, who begged for food, but gradually monasteries evolved from groups of huts to substantial buildings. Monasteries are most important in Theravada Buddhism: according to its creed only monks can reach *nirvana*.

The earliest Buddhist monuments date from the 3rd century BC, when Asoka, the Mauryan emperor of India (*page 188*), erected great stone columns surmounted by figures of animals and the Wheel of the Buddhist Law throughout his empire, and built *stupas*, the most famous of which is at Sanchi. The principal forms of early Buddhist art derived primarily from symbolic depictions of the events of Gautama's life. With the development of the Mahayana doctrine in the 1st century AD, which offered universal salvation, images of the Buddha began to appear in human form, notably in central India (Mathura), where the Buddha is shown preaching or meditating. The making of images was in itself considered a meritorious deed, so these images were repeated in great numbers wherever Buddhism spread, and many are still standing today, reflecting the adoption and dissemination of Buddhism.

The Silk Road, important since 200 BC, contributed to the spread of Buddhism in the north. By the 6th century AD monasteries, functioning as resting places and banks for travellers, were established all along the route through Central Asia to China. Some Silk Road towns consisted almost exclusively of monasteries and *stupas*. Between the 4th and 14th centuries AD, cave temples were cut into the cliffs of this region and adorned with splendid wall paintings and polychrome clay or stucco images of the Buddha and the Mahayana pantheon. Many of these cave-temple complexes survive today. At Dunhuang, for example, there are some 460 caves filled with images.

Further east, in Korea, an artificial cave-temple was built in the 8th century at Sokkuram near the Shilla capital of Kyongju, housing a magnificent granite Buddha and with attendant images in low relief on the walls.

The Chinese capitals of Luoyang and Chang'an once boasted Buddhist monasteries of unparalleled magnificence, but these were destroyed during phases of persecution, and only a handful of wooden buildings of early date survive. More evidence for the wooden architecture of Buddhist temples is to be found in Japan, such as the 7th century five-storey pagoda and Golden Hall of the Horyuji at Nara.

No less impressive are the Buddhist monuments of South-East Asia and Indonesia: the terraces of Borobudur on Java; at Angkor in Cambodia (*see page 258*), vast stone temples survive from the Khmer civilisation of the 12th and 13th centuries. At Pagan in Burma several thousand temples stood within 41 square kilometres – 2000 are still standing. In Thailand, the gilded images at Ayutthaya show influence both from Burma and from the Khmer. Further north in Tibet, the Potala Palace at Lhasa survives as a showpiece, but many other monasteries of Lamaistic Buddhism have been destroyed in the present century.

Buddhism has remained an important religion to this day in Ceylon (Sri Lanka), Burma, Thailand, Japan and Korea. Japan has the most Buddhists, and still has 80,000 temples, many in wood, which have been constantly restored. Elsewhere, despite a slight revival in India and the West, only archaeological remains and museum exhibits tell the story of Buddhism.

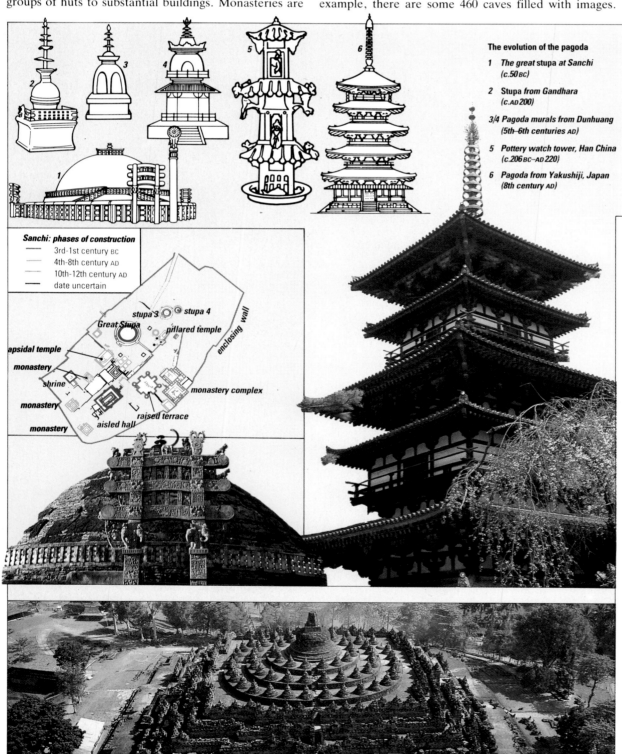

The evolution of the pagoda

1 *The great stupa at Sanchi* (*c.50 BC*)

2 *Stupa from Gandhara* (*c.AD 200*)

3/4 *Pagoda murals from Dunhuang* (*5th–6th centuries AD*)

5 *Pottery watch tower, Han China* (*c.206 BC–AD 220*)

6 *Pagoda from Yakushiji, Japan* (*8th century AD*)

Sanchi: phases of construction
— 3rd-1st century BC
— 4th-8th century AD
— 10th-12th century AD
— date uncertain

stupa 3
stupa 4
Great Stupa
pillared temple
enclosing wall
apsidal temple
monastery
shrine
monastery
monastery complex
raised terrace
aisled hall

2 BUDDHIST MONUMENTS: STUPAS AND PAGODAS

The Indian *stupa* (ritual centre of a monastery) consists of a square base surmounted by a hemispherical mound with a central mast, crowned with *chatras* or ceremonial umbrellas. The whole may be surrounded by an enclosure, as at Sanchi (*lower left*). The pagoda of East Asia consists of several storeys and is based partly on the Chinese watch tower form, but its central mast crowned by a finial preserves the original *stupa* form of a square base and hemispherical dome, with multiple *chatras* at the top. Most surviving wooden pagodas are in Japan, such as the 8th century pagoda at the Yakushiji temple (*lower left*). At Borobudur in Java, the square base of the *stupa* takes on a more complex form of five square and four circular terraces, forming a three-dimensional *mandala* or cosmic diagram (*bottom*).

3 BUDDHIST ART

The cave-temples of India, Central Asia and China are amongst the most important Buddhist monuments. Those of Ajanta in India (*page 188*), dating from the 6th and 7th centuries AD, contain wall paintings of the highest quality, such as the *Bodhisattva* shown here. The largest complexes, such as the Fengxiansi at the Longmen cave-temples near Luoyang in Henan province, completed in 672–675, were undertaken with imperial or state patronage.

A *Wall painting of Bodhisattva from Ajanta cave-temple, India. 6th–7th century AD, height of figure 130cm.* B *Korean decorated bell with a dragon-shaped suspension loop Koryo period, bronze, 13th century AD, height 1.4m.*

C *Carved Buddha from the Longmen cave-temples near Luoyang in Henan province, China. AD 672–675, height of figure 16m.*

A

B

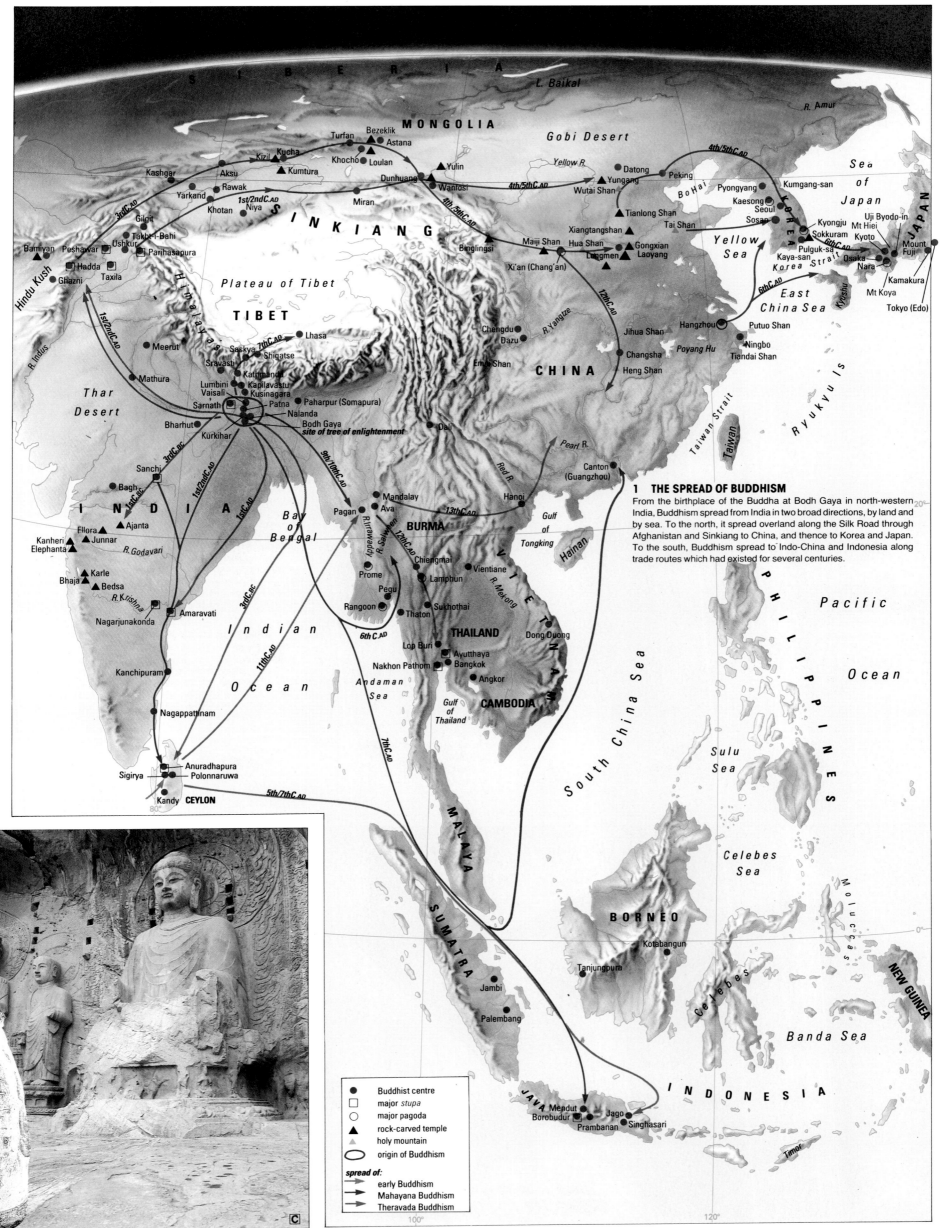

SIBERIA

L. Baikal

R. Amur

MONGOLIA

Gobi Desert

Turfan
Bezeklik
Astana
Kizil
Kucha
Kumtura
Khocho
Loulan
Yulin
Datong
Peking
Yungang
Wutai Shan
4th/5thC.AD

Kashgar
Aksu
Rawak
Yarkand
Khotan
Niya
Dunhuang
Wanfosi
Miran
4th/5thC.AD
4th/5thC.AD

Gilgit
Ushkur
Bamiyan
Peshawar
Takht-i-Bahi
Parihasapura
Hadda
Ghazni
Taxila

Hindu Kush

1st/2ndC.AD

Tianlong Shan
Maiji Shan
Binglingsi
Xiangtangshan
Hua Shan
Gongxian
Laoyang
Xi'an (Chang'an)
Longmen

Pyongyang
Kumgang-san
Kaesong
Seoul
Sosan
Kyongju
Sokkuram
Pulguk-sa
Kaya-san
Kyushu

Uji Byodo-in
Mt Hiei
Kyoto
Osaka
Nara
Mt Koya
Kamakura
Tokyo (Edo)
Mount Fuji

JAPAN

Sea of Japan

Yellow Sea

Korea Strait

6thC.AD

East China Sea

6thC.AD

Plateau of Tibet

TIBET

Lhasa
Saskya
Shigatse
7thC.AD

Meerut
Mathura
Sravasti
Kathmandu
Lumbini
Kapilavastu
Vaisali
Sarnath
Kusinagara
Patna
Paharpur (Somapura)
Nalanda
Bodh Gaya
site of tree of enlightenment
Bharhut
Kurkihar

Thar Desert

INDIA

1st/2ndC.AD

Chengdu
Dazu
Emei Shan
Changsha
Heng Shan

CHINA

Jihua Shan
Hangzhou
Putuo Shan
Ningbo
Tiandai Shan

R. Yangtze

12thC.AD

Ryukyus

3rdC.BC

Sanchi
Bagh

1st/2ndC.AD
1stC.AD

Bay of Bengal

Pagan
Mandalay
Ava
BURMA

13thC.AD

Hanoi

Canton (Guangzhou)

Pearl R.

Red R.

Gulf of Tongking

Hainan

1 THE SPREAD OF BUDDHISM

From the birthplace of the Buddha at Bodh Gaya in north-western India, Buddhism spread from India in two broad directions, by land and by sea. To the north, it spread overland along the Silk Road through Afghanistan and Sinkiang to China, and thence to Korea and Japan. To the south, Buddhism spread to Indo-China and Indonesia along trade routes which had existed for several centuries.

Ellora
Ajanta
Kanheri
Junnar
Elephanta
Karle
Bhaja
Bedsa

R. Godavari

R. Krishna

Amaravati
Nagarjunakonda

9th/10thC.AD

Irrawaddy

Prome
Pegu
Rangoon
Thaton

12thC.AD

R. Salween

Chiengmai
Lamphun
Sukhothai

Vientiane

R. Mekong

VIETNAM

Indian Ocean

3rdC.BC

6th C.AD

11thC.AD

Kanchipuram

Nagappatinam

Andaman Sea

Lop Buri
Nakhon Pathom
Ayutthaya
Bangkok
Angkor

THAILAND

Dong Duong

CAMBODIA

Gulf of Thailand

Pacific Ocean

South China Sea

PHILIPPINES

Sulu Sea

7thC.AD

Sigirya
Anuradhapura
Polonnaruwa
Kandy CEYLON

5th/7thC.AD

MALAYA

SUMATRA

Celebes Sea

BORNEO

Kotabangun

Tanjungpura

Moluccas

NEW GUINEA

Jambi

Palembang

JAVA
Mendut
Borobudur
Prambanan
Jago
Singhasari

INDONESIA

Banda Sea

Celebes

Timor

● Buddhist centre
□ major *stupa*
○ major pagoda
▲ rock-carved temple
▲ holy mountain
⬭ origin of Buddhism

spread of:
→ early Buddhism
→ Mahayana Buddhism
→ Theravada Buddhism

Tang and Sung China

China was finally unified under the Tang in 618, having undergone a long period of instability and vulnerability after the collapse of the Han dynasty (*page 194*). Both under the Tang and its successor, the Sung (Song) dynasty, China was to reach new cultural heights.

The vast empire of the Tang, extending into Central Asia, with a population of c.60 million people, has left surprisingly few remains. Most impressive are the colossal royal tombs to the north of Chang'an, which are yet to be excavated. The visible remains also include a series of highly decorated cave temples in the Central Asian territories, a few stone buildings, and a handful of wooden monastic buildings. However, excavations at one of Tang China's two great capital cities, Chang'an, have revealed many details of its plan, walls, gates, markets, streets and public buildings, which can be correlated with literary evidence to build up a detailed picture of the ancient city. Among the most important discoveries are the remains of the royal palace, and three royal tombs which contained rich funerary objects and magnificent wall paintings of court life.

To the west of Chang'an was a great Tang monastery. In the treasury were found Buddhist reliquaries, known from contemporary literature, together with a huge and well-preserved hoard of textiles, garments, silverware and ceramics. Outside the capital, excavations of abandoned cities in the Tarim Basin reveal completely lost Indo-European and Persian cultures, with beautiful sculpture, wall paintings and written documents that show the links between China and Central Asia. Also of immense importance is the caravan city and centre of Buddhist pilgrimage at Dunhuang, where hundreds of elaborately decorated cave shrines survive. Dunhuang also yielded up a huge cache of books and documents, hidden during an 11th-century invasion, which included the oldest examples of printing yet discovered in China.

The Tang was a period in which China was still rooted politically and economically in the north. After about 755, partly because of political developments – including

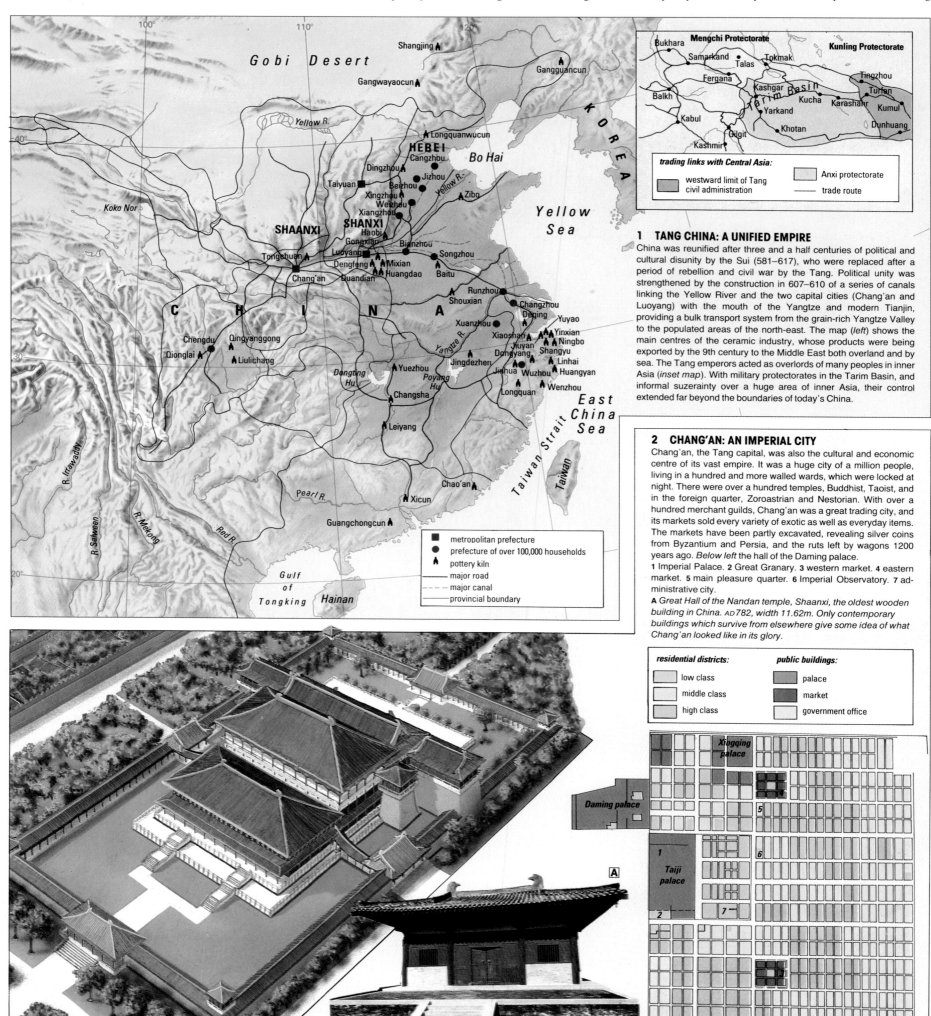

1 TANG CHINA: A UNIFIED EMPIRE

China was reunified after three and a half centuries of political and cultural disunity by the Sui (581–617), who were replaced after a period of rebellion and civil war by the Tang. Political unity was strengthened by the construction in 607–610 of a series of canals linking the Yellow River and the two capital cities (Chang'an and Luoyang) with the mouth of the Yangtze and modern Tianjin, providing a bulk transport system from the grain-rich Yangtze Valley to the populated areas of the north-east. The map (*left*) shows the main centres of the ceramic industry, whose products were being exported by the 9th century to the Middle East both overland and by sea. The Tang emperors acted as overlords of many peoples in inner Asia (*inset map*). With military protectorates in the Tarim Basin, and informal suzerainty over a huge area of inner Asia, their control extended far beyond the boundaries of today's China.

2 CHANG'AN: AN IMPERIAL CITY

Chang'an, the Tang capital, was also the cultural and economic centre of its vast empire. It was a huge city of a million people, living in a hundred and more walled wards, which were locked at night. There were over a hundred temples, Buddhist, Taoist, and in the foreign quarter, Zoroastrian and Nestorian. With over a hundred merchant guilds, Chang'an was a great trading city, and its markets sold every variety of exotic as well as everyday items. The markets have been partly excavated, revealing silver coins from Byzantium and Persia, and the ruts left by wagons 1200 years ago. *Below left* the hall of the Daming palace.

1 Imperial Palace. 2 Great Granary. 3 western market. 4 eastern market. 5 main pleasure quarter. 6 Imperial Observatory. 7 administrative city.

A *Great Hall of the Nandan temple, Shaanxi, the oldest wooden building in China. AD782, width 11.62m. Only contemporary buildings which survive from elsewhere give some idea of what Chang'an looked like in its glory.*

trading links with Central Asia:

westward limit of Tang civil administration	Anxi protectorate
	trade route

metropolitan prefecture
prefecture of over 100,000 households
pottery kiln
major road
major canal
provincial boundary

residential districts:
low class
middle class
high class

public buildings:
palace
market
government office

the loss of the north-west and the dominions in Central Asia – China began to be oriented more and more towards the south. Foreign contacts continued, but the shipping routes from China to India and the Persian Gulf were now far more important than the camel caravans on the old Silk Road. By the Sung period China was a major maritime power, and her shipping ranged freely throughout South-East Asia and the Indian Ocean. Chinese coins and porcelain have been found on the coasts of the Straits of Hormuz and Arabia. One reason for this was the Chinese invention of the mariner's compass. Yet Sung China was far more remote from the outside world than during the Tang. Then foreign influences, from Buddhist philosophy to grape wine and Central Asian music were everywhere. While Sung culture was inward looking, suspicious of the world beyond China.

Sung China was nevertheless much richer and more populous than the Tang. The majority of more than 100 million people lived in the Yangtze Valley or in the south. Regions such as Fujian, backwaters in the 8th century, now became major centres of sophisticated culture. Unfortunately, most of the great Sung cities have remained important urban centres until today, making systematic archaeological investigations impossible. Moreover, burial practices changed, and the tombs of even the most important men were no longer the strong and extensive structures of early Tang times. Nor were their funerary furnishings as lavish. However, many Sung buildings and artefacts of all sorts have survived, and there is still a rich body of Sung painting, ceramics and printed books.

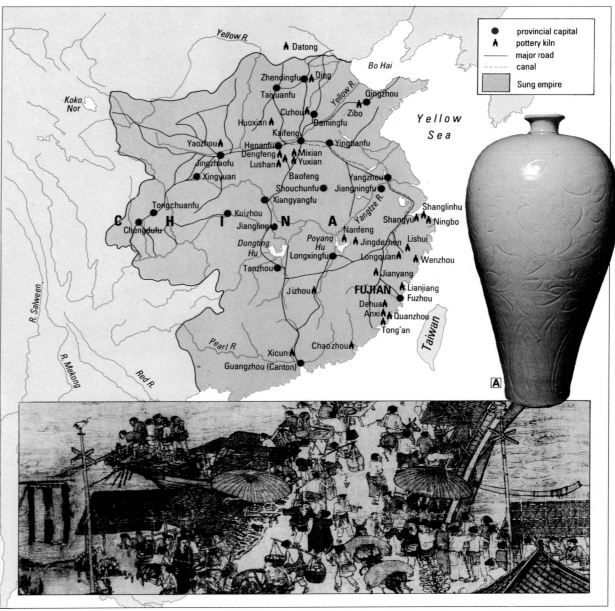

4 SUNG CHINA

The Sung capital, Kaifeng, was a great mercantile city adopted as a capital, whereas Tang Chang'an was purpose-built as a symbolic seat of power. Kaifeng was on the canal to the south, and the centre of a major industrial region, with an iron industry using coal for smelting. The Sung even manufactured prefabricated cast-iron pagodas. During the Sung period, China's 'centre of gravity' – political, cultural and economic alike – moved from northern China to the Yangtze. The network of trade still included camel caravans to inner Asia, but water-borne traffic became more dominant. The Spring festival scroll (right) drawn in about 1120, illustrates the bustling life of Kaifeng and its water-borne traffic. Perhaps the most beautiful Sung artefacts are ceramics.

A *Ding vase with carved decoration from Hebei province. c.11th–12th century AD, porcelain, height 36.3cm.*

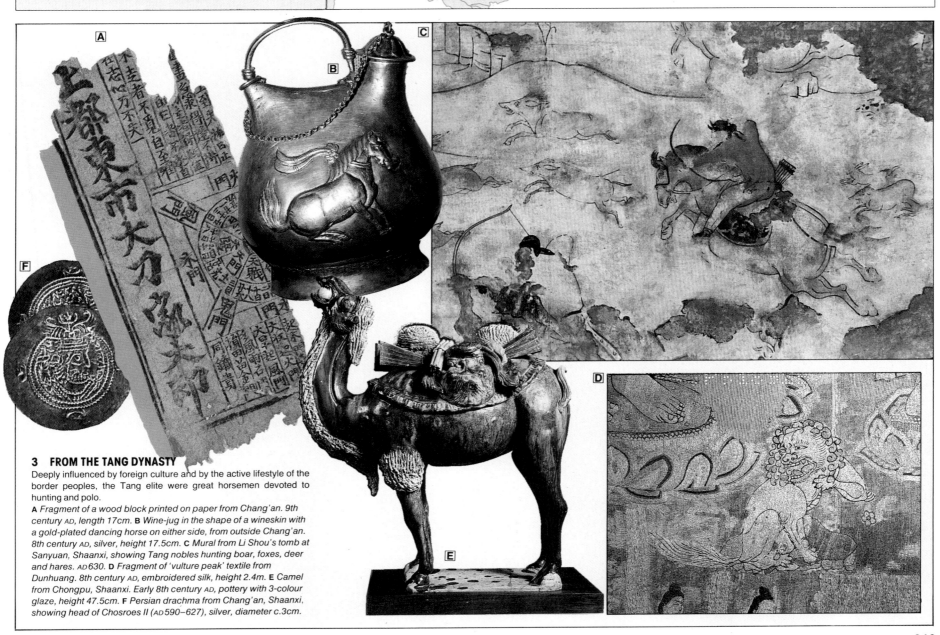

3 FROM THE TANG DYNASTY

Deeply influenced by foreign culture and by the active lifestyle of the border peoples, the Tang elite were great horsemen devoted to hunting and polo.

A *Fragment of a wood block printed on paper from Chang'an. 9th century AD, length 17cm.* B *Wine-jug in the shape of a wineskin with a gold-plated dancing horse on either side, from outside Chang'an. 8th century AD, silver, height 17.5cm.* C *Mural from Li Shou's tomb at Sanyuan, Shaanxi, showing Tang nobles hunting boar, foxes, deer and hares. AD 630.* D *Fragment of 'vulture peak' textile from Dunhuang. 8th century AD, embroidered silk, height 2.4m.* E *Camel from Chongpu, Shaanxi. Early 8th century AD, pottery with 3-colour glaze, height 47.5cm.* F *Persian drachma from Chang'an, Shaanxi, showing head of Chosroes II (AD 590–627), silver, diameter c.3cm.*

Ming China

Founded in 1368 by an itinerant Buddhist monk turned soldier, the Ming was the last native dynasty to rule China. Its predecessor, the Sung (Song), fell first to the incursions of a northern people called the Jurchen and finally to the Mongols, who had conquered most of China by 1280. The Mongol occupation of China was short-lived. In less than a century Mongol power over the central provinces of China began to slacken; rebellions and uprisings became common by the 1350s. It was under these conditions that the first Ming emperor came to power. He established a despotic imperial regime that endured for almost three centuries until the Manchu, another northern people, occupied Peking, the Ming capital, in 1644 and established the Ching dynasty (1644–1911).

By far the most important and spectacular Ming site excavated to date is the tomb of Wanli, the emperor between 1573 and 1620, one of 13 imperial tombs in the valley of the Ming tombs north of Peking, and one of the largest. The entrance to the burial chamber was discovered by chance. Noticing that some bricks in an outer wall of the burial complex were loose, archaeologists removed them and found an archway leading to a tunnel filled with earth. The tunnel ended at a small stela with directions to the main entrance of the burial chamber. The stela had apparently been inadvertently left in place when the tomb was closed for the last time. The great self-locking marble doors of the burial chamber were opened by inserting a strong but flexible strip of metal through the doors and using it to dislodge marble columns that had fallen into place behind the doors when they were shut for the last time. The grave-goods from this imperial tomb were particularly rich. They included numerous gold and silver utensils, brocade fabrics, clothing and personal effects of the emperor and his consorts, and the imperial regalia. The 'phoenix crown' of the empress stands out as one of the most remarkable objects from the tomb.

A number of tombs belonging to **princes** and other members of the Ming imperial clan have also been excavated. At Zouxian, the tomb of Zhu Tan (1370–1390), the tenth son of the first Ming emperor, contained clothing, lacquer furniture, several scroll paintings on silk, an antique zither dated 1164, a number of rare 13th- and 14th-century printed books, and an elaborately carved retinue of over 400 small wooden figures. His tomb and grave-goods are typical of the relatively sumptuous princely burials of the early Ming period. The tomb of Zhu Yuelian at Fenghuang Shan, the most elaborate princely tomb discovered to date, contained a full-scale multicoloured ceramic facade of an ancestral hall as well as a collection of over 500 glazed ceramic figurines comprising the prince's retinue, all ranged about a ceramic model of his carriage. During the course of the 16th century princely burials became less elaborate, but the grave-goods often included exquisite objects from the early Ming period.

Several other Ming tombs have yielded objects of value to the history of medicine, clothing, commerce and daily life in Ming China. The tomb of Xia Quan (1348–1411), a 14th-century doctor, at Jiangyin, contained a collection of medical instruments and texts that shed new light on 14th-century medical practices. At Nanyuan the tomb of Xia Ru (1467–1515), father-in-law of the tenth Ming emperor, contained over 83 articles of clothing and bedding in a state of near-perfect preservation, the most important find of Ming clothing and textiles to date. Articles of clothing from this and other Ming tombs indicate that male members of the Ming imperial clan wore a Mongolian style of dress. The tomb of Wei Quan (d.1495), the eunuch administrator of maritime trade at Canton from 1476 to 1488, contained several foreign coins, including a Venetian silver coin minted between 1457 and 1462, indicating that China had commercial relations with the Mediterranean world before the end of the 15th century.

Recent excavations have also confirmed the official records of great maritime expeditions in the early 15th century. Between 1405 and 1433 at least six expeditions sailed from Ming China to South-East Asia, India, and Arabia; on at least two occasions parts of the fleet reached the east coast of Africa. According to the records, the largest ships were reported to have exceeded 122 metres in length. In 1957 a wooden rudder beam 11 metres long was excavated at the site of the shipyards where these ships were built, and it has been calculated that the ship for which this rudder was fashioned must have been between 146 and 160 metres long, confirming that the figures in the official history are not exaggerated.

Many known Ming sites and tombs remain untouched, but the small proportion which have been excavated give a clear indication of the splendour of the Ming court, and hint at the great wealth of information about the Chinese past which lies, as yet, undisturbed.

5 COURTLY SPLENDOUR

A The phoenix crown of Empress Xiaoqing, from the tomb of the emperor Wanli. c. AD 1613, frame of lacquered bamboo, surmounted by gold, kingfisher feathers, precious and semi-precious stones, diameter 23.7 cm. **B** Miniature furnishings from the tombs of Pan Hui (d. 1587) and Pan Yunzheng (d. 1589). **Left** wooden bed with woven mat, height 36 cm. **Right** low table with traces of red lacquer, height 3.7 cm and brass pot with lid, height 7 cm. These furnishings were probably typical of a middle-class Shanghai household. **C** Portrait of Zhu Yijun (1563–1620), the emperor Wanli, whose 48-year reign was the longest in the Ming dynasty. **D** Blue and white vase with bird from Jingdezhen. Early 15th century AD, porcelain, height 10.8 cm. **E** The multifarious splendours of the imperial capital, a handscroll depicting life in Peking. This detail shows vendors' stalls set up by the city's main southern gate. c. AD 1609, painted silk, total length 21 m.

Dingling: the emperor Wanli's tomb

platform with 3 coffins and treasure chests — *burial chamber* — *exit corridor* — *platform for coffin* — *central hall* — *outer hall* — *marble thrones* — *exit corridor* — *side chamber* — *marble door with self-locking mechanism* — *marble door* — *antechamber* — *entrance*

4 DINGLING: THE EMPEROR WANLI'S TOMB

The emperor Wanli selected the site for his final resting place in 1583, when he was still in his early twenties. The entire tomb complex, including both the underground vaults and the halls and ritual buildings above ground, was built between 1583 and 1590, for the enormous sum of 227 tonnes of silver. 30 years later in 1620 the emperor was buried in his magnificent tomb with two women whom he was never fond of in life: his first empress, and the mother of his eldest son and successor, who was raised to imperial status by her son when he became emperor.

The valley of the Ming tombs

1 Deling
2 Jingling
3 Xianling
4 Qingling
5 Yuling
6 Maoling
7 Tailing
8 Kangling
9 Zhaoling
10 concubine cemeteries
11 Siling

Changling — *Yongling* — *Dingling* — *reservoir*

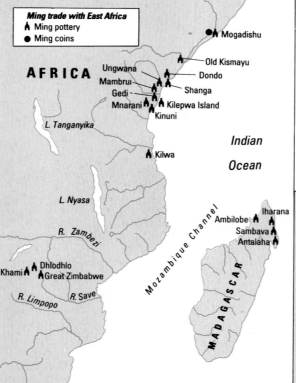

Ming trade with East Africa
🏺 Ming pottery
⬤ Ming coins

AFRICA — Mogadishu — Old Kismayu — Ungwana — Dondo — Mambrui — Shanga — Gedi — Mnarani — Kilepwa Island — Kinuni — Kilwa — L. Tanganyika — L. Nyasa — R. Zambezi — Khami — Dhlodhlo — Great Zimbabwe — R. Limpopo — R. Save — Indian Ocean — Mozambique Channel — Ambilobe — Iharana — Sambava — Antalaha — MADAGASCAR

International trade: finds of Ming porcelain

NORTH AMERICA — EUROPE — AFRICA — CHINA — Pacific Ocean — Acapulco — Pacific Ocean — Atlantic Ocean — Indian Ocean — Manila

3 THE MING: WORLDWIDE TRADE

At least two of the great Chinese naval expeditions of the early 15th century reached the east coast of Africa. While these voyages were undertaken primarily for political and diplomatic reasons, they had great ramifications for international trade, because the rudders and navigational charts developed during these voyages enabled maritime trade routes to be opened up and charted from the coast of China to the coast of Africa.

Although Chinese porcelain from earlier periods has been found on the east coast of Africa, much of it dates from the 14th century and later, when a flourishing trade developed (*see map left*). Chinese porcelain has been found far inland at Great Zimbabwe as well as all along the coast south from Mogadishu. After the Spanish reached Manila in the 1560s, another trade route was opened across the Pacific, and vast quantities of Ming porcelain were shipped via Acapulco to Europe (*see map above*).

2 PEKING: AN IMPERIAL CITY

From about 1400 to 1600 Peking, the principal capital of the Ming empire, was the largest and most populous city on earth. Detailed studies based on excavations, literary and visual records and later maps have enabled archaeologists to reconstruct the city as it stood in about 1600 (*plan right*). An imperial capital has stood on or near the site of modern Peking since the 10th century; the present city preserves the basic plan of the Ming capital. The Ming capital originally comprised three walled enclosures. At the centre was the palace city (now called the Forbidden City), which contained the imperial residential and audience palaces. Around it was the imperial city, which contained the offices of the eunuch bureaucracy, gardens, parks, storehouses, and factories. A hard-tamped earth wall faced with brick surrounded the entire city. In 1553 another wall was built to protect the southern suburbs of the city and the Altar to Heaven, which had been pillaged by the Mongols when they raided Peking in 1550. Thereafter the northern part of the city was called the inner city and the southern part enclosed by the new wall, the outer city. The walls of the northern city ran about 6.5 kilometres east to west and 5.5 kilometres north to south. The walls of the southern city ran about 8 kilometres east to west and 3 kilometres north to south.

To the west of the palace city were the lakes and gardens of the imperial park. After 1500 many Ming emperors chose to reside in this park rather than in the palace city. Most offices of the eunuch bureaucracy were located to the north and north-east of the palace city, while the main offices of the civil and military arms of the imperial government were immediately to the south of it. The military and civil offices stood on either side of the main avenue that ran between the main gate of the northern city and the main gate of the palace city. Audiences were usually held in the southernmost courtyard of the palace city (*see photograph above*). The main commercial centre of the city was located to the south of the inner city. Much more space within the city was devoted to commerce and residential areas than in Han or Tang times, reflecting a trend begun in the Sung period.

1 RECOVERY UNDER THE MING

After the devastation of both population and land under Mongol rule, the Ming emperors set about reviving agriculture, introducing large-scale irrigation, drainage and reafforestation programmes. As a result, the population grew from less than 60 million in 1350 to almost 200 million by 1550. Taxation was reformed, partly to encourage small landowners while a new bureaucratic system was developed to ease provincial administration. Large-scale public works such as canal building and the reconstruction of the Great Wall reflected consolidation and political stability. Industry, especially silk and cotton textiles and ceramics, was developed and trade boomed, easily meeting the challenge of a world market when European traders began to appear in the 17th century.

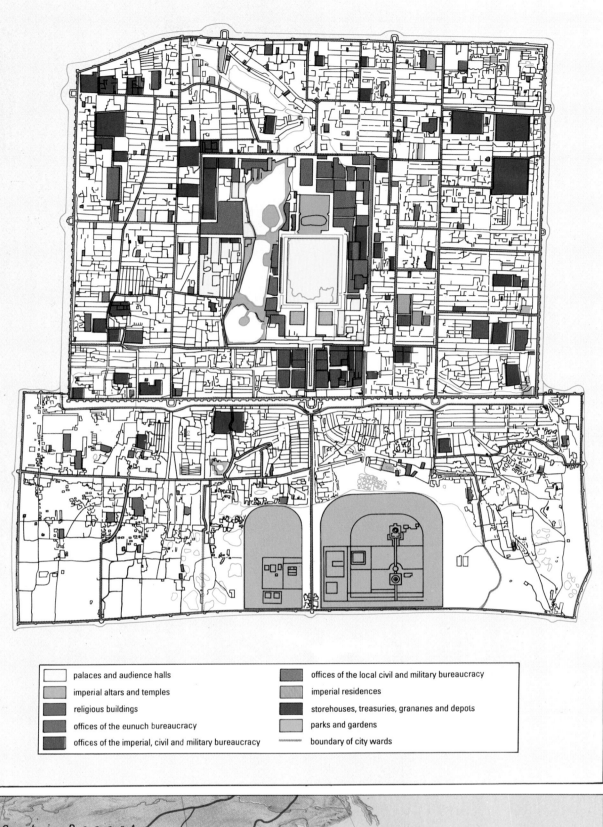

⬜ palaces and audience halls	🟥 offices of the local civil and military bureaucracy
🟩 imperial altars and temples	🟫 imperial residences
🟥 religious buildings	🟥 storehouses, treasuries, granaries and depots
🟥 offices of the eunuch bureaucracy	🟦 parks and gardens
🟥 offices of the imperial, civil and military bureaucracy	— boundary of city wards

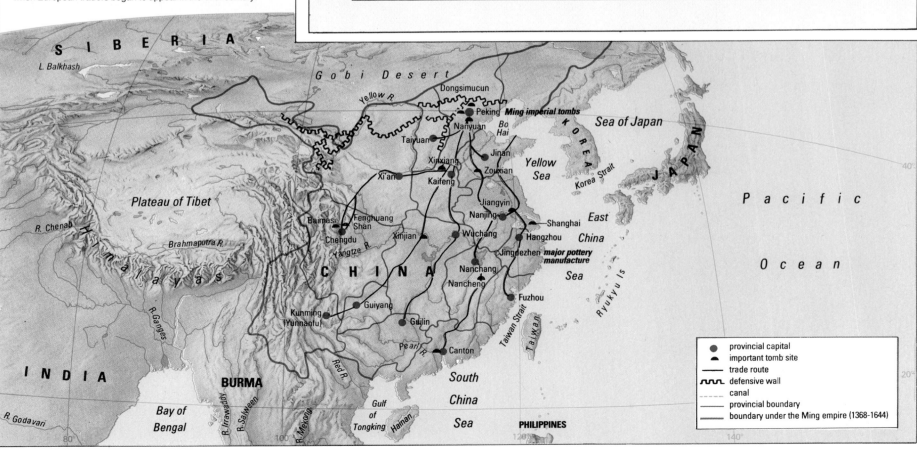

●	provincial capital
▲	important tomb site
—	trade route
ᨃᨃᨃ	defensive wall
- - -	canal
—	provincial boundary
—	boundary under the Ming empire (1368-1644)

Feudal Japan

On both the Korean peninsula and the Japanese islands, the late 7th century AD witnessed the establishment of single, powerful states. Korea was unified under Shilla (*page 196*), and a strong Buddhist state was established lasting until the Koryo period (935–1392). In 1392 Koryo gave way to the Confucian rule of the Yi dynasty which continued for the next five centuries.

In Japan, the consolidation of the Yamato state set the stage for centralised bureaucratic government through the Nara (710–784) and Heian (784–1185) periods. A manorial system of land-holding, however, gave rise to powerful local lords who contributed to the collapse of centralised administration in 1185. A feudal system of government then came into being as the Kamakura shogunate (1185–1333), which operated in addition to the imperial court still located at the Heian capital in present day Kyoto. Vicious internecine rivalry characterised relationships between feudal lords throughout the ensuing Muromachi (1333–1573) and Momoyama (1573–1603) periods until the powerful figure of Tokugawa Ieyasu brought peace and unification, establishing the Tokugawa shogunate in Edo (modern Tokyo) in 1603.

The early rulers of united Shilla and Yamato both followed Chinese models in developing their new political systems. In Japan, the institution of this new system, called Ritsuryo, resulted in enormous changes to the urban landscape: palaces and capital cities were laid out grid-style on a grand scale imitating the Tang capital of Chang'an. The 8th-century Heijo palace at Nara covered more than 4 hectares, and the city around it spread over several square kilometres. Nara is estimated to have housed a population of 200,000, mainly consisting of aristocrats and functionaries employed at court. The Heijo palace was made the centre of the administrative hierarchy, and a parallel religious hierarchy was also created, centred on the Todaiji Temple in Nara. The latter acted as the headquarters of a network of Buddhist monasteries and nunneries, which were constructed near every provincial capital according to a decree promulgated in 742. The Imperial Treasure House, the Shoso-in, was located at the Todaiji itself and is still standing today, complete with its rare 8th-century treasures, many of which were imported from Tang China and places further west via the Silk Road.

Buddhism was adopted by the court in the mid-6th century. Seeking power and prestige the elite immediately began to replace mounded tomb construction with temple building. Several rulers also opted for Buddhist cremation, but as a faith, the esoteric aspects of Buddhism found few adherents. At the same time the native faith, later called Shinto, became more formalised, with its own architectural style, evident in Shinto shrines.

The political use of Buddhism to bolster the power of the state failed when Buddhist monks almost usurped the throne in the late 8th century. To escape the immediate threat of the many monks in the Nara capital, the palace was moved to the Kyoto basin in 784, where the Heian Palace, once established, continued as the imperial seat of government until 1868. *Sutra* texts (discourses of the Buddha) were buried in great numbers in *Sutra* mounds during the late Heian period as the prophesied Buddhist apocalypse grew near. These finds attest to the growth of Buddhism as a mass religion from the 12th century, when Jodo-shinshu developed as a non-esoteric, popular Buddhist sect.

Throughout the Heian period there were changes in the organisation of crafts and industry, leading to the development of market and production-oriented cities in the Kamakura period. The Sue stoneware tradition, which began providing funerary wares in the late 5th century, came to supply the table and service ware needs of palace and temple in the 7th and 8th centuries. Kilns for Sue ware and roof tile manufacture were established near many provincial centres. Sue stoneware inspired the development of several native ceramic traditions, referred to as the Six Old Kilns. These produced rustic, unglazed or ash-glazed wares. Following warlord Hideyoshi's ravaging of the Korean peninsula in the late 16th century, Korean ceramicists were forcibly transplanted to create fine porcelain for Japanese feudal lords.

The development of the warrior code, or *Bushido*, coincided with the introduction of Zen Buddhism and the tea ceremony from China. A set of kilns near present day Nagoya, collectively known as Sanage, specialised in the mass-production of pottery, and demand for tea equipment, particularly bowls, resulted in the establishment of over 400 kilns for firing Yamachawan tea bowls. An important city which grew up in this period was Sakai (near modern Osaka), a port and merchandising centre for western Japan with trade connections to Korea, Okinawa, China and beyond.

3 CRAFTS OF JAPAN

A *Tax tallies from the Heijo Palace in Nara, documenting seaweed sent to the court from Oki Province. They were tied onto the goods during transport. c.AD 717, wooden, length 17cm.* B *The main building of the Todaiji Temple in Nara houses one of the largest bronze Buddha figures in the world. Aristocratic Yamato women were asked to donate their fine bronze mirrors for recasting into the statue. 8th century AD.* C *Tang dynasty lute from the Shoso-in, Nara. c.8th century AD, lacquered with mother-of-pearl inlay, length 100cm.* D *Karatsu ware urn from the Sanage kilns. 13th-14th century AD, natural ash glaze characterises wares of the Heian period, stoneware, height 25.4cm.* E *'Korean Ware' bottle with white and brown glazes from the Karatsu kilns. c.AD 1590-1630, stoneware, height 24.8cm.*

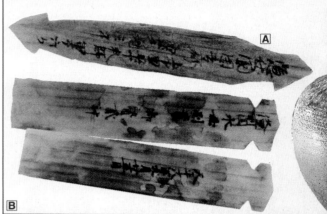

2 YAJIMA-YAKATA: A SAMURAI MANSION

The rise of feudalism from the 12th century in Japan was accompanied by the appearance of the *yakata* type of manor house which housed the warrior elite. Often surrounded by moats, these manor houses consisted of a compound of several buildings. The samurai mansion of Yajima-yakata dates from the 14th century AD and was the residence of an aristocratic samurai warrior. The ditched enclosure measures 150 metres east–west and over 200 metres north–south, and within it were found remains of several buildings, the largest up to eight metres long. Water was obtained from wells.

1 JAPAN UNDER THE SHOGUNS

The territorial hierarchy of the Ritsuryo state focused on main roads (*do*) leading from Nara to the newly designated provinces, some 60 in number. New provincial capitals were built in one-hectare units and manned by central appointees. County centres manned by the local elite were established specifically to gather in the taxes levied by the new administration, which were either stored at the provincial centres or moved to the capital. This territorial system did not extend at first into the northern part of Honshu island, which was occupied by an aboriginal group historically known as Emishi. State expansion into this area was carried out by armed aggression during the 8th and 9th centuries from a series of fortresses established throughout the north and financed from nearby provincial stores. The inset map shows the locations of porcelain kilns established by Korean potters in western Japan after Hideyoshi's continental raids.

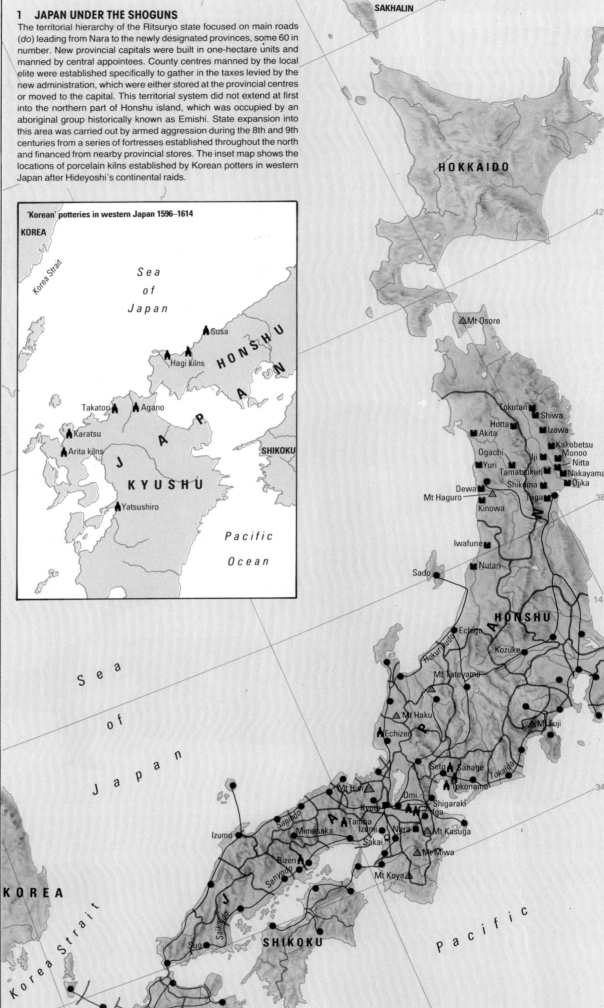

'Korean' potteries in western Japan 1596–1614

	capital
●	provincial capital (only excavated sites named)
—	provincial boundary
△	holy mountain
ᛘ	fortress
⚔	pottery kiln
	road (major roads named)

Islands of Polynesia

Although Lapita settlers reached the Tongan and Samoan Islands of Western Polynesia by at least 1000 BC (*page 200*) it was not until the 1st millennium AD that most of the far-flung islands beyond, extending as far as Hawaii, Easter Island and New Zealand, were first reached by Polynesian colonists. All the major island groups, with the possible exception of New Zealand (*page 270*), were discovered by AD 650, and subsequent Polynesian dispersal in tropical latitudes seems to have been confined to the founding of small island colonies in Melanesia, and to the establishment of temporary settlements on many of the tiny isolated islands of Polynesia which were not close to the major island groups.

Because of their unified and relatively recent origin from Lapita forebears the Polynesians at the time of European contact still retained a high degree of their original physical and linguistic homogeneity. About 35 quite closely related languages had evolved out of the common Proto-Polynesian ancestor, which probably continued as a single language well into the 1st millennium BC. There were marked similarities in religion and society throughout Polynesia. All Polynesian societies had religiously-sanctioned chiefly offices which were inherited within high-ranking families. Certain of the more densely populated islands, such as the Tongan, Samoan, Society and Hawaiian groups, allowed the ruling chiefs surprisingly wide powers to exact deference, labour and tribute from the common folk.

The differences which distinguished Polynesian societies one from another appear to have developed in the conditions of relative isolation which occurred after the initial dispersal. Some of these differences reflect the influences of environment, which ranged from dry atoll to lush fertile volcanic island. In addition, isolation allowed random and idiosyncratic cultural changes to accumulate through time, accounting for the florescence of statue carving on Easter Island, the remarkable reliance on naval warfare in 18th century Tahiti, and the economic dependence on the cultivation of the taro tuber on irrigated terraces in the Hawaiian Islands.

Although pottery making was abandoned with the fading of the Lapita culture early in the 1st millennium AD, and metallurgy never penetrated the Pacific further than western New Guinea, the archaeological record is often very rich and varied. The fact that many remains are relatively recent, and that fully prehistoric lifestyles continued up until the 18th century, means that house and temple foundations of stone and earth still survive. The terraces constructed for taro cultivation across valleys and lowlands in the Hawaiian and Cook Islands lend themselves to intensive archaeological investigation, and the economy of many sites is evident in the bones of fish, shellfish, pig, chicken and dog. But the tropical climate does not often encourage the survival of plant remains, and Polynesian plant staples such as banana, taro, yam, breadfruit and sweet potato (a plant of Andean origin, and evidence for at least some prehistoric contact between Polynesia and South America) rarely leave traces. Cereals such as rice and millet were never carried beyond the western borders of Oceania in prehistoric times.

Artefacts which occur widely at sites throughout Polynesia include shell fishhooks (often of highly nacreous pearl shell), finely flaked and polished stone adzes, and food preparation tools such as stone pounders and shell coconut graters. Recently, excavations in a waterlogged site at Vaitootia on Huahine (Society Islands) have brought to light wooden hand clubs similar to 18th century Maori *patu*, adze handles, bark-cloth beaters, cordage, pieces of coconut and gourd, a canoe steering paddle 3.8 metres long, and even planks from a double canoe. These artefacts date to c. AD 800, and form the oldest collection of organic items so far recovered in Polynesia.

One major feature of the eastern Polynesian archaeological landscape is the type of religious structure commonly termed a *marae*, or *heiau* in Hawaii and *ahu* in Easter Island. *Marae* are generally open-air structures consisting of paved terraces and courts, walls, platforms (sometimes stepped like truncated pyramids), and upright slabs of stone. The Easter Island *ahu*, surmounted by their huge statues, are undoubtedly the best-known of these structures.

Apart from the monuments, the most striking aspect of the Polynesian story is that every island in the tropical Pacific within the great triangle formed by Hawaii, Easter Island and New Zealand, no matter how isolated, was reached at some time by prehistoric Polynesian voyagers. Their achievement stands as perhaps the greatest geographical conquest of human prehistory.

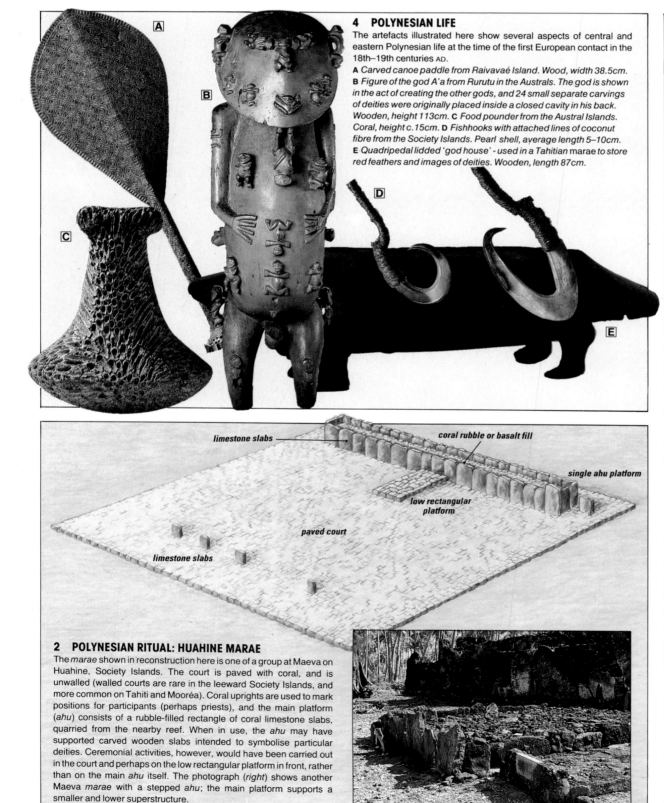

4 POLYNESIAN LIFE
The artefacts illustrated here show several aspects of central and eastern Polynesian life at the time of the first European contact in the 18th–19th centuries AD.
A *Carved canoe paddle from Raivavaé Island. Wood, width 38.5cm.*
B *Figure of the god A'a from Rurutu in the Australs. The god is shown in the act of creating the other gods, and 24 small separate carvings of deities were originally placed inside a closed cavity in his back. Wooden, height 113cm.* C *Food pounder from the Austral Islands. Coral, height c.15cm.* D *Fishhooks with attached lines of coconut fibre from the Society Islands. Pearl shell, average length 5–10cm.* E *Quadripedal lidded 'god house' - used in a Tahitian marae to store red feathers and images of deities. Wooden, length 87cm.*

limestone slabs
coral rubble or basalt fill
single ahu platform
low rectangular platform
paved court
limestone slabs

2 POLYNESIAN RITUAL: HUAHINE MARAE
The *marae* shown in reconstruction here is one of a group at Maeva on Huahine, Society Islands. The court is paved with coral, and is unwalled (walled courts are rare in the leeward Society Islands, and more common on Tahiti and Mooréa). Coral uprights are used to mark positions for participants (perhaps priests), and the main platform (*ahu*) consists of a rubble-filled rectangle of coral limestone slabs, quarried from the nearby reef. When in use, the *ahu* may have supported carved wooden slabs intended to symbolise particular deities. Ceremonial activities, however, would have been carried out in the court and perhaps on the low rectangular platform in front, rather than on the main *ahu* itself. The photograph (*right*) shows another Maeva *marae* with a stepped *ahu*; the main platform supports a smaller and lower superstructure.

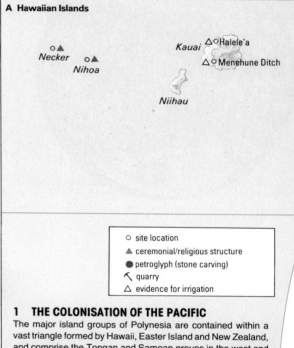

A Hawaiian Islands

Necker
Nihoa
Niihau
Kauai
Halele'a
Menehune Ditch

○ site location
▲ ceremonial/religious structure
● petroglyph (stone carving)
⌐ quarry
△ evidence for irrigation

1 THE COLONISATION OF THE PACIFIC
The major island groups of Polynesia are contained within a vast triangle formed by Hawaii, Easter Island and New Zealand, and comprise the Tongan and Samoan groups in the west and the Cook, Society, Austral, Tuamotu and Marquesas groups in the centre. The islands of New Zealand, Easter Island and Hawaii were settled between one and two thousand years later than Tonga and Samoa, and in general share a high degree of cultural homogeneity.

Archaeological sites in Polynesia include shell middens, remains of houses (generally of timber, but sometimes on stone platforms or pavements; stone corbelled houses only occur on Easter Island), temples (*marae*), burial mounds and cairns (mainly Tonga and Hawaii), stone walled or terraced field systems, adze quarries, and petroglyph fields. The latter are especially common in Hawaii and Easter Island, and the island of Hawaii also has an extensive adze quarry high on the slopes of Mauna Kea. *Marae* are characteristically eastern Polynesian, but the Pulemelei in Western Samoa is also a very large stone platform which may have supported a temple or council house, and the Tongans invested equivalent labour in constructing chiefly burial mounds (Mu'a and Feletoa).

NEW GUINEA
AUS
M E
M

I Tonga
Vava'u
Feletoa
Ha'apai Group

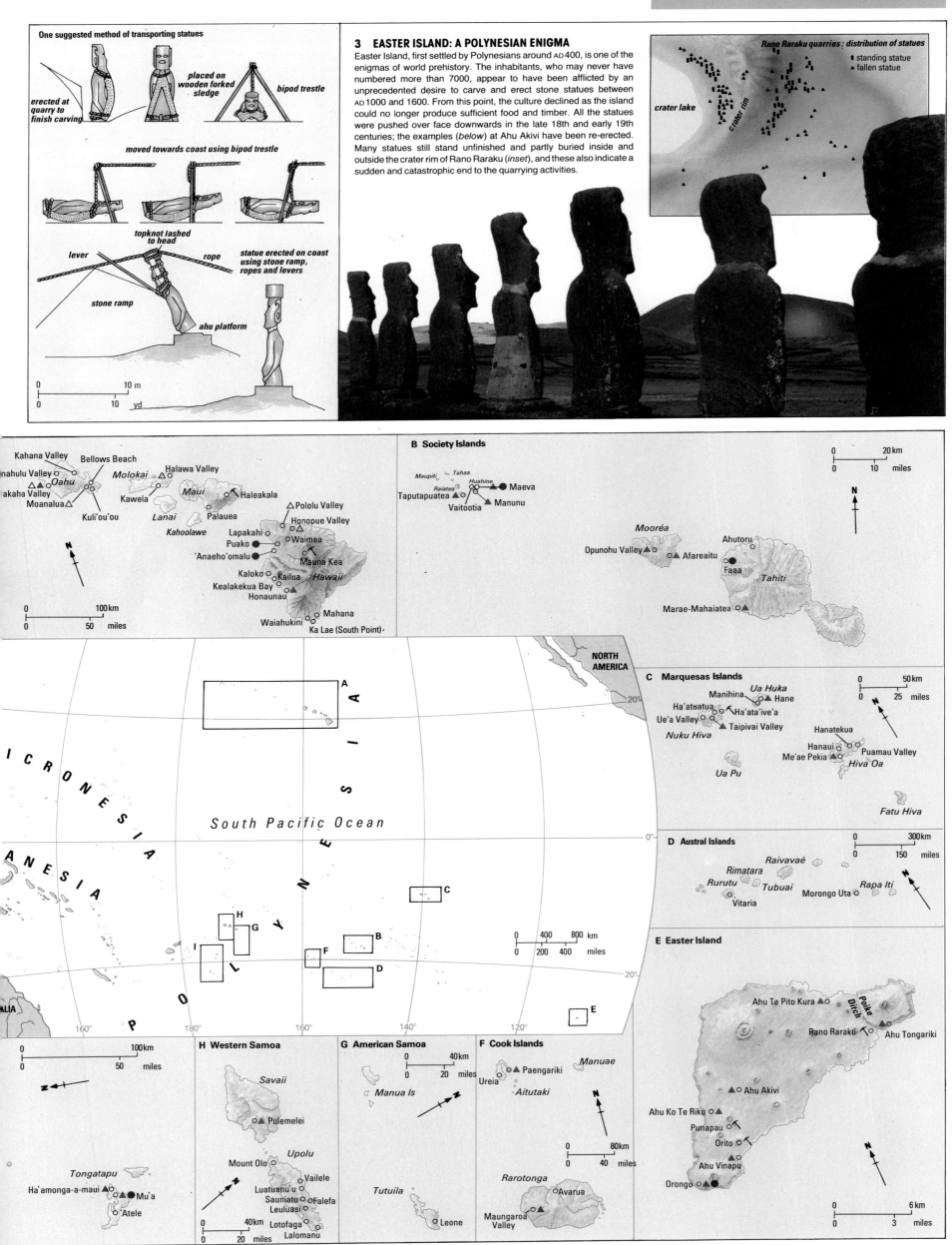

One suggested method of transporting statues

erected at quarry to finish carving — *placed on wooden forked sledge* — **bipod trestle**

moved towards coast using bipod trestle

topknot lashed to head

lever — *rope*

statue erected on coast using stone ramp, ropes and levers

stone ramp — *ahu platform*

0 — 10 m
0 — 10 yd

3 EASTER ISLAND: A POLYNESIAN ENIGMA

Easter Island, first settled by Polynesians around AD 400, is one of the enigmas of world prehistory. The inhabitants, who may never have numbered more than 7000, appear to have been afflicted by an unprecedented desire to carve and erect stone statues between AD 1000 and 1600. From this point, the culture declined as the island could no longer produce sufficient food and timber. All the statues were pushed over face downwards in the late 18th and early 19th centuries; the examples (*below*) at Ahu Akivi have been re-erected. Many statues still stand unfinished and partly buried inside and outside the crater rim of Rano Raraku (*inset*), and these also indicate a sudden and catastrophic end to the quarrying activities.

Rano Raraku quarries: distribution of statues
- ■ standing statue
- ▲ fallen statue
crater lake — *crater rim*

B Society Islands

0 — 20 km
0 — 10 miles

Maupiti — Tahaa — Huahine — Maeva
Raiatea — Manunu
Taputapuatea — Vaitootia

Mooréa — Ahutoru
Opunohu Valley — Afareaitu
Faaa — Tahiti
Marae-Mahaiatea

Kahana Valley — Bellows Beach
nahulu Valley — Halawa Valley
Oahu — Molokai
akaha Valley — Kawela — Maui — Haleakala
Moanalua — Lanai — Pololu Valley
Kuli'ou'ou — Kahoolawe — Palauea — Honopue Valley
Lapakahi — Waimea
Puako — Mauna Kea
'Anaeho'omalu — Hawaii
Kaloko — Kailua
Kealakekua Bay — Honaunau
Mahana
Waiahukini — Ka Lae (South Point)

0 — 100 km
0 — 50 miles

C Marquesas Islands

0 — 50 km
0 — 25 miles

Ua Huka
Manihina — Hane
Ha'atuatua — Ha'ata'ive'a
Ue'a Valley — Taipivai Valley
Nuku Hiva — Hanatekua
Hanaui — Puamau Valley
Me'ae Pekia — Hiva Oa
Ua Pu
Fatu Hiva

D Austral Islands

0 — 300 km
0 — 150 miles

Raivavaé
Rimatara
Ru>rutu — Tubuai — Rapa Iti
Morongo Uta
Vitaria

NORTH AMERICA

A
20°

MICRONESIA
MELANESIA
POLYNESIA

South Pacific Ocean

0°

C

H
G
B
I
F
D
20°

0 — 400 — 800 km
0 — 200 — 400 miles

E

160° — 180° — 160° — 140° — 120°

E Easter Island

Ahu Te Pito Kura
Poike Ditch
Rano Raraku — Ahu Tongariki
Ahu Akivi
Ahu Ko Te Riku
Punapau
Orito
Ahu Vinapu
Orongo

0 — 6 km
0 — 3 miles

0 — 100 km
0 — 50 miles

H Western Samoa

Savaii
Pulemelei
Upolu
Mount Olo — Vailele
Luatuanu'u — Sauniatu — Falefa
Leuluasi
Lotofaga
Lalomanu

0 — 40 km
0 — 20 miles

G American Samoa

0 — 40 km
0 — 20 miles

Manua Is
Tutuila
Leone

F Cook Islands

Manuae
Paengariki
Ureia — Aitutaki

Rarotonga
Avarua
Maungaroa Valley

0 — 80 km
0 — 40 miles

Tongatapu
Ha'amonga-a-maui — Mu'a
Atele

Maori New Zealand

New Zealand was probably the last major landmass in Polynesia to be settled. It was colonised towards the end of the 1st millennium AD by Polynesian agriculturalists, the ancestors of the Maoris. It is not known exactly which island the first settlers came from, but the Cook, Society and Marquesas Islands are the most likely region.

New Zealand is larger than all other islands of Polynesia put together, and has a temperate climate spanning 12 degrees of latitude. Although the first settlers probably tried to introduce a broad range of tropical plant foods and animals, only the sweet potato and the dog were truly successful, while a few other plants, including yam, taro and gourd acquired tenuous footholds in the warmer North Island. The cool climate made agriculture impossible in most of South Island, so here and in the remote Chatham Islands (settled from New Zealand) small mobile populations existed throughout prehistory who were dependent upon fishing, fowling and native plants. In the warmer northern regions, and particularly the central and northern coasts of the North Island, quite dense agricultural populations ultimately evolved, with an economy based on cultivation of the sweet potato and the rhizome of the native bracken fern.

Throughout the country the first settlers and their immediate descendants were able to exploit the advantages of an environment previously without humans, well-stocked with easily caught populations of moas (flightless birds, now extinct), forest birds, sea mammals (especially seals) and shellfish. Consequently, agriculture was for a time not important in those northern regions, although it was never entirely abandoned – as archaeological discoveries of field boundary systems and sweet potato storage pits, some dating to as early as AD 1100, attest. The population of the northern and central North Island apparently came to depend more on agriculture after about 1300, owing in part to a drastic decline in the availability of wild resources. No less than 13 species of moas and 20 other birds were well on the way to extinction by this time. The increasing dependence on agriculture

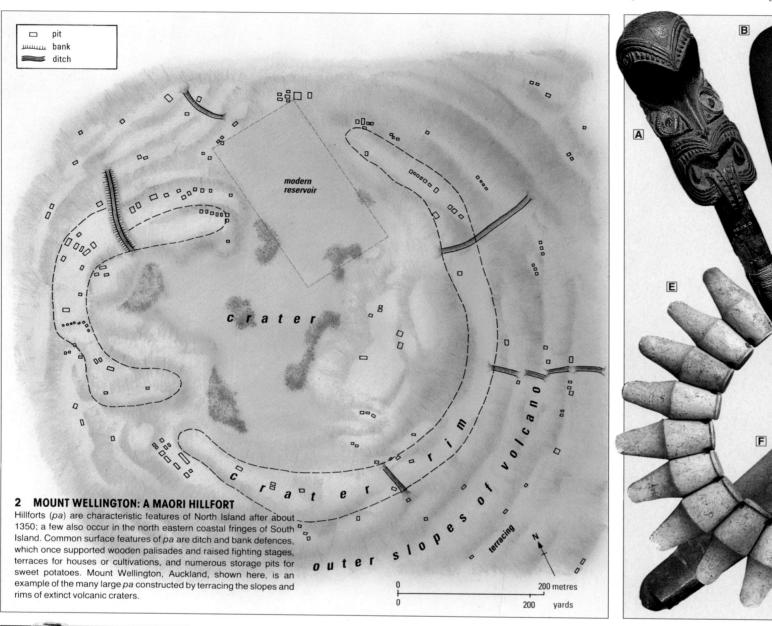

2 MOUNT WELLINGTON: A MAORI HILLFORT

Hillforts (pa) are characteristic features of North Island after about 1350; a few also occur in the north eastern coastal fringes of South Island. Common surface features of pa are ditch and bank defences, which once supported wooden palisades and raised fighting stages, terraces for houses or cultivations, and numerous storage pits for sweet potatoes. Mount Wellington, Auckland, shown here, is an example of the many large pa constructed by terracing the slopes and rims of extinct volcanic craters.

Legend:
- □ pit
- bank
- ditch

Labels: modern reservoir · crater · crater rim · outer slopes of volcano · terracing

0 — 200 metres
0 — 200 yards

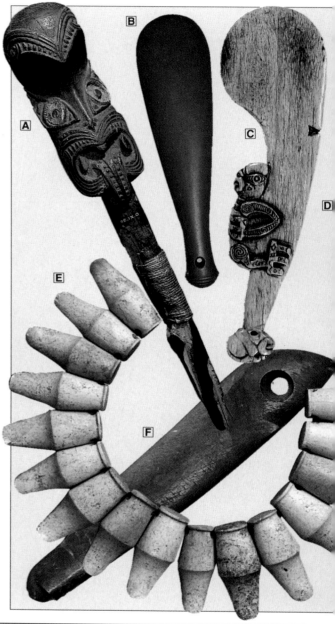

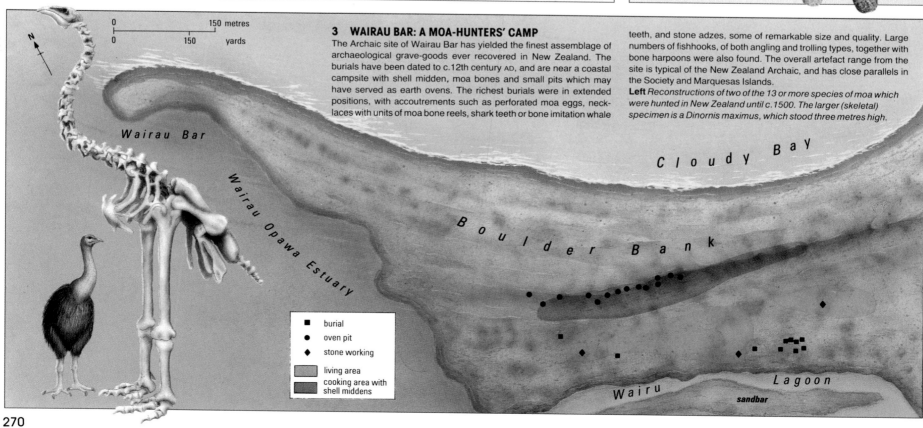

3 WAIRAU BAR: A MOA-HUNTERS' CAMP

The Archaic site of Wairau Bar has yielded the finest assemblage of archaeological grave-goods ever recovered in New Zealand. The burials have been dated to c.12th century AD, and are near a coastal campsite with shell midden, moa bones and small pits which may have served as earth ovens. The richest burials were in extended positions, with accoutrements such as perforated moa eggs, necklaces with units of moa bone reels, shark teeth or bone imitation whale teeth, and stone adzes, some of remarkable size and quality. Large numbers of fishhooks, of both angling and trolling types, together with bone harpoons were also found. The overall artefact range from the site is typical of the New Zealand Archaic, and has close parallels in the Society and Marquesas Islands.

Left Reconstructions of two of the 13 or more species of moa which were hunted in New Zealand until c.1500. The larger (skeletal) specimen is a Dinornis maximus, which stood three metres high.

Labels: Wairau Bar · Wairau Opawa Estuary · Cloudy Bay · Boulder Bank · Wairu · Lagoon · sandbar

Legend:
- ■ burial
- ● oven pit
- ◆ stone working
- living area
- cooking area with shell middens

0 — 150 metres
0 — 150 yards

probably went hand-in-hand with a rise in human population and warfare in the North Island after 1300. On the South Island the population and site numbers declined in later prehistory, evidently because the depletion of natural resources could not be compensated for by agriculture.

This period between c.AD 1000 and 1350 is termed Archaic, while the phase after c.1350 in the North Island, and after c.1650 in the eastern South Island, is called Classic Maori. The North Island Classic is characterised by massive earthwork fortifications and agricultural systems, features which occur only rarely in the South Island. Archaic artefact assemblages are often very similar to those from contemporary central Polynesia, and include items such as polished adzes, fish-hooks of bone, stone and shell, bone pendants and necklaces, bone harpoons and tattooing needles. Richly furnished burials, with grave-goods including such artefacts as well as moa egg water bottles, have been recovered from the site of Wairau Bar in the northern South Island, evident testimony of a society with hereditary social ranking.

During the Classic phase the population increased rapidly, accompanied by a continuing growth of intertribal warfare. Fortresses (*pa*) with terraces, ditches and palisades were constructed on the sides of extinct volcanoes, on steep-sided ridges and promontories, on fairly flat land and in swamps. *Pa* tended to become more numerous and more powerfully defended over time, and accounts of them from the late 18th century describe houses and storehouses around central open spaces (*marae*), and sometimes even cultivation plots within the defences. Waterlogged conditions at *pa* situated in or near swamps have preserved many wooden artefacts, ranging from canoes and house planks to finely carved weapons and hair combs.

Despite their tropical Polynesian origins, so obvious in language, physique and social structure, the Maoris, partly by virtue of their unique temperate environment, succeeded in creating a culture quite different from those of their tropical cousins. The Classic phase in particular, with its fortifications, art, single-hulled canoes and weapon styles, was a striking cultural development. The South Island and Chatham Island Polynesians occupy an interesting position in world anthropology, since they were one of the few populations on record to switch from an agricultural to a hunting and gathering economy.

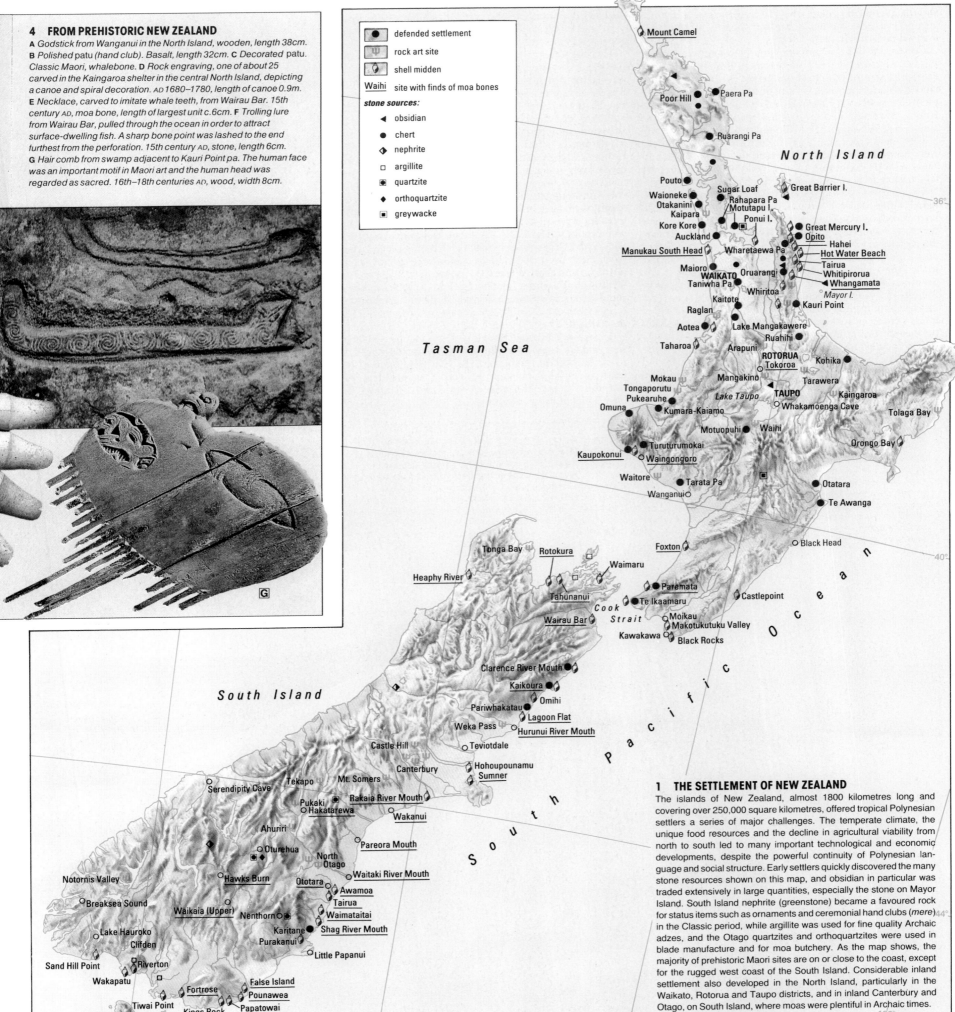

4   FROM PREHISTORIC NEW ZEALAND

A Godstick from Wanganui in the North Island, wooden, length 38cm. **B** Polished patu (hand club). Basalt, length 32cm. **C** Decorated patu. Classic Maori, whalebone. **D** Rock engraving, one of about 25 carved in the Kaingaroa shelter in the central North Island, depicting a canoe and spiral decoration. AD 1680–1780, length of canoe 0.9m. **E** Necklace, carved to imitate whale teeth, from Wairau Bar. 15th century AD, moa bone, length of largest unit c.6cm. **F** Trolling lure from Wairau Bar, pulled through the ocean in order to attract surface-dwelling fish. A sharp bone point was lashed to the end furthest from the perforation. 15th century AD, stone, length 6cm. **G** Hair comb from swamp adjacent to Kauri Point pa. The human face was an important motif in Maori art and the human head was regarded as sacred. 16th–18th centuries AD, wood, width 8cm.

Legend:
- defended settlement
- rock art site
- shell midden
- Waihi — site with finds of moa bones

stone sources:
- obsidian
- chert
- nephrite
- argillite
- quartzite
- orthoquartzite
- greywacke

1   THE SETTLEMENT OF NEW ZEALAND

The islands of New Zealand, almost 1800 kilometres long and covering over 250,000 square kilometres, offered tropical Polynesian settlers a series of major challenges. The temperate climate, the unique food resources and the decline in agricultural viability from north to south led to many important technological and economic developments, despite the powerful continuity of Polynesian language and social structure. Early settlers quickly discovered the many stone resources shown on this map, and obsidian in particular was traded extensively in large quantities, especially the stone on Mayor Island. South Island nephrite (greenstone) became a favoured rock for status items such as ornaments and ceremonial hand clubs (*mere*) in the Classic period, while argillite was used for fine quality Archaic adzes, and the Otago quartzites and orthoquartzites were used in blade manufacture and for moa butchery. As the map shows, the majority of prehistoric Maori sites are on or close to the coast, except for the rugged west coast of the South Island. Considerable inland settlement also developed in the North Island, particularly in the Waikato, Rotorua and Taupo districts, and in inland Canterbury and Otago, on South Island, where moas were plentiful in Archaic times.

The Arctic world

As the ice-sheet retreated at the end of the last Ice Age, groups of hunters began to move into the desolate tundras and taigas of the Arctic north. From c.10,000 BC people who seem to have originated in Central Asia migrated across the Bering land bridge into Arctic America. The Inuit (or Eskimo) are either their direct descendants or are a separate group who came across the Bering Sea at a later stage, in the 3rd millennium BC. Remains of the Inuit are found from Siberia to the eastern coast of Greenland. A parallel development took place in Europe, where hunting groups moved from the east, south and west into Lappland, an area comprising northern Norway, Sweden, Finland and the Kola peninsula of Russia. While the Inuit and the Saami (the inhabitants of Lappland) were distinct groups and there was no contact between them, there are many similarities in their cultures.

Conditions in Lappland are slightly less severe than in Arctic America owing to the warming effect of the Gulf Stream: much of the coast is ice-free in winter, and the land is able to support a variety of fauna, although edible plants are scarce. The Saami lived by hunting, fowling and fishing. Both sea and river fish were caught, as well as some large sea mammals. Elk and bear were frequently hunted, and from the later prehistoric period reindeer were hunted, herded and even used for traction. Elk and reindeer were commonly caught by driving them into pits, which were sometimes reinforced with fences and walls.

The earliest tools used by the Saami were microliths (small stone blades). Gradually new technologies were introduced, many from the east; slate tools, straight-based arrowheads and asbestos-tempered pottery. Comb-dented pottery arrived from the east as early as 3200 BC, and some linguists think that the Saami language, which is in the Finno-Ugrian group, may have accompanied it. The 1st millennium BC saw the arrival of bronzes and moulds, followed by the introduction of iron. Sacrificial sites from historical times have been found with quantities of metal items – coins, brooches, rings and crucifixes from Russia, the eastern Baltic and north-west Europe.

The remains of the Saami can be distinguished by the engraved ornamentation on pottery, wood, antler and bone. At Alta, a large number of rock engravings have been discovered dating to between approximately 4200 BC and 500 BC. Shamanism was the main Saami religion. The

shaman was frequently given special burial, and ritual items, such as shaman's drums, have been discovered. The bear was regarded as sacred, and there was a cult in which the animal was killed, the meat consumed and the bones buried with the skull at the top. Animal sacrifices were also carried out next to unusual trees and stones.

The early Inuit, like the first Saami, used flint micro-lithic tools for cutting and carving bone. They formed a culture known as the Arctic Small Tool tradition, which is found throughout Siberia, Alaska, Canada and Greenland from about 2000 BC. Other stone tools included harpoons, fish spears, small knives and arrowheads. Throughout the prehistoric period, new technologies were introduced: slate and bone tools, pottery, improved harpoons and blubber lamps. Such innovations were often lost, however, only to reappear a few centuries later. Special adaptations to the cold, icy climate were necessary, and this is reflected in finds of bone sledges, snow goggles and ice-creepers.

The dwellings of the early Inuit were generally insubstantial. Many sites, marked by hearths of stone slabs, are located on former beaches. It is thought that they camped there in hide tents, with sleeping places of levelled gravel. By the time of the Dorset culture (AD 800–1000), there had been great improvements. Settlements grew larger, and semi-subterranean winter houses have been excavated which could have accommodated 2–3 families. Fishing and the hunting of sea-mammals and caribou were carried out in season, with improved spears and harpoon heads. In a short space of time, however, the Dorset culture completely disappeared. This could have been the result of changes in food supply, or to their displacement by or incorporation into another group, such as the Thule communities. The Early Thule are found in Alaska, and had a successful economy in which whaling played a large part. They used dog sledges, boats such as kayaks and pottery, and had a settled, permanent lifestyle with well-insulated winter homes. Around AD 1100 there was a rapid expansion eastwards and Thule culture could be found from the east Siberian coast to Greenland. Their descendants are the modern Inuit (Eskimo).

The archaeological remains of the Arctic reflect the tremendous ingenuity of human groups in adapting to the most inhospitable environments. The continuity of their existence is being broken only today, as outsiders try to introduce them to the modern world and discourage their traditional hunting activities.

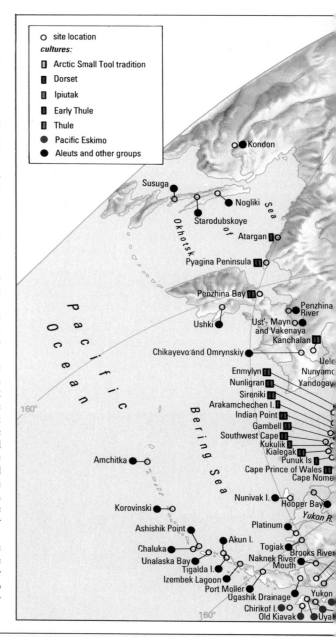

Key:
- ○ site location
- *cultures:*
- Arctic Small Tool tradition
- Dorset
- Ipiutak
- Early Thule
- Thule
- ● Pacific Eskimo
- ● Aleuts and other groups

2 THE SAAMI CULTURE OF LAPPLAND

Archaeological remains in Lappland have given us a good view of the different aspects of Saami life (*see map right*). The portable Saami tent (*below*), known as a *kåta*, would have been used from the 16th century AD, with the advent of migratory reindeer pastoralism. The four curved birch poles locked together by three cross-pieces provided more headroom than a simple conical tent, and a kettle or pot suspended over the hearth gave added stability. The *kåta* is divided into two sections: the sleeping area at the front, and the sacred kitchen with hearth at the back.

Krankmårtenhögen (*right*) is a cemetery site dated AD 1–200. The cremation graves are marked by triangular stone settings, and unburnt bones and antlers were found on top, probably representing animal sacrifices. This type of stone-setting reflects contact with the Scandinavian Iron Age to the south; some Viking cemeteries are similar.
A Part of ski with typical Saami carved decoration. AD 1100, wooden, length 14.7cm. **B** Metal bird deposited at the sacrificial site of Gråträsk, probably imported from Russia. AD 1000–1300. **C** Bear skull from bear cult grave at Värjaren. A metal chain hung from the skull. c. AD 1700.

birch poles

cross-piece

bowed frame

grey felt

kitchen area

cooking pot

stone hearth

reindeer skins

birch twigs

entrance

A

B

C

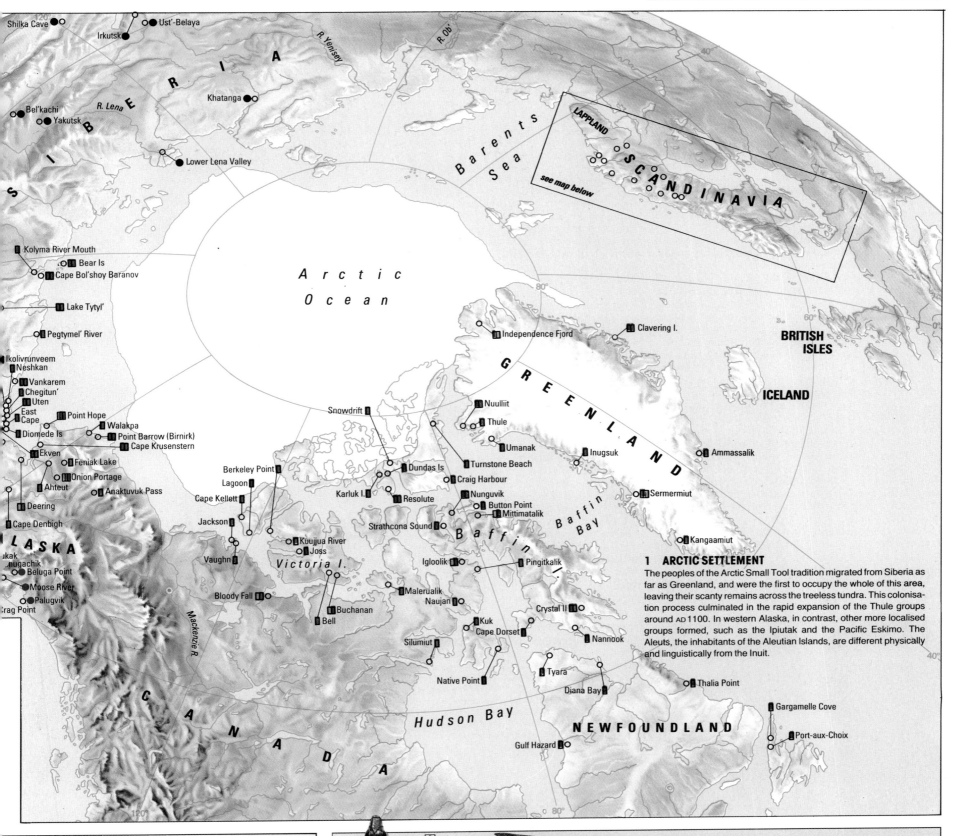

Map 1 labels:

Shilka Cave · Ust'-Belaya · Irkutsk · Bel'kachi · Yakutsk · Khatanga · Lower Lena Valley · R. Yenisey · R. Ob' · R. Lena

Barents Sea · LAPPLAND · SCANDINAVIA · see map below · BRITISH ISLES · ICELAND

Kolyma River Mouth · Bear Is · Cape Bol'shoy Baranov · Lake Tytyl' · Pegtymel' River · Ikolivrunveem · Neshkan · Vankarem · Chegitun' · Uten · East Cape · Point Hope · Walakpa · Diomede Is · Point Barrow (Birnirk) · Cape Krusenstern · Ekven · Feniak Lake · Onion Portage · Ahteut · Anaktuvuk Pass · Deering · Cape Denbigh

Arctic Ocean

Independence Fjord · Clavering I. · GREENLAND · Nuulliit · Thule · Snowdrift · Umanak · Inugsuk · Ammassalik · Turnstone Beach · Dundas Is · Craig Harbour · Sermermiut · Berkeley Point · Karluk I. · Resolute · Nunguvik · Button Point · Mittimatalik · Lagoon · Cape Kellett · Jackson · Strathcona Sound · Kangaamiut · Baffin Bay · Kuujjua River · Joss · Igloolik · Pingitkalik · Vaughn · Victoria I. · Malerualik · Naujan · Bloody Fall · Buchanan · Bell · Kuk · Cape Dorset · Crystal II · Silumiut · Nannook · Native Point · Tyara · Diana Bay · Thalia Point

Mackenzie R. · CANADA · Hudson Bay · NEWFOUNDLAND · Gulf Hazard · Gargamelle Cove · Port-aux-Choix

nugachik · Beluga Point · Moose River · Palugvik · rag Point · ALASKA

1 ARCTIC SETTLEMENT

The peoples of the Arctic Small Tool tradition migrated from Siberia as far as Greenland, and were the first to occupy the whole of this area, leaving their scanty remains across the treeless tundra. This colonisation process culminated in the rapid expansion of the Thule groups around AD 1100. In western Alaska, in contrast, other more localised groups formed, such as the Ipiutak and the Pacific Eskimo. The Aleuts, the inhabitants of the Aleutian Islands, are different physically and linguistically from the Inuit.

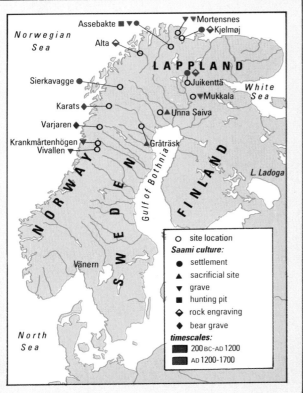

Lappland map labels:

Norwegian Sea · Assebakte · Mortensnes · Alta · Kjelmøj · LAPPLAND · Sierkavagge · Juikenttä · Karats · Mukkala · White Sea · Varjaren · Unna Saiva · Krankmårtenhögen · Vivallen · Gråträsk · NORWAY · SWEDEN · FINLAND · Gulf of Bothnia · L. Ladoga · Vänern · Vänern · North Sea

○ site location

Saami culture:
- ● settlement
- ▲ sacrificial site
- ▼ grave
- ■ hunting pit
- ◇ rock engraving
- ◆ bear grave

timescales:
- 200 BC–AD 1200
- AD 1200–1700

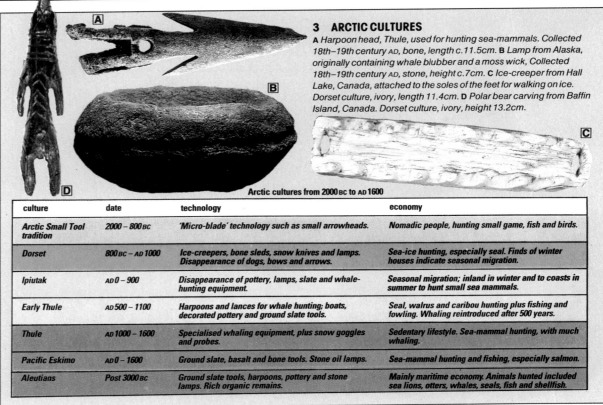

3 ARCTIC CULTURES

A *Harpoon head, Thule, used for hunting sea-mammals. Collected 18th–19th century AD, bone, length c.11.5cm.* B *Lamp from Alaska, originally containing whale blubber and a moss wick, Collected 18th–19th century AD, stone, height c.7cm.* C *Ice-creeper from Hall Lake, Canada, attached to the soles of the feet for walking on ice. Dorset culture, ivory, length 11.4cm.* D *Polar bear carving from Baffin Island, Canada. Dorset culture, ivory, height 13.2cm.*

Arctic cultures from 2000 BC to AD 1600

culture	date	technology	economy
Arctic Small Tool tradition	2000 – 800 BC	'Micro-blade' technology such as small arrowheads.	Nomadic people, hunting small game, fish and birds.
Dorset	800 BC – AD 1000	Ice-creepers, bone sleds, snow knives and lamps. Disappearance of dogs, bows and arrows.	Sea-ice hunting, especially seal. Finds of winter houses indicate seasonal migration.
Ipiutak	AD 0 – 900	Disappearance of pottery, lamps, slate and whale-hunting equipment.	Seasonal migration; inland in winter and to coasts in summer to hunt small sea mammals.
Early Thule	AD 500 – 1100	Harpoons and lances for whale hunting; boats, decorated pottery and ground slate tools.	Seal, walrus and caribou hunting plus fishing and fowling. Whaling reintroduced after 500 years.
Thule	AD 1000 – 1600	Specialised whaling equipment, plus snow goggles and probes.	Sedentary lifestyle. Sea-mammal hunting, with much whaling.
Pacific Eskimo	AD 0 – 1600	Ground slate, basalt and bone tools. Stone oil lamps.	Sea-mammal hunting and fishing, especially salmon.
Aleutians	Post 3000 BC	Ground slate tools, harpoons, pottery and stone lamps. Rich organic remains.	Mainly maritime economy. Animals hunted included sea lions, otters, whales, seals, fish and shellfish.

Towards a world economy

The ten years following 1490 were one of the most momentous decades in history, when Europeans first discovered routes around the rest of the world. In 1497–8 Vasco da Gama rounded southern Africa and sailed on to India, thus opening up the European sea route to the riches of the Far East, and in 1498 Columbus first sighted the mainland of America, the New World. These voyages led to Magellan's heroic first circumnavigation of the world, which was completed in 1522, though he himself had died before it ended. From then onwards, the European vision of the world changed from one bounded by Europe to one encompassing the whole.

The new trading colonies which mark this development and the distribution of shipwrecks and their contents, reflect a distinct geo-historical pattern. In 1494 an agreement on a division of the world for the purpose of exploration and settlement was established through the Pope. Access to lands east of a longitude line through the Atlantic would be restricted to Portugal, and west of the line would belong to Spain, an interpretation which extended to Spanish settlements in the Philippines. During the 16th century Spain found seemingly limitless quantities of gold, silver and other wealth in Central and southern America, together with ample native Indian labour to undertake mining under their domination. On the other side of the world the Portuguese found rich trading profits in India, the Indies and China.

By the end of the 16th century the English and Dutch, excluded by Spanish power from the new Atlantic routes, had followed the Portuguese route around southern Africa, and were taking out trade goods and bullion and returning with spices, silks and porcelain. The powerful Dutch East India Company, founded in 1602, had ousted the English in their efforts to trade with the Moluccas, the fabled Spice Islands. Within three years the Dutch had even driven the Portuguese from the Moluccas. By 1623 the pattern for the future in the East was established: the Moluccas, Java and Japan had to be abandoned by the English in favour of the Dutch; the English concentrated on India and Persia, where intercontinental seaborne trade was still undeveloped.

Precious metals, pearls, dyestuffs and sugar were among the commodities that were shipped from Central America to Spain in the annual *flota* or Plate Fleet. Ships carried the rich cargoes, primarily from Veracruz and Portobello, to Havana in Cuba, where the main convoy set sail across the Atlantic for Spain. Chinese silks were purchased with American silver and shipped from Manila across the Pacific to Acapulco for trans-shipment to Veracruz. There were many hazards – pirates inhabited the Caribbean islands, and hurricanes were responsible for the loss of whole fleets off Florida in 1715 and 1733, causing economic crises for Spain. The wrecks of Spanish ships have provided a detailed insight into the forms of gold and silver. There were ingots in various shapes – buns, fingers and wedges – as well as coins such as gold doubloons and silver *reales* or 'pieces-of-eight'.

As the Plate ships arrived in Seville, the Dutch and English trading ships stood ready to carry some of the precious metals on to Amsterdam and London, to be used in their trade with the Far East. The remarkable efficiency in moving the bullion from continent to continent is indicated by some pieces-of-eight found in the Dutch East Indiaman *Hollandia* wrecked off the Isles of Scilly, England. Although the coins had been minted in Mexico in 1742, they had been carried overland to Veracruz, shipped across the Atlantic to Seville, trans-shipped up to Amsterdam, and finally loaded on board the *Hollandia* which set sail for Java in July, 1743. All on board died when the ship had her bottom ripped open on a reef.

Bullion was in great demand by Asian merchants, and the large, heavily armed East Indiamen often carried tons of precious metals. Silver had a value in the East which was much greater than its value in Europe; gold was not so useful in this respect, for its value in the East was much the same as its value in Europe.

European countries in the 17th century tended to have a silver-based standard of monetary value, but a major reduction in the availability of silver during the early 18th century was a major contributory factor in the change from a silver- to a gold-based standard in the 18th century. At the same time, the sheer inconvenience and danger of loss in transporting tons of bullion between countries encouraged a more developed banking and trading system in Europe. The coins and ingots found in historic shipwrecks are, therefore, a vital clue to understanding the beginnings of intercontinental trade, the world economy and the stimulus for a world banking system.

3 FROM THE WRECKS OF EAST INDIAMEN
A *Spanish–American silver coins: 8, 4 and 2 reales, minted in Mexico, from the Hollandia, wrecked off the Isles of Scilly in 1743. The 8 real coin (left) is the famous piece-of-eight, diameter 38mm.*
B *A bottle filled with red wine, from the outward-bound Amsterdam, wrecked in 1749. Analysis suggests the wine is French. Height of bottle 18.7cm.* C *A tureen or soup bowl of Chinese porcelain, from the Geldermalsen, sunk in the South China Sea in 1752. Height 17.5cm.*
D *Clay pipes from the Vergulde Draeck wrecked off Western Australia in 1656. Length of longest pipe 38cm.*

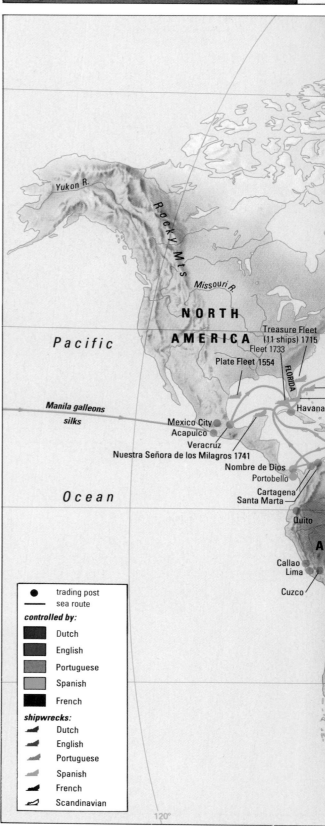

trading post
sea route
controlled by:
Dutch
English
Portuguese
Spanish
French
shipwrecks:
Dutch
English
Portuguese
Spanish
French
Scandinavian

Yukon R.

Rocky Mts

Missouri R.

NORTH AMERICA

Pacific

Ocean

Treasure Fleet (11 ships) 1715
Fleet 1733
Plate Fleet 1554
FLORIDA
Havana

Manila galleons
silks

Mexico City
Acapulco
Veracruz
Nuestra Señora de los Milagros 1741
Nombre de Dios
Portobello
Cartagena
Santa Marta

Quito

Callao
Lima

Cuzco

2 THE AMSTERDAM: WRECK OF AN EAST INDIAMAN

The *Amsterdam* (right) is the most complete surviving Dutch East Indiaman known in the world. She was run ashore on 26 January 1749, near Hastings, on the south coast of England, while on her maiden voyage from the Netherlands to Batavia in Java. Carrying a mixed cargo which included a huge quantity of cloth, bottled wines, and over 2.5 tonnes of silver, she was home for over 300 people for the nine months voyage.

During severe gales she lost her rudder in the English Channel. Due to disease on board 50 men had already died, and 40 more were sick and dying. Rather than wait for the ship to be taken into port, the crew apparently mutinied and forced the captain to run her ashore. The ship sank about eight metres into the soft clay seabed and quickly filled with silt and quicksand before it was possible to salvage anything other than the silver. When excavated she contained intact much of her cargo and stores, and many personal possessions of her crew.

Left *A view of the* Amsterdam *wreck at low tide near Hastings.*

'Amsterdam': probable cargo and supplies

16,000 silver ducatons (salvaged 1749)	*casks of beer*	*sulphur*
1200 silver bars (salvaged 1749)	*cheese from Edam*	*carpets*
*cases of French and Rhine wines**	*clay pipes**	*tar*
bacon from Groningen	*talcum in barrels*	*hats*
*butter, both Frisian and Irish**	*iron pots and tools*	*Marseille soap*
bottles of gin and brandy	*pots of Delftware*	*cow hair*
gold and silver lace	*wood including oak*	*pig iron*
drape, canvas and linen	*unground vermillion*	*glue*
medicines and oils	*velvet cloth**	*starch*
muskets, bayonets and gunpowder	*sewing yarn*	*cartridge paper*
copper pots and wire	*glass cups*	*mercury*
rolls of Moscovian leather	*paints*	*wooden tools*
'Poelse', linseed and rape oil	*barrels of food**	
* some discovered		

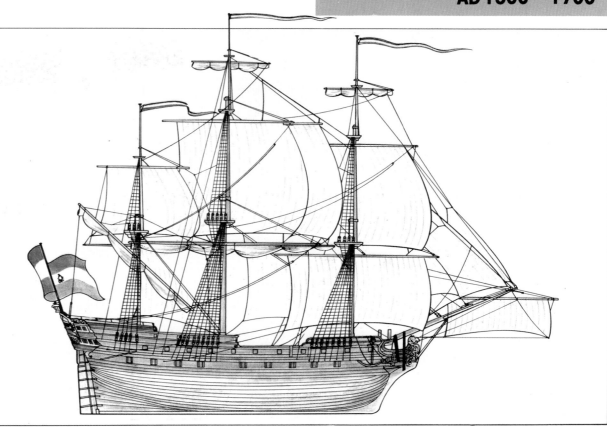

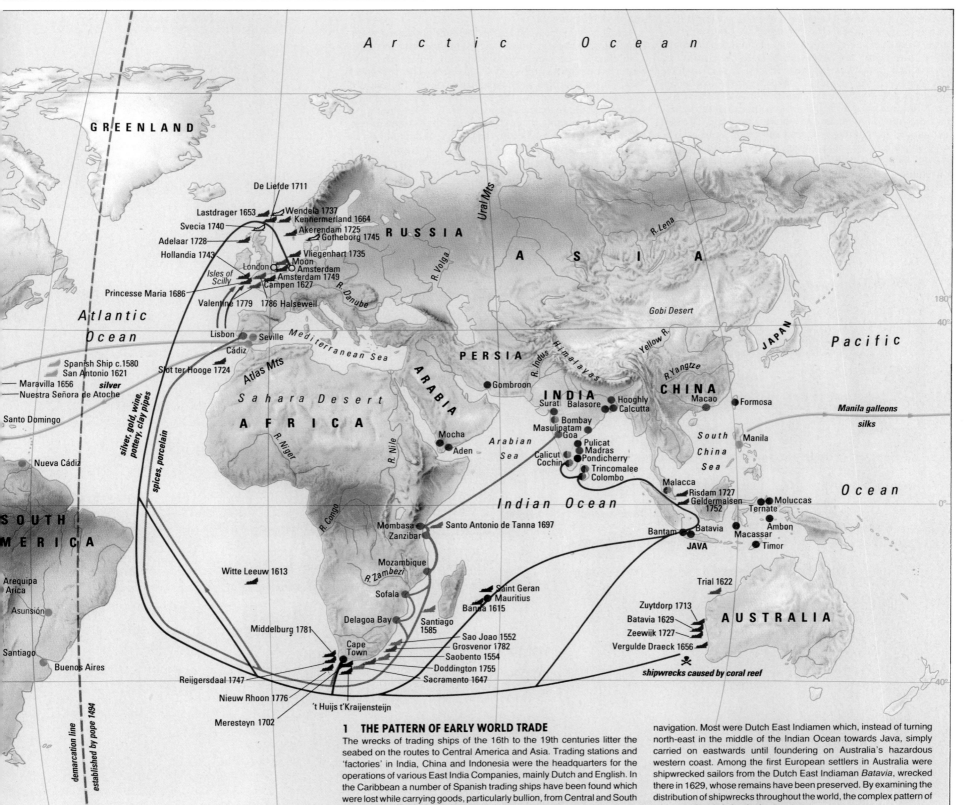

1 THE PATTERN OF EARLY WORLD TRADE

The wrecks of trading ships of the 16th to the 19th centuries litter the seabed on the routes to Central America and Asia. Trading stations and 'factories' in India, China and Indonesia were the headquarters for the operations of various East India Companies, mainly Dutch and English. In the Caribbean a number of Spanish trading ships have been found which were lost while carrying goods, particularly bullion, from Central and South America to Spain. The wrecks off western Australia represent faulty navigation. Most were Dutch East Indiamen which, instead of turning north-east in the middle of the Indian Ocean towards Java, simply carried on eastwards until foundering on Australia's hazardous western coast. Among the first European settlers in Australia were shipwrecked sailors from the Dutch East Indiaman *Batavia*, wrecked there in 1629, whose remains have been preserved. By examining the distribution of shipwrecks throughout the world, the complex pattern of early world trade is beginning to emerge.

Towards an industrial economy

The Industrial Revolution, which marks the arrival of the modern age, began in Britain in the 18th century. In its early stages it made only minor changes to the British landscape. During this period, the principal towns owed their importance not so much to their size as to the fact that they were economic centres. A town of 20–30,000 people served a number of villages or smaller towns within a radius of about 65 kilometres. Within this area there might be considerable industrial growth, but there were fields and trees between the factories and the workshops. Before 1800 regions such as the West Riding to Yorkshire, south Lancashire and the West Midlands had very little genuinely urban development. Industrialisation in the 18th century was characterised by a very gradual thickening of still rural industrial settlements, not by conurbations, which were a 19th-century phenomenon.

The localisation of industry was only just beginning in 1800. The manufacture of woollen textiles was widely distributed, although there was some local specialisation, determined mainly by the amount of water available. Broadcloths and serges needed fulling, which demanded large quantities of water, whereas the manufacture of blankets, flannels and worsteds required very little. The cotton industry became established in Lancashire because the climate was damp, the guilds were less powerful than elsewhere, ports were close at hand to bring the raw cotton from overseas and there was a labour force already skilled in working flax and wool. In both the cotton and the woollen industries the new machines had to have water power to drive them before the arrival of steam engines gave manufacturers a wider choice of location.

In 1700, outside the London area, population density was determined mainly by the woollen industry. By 1750, even before the coming of canals and turnpike roads, the distribution of the population was changing rapidly. Textiles were moving north and the areas where coal and iron were easily available were beginning to be more thickly settled. Between 1700 and 1800 the total population of Britain increased from about six million to nine million, an average growth of approximately 30,000 a year. Thereafter, the increase was much more rapid. Between 1811 and 1821 the total went up from ten to twelve million, a rate of increase five times as great as in the previous century. In the major industrial centres the change was even more striking. Manchester had 90,000 people in 1801, 237,000 in 1831 and 400,000 in 1861.

This unprecedented increase in the population was one reason for the huge rise in industrial and agricultural production during the 18th and 19th centuries. The needs of the extra millions had to be met. Another was war, always a prodigious consumer of iron and iron products. In 1790 the British production of iron was no more than 79,000 tons. In 1820, as a result of the Napoleonic Wars, it had risen to 400,000 tons.

With rising population, demand for market products grew. Wages were low so new inventions were required, not only to allow manufacturers to produce more, but also to bring prices down. Kay's flying shuttle in 1733, Hargreaves' spinning jenny in 1770, Crompton's spinning mule in 1778 and Cartwright's power loom in 1785 were among the developments which transformed the textile industry. In ironmaking, the most important pioneers were Abraham Darby, who in 1709 succeeded in discovering how to use coal instead of charcoal for smelting iron, and Henry Cort, who in 1784 introduced the puddling process for making wrought iron. Mining and all forms of manufacturing benefited from the invention and improvement of the steam-engine, through a series of developments from Newcomen's atmospheric engine of 1712 to Watt's engines of the 1770s and 1780s, and Trevithick's high-pressure engines introduced during the first 20 years of the 19th century.

It was of little use to be able to produce goods in greater quantities, however, unless they could be moved easily and cheaply to their customers and unless the raw materials could be delivered to factories. The Industrial Revolution was also a transport revolution. During the 17th and 18th centuries, the roads deteriorated so badly because of the increase in wheeled traffic that they were practically unusable by anything other than riding horses and packhorse trains. Before the coming of the railways in the 1830s the only dependable way to transport heavy loads was by water. Considerable investment was made in constructing canals during the second half of the 18th century, but the momentum fell away as soon as the potential of railways began to be realised.

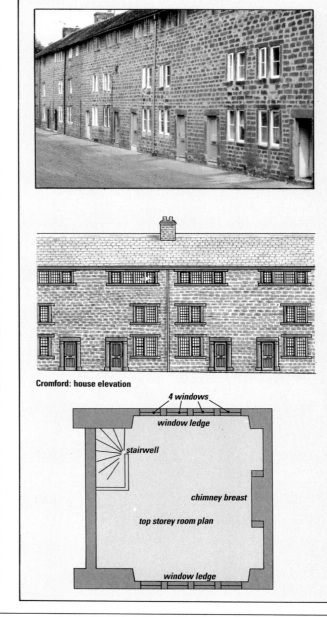

Cromford: house elevation

4 windows
window ledge
stairwell
chimney breast
top storey room plan
window ledge

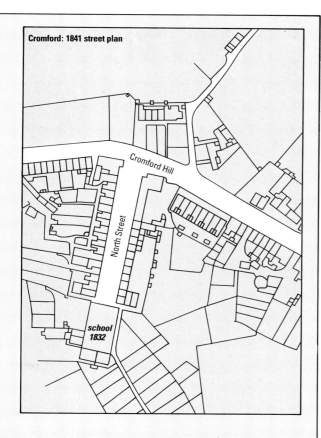

Cromford: 1841 street plan

Cromford Hill

North Street

school 1832

3   CROMFORD: A PLANNED WORKERS' VILLAGE

In 1769 Samuel Arkwright patented a spinning machine, his famous 'water-frame', and in 1771 he began to build the first water-powered cotton-spinning mill in the world at Cromford in Derbyshire, by the side of the River Derwent. As the mill became successful, he built homes for his workers. The resulting village of Cromford (*plan above*) was the earliest such settlement of any note. It remains virtually unaltered and is protected by a conservation order. The best-preserved houses are in North Street (*above left*). Built of stone in 1777, they are three storeys high. The top storey is often connected by a door to the adjacent house. This was used by Arkwright's employees in the evenings for making stockings. Apart from the houses, Arkwright also built community facilities, a school, a chapel and an inn, The Greyhound. In 1777 Cromford Mill employed 200 people.

2   QUARRY BANK MILL

Water supply determined the location of many early cotton mills, and owners developed factory communities around them. Samuel Greg began Quarry Bank Mill at Styal, in Cheshire, in 1783. A second waterwheel was installed in 1801, when the length of the original mill was doubled and an attic storey added. The problem of erratic water supply was overcome in 1796 by installing a steam engine to supplement power from the River Bollin.

4   STEAM, IRON AND MACHINERY

The Industrial Revolution was based on the use of coal, steam and iron. The first steam-engines were used to pump water from mines, not to drive machinery. The pioneer was Thomas Newcomen, who installed his first atmospheric steam pumping engine in 1712, at a coalmine in Staffordshire (*illustration* **B**). Hargreaves' spinning jenny (**A**), is a fine example of innovation in the textile industry. One of the best-known *in situ* achievements of the Industrial Revolution is at Ironbridge on the River Severn, where the first iron bridge in the world was erected in 1779 (**C**).

The Engine to raise Water by Fire

Printed for J.Hinton at the Kings Arms St Pauls Church Yard. 1747.

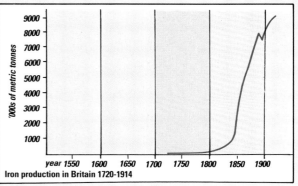

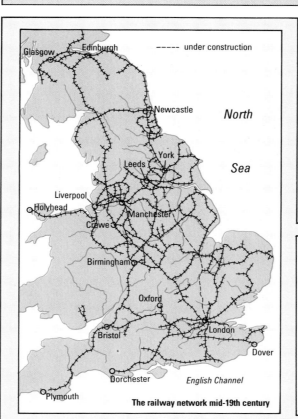

The railway network mid-19th century

----- under construction

Glasgow, Edinburgh, Newcastle, York, Leeds, Liverpool, Holyhead, Manchester, Crewe, Birmingham, Oxford, Bristol, London, Dover, Dorchester, Plymouth

North Sea

English Channel

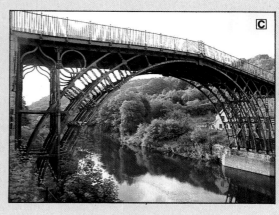

Iron production in Britain 1720-1914

'000s of metric tonnes

9000, 8000, 7000, 6000, 5000, 4000, 3000, 2000, 1000

year 1550, 1600, 1650, 1700, 1750, 1800, 1850, 1900

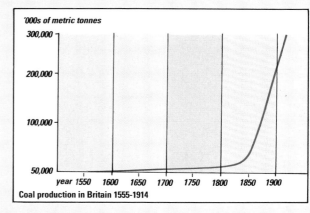

Coal production in Britain 1555-1914

'000s of metric tonnes

300,000, 200,000, 100,000, 50,000

year 1550, 1600, 1650, 1700, 1750, 1800, 1850, 1900

The waterway system 1789

Carlisle, Hull, Manchester, Liverpool, Chester, Trent & Mersey canal, Nottingham, Coventry canal, Birmingham, Norwich, Oxford canal, Oxford, Severn and Thames canal, London

North Sea

English Channel

1   THE TRANSPORT REVOLUTION

The graphs (*above*) illustrate the rising output of both coal and pig-iron, but this increased productivity had to be accompanied by improved transportation. Between the 1750s and the middle of the 19th century about 4800 kilometres of canals were added to the existing 1600 kilometres of navigable rivers in Britain. After 1850, with the advent of the railways, very little was done to improve the system, although Britain's largest canal, the Manchester Ship Canal, was not opened until 1894.

The predecessors of the railways were horse-drawn wagonways and tramroads associated with the mining and smelting industries. After about 1773 many of them were used as feeders to canals. Railways, in the modern sense of the word, began to be built c.1830. In the early days, their main purpose was to move heavy and bulky freight, not passengers. The network was substantially completed by the 1870s, although lines continued to be built until well into the present century.

ACKNOWLEDGEMENTS

Page Credit

22 Goethe Museum (photo courtesy of The Folio Society)
24 *above*
A York Archaeological Trust
B British Museum
below
A Ashmolean Museum, Oxford
B Courtesy of the Vindolanda Trust/© University of Newcastle-upon-Tyne
25 B British Museum (Michael Holford)
Left Ardea London Ltd.
Above Research Laboratory for Archaeology, Oxford
26 A Bolton Museum & Art Gallery, Bolton Metropolitan Borough Council
B Novosti Press Agency
C Schweizerisches Landesmuseum, Zurich
27 A Dr. Georg Gerster, John Hillelson Agency Ltd.
B–C R. W. Agache, Service des Fouilles, Abbeville
35 *above*
A–B Founders Society, Detroit Institute of Arts (photo: Dirk Bakker)
C Museum of the American Indian, Heye Foundation, New York
below
A Dr. Roger Joussaume
B Dr. Chris Scarre
37 A National Museums of Scotland
B National Maritime Museum
Above Planet Earth Pictures
38 A Ferdinand Anton, Munich
B–C British Museum (Michael Holford)
D Mansell Collection
40 A Dumbarton Oaks Research Collection, Washington DC
B Danish National Museum (Neils Elswing)
C Danish National Museum (John Lee)
41 Metropolitan Museum of Art, New York, Rogers Fund, 1933
42 A University Museum of Archaeology & Anthropology, Cambridge
B National Museum of Anthropology, Mexico (Don Brothwell, Institute of Archaeology, London)
43 A–D Dr. A. R. David, Manchester Museum
45 US National Park Service, Mid-West Archaeological Center, Nebraska
46 *above left to right*
The Ancient Art & Architecture Collection
Manchester Museum
Danish National Museum (L Larsen)
Ancient Art & Architecture Collection
British Museum (Michael Holford)
Below University Museum of Archaeology & Anthropology, Cambridge
47 A British Museum (Michael Holford)
B University Museum of Archaeology & Anthropology, Cambridge
C University Museum of Archaeology & Anthropology, Cambridge (Michael Holford)
D Fitzwilliam Museum, Cambridge (Michael Holford)
48 A–C © Peabody Museum, Harvard University (photos: Hillel Burger)
49 Robert Harding Picture Library
50 Colorphoto Hinz SWB, Switzerland
53 A–B Peter Andrews, Natural History Museum: © David Pilbeam, Harvard University
C W. Sacco & David Pilbeam, Harvard University
55 A–D John Reader
Below John Reader
56 John Reader
58 Planet Earth Pictures
59 Natural History Museum
61 A Courtesy Department Library Services, American Natural History Museum: Trans. No. T.626
B–C Peter Andrews, Natural History Museum
63 A–E British Museum
64 A–G British Museum

H John Reader
I Natural History Museum
65 Dr. Yoel Rak, Tel Aviv University
66 A Dr. Chris Stringer, Natural History Museum
B–C Pitt Rivers Museum, Oxford
D John Wymer, Norfolk Museums Service (photo courtesy of University of Chicago)
68 B Western Australia Museum, Perth
C Prof. D. J. Mulvaney, The Australian National University, Canberra
D Prof. R. Wright, University of Sydney
Above Prof. R. Wright, University of Sydney
70 A Prof. T. F. Lynch, Cornell University, New York
B Dr. Nième Guidon, Ecole des Hautes-Etudes en Sciences Sociales, Paris
C Prof. T. F. Lynch, Cornell University, New York
D Prof. J. M. Adovasio, University of Pittsburgh
E British Museum
72 A–F British Museum
75 *above*
A–C Michael Holford
below
A Ancient Art & Architecture Collection
B–C Jean Vertut, Issy-les-Moulineaux
D Institute of Archaeology, Leningrad
76 Dr. R. Rodden
79 A R. S. Peabody Foundation for Archaeology, Mass.
80 A Ashmolean Museum, Oxford
B Andrew Lawson, Oxford
C–D Ekdotike Athenon, Athens
81 Sonia Halliday Photographs
83 A–D James Mellaart
E Turkish National Museums (Michael Holford)
85 *above*
A–C British Museum
Below Museum of Archaeology, Belgrade (Scala, Florence)
86 A Ashmolean Museum, Oxford
D Rheinisches Landesmuseum, Bonn
E Jus Autor, Bulgaria
88 A J-F. Jarrige, Musée Guimet, Paris
B Dr. R. Allchin, The Ancient India & Iran Trust, Cambridge
C J-F. Jarrige, Musée Guimet, Paris
91 A–F Dr. Ian Glover
92 B Robert Harding Picture Library
C British Museum
E Museum of Far Eastern Antiquities, Stockholm
94 Henri Lhote, Paris
95 *Above left* Henri Lhote, Paris
A–C University Museum of Archaeology & Anthropology, Cambridge
E Pitt Rivers Museum, Oxford
F University Museum of Archaeology & Anthropology, Cambridge
97 *above*
A British Museum
B Frobenius-Institut, Frankfurt
C Museum of Victoria, Melbourne
D University Museum of Archaeology & Anthropology, Cambridge
E–F South Australia Museum, Adelaide
G Dr. Geoff Bailey
97 *below*
A–B South Australia Museum, Adelaide
98 Dr. Joan Oates
99 A–B Dr. Joan Oates
C Baghdad Museum (Scala, Florence)
D Hirmer Fotoarchiv, Munich
E Ashmolean Museum, Oxford
101 A Machida City Educational Board, Japan
B British Museum
C University College, London
D Robert Harding Picture Library
102 Robert Harding Picture Library
104 Sonia Halliday Photographs
105 A Robert Harding Picture Library
B–C Werner Forman Archive

106 *Above* Aerofilms Ltd
A Dr. Chris Scarre
B Salisbury & South Wiltshire Museum
C Anthony Weir, Janet & Colin Bord
D Danish National Museum (Lennart Larsen)
E Prof. Glyn Daniel
107 Dr. Chris Scarre
108 Aerofilms Ltd.
109 A Fay Godwin, Barbara Heller Photograph Library
B Anthony Weir, Janet & Colin Bord
C Janet & Colin Bord
D Mick Sharp
110 A Jus Autór, Bulgaria
B National Museums of Scotland
C History Museum of Transylvania, Romania
D Magyar Nemzeti Museum, Budapest
E Museum of Archaeology, Poznan
111 A Magyar Nemzeti Museum, Budapest
B Ashmolean Museum, Oxford
C Magyar Nemzeti Museum, Budapest
F National Museums of Scotland
112 B British Museum
C Susan Griggs Agency
D Museo Arquelogico, Madrid
E Photoresources
F Ekdotike Athenon, Athens
114 *above*
A Salzburger Museum Carolino-Augusteum
B Museo Provinciale d'Arte, Provincia Autonoma di Trento, Italy
C Devizes Museum
D Museum für Ur-und Frühgeschichte, Potsdam
E University of Magdeburg
below
C–D Federseemuseum, West Germany
116 *above*
A Danish National Museum (Lennart Larsen)
B Werner Forman Archive
below
B–D Danish National Museum (Lennart Larsen)
117 C–G Danish National Museum (Lennart Larsen)
118 *Above* Susan Griggs Agency
A–B F. van Noten
C–D Prof. C. Thurstan Shaw
119 *Above* Robert Harding Picture Library
Below Susan Griggs Agency
120 B Salzburger Museum Carolino-Augusteum
C Michael Holford
121 D Peter Clayton
E Hirmer Fotoarchiv, Munich
Centre Museum of Far Eastern Antiquities, Stockholm
Below Museum für Urgeschichte Asparn/Zaya, Niederösterreich (Franz Hampl)
122 The Bridgeman Art Library
123 A The Louvre, Paris (Photographie Giraudon)
B The MacQuitty International Photographic Collection
C Bibliothèque Nationale, Paris
D Robert Harding Picture Library
125 A Réunion des Musées Nationaux, Paris
B British Museum
C Photo by Victor J. Boswell Jr., National Geographic Society © 1983 Oriental Institute of the University of Chicago
D Iraq Museum, Baghdad (Scala, Florence)
Below Hirmer Fotoarchiv, Munich
126 British Museum
127 A British Museum (Michael Holford)
B British Museum (Hirmer Fotoarchiv, Munich)
C British Museum (Michael Holford)
D British Museum
Below Dr. Georg Gerster, John Hillelson Agency
128 Michael Holford

129 A Ashmolean Museum, Oxford
B British Museum (Michael Holford)
C Dr. Bernard Fielden
D Robert Harding Picture Library
Below Dr. Chris Scarre
131 A The MacQuitty International Photographic Collection
B Josephine Powell, Rome
C Robert Harding Picture Library
D British Museum
E Robert Harding Picture Library
Below The MacQuitty International Photographic Collection
133 A British Museum
B Hirmer Fotoarchiv, Munich
C Missione Archaeologica Italiana, Syria/University of Rome
D Ashmolean Museum, Oxford
E British Museum
F Hirmer Fotoarchiv, Munich
134 A Dr. J. N. Postgate Aleppo Archaeological Museum, Syria, copied by Lucien Cavro
135 A Charles Aylmer, Cambridge University Library
136 Werner Forman Archive
137 A Uni-Dia Verlag, Germany
B British Museum
C–E Robert Harding Picture Library
138 A–C Egyptian Museum, Turin (Chomon Perino)
139 *above*
A British Museum (Michael Holford)
B–E British Museum
F Kunsthistorisches Museum, Vienna (Meyer)
G–H British Museum (M Holford)
below
A British Museum
B–C British Museum (M Holford)
140 Prof. Raymond Schoder, Loyola University, Chicago
141 A Ekdotike Athenon, Athens
B Photoresources
C Ekdotike Athenon, Athens
D Peter Clayton
E Photoresources
F Ekdotike Athenon, Athens
142 *Below* Hirmer Fotoarchiv, Munich
A Courtesy of The Oriental Institute of the University of Chicago
C Sonia Halliday Photographs
143 B Michael Holford
D The Louvre, Paris (Photographie Giraudon)
E Hirmer Fotoarchiv, Munich
Below British Museum (M Holford)
144 A The Ancient Art & Architecture Collection
B–C Ekdotike Athenon, Athens
D British Museum (Michael Holford)
E Ekdotike Athenon, Athens
147 A–B British Museum
C British Museum (Michael Holford)
D Robert Harding Picture Library
E British Museum (Michael Holford)
148 A–B The Hermitage Museum, Leningrad (Prof. Stuart Piggott)
C Les Editions Nagel S.A., Geneva
Below The Historical Museum, Erevan, Armenian ASR (Prof. Stuart Piggott)
150 *above*
A–B University Museum of Pennsylvania
C Smithsonian Institution, Washington DC
D R. Suppo, Fuocofisso, Turin
E Muzium Negara, Malaysia/Arts of Asia Publications Ltd.
below
A–D Prof. C. F. W. Highham, University of Otago, New Zealand
151 F Prof. C. F. W. Highham, University of Otago, New Zealand
152 Museo di Villa Giulia, Rome (Leonard von Matt, Switzerland)
154 A Zefa Picture Library
B The Ancient Art & Architecture Collection
C Robert Harding Picture Library
D The Ancient Art & Architecture Collection
156 A British Museum
B British Museum (Michael Holford)
C Holle Bildarchiv, West Germany
D British Museum
Below Sonia Halliday Photographs

157 Dr. Georg Gerster, John Hillelson Agency
158 **A–B** British Museum
C Dr. J. N. Postgate
159 Robert Harding Picture Library
160 **A** British Museum
B National Museum, Athens (Scala, Florence)
C Zefa Picture Library
D Danish National Museum (Lennart Larsen)
E The Louvre, Paris (Photographie Giraudon)
162 **A** Ekdotike Athenon, Athens
B British Museum (Michael Holford)
C British Museum
D Ekdotike Athenon, Athens
Right Zefa Picture Library
165 **A** Museo delle Terme, Rome (Scala, Florence)
B Sonia Halliday Photographs
C Paul Bernard
D Elsie Timbey Collection/Society for Cultural Relations with the USSR
167 *above*
A Gloucestershire Museum
B Ulster Museum, Belfast
C Rheinisches Landesmuseum, Bonn
D Musée Archéologique de Dijon
E British Museum
F Württembergisches Landesmuseum, Stuttgart
below
A–B Prähistorische Staatssamlung, Munich
Right National Monuments Record
168 **A–B** British Museum
C Antiquarium del Foro, Rome (Scala, Florence)
D Werner Forman Archive
E The Prado, Madrid (Scala, Florence)
169 **F** British Museum
G Museo di Villa Giulia, Rome (Scala, Florence)
170 **A–B** Michael Holford
C The Ancient Art & Architecture Collection
D Photoresources
172 **A–B** Michael Holford
C Scala, Florence
D Michael Holford
174 **A–B** Landos Museum, Trier
C Rheinisches Landesmuseum, Trier
D Ashmolean Museum, Oxford
177 **A** Mansell Collection
B Leonard von Matt, Switzerland
C The Ancient Art & Architecture Collection
D National Museum, Naples (Scala, Florence)
Centre Mansell Collection
178 **A** Michael Vickers, Ashmolean Museum, Oxford
B Prof. Gunther Gabrecht, Leichtweiss-Institut for Water Research, Braunschweig
C Michael Holford
179 **A** Museo Arquelogica Nacional, Madrid
D The Ancient Art & Architecture Collection
180 **G** British Museum
H British Museum (Michael Holford)
181 **A** Silkeborg Museum, Denmark
B Danish National Museum (Lennart Larsen)
C Schleswig-Holsteinisches Museum für Vor-und Frühgeschichte, West Germany
D Ashmolean Museum, Oxford
E–F British Museum (Michael Holford)
182 **A** Photoresources
C The Ancient Art & Architecture Collection
D Photoresources
183 **A–E** Photoresources
185 **A** Ashmolean Museum, Oxford
B British Museum
C K. Schmitt-Korte, West Germany
D British Museum
Right Alan Hutchison Library Ltd.
187 **A** Staatliche Museen/Bildarchiv Preussicher Kulturbesitz, Berlin
C Novosti Press Agency
D The Ancient Art & Architecture Collection
E British Museum
Below Robert Harding Picture Library
188 **A** British Museum

B British Museum (Michael Holford)
C–D British Museum
E Ann & Bury Peerless Slide Resources & Picture Library
F Dr. Chris Scarre
Above Robert Harding Picture Library (both photos)
190 **A** Josephine Powell, Rome
B Musée Guimet (Réunion des Musées Nationaux)
191 **C** Kabul Museum (Photographie Giraudon)
193 **B** Museum of Far Eastern Antiquities, Stockholm
C–D British Museum
F British Museum
G Xinhua (Zefa Picture Library)
H British Museum
195 *above*
A The MacQuitty International Photographic Collection
B Werner Forman Archive
C Robert Harding Picture Library
below
D Sunday Times
196 **A** The Ancient Art & Architecture Collection
B Kyoto National Museum, Japan
C Werner Forman Archive
D Kodansha Ltd, Tokyo
E Toro Museum, Japan
Below Dr. Georg Gerster, John Hillelson Agency
198 **A** Museum Rietberg, Zurich
B Dr. Ian Glover
C Victoria & Albert Museum
D British Museum
E Dr. Elizabeth Moore
201 **A** Walter Meayers Edwards © National Geographic Society
B W. Ambrose, Australian National University, Canberra (photo: D. Markovic)
C Dr. R. C. Green, University of Auckland
D Dr. J. Poulsen, Institut for Forhistorisk Arkaeologi, Denmark
E Dr. Yoshiko Sinoto, Bernice Pauahi Bishop Museum, Hawaii
202 **A** British Museum (Michael Holford)
B Alan Hutchison Library
Below Dr. D. W. Phillipson
203 **C** University Museum of Archaeology & Anthropology, Cambridge
D National Museum of Kenya, Nairobi
E Henri Lhote, Paris
204 Michael Holford
206 **A–B** Prof. D. Metcalfe, Archaeological Center, University of Utah
C–F Prof. George C. Frison, University of Wyoming
G British Museum
209 **A–B** Prof. Kent V. Flannery, University of Michigan
210 **A** Peabody Museum of Archaeology & Ethnology, Harvard University
B R. Feldman, Field Museum of Natural History, Chicago
C University Museum of Archaeology & Anthropology, Cambridge
D R. Feldman, Field Museum of Natural History, Chicago
E Founders Society, Detroit Institute of Arts (photo: Dirk Bakker)
211 **F** American Museum of Natural History
213 **A** Ferdinand Anton, Munich
B Peabody Museum, Harvard University (photo: Hillel Burger: Trans. No. T.616)
C Ferdinand Anton, Munich
D Courtesy of Museum of the American Indian, Heye Foundation, New York, Photo No. 3803
214 Ferdinand Anton, Munich
215 **A** Dumbarton Oaks Research Collection, Washington DC
B E-T Archive
C–E Ferdinand Anton, Munich
216 © 1965 Prof. René Millon
217 **A** University Museum, Pennsylvania
B Ferdinand Anton, Munich
C British Museum
D Werner Forman Archive
218 **A–B** Ferdinand Anton, Munich
219 **C** University Museum, Pennsylvania
D Ferdinand Anton, Munich
Right Ferdinand Anton, Munich
221 **A** Museum of the American Indian, Heye Foundation, New York

B Ohio Historical Society, Columbus
C British Museum
D Field Museum of Natural History, No. 110024C, Chicago
222 *Above* Mike Andrews, Susan Griggs Agency
Below Dr. Georg Gerster, John Hillelson Agency
223 **A** Staatliches Museum für Volkerkünde, Munich
B The Royal Pavillion Art Gallery & Museums, Brighton
C Ferdinand Anton, Munich
D British Museum
E Collection Mujica Gallo, Lima (Michael Holford)
225 *left*
A–B British Museum
right
A Iris Barry
B–C Dr. Warwick Bray
D Iris Barry
Above Anna Roosevelt, New York
227 **A** Michael Holford
B Jean Bottin, Paris
C Elizabeth Baquedano
D Biblioteca Nazionale, Florence (Scala, Florence)
E British Museum
Below Zefa Picture Library
229 **A–B** Werner Forman Archive
C University Museum of Archaeology & Anthropology, Cambridge
D Werner Forman Archive
Centre Arizona State Museum, University of Arizona
231 **A** Museum of the American Indian, Heye Foundation, New York
B Peabody Museum, Harvard University (photo: Hillel Burger: Trans. No. T.10/21542)
C–D Museum of the American Indian, Heye Foundation, New York
233 **A–B** Ruth & Louis Kirk
C Yasu Osawa
D–F Ruth & Louis Kirk
234 *above*
A The Florida State Museum
below
A–D I. Noël Hume, Colonial Williamsburg Foundation
235 **B–D** The Florida State Museum
Below The Florida State Museum
236 Robert Harding Picture Library
238 **A** Sonia Halliday Photographs
B Barber Institute of Fine Arts
C The Harvard University Art Museums (Arthur M. Sackler Museum): Bequest – Thomas Whittemore
D Bibliothèque Nationale, Paris (Clam!)
240 **A** The Keir Collection, London
B Werner Forman Archive
C Victoria & Albert Museum (Eileen Tweedy)
D The Keir Collection, London
E Victoria & Albert Museum (Michael Holford)
Right Zefa Picture Library
243 **A** University Museum of National Antiquities, Oslo
B Statens Historiska Museum, Stockholm
C British Museum
D Statens Historiska Museum, Stockholm
E Photoresources
F Susan Griggs Agency
245 **A** Jean Dieuzaide, Toulouse
B Sonia Halliday Photographs
C Colchester & Essex Museum
D Colin Platt
E British Museum
246 **A** Yorkshire Museum of Farming
B Rotunda Museum, Scarborough Borough Council
C Wharram Percy Research Project, University of York
D Judges Postcards Ltd.
E British Library
248 **A** Prof. Frank Willett, Glasgow
B Prof. C. Thurstan Shaw (Doig Simmonds)
C Prof. Frank Willett, Glasgow
D Prof. C. Thurstan Shaw
Below Michael & Aubine Kirtley © 1982 National Geographic Society
250 **A** Prof. Frank Willett, Glasgow
B–E British Museum (Michael Holford)
F Robert Estall

252 **A** Dr. P. de Maret
B British Museum
C J. E. G. Sutton, The British Institute in Eastern Africa, Nairobi
253 **D** Dr. Georg Gerster, John Hillelson Agency
Above Dr. Georg Gerster, John Hillelson Agency
254 **A** Musée Guimet (Michael Holford)
B Robert Harding Picture Library
255 **A** Michael Holford
B Robert Harding Picture Library
Above Ann & Bury Peerless, Slide Resources & Picture Library
Below John Gollings
256 Michael Holford
257 **A** Victoria & Albert Museum (Michael Holford)
B British Museum
D The Bridgeman Art Library
E Robert Harding Picture Library
F British Museum
258 Colorphoto Hinz SWB, Switzerland
259 **A** Rijksmuseum voor Volkenkunde, The Netherlands
B Douglas Dickens
C Musée Guimet, Paris (Michael Holford)
D *Vietnamese Ceramics* by Arts of Asia
260 *Left* Robert Harding Picture Library
Right Douglas Dickins
Below Brian Brake, John Hillelson Agency
A Douglas Dickins
B Embassy of the Republic of Korea
261 **C** Werner Forman Archive
263 *above*
A Percival David Foundation of Chinese Art
below
A British Library
B The MacQuitty International Photographic Collection
D British Museum
E Robert Harding Picture Library
264 **A** Charles Aylmer, Cambridge University Library
B School of Oriental and African Studies, London
C National Palace Museum, Taiwan
D Percival David Foundation of Chinese Art
E Charles Aylmer, Cambridge University Library
265 Robert Harding Picture Library
266 **A** Taku Tanaka, Nara National Cultural Properties Committee, Japan
B Douglas Dickins
267 **D** Victor Harris, Department of Oriental Antiquities, British Museum
E Victoria & Albert Museum
268 **A** University Museum of Archaeology & Anthropology, Cambridge
B British Museum (Michael Holford)
C–D University Museum of Archaeology & Anthropology, Cambridge
E British Museum
Below Christian Pinson, Tahiti
269 Robert Harding Picture Library
270 **A–B** University Museum of Archaeology & Anthropology, Cambridge
C National Museum of New Zealand
271 **D** Michael Trotter & Beverley McCulloch, Canterbury Museum, New Zealand
E–F Wairau Bar Collection, Canterbury Museum, New Zealand
G Wilfred Shawcross, Australian National University, Canberra (Arts Photographic Unit, ANU)
272 *Above* Dr. Björn Ambrosianni, Statens Historiska Museum, Stockholm
A Vasterbotten Museum, Sweden
B–C Antikvarisk-Topografiska Arkivet, Sweden
273 **A–B** University Museum of Archaeology & Anthropology, Cambridge
C–D Canadian Museum of Civilisation, Ottawa
274 *Above* Peter Marsden
A–B Peter Marsden
C Groninger Museum, The Netherlands
D Western Australia Museum, Perth
276 The Arkwright Society, Cromford
277 **A** Lancashire County Council
B Ann Ronan Picture Library
C Michael Holford

GLOSSARY

ACERAMIC Pertaining to a society which does not use pottery, but instead may use leather, basketry, bark, gourds etc. for making containers.

ACHEULIAN The time period of the Palaeolithic which followed the Oldowan and was named after the type-site at St. Acheul in France. The term Acheulian is often used to describe the stone tools, particularly handaxes, of the period.

ACROPOLIS The elevated, most strongly defended part of a city serving as the last refuge in case of assault.

ADOBE Sun-dried, unfired clay-brick building material.

ADZE A woodworking tool which has its working edge perpendicular to the long axis of the haft. It therefore contrasts with an axe, the working edge of which is parallel with the plane of the haft.

AERIAL PHOTOGRAPHY The detection and photographic recording of sites from satellites, aircraft or balloons can help to understand the shape of large sites which are not clear from the ground. Vertical aerial photographs, taken from greater heights, are useful for surveys of large areas especially for *crop marks* and similar phenomena. Oblique aerial photographs, from lower altitudes, and normally of specific areas, detect shadows created by slight earthworks and permit more detailed interpretations of known sites.

AGGER A Roman bank or dyke of earth, used for protection from enemies or from flooding or as the foundation for a road.

AGORA A complex of buildings around a market-place which provided the focus for civil and commercial administration in an ancient Greek city.

AHU See *marae*.

ALEMBIC The upper part of a two-piece round container used in distillation. A downward-sloping spout allows a condensed distillate to run into another vessel.

AMPHITHEATRE A Roman building open to the elements with an arena surrounded by tiers of seats. Public spectacles were held in the arena.

AMPHORA A large two-handled jar with a narrow mouth, suitable for the storage and transportation of liquids such as olive oil or wine.

APADANA The principal audience hall of a Persian palace.

AQUEDUCT An artificial conduit used to supply water to a city from a source some distance away.

ARD A simple form of plough, usually made of wood, which has no mould-board, coulter or wheels. The share (point) is dragged through the soil, parting it rather than turning it over.

ARROYO The dry bed of a seasonal stream.

ATRIUM A hall with a central roof-opening and a pond or basin to collect rainwater, around which the rooms of a Roman town-house were arranged.

AWL A hand-held tool of stone or metal with a strong, sharp point used for perforating or scoring different materials.

AXE FACTORY An often isolated source of high quality stone which was intensively exploited for the production of stone axes.

BACKED BLADE In stone tools, a blade which has been blunted by further chipping along one edge to provide a finger-rest or to ease hafting.

BALUSTRADE A row of ornamented supports to a railing or low colonnade.

BAND A group of families forming a small-scale social unit; characteristic of communities which live by hunting and gathering. Sexual division of labour is common, though there are usually no other marked status differences.

BANDKERAMIK Hemispherical pottery decorated with incised linear designs such as spirals and meanders, which gives its name to the earliest farming communities of central Europe.

BARROW An earthen mound constructed over a burial (individual or communal). Round barrows are also known as *tumuli*.

BASILICA The main administrative building in a Roman city, the aisled-hall plan of which was adopted by many early Christian churches.

BAS-RELIEF A technique of sculpture in which subjects are defined by being slightly raised from a flat background. Also known as *low-relief*.

BEDDING TRENCH A straight slot dug in the ground into which a large timber is laid so that wall posts can be recessed into it and thus held securely in place.

BIER A movable wooden platform on which corpses are laid, sometimes together with grave-goods, and eventually carried to a burial place.

BIFACE A stone tool usually pointed at one end and flaked on both flat faces until the tool was thin and sharp-edged.

BIVALVE MOULD In metalworking, a simple form of mould comprising two halves held in place by dowels whilst the molten metal is poured in. The mould is parted to release the cast object once the metal has cooled.

BLACK DEATH A particularly severe outbreak of plague which crossed Europe between AD 1346 and 1350, probably a combination of bubonic and pneumonic plagues.

BLADE In stone tools, a particular form of *flake* which is more than twice as long as it is wide. Blades are useful because of their long, sharp cutting edges.

BOG BODY A human corpse preserved in waterlogged conditions such that skin and hair often survive but most internal organs and bones decay. Clothing also sometimes survives in such circumstances.

BOG OAK The fallen trunk of an oak tree killed by waterlogging but subsequently preserved in the peat which formed as a result of the wet conditions.

BORROW PIT A small quarry-pit from which clay, earth or mud is taken, usually for building purposes.

BOULEUTERION The council chamber of an ancient Greek city.

BP The suffix attached to a scientifically-derived date to indicate that it is expressed in years before present. The present is always taken as 1950.

BRICK-RELIEF A technique of sculpture in which subjects are left in *bas-relief* on a brick-built surface or wall.

BULLA (PL. BULLAE) In the Near East, a hollow clay ball which contained tokens representing goods despatched or exchanged and was thus part of a system of accounts.

BURIAL URN A vessel in which the cremated ashes of one or more individuals are placed.

BURIN In stone tools, a *flake* which has been shaped deliberately so that it has a strong, sharp corner with which to make grooves in bone, wood or antler, either for decorative purposes or to detach a long splinter of the material.

BURNISH The action of rubbing the surface of a partially dried, unfired pot with an instrument such as a pebble or a bone. This gives the pot a smooth, faintly lustrous appearance.

CACHE A collection of items similar to a *hoard*, but more likely to have been intended for recovery.

CALABASH A gourd used as a storage or drinking vessel.

CALIBRATION Fluctuations in the amount of Carbon-14 in the atmosphere mean that *radiocarbon dating* is not completely accurate. By obtaining radiocarbon dates for wood of known *dendrochronological* date from very long-lived trees, a correction factor can be introduced to calibrate radiocarbon dates.

CALIPHS The successors of Mohammed as rulers and religious leaders of the Islamic world, the most powerful being those of the Umayyad and Abbasid dynasties.

CANOPIC JAR An ancient Egyptian container of stone or pottery used for holding the entrails of an embalmed body.

CAPITOL The principal hill at Rome, site of the temple of Jupiter Optimus Maximus.

CARAVANSERAI A staging-post on a camel caravan route where rest and refreshment was available. Also known as a *khan*.

CARBONISATION The burning or scorching of organic materials, particularly plant remains such as seeds or grains, in conditions of insufficient oxygen which results in their preservation. Charcoal is a widely-known example.

CARDIAL POTTERY The earliest pottery of the west Mediterranean, named after its characteristic cockle shell (*Cardium*) decoration.

CARYATID A sculpted female figure used as a column to support an entablature (elaborate roofing).

CASTING In metalworking, the use of clay or stone moulds into which molten metal is poured to produce an object.

CASTING-ON TECHNIQUE A method used in a secondary stage of making metal objects in which a clay mould is made around part of an existing object. Molten metal is then poured in and fuses onto the original object. Used in adding handles, legs and hilts to complex artefacts.

CATACOMB An underground cemetery comprising a complex of passageways and recessed chambers.

CATAFALQUE A decorated wooden platform in which a *sarcophagus* was temporarily placed before burial.

CAUSEWAYED CAMPS A type of Neolithic enclosure found in north-west Europe, characterised by frequent breaks or causeways in the surrounding ditch. These enclosures probably had a continuous bank inside the ditch, and are believed to have served a variety of functions including as centres of exchange and sometimes as settlements.

CELLA The inner sanctum of a temple.

CELT An alternative name for an axe head of metal or stone, which was hafted on a wooden handle.

CENTURION The commanding officer of the smallest unit of the Roman imperial army (century), which comprises about 80 soldiers.

CHAIN MAIL Protective armour in the form of interlinked metal rings.

CHINAMPA An area of agricultural land created by the Aztecs by constructing a *wattle* enclosure on the edge of a lake and filling it with earth and mud to reclaim the land.

CIRE PERDUE See *lost-wax casting technique*.

CIST A box-like chamber for burial, made using stone slabs set on edge, which may be buried and/or covered by a mound.

CITADEL A strongly fortified structure, especially within a city. See *acropolis*.

CITY-STATE A social and political unit which consisted of a single urban centre and its hinterland. It had its own government and was not subject to any outside authority.

CLEAVER A stone tool of the Lower Palaeolithic period with a straight, sharp working edge in contrast to the pointed *handaxe*.

COHORT A subdivision of a Roman imperial *legion* which formed a tactical unit in battle.

COIL-BUILT POTTERY A technique whereby a pot is formed gradually by adding to a spiral of thin, sausage-like clay coils, which are smoothed out afterwards to form the walls of the pot.

COLUMN CAPITAL The uppermost, often decorated, part of a column.

COMMANDERY A military province in Han China.

COMPOSITE BOW A short but powerful bow made by binding laminae of different materials together to combine properties of strength, durability and power.

COMPOSITE TOOL A tool which combines different materials such as a bone harpoon with stone points and barbs set in it, or a wooden arrow with a shaped stone point at the tip (see *microlith*).

CONTINENTAL PLATES Giant slabs of the Earth's crust which are believed to move slowly in relation to each other.

CORBELLING A technique of roofing whereby successive courses of bricks or slabs are allowed to project a little further inwards than the course below until a curved or domed ceiling is achieved.

CORDIFORM Heart-shaped.

CORDUROY Made from short logs laid parallel and side-to-side, thus forming a continuous corrugated surface.

CORE In stone-tool manufacture, the block of stone from which useful flakes (of stone) are produced when hit accurately using a pebble, antler or bone hammer.

CORE-TOOL A relatively large stone tool shaped by flaking away unwanted stone using a pebble, antler or bone hammer.

CORINTHIAN STYLE Greek architectural style characterised by columns with a diameter-to-height ratio of one-to-ten, and an enlarged capital (uppermost part) decorated with sculptured foliage, often acanthus leaves. This style was extensively used by the Romans.

CORNICE The uppermost projecting element of a Classical building, immediately below the roof line.

CROP MARK A telltale difference in the growth and ripeness of a patch of cereal crop which results from buried archaeological features such as walls (which stunt crop growth) or ditches (which increase crop growth).

CRUCIBLE A small clay bowl used for remelting *smelted* metal so that it can be poured into a mould.

CUIDADELA A royal compound belonging to a king of the Inca empire, which also served as a *mausoleum* after his death.

CUIRASS A piece of armour designed to protect the torso. It comprised both breast- and back-armour, sometimes shaped to the contours of the chest and back muscles (muscled cuirass). Variously made of laminated linen, leather, sheet-bronze or -iron, or scales of horn, hide or metal.

CULTURE 'A culture' is the term used by archaeologists to define regional groupings of similar artefacts and other features, which are often then equated with an hypothesised social group. Thus the Bandkeramik culture of Neolithic Europe is an hypothesised social group characterised by its use of a particular type of pottery, houses, etc.

CUNEIFORM Literally 'wedge-shaped', cuneiform is the name given to a writing system comprising reed-impressions in tablets of clay. It was used throughout Mesopotamia for a number of languages from the 3rd to the 1st millennium BC.

CYCLOPEAN WALL A massive stone wall in which the gaps between the inner and outer faces of the huge stone boulders are filled with small stones and clay.

CYLINDER SEAL A Mesopotamian/Mediterranean small stone cylinder incised with reversed designs so that when it was rolled over a soft surface the design appeared in relief. These seals were used among other things to mark property and to legalise documents.

DEEP-SEA CORE A narrow column of sediments taken by drilling from the sea bed which contains a record of climatic changes through its sequence of superimposed layers.

DENDROCHRONOLOGY Otherwise known as tree-ring dating. This method is used to date wooden structures and objects from archaeological sites by comparing the pattern of growth rings with an established master sequence for tree-ring width over the last 7000 years.

DIADEM A plain or decorated headband of man-made or natural materials.

DIGGING STICK A straight stick, the end of which is often hardened by charring, which can be used to lever and dig out edible roots and plants or to break up the earth prior to planting.

DIVAN A bed or low couch in box form.

DOLMEN A simple arrangement of large stones used to create a chamber for the burial of one or more people. See also *megalithic tomb*.

DORIC STYLE Greek architectural style characterised by fluted columns with a diameter-to-height ratio of one-to-eight and an unelaborated capital. See also *Corinthian style* and *Ionic style*.

DUGOUT CANOE A simple form of canoe made from a single tree, the hollow in which is created by burning or chopping out the unwanted wood.

DYNASTY A line of rulers whose right to power is inherited.

EAR-FLARE A large circular ear-ornament, flared like the bell of a trumpet, which was often made of jade. The ear-flare was an elaborate form of *ear spool*.

EAR SPOOL An ornament worn in the ear lobe sometimes of such weight that the ear might be stretched to shoulder-length.

ECOSYSTEM The set of relationships between living and non-living things in nature, or a specific natural community, including the interactions of climate, soils, rivers and all forms of animals and plants.

ELECTRON MICROSCOPY A way of studying materials at extremely high magnification using electrons instead of light. It is useful for identifying a range of things including bone diseases and residues on the edges of used stone tools.

ELITE See *stratified society*.

EMPORIUM (PL. EMPORIA) A centre of commerce characterised by a wide range of goods, often from far afield.

ENTREPOT A trading town or city, often a port, strategically situated for the redistribution of goods from a variety of sources.

FACADE The main front of a structure, often elaborated and visually impressive.

FALSE-COLOUR SATELLITE IMAGERY A form of *aerial photography* performed at very high altitudes using infra-red sensitive film. It allows the mapping of ancient man-made features such as irrigation systems and roads by detecting differences in the reflected heat of the earth.

FEUDALISM A strictly hierarchical political and economic system in which land is granted in return for military or labour services.

FIBULA A brooch or fastener (similar to a 'safety-pin') made of bronze or iron consisting of a bow, pin and catch.

FIGURINE A small modelled human or animal form usually of clay, stone or metal.

FLAKE A thin chip of stone, usually with useful sharp edges, removed from a *core*.

FLAKED STONE TOOL Stone tool made by removal of thin *flakes* of stone with blows from a *hammerstone*.

FLARE See *ear-flare*.

FLAT GRAVE A burial consisting of a simple oval or rectangular pit containing an inhumed individual. The pit was infilled but not marked by a mound or other earthwork.

FLYING BUTTRESS An arched supporting pier outside a building which takes most of the weight of the roof, allowing the walls to be devoted to window-space rather than being used to support the roof.

FORGING In metalworking, the shaping of a piece of metal by heating, to soften it, and then hammering.

FORUM (PL. FORA). A square which served as a meeting- and/or market-place.

FRESCO A watercolour painting on a wall or ceiling completed before the plaster is dry.

FRIEZE A band of decoration on a wall or vessel, which may be painted or in *bas-relief*.

FRONTLET The upper skull and antlers of a deer or stag.

GILDING The application of a thin layer of gold paint or gold leaf.

GLAZE A transparent paint used to create a glassy, waterproof surface on a pot when fired.

GLYPH A carved figure, character or picture incised, painted or in relief. The system of picture-writing is known as *hieroglyphics*.

GORGET A piece of armour for protecting the throat region.

GREAVE A piece of leg armour designed to protect the lower leg. It originally covered the shin only, but in mediaeval Europe there was also a closed greave which protected both the shin and the calf.

GRINDING STONE Any stone, usually with at least one flat surface, used for grinding foodstuffs, medicines, cosmetics or colourants.

GROUND STONE TOOL A stone tool given a smooth final form by grinding it against another, more abrasive rock.

GUI An early Chinese handled bronze bowl which often bore writing as well as complex designs.

GYMNASIUM A public sports complex.

HAFT The handle section of an implement such as an *adze* or an *awl*.

HALBERD A metal blade attached at right angles to the end of a narrow staff and used as a weapon.

HAMMERSTONE In stone-tool production, the usual instrument used to detach *flakes* from a *core*.

HANDAXE A general purpose stone *core-tool* dating to the older stages of the Palaeolithic period which was shaped by the removal of *flakes* from both faces often into a rough flattened pear-shape with a point at one end.

HARPOON A type of spear adapted for hunting fish, seals, whales etc. which features prominent barbs to prevent the point of the harpoon being dislodged, and also a line for retrieving the prey.

HELLENISTIC PERIOD Period of widest Greek influence, beginning with the unification of Macedonia and the Greek states of Philip II of Macedon in 336BC, greatly extended by the conquests of Alexander the Great. Hellenistic cultural influence continued to be a powerful force in the Roman and Parthian empires during the early centuries AD.

HENGE A type of enclosure with one or two entrances and an earthen bank outside its ditch. Henges are believed to have been focal points for 'ritual' activity. Found in Britain during the later Neolithic period, but occasional examples still in use in the Bronze Age, e.g. Stonehenge.

HIERARCHICAL SOCIETY See *stratified society*.

HIEROGLYPH See *glyph*.

HIPPODROME A stadium for chariot racing.

HOARD A deliberate deposit of complete and/or broken objects buried in the ground for subsequent recovery or as a symbolic act.

HOMINID Humans of both modern and extinct forms including the genera *Australopithecus* and *Homo*.

HOMINOID A broad family of primates which includes apes and humans and their evolutionary forerunners.

HYPOCAUST A raised floor beneath which hot air from a furnace circulated to heat the room above.

ICONOGRAPHY A system of illustrations, usually of a symbolic and metaphorical nature, concerning a particular subject.

INGOT A shaped mass of smelted but unworked metal.

INSULA (PL. INSULAE) A rectangular residential block in a town surrounded on all sides by streets.

IONIC STYLE Greek architectural style characterised by columns with a diameter-to-height ratio of between one-to-eight and one-to-ten. The flutes on the columns have flattened edges and the capital stone at the top of the column is scroll-like.

IWAN A vaulted, open-fronted hall or reception room facing onto a courtyard in a Persian palace.

KABAL A simple turntable used in pottery manufacture in the New World.

KHAN See *caravanserai*.

KIN-GROUP A group of people related by blood rather than, for example, age or gender.

KIVA A circular or rectangular subterranean room in a *pueblo* used for ceremonies and meetings, particularly by men.

LACQUER WARE A range of ornate domestic and funerary vessels manufactured by coating a wooden or fabric pre-form with sap from the lacquer tree, which slowly hardens on exposure to air.

LAKE VILLAGES Settlements which were originally built on dry land at the edges of lakes or on islands within them, but which were subsequently inundated by rising water levels.

LAMINATING The production of a high-quality metal tool or weapon by repeatedly forging out a blank form, folding the metal over and forging it again so that qualities of malleability and hardness can be combined.

LA TÈNE ART A style current from the 5th–1st centuries BC in western Europe showing influences from Scythian and Mediterranean art but also local originality using bold abstract curvilinear designs with infilled zones.

LATIFUNDIA Large planned agricultural estates geared to efficient production and high profits through the use of cheap, often slave labour. Although strictly a Roman term, its use extends to agricultural estates in general where production is at an industrial level.

LEGION The main unit of the Roman imperial army comprising 5000–6000 foot soldiers and a small number of mounted men and officers.

LEVALLOIS FACIES Aspect of stone-tool production using the *prepared-core technique*, specific to the Middle Palaeolithic period.

LINEAGE A kin-group defined through a number of generations by a specific line of descent, either through the male side (patrilineal) or the female side (matrilineal).

LIVING FLOOR An area within a cave or structure, or out in the open, on which everyday human activities took place. Ancient living floors have occasionally been preserved through the accumulation of soil and debris over them.

LOESS Wind-blown glacial sand which forms a rich and easily-worked soil.

LOST-WAX CASTING TECHNIQUE Also known as *cire perdue*. A method of casting intricate metal shapes by first modelling the required form in wax, then surrounding the wax with clay, firing it and draining out the melted wax. This leaves a high-quality mould for a single casting.

LOW-RELIEF See *bas-relief*.

LURER Scandinavian Bronze Age horn-shaped musical instruments.

LYNCHET A small-scale terracing effect visible particularly in ancient field-systems which is caused by accumulation of soil against an obstruction such as a field boundary.

MACE A club-like instrument which has a perforated stone or metal head and is used as a weapon or ceremonial item.

MAGNETOMETER A portable device for measuring variations in the Earth's magnetic field, able to detect signs of human activity such as hearths and kilns.

MANO In the New World, a cylindrically-shaped grinding stone used in the hand and in conjunction with a smooth *metate*, a bottom- or nether-stone.

MANUPORT An unmodified stone carried to its findspot from elsewhere by human agency.

MARAE Polynesian temples comprising courtyards and altar-like *ahu*, before which ceremonies took place.

MASTABA A flat-topped, bench-like Egyptian tomb structure under which rulers, high-ranking officials and priests were buried.

MATCHLOCK A type of musket which used an attached burning taper to light the gunpowder.

MAUSOLEUM A storage structure for the dead which was above ground.

MEALING BIN A small *adobe*- or stone-lined pit in which was placed a *metate*, used for grinding maize.

MEGALITH A very large stone, sometimes free-standing, sometimes part of a structure. Also an abbreviated form of *megalithic tomb*.

MEGALITHIC TOMB A large tomb which used *megaliths* to create passages and chambers in which burials of one or more people could be placed.

MEGARON A tripartite rectangular building found mainly in Bronze Age Greece with an entrance porch at one narrow end, a vestibule and, within the inner room, a central hearth surrounded by four columns.

MENHIR See *monolith*.

METATE See *mano*.

MICROBLADE A very small, narrow *blade*.

MICROLITH A small stone tool, shaped into either a point or a barb, for use in composite hunting weapons such as harpoons and arrows.

MIDDEN Any heap of rubbish adjacent to a dwelling or other site. See also *shell midden*.

MIDDLE KINGDOM The period of Egyptian history beginning with the reunification of Upper and Lower Egypt by the 11th Dynasty king Nebhepetre Mentahopte II ushering in 260 years of stability and prosperity (c.2040–1783 BC).

MIT'A A tax or duty exacted from the people of the Inca empire by the state, payable in the form of labour.

MONOLITH A single, large, isolated stone, often shaped and usually standing upright. Synonymous with *menhir* in the Neolithic of north-west Europe.

MORTUARY HOUSE A simple timber structure in which one or more corpses was placed, perhaps with some grave-goods. In some instances an earthen mound (*barrow*) was raised over the mortuary structure.

MOSAIC A wall or floor decoration made up of many cubical clay blocks (tesserae) of different colours.

MOTIF An element in a (usually) complex design. It may be non-representational or pictorial.

MULLER A small grinding stone, often for use with pigments but also grains, ores and drugs.

MUMMIFICATION The technique of preserving a body whereby the viscera and brain are extracted from the dried body prior to embalming it in sodium carbonate and finally wrapping it in bandages and a canvas shroud.

NECROPOLIS An area of tombs, temples and pathways which amounted to a city set aside for the dead.

NET SINKER A perforated stone weight used to keep a gill-net vertical in the water.

NEW KINGDOM The Egyptian period following the expulsion of Asiatic Hyksos rulers and the subsequent reunification under the kings of the 18th to 21st Dynasties including Tuthmoses I–IV, Akhenaten, Tutankhamun and Ramesses I–XI. To this period belongs much of the monumental architecture of Egypt.

NURAGHE (PL. NURAGHI) A small Sardinian drystone fortress characterised by a tower in the form of a truncated cone.

NYMPHAEUM A public drinking fountain. Nymphs were associated with a range of natural features such as water, mountains and trees.

OBSIDIAN A glassy black rock of volcanic origin which is suitable for making sharp-edged stone tools.

ODEUM A small theatre or roofed hall for holding music concerts.

OLD KINGDOM The period preceding the *Middle Kingdom* during which four dynasties of kings ruled over Egypt and were buried in colossal stone pyramids.

OLDOWAN Earliest stone tools from the Olduvai Gorge, consisting of simple chipped pebbles, and found at other sites of the period 2–1.5 million years ago.

OPEN-WORK A decorative technique in which gaps or interstices are left around a pattern, sometimes to be filled in with a different material.

OPPIDUM (PL. OPPIDA) Large permanent settlements of Iron Age Celtic Europe which served as centres for administration, trade, craft production and religion.

ORACLE BONES The bones, usually cattle shoulder blades, used in Chinese divination rituals during the Shang and early Chou periods. The cracks resulting from the application of a heated point formed the basis of the divination.

OSTRACA Fragments of soft stone or pottery which bear jottings or exercise writing.

OXYGEN ISOTOPE A molecular variant of normal oxygen which varies in proportion to the normal type according to the temperature, thus allowing climatic reconstruction.

PA A Maori defended settlement.

PADDIES Fields for the intensive cultivation of rice, flooded naturally or by irrigation.

PAGODA A Buddhist temple tower of several storeys, common in East Asia.

PALAEOPATHOLOGY The study of ancient diet, diseases and traumatic injuries through the analysis of preserved bones.

PALAESTRA A Roman building which consisted of a large central sand-covered courtyard surrounded by changing rooms and washrooms, used for wrestling, gymnastics and military training.

PALISADE A stake-built defensive barrier, often on top of an embankment or rampart.

PANTHEON A temple dedicated to a range of gods. Also used to refer to the gods of a people.

PAPYRUS The main writing medium in use in Egypt from the 5th Dynasty (*Old Kingdom*) through to early Christian times. It was made from sheets of compressed and dried slices of reed stems.

PAROIKOI The dependent peasants of a Byzantine monastic economy.

PASTORALISM An economy in which the bulk of the food supply is derived from domesticated animals, usually in the form of secondary products such as milk, yoghurt and cheese.

PATRIARCHATE An area of ecclesiastical administration under the jurisdiction of one of the four principal sees of the eastern Church: Antioch, Jerusalem, Alexandria and Constantinople.

PATU A Polynesian short club-like weapon, made of a variety of materials including wood and whalebone (paroa).

PECTORAL A decorative and/or protective plate which covers the chest.

PERISTYLE COURT An enclosed area surrounded by columns, central to a villa using a courtyard plan.

PETROGLYPH A picture or symbol (*glyph*) carved into rock.

PHARAOH The title taken by the rulers of ancient Egypt.

PIECE MOULD In metalworking, a clay mould, made of a number of separate pieces fitting together, for casting intricately-shaped objects.

PILASTER A rectangular column attached to a wall.

PITHOS (PL. PITHOI) A large ancient Greek storage jar for liquids.

PIT HOUSE A dwelling in which the floor level is below the surrounding ground level so that often all that remains to be detected of such a house on an archaeological site is a large shallow pit.

PLATE ARMOUR Protective armour in the form of sheet-iron fittings tailored to the shape of the body and strapped in position. This type of armour was current in 15th–16th century AD Europe.

PLAZA An open square in ancient cities of the New World, similar to the Roman *forum*, which was the focus for meetings and events.

PNYX An ancient Greek open-air auditorium for public assemblies.

POLIS A city or *city-state* of ancient Greece.

POLLEN CORE A column of soil or peat extracted from the ground containing a continuous record of pollen grains representative of changing vegetation over a period of time: the deeper the core, the older the pollen.

POLYCHROME Decoration using several differently-coloured pigments.

PORCELAIN A fine form of pottery which is fired to a very high temperature in order to vitrify the clay.

PORTICO A colonnaded annexe or entrance.

POSTHOLE A rock- or earth-cut socket which at one time held the upright post of a structure.

POTASSIUM-ARGON DATING A technique similar to *radiocarbon dating* but applicable to much older deposits. It dates not the objects themselves, but the rock strata between which they lie by measuring the ratio of radioactive Potassium-40 to stable Argon-40 in certain types of volcanic rock.

POTSHERD A fragment of broken pottery.

POZZOLANA Concrete, made from volcanic ash, which hardens under water.

PREFECTURE A unit of civic administration, e.g. in Tang and Sung China.

PREPARED-CORE TECHNIQUE Method of stone-tool production whereby cores themselves were shaped in order to produce flakes of a desired form, instead of the *flakes* being shaped after their removal from the *core*.

PRESSURE-FLAKING A technique for removing small, narrow flakes whereby pressure is applied to a core at the correct point simply by pressing, rather than striking, using the tip of an antler.

PROCURATOR A Roman civil administrative position with responsibilities ranging from estate management to governorship of minor provinces.

PROJECTILE POINT The tip of a spear or arrow, often made of a material which is different from that of the shaft. Thus a stone projectile point may be hafted in a wooden shaft.

PROTOHISTORIC ERA The earliest time period during which writing appears in a given region.

PROTO-NEOLITHIC The early stages of the adoption of characteristic Neolithic traits such as animal and plant domestication, and the manufacture of pottery.

PRYTANEION The town hall of a Greek or Hellenistic city.

PUEBLO A stone- or brick-built dwelling in the Southwest USA, usually occurring as a complex agglomeration of individual houses and other structures. Many of the rooms were entered via a trap-door in the roof.

PYRAMID A type of large stone structure which either had four smooth sides culminating in a point (in Egypt only), or a stepped profile. In Egypt pyramids were used as tombs, whereas in Mesopotamia, Mesoamerica and South America they were temple-platforms.

QUENCHING In metalworking, the plunging of a red-hot iron implement into cold water or brine to harden it.

QUINQUEREME A Roman and Hellenistic warship which was larger and more powerful than its predecessor, the *trireme*.

RADIOCARBON DATING A dating technique which measures the length of time which has elapsed since any living thing died by analysing the ratio of normal Carbon-12 to radioactive Carbon-14 in its remains. This technique is used to date bone, wood, shell, charcoal and other materials.

RADIOGRAPHY The palaeopathological study of preserved body tissues using X-ray photography. It is especially useful for studying *bog bodies* and bodies preserved by *mummification*.

REFLEX BOW A small but powerful bow made such that, until strung, the ends of the bow project forwards rather than backwards.

RELIEF See *bas-relief*.

REMOTE SENSING The detection of hidden archaeological features such as walls, pits or roads by means of sound or radar impulses passed through the ground. Unlike *aerial photography*, remote sensing is not normally used to detect new sites but only to explore known ones.

REPOUSSE Metalworking technique whereby a design is raised or embossed by hammering the metal out from behind.

ROCK ART Any carving or painting on a rock surface, whether in a cave or in the open, pictorial or abstract.

ROCK-CUT TOMB A burial chamber quarried wholly or partly into rock.

ROMAN PERIOD The period of Roman political and military control, generally between 200 BC and AD 400, but varying from region to region, depending on the date of conquest.

RUNES A system of writing consisting of simple strokes devised by Germanic peoples through contact with Mediterranean scripts in the 3rd century AD. Runes were used throughout northern Europe up to the Middle Ages as a result of Viking expansion, most commonly in dedications on jewellery and on free-standing memorial stones (runestones).

SARCOPHAGUS A stone, lead, wooden or terracotta coffin, frequently highly decorated.

SCAR In stone tools, this is the negative impression left after the removal of a flake.

SCRAPER In stone tools, a *flake* which has been shaped deliberately to provide a sharp, rounded edge with which to scrape unwanted fat from the insides of animal skins without damaging the skin, or to shape wood or bone artefacts.

SEAL A device for impressing characteristic marks into a soft surface, often to indicate ownership. Seals may be in the form of stamps or *cylinder seals*.

SEDENTARY LIFESTYLE One based in a single location rather than involving moving camp at regular intervals.

SHAFT-HOLE AXE An axe-head of metal or stone with a hole through it for hafting.

SHAMAN A medicine man in 'primitive' societies, often with supernatural powers, who was capable of healing or harming.

SHELL MIDDEN An extensive rubbish heap consisting largely of shells, the result of many years of exploitation of marine resources as a main or supplementary food source. Shell middens are found in many different parts of the world.

SITE CATCHMENT The area around a site from which the different types of resources utilised at the site (e.g. crops, stone, clay) were derived.

SITE EXPLOITATION TERRITORY The area around a particular site which would have been most intensively or frequently exploited for resources such as food.

SITULA ART Embossed or incised decoration of Early Iron Age date in south-central Europe, the medium for which was usually a bronze shouldered bucket-shaped vessel (situla).

SLAG The non-metal residue left behind after the *smelting* of a metal ore.

SLASH AND BURN AGRICULTURE A farming technique in which patches of forest are cleared for agriculture by cutting and burning the undergrowth, but are abandoned after a few seasons in favour of freshly-cleared areas.

SLIP A thin coat of watery clay mixture applied to a pot prior to firing which gives a smooth surface and often a different colour to the finished article.

SMELTING The extraction of usable metal from an ore by heating to extreme temperatures in a furnace.

SOCKETED IMPLEMENT A bronze or iron weapon or tool cast so that it was hollow and open at the butt-end to allow a haft to be inserted.

SPINDLE WHORL A small, perforated disc of stone or pottery which acts as a flywheel, maintaining the momentum of the spindle rotated by the spinner whilst he or she teases more fibres out of a fleece.

STADION An ancient Greek open-air stadium for sports.

STAKE-HOLE The cavity left behind in the ground after the removal or decay of a stake or post, which would usually have been part of a structure or fence. The cavity becomes filled with soil of a slightly different colour or texture from that into which the stake-hole was originally cut, thus allowing its detection by archaeologists. See also *posthole*.

STAVE BOW A simple form of bow made from a single piece of wood, such as yew.

STELA (PL. STELAE) A small carved stone slab widely used as a monument, milestone or gravestone, often inscribed pictorially or with writing.

STOA A colonnaded market-hall in an ancient Greek city.

STRATIFIED SOCIETY A society in which competing groups have unequal access to power and/or resources, some groups being subordinate to others. The uppermost stratum is termed an '*elite*'.

STRATIGRAPHY The layering of soils one above another which allows archaeologists to trace the development of a site and to place a range of archaeological remains (e.g. artefacts) within the layers into a time sequence.

STUCCO Decorative plaster-work.

STUPA A South Asian Buddhist monument consisting of a hemispherical mound of earth, brick or stone, containing burials or relics, often the focus of a monastery.

STYLUS A pointed writing instrument which can be made from a variety of materials: reed stem, bone or metal.

TELL A mound formed by the massive accumulation of debris from derelict mud and/or wattle houses of a town or city over a long period of time.

TEMENOS A temple precinct.

TEMPER In pottery manufacture, temper is an additive to the raw clay such as sand or finely crushed stone which helps to prevent the pot shrinking or cracking during firing.

TERP (PL. TERPEN) An artificial mound, similar to a *tell*, found in late prehistoric north-west Europe, which was created by the continual remaking of clay floors and deposition of rubbish. Terpen, or 'Wierden' in Germany, provided opportune sites for settlement in areas which were threatened by flooding.

TERRACOTTA Baked clay.

TERRA SIGILLATA Roman mass-produced pottery with a range of forms but characterised by a red, shiny, glaze-like slip. Exported throughout the western Empire, it can be a very accurate chronological indicator.

TETRAPYLON A four-arched crossing.

THEMATA Large units of the Byzantine armed forces found between the 7th and 10th centuries AD.

THERMOLUMINESCENCE DATING A dating technique which measures the amount of time which has elapsed since an object was last heated by the amount of light it emits when re-heated. This technique is especially useful for dating pottery.

THOLOS (PL. THOLOI) A beehive-shaped chamber of stone.

THREE AGE SYSTEM The theoretical division of prehistory into three successive technological stages characterised by the use of stone, bronze and iron.

TORC A neck-ring, often spirally-twisted, of bronze or gold.

TOURNETTE A pivoted platter which can be rotated manually to ease the manufacture of a pot, but which is not turned mechanically and so is not a potter's wheel.

TREPANATION A world-wide and long-lived crude operation to remove a disc or roundel of skull bone, perhaps to relieve pressure after the fracturing of the skull, or to try to combat headaches or epilepsy. In many cases the patient's skull healed completely and the person survived.

TRICLINIUM A Roman dining room, often with an arrangement of three couches in a horseshoe-shape.

TRILITHON An arrangement of often very large stones, comprising two uprights and a lintel, as at Stonehenge.

TRIREME The earliest type of Greek warship which used a battering ram in the prow as its main weapon. Named after the three banks of oars by which it was propelled.

TROLLING LURE A fishing device which is towed behind a moving boat.

TUMULUS (PL. TUMULI) See *barrow*.

TUYERE In metalworking, a tube through which air can be blown in order to increase the heat in a furnace.

URNFIELD A group or cemetery of inurned cremations buried in the ground.

URNFIELD PERIOD The Later Bronze Age in central Europe (c.1300–700 BC) which was characterised not only by its cremation cemeteries but also by its fortified settlements and sheet-bronze metalworking.

VARVES Alternate layers of coarse and fine muds laid down on lake beds by melting glaciers in spring and summer each year. The layers can be counted back year by year from the present.

VAULT A form of roofing in stone or brick using the principle of gravity to lock the materials together. The barrel vault is continuous and of semi-circular section, whilst with the rib vault the weight of the roof is carried by ribs.

VENUS FIGURINE A stylised figurine of Upper Palaeolithic date representing a woman with exaggerated sexual characteristics such as breasts, hips and stomach.

VERNACULAR The writing, speech, architecture etc. common among the indigenous people of a country or region.

VICUS (PL. VICI) A small unit of settlement in the Roman landscape, either a country village (sometimes attached to a military fort) or a district of a town.

VILLA In a Roman context, this comprised a farmstead with ancillary buildings, usually with one main residential structure. Later the term was also used to mean a country house. In a Minoan context a villa was a rural residence with some local administrative functions.

VIZIER Prime minister or right-hand man to the king.

WATTLE AND DAUB Interwoven hazel rods (wattle) coated with a mixture of clay, straw, dung and other materials. It was used for, among other things, house walls, ovens and simple pottery kilns.

WRISTGUARD A thin stone plaque which is strapped on to the inner forearm of an archer to prevent it from being grazed when the bowstring is released.

ZIGGURAT A Mesopotamian stepped or terraced temple-platform or tower.

BIBLIOGRAPHY

Dating the past p.24

M.G.L Baillie: *Tree-ring dating and archaeology* London, 1982
S. Fleming: *Dating in Archaeology. A Guide to Scientific Techniques* London, 1976
S. Fleming: *Thermoluminescence Techniques in Archaeology* Oxford, 1979
E. Hollstein: *Mitteleuropäische Eichenchronologie* Mainz am Rhein, 1980
C. Renfrew: *Before Civilization: the radiocarbon revolution and prehistoric Europe* London, 1973

Survival from the past p.26

J. Coles: *The Archaeology of Wetlands* Edinburgh, 1984
D.R. Wilson (ed.): *Aerial Reconnaissance for Archaeology* London, 1975

Excavation p.28

P. Barker: *Techniques of Archaeological Excavation* London, 1977
J.G. Evans: *Land Snails in Archaeology* London, 1972
J.G. Evans: *An Introduction to Environmental Archaeology* London, 1978
E.C. Harris: *Principles of Archaeological Stratigraphy* London, 1979
J. McIntosh: *The Archaeologist's Handbook* London, 1986
S. Piggott: *Ancient Europe* Edinburgh, 1965
I.M. Stead: *Excavations at Winterton Roman Villa and Other Roman Sites in North Lincolnshire 1958–67* London, 1976

Settlement p.30

J. Hawkes (ed.): *Atlas of Ancient Archaeology* London, 1974
J.N. Hill: *Broken K Pueblo: prehistoric social organization in the American Southwest* Tucson, 1970
B.J. Kemp: *Amarna Reports Vols 1–4* Cambridge, 1984–87
H. de Lumley: *Une Cabane Acheuléene dans la Grotte du Lazaret (Nice)* Paris, 1969
W. Stevenson Smith: *The Art and Architecture of Ancient Egypt* Harmondsworth, 1958

Settlement patterns p.32

J-P. Demoule and M. Ilett: 'First Millennium Settlement and Society in Northern France: a case study from the Aisne Valley' in J.V.S. Megaw and T.C. Champion (eds) *Settlement and Society: Aspects of West European Prehistory in the First Millennium* BC pp.193–221, Leicester, 1985
R.S. MacNeish (ed.): *The Prehistory of the Tehuacán Valley, Vol.5: Excavation and Reconnaissance* Austin, 1972
G.R. Willey: *The Virú Valley, Peru* Washington, 1953

Burials p.34

O.N. Bader: 'Les Sépultunes au Paléolithique Avancé et un Tombeau dans la Station Sounghir' in *Sovetskaya Arkheologiya* part 3, pp.142–159, 1957
R. Joussaume: *Des Dolmens pour les Morts* Paris, 1985
C.S. Peebles and S.M. Kus: 'Some Archaeological Correlates of Ranked Societies' in *American Antiquity* Vol.42, pp.421–448, 1977
A. Salamon and I. Lengyel: 'Kinship Interrelations in a 5th Century "Pannonian" Cemetery' in *World Archaeology* Vol.12, pp.93–104, 1980
V. Steponaitis: *Ceramics, Chronology and Community Patterns at Moundville, a late Prehistoric Site in Alabama* New York, 1983

Underwater sites p.36

G. Bass: *Archaeology Under Water* London, 1966
D.L. Hamilton: 'Preliminary Report on the Archaeological Investigations of the Submerged Remains of Port Royal, Jamaica, 1981–2, in *The International Journal of Nautical Archaeology* Vol.13, pp.11–25, 1984
C.J.M. Martin: 'The Dartmouth, a British Frigate Wrecked off Mull 1690' in *The International Journal of Nautical Archaeology* Vol.7, pp. 29–58, 1978
K. Muckelroy: *Maritime Archaeology* Cambridge, 1978
K. Muckelroy (ed.): *Archaeology Under Water* New York, 1980
M. Pawson and D. Buisseret: *Port Royal Jamaica* Oxford, 1976

Food p.38

H.G. Baker: *Plants and Civilization* Belmont, California, 1965
D. & P. Brothwell: *Food in Antiquity* London, 1969
W.J. Darby, P. Ghalioungui and L. Grivetti: *Food: The Gift of Osiris* London and New York, 1977
C.B. Heiser, Jnr: *Seed to Civilization. The Story of Man's Food* San Francisco, 1973
L.K. Napton: *Archaeological and Paleobiological Investigations in Lovelock Cave, Nevada; further analysis of human coprolites* Berkeley, 1969
D. Zohary and M. Hopf: *Domestication of Plants in the Old World* Oxford, 1988

Textiles p.40

E. Broudy: *The Book of Looms: a history of the handloom from ancient times to the present* London, 1979
M. Hald: *Olddanske Tekstiler* Copenhagen, 1950
M. Hoffmann: *The Warp-Weighted Loom* Oslo, 1964
A. Lucas: *Ancient Egyptian Materials and Industries* London, 1948 (3rd ed.)
I.L. Mason: *Evolution of Domesticated Animals* London, 1984
K. Peck Kent: 'The Cultivation and Weaving of Cotton in the Prehistoric Southwestern United States' in *Transactions of the American Philosophical Society* Vol.47, part 3, pp.457–732, 1957
J.P. Wild: *Textile Manufacture in the Northern Roman Provinces* Cambridge, 1970

Disease p.42

D.R. Brothwell and A.T. Sandison (eds): *Diseases in Antiquity* Springfield, Illinois, 1967
A. Cockburn and E. Cockburn (eds): *Mummies, Disease and Ancient Cultures* Cambridge, 1980
R. David and E. Tapp (eds): *Evidence Embalmed – modern medicine and the mummies of Ancient Egypt* Manchester, 1984
C. Wells: *Bones, Bodies and Disease* London, 1964
M.R. Zimmerman and M.A. Kelley: *Atlas of Human Palaeopathology* New York, 1982

Warfare p.44

A. Azzaroli: *An Early History of Horsemanship* Leiden, 1985
R. Law: *The Horse in West African History* Oxford, 1980
M.A. Littauer: 'Early Stirrups' in *Antiquity* Vol.55, pp.99–105, 1981
P.R.S. Moorey: 'The Emergence of the Light Horse-drawn Chariot in the Near East, c.2000–1500 BC' in *World Archaeology* Vol.18, pp.196–215, 1986
L. White: *Medieval Technology and Social Change* Oxford, 1962

Valuables p.46

J.G.D. Clark: *Symbols of Excellence* Cambridge, 1986
J.W. Leach and E. Leach (eds): *The Kula: new perspectives on Massim exchange* Cambridge, 1983
B. Malinowski: *Argonauts of the Western Pacific* London, 1922

Ritual p.48

I.E.S. Edwards: *The Pyramids of Egypt* Harmondsworth, 1976 (revised ed.)
J. Garanger: *Archéologie des Nouvelles-Hébrides, contribution à la connaissances des îles du centre* Paris, 1972
R. Ghirshman: *Tchoga Zanbil, I: La Ziggurat* Paris, 1966
A.M. Iozzer: *Chichén Itzá and its Cenote of Sacrifice* Cambridge, Mass., 1957
F. Robicsek: *The Smoking Gods. Tobacco in Maya Art, History and Religion* Norman, 1978

Africa pp.54/56

M.D. Leakey: *Olduvai Gorge: Vol.3. Excavation in Beds I and II 1960–63* Cambridge, 1971

Climate p.58

A.G. Sutcliffe: *On the track of the Ice Age mammals* London, 1985

Early hominids: E. Africa p.60

The Atlas of Primitive Man in China Peking, 1980

Early hominids: Europe p.62

D. Mania and A. Dietzel: *Begegnung mit dem Urmenschen: die funde von Bilzingsleben* Leipzig, 1980

The Neanderthals p.64

M. Shackley: *Neanderthal Man* London, 1980
E. Trinkaus and W.W. Howells: 'The Neanderthals' in *Scientific American*, pp.94–105, Vol.241, No.6, 1979

First modern humans p.66

R. Singer and J. Wymer: *The Middle Stone Age of Klassies River Mouth in South Africa* Chicago, 1982

Peopling of Australia p.68

R.V.S. Wright (ed.): *Archaeology of the Gallus site, Koonalda Cave* Canberra, 1971
J.P. White and J.F. O'Connell: *A Prehistory of Australia, New Guinea and Sahul* New York, 1982

Peopling of the Americas p.70

T.D. Dillehey: 'A late Ice Age Settlement in Southern Chile' in *Scientific American* 251, part 4, pp.106–113, 1984

European hunter-gatherers p.72

A. Leroi-Gourhan: *Pincevent: Campement Magdalenien de Chasseurs de Rennes* Paris, 1984
O. Soffer: *The Upper Palaeolithic of the central Russian plain* New York, 1985

Art of hunter-gatherers p.74

P.G. Bahn and J. Vertut: *Images of the Ice Age* London, 1988
H. Breuil and H. Obermaier: *The cave of Altamira at Santillana del Mar, Spain* Madrid, 1935
L'art des Cavernes: Atlas des grottes ornées paléolithiques Françaises Paris, 1984

Birth of agriculture p.78

J. Clutton-Brock: *Domesticated Animals: from early times* London, 1981
J.R. Harlan: *Crops and Man* Madison, 1975
E. Isaac: *Geography of Domestication* Englewood Cliffs, N.J., 1970
R.B. Lee and I. de Vore: *Man the Hunter* Chicago, 1968
P.C. Mangelsdorf: *Corn: its origin, evolution and improvement* Cambridge, Mass., 1974
I.L. Mason: *Evolution of Domesticated Animals* London, 1984
C.A. Reed: *Origins of Agriculture* The Hague, 1977
N.W. Simmonds (ed.): *Evolution of Crop Plants* London, 1979

Farmers of the Near East p.80

J.R. Harlan and D. Zohary: 'Distribution of Wild Wheats and Barley' in *Science* Vol.153, pp.1074–1080, 1966
K. Kenyon: *Excavations at Jericho* Vols 3 and 4, London, 1981–2
J. Mellaart: *The Neolithic of the Near East* London, 1975
D. and J. Oates: *The Rise of Civilization* Oxford, 1976
C. Redman: *The Rise of Civilization: from early farmers to urban society in the ancient Near East* San Francisco, 1978
P. Singh: *Neolithic Cultures of West Asia* London, 1974
Tübinger Atlas des Vorderen orients Wiesbaden, 1977
C. Vita-Finzi and E.S. Higgs: 'Prehistoric Economy in the Mount Carmel Area of Palestine: Site Catchment Analysis' in *Proceedings of the Prehistoric Society* Vol.37, pp.1–37, 1970

Çatal Hüyük p.82

O. Erol: 'The Quaternary History of the Lake Basins of Central and Southern Anatolia' in W.C. Brice (ed.) *The Environmental History of the Near and Middle East Since the Last Ice Age* pp.111–139, London, 1978
J. Mellaart: *Çatal Hüyük, a Neolithic town in Anatolia* London, 1967

Europe after the ice p.84

G.N. Bailey: 'Shell Middens as Indicators of Postglacial Economies: a territorial perspective' in P. Mellars (ed.) *The Early Postglacial Settlement of Northern Europe* pp.37–63, London, 1978
T. Champion, C. Gamble, S. Shennan and A. Whittle: *Prehistoric Europe* London, 1984
J.G.D. Clark: *Excavations at Star Carr* Cambridge, 1954
J.G.D. Clark: *The Earlier Stone Age Settlement of Scandinavia* Cambridge, 1975
B. Huntley and H.J.B. Birks: *An Atlas of Past and Present Pollen Maps for Europe: 0–13,000 years ago* Cambridge, 1983
A. Morrison: *Early Man in Britain and Ireland* London, 1980
J. Shackleton, T. van Andel and C. Runnels: 'Coastal Paleogeography of the Western Mediterranean during the last 125,000 years' in *Journal of Field Archaeology* Vol.11, pp.307–314, 1984
D. Srejovic: *Lepenski Vir* London, 1972

Farming in Europe p.86

G. Barker: *Prehistoric Farming in Europe* Cambridge, 1985
J.P. Farrugia, R. Kuper, J. Lüning and P. Stehli: 'Der Band- Keramische Siedlungsplatz Langweiler 2' in *Rheinische Ausgrabungen* Vol.13, 1973
S. Milisauskas: *European Prehistory* New York, 1978
A. Sargent: 'The Carbon-14 Chronology of the Early and Middle Neolithic of Southern Italy' in *Proceedings of the Prehistoric Society* Vol.51, pp.31–40, 1985
R. Tringham: *Hunters, Fishers and Farmers of Eastern Europe 6000–3000* BC London, 1971
A. Whittle: *Neolithic Europe: a survey* Cambridge, 1985

Farming in South Asia p.88

B. and F.R. Allchin: *The Rise of Civilization in India and Pakistan* Cambridge, 1982
B. Allchin (ed.): Section on 'Mehrgarh' in *South Asian Archaeology 1981*, pp.21–61, Cambridge, 1984
J-F. Jarrige and M. Lechevallier: 'Excavations at Mehrgarh, Baluchistan: their significance in the prehistorical context of the Indo-Pakistani borderlands' in M. Taddei (ed.) *South Asian Archaeology 1977* Naples, 1979
M.S. Randhawa: *A History of Agriculture in India* Vol.1, New Delhi, 1980
G.R. Sharma: *Beginnings of Agriculture* Allahabad, 1980

Farming in S.E. Asia p.90

J. Allen, J. Golson and R. Jones (eds): *Sunda and Sahul* London, 1977
P. Bellwood: *Prehistory of the Indo-Malaysian Archipelago* Australia, 1985
R. Fox: *The Tabon Cave* Manila, 1970
I. Glover: 'The Hoabinhian: hunter-gatherers or early agriculturalists in South-East Asia?' in J.V.S. Megaw (ed.) *Hunters, Gatherers and First Farmers Beyond Europe* pp.145–165, Leicester, 1977
I. Glover: 'The Late Stone Age in eastern Indonesia' in *World Archaeology* Volume IX (1), pp.42–61, 1977
C. Gorman: 'The Hoabinhian and after: subsistence patterns in Southeast Asia during the Late Pleistocene and early Recent periods' in *World Archaeology* Volume II (3), pp.300–320, 1971
R. Mourer: 'Laang Spean and the prehistory of Cambodia' in *Modern Quaternary Research in Southeast Asia* Vol.3, pp.29–57, Rotterdam, 1977
Ha Van Tan: 'Nouvelles Recherches Prehistoriques et Protohistoriques au Vietnam' in *Bulletin de l'Ecole Française d'Extreme Orient* Tome LXVIII, pp.115–143, Paris

Farming in East Asia p.92

C.M. Aikens and T. Higuchi: *The Prehistory of Japan* New York, 1982
T. Akazawa: 'Cultural Change in Prehistoric Japan: receptivity to rice agriculture in the Japanese Archipelago' in F. Wendorf and A.E. Close (eds) *Advances in World Archaeology* Vol.1, pp.151–211, New York, 1982
F. Bray: 'Agriculture' in J. Needham (ed.) *Science and Civilization in China* Vol.6, part 2, Cambridge, 1984
Kwang-chih Chang: *The Archaeology of Ancient China* New Haven and London, 1986 (4th ed.)
C.S. Chard: *Northeast Asia in Prehistory* Madison, 1974
I. Glover: 'Agricultural Origins in East Asia' in A. Sherratt (ed.) *The Cambridge Encyclopedia of Archaeology* pp.152–161, Cambridge, 1980
Hsi-an Pan-P'o (The Neolithic Village at Pan P'o, Sian) The Institute of Archaeology, Academia Sinica and the Pan P'o Museum, Sian. Peking, 1963
S.M. Nelson: 'Recent Progress in Korean Archaeology' in F. Wendorf and A.E. Close (eds) *Advances in World Archaeology* Vol.1, pp.99–149, New York, 1982
Ping-ti Ho: 'Loess and the Origin of Chinese Agriculture' in *The American Historical Review* Vol.75, pp.1–36, 1969
Xia Nai, An Zhimin, Zhang Changshou and Xu Pingfang: *Recent Archaeological Discoveries in the People's Republic of China* Tokyo, 1984

Africa p.94

J. Desmond Clark and Steven A. Brandt (eds): *From Hunters to Farmers. The Causes and Consequences of Food Production in Africa* Berkeley, 1984

P.M. Hobler and J.J. Hester: 'Prehistory and environment in the Libyan Desert' in *South African Archaeological Bulletin* 23, pp.120–130, 1969

D.W. Phillipson: *The Later Prehistory of Eastern and Southern Africa* London, 1977

D.W. Phillipson: *African Archaeology* Cambridge, 1985

B.D. Shaw: 'Climate, environment and prehistory in the Sahara' in *World Archaeology* 8, pp.133–149, 1976

J.E.G. Sutton: 'The Aquatic Civilization of Middle Africa' in *Journal of African History* 15, pp.527–546, 1974

A.R. Willcox: *The rock art of Africa* London, 1984

M.A.J. Williams and H. Faure (eds): *The Sahara and the Nile* Rotterdam, 1980

Aboriginal Australia p.96

J.C.R. Camm and J.McQuilton: *Australians: A Historical Atlas* New South Wales, 1987

R. Edwards: *Australian Aboriginal Art: the art of the Alligator Rivers region, Northern Territory* Canberra, 1979

J. Flood: *Archaeology of the Dreamtime* Sydney, 1983

D.J. Mulvaney: *The Prehistory of Australia* London, 1969

D.J. Mulvaney: 'The Chain of Connection' in N. Peterson (ed.) *Tribes and Boundaries in Australia* pp.72–94, Canberra, 1976

G. Pretty: 'The Cultural Chronology of Roonka Flat' in R.V.S. Wright (ed.) *Stone Tools as Cultural Markers* pp.288–331, Canberra, 1977

Mesopotamian civilisations p.98

S. Lloyd: *The Archaeology of Mesopotamia* London, 1984 (revised ed.)

J. Oates, T.E. Davidson, D. Kamilli and H. McKerrell: 'Seafaring Merchants of Ur?' in *Antiquity* Vol.51, pp.221–234, 1977

J.N. Postgate: *The First Empires* Oxford, 1977

M. Roaf: 'The Hamrin Sites' in J. Curtis (ed.) *Fifty Years of Mesopotamian Discovery* pp.40–47, London, 1982

M. Roaf: 'Excavations at Tell Madhhur: the results of the third season' in *Sumer* Vol.40, pp.144–148, 1984

W. Yasin: 'Excavations at Tell es-Sawwan, 1969' in *Sumer* Vol.26, pp.3–20, 1970

Ceramics p.100

C.M. Aikens and T. Higuchi: *The Prehistory of Japan* New York, 1982

A.C. Anderson: *Interpreting Pottery* London, 1984

Kwang-chih Chang: *The Archaeology of Ancient China* New Haven, 1986 (4th ed.)

C.F. Fangraw: 'Early Chinese Ceramics and Kilns' in *Archaeology* Vol.30, pp.382–393, 1977

Hsi-an Pan-P'o (The Neolithic Village at Pan P'o, Sian) (ed.), The Institute of Archaeology, Academia Sinica and the Pan P'o Museum, Sian. Peking, 1963

Y. Majidzadeh: 'The Development of the Pottery Kiln in Iran from Prehistoric to Historical Periods' in *Paléorient* Vol.3, pp.207–219, 1975

P.M. Rice: *Pottery Analysis* Chicago, 1987

A. Rieth: *5000 Jahre Töpferscheibe* Konstanz, 1960

A. Sargent: 'The Carbon-14 Chronology of the Early and Middle Neolithic of Southern Italy' in *Proceedings of the Prehistoric Society* Vol.51, pp.31–40, 1985

Agriculture p.104

G. Barker: *Prehistoric Farming in Europe* Cambridge, 1985

K.W. Butzer: *Early Hydraulic Civilization in Egypt* Chicago, 1976

H.C. Conklin: *Ethnographic Atlas of Ifugao* New Haven, 1980

R.A. Donkin: *Agricultural Terracing in the Aboriginal New World* Tucson, 1979

D. Eisma: 'Stream Deposition and Erosion by the Eastern Shore of the Aegean' in W.C. Brice (ed.) *The Environmental History of the Near and Middle East since the Last Ice Age* pp.67–81, London, 1978

C.F. Higham, A. Kijngam, B.F. Manly and S.J. Moore: 'The Bovid Third Phalanx and Prehistoric Ploughing' in *Journal of Archaeological Science* Vol.8, pp. 353–365, 1981

T. Jacobsen: *Salinity and Irrigation Agriculture in Antiquity: Diyala Basin Archaeological Projects, reports on essential results 1957–8* Malibu, 1982

A. Sherratt: 'Plough and Pastoralism: aspects of the secondary products revolution' in I. Hodder, G. Isaac and N. Hammond (eds) *Pattern of the Past: studies in honour of David Clarke* pp.261–306, Cambridge, 1981

Megalithic Europe p.106

T. Champion, C. Gamble, S. Shennan and A. Whittle: *Prehistoric Europe* London, 1984

H. Godwin: *The History of the British Flora* Cambridge, 1975 (2nd ed.)

B. Huntley and H.J.B. Birks: *An atlas of past and present pollen maps for Europe: 0–13,000 years ago* Cambridge, 1983

S. Piggott: *The West Kennet Long Barrow: excavations 1955–6* London, 1962

C. Renfrew (ed.): *The Megalithic Monuments of Western Europe* London, 1983

E.S. Twohig: *The Megalithic Art of Western Europe* Oxford, 1981

A. Whittle: *Neolithic Europe: A Survey* Cambridge, 1985

Standing stones p.108

R.J.C. Atkinson: *Stonehenge* Harmondsworth, 1979 (2nd ed.)

A. Burl: *The Stone Circles of the British Isles* New Haven and London, 1976

A. Burl: *Megalithic Brittany* London, 1985

C. Chippendale: *Stonehenge complete* London, 1983

W. Startin and R. Bradley: 'Some notes on work organisation and society in prehistoric Wessex' in C.L.N. Ruggles and A.W.R. Whittle (eds) *Astronomy and Society in Britain during the period 4000–1500 BC* pp.289–296, Oxford, 1981

A. and A.S. Thom: *Megalithic Remains in Britain and Brittany* Oxford, 1978

Copper Age Europe p.110

I. Bognar-Kutzian: *The Copper Age Cemetery of Tiszapolgár-Basatanya* Budapest, 1963

T. Champion, C. Gamble, S. Shennan and A. Whittle: *Prehistoric Europe* London, 1984

R. Harrison: *The Beaker Folk* London, 1980

C. Renfrew: 'The Autonomy of the South-East European Copper Age' in *Proceedings of the Prehistoric Society* 35, pp.12–47, 1969

C. Renfrew: 'Varna and the social context of early metallurgy' in *Antiquity* 52, pp.199–203, 1978

R. Tringham: *Hunters, Fishers and Farmers of Eastern Europe 6000–3000 BC* London, 1971

A. Whittle: *Neolithic Europe: A Survey* Cambridge, 1985

Mediterranean civilisation p.112

C.W. Blegen: *Troy: The Excavations conducted by the University of Cincinnati 1932–1938* 4 vols, Princeton, 1950–58

K. Branigan: *Aegean Metalwork of the Early and Middle Bronze Age* Oxford, 1974

G. Camps: *Aux origines de la Berbérie.. Monuments et rites funéraires protohistoriques* Paris, 1962

J.D. Evans: 'Bossed Bone Plaques of the Second Millennium' in *Antiquity* 30, pp.80–93, 1956

C. Renfrew: *The Emergence of Civilization: The Cyclades and the Aegean in the Third Millennium BC* London, 1972

C. Renfrew and R. Whitehouse: 'The Copper Age of Peninsular Italy and the Aegean' in *Annual of the British School at Athens* 69, pp.343–390, 1974

C. Renfrew (ed.): *The Megalithic Monuments of Western Europe* London, 1983

H.N. Savory: *Spain and Portugal* London, 1968

J. Thimme (ed.): *Art and culture of the Cyclades in the third millennium BC* Chicago, 1977

Bronze Age Europe p.114

J.G.D. Clark: *Prehistoric Europe: the Economic Basis* London, 1952

J.M. Coles and A.F. Harding: *The Bronze Age in Europe* London, 1979

M. Gimbutas: *Bronze Age Cultures in Central and Eastern Europe* The Hague, 1965

W. Kimmig: 'Buchau' in *Reallexikon der Germanischen Altertumskunde* Vol.4, pp.37–55, Berlin, 1981 (2nd ed.)

H. Müller-Karpe: *Handbuch der Vorgeschichte* Munich, 1966

H. Reinerth: *Das Federseemoor als Siedlungsland des Vorseitmenschen* Leipzig, 1936

Bronze Age Scandinavia p.116

V. Boye: *Fund af Egekister fra Bronzealderen i Danmark* Copenhagen, 1896

H.C. Broholm: *Danmarks Bronzealder* 4 vols, Copenhagen, 1953–1949

H.C. Broholm, W.P. Larsen and G. Skjerne: *The Lures of the Bronze Age* Copenhagen, 1949

J. Brondsted: *Danmarks Oldtid II: Bronzealderen* Copenhagen, 1958

J.M. Coles and A.F. Harding: *The Bronze Age in Europe* London, 1979

P.V. Glob: *The Mound People. Danish Bronze-Age Man Preserved* London, 1974

M. Stenberger: *Sweden* London, 1962

Farming in Africa p.118

J.D. Clark and S.A. Brandt (eds): *From Hunters to Farmers. The Causes and Consequences of Food Production in Africa* Berkeley, 1984

B.M. Fagan and F. van Noten: *The Hunter-Gatherers of Gwisho* Tervuren, 1971

J.R. Harlan, J.M.J. de Wet and A.B. Stemler (eds): *Origins of African Plant Domestication* The Hague, 1976

R. Inskeep: 'The Final Stages of Hunting and Gathering in Africa' in A. Sherratt (ed.) *The Cambridge Encyclopedia of Archaeology* pp.174–178, Cambridge, 1980

D.W. Phillipson: *The Later Prehistory of Eastern and Southern Africa* London, 1977

D.W. Phillipson: *African Archaeology* Cambridge, 1985

T. Shaw: *Nigeria: its archaeology and early history* London, 1978

T. Shaw: 'Agricultural Origins in Africa' in A. Sherratt (ed.) *The Cambridge Encyclopedia of Archaeology* pp.179–184, Cambridge, 1980

Metallurgy p.120

N. Barnard and T. Tamotsu: *Metallurgical Remains of Ancient China* Tokyo, 1975

J.G.D. Clark: *Prehistoric Europe; the economic basis* London, 1952

R. J. Forbes: *Metallurgy in Antiquity* Leiden, 1950

P. Knauth: *The Metalsmiths* New York, 1974

R. Maddin, J.D. Muhly and T.S. Wheeler: 'How the Iron Age Began' in *Scientific American* Vol.237, pp.122–131, 1977

J. Rawson: *Ancient China: art and archaeology* London, 1980

R.R. Shepherd: *Prehistoric Mining and Allied Industries* London, 1980

C.J. Singer, E.J. Holmyard and A.R. Hall: *A History of Technology* Vol.1, Oxford, 1954

R.F. Tylecote: *A History of Metallurgy* London, 1976

T.A. Wertime and J.D. Muhly (eds): *The Coming of the Age of Iron* New Haven, 1980

First civilisations p.122

B. and F.R. Allchin: *The Rise of Civilization in India and Pakistan* Cambridge, 1982

Kwang-chih Chang: *Shang Civilization* New Haven and London, 1980

Kwang-chih Chang: *The Archaeology of Ancient China* New Haven and London, 1986 (4th ed.)

S. Lloyd: *The Archaeology of Mesopotamia* London, 1984 (revised ed.)

P.R.S. Moorey: *Materials and Manufacture in Ancient Mesopotamia: the evidence of archaeology and art* Oxford, 1985

J.N. Postgate: *The First Empires* Oxford, 1977

C.L. Woolley: *Ur Excavations Vol.2: The Royal Cemetery* London and Philadelphia, 1934

Mesopotamian cities p.124

H. Frankfort: *The Art and Architecture of the Ancient Orient* Harmondsworth, 1970 (4th revised ed.)

H. Lenzen: *Vorläufiger Bericht Über die von dem Deutschen Archäologischen Institut aus Mitteln der Deutschen Forschungsgemeinschaft Unternommen Ausgrabungen in Uruk-Warka* Vols 12–25, Berlin, 1956–74

ibid. J. Schmidt, Vols 26–33, Berlin, 1972–83

D. and J. Oates: *The Rise of Civilization* Oxford, 1976

Ur: a Sumerian city p.126

S. Lloyd: *The Archaeology of Mesopotamia* London, 1984 (revised ed.)

J.N. Postgate: *The First Empires* Oxford, 1977

L. Woolley: *Ur 'of the Chaldees'* (revised and updated by P.R.S. Moorey) London, 1982

L. Woolley and others: *Ur Excavations, vol.2: The Royal Cemetery* 2 vols, London and Philadelphia, 1934

L. Woolley and others: *Ur Excavations, vol.5: The Ziggurrat and its surroundings* London and Philadelphia, 1939

L. Woolley and others: *Ur Excavations, vol.6: The Buildings of the Third Dynasty* London and Philadelphia, 1974

Egypt: the pyramid age p.128

B. Bell: 'The oldest records of the Nile floods' in *Geographical Journal* 136, pp.569–573, 1970

I.E.S. Edwards: *The Pyramids of Egypt* Harmondsworth, 1972 (revised ed.)

G.A. Reisner: *A History of the Giza Necropolis, Vol.1* Cambridge, Mass., 1942

B. Trigger, B. Kemp, D. O'Connor and A. Lloyd: *Ancient Egypt: A Social History* Cambridge, 1983

Cities of the Indus p.130

B. Allchin and F.R. Allchin: *The Rise of Civilization in India and Pakistan* Cambridge, 1982

E.J.H. Mackay: *Further Excavations at Mohenjo-daro* 2 vols, New Delhi, 1938

J. Marshall: *Mohenjo-daro and the Indus Civilization* 3 vols, London, 1931

G.L. Possehl (ed.): *Harappan Civilization: a contemporary perspective* New Delhi, 1982

S.R. Rao: *Lothal and the Indus Civilization* New York, 1973

M. Wheeler: *The Indus Civilization* Cambridge, 1968

Mesopotamia: palace-cities p.132

S. Lloyd: *The Archaeology of Mesopotamia* London, 1984 (revised ed.)

A. Parrot: *Mission archéologique de Mari* 4 vols, Paris, 1956–1967

P. Matthiae: *Ebla. An Empire Rediscovered* English edition, London, 1980

J.N. Postgate: *The First Empires* Oxford, 1977

'Eblouissante richesse de Mari' in *Histoire et Archéologie* No.80, February 1984

L. Orlin: *Assyrian colonies in Cappadocia* 1970

J. Hawkes (ed.): *Atlas of Ancient Archaeology* London, 1974

Writing p.134

D. Diringer: *Writing* London, 1962

D. Diringer: *The Alphabet: a key to the history of mankind* London, 1968 (3rd revised ed.)

I.J. Gelb: *A Study of Writing* Chicago, 1963 (revised ed.)

P. Matthiae: *Ebla: an empire rediscovered* London, 1980

J. Oates (ed.): 'Early Writing Systems' in *World Archaeology* Vol.17, no.3, 1986

G. Pettinato: *Ebla: un impero inciso nell' argilla* Milan, 1979

D. Schmandt-Besserat: 'The Earliest Precursor of Writing' in *Scientific American* Vol.238, pp.38–47, 1978

Egypt pp.136–138

M. Bierbrier: *The tomb-builders of the pharaohs* London, 1982

B. Bruyère: *Rapport sur les Fouilles de Deir el Médineh (1934–35) Part III* Cairo, 1939

H. Carter: *The Tomb of Tutankhamen* 3 vols, London, 1923–33

C. Desroches-Noblecourt: *Tutankhamen* London, 1963

T.G.H. James: *Pharaoh's People* Oxford, 1985

A. Spencer: *Death in Ancient Egypt* Harmondsworth, 1982

B. Trigger, B. Kemp, D. O'Connor and A. Lloyd: *Ancient Egypt: a Social History* Cambridge, 1983

Minoan Crete p.140

K. Branigan: *The foundations of palatial Crete: a survey of Crete in the Early Bronze Age* London, 1970

G. Cadogan: *Palaces of Minoan Crete* London, 1976

J. Chadwick, J.T. Killen and J-P. Olivier: *The Knossos Tablets. A Transliteration* Cambridge, 1971 (4th ed.)

C. Doumas: *Thera: Pompeii of the Ancient Aegean* London, 1983

S. Hood: *The Minoans* London, 1971

S. Hood: *The Arts in Prehistoric Greece* Harmondsworth, 1978

C. Renfrew: *The Emergence of Civilization: The Cyclades and the Aegean in the Third Millennium BC* London, 1972

Struggle for the Levant p.142

G.F. Bass *et al.*: 'Cape Gelidonya: A Bronze Age Shipwreck' in *Transactions of the American Philosophical Society* Vol.57, Part 8, 1967

K. Bittel: *Hattusha, the Capital of the Hittites* New York, 1970

I.E.S. Edwards, C.J. Gadd, N.G.L. Hammond and E. Sollberger (eds): *The Cambridge Ancient History* Vol.2, Cambridge, 1973 (3rd ed.)

O.R. Gurney: *The Hittites* Harmondsworth, 1981 (2nd ed.)

J.G. Macqueen: *The Hittites and their Contemporaries in Asia Minor* London, 1975

J.B. Pritchard: *The ancient Near East in Pictures relating to the Old Testament* Princeton, 1969 (2nd ed.)

Mycenaean Greece p.144

J. Bintliff: *Natural environment and human settlement in prehistoric Greece* Oxford, 1977

S. Hood: *The Arts in prehistoric Greece* Harmondsworth, 1978

R.H. Simpson: *Mycenaean Greece* Park Ridge, NJ, 1981

G.E. Mylonas: *Mycenae and the Mycenaean Age* Princeton, 1966

Taylour, Lord William: *The Mycenaeans* London, 1983

A.J.B. Wace: *Excavations at Mycenae 1939–1955* London, 1980

A.J.B. Wace: *Mycenae: an archaeological history and guide* Princeton, 1949

Shang China p.146

J. Rawson: *Ancient China, Art and Archaeology* London, 1980
H. Garner: *Chinese Lacquer* London, 1979
Wen Fong (ed.): *The Great Bronze Age of China* New York, 1980
N. Barnard and S. Tamotsu: *Metallurgical Remains of Ancient China* Tokyo, 1975
Kwang-chih Chang: *Shang Civilization* New Haven and London, 1980
Kwang-chih Chang: *The Archaeology of Ancient China* New Haven and London, 1986 (4th ed.)
Shandong Province Museum: 'Shandeng idu Subutun ti'ihao nuli xunzang mu' in *Wenwu* (8), pp.17–30, 1972
'An Chin-huai: The Shang City at Cheng-chon and Related Problems' in Kwang-chih Chang (ed.) *Studies of Shang Archaeology*, pp.15–48, New Haven and London, 1987

The Steppes p.148

M. Gimbutas: *Bronze Age Cultures in Central and Eastern Europe* The Hague, 1965
M.P. Gryaznov: *South Siberia* London, 1969
M.A. Littauer: 'Rock Carvings of Chariots in Transcaucasia, Central Asia and Outer Mongolia' in *Proceedings of the Prehistoric Society* Vol.43, pp.243–262, 1977
E.D. Phillips: *The Royal Hordes: nomad peoples of the Steppes* London, 1965
S. Piggott: 'The Earliest Wheeled Vehicles and the Caucasian Evidence' in *Proceedings of the Prehistoric Society* Vol.34, pp.266–318, 1968
S. Piggott: 'Chinese Chariotry: An outsider's view' in P. Denwood (ed.) *Arts of the Eurasian Steppelands* pp.32–51, London, 1978
S. Piggott: *The Earliest Wheeled Transport* London, 1983
M. Zvelebil: 'The Rise of the Nomads in Central Asia' in A. Sherratt (ed.) *The Cambridge Encyclopedia of Archaeology* pp.252–256, Cambridge, 1980

Bronze Age S.E. Asia p.150

D. Bayard: *Southeast Asian Archaeology at the XV Pacific Science Congress: The origins of agriculture, metallurgy, and the state in Mainland Southeast Asia.* University of Otago Studies in Prehistoric Anthropology, Vol.16
P. Bellwood: *Prehistory of the Indo-Malaysian Archipelago* Australia, 1985
Kwang-chih Chang: 'The beginnings of agriculture in the Far East' in *Antiquity* Vol.44, pp.175–84
C. Gorman: 'A Priori Models and Thai Prehistory: a reconsideration of the beginnings of agriculture in Southeastern Asia' in Redd (ed.) *Origins of Agriculture* pp.321–55
C. Gorman and C. Pisit: 'Ban Chiang: A Mosaic of Impressions from the First Two Years' in *Expedition* Vol.18(4), pp.14–26
C. Higham and A. Kijngam: *Prehistoric Investigations in Northeastern Thailand* B.A.R. International Series 231 (i, ii, iii), Oxford, 1984
R.B. Smith and W. Weston (eds): *Early South East Asia* Oxford, 1979
M.W.F. Tweedie: *Prehistoric Malaya* Singapore, 1957
J. White: *Ban Chiang, Discovery of a Lost Bronze Age* Philadelphia, 1982

Archaeology of empire p.154

P. Albenda: *The Palace of Sargon King of Assyria* Paris, 1986
A. Herrmann: *An Historical Atlas of China* Edinburgh, 1966
M.T. Larsen (ed.): *Power and propaganda: a symposium on ancient empires* Copenhagen, 1979
S. Lloyd: *The Archaeology of Mesopotamia* London, 1984 (revised ed.)
J.E. Schwartzberg (ed.): *A Historical Atlas of South Asia* Chicago, 1978

The Assyrian empire p.156

H. Frankfort: *The Art and Architecture of the Ancient Orient* Harmondsworth, 1970 (revised ed.)
D.B. Harden: *The Phoenicians* Harmondsworth, 1980 (revised ed.)
D. Marshall Lang: *Armenia: Cradle of Civilization* London, 1980 (3rd ed.)
S. Lloyd: *The Archaeology of Mesopotamia* London, 1984 (revised ed.)
M. Mallowan: *Nimrud and its Remains* London, 1966
J.N. Postgate: 'The Economic Structure of the Assyrian Empire' in M.T. Larsen (ed.) *Power and propaganda: a symposium on ancient empires* pp.193–221, Copenhagen, 1979
J.N. Postgate: *The First Empires* Oxford, 1977
Y. Yadin: 'Megiddo' in M. Avi-Yonah (ed.) *Encyclopedia of Archaeological Excavations in the Holy Land* 4 vols, pp.830–856, London, 1975–1978

First Persian empire p.158

J.M. Cook: *The Persian Empire* London, 1983
O.M. Dalton: *The Treasure of the Oxus* London, 1964
B. Dicks: *The Ancient Persians* Newton Abbot, 1979
G.R. Driver: *Aramaic Documents of the Fifth Century BC* Oxford, 1957
H. Frankfort: *The Art and Architecture of the Ancient Orient* Harmondsworth, 1954
R.T. Hallock: *The Evidence of the Persepolis Tablets* (*Cambridge History of Iran* fascicule) Cambridge, 1971
S. Matheson: *Persia: An Archaeological Guide* London, 1976 (2nd ed.)
M. Roaf: *Sculptures and Sculptors at Persepolis (Iran XXI)*, 1983
E.F. Schmidt: *Persepolis* 3 vols, Chicago, 1953–70
D. Stronach: *Pasargadae* Oxford, 1978

Classical Greece p.160

D. Adamesteanu: *Basilicata Antica* Cava dei Tirreni, 1974
J. Boardman: *The Greeks Overseas* London, 1980 (3rd ed.)
J. Collis: *The European Iron Age* London, 1984
R.A. Higgins: *Greek Terracottas* London, 1967
M. Robertson: *A Shorter History of Greek Art* Cambridge, 1981
A. Wasowicz: *Olbia pontique et son territoire* Paris, 1975

Athens p.162

M.I. Finley (ed.): *Atlas of Classical Archaeology* London, 1977
R. Osborne: *'Demos': the discovery of Classical Attika* Cambridge, 1985
M. Petropoulakou and E. Pentrazos: *Attika: Ekistic elements – first report* Athens, 1973
M. Robertson: *A Shorter History of Greek Art* Cambridge, 1981
A. Snodgrass: *Archaic Greece: the age of experiment* London, 1980
J. Travlos: *Pictorial Dictionary of Ancient Athens* London, 1971

Hellenism in Asia p.164

F.R. Allchin and N. Hammond (eds): *The archaeology of Afghanistan: from earliest times to the Timurid period* London, 1978
G.E. Bean: *Aegean Turkey: an archaeological guide* London, 1966
J.M. Cook: *The Greeks in Ionia and the East* London, 1962
C.M. Havelock: *Hellenistic art* New York, 1981 (2nd ed.)
M.I. Rostovtzeff: *The Social and Economic History of the Hellenistic World* (3 vols), Oxford, 1941
M. Schede: *Die Ruinen von Priene: kurze Beschreibung* Berlin, 1964
R. Stillwell, W.L. Macdonald and M. Holland McAllister (eds): *The Princeton Encyclopedia of Classical Sites* Princeton, 1976

Celtic Europe p.166

J.V.S. Megaw: *Art of the European Iron Age: a study of the elusive image* Bath, 1970
J. Collis: *The European Iron Age* London, 1984
W. Kramer and F. Schubert: *Die Ausgrabungen in Manching 1955–61. Einführung und Fundstellungübersicht* Wiesbaden, 1970
J.M. de Navarro: *The Finds from the Site of La Tène – I. Scabbards and the swords found in them* London, 1972
B.W. Cunliffe: *Danebury: Anatomy of an Iron Age Hillfort* London, 1983
B.W. Cunliffe: *Iron Age Communities in Britain* London, 1978 (2nd ed.)

Rome pp.168–172

L. Barfield: *Northern Italy before Rome* London, 1971
A. Boethius: *Etruscan and Early Roman Architecture* Harmondsworth, 1978
E. Gjerstad: *Early Rome* (6 vols), Lund, 1953–1973
D. Harden: *The Phoenicians* London, 1962
H. Hurst and L.E. Stager: 'A metropolitan landscape: the Late Punic port of Carthage' in *World Archaeology* 9, pp.334–346, 1978
K. Muckelroy: *Maritime archaeology* Cambridge, 1978
I. Reich: *Italy before Rome* Oxford, 1979

A Roman landscape p.174

E.M. Wightman: *Roman Trier and the Treveri* London, 1970
H. Cleere and J. du Plat Taylor (eds): *Roman shipping and trade: Britain and the Rhine provinces* London, 1978
P. Steiner: *Römische Landhäuser im Trierer Bezirk* Berlin, 1923
F. Fremersdorf: *Der Römische Gutshof Köln-Müngersdorf* Berlin and Leipzig, 1933

Pompeii p.176

U. Cappelletti: *Pompeii: 24 Agosto – anno 79 d.C.* Florence, 1979
H. Eschebach: *Die Städtbauliche Entwicklung des Antiken Pompeji* Heidelberg, 1970
M. Grant: *Cities of Vesuvius: Pompeii and Herculaneum* Harmondsworth, 1976
W.F. Jashemski: *The Gardens of Pompeii* New Rochelle, 1979
Pompeii AD 79. Exhibition catalogue by J. Ward-Perkins and A. Claridge, London, 1976
H.B. Van der Poel: *Corpus Topigraphicum Pompeianum* Rome, 1977

Greek and Roman technology p.178

F. Benoit: 'L'usine de meunerie hydraulique de Barbegal (Arles)' in *Revue Archéologique* 15, pp.19–80, 1940
K.W. Butzer: *Early Hydraulic Civilization in Egypt: a study in cultural ecology* Chicago, 1976
D.B. Hague and R. Christie: *Lighthouses: their architecture, history and archaeology* Llandysul, 1975
J.F. Healy: *Mining and Metallurgy in the Greek and Roman World* London, 1978
J.G. Landels: *Engineering in the Ancient World* London, 1978
E. Lyding Will: 'The Sestius Amphoras: a Reappraisal' in *Journal of Field Archaeology* 6, pp.339–350, 1979
K.D. White: *Roman Farming* London, 1970

The Germanic world p.180

A. Burl: *Rings of Stone: Prehistoric Stone Circles of Britain and Ireland* London, 1979
A.C. Evans: *The Sutton Hoo Ship Burial* London, 1986
A. Dieck: *Die europaïschen Moorleichenfunde (Hominidenmoorfunde)* Neumunster, 1965
P. Dixon: *Barbarian Europe* Oxford, 1976
V.I. Evison: 'Anglo-Saxon Glass Claw-beakers' in *Archaeologia* 107, pp.43–76, 1982
P.V. Glob: *The Bog People. Iron-Age Man Preserved* London, 1969
W. Haarnagel: *Die Grabung Feddersen Wierde* Wiesbaden, 1979
J. Jensen: *The Prehistory of Denmark* London, 1982
M. Todd: *The Northern barbarians 100 BC–AD 300* London, 1975

The Steppe nomads p.182

M.I. Artamonov: *Treasures from Scythian tombs in the Hermitage Museum, Leningrad* London, 1969
E.D. Phillips: *The Royal Hordes; nomad peoples of the Steppes* London, 1965
S.I. Rudenko: *Frozen Tombs of Siberia. The Pazyryk Burials of Iron Age Horsemen* London, 1970
O.J. Maenchen-Helfen: *The world of the Huns; studies in their history and culture* Berkeley, 1973
T. Sulimirski: *The Sarmatians* London, 1970
T. Talbot-Rice: *The Scythians* London, 1957
I. Kiszely: *The Origins of Artificial Cranial Formation in Eurasia from the Sixth Millennium BC to the Seventh Century AD* Oxford, 1978
M. Zvelebil: 'The Rise of the Nomads in Central Asia' in A.G. Sherratt (ed.) *Cambridge Encyclopedia of Archaeology* pp.252–256, Cambridge, 1980

Red Sea states p.184

I. Browning: *Petra* London, 1982
R.E. Brünnow and A. von Domaszewski: *Die Provincia Arabia* Vol.I, Strassburg, 1904
B. Doe: *Southern Arabia* London, 1971
B. Doe: *Monuments of South Arabia* Cambridge and New York, 1983
N. Groom: *Frankincense and myrrh: a study of the Arabian incense trade* London, 1981
R.G. Khouri: *Petra* Harlow, 1986
Y.M. Kobishchanov: *Axum* University Park, 1979
M. Lindner (ed.): *Petra und das Königreich der Nabatäer: Lebensraum, Geschichte und Kultur eines arabischen Volkes der Antike* München, 1980
H. von Wissmann: 'Die Geschichte des Sabäerreichs und der Feldzug des Aelius Gallus' in H. Temporini and W. Haase (eds) *Aufstieg und Niedergang der römischen Welt* Vol.9:1, pp.308–544, Berlin, 1976

Imperial Persia p.186

R.McC. Adams: *Land Behind Baghdad* Chicago, 1965
A. Bruno: 'The Preservation and Restoration of Taq-Kisrā' in *Mesopotamia* Vol.1, pp.89–108, 1966
A. Christensen: *L'Iran sous les Sassanides* Copenhagen, 1944
R.N. Frye: 'The Sasanian System of Walls for Defense' in R.N. Frye *Islamic Iran and Central Asia (7th–12th centuries)* London, 1979
P.O. Harper and P. Meyers: *Silver vessels of the Sasanian Period* Vol.1, New York, 1981
G. Herrmann: *The Iranian Revival* Oxford, 1977
J. Kroger: *Sasanidischer Stuckdekor* Mainz am Rhein, 1982
K. Schippmann: *Die Iranischen Feuerheiligtümer* Berlin, 1971

Mauryan India p.188

B. and F.R. Allchin: *The Rise of Civilization in India and Pakistan* Cambridge, 1982
H. Bechert and R. Gombrich: *The World of Buddhism* London, 1984
K.M. De Silva: *A History of Sri Lanka* London, 1981
J.C. Harle: *The Art and Architecture of the Indian Subcontinent* Harmondsworth, 1986
J.E. Schwartzberg (ed.): *A Historical Atlas of South Asia* Chicago, 1978
R.E.M. Wheeler: *Rome Beyond the Imperial Frontiers* London, 1954
G. Yazdani *et al.*: *Ajanta* 3 vols, Oxford, 1931–46
W. Zwalf: *The Shrines of Gandhara* London, 1979

Trans-Asian trade p.190

J. Hackin: *Rencontre de Trois Civilisations, Inde, Grèce, Chine: Nouvelle Recherches archéologiques à Begram* Paris, 1954
R. Hayashi: *The Silk Road and the Shoso-in* New York, 1975
G.W.B. Huntingford: *The Periplus of the Erythraean Sea* London, 1980
J.I. Miller: *The Spice Trade of the Roman Empire* Oxford, 1969
M.G. Raschke: 'New Studies in Roman Commerce with the East' in H. Temporini (ed.) *Aufstieg und Niedergang Der Römischen Welt* pp.604–1378, Berlin, 1978
R.E.M. Wheeler: *Flames Over Persepolis: turning point in history* London, 1968
J.P. Wild and H. Granger-Taylor: 'Some Ancient Silk from the Crimea in the British Museum' in *The Antiquaries Journal* Vol.61, pp.302–306, 1981

Han China p.194

Ch'ang-sha Ma-wang-tui i-hao Han-mu (The Han tomb no.1 at Mawangdui, Changsha) by Hunan Provincial Museum and the Institute of Archaeology, Peking, 1973
P. Fitzgerald: *Ancient China* Oxford, 1978
The Genius of China. Exhibition catalogue with text by W. Watson, London, 1973
Qian Hao: *Out of China's Earth* London, 1981
M. Loewe and D. Twitchett (eds): *Cambridge History of China, Vol.1: The Ch'in and Han Empires* Cambridge, 1986
M. Pirazzoli-t'Serstevens: *The Han Civilization of China* Oxford, 1982
Z. Wang: *Han Civilization* New Haven, 1982

Korea and Japan p.196

C.M. Aikens and T. Higuchi: *The Prehistory of Japan* New York, 1982
T. Akazawa: 'Cultural Change in Prehistoric Japan: Receptivity to Rice Agriculture in the Japanese Archipelago' in F. Wendorf and A.E. Close (eds) *Advances in World Archaeology* Vol.1, pp.151–211, New York, 1982
G.L. Barnes: 'Jiehao Tonghao: Peer Relations in East Asia' in C. Renfrew and J.F. Cherry (eds) *Peer Polity Interaction* pp. 79–91, Cambridge, 1986
R. Goepper and R. Whitfield: *Treasures from Korea* London, 1984
J.E. Kidder: *Ancient Japan* Oxford, 1977
S. Nelson: 'Recent Progress in Korean Archaeology' in F. Wendorf and A.E. Close (eds) *Advances in World Archaeology* Vol.1, pp.99–149, New York, 1982
M. Suenaga: *Nihan No Kofun* (Aerial Observations on Ancient Tombs of Japan) Tokyo, 1961

South-East Asia p.198

B. Bronson: *Asian Perspectives* Vol.XII, pp.142–143
P. Charoenwongsa and M.C. Sudhadradis Diskul: *Thailand* Geneva, 1978
I. Glover: 'Ban Don Ta Phet and its relevance to problems in the pre- and protohistory of Thailand' in *Bulletin of the Indo-pacific Prehistory Association* (2), pp.16–30
B. Groslier: *Indochina* London, 1966
L. Malleret: *L'Archéologie du delta du Mekong* Paris
R.B. Smith and W. Watson (eds): *Early South-East Asia* Oxford, 1979
A. Thaw: *Beikthano* Rangoon, 1968
A. Thaw: *Historical Sites in Burma* Rangoon, 1972
P. Wheatley: *Nagara and Commandery* The University of Chicago, Department of Geography, Research Paper Nos 207–208, 1983

Polynesian settlements p.200

P. Bellwood: *Man's Conquest of the Pacific: the prehistory of Southeast Asia and Oceania* Auckland, 1978
P. Bellwood: *The Polynesians* London, 1987 (revised ed.)
B.R. Finney: 'Voyaging' in J.D. Jennings (ed.) *The Prehistory of Polynesia* pp.323–351, Cambridge, Mass., 1979
R.C. Green: 'Lapita' in J.D. Jennings (ed.) *The Prehistory of Polynesia* pp.27–60, Cambridge, Mass., 1979
A.C. Haddon and J. Hornell: 'The Canoes of Oceania' in *Bernice P. Bishop Special Publication* No.27–29, Honolulu, 1936–38

Iron Age Africa p.202

B. Fagg: *Nok Terracottas* London, 1979
R.J. Mason: 'Early Iron Age Settlement at Broederstroom 24/73, Transvaal, South Africa' in *South African Journal of Science* Vol.77, pp.401–416, 1981
R. Mauny: 'Trans-Saharan Contacts and the Iron Age in West Africa' in J.D. Fage (ed.) *Cambridge History of Africa* Vol.2, Cambridge, 1978
D.W. Phillipson: *The Later Prehistory of Eastern and Southern Africa* London, 1977
D.W. Phillipson: *African Archaeology* Cambridge, 1985
D.W. Phillipson: 'An Archaeological Reconsideration of Bantu Expansion' in *Muntu* Vol.2, pp.69–84, 1985
J. Rudner and I. Rudner: *The Hunter and his Art* Cape Town, 1970
J. Vansina: 'Western Bantu Expansion' in *Journal of African History* Vol.25, pp.129–145, 1984
A.R. Willcox: *The Rock Art of South Africa* Johannesburg, 1963

N. America after the ice p.206

G.C. Frison: *The Casper Site: A Hell Gap Bison Kill on the High Plains* New York, 1974
J.L. Phillips and J.A. Brown: *Archaic Hunters and Gatherers in the American Midwest* New York, 1983
S. Struever and F. Antonelli Holton: *Koster: Americans in search of their past* New York, 1979

Farmers of the Americas p.208

W. Bray: 'Early Agriculture in the Americas' in A. Sherrat (ed.) *The Cambridge Encyclopedia of Archaeology* Cambridge, 1980
D.S. Byers and R.S. Macneish (eds): *The Prehistory of the Tehuacán Valley* Austin, 1967–77
K.V. Flannery: *Guilá Naquitz*
H.G. Wilkes: 'Maize and its Wild Relatives' in *Science* 177, 1972

Villages of the Americas p.210

D.S. Byers and R.S. Macneish (eds): *The Prehistory of the Tehuacán Valley* Austin, 1967–77
C.B. Donnan: *Early Ceremonial Architecture in the Andes* Washington, 1985
K.V. Flannery: *The Early Mesoamerican Village* New York, 1976
M.E. Moseley: *The Maritime Foundations of Andean Civilization* California, 1975

The Andes p.212

G. Bankes: *Peru Before Pizarro* Oxford, 1977
E.P. Benson (ed.): *Dumbarton Oaks Conference on Chavín* Washington, 1971
E.P. Benson: *The Mochica* New York, 1972
C.B. Donnan: *Moche Art of Peru* Los Angeles, 1978
A.L. Kolata: 'Tiwanaku: Portrait of an Andean Civilization' in *Field Museum of Natural History Bulletin* 53 (8), pp.13–28, Chicago, 1982
A.L. Kolata: 'The Agricultural Foundations of the Tiwanaku State: A View from the Heartland' in *American Antiquity* 51 (4), 1986
A.C. Paulsen: 'The Thorny Oyster and the Voice of God: *Spondylus* and *Strombus* in Andean Prehistory' in *American Antiquity* 39 (4), 1974
J. Reinhard: *The Nazca Lines: a New Perspective on their Origin and Meaning* Lima, 1985

Central America p.214

E.P. Benson (ed.): *The Olmec and their Neighbours* Washington, 1981
M. Coe and R. Diehl: *In the Land of the Olmec* 2 Vols, Austin, 1980
M.D. Coe: *Mexico* London, 1984
D.C. Grove: *Chalcatzingo, Excavations on the Olmec Frontier* London, 1984

Teotihuacán p.216

R. Millon: 'Teotihuacán: city, state and civilization' in Bricker and Sabloff (eds) *Handbook of Middle American Indians* Supplement I, 1981
R. Millon: *Urbanization at Teotihuacán, Mexico* Austin, 1973

The Maya p.218

M.D. Coe: *The Maya* London, 1984
N. Hammond: *Ancient Maya Civilization* Cambridge, 1982
L. Schele and M.E. Miller: *The Blood of Kings: Dynasty and Ritual in Maya Art* Fort Worth, 1986

North America p.220

D.S. Brose, A. Brown and D.W. Penney: *Ancient Art of the American Woodland Indians* New York, 1986
D.S. Brose and N. Greber: *Hopewell Archaeology: The Chillicothe Conference* Kent, Ohio, 1979
L.S. Cordell: *Prehistory of the Southwest* New York, 1984
A. Ortiz: *Southwest, Handbook of North American Indians* Vol.9, Washington, 1979
A. Ortiz: *Southwest, Handbook of North American Indians* Vol.10, Washington, 1983

Empires of the Andes p.222

G. Bankes: *Peru Before Pizarro* Oxford, 1977
J. Henning and E. Ranney: *Monuments of the Inca* Boston, 1982
J. Hyslop: *The Inka Road System* London, 1984
A.L. Kolata: 'Chan Chan and Cuzco: On the Nature of the Ancient Andean City' in A.L. Kolata (ed.) *Civilizations in the Ancient Americas* 1983
M. Moseley and K.C. Day: *Chan Chan* Albuquerque, 1982
M.P. Weaver: *The Aztecs, Maya and their Predecessors* New York, 1981

Farmers of the Amazon p.224

W. Denevan and A. Zucchi: 'Ridged-Field Excavations in the Central Orinoco Llanos, Venezuela' in D. Browman (ed.) *Advances in Andean Archaeology* The Hague, 1978
D.W. Lathrap: *The Upper Amazon* London, 1970
A.C. Roosevelt: 'Chiefdoms in the Amazon and Orinoco' in R.D. Drennan and C.A. Uribe (eds) *Chiefdoms in the Americas* New York, 1987
A.C. Roosevelt: *Parmana: Prehistoric Maize and Manioc Subsistence Along the Amazon and Orinoco* New York, 1980

Aztecs and their ancestors p.226

N. Davies: *The Ancient Kingdoms of Mexico* London, 1982
N. Davies: *The Aztecs* London, 1973
R.A. Diehl: *The Toltec Capital of Ancient Mexico* London, 1983
H.B. Nicholson and E. Quiñones: *Art of Aztec Mexico* Washington, 1983

Farmers of the Southwest p.228

L.C. Cordell: *Prehistory of the Southwest* New York, 1984
E.W. Haury: *The Hohokam, Desert Farmers and Craftsmen: Excavations at Snaketown, 1964–1965* Tucson, 1976
R.H. and F.C. Lister: *Chaco Canyon* Albuquerque, 1981
A. Ortiz (ed.): *Southwest, Handbook of North American Indians* Vol.9, Washington, 1979
A. Ortiz (ed.): *Southwest, Handbook of North American Indians* Vol.10, Washington, 1983

Mississippian cultures p.230

J.A. Brown: 'Piro Art in its Mortuary Contexts' in E.P. Benson (ed.) *Death and the Afterlife in Pre-Columbian America* Washington, 1975
M.L. Fowler: *Cahokia: Ancient Capital of the Midwest* California, 1974
V.J. Knight Jr.: 'The Institutional Organization of Mississippian Religion' in *American Antiquity* 51 (4), 1986
D.F. and P.A. Morse: *Archaeology of the Central Mississippi Valley* New York, 1982
B.D. Smith (ed.): *Mississippian Settlement Patterns* Orlando, 1978

Ozette p.232

R. Kirk and R.D. Daugherty: *Exploring Washington Archaeology* Seattle, 1978
R. Kirk and R.D. Daugherty: *Hunters of the Whale* New York, 1974

European settlements p.234

K.A. Deagan: *Spanish St. Augustine* New York, 1983
I. Noël Hume: 'First look at a lost Virginia settlement' in *National Geographic* Vol.155, pp.735–767, 1979

I.N. Hume: 'New Clues to an Old Mystery' in *National Geographic* Vol.161, pp.53–77, 1982
I.N. Hume: *Martin's Hundred* London, 1982

Byzantine empire p.238

C. Foss and P. Magdalino: *Rome and Byzantium* Oxford, 1977
P. Grierson: *Byzantine Coins* London, 1982
R. Janin: *Constantinople Byzantine* Paris, 1950
R. Krautheimer: *Early Christian and Byzantine Architecture* Harmondsworth, 1979 (3rd ed.)
M. MacLagan: *The City of Constantinople* London, 1968
C. Mango: *Le Development Urbain de Constantinople* Paris, 1985
P.D. Whitting (ed.): *Byzantium: an introduction* Oxford, 1981

The Islamic world p.240

K.A.C. Creswell: *Early Muslim Architecture* Oxford, 1969
E.E. Herzfeld: *Geschichte der Stadt Samarra* Hamburg, 1948
A.H. Hourani and S.M. Stern (eds): *The Islamic City* Oxford, 1970
H. Kennedy: *The Prophet and the Age of the Caliphates* London and New York, 1986
G. Michell (ed.): *Architecture of the Islamic World: its history and social meaning* London, 1978
G. Michell and D. Jones (eds): *The Arts of Islam* London, 1976
A. Northedge: 'Planning Samarra: A Report for 1983–4' in *Iraq* Vol.47, pp.109–128, 1985
H. Philon: *Early Islamic Ceramics* London, 1980
J.M. Rogers: 'Samarra, a Study in Medieval Town-Planning' in Hourani and Stern (eds) *The Islamic City* pp.119–155, Oxford, 1970
U. Scerrato: *Islam* London, 1976

The Viking world p.242

J. Brøndsted: *The Vikings* Harmondsworth, 1965
J. Graham-Campbell: *The Viking World* London, 1980
J. Graham-Campbell and D. Kidd: *The Vikings* London, 1980
R. Hodges: *Dark Age Economics* London, 1982
H. Jankuhn: *Die Ausgrabungen in Haithabu* Berlin, 1943
K. Randsborg: *The Viking Age in Denmark* London, 1980

Mediaeval Christendom p.244

W. Braunfels: *Monasteries of Western Europe* London, 1972
K.J. Conant: *Cluny: les églises et la maison du chef d'ordre* Cambridge, Mass., 1968
K.J. Conant: *Carolingian and Romanesque Architecture 800–1200 AD* Harmondsworth 1974 (2nd revised ed.)
D.B. Hague and R. Christie: *Lighthouses: their architecture, history and archaeology* Llandysul, 1975
G. Jackson: *The Making of Medieval Spain* London, 1972
R.S. Lopez: *The Birth of Europe* London, 1967

Feudal Yorkshire p.246

D.D. Andrews and G. Milne (eds): *Wharram: a study of settlement on the Yorkshire Wolds* Vol.1, London, 1979
M.W. Beresford and H.P.R. Finberg: *English Medieval Boroughs* Newton Abbot, 1973
H. Clarke: *The Archaeology of Medieval England* Oxford, 1984
J.G. Hurst: 'The Topography of Wharram Percy Village' in B.K. Roberts and R.E. Glasscock (eds) *Villages, Fields and Frontiers* Oxford, 1983
J.G. Hurst: 'The Wharram Research Project: Results to 1983' in *Medieval Archaeology* Vol.28, pp.77–111, 1984
D.J.C. King: *Castellarium Anglicanum* New York, 1982
D. Knowles and R.N. Hadcock: *Medieval Religious Houses: England and Wales* London, 1953
R. Midmer: *English Medieval Monasteries* London, 1979
C. Platt: *The Monastic Grange in Medieval England: a reassessment* London, 1969
P.H. Sawyer (ed.): *English Medieval Settlement* London, 1979
A. Sorrell: 'England before the sheep farming revolution: the deserted village of Wharram Percy reconstructed' in *The Illustrated London News* Vol.243, pp.816–817, 1963

Saharan trade p.248

M. Bloch: 'The Social Influence of Salt' in *Scientific American* Vol.209, pp.88–98, 1963
J.D. Fage: *An Atlas of African History* London, 1978
N. Levtzion: *Ancient Ghana and Mali* London, 1973

S.K. and R.J. McIntosh: *Prehistoric Investigations in the region of Jenné, Mali* Oxford, 1980
S.K. and R.J. McIntosh: 'Finding West Africa's Oldest City' in *National Geographic* Vol.162, pp.396–418, 1982
T. Shaw: *Igbo-Ukwu* London, 1970
T. Shaw: *Nigeria: its archaeology and early history* London, 1978
G. Thilmans, C. Descamps, B. Khayat: *Protohistoire du Senegal: recherches archéologiques T1: Les Sites Mégalithiques* Dakar, 1980

West Africa p.250

J. Anquandah: *Rediscovering Ghana's Past* London, 1982
G. Connah: *3,000 years in Africa* Cambridge, 1981
T.F. Garrard: *Akan Weights and the Gold Trade* London, 1980
A. W. Lawrence: *Trade, Castles and Forts in West Africa* London, 1963
R. Mauny: *Tableau Géographique de l'Ouest Africain au Moyen Âge* Dakar, 1961

East African kingdoms p.252

D.R. Buxton: *The Abyssinians* London, 1970
G. Caton-Thompson: *The Zimbabwe Culture* Oxford, 1971
H.N. Chittick: *Kilwa* Nairobi, 1974
P.S. Garlake: *Great Zimbabwe* London, 1973
P.S. Garlake: *The Kingdoms of Africa* Oxford, 1978
P. de Maret: 'Sanga: new excavations, more data and some related problems' in *Journal of African History* Vol.18, pp.231–337, 1977
D.W. Phillipson: *The Later Prehistory of Eastern and Southern Africa* London, 1977
D.W. Phillipson: *African Archaeology* Cambridge, 1985

India and Ceylon p.254

J.M. Fritz, G. Michell and M.S. Nagaraja Rao: *Where Kings and Gods Meet: the Royal centre at Vijayanagara, India* Tucson, 1984
J.C. Harle: *The Art and Architecture of the Indian Subcontinent* Harmondsworth, 1986
B. Rowland: *The Art and Architecture of India* Harmondsworth, 1977
'Sigiriya Project' (Ministry of Cultural Affairs) Colombo, 1984
R. Thapar: *A History of India* Vol.1, Harmondsworth, 1966

Islamic empires p.256

I. Artuk: *Kanuni Sultan Suleyman Adina Basilan Sikkeler* Ankara, 1972
O. Aslanapa: *Turkish Art and Architecture* London, 1971
W.C. Brice: *An Historical Atlas of Islam* Leiden, 1981
H.C. Darby and H. Fullard (eds): *The New Cambridge Modern History* Vol.14, Cambridge, 1970
G. Michell (ed.): *Architecture of the Islamic World* London, 1978
N. Pere: *Osmanlilarda Madeni Paralar* Istanbul, 1968
Y. Petsopoulos (ed.): *Tulips, Arabesques and Turbans: Decorative arts from the Ottoman Empire* London, 1982
A.C. Schaendlinger: *Osmanische Numismatik* Braunschweig, 1973
J.E. Schwartzberg (ed.): *A Historical Atlas of South Asia* Chicago, 1978
E.W. Smith: *The Moghal Architecture of Fathpur Sikri* Allahabad, 1894

Kingdoms of S.E. Asia p.258

A.J. Bernet Kempers: *Ancient Indonesian Art* Cambridge, Mass., 1959
G. Coedès: *Angkor: an introduction* Hong Kong, 1963
B. Groslier: *Angkor: art and civilization* London, 1966 (revised ed.)
B. Groslier: *Indochina* London, 1966
B. Groslier: 'La Cité Hydraulique Angkorienne' in *Bulletin de l'école Française de l'extrême Orient* Vol.66, pp.161–202, 1979
W.J. van Liere: 'Traditional Water Management in the Lower Mekong Basin' in *World Archaeology* Vol.11, pp.265–280, 1980
P.T. White: 'The Temples of Angkor: Ancient Glory in Stone' in *National Geographic* Vol.161, pp.552–589, 1982

Buddhist Asia p.260

H. Bechert and R. Gombrich: *The World of Buddhism* London, 1984
J.H. Marshall: *A Guide to Sanchi* Calcutta, 1918
J.H. Marshall and A. Foucher: *The Monuments of Sanchi* Calcutta, 1940
D. Mitra: *Buddhist Monuments* Calcutta, 1971
D. Seckel: *The Art of Buddhism* London, 1964
M. Singh: *The Cave Paintings of Ajanta* London, 1965

W. Willetts: *Chinese Art* Harmondsworth, 1958
E. Zürcher: *Buddhism: its origin and spread in words, maps and pictures* London, 1962
W. Zwalf: *Buddhism: Art and Faith* London, 1985

Tang and Sung China p.262

A. Herrmann: *An Historical Atlas of China* Edinburgh, 1966
M. Tregear: *Song Ceramics* London, 1982
D. Twitchett (ed.): *Cambridge History of China, Vol.3: Sui and Tang China 589–906 AD* Cambridge, 1979
W. Watson: *Tang and Liao Ceramics* London, 1984

Ming China p.264

H. Deschamps: *Histoire de Madagascar* Paris, 1960
A. Hulsewé: 'Mélanges' in *T'oung Pao* Vol.47, pp.81–83, 1959
J.S. Kirkman: *The Tomb of the Dated Inscription at Gedi* London, 1960
J. Needham (ed.): *Science and Civilization in China* Cambridge, 1954
Zhong guo bo wu guan (The Museums of China) Vol.1, Peking, 1983

Feudal Japan p.266

R. Hempel: *The Heian Civilization of Japan* Oxford, 1983
R.S. Jenyns: *Japanese Pottery* London, 1971
J.E. Kidder: *Early Buddhist Japan* London, 1972
J.E. Kidder: *Ancient Japan* Oxford, 1977
T. Mikami: *The Art of Japanese Ceramics* Tokyo, 1972
R. Takeuchi *et al.* (eds): *The Historical Atlas of Japan* Tokyo, 1982

Islands of Polynesia p.268

T. Barrow: *The Art of Tahiti* London, 1979
P. Bellwood: *The Polynesians* London, 1987 (revised ed.)
K.P. Emory: 'Stone Remains in the Society Islands' in *Bernice P. Bishop Museum Bulletin* No.16, Honolulu, 1933
J.D. Jennings (ed.): *The Prehistory of Polynesia* Cambridge, Mass., 1979
W. Mulloy: 'A speculative reconstruction of techniques of carving, transporting and erecting Easter Island Statues' in *Journal of Archaeology and Physical Anthropology in Oceania* Vol.5, pp.1–23, 1970

Maori New Zealand p.270

P. Bellwood: *Man's Conquest of the Pacific* Auckland, 1978
J.M. Davidson and F. Leach: *Archaeological Studies of Pacific Stone Resources* Oxford, 1981
J.M. Davidson: *The Prehistory of New Zealand* Auckland, 1984
R.S. Duff: *The Moa-hunter Period of Maori Culture* Wellington, 1956
Fox, Lady A.: *Maori Fortifications in the North Island of New Zealand* Auckland, 1976
M.M. Trotter and B. McCulloch: *Prehistoric Art of New Zealand* Wellington, 1971

The Arctic world p.272

H-G. Bandi: *Eskimo Prehistory* London, 1969
D.E. Dumond: *The Eskimos and Aleuts* London, 1977
D. Damas (ed.): *Handbook of North American Indians, Vol.5: The Arctic* Washington, 1984

World economy p.274

J.N. Green: *The Loss of the V.O.C. Jacht 'Vergulde Draecke', Western Australia, 1656* Oxford, 1977
P. Marsden: *The Wreck of the 'Amsterdam'* London, 1974
P. Marsden: 'A Reconstruction of the Treasure of the 'Amsterdam' and the 'Hollandia' and their Significance' in *The International Journal of Nautical Archaeology* Vol.7, pp.133–148, 1978
K. Muckelroy: *Maritime Archaeology* Cambridge, 1978
K. Muckelroy (ed.): *Archaeology Under Water* New York, 1980

Industrial economy p.276

C. Hadfield: *British Canals: an illustrated history* London, 1959 (2nd ed.)
W.G. Hoffmann: *British Industry 1700–1950* Oxford, 1955
K. Hudson: *Industrial Archaeology; a new introduction* London, 1976
K. Hudson: *World Industrial Archaeology* Cambridge, 1979
J. Simmons: *The Railways of Britain* London, 1986 (3rd ed.)

INDEX

Places of archaeological interest fall into two broad categories. In many of the lands of the Old World – the first states of the Middle East, Greece, the Roman empire, as well as the early empires of India and China – written records survive which allow us to know the original names of the ancient towns and cities whose remains and artefacts can be studied in a known historical context. It is therefore as convenient for archaeology as it is for history to refer to these places by their ancient rather than their modern names, and this is the practice generally followed on the maps in the Atlas, i.e. they show Byzantium or Constantinople (as historically appropriate) rather than Istanbul, Uruk rather than Warka.

Into the second broad category fall those sites from earlier civilisations and cultures whose original names will remain forever unknown and which can only be referred to by the modern names they have been given, most often those of nearby places or features. The spelling of these names in the Atlas follows the form used in the language of the country in which they are now situated, though some translation of generic terms has been introduced in the interest of simplicity. Diacritics have been omitted only in spellings derived by transliteration from non-Roman languages, e.g. Sana rather than Şan'ā'. Chinese names appear for the most part in Pinyin form. The exception to these are historically conventional names, where the modern Pinyin form seems inappropriate. This is true of some major cities, and all dynasty names, e.g. Peking rather than Beijing, Chou rather than Zhou.

The modern names of ancient places are given in brackets after the main entry, as are any other variant names that may be of interest or use to the reader. Places are located generally by reference to the country in which they lie (exceptionally by reference to island groups or sea areas), narrowed down as necessary by location as E(ast), N(orth), C(entral), etc. Reference will normally be to the modern state in which the place now falls except where an historical name seems more appropriate in the archaeological context, e.g. Anatolia rather than Turkey, Mesopotamia rather then Iraq, Persia rather than Iran.

The index also includes broad geographical entries by continent, region and country where references can be found to those maps which cover the area concerned in particular detail. There are, finally, subject headings which will enable readers to focus on particular epochs, cultures or aspects of archaeology, e.g. boat-burials, Hassuna pottery, Mughal empire, Natufian sites, Shang dynasty.

Abbreviations

a/c	also called	f/c	formerly called	mod.	modern
Akk.	Akkadian	form.	formerly	N.	North(ern)
anc.	ancient	Fr.	French	n/c	now called
a/s	also spelled	f/s	formerly spelled	n/s	now spelled
Bibl.	Biblical	Gk.	Greek	S.	South(ern)
C.	Central	I(s)	Island(s)	s/c	sometimes called
Du.	Dutch	It.	Italian	U.	Upper
E.	East(ern)	Lat.	Latin	var.	variant
Eng.	English	L.	Lower	W.	West(ern)
		med.	mediaeval		

A

Amnisos — Avaldsnes

Amnisos *N.Crete* Linear B tablets 141
Åmose *E.Denmark* pollen core site 107
Åmøy *S.W.Norway* rock art 117
Amphiareion *S.E.Greece* theatre 161; Athenian sanctuary 163
Amri *N.W.India* Indus Valley settlement 89; early city 123; Harappan site 130
Amrit *Lebanon* Neanderthal site 65
Amsa-dong *C.Korea* shell mound 93
Amsterdam *Holland* early trade 275
Amud *N.Israel* Neanderthal site 65
An Carra *N.W.Scotland* menhir 108
An Najaf *S.Mesopotamia* holy city 257
An Nhon (a/c Binh Dinh, f/c Vijaya) *S.Vietnam* early site 259
Ana *Iraq* Islamic town 241
'Anaeho'omalu *Hawaiian Is* petroglyph 269
Anahulu Valley *Hawaiian Is* early site 269
Anaktuvuk Pass *Alaska* Ipiutak site 273
Ananatuba *E.Brazil* early horticultural village 224
Anaphlystus *S.E.Greece* Athenian settlement 163
Anasazi culture *S.W.USA* 228–229
Anatolia early hominids 62; Neolithic and Palaeolithic settlement 82–83; early farming 87; early pottery 101; Bronze Age 113; early civilisation 122; Assyrian empire 133, 157; early writing 134–135; Achaemenid empire 158; Greek colonies 161; Hellenistic influence 165; Roman cities and fortresses 171; Byzantine empire 239; Ottoman empire 256–257
Anaz *E.Anatolia* Assyrian stela 157
Ancón *C.Peru* early farming 208; preceramic site 211; Chavín site 213; Inca centre 223
Ancona *C.Italy* Roman city 169
Ancylus Lake *Baltic* 84
Ancyra (mod. Ankara) *C.Anatolia* Roman provincial capital 171; Byzantine walled town 239
Andernach (anc. Antunnacum) *W.Germany* hunter-gatherer site 72; hunter-gatherer art 74; Roman village 174
Andrews *N.USA, Michigan* Archaic site 207
Andronovo *S.Siberia* Steppe settlement 149
Andronovo culture *Russia* 148–149
Angel *E.USA* temple-mound 230
Angers *N.W.France* monastery 245
Anghelu Ruju *N.Sardinia* rock-cut tomb 113
Angkor *Indo-China, Cambodia* early monumental site 199; Khmer capital 258, 259; Buddhist centre 261
Angkor Borei *Cambodia* early monumental site 199
Angkor Wat *Cambodia* temple complex 258
Angles-sur-l'Anglin *C.France* Neanderthal site 64; hunter-gatherer art 74
Aniba *U.Egypt* fortification 137, 143
Anjar *Syria* Islamic town 241
Anjira *N.W.India* early farming village 89; Harappan site 130
Ankara (anc. Ancyra) *W.Anatolia* Islamic town 241; Sinan mosque 256
Anlu *N.China* early settlement 92
Annagassan *N.Ireland* Viking centre 242
Annapolis *E.USA, Maryland* colonial settlement 235
Annau *C.Asia* Steppe settlement 149
Anopolis *N.Crete* Minoan village 141
Ano Zakro *E.Crete* Minoan village 141
Anta de Marquesa *C.Portugal* megalithic tomb 107
Anta dos Gorgions *S.Portugal* megalithic tomb 107
Antalaha *Madagascar* Ming pottery 264
Antinoe *L.Egypt* silk find 190
Antioch (Lat. Antiochia, mod. Antakya) *S.E. Anatolia* Hellenistic city 165; Roman provincial capital 171; Roman empire 178; early trading capital 190; Byzantine walled town 239
Antium (mod.Anzio) *C.Italy* Roman colony 169
Antonine Wall *S.Scotland* 170
Antwerp (Fr. Anvers) *Belgium* Viking mint 242
Anuradhapura *N.Ceylon* early city 189; early capital and Buddhist centre 255; Buddhist stupa 261
Anxi *N.W.China* early trade centre 191
Anxi *S.E.China* Sung kiln 263
Anyang *N.China* early city 123; early writing 135; Shang capital 146; Steppe bronzes 149
Anyar *W.Java* early metal site 199
Anza *W.Bulgaria* farming site 87; early pottery 100
Aotea *New Zealand, North I.* defended settlement 271
Apa *N.Romania* metal hoard 115
Apache Creek *S.W.USA* Pueblo farming site 228
Apamea *W.Syria* Hellenistic city 165
Apan *C.Mexico* early town 217
Apatzingán *C.Mexico* early town 226
Apaxco *C.Mexico* Aztec centre 227
Aphidna *S.E.Greece* Athenian settlement 163
Aphrodisias *S.W.Anatolia* Neolithic site 83; Roman city 171
Apizaco *C.Mexico* early town 217
Apodhoulou *C.Crete* Minoan village 140
Apollo 11 Cave *S.W.Africa, Namibia* Stone Age tools 67; Stone Age site 253
Apollonia *N.E.Africa* Greek colony 161
Apollonia (mod.Sozopol) *E.Bulgaria* Greek colony 161
Apollonia *N.W.Greece* Greek colony 160
Apollonis *W.Anatolia* Hellenistic city 165
Apologos *S.Mesopotamia* early trade 191
Aptera *N.W.Crete* Linear B tablet 140
Apulum (mod.Alba Iulia) *Romania* Roman city and legionary fortress 171
Aquateca *C.Guatemala* Maya settlement 218
Aquileia (med.Aglar) *N.E.Italy* Roman city 171; archbishopric 245
Aquiles Serdán *S.E.Mexico* Pre-Classical site 214
Aquincum (mod.Budapest) *Hungary* Roman provincial capital and legionary fortress 171; silk find 190
Arabia early civilisation 122; early states 184; early maritime trade 190–191, 275; Islam 240–241; Ottoman empire 257
Arabians under Achaemenid empire 158
Arachosians ancient people of Afghanistan 159
Aracu *W.Brazil* early settlement 224
Aradus (a/c Ruad, Arvad) *W.Syria* Phoenician city 157
Arago *S.W.France* early tools and human remains 62
Arakamchechen I. *E.USSR* Thule site 272
Araouane *W.Africa, Mali* early town 251
Araphen *S.E.Greece* Athenian sanctuary 163
Arapuni *New Zealand, North I.* rock art 271
Araxos *C.Greece* Mycenaean fortress 145
Araya *C.Japan* early man 69
Arbela (f/c Nad Ardashir, mod. Arbil) *N.Mesopotamia* Sasanian city 186
Arbil (a/s Irbil, anc. Arbela, Arba'ilu) *N.Mesopotamia* Mitannian city 143; Assyrian provincial capital 157
Arcadia region of S.Greece 163
Archaic Stage culture *N.America* 206–207
Archanes (a/s Arkhanes) *C.Crete* Minoan village 141
Arctic cultures 272–273
Arcy-sur-Cure *N.E.France* Neanderthal site 64; hunter-gatherer site 72
Ardabil *N.Persia* Islamic town 241
Ardales *S.Spain* hunter-gatherer art 74
Arelate (mod.Arles) *S.France* Roman city 171
Arene Candide *N.W.Italy* hunter-gatherer site 72, hunter-gatherer 74; farming settlement 87, 107
Arequipa *S.Peru* early trade 274
Arezzo *N. Italy* early university 245
Argalykty *E.USSR* barrow burial 183
Argaru (mod.Tiruchchirappalli) *S.India* early trade 191
Argentina early settlement 70–71
Argentoratum (mod.Strasbourg) *N.E.France* Roman legionary fortress 171
argillite *New Zealand* 271
Argissa *N.Greece* farming site 87; early pottery 100
Argoeuvres *N.France* early tools 62
Argolis region of S.Greece 163
Argos *S.Greece* Mycenaean fortress 145; Hellenistic city 165; city-state 161
Arguin *W.Africa, Mauritania* early town 251
Århus *C.Denmark* Viking centre 243
Arians ancient people of Afghanistan 159
Arica *N.Chile* maritime trade 274
Aridos *C.Spain* early tools 62
Ariendorf *N.W.Germany* early tools 62
Arikamedu (anc. Poduca) *S.India* early city 189
Ariminum (a/s Ariminium, mod. Rimini) *N.Italy* Roman city 171
Arinberd *Armenia* Urartian fortress 157; Achaemenid city 158
Aristé *N.E.Brazil* early settlement 224
Arita kilns *W.Japan* Korean pottery 267
Ariuşd *Romania* Cucuteni-Tripolye village 111
Arizona Pueblo farmers 228
Arkalochori (a/s Arkalokhorion) *C.Crete* sacred cave 141
Arkharinskiy *S.W.Russia* Steppe settlement 149
Arkin *U.Egypt* Acheulian tools 57
Arkin 5–6A *N.E.Africa, Egypt* Stone Age tools 67
Arkines *S.W.Greece* tholos tomb 145
Arklow *E.Ireland* Viking centre 242
Arkoudiotissa *N.W.Crete* sacred cave 140
Arku Cave *N.Philippines* Neolithic settlement 151
Arles *S.France* archbishopric 245
Arlit *N.Africa, Niger* early livestock 119
Arlon (anc.Orolaunum) *S.Belgium* Roman village 174
Armagh *N.Ireland* archbishopric 245
Armant (a/c Hermonthis) *U.Egypt* ancient cemetery 129; ancient city 137
Armavir-Blur *Armenia* Urartian fortress 157
Armenia Assyrian empire 157
Armenians under Achaemenid empire 158
Armstrong *C.Canada, Ontario* Archaic site 207
Aromaton Emporion (a/c Mart of Spices) *N.E.Africa* early trade 191
Arpa Valley *C.Asia* Steppe settlement 149
Arpachiyah *N.Mesopotamia* pottery remains 99
Arpad (mod.Tel Rifaat) *Syria* Assyrian provincial capital 157
Arpi *S.Italy* Roman empire 169
Arrapkha (mod.Kirkuk) *N.Mesopotamia* early town 133; Assyrian provincial capital 157
Arras *N.England* Celtic art 166
Arras *N.France* Frankish pottery kiln 242
Arretium (mod.Arezzo) *C.Italy* Etruscan and Roman city 169
Arslantaş *N.W.Mesopotamia* Assyrian city 157
Artajona *N.Spain* megalithic tomb 107
Artemita (a/c Chalasar) *C.Mesopotamia* Hellenistic city 165; Parthian city 186
Artik *S.W.USSR* Steppe settlement 149
Arvad *W.Syria* Egyptian control 143
Arvi *S.Crete* Minoan village 141
Arzhan Kurgan *E.USSR* barrow burial 183
Asabon *S.E.Arabia* early trade 191
Asahitokoro *N.Japan* rice farming site 197
Asejire *W.Africa, Nigeria* hunter-gatherers 119
Ashdod *S.Palestine* early port 143; Assyrian provincial capital 157
Ashishik Point *Aleutian Is* Arctic culture 272
Ashkelon (Akk.Ashqaluna) *Palestine* Egyptian control 143
Ashur *N.Mesopotamia* pyramid 49; early city 122, 124, 133; early writing 134; Mitannian city 143; Assyrian capital 155, 157; Parthian city 186
Asia disease 42; early maritime trade 191, 274; Buddhism 260–261
Asia, Central trade routes 38–39, 191, 262, 264; Steppe settlements 149; Islam 240–241
Asia, South-East early settlement 90–91; Neolithic settlement 151; early trade 190–191; early kingdoms 258–259 (see also entries for the various countries and islands of South-East Asia)
Aşikli Hüyük *C.Anatolia* Neolithic site 81,83
Asine *S.E.Greece* Mycenaean tomb 145
Askitario *E.Greece* ancient fortress 113
Askiz *S.Siberia* Steppe settlement 149
Aspendus *S.W.Anatolia* Hellenistic city 165; Roman city 171; aqueduct 178
Aspero *S.Peru* pyramid 49; platform mounds 210–211
Asprokhaliko *C.Greece* Neanderthal site 65
Aspropirgos *S.E.Greece* Athenian settlement 163
Assebakte *N.Norway* Saami settlement 273
Asselar *N.Africa, Algeria* bone harpoons 94
Assos *N.W.Anatolia* Greek temple 161; Hellenistic city 165
Assyrian empire 154–157
Assyrians ancient people of Mesopotamia 158
Astakapra *N.W.India* early trade 191
Astana *N.W.China* Buddhist centre 261
Asuka-Itabuki *C.Japan* Yamato palace 197
Asunción *Paraguay* early trade 27
Aswan (anc.Syene) *U.Egypt* granite site 129; ancient mine 137; Islamic town 240–241; gold 256
Asyut *U.Egypt* noble's tomb 129; ancient city 137
Atapuerca *N.Spain* early human remains 62
Atargan *E.USSR* Thule site 272
Atashgah *N.Persia* fire–temple 186
'Atele *Tonga* early site 269
Aterian tools *Africa* 67
Atfih *U.Egypt* early capital 139
Athens (Lat. Athenae) *S.E.Greece* Mycenaean settlement 145; city–state 161–163; Hellenistic city 165; Roman empire 169, 171, 178; silk find 190; Byzantine town 239
Athens agora *(S.E.Greece)* marbled bronze artefacts 113
Athos *N.E.Greece* Byzantine monastery 239
Athr *Arabia* Islamic town 241
Athribis *L.Egypt* ancient city 137
Atlihuayan *C.Mexico* Pre–Classical site 214
Atlixco *C.Mexico* early town 217
Atranjikhera *N.India* early city 189
Atsinna *S.W.USA* Pueblo farming site 228
Attalia (mod.Antalya) *S.W.Anatolia* Hellenistic city 165; Roman city 171
Attica ancient country of S.E.Greece 145, 161, 163
Attigny *N.France* Viking mint 242
Attock *N.W.India* Harappan site 130
Atwetwebooso *W.Africa, Ghana* Iron Age site 203
Atzcapotzalco *C.Mexico* early town 217; Aztec town 226;
Auch *S.W.France* archbishopric 245
Auckland *New Zealand, North I.* defended settlement 271
Augusta Praetoria (mod. Aosta) *N.Italy* Roman city 171
Augusta Treverorum (mod. Trier) *N.Germany* Roman city 171
Augusta Vindelicorum (mod. Augsburg) *S.Germany* Roman city 171
Augustodunum (mod. Autun) *E.France* Roman city 171
Aulnat *E.France* Celtic site 166
Aulnay–aux–Planches *N.E.France* Bronze Age settlement 115
Aurangabad *C.India* Mughal mint 257
Aurar *N.W.India* Harappan site 130
Aurignac *S.France* hunter–gatherer site 72
Ausculum (mod.Ascoli Satriano) *C.Italy* Roman empire 169
Australia disease 42–43; first peopling 68; Aboriginal settlement 96–97; early shipwrecks 275
Austral Is early settlement 269
Australopithecines 54–55
Austrheim *W.Norway* rock art 117
Austria early hominids 62; Neanderthals 65; hunter–gatherers 72; megalithic period 107; Celts 166–167; Roman cities and fortresses 171
Austronesian language group 201
Auvernier *W.Switzerland* Corded ware settlement 110
Auximum *C.Italy* Roman colony 169
Ava *N.Burma* Buddhist centre 261
Avakana *C.Ceylon* Buddhist site 189
Avaldsnes *S.W.Norway* early settlement 180

Avalites — Berry-au-Bac

Avalites (a/s Aualites) *N.E.Africa, Somalia* ancient port 184; early trade 191
Avarua *Cook Is* early site 269
Avdeyevo *C.USSR* hunter–gatherer art 74
Avebury *S.England* stone circle and henge 108
Avennes *N.France* flint mine 107
Avrillé *W.France* menhir 108
Avukana *N.Ceylon* Buddhist remains 255
Awal *N.Mesopotamia* early writing 134
Awamoa *New Zealand, South I.* moa bones 271
Awatobi *S.W.USA* Pueblo farming site 228
Awdaghost *W.Africa, Mauritania* Islamic trade 240; urban centre 249
Awlil *W.Africa, Mauritania* early settlement 249
Axim *W.Africa, Ghana* early port 251
Axima *S.E.France* Roman provincial capital 171
Axum *N.E.Africa, Ethiopia* early state 184; early trade 190; rock–cut churches 253
Ayacucho *Peru* early farming 208
Ayaviri *E.Peru* Inca centre 223
Ayia Gala *S.Aegean* Neolithic site 83
Ayia Irini *S.E.Greece* Mycenaean fortress 145
Ayia Marina *N.E.Greece* Mycenaean fortress 145
Ayios Ilias *W.Greece* tholos tomb 145
Ayios Ioannis *N.E.Greece* Mycenaean fortress 145
Ayios Nikolaos *S.W.Greece* tholos tomb 145
Ayios Theodhoros *N.Greece* tholos tomb 145
Ayutthaya *C.Thailand* Buddhist stupa 261
Azaila *N.E.Spain* native settlement 169
Azanqaro *C.Peru* Inca centre 223
Azmak *S.W.Bulgaria* farming site 87; early pottery 101
Azmaska Mogila *C.Bulgaria* tell settlement 111
Aznavur (a/c Patnos) *E.Anatolia* Urartian fortress 157
Aztalan *N.USA* temple - mound 230
Aztec empire 226–227
Aztec Ruins *S.W.USA* Pueblo farming site 228
Azykh Cave *S.USSR* early tools 62; Neanderthal site 65

B

Ba *W.China* Han city 195
Babadan *N.Japan* early man 69
Babil *N.Mesopotamia* Assyrian stela 157
Babino *S.W.Russia* Steppe settlement 149
Babueski *N.W.Turkey* Sinan mosque 256
Babylon *C.Mesopotamia* pyramid 49; early city 122, 133; Assyrian capital 157; Achaemenid palace 158; Hellenistic city 165; Parthian city 186
Babylon Fossatum *(L.Egypt)* Roman legionary fortress 171
Babylonians ancient people of Mesopotania 158
Bacare (a/s Bakare, a/c Porakad) *S.India* early trade 191
Bac Son *N.Indo–China ,Vietnam* cave site 90
Bactra (a/c Zariaspa, mod. Balkh) *Afghanistan* Achaemenid city 159; Hellenistic city 165; early trade centre 191
Bactrians ancient people of Afghanistan 159
Bad Bertrich *W.Germany* pagan shrine 174
Bad Nauheim *C.Germany* Celtic site 166
Bada *N.Celebes* early metal site 199
Badagri *W.Africa, Nigeria* early town 251
Badegoule *C.France* hunter–gatherer art 74
Badopal *N.W.India* Harappan site 130
Badorf *N.Germany* Rhenish pottery kiln 243
Bad–tibira *S.Mesopotamia* early city 125
Badulla *S.Ceylon* Buddhist remains 255
Baeterrae *S.France* native settlement 169
Bagarre *N.France* early tools 62
Bagh *C.India* Buddhist centre 261
Baghdad *C.Mesopotamia* Islamic town 240–241; Sinan mosque 257
Baghouz *E.Syria* pottery remains 99
Bagneux *N.W.France* megalithic tomb 107
Bagor *N.India* Mesolithic site 89
Bagum *C.Mesopotamia* pottery remains 99
Bagumbayan *C.Philippines* Neolithic settlement 151
Bahariya Oasis *W.Egypt* early cultivation 129
Bahrain *Persian Gulf* early trade 122
Baia Farta *S.W.Africa, Angola* Acheulian tools 57
Baijiacun *N.China* E.Chou cemetery 192
Băile Herculane *Romania* Mesolithic settlement 84
Bailongdong *N.China* Homo erectus 60
Baimasi *W.China* E.Chou burial 192; Ming tomb 265
Baimiaofancun *N.China* E.Chou bronze hoard 192
Bairat *N.India* early city 189
Baishizidi *E.China* E.Chou burial 192
Baitu *N.China* Tang kiln 262
Baker's Hole *S.E.England* early tools 62
Baksei Chamkrong *Cambodia* transitional settlement 151
Bala *W.Egypt* temple 137
Balakot *N.W.India* Indus Valley settlement 89; early city 123; Harappan site 130
Balasore *E.India* early trade 275
Balat *W.Egypt* noble's tomb 129
Baldegg *Switzerland* lake dwelling 115
Balfarg *N.E.Scotland* stone circle and henge 108
Bali *E.Indies* early site 259
Balita (mod.Varkkallai) *S.India* early trade 191
Balkåkra *S.Sweden* metalwork 117
Balkh (anc. Bactra, a/c Zariaspa) *Afghanistan* Islamic town 241; early trade 262
Ballmoos *E.Switzerland* pollen core site 107
Ballochroy *W.Scotland* stone circle 108–109
Ballynagilly *N.Ireland* pollen core site 107
Ballynoe *N.E.Ireland* stone circle 108
Ballyscullion *N.Ireland* pollen core site 107
Balmori *N.Spain* shell midden 84
Balomir *C.Romania* copper 111
Baltimore *N.W.USA, Maryland* colonial settlement 235
Baluchistan Indus civilisation 130
Balve Höhle *W.Germany* Neanderthal site 65
Balyma *C.Russia* Steppe settlement 149
Bamako *W.Africa, Mali* Islamic trade 240; early settlement 249; early town 251
Bambata Cave *S.E.Africa, Zimbabwe* Stone Age tools 67; Stone Age site 203
Bamiyan *Afghanistan* Buddhist site 189; rock - carved temple 261
Bampur *S.E.Persia* Achaemenid city 158
Ban Chiang *N.E.Thailand* early plough 105; transitional settlement 151; moated site 199
Ban Don Ta Phet *C.Thailand* early site 199
Ban Kao Caves *S.Thailand* cave site 90
Ban Kao *C.Thailand* early metal site 151
Ban Muang Fai *C.Thailand* moated site 199
Ban Na Di *N.Thailand* transitional settlement 151
Ban Prasat *N.Thailand* transitional settlement 151
Ban Ta Luang *N.Thailand* transitional settlement 151
Ban Tamyae *C.Thailand* transitional settlement 151; moated site 199
Ban Thamen Chai *C.Thailand* moated site 199
Banahilk *N.Mesopotamia* pottery remains 99
Banavali *N.India* Indus Valley settlement 89; Harappan site 130
Banavasi *W.India* Deccan city 189
Banbhore *N.W.India* Islamic port 240–241
Bandarawela *S.Ceylon* Mesolithic site 89
Bandwai *N.Mesopotamia* Assyrian rock relief 157
Banepi (a/c Ngalo) *Solomon Is* Lapita site 201
Bangkok (n/c Krung Thep) *C.Thailand* Buddhist centre 261
Banjul see Bathurst
Banks I. *Solomon Is* Lapita obsidian 201
Bañolas *N.Spain* Neanderthal site 65
Banpo *N.China* early settlement 92–93; early kiln 101
Bantam *E.Indies, Java* maritime trade 275
Banteay Prei Nokor *Cambodia* early monumental site 199
Banting *S.E.Canada* fluted points 71
Bantu languages 202–203
Baofeng *N.China* Sung kiln 263
Baoji *N.China* Chou burial 192
Baozitou *S.W.China* early pottery 101
Baqitun *N.China* E.Chou cemetery 192
Bara - Bahou *C.France* hunter–gatherer art 74
Barakaccha *N.E.India* Mesolithic site 89
Barake *N.W.India* early trade 191
Barapedi cave *S.India* Mesolithic site 89
Barasimla *C.India* Mesolithic site 89
Barbaricum (a/s Barbarikon) *N.W.India* early trade centre 191
Barbas *C.France* Neanderthal site 65
Barbegal *S.France* Roman water mill 178–179
Barca *Czechoslovakia* hunter - gatherer site 72; fortified site 115
Barca (a/s Barke) *N.E.Africa* Greek colony 161
Barcelona *N.E.Spain* mediaeval trade 244
Barclodiad y Gawres *N.Wales* megalithic tomb 107
Bard - i Nishandah *W.Persia* fire - temple 186
Barger - Oosterveld *N.Holland* early temple 115
Bärhorst *E.Germany* early settlement 180
Bari *S.Italy* archbishopric 245
Baringo *E. Africa, Kenya* early man 54
Barium (mod.Bari) *S.Italy* Roman empire 169
Barleben *E.Germany* early tools 62
Barlovento *N.Colombia* early settlement 224
Barm–i Dalak *S.Persia* rock relief 186
Barnack *E.England* Beaker burial 110
Barnaul *S.Siberia* Steppe settlement 149
Barnenez (a/s Barnénès) *N.W.France* megalithic tomb 107
Baror *N.W.India* Harappan site 130
Barqa *N.Africa, Libya* Islamic town 241
Barrancas *C.Venezuela* early horticultural village 224
Barranc Blanc *E.Spain* hunter–gatherer site 72
Barton Ramie *Belize* Maya settlement 218
Barumini *Sardinia* fortified site 115
Barus *N.Sumatra* early port 259
Barygaza (Eng. Broach, n/s Bharuch) *N.W.India* early trade 191
Basi *Corsica* farming site 87; early pottery 100
Basketmaker culture *N.America* 220–221
Basra *S.Mesopotamia* Islamic port 240–241; Sinan mosque 257
Bass Point *S.E.Australia* early man 69
Bassae *S.W.Greece* temple 161
Basse - Yutz *N.E.France* Celtic site 166
Bastam *E.Anatolia* Urartian fortress 157
Bastura Chai *N.Mesopotamia* tunnel 157
Bat Cave *S.W.USA, New Mexico* Archaic site 207; Pueblo farming site 228
Báta *C.Hungary* Celtic site 167
Batavia (n/c Jakarta) *E.Indies, Java* early trade 275
Bathurst (n/c Banjul) *W.Africa, Sierra Leone* early port 251
Bathurst Head *N.E.Australia* Aboriginal site 96
Batu Buruk *C.Malaya* transitional settlement 151
Batu Ejaya *S.Celebes* early metal site 199
Batungan *C.Philippines* Neolithic settlement 151
Bau Tro *N.Vietnam* Neolithic settlement 151
Bau - de - l'Aubesier *S.E.France* Neanderthal site 65
Baulmes *Switzerland* Mesolithic settlement 84
Baum *E.USA* temple–mound 230
Baume - Bonne *S.E.France* early tools 62; Neanderthal site 65
Baumhoff's Rock Shelter *S.W.USA, Nevada* prehistoric diet 39
Baz - i Hur *N.E.Persia* fire–temple 186
Bazitou *S.W.China* cave site 92
Beaker burials 29; *Europe* 110
bear graves *Lappland* 273
Bear Is *E.USSR* Thule site 273
Beaumetz - lès - Loges *N.France* early tools 62
Beaurieux *N.E.France* Iron Age cemetery 33
Beauvais *N.France* Viking mint 242
Becan *E.Mexico* Maya centre 217, 218
Bédeilhac *S.W.France* hunter-gatherer art 74
Bedford *C.USA, Illinois* Hopewell site 220
Bedsa *S.India* rock-carved temple 216
Begho *W.Africa, Ghana* early city 251
Beginners Luck Cave *S.E.Australia* early man 69
Begram (a/s Bagram, anc.Kapisa) *Afghanistan* Graeco-Bactrian city 165; early trade centre 190–191
Behistun (a/c Bisitun) *N.W.Persia* rock-inscription 159; Hercules relief 165; rock relief 186
Beicaogou *E.China* E.Chou burial 192
Beicaopo *N.China* Chou burial 192
Beidha *S.Palestine* Natufian and Neolithic site 81
Beisamoun *S.Syria* Neolithic site 81
Beishouling *N.China* early settlement 92
Beit el-Wali *U.Egypt* temple 137
Beixinbao *N.E.China* E.Chou cemetery 192
Beiyinyangying *E.China* early settlement 92; Longshan site 147
Beizhou *N.China* Tang prefecture 262
Békásmegyer *E.Hungary* Copper Age cemetery 110
Bel'kacha *E.USSR* Arctic culture 273
Belbaşi *S.W.Anatolia* Palaeolithic site 83; early pottery 101
Belcher *S.USA* temple-mound 230
Beldibi *S.W.Anatolia* Palaeolithic site 83; early pottery 101
Belém *C. Portugal* early university and bishopric 245
Belevi *W.Anatolia* Hellenistic mausoleum 165
Belgium Megalithic Age 107; Roman empire 174
Belgrade *Yugoslavia* Ottoman mint 256
Belize early farming 208, 222; Maya settlement 218
Bell *N.Canada* Thule site 273
Bella *N.England* mediaeval village 246
Bellefonds *C.France* Mesolithic settlement 84
Belle-Roche *Belgium* early tools 62
Bellona I. *Solomon Is* Lapita site 201
Bellote *E.Mexico* Maya settlement 218
Bellows Beach *Hawaiian Is* early site 201, 269
Bellsås *N.Sweden* Mesolithic settlement 84
Belsk *Ukraine* Greek imports 161
Beluga Point *Alaska* Pacific Eskimo site 273
Belur *S.India* Hindu religious site 254
Bendemeer *E.Australia* Aboriginal site 96
Ben Do *S.Vietnam* Neolithic settlement 151
Benevento (Lat. Beneventum) *C.Italy* archbishopric 245
Beneventum (mod.Benevento) *C.Italy* Roman empire 169
Benguela *S.W.Africa, Angola* Acheulian tools 57
Beni Hasan *U.Egypt* noble's tomb 129, 137
Benin *W.Africa, Nigeria* early town 251
Bennekom *S.Holland* Corded Ware burial 110
Bent *N.E.USA, New York* Archaic site 207
Benten *N.Japan* Ainu hillfort 197
Berbati *S.Greece* tholos tomb 145
Berdyzh *W.USSR* hunter-gatherer site 72
Bërëlëkh *E.USSR* hunter-gatherer art 74
Berenice *Red Sea* ancient port 184; early trade centre 190
Berestnyagi *Ukraine* Greek imports 161
Berezan *Ukraine* Greek imports 161
Berezhnovka *C.Russia* Steppe settlement 149
Berezovka *E.USSR* barrow burial 183
Bergamo *N.Italy* Celtic oppidum 166
Beringia *Asia-America* land bridge 70–71
Berkeley Point *N.W.Canada* Thule site 273
Berkhat-Ram *S.Syria* early tools 62
Bern-Engelhalbinsel *C.Switzerland* Celtic oppidum 166
Bernifal *C.France* hunter-gatherer art 74
Beroea (mod.Aleppo) *C.Syria* Hellenistic city 165
Berry-au-Bac *N.E.France* Iron Age settlement 33; defensive enclosure 107

Berytus — Cádiz

Berytus (a/c Beruta, mod.Beirut) *Lebanon* Egyptian control 143; Phoenician city 157
Berzine *W.Syria* early tools 62
Besançon *E.France* Celtic oppidum 166; archbishpric 245
Beshtasheni *S.W.Russia* Steppe settlement 149
Besuki *E.Java* early metal site 199
Betatakin *S.W.USA* Pueblo farming site 228
Beth-shan (a/s Beth-shean a/c Scythopolis) *N.Palestine* Egyptian fortress 143; Levantine city and temple 157
Beth-zur *S.Palestine* ivory 157
Betijoque *N.W.Venezuela* early settlement 224
Betulov Spodmol *Yugoslavia* Mesolithic settlement 84
Beune Valley *C.France* pollen core site 107
Beverley *N.England* mediaeval town 247
Beycesultan *W.Anatolia* farming site 87
Bezeklik *N.W.China* rock-carved temple 261
Bhagatrav *N.W.India* Harappan site 130
Bhaja *S.India* rock-carved temple 261
Bharhut *N.E.India* Buddhist site 189; Buddhist centre 261
Bhattiprolu *S.India* Buddhist site 189
Bhimbetka *C.India* Mesolithic site 89
Bhogavardhana *W.India* Deccan city 189
Biache-Saint-Vaast *N.France* early tools and human remains 62
Bianzhou *N.China* Tang prefecture 262
Biepi *W.Africa, Nigeria* early town 251
Bigo *E.Africa, Uganda* Iron Age site 253
Bihourel *N.France* early tools 62
Bilbilis (mod.Catalayud) *C.Spain* native settlement 169
Billig (anc.Belgica) *W.Germany* Roman village 174
Bilma *C.Africa, Niger* Acheulian tools 57; early settlement 249; early town 251
Bilzingsleben *E.Germany* early tools and human remains 62–63
Bimaran *N.India* Buddhist site 189
Bingley *N.England* mediaeval town 247
Binglingsi *N.W.China* rock-carved temple 261
Birbhanpur *E.India* Mesolithic site 89
Birch *N.USA, Michigan* Archaic site 207
Birdlip *W.England* Celtic oppidum 166
Birdsall *N.England* mediaeval village 246
Birka *S.Sweden* Islamic trade 240; Viking trading emporium 243
Birkalein *E.Anatolia* tunnel 157
Birkenfeld *W. Germany* Roman village 174
Birket Habu *U.Egypt* artificial harbour 136
Birmingham *C.England* canal and railway development 277
Birnin Gazargamu *W.Africa, Nigeria* early town 251
Bir Sahara *N.E.Africa, Egypt* Acheulian tools 57; Stone Age tools 67
Birsay *Orkney Is* Viking centre 242
Birsmatten *Switzerland* Mesolithic settlement 84; megalithic site 87
Bir Tarfawi *N.E.Africa, Egypt* Acheulian tools 57; Stone Age tools 67
Bisceglie *S.Italy* Neanderthal site 65; megalithic tomb 113
Bishapur *S.W.Persia* Sasanian city 186
Bismantova *N.Italy* urnfield 115
bison kill sites *N.America* 207
Bisovaya *C.USSR* hunter-gatherer site 72
Bissau *W.Africa, Guinea-Bissau* early port 251
Bitburg (anc.Beda) *W.Germany* Roman village 174
Bitorri Cave *C.Africa, Congo* hunter-gatherers 119
Biyoko see Fernando Po
Biysk *S.Siberia* Steppe settlement 149
Bizen *C.Japan* pottery kiln 267
Bizerta *N.Tunisia* Carthaginian city 169
Bjerre *N.Denmark* flint mine 107
Black Head *New Zealand, North I.* early site 271
Black Patch *S.E.England* flint mine 107
Black Rocks *New Zealand, North I.* shell midden 271
Black Sea Greek colonies 161
Blackburn *S.Africa* Iron Age site 253
Blackwater Draw *S.USA, Texas* Palaeo-Indian site 207
Blaka Kallia *N.Africa, Chad* Acheulian tools 57
Blea Tarn *N.W.England* pollen core site 107
Blisnietsova Cave *C.USSR* hunter-gatherer site 72
Blistrup *E.Denmark* musical instruments 117
Bloody Fall *N.Canada* Thule site 273
Blučina *W.Czechoslovakia* fortified site 115
Bluefish Cave *N.W.Canada* early settlement 71
Blue Jay *E.Africa, Zimbabwe* Iron Age site 253
Bluff *S.W.USA* Pueblo farming site 228
boat-burials *N.Europe* 180
Bobo Dioulasso *W.Africa, Burkina* early town 251
Boca del Río *S.E.Mexico* early farming site 211
Bockstein *S.Germany* Neanderthal site 65
Bodh Gaya *N.India* site of tree of enlightenment 261
Bodo *N.E.Africa, Ethiopia* Homo erectus 57
Boelkilde *S.W.Germany* bog body 180
Boeotia ancient country of C. Greece 145, 161, 163
Boğazköy *C.Anatolia* Assyrian colony 133; early writing 135; Hittite city 142–143
bog bodies *N.Europe* 180
Bogdanovka *C.USSR* barrow burial 183
Bogong Cave *S.E.Australia* Aboriginal site 96
Bogotá (f/c Santa Fé de Bogotá) *Colombia* early farming 208
Bohai *N.China* Han city 195
Boirra *New Caledonia* Lapita site 201
Bois du Rocher *N.W.France* Neanderthal site 64
Bolivia Inca empire 223; colonial settlement 235
Bolkar Dağ *S.Anatolia* Neolithic site 83
Bologna *N.Italy* early university 245
Bol'shaya Rechka *S.Siberia* Steppe settlement 149
Bol'shoy Ulagan *E.USSR* barrow burial 183
Bolton *N.England* mediaeval town 247
Bolu *N.Anatolia* Sinan mosque 256
Bolvadin *W.Anatolia* Sinan mosque 256
Bomaderry *S.E.Australia* Aboriginal site 96
Bombay *W.India* maritime trade 275
Bombo Kaburi *E.Africa, Tanzania* Iron Age site 203
Bonampak *E.Mexico* Maya settlement 218
bone plaques *Mediterranean* 112–113
Bonna (mod.Bonn) *N.W.Germany* Roman legionary fortress 171
Bono Manso *W.Africa, Ghana* early town 251
Bononia (mod.Bologna) *N.Italy* Roman city 171
Bonteberg *S.Africa* Stone Age site 253
Boomborg-Hatzum *N.E.Holland* terp settlement 180
Boomplaas *S. Africa* Stone Age tools 67
Boone *N.USA, Iowa* Hopewell site 220
Boppard (anc.Boudobriga) *W.Germany* Roman village 174
Boqer Takhtit *Israel* Stone Age tools 67
Borax Lake *W.USA, California* Archaic site 207
Borazjan *S.Persia* Achaemenid palace 159
Borba *C.Brazil* early settlement 224
Bordeaux *W.France* mediaeval trade 244; archbishopric 245
Border Cave *S.Africa* Stone Age tools 67
Borg in-Nadur *Malta* fortified site 115
Borj Qinnarit *Lebanon* early tools 62
Borneo early settlement 69, 90–91; early metal sites 199; early ports 259; Buddhism 261
Borno *W.Africa, Nigeria* early state 251
Borobudur *C.Java* Buddhist site 259; Buddhist stupa 261
Borodayevka *C.Russia* Steppe settlement 149
Borodino *S.W.USSR* metal hoard 115
Boroughbridge *N.England* mediaeval town 247
Borremose *N.W.Denmark* early settlement 180
Borum Eshøj *W.Denmark* barrow burial 116–117
Bosa *Sardinia* Carthaginian city 169
Boston *N.E.USA, Massachusetts* colonial settlement 235
Bostra (mod.Busra) *S.Syria* Roman provincial capital 171; early trade 184
Bosumpra Cave *W.Africa, Ghana* early food 119
Bouar *C.Africa* early settlement 249
Bouga *C.Greece* tholos tomb 145
Bougon *W.France* megalithic tomb 107
Boun Marcou *S.France* Beaker burial 110
Bou Nouara *N.E.Algeria* megalithic tomb 112
Bouqras *S.E.Syria* Neolithic site 81,83; early pottery 101
Bourges *C.France* archbishopric 245
Boussargues *S.France* ancient fortress 113
Boviolles *N.E.France* Celtic oppidum 166
Boxgrove *S.England* early tools 62
Boy Tepe *E.Anatolia* Neolithic site 83
Bradford *N.England* mediaeval town 247
Braga *N.Portugal* archbishopric 245
Brahmagiri *S.India* megalithic tomb 189
Branč *E.Czechoslovakia* Copper Age cemetery 110
Brand *C.USA, Arkansas* Archaic site 207
Brandsby *N.England* mediaeval town 247
Brandskogen *C.Sweden* rock art 117
Brankysek *W.Czechoslavakia* Corded Ware burial 110
Brass *W.Africa, Nigeria* early town 251
Brassempouy *S.W.France* hunter-gatherer art 74
Bratislava *C.Czechoslovakia* Celtic site 167
Braughing *E.England* Celtic oppidum 166
Braunsberg *E.Austria* Celtic oppidum 167
Brauron *S.E.Greece* ancient harbour 163
Brazil Early settlement 70–71; early farming 224–225
Bredmose *N.W.Denmark* bog body 180
Breisach (Hochstetten) *W.Germany* Celtic site 166
Bremen *N.Germany* archbishopric 245
Brenig *N.Wales* barrow burial 115
Breść Kujawski *E.Poland* farming site 87
Brescia *N.Italy* Celtic oppidum 166
Bretteville-le-Rabet *N.France* flint mine 107
Briar Hill *C.England* defensive enclosure 107
Bridlington *N.England* mediaeval town 247
Brigetio (mod.Szőny) *Hungary* Roman legionary fortress 171
Brili *S.W.Russia* Steppe settlement 149
Brillenhöhle *W.Germany* hunter-gatherer site 72
Brindisi *S.Italy* archbishopric 245
Britain Megalithic Age 107; Roman cities and fortresses 170 (see also England, Scotland and Wales)
Brno *Czechoslovakia* hunter-gatherer 72; hunter-gatherer art 74
Broach (anc. Barygaza) *W.India* early city 189
Broadbeach *E.Australia* Aboriginal site 96
Brodgar, Ring of *Orkney Is* stone circle and henge 108
Broederstroom *S.Africa* Iron Age site 203
Brohm *C.Canada, Ontario* Archaic site 207
Broken K Pueblo *S.W.USA* early settlement 30; Pueblo farming site 228
Bronocice *S.Poland* Corded Ware burial 110
bronze hoards *Chou China* 192; *Europe* 115; *Steppes* 148–149
Brooks River *Alaska* Arctic culture 273
Broom *S.England* early tools 62
Brough *N.England* mediaeval town 247
Broxbourne *S.E.England* Mesolithic settlement 84
Brundisium (mod.Brindisi) *S.Italy* Roman city 171
Bruniquel *S.E.France* hunter-gatherer site 72
Bryncelli Ddu *N.Wales* megalithic tomb 107
Buang Bep *S.Thailand* early metal site 151
Bubanj Hum *E.Yugoslavia* tell settlement 110
Bubastis *L.Egypt* ancient city 137, 143
Buchanan *N.Canada* Dorset site 273
Bucy-le-Long *N.E.France* Iron Age settlement 33
Budakalász *W.Hungary* Copper Age cemetery 110
Buddhism *Ceylon* 255; *Asia* 260–261
Büdelsdorf *N.Germany* defensive enclosure 107
Budino *N.Spain* early tools 62
Budugalge *S.Ceylon* Buddhist remains 255
Buduruwagala *S.Ceylon* Buddhist remains 255
Buenos Aires *Argentina* colonial settlement 235; maritime trade 275
Buhen *U.Egypt* early city 122; ancient city 129; fortification 137, 143
Bui Ceri Uato *S.E.Indonesia, Timor* cave site 90–91; Neolithic settlement 151
Bukhara *C.Asia* Islamic town and fortress 241; early trade 262
Bukit Chuping *N.Malaya* cave site 90
Bukit Tengu Lembu *N.Malaya* early metal site 151; early site 199
Bulbjerg *N.Denmark* Bronze Age settlement 117
Bulgaria early farming 97; tell settlements 110; Bronze Age 115; Roman cities and fortresses 171; Ottoman empire 256
Bull Brook *N.E.USA, Massachusetts* Palaeo-Indian site 207
Bulltofta *S.W.Sweden* barrow burial 117
Buluk *Kenya* Proconsul and Kenyapithecus 56
Buni Complex *W.Java* early metal site 199
Bünyan *C.Anatolia* religious site 158
Burdale *N.England* mediaeval village 246
Burdigala (mod.Bordeaux) *W.France* Roman provincial capital 170
Buret *E.USSR* hunter-gatherer site 73; hunter-gatherer art 74
Bürgäschisee-Süd *N.W.Switzerland* farming settlement 107
Burgos *N.Spain* archbishopric 245
Burhanpur *C.India* Mughal mint 257
Burke's Cave *C.Australia* Aboriginal site 96
Burma early settlement 90–91; Neolithic settlement 151; early monumental sites 199; early kingdoms 259; Buddhism 261
Burrill Lake *S.E.Australia* early man 69
Burzahom *N.India* later farming village 89
Bush Barrow *S.England* barrow burial 115
Bushman Rockshelter *S. Africa* Stone Age tools 67
Bussa *W.Africa, Nigeria* early town 251
Bust *Afghanistan* Parthian/Sasanian city 186
Butkara *N.India* Gandharan art 189
Buto *L.Egypt* ancient city 137
Button Point *N.E.Canada* Dorset site 273
Buxentum (Gk.Pyxous, a/s Pyxus) *S.Italy* Roman colony 169
Büyükkale *C.Anatolia* citadel of Boğazköy 142
Büyükkaya *C.Anatolia* hill of Boğazköy 142
Buzhaozhai *N.China* Longshan site 147
Bwana Mkubwa *C.Africa, Zambia* Iron Age site 253
Bweyorere *E. Africa, Uganda* Iron Age site 253
Byblos (Akk. Gubla) *S.W.Syria* Neolithic site 83; early trade 122; early town 133; early port 143; Phoenician city 157; Achaemenid city 158
Býčí Skála *C.Czechoslovakia* vehicle burial 167
Bykovo *C.Russia* Steppe settlement 149
Byland Abbey *N.England* 247
Bylany *Czechoslovakia* farming site 87
Bynum *S.USA, Mississippi* Hopewell site 220
Bytyń *C.Poland* copper models 110
Byzantine empire 238-239
Byzantion (a/s Byzantium, mod. Viyajadrug) *W.India* 191
Byzantium (later Constantinople, mod. Istanbul) *N.W. Turkey* Achaemenid city 158; Greek colony 161; Hellenistic city 165; Roman empire 171

C

Caballito Blanco *C.Mexico* stone source 209
Cabeço da Arruda *C.Portugal* megalithic tomb 107
Cabeza del Plomo *S.E.Spain* ancient fortress 112
Cacamahuilpa *C.Mexico* Pre-Classical site 214
Cacheu *W.Africa, Guinea-Bissau* early port 251
Caddington *S.England* early tools 62
Caddoan culture *N.America* 230–231
Cádiz (anc.Gades) *S.W.Spain* Islamic trade 240; maritime trade 275

Caere — Chengqiao

Caere (mod.Cerveteri) *C.Italy* Etruscan city 169
Caesaraugusta (mod.Zaragoza) *N.E.Spain* Roman city 170
Caesarea (mod.Cherchell) *N.Algeria* Roman provincial capital 170
Caesarea Cappadociae (mod.Kayseri) *C.Anatolia* Roman provincial capital 171; Byzantine bishopric 239
Caesarea Maritima *W.Palestine* Roman provincial capital 171
Caf Taht el Ghar *Morocco* farming site 87; Beaker burial 110
Cafer Hüyük *E.Anatolia* Neolithic site 83
Cagny-la-Garenne *N.France* early tools 62
Cahokia *C.USA* temple-mound 230–231
Cahuachi *S.Peru* Paracas site 213
Cahyup *C.Guatemala* Maya settlement 218
Caimito *N.Peru* early settlement 224
Cairnpapple *E.Scotland* stone circle 108
Cairo *L.Egypt* Ottoman mint 256
Cajamarca *N.Peru* Middle Horizon site 213; Inca centre 223
Cajamarquilla *C.Peru* pyramid 49; Middle Horizon site 213; Inca centre 223
Čaka *E.Czechoslovakia* barrow burial 115
Calabar *W.Africa, Nigeria* early town 251
Calakmul *Mexico,Yucatán* Maya settlement 218
calcite sources *Egypt* 129
Calcutta *E.India* maritime trade 275
Calico Hills *S.W.USA* early settlement 71
Calicut (n/c Kozhikode) *S.W.India* Mesolithic site 89; maritime trade 275
Calixtlahuaca *C.Mexico* pyramid 49; Pre-Classical site 214; Aztec town 226
Callanish *N.W.Scotland* stone circle and alignment 108
Callao *Peru* maritime trade 274
Calleva (mod.Silchester) *S.England* Roman city 170
Callipolis *S.Thrace* Byzantine town 238
Calpulalpan *C.Mexico* early town 217
Calydon *C.Greece* temple 161
Camargo *N.W.Spain* hunter-gatherer site 72
Camarina (a/s Kamarina) *S.Sicily* Greek colony 160, 169
Cambodia early settlement 90–91; Neolithic settlement 151; monumental sites 199; Khmer empire 256–259
Cambous *S.France* farming settlement 107; early setttlement 112
Cambridge *E.England* early university 245
Cameixa *N.Portugal* native settlement 169
Cameron Creek *S.W.USA* Pueblo farming site 228
Camerota *S.Italy* Neanderthal site 65
Caminade *C.France* Neanderthal site 65
Caminero *C.France* Neanderthal site 65
Camirus *E.Mediterranean* Hellenistic city 165
Camp d'Artus *N.W.France* Celtic oppidum 166
Camp de Caledon *N.E.France* Celtic oppidum 166
Camp de Laure *S.E.France* ancient fortress 113
Camprafaud *S.W.France* farming site 87
Camster Long *N.Scotland* megalithic tomb 107
Camulodunum (mod.Colchester) *S.E.England* Roman city 170
Camutins *E.Brazil* early settlement 224
Can Llobateres *N.E.Spain* Dryopithecus 53
Can Ponsic *N.E.Spain* Dryopithecus 53
Canada early settlement 70–71; early cultures 207, 221; colonial settlement 235; Arctic cultures 272–273
Canca *E.Anatolia* Ottoman mint 257
Cancuén *C.Guatemala* Maya settlement 218
Candamo *N.W.Spain* hunter-gatherer art 74
Çandir *N.Anatolia* Ramapithecus and Sivapithecus 53
Cane *S.W.Arabia* early trade 191
Canegrate *N.Italy* urnfield 115
Cañete *S.Peru* Paracas site 213
Cangzhou *N.China* Tang prefecture
Canhasan *S.Anatolia* Neolithic site 81, 83; farming site 87
Cannonball Island *NW USA* midden 232
Cañon de la Mano *C.Mexico* Pre-Classical site 214
Cantalouette *C.France* early tools 62
Canterbury *New Zealand, South I.* rock art 271
Canterbury *S.E.England* archbishopric and pilgrimage centre 245
Canton (a/c Guangzhou) *S.China* early trade centre 191; Islamic trade 240; Buddhist centre 261; Ming provincial capital 265
Canusium (mod.Canosa di Puglia) *S.Italy* Roman empire 169
Canyon de Chelly *S.W.USA* Pueblo farming site 228
Caoxieshan *E.China* early settlement 92; rice farming site 197
Cap Blanc *C.France* hunter–gatherer site 72; hunter gatherer art 74
Cap Blanc *N.Africa, Tunisia* Stone Age tools 67
Cap Ragnon *S.France* early pottery 100
Capacna *C.Mexico* early farming site 211
Cape Andreas *Cyprus* Neolithic site 83
Cape Bol'shoy Baranov *E.USSR* Thule site 273
Cape Bon *N.Tunisia* Carthaginian site 169
Cape Coast Castle *W.Africa, Ghana* early port 251
Cape Denbigh *Alaska* Thule site 273
Cape Dorset *E.Canada* Dorset site 273
Cape Hangklip *S.Africa* Acheulian tools 57
Cape Kellett *N.W.Canada* Thule site 273
Cape Krusenstern *Alaska* Thule site 273
Cape Nome *Alaska* Thule site 272
Cape Prince of Wales *Alaska* Thule site 272
Cape Town *S.Africa* maritime trade 275
Capelletti *N.Africa, Algeria* early cattle 94, 119
Capertee *S.E.Australia* Aboriginal site 96
Cappadocians ancient people of E.Anatolia 158
Capsa (mod.Gafsa) *S.Tunisia* Roman city 171
Capua *C.Italy* Roman city 169; archbishopric 245
Caracas *Venezuela* colonial settlement 235
Caracol *Belize* Maya settlement 218
Caralis (a/s Carales, mod.Cagliari) *S.Sardinia* Greek colony 161
Carapito *N.Portugal* megalithic tomb 107
Carchemish *E.Anatolia* early city 133, 143; Assyrian provincial capital 157
Cardia (a/s Kardia) *N.W.Turkey* Greek colony 161
Carenque *W.Portugal* rock-cut tomb 112
Caria ancient country of S.W.Anatolia 161
Carians ancient people of S.W.Anatolia 158
Carigüela *S.Spain* Neanderthal site 64
Carigüela de Piñar *S.Spain* farming settlement 107
Çark'in *S.W.Anatolia* Palaeolithic site 83; early pottery 101
Carlisle *N.England* monastery 245
Carnac *N.E.France* stone circle and alignment 108
carnelian *Mesopotamia* 124–125
Carnuntum (mod.Deutschaltenburg) *Austria* Roman provincial capital and legionary fortress 171
Carolingian empire trade 243
Carrhae (mod.Harran) *N.Mesopotamia* 186
Carrión de los Condes *N.Spain* monastery 245
Carrowmore *W.Ireland* megalithic tomb 107
Cartagena *Colombia* maritime trade 274
Carthage (Lat. Carthago) *N.Tunisia* Phoenician city 161; Carthaginian city 169; Roman provincial capital 171; Roman aqueduct 178; early iron 203; early trade 249
Carthago Nova (mod.Cartagena) *S.E.Spain* Roman city 170
Casa Grande *S.W.USA* Pueblo farming site 228
Casa San Paolo *S.Italy* early pottery 100
Casainhos *W.Portugal* megalithic tomb 112
Casarabe *C.Brazil* early settlement 224–225
Cashel *S.Ireland* archbishopric 245
Casma *C.Peru* Chavín site 213
Casmenae (a/s Kasmenai) *E.Sicily* Greek colony 160, 169
Casper *W.USA, Wyoming* bison kill site 206–207
Caspians ancient people of C.Asia 159
Cassenga *C.Africa, Angola* Oldowan tools 57
Cassington *S.England* Beaker burial 110
Castelluccio *Sicily* rock-cut tomb and bone artefacts 113
Castillo *N.W.Spain* early tools 62; hunter-gatherer site 72; hunter-gatherer art 74
Castillon *N.France* Celtic oppidum 166
Castle Cavern *S.Africa* Iron Age site 203
Castle Eden *N.E.England* claw beaker 180
Castle Hill *New Zealand, South I.* rock art 271
Castlepoint *New Zealand, North I.* shell midden 271
Castlerigg *N.W.England* stone circle 108
Castlerock *N.Ireland* bog body 180
Castrum Novum *C.Italy* Roman empire 169
Catacomb Grave culture Steppes 148
Çatal Hüyük *S.Anatolia* Neolithic site 82–83; early pottery 101
Çatalca *N.W.Turkey* Sinan mosque 256
Catana (a/s Katana, mod.Catania) *E.Sicily* Greek colony 160
Cathedral Cave *E.Australia* Aboriginal site 96
Catigny *N.France* Neanderthal site 64
cattle-pen sites *India* 89
Cau Sat *S.Vietnam* Neolithic settlement 151
Caucasus early hominids 62
Caulonia (a/s Kaulonia) *S.Italy* Greek colony 160, 169
Caúma *C.Africa, Angola* Oldowan tools 57
Caunus *S.W.Anatolia* Hellenistic city 165
Cava Pompi *C.Italy* early tools and human remains 62
Çavdarhisar *W.Anatolia* Roman dam 178
Cave Bay Cave *S.E.Australia* early man 69
Cave Creek *S.W.USA* Pueblo farming site 228
Cave of Hearths *S.Africa* early man 57; Stone Age tools 67
Ca'Verde *N.Italy* Neanderthal site 65
cave stratigraphy 29
Çavuştepe *E.Anatolia* Urartian fortress 157
Çayönü *E.Anatolia* Neolithic site 81,83
Cedral *N.Mexico* early settlement 71
Ceiba Grande *S.E.Mexico* Pre-Classical site 214
Cejkov *Czechoslovakia* hunter-gatherer site 72
Celebes early settlement 90–91; Neolithic settlement 151
Cellino San Marco *S.E.Italy* rock-cut tomb 113
Celts *Europe* 166–167
Cemenelum *S.E.France* Roman provincial capital 171
Cempoala *C.Mexico* pyramid 49; Aztec town 226
Centenillo *C.Spain* Roman mines 178
Centumcellae (mod.Civitavecchia) *C.Italy* Roman city 171
Cephisia (a/s Kephissia) *S.E.Greece* Athenian settlement 163
Cercinitis (a/s Kerkinitis) *S.Russia* Hellenistic city 165
Cernavodă *E.Romania* Copper Age cemetery 111
Cernica *C.Romania* Copper Age cemetery 111
Cerrig Duon *S.Wales* stone alignment 108
Cerro Baúl *S.Peru* Inca centre 223
Cerro Chivateros *Peru* early settlement 71
Cerro de la Bomba *S.E.Mexico* early farming site 211
Cerro de las Mesas *C.Mexico* early town 217
Cerro de Real *S.Spain* Bronze Age settlement 115
Cerro Mangote *C.America, Panama* early pottery 211
Cerro Narrío *Ecuador* early farming site 211
Cerros *Belize* Maya settlement 218
Čertova Dira *Czechoslovakia* Neanderthal site 65
České Lhotice *W.Czechoslovakia* Celtic site 167
Ceylon (a/c Sri Lanka) Buddhism 189, 255, 261; early maritime trade 275
Chacmool *Mexico,Yucatán* Maya settlement 218
Chaco Canyon *S.W.USA* Pueblo farming site 228
Chaculá *C.Guatemala* Maya settlement 218
Chad pottery 94
Chaganak *C.Asia* Steppe settlement 149
Chagar Bazar *N.Mesopotamia* pottery remains 99; early town 133; early writing 134; Mitannian city 143
Chahar Qapu *W.Persia* fire-temple 186
Chaillot-de-la-Jard *W.France* defensive enclosure 107
Chaiya (a/s Jaya) *S.Thailand* early site 199, 259
Chak Purbane Syal *N.W.India* Harappan site
Chakipamka *S.Peru* Middle Horizon site 213
Chalcatzingo *C.Mexico* Pre-Classical site 214
Chalcedon (mod.Kadiköy) *N.Anatolia* Greek colony 161; Byzantine town 238
Chalchihuites *C.Mexico* early town 217, 226
Chalchuapa *El Salvador* Pre-Classical site 214; Maya settlement 218
Chalcis *S.E.Greece* city-state 161
Chalco *C.Mexico* Aztec centre 226
Chale Gar *W.Persia* early copper mine 120
Chalk Hollow *S.USA, Texas* Archaic site 207
Challans *W.France* metal hoard 115
Chalon *E.France* Celtic site 166
Chaluka *Aleutian Is* Arctic culture 272
Chamá *C.Guatemala* Maya settlement 218
Champ Durand *W.France* defensive enclosure 107
Champotón *Mexico,Yucatán* Maya settlement 218; early town 226
Chan Chan *N.W.Peru* pyramid 49; Inca capital 222–223
Chan Sen *N.Thailand* transitional settlement 151; moated site 199; early site 259
Chanapata *S.E.Peru* early farming site 211
Chancelade *C.France* hunter-gatherer site 72
Chandragiri *S.India* Vijayanagara centre 254
Chang'an (a/c xi'an) *N.China* early trade capital 191; Han city 195; Islamic trade 240; Tang capital 262
Changbong-do *N.Korea* early settlement 93
Changge *N.China* early settlement 92
Changling *N.E.China* Ming tomb 264
Changsha *C.China* Han kingdom 195; Buddhist centre 261; Tang kiln 262
Changshan *N.China* Han city 195
Changtaiguan *C.China* E.Chou burial 192
Changzhou *E.China* Tang prefecture 262
Chanhu-Daro *N.W.India* early city 123; Harappan site 130
Channel Is standing stones 108
Chantsa *N.E.Greece* Mycenaean fortress 145
Chao'an *S.E.China* cave site 92; Tang kiln 262
Chaozhou *S.China* Sung kiln 263
Charakopio *S.W.Greece* tholos tomb 145
Charanke *N.Japan* Ainu hillfort 197
Charavines *S.E.France* farming settlement 107
Charax *S.Mesopotamia* Hellenistic city 165
chariot-carvings *Africa* 202–203
Charleston *E.USA, S.Carolina* colonial settlement 235
Charlottetown *E.Canada, Prince Edward I.* colonial settlement 235
Charsadda (a/s Charsada) *N.W.India* Achaemenid city 159; Graeco-Bactrian city 165; early city 189; early trade centre 191
Chartres *N.France* archbishopric 245
Charukorohoi *N.Japan* Ainu hillfort 197
Chassemy *N.E.France* Iron Age settlement 33
Chassey *E.France* defensive enclosure 107
Châteauneuf-lès-Martigues *S.E.France* Mesolithic settlement 84; farming site 87
Châteauneuf-sur-Charente *C.France* Neanderthal site 65
Châtelperron *E.France* hunter-gatherer site 72
Chau Say Tevoda *Cambodia* Neolithic settlement 151
Chavez Pass Ruins *S.W.USA* Pueblo farming site 228
Chavín culture *Andes* 212–213
Chavín de Huantar *C.Peru* pyramid 49; Chavín site 213
Chedzurgwe *E.Africa, Zimbabwe* Iron Age site 253
Chegitun *E.USSR* Thule site 273
Chekka Jdidé *Lebanon* Neanderthal site 65
Chelles *N.France* early tools 62
Chelyabinsk *C.USSR* Steppe settlement 149
Chemagal *E.Africa, Kenya* Iron Age site 253
Chemeron *E.Africa, Kenya* Australopithecus 54
Chenachane *N.Africa Algeria* wavy-line pottery 94
Chengdu *W.China* Han city 195; Buddhist centre 261; Tang prefecture 262; Ming provincial capital 265
Chengdufu *W.China* provincial capital 263
Chengqiao *E.China* E.Chou burial 192

Cuzco — Ebla

Cuzco *S.Peru* Paracas site 213; Inca capital 223; trade 274
Cycladic frying-pans *Greece* 113
Cycladic marble figurines *Greece* 113
Cynosura (a/s Kynosoura) *S.E.Greece* Athenian settlement 163
Cypriots under Achaemenid empire 158
Cyprus early trade 133
Cyrene (a/s Kyrene, mod. Shahhat) *N.E.Africa* Greek colony 161; Roman provincial capital 171
Cyrrhus (a/s Kyrrhos) *S.E.Anatolia* Hellenistic city 165; Roman city and legionary fortress 171
Cys-la-Commune *N.E.France* Iron Age cemetery 33
Cyzicus *N.W.Anatolia* Byzantine town 238
Czechoslovakia early hominids 62; Neanderthals 65; hunter-gatherers 72; Palaeolithic art 74; Mesolithic settlement 84; Bronze Age 115; Celts 166–167; Germanic settlement 180

D

Da But *N.Vietnam* Neolithic settlement 151
Dabaotai *N.E.China* Han burial 195
Dabarkot *N.W.India* Harappan site 130
Daboya *W.Africa, Ghana* early town 251
Dacun *N.China* early settlement 92
Dadianzi *N.E.China* E.Chou cemetery 192
Dadiwan *N.W.China* early pottery 101
Dadongze *N.China* early settlement 92
Dahan-i Ghulaman *E.Persia* Achaemenid palace 159
Dahe *N.China* Han city 195
Dahecun *N.China* early settlement 92
Dahlak Is *Red Sea* monolith 253
Dahshur *L.Egypt* pyramids 49, 129; burial 122; royal capital 137
Daigi-gakoi *N.E.Japan* early settlement 93
Daima *W.Africa, Nigeria* early livestock 119; Iron Age site 203; urban centre 249; early town 251
Dainzu *S.E.Mexico* early farming site 211; Pre-Classical site 214
Dakhla Oasis *N.E.Africa, Egypt* Stone Age tools 57, 67; early cultivation 129
Dal'verzin *C.Asia* Steppe settlement 149
Dali *N.China* early man 69
Dali *W.China* Buddhist centre 261
Dalkey Island *E.Ireland* shell midden 84
Dalles, *N.W.USA, Washington* Archaic site 207
Dalton *C.USA, Missouri* Palaeo-Indian site 207
Daly River *N.Australia* Aboriginal site 96
Damascus *S.Syria* early town 133; Egyptian control 143; Assyrian provincial city 157; Hellenistic city 165; Roman city 171; early trade 184, 190; Islamic town 241; Sinan mosque 256
Damb Sadaat *N.W.India* Harappan site 130
Dambarare *E.Africa, Zimbabwe* Iron Age site 253
Dambwa *C.Africa, Zimbabwe* Iron Age site 203
Damghan *N.E.Persia* Islamic town 240–241
Damingfu *N.China* provincial capital 263
Dammwiese *W.Austria* Celtic site 166
Dandara (a/c Dendara, a/c Tentyra) *U.Egypt* ancient cemetery 129
Danebury *S.England* Celtic hillfort 167
Danevirke *S.Denmark* Frontier dyke 243
Danger Cave *W.USA, Utah* Archaic site 207
Daojali Hading *E.India* later farming village 89
Dar es-Soltane *N.W.Africa, Morocco* Stone Age tools 67
Dara *S.W.Greece* tholos tomb 145
Dara *U.Egypt* pyramid 49, 129
Dara-i-Kur *C.Asia* later farming village 89
Darabgird *S.Persia* Sasanian city 186
Dariush Kabir *S.W.Persia* remains of bridge 159
Dastagird *C. Mesopotamia* Sasanian city 186
Datong *N.China* Buddhist centre 261; Sung kiln 263
Daura *W.Africa, Nigeria* early town 251
Davding *W.Denmark* musical instruments 117
Davis *.USA* temple-mound 230
Dawenkou *N.E.China* early settlement 92; early kiln 101; Longshan site 147
Dawu *W.Africa, Ghana* early town 251
Daxi *N.China* early settlement 92
Dazu *W.China* Buddhist centre 261
De Hangen *S.Africa* hunter-gatherers 95; Stone Age site 253
Debert *E.Canada, Nova Scotia* Palaeo-Indian site 207
Decelea (a/s Dekeleia) *S.E.Greece* Athenian settlement 163
Dedan *W.Arabia* early trade 184
Deepcar *C.England* Mesolithic settlement 84
Deering *Alaska* Ipiutak site 273
Deh Morasi Ghundai *Afghanistan* later farming village 89
Dehua *S.E.China* Sung kiln 263
Deir el-Bersha *U.Egypt* 137
Deir el-Gabrawi *U.Egypt* noble's tomb 129
Deir el-Malik *U.Egypt* noble's tomb 129
Deir el-Medina *U.Egypt* workmen's village 136, 138
Delagoa Bay *S.E.Africa, Mozambique* maritime trade 275
Délébo *C.Africa, Chad* wavy-line pottery 94
Delhi *C.India* Mughal capital 257
Deling *N.E.China* Ming tomb 264
Delos *S.Aegean* harbour and temple 161; Hellenistic city 165
Delphi *C.Greece* theatre and temple 161; sanctuary 165
Demetrias *N.Greece* Hellenistic city 165
Dendenchofu *C.Japan* mound cemetery 197
Dendera *U.Egypt* Ptolemaic temple 165
Dendra *S.Greece* Mycenaean fortress 145
Dengfeng *N.China* early settlement 92; Tang kiln 262; Sung kiln 263
Dengkil *C.Malaya* early metal site 151
Denmark mesolithic sites 87; Megalithic Age 107; Bronze Age 115–117; early settlement 180; Vikings 243
Dent *W.USA, Colorado* Palaeo-Indian site 207
Deqing *E.China* Tang kiln 262
Der (n/c Badra) *E.Mesopotamia* early city 124; Assyrian provincial capital 157
Derby *C.England* Viking centre 242
Dereivka *S.W.Russia* Steppe settlement 149
Derenberg *N.Germany* defensive enclosure 107
Derry *N.Ireland* monastery 245
Derrynahinch *S.E.Ireland* megalithic tomb 107
Dertona (mod.Tortona) *N.Italy* Roman empire 169
Desalpur *N.W.India* early city 123; Harappan site 130
Deszk-Olajkút *Hungary* farming site 87
Detzem (anc.Ad Quintum) *W.Germany* Roman village 174
Deva (mod.Chester) *N.England* Roman legionary fortress 171
Deve Hüyük *S.E.Anatolia* cemetery 158
Devil's Dyke *S.England* Celtic hillfort 167
Devil's Lair *S.W.Australia* early man 69; Aboriginal site 96
Devil's Tower *Gibraltar* Neanderthal site 64
Devínská Nová Ves (Ger.Neudorf and der March) *Czechoslovakia* Sivapithecus 53
Devnimori *E.India* Buddhist site 189
Devon Downs *S.Australia* Aboriginal site 96
Dewa *N.Japan* Heian fortress 267
Dhal *N.W.India* Harappan site 130
Dhank *W.India* Buddhist site 189
Dharanikota *S.India* Deccan city 189
Dhlodhlo *E.Africa, Zimbabwe* Iron Age site 253; Ming pottery 264
Dhokathismata *S.E.Greece* bronze daggers 113
Dia *N.Crete* ancient port 141
diamonds 46
Diana Bay *E.Canada* Dorset site 273
Diara *W.Africa, Mauritania* early town and kingdom 251
Diaurum *S.E.Brazil* early settlement 224
Díaz Ordaz *C.Mexico* stone source 209
Dickson *C.USA* temple-mound 230
Dictaean *E.Crete* sacred cave 141
Didyma *S.W.Anatolia* Greek temple 161; Hellenistic city 165
Die Kelders *S.Africa* Stone Age tools 67; Stone Age site 203
Dieng (a/s Dijeng) *W.Java* early site 259
Dieng Plateau *C.Java* early monumental site 199
Dieskau *N.Germany* metal hoard 115
Dighavapi *S.Ceylon* Buddhist site 189
Diji-li-takri *N.W.India* Harappan site 130
Dikbosch *S.Africa* Stone Age site 203
Dimbulagala *N.Ceylon* Buddhist remains 255
Dimolit *N.Philippines* Neolithic settlement 151
Ding (n/c Dingxian) *N.China* Sung kiln 263
Dingcun *N.E.China* early man 69
Dingling *N.E.China* Ming tomb 264
Dinorben *N.Wales* fortified site 115
Diomede Is *Alaska/USSR* Thule site 273
diorite sources *Egypt* 129
Dioscurias (mod.Sukhumi) *S.Russia* Greek colony 161
Dire Dawa (Porc Epic Cave) *E.Africa, Ethiopia* Stone Age tools 67
Direkli Cave *E.Anatolia* Palaeolithic site 83
Dishasha *U.Egypt* noble's tomb 129
Divostin *C.Yugoslavia* farming site 87
Diyarbakir *E. Anatolia* Sinan mosque 257
Djado *C.Africa* early settlement 249
Djanak *C.Asia* Steppe settlement 149
Djebila *N.W.Morocco* Carthaginian cemetery 169
Djeitun *C.Asia* Steppe settlement 149
Djénné see Jenne
Djougou *W.Africa, Benin* early town 251
Dobranichevka *W.USSR* hunter-gatherer site 72
Doc Chua *S.Vietnam* transitional settlement 151
Dodona *N.W.Greece* Greek temple 161; sanctuary 165
Doerschuk *S.E.USA, North Carolina* Archaic site 207
Dog River *Lebanon* Assyrian rock relief 157
Doğubayazit *E.Anatolia* Urartian fortress 157
Dogunbaden *S.W.Persia* fire-temple 186
Dölauer Heide *N.Germany* defensive enclosure 107
Dolmen de Soto *S.W.Spain* megalithic tomb 107
Dolní Věstonice *Czechoslovakia* hunter-gatherer site 72; hunter-gatherer art 74
Domburg *Holland* Viking trading emporium 242
Domebo *S.USA, Texas* Palaeo-Indian site 207
Domu s'Orku *S.Sardinia* dry-stone fortress 169
Domuztepe *S.E.Anatolia* Neolithic site 83
Doña Clotilde *E.Spain* Mesolithic settlement 84
Doncaster *N.England* mediaeval town 247
Dondo *E.Africa, Kenya* Ming pottery 264
Dong *N.China* Han city 195
Dong Dau *N.Vietnam* transitional settlement 151
Dong Duong *Indo-China, S.Vietnam* early site 259; Buddhist centre 261
Dong Lakhon *C.Thailand* moated site 199; early site 259
Dong Son *N.Vietnam* transitional settlement 151; early site 199
Donghai *N.China* Han city 195
Dongshankou *N.E.China* E.Chou cemetery 192
Dongsimucun *N.E.China* Ming tomb 265
Dongsunba *W.China* E.Chou cemetery 192
Dongxiang *N.W.China* Shang copper source 147
Dongxing *S.W.China* cave site 92
Dongyang *E.China* Tang kiln 262
Dongzhuangcun *N.China* early settlement 92
Donja Slatina *S.W.Yugoslavia* fortified site 115
Donnersberg *C.Germany* Celtic oppidum 166
Doornlaagte *S.Africa* Acheulian tools 57
Dorasamudra (n/c Halebid) *S.India,* Hoysala capital 254
Dorchester *S.W.England* railway development 277
Dorestad *N.Holland* Viking trading emporium 243
Dorginarti I. *U.Egypt* fortress 143
Dorset culture *Arctic* 272–273
Dortmund *N.W.Germany* ritual metalwork 180
Doruthy *S.W.France* hunter-gatherer site 72
Døstrup *N.W.Denmark* scratch ploughs 117
Douara Cave *S.Syria* early tools 62
Double Adobe *S.W.USA, Arizona* Archaic site 207
Dougga *N.Tunisia* megalithic tomb 113
Dover (Lat. Dubris) *S.E.England* Roman city 170; railway development 277
Downpatrick *N.Ireland* Bronze Age settlement 115; monastery 245
Dowris *C.Ireland* metal hoard 115
Dowth *E.Ireland* megalithic tomb 107
Dragonby *E.England* Celtic site 166
Dramont *S.France* Roman shipwreck 178
Drangianians ancient people of Afghanistan 159
Draved *S.Denmark* pollen core site 107
Drehem *C.Mesopotamia* early writing 134
Drunken Point *C.Canada, Ontario* Archaic site 207
Dry Creek *Alaska* early settlement 71
Dryopithecus 52-53
Duandian *N.China* Tang kiln 262
Dublin *E.Ireland* Viking centre 242; archbishopric 245
Dubris (mod.Dover) *S.England* Roman city 170
Duggleby *N.England* mediaeval village 246
Dülük *E.Anatolia* early tools 62
Dumat al Jandal (a/c Al Jawf) *N.Arabia* Islamic town 241
Dunbar *S.Scotland* Celtic fortress 242
Dundas Is *N.E.Canada* Dorset site 273
Dunhuang *N.W.China* early trade 191, 262; Han frontier port 195; rock-carved temple 261;
Dünsberg *C.Germany* Celtic oppidum 166
Dur Kurigalzu *C.Mesopotamia* pyramid 49
Dura-Europos (mod.Salahiyah) *E.Syria* early trade centre 191; Roman city 171; Hellenistic city 165
Durango *S.W.USA, Colorado* Basketmaker site 220
Durham *N.England* monastery 245
Durkhumid *E.Anatolia* Assyrian colony 133
Durocortorum (mod.Rheims) *N.E.France* Roman provincial city 171
Durostorum (mod.Silistra) *N.Bulgaria* Roman legionary fortress 171
Durovka *W.USSR* barrow burial 182
Durras North *S.E.Australia* Aboriginal site 96
Durrington Walls *S.England* stone circle 108
Dürrnberg *E.Austria* Celtic site 167
Dushizi *S.China* cave site 92
Dust Devil Cave *S.W.USA, Utah* Archaic site 207
Dutchess Cave *E.USA, New York* Palaeo-Indian site 207
Dutchess Quarry *N.E.USA* fluted points 71
Dutton *C.USA* fluted points 71
Duvensee *W.Germany* Mesolithic settlement 84
Duyong Caves *W.Philippines* cave site 90; Neolithic settlement 151
Dyer *C.USA, Indiana* Archaic site 207
Dyrholm *Denmark* Mesolithic settlement 84
Dyrrhachium (It.Durazzo, mod Durrës) *Albania* Roman city 171; Byzantine walled town 239
Dzhruchula *S.USSR* Neanderthal site 65
Dzibilchaltún *Mexico, Yucatán* Maya settlement 217, 218; early town 226
Dzibilnocac *Mexico,Yucatán* Maya settlement 218
Dzvonetskaya Balka *S.W.Russia* Steppe settlement 149

E

Early Indus period 130–131
Early Khartoum *N.E.Africa, Sudan* hunter-gatherers 95; early pottery 101
Early Thule culture *Arctic* 272–273
East Cape *Alaska* Thule sites 273
East Indies early maritime trade 191, 275
Easter I. *S.Pacific* Polynesian settlement 201, 269
Ebbou *E.France* hunter-gatherer art 74
Ebla *W.Syria* early city 122; early writing 134

F

G

Megara Hyblaea — Mpulungu

Megara Hyblaea *E.Sicily* Greek colony 160, 169
Megaris district of S.E.Greece 163
Megiddo *C.Palestine* early town 133; Egyptian fortress 143; Royal fortress of Israel 156–157
Mehi *N.W.India* Harrappan site 130
Mehrgarh *N.W.India* early farming village 88–89; early city 123; Harappan site 130
Meinarti, Island of *U.Egypt* fortress 143
Meir *U.Egypt* noble's tomb 129, 137
Mejiro *W.Africa, Nigeria* hunter-gatherers 95
Mejlgård *N.Denmark* shell midden 84
Melanesia *W.Pacific* early settlement 201
Meldon Bridge *S.E.Scotland* defensive enclosure 107
Meliddu (a/c Melitene, mod.Malatya) *E.Anatolia* Assyrian provincial city 157
Melilli *Sicily* ancient fortress 113
Melitene (anc.Meliddu, mod.Malatya) *E.Anatolia* Roman legionary
fortress 171
Melitopol *S.W.USSR* barrow burial 182
Melizeigara *W.India* early trade 191
Melka Kunture (a/s Kontoure) *E.Africa, Ethiopia* early man 57; Stone Age tools 67; hunter-gatherers 95
Melkhoutboom *S.Africa* Stone Age site 253
Melolo *S.Indonesia* early metal site 199
Melos *S.Aegean* Greek city 161
Melville Koppies *S.Africa* Iron Age site 203
Memphis *L.Egypt* early city 122, 143; ancient city 129, 137; Achaemenid city 158; Hellenistic city 165; early iron 203
Menard *S.USA* temple-mound 230
Mende *N.E.Greece* Greek colony 161
Mendut *C.Java* Buddhist centre 261
Menehune Ditch *Hawaiian Is* 268
Menelaion *S.Greece* Mycenaean settlement 145
Mengchi Protectorate *C.Asia* trade with China 262
Mengxi *C.China* Longshan site 147
menhirs *W.Europe* 108–109
Menidi *E.Greece* tholos tomb 145
Meniet *N.Africa, Algeria* bone harpoons 94; early livestock 119
Menneville *N.E.France* Iron Age cemetery 33
Mercin-et-Vaux *N.E.France* Iron Age cemetery 33
Mérida *W.Spain* Roman aqueduct 178; Islamic town 240
Merimda *N.E.Africa, Egypt* early cereals 119
Merkour *S.E.Greece* Athenian settlement 163
Meroë *N.E.Africa, Sudan* temple remains 184; early trade 190; early iron 203
Merrivale *S.W.England* stone alignment and menhir 108
Merry Maidens (a/c Dawns Men) *S.W.England* stone circle 108
Mersa Gawasis *Red Sea* temple 137
Mersin *S.E.Anatolia* Neolithic site 83; farming site 87; early pottery 101
Merv (a/c Margush, anc. Alexandria, mod. Mary) *C.Asia* Achaemenid city 159; Parthian/Sasanian city 186; early trade centre 191; Islamic town 241
Mesa Verde *S.W.USA* Pueblo farming site 228
Mesas de Asta *S.W.Spain* early settlement 112
Mesembria *Bulgaria* Greek colony 161; Byzantine walled town 239
Meshed *N.E.Persia* holy city 257
Mesoamerica see Mexico, Guatemala
Mesopotamia pyramids 49; Neolithic sites 81–83; prehistoric settlement 98–99; early pottery 101; early agriculture 104–105; early civilisation 122; early cities 124–125; Sumer 126–127; early writing 134–135; Assyrian empire 154–157; Achaemenid empire 158; Hellenistic influence 165; Parthian and Sasanian empires 186; Islam 241; Ottoman empire 257
Messene *S.Greece* theatre and temple 161
Messenia region of S.W.Greece 163
Messina *Sicily* archbishopric 245
Mesvin IV *Belgium* early tools 62
Metapontum (a/s Metapontion) *S.Italy* Greek colony 160, 161, 169
Metaurus *S.Italy* Greek colony 169
Methone *N.E.Greece* Greek colony 161
Metmenge *S.E.Anatolia* early tools 62
Metz *E.France* Roman aqueduct 178
Mexicaltzingo *C.Mexico* Aztec centre 226
México (mod.Mexico City) *C.Mexico* colonial settlement 235; early trade 274
Mexico early settlement 32–33, 70–71; ritual 48; pyramids 49; early writing 134–135; early farming 208–211; early civilisations 214–215; Teotihuacán empire 215–217; Maya empire 217; Aztec empire 226–227; colonial settlement 235
Mextitlán early state of Mexico 226
Mezcala *C.Mexico* early farming site 211; Pre-Classical site 214
Mezhirich' *C.USSR* hunter-gatherer site 72; hunter-gatherer art 74
Mezin *W.USSR* hunter-gatherer site 72; hunter-gatherer art 74
Miami *S.USA, Texas* Palaeo-Indian site 207
Miaodigou *N.China* Longshan site 147
Miaoqiancun *N.China* E.Chou cemetery 192
mica *N.America* 220
Micoquian tools *Europe* 64–65
Micronesia *N.W.Pacific* early settlement 201
Mid Clyth *N.E.Scotland* stone alignment 108
Middle Stone Age *Africa* 66–67
Midhen *S.W.Greece* tholos tomb 145
Miesenheim *W.Germany* early tools 62
Mihintale *N.Ceylon* Buddhist site 189; Buddhist remains 255
Mikhaylovka *S.W.USSR* Steppe settlement 149
Mikhaylovo-Apostolovo *Ukraine* Greek imports 161
Mikonos (a/s Mykonos) *S.E.Greece* ancient fortress 113
Mikro Kavouri *S.E.Greece* Athenian settlement 163
Mila Mergi *N.Mesopotamia* Assyrian rock relief 157
Mila *N.W.Greece* tholos tomb 145
Milan (It.Milano) *N.Italy* Celtic oppidum 166; mediaeval trade 244; archbishopric 245
Miletus *W.Anatolia* Classical state 105; early port 143; Achaemenid city 158; Greek city 161; Hellenistic city 165; Roman city 171
Miller *S.USA, Mississippi* Hopewell site 220
Millstream *W.Australia* Aboriginal site 96
Mimasaka *C.Japan* shogunate provincial capital 267
Mimbres culture *S.W.USA* 228–229
Mimot *Cambodia* Neolithic settlement 151
Mina Perdida *S.Peru* early farming site 211
Mina *E.Brazil* shell midden 224
Mindeddu *E.Sardinia* dry-stone fortress 169
Mindif *W.Africa, Cameroon* Stone Age tools 67
Ming dynasty *China* 264–265
Minisink *E.USA, Delaware* Palaeo-Indian site 207
Minoa (a/c Heraclea Minoa) *W.Sicily* Greek colony 160
Minoans 140–141
Minturnae (mod.Minturno) *C.Italy* Roman colony 169
Mirabib *S.W.Africa, Namibia* Stone Age site 203
Mirador *S.E.Mexico* Pre-Classical site 214
Miran *N.W.China* Buddhist centre 261
Mirgissa *U.Egypt* fortification 137
Miriwun *N.Australia* early man 69
Mirpur Khas *N.W.India* Buddhist site 189
Misa-ri *C.Korea* early settlement 93
Mison *C.Vietnam* early monumental site 199
Mississippian culture 230–231
Miswar *S.W.Arabia* early capital 184
Mitannian empire 142–143
Mitathal (a/s Mitahal) *N.W.India* Indus Valley settlement 89; Harappan site 130
Mitha Deheno *N.W.India* Harappan site 130
Mitla *C.Mexico* pyramid 49; Pre-Classical site 214; Aztec town 226
Mitla Fortress *C.Mexico* stone source 209
Mitli *N.W.India* Mesolithic settlement 89
Mitropolis *S.Crete* Minoan villa 141
Mitterberg *W.Austria* copper mine 115, 120–121
Mittimatalik *N.E.Canada* Dorset site 273
Mivath *N.India* Mughal mint 257
Miwa,Mt. *C.Japan* holy mountain 267
Mixco Viejo *S.Guatemala* Maya settlement 218; early town 226
Mixian *N.China* Tang kiln 262; Sung kiln 263
Mixnitz *Austria* Neanderthal site 65
Mixquic *C.Mexico* Aztec centre 226
Mixtec kingdoms *C.Mexico* 226
Mizukamidani *C.Japan* early settlement 93
Mlu Prei *Cambodia* transitional settlement 151
Mnarani *E.Africa, Kenya* Ming pottery 264
moa bones *New Zealand* 271
Moanalua *Hawaiian Is* early irrigation 269
Mocha *S.W.Arabia, Yemen* maritime trade 275
Moche civilisation *Andes* 212–213
Moche *N.W.Peru* pyramid 49; pre-Inca centre 223
Mochlos (a/s Mokhlos) *N.E.Crete* Minoan town 141
Modoc *C.USA, Illinois* Archaic site 207
Moel Ty Uchaf *N.Wales* stone circle 108
Mogadishu (n/s Muqdisho) *E.Africa, Somalia* Islamic trade 240; Iron Age site 253; Ming pottery 264
Mogador (mod. Essaouira) *N.W.Africa, Morocco* Phoenician city 161; early iron 203
Mogara *N.India* Mesolithic settlement 89
Mogen *S.Norway* early settlement 180
Moghogha Sura *N.W.Morocco* Carthaginian cemetery 169
Mogollon culture *SW.USA* 228–229
Mogollon Village *S.W.USA* Pueblo farming site 228
Mogontiacum (mod.Mainz) *W.Germany* Roman legionary fortress 171
Mohameriya *U.Egypt* ancient cemetery 129
Mohelnice *Czechoslovakia* farming site 87
Mohenjo-Daro *N.W.India* early city 123, 130–131; early writing 135; Buddhist site 189
Moho Cay *E.Mexico* Maya centre 217
Moikau *New Zealand, North I.* early site 271
Mokau *New Zealand, North I.* rock art 271
Mokrin *N.E.Yugoslavia* Bronze Age cemetery 115
Molino Casarotto *N.Italy* farming settlement 87, 107
Molodovo *S.USSR* Neanderthal site 65; hunter-gatherer site 72; hunter-gatherer art 74
Moluccas (a/c Spice Islands) early maritime trade 275
Mombasa *E.Africa, Kenya* maritime trade 275
Monagrillo *C.America, Panama* early pottery 211
Monamore *W.Scotland* megalithic tomb 107
monasteries *Buddhist India* 188-189; *mediaeval Europe* 245; *England* 247
Monastir *N.W.Africa, Tunisia* Islamic fortress 240
Monastiraki *C.Crete* Minoan villa 140
Mongolia early civilisation 124; Steppe nomads 183
Mongonu *W.Africa, Nigeria* early town 251
Monk Bretton *N.England* mediaeval town 247
Monks Mound *C.USA* temple-mound 231
Monoo *N.Japan* Heian fortress 267
Monreale *W.Sicily* archbishopric 245
Monsempron *C.France* Neanderthal site 65
Monsheim *C.Germany* defensive enclosure 107
Mont Auxois *E.France* Celtic oppidum 166
Mont Bégo *S.E.France* rock art 115
Mont Beuvray *E.France* Celtic oppidum 166
Mont Lassois *E.France* Hallstatt site 166
Mont-Dol *N.W.France* Neanderthal site 64
Mont-St.Michel *N.W.France* monastery 245
Montagu Cave *S.Africa* Acheulian tools 57; Stone Age tools 67
Montclus *S.France* Mesolithic settlement 84
Monte Albán *C.Mexico* pyramid 49; early writing 135; early farming site 211; Zapotec site 214; early town 217; Aztec town 226
Monte Alto *S.Guatemala* Maya settlement 218
Monte Aquilone *S.Italy* defensive enclosure 107
Monte Bernorio *N.Spain* native settlement 169
Monte sa Idda *S.Sardinia* metal hoard 115
Monte Sant'Angelo *C.Italy* archbishopric 245
Monte Sirai *S.Sardinia* Carthaginian site 169
Monte Verde *C.Chile* early settlement 70–71
Montenegro *C.Mexico* Pre-Classical site 214
Monteoru *N.E.Romania* fortified site 115
Montgaudier *C.France* hunter-gatherer art 74
Montières *N.France* early tools 62
Montmaurin *C.France* early tools 62
Montpellier *S.France* monastery 245
Monzú *Colombia* early pottery 211
Moor Park *S.Africa* Iron Age site 253
Moore Creek *E.Australia* Aboriginal site 96
Moose River *Alaska* Pacific Eskimo site 273
Mopti *W.Africa* early settlement 249
Morales *E.Mexico* Maya settlement 218
Moravany *Czechoslovakia* hunter-gatherer site 72; hunter-gatherer art 74
Morgedal *S.Norway* iron-working site 180
Morhana Pahar *N.E.India* Mesolithic settlement 89
Morocco early man 67; early farming 87; early pottery 94; Beaker burials 110; Bronze Age 112; Roman cities and fortresses 170; early trade 249
Morongo Uta *Austral Is* early site 269
Moroto *Uganda* Proconsul 53
Morrisons Islands *C.Canada, Ontario* Archaic site 207
Mortensnes *N.Norway* Saami grave 273
Morton *E.Scotland* shell midden 84; megalithic site 87
Moscha (a/s Moskha) *S.Arabia* early trade 191
Moschi ancient people of E.Anatolia 158
Moshebis *S.Africa* Stone Age site 253
Mosselbaai *S.Africa* Stone Age tools 67
Mossgiel *S.E.Australia* early man 69
Mostar *Yugoslavia* Sinan mosque 256
Mosul (f/c Nud Ardashir) *N.Mesopotamia* Sasanian city 186; Islamic town 240-241
Mosyllon (a/s Mosullon) *N.E.Africa, Somalia* ancient port 184; early trade 191
Mother Grundy's Parlour *C.England* hunter-gatherer site 72
Motuopuhi *New Zealand, North I.* early settlement 271
Motutapu Island *New Zealand, North I.* defended settlement 271
Motya (a/s Motye) *W.Sicily* Phoenician city 161; Carthaginian city 169
Mouchi Sounosso *N.Africa, Chad* early man 57
Mouila *W.Africa, Gabon* early iron 203
Mouliana *E.Crete* Minoan village 141
Mound City *N.E.USA, Ohio* Hopewell site 221
Moundville *S.E.USA* burial site 35; temple-mound 230
Mount Burr *S.Australia* Aboriginal site 96
Mount Caburn *S.England* Celtic hillfort 167
Mount Camel *New Zealand, North I.* moa bones 271
Mount Horeb *N.E.USA, Kentucky* Hopewell site 221
Mount Olo *Western Samoa* early site 269
Mount Pleasant *S.England* henge 108
Mount Rowland *Tasmania* Aboriginal site 96
Mount William *S.E.Australia* Aboriginal site 96
Mount's Bay *S.W.England* axe factory 107
Mountain Cow *Belize* Maya settlement 218
Mountsandel *N.Ireland* Mesolithic settlement 84
Mousterian tools *Europe* 64–65; *Africa* 67
Mowthorpe *N.England* mediaeval village 246
Moxby *N.England* mediaeval town 247
Mozambique *S.E.Africa* maritime trade 275
Mözs *C.Hungary* early cemetery 34
Mozu *C.Japan* mound cemetery 196–197
Mpulungu *C.Africa, Zambia* hunter-gatherers 95

Q

R

Ras Beyrouth — San Simon

Ras Beyrouth *Lebanon* early tools 62; Neanderthal site 65
Ras el'Amiya *C.Mesopotamia* pottery remains 99
Ras el Ma *W.Africa, Mali* early settlement 249
Ras el-Kelb *Lebanon* Neanderthal site 65
Ras el-Lados *Lebanon* Neanderthal site 65
Ras Shamra (anc.Ugarit) *N.W.Syria* Neolithic site 81,83; early pottery 101; Achaemenid burial 158
Rat Buri *C.Thailand* early site 259
Ratiaria (mod.Archar) *N.Bulgaria* Roman legionary fortress 171
Räuberhöhle *S.Germany* Neanderthal site 65
Ravenna *N.Italy* archbishopric 245
Ravensburg *N.W.Germany* early tools 62
Ravnholt *C.Denmark* bog body 180
Rawak *C.Asia* Buddhist centre 261
Ray (a/s Rai mod.Tehran) *N.Persia* Parthian/Sasanian city 186
Razet *N.E.France* rock-cut tombs 107
Real Alto *W.Ecuador* pyramid 49; early farming site 211
Red Mountains *S.W.USA* Pueblo farming site 228
Red Sea states 184–185
Redkin Lager *S.W.USSR* Steppe settlement 149
Reggio (di Calabria) *S.Italy* archbishopric 245
Reggio (nell'Emilia) *N.Italy* early university 245
Regourdou *C.France* Neanderthal site 65
Reigh *N.USA, Wisconsin* Archaic site 207
Relilaia *N.Africa, Algeria* hunter-gatherers 94
Remagen (anc.Rigomagus) *W. Germany* Roman village 174
Remedello *N.Italy* Copper Age cemetery 110
Remojadas *C.Mexico* early farming site 211
René Simard *C.France* Neanderthal site 65
Rennell I. *Solomon Is* Lapita site 201
Renner *C.USA, Missouri* Hopewell site 220
Reric *N.Germany* Viking trading emporium 243
Resolute *N.E.Canada* Thule site 273
Retoka *S.Pacific* burial site 48
Revheim *S.W.Norway* musical instruments 117
Rhaedestus *E.Thrace* Byzantine town 238
Rhamnus *S.E.Greece* theatre and temple 161; Athenian settlement 163
Rhegium (a/s Rhegion, mod.Reggio di Calabria) *S.Italy* Greek colony 160–161; Roman city 171
Rheims (Fr.Reims) *N.France* Viking centre 242; archbishopric 245
Rheindahlen *N.W.Germany* early tools 62; Neanderthal site 65
Rheingönheim *W.Germany* silk trade 190
Rhodes *E.Mediterranean* Hellenistic city 165
Rhos-y-beddau *N.W.Wales* stone alignment 108
Ribblehead *N.E.Ireland* Viking centre 242
Ribe *W.Denmark* early settlement 180; Viking trading emporium 243
Richmond *N.England* mediaeval town 247
Richu *C.Japan* Yamato tomb 196
Rickeby *E.Sweden* rock art 117
Rievaulx *N.England* monastery 245; Cistercian abbey 247
Rigabe *S.E.France* early tools 62; Neanderthal site 65
Rijkholt (-Sint-Geertruid) *S.Holland* flint mine 107
Rim *W.Africa Mali* hunter-gatherers 119; Iron Age site 203
Rinaldone *C.Italy* Copper Age cemetery 110
Ringkloster *N.Denmark* Mesolithic settlement 84; megalithic site 87
Río Azul *N.Guatemala* Maya settlement 218
Río Bec *Mexico, Yucatán* Maya settlement 218
Río Chiquito *C.Mexico* Olmec site 214
Rio de Janeiro *Brazil* colonial settlement 235
Río Seco *S.Peru* early public building 211
Río Tinto *S.Spain* early copper mine 120
Ríofrío *N.Spain* pollen core site 107
Riol (anc.Rigodulum) *W. Germany* Roman village 174
Ripabianca *C.Italy* farming site 87
Riparo Blanc *C.Italy* shell midden 84
Ripiceni-Izvor *Romania* Neanderthal site 65
Ripoli *C.Italy* defensive enclosure 107
Ripon *N.England* mediaeval town 247
Rishahr (f/c Rev Ardashir) *S.W.Persia* Sasanian city 186
Rissori *Belgium* early tools 62
Rithymna (mod.Rethimnon) *N.Crete* Minoan village 140
ritual 48–49
Riverton *C.USA, Illinois* Archaic site 207
Riverton *New Zealand, South I.* shell midden 271
Rixheim *E.France* farming site 87; urnfield 115
Roaix *S.E.France* rock-cut tomb 107
Roanne *E.France* Celtic site 166
Robbins *N.E.USA, Kentucky* Adena site 221
Roberts Drift *S.Africa* Iron Age site 253
Robin Hood's Cave *C.England* hunter-gatherer site 72
Robinson *N.E.USA, New York* Archaic site 207
Roc de Marsal *C.France* Neanderthal site 65
Roc de Sers *N.W.France* hunter-gatherer site 72; hunter-gatherer art 74
Roc-en-Pail *N.W.France* Neanderthal site 64
Rock Eagle *S.E.USA* temple-mound 230
rock edicts *Asokan India* 155, 189
rock inscriptions Assyrian empire 157; Achaemenid empire 158–159
rock reliefs *Parthian and Sasanian Persia* 186
Rockmarshall *N.Ireland* shell midden 84
Rocky Cape *Tasmania* Aborginal site 96
Rocourt *Belgium* Neanderthal site 64
Rodgers Shelter *C.USA, Missouri* Archaic site 207
Roersdam *C.Denmark* bog body 180
Rognac *S.France* native settlement 169
Rohira *N.W.India* Harappan site 130
Roi Et Sites *N.E.Thailand* early sites 199
Rojadi *N.W.India* Harappan site 130
Rollright Stones *C.England* stone circle 108
Roluos *Indo-China, Cambodia* early site 259
Romagnano *N.Italy* Mesolithic settlement 84; farming site 87
Roman empire 168–177; roads 155; technology 178–179
Romanelli *S.Italy* hunter-gatherer site 72; hunter-gatherer art 74
Romania Neanderthals 65; Mesolithic sites 84, 87; tell settlements 110–111; Bronze Age 115, Roman cities and fortresses 171
Rome *(Lat. and mod. Roma) C.Italy* 168–173; early writing 135; Roman city 171; aqueduct 178; early trading capital 190; mediaeval trade 244; archbishopric and pilgrimage centre 245
Romeral *S.Spain* megalithic tomb 107
Rønbjerg *N.W.Denmark* bog body 180
Ronquín *C.Venezuela* early horticultural village 224
Rooidam *S.Africa* Acheulian tools 57
Roonka Flat *S.Australia* Aboriginal site 96
Roosevelt *S.W.USA* Pueblo farming site 228
Ropp *W.Africa, Nigeria* hunter-gatherers 95
Roquepertuse *S.France* Celtic site 166
Rørbaek *N.W.Denmark* bog body 180
Rosetta Stone *L.Egypt* 165
Rosh Horesha *S.Palestine* Natufian site 81
Rosh Zin *S.Palestine* Natufian site 81
Roskilde *N.Denmark* Viking centre 243
Ross *S.Ireland* monastery 245
Rossano *S.Italy* archbishopric 245
Rossum Praestegård *S.Norway* musical instruments 117
Rotokura *New Zealand, South I.* shell midden and moa bones 271
Roudo *W.Syria* early tools 62
Rouen *N.France* Viking trading emporium 242; archbishopric 245
Rouffignac *C.France* hunter-gatherer art 74; Mesolithic settlement 84
Rough Island *N.Ireland* shell midden 84
Roum *N.W.Denmark* bog body 180
Round Green *S.England* early tools 62
Roundway *S.England* Beaker burial 110
Royal Road *Persia* 158–159
Ruahihi *New Zealand, North I.* defended settlement 271
Ruanga *E.Africa, Zimbabwe* Iron Age site 253
Ruarangi Pa *New Zealand, North I.* defended settlement 271
Rudabánya *Hungary* Dryopithecus 53
Rudki *W.Poland* iron-working site 180
Rudna Glava *C.Yugoslavia* early copper mine 110, 120
Rudston *N.E.England* Beaker burial 110
Runan *C.China* Han city 195
runestones *Denmark* 243
Runnymede *S.England* Bronze Age settlement 115
Runzhou *E.China* Tang prefecture 262
Rupar *N.W.India* early city 123; Harappan site 130
Rupnath *C.India* rock edict 189
Rupununi *Guyana* early settlement 224
Rusahinili *E.Anatolia* Urartian city 157
Ruše *N.Yugoslavia* urnfield 115
Rusellae *N.Italy* Etruscan city 169
Rusinga Island *Kenya* Proconsul 53
Russell Cave *S.E.USA, Tennessee* Archaic site 207
Russia early graves 34; disease 42; hunter-gatherers 72; early agriculture 78–79; Mesolithic sites 87; Steppe settlements 148–149; Roman cities and fortresses 171; Steppe nomads 182–183; Chinese silks and mirrors 191; Byzantine empire 239 (see also USSR)
Rustenburg *S.Africa* Iron Age site 253

S

Sa Huynh *S.Vietnam* transitional settlement 151; early site 199
Saaide *W.Syria* Natufian site 81
Saaifontein see Zaayfontein
Saalburg *N.W.Germany* Roman water mill 178
Saami culture *Scandinavia* 273
Saarbrücken *W. Germany* Roman village 174
Sab Champa *C.Thailand* moated site 199
Saba 'a *N.W. Mesopotamia* Assyrian stela 157
Sabaea *S.W.Arabia* early state 184
Sabancheyevo *C.USSR* Steppe settlement 149
Sabrata *W.Libya* Roman city 171
Saccopastore *C.Italy* Neanderthal site 65
Sacrificios Island *C.Mexico* Aztec town 226
Sacsayhuamán *C.Peru* Inca fortress 223
Sadanoyama *C.Japan* Yamato tomb 196
Sadhaura *N.India* Mughal mint 257
Sado middens *S.Portugal* 84
Sado *N.Japan* shogunate provincial capital 267
Saeth Maen *S.Wales* stone alignment 108
Safavid empire 256–257
Sagaholm *S.Sweden* rock art 117
Sagartians ancient people of S.Persia 159
Saguntum (mod. Sagunto) *E.Spain* native settlement 169
Ságvár *Hungary* hunter-gatherer site 72
Sahul-land early land-bridge 69
Sai Yok *S.Thailand* cave site 90; early metal site 151
Sai, Island of *U.Egypt* fortress 143
Said Qala Tepe *Afghanistan* later farming village 89
Saikaido *C.Japan* early highway 267
Saint-Eugène *S.France* Beaker burial 110
Saint-Gaudens *S.W.France* Dryopithecus 53
Sais *L.Egypt* ancient city 137
Saitobaru *S.W.Japan* mound cemetery 197
Sakcagözü *S.E.Anatolia* pottery remains 99; Assyrian city 157
Saki *C.Japan* mound cemetery 197
Sakitama *C.Japan* mound cemetery 197
Šal'a *Czechoslovakia* Neanderthal site 65
Saladero *C.Venezuela* early horticultural village 224
Salaga *W.Africa, Ghana* early town 251
Salamanca *N.Spain* monastery 245
Salamis *Cyprus* ivory 157
Salamis *S.E.Greece* Athenian settlement 163
Salapia *C.Italy* Roman empire 169
Salcombe *S.W.England* ancient shipwreck 115
Saldae (Fr.Bougie, mod.Bejaia) *N.W.Africa* Phoenician city 161
Salé *N.W.Africa, Morocco* Homo erectus 57
Salemas *Portugal* Neanderthal site 64
Salerno (Lat. Salernum) *S.Italy* Roman colony 169; archbishopric 245
Salgir River *S.W.USSR* Steppe settlement 149
Salinas la Blanca *S.E.Mexico* Maya settlement 218
Salinelles *S.E.France* flint mine 107
Salipetaka *E.India* Buddhist site 189
Salmas *N.W.Persia* rock relief 186
Salmendingen *W.Germany* Dryopithecus 53
Salonae (mod.Solin) *N.Yugoslavia* Roman provincial capital 171
Salts Cave *C.USA, Kentucky* Archaic site 207
Salzburg *W.Austria* archbishopric 245
Salzgitter-Lebenstedt *N.Germany* Neanderthal site 65
Samandağ Cave *S.Anatolia* Palaeolithic site 83
Samanli *W.Anatolia* Sinan mosque 256
Samapa *E.India* rock edict 189
Samaria *N.Palestine* Royal fortress of Israel 157; Achaemenid city 158; Hellenistic city 165
Samarkand (anc.Maracanda) *C.Asia* Achaemenid city 159; early trade centre 191; Islamic town 241; early trade 262
Samarra *C.Mesopotamia* pottery remains 99; Abbasid capital 240–241; holy city 257
Samarra pottery *Mesopotamia* 99
Sambava *Madagascar* Ming pottery 264
Sambor Prei Kuk *Cambodia* Neolithic settlement 151; early monumental site 199
Samburu Hills *Kenya* Kenyapithecus 53
Samhar *S.Arabia* ancient port 184
Samoa Lapita culture 201; early settlement 269
Samos *S.E.Aegean* Greek city 161; Greek aqueduct 178
Samosata (mod.Samsat) *E.Anatolia* Roman legionary fortress 171
Samothrace *N.Aegean* sanctuary 165
Samrong Sen *Cambodia* transitional settlement 151
Samun Dukiya *W.Africa, Nigeria* Iron Age site 203
San Antonio *S.USA, Texas* colonial settlement 235
San Augustín *E.Mexico* Maya settlement 218
San Biagio *S.Italy* Greek shrine 161
San Carla *Balearic Is* fortified site 115
San Cosmos *S.W.USA* Pueblo farming site 228
San Diego *S.W.USA* early settlement 71
San Felipe *E.Guatemala* Maya settlement 218
San Fernando de Apure *Venezuela* early settlement 224
San Gervasio *Mexico, Yucatán* Maya settlement 218
San Isidro *C.Spain* early tools 62
San Isidro *N.Mexico* early settlement 71
San Isidro *S.E.Mexico* Pre-Classical site 214
San Jerónimo *C.Mexico* early farming site 211; Pre-Classical site 214
San Jose *Belize* Maya settlement 218
San Jose Mogote *C.Mexico* early farming site 211; early hieroglyphs 214
San Lorenzo *C.Mexico* early public building 211; Olmec centre 214–215
San Marco *S.Italy* monastery 245
San Marcos *C.Mexico* early settlement 209
San Martín de Castaneda *N.W.Spain* monastery 245
San Martín Pajapán *C.Mexico* Olmec site 214
San Miguel *E.Mexico* Maya settlement 218
San Miguel Amuco *C.Mexico* Pre-Classical site 214
San Pablito *C.Mexico* Pre-Classical site 214
San Pedro de Atacama *S. Bolivia* 212
San Simon *S.W.USA* Pueblo farming site 228

U

V

Virú Valley — Yarm

Virú Valley *Peru* pre-Columbian settlement 32
Virunum *S.Austria* Roman provincial capital 171
Virupaksha temple of Vijayanagara 254
Visadi *N.W.India* Mesolithic site 89
Vistahermosa *S.E.Mexico* Pre-Classical site 214
Viste Cave *S.Norway* Mesolithic settlement 84
Vitaria *Austral Is* early site 269
Vivallen *N.Norway* Saami grave 273
Vix *E.France* Greek bronze 161; Hallstatt site 166
Vladimirovka *S.W.USSR* Cucuteni-Tripolye village 111; Steppe settlement 149
Vo Canh *S.Vietnam* early site 199
Vogelherd *S.Germany* Neanderthal site 65; hunter-gatherer art 72; hunter-gatherer site 74
Volaterrae (mod. Volterra) *N.Italy* Etruscan city 169
Voldtofte *S.Denmark* Bronze Age settlement 117
Volgu *E.France* hunter-gatherer site 72
Volsinii (mod. Bolsena) *N.Italy* Etruscan city 169
Volturnum *C.Italy* Roman colony 169
Vorou *C.Crete* tholos tomb 141
Vorukh *C.Asia* Han mirror find 191
Vouni *Cyprus* Achaemenid palace 158
Vourvoura *S.Greece* tholos tomb 145
Vrana *E.Greece* tholos tomb 145; Athenian settlement 163
Vrevskiy *C.Asia* Han mirror find 191
Vromopousi *S.E.Greece* Athenian settlement 163
Vroue *N.Denmark* Corded Ware burial 110
Vršnik *S.Yugoslavia* farming site 87
Vrysinas (a/s Vrisinas) *W.Crete* peak sanctuary
Vulci *N.Italy* Etruscan city 169

W

Wa *W.Africa, Ghana* early town 251
Wadan (a/s Ouadane) *W.Africa, Mauritania* early town 251
Wadi Caam *N.Libya* Roman dam 178
Wadi Djidiouia *N.Algeria* Roman dam 178
Wadi el Boul *C.Tunisia* Roman dam 178
Wadi el-Hudi *U.Egypt* ancient mine 137
Wadi el-Sheikh *L.Egypt* flint 129
Wadi Ganima *N.Libya* Roman dam 178
Wadi Garawi *L.Egypt* calcite 129
Wadi Labdah *N.Libya* Roman dam 178
Wadi Maghara *Sinai* graffiti 129; copper mine 137
Wadi Megenin *N.Libya* Roman dam 178
Wadi Mina *N.Algeria* Roman dam 178
Wadi Shaw *N.Sudan* early pottery 101
Wadi Wassa' *U.Egypt* early pottery 101
Wagadugu see Ouagadougou
Wahlitz *N.Germany* Corded Ware burial 110
Waiahukini *Hawaiian Is* early site 201, 269
Waihi *New Zealand, North I.* rock art 271
Waikaia (Upper) *New Zealand, South I.* moa bones 271
Waimaru *New Zealand, South I.* shell midden 271
Waimataitai *New Zealand, South I.* moa bones 271
Waimea *Hawaiian Is* early site 269
Waingongoro *New Zealand, North I.* shell midden 271
Waioneke *New Zealand, North I.* defended settlement 271
Wairau Bar *New Zealand, South I.* early site 201; moa hunter's camp 270–271
Waitaki River Mouth *New Zealand, South I.* moa bones 271
Waitore *New Zealand, North I.* rock art 271
Wajak *Java* early man 69
Wakanui *New Zealand, South I.* moa bones 271
Wakapatu *New Zealand, South I.* shell midden 271
Wakefield *N.England* mediaeval town 247
Wakhshushana *E.Anatolia* Assyrian colony 133
Walakpa *Alaska* Thule site 273
Walata (Fr.Oualata) *W.Africa, Mauritania* early settlement 249; early town 251
Waldalgesheim *N.Germany* vehicle burial 166
Waldfischbach *W. Germany* Roman village 174
Wales early hominids 62; Megalithic Age 107; standing stones 108; Bronze Age 115
Wallacea *E.Indies* 90
Walls *S.E.USA* temple-mound 230
Walpi *S.W.USA* Pueblo farming site 228
Walsingham *S.England* pilgrimage centre 245
Wanbaoting *N.E.China* early stirrups 44
Wanfosi *N.W.China* Buddhist centre 261
Wangdu *N.China* Han burial 195
Wangshan *C.China* E.Chou burial 192
Wangwan *N.China* Longshan site 147
Wangyandong *S.China* cave site 92
Wanlek *E.New Guinea* swamp site 90
Waramuri *Guyana* early settlement 224
Warka (anc. Uruk) *S.Mesopotamia* pottery remains 99
Warm Mineral Springs *S.E.USA* fluted points 71
Warri *W.Africa, Nigeria* early town 251
Warter *N.England* mediaeval town 247
Washpool *New Zealand, North I.* early site 201
Washshukanni *E.Anatolia* Mitannian city 143
Wasit *Iraq* Islamic town 241
Wasserbillig *W. Germany* Roman village 174
Wasserburg *S.Germany* Bronze Age settlement 114–115
Wat Phu *Indo-China, Laos* monumental site 199; early site 259
Wat's Dyke *W.England* 242
Waterford *S.Ireland* Viking centre 242
Watertown Arsenal *N.E.USA, Massachusetts* Archaic site 207
Watton *N.England* mediaeval town 247
Wawcott *S.W.England* megalithic site 87
Wei *N.China* Han city 195
Weifang *N.China* Shang pottery 146
Weipa *N.E.Australia* Aboriginal site 96
Weis *N.W.USA, Montana* Archaic site 207
Weizhou *N.China* Tang prefecture 262
Weka Pass *New Zealand, South I.* rock art 271
Weligama *S.Ceylon* Buddhist remains 255
Wellington, Mount *New Zealand, North I.* Maori hillfort 270
Wells Crater *C.USA, Kentucky* Palaeo-Indian site 207
Wenchi *W.Africa, Ghana* early town 251
Wengyuan *S.China* cave site 92
Wenzhou *E.China* Tang kiln 262; Sung kiln 263
Weris *E.Belgium* megalithic site 107
West Athens Hill *N.E.USA, New York* Palaeo-Indian site 207
West Kennet *S.England* longbarrow 106-107
West Point *Tasmania* Aboriginal site 96
West Stow *S.E.Denmark* claw beaker 180
Westeregeln *E.Germany* farming site 87
Western Samoa early settlement 269
Westernschouwen *Holland* Viking trading emporium 242
Westness *Orkney Is* Viking centre 242
Westward Ho *S.W.England* shell midden 84
Wet *S.W.USA* Pueblo farming site 228
Wetwang *N.England* mediaeval village 246
Wetzikon *Switzerland* Mesolithic settlement 84
Wexford *S.Ireland* Viking centre 242
Whakamoenga Cave *New Zealand, North I.* early site 271
Whangamata *New Zealand, North I.* shell midden and moa bones 271
Wharetaewa Pa *New Zealand, North I.* defended settlement 271
Wharram Grange *N.England* mediaeval village 246
Wharram Percy *N.England* mediaeval village 246
Wharram-le-Street *N.England* mediaeval village 246
Wheathampstead *N.England* Celtic site 166
Whiritoa *New Zealand, North I.* rock art 271
Whitby *N.England* mediaeval town 247
White Mound Village *S.W.USA* Pueblo farming site 228
Whitipirorua *New Zealand, North I.* shell midden 271
Whitsbury *S.England* Celtic hillfort 167
Wichquana *S.E.Peru* early farming settlement 211
Wicklow *E.Ireland* Viking centre 242
Wiesbaden (anc.Aquae) *W. Germany* Roman town 174
Wietrzychowice *W.Poland* megalithic tomb 107
Wilberfoss *N.England* mediaeval town 247
Wildscheuer *N.Germany* Neanderthal site 65; hunter-gatherer site 72
Wilgie Mia *W.Australia* Aboriginal site 96
Willendorf *Austria* hunter-gatherer site 72; hunter-gatherer art 74
Williamsburg *E.USA, Virginia* colonial settlement 235
Williamson *E.USA, Virginia* Palaeo-Indian site 207
Wilsford *S.England* Celtic religious site 166
Wilson Butte *N.W.USA, Idaho* Archaic site 207
Wilson Butte Cave *N.W.USA* fluted points 71
Wilson Mound *C.USA* temple-mound 231
Wilson's Promontory *S.E.Australia* Aboriginal site 96
Wilton *S. Africa* hunter-gatherers 95, 119; Stone Age site 203, 253
Wimereux *N.France* early tools 62
Winay Wayna *S.Peru* pre-Inca centre 223
Winchester *S.England* Viking mint 242
Windeby Bog *N.Germany* bog body 180
Windhoek *S.W.Africa, Namibia* Stone Age tools 67
Windmill Hill *S.England* defensive enclosure 107
Winnall Moors *S.England* pollen core site 107
Winona and Ridge Ruins *S.W.USA* Pueblo farming site 228
Winterville *S.USA* temple-mound 230
Wisconsin glaciers 207
Witów *S.Poland* Mesolithic settlement 84
Wittnauer Horn *N.Switzerland* fortified site 115
Wolstenholme *E.USA, Virginia* colonial settlement 234
Wombah *E.Australia* Aboriginal site 96
Wonderboom *S.Africa* Acheulian tools 57
Woodchuck Cave *S.W.USA* Pueblo farming site 228
Woodlark I. *New Guinea* Kula gift exchange 46
wool early cultivation 40; mediaeval Europe 244
Woolbury *S.England* Celtic hillfort 167
Woollandale *E.Africa, Zimbabwe* Iron Age site 253
Worcester *C.England* monastery 245
Worms (anc.Borbetomagus) *W. Germany* Roman town 174
Wright *N.E.USA, Kentucky* Hopewell site 221
Wu'an *N.China* early settlement 92
Wuchang *E.China* Ming provincial capital 265
Wucheng *C.China* early city 123; Shang city 146
Wupatki *S.W.USA* Pueblo farming site 228
Wuping *S.E.China* Longshan site 147
Wutai Shan *N.China* rock-carved temple 261
Wuwei *N.W.China* early trade centre 191; Han burial 195
Wuzhou *E.China* Tang prefecture 262
Wykeham *N.England* mediaeval town 247
Wyrie Swamp *S.Australia* Aboriginal site 96

X

Xalitla *C.Mexico* Pre-Classical site 214
Xaltocán *C.Mexico* Aztec centre 226
Xanthus *S.W.Anatolia* rock inscription 158; Hellenistic city 165
Xcocha *Mexico, Yucátan* Maya settlement 218
Xelhá *Mexico, Yucátan* Maya settlement 218; early town 226
Xerovrysi *S.W.Greece* tholos tomb 145
Xi'an (a/c Chang'an) *N.China* early settlement 92; Buddhist pagoda 261; Ming provincial capital 265
Xiachuan *N.E.China* early man 69
Xiangyangfu *C.China* provincial capital 263
Xiangzhou *N.China* Tang prefecture 262
Xianling *N.E.China* Ming tomb 264
Xianmengcun *N.China* early settlement 92
Xianrendong *S.E.China* early settlement 92; early pottery 101
Xiaolinding *N.China* early settlement 92
Xiaonanhai *N.E.China* early man 69
Xiaoshan *E.China* Tang kiln 262
Xiapanwang *N.China* early settlement 92
Xiasi *N.China* E.Chou cemetery 192
Xiawanggang *N.China* Longshan site 147
Xibeigang *N.China* early burial 123
Xicalango *E.Mexico* Maya settlement 218; Aztec trade centre 226
Xicun *S.China* Tang kiln 262; Sung kiln 263
Xigong *N.China* E.Chou burial 192
Xihanzhuang *N.China* early settlement 92
Xilingxia *N.China* early settlement 92
Ximen *E.China* E.Chou burial 192
Xingtai *N.China* early city 123; Shang city 146
Xingyuan *N.China* provincial capital 263
Xingzhou *N.China* Tang prefecture 262
Xinxiang *N.China* Ming tomb 265
Xishishan *E.China* E.Chou burial 192
Xixiahou *N.China* early settlement 92
Xiyincun *N.China* early settlement 92
Xoc *S.E.Mexico* Pre-Classical site 214
Xochicalco *C.Mexico* pyramid 49; early town 217; Aztec town 226
Xochimilco *C.Mexico* Aztec centre 226
Xochipala *C.Mexico* Pre-Classical site 214
Xpuhil *Mexico, Yucatán* Maya settlement 218
Xuantu *N.E.China* Han city 195
Xuanzhou *E.China* Tang prefecture 262
Xueguan *N.China* early man 69
Xujiayao *N.E.China* early man 69

Y

Yabrud *Syria* Neanderthal site 65
Yaco (a/s Iiaco) *W.Brazil* early settlement 224
Yagala *W.Africa, Sierra Leone* early food 119
Yagodnoye *C.USSR* Steppe settlement 149
Yagul *C.Mexico* pyramid 49; early settlement 209
Yajima-yakata *Japan* Samurai mansion 266–267
Yakutsk *E.USSR* Arctic culture 273
Yala Alego *E.Africa, Kenya* Iron Age site 203
Yamada-Uenodai *N.Japan* early man 69
Yamama *E.Arabia* Islamic town 241
Yamato *C.Japan* early state 196–197
Yanagimata *C.Japan* early settlement 93
Yandogay *E.USSR* Thule site 272
Yangjia *S.China* E.Chou bronze hoard 192
Yangshao *N.China* Longshan site 147
Yangshaocun *N.Japan* early settlement 92
Yangzhou *E.China* Islamic trade 240; provincial capital 263
Yanjiamatou *N.China* early settlement 92
Yanling *N.China* early settlement 92
Yanshi *N.China* early settlement 92
Yanuca (a/s Yanutha) *Fiji* Lapita site 201
Yanxiadu *N.E.China* E.Chou cemetery 192
Yaojiagang *N.China* E.Chou bronze hoard 192
Yaotougou *N.China* early man 69
Yaozhou (n/c Yaoxian) *N.W.China* Sung kiln 263
Yapahuwa *N.Ceylon* Buddhist remains 255
Yarang *S.W.Thailand* early site 259
Yarar *N.Australia* Aboriginal site 96
Yarim Tepe *N.Mesopotamia* pottery remains 99
Yarinococha *N.Peru* early horticultural village 224
Yarkand (a/s Yarkant) *N.W.China* Buddhist centre 261; early trade 262
Yarm *N.England* mediaeval town 247

Z